The World
Bibliography of
Sherlock Holmes
and Dr. Watson

Sherlock Holmes.
Drawing by Frederic Dorr Steele.

THE WORLD BIBLIOGRAPHY OF SHERLOCK HOLMES AND DR. WATSON

A Classified and Annotated List of Materials Relating to Their Lives and Adventures

RONALD BURT DE WAAL

Bramhall House · New York

A NOTE ON TITLES AND AUTHORS' NAMES

In this Bibliography, the titles of items in serial publications or a series (newspapers, periodicals, radio and television programs, etc.), and items such as chapters of books, are in quotation marks. The titles of items that have appeared as separate publications or productions (books, pamphlets, films, plays, etc.) appear in italics. Information taken from part of a book other than the title page, or information obtained from another source, is in brackets. Translations of titles first published in a foreign language are in brackets and follow the original title. If the title is part of a series, the name of the series and the number of the part in question are in parentheses as the last item in the entry.

Authors' names are usually given as they have been used by those authors. Full names, when known, are listed in the Index of Personal Names. The real names of pseudonymous and anonymous authors are also given, when known, and are in brackets. Authors who have consistently written under one pseudonym are usually listed under that name. A cross-reference from the real name to the pseudonym will be found in the Index. If an author's name does not appear after the title of a book, it can be assumed that the book or item cited from the book was written by the author listed as the main entry.

Copyright © MCMLXXIV by Ronald Burt De Waal
Library of Congress Catalog Card Number: 72-80900

This edition is published by Bramhall House
a division of Clarkson N. Potter, Inc., distributed by Crown Publishers, Inc.
by arrangement with Little, Brown, and Company
a b c d e f g h

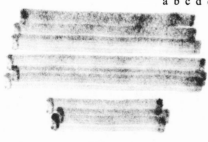

For my Mother,

who first introduced me

to

Sherlock Holmes

and

Dr. Watson

Acknowledgments

The idea of compiling a bibliography on Sherlock Holmes occurred to me after reading the late William S. Baring-Gould's article, " 'A Singular Set of People' " (item 4639), in the January 1966 issue of *Esquire*. From it I first learned about the Baker Street Irregulars, and the discovery led to my attending their annual dinners in New York and eventually being invested with the title of "Lomax, the Sub-Librarian." Baring-Gould's article rekindled the interest I had felt, but unfortunately let lapse, when, as a child, in the company of my brother and my mother (who has always been a great mystery story enthusiast), I thrilled to the incomparable performances of Basil Rathbone and Nigel Bruce on both screen and radio. Had it not been for my mother, I probably never would have developed an interest in Sherlock Holmes; had it not been for Baring-Gould's article, I might never have re-entered the world of Sherlock Holmes and compiled this bibliography.

I should like to thank the many Sherlockians around the world who have written and spoken words of encouragement and who have furnished information for the bibliography. I would particularly like to express my gratitude to Carl Anderson, Bliss Austin, Mrs. Cecil Baring-Gould, Nathan L. Bengis, the late Anthony Boucher, Dean Dickensheet, Irving Fenton, James C. Iraldi, John Bennett Shaw, and Julian Wolff for letting me come into their homes (sometimes even staying for several days) to work with their magnificent collections of Sherlockiana. This bibliography could never have been compiled without access to these collections which, along with other libraries, are listed and described in Appendix II.

No work of this sort is ever accomplished without immense obligation to those who have gone before, and my debt to Edgar W. Smith, Julian Wolff, Nathan L. Bengis, John Bennett Shaw, and other Sherlockians for their bibliographical studies is obvious.

I am also greatly indebted to Bjarne Nielsen and Aage Rieck Sørensen of Denmark, to Nils Norberg and E. A. Wangensten of Norway, and to Ted Bergman of Sweden for their invaluable contributions to the Danish, Norwegian, and Swedish portions of the bibliography. William Lewus of the Department of Foreign Languages at Colorado State University was extremely helpful in translating the bibliographical information generously furnished by the All-Union State Library of Foreign Literature in Moscow.

My research was considerably aided by two grants from the Faculty Improvement Committee of the Colorado State University. They helped finance several trips to various parts of the country to examine library holdings and private collections.

Special thanks must go to Mrs. Eleanor Hard and Mrs. Loretta Saracino, of the CSU Libraries' Interlibrary Loan Department, who were so unfailingly helpful in securing several hundred books, microfilm reels, and photocopies of articles and reviews from numerous libraries in this country and in England.

I would be remiss if I failed to note my deep appreciation to LeMoyne W. Anderson, Director of the Colorado State University Libraries, and to Richard D. Hershcopf, Assistant Director, for their continuing interest in my project and for granting me several leaves of absence to visit and obtain information from many private and institutional collections of Sherlockiana.

Finally, I am grateful to Ben Wolf, president of the George S. MacManus Company of Philadelphia, for being the first publisher to express an interest in the bibliography and for bringing it to the attention of the New York Graphic Society.

Contents

Contents

Contents

List of Illustrations

Preface

This bibliography is a comprehensive record of the various appearances in periodicals, newspapers, and books of the Canonical tales (fifty-six short stories and four novels) and Apocrypha written by Sir Arthur Conan Doyle between 1887 and 1927, together with the translations of these tales into fifty languages, the higher criticism, or writings about the Writings, the films, musicals, plays, radio and television programs, phonograph records, parodies and pastiches, and a multitude of other items (from figurines to Christmas cards) that have accumulated throughout the world on the two most famous "fictional" characters of all time.

The bibliography is divided into ten parts and twenty-nine sections. The table of contents lists the subject headings used, and the two indexes list personal names (except characters and reviewers) and titles. Most of the parts and some sections are preceded by a brief introductory note covering arrangement, sources, acknowledgments, and other matters. There are also a number of important cross references under many subject headings.

That there is a need for such a bibliography is evident from the comments of two eminent Sherlockians. In the Winter 1964 issue of *The Sherlock Holmes Journal*, S. Tupper Bigelow wrote:

> *One of the greatest difficulties confronting a contributor to the writings upon the Writings is his doubt that no matter how brilliant and coruscating his idea may be—and it is certainly original to him—is it, in fact, original? Has the matter ever been dealt with before?*
>
> *What he does, I suppose, is guess that it hasn't, writes his piece and submits it, and perhaps it is published. And while he is preening himself on his Sherlockian scholarship, and reads his contribution in print—a heady emotion, to be sure—many of his Sherlockian correspondents write later to tell him that old So-and-So wrote much the same thing X years before.*

To help eliminate such wasteful and frustrating duplication, T. S. Blakeney suggested in a letter published in the Spring 1967 issue of the same journal that "what we need . . . is a work that brings together the references that bear upon each story in the Canon, a thorough combing and collation of, for example, the *SHJ* and the *BSJ*."

Two standard Sherlockian bibliographies by Edgar W. Smith have been the most important sources of bibliographical information on the Sacred Writings and the writings about the Writings:

1. *The Baker Street Inventory* (item 3742) lists the more important criticisms and parodies and pastiches in the English language up to the time of its publication (in a limited edition of 300 copies) in 1946. This bibliography has been supplemented (by Mr. Smith until 1961 and since then by Dr. Julian Wolff) with a regularly annotated listing in *The Baker Street Journal*. The *BSJ* "Inventory" does not attempt to list and annotate the numerous writings that appear in the Sherlockian periodicals, which of course contain most of the contributions to the literature. It confines itself rather to books and articles published elsewhere, with occasional mention of miscellaneous items.
2. *Sherlock Holmes: The Writings of John H. Watson, M.D.* (item 3744), published shortly after Edgar Smith's death in 1960, is a *descriptive* list of the first and most important appearances of the Canonical tales in the English language.

The present compilation attempts to consolidate and classify the items in these and other bibliographies and checklists, and to provide an inventory of the many items which have never been listed before.

Preface

It is hoped that this reference work will prove useful not only to scholars of the Canon and of London in the Victorian era, but also to collectors of Sherlockiana and to high school and college students who, along with others, would like to know more about Sherlock Holmes. The bibliography can be used by students as a starting point for their own interpretations of the Sacred Writings.

It was at first the ambitious intention of the compiler to provide an exhaustive annotated listing of every item that has appeared in all countries of the world on Holmes and Watson. Knowledgeable Sherlockians will realize the immensity, if not impossibility, of such an undertaking. Were there a definitive Sherlock Holmes collection (none, of course, exists), then and only then would it have been possible to compile such a listing. Considerations of time would, however, still have precluded the possibility of fully describing or summarizing all the variant printings and foreign language editions of the Canon; the many different performances of the plays, the radio programs, and so on, for the various countries of the world. Every effort has been made to track down as many items as possible; indeed one Sherlockian has expressed the opinion that the compiler has probably seen and examined more Sherlockiana than anyone before him.

Two five-year supplements to this bibliography are being planned, as is a second edition in 1987 to commemorate the centennial of the Sacred Writings. The entry numbers in the supplements will be a continuation of the numbering sequence used here. It would be extremely helpful if interested persons would send additional information and suggestions for the improvement of the bibliography to the compiler so that such information and improvements can be incorporated in the projected supplements and the revised edition.

If Doyle were to return today, he would be astonished by the continued popularity of the Sherlock Holmes stories and by the vast amount of material that has appeared about them. (In response to a recent order he sent to the Covent Garden Bookshop in London, the compiler was informed that "of all our customers, every second person is a collector of A. Conan Doyle"! The order went unfilled because every title requested had been completely sold out.)

The sixty tales represent but a small and, according to Doyle, incidental part of his total literary output. Even his son Adrian tended to minimize the importance of the stories as compared to his father's "major" works.

As a mild form of chastisement of Sir Arthur for his disparaging remarks about these stories, as well as to help maintain the reality of Holmes, Sherlockians take delight in pretending that it was actually Dr. Watson who recorded the adventures and that Doyle was merely acting as the literary agent. They have attributed the four novels and fifty-two of the short stories to Watson, "The Adventure of the Blanched Soldier" and "The Adventure of the Lion's Mane" to Sherlock Holmes himself, and "His Last Bow" to Sherlock's older brother Mycroft. Doyle is credited with having written only "The Adventure of the Mazarin Stone," an adaptation from his one-act play *The Crown Diamond*, and Part II of *A Study in Scarlet*.

At the annual dinners of the Baker Street Irregulars, Sir Arthur's name is seldom mentioned. There are toasts to Sherlock Holmes, to Dr. Watson, to Mrs. Hudson, even to the hypothetical second wife of Dr. Watson —but never to Sir Arthur. And so the pretense is carried on, in what in Sherlockian parlance are called the writings about the Writings, or the Sacred Writings. And sacred they are to anyone who is a frequent visitor at 221B Baker Street.

These tales of mystery and high moral purpose have brought untold pleasure and excitement into the humdrum lives of young and old alike in all parts of the world. What greater contribution could any writer make? *And so to you, Sir Arthur Conan Doyle, a long overdue toast from all of us for having created the best and most exciting of all possible worlds—the world of Sherlock Holmes and Dr. Watson!*

R.B.D.

The World Bibliography of Sherlock Holmes and Dr. Watson

I | *The Sacred Writings*

The sixty tales are arranged in three sections. In Section A, the *Individual Tales* are listed alphabetically according to the standard abbreviations devised by Jay Finley Christ (see Appendix I) and then by date of appearance. With the exception of a few anthologies, books in which two or more tales appear are listed in Section B or C. In Section B, the *Collected Tales* are arranged alphabetically and then chronologically, and the contents are noted for the first edition of each of the five collected editions. The editions are complete unless otherwise indicated. In Section C, the *Selected and Complete Tales* are also listed alphabetically and then chronologically or by publisher's name when the date of publication is unknown. In all three sections books that do not have a publication date are usually listed after those with the same title having a date.

Because of the difficulty involved in physically describing and distinguishing different and variant printings of the same book, several of these editions could not be identified adequately enough to list in this enumerative bibliography. Nathan L. Bengis and Edgar W. Smith have made important contributions in this area (see items 2685 and 3744), and perhaps other Sherlockian bibliophiles will make still further contributions.

A | *Individual Tales*

THE ADVENTURE OF THE ABBEY GRANGE

1. "The Adventure of the Abbey Grange," [Illustrated by Sidney Paget]. *The Strand Magazine*, 28, No. 165 (September 1904), 242-256. (The Return of Sherlock Holmes, No. 12)

2. ———, Illustrated by Frederic Dorr Steele. *Collier's, 34*, No. 14 (December 31, 1904), 10-12, 23, 25-26. (The Return of Sherlock Holmes, No. 12)

3. ———. The Boston Sunday *Post*, [1911]. 14 p. illus. (Masterpieces of Sherlock Holmes)

4. ———. [New York]: Sunday *World* Fiction Section, [1911]. 14 p. illus.

THE ADVENTURE OF THE BERYL CORONET

5. "The Adventure of the Beryl Coronet," [Illustrated by Sidney Paget]. *The Strand Magazine*, 3, No. 17 (May 1892), 511-525. (The Adventures of Sherlock Holmes, No. 11)

THE ADVENTURE OF BLACK PETER

6. "The Adventure of Black Peter," Illustrated by Frederic Dorr Steele. *Collier's*, 32, No. 21 (February 20, 1904), 18-20, 22-25. (The Return of Sherlock Holmes, No. 6)

7. ———, [Illustrated by Sidney Paget]. *The Strand Magazine,* 27, No. 159 (March 1904), 242-255. (The Return of Sherlock Holmes, No. 6)

8. ———. [New York]: Sunday *World* Fiction Section, [1911]. 15 p. illus.

THE ADVENTURE OF THE BLANCHED SOLDIER

9. "The Adventure of the Blanched Soldier," Pictures by Frederic Dorr Steele. *Liberty*, 3, No. 24 (October 16, 1926), 12-14, 17, 19, 21.

10. ———, Illustrated by Howard K. Elcock. *The Strand Magazine*, 72, No. 431 (November 1926), 422-434.

11. ———, Illustrated by Frederic Dorr Steele. *Los Angeles Times Sunday Magazine* (January 30, 1927), 16-18.

12. ———, *Great Detective Stories About Doctors*. Edited, with an introduction by Croff Conklin and Noah D. Fabricant. New York: Collier Books, [1965]. p. 59-77.

THE ADVENTURE OF THE BLUE CARBUNCLE

13. "The Adventure of the Blue Carbuncle," [Illustrated by Sidney Paget]. *The Strand Magazine*, 3, No. 13 (January 1892), 73-85. (The Adventures of Sherlock Holmes, No. 7)

14. "Story of the Blue Carbuncle," *Pennsylvania Grit Story Companion* [Williamsport], 23, No. 3, Story Companion No. 518 (December 18, 1904), 1-5. 12. illus.

15. "The Adventure of the Blue Carbuncle," *Century of Thrillers*. New York: President Press, [1937]. Vol. 1, p. 69-88.

16. ———. With an introduction by Christopher Morley. Edited and with a bibliographical note by Edgar W. Smith. New York: The Baker Street Irregulars, 1948. 64 p. illus.
    ———. [Deluxe ed.] New York: The Baker Street Irregulars, 1948. 75 p. illus.
    At head of title: The Adventures of Sherlock Holmes. Cover title: The Blue Carbuncle.
    The first and only separate appearance, in book form, of this Christmas story which Christopher Morley, in his introduction, describes as "a far better work of art than the immortal *Christmas Carol* [by Charles Dickens]."
    Reviews: *New York Herald Tribune Weekly Book Review* (December 12, 1948), 14 (Will Cuppy); *San Francisco Chronicle* (December 18, 1948), 10 (J. H. Jackson).

17. ———, *Ellery Queen's Mystery Magazine*, 17 (April 1951), 37-52.

18. ———, *Famous Mysteries*. Edited by Mary Yost Sandrus and illustrated by Don Merrick. Chicago: Scott, Foresman and Co., [1955]. p. 36-63.

19. ———. [New York: The Benjamin Co. for Flint Laboratories, 1970.] 31 p.
    A promotional booklet distributed only to physicians in the U.S.

20. "Adventure of the Blue Carbuncle: A Classic Sherlock Holmes Mystery," Illustrations by William Shields. [With an afterword "Was Sherlock Holmes Wrong?" by Louis Zara.] *Mineral Digest*, 1, No. 1 (1970), 33-48.
    Beautifully printed with three magnificent colored illustrations, one of which folds out to 32 inches.

THE BOSCOMBE VALLEY MYSTERY

21. "The Boscombe Valley Mystery," [Illustrated by Sidney Paget]. *The Strand Magazine*, 2, No. 10 (October 1891), 401-416. (The Adventures of Sherlock Holmes, No. 4)

22. ———, *The Great Detective Stories: A Chronological Anthology*. Compiled and edited, with an introduction by Willard Huntington Wright. New York: Charles Scribner's Sons, 1927. p. 147-169.

23. ———, *The World's Great Detective Stories: A Chronological Anthology*. Compiled and edited, with an introduction by S. S. Van Dine [Willard Huntington Wright]. New York: Blue Ribbon Books, [c. 1931]. p. 147-169.

24. ———, *Famous Mysteries*. Edited by Mary Yost Sandrus and illustrated by Don Merrick. Chicago: Scott, Foresman and Co., [1955]. p. 64-95.

THE ADVENTURE OF THE BRUCE-PARTINGTON PLANS

25. "The Adventure of the Bruce-Partington Plans," [Illustrated by Arthur Twidle]. *The Strand Magazine*, 36, No. 216 (December 1908), 689-705.

26. "The Adventure of the Bruce-Partington Plans: A Reminiscence of Mr. Sherlock Holmes," [Illustrated by Frederic Dorr Steele]. *Collier's*, 42, No. 12 (December 12, 1908), 15-18, 28, 30, 33-34.

27. "The Adventure of the Bruce-Partington Plans," *Tellers of Tales: 100 Short Stories from the United States, England, France, Russia and Germany*. Selected and with an introduction by W. Somerset Maugham. New York: Doubleday, Doran & Co., 1939. p. 326-348.

28. ———, *World's Great Spy Stories*. Edited, with an introduction by Vincent Starrett. Cleveland and New York: The World Pub. Co., [1944]. p. 169-192.

29. ———, *Best Secret Service Stories*. Edited by John Welcome [John Brennan]. London: Faber and Faber, [1960]. p. 87-115.

30. ———, *Alfred Hitchcock's Sinister Spies*. Illustrated by Paul Spina. New York: Random House, [1966]. p. 31-64.

31. "The Bruce Partington Plans," *Ten Tales of Detection*. Chosen and introduced by Roger Lancelyn Green. With colour frontispiece and line drawings in the text by Ian Ribbons. London: J. M. Dent & Sons Ltd.; New York: E. P. Dutton & Co. Inc., [1967]. p. 61-89. (Children's Illustrated Classics, No. 72)

32. ———, *Great Spy Stories from Fiction*. Edited by Allen Dulles. New York and

Evanston: Harper & Row, [1969]. p. 119-144. (A Ginger Book)

THE ADVENTURE OF
THE CARDBOARD BOX

33. "The Adventure of the Cardboard Box," [Illustrated by Sidney Paget]. *The Strand Magazine*, 5, No. 25 (January 1893), 61-73. (The Adventures of Sherlock Holmes, No. 14)

34. "The Adventure of the Card-Board Box," [Illustrated by W. H. Hyde]. *Harper's Weekly*, 37, No. 1882 (January 14, 1893), 29-31. (The Adventures of Sherlock Holmes)

THE ADVENTURE OF
CHARLES AUGUSTUS MILVERTON

35. "The Adventure of Charles Augustus Milverton," Illustrated by Frederic Dorr Steele. *Collier's*, 32, No. 26 (March 26, 1904), 13-15, 19-20. (The Return of Sherlock Holmes, No. 7)

36. ———, [Illustrated by Sidney Paget]. *The Strand Magazine*, 27, No. 160 (April 1904), 373-383. (The Return of Sherlock Holmes, No. 7)

37. ———. [New York]: Sunday *World* Fiction Section, May 21, 1911. 14 p. illus.

THE ADVENTURE OF
THE COPPER BEECHES

38. "The Adventure of the Copper Beeches," [Illustrated by Sidney Paget]. *The Strand Magazine, 3, No. 18* (June 1892), 613-628. (The Adventures of Sherlock Holmes, No. 12)

39. ———, Illustrated by Ben Denison. *Playboy*, 1, No. 3 (February 1954), 20-21, 24, 35-36, 45-46, 49-50.

THE ADVENTURE OF
THE CREEPING MAN

40. "The Adventure of the Creeping Man," Illustrated by Howard Elcock. *The Strand Magazine*, 65, No. 387 (March 1923), 210-224.

41. "The Creeping Man," Illustrations by Frederic Dorr Steele. *Hearst's International*, 43, No. 3 (March 1923), 8-13, 116, 118, 120.

42. "The Adventure of the Creeping Man," [Illustration by Frederic Dorr Steele]. *The Courier-Journal*, Magazine Section [Louisville, Ky.] (March 15, 1925), 2, 8.

43. ———, [Illustrated by Criswell]. *Los Angeles Times Sunday Magazine* (March 22, 1925), 7, 19-20.

THE CROOKED MAN

44. "The Adventure of the Crooked Man," [Illustrated by Sidney Paget]. *The Strand Magazine*, 6, No. 31 (July 1893), 22-32. (The Adventures of Sherlock Holmes, No. 20)

45. ———, [Illustrated by W. H. Hyde]. *Harper's Weekly*, 37, No. 1907 (July 8, 1893), 645-647. (The Adventures of Sherlock Holmes)

46. "The Crooked Man," *The Great Detectives*. London: Hennel Locke Ltd., [1947]. p. 31-51.

THE ADVENTURE OF
THE DANCING MEN

47. "The Adventure of the Dancing Men," [Illustrated by Sidney Paget]. *The Strand Magazine*, 26, No. 156 (December 1903), 602-617. (The Return of Sherlock Holmes, No. 3)

48. ———, Illustrated by Frederic Dorr Steele. *Collier's*, 32, No. 10 (December 5, 1903), 11-14. (The Return of Sherlock Holmes, No. 3)

49. ———. [New York]: Sunday *World* Fiction Section, [1911]. 15 p. illus.

50. ———, *The Pocket University*. Edited by Hamilton W. Mabie. Volume 22, Part 1. *Fiction*. Garden City, N.Y.: Doubleday, Page & Co., 1924. p. 63-100.

51. ———, *Famous Stories of Code and Cipher*. Edited by Raymond T. Bond. New York; Toronto: Rinehart and Co., 1947. p. 135-160.

52. ———, *A Cavalcade of Collier's*. Edited by Kenneth McArdle. New York: A. S. Barnes & Co., [1959]. p. 56-72.

53. ———, *Great Tales of Action and Adventure*. Edited by George Bennett. [New York: Dell Pub. Co., June 1959.] p. 124-152. (Laurel TM 674623)

54. ———, *Famous Stories of Code and Cipher*. Edited by Raymond T. Bond. New York: Collier Books, [1965]. Chap. 7, p. 171-198.

THE ADVENTURE OF
THE DEVIL'S FOOT

55. "The Adventure of the Devil's Foot: A Reminiscence of Sherlock Holmes," Illustrated by Gilbert Holiday. *The Strand Magazine*, 40, No. 240 (December 1910), 638-653.

56. ———, Illustrated by Gilbert Holiday. *The Strand Magazine* [New York], 40, No. 240

(January 1911), 722-730; 41, No. 241 (February 1911), 2-9.

57. *The Adventure of the Devil's Foot.* The Boston Sunday *Post*, [1911]. 14 p. illus. (Masterpieces of Sherlock Holmes)

THE ADVENTURE OF THE DYING DETECTIVE

58. "The Adventure of the Dying Detective: A New Sherlock Holmes Story," Illustrated by Frederic Dorr Steele. *Collier's*, 52, No. 10 (November 22, 1913), 5-7, 24-25.

59. *The Adventure of the Dying Detective.* [New York]: Advertising Department, Collier's Weekly, [1913]. 38 p. (Vol. 4)

60. ———, Illustrated by Wal. Paget. *The Strand Magazine*, 46, No. 270 (December 1913), 604-614.

THE ADVENTURE OF THE EMPTY HOUSE

61. "The Adventure of the Empty House," Illustrated by F. D. Steele. *Collier's*, 31, No. 26 (September 26, 1903), 12-16. (The Return of Sherlock Holmes, No. 1)

62. ———, [Illustrated by Sidney Paget]. *The Strand Magazine*, 26, No. 154 (October 1903), 362-376. (The Return of Sherlock Holmes, No. 1)

63. "The Empty House," *Murder Mixture: An Anthology of Crime Stories.* Selected by Elizabeth Lee. London: Elek Books, [1963]. p. 145-164.

THE ADVENTURE OF THE ENGINEER'S THUMB

64. "The Adventure of the Engineer's Thumb," [Illustrated by Sidney Paget]. *The Strand Magazine*, 3, No. 15 (March 1892), 276-288. (The Adventures of Sherlock Holmes, No. 9)

65. "The Engineer's Thumb," *Great Horror Stories.* Compiled by Rosamund Morris. Illustrated by Hamilton Greene. New York: Hart Pub. Co., [1965]. p. 43-87. (Sunrise Library)

66. ———, *Masterpieces of Horror.* Compiled by Rosamund Morris. New York: Hart Pub. Co., [1966]. p. 25-55.

67. *The Adventure of the Engineer's Thumb.* [New York: The Benjamin Co. for Flint Laboratories, 1970.] 32 p.
A promotional booklet distributed only to physicians in the U. S.

THE FINAL PROBLEM

68. "The Adventure of the Final Problem," [Illustrated by Sidney Paget]. *The Strand Magazine*, 6, No. 36 (December 1893), 558-570. (The Adventures of Sherlock Holmes, No. 24)

69. "The Adventure of the Final Problem: The Last Episode in the Life of Sherlock Holmes," [Illustrated by H. C. Edwards]. *McClure's Magazine*, 2, No. 1 (December 1893), 99-112.

70. *The Final Problem.* A privately printed edition designed and printed by Mo Lebowitz, proprietor of The Antique Press. Annotated by the late William S. Baring-Gould in the Clarkson N. Potter book, *The Annotated Sherlock Holmes.* [North Bellmore, Long Island]: The Antique Press, Summer 1969. 23 p. 18 x 6 in.
Limited to 75 copies.

THE FIVE ORANGE PIPS

71. "The Five Orange Pips," [Illustrated by Sidney Paget]. *The Strand Magazine*, 2, No. 11 (November 1891), 481-491. (The Adventures of Sherlock Holmes, No. 5)

72. ———, *Masterpieces of Mystery & Detection.* Compiled by Rosamund Morris. New York: Hart Pub. Co., [1965]. p. 165-188.

73. ———. [New York: The Benjamin Co. for Flint Laboratories, 1970.] 31 p.
A promotional booklet distributed only to physicians in the U. S.

THE "GLORIA SCOTT"

74. "The Adventure of the 'Gloria Scott,'" [Illustrated by Sidney Paget]. *The Strand Magazine*, 5, No. 28 (April 1893), 395-406. (The Adventures of Sherlock Holmes, No. 17)

75. ———, [Illustrated by W. H. Hyde]. *Harper's Weekly*, 37, No. 1895 (April 15, 1893), 345-347. (The Adventures of Sherlock Holmes)

76. "The Gloria Scott," *Suspense . . . A Treasury for Young Adults.* Edited by Seon Manley and Gogo Lewis. New York: Funk & Wagnalls, [1966]. p. 47-68.

THE ADVENTURE OF THE GOLDEN PINCE-NEZ

77. "The Adventure of the Golden Pince-Nez," [Illustrated by Sidney Paget]. *The Strand Magazine*, 28, No. 163 (July 1904), 2-16. (The Return of Sherlock Holmes, No. 10)

78. ———, Illustrated by Frederic Dorr Steele. *Collier's,* 34, No. 5 (October 29, 1904), 15, 18-19, 27-30. (The Return of Sherlock Holmes, No. 10)

79. ———. The Boston Sunday *Post,* [1911]. 14 p. illus. (Masterpieces of Sherlock Holmes)

80. ———. [New York]: Sunday *World* Fiction Section, [1911]. 15 p. illus.

THE GREEK INTERPRETER

81. "The Adventure of the Greek Interpreter," [Illustrated by Sidney Paget]. *The Strand Magazine,* 6, No. 33 (September 1893), 296-307. (The Adventures of Sherlock Holmes, No. 22)

82. "The Greek Interpreter," [Illustrated by W. H. Hyde]. *Harper's Weekly,* 37, No. 1917 (September 16, 1893), 887, 890-892. (The Adventures of Sherlock Holmes)

83. ———, *Stories of To-day and Yesterday: Thirty Selected Short Stories; Nine Imitative Stories by Students; Questions for Class Discussion; Directions for Creative Narration.* Edited by Frederick Houk Law. New York; London: The Century Co., [1930]. p. 66-87.

84. ———, *Best Mystery Stories.* Edited, with an introduction by Maurice Richardson. London: Faber and Faber, [1968]. p. 44-62.

THE HOUND OF THE BASKERVILLES

85. "The Hound of the Baskervilles: Another Adventure of Sherlock Holmes," [Illustrated by Sidney Paget]. *The Strand Magazine,* 22, No. 128 (August 1901), 122-132; 22, No. 129 (September 1901), 242-254; 22, No. 130 (October 1901), 362-373; 22, No. 131 (November 1901), 495-506; 22, No. 132 (December 1901), 602-612; 23, No. 133 (January 1902), 2-15; 23, No. 134 (February 1902), 122-130; 23, No. 135 (March 1902), 242-252; 23, No. 136 (April 1902), 362-372.

86. ———, [Illustrated by Sidney Paget]. *The Strand Magazine* [New York], 22, No. 128 (September 1901), 122-132; 22, No. 129 (October 1901), 242-254; 22, No. 130 (November 1901), 362-373; 22, No. 131 (December 1901), 495-506; 22, No. 132 (January 1902), 602-612; 23, No. 133 (February 1902), 2-15; 23, No. 134 (March 1902), 122-130; 23, No. 135 (April 1902), 242-252; 23, No. 136 (May 1902), 362-372.

87. ———. [Illustrated by Sidney Paget.]

Frederic Dorr Steele's cover illustration for "The Adventure of the Golden Pince-nez," Collier's, *October 29, 1904* (78).

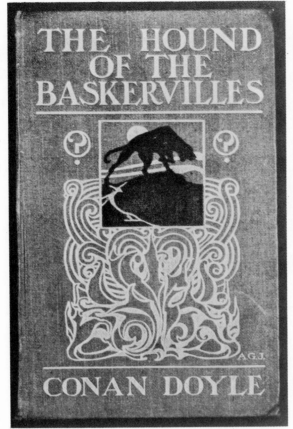

First hardcover edition of The Hound of the Baskervilles, *published in 1902 by George Newnes Ltd., London* (**87**).

London: George Newnes, Ltd., 1902. 358, [1] p.

Contents: 1. Mr. Sherlock Holmes. - 2. The Curse of the Baskervilles. - 3. The Problem. - 4. Sir Henry Baskerville. - 5. Three Broken Threads. - 6. Baskerville Hall. - 7. The Stapletons of Merripit House. - 8. First Report of Dr. Watson. - 9. [Second Report of Dr. Watson] The Light Upon the Moor. - 10. Extract from the Diary of Dr. Watson. - 11. The Man on the Tor. - 12. Death on the Moor. - 13. Fixing the Nets. - 14. The Hound of the Baskervilles. - 15. A Retrospection.

88. ———. [Illustrated by Sidney Paget.] New York: McClure, Phillips & Co., 1902. 248 p.
First American edition.

89. ———. [Illustrated by Sidney Paget.] New York: The American News Co., [March 1902]. 248 p.
At head of title: A Special Limited Edition.

90. ———. Garden City, N.Y.: Doubleday, Page & Co., [c. 1902]. 248 p.

91. ———. [Frontispiece by Sidney Paget.] New York: Grosset & Dunlap, Publishers, [c. 1902]. 248 p.
At head of title: A Special Limited Edition.

92. ———. London and Bombay: Longmans, Green, and Co., 1902. 358 p. (Longmans' Colonial Library)

93. ———. Toronto: George N. Morang & Co., 1902. 248 p.

94. ———, *The Pittsburgh Gazette* (July 6, 1902), 6-7; (July 13, 1902), 4-5; (July 20, 1902), 4; (July 27, 1902), 2; (August 3, 1902), 2; (August 10, 1902), 2; (August 17, 1902), 2; (August 24, 1902), 2; (August 31, 1902), 2; (September 7, 1902), 2; (September 14, 1902), 2.
The first installment appeared, curiously, in the Woman's Section of the Sunday edition; the remainder were published in the Magazine Section. The story was illustrated with rather crude reproductions of some of the Sidney Paget illustrations, though no credit is given, and the SP initials are missing.

95. ———. Copyright edition. Leipzig: Bernhard Tauchnitz, 1902. 270 p. (Tauchnitz Edition, Vol. 3571) (A. Conan Doyle, No. 29)

96. ———. Illustrated [by Sidney Paget]. New York: McClure, Phillips & Co., 1903. 248 p.
On spine: Special edition.

97. *The Hound of the Baskervilles.* London: George Newnes, Ltd., [1912]. 126 p. (Newnes' Sixpenny Copyright Novels)

98. *The Hound of the Baskervilles: Another Adventure of Sherlock Holmes.* [Illustrated by Sidney Paget.] London: Smith, Elder & Co., 1913. 358 p.

99. *The Hound of the Baskervilles.* London: Thomas Nelson & Sons, [1915]. 373 p. (Nelson's Library)

100. *The Hound of the Baskervilles: Another Adventure of Sherlock Holmes.* London: John Murray, [1918]. 248 p.

101. ———. London: John Murray, [June 1922]. 315 p.
First "cheap ed."

102. *The Hound of the Baskervilles.* With an introduction by Frank Condie Baxter. Garden City, N.Y.: Doubleday, Page & Co., 1926. xviii, 248 p. (The Lambskin Library, No. 53)

103. ———, *Famous Dogs in Fiction.* Edited by J. Walker McSpadden. [Illustrated by Margaret S. Johnson.] Revised ed. New York: Thomas Y. Crowell Co., [1930]. p. 266-287.
Contains a summary of the first thirteen chapters, followed by the complete text of chapter 14.

104. ———. The G. Washington Edition. [Vol. 2] New York: Doubleday, Doran & Co., [c.1930]. 191 p.
Includes a frontispiece of Richard

Gordon, the celebrated actor who played the title role in a radio dramatization of the tales.

105. ———. London: Penguin Books, 1937. 249 p. (No. 111)

106. ———. Harmondsworth, Middlesex, England: Penguin Books Ltd., [August 1937]. vii, 216 p.

107. ———. Abridged and edited by B. M. Chester. With 4 illustrations by M. Buchanan. London: Oxford University Press, 1938. vi, 130 p.

108. ———. Berne [Switzerland]: Phoenix Pub. Co. Ltd., [1947]. 219 p. (Scherz Phoenix Books, No. 97)

109. ———. New York: Bantam Books, [March 1949]. 181 p. (No. 366)

110. ———. London: Pocket Books (G. B.) Ltd., [1950]. 199 p. (Pocket Book, No. B7)

111. ———. Abridged and edited by B. M. Chester. With four illustrations by Mina Buchanan. London: Oxford University Press, [1951]. vi, 130 p. (Stories Told and Retold)

112. ———. With an introduction by B. A. Marsh and illustrations by Shirley Hughes. London: John Murray, [1957]. xiv, 230 p. (The School Library of Famous Books) Includes Notes and Exercises, p. 225-230.

113. ———, *An Omnibus of British Mysteries.* Condensed. [Edited by George Bisserov.] New York: Juniper Press, [1959]. p. 137-263. (The Classics of Mystery, Vol. 5)

114. ———. Chicago: Henry Regnery Co., 1959. 242 p. (Gateway Editions, No. 6050) At head of title: An Adventure of Sherlock Holmes.

115. ———. New York: Dell Pub. Co., [August 1959]. 224 p. (The Dell Great Mystery Library, No. 24) (D302)

116. ———. Illustrated by Gil Walker. New York: Looking Glass Library; distributed by Random House, [1961]. 282 p. (Looking Glass Library, No. 26)

117. ———. New York: Collier Books, 1962. 185 p. (HS41V)

118. ———. [New York]: Berkley Pub. Corp., [December 1963]. 174 p. (Berkley Medallion, F858)

119. ———, *Four Complete Adventure Novels.* [Compiled by] Jessie Alford Nunn. New York: Globe Book Co., [1964]. p. 489-675. illus.

120. ———. [With a word to the reader by Herbert Brean.] New York: Scholastic Book Services, [March 1964]. ix, 244 p. (Scholastic Library Edition, T590)

121. ———. [New York: Dell Pub. Co., Eighth Dell printing, October 1964.] 224 p. (Laurel-Leaf Library, No. 3758)

122. ———. [Introduction by Isidore Goldstein.] New York: Airmont Pub. Co., [1965]. 128 p. (Classics Series, CL62)

123. ———. New York: Lancer Books, [1967]. 255 p. (Magnum Easy Eye Books, 13-407)

124. ———. With an introduction by William S. Baring-Gould. [New York]: The New American Library, [June 1967]. xx, 176 p. (Signet Classics, CD337)

125. *The Hound of the Baskervilles: Another Adventure of Sherlock Holmes.* With biographical illustrations and pictures from early editions of the novel, together with an introduction by James Nelson. New York: Dodd, Mead & Co., [1968]. xi, 204 p. (Great Illustrated Classics)

126. *The Hound of the Baskervilles.* Unabridged. Illustrated by Hal Frenck. Cover by Shannon Stirnweis. Racine, Wis.: Whitman Pub. Div., Western Pub. Co., [1968]. 212 p. (Whitman Classics)

127. ———. Illustrated [with a frontispiece by Sidney Paget]. New York: P. F. Collier & Son, [n.d.] 248 p. At head of title: The latest books of Conan Doyle by special arrangement with the author.

128. ———. Garden City, N.Y.: Doubleday & Co., [n.d.] 198 p. (Dolphin Books, C127)

129. ———. New York: Grosset & Dunlap, [n.d.] 249 p. (The Ferret Library. Bennett A. Cerf, editor)

130. *The Hound of the Baskervilles: Another Adventure of Sherlock Holmes.* London: Eveleigh Nash & Grayson Ltd., [n.d.] 315 p. (Nash's Library of Thrillers)

A CASE OF IDENTITY

131. "A Case of Identity," [Illustrated by Sidney Paget]. *The Strand Magazine,* 2, No. 9 (September 1891), 248-259. (The Adventures of Sherlock Holmes, No. 3)

132. ———. New York: Optimus Printing Co., [1895]. 30 p. (The Handy Classic Series, Choice Stories by Famous Authors, No. 10)

133. ———. London; New York: F. Tennyson Neely, Publisher, 1899. 93 p. (Neely's Booklet Series, No. 16, April 17, 1899)

Individual Tales

134. ———, *The Lock and Key Library: Classic Mystery and Detective Stories.* Edited by Julian Hawthorne. New York: The Review of Reviews Co., 1909. Vol. 8, p. 42-61.

135. ———. Philadelphia: Royal Pub. Co., [190-?] (The Sherlock Holmes Detective Library, No. 425)

136. ———. The Boston Sunday *Post,* [1911]. 14 p. illus. (Masterpieces of Sherlock Holmes)

137. ———, *The 101 World's Great Mystery Stories.* New York: Blue Ribbon Books, [1928]. p. 131-143.

138. ———, *World's Great Detective Stories.* New York: Black's Readers Service Co., 1928. p. 131-143.

139. ———. [Chicago: Bertha M. Clay, n.d.] 45-82, 3-75 p. (Atlantic Library, No. 44)
     Cover title: A Case of Identity or Sherlock Holmes the Detective.
     Also contains: For Himself Alone.

140. *A Case of Identity and Other Stories.* New York: Optimus Printing Co., [n.d.] 30, 30, 30, 30 p.
     On spine: Rosebud Edition.
     Also contains: The Man from Archangel. - The Captain of the "Pole-Star". - John Barrington Cowles.

141. *A Case of Identity: A Sherlock Holmes Story.* Baltimore: I. & M. Ottenheimer, [n.d.] 227-255, 5-61 p. (Old Sleuth's Series, No. 10)
     On cover: A Case of Identity or A Detective's Wonderful Narrative, by Old Sleuth.
     Also contains: Romeo and Juliet.

142. ———. Baltimore: I. & M. Ottenheimer, [n.d.] 227-255, 5-61 p. (The Sherlock Holmes Detective Library)
     Also contains: Romeo and Juliet.

143. ———. Cleveland, Ohio: The Arthur Westbrook Co., [n.d.] 227-255, 115 p. (American Detective Series, No. 4)
     Also contains: The American Monte-Cristo.

THE ADVENTURE OF THE ILLUSTRIOUS CLIENT

144. "The Adventure of the Illustrious Client," Illustrated by John Richard Flanagan. *Collier's,* 74, No. 19 (November 8, 1924), 5-7, 30, 32, 34.

145. ———, [Illustrated by Howard K. Elcock]. *The Strand Magazine,* 69, No. 410 (February 1925), 108-118; 69, No. 411 (March 1925), 259-266.

146. ———, [Illustrated by Frederic Dorr Steele]. *Los Angeles Times Sunday Magazine* (April 5, 1925), 7-8, 22.

THE DISAPPEARANCE OF LADY FRANCES CARFAX

147. "The Disappearance of Lady Frances Carfax," Illustrated by Alec Ball. *The Strand Magazine,* 42, No. 252 (December 1911), 602-614.

148. ———, Illustrations by Frederic Dorr Steele. *The American Magazine,* 73, No. 2 (December 1911), 130-142.

149. ———, *Ellery Queen's Challenge to the Reader: An Anthology.* New York: Frederick A. Stokes Co., 1938. p. 458-478.
     ———. ———. New York: Blue Ribbon Books, [1940]. p. 458-478.
     ———, ———. New York: The American Mercury, [n.d.] p. 109-125. (Mercury Mysteries, No. 68)
     The names of Holmes and Watson have been changed to Pharaoh Jones and Dr. Dover, and the reader is asked to identify the author and detective.

HIS LAST BOW

150. "His Last Bow: The War Service of Sherlock Holmes," Illustrated by A. Gilbert. *The Strand Magazine,* 54, No. 321 (September 1917), 226-236.

151. ———, Illustrated by Frederic Dorr Steele. *Collier's, 60. No. 2* (September 22, 1917), 5-7, 47-49.

152. "His Last Bow: An Epilogue of Sherlock Holmes," *Best Secret Service Stories 2.* Edited, with an introduction by John Welcome [John Brennan]. London: Faber and Faber, [1965]. p. 109-124.

THE ADVENTURE OF THE LION'S MANE

153. "The Adventure of the Lion's Mane," Pictures by Frederic Dorr Steele. *Liberty,* 3, No. 30 (November 27, 1926), 18, 21, 23, 25-26, 29, 31.

154. ———, Illustrated by Howard K. Elcock. *The Strand Magazine,* 72, No. 432 (December 1926), 539-550.

155. ———, [Illustration by Frederic Dorr Steele]. *The Courier-Journal,* Magazine Section [Louisville, Ky.] (February 6, 1927), 3-4.

156. ———, *Los Angeles Times Sunday Magazine* (February 6, 1927), 16-18. illus.

THE ADVENTURE OF
THE MAZARIN STONE

157. "The Adventure of the Mazarin Stone," Illustrated by A. Gilbert. *The Strand Magazine,* 62, No. 370 (October 1921), 288-298.

158. ———, Illustrated by Frederic Dorr Steele. *Hearst's International,* 40, No. 5 (November 1921), 6-8, 64-65.

159. ———, *The Faber Book of Stories.* Edited by Kathleen Lines. London: Faber and Faber, [1960]. p. 73-90.

THE ADVENTURE OF
THE MISSING THREE-QUARTER

160. "The Adventure of the Missing Three-Quarter," [Illustrated by Sidney Paget]. *The Strand Magazine,* 28, No. 164 (August 1904), 122-135. (The Return of Sherlock Holmes, No. 11)

161. ———, Illustrated by Frederic Dorr Steele. *Collier's,* 34, No. 6 (November 26, 1904), 15, 18, 27-30. (The Return of Sherlock Holmes, No. 11)

162. ———. The Boston Sunday *Post,* [1911]. 15 p. illus. (Masterpieces of Sherlock Holmes)

163. ———, *Collier's Greatest Sports Stories.* Edited by Tom Meany. New York: A. S. Barnes and Co., [1955]. p. 20-39.

THE MUSGRAVE RITUAL

164. "The Adventure of the Musgrave Ritual," [Illustrated by Sidney Paget]. *The Strand Magazine,* 5, No. 29 (May 1893), 479-489. (The Adventures of Sherlock Holmes, No. 18)

165. ———, [Illustrated by W. H. Hyde]. *Harper's Weekly,* 37, No. 1899 (May 13, 1893), 453-455, 458. (The Adventures of Sherlock Holmes)

166. "The Musgrave Ritual," *Pennsylvania Grit Story Companion* [Williamsport], 23, No. 7, Story Companion No. 522 (January 15, 1905), 9-13.

167. ———, *Horizons.* Vol. 3. *In Silent Rooms.* [Compiled by] Patricia A. Guthrie, Anne Patricia Campbell, [and] C. Helen Pielmeier. Revised edition. [Boston]: Ginn and Co., [1970]. p. 70-93. illus. (Faith and Freedom Basic Readers)
———, *Independent Student Activities from Manual for Teaching.* p. 30-32.

———, *Manual for Horizons.* p. 283-295.
———, *Workbook and Tests to Accompany Horizons.* p. 59-60.

THE NAVAL TREATY

168. "The Adventure of the Naval Treaty," [Illustrated by Sidney Paget]. *The Strand Magazine,* 6, No. 34 (October 1893), 392-403; 6, No. 35 (November 1893), 459-468. (The Adventures of Sherlock Holmes, No. 23)

169. "The Naval Treaty," [Illustrated by W. H. Hyde]. *Harper's Weekly,* 37, No. 1921 (October 14, 1893), 978-980; 37, No. 1922 (October 21, 1893), 1006-1007, 1010. (The Adventures of Sherlock Holmes)

170. ———, *Pennsylvania Grit Story Companion* [Williamsport], 23, No. 25, Story Companion No. 540 (May 21, 1905), 1-8. illus.

THE ADVENTURE OF
THE NOBLE BACHELOR

171. "The Adventure of the Noble Bachelor," [Illustrated by Sidney Paget]. *The Strand Magazine,* 3, No. 16 (April 1892), 386-399. (The Adventures of Sherlock Holmes, No. 10)

172. ———. [New York: The Benjamin Co. for Flint Laboratories, 1970.] 32 p.
A promotional booklet distributed only to physicians in the U. S.

THE ADVENTURE OF
THE NORWOOD BUILDER

173. "The Adventure of the Norwood Builder," Illustrated by F. D. Steele. *Collier's, 32, No. 5 (October 31, 1903),* 16-18, 28-31. (The Return of Sherlock Holmes, No. 2)

174. ———, [Illustrated by Sidney Paget]. *The Strand Magazine,* 26, No. 155 (November 1903), 482-496. (The Return of Sherlock Holmes, No. 2)

175. ———. [New York]: Sunday *World* Fiction Section, [1911]. 15 p. illus.

176. ———, *Beacon Lights of Literature.* Book One. Edited by Rudolph W. Chamberlain and Edwin B. Richards. Syracuse, N.Y.: Iroquois Pub. Co., [c. 1931]. p. 85-110.
Includes a note on the author and story, fourteen questions and five exercises.

177. ———, *Prose and Poetry for Enjoyment.* Edited by H. Ward McGraw. Catholic edition edited by Julian L. Maline and

William J. McGucken. Illustrated by Guy Brown Wiser. Syracuse; Chicago; Dallas: The L. W. Singer Co., [1940]. p. 95-119. (The New Prose and Poetry Series, [3])

178. ———, ———. Edited by Elizabeth Frances Ansorge, Harriet Marcelia Lucas, Raymond F. McCoy, [and] Donald MacLean Tower. Design and illustrations by Guy Brown Wiser. Syracuse, N.Y.: The L. W. Singer Co., [1942]. p. 606-630.

THE ADVENTURE OF THE PRIORY SCHOOL

179. "The Adventure of the Priory School," Illustrated by Frederic Dorr Steele. *Collier's*, 32, No. 18 (January 30, 1904), 18-20, 25, 27-30. (The Return of Sherlock Holmes, No. 5)

180. ———, [Illustrated by Sidney Paget]. *The Strand Magazine*, 27, No. 158 (February 1904), 122-140. (The Return of Sherlock Holmes, No. 5)

181. ———. [New York]: Sunday *World* Fiction Section, May 7, 1911. 15 p. illus.

182. ———, *The Great Short Stories of Detection, Mystery and Horror*. Edited by Dorothy L. Sayers. London: Victor Gollancz Ltd., 1928. p. 178-207.
———, With title: *The Omnibus of Crime*. Edited by Dorothy L. Sayers. New York: Payson and Clarke Ltd., 1929. p. 161-190.
———, ———. New York: Harcourt, Brace & Co., 1929. p. 127-150. Reissued in 1961.

183. ———, *The Saint Detective Magazine*, 8, No. 5 (November 1957), 54-80.

184. ———, *30 Stories to Remember*. Selected by Thomas B. Costain and John Beecroft. Garden City, N.Y.: Doubleday & Co., [1962]. p. 547-568.

185. ———, *Tales of Detection and Mystery from "The Omnibus of Crime."* Edited by Dorothy L. Sayers. New York: Macfadden-Bartell Corp., 1962. p. 67-93. (Macfadden Books, No. 50-143)

186. ———, *My Favorite Mystery Stories*. Selected and edited by Maureen Daly. New York: Dodd, Mead & Co., [1966]. p. 86-128.

THE ADVENTURE OF THE RED CIRCLE

187. "The Adventure of the Red Circle: A Reminiscence of Sherlock Holmes," Illustrated by H. M. Brock & Joseph Simpson [Part I] and by Joseph Simpson [Part 2]. *The Strand Magazine*, 41, No. 243 (March 1911), 258-266; 41, No. 244 (April 1911), 428-434.

188. ———, *The Strand Magazine* [New York], 41, No. 243 (April 1911), 290-298; 41, No. 244 (May 1911), 472-478.

189. *The Adventure of the Red Circle*. The Boston Sunday *Post*, [1911]. 14 p. illus. (Masterpieces of Sherlock Holmes)

THE RED-HEADED LEAGUE

190. ["The Red-Headed League," [Illustrated by Sidney Paget]. *The Strand Magazine*, 2, No. 8 (August 1891), 190-204. (The Adventures of Sherlock Holmes, No. 2)

191. ———, *Library of the World's Best Literature: Ancient and Modern*. Charles Dudley Warner, editor. New York: R. S. Peale and J. A. Hill, Publishers, [1897]. Vol. 8, p. 4815-4838.

192. ———, ———. Memorial edition de luxe. New York: J. A. Hill & Co., [1902]. Vol. 12, p. 4815-4838.

193. ———, *The Lock and Key Library: Classic Mystery and Detective Stories*. Edited by Julian Hawthorne. New York: The Review of Reviews Co., 1909. Vol. 8, p. 87-113.

194. ———. Philadelphia: Royal Pub. Co., [190?] (The Sherlock Holmes Detective Library, No. 449)

195. ———. The Boston Sunday *Post*, [1911]. 14 p. illus. (Masterpieces of Sherlock Holmes)

196. ———, *The Warner Library: The World's Best Literature*. Editors: John W. Cunliffe [and] Ashley H. Thorndike. New York: Printed at the Knickerbocker Press for the Warner Library Co., 1917. Vol. 8, p. 4815-4838.

197. ———, *Modern Short Stories*. Edited, with introduction and notes by Frederick Houk Law. New York: The Century Co., [1918]. p. 164-191.

198. ———, *Short Stories of Various Types*. Edited, with an introduction and notes by Laura F. Freck. New York and Chicago: Charles E. Merrill Co., [1920]. p. 203-237. (Merrill's English Texts)

199. ———, *Great Detective Stories*. Edited by Joseph Lewis French. [Vol. 3] *From Costello to Stevenson*. New York: Lincoln MacVeagh; The Dial Press, 1924. p. 247-287. (The Dial Detective Library)

200. "The Adventure of the Red-Headed League," *Crime and Detection*. With an introduction by E. M. Wrong. Oxford

University Press, Humphrey Milford, 1926. p. 75-107.

201. "The Red-Headed League," *Fourteen Great Detective Stories*. Edited, with an introduction by Vincent Starrett. New York: The Modern Library, [1928]. p. 21-46.

202. ——, *Great Moments from Great Stories*. Edited, with notes and an introduction by Thomas L. Doyle. New York: Globe Book Co., [1928]. p. 219-243.

203. ——, *Great Detective Stories of the World*. Edited by Joseph Lewis French. New York: The Dial Press, 1929. Part 3, p. 247-287.

204. ——, ——. [N.p.]: Albert & Charles Boni, [c.1929]. Part 3, p. 247-287.

205. ——, *Representative Modern Short Stories*. Edited by Alexander Jessup. New York: The Macmillan Co., 1929. p. 507-524.

206. ——, *Interest Trails in Literature*, by Helene Willey Hartley. *Book Three*. New York; Chicago: Charles E. Merrill Co., [1936]. p. 7-36.
Includes ten questions at the end of the story.

207. ——, *Theme and Variation in the Short Story*. Edited by De Lancey Ferguson, Harold A. Blaine, [and] Wilson R. Dumble. New York: The Cordon Co., [1938]. p. 278-304.

208. ——, *Literature and Life*. Book Two, by Dudley Miles, Clarence Stratton and Robert C. Pooley. Chicago: Scott, Foresman and Co., [1941]. p. 36-51. illus. (Life-Reading Service)

209. ——, *The Pocket Book of Great Detectives: Seventeen American and English Masterpieces of Detective Fiction*. With an introduction by Alfred Hitchcock. Edited by Lee Wright. New York: Pocket Books, Inc., [May 1941]. p. 185-214. (No. 103)

210. "The Red-Headed League: A Sherlock Holmes Thriller," *The Chillers*, by Dorothy Sayers, W. W. Jacobs, Amelia B. Edwards, [and] A. Conan Doyle. Illustrated ed. Chicago: Royce Publishers, 1943. p. 87-128. (Quick Readers)

211. "The Red-Headed League," *The Golden Argosy: A Collection of the Most Celebrated Short Stories in the English Language*. Edited and with comments by Charles Grayson and Van H. Cartmell. New York: Dial Press, 1947. p. 147-166.

212. ——, *A Treasury of Short Stories*.

Edited by Bernardine Kielty. New York: Simon and Schuster, 1947. p. 169-185.

213. ——, *Fourteen Great Detective Stories*. Edited by Howard Haycraft. Revised ed. New York: The Modern Library, [1949]. p. 25-52.

214. ——, *Great Short Stories*. Edited by Wilbur Schramm. New York: Harcourt, Brace and Co., [1950]. p. 382-407.

215. ——, *Ellery Queen's Mystery Magazine*, 15 (March 1950), 93-112.
Selected by a Blue Ribbon Jury of experts as one of the twelve best detective short stories ever written.

216. ——, *Adventures in Reading*. Mercury Edition. [Edited by] Jacob M. Ross, Blanche Jennings Thompson, [and] Evan Lodge. New York; Chicago: Harcourt, Brace and Co., [1952]. p. 94-110. illus.

217. ——, *Great Mystery Stories*. Compiled by Eleanor M. Edwards. Illustrated by David Stone. New York: Hart Pub. Co., [1960]. p. 115-161. (A World-Famous Book, No. 202)

218. ——, *Alfred Hitchcock's Haunted Houseful*. Illustrated by Fred Banbery. New York: Random House, [1961]. p. 109-134.

219. ——, *Ellery Queen's Mystery Magazine*, 39 (January 1962), 59-78.

220. ——, *Masterpieces of Mystery & Detection*. Compiled by Rosamund Morris. New York: Hart Pub. Co., [1965]. p.189-222.

221. ——. [New York: The Benjamin Co. for Flint Laboratories, 1970.] 32 p.
A promotional booklet distributed only to physicians in the U. S.

222. ——. [Chicago: Bertha M. Clay, n. d.] 21, 104 p. (Atlantic Library, No. 42)
Also contains: The Dark House.

223. *The Red-Headed League: A Sherlock Holmes Story*. Cleveland, Ohio: The Arthur Westbrook Co., [n.d.] 23, 134 p. (American Detective Series, No. 6)
Also contains: The Great Hesper: A Novel, by Frank Barrett.

224. ——. Cleveland, Ohio: The Arthur Westbrook Co., [n.d.] 23, 134, 38 p. (American Detective Series, No. 6)
Also contains: The Great Hesper. - First three chapters of Sign.

THE REIGATE PUZZLE

225. "The Adventure of the Reigate Squires,"

[Illustrated by Sidney Paget]. *The Strand Magazine*, 5, No. 30 (June 1893), 601-612. (The Adventures of Sherlock Holmes, No. 19)

226. "The Reigate Puzzle," [Illustrated by W. H. Hyde]. *Harper's Weekly*, 37, No. 1904 (June 17, 1893), 574-576. (The Adventures of Sherlock Holmes)

227. ──────, *Mack's Pocket Detective Stories Magazine*, 1, No. 1 (November 1930), 17-36.

THE RESIDENT PATIENT

228. "The Adventure of the Resident Patient," [Illustrated by Sidney Paget]. *The Strand Magazine*, 6, No. 32 (August 1893), 128-138. (The Adventures of Sherlock Holmes, No. 21)

229. "The Resident Patient," [Illustrated by W. H. Hyde]. *Harper's Weekly*, 37, No. 1912 (August 12, 1893), 761-763. (The Adventures of Sherlock Holmes)

THE ADVENTURE OF
THE RETIRED COLOURMAN

230. "The Adventure of the Retired Colourman," Pictures by Frederic Dorr Steele. *Liberty*, 3, No. 33 (December 18, 1926), 7-11.

231. ──────, Illustrated by Frank Wiles. *The Strand Magazine*, 73, No. 433 (January 1927), 3-12.

232. ──────, *Los Angeles Times Sunday Magazine* (May 22, 1927), 16-18. illus.

A SCANDAL IN BOHEMIA

233. "A Scandal in Bohemia," [Illustrated by Sidney Paget]. *The Strand Magazine*, 2, No. 7 (July 1891), 61-75. (The Adventures of Sherlock Holmes, No. 1)

234. ──────. New York: Optimus Printing Co., [1895]. 32 p. (The Handy Classic Series, Choice Stories by Famous Authors, No. 13)

235. ──────. New York: George Munro's Sons, [1895]. 57, 39-95 p. (Seaside Library. Pocket ed., No. 2093)
Also contains: J. Habakuk Jephson's Statement. - The Great Keinplatz Experiment.

236. ──────. New York: George Munro's Sons, [1896]. 57, 39-95 p. (Munro's Library of Popular Novels, No. 133)
Contents same as above.

237. ──────. Chicago: Donohue, Henneberry & Co., [ca. 1897]. 191-229, 45-156 p. (Gem Edition)

Also contains: At the Green Dragon, by Beatrice Harraden.

238. *Beaten by Woman's Wit, or The Mystery of a Photograph*, by "Old Sleuth." Philadelphia, Pa.: Royal Pub. Co., 1903. 187-224, 9-54 p. (The Sherlock Holmes Detective Library, No. 426)
Contents: Scan. - A Tale of Three Lions, by H. Rider Haggard.

239. "A Scandal in Bohemia," *Pennsylvania Grit Story Companion* [Williamsport], 23, No. 19, Story Companion No. 534 (April 9, 1905), 9-14.

240. ──────, *Great Short Stories*. Edited by William Patten. Vol. 1. *Detective Stories*. New York: P. F. Collier & Son, [1906]. p. 235-261.

241. ──────, *The Lock and Key Library: Classic Mystery and Detective Stories*. Edited by Julian Hawthorne. New York: The Review of Reviews Co., 1909. Vol. 8, p. 61-87.

242. ──────. The Boston Sunday *Post*, [1911]. 11 p. (Masterpieces of Sherlock Holmes)

243. ──────, *Greatest Short Stories*. New York: P. F. Collier & Son, [1915]. Vol. 5, p. 179-214.

244. ──────, *Famous Detective Stories*. Edited by J. Walker McSpadden. New York: Thomas Y. Crowell Co., [1920]. p. 57-91.

245. ──────, *Masterpieces of Mystery in Four Volumes*. Edited by Joseph Lewis French. [Vol. 1] *Detective Stories*. Garden City, N.Y.: Doubleday, Page & Co., 1924. p. 164-199.

246. ──────, [Illustrations by Sidney Paget]. *The Strand Magazine*, 80, No. 477 (September 1930), 231-243.

247. ──────, *The Omnibus of Romance*. Edited by John Grove [John R. Colter]. New York: Dodd, Mead & Co., 1931. p. 467-488.

248. ──────, ──────. Edited by John Grove. New York: The Junior Literary Guild, Inc., 1931. p. 467-488.

249. ──────, *Great Love Stories by Famous Authors*. Edited by John Grove. New York: Halcyon House, [1931]. p. 467-488.

250. ──────, *Masterpieces of Mystery*. Edited by Joseph Lewis French. [Vol. 1] *Detective Stories*. Garden City, N.Y.: Garden City Pub. Co., [1937]. p. 164-199.

251. ──────, *Famous Mystery and Detective*

Stories. Edited by J. Walker McSpadden. New York: Blue Ribbon Books, [1938]. Part 2, p. 57-91.

252. ———, *For Men Only: A Collection of Short Stories.* Edited, with an introduction by James M. Cain. Cleveland and New York: The World Pub. Co., [1944]. p. 284-309.

253. ———, *With All My Love: An Anthology.* Compiled by R. M. Barrows. Chicago, Ill.: Consolidated Book Publishers, 1945. p. 32-51.

254. ———, Illustrated by William L. Marsh. *Playboy,* 1, No. 2 (January 1954), 22-23, 25-26, 28, 44, 46, 49.

255. ———, *Great Detective Stories.* Compiled by Rosamund Morris. Illustrated by Frank Kramer. New York: Hart Pub. Co., [1965]. p. 109-153. (Sunrise Library)

256. ———, Masterpieces of Mystery & Detection. Compiled by Rosamund Morris. New York: Hart Pub. Co., [1966]. p. 223-256.

257. ———. [Chicago: Bertha M. Clay, n.d.] 1-57, 71-106 p. (Atlantic Library, No. 41) Cover title: A Scandal in Bohemia or Caught by Sherlock Holmes.
   Cover title: A Scandal in Bohemia or Caught by Sherlock Holmes.

258. *A Scandal in Bohemia and Other Stories.* New York: The Happy Hour Library, Inc., [n.d.] 96 p.
   Also contains: The Ring of Thoth. - The Fall of the House of Usher.

259. *A Scandal in Bohemia.* New York: George Munro's Sons, Publishers, [n.d.] 57, 39-75 p. (The Victor Series of Paper Books, No. 67)
   Also contains: J. Habakuk Jephson's Statement.

260. ———. [Chicago: Max Stein, Publisher, n.d.] 57, 71-106 p. (Atlantic Library, No. 41)
   Cover title: A Scandal in Bohemia or Caught by Sherlock Holmes.
   Also contains: The Mail-Cart Robbery, by Mrs. Henry Wood.

261. *A Scandal in Bohemia: A Sherlock Holmes Story.* Cleveland, Ohio: The Arthur Westbrook Co., [n.d.] 188-224, 21-120 p. (American Detective Series, No. 5)
   Also contains: The Chadwick Case.

262. ———. Cleveland, Ohio: The Arthur Westbrook Co., [n.d.] 187-224, 21-120, 23, 31 p. (American Detective Series, No. 5)
   Also contains: The Chadwick Case. - RedH. - First four chapters and one page of chapter 5 of The Great Hesper, by Frank Barrett.

THE ADVENTURE OF THE SECOND STAIN

263. "The Adventure of the Second Stain," [Illustrated by Sidney Paget]. *The Strand Magazine,* 28, No. 168 (December 1904), 602-617. (The Return of Sherlock Holmes, No. 13)

264. ———, [Illustrated by Frederic Dorr Steele]. *Collier's,* 34, No. 18 (January 28, 1905), 13-15, 28-30. (The Return of Sherlock Holmes, No. 13)

265. ———. The Boston Sunday *Post,* [1911]. 14 p. illus. (Masterpieces of Sherlock Holmes)

266. ———. [New York]: Sunday *World* Fiction Section, [1911]. 15 p. illus.

THE ADVENTURE OF SHOSCOMBE OLD PLACE

267. "The Adventure of Shoscombe Old Place," Pictures by Frederic Dorr Steele. *Liberty,* 3, No. 44 (March 5, 1927), 39, 41-42, 45-46, 51, 53.

268. ———, Illustrated by Frank Wiles. *The Strand Magazine,* 73, No. 436 (April 1927), 316-327.

269. ———, *Los Angeles Times Sunday Magazine* (May 29, 1927), 16-17.

THE SIGN OF THE FOUR

270. "The Sign of the Four," [Illustration by H. D.] *Lippincott's Monthly Magazine* [London], 45, No. 266 (February 1890), 147-223.

271. "The Sign of the Four; or, The Problem of the Sholtos," [Illustration by H. D.] *Lippincott's Monthly Magazine* [Philadelphia], 45, No. 266 (February 1890), 147-223.

272. "The Sign of Four," [Illustrated by R.] *The Bristol Observer* (May 17, 24, 31; June 7, 14, 21, 28; July 5, 1890).

273. ———, *The Hampshire Telegraph & Sussex Chronicle* (July 5, 12, 19, 26; August 2, 9, 16, 23, 30, 1890).

274. ———, *The Birmingham Weekly Mercury* (August 2, 9, 16, 23, 30; September 6, 13, 20, 1890).

275. "The Sign of the Four," *Five Complete Novels by Famous Authors, from Lippincott's Monthly Magazine, with Short Stories, Essays (Critical and Biographical), Poetry and Articles on Miscellaneous Subjects.* London, New York and

Melbourne: Ward, Lock & Co., [1890]. p. 147-223.

276. ———, *Six Complete Novels by Famous Authors, from Lippincott's Monthly Magazine, with Short Stories, Essays (Critical and Biographical), Poetry and Articles on Miscellaneous Subjects.* London, New York and Melbourne: Ward, Lock & Co., [1890]. p. 147-223.

277. ———, *Lippincott's Monthly Magazine.* Volume XLV, January-June 1890, Being Volume I of the Special English Edition. London: Ward, Lock & Co.; Philadelphia: J. B. Lippincott Co., 1890. p. 147-223.

278. ———, *Lippincott's Monthly Magazine: A Popular Journal of General Literature, Science, and Politics.* Volume XLV, January to June, 1890. Philadelphia: J. B. Lippincott Co., 1890. p. 147-223.

279. *The Sign of Four.* London: Spencer Blackett, 1890. 283, 32 p. of advertisements. Frontispiece by Charles Kerr.
On spine: Spencer Blackett's Standard Library.
    Contents: 1. The Science of Deduction. - 2. The Statement of the Case. - 3. In Quest of a Solution. - 4. The Story of the Bald-Headed Man. - 5. The Tragedy of Pondicherry Lodge. - 6. Sherlock Holmes Gives a Demonstration. - 7. The Episode of the Barrel. - 8. The Baker Street Irregulars. - 9. A Break in the Chain. - 10. The End of the Islander. - 11. The Great Agra Treasure. - 12. The Strange Story of Jonathan Small.

280. ———. London: Spencer Blackett, 1890. 283 p.
    On spine: Griffith Farran & Cos. Standard Library.

281. ———. New York : P. F. Collier, Publishers, 1891. 124 p. (Once a Week Library, 2, No. 16, March 15, 1891)
    Also contains: The Siege of Sunda Gunge.

282. ———. Copyright edition. Leipzig: Bernhard Tauchnitz, 1891. 278 p. (Tauchnitz Edition, Vol. 2698) (A. Conan Doyle, No. 1)

283. ———. London: George Newnes, Ltd., 1892. 283 p.
    On spine: Griffin Farran.

284. ———. Second edition. London: George Newnes, Ltd., 1892. 283 p.

285. ———. Third edition. London: George Newnes, Ltd., 1893. 283 p.

286. ———. Philadelphia: J. B. Lippincott Co., 1893. 283 p.
    First American edition.

287. ———. Philadelphia: J. B. Lippincott Co., [October 1893]. 283 p. (Lippincott's Select Novels, No. 150)

288. ———. New edition. London: George Newnes, Ltd., 1894. 283, 8 p. of advertisements.

289. "The Sign of the Four," *The Surgeon of Gaster Fell*, by A. Conan Doyle. New York: M. J. Ivers & Co., 1895. 53, 176, 12 p. of advertisements. (American Series, No. 362)

290. ———. New York: George Munro's Sons, [March 9, 1896]. 109, 19 p. of advertisements. (Munro's Library of Popular Novels, No. 134)

291. *The Sign of the Four: A Novel.* New York: Street & Smith, Publishers, [Jan. 21, 1898]. 176, [16] p. of advertisements. (Arrow Library, No. 17)

292. *The Sign of Four.* London: George Newnes, Ltd., 1899. 128 p. (The Sixpenny Series)

293. ———. Philadelphia: J. B. Lippincott Co., 1901. 283 p.

294. ———. Souvenir edition. London: George Newnes, Ltd., 1901. 285, 32 p. of advertisements.

295. ———. Souvenir edition. London: George Newnes, Ltd., 1902. 285 p.

296. ———. Souvenir edition. [Illustrated by F. H. Townsend.] London: George Newnes, Ltd., [1903]. 285 p.

297. "The Sign of the Four," *Great Short Stories.* Edited by William Patten. Vol. 1. *Detective Stories.* New York: P. F. Collier & Son, [1906]. p. 119-234.

298. ———. New York: Hurst and Co., Publishers, [n.d.] 176 p. (The Hawthorne Library, No. 169, Tri-Weekly, March 4, 190?)

299. ———. Philadelphia: Royal Pub. Co., [190-?] (The Sherlock Holmes Detective Library, No. 450)

300. *The Sign of Four.* London and Edinburgh: T. Nelson & Sons, [December 1912]. (Sevenpenny Library Edition)
    Frontispiece by Harold C. Earnshaw.

301. ———. Philadelphia: J. B. Lippincott Co., 1913. 283 p.

302. ———. London: John Murray, 1917. 154 p.

303. ———. [London]: John Murray, [May

1922]. 285 p. (Murray's Fiction Library)
"Reprinted (Cheap Edition)."

304. *The Sign of the Four,* by A. Conan Doyle. With *Markheim,* by Robert Louis Stevenson. [Racine, Wis.: Whitman Pub. Co., 1922.] 189 p.

305. "The Sign of Four," Illustrated by Frederick R. Reinert. *Police Stories* [Police Pub. Co., New York], 4, No. 4 (April 1926), 10-13, 64, 66, 68; continued.

306. *The Sign of Four,* by A. Conan Doyle. *The Big Bow Mystery,* by Israel Zangwill. New York: Charles Scribner's Sons, 1928. 306 p. (The S. S. Van Dine Detective Library)

307. *The Sign of Four.* London: Gryphon Books Ltd., [1949]. 153 p.

308. ———. London: Royle Publications Ltd., in association with Gryphon Books Ltd., [1949]. 153 p.

309. "Introducing Sherlock Holmes," Illustrated by William L. Marsh. *Playboy,* 1, No. 1 (December 1953), 22-25.
Chapter 1. The Science of Deduction.

310. *The Sign of the Four.* [Abridged edition] Illustrated by Leonard Vosburgh. Under the general editorship of Elizabeth Fowler. New York: Hart Pub. Co., [1960]. 191 p. col. illus. (A World-Famous Book, No. 207)

311. ———. [Abridged edition] Illustrated by Leonard Vosburgh. New York: Hart Pub. Co., [1962]. 191 p. illus. (Sunrise Library)

312. *The Sign of Four.* With an introduction by A. E. Smith and illustrations by Anne Linton. [London]: John Murray, [1961]. xiii, 162 p. (The School Library of Famous Books)
Includes Notes and Exercises, p. 157-162.

313. ———. London: John Murray, [1962]. 144 p.

314. ———, *First of the Great Detective Stories.* Edited by John T. Yount. Volume I, by Edgar Allan Poe [and] Sir Arthur Conan Doyle. San Angelo, Texas: Archive Publishers, 1971. p. 119-234.

315. *The Sign of the Four.* New York: William L. Allison Co., [n.d.] 176 p.
On spine: New Albion.

316. ———. New York: W. L. Allison Co., [n.d.] 212 p.
On cover and spine: Arundel Edition.

317. ———. Philadelphia: Henry Altemus, [n.d.] 176 p.

318. ———. New York and Boston: H. M. Caldwell Co., [n.d.] 189 p.

Frontispiece of Dr. A. Conan Doyle and four anonymous illustrations.

319. *Sherlock Holmes and the Great "Agra" Treasure; or, The Sign of the Four.* [Chicago: Bertha M. Clay, n.d.] 109 p. (Atlantic Library, No. 43)

320. *The Sign of the Four.* Chicago: W. B. Conkey Co., [n.d.] 202 p.
Frontispiece of A. Conan Doyle.

321. ———. Chicago: W. B. Conkey Co., [n.d.] 202 p. (Amaranth Series, No. 131)

322. ———. Chicago: W. B. Conkey Co., [n.d.] 176 p.

323. ———. Chicago and New York: M. A. Donohue & Co., [n.d.] 189 p. (Flashlight Detective Series, No. 44)

324. ———. Chicago and New York: M. A. Donohue & Co., [n.d.] 189 p. (The Modern Authors' Library)

325. ———. New York: The Edward Pub. Co., [n.d.] 212 p.

326. ———. New York: The Federal Book Co., Publishers, [n.d.] 176 p.

327. *The Sign of Four.* New York: Grosset & Dunlap, Publishers, [n.d.] 283 p.
On spine: The Sign of Four: A Sherlock Holmes Story.

328. *The Sign of the Four: A Sherlock Holmes Detective Story.* Girard, Kansas: Haldeman-Julius Publications, [n.d.] 84 p. (Big Blue Book, No. B-31)

329. *The Sign of the Four.* Chicago and New York: The Henneberry Co., [n.d.] 202 p.
Frontispiece of Dr. A. Conan Doyle and three illustrations by Charles A. Cox.

330. ———. New York: Hurst & Co., [n.d.] 176 p.

331. ———. [New York]: The F. M. Lupton Pub. Co., [n.d.] 176 p. (The White Series)

332. ———. New York: F. M. Lupton, Publisher, [n.d.] 64 p. (The Arm Chair Library)
Also contains four stories by other authors.

333. ———. New York: The Mershon Co., Publishers, [n.d.] iii, 189 p.

334. ———. New York: George Munro's Sons, Publishers, [n.d.] 109 p. (The Seaside Library, Pocket Edition, No. 2094)

335. ———. New York: George Munro's Sons, Publishers, [n.d.] 109, 122 p.

Individual Tales

On spine: The American Edition.
Also contains: The Captain of the "Pole-Star". - J. Habakuk Jephson's Statement. - The Great Keinplatz Experiment. - The Man from Archangel.

336. ———. New York: George Munro's Sons, [n.d.] 109, 122 p. (The Majestic Series, No. 395)
Contents same as above.

337. *The Sign of Four.* London and Edinburgh, Paris: Thomas Nelson and Sons, [n.d.] 286 p. (Nelson's 1 / 6 Net Library)

338. ———. London: George Newnes, Ltd., [n.d.] 124 p. (Newnes's Copyright Novels)
Cover illustrated by Norman Keene.

339. ———. London: George Newnes, Ltd., [n.d.] 78 p. (The Penny Library of Famous Books, No. 9)

340. ———. London: George Newnes, Ltd., [n.d.] 128 p. (Newnes' Popular Sixpenny Novels)

341. ———. London: George Newnes, Ltd., [n.d.] 124 p.
Cover illustrated by Herbert Cole and dated 1903.

342. *The Sign of the Four.* New York: J. S. Ogilvie Pub. Co., [n.d.] 176 p. (Eureka Detective Series, No. 19)

343. ———. New York: J. S. Ogilvie Pub. Co., [n.d.] 176 , 16 p. of advertisements. (Sunset Series, No. 261)

344. ———. New York: Optimus Printing Co., [n.d.] 176 p.

345. ———. Baltimore: I. & M. Ottenheimer, [n.d.] (The Sherlock Holmes Detective Library, No. 450)

346. ———. Philadelphia: Royal Pub. Co., [n.d.] (The Drama Series, No. 119)

347. ———. Philadelphia: Royal Pub. Co., [n.d.] 212 p. (The Sherlock Holmes Library, No. 204)

348. ———. New York & Chicago: Siegel-Cooper Co., [n.d.] 176 p.

349. ———. New York; Chicago: Siegel, Cooper Co., [n.d.] 193 p.
On spine: Geo. M. Hill.

350. ———. Philadelphia: Strawbridge & Clothier, [n.d.] 189 p.

351. ———. New York and London: Street & Smith Pub. Co., [n.d.] 176 p.
On cover: Select Fiction Library.

352. *The Sign of the Four: A Novel.* New York and London: Street & Smith, Publishers, [n.d.] 176 p.

353. ———. New York and London: Street & Smith, Publishers, [n.d.] 176, 42 p.
Also contains: A Night Among the Nihilists. - Cyprian Overbeck Wells.

354. *The Sign of the Four.* Chicago: Thompson & Thomas, [n.d.] 176 p.

355. ———. Cleveland, Ohio: The Arthur Westbrook Co., [n.d.] 212, 11 p. of advertisements. (American Detective Series, No. 7)

356. ———. Cleveland, Ohio: The Arthur Westbrook Co., [n.d.] 212, 44 p. (American Detective Series, No. 7)
Also contains: The Giant Detective in France.

SILVER BLAZE

357. "The Adventure of Silver Blaze," [Illustrated by Sidney Paget.] *The Strand Magazine,* 4, No. 24 (December 1892), 645-660. (The Adventures of Sherlock Holmes, No. 13)

358. ———, [Illustrated by W. H. Hyde]. *Harper's Weekly,* 37, No. 1888 (February 25, 1893), 181-184. (The Adventures of Sherlock Holmes)

359. "Silver Blaze," *Pennsylvania Grit Story Companion* [Williamsport], 23, No. 5, Story Companion No. 520 (January 1, 1905), 1-7. illus.

360. ———. *The Detective in Fiction: A Posse of Eight.* Selected from the stories of well-known writers and introduced by E. A. Seaborne. London: G. Bell & Sons Ltd., 1931. Chap. 2, p. 82-113. (Bell's English Language and Literature Series)

361. ———, *Sleuths: Twenty-Three Great Detectives of Fiction and Their Best Stories.* Edited by Kenneth Macgowan. New York: Harcourt, Brace and Co., [1931]. p. 37-61.

362. ———, *Hidden Treasures in Literature.* Book One. [Edited by] Luella B. Cook, George W. Norvell, [and] William A. McCall. New York; Chicago: Harcourt, Brace and Co., [1934]. p. 150-171.

363. ———, *Sporting Blood: The Great Detective Stories.* Edited by Ellery Queen. Introduction by Grantland Rice. Boston: Little, Brown and Co., 1942. p. 3-27.

364. ———, *The Great Sports Detective Stories: Sporting Blood.* Edited by Ellery

Queen. Garden City, N.Y.: Blue Ribbon Books, [1946]. p. 3-27.

365. ———, *The Great Horse Omnibus: From Homer to Hemingway,* by Thurston Macauley. Introduction by Bing Crosby. Chicago; New York: Ziff-Davis Pub. Co., 1949. p. 59-87.

366. ———, *Great Stories from the World of Sport.* Edited by Peter Schwed and Herbert Warren Wind. New York: Simon and Schuster, 1958. Vol. 1, p. 283-304.

367. ———, ———. Edited by Peter Schwed and Herbert Warren Wind. London: Heinemann, [1960]. p. 83-104.

368. *Silver Blaze — From the Memoirs of Sherlock Holmes.* [New York: Springbok Editions, 1966.] 16 p.
   With a separately published solution. 3 p. Included in Springbok Circular Jigsaw Puzzle, C932 (item 4922).

369. "The Adventure of Silver Blaze," *Ten Tales of Detection.* Chosen and introduced by Roger Lancelyn Green. With colour frontispiece and line drawings in the text by Ian Ribbons. London: J. M. Dent & Sons Ltd.; New York: E. P. Dutton & Co., [1967]. p. 35-60. (Children's Illustrated Classics, No. 72)

THE ADVENTURE OF
THE SIX NAPOLEONS

370. "The Adventure of the Six Napoleons," Illustrated by Frederic Dorr Steele. *Collier's,* 33, No. 5 (April 30, 1904), 14-15, 28-31. (The Return of Sherlock Holmes, No. 8)

371. ———, [Illustrated by Sidney Paget]. *The Strand Magazine,* 27, No. 161 (May 1904), 482-495. (The Return of Sherlock Holmes, No. 8)

372. ———. [New York]: Sunday *World* Fiction Section, [1911] . 15 p. illus.

373. ———. Reprinted from the sixty-two novels, novelettes and short stories that make up the ten volumes of Sir Arthur Conan Doyle's great stories. New York: P. F. Collier & Son, [1917?]. [209]-236 p.

374. ———, *Exploring Life Through Literature,* by Robert C. Pooley, Irvin C. Poley, Jean Cravens Leyda, [and] Lillian J. Zellhoefer. Chicago: Scott, Foresman and Co., [1951]. p. 12-26. illus. (America Reads, 2)

375. ———, *Masterpieces of Surprise.* Compiled by James L. Monahan. New York: Hart Pub. Co., [1966]. p. 203-233.

THE ADVENTURE OF
THE SOLITARY CYCLIST

376. "The Adventure of the Solitary Cyclist," Illustrated by Frederic Dorr Steele. *Collier's,* 32, No. 13 (December 26, 1903), 16-17, 20-21. (The Return of Sherlock Holmes, No. 4)

377. ———, [Illustrated by Sidney Paget]. *The Strand Magazine,* 27, No. 157 (January 1904), 2-14. (The Return of Sherlock Holmes, No. 4)

378. ———. [New York]: Sunday *World* Fiction Section, [1911]. 15 p. illus.

THE ADVENTURE OF
THE SPECKLED BAND

379. "The Adventure of the Speckled Band," [Illustrated by Sidney Paget]. *The Strand Magazine,* 3, No. 14 (February 1892), 142-157. (The Adventures of Sherlock Holmes, No. 8)

380. ———, *Great Short-Stories.* With introductory essays on the great story writers by William J. Dawson and Coningsby W. Dawson. Two volumes in one. New York and London: Harper & Brothers, [1910]. Vol. 2, p. 89-122.

381. ———, *The Short Story: A Technical and Literary Study,* by Ethan Allen Cross. Chicago: A. C. McClurg & Co., 1914. p. 241-276.

382. ———, *Progressive Readings in Prose.* Edited by Rudolph W. Chamberlain and Joseph S. G. Bolton. Garden City, N.Y.: Doubleday, Page & Co., 1923. p. 313-327.

383. ———, *Short Stories.* Edited by H. C. Schweikert. New York: Harcourt, Brace and Co., [1925]. p. 299-325.

384. ———, Drawings by John Alan Maxwell. *The Golden Book Magazine,* 12, No. 72 (December 1930), 85-94, 107, 110-111.

385. ———, *Study and Appreciation of the Short Story: With Representative Readings,* by Roy Ivan Johnson, Esther Marshall Cowan, [and] Mary Safford Peacock. New York: Silver, Burdett and Co., [1930]. p. 144-171.

386. ———, *A Book of the Short Story.* Selected and edited . . . by E. A. Cross. New York: American Book Co., [1934]. p. 520-540.

387. ———, *A Century of Thrillers: From Poe to Arlen.* With a foreword by James Agate. [Illustrated by MacKay.] London: Daily Express Publications, 1934. p. 137-163.

Individual Tales

388. ——, *The Mystery Book.* Edited by H. Douglas Thompson. [Illustrated by Ernest Wallcousins.] London: Odhams Press Ltd., [1934]. p. 464-489.

389. ——, *Short Stories.* Edited by H. C. Schweikert. Enlarged edition. New York; Chicago: Harcourt, Brace and Co., [1934]. p. 351-377.

390. ——, *Century of Thrillers.* New York: President Press, [1937]. Vol. 1, p. 44-68.

391. ——, *The Boys' Book of Great Detective Stories.* Edited by Howard Haycraft. New York and London: Harper & Brothers, [1938]. p. 19-46.

392. ——, *Contemporary Literature.* [Edited by] Russell Blankenship, Rollo L. Lyman, [and] Howard C. Hill. New York: Charles Scribner's Sons, [1938]. p. 930-953.

393. ——, *The Bedside Book of Famous British Stories.* Edited by Bennett A. Cerf and Henry C. Moriarty. With an introduction by Bliss Perry. New York: Random House, [1940]. p. 343-364.

394. ——, ——. New York: The Literary Guild of America, Inc., [1940]. p. 343-364.

395. ——, *Prose and Poetry for Appreciation.* Edited by Elizabeth Frances Ansorge, Harriet Marcelia Lucas, Raymond F. McCoy, [and] Donald MacLean Tower. Design and illustrations by Guy Brown Wiser. Syracuse, N.Y.: The L. W. Singer Co., [1942]. p. 670-696. (The Prose and Poetry Series)

396. ——, Condensed from *The Complete Sherlock Holmes. The Reader's Digest,* 41, No. 243 (July 1942), 139-153.

397. ——, *Short Stories: A Collection for High School Students.* Edited by Henry I. Christ [and] Jerome Shostak. New York: Oxford Book Co., [1948]. p. 22-51.
    Includes an editorial introduction, vocabulary, words to learn, objective questions, and discussion questions.

398. ——, *An Anthology of Famous British Stories.* Edited by Bennett A. Cerf and Henry C. Moriarty. With an introduction by Bliss Perry. [1st Modern Library Giant edition.] New York: The Modern Library, [1952]. p. 343-364.

399. ——, *The Family Book of Best Loved Short Stories.* Edited by Leland W. Lawrence [Lawrence Lamb]. Garden City, N.Y.: Hanover House, [1954]. p. 355-378.

400. ——, *Treasury of Snake Lore.* Edited by Brandt Aymar. New York: Greenberg: Publisher, [1956]. p. 177-196.

401. ——, *Stories to Remember.* Edited by Joyce McMaster. Vancouver: The Copp Clark Pub. Co., [1957]. p. 41-71.

402. ——, *Favorite Short Stories.* Selected and edited by Lewis G. Sterner. New York: Globe Book Co., [1958]. p. 233-273. illus.
    A collection of short stories for high school students that also contains a section at the end of each story on Vocabulary, Questions for Comprehension, and Doing Things.

403. ——, *A Book of Stories.* Brother H. Raphael, Editor. New York: The Macmillan Co., [1960]. p. 146-173.

404. "The Speckled Band," *Junior Catholic Messenger,* 27, No. 15 (January 6, 1961), 6-7; 27, No. 16 (January 13, 1961), 6-7; 27, No. 17 (January 20, 1961), 6-7.
    A simplified version for middle grades.

405. ——, *Great Suspense Stories.* Compiled by Rosamund Morris. Illustrated by Raymond Burns. New York: Hart Pub. Co., [1962]. p. 9-51. (Sunrise Library)

406. "The Adventure of the Speckled Band," *The Boys' Book of Great Detective Stories.* Edited by Howard Haycraft. New York and Evanston: Harper & Row, [September 1965]. p. 19-46.

407. "The Speckled Band," *Masterpieces of Horror.* Compiled by Rosamund Morris. New York: Hart Pub. Co., [1966]. p. 57-91.

408. *The Adventure of the Speckled Band.* [New York]: Associated Educational Services Corp., [1967]. 32 p. (Papertexts) (30078 ES / 2)
    Includes Ideas Worth Discussing, Vocabulary Review, and Suggested Composition Activities.

409. "Dr. Watson Records Another Adventure: Beginning of 'The Speckled Band,' from Adventures of Sherlock Holmes," *An Editor's Treasury: A Continuing Anthology of Prose, Verse, and Literary Curiosa.* Edited by Herbert R. Mayes. New York: Atheneum, 1968. Part 1, Vol. 1, p. 521-522

410. "The Adventure of the Speckled Band," Illustrations by Alan Magee. *Scholastic Scope,* 13, No. 10 (November 16, 1970), 8-11, 22.
    A simplified dramatization for high school students.

THE STOCKBROKER'S CLERK

411. "The Adventure of the Stockbroker's Clerk," [Illustrated by Sidney Paget]. *The Strand Magazine,* 5, No. 27 (March 1893), 281-291. (The Adventures of Sherlock Holmes, No. 16)

412. "The Adventure of the Stock-Broker's Clerk," [Illustrated by W. H. Hyde]. *Harper's Weekly*, 37, No. 1890 (March 11, 1893), 225-227. (The Adventures of Sherlock Holmes)

413. "The Stockbroker's Clerk," *Great English Short Stories*. Edited by Lewis Melville [Lewis Saul Benjamin] and Reginald Hargreaves. New York: The Viking Press, 1930. p. 717-732.

414. ———, ———. New York: Blue Ribbon Books, Inc., [1933]. p. 717-732.

A STUDY IN SCARLET

415. "A Study in Scarlet," *The Reminiscences of John H. Watson, M.D.* [London, 1887?]
   A book so scarce that it has yet to be located; it is mentioned in *Beeton's Christmas Annual* for 1887. The first of Trevor H. Hall's *Ten Literary Studies* (item 2754) is devoted to this and the second appearance, in *Beeton's*, of Dr. Watson's first recorded adventure of Sherlock Holmes.

416. ———. Containing Also Two Original Plays for Home Performance. I. "Food for Powder," by R. André. II. "The Four-Leaved Shamrock," by C. J. Hamilton. With Numerous Original Engravings, by D. H. Friston, R. André, and Matt Stretch. London; New York: Ward, Lock and Co., [1887], 168 p. (Beeton's Christmas Annual, No. 28)

The cover of Beeton's Christmas Annual *for 1887, in which appeared the first Sherlock Holmes story, "A Study in Scarlet."* (415).

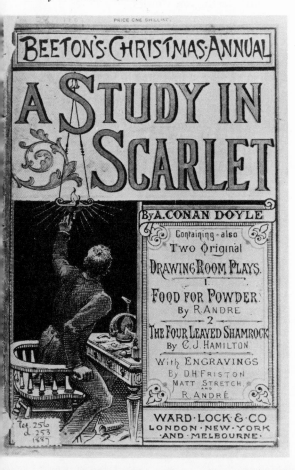

Contents: Part I. Being a reprint from the reminiscences of John H. Watson, M.D., late of the Army Medical Department: 1. Mr. Sherlock Holmes. - 2. The Science of Deduction. - 3. The Lauriston Gardens Mystery. - 4. What John Rance Had to Tell. - 5. Our Advertisement Brings a Visitor. - 6. Tobias Gregson Shows What He Can Do. - 7. Light in the Darkness. - Part II. The Country of the Saints: 1. On the Great Alkali Plain. - 2. The Flowers of Utah. - 3. John Ferrier Talks with the Prophet. - 4. A Flight for Life. - 5. The Avenging Angels. - 6. A Continuation of the Reminiscences of John Watson, M.D. - 7. The Conclusion.

417. ———. London; New York: Ward, Lock and Co., 1888. 169 p.
   Includes a Publisher's Preface and six original illustrations by the author's father, Charles Doyle.
   First separate edition.

418. ———. London; New York: Ward, Lock & Co., 1888. 169, 155, 134, 160, 196 p.
   Also contains four other stories by various authors.

419. ———. Philadelphia: J. B. Lippincott Co., 1890. 214 p. (Lippincott's Series of Select Novels, No. 107)
   First American edition.

420. ———. A new edition. With forty illustrations by Geo. Hutchinson. London, New York, and Melbourne: Ward, Lock, Bowden & Co., 1891. vii, 224, [24] p. of advertisements.

421. *A Study in Scarlet: The First Book About Sherlock Holmes.* London, Melbourne and Toronto: Ward, Lock & Co., [ca. 1892]. 255 p.
   Frontispiece by Geo. Hutchinson.
   Includes a Publishers' Note and an introductory note entitled "Mr. Sherlock Holmes" by Dr. Joseph Bell.

422. *A Study in Scarlet: A Detective Story.* A new edition. With forty illustrations by Geo. Hutchinson. Port Sunlight, near Birkenhead: Lever Brothers, Ltd., [ca. 1893]. 224 p.

423. *A Study in Scarlet.* Illustrated [by George Hutchinson]. Philadelphia: J. B. Lippincott Co., 1893. 214 p.

424. ———. New York: F. M. Lupton, April 22, 1893. 61 p. (The Arm Chair Library, No. 16)
   Also contains: Hinton Hall, by Mrs. May Agnes Fleming.

425. ———. A new edition, with a note on Sherlock Holmes by Dr. Joseph Bell, and forty illustrations by Geo. Hutchinson. London; New York; Melbourne: Ward, Lock & Bowden, Ltd., 1893. xx, 224 p.

A STUDY IN SCARLET.

PART I.

(*Being a reprint from the reminiscences of* John H. Watson, M.D., *late of the Army Medical Department.*)

CHAPTER I.

MR. SHERLOCK HOLMES.

 N the year 1878 I took my degree of Doctor of Medicine of the University of London, and proceeded to Netley to go through the course prescribed for surgeons in the army. Having completed my studies there, I was duly attached to the Fifth Northumberland Fusiliers as Assistant Surgeon. The regiment was stationed in India at the time, and before I could join it, the second Afghan war had broken out. On landing at Bombay, I learned that my corps had advanced through the passes, and was already deep in the enemy's country. I followed, however, with many other officers who were in the same situation as myself, and succeeded in reaching Candahar in safety, where I found my regiment, and at once entered upon my new duties.

The campaign brought honours and promotion to many, but for me it had nothing but misfortune and disaster. I was removed from my brigade and attached to the Berkshires, with whom I served at the fatal battle of Maiwand. There I was struck on the shoulder by a Jezail bullet, which shattered the bone and grazed the subclavian artery. I should have fallen into the hands of the murderous Ghazis had it not been for the devotion and courage shown by Murray, my orderly, who threw me across a pack-horse, and succeeded in bringing me safely to the British lines.

Worn with pain, and weak from the prolonged hardships which I

1

Frontispiece and opening page of "A Study in Scarlet" in Beeton's Christmas Annual *for 1887* (**415**). *Photograph courtesy of The House of El Dieff, Inc., New York.*

426. ———. With a note on Sherlock Holmes by Dr. Joseph Bell. Illustrated [by George Hutchinson]. London and Melbourne: Ward, Lock & Co., [1893]. xx, 224, 14 p. of advertisements.

427. ———. New York: George Munro's Sons, Publishers, [October 16, 1895]. 177 p. (Munro's Library of Popular Novels, No. 14)

428. *A Study in Scarlet: A Novel.* New York: Optimus Printing Co., [1895]. 175 p.

429. ———. Philadelphia: Strawbridge & Clothier, [1895]. iii, 216 p.

430. *A Study in Scarlet.* Illustrated by James Greig. London: Ward, Lock & Bowden, Ltd., 1895. 64 p.
"Issued as a Supplement to the Windsor Magazine, Xmas, 1895."

431. ———. Chicago: Donohue, Henneberry & Co., [1896]. 198 p. (The Modern Authors' Library, No. 16. Issued Tri-weekly, February 21, 1896)

432. ———. New edition, with a note on Sherlock Holmes by Dr. Joseph Bell, and forty illustrations by George Hutchinson. London, New York and Melbourne: Ward, Lock & Bowden, Ltd., [1896]. xx, 224, 10 p. of advertisements.

433. ———. New York: George Munro's Sons, [April 12, 1898]. 177, 173-233 p. (Royal Series, No. 44)
Also contains: Cyprian Overbeck Wells. - John Barrington Cowles.

434. ———. New York: Prudential Book Co., 1899. 128 p. (The Brookfield Series, No. 1)

435. ———. With a note on Sherlock Holmes by Dr. Joseph Bell. Illustrated by George Hutchinson. London: Ward, Lock & Co., [1901]. xx, 224, [12] p. of advertisements.

436. ———. Souvenir edition. [Illustrated by George Hutchinson and James Greig.] London: George Newnes, Ltd., 1902. xx, 224 p.

437. ———. With a note on Sherlock Holmes by Dr. Joseph Bell. Illustrated by George Hutchinson. London: Ward, Lock and Co., [1903?] 96 p.

438. ———. Souvenir edition. [Illustrated by George Hutchinson and James Greig.] London: George Newnes, Ltd., 1904. 224 p.

439. ———. London: George Newnes, Ltd., 1905. xx, 224 p.

440. *A Study in Scarlet: A Novel.* New York:

A. L. Burt, [190-?] 365 p. (The Home Library)

441. *A Study in Scarlet.* Philadelphia: Royal Pub. Co., [190-?] (The Sherlock Holmes Detective Library, No. 420)

442. *A Study in Scarlet: The First Book About Sherlock Holmes.* Illustrated [by George Hutchinson]. London, Melbourne and Toronto: Ward, Lock & Co., 1911. xx, 224, 16 p. of advertisements.

443. ———. London and Melbourne: Ward, Lock & Co., 1920. 255 p.

444. *A Study in Scarlet: A Sherlock Holmes Detective Story.* Girard, Kansas: Haldeman-Julius Publications, [192-?] 88 p. (Big Blue Book, No. B-35)

445. "The Avengers," *Tales of Terror.* Edited by Joseph L. French. Boston: Small, Maynard & Co., [1925]. p. 172-224.
Contains chapters 1-5 of part 2: The Country of the Saints.

446. "A Study in Scarlet," *Types of English Fiction.* Edited by Hardin Craig and John W. Dodds. New York: The Macmillan Co., 1940. p. 650-685.
Contains an introduction; chapters 3, 6, and 7 of part 1; chapter 7 of part 2; and brief summaries of other chapters.

447. ———, *Readings for Our Times,* by Harold Blodgett and Burges Johnson. Boston: Ginn and Co., [1942]. p. 6-95.

448. ———, *Beeton's Christmas Annual,* No. 28 (1887), 1-95. [Morristown, N. J.: The Baker Street Irregulars, 1960.]
A facsimile edition of 500 copies produced jointly by Edgar W. Smith and Lord Donegall. Includes a Publishers' Note, dated Christmas 1960, by Mr. Smith.
Reviews: SHJ, 5, No. 1 (Winter 1960), 2-3 (Lord Donegall); SHJ, 8, No. 4 (Summer 1968), 106 (Lord Donegall).

449. ———. London: John Murray, [1967]. 143 p.

450. *A Study in Scarlet: A Novel.* New York: William L. Allison Co., [n.d.] 188 p.
On cover and spine: Arundel Edition.

451. *A Study in Scarlet.* New York: American Publishers Corp., [n.d.] 213, 13 p. of advertisements. (Delphic Series, No. 91)

452. *A Study in Scarlet: A Sherlock Holmes Story.* London: Brown, Watson Ltd., [n.d.] 159 p. (Digit Books, No. R604)

453. *A Study in Scarlet: A Novel.* New York: A. L. Burt Co., [n.d.] 365 p.
Frontispiece by J. Watson Davis.

454. *A Study in Scarlet.* New York: Thomas Y. Crowell & Co., [n.d.] 213 p.
Frontispiece of Sir Arthur Conan Doyle.

455. *A Study in Scarlet: A Novel.* Chicago; New York: Donohue Brothers, [n.d.] 188 p.

456. ———. New York: The Federal Book Co., [n.d.] 175 p.

457. *Tales of Sherlock Holmes.* New York: Grosset & Dunlap, [n.d.] 131 p.
Contents: Stud.

458. *A Study in Scarlet: A Novel.* New York: The Mershon Co., [n.d.] iii, 216 p.

459. ———. New York: Hurst and Co., [n.d.] 176 p. (Arlington Edition)

460. ———. New York: The Mershon Co., [n.d.] iii, 216 p.

461. ———. Rahway, N.J.; New York: The Mershon Co., [n.d.] iii, 216, [4] p.

462. *A Study in Scarlet.* New York: George Munro's Sons, [n.d.] 177, 20, 97-122 p. (The American Edition)
Also contains: My Friend the Murderer. - The Man from Archangel.

463. *A Study in Scarlet: A Novel.* New York: J.S. Ogilvie Pub. Co., [n.d.] 176, 16 p. of advertisements. (The Sunset Series, No. 99)

464. *Sherlock Holmes: A Novel.* New York: J.S. Ogilvie Pub. Co., [n.d.] 176 p. (The Sunset Series, No. 279)
Contents: Stud.

465. *A Study in Scarlet.* New York: The Prudential Book Co., [n.d.] 128 p. (Wakefield Series, No. 9)

466. ———. New York: Readers' League of America, [n.d.] 244 p.

467. ———. New York: J. H. Sears & Co., [n.d.] 244 p.

468. *A Study in Scarlet: A Novel.* New York and London: Street & Smith, Publishers, [n.d.] 175, [9] p. of advertisements. (Select Fiction Library)

469. *A Study in Scarlet.* New York: "Tarry at the Taft," [n.d.] 244 p.
On cover: "Compliments of the Hotel Taft, New York."

470. *A Study in Scarlet: A Novel.* Chicago: Thompson & Thomas, [n.d.] 176 p.

471. *A Study in Scarlet: The First Book About Sherlock Holmes.* London and Melbourne: Ward, Lock & Co. Ltd., [n.d.] 160 p. (Master Novelist Series, No. 17)

472. *A Study in Scarlet.* With a note on Sherlock Holmes by Dr. Joseph Bell. Illustrated by George Hutchinson. London and Melbourne: Ward, Lock & Co. Ltd., [n.d.] 96 p. (Sixpenny Edition)

473. ———. Chicago: E. A. Weeks & Co., [n.d.] 201 p.

474. *Sherlock Holmes Detective Stories.* Cleveland, Ohio: The Arthur Westbrook Co., [n.d.] 188 p. (Great American Detective Series, No. 1)
Contents: Stud.

475. *A Study in Scarlet: A Novel.* Cleveland, Ohio: The Arthur Westbrook Co., [n.d.] 176, 17 p. (American Detective Series, No. 2)
Also contains: Beyond the City (chap. 1-2), by A. Conan Doyle.

476. *A Study in Scarlet.* Deposit, N.Y.: The A. S. Wickwire Press, [n.d.] 175 p. (American Series of Famous Fiction. Edited by Dr. Jno. Rudd)

**THE ADVENTURE OF
THE SUSSEX VAMPIRE**

477. "The Adventure of the Sussex Vampire," Illustrated by H. K. Elcock. *The Strand Magazine,* 67, No. 397 (January 1924), 3-13.

478. "The Sussex Vampire," Illustrations by W. T. Benda. *Hearst's International,* 45, No. 1 (January 1924), 30-36.

479. "The Adventure of the Sussex Vampire," [Illustrated by Frederic Dorr Steele]. *The Courier-Journal,* Magazine Section [Louisville, Ky.] (March 8, 1925), 2.

480. ———, [Illustrated by Frederic Dorr Steele]. *Los Angeles Times Sunday Magazine* (March 15, 1925), 16-17, 31.

481. ———, *Great Tales of Mystery.* Edited by R. C. Bull. Illustrated by Edward Pagram. New York: Hill and Wang, [1960]. p. 66-84.

**THE PROBLEM OF
THOR BRIDGE**

482. "The Problem of Thor Bridge," Illustrated by A. Gilbert. *The Strand Magazine,* 63, No. 374 (February 1922), 94-104; 63, No. 375 (March 1922), 211-217.

483. ———, Illustrated by G. Patrick Nelson. *Hearst's International,* 41, No. 2 (February 1922), 6-7, 69; 41, No. 3 (March 1922), 14-15, 60-62.

484. ———, *The Second Century of Detective Stories.* Edited by E. C. Bentley. London: Hutchinson & Co., [1938]. p. 317-345.

**THE ADVENTURE OF
THE THREE GABLES**

485. "The Adventure of the Three Gables," Pictures by Frederic Dorr Steele. *Liberty,* 3, No. 20 (September 18, 1926), 9-14.

486. ———, Illustrated by Howard Elcock. *The Strand Magazine,* 72, No. 430 (October 1926), 318-328.

487. ———, [Illustration by Frederic Dorr Steele]. *The Courier-Journal,* Magazine Section [Louisville, Ky.] (February 13, 1927), 3-4.

**THE ADVENTURE OF
THE THREE GARRIDEBS**

488. "The Adventure of the Three Garridebs," Illustrated by John Richard Flanagan. *Collier's,* 74, No. 17 (October 25, 1924), 5-7, 36-37.

489. ———, Illustrated by John Richard Flanagan. *Current Opinion,* 77, No. 6 (December 1924), 724-731, 796, 798-799.

490. ———, Illustrated by Howard Elcock. *The Strand Magazine,* 69, No. 409 (January 1925), 2-14.

491. ———, [Illustration by Frederic Dorr Steele]. *The Courier-Journal,* Magazine Section [Louisville, Ky.] (March 22, 1925).

492. ———, [Illustrated by Frederic Dorr Steele]. *Los Angeles Times Sunday Magazine* (March 29, 1925), 16-17.

**THE ADVENTURE OF
THE THREE STUDENTS**

493. "The Adventure of the Three Students," [Illustrated by Sidney Paget]. *The Strand Magazine,* 27, No. 162 (June 1904), 602-613. (The Return of Sherlock Holmes, No. 9)

494. ———, Illustrated by Frederic Dorr Steele. *Collier's,* 33, No. 26 (September 24, 1904), 14-15, 27-29. (The Return of Sherlock Holmes, No. 9)

495. ———. New York: Sunday *Post,* [1911?] 8 p. (Masterpieces of Sherlock Holmes)

496. ———. [New York]: Sunday *World* Fiction Section, [1911]. 15 p. illus.

497. ———, *Literature We Like.* [Edited by] Russell Blankenship [and] Winifred H. Nash. New York: Charles Scribner's Sons, [1939]. p. 475-491.

498. ———, *The Short Story Reader.* Edited by Rodney A. Kimball. New York: The Odyssey Press, [1946]. p. 51-70.

THE MAN WITH THE TWISTED LIP

499. "The Man with the Twisted Lip," [Illustrated by Sidney Paget]. *The Strand Magazine*, 2, No. 12 (December 1891), 623-637. (The Adventures of Sherlock Holmes, No. 6)

THE VALLEY OF FEAR

500. "The Valley of Fear," Illustrated by Frank Wiles. *The Strand Magazine*, 48, No. 285 (September 1914), 240-252; 48, No. 286 (October 1914), 362-375; 48, No. 287 (November 1914), 482-491; 48, No. 288 (December 1914), 602-613; 49, No. 289 (January 1915), 2-15; 49, No. 290 (February 1915), 176-187; 49, No. 291 (March 1915), 257-267; 49, No. 292 (April 1915), 449-461; 49, No. 293 (May 1915), 543-556.

501. ———, [Illustrated by Arthur I. Keller]. *The Philadelphia Press* (September 6-November 22, 1914).

502. ———, Drawings by Arthur I. Keller. *Boston Sunday Post*, Magazine Section (September 20-November 22, 1914). 10 issues.

503. ———. With a frontispiece by Frank Wiles. London: Smith, Elder & Co., 1915. 306 p.
Contents: Part I. The Tragedy of Birlstone: 1. The Warning. - 2. Mr. Sherlock Holmes Discourses. - 3. The Tragedy of Birlstone. - 4. Darkness. - 5. The People of the Drama. - 6. A Dawning Light. - 7. The Solution. - Part II. The Scowrers: 1. The Man. - 2. The Bodymaster. - 3. Lodge 341, Vermissa. - 4. The Valley of Fear. - 5. The Darkest Hour. - 6. Danger. - 7. The Trapping of Birdy Edwards. - Epilogue.

504. ———. London: Geo. Bell & Son, [March 1915]. (Colonial Edition)

505. *The Valley of Fear: A Sherlock Holmes Novel.* Illustrated by Arthur I. Keller. New York: George H. Doran Co., [1915]. 320 p. First American edition.

506. ———. With four illustrations by Arthur I. Keller. New York: A. L. Burt Co., [1920]. 320 p.

507. *The Valley of Fear.* London: John Murray, 1922. 306 p.

508. *The Valley of Fear: A Sherlock Holmes Novel.* [Introduction by John Dickson Carr.] New York: Bantam Books, [March 1950]. 181 p. (No. 733)

509. *The Valley of Fear.* London: Pan Books Ltd., [1915]. 185 p. (No. 177)

510. ———. London: John Murray, [1960]. 192 p.

511. ———. [New York]: Berkley Pub. Corp., [March 1964]. 175 p. (Berkley Medallion, F890)

512. ———. London: George Newnes, Ltd., [n.d.] 144 p. (Newnes' New-Size Novels)

513. *The Valley of Fear: A Sherlock Holmes Novel.* New York: The Review of Reviews Co., [n.d.] 320 p.

THE ADVENTURE OF THE VEILED LODGER

514. "The Adventure of the Veiled Lodger," Pictures by Frederic Dorr Steele. *Liberty*, 3, No. 38 (January 22, 1927), 7-10.

515. ———, Illustrated by Frank Wiles. *The Strand Magazine*, 73, No. 434 (February 1927), 108-116.

THE ADVENTURE OF WISTERIA LODGE

516. "The Singular Experience of Mr. J. Scott Eccles: A Reminiscence of Mr. Sherlock Holmes," [Illustrated by Frederic Dorr Steele]. *Collier's*, 41, No. 21 (August 15, 1908), 15-20.

517. ———, [Illustrated by Arthur Twidle]. *The Strand Magazine*, 35, No. 213 (September 1908), 242-250; Concluded, with title: "The Tiger of San Pedro," 35, No. 214 (October 1908), 362-373.

THE YELLOW FACE

518. "The Adventure of the Yellow Face," [Illustrated by Sidney Paget]. *The Strand Magazine*, 5, No. 26 (February 1893), 162-172. (The Adventures of Sherlock Holmes, No. 15)

519. ———, [Illustrated by W. H. Hyde]. *Harper's Weekly*, 37, No. 1886 (February 11, 1893), 125-127. (The Adventures of Sherlock Holmes)

B Collected Tales

THE ADVENTURES OF SHERLOCK HOLMES

520. *The Adventures of Sherlock Holmes.* [Illustrations by Sidney Paget.] London: George Newnes, Ltd., 1892. 317 p. (The Strand Library)
Contents: 1. Scan. - 2. RedH. - 3. Iden. - 4. Bosc. - 5. Five. - 6. Twis. - 7. Blue. - 8.

Spec. - 9. Engr. - 10. Nobl. - 11. Bery. - 12. Copp.

521. *Adventures of Sherlock Holmes.* Illustrated [by Sidney Paget]. New York and London: Harper & Brothers, [1892]. 307 p. First American edition.

522. *The Adventures of Sherlock Holmes.* Second edition. London: George Newnes, Ltd., 1893. 317 p. (The Strand Library)

523. ———. Third edition. London: George Newnes, Ltd., 1894. 317 p. (The Strand Library)

524. ———. Illustrations by Sidney Paget. Fourth edition. London: Longmans, Green, and Co., 1894. 343, 24 p. of advertisements. (Longmans' Colonial Library)

525. ———. Illustrations by Sidney Paget. Thirty-fourth thousand. London: George Newnes, Ltd., 1895. 243 p.

526. ———. [London]: John Murray, [December 1898]. 293 p.
"Cheaper edition."

527. ———. Illustrations by Sidney Paget. New edition. London: George Newnes, Ltd., 1898. 343, 32 p. of advertisements.

528. ———. Illustrations by Sidney Paget. Fifth edition. London: George Newnes, Ltd., 1898. 343 p.

529. *Adventures of Sherlock Holmes.* London: George Newnes, Ltd., 1898 [sic] [1899]. 157 p. (The Sixpenny Series of Copyright Books)

530. ———. New York and London: Harper & Brothers Publishers, 1900. 307 p.
"Special Edition, Limited to 50,000 Copies."

531. *The Adventures of Sherlock Holmes.* Souvenir edition. [Illustrated by Sidney Paget.] London: George Newnes, Ltd., 1901. 343, 28 p. of advertisements.

532. ———. Souvenir edition. [Illustrated by Sidney Paget.] London: George Newnes, Ltd., 1902. 343, 32 p. of advertisements.

533. ———. Souvenir edition. [Illustrated by Sidney Paget.] London: George Newnes, Ltd., 1902. 341 p.

534. *Adventures of Sherlock Holmes.* Illustrated [by Sidney Paget]. New York and London: Harper & Brothers Publishers, 1902. 307 p.

535. ———. New York and London: Harper & Brothers Publishers, 1903. 307 p.
"Special limited edition."

On cover: "First use of picture of Gillette as Holmes in book."

536. ———. London: John Murray, 1903. ix, 419 p.

537. *The Adventures of Sherlock Holmes.* Illustrated by Sidney Paget. London: George Newnes, Ltd., 1905. 341 p.

538. ———. Illustrated by Sidney Paget. London: George Newnes, Ltd., 1906. 341 p.

539. ———. Illustrated by Sidney Paget. New edition. London: Smith, Elder & Co., 1907. 341 p.

540. ———. London: Thomas Nelson, Publisher and Sons, [1913]. 379 p. (Nelson's Library)

541. ———. London and Edinburgh: Thomas Nelson & Sons, [1914]. 379 p. (W 14-9)

542. *Adventures of Sherlock Holmes.* With four illustrations [by Sidney Paget]. New York: A. L. Burt Co., Publishers, [October 1914]. 307 p.

543. ———. Illustrated [by Sidney Paget]. New York and London: Harper & Brothers Publishers, [April 1917]. 307 p.

544. *The Adventures of Sherlock Holmes.* New impression. Illustrated by Sidney Paget. London: John Murray, 1918. 293 p.

545. ———. London: George Newnes, 1918. 157 p. (Newnes' Sixpenny Copyright Novels)

546. *Adventures of Sherlock Holmes.* With four illustrations [by Sidney Paget]. New York: A. L. Burt Co., [1920]. 307 p.

547. ———. New York and London: Harper & Brothers Publishers, [1920]. 307 p.
Frontispiece by Sidney Paget.

548. ———. New York: A. L. Burt Co., Publishers, [December 1922]. 307 p.

549. ———. New York and London: Harper & Brothers Publishers, [April 1924]. 307 p.
Frontispiece by Sidney Paget.

550. *The Adventures of Sherlock Holmes.* London: John Murray, [1924]. 293 p.
"First thin paper edition."

551. ———. London: George Newnes, [1928]. 128 p.

552. *Adventures of Sherlock Holmes.* With an introduction by John B. Opdycke. New York and London: Harper & Brothers Publishers, [1930]. liii, 307 p. (Harper's Modern Classics)

Includes a frontispiece of Sir Arthur Conan Doyle and three other photographs, of Scotland Yard, William Gillette, and Clive Brook.

553. ———. New York, Evanston, and London: Harper & Row, Publishers, [1930]. 307 p.

554. ———. Eight popular stories, especially selected and edited. Illustrated by Cheslie D'Andrea. Racine, Wis.: The Whitman Pub. Co., [1955]. 282 p. (Classics)
   Contents: RedH. - Bosc. - Five. - Blue. - Engr. - Nobl. - Bery. - Copp.

555. *The Adventures of Sherlock Holmes.* London: John Murray, [1957]. 248 p.

556. ———. Drawings by Paul Hogarth. [Introduction by Brian A. Marsh.] [London]: The Folio Society, 1958. 291 p.

557. ———. New York: Popular Library, [November 1960]. 253 p. (Popular Giant, G486)

558. *Adventures of Sherlock Holmes.* New York: Collier Books, 1962. 279 p. (HS42V)

559. *The Adventures of Sherlock Holmes.* [New York]: Berkley Pub. Corp., [August 1963]. 304 p. (A Berkley Medallion Book, X808)

560. *Adventures of Sherlock Holmes.* New York: Award Books, Inc., [1964]. 190 p. (Best Seller Classics, CL 455)
   Contents: RedH. - Bosc. - Five. - Engr. - Nobl. - Bery. - Copp.

561. *The Adventures of Sherlock Holmes.* New York: Scholastic Book Services, [December 1964]. 376 p. (T677)

562. *Adventures of Sherlock Holmes.* [Cover: Lynn Sweat.] New York: Collier Books, [Third printing, 1965]. 279 p. (01959)

563. ———. With an introduction by U. Harold Males. Evanston, Ill.: Harper & Row, [1965]. 318 p.

564. ———. Illustrated by Jo Polseno. New York: Golden Press, [1965]. 254 p.
   Contents: RedH. - Bosc. - Five. - Blue. - Engr. - Nobl. - Bery. - Copp.

565. ———. Illustrated by Jo Polseno. Racine, Wis.: The Whitman Pub. Co., [1965]. 254 p. (The Whitman Classics Library)
   Contents same as above.

566. ———. Eight popular stories by A. Conan Doyle especially selected and edited. Illustrated by Cheslie D'Andrea. Racine,

Wis.: Whitman Pub. Co., [1965]. 282 p. (Whitman Classics)
   Contents same as above.

567. *The Adventures of Sherlock Holmes.* [Introduction by Robert A. W. Lowndes.] New York: Airmont Pub. Co., [1966]. 223 p. (Classics Series, CL97)

568. *Adventures of Sherlock Holmes.* Introduction by U. Harold Males. New York: Harper & Row, [1966]. xx, 281 p. (Perennial Classic, P3059C)

569. ———. New York: Lancer Books, [1968]. 382 p. (Magnum Easy Eye Books, 14-614, No. 36)
   Contents: Scan. - RedH. - Iden. - Bosc. - Five. - Twis. - Blue. - Spec. - Nobl. - Bery. - Copp.

570. *The Great Adventures of Sherlock Holmes.* Edited by Harry Shefter. New York: Washington Square Press, [January 1972]. 294 p. illus. (Pocket Books)
   An Enriched Edition with a Reader's Supplement, including eighteen drawings and photographs (48 p.).

571. ———. New York: Grosset & Dunlap, [n.d.] 307 p.

572. *The Adventures of Sherlock Holmes.* London and Edinburgh: Thomas Nelson & Sons, [n.d.] 379 p. (Nelson's Library) Frontispiece by Noel Pocock.

THE CASE BOOK OF SHERLOCK HOLMES

573. *The Case-Book of Sherlock Holmes.* London: John Murray, [1927]. 320 p.
   Contents: Preface, by Arthur Conan Doyle. - 1. Illu. - 2. Blan. - 3. Maza. - 4. 3Gab. - 5. Suss. - 6. 3Gar. - 7. Thor. - 8. Cree. - 9. Lion. - 10. Veil. - 11. Shos. - 12. Reti.

574. *The Case Book of Sherlock Holmes.* New York: George H. Doran Co., [1927]. vii, 320 p.
   First American edition.

575. ———. New York: A. L. Burt Co., [c.1927]. vii, 320 p.

576. ———. Toronto: The Ryerson Press, [c.1927]. vii, 320 p.

577. *The Case-Book of Sherlock Holmes.* Copyright edition. Leipzig: Bernhard Tauchnitz, 1927. 296 p. (Tauchnitz Edition, Vol. 4790) (A. Conan Doyle, No. 42)

578. ———. Copyright edition. Leipzig: Bernhard Tauchnitz, 1927. 296, [32] p. of advertisements. (Tauchnitz Edition, Vol. 4790) (A. Conan Doyle, No. 42)

Collected Tales

579. ———. London: John Murray, [February 1930]. 320 p.
"Uniform edition."

580. *The Case Book of Sherlock Holmes.* New York: Pocket Books, Inc., [February 1950]. vii, 262 p. (No. 670)

581. *The Case-Book of Sherlock Holmes.* Harmondsworth, Middlesex: Penguin Books, [1951]. 254 p. (No. 805)

582. *The Case Book of Sherlock Holmes.* [New York]: Berkley Pub. Corp., [July 1964]. 254 p. (A Berkley Medallion Book, X946)

583. *The Case-Book of Sherlock Holmes.* Leicester: Ulverscroft [F. A. Thorpe, April 1967]. 252 p. (Ulverscroft Large Print Series)

HIS LAST BOW

584. *His Last Bow: Some Reminiscences of Sherlock Holmes.* London: John Murray, 1917. vii, 305 p.
Contents: Preface, by John H. Watson, M.D. - 1. Wist. - 2. Card. - 3. RedC. - 4. Bruc. - 5. Dyin. - 6. Lady. - 7. Devi. - 8. Last.

585. *His Last Bow: A Reminiscence of Sherlock Holmes.* New York: George H. Doran Co., [1917]. vii, 308 p.
First American edition.

586. ———. New York: A. L. Burt Co., [1920]. 308 p.

587. ———. Garden City, N.Y.: Doubleday, Doran & Co., 1933. 208 p.

588. *His Last Bow.* Garden City, N.Y.: The Sun Dial Press, [1937]. 208 p.
"Hampton Court edition."

589. *His Last Bow: Some Reminiscences of Sherlock Holmes.* London: Pan Books Ltd., [1955]. 188 p. (No. 333)

590. ———. London: John Murray, 1960. 305 p.

591. ———. London: John Murray, [1962]. 205 p.

592. *His Last Bow.* [New York]: Berkley Pub. Corp., [May 1964]. 191 p. (A Berkley Medallion Book, F912)

593. ———. [New York]: Berkley Pub. Corp., [February 1968]. 191 p. (A Berkley Medallion Book, X1576)

594. *His Last Bow: Some Reminiscences of Sherlock Holmes.* London: George Newnes, Ltd., [n.d.] 160 p. (Newnes Copyright 1 / - Novels)
Cover illustrated by Frank Wrig.

595. *His Last Bow: A Reminiscence of Sherlock Holmes.* New York: The Review of Reviews Co., [n.d.] vii, 308 p.

THE MEMOIRS OF SHERLOCK HOLMES

596. *The Memoirs of Sherlock Holmes.* Illustrations by Sidney Paget. London: George Newnes, Ltd., 1894. 279 p. (The Strand Library)
Contents: 1. Silv. - 2. Yell. - 3. Stoc. - 4. Glor. - 5. Musg. - 6. Reig. - 7. Croo. - 8. Resi. - 9. Gree. - 10. Nava. - 11. Fina.

597. *Memoirs of Sherlock Holmes.* Illustrated [by W. H. Hyde and Sidney Paget]. New York: Harper & Brothers Publishers, 1894. vi, 281 p.
Running title: The Adventures of Sherlock Holmes [sic].
This is the only edition of the *Memoirs* that contains the suppressed "The Adventure of the Cardboard Box." It was later included in *His Last Bow.*
First American edition.

598. ———. Illustrated [by W. H. Hyde and Sidney Paget]. New and revised edition. New York: Harper & Brothers Publishers, 1894. vi, 259 p.

599. *The Memoirs of Sherlock Holmes.* Copyright edition. Leipzig: Bernhard Tauchnitz, 1894. 2 v. (280, 253 p.) (Tauchnitz Edition, Vol. 2972, 2973) (Doyle, No. 15)

Illustrator Arthur Twidle's conception of the struggle between Sherlock Holmes and Professor Moriarty at the Reichenbach Falls.

600. *The Last Adventures of Sherlock Holmes: Being a New Edition of His "Memoirs."* Illustrations by Sidney Paget. London: George Newnes, Ltd., 1897. 296 p.

601. ———. Illustrations by Sidney Paget. Twenty-Second Thousand. London: George Newnes, Ltd., 1897. 296, 12 p. of advertisements.

602. ———. Illustrations by Sidney Paget. Twenty-Ninth Thousand. London: George Newnes, Ltd., 1898. 296 p.

603. *Memoirs of Sherlock Holmes.* Illustrated [by W. H. Hyde and Sidney Paget]. New and revised edition. New York and London: Harper & Brothers Publishers, 1900 vi, 259 p.

604. ———. London: George Newnes, Ltd., 1901. 157 p. (The Sixpenny Series of Copyright Books)
Printed in double columns.

605. *The Last Adventures of Sherlock Holmes.* Souvenir edition. [Illustrations by Sidney Paget.] London: George Newnes, Ltd., 1902. 296 p.

606. *Memoirs of Sherlock Holmes.* Illustrated [by W. H. Hyde and Sidney Paget]. New and revised edition. New York and London: Harper & Brothers Publishers, 1903. vi, 259 p.

607. *The Memoirs of Sherlock Holmes.* Illustrated by Sidney Paget. London: George Newnes, Ltd., 1906. 296 p.

608. ———. With a frontispiece [by Sidney Paget]. London: Smith, Elder & Co., 1911. 248 p.

609. ———. New edition. Illustrated by Sidney Paget. London: Smith, Elder & Co., 1912. 248 p.

610. ———. London: Thomas Nelson & Sons, [1913]. 384 p. (Nelson's Library)

611. *Memoirs of Sherlock Holmes.* With four illustrations [by W. H. Hyde]. New York: A. L. Burt Co., [January 1918]. 259 p.

612. *The Memoirs of Sherlock Holmes.* London: John Murray, [1924]. 248 p.
"First thin paper edition."

613. ———. London: John Murray, [June 1925]. 313 p.
First "uniform edition."

614. *Memoirs of Sherlock Holmes.* [Illustrated by W. H. Hyde.] New York: A. L. Burt Co., [1925]. 259 p.

"*The death of Sherlock Holmes*" in "*The Final Problem,*" as depicted by Sidney Paget. This drawing became the frontispiece of The Memoirs of Sherlock Holmes., *1894* (**596**).

615. *The Memoirs of Sherlock Holmes.* [London]: John Murray, [October 1930]. 313 p.

616. *Memoirs of Sherlock Holmes.* New York: Bantam Books. [August 1949]. 250 p. (No. 704)

617. *The Memoirs of Sherlock Holmes.* Harmondsworth, Middlesex: Penguin Books, [1950]. 255 p. (No. 785)

618. *Memoirs of Sherlock Holmes.* New York: Collier Books, 1963. 254 p. (AS498V)

619. *The Memoirs of Sherlock Holmes.* [New York]: Berkley Pub. Corp., [September 1963]. 255 p. (A Berkley Medallion Book, X819)

620. ———. Leicester: Ulverscroft [F. A. Thorpe, September 1966]. 251 p. (Ulverscroft Large Print Series)

621. *Memoirs of Sherlock Holmes.* Garden City, N.Y.: Doubleday & Co., [n.d.] 273 p. (Dolphin Books, C126)

622. *The Memoirs of Sherlock Holmes.* London and Edinburgh: Thomas Nelson & Sons, [n.d.] 384 p. (Nelson's Library)

623. *Memoirs of Sherlock Holmes.* London: George Newnes, Ltd., [n.d.] 10, 160 p. (Newnes' Copyright Novels, No. 21)
Printed in double columns.

624. ———. London: George Newnes, Ltd.,

[n.d.] 157 p. (Newnes' Famous Sixpenny Novels, No. 21)
Printed in double columns.

THE RETURN OF SHERLOCK HOLMES

625. *The Return of Sherlock Holmes.* Illustrated by Sidney Paget. London: George Newnes, Ltd., 1905. 403 p.
Contents: 1. Empt. - 2. Norw. - 3. Danc. - 4. Soli. - 5. Prio. - 6. Blac. - 7. Chas. - 8. SixN. - 9. 3Stu. - 10. Gold. - 11. Miss. - 12. Abbe. - 13. Seco.

626. ———. Illustrated by Charles Raymond Macauley. New York: McClure, Phillips & Co., 1905. 381 p.
First American edition.

627. ———. Illustrated by Charles Raymond Macauley. New York: McClure, Phillips & Co., 1905. 381 p.
On spine: Special edition.

628. ———. Toronto: Morang & Co., [1905]. 381 p.

629. *The Return of Sherlock Holmes: Detective Stories.* Three Owls edition. New York: W. R. Caldwell & Co., [February 1905]. 381 p. illus. (The International Adventure Library)

630. *The Return of Sherlock Holmes.* Illustrated by Charles Raymond Macauley. New York: A. Wessels Co., 1907. 381 p.

631. ———. Illustrated by Charles Raymond Macauley. New York: Doubleday, Page & Co., 1910. 381 p.

632. ———. New edition. Illustrated by Sidney Paget. London: Smith, Elder & Co., 1911. 403 p.

633. ———. Illustrated by Charles Raymond Macauley. Garden City, N.Y.: Doubleday, Page & Co., 1915. 381 p.

634. ———. Illustrated by Sidney Paget. New impression. London: John Murray, 1918. 403 p.

635. ———. Garden City, N.Y., and Toronto: Doubleday, Page & Co., 1921. 381 p.
Frontispiece by Charles Raymond Macauley.

636. ———. London: John Murray, [1924]. 316 p.
"First thin paper edition."

637. ———. Garden City, N.Y.: The Sun Dial Press, [1937]. 381 p.
"Hampton Court edition."

638. ———. New York: Triangle Books, [1941]. 381 p.

639. ———. London: John Murray, [September 1949]. 312 p.
"Uniform edition."

640. ———. London: Pan Books Ltd., 1954. 252 p. (No. 286)

641. ———. [New York]: Berkley Pub. Corp., [October 1963]. 320 p. (A Berkley Medallion Book, X830)

642. ———. Leicester: Ulverscroft [F. A. Thorpe, August 1967]. 238 p. (Ulverscroft Large Print Series)
Contents: Empt. - Norw. - Danc. - Soli. - Prio. - Blac. - Chas. - SixN. - 3Stu. - Gold.

643. ———. Illustrated. New York: P. F. Collier & Son, [n.d.] 381 p.
Frontispiece of Mr. William Gillette as "Sherlock Holmes."

C *Selected and Complete Tales*

---

644. *The Adventure of the Speckled Band and Other Stories of Sherlock Holmes.* With an introduction and notes by William S. Baring-Gould. [New York]: The New American Library, [October 1965]. xv, 287 p. (Signet Classic, CD324)
Contents: Introducing Mr. Sherlock Holmes, by William S. Baring-Gould. - Spec. - Scan. - RedH. - Blue. - Musg. - Nava. - Silv. - Fina. - Empt. - Bruc. - Danc. - SixN. - Notes. - Selected Bibliography.
Review: SHJ, 7, No. 3 (Winter 1965), 91-92 (Lord Donegall).

645. *The Adventures and Memoirs of Sherlock Holmes.* New York: The Modern Library, [1946]. vi, 612 p. (Modern Library of the World's Best Books, No. 206)

646. *Adventures and Memoirs of Sherlock Holmes and Sign of Four.* Preston: James Askew & Son, [n.d.] 157, 157, 124 p.
Consists of the three paperbacks published by George Newnes in the Sixpenny Novels Series. *Adventures* is illustrated by Sidney Paget and *Sign* by F.H. Townsend.

647. *Adventures of Sherlock Holmes.* Girard, Kansas: Haldeman-Julius Co., [n.d.] 64 p. (Little Blue Book, No. 1029)
Cover title: Two Adventures of Sherlock Holmes.
Contents: Spec. - Nobl.

648. *The Adventures of Sherlock Holmes.* London: John Murray, [November 1923]. 188 p. (Modern English Series)

Contents: Preface, by R. B. L. and R. B. M. - RedH. - Five. - Blue. - Spec. - Reig. - Fina. - Glossary. - Questions.

649. ———. Illustrated by Sidney Paget. London: George Newnes, Ltd., [n.d.] 157, 157, 124 p.
Also contains: Memoirs. - Sign.

650. ———. Adapted by Olive Eckerson. Edited by Wallace R. Murray. New York: Globe Book Co., [1950]. viii, 255 p.
Illustrated with photographs from the Twentieth Century-Fox film version of *The Adventures of Sherlock Holmes.* Includes study questions at the end of each story.
Contents: To the Teacher, by O. E. - To the Reader, by O. E. - A Word from Doctor Watson. - 1. Spec. - 2. Twis. - 3. Blue. - 4. Fina. - 5. The Return of Sherlock Holmes. - 6. Empt. - 7. Prio. - 8. SixN. - 9. The Adventure of the Lion's Mane: A Radio Play. - A Few Words About Sir Arthur Conan Doyle.

651. ———. Illustrated by Richard M. Powers. Garden City, N.Y.: Junior Deluxe Editions (Nelson Doubleday), [1956]. 312 p.
Contents: Scan. - RedH. - Iden. - Bosc. - Five. - Twis. - Blue. - Sign.

652. ———. New York: Parents' Magazine Press, [1964]. 422 p.
Jacket and cover design by Albert J. Nagy.
Contents: Preface, by Irene Smith. - Stud. - Sign. - Scan. - Bosc. - Iden. - RedH.

653. *"The Adventures of Sherlock Holmes and Doctor Watson."* [New York: The Benjamin Co. for Flint Laboratories, 1970.] [158] p.
Contents: Five. - Engr. - Blue. - Nobl. - RedH.
A promotional booklet distributed only to physicians in the U.S.

654. *The Annotated Sherlock Holmes.* The four novels and the fifty-six short stories complete, by Sir Arthur Conan Doyle. Edited, with an introduction, notes, and bibliography by William S. Baring-Gould. Illustrated with maps, diagrams, coats-of-arms, photographs, and drawings by Charles Doyle, Howard K. Elcock, D. H. Friston, A. Gilbert, James Grieg, George Hutchinson, William H. Hyde, Charles Raymond Macauley, Sidney Paget, Frederic Dorr Steele, Arthur Twidle, Frank Wiles, and numerous others. New York: Clarkson N. Potter, Inc./ Publisher, [1967]. 2 v. (688, 824 p.)
———. London: John Murray, [1968]. 2 v. (688, 824 p.)
Nineteen chapters of the late Sherlockian scholar's brilliant and "definitive" study of the Sacred Writings are devoted to an examination of the following topics: 1. Conan Doyle and the tales. - 2. The translations, parodies and pastiches. - 3. The writings about the Writings. - 4. Stage and film versions of the tales. - 5. The illustrators and illustrations. - 6. The Societies. - 7. Exhibitions and memorials. - 8. Sherlock Holmes. - 9. Dr. Watson. - 10. Professor Moriarty. - 11. 221B Baker Street. - 12. "What Is It That We Love in Sherlock Holmes," by Edgar W. Smith. - 16. The three chronological breaks in the Holmes-Watson partnership. - 18. Dr. Roylott's messenger of death. - 22. Dr. Watson's *three* marriages and wives. - 34. Dr. Watson's *two* wounds. - 48. The Great Hiatus and Reichenbach. - 75. On "The Adventure of the Mazarin Stone". - 77. Holmes's retirement. (These chapters are also listed separately under the appropriate subject.)

The remaining chapters comprising the John Murray text of the sixty tales are arranged in chronological order, according to Baring-Gould's chronology, and contain copious marginal notes and illustrations.

The two volumes were offered by The Mystery Guild as an inducement to membership in its book club (a full-page advertisement appeared on page 52 of *The New York Times Book Review* for February 22, 1970).

Reviews: AB Bookman's Weekly, 41 (April 1-8, 1968), 1274; *American Book Collector,* 19 (September 1968), 17-18 (Thomas M. McDade); *American Scholar,* 37 (Autumn 1968), 680-684 (Jacques Barzun), and reprinted in *CPBook,* 4, No. 16 (Fall 1968), 312-314; *Booklist,* 64 (May 15, 1968), 1082; *Christian Science Monitor* (February 15, 1968), 12 (Patience M. Daltry); *Library Journal,* 93 (February 15, 1968), 753 (Malcolm M. Ferguson); *Life,* 63 (December 15, 1967), R4 (Herbert Kupferberg); *Listener,* 80 (July 4, 1968), 21-22 (Richard Usborne); *Los Angeles Times* (January 7, 1968), 24 (Robert Kirsch), and reprinted in *CPBook,* 4, No. 14 (Winter 1968), 268-269; *Nation,* 207 (August 9, 1968), 122-123 (Theodore Roszak); *New York Times Book Review* (January 21, 1968), 1, 32-33 (Anthony Boucher), and reprinted in *CPBook,* 4, No. 14 (Winter 1968), 266-268; *Observer* (May 5, 1968), 26 (Maurice Richardson); *Philadelphia Inquirer* (January 7, 1968) (Robert Cromie); *San Francisco Sunday Examiner & Chronicle* (March 24, 1968), 34 (Leonore Glen Offord); *Saturday Review,* 51 (June 29, 1968), 30 (Sergeant Cuff); *SOS,* 2, No. 3 (February 1968), 2 (Bruce Kennedy); *SHJ,* 8, No. 4 (Summer 1968), 133-135 (Lord Donegall); *Sherlockiana,* 13, Nr. 1-2 (1968), 1-2 (H.L.); *Startling Mystery Stories,* 2, No. 4 (Fall 1968), 4-5, 123-127 (Robert A. W. Lowndes); *Telegraph* (April 21, 1968) (Roger Lancelyn Green), and reprinted in *CPBook,* 5, No. 17 (Winter 1969), 330, and in *Sherlockiana,* 13, Nr. 1-2 (1968), 3; *Times Literary Supplement* (May 9, 1968), 472; *VH,* 2, No. 1 (January 1968), 9.

655. *The Best of Sherlock Holmes.* New York: Grosset & Dunlap, Publishers, [n.d.] 339 p.
Contents: Stud. - Scan. - RedH. - Sign. - Bosc.

656. *The Book of Sherlock Holmes.* Illustrated by Charlotte Ross. Introduction by May Lamberton Becker. Cleveland and New York: The World Pub. Co., [1950]. 320 p. (Rainbow Classics, R28)
Also published in a deluxe box edition. (DLR-28)
Contents: Stud. - Sign. - Scan. - RedH. - Iden. - Bosc.

657. *The Boys' Sherlock Holmes.* A selection from the works of A. Conan Doyle. Arranged by Howard Haycraft. New York and London: Harper & Brothers, 1936. xix, 336 p. illus.
Contents: Introduction: The True Story of Sherlock Holmes, by Howard Haycraft. - 1. Stud. - 2. The Original of Sherlock Holmes, by Dr. H. E. Jones. - 3. Sign. - 4. Selected Short Stories: Spec. - Nobl. - Bery. - Copp. - Blue.

658. ———. A selection from the works of A. Conan Doyle. Arranged, with introduction by Howard Haycraft. New and enlarged edition. New York and Evanston: Harper & Row, [1961]. xix, 524 p. illus.
Contents: Introduction: The True Story of Sherlock Holmes, by Howard Haycraft. - 1. Stud. - 2. The Original of Sherlock Holmes, by Dr. H. E. Jones. - 3. Sign. - 4. Selected Short Stories: Spec. - Silv. - RedC. - Scan. - Musg. - Blue. - 5. Houn.

659. *A Case of Identity.* Chicago: Donohue, Henneberry & Co., [n.d.] 201-230, 5-189 p.
Also contains: Sign.

660. *A Case of Identity: A Sherlock Holmes Story.* Cleveland, Ohio: The Arthur Westbrook Co., [n.d.] (American Detective Series, No. 4)
Partial contents: Iden. - RedH.

661. *Casebook of Sherlock Holmes.* Illustrated by Don Irwin. Santa Rosa, Calif.: Classic Press, Inc., [1968]. 281 p. (Educator Classic Library, No. 7)
Large type edition.
Includes marginal definitions and illustrations.
Contents: Stud (pt. 1 and chap. 13-14 of pt. 2). - Spec. - Scan. - Blue. - Houn. - Backword (about Conan Doyle and the document detectives).

662. *Cases of Sherlock Holmes.* Adapted by William Kottmeyer, Superintendent of Instruction, St. Louis Public Schools. Illustrated by Joseph Camana. St. Louis: Webster Division, McGraw-Hill Book Co., [1947]. 118 p. (The Webster Everyreaders)

Contents: Spec. - RedH. - SixN. - Empt. - Something About the Author, by William Kottmeyer.

663. *The Complete Sherlock Holmes.* Authorized Edition in Eight Volumes. New York: P. F. Collier & Son Co., [c.1928]. 8 v.
On spine: Sherlock Holmes.
Volumes unnumbered.
Contents: [Vol. 1] Stud. - Sign. - [Vol. 2] Adventures. - [Vol. 3] Memoirs. - [Vol. 4] Houn. - [Vol. 5] Return. - [Vol. 6] Vall. - [Vol. 7] His Last Bow. - [Vol. 8] Case Book.

664. *The Complete Sherlock Holmes in Six Volumes.* Authorized Edition. New York: P.F. Collier & Son Corp., [1936]. 6 v.

665. *The Complete Sherlock Holmes.* The A. Conan Doyle Memorial Edition. With a preface by Christopher Morley. Garden City, N.Y.: Doubleday, Doran & Co., 1930. 2 v. (xviii, 1323 p.)
The first American collected edition, in two volumes.
Contents: Vol. 1. Stud. - Sign. - Adventures. - Memoirs. - Vol. 2. Return. - Houn. - Vall. - His Last Bow. - Case Book.
Reviews: Booklist, 27 (December 1930), 164; *Bookman,* 72 (September 1930), xx; *Chicago Daily Tribune* (October 4, 1930), 13; *New York Herald Tribune Books* (September 7, 1930), 10 (Will Cuppy); *New York Times Book Review* (October 19, 1930), 33; *Saturday Review of Literature,* 7 (September 13, 1930), 122.

666. ———. With a preface by Christopher Morley. New York: The Literary Guild, 1936. xvi, 1323 p.
The first one-volume collected edition.

667. ———. With a preface by Christopher Morley. Garden City, N.Y.: Doubleday, Doran & Co., 1936. xvi, 1323 p.

668. ———. With a preface by Christopher Morley. De luxe edition. New York: Garden City Pub. Co., [1938]. xvi, 1323 p. illus.

669. ———. With a preface by Christopher Morley and an introduction by John Dickson Carr. New York: Doubleday & Co., 1953. 2 v. (xvii, 1323 p.)
Limited and signed edition of 147 copies.

670. ———. With a preface by Christopher Morley. Garden City, N.Y.: Doubleday & Co., [1960]. 1122 p.

671. ———. With a preface by Christopher Morley. Garden City, N.Y.: Doubleday & Co., [1960]. 2 v. (1122 p.)

672. *Conan Doyle Stories: Six Notable Adventures of Sherlock Holmes.* New York: Platt & Munk, [1960]. 494 p. (Platt & Munk Great Writers Collection)

Contents: Stud. - Sign. - Iden. - RedH. - Scan. - Bosc. - About A. Conan Doyle: Biographical Notes.

673. *Conan Doyle's Best Books in Three Volumes.* Illustrated. Sherlock Holmes Edition. New York: P. F. Collier & Son, Publishers, [190-?] 3 v. (xii, 414; 558; iv, 466 p.)
    Contents: Vol. 1. The Original of Sherlock Holmes, by Dr. Harold Emery Jones. - Stud. - Scan. - Iden. - Vol. 2. Sign. - Vol. 3. The White Company. - Beyond the City.

674. *Conan Doyle's Stories for Boys.* Illustrated. New York: Cupples & Leon Co., [1938]. v, 491 p.
    Contents: Stud. - Sign. - Iden. - RedH. - Scan. - Bosc.

675. *The Devil's Foot.* London: George Newnes, Ltd., [1921]. 128 p. (Newnes' Sevenpenny Novels, No. 31)
    Also contains: Scan. - Yell. - Copp.

676. *The Doings of Raffles Haw,* by A. Conan Doyle. New York: Lovell, Coryell & Co., [1891]. 255 p.
    Also contains: RedH. - Bosc. - Scan. - Iden.

677. ———. New York: United States Book Co., [c. 1891]. 199, 213 p.
    Also contains: RedH. - Bosc. - Stud.

678. ———. New York: Lovell, Coryell & Co., [July 1892]. 199 p. (The Belmore Series, No. 5)
    Also contains: RedH. - Bosc.

679. ———. New York: F. M. Buckles & Co., 1903. 199, 22 p. of advertisements. (Century Series, No. 46)
    Contents same as above.

680. *The Doings of Raffles Haw and Other Stories,* by A. Conan Doyle. New York: George H. Doran Co., [1919]. 199 p.
    Contents same as above.

681. *The Doings of Raffles Haw,* by Sir Arthur Conan Doyle. Freeport, N.Y.: Books for Libraries Press, [1969]. 199 p. (Short Story Index Reprint Series)
    Contents same as above.

682. *The Empty House.* London: George Newnes, Ltd., [1921]. 128 p. (Newnes' Sevenpenny Novels, No. 33)
    Also contains: Iden. - The Tiger of San Pedro [Wist]. - Soli.

683. *Famous Tales of Sherlock Holmes.* With biographical illustrations and pictures from early editions of the stories, together with an introduction by William C. Weber. New York: Dodd, Mead & Co., [1958]. viii, 339 p. (Great Illustrated Classics)
    Contents: Stud. - Scan. - RedH. - Sign. - Bosc.

684. *Five Sherlock Holmes Detective Stories.* New York: J. S. Ogilvie Pub. Co., [n.d.] 186 p. (Eureka Detective Stories, No. 32)
    Contents: RedH. - Iden. - Scan. - That Little Square Box. - John Barrington Cowles.

685. ———. New York: J. S. Ogilvie Pub. Co., [n.d.] 186 p. (Sunset Series, No. 290)
    Contents same as above.

686. *Further Adventures of Sherlock Holmes.* Girard, Kansas: Haldeman-Julius Co., [n.d.] 64 p. (Little Blue Book, No. 266)
    Contents: Bery. - Stoc.

687. "Great Cases of Sherlock Holmes," Illustrated by Guy Deel. *Best Loved Books for Young Readers.* Selected and condensed by the editors of The Reader's Digest. Pleasantville, N.Y.: The Reader's Digest Association, [1966]. Vol. 4, p. 185-360.
    Contents: Prologue (from Stud). - Copp. - Danc. - Silv. - Spec. - Reig. - Blue. - Twis. - RedH.

688. *Great Stories.* Selected by John Dickson Carr. New York: London House and Maxwell, [1959]. 256 p.
    Partial contents: Twis. - Lost. - Silv.

689. ———. Selected by John Dickson Carr. London: John Murray, [1959]. 256 p.
    Contents same as above.

690. *Great Stories of Sherlock Holmes.* [New York: Dell Pub. Co., May 1962.] 287 p. (F169)
    Contents: Thor. - Reig. - Danc. - Silv. - Stoc. - Gree. - Abbe. - Blac. - Chas. - SixN. - Devi. - Shos.

691. *The Man with the Twisted Lip.* London: George Newnes, Ltd., [1921]. 128 p. (Newnes' Sevenpenny Novels, No. 32)
    Also contains: Dyin. - Prio. - RedH.

692. *Memoirs and Adventures of Sherlock Holmes. Sign of Four, Memoirs and Adventures.* Preston: James Askew and Son, [1900?] 157, 157, 124 p.
    Frontispiece of A. Conan Doyle.

693. *My Friend the Murderer and Other Mysteries and Adventures,* by A. Conan Doyle. New York: International Book Co., [1893]. 288, 199 p. (Works of A. Conan Doyle) (Popular Edition)
    Partial contents: RedH. - Bosc.

694. *Original Adventures of Sherlock Holmes.* New York: R. F. Fenno & Co., [190-?] 431 p.
    At head of title: Special limited edition.

Illustrated with scenes from the play *Sherlock Holmes* by William Gillette.
Contents: Stud. - Sign. - Scan. - RedH. - Iden. - Bosc.

695. *The Red-Headed League and The Adventure of the Speckled Band.* Illustrated by Paul Spina. New York: Franklin Watts, Inc., [1968]. 85 p.

696. *The Resident Patient.* London: George Newnes, Ltd., [1921]. 128 p. (Newnes' Sevenpenny Novels)
Also contains: Bery. - Nobl.

697. *Selected Adventures of Sherlock Holmes.* Leicester: Ulverscroft [F. A. Thorpe, March 1966]. 243 p. (Ulverscroft Large Print Series)
Contents: Scan. - RedH. - Iden. - Bosc. - Five. - Twis. - Blue. - Spec. - Engr.

698. *Sherlock Holmes.* New York: Street & Smith, [1897]. 2 v. (226, 215 p.) (Magnet Library, No. 322, 323)
Cover title: Sherlock Holmes Detective Stories in Two Volumes.
Contents: Vol. 1. Scan. - Iden. - RedH. - Stud. - Vol. 2. Sign. - Bosc.

699. ———. New York: R. F. Fenno & Co., [1903]. 431 p. illus.
Contents: Sherlock Holmes (from Stud). - Sign. - Scan. - RedH. - Iden. - Bosc.

700. ———. The G. Washington Edition. [Vol. 1] New York: Doubleday, Doran & Co., [c.1932]. 190 p.
Includes a frontispiece of Leigh Lovell, who portrayed Dr. Watson in the radio series *Adventures of Sherlock Holmes* (items 5451-5456).
Contents: Illu. - Blan. - Maza. - 3Gab. - Cree. - Suss. - Veil.

701. [*Sherlock Holmes.*] A definitive text, corrected and edited by Edgar W. Smith, and illustrated with a selective collation of the original illustrations by Frederic Dorr Steele, Sidney Paget & others. New York: The Limited Editions Club, [1950-1952]. 8 v. (1777 p.)
Title from spine.
Limited to 1500 numbered copies.
Contents: The Adventures of Sherlock Holmes. Vol. 1. Introduction, by Vincent Starrett. - Notes on the Collation, by Edgar W. Smith. - Stud. - Sign. - Vol. 2. Adventures. - Vol. 3. Memoirs. - *The Later Adventures of Sherlock Holmes.* Vol. 1. Introduction, by Elmer Davis. - Return. - Vol. 2. Introduction, by Fletcher Pratt. - Houn. - Vol. 3. Introduction, by Rex Stout. - His Last Bow. - *The Final Adventures of Sherlock Holmes.* Vol. 1. Introduction, by Anthony Boucher. - Vall. - Vol. 2. Introduction, by Christopher Morley. - Case Book. - Epilogue, by Edgar W. Smith.

702. [———.] A definitive text, corrected and edited by Edgar W. Smith, with an introduction by Vincent Starrett, and illustrated with a selective collation of the original illustrations by Frederic Dorr Steele and others. New York: The Heritage Press, [1952 (Vol. 1)-1957 (Vol. 2-3). 3 v. (xxiii, 1777 p.)
Vol. 1 was reprinted by The Heritage Press in October 1971, Vol. 2 in May 1972.
Title from spine; each volume has a special title page.
Contents: Vol. 1. *The Adventures of Sherlock Holmes.* Introduction, by Vincent Starrett. - Notes on the Collation, by Edgar W. Smith. - Stud. - Sign. - Adventures. - Memoirs. - Vol. 2. *The Later Adventures of Sherlock Holmes.* Return. - Houn. - Vol. 3. *The Final Adventures of Sherlock Holmes.* His Last Bow. - Vall. - Case Book.

703. ———. Especially edited and abridged for The Golden Picture Classics by Charles Verral. Illustrated by Tom Gill. New York: Simon and Schuster, [1957]. 96 p. (Golden Picture Classics, CL-108)
Contents: Introduction. - I Meet Mr. Sherlock Holmes (from Stud). - Spec. - Nava. - Iden. - Blue. - RedH. - Fina. - Epilogue.

704. ———. Especially edited and abridged by Charles Verral. [New York: The Nestle Co., 1968.] 95 p.
———. Especially edited and abridged by Charles Verral. [New York: The Nestle Co., 1968.] 96 p.
"Free with purchase of 2 lb. Nestle's Quik."
Contents same as above.

705. ———. Art-type edition. New York: Books, Inc., [n.d.] (University Library of Classics)
On spine: Sherlock Holmes Detective Stories.
Partial contents: Stud. - Sign. - Scan. - Iden.

706. ———. New York, N.Y.: Caxton House, Inc., [n.d.] (Popular Classics of the World)
Contents same as above.

707. *Sherlock Holmes: A Study in Scarlet and The Red-Headed League.* Abridged for young readers by Felix Sutton. Illustrated by H. B. Vestal. New York: Wonder Books, [1957]. 64 p. (Young Readers Wonder Books, No. 2549)

708. *Sherlock Holmes: A Study in Scarlet, The Sign of Four.* Leicester: Ulverscroft [F. A. Thorpe, February 1969]. 250 p. (Ulverscroft Large Print Series)

709. *Sherlock Holmes: A Study in Scarlet, The*

Sign of Four, The Hound of the Basker-villes, The Valley of Fear: The Complete Long Stories. London: John Murray, [1929]. ix, 639 p.

The first English edition of the long stories in one volume.

710. *Sherlock Holmes and Dr. Watson: A Textbook of Friendship.* Edited by Christopher Morley. New York: Harcourt, Brace and Co., [1944]. 366 p.

The first annotated textbook on Sherlock Holmes, intended primarily for high school students. Each story is followed by a "Topics for Discussion" section.

Contents: Memorandum, by C. M. - Introduction, by Christopher Morley. - Stud (chapters 1-5 of part 2 have been omitted but are briefly summarized). - Sign. - Fina. - Empt. - Bruc. - A Guide to the Complete Sherlock Holmes, by Christopher Morley. - Note for Advanced Students.

Reviews: Booklist, 40 (May 1, 1944), 304; *Chicago Sun Book Week* (April 9, 1944), 4 (Elizabeth Bullock); *Chicago Tribune* (April 9, 1944), VII, 10 (Vincent Starrett); *Kirkus,* 12 (April 1, 1944), 154; *New York Herald Tribune Weekly Book Review* (April 9, 1944), 4 (M. L. Becker); *New York Times Book Review* (April 2, 1944), 15; *New Yorker,* 20 (April 8, 1944), 92; *Saturday Review of Literature,* 27 (April 1, 1944), 26; *School and Society,* 59 (April 8, 1944), 256; *Wisconsin Library Bulletin,* 40 (June 1944), 85.

711. *Sherlock Holmes and Other Detective Stories.* Wood-engravings by John Musacchia. New York: Illustrated Editions Co., [1941]. 176 p.

Partial contents: RedH. - Iden. - Scan. - Sign.

712. *Sherlock Holmes Crime Stories.* Girard, Kansas: Haldeman-Julius Co., [n.d.] 64 p. (Little Blue Book, No. 1028)

Contents: Twis. - Blue.

713. *Sherlock Holmes, Detective: Eight of His Famous Adventures.* Arranged for young readers, with a preface by Raymond T. Bond. With photographs and illustrations from the original editions. New York: Dodd, Mead & Co., [1965]. vi. 240 p.

Contents: Twis. - Engr. - Spec. - Bery. - Copp. - Bosc. - Fina. - Empt.

714. *Sherlock Holmes Detective Stories.* New York: Books, Inc., Publishers, [n.d.]

On spine: Dean Press.

Contents: Stud. - Sign. - The Ring of Thoth. - Scan. - A Case, The Surgeon of Gaster Fell. - The Captain of the "Pole Star". - J. Habakuk. - Keinplatz. - Square Box.

715. *The Sherlock Holmes Detective Stories.*

New York: F. M. Lupton, Publisher, October 1896. 60 p. (The People's Handbook Series, No. 48)

Printed in double columns.

Contents: Sign. - Scan. - Iden. - RedH.

716. *Sherlock Holmes Detective Stories.* New York: Readers League of America, [n.d.] iii, 239 p.

Contents: Sign. - Scan. - The Ring of Thoth. - Iden. - The Surgeon of Gaster Fell.

717. ———. New York: J. H. Sears & Co., [c.1923]. 239 p. (The Reader's Library)

Contents same as above.

718. ———. New York: "Tarry at the Taft," [n.d.] iii, 239 p.

On cover: "Compliments of the Hotel Taft, New York."

Contents same as above.

719. ———. New York: Court Book Co., May 1941. iii, 239 p.

Contents same as above.

720. ———. Boston, Mass.: Leslie Pub. Co., 1930. 239, 244 p.

With a frontispiece of the author.

Contents: Sign. - Scan. - The Ring of Thoth. - Iden. - The Surgeon of Gaster Fell. - Stud.

721. ———. New York: Murray Book Corp., 1930. 239, 244 p.

Contents same as above.

722. ———. New York: Three Pay Sales Corp., 1930. 239, 244 p.

Contents same as above.

723. ———. Girard, Kansas: Haldeman-Julius Co., [n.d.] 64 p. (Little Blue Book, No. 1026)

Contents: RedH. - Five.

724. ———. New York: Mayfair Pub. Co., [n.d.] 95 p.

Contents: Sign. - Stud.

725. ———. New York: Street & Smith, [n.d.] 215 p. (Magnet Library, No. 323)

Vol. 2 of a two-volume set.

Contents: Sign. - Bosc.

726. *Sherlock Holmes Detective Stories: 10 Complete in One Volume.* New York; Boston: Gordon & Payne, [n.d.] 1 v. (various pagings)

Partial contents: Stud. - Sign. - Scan. - Iden.

727. *Sherlock Holmes' Greatest Cases.* Introduction by Howard Haycraft. Large type edition complete and unabridged. New York: Franklin Watts, Inc., [1966]. 463 p. (Keith Jennison Books)

Contents: Houn. - RedH. - Spec. - Scan. - Musg. - Silv. - Blue.

728. ———. Introduction by Howard Haycraft. New York: Bantam Books, [September 1968]. 278 p. (N3825)
Contents same as above.

729. *Sherlock Holmes: His Adventures, Memoirs, Return, His Last Bow, & The Case-Book: The Complete Short Stories.* London: John Murray, [1928]. xi, 1335 p.
The first English edition of all the short stories in one volume.

730. ———. London: John Murray, 1952. xi, 1336 p.

731. *Sherlock Holmes Investigates.* Stories by Sir Arthur Conan Doyle. Selected and introduced for new readers by Michael & Mollie Hardwick. [Illustrations by Sidney Paget.] [London]: John Murray, [1963]. 232 p.
Contents: Who Is Sherlock Holmes? - Sherlock Holmes's London. - 1. Mr. Sherlock Holmes Meets Dr. Watson. - 2. Twis. - 3. Spec. - 4. RedH. - 5. Engr. - 6. Reig. - 7. Blue. - A Final Word.
Review: SHJ, 6, No. 2 (Spring 1963), 61 (Lord Donegall).

732. ———. Selected and introduced by Michael and Mollie Hardwick. With Sidney Paget illustrations. New York: Lothrop, Lee & Shepard Co., [1967]. 232 p.
Contents same as above.

733. *Sherlock Holmes Mystery Stories.* Girard, Kansas: Haldeman-Julius Co., [n.d.] 64 p. (Little Blue Book, No. 1027)
Contents: Bosc. - Engr.

734. *The Sherlock Holmes Pocket Book.* New York: Pocket Books, Inc., [February 1941]. 355, 8 p. of advertisements. (No. 95)
Contents: Stud. - Sign. - Scan. - Iden. - RedH.

735. *Sherlock Holmes Problem Stories.* Girard, Kansas: Haldeman-Julius Co., [n.d.] 64 p. (Little Blue Book, No. 1101)
Contents: Copp. - Croo.

736. *Sherlock Holmes: Selected Stories.* With an introduction by S. C. Roberts. London: Oxford University Press, [1951]. xxiii, 435 p. (The World's Classics, No. 528)
Contents: Silv. - Spec. - Sign. - Scan. - Nava. - Blue. - Gree. - RedH. - Empt. - Miss. - Last.

737. *Sherlock Holmes Stories.* Introduced by H. M. King. London: John Murray, 1950. 3 v. (vii, 113; vii, 112; vii, 119 p.) illus.
A simplified adaptation for use in British schools.

Each volume includes the same introduction and a note on Sherlock Holmes and Dr. Watson, as well as notes and questions at the end of each story.
Contents: [Vol. 1] *The First Book of Sherlock Holmes.* Silv. - Stoc. - Fina. - [Vol. 2] *The Second Book of Sherlock Holmes.* Empt. - RedH. - Dyin. - [Vol. 3] *The Third Book of Sherlock Holmes.* Twis. - Danc. - Last.

738. *The Sherlock Holmes Stories.* New York and London: Street & Smith, Publishers, [n.d.] 87, 42, 96 p. (Select Fiction Library)
Partial contents: Scan. - Iden. - RedH.

739. *Sherlock Holmes Tales.* Girard, Kansas: Haldeman-Julius Co., [n.d.] 64 p. (Little Blue Book, No. 102)
Contents: Iden. - Scan.

740. *The Sign of the Four; or, The Problem of the Sholtos.* New York: American Publishers Corp., [n.d.] 224 p.
Also contains: Scan.

741. ———. New York: American Pub. Corp., [n.d.] 224 p. (Delphic Series)
Contents same as above.

742. *The Sign of the Four.* New York: American Publishers Corp., [n.d.] 224 p. (Conan Doyle's Works)
On spine: Aldine Edition.
Contents same as above.

743. ———. New York: Thomas Y. Crowell & Co., [n.d.] 255 p.
Frontispiece of the author.
On cover and spine: At the Sign of the Four.
Also contains: Scan. - Iden.

744. ———. Chicago: M. A. Donohue & Co., [n.d.] 229 p.
Also contains: Scan.

745. ———. Chicago: Donohue, Henneberry & Co., [n.d.] 229 p. (Modern Authors Series, No. 7)
Contents same as above.

746. ———. Chicago: Donohue, Henneberry & Co., [n.d.] 229, 180 p.
Also contains: Scan. - Beyond the City.

747. ———. Chicago: Donohue, Henneberry & Co., [n.d.] 229, 159-192 p.
On spine: Advance Edition.
Also contains: Scan. - An Idyll of London, by Beatrice Harraden.

748. *The Sign of the Four; or, The Problem of the Sholtos.* New York: International Book Co., [n.d.] 255, 213 p. (A. Conan Doyle's Works)

On spine: The Sign of the Four. A Study in Scarlet.
Also contains: Scan. - Iden. - Stud.

749. *The Sign of Four.* Philadelphia: J. B. Lippincott, 1894. 283, 214 p.
On spine: The Sign of Four and A Study in Scarlet.
Stud has separate title page and is dated 1890.

750. *The Sign of the Four; or, The Problem of the Sholtos.* New York: Lovell, Coryell & Co., [n.d.] 255 p.
On spine: The Sign of the Four. A Scandal in Bohemia.
Also contains. Scan. - Iden.

751. *The Sign of the Four.* Chicago: F. Tennyson Neely, [July 1895]. 229 p. (Neely's Popular Library, No. 45)
Also contains: Scan.

752. ———. Chicago and New York: Rand, McNally & Co., [n.d.] 235 p.
Also contains: Scan.

753. ———. Chicago and New York: Rand, McNally & Co., [n.d.] 235 p. (The Parkside Library, No. 9)
On cover: The Continental Pub. Co., Chicago and New York.
Contents same as above.

754. *The Sign of the Four; or, The Problem of the Sholtos.* New York; Chicago: United States Book Co., [1891?] 224 p.
On spine: Linwood Edition.
Contents same as above.

755. ———. New York; Chicago: United States Book Co., [1894]. 255 p.
Also contains: Scan. - Iden.

756. *The Sign of the Four and A Scandal in Bohemia.* Chicago: Geo. M. Hill Co., [1898]. 235 p.

757. ———. Chicago and New York: Rand, McNally & Co., Publishers, [n.d.] 235 p. illus. (Alpha Library)

758. ———. Philadelphia and New York: John Wanamaker, [n.d.] 235 p. (Columbine Library)

759. ———. Chicago: E. A. Weeks & Co., [n.d.] 235 p.

760. ———. Chicago: E. A. Weeks & Co., [n.d.] 235 p. (Marguerite Series, No. 41)

761. ———. Chicago and New York: The Werner Co., [n.d.] 235 p.

762. *The Sign of the Four, A Scandal in Bohemia, and Other Stories.* New York: A. L. Burt Co., [n.d.] 364 p.
Also contains: Iden. - My Friend the Murderer. - The Ring of Thoth. - The Surgeon of Gaster Fell. - John Huxford's Hiatus.

763. ———. New York: A. L. Burt Co., [1900?] 364 p. (The Home Library)
Frontispiece by J. Watson Davis.
Contents same as above.

764. *The Sign of the Four and A Study in Scarlet.* New York: Lovell, Coryell & Co., [n.d.] 183, 213 p.

765. ———. New York: Lovell, Coryell & Co., [June 1893]. 255, 213 p. (The Belmore Series, No. 21)
Also contains: Scan. - Iden.

766. ———. New York: Lovell, Coryell & Co., [1893?] 255, 213 p.
Contents same as above.

767. *Some Adventures of Sherlock Holmes.* Abridged and slightly simplified by W. J. Hoggett. Illustrated by Stein. London: Longmans, Green and Co., [1949]. ix, 182 p. (The Bridge Series)
Contents: Copp. - 3Stu. - Spec. - RedH. - Twis. - Dyin. - Glossary.

768. *Stories of Sherlock Holmes.* Illustrated [by Sidney Paget and W. H. Hyde]. New York and London: Harper & Brothers Publishers, 1904. 3 v. (xv, 287; 307; 259 p.) (Sherlock Holmes Series)
Contents: Vol. 1. The Creator of Sherlock Holmes, by James MacArthur. - Stud. - Sign. - Vol. 2. Adventures. - Vol. 3. Memoirs.

769. *A Study in Scarlet.* New York: American Publishers Corp., [n.d.] 213, [227]-255 p.
Also contains: Iden.

770. *A Study in Scarlet and A Case of Identity.* Chicago and New York: Rand, McNally & Co., 1894. 232 p. (Globe Library, Vol. 1, No. 192, October 29, 1894)

771. ———. Chicago: Rand, McNally & Co., [190-?] 232 p. (The Antique Library)

772. ———. Chicago: E. A. Weeks & Co., [n.d.] 232 p.

773. *A Study in Scarlet and The Sign of the Four.* New York and London: Harper & Brothers Publishers, 1904. xv, 287 p.
Includes an introduction by James MacArthur.

774. *A Study in Scarlet & The Sign of Four.* Garden City, N.Y.: Doubleday & Co.,

[January 1961]. 232 p. (Dolphin Books, C124)

775. *A Study in Scarlet and The Sign of Four.* [New York]: Berkley Pub. Corp., [July 1963]. 253 p. (A Berkley Medallion Book, F798)

776. ———. [New York]: Berkley Pub. Corp., [February 1968]. 253 p. (A Berkley Medallion Book, X1575)

777. *Tales of Sherlock Holmes.* With an introduction by G. Mercer Adam. Illustrated by J. Watson Davis. New York: A. L. Burt Co., [1906]. iv, 415 p.
Contents: Stud. - Sign. - Scan. - Iden.

778. ———. With an introduction by G. Mercer Adam. New York: A. L. Burt Co., [n.d.] iv, 415 p.
Contents same as above, except that three of the four illustrations have been omitted.

779. ———. With an introduction by G. Mercer Adam. New York: A. L. Burt Co., [n.d.] iv, 415 p.
Contents same as above, but without the four illustrations.

780. ———. New York: Grosset & Dunlap, [1915]. 359 p.
Illustrated with scenes from the play *Sherlock Holmes* by William Gillette.
Contents: Stud. - Iden. - Scan. - RedH. - Bosc. - Sign.

781. ———. Boston: Human Life Pub. Co., [n.d.] 359 p.
Contents same as above.

782. ———. Boston: The Mutual Book Co., [n.d.] 359 p.
Contents same as above.

783. ———. Washington, D. C.: National Home Library Foundation, [1932]. 259 p. (Jacket Library, No. 10)
Contents: Stud. - Sign. - Scan.

784. ———. New York: Triangle Books, [May 1938]. iv, 415 p.
Contents: Introduction, by G. Mercer Adam. - Stud. - Sign. - Scan. - Iden.

785. ———. Illustrated by Harvey Dinnerstein. Afterword by Clifton Fadiman. New York: The Macmillan Co., 1963. ix, 608 p. (Macmillan Classics, No. 24)
Contents: Stud. - Sign. - Bery. - Scan. - Iden. - Spec. - Silv. - RedH. - Musg. - Houn.

786. [———.] New York: American Publishers Corp., [n.d.] 2 v. (255, 213, 138-199 p.)
Title from spine.
Also on spine: Popular Edition.
Contents: Vol. 1. *The Sign of the Four; or, The Problem of the Sholtos.* Sign. - Scan.

- Iden. - Vol. 2. *A Study in Scarlet.* Stud. - RedH. - Bosc.

787. ———. New York: Grosset & Dunlap, [n.d.] 311 p.
Contents: Stud. - Scan. - RedH. - Sign.

788. ———. Girard, Kansas: Haldeman-Julius Co., [n.d.] 96 p. (Ten Cent Pocket Series, No. 102)
Contents: Iden. - Scan. - RedH.

789. ———. New York: Little Leather Library Corp., [n.d.] 96 p.
Contents: Iden. - Scan.

790. *Tales of Sherlock Holmes: Detective Stories.* Three Owls edition. New York: W. R. Caldwell & Co., [n.d.] 359 p. (The International Adventure Library)
Contents: Stud. - Iden. - Scan. - RedH. - Bosc. - Sign.

791. *Three Sherlock Holmes Stories.* Edited and with an introduction by Leslie Sherwood. London; New York; Toronto: Longmans, Green & Co., [1949]. x, 86 p. (Essential English Library)
Simplified versions.
Contents: Introduction. - Blue. - Spec. - Silv. - Glossary.

792. *A Treasury of Sherlock Holmes.* Selected and with an introduction by Adrian Conan Doyle. Garden City, N.Y.: Hanover House, [1955]. xiv, 686 p.
Contents: Stud. - Houn. - RedH. - SixN. - Fiña. - Five. - Danc. - Dyin. - Blue. - Nava. - Bery. - Silv. - Musg. - Spec. - Blac. - Reig. - Chas. - Engr. - Seco. - Abbe. - Maza. - Thor. - Shos. - Devi. - Gree. - Glor. - Prio. - Empt. - Last.
Reviews: New York Herald Tribune Book Review (March 13, 1955), 12 (James Sandoe); *New York Times Book Review* (February 6, 1955), 25 (Anthony Boucher); *San Francisco Chronicle* (January 26, 1955), 15 (J. H. Jackson); *Springfield Republican* (March 13, 1955), 6C.

793. ———. Selected and with an introduction by Adrian Conan Doyle. [Deluxe edition.] Garden City, N.Y.: International Collectors Library, [1955]. xiv, 686 p.
Contents same as above.

794. *Works of Arthur Conan Doyle.* With preface, notes, and hand-colored photogravure illustrations. New York: D. Appleton and Co., [c.1902]. 14 v. (Author's edition)
Illustrations by Arthur Twidle.
Limited to 50 sets.
Partial contents: Stud. - Sign. - Adventures. - Memoirs. - Houn.

795. ———. With preface and notes by the

author and photogravure illustrations. New York: D. Appleton and Co., [c. 1902]. 13 v. (Author's edition)

Illustrations by Arthur Twidle.
Limited to 1000 sets.
Contents same as above.

796. [———.] Illustrated. London: Smith, Elder & Co., 1903. 12 v. (Author's edition)
Illustrations by Arthur Twidle.
Limited to 1000 signed sets.
[———.] Also published under the John Murray imprint, dated 1903, but not actually issued until 1917, the year Smith, Elder's business was amalgamated with John Murray's. The sets were the unused portion of the original 1000.
Partial contents: Stud. - Sign. - Adventures. - Memoirs.

797. *The Works of A. Conan Doyle.* One volume edition. New York: Walter J. Black, Inc., [1928?] 1020 p.
Partial contents: Scan. - Bosc. - Iden. - RedH. - Sign. - Stud.

798. ———. One volume edition. Roslyn, N.Y.: Black's Readers Service Co., [n.d.] 621 p.
Partial contents: Scan. - Bosc. - Iden. - RedH. - Sign.

799. ———. One volume edition. New York: P. F. Collier & Son., [n.d.] 1020 p.
Partial contents: Scan. - Bosc. - Iden. - RedH. - Sign. - Stud.

800. ———. New York: P. F. Collier & Son, [n.d.] 10 v.
Also published in a deluxe edition.
Partial contents: Vol. 1. The Original of Sherlock Holmes, by Dr. Harold Emery Jones. - Stud. - Scan. - Iden. - Vol. 2. Sign. - Vol. 6. Houn. - Vol. 8. Return.

801. [*The Works of Sir Arthur Conan Doyle.*] The Crowborough Edition. Garden City, N.Y.: Doubleday, Doran & Co., 1930. 24 v.
Limited to 760 signed and numbered sets.
Partial contents: Vol. 15. Stud. - Vall. - Introduction, by Dr. Joseph Bell. - Vol. 16. Sign. - Houn. - Vol. 17. Adventures. - Vol. 18. Memoirs. - Vol. 19. Return. - Vol. 20. His Last Bow. - Case Book. - Vol. 22. ManW. - Lost. - Vol. 24. Memories and Adventures.

D Braille Editions

802. *The Adventures of Sherlock Holmes.* London: The Royal National Institute for the Blind, 1920. 3 v. (Catalogue No. 4922, 4923, 4924)

803. *Cases of Sherlock Holmes.* Adapted by

[William] Kottmeyer. Louisville, Ky.: American Printing House for the Blind, 1965. 1 v. (Everyreader Series)
"Braille Grade 2, F."
Contents: Spec. - RedH. - SixN. - Empt. - Something About the Author, by William Kottmeyer.

E Shorthand Editions

804. "The Adventures of Sherlock Holmes," *Pitman's Shorthand Weekly,* Vol. 4, No. 6- Vol. 6 (1894?) illus.
"The Strand Library Edition (Geo. Newnes, Ltd.) 6s., forms a Key."

805. *The Return of Sherlock Holmes.* Engraved in the advanced style of Pitman's shorthand, by permission of the author. A selection of the stories from the edition published by George Newnes, Ltd., which forms the key to the shorthand. London: Sir Isaac Pitman & Sons, Ltd., [1915?] 3 v. illus.
Contents: Vol. 1. Danc. - Soli. - Prio. - Vol. 2. Empt. - Blac. - Chas. - Vol. 3. Gold. - SixN. - Seco.

806. ———. Engraved in the advanced stage of Pitman's shorthand. New Era Edition. London: Sir Isaac Pitman & Sons, Ltd., [n.d.] 3 v. (120, 130, 120 p.)
Volumes 2 and 3 are illustrated with drawings by Sidney Paget.
Contents same as above.

807. *The Sign of Four.* Engraved in the easy reporting style of Pitman's shorthand. Twentieth Century Edition. London: Sir I. Pitman & Sons, [ca. 1890]. 171 p.

808. ———. Engraved in the easy reporting style of Pitman's shorthand. London: Sir Isaac Pitman & Sons, 1898. 171 p. (Pitman's Shorthand Library, 4)

809. ———. Engraved in the advanced style of Pitman's shorthand. London: Sir Isaac Pitman & Sons, Ltd., [1916]. 171 p.
On cover: Centenary Edition.

810. ———. Printed in the advanced stage of Pitman's shorthand. New Era Edition. London: Sir Isaac Pitman & Sons, Ltd., 1925. 170 p.

811. ———. Printed in the advanced stage of Pitman's shorthand. New Era Edition. New York: Pitman Pub. Corp., [n.d.] 170 p.

812. *The Sign of the Four.* Printed in Gregg shorthand. New York; Chicago; San Francisco: The Gregg Pub. Co., [1918]. 188 p.
"Shorthand plates written by Alice Rinné Hagar."

Round the Fire.

II.—THE STORY OF THE MAN WITH THE WATCHES.

By A. Conan Doyle.

THERE are many who will still bear in mind the singular circumstances which, under the heading of the Rugby Mystery, filled many columns of the daily Press in the spring of the year 1892. Coming as it did at a period of exceptional dulness, it attracted perhaps rather more attention than it deserved, but it offered to the public that mixture of the whimsical and the tragic which is most stimulating to the popular imagination. Interest drooped, however, when, after weeks of fruitless investigation, it was found that no final explanation of the facts was forthcoming, and the tragedy seemed from that time to the present to have finally taken its place in the dark catalogue of inexplicable and unexpiated crimes. A recent communication (the authenticity of which appears to be above question) has, however, thrown some new and clear light upon the matter. Before laying it before the public it would be as well, perhaps, that I should refresh their memories as to the singular facts upon which this commentary is founded. These facts were briefly as follows :—

At five o'clock upon the evening of the 18th of March in the year already mentioned a train left Euston Station for Manchester. It was a rainy, squally day, which grew wilder as it progressed, so it was by no means the weather in which anyone would travel who was not driven to do so by necessity. The train, however, is a favourite one among

" THE TWO MIGHT VERY WELL HAVE PASSED AS FATHER AND DAUGHTER."

Manchester business men who are returning from town, for it does the journey in four hours and twenty minutes, with only three stoppages upon the way. In spite of the inclement evening it was, therefore, fairly well filled upon the occasion of which I speak. The guard of the train was a tried servant of the company—a man who had worked for twenty-two years without blemish or complaint. His name was John Palmer.

The station clock was upon the stroke of five, and the guard was about to give the customary signal to the engine-driver, when he observed two belated passengers hurrying down the platform. The one was an exceptionally tall man, dressed in a long black overcoat with an astrakhan collar and cuffs. I have already said that the evening was an inclement one, and the tall traveller had the high, warm collar turned up to protect his throat against the bitter March wind. He appeared, as far as the guard could judge by so hurried an inspection, to be a man between fifty and sixty years of age, who had retained a good deal of the vigour and activity of his youth. In one hand he carried a brown leather Gladstone bag. His companion was a lady, tall and erect, walking with a vigorous step which outpaced the gentleman beside her. She wore a long, fawn - coloured dustcloak, a black, close-fitting toque, and a dark veil which concealed the greater part of her face. The two might very well have passed as father and daughter. They walked swiftly down the line of carriages, glancing in at the

First page of "The Story of the Man with the Watches," The Strand Magazine, July 1898 (829).

II | *The Apocrypha*

The writings attributed to Dr. Watson's contemporary, Sir Arthur Conan Doyle, are referred to as the Apocrypha. They resemble the Sacred Writings, but not so closely that they are likely to be admitted to the Canon.

Among the items included in the Apocrypha are three plays: 1. an unpublished play entitled *Angels of Darkness* (listed in Part III), based upon the Mormon flashback in *A Study in Scarlet*; 2. *The Speckled Band*, based upon Dr. Watson's adventure by the same name; 3. *The Crown Diamond*, which was later turned into "The Adventure of the Mazarin Stone," a story that, as has already has been noted, is attributed to the literary agent. Performances of plays 2 and 3 are listed in Part IX, Section E.

In addition, Doyle wrote two short parodies, "The Field Bazaar" and "How Watson Learned the Trick," which take the form of the familiar breakfast-table scene. Holmes is also believed to figure prominently in two other stories: "The Man with the Watches" and "The Lost Special."

Other writings by Doyle that are considered part of the Apocrypha appear in Part V, Section F, under *The Literary Agent*. Critical articles about the Apocrypha are listed in the same section under *The Apocrypha*.

THE CROWN DIAMOND

813. *The Crown Diamond: An Evening with Sherlock Holmes: A Play in One Act.* New York: The Baskerrette Press, 1958. [32] p.
Includes a foreword and three illustrations by Edgar W. Smith.
Limited to 59 copies.
"An unbelievably corny play printed for the first time because a decent respect for the opinions of mankind—and especially that segment of mankind distinguished as the Baker Street Irregulars—demands that censorship unaccountably imposed upon it for more than thirty-seven years be arbitrarily rescinded." (Edgar W. Smith)

THE FIELD BAZAAR

814. "The Field Bazaar," *The Student, Edinburgh University Magazine* (NS), Bazaar Number (November 20, 1896), 35-36.

815. ———. London: The Athenaeum Press [A. G. Macdonell], [1934]. [2] p.
Limited to 100 copies.

816. ———, *221B: Studies in Sherlock Holmes.* Edited by Vincent Starrett. New York: The Macmillan Co., 1940. p. 1-4.
Also published in a facsimile edition by the Baker Street Irregulars, 1956.

817. *The Field Bazaar: A Sherlock Holmes Pastiche.* Summit, N.J.: The Pamphlet House, 1947. 15 p.
Includes an introduction by Edgar W. Smith.
Limited to 250 copies.

818. "Basaren i Edinburgh," [Oversat af A. D. Henriksen]. *Sherlock Holmes Årbog* I (1965): 12-15.

819. "The Field Bazaar," *The Daily Californian Weekly Magazine,* 4, No. 9 (January 14, 1969), 11.

820. "Kricket-basaren," *BSCL,* No. 7 (1969), 9-12.

HOW WATSON LEARNED THE TRICK

821. "How Watson Learned the Trick," *The Book of the Queen's Dolls' House Library.* Edited by E. V. Lucas. London: Methuen & Co. Ltd., 1924. Vol. 2, p. 92-94.
Limited to 1500 copies.

822. ———, *The New York Times* (August 24, 1924), III, 3.

823. ———. Chicago: Camden House, 1947. 4 p.

The Apocrypha

Includes a bibliographical note by Vincent Starrett.
Limited to 60 copies.

824. ———, *BSJ*, 1, No. 2 (April 1951), 63-65.

825. ———, *The Incunabular Sherlock Holmes*. Edited by Edgar W. Smith. Morristown, N.J.: The Baker Street Irregulars, 1958. p. 97-100.

826. "Hvorledes Watson laerte tricket," [Oversat af A. D. Henriksen]. *Sherlock Holmes Årbog* II (1966), 15-17.

827. "How Watson Learned the Trick," *The Daily Californian Weekly Magazine*, 4, No. 9 (January 14, 1969), 11.

828. "Hur Watson lärde sig knepet," *BSCL*, No. 7 (1969), 13-14.

THE MAN WITH THE WATCHES, AND THE LOST SPECIAL

829. "The Story of the Man with the Watches," [Illustrations by Frank Craig]. *The Strand Magazine*, 16, No. 91 (July 1898), 33-43. (Round the Fire, 2)

830. "The Story of the Lost Special," [Illustrations by Max Cowper]. *The Strand Magazine*, 16, No. 92 (August 1898), 153-162. (Round the Fire, 3)

831. *Round the Fire Stories*, by Arthur Conan Doyle. London: Smith, Elder & Co., 1908. 372 p.
Partial contents: ManW. - Lost.

832. ———. New York: The McClure Co., 1908. 356 p.

833. *Tales of Terror and Mystery*, [by] A. Conan Doyle. [London]: John Murray, [July 1922]. 310 p.
Partial contents: Lost. - ManW.

834. ———. London: John Murray, [1963]. 190 p.

835. *The Black Doctor and Other Tales of Terror and Mystery*, by A. Conan Doyle. New York: George H. Doran Co., [1925]. 279 p.
Partial contents: Lost. - ManW.

836. *The Conan Doyle Stories*. London: John Murray, [1929]. xiii, 1201 p.
Partial contents: Lost. - ManW.

837. *Letters from Baker Street*. Edited by Edgar W. Smith. New York: The Pamphlet House, 1942. 60 p.
Partial contents: Lost. - ManW.

838. "The Man with the Watches," *MacKill's Mystery Magazine*, 3, No. 6 (April 1954), 109-122.

839. "The Lost Special," *When the World Screamed and Other Stories*, [by] Sir Arthur Conan Doyle. London: John Murray, [1968]. Chap. 2, p. 41-61.

840. *The Sherlockian Doyle: Sir Arthur Conan Doyle's The Man with the Watches and The Lost Special*. With a special introduction by Lord Donegall, B.S.I.; original illustrations by Roy Hunt. [Culver City, Calif.: Luther Norris, October 1968.] 46 p.
Limited to 500 copies.
Reviews: New York Times Book Review (November 24, 1968), 75 (Allen J. Hubin); *SOS*, 3, No. 2 (July 1969), 3-5 (Bruce Dettman); *SHJ*, 9, No. 1 (Winter 1968), 28 (Lord Donegall); *Sherlockiana*, 13, Nr. 4 (1968), 16.

A PLOT FOR A SHERLOCK HOLMES STORY

841. "A Plot for a Sherlock Holmes Story," *Conan Doyle: His Life and Art*, by Hesketh Pearson. London: Methuen & Co., [1943]. p. 93-95.
A short scenario for an uncompleted tale of Dr. Watson's which Mr. Pearson discovered among Conan Doyle's papers.

842. ———, ———. London: Published for the British Publishers Guild by Methuen and Co., [1946]. p. 105-107.

843. ———, ———. New York: Walker & Co., [1961]. p. 131-133.

844. ———, *A Baker Street Four-Wheeler*. Edited by Edgar W. Smith. [Maplewood, N.J., and New York: The Pamphlet House, 1944.] p. 14-15.

845. "Plan för Sherlock Holmes-skildring," [Tr. into Danish by Ted Bergman]. *BSCL*, No. 8 (1970), 26-28.

THE SPECKLED BAND

846. *The Speckled Band: An Adventure of Sherlock Holmes*. London; New York: Samuel French, Ltd., 1912. 124 p. (French's Acting Edition, No. 2558)
A play in three acts, first produced at the Adelphi Theatre, London, on June 4, 1910. See also items 5189-5200.

847. ———. New York; London: Samuel French, 1912. 124 p. (The Dramatic Works of Arthur Conan Doyle)

40

 # III Manuscripts

In this part are listed the manuscripts of the Sacred Writings and the Apocrypha now known to be located in various college and public libraries and in private collections. They are all holographs written in the neat, precise hand of the author. The information was obtained primarily from the compilations of David A. Randall and Peter E. Blau, from catalogs, and from a personal examination of several of the manuscripts. Of the forty manuscripts and fragments, twelve are owned by libraries. Articles about the manuscripts are listed under *Manuscripts* in Part V, Section F.

THE SACRED WRITINGS

848. *The Adventure of the Abbey Grange.* [1904] 26 p.
Auction: New York: February 13, 1923. $105. New York: Sold by Scribner's to a California dealer. New York: Parke-Bernet Galleries, March 22, 1966. $5,400.
Location: Unknown.

849. *The Adventure of the Blanched Soldier.* Signed and dated Jan. 1926. 26 p.
Bound in vellum and signed on front cover.
Auction: New York: January 1944. $310.
Location: Berg Collection, New York Public Library.

850. *The Adventure of Charles Augustus Milverton.* [1904] 21 p. (6,800 words)
Here entitled: *The Adventure of the Worst Man in London.*
Bound in vellum by Spealls with a red slipcase.
The first page is reproduced on the Milvertonians' Christmas card, 1963.
Auction: January 30, 1923. $70. New York: Scribner's Sherlock Holmes catalogue, 1943. $450.
Location: Carl Anderson, Philadelphia.

851. *The Adventure of the Creeping Man.* [1923] 44 p.
Bound in white linen.

Auction: None.
Location: Lady Bromet (Air Cmdt. Dame Jean Conan Doyle)

852. *The Adventure of the Crooked Man.* (1893]
Note: Col. James Barclay is written as Col. Robert Barker; Miss Nancy Devoy as Miss Annie Devoy.
Auction: The first four pages were sold by Christie's in London on April 28, 1966. L260.
Location: Unknown.

853. *The Adventure of the Dancing Men.* [1903]
Auction: London: April 22, 1918. Donated by Doyle to the Red Cross Charity Sale. L10.10. New York: February 13, 1923. $105. London: January 28, 1925. Sold with Prio and Soli in one lot. L66.
Location: Unknown.

854. *The Adventure of the Devil's Foot.* Signed at end. [1910] 2 exercise books (58 p.)
"Sherlock Holmes Series" inscribed on title page by Doyle.
Bound in vellum and signed on front cover.
Auction: None.
Location: Berg Collection, New York Public Library. Presented by Lucius Wilmerding.

855. *The Adventure of the Dying Detective.* Signed and dated July 27 / 13. 18 p.
The title page containing "Sherlock Holmes Series. A. Conan Doyle. The Adventure of the Dying Detective. Original Mss," is not included in the 18 pages. Three pages are not in Doyle's writing.
The first page is reproduced in Christie's catalogue; the last page in *Sir Arthur Conan Doyle Centenary 1859-1959* (London: John Murray, 1959, p. 105) (Garden City, N.Y.: Doubleday & Co., n.d., p. 105).
Note: Mr. Culverton Smith is written as Mr. Colverton Smith.

Manuscripts

Auction: London: Christie, Manson & Woods, April 28, 1966.
Location: Unknown.

856. *The Adventure of the Empty House.* [1903] 3 exercise books (47 p.)
"Sherlock Holmes Series" inscribed on title page by Doyle.
Bound in vellum and signed on front cover.
One page is reproduced in Maggs Bros. catalogue no. 436 (1923), plate 8.
Auction: None.
Location: Rosenbach Foundation, Philadelphia.

857. *The Final Problem.* [1893] 1 leaf, with the first three sentences of Holmes's letter to Watson regarding his last meeting with Moriarty.
The letter, with a commentary by "Prof. James Moriarty," is reproduced in *BSG,* 1, No. 2 (1961), 34.
Auction: Philadelphia: December 8, 1915.
Location: Lilly Library, University of Indiana, Bloomington.

858. *The Adventure of the Golden Pince-nez.* [1904] 55 p.
"The Sherlock Holmes Series" inscribed on title page and above it on the first page of text, "The Return of Sherlock Holmes, IX."
Bound in parchment with the original wrappers of one book bound in, signed four times and inscribed on the front cover: "Sherlock Holmes Original MS. from Arthur Conan Doyle to H. Greenhough Smith - A Souvenir of 20 years of collaboration. Feb. 8 / 16." (Mr. Smith was editor of *The Strand Magazine* from its beginning in 1891 to the mid-twenties.) Includes the bookplate of Alain de Suzannet, Undershaw, Hindhead [1904].
The first page is reproduced in *The Strand Magazine,* 68 (December 1924), 644; the cover in Feldman's catalog *Seventy.*
Auction: London: April 18, 1932. L88. London: March 26, 1934. L120. London: Sotheby & Co., July 12, 1967. L900. New York: House of El Dieff, Feldman's catalog. $7,500.
Location: University of Texas Library, Austin.

859. *The Adventure of the Greek Interpreter.* Signed. [1893] 34 p.
The first page is reproduced in *SHJ,* 7, No. 2 (Summer 1965), 34.
Auction: London: Christie, Manson & Woods, December 18, 1964. L4,500 ($12,600). Offered as part of the Sir Arthur Conan Doyle Archives by Lew David Feldman in 1971.
Location: New York: House of El Dieff.

860. *The Hound of the Baskervilles.* "Chapter XI. The Man on the Tor." [1901] 16 p. (4,300 words)

Auction: New York: March 18, 1936. $115.
Location: Berg Collection, New York Public Library.

861. *The Adventure of the Illustrious Client.* [1924] 35 p.
Bound in white linen.
Auction: None.
Location: Lady Bromet (Air Cmdt. Dame Jean Conan Doyle)

862. *His Last Bow: An Epilogue of Sherlock Holmes.* Corrected, signed and dated March 7 / 17. 13 p. (incomplete)
Auction: None. Offered as part of the Sir Arthur Conan Doyle Archives by Lew David Feldman in 1971.
Location: New York: House of El Dieff.

863. *The Disappearance of Lady Frances Carfax.* [1911] 28 p. (7,500 words)
Bound in vellum.
Auction: New York: February 5, 1929. $285.
Location: Unknown.

864. *The Adventure of the Lion's Mane.* Signed at end A. Conan Doyle. Crowborough. [1926]. 42 p., with corrections and deletions.
Bound in vellum.
Auction: London: Christie, Manson & Woods, April 28, 1966.
Location: Unknown.

865. *The Adventure of the Mazarin Stone.* 19 p., with corrections.
Here entitled: *The Adventure of the Mazarin Diamond.*
Bound in white cloth.
Auction: London: Sotheby & Co., December 14-15, 1970. L400.
Location: Unknown.

866. *The Adventure of the Missing Three-Quarter.* [1904] 25 p. (8,000 words)
Bound in vellum by Spealls. Includes the bookplate and signature of Vincent Starrett.
The first page is reproduced in *BSJ,* 5, No. 1 (January 1955), 25; in *The Annotated Sherlock Holmes* (1967), Vol. 2, p. 490; in *SHJ,* 10, No. 2 (Summer 1971), 55.
Auction: New York: January 30, 1923. $130. New York: Scribner's Sherlock Holmes catalogue, 1943. $450.
Location: British Museum. Presented May 22, 1959, by J. Bliss Austin, L. David Feldman, E. T. Guymon, Jr., Rollin V. N. Hadley, Jr., Edgar W. Smith, the Sherlock Holmes Society of London, and the Friends of the National Libraries.

867. *The Adventure of the Norwood Builder.* Signed at end. [1903] 50 p. (9,500 words), with numerous corrections.
"Sherlock Holmes Series" inscribed on title page by Doyle.

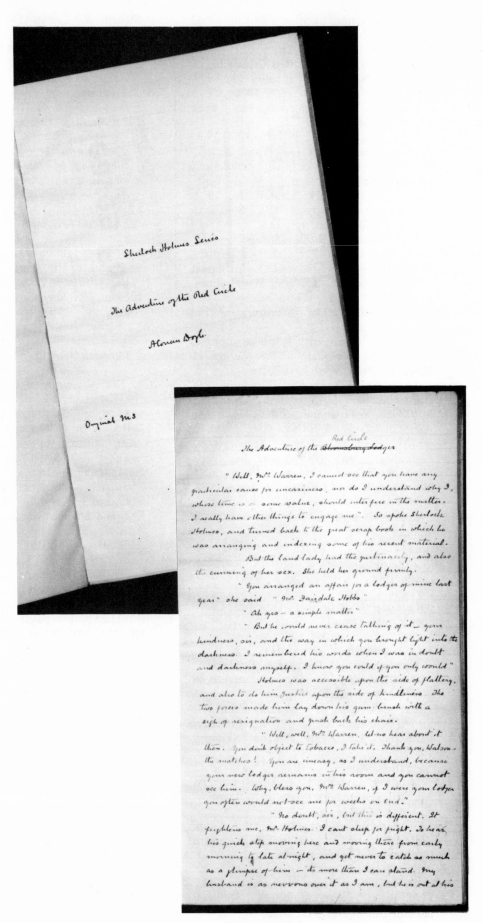

Title page and opening of "The Adventure of the Red Circle"
(869). Photograph courtesy of The House of El Dieff, Inc., New
York.

Manuscripts

Bound in vellum by Spealls and inscribed on the binding: "Anno Belli germanici IV."
Auction: London: April 22, 1918. Donated by Doyle to the Red Cross Charity Sale. L12. New York: February 13, 1923. $100. New York: February 8, 1926. $60.
Location: Berg Collection, New York Public Library.

868. *The Adventure of the Priory School.* [1903] 71 p. (13,500 words), with corrections and cancellations.
Auction: New York: January 26, 1922. $155. London: January 28, 1925. Sold with Danc and Soli in one lot. L66.
Location: Leigh Block, Chicago.

869. *The Adventure of the Red Circle.* Signed at end Arthur Conan Doyle, Windlesham, Crowborough. [1911] 23 p.
Here entitled: *The Adventure of the Bloomsbury Lodger.*
Bound in vellum with a brown slipcase. Includes the bookplate and signature of Vincent Starrett.
The first page is reproduced in *BSJ Christmas Annual,* No. 1 (1956), 46; in part in *BSJ,* 10, No. 1 (January 1960), 41; in *The Annotated Sherlock Holmes* (1967), Vol. 2, p. 704; in Feldman's catalog *Seventy One.*
Auction: None. New York: Scribner's Sherlock Holmes catalogue, 1943. $450. New York: House of El Dieff catalog, 1971. $8,000.
Location: Lilly Library, University of Indiana.

870. *The Adventure of the Retired Colourman.* [1926] 18 p.
Auction: None.
Location: Lady Bromet (Air Cmdt. Dame Jean Conan Doyle)

871. *A Scandal in Bohemia.* [1891] 30 p.
Here entitled: *A Scandal of Bohemia.*
Bound in blue full morocco; lettered in gold on front cover and spine.
The first page is reproduced in *The Strand Magazine* (October 1946); in Henry Lauritzen's *Min Kaere Watson* (Aalborg: 1954, p. 21).
Auction: None.
Location: University of Texas Library, Austin. Presented by Frederic A. Dannay.

872. *The Adventure of the Second Stain.* [1904] 31 p. (five and one half pages are in the hand of Doyle's secretary)
Bound in vellum.
Auction: New York: January 26, 1922. $170. New York: Scribner's Sherlock Holmes catalogue, 1943. $450.
Location: Haverford College Library, Haverford, Pa. Presented by Christopher Morley.

873. *The Adventure of Shoscombe Old Place.*
Signed A. Conan Doyle, Crowborough, Sussex. [1927] 21 p.
Here entitled: *The Adventure of Shoscombe Abbey.*
Bound in cloth.
Auction: None.
Location: Doyle Estate. On display at "The Sherlock Holmes" in London.

874. *The Sign of the Four.* [1890] 160 leaves.
Inlaid with portrait and printed title page. Bound in levant morocco.
Auction: New York: December 9, 1909. $105.
Location: Unknown.

875. ———. [1890] 1 leaf (220 words), the beginning of the story.
Reproduced in *BSJ,* 4, No. 2 (April 1954), 126; in *The Annotated Sherlock Holmes* (1967), Vol. 1, p. 688.
Auction: New York: November 22, 1929. $50.
Location: Unknown.

876. *The Adventure of the Solitary Cyclist.* [1903] 2 exercise books, about 7,900 words, with cancellations and insertions (40 p.)
Bound in vellum by Spealls with half green morocco slipcase.
The second page is reproduced in *BSJ,* 22, No. 2 (June 1972), 73.
Auction: New York: January 26, 1922. $120. London: January 28, 1925. Sold with Prio and Danc in one lot. L66. New York: April 25, 1927. $160.
Location: Olin Library, Cornell University, Ithaca, N.Y. Presented in 1967 by William G. Mennen.

877. *The Adventure of the Speckled Band.* [1891] 33 p. (two pages are in the hand of a secretary but contain corrections by Doyle)
Note: In the manuscript Helen Stoner is Helen Roylott, the daughter of Dr. Grimesby Roylott.
Auction: London: March 26, 1934. L82. New York: Sold by Scribner's to a Chicago dealer in 1935.
Location: Unknown.

878. *A Study in Scarlet.* [1887] 1 leaf.
The earliest page relating to the creation of "Sherrinford Holmes" and "Ormond Sacker" of "221B Upper Baker Street."
Reproduced in Vincent Starrett's *The Private Life of Sherlock Holmes* (New York: The Macmillan Co., 1933, p. 11); in revised ed. (The University of Chicago Press, 1960, p. 6); in *Sir Arthur Conan Doyle Centenary 1859-1959* (p. 104); in part in *BSJ,* 12, No. 4 (December 1962), 218; 19, No. 1 (March 1969), 49; in *The Annotated Sherlock Holmes* (1967), Vol. 1, p. 11; on cover of Lew David Feldman's *Sir Arthur Conan Doyle Archives* (New York: House of El Dieff, 1970); *In the Footsteps of Sherlock Holmes*

[Revised ed.] (David & Charles, 1971) (Drake, 1972), facing p. 37.
   Auction: None
   Location: New York: House of El Dieff.

879. *The Problem of Thor Bridge.* [1922] 47 p., signed and corrected.
   Here entitled: *The Problem of Thor's Bridge.*
   Auction: None. Offered as part of the Sir Arthur Conan Doyle Archives by Lew David Feldman in 1971.
   Location: New York: House of El Dieff.

880. *The Adventure of the Three Gables.* Signed at end A. Conan Doyle, Crowborough. [1926] 31 p.
   Bound in vellum and lettered in gold on front cover, with a red half-morocco slipcase.
   Auction: None.
   Location: Walter Pond, New York.

881. *The Adventure of the Three Garridebs.* Signed twice and dated June 1924. 22 p.
   Auction: None. Offered as part of the Sir Arthur Conan Doyle Archives by Lew David Feldman in 1971.
   Location: New York: House of El Dieff.

882. *The Adventure of the Three Students.* [1904] 21 p.
   "The Return of Sherlock Holmes, IX" inscribed above title.
   Auction: None.
   Location: Houghton Library, Harvard University. Presented in 1925 by Norton Perkins.

883. *The Valley of Fear.* [1914] 185 p., with many deletions, corrections, additions, etc.
   The manuscript was dismembered and the chapters were sold separately in 1950. It is now reassembled except for the missing "Epilogue." Chapters 1 and 7, 2, 4, 11 are bound separately; the other chapters remain unbound.
   The first page is reproduced in *The Strand Magazine*, 48 (August 1914), 227; and an unpublished fragment in Bliss Austin's *A Baker Street Christmas Stocking*, 1956.
   Auction: New York: January 30, 1923.

$275. New York: Scribner's Sherlock Holmes catalogue, 1943. $1,100.
   Location: James Bliss Austin, Pittsburgh.

884. *The Adventure of the Veiled Lodger.* Signed and dated at end A. Conan Doyle, Windlesham, Crowborough, Oct. 3 / 26. 15 p.
   Bound in white cloth and lettered in gold on front cover, with a green half-morocco slipcase.
   Auction: None.
   Location: Walter Pond, New York.

THE APOCRYPHA

885. *Angels of Darkness.* [1889-1890] 5 quarto notebooks (67, 32, 52, 15, 21 p.)
   An unpublished play in three acts that is briefly discussed by John Dickson Carr in his *Life of Sir Arthur Conan Doyle* (John Murray, p. 92-93; Harper, p. 70). The play is a reconstruction of the Utah scenes from *A Study in Scarlet*. Holmes is not present but a black Watson has the lead! Two revelations of Mr. Carr's are that Watson practiced medicine in San Francisco and that he apparently had a wife *before* he married Mary Morstan. Perhaps the world is at last prepared for these new and disturbing insights into Watson's life!
   Auction: None. Offered by Lew David Feldman in 1971.
   Location: New York: House of El Dieff.

886. *The Crown Diamond.* [1921] 25 p., in small notebook, corrected and signed on cover.
   Auction: None. Offered by Lew David Feldman in 1971.
   Location: New York: House of El Dieff.

887. *Memories and Adventures.* [1923] [?] unnumbered leaves.
   Auction: None.
   Location: James Bliss Austin, Pittsburgh.

888. *Some Personalia About Mr. Sherlock Holmes.* [1917] 10 p., corrected and signed.
   Auction: None. Offered by Lew David Feldman in 1971.
   Location: New York: House of El Dieff.

Foreign-language editions include the ten-volume Oeuvres complètes **(1120)**.

IV | Foreign-Language Editions

This part proved to be the most difficult but at the same time the most interesting and challenging to compile. Fifty languages into which the Canon has been translated are included here, and undoubtedly the tales have been translated into still other languages. Also listed are English readers, as well as parodies and pastiches that made their original appearance in the language shown. Translations of these mock stories (some of them outright plagiarisms) are also given. Translations of the parodies and pastiches written by American and British authors appear in Part X.

Bibliographical information for the foreign-language editions is given in either the language into which they have been translated, in a transliteration, or, when it has been expedient to do so, in English. All information not in the original language or on the title page has been placed in brackets. It should also be noted that many countries do not distinguish between the words *edition* and *printing* and usually refer to a "3rd printing," for instance, as a "3rd edition."

Most of the information about foreign-language editions was obtained from the private collections of Sherlockians, and particularly from Irving Fenton, who contributed his knowledge and shared his outstanding collection of foreign editions. Other persons who helped furnish information were Ted Bergman of Sweden, Rudolf Čechura of Czechoslovakia, Cornelis Helling of Holland, and Nils Nordberg and E. A. Wangensten of Norway. Some information was also obtained from UNESCO's *Index Translationum* and from the printed catalogs and bibliographies of the respective countries. Because it was not possible to examine certain books listed in these printed sources, information concerning them is not always complete.

The Sherlock Holmes stories obviously enjoy a great popularity in many countries, including the Soviet Union, where the latest collected edition of Doyle's works (item 1542) was completely sold out within a few months of its publication. In the Spanish-speaking countries, interest in Sherlock Holmes no doubt resulted from the translations, but wide popularity was due to a series of pulp and paperback pastiches entitled *Memorias íntimas de Sherlock Holmes*, first published in Berlin in 1907 with the title *Detektiv Sherlock Holmes und seine welberühmten Abenteuer*, etc. Many of the stories in these series appeared with Doyle's name on the cover or the title page, or both, but most of them are "original" stories by anonymous authors. Sherlock Holmes's name remains intact, but the names of the other characters have been changed, including Dr. Watson's (Harry Taxon) and Mrs. Hudson's (Mrs. Bonnet). These same series have also been published in Portuguese with the title *Aventuras extraordinarias d'um policia secreta* and in Swedish with the title *Sherlock Holmes detektiv-historier*. It would be interesting to know more about the history of these stories and to have more of them translated into English.

Among the better-known foreign imitations are those by Maurice Leblanc who, in three widely translated books, has pitted Herlock Sholmès, the world's greatest detective, against the master rogue, Arsène Lupin.

AFRIKAANS

889. *Die Avonture van Sherlock Holmes.* [Vertaling van Jacques van Zijl.] Pretoria: J. L. van Schaik, Bpk, 1953. 195 p. (Die Libri-Reeks, 10)

Contents: Blue. - Spec. - Engr. - Nobl. - Bery. - Copp.

890. *Sherlock Holmes op die Spoor.* [Vertaling van Jacques van Zijl.] Pretoria: J. L. van Schaik, Bpk, 1953. 186 p. (Die Libri-Reeks, 13)

Contents: Scan. - RedH. - Iden. - Bosc. - Five. - Twis.

Foreign-Language Editions

ARABIC

891. [*Awdat Sharlūk Hūlmz.* al-Qāhirah: al-Dār al-Qawmīyah, 1967.] 127 p.
Contents: Adventures.

892. [*Al-jarīmat al-khafīyah.* Tr. by 'Abd al-Rahman al-Ghamrāwī. al-Qāhirah: 1923.] 266 p. (Waqā'i . . . Sharlūk Hūlmz)
Contents: Stud.

893. [*Kalb āl-Bāskarfīl.* Tr. by Hasan Muhammad Jūhar et al. al-Qāhirah: Mu'assasit al-Matbū'āt al'Hadīthah, 1960.] 126 p.
Contents: Houn.

894. [*Al-Kalb al-Juhannamī.* Tr. by Mahmūd Mas'ūd. al-Qāhirah: al-Dār al-Qawmīyah, 1967.] 158 p.
Contents: Houn.

895. [*Mughāmarat Sharlūk Hūlmz.* al-Qāhirah: al-Dār al-Hilal, 1956.] 162 p.
Contents: Adventures.

896. [———. Tr. by Sādiq Rāshid. al-Qāhirah: al-Dār al-Qawmīyah lel-Tibā'ah wa al-Nashr, 1959.] 126 p.

897. [*The Police-King; or, The Adventures of Sherlock Holmes.* Pt. 1-3. Beirut: 1911.]

ARMENIAN

898. [*Zapiski o Šerloke Holmse.* Erevan: Ajpetrat, 1958.] 536 p. illus.
Contents: Memoirs.

Parodies and Pastiches

899. [*Abdul Hamid and Sherloc Holmes,* by "Detective." Constantinople: 1911.]

900. [*Enver, Taleat, Jemal and Sherloc Holmes,* by "Detective." Constantinople: 1920.]

AZERBAIJANI

901. [*Baskervillorin iti.* Tr. by Bejdulla Musaev. Baku: Detjunizdat, 1958.] 319 p. illus.
Contents: Houn.

BENGALI

902. [*Ayādbhencār ab Śarlak Homs.* Edited by Amiyakumār Cakrabartī. Calcutta: Abhyuday Prakaš Mandir, 1964.] iv, 320 p.
Contents: Adventures.

903. [*Di hāund ab di Bāskārbhils.* Tr. by Amalendu Sen. Calcutta: Abhyuday Prakaš Mandir, 1963.] ii, 232 p.
Contents: Houn.

904. [*Śarlak Homs phire elen.* Tr. by Adriš Bardhan. Calcutta: Alpha-Beta, 1963.] 517 p.

BULGARIAN

905. [*Baskervilskoto kuče.* Tr. by Todor Vålčev. Sofia: Narodna Kultura, 1956.] 167 p.
Tr. from the Bernhard Tauchnitz edition of 1902 (item 95).

906. [*Seste Napoleonovci: Razkazi.* Tr. by P. Petrov. Sofia: Naroden Strazh, 1949.] 60 p.
From the Russian translation (item 1604).

907. [*Tajnata na Boskomskata dolina: Razkari za Šerlok Holms.* Tr. by Kiril Havezov. Sofia: Dårž. voen. izd, 1965.] 93 p.

CHINESE

908. [*Complete Collection of Famous Detective Stories.* Taipei: World Book Co., 1953.] 8 v. illus.
Contents: Vol. 1. Stud. - Vol. 2. Sign. - Vol. 3 Houn. - Vol. 4. Vall. - Vol. 5. Adventures. - Vol. 6. Memoirs. - Vol. 7. Return. - Vol. 8. His Last Bow. - Case Book.

909. [*The Hound of the Baskervilles.* Hong Kong: R. H. Sin Book Co., 1953.] 256 p.
Includes five full-page illustrations of rather crude copies of the Paget illustrations and a number of footnotes in Chinese explaining some of the terms used in the story.

910. [*Memoirs of Sherlock Holmes.* Hong Kong: Tse Ming Book Co., n.d.] 311 p.

911. [*Sherlock Holmes.* Hong Kong: Tse Ming Book Co., n.d.] 27 (?) v.
Contents: Vol. 1. Blan. - Vol. 2. Blue. - Vol. 3. Chas. - Vol. 4. Copp. - Vol. 5. Cree. - Vol. 6. Danc. - Vol. 7. Devi. - Vol. 8. Empt. - Vol. 9. Engr. - Vol. 10. Fina. - Vol. 11. Five. - Vol. 12. Glor. - Vol. 13. Gree. - Vol. 14. Maza. - Vol. 15. Miss. - Vol. 16. Prio. - Vol. 17. Thor. - Vol. 18. RedH. - Vol. 19. Reig. - Vol. 20. Resi. - Vol. 21. Scan. - Vol. 22. Shos. - Vol. 23. Silv. - Vol. 24. Suss. - Vol. 25. 3Gar. - Vol. 26. 3Stu. - Vol. 27. Wist.

912. [*A Study in Scarlet.* Hong Kong: R. H. Sin Book Co., n.d.] 175 p.

913. [*Tales of Sherlock Holmes.* Tr. by Hsich Hsin Fa. Taipei: Kuo Yü Book Co., 1963.] 244 p.

914. [*The Valley of Fear.* Shanghai: Chung Hwa Book Co., 1933.]

915. [*Various Tales.* Hong Kong: Li Li Pub. Co., n.d.]
Partial contents: Thor. - Card. - Suss. - Cree. - Norw.

CZECH

916. *Aféra K. A. Milvertona.* Z. angličtiny přeložil Josef Pachmayer. Praha: Josef R. Vilímek, [1906]. 44 p. illus. (Z dobrodružství detektiva Sherlocka Holmesa)
Contents: Chas.

917. *Berylový diadém.* Z angličtiny přeložil Josef Pachmayer. Praha: Josef R. Vilímek, [1906]. 56 p. illus. (Z dobrodružství detektiva Sherlocka Holmesa)
Contents: Bery.

918. *Dobrodružství černého Petra.* Z angličtiny přeložil Josef Pachmayer. Praha: Josef R. Vilímek, [1906]. 44 p. illus. (Z dobrodružství detektiva Sherlocka Holmesa)
Contents: Blac.

919. *Dobrodružství cyklistky.* Z angličtiny přeložil Josef Pachmayer. Praha: Josef R. Vilímek, [1907]. 44 p. illus. (Z dobrodružství detektiva Sherlocka Holmesa)
Contents: Soli.

920. *Dobrodružství detektiva Sherlocka Holmesa.* Z angličtiny přeložil Josef Pachmayer. S ilustr. J. Friedricha. Praha: Josef R. Vilímek, [1907]. 315 p. (Detektivní romány a novely)
Contents: Adventures.

921. ———. Z angličtiny přeložil Karel Weinfurter a Josef Pachmayer. Praha: Hokr, 1925. 235 p. (Záhady, 3)

922. *Dobrodružství se zlatým skřipcem.* Z angličtiny přeložil Josef Pachmayer. Praha: Josef R. Vilímek, [1906]. 48 p. illus. (Z dobrodružství detektiva Sherlocka Holmesa)
Contents: Gold.

923. *Dobrodružství tří studentu.* (Z angličtiny přeložil Josef Pachmayer. Praha: Josef R. Vilímek, [1906]. 40 p. illus. Z dobrodružství detektiva Sherlocka Holmesa)
Contents: 3Stu.

924. *Dobrodružství v soukromé škole.* Z angličtiny přeložil Josef Pachmayer. Praha: Josef R. Vilímek, [1906]. 64 p. illus. (Z dobrodružství detektiva Sherlocka Holmesa)
Contents: Prio.

925. *Druhá skvrna.* Z angličtiny přeložil Josef Pachmayer. Praha: Josef R. Vilímek, [1906]. 52 p. illus. (Z dobrodružství detektiva Sherlocka Holmesa)
Contents: Seco.

926. *Inženýruv palec.* Z angličtiny přeložil Josef Pachmayer. Praha: Josef R. Vilímek, [1906]. 52 p. illus. (Z dobrodružství detektiva Sherlocka Holmesa)
Contents: Engr.

927. *Liga zrzavých.* Z angličtiny přeložil Josef Pachmayer. S ilustr. Sidney Pageta. Praha: Josef R. Vilímek, [1906]. 56 p. (Z dobrodružství detektiva Sherlocka Holmesa)
Contents: RedH.

928. *Modrý Korund.* Z angličtiny přeložil Josef Pachmayer. Praha: Josef R. Vilímek, [1906. 52 p. illus. (Z dobrodružství detektiva Sherlocka Holmesa)
Contents: Blue.

929. *Muž se skřiveným rtem.* Z angličtiny přeložil Josef Pachmayer. Praha: Josef R. Vilímek, [1906]. 54 p. illus. (Z dobrodružství detektiva Sherlocka Holmesa)
Contents: Twis.

930. *Paměti detektiva Sherlocka Holmesa.* Z angličtiny přeložil Josef Pachmayer. S ilustr. Sidney Pageta. Praha: Josef R. Vilímek, [1906]. 271 p. (Vilímkova knihovna)
Contents: Memoirs.

931. *Pes Baskervillský: Kriminální román.* Anglicky napsáno. Přeložil Karel Kukla. Praha: Svět zvířat, 1903. 100 p.

932. *Pes Baskervillský.* Z angličtiny přeložil Josef Pachmayer. S ilustr. Sidney Pageta. Praha: Josef R. Vilímek, [1905]. 353 p. (Vilímkova knihovna, 47)

933. ———. Přeložil František Gel. Praha: Hudby a Umění, 1958. 241 p.

934. ———. Přeložil František Gel. Praha: Státní Nakladatelství Krásné Literatury a Umění, 1958. 241 p.

935. *Pes Baskervillský: Další dobrodružství Sherlocka Holmesa.* Přeložil František Gel. Praha: Státní Nakladatelství Détske Knihy, 1964. 194 p. illus.

936. ———. [Přeložil František Gel. Ilustroval Karel Vaca.] [Praha]: Albatros, [1969]. 187 p.

937. *Pohřešovaný.* Z angličtiny přeložil Josef Pachmayer. Praha: Josef R. Vilímek, [1906]. 44 p. illus. (Z dobrodružství detektiva Sherlocka Holmesa)

938. *Příhoda s pěti pomorančovými jadérky.* Z angličtiny přeložil Josef Pachmayer. S ilustr. Sidney Pageta. Praha: Josef R. Vilímek, [1906]. 44 p. (Z dobrodružství detektiva Sherlocka Holmesa)
Contents: Five.

939. *Příhoda se šesti Napoleony.* Z angličtiny přeložil Josef Pachmayer. Praha: Josef R. Vilímek, [1906]. 48 p. illus. (Z dobrodružství detektiva Sherlocka Holmesa)
Contents: SixN

940. *Příhoda v Abbey Grange.* Z angličtiny přeložil Josef Pachmayer. Praha: Josef R. Vilímek. [1906]. 52 p. illus. (Z dobrodružství detektiva Sherlocka Holmesa)

941. *Příhoda v prazdném domě.* Z angličtiny přeložil Josef Pachmayer. Praha: Josef R. Vilímek. [1907]. 48 p. illus. (Z dobrodružství detektiva Sherlocka Holmesa)
Contents: Empt.

942. *Případ podivuhodné záměny.* Z angličtiny přeložil Josef Pachmayer. S ilustr. Sidney Pageta. Praha: Josef R. Vilímek, [1906]. (Z dobrodružství detektiva Sherlocka Holmesa)

943. *Sherlock Holmes vítězí.* Z angličtiny přeložil Josef Pachmayer. Praha: Josef R. Vilímek, [1906]. 328 p.

944. *Skandální příhoda.* Z angličtiny přeložil Josef Pachmayer. S ilustr. Sidney Pageta. Praha: Josef R. Vilímek, [1906]. 56 p. (Z dobrodružství detektiva Sherlocka Holmesa)

945. *Skvrnitý pás.* Z angličtiny přeložil Josef Pachmayer. Praha: Josef R. Vilímek, [1906]. 58 p. illus. (Z dobrodružství detektiva Sherlocka Holmesa)
Contents: Spec.

946. *Studie o krvavých barvách.* [Study of a Bloody Color.] Přeložil František Havránek. Praha: Sotek, 1925. 197 p.
Contents: Stud.

947. *Studie v šarlatové.* Přeložil Vladimír Henzl. Praha: Práce, 1964. 95 p.
Contents: Stud.

948. *Tajemství údolí Boscombského.* (Z angličtiny přeložil Josef Pachmayer. S ilustr. Sidney Pageta. Praha: Josef R. Vilímek. [1906]. 60 p. Z dobrodružství detektiva Sherlocka Holmesa)
Contents: Bosc.

949. *Tančicí mužíci.* Z angličtiny přeložil Josef Pachmayer. Praha: Josef R. Vilímek, [1907]. 40 p. illus. (Z dobrodružství detektiva Sherlocka Holmesa)

Contents: Danc.

950. *Údolí. bázně.* Autorisovaný překlad. Z angličtiny přeložil Karel Weinfurther. Praha: Slaboch, 1922. 238 p.
Contents: Vall.

951. *Vzkříšení Sherlocka Holmesa: Detektivní novely.* Z angličtiny přeložil Josef Pachmayer. Praha: Josef R. Vilímek, [1907]. 308 p. illus.
Contents: Return.

952. *Záhadné zmizení Lady Carfaxové.* Přeložil Oskar Reindl. Praha: Tožička, [1923]. 32 p. (Dobrodružné novely, 8)

953. *Znamení čtyř.* Z angličtiny přeložil Jaromír Zajíček-Horský. Praha: Josef R. Vilímek, [1906]. 290 p. illus. (Vilímkova knihovna, 51)
Contents: Sign.

954. ———. Z angličtiny přeložil Jaromír Zajíček-Horský. Nové vydáni. Praha: Josef R. Vilímek, 1907. 216 p. illus. (Detektivni romány)

955. *Ztracená stopa.* Z angličtiny přeložil Josef Pachmayer. Praha: Josef R. Vilímek, [1906]. 48 p. illus. (Z dobrodružství detektiva Sherlocka Holmesa)

956. *Ztracená stopa: Dobrodružství Sherlocka Holmesa.* Z angličtiny přeložil Josef Pachmayer. S ilustr. J. Friedricha. Praha: Josef R. Vilímek, 1906]. 297 p. (Vilimkova knihovna, 106)

957. *Ztracená stopa.* Z angličtiny přeložil Josef Pachmayer. [2. yvdáni] Praha: Hoko, 1925. 255 p. (Z dobrodružství detektiva Sherlocka Holmesa) (Záhady, 4)

958. *Zvláštní příhoda ve venkovském sídle.* Z angličtiny přeložil Josef Pachmayer. Praha: Josef R. Vilímek, [1906]. 48 p. illus. (Z dobrodružství detektiva Sherlocka Holmesa)

Apocrypha

959. *Tajuplné přiběhy.* [Round the Fire Stories.] Přeložil dr. Stanislav Chitussi. Ilustroval Josef Koči. Praha: Josef R. Vilímek, [1913]. 304 p. (Vilímkova knihovna, XVI, 4, 117)
Partial contents: Lost. - ManW.

Parodies and Pastiches

960. Čechura, Rudolf. *Nikdo nemá alibi.* [Nobody Has an Alibi.] [Illustroval Jan Javorsky.] Praha: Práce, 1969. [109] p. (Románo novinky, číslo 172)
Also contains: Sherlock Holmes' Story.
A young Czech policeman named Tomáš Klíma wins a big lottery prize and decides to spend the money in London, literally in the footsteps of Sherlock Holmes. He advertises in *The Times* for a manservant, whose name *must* be Watson, so that he can set up a "Holmes and Watson Private Detective Agency." A man whose real name is Dr. John Watson goes into partnership with "Mr. Holmes." They solve a case that has arisen out of the Great Train Robbery. Only at the end of the story does Mr. Klíma realize that his manservant Dr. Watson is actually a superintendent of Scotland Yard.
Review: SHJ, 9, No. 3 (Winter 1969), 106-107 (Lord Donegall).

961. Honzík, Miroslav, a Ilja Kučera. *Omyl Sherlocka Holmese.* [Ilustroval Ivan Strnad.] Praha: Státní Nakladatelství Dětské Knihy, 1968. 226 p.

Contents: Sh přichází. - Případ jedné noci. - Alibi na minutu. - Zločin na šedavě. - Záhada modré komnaty. - Rameno spravedlnosti (Karel Grundloch, a Josef Jelínek).

962. Tafel, Jaroslav. *Prázdniny se Sherlockem Holmesem.* [Ilustroval Dobroslav Foll.] Praha: Státní Nakladatelství Dětské Knihy, [1966]. 267 p.
Contents: Pozvání od Sherlocka Holmese. - Zmizení jednoho lorda. - Létající mrtvola. - Vražda v přístavu. - Trápení tlusté paní. - Tajuplný meloun. - Zločin v mlze. - Podezřelý kouzelník. - Ztracený poklad. - Únos nebohého sirotka. - Nejslavnější případ Sherlocka Holmese. - Případ s dvouhrbým velbloudem. - Nestvůra chewinggumská. - Housky pro Její Veličenstvo. - Ukradený diamant.

DANISH

963. *Baskervilles hund.* Oversat af Iver Gudme. København]: Gyldendal, 1944. 176 p.

964. *Baskerville-hunden.* Paa dansk ved Verner Seemann. [København]: Martins Forlag, 1954. 222 p.
———. København: Martins Forlag, [1964]. 197 p.

965. *Baskervilles hund.* Ved Else Schiøler. [Illustreret af Alex Secher.] [København]: G.E.C. Gads Forlag, 1962. 203 p.
A simplified and abbreviated edition.

966. *Baskervilles hund: Sherlock Holmes opdagelser.* [Oversat af Peter Jerndorff-Jessen.] København: Gyldendalske Boghandel, Nordisk Forlag, [n.d.] 247 p.

967. "Den blaa karfunkel," Oversat af Verner Seeman. *Mord til Jul.* Udvalgt og indledt af Tage la Cour. [København]: Carit Andersens Forlag, 1952. p. 7-51.

968. *Den blaa karfunkel og andre noveller.* Paa dansk ved Verner Seemann. [København]: Martins Forlag, 1954. 214 p.
———. København: Martins Forlag, [1964]. 189 p.
Contents: Empt. - Blue. - RedH. - Twis. - Norw. - Engr. - Seco.

969. "Det brogede bånd," Oversat af Poul Ib Liebe. *Mord i Gaslys.* Udvalgt og indledt af Tage la Cour. Illustreret af Palle Nielsen. [København]: Carit Andersens Forlag, [1953]. p. 141-189.
Contents: Spec.

970. "Det brogede bånd: Et Sherlock Holmes mysterium," *Det Bedste fra Reader's Digest* [København]: (May 1967), 163-184.

971. *De dansende maend og andre noveller.* Paa dansk ved Kay Nielsen. [København]: Martins Forlag, 1962. 212 p.
———. København: Martins Forlag, [1966]. 196 p.
Contents: Danc. - Five. - Yell. - Stoc. - Croo. - Resi. - Soli. - Blac. - Chas. - Gold.

972. *Djaevlefoden.* Paa dansk ved Kay Nielsen. [København]: Martins Forlag, 1959. 182 p.
———. København: Martins Forlag, [1965]. 178 p.
Contents: His Last Bow.

973. *Dommerens hemmelighed.* København: Universal-forlaget, 1911. 96 p.
Contents: Glor. - Yell. - Silv.

974. *De fires tegn: Roman.* Oversat af Iver Gudme. [København]: Gyldendal, 1944. 159 p.
Contents: Sign.

975. *De fires tegn.* Paa dansk ved Verner Seemann. [København]: Martins Forlag, 1954. 219 p.
———. København: Martins Forlag, 1963. 160 p.

976. "Den fornemme klient," Oversat af Tage la Cour. *Kriminalhistorier fra hele Verden.* Udvalgt og indledt af Tage la Cour. [København]: Carit Andersens Forlag, [1955]. p. 246-269.
Contents: Illu.

977. *Frygtens dal.* Paa dansk ved P. Engelstoft. [København]: Martins Forlag, 1957. 189 p.
———. København: Martins Forlag, 1964. 180 p.
Contents: Vall.

978. "Guldlorgnetterne," Oversat af Poul Ib Liebe. *Detektivhistorier fra Sherlock Holmes til Hercule Poirot.* Udvalgt og indledt af Tage la Cour. [København]: Carit Andersens Forlag, [1956]. p. 322-345.
Contents: Gold.

979. *Den krybende mand og andre noveller.* Paa dansk ved Kay Nielsen. [København]: Martins Forlag, 1960. 222 p.
———. København: Martins Forlag, [1965]. 222 p.
Contents: Case Book.

980. "Manden med hareskaaret," *Verdens bedste kriminalhistorier.* Samlet af Jens Anker. [København]: Politikens Stjernehaefte, Nr. 32 [1946]. p. 1-10.
Contents: Twis.

981. "Mordet på Abbey Grange," [Oversat af P. Engelstoft. Illustreret af Henry Lauritzen]. *Sherlock Holmes Arbog* III (1967), 7-35.

982. "Mysteriet i Boscombe-Dalen," *Engelske kriminalhistorier.* Samlet af Jens Jensens. [København]: Politikens Stjernehaefte, Nr. 40 [1946]. p. 1-10.

983. *Mysteriet paa Birlstone Herregaard.* **Oversat af P. Engelstoft. København: Forlagt af H. Aschehoug og Co., [1916].** 192 p.
Contents: Vall.

984. "Papaesken," Oversat af Kay Nielsen. *Poe-klubbens yndlingslaesning.* Udvalgt af Svend Aage Lund. København: Stig Vendelkaers Forlag, 1966. p. 85-108.
Contents: Card.

985. "De rødhåredes klub," På dansk ved Poul Ib Liebe. *Ungdommens Detektivbog.* Udvalgt og indledt af Tage la Cour. [København]: Steen Hasselbalchs Forlag, 1956. p. 55-73.
Contents: RedH.

986. *San Pedros Tiger og andre Sherlock Holmes fortaellinger.* Autoriseret oversaettelse ved P. Engelstoft. København: Forlagt of H. Aschehoug & Co., 1919. 136 p.
Contents: Wist. - Card. - Dyin. - Lady. - Abbe.

987. *Sherlock Holmes.* Oversat ved A. Petersen. København: Nordens Forlag, [n.d.] 4 v. (400, 400, 416, 378 p.) illus.
Contents: Sign. - Nobl. - Bery. - RedH. - Spec. - Bosc. - Musg. - Norw. - Copp. - Stoc. - Twis. - Scan. - Engr. - Croo. - Card. - Nava. - Stud. - Gree. - Yell. - Glor. - Reig. - Iden. - ManW. - Fina.
In this edition "The Man with the Watches" is a real Sherlock Holmes story and the name of Sherlock Holmes is mentioned four times.

988. ———. [På dansk ved Kris Winther.] København: Erling Zinglersens Forlag og Central Forlaget, 1944. 7 v. (72, 68, 48, 48, 48, 48, 48 p.)
Contents: Vol. 1-2. Houn. - Vol. 3-7. Reig. - Resi. - Musg. - Croo. - Stoc. - Gree. - Nava. - Silv. - Chas. - Blac. - 3Stu. - Prio. - SixN.
This cheap edition was planned for twenty volumes but only seven were published.

989. ———. Med illustrationer af V. Setoft. [På dansk ved Verner Seemann.] København: Forlaget Nyttebøger, [1945]. 6 v.
Contents: Vol. 1. *En studie i rødt.* [Introduction by Verner Seemann.] 293 p. [Stud.] - Vol. 2. *De fires tegn.* 233 p. [Sign.] - Vol. 3. *Baskerville-slaegtens hund.* 325 p. [Houn.] - Vol. 4. "*Skandale i Bøhmen*" og *andre fortaellinger.* 277 p. [Scan. - RedH. - Twis. - Blue. - Engr. - Copp.] - Vol. 5. *Fra "Silver Blaze" til "det afsluttende problem."* 271 p. [Silv. - Glor. - Reig. - Gree.

- Nava. - Fina.] - Vol. 6. *Atter i arbejde.* 255 p. [Empt. - Norw. - Danc. - Prio. - SixN. - Seco.]

990. *Sherlock Holmes dør - og vender tilbage!* Oversat af P. Engelstoft, Erich Erichsen, og Ellen Kirk. [København]: Politikens Stjernehaefte, Nr. 14 [1944]. 56, 8 p.
Contents: Fina. - Empt. - Abbe. - RedH. - Lady. - Blac. - Devi.

991. *Sherlock Holmes historier.* [Udvalgt af Tage la Cour. Oversat af Poul Ib Liebe, Tage la Cour, og Verner Seemann.] [København]: Carit Andersens Forlag, [1959]. 317 p.
———. [København]: Carit Andersens Forlag, [1963]. 311 p.
Contents: Scan. - Iden. - Bosc. - Twis. - Blue. - Spec. - Engr. - Nobl. - Bery. - Fina.

992. *Sherlock Holmes i arbejde.* Paa dansk ved Erich Erichsen. København: Forlagt af H. Aschehoug & Co., 1917. 160 p.
Contents: Empt. - Norw. - Danc. - Soli. - Prio. - Blac.

993. *Sherlock Holmes mesterstykker.* Udvalgt af Tage la Cour. [Oversat af Tage la Cour og Verner Seemann.] [København]: Carit Andersens Forlag, [1959]. 323 p.
———. [København]: Carit Andersens Forlag, [1964]. 313 p.
Contents: Empt. - Copp. - Silv. - Musg. - Nava. - Prio. - SixN. - 3Stu. - Miss. - Thor.

994. *Sherlock Holmes' nye bedrifter.* [København]: E. Jespersens Forlag, 1910.
———. [København]: Jespersen og Pios Forlag, 1926. p. 5-102.
A collection of Conan Doyle stories.
Partial contents: Wist. - Bruc.

995. "Sherlock Holmes - og historien om den graeske tolk!" *Mandens Blad* [København]: (March 1963), 12-14, 45-46.
Contents: Gree.

996. *Sherlock Holmes' opdagelser:* "De fires tegn," Oversat af Mette **Budtz-Jørgensen.** [København]: Politikens Stjernehaefte, Nr. 5 [1944], 1-38.
Contents: Sign.

997. *Sherlock Holmes' opdagelser: Forbryderfortaellinger.* Paa dansk ved P. Jerndorff-Jessen. Aarhus: Jydsk Forlags-Forretning, [1893-1898]. 8 v.
Contents: Vol. 1. *En studie i rødt.* 1893. 222 p. [Stud.] - Vol. 2. *Lys i morket.* [Introduction by P. Jerndorff-Jessen.] 1894. 184 p. [RedH. - Bosc. - Twis. - Spec.] - Vol. 3. *De fires tegn.* 1894. 196 p. [Sign.] - Vol. 4. *Rødbøgene* og andre *fortaellinger.* 1895. [Copp. - Glor. - Bery. - Scan.] - Vol. 5. *Den blaa karfunkel og andre fortaellinger.* 1896. [Silv. - Musg. - Stoc. - Blue.] - Vol. 6. *Den*

forsvundne brud og andre fortaellinger. 1897. 169 p. [Engr. - Reig. - Nobl. - Iden.] - Vol. 7. *Det gule ansigt og andre fortaellinger.* 1897. 142 p. [Gree. - Yell. - Nava.] - Vol. 8. *Sherlock Holmes dod og andre fortaellinger.* 1898. 154 p. [Five. - Croo. - Resi. - Fina.]

998. ———. 2. Oplag. Aarhus: Jydsk Forlags-Forretning og Det Jydske Forlag, [1898-1902]. 9 v.
   Contents: Vol. 1-8. Same as above. - Vol. 9. *Baskervilles hund.* 1902. 247 p.

999. ———. 3. Oplag. Autoriseret oversaettelse ved P. Jerndorff-Jessen. København: Gyldendalske Boghandel, Nordisk Forlag, [1905-1907]. 9 v.
   Contents: Same as above but the numbers of the volumes are changed. Vol. 1. *En studie i rødt.* 1905. 192 p. - Vol. 2. *De fires tegn.* 1905. 166 p. - Vol. 3. *Lys i mørket.* 1905. 162 p. - Vol. 4. *Den blaa karfunkel.* 1906. 152 p. - Vol. 5. *Rødbøgene.* 1906. 152 p. - Vol. 6. *Den forsvundne brud.* 1906. 144 p. - Vol. 7. *Det gule ansigt.* 1906. 126 p. - Vol. 8. *Baskervilles hund.* 1906. 247 p. - Vol. 9. *Sherlock Holmes' død.* 1907. 132 p.
   This edition was also published in four volumes.

1000. *Sherlock Holmes' sidste bedrifter.* Kobenhavn og Oslo: Jespersen og Pios Forlag, 1931. p. 5-84.
   Contents: Wist. - Bruc.

1001. *Sherlock Holmes udvalgte fortaellinger.* Oversat af Iver Gudme. [København]: Gyldendal, [1944]. 2 v. (206, 192 p.)
   Contents: Vol. 1. Glor. - Musg. - Spec. Nava. - Croo. - RedH. - Fina. - Vol. 2. Empt. - Norw. - Silv. - Prio. - 3Gar. - Thor.

1002. *Silver Blaze og andre noveller.* Paa dansk ved Verner Seemann. [København]: Martins Forlag, 1954. 218 p.
   ———. København: Martins Forlag, [1965]. 193 p.
   Contents: Silv. - Glor. - Reig. - Gree. - Nava. - SixN. - Fina.

1003. *En studie i rødt: Roman.* Oversat og indledet af Iver Gudme, med en fortale af C. A. Bodelsen. [København]: Gyldendal, [1944]. 160 p.
   Contents: Stud.

1004. *En studie i rødt.* [With an introduction by Verner Seemann.] Paa dansk ved Verner Seemann. [København]: Martins Forlag, 1954. 224 p.
   Contents: Stud. - Danc.

1005. ———. [With an introduction by Verner Seemann.] Paa dansk ved Verner Seemann. [København]: Martins Forlag, 1963. 188 p.
   ———. København: Martins Forlag, 1967. 160 p.
   Contents: Stud.

1006. "De tre studenter," *Detektiv historier.* Udvalgt af Tage la Cour. København: Carit Andersens Forlag, [n.d.] p. 203-223.
   Contents: 3Stu.

1007. "En udvalgt samling af Sherlock Holmes' eventyr," [Oversat af P. Jerndorff-Jessen.] *I ledige timer.* København: Forlagt af Carl Allers Etablissement, 1902. Vol. 29, p. 1-476.
   Contents: Adventures. - Sign.
   The Adventures are illustrated with all the illustrations of Sidney Paget.

English Readers

1008. *The Hound of the Baskervilles.* Abbreviated and simplified for use in schools. [Copenhagen]: Grafisk Forlag, 1944. 62 p. (Easy Readers, Series C, Nr. 4)

1009. ———. New edition. [Cover design: Ib Jorgensen. Illustrations: Oscar Jorgensen.] [Copenhagen]: Grafisk Forlag, [1967]. 96 p. (Easy Readers, Series C)
   The vocabulary of this series has been chosen from among the most common 1,800 words in English.

1010. *Silver Blaze: Memoirs of Sherlock Holmes.* Adapted and supplied with notes for school use by W. F. Larsen. København: Trykt i det danske Selskabs Skole, 1903. 38 p.

1011. *The Speckled Band: A Sherlock Holmes Story.* Simplified for use in schools. [Copenhagen]: Grafisk Forlag, 1958. 16 p. illus. (Easy Readers, Series A, Nr. 25)

1012. ———. New edition. [Cover design: Ib Jørgensen. Illustrations: Oscar Jorgensen.] [Copenhagen]: Grafisk Forlag, [1967]. 48 p. (Easy Readers, Series A)
   The vocabulary of this series has been chosen from among the most common 500 words in English.

Parodies and Pastiches

1013. Becker, Tage. *Sherlock Holmes contra Silver Blaze: En skandale i sort og rødt.* [Sherlock Holmes versus Silver Blaze: A Scandal in Black and Red.] København: Rosenkilde og Bagger, 1961. 97 p.

1014. Christensen, Severin. "Den forsvundne herskabstjener" ["The Vanished Footman"], *Maaneds-Magasinet* [København]: (June 1910).

1015. *Detektivkongen Sherlock Holmes - Forbrydernes Skraek.* [The Detective-King Sherlock Holmes - The Dread of the Criminals.] [København: n.d.]
   A series of "dime novels" *a la* Nick Carter.

1016. Lauritzen, Henry. *Detektivernes fest.* [Feast of the Detectives.] Aalborg: Aksel Schølins Bogtrykkeri, [1966]. [24] p. illus. Limited to 400 copies.

"A tale in Danish involving the great detectives of literature, with much prominence given to Sherlock Holmes, of course. The illustrations by the author are one of the delightful features of this excellent booklet." (Julian Wolff)

Review: SHJ, 8, No. 2 (Spring 1967), 66 (Lord Donegall).

1017. Muusmann, Carl. "Sherlock Holmes paa Marienlyst," *Beridernes konge og andre fortaellinger,* [af] Carl Muusmann. Illustreret af Carsten Ravn. København: Fh. A. Christiansens Forlag, 1906. p. 41-146.

1018. ———. *Sherlock Holmes at Elsinore.* Illustrated by Carsten Ravn. Translated by Poul Ib Liebe. With an introduction by Tage la Cour. New York: The Baker Street Irregulars, 1956. 77 p.

A pastiche in which Holmes solves a baffling mystery while on a visit to a fashionable Danish seaside hotel.

1019. Petersen, Robert Storm. "Holm og Madsen: En detektiv-historie," *Ugler i mosen,* [af] Robert Storm Petersen. København: Jespersen og Pios Forlag, 1929. p. 23-40.

———. ———, *Gemylige Folk,* af Robert Storm Petersen. København: Poul Branners Forlag, 1943. p. 153-166.

Detective: Charles Holm. Narrator: Dr. Madsen.

1020. ———. "En pibe tobak," *Den udvikler sig,* [af] Robert Storm Petersen. København: Poul Branner - Nørregade, 1933. p. 86-93. illus.

———. ———, *I Fred og Ro,* af Robert Storm Petersen. København: Poul Branners Forlag, 1945. p. 150-154.

———. ———, *Stop* [København]: 2, Nr. 6 (1965), 21-22, 25.

———. "A Pipe of Tobacco," *Tobacco Talk in Baker Street,* by Robert Storm Petersen and Tage la Cour. New York: The Baker Street Irregulars, 1952. p. 7-15.

1021. ———. "Den usynlige atlet og andre smaating" ["The Invisible Athlete and Other Trifles"], *Det er ikke muligt!* af Robert Storm Petersen. København: Jespersen og Pios Forlag, 1932. p. 77-92.

———. ———, *Det var dengang,* af Robert Storm Petersen. København: Poul Branners Forlag, 1944. p. 28-39.

1022. "Sherlock Holmes' overmand" ["A Match for Sherlock Holmes"], *Maaneds-Magasinet* [København]: (June 1911).

DUTCH

1023. *De Agra-schat.* Rijswijk (Z.-H.): Blankwaardt & Schoonhoven, [n.d.]
Contents: Sign.

1024. ———. Amsterdam: N. J. Boon, [n.d.] 151 p. illus.

1025. *Die avonturen van Sherlock Holmes.* Vertaling van Jacques van Zijl. Pretoria: J. L. van Schaik, Bpk., 1960. 195 p. (Die Libri-Reeks, 10)
Contents: Blue. - Spec. - Engr. - Nobl. - Bery. - Copp.

1026. *De avonturen van Sherlock Holmes.* [Geillustreerd door Sidney Paget.] Amsterdam: N. J. Boon, [n.d.] 170 p.
Contents: Nobl. - Bery. - RedH. - Bosc. - Musg.

1927. *Avonturen van Sherlock Holmes.* Vertaald door Simon Vestdijk. Amsterdam en Antwerpen: Contact, [1956]. 236 p. (De Contactboekerij)
Contents: RedH. - Spec. - Bosc. - Twis. - Five. - Soli. - Engr. - Scan. - Blue. - Reig.

1028. *Het avontuur van Abbey Grange.* Rijswijk (Z.-H.): Blankwaardt & Schoonhoven, [n.d.] 28, 28, 12 p. (Sherlock Holmes Serie, 12)
Contents: Abbe. - Blac. - Beschouwingen over Sherlock Holmes.

1029. *Het dal der verschrikking.* [Vertaald door H. Roduin.] Amsterdam / Antwerpen: Uitgeverij Contact, [1962]. 208 p. (Contactboekerij)
Contents: Vall.

1030. *De Dood van Sherlock Holmes.* [Geillustreerd door Sidney Paget.] Amsterdam: N. J. Boon, [n.d.] 150 p.
Contents: Croo. - Card. - Stoc. - Nava. - Fina.

The cover is reproduced in *SHJ,* 5, No. 3 (Winter 1961), 91.

1031. *Een Godsgericht.* [An Ordeal.] [Geillustreerd door Sidney Paget.] Amsterdam: N. J. Boon, [n.d.]
Contents: Stud.

1032. *De Grieksche Tolk.* [Geillustreerd door Sidney Paget.] Amsterdam: N. J. Boon, [n.d.] 160 p.
Contents: Gree. - Resi. - Silv. - Glor. - Reig. - Yell.

1033. *Herinneringen aan Sherlock Holmes.* [Reminiscences of Sherlock Holmes.] [Geillustreerd door Arthur Twidle en L. J. Jordaan.] Amsterdam: N. J. Boon, [n.d.] 144 p.

Contents: Wist. - Bruc. - [Two pastiches]. - [An adaptation of Sherlock Holmes and His Creator, by Arthur Bartlett].

1034. *De hond van de Baskervilles.* Geillustreerd [door Sidney Paget]. Rijswijk (Z.-H.): Blankwaardt & Schoonhoven, [n.d.] 192, 120 p.
Contents: Houn. - 3Stu. - Gold. - Miss. - Abbe.

1035. ——. Vertaald door Simon Vestdijk. Amsterdam en Antwerpen: Uitgeverij Contact, [1957]. 173 p. (Contactboekerij)

1036. ——. Vertaald door S. Vestdijk. Amsterdam: Uitgeverij Contact, [1969]. 170 p. (Contactboekerij)

1037. *De Jachthond van de Baskervilles.* [Geillustreerd door Sidney Paget.] Amsterdam: N. J. Boon, [n.d.] 192 p.

1038. *De Liefde eener Vrouw.* [The Love of a Woman.] [Geillustreerd door Sidney Paget.] Amsterdam: N. J. Boon, [n.d.] 142 p.
Partial contents: Seco. - Iden. - Blue.

1039. *Meesterwerken van Sir Arthur Conan Doyle.* [Met 31 foto's uit de BBC-televisiefilms.] Amsterdam: Uitgeverij Contact, [1969-1970]. 2 v. (618, 507 p.)
Contents: Vol. 1. Houn, vertaald door S. Vestdijk. - Stud, vertaald door Jean A. Schalekamp. - Sign, vertaald door H. W. J. Schaap. - Vall, vertaald door H. Roduin. - Vol. 2. *Twintig avonturen van Sherlock Holmes* (RedH. - Twis. - Spec. - Engr. - Copp. - Silv. - Nava. - Danc. - Soli. - SixN. - Bosc. - Five. - Blue. - Prio. - Chas. - Thor. - Gree. - Fina. - Empt. - Seco.) Vertaald door S. Vestdijk en Jean A. Schalekamp.

1040. *De moordenaar kwam naar Londen: Een onbekend avontuur van Sherlock Holmes.* [The Murderer Came to London: An Unknown Adventure of Sherlock Holmes.] Uit het Engels bewerkt door L. W. van Giessen. Amsterdam; Engelhard: van Embden & Co., [1949]. 180 p.
Contents: Stud. - "Sherlock Holmes, de grootste detective der wereld," door H. P. v. d. Aardweg.

1041. *Nieuwe Avonturen van Sherlock Holmes.* [Geillustreerd.] Rijswijk (Z.-H.): Blankwaardt & Schoonhoven, [n.d.] 220 p.
Contents: Empt. - Norw. - Danc. - Soli. - Lady. - Devi. - RedC.

1042. ——. Vertaald door S. Vestdijk. Amsterdam en Antwerpen: Uitgeverij Contact, 1959. 195 p. (Contactboekerij)
Contents: Nava. - Copp. - SixN. - Danc. - Silv. - Prio. - Chas.

1043. ——. Vertaald door Simon Vestdijk. Amsterdam: Contact, 1961. 2 v. (200, 236 p.)
Contents: Adventures. - Memoirs. - Return.

1044. *Nieuwe verhalen van Sherlock Holmes.* [Vertaald door Jean A. Schalekamp.] Amsterdam: Uitgeverij Contact, [1968]. 112 p. (Contactboekerij)
Contents: Gold. - Miss. - Abbe. - Seco.

1045. *Sherlock Holmes, de Detective.* [Geillustreerd door Sidney Paget.] Amsterdam: N. J. Boon, [n.d.] 158 p.
Contents: Copp. - Scan. - Five. - Twis. - Spec. - Engr.

1046. *Sherlock Holmes Omnibus.* Amsterdam / Antwerpen: Uitgeverij Contact, [1962-1964]. 2 v. (630, 443 p.)
Contents: Vol. 1. Sherlock Holmes-verhalen (RedH. - Twis. - Spec. - Engr. - Copp. - Silv. - Nava. - Danc. - Soli. - SixN.), vertaald door S. Vestdijk. - Houn, vertaald door S. Vestdijk. - Vall, vertaald door H. Roduin. - Vol. 2. Stud, vertaald door Jean A. Schalekamp. - Sign, vertaald door H. W. J. Schaap. - Sherlock Holmes-verhalen (Five. - Blue. - Scan. - Fina. - Empt. - Prio. - Chas), vertaald door S. Vestdijk.

1047. [*De Sherlock Holmes Serie.*] Rijswijk (Z.-H.): Blankwaardt & Schoonhoven, [n.d.] 26 v.
The cover (the same for each volume) is reproduced in *SHJ*, 5, No. 3 (Winter 1961), 91.

1048. *Sherlock Holmes-verhalen.* [Vertaald door Jean A. Schalekamp.] Amsterdam: Uitgeverij Contact, [1968]. 124 p. (Contactboekerij)
Contents: Iden. - Nobl. - Bery. - Blac. - 3Stu.

1049. *Een studie in rood.* [Vertaald door Jean A. Schalekamp.] Amsterdam / Antwerpen: Uitgeverij Contact, [1964]. 127 p. (Contactboekerij)
Contents: Stud.

1050. *Het teken van de vier.* [Vertaald door H. W. J. Schapp.] Amsterdam / Antwerpen: Uitgeverij Contact, [1963]. 126 p. (Contactboekerij)
Contents: Sign.

1051. *De Terugkeer van Sherlock Holmes.* [Geillustreerd door Sidney Paget.] Amsterdam: N. J. Boon, [n.d.] 144 p.
Contents: Empt. - Norw. - Danc. - Soli.

1052. ——. Amsterdam: N. V. Uitgevers Maatschappij "Minerva," [n.d.] 328 p.
Contents: RedH. - Bosc. - Musg. - Card. - Nava. - Blac. - Abbe.

1053. *De twaalf laatste avonturen.* [The Twelve Last Adventures.] Amsterdam: Allert de Lange, [ca. 1930]. 230 p.
Contents: Case Book.

1054. *De Verdwenen Dame.* [The Lady Who Disappeared.] [Geillustreerd door Sidney Paget.] Amsterdam: N. J. Boon, [ca. 1906]. 120 p.
Contents: 3Stu. - Gold. - Miss. - Abbe.

1055. *De Wraak eener Vrouw.* [A Woman's Revenge.] [Geillustreerd door Sidney Paget.] Amsterdam: N. J. Boon, [n.d.] 139 p.
Contents: Prio. - Blac. - Chas. - SixN.

English Readers

1056. *The End and the Beginning.* [Adapted and annotated by H. Otto Levenbach.] Amsterdam: J. M. Meulenhoff, [1955]. x, 52 p. (Meulenhoff's English Library, 43)
Contents: Aan de Lezer [Introduction]. - Fina. - Empt.
The vocabulary is published in a separate booklet. 8 p.

1057. *The Hound of the Baskervilles.* Adapted and annotated by H. J. Hendriksen. Illustrated by J. Bouman. 13th ed. Amsterdam: W. Versluys, [1969]. 125 p.

1058. *The Sign of Four.* With explanatory notes [by] J. Bouten. 11th ed., by I. A. S. Fischer. Zwolle: W. E. J. Tjeenk Willink, 1968. 108 p. (Stories and Sketches, 4)

1059. *The Speckled Band.* Adapted and annotated for the use of schools by C. Apeldoorn and E. Inglis Arkell. 18th ed. Purmerend: J. Muusses, [1968]. 47 p.
Also includes forty questions.
"This reader is intended for pupils of 15 ,or 16 years of age who have mastered the rudiments of English grammar." (Preface, dated November 15, 1927)
The vocabulary is published in a separate booklet. 16 p.

Parodies and Pastiches

1060. Glens, Owen. *De Ontvoering.* [The Abduction.] Amsterdam: "Vivat," [ca. 1900].

1061. ———. *Sherlock Holmes in Doodsgevaar.* [Sherlock Holmes in Peril of Death.] [Adapted from the play by Conan Doyle and William Gillette. Illustrated by A. Rovers.] Amsterdam: "Vivat," 1902. 159 p.
Reviews: SHJ, 9, No. 3 (Winter 1969), 108-109 (Cornelis Helling).

1062. Stratenus, Louise. *Een verborgen bladzijde uit het leven van Sherlock Holmes.* [A Secret Page from the Life of Sherlock Holmes.] Amsterdam: "Vivat," [ca. 1900]. 168 p.

Review: SHJ, 7, No. 1 (Winter 1964). 30 (Cornelis Helling).

1063. Veth, Cornelis. *De allerlaatste avonturen van Sir Sherlock Holmes.* [The Last Adventures of Sir Sherlock Holmes.] Bussum: C. A. J. van Dishoeck, 1912. 46 p. illus. (Prikkel-Idyllen, 1)
———. ———, *Prikkel-Idyllen,* door Cornelis Veth. Eerste deel. Bussum: C. A. J. van Dishoeck, 1926. p. 1-41.
Contents: 1. Het Bioscope Theater [The Moving Picture Theater]. - 2. Het avontuur van het bloedige postpakket [The Adventure of the Bloody Parcel Post]. - 3. Het avontuur van de zonderlinge advertentie [The Adventure of the Singular Advertisement]. - 4. Het avontuur van den geheimzinnigen kater [The Adventure of the Mysterious Tomcat].

1064. [Willink, Luc.] *De nalatenschap van Sherlock Holmes.* [The Legacy of Sherlock Holmes], door Clifford Semper [pseud.] Amsterdam: Andries Blitz, [n.d.] 253 p.
Contents: Vol. 1. De blikken trommel [The Tin Can], door De Schrijver. - Vol. 2. Het avontuur met den Franschen commissaris [The Adventure of the French Police Commissioner]. - Vol. 3. Het mysterie van den blanco brief [The Mystery of the Blank Letter]. - Vol. 4. Het avontuur van den vermoeiden kapitein [The Adventure of the Tired Captain]. - Vol. 5. De onoplettende kaartspelers [The Absent-Minded Card Players]. - Vol. 6. De Zeven roode rozen [The Seven Red Roses]. - Vol. 7. Een daad van rechtvaardigheid [A Deed of Justice]. - Vol. 8. De Goden van Briton Hall [The Gods of Briton Hall]. - Vol. 9. Het schot in het duister [The Shot in the Dark].

FINNISH

1065. *Baskervillen koira.* Porvoo; Helsinki: Werner Söderström, 1957. 159 p. (Punainen sulka, 1)

1066. *Punatukkaisten Yhdistys.* Hameenlinna: Nide, [1953]. 122 p. (Maailmankuuluja jännitys-novelleja!)
Contents: RedH. - Gree. - Vihreä Mamba, by Edgar Wallace. - Yöpikajunan Salaisuus, by Freeman Wills Crofts.

1067. *Sherlock Holmes seikkailut.* [O. E. Juurikorven uudistettu suomennos.] Porvoo; Helsinki: Werner Söderström, [1957]. 2 v. (427, 421 p.)
Contents: Adventures. - Memoirs. - Return..

1068. *Valliosalaisuns ynnä muita salapoliisikertomuksia.* Malmö: Skandinaviska Bokförlagets tryckeri, [1927]. 94 p.
Contents: Seco. - Abbe. - 3Stu.

FRENCH

1069. *L'Abbaye de Grange.* Paris: Société d'Edition et de Publications, [n.d.] [90] p. illus. (Les Oeuvres de Conan Doyle. Collection Rouge, 16)
Contents: Abbe. - Miss.

1070. *Archives sur Sherlock Holmes.* Traduction de Evelyn Colomb. [Paris]: Robert Laffont, [1956]. 446 p. (Le Livre de Poche policier, 1546-1547)
Contents: Case Book.

1071. *L'Association des hommes roux.* Paris: Société d'Edition et de Publications, [n.d.] [90] p. illus. (Les Oeuvres de Conan Doyle. Collection Rouge, 11)
Contents: RedH. - Fina.

1072. *Les Aventures de Sherlock Holmes.* Traduit de l'anglais par P. O. Paris: Félix Juven, 1902. vii, 275 p. (Librairie Félix Juven)
Contents: Preface. - Blue. - Spec. - Engr. - Nobl. - Bery. - Copp.

1073. ———. Traduit par P. O. Paris: La Renaissance du Livre, 1932. 256 p. (Le Disque rouge)

1074. ———. Traduction de René Lécuyer. Paris: Editions R. Simon, 1935. 253 p. (Collection Police-Secours)

1075. ———. Traduction nouvelle de René Lécuyer. Paris: Editions R. Simon, [1939]. 221 p. (Collection Police-Secours)
Contents: Blue. - Spec. - Engr. - Nobl. - Bery. - Copp.

1076. ———. Traduction de Bernard Tourville. [Paris]: Robert Laffont, [1956]. 438 p. (Le Livre de Poche policier, 1070-1071)
Contents: Adventures.

1077. *La Bande mouchetée.* Paris: Société d'Edition et de Publications, [n.d.] [92] p. illus. (Les Oeuvres de Conan Doyle. Collection Rouge, 1)
Contents: Spec. - Glor.

1078. ———. Traduction et adaptation de Louis Labat. [Paris]: Librairie Hachette, [1928].

1079. ———. Traduit de l'anglais par Lucien Maricourt. [Givors]: André Martel, 1947. 249 p.
Contents: Spec. - Bosc. - Iden. - Five. - Twis. - RedH.

1080. *Le Cercle rouge.* Traduit de l'anglais par Michel le Houbie. [Givors]: André Martel, 1949. 254 p.
Contents: RedC. - Dyin. - Blue. - Nava. - Veil. - Miss. - Fina.

1081. *Le Chien des Baskerville: Roman anglais.* Traduit de l'anglais par A. de Jassaud. Paris: Librairie Hachette, 1905. 265 p. (Bibliothèque des meilleurs romans étrangers)

1082. *Le Chien des Baskerville.* Traduit par A. de Jassaud. Paris: Pierre Lafitte, 1933. 192 p. (Le Point d'interrogation. Collection de romans d'aventures)

1083. ———. Traduit par A. de Jassaud. Paris: Librairie Hachette, [1939]. 192 p. illus. (Bibliothèque de la jeunesse)

1084. ———. Traduit de l'anglais par Lucien Maricourt. [Givors]: André Martel, 1947. 276 p.

1085. ———. Traduction de Bernard Tourville. [Paris]: Robert Laffont, [1956]. 254 p. (Le Livre de Poche policier, 1630)

1086. ———. Traduit de l'anglais par Bernard Tourville. Paris: Ditis, 1959. 256 p. (Collection "J'ai lu," 51)

1087. ———. Traduction de Bernard Tourville. [Illustrations de Pietro Sarto.] Lausanne: La Guilde du livre, [1960]. 207 p. (Collection La Guilde du livre, 354)

1088. ———. Traduit de l'anglais par Bernard Tourville. [Paris: Robert Laffont, 1961.] 248 p. (Collection "J'ai lu," 51)

1089. ———. Traduit de l'anglais par Bernard Tourville. Paris: Ditis, 1964. 224 p. (J'ai lu Policier, 3)

1090. *Chronique de Sherlock Holmes.* Paris: Librairie des Champs-Elysées, 1929. 256 p. (Le Masque)

1091. *Les Cinq pépins d'orange.* Paris: Société d'Edition et de Publications, [n.d.] [88] p. illus. (Les Oeuvres de Conan Doyle. L'Illustre policier anglais, 4)
Contents: Five. - Reig.

1092. *Un Crime étrange.* Traduit de l'anglais. [Paris]: Pierre Lafitte, [1933]. 191 p. ("Le Point D'interrogation." Collection de romans d'aventures, 32)
Contents: Sign.

1093. *La Cycliste solitaire.* Paris: Société d'Edition et de Publications, [n.d.] [88] p. illus. (Les Oeuvres de Conan Doyle. L'Illustre policier anglais, 3)
Contents: Soli. - 3Stu.

1094. "Les Danseurs," *Je sais tout* [Paris], 1, No. 5 (15 Juin 1905), 578-586. illus.
Contents: Danc.

1095. *Les Débuts de Sherlock Holmes.* Traduction d'Albert Savine. Paris: F. Rouff,

Foreign-Language Editions

57

1914. 36 p. (Grande Collection nationale, 28)
Contents: Stud.

1096. ———. Traduction par Albert Savine. Nouvelle édition. Paris: Albin Michel, 1922. 255 p.

1097. *Les Débuts de Sherlock Holmes: Roman.* Traduit de l'anglais par Albert Savine. Paris: Albin Michel, [1941]. 249 p. (Collection des maîtres de la littérature étrangère)

1098. *Les Débuts de Sherlock Holmes.* Traduit de l'anglais par Albert Savine. Frontispice de Colette Pettier. Paris: Les Compagnons du Livre, 1951. 259 p.

1099. *Un Echec de Sherlock Holmes.* Traduit par Lucien Maricourt. [Givors]: André Martel, 1948. 250 p.
Contents: Yell. - Silv. - Glor. - Musg. - Croo. - Resi. - Gree.

1100. *L'Escarboucle bleue.* Paris: Société d'Edition et de Publications, [n.d.] [92] p. illus. (Les Oeuvres de Conan Doyle. Collection Rouge, 9)
Contents: Blue. - Bery.

1101. *Une Etude en rouge.* Précédé d'une préface par L. Brandin. Traduit par Mme Charleville. Paris: C. Delagrave, [1903]. xiii, 256 p. (Bibliothèque des meilleurs romans anglais contemporains publiée sous la direction de M. L. Brandin)
Contents: Stud.

1102. ———. Traduit par Mme Charleville. Paris: C. Delagrave, [1933]. 254 p. (Bibliothèque Juventa)

1103. ———. Traduit par René Lécuyer. Paris: Librairie des Champs-Elysées, [1933]. 246 p. (Collection Le Masque)

1104. ———. Traduit de l'anglais par Lucien Maricourt. [Givors]: André Martel, 1946. 266 p.

1105. ———. Traduit de l'anglais par Lucien Maricourt. [Givors]: André Martel, 1947. 272 p.
Contents: Stud. - Scan.

1106. "Les Hetres pourpres (suite)," Traduit de l'anglais par P. O. J. *Le Journal* [Paris] (28 Septembre 1905), 2. (Nouvelles aventures de Sherlock Holmes)
Contents: Copp.

1107. *L'Homme à la lèvre retroussée.* Paris: Société d'Edition et de Publications, [n.d.] [90] p. illus. (Les Oeuvres de Conan Doyle. Collection Rouge, 10)
Contents: Twis. - Yell.

58   1108. *La Marque des quatre: Roman anglais.*

Huitième édition. Paris: Librairie Hachette, 1896. 244 p. (Bibliothèque des meilleurs romans étrangers)
Contents: Sign.

1109. *La Marque des quatre.* Paris: Pierre Lafitte, 1923. 79 p.

1110. ———. Traduit de l'anglais. [Paris]: Pierre Lafitte, [1934]. 190 p. ("Le Point d'interrogation." Collection de romans d'aventures, 35)

1111. ———. Paris: Librairie Hachette, [1941]. 190 p. (Collection L'Enigme)

1112. *Nouveaux exploits de Sherlock Holmes.* Paris: Félix Juven, [1905]. 276 p.
Contents: Croo. - Soli. - 3Stu. - Reig. - Gree. - Resi. - Fina.

1113. ———. Traduit par F. G. Paris: La Renaissance du Livre, 1911. 276 p.

1114. ———. Traduit par F. G. Paris: La Renaissance du Livre, [1925]. 190 p.
Contents: Croo. - Soli. - 3Stu. - Reig. - Gree. - Resi. - Fina.

1115. ———. Traduit par F. G. Paris: La Renaissance du Livre, 1932. 256 p. (Le Disque rouge)

1116. *La Nouvelle Chronique de Sherlock Holmes.* Traduit avec l'autorisation de l'auteur par Louis Labat. Paris: Pierre Lafitte, [1922]. 223 p.
Contents: His Last Bow.

1117. ———. Traduit par Louis Labat. Paris: Librairie des Champs-Elysées, [1929]. 252 p. (Collection Le Masque)

1118. *Les Nouvelles Aventures de Sherlock Holmes.* Traduit de l'anglais par F. O. Paris: Félix Juven, [1903]. 279 p.

1119. ———. Traduit par F. O. Paris: La Renaissance du Livre, [1919]. 251 p. (Le Disque rouge)
Contents: Scan. - RedH. - Iden. - Vall. - Five. - Twis.

1120. *Oeuvres complètes.* Collection dirigée par André Algarron. Paris: Robert Laffont, [1956-1958]. 10 v. (Sherlock Holmes, 1, 2, 3, 4)
Partial contents: Vol. 1 Advertissement au lecteur [Introduction]. - Stud, Traduction de Pierre Baillargeon. - Sign, Tr. de Michel Landa. - Adventures, Tr. de Bernard Tourville. 634 p. - Vol. 4. Memoirs, Tr. de Bernard Tourville. - Return, Tr. de Robert Latour. 666 p. - Vol. 7. Houn, Tr. de Bernard Tourville. - His Last Bow, Tr. de Gilles Vauthier. - Case Book, Tr. de Evelyn Colomb. 716 p. - Vol. 10. Vall, Tr. de Robert Latour. - Lost, Tr. de Evelyn Colomb. -

ManW, Tr. de Evelyn Colomb. - Exploits, de Adrian Conan Doyle et John Dickson Carr. Tr. de Gilles Vauthier. 660 p.

1121. ———. Kapellen [Belgique]: Walter Beckers, [1966-1967]. 24 v. illus. (Collection Les Immortels de la littérature. Série Criminologie)
Partial contents: Vol. 5. Houn. - His Last Bow. 445 p. - Vol. 6. Case Book. 302 p. - Vol. 7. Vall. - Lost. - ManW. 365 p. - Vol. 8. Exploits, de Adrian Conan Doyle et John Dickson Carr. 329 p.

1122. *Oeuvres littéraires complètes.* Préface et notes de Gilbert Sigaux. Lausanne [Suisse]: Editions Recontre, [1966-1968]. 20 v.
Partial contents: Vols. 2-6. *Le cycle de Sherlock Holmes:* Vol. 2. Stud, Traduction de Pierre Baillargeon. - Sign, Tr. de Michel Landa. - Adventures, Tr. de Bernard Tourville. 631 p. - Vol. 3. Memoirs, Tr. de Bernard Tourville. - Houn, Tr. de Bernard Tourville. 493 p. - Vol. 4. Return, Tr. de Robert Latour. 419 p. - Vol. 5. Vall, Tr. de Robert Latour. - His Last Bow, Tr. de Gilles Vauthier. 437 p. - Vol. 6. Case Book, Tr. de Evelyn Colomb. - Exploits, de Adrian Conan Doyle et John Dickson Carr. Tr. de Gilles Vauthier. 589 p. - Vol. 13. Lost, Tr. de Evelyn Colomb (p. 267-287). - ManW, Tr. de Evelyn Colomb (p. 308-327). - Vol. 20. Memories and Adventures, Tr. de Gilbert Sigaux. 485 p.

1123. *Le Pince-nez d'or.* [Paris]: Grande librairie univers, 1928. 252 p. (Collection Dilecta)

1124. "Les Plans du Bruce-Partington," Traduit de Lucie Paul Margueritte. *Je Sais Tout* [Paris].

1125. *Premières aventures de Sherlock Holmes.* [Traduit par P. O.] Illustrations de G. da Fonseca. Paris: Librairie Félix Juven, [1909]. 126 p. (Bibliothèque Illustrée)
Contents: Blue. - Spec. - Engr. - Nobl. - Bery. - Copp. - Scan.

1126. ———. Illustrations de G. da Fonseca. [Paris]: E. Flammarion, 1913. 120 p. (Collection Flammarion, 34)

1127. *La Résurrection de Sherlock Holmes.* Paris: Félix Juven, 1905. 271 p.

1128. ———. Paris: La Renaissance du Livre, [1918]. 252 p. (Le Disque rouge)
Contents: Empt. - Norw. - Danc. - Prio. - Blac.

1129. ———. Traduction de Robert Latour. Paris: Robert Laffont, 1956. 422 p. (Le Livre de Poche policier, 1322-1323)
Contents: Return.

1130. *Le Retour de Sherlock Holmes.* Traduit de l'anglais par Louis Chantemele. [Givors]: André Martel, 1949. 254 p. (Collection Les Aventures de Sherlock Holmes)
Contents: Empt. - Soli. - Prio. - Blac. - Chas. - SixN.

1131. "La Rivale: Extrait des mémoires inédits du Dr. Watson sur Sherlock Holmes: Nouvelle inédite," Traduit de l'anglais par Louis Labat. *Les Oeuvres libres: Recueil littéraire mensuel ne publiant que de l'inédit.* Paris: Arthème Fayard, [1922]. Vol. 14., p. 317-350.
Contents: Thor.

1132. "Un Scandale en Bohême," *BSJ* [OS], 1, No. 2 (April 1946), 163-185.
Reprinted from the Félix Juven edition of 1909 (item 1125).

1133. *Un Scandale en Bohême.* Paris: Société d'Edition et de Publications, [n.d.] [90] p. illus. (Les Oeuvres de Conan Doyle. L'Illustre policier anglais, 5)
Contents: Scan. - Iden.

1134. *Sept aventures de Sherlock Holmes: Un Scandale en Bohême. La Ligue des rouquins. Les Cinq pépins d'orange. L'Escarboucle bleue. Le Ruban moucheté. Un Aristocrate célibataire. Les Hêtres rouges.* Traduit par Bernard Tourville. Verviers: Marabout, 1959. 187 p.
Contents: Scan. - RedH. - Five. - Blue. - Engr. - Nobl. - Copp.

1135. *Sherlock Holmes: Etude en rouge. Le Signe des quatre.* Préface de Germaine Beaumont. [Traduit de Pierre Baillargeon et Michel Landa.] [Paris: Robert] Laffont, [1956]. 447 p. (Le Livre de Poche policier, 885—886)
Contents: Stud. - Sign.

1136. *Sherlock Holmes triomphe!* Traduction de Henry Evie. Paris: Félix Juven, [1905]. 277 p.

1137. ———. Traduit par Henry Evie. Paris: La Renaissance du Livre, 1932. 256 p. (Le Disque rouge, 15)

1138. *Le Signe des quatre.* Traduit de l'anglais par Lucien Maricourt. [Givors]: André Martel, 1946. 214 p.

1139. *Les six "Napoléons."* Paris: Société d'Edition et de Publications, [n.d.] [92] p. illus. (Les Oeuvres de Conan Doyle. Collection Rouge, 13)
Contents: SixN. - Norw.

1140. *Son dernier coup d'archet.* Traduction de Gilles Vauthier. [Paris]: Robert Laffont, [1956]. 253 p. (Le Livre de Poche policier, 2019)
Contents: His Last Bow.

1141. *Souvenirs de Sherlock Holmes.* Traduit de l'anglais par P. O. [Paris]: Librairie Félix Juven, [1904]. 265 p.
    Contents: Silv. - Nava. - Glor. - Yell. - Musg. - Stoc.

1142. ———. Traduit par F. O. Paris: La Renaissance du Livre, 1913. 264 p.

1143. *Souvenirs sur Sherlock Holmes.* Traduction de Bernard Tourville. [Paris]: Robert Laffont, [1956]. 446 p. (Le Livre de Poche policier, 1238-1239)
    Contents: Memoirs.

1144. *La Vallée de la peur: Roman.* Traduction de l'anglais par Louis Labat. Paris: Pierre Lafitte, [1920]. 256 p.

1145. *La Vallée de la peur: Une aventure de Sherlock Holmes.* Traduit par Louis Labat. Paris: Librairie des Champs-Elysées, 1929. 256 p. (Collection Le Masque)

1146. *La Vallée de la peur.* Traduit de l'anglais par Lucien Maricourt. [Givors]: André Martel, 1948. 250 p.

1147. ———. Traduction de Robert Latour. [Paris]: Robert Laffont, [1956]. 254 p. (Le Livre de Poche policier, 1433)

English Readers

1148. *Four Adventures of Sherlock Holmes.* Avec une introduction, des notes et des exercices de G. Bouvet. Paris; Bruxelles: Didier, 1955. 144 p. (The Rainbow Library, 40)
    Contents: Glor. - Musg. - Copp. - Fina.

1149. ———. Edited by G. Bouvet. Paris: Didier, [1958]. 96 p. (The Rainbow Library, 40)
    Contents same as above. The introduction, notes and exercises are published in a separate booklet. 48 p.

1150. *Sherlock Holmes (Conan Doyle's Famous Creation): Quelques Chapitres de Sa Vie; A Few Chapters of His Life; Avec Questions et Réponses; With Questions and Answers.* Philadelphia: Edward Roth, 1902. 94 p.
    At head of title: Système à deux cahiers. Two copy-book systems. Matière pour la conversation française. Material for French conversation.
    Contains an introduction in English, the first two chapters of *A Study in Scarlet* in French and English, and questions and answers in French and English.

Parodies and Pastiches

1151. *Les Aventures du fils de Sherlock Holmes.* [The Adventures of the Son of Sherlock Holmes.] Racontées par le Docteur Watson. Paris: Publications Richonnier, [ca. 1914].
    Review: Saturday Review of Literature, 10 (May 26, 1934), 715 (Christopher Morley).

1152. [Giraudoux, Jean.] "D'un cheveu," par Jean Cordelier et Ch. Aivrard [pseud.] *Le Matin* (9 Novembre 1908).
    ———. ———, *Les Contes d'un matin,* [par] Jean Giraudoux. [Paris]: Gallimard, [1952]. p. 59-71.
    ———. "Il S'en Fallut d'un cheveu," *Lectures pour Tous* [Paris] (Décembre 1960).
    ———. "Et haar," Oversat af A. Nicolet. *Sherlockiana,* 5, Nr. 1-2 (1960), 2-4.
    ———. "By a Hair," Tr. by Kai-Ho Mah. With an introductory note by Ronald De Waal. *BSJ,* 20, No. 1 (March 1970), 48-51.
    The author's humorous imitation presents the narrator (Watson?) as the adulterous lover of Mrs. Sherlock Holmes. The tale-teller meets the Master, who seems to penetrate the truth of the affair by using a single hair as evidence, but in the end Holmes turns out to be quite wrong in his deductions.

1153. Hansen. *Petzi et le détective.* [Tournai, Belgique]: Casterman, [1965]. 32 p. illus.
    A book for children.

1154. Jacquin, J[oseph], et A[ristide] Fabre. *Le Chien de Serloc Kolmes.* Ouvrage illustré de 102 gravures. Deuxième édition. Paris: Librairie Hachette, 1914. 196 p. (Bibliothèque des écoles et des familles)

1155. Leblanc, Maurice. *L'Aiguille creuse.* Paris: Pierre Lafitte, 1909. 344 p. (Les Aventures extraordinaires d'Arsène Lupin, 3)
    ———. ———. Paris: Pierre Lafitte, [1912]. 224 p.
    ———. ———, *Les Aventures d'Arsène Lupin, Gentleman-Cambrioleur.* [Paris]: Hachette / Gallimard, [1961]. Vol. 2, p. 243-464.
    ———. *La Comtesse de Cagliostro. L'Aiguille creuse. Le Secret des rois de France.* Paris: Club du Livre Policier, 1959. 416 p.
    ———. *Frankrigs Hemmelighed: Arsène Lupins sidste Bedrifter.* København: Fr. Hegels Forlag, 1909. 182 p.
    ———. [*Kigan-jô.* Tr. by Tatsuo Hoshino. Tokyo: Mikasa Shobô, 1958.] 234 p. (Lupin Zenshu, 4)
    ———. *The Hollow Needle: Further Adventures of Arsène Lupin.* Tr. by Alexander Teixeira de Mattos. Illustrated by J. W. Robson. New York: Doubleday, Page & Co., 1910. 325 p.
    ———. ———. London: Amalgamated Press, 1910.
    ———. ———. London: Eveleigh Nash, 1911. v, 301 p.
    ———. ———. Three Owls edition. New York: W. R. Caldwell & Co., [ca. 1910]. 325

p. (The International Adventure Library)
———. ———. New York: Grosset & Dunlap, 1912. 325 p.
———. ———. London: George Newnes, 1913. 253 p.
———. ———. London: George Newnes, 1915. 124 p. (Newnes' Sixpenny Copyright Novels)
———. ———. New York: Macaulay Co., 1929. 253 p.
———. ———. [Introduction by Maurice Richardson.] London: The Bodley Head, [1960]. 224 p.
———. ———. Chester Springs, Pa.: Dufour Editions, 1962.

Less than halfway through the book Sherlock Holmes appears almost in person under the name of Holmlock Shears, called in by the Comte de Gesvres, who believes that Inspector Ganimard is out of his depth.

Reviews: Book Review Digest, 6 (1910), 234; *Nation*, 91 (October 13, 1910), 340; *New York Times* (November 26, 1910), 672; *SHJ*, 5, No. 3 (Winter 1961), 90 (Lord Donegall).

1156. ———. *Arsène Lupin contre Herlock Sholmès*. Paris: Pierre Lafitte, 1908. 322 p. (Les Aventures extraordinaires d'Arsène Lupin, 2)
———. ———. [Paris]: Pierre Lafitte, [1932]. 192 p. ("Le Point d'interrogation." Collection de romans d'aventures)
———. ———. [Paris]: Club des Jeunes Amis du Livre, [1957]. 291 p.
———. ———. *Les Aventures d'Arsène Lupin, Gentleman-Cambrioleur*. [Paris]: Hachette / Gallimard, [1961]. Vol. 2, p. 1-239.
———. ———. Paris: [Robert Laffont], 1963. 247 p. (Le Livre de Poche policier, 999)
———. *Arsène Lupin contra Sherlock Holmes*. [København]: Gyldendalske Boghandel, Nordisk Forlag, 1910. 258 p.
———. [*Goto shinshi Lupin*. Tr. by Shin'ichiro Nakamura. Tokyo: Hayakawa Shobo, 1958.] 198 p.
———. [*Kaijin tai kyojin*. Tr. by Tatsuo Hoshino. Tokyo: Mikasa Shobo, 1958.] 240 p. (Lupin Zenshu, 7)
———. *Arsène Lupin contra Herlock Sholmes: Romance*. Traducao de Educardo de Lima Castro. Rio de Janeiro: Casa Editora Vecchi Ltda, 1959. 203 p. ("Os mais célebres romances policiais," 2)
———. *Arsenio Lupin contra Herlock Sholmes*. Traduccion de Carlos Docteur. México, D. F.: Editora Nacional, 1952. 299 p. (Aventuras extraordinarias de Arsenio Lupin. Coleccion economica, 385)
———. *The Fair-Haired Lady*. Tr. by Alexander Teixeira de Mattos. London: Grant Richards, 1909. 271 p.
———. *Arsène Lupin versus Herlock Sholmes*. Tr. by George Morehead. Chicago: M. A. Donohue & Co., [c.1910]. 350 p. (The Extraordinary Adventures of Arsène Lupin)
———. *Arsène Lupin versus Holmlock Shears*. Tr. by Olive Harper [pseud.] New York: J. S. Ogilvie Pub. Co., [c.1910]. 282 p.
———. *The Blonde Lady: Being a Record of the Duel of Wits Between Arsene Lupin and the English Detective*. Tr. by Alexander Teixeira de Mattos. Illustrated by H. Richard Boehm. New York: Doubleday, Page & Co., 1910. 345 p.
———. *The Arrest of Arsene Lupin*. Tr. by Alexander Teixeira de Mattos. London: **Eveleigh Nash & Grayson Ltd.**, [1911]. 256 p.
———. *Sherlock Holmes versus Arsène Lupin: The Case of the Golden Blonde*. Adapted into English by Jacob Brussell. **New York: Atomic Books, Inc.**, [1946]. 128 p.

1157. ———. "Herlock **Sholmès** arrive trop tard," *Arsène Lupin, Gentleman-Cambrioleur*. Préface de Jules Clareitie. Paris: Pierre Lafitte, 1907. p. 267-307. (Les Aventures extraordinaires d'Arsène Lupin, 1)
———. ———, *Les Aventures d'Arsène Lupin, Gentleman-Cambrioleur*. [Paris]: Hachette / Gallimard, [1961]. Vol. 1, p. 455-485.
———. "Herlock Sholmès przybywa za późno," *Arsène Lupin dżentelmen-włamywacz*. Prełożył Tadeusz Evert. Warszawa: Iskry. 1957. p. 207-242.
———. "Holmlock Shears Arrives Too Late," *The Exploits of Arsène Lupin*. Tr. by Alexander Teixeira de Mattos. New York and London: Harper & Brothers, 1907. Chap. 9, p. 273-314.
———. ———, ———. New York: P. F. Collier & Son Co., [c.1907]. Chap. 9, p. 273-314.
———. ———, ———. London: Cassell & Co., 1909.
———. ———, *The Extraordinary Adventures of Arsène Lupin, Gentleman-Burglar*. Tr. from the French by George Morehead. Chicago: M. A. Donohue & Co., [c.1910]. Chap. 9, p. 265-308.
———. ———, *The Misadventures of Sherlock Holmes*. Edited by Ellery Queen. Boston: Little, Brown and Co., 1944. p. 14-38.
———. ———, *The Exploits of Arsene Lupin*. London: The Bodley Head, 1960.

FRISIAN

1158. *De houn fan de Baskervilles*. [Tr. by Inne de Jong.] Bolsward: Osinga, 1960. 190 p.

GEORGIAN

1159. [*Priključenija Šerloka Holmsa*. Tr. by E. Magradze. Tbilisi: Literatura da helovneba, 1966.] 687 p.

1160. [*Sobaka Baskervilej*. Tr. by É.

Magradze. Tbilisi: Sabčota Sakartvelo, 1964.] 165 p.

GERMAN

1161. *Abenteuer des Doktor Holmes: 9 Detektivgeschichten.* Autorisiert Uber-setzung von Louis Ottmann und Margarete Jacobi. Stuttgart: Robert Lutz, [1910]. 250 p. (Lutz' Kriminal-und Detektiv-Romane, 12)

1162. *Als Sherlock Holmes aus Lhassa kam: 7 neue Detektivgeschichten.* Ubers. von Rudolf Lautenbach und Adolf Gleiner. Illustriert von Richard Gutschmidt. Stuttgart: Robert Lutz, [1906]. 310 p. (Sherlock Holmes-Serie, 7)
  Contents: Empt. - Norw. - Yell. - Glor. - Gree. - Gold. - Soli.

1163. *Der Baumeister von Nordwood und andere Geschichten.* Ubers. von Rudolf Lautenbach und Adolf Gleiner. Berlin: Neufeld & Henius, [1930]. 181 p. (Lutz' Kriminal-Romane, 3)

1164. *Der blaue Karfunkel.* München: Droemer, [1949]. 321 p. (Die Abenteuer des Sherlock Holmes, 1) (Romane der Welt)

1165. *Der blaue Karfunkel und andere Sherlock Holmes Stories.* [Ubers. von Hans Herlin et al.] Gütersloh: Bertelsmann; Stuttgart: Europäischer Buch-u. Phonoklub, 1968. 663 p. illus.

1166. *Der Bund der Rothaarigen und andere Detektivgeschichten.* Autor. Ubers. von Louis Ottmann und Margarete Jacobi. Mit Illustrationen. Stuttgart: Robert Lutz, [1906]. 319 p. (Sherlock Holmes-Serie, 3)
  Contents: RedH. - Scan. - Iden. - Bosc. - Stoc. - Twis. - Blue.

1167. ———. Stuttgart: Franckh'sche Verlagshandlung, [1936]. 186 p.

1168. *Die drei Giebel und andere Abenteuer von Sherlock Holmes.* [Ubers. von Eve Fritsche.] Berlin: H. Wille, [1927]. 135 p. (Wille's Illustrierte Kriminalbücherei, 32)

1169. *Erinnerungen an Sherlock Holmes.* 1. Teil. *5. Detektivgeschichten.* Autor. Ubers. von R[udolf] Lautenbach und M. Pannwitz. Stuttgart: Robert Lutz, [1910]. 208 p. (Lutz' Kriminal-und Detektiv-Romane, 56)

1170. ———. 2. Teil. *4 Detektivgeschichten.* Autor. Ubers. von R[udolf] Lautenbach. Stuttgart: Robert Lutz, [1912]. 201 p. (Lutz' Kriminal-und Detektiv-Romane, 62)

1171. ———. 3. Teil. *5 Detektivgeschichten.* Autor. Ubers. von R[udolf] Lautenbach. Stuttgart: Robert Lutz, [1914]. 238 p. (Lutz' Kriminal-und Detektiv-Romane, 68)

1172. *Fünf Apfelsinenkerne und andere Detektivgeschichten.* Autor. Ubers. von Margarete Jacobi und Louis Ottmann. Mit Illustrationen. Stuttgart: Robert Lutz, [1906]. 312 p. (Sherlock Holmes-Serie, 5)
  Contents: Five. - Musg. - Reig. - Croo. - Resi. - Nava. - Fina.

1173. ———. Stuttgart: Franckh'sche Verlagshandlung, [1936]. 173 p.

1174. *Das Gesicht am Fenster: Neue Sherlock-Holmes Abenteuer.* [Ubers. von Eve Fritsche.] Berlin: Aufwärts-Verlag, [1939]. 96 p. (Der Dreissig-Pfennig-Roman, 127)

1175. *Das getupfte Band und andere Detektivgeschichten.* Ubers. von Margarete Jacobi und Louis Ottmann. Mit Illustrationen. Stuttgart: Robert Lutz, [1906]. 314 p. (Sherlock Holmes-Serie, 4)
  Contents: Spec. - Engr. - Nobl. - Bery. - Copp. - Silv.

1176. ———. Stuttgart: Franckh'sche Verlagshandlung, [1938]. 195 p.

1177. "Der Hund von Baskerville," *Volksblatt und Freiheits-Freund* [Neeb-Hirsch Pub. Co., Pittsburgh] (September 26-November 18, 1904).
  Newspaper in German script.

1178. *Der Hund von Baskerville.* [Übertragen von George Meyer.] Milwaukee, Wis.: The Herald Co., 1904. 115 p. illus. (Sherlock Holmes Serie) (Herald Bibliothek, No. 7)

1179. *Der Hund von Baskerville: Roman.* Ubers. von Heinrich Darnoc. Mit Illustrationen von Richard Gutschmidt. Stuttgart: Robert Lutz, [1906]. 324 p. (Sherlock Holmes-Serie, 6)

1180. ———. Übers. von Heinrich Darnoc. Stuttgart: Robert Lutz, [1913]. 310 p. (Lutz' Kriminal-und Detektiv-Romane, 41)

1181. ———. [Übers. von Heinrich Darnoc. Illustriert von Hans Anton Aschenborn.] Stuttgart: Franckh'sche Verlagshandlung, [1935]. 295 p. (Sherlock-Holmes-Romane, 6)

1182. *Der Hund von Baskerville.* Bern: Alfred Scherz Verlag, [1947]. 225 p. (Sherlock Holmes, 1) (Die schwarzen Kriminalromane, 5)

1183. *Der Hund von Baskerville: Roman.* München: Droemersche Verlagsanstalt, [1950]. 310 p.

1184. *Der Hund von Baskerville: Kriminalroman.* [Berlin]: Verlag: Das Neue Berlin, [1955]. 213 p. (NB-Romane, 13)

1185. ———. [Übertragen von Heinz Kott-

haus.] [Hamburg]: SM-Bücher, [1960]. 188
p. (28 K)

1186. *Der Hund von Baskerville*. Übers. von
Heinz Kotthaus. [Gütersloh]: Bertelsmann-
Lesering, 1960. 196 p.

1187. ———. Übers. von Heinz Kotthaus.
Gütersloh: S. Mohn, 1961. 188 p.

1888. ———. [Übers. von Heinz Kotthaus.]
Hamburg: Blüchert Verlag, 1963. 182 p.
(Gesammelte Werke in Einzelausgaben, 2.
Hrsg. von Nino Erné)

1189. ———. [Übertragen von Heinz Kotthaus.] Gütersloh: Signum, 1964. 188 p.

1190. ———. Übers. von Heinz Kotthaus.
Hamburg: Mosaik Verlag, 1966. 196 p.
(Gesammelte Werke in Einzelausgaben, 2.
Hrsg. von Nino Erné)

1191. ———. Übers. von Heinz Kotthaus.
Frankfurt / M., Berlin: Ullstein, 1967. 168
p. (Ullstein-Bücher, 2602)

1192. *Des Löwen Mähne und andere Aben-
teuer von Sherlock Holmes*. [Übers. von Eve
Fritsche und Else Baronin von Werkmann.]
Berlin: H. Wille, [1928]. 143 p. (Wille's
Illustrierte Kriminalbücherei, 33)

1193. *Der Mazarin-Diamant und andere
Abenteuer von Sherlock Holmes*. [Übers.
von Eve Fritsche und Else Baronin von
Werkmann.] Berlin: H. Wille, [1928]. 142 p.
(Wille's Illustrierte Kriminalbücherei, 34)

1194. *Neue Abenteuer des Doktor Holmes*.
Übers. von Margarete Jacobi und L[ouis]
Ottmann. Stuttgart: Verlag von Robert
Lutz, [1910]. 299 p. (Lutz' Kriminal-und
Detektiv-Romane, 20)
Contents: Silv. - Stoc. - Musg. - Reig. -
Croo. - Resi. - Nava. - Engr. - Fina.

1195. *Das Rätsel der Thor-Brücke und andere
Abenteuer von Sherlock Holmes*. [Übers.
von Else Baronin von Werkmann.] Berlin:
H. Wille, [1928]. 144 p. (Wille's Illustrierte
Kriminalbücherei, 35)

1196. *Sämtliche Sherlock Holmes Stories*. Mit
Zeichnungen von Stefan Lemke und Marie-
Luise Pricken. [Herausgegeben von Nino
Erné. Deutsch von Hans Herlin, Rudolf
Rocholl, Beatrice Schott und Tanja Terek.]
Hamburg: Mosaik-Verlag, [1967]. 2 v. (663,
745 p.) illus.
Deluxe edition (full leather).

1197. ———. [Gütersloh]: C. Bertelsmann
Verlag, [n.d.] 2 v. (663, 745 p.) illus.
Contains the fifty-six short stories,
arranged chronologically, with an in-
troduction on the chronology by Nino Erné.
The German translation is based on the

John Murray omnibus edition and the 107
drawings are in modern style. (The deluxe
edition was considered one of the fifty most
beautifully bound books published in
Germany during 1967.)
Review: SHJ, 9, No. 1 (Winter 1968), 29
(Lord Donegall).

1198. *Sherlock Holmes: Sämtliche Romane*.
[Nach der Übers. von Beatrice Schott,
Tatjana Wlassow und Heinz Kotthaus.
Revidiert und Herausgegeben von Nino
Erné.] Hamburg: Blüchert Verlag, [1963].
639 p.
Contents: Stud. - Sign. - Houn. - Vall.

1199. ———. Hamburg: Mosaik-Verlag,
[1967]. 596 p.
Contents same as above.

1200. *Sherlock Holmes: Sämtliche Romane:
Studie in Scharlachrot. Im Zeichen der Vier.
Der Hund von Baskerville. Das Tal der
Furcht*. [Übers. von Beatrice Schott, Tatjana
Wlassow und Heinz Kotthaus.] Zürich:
Buchclub Ex Libris, 1967. 626 p.

1201. *Sherlock Holmes' Abenteuer*. [Über-
tragen von Alexandra Brun.] Bern: Alfred
Scherz Verlag, [1953]. 2 v. (192, 191 p.) (Die
schwarzen Kriminalromane, 53, 60)
Contents: Vol. 1. Scan. - RedH. - Iden. -
Bosc. - Five. - Twis. - Blue. - Spec. - Vol. 2.
Engr. - Nobl. - Bery. - Copp. - Wist. - Card. -
RedC.

1202. ———. Übers. von Hans Herlin.
Hamburg: Blüchert Verlag, 1959. 195 p.
(Gesammelte Werke in Einzelausgaben, 1.
Hrsg. von Nino Erné)
Contents: Scan. - Bosc. - Blue. - Five. -
Twis. - Nobl. - Spec. - Copp.

1203. ———. [Übertragen von Hans Herlin.]
[Gütersloh]: Bertelsmann-Lesering, 1960.
195 p.

1204. ———. [Hrsg. von Nino Erné. Übers.
von Hans Herlin. Lizenzausg.] Zürich:
Buchclub Ex Libris, [1964]. 200 p.

1205. ———. Übers. von Hans Herlin. Frankfurt / M., Berlin: Ullstein, 1967. 172 p.
(Ullstein-Bücher, 2630)

1206. *Sherlock Holmes' Abenteuer:
Kriminalstories*. [Hamburg]: SM Signum
Taschenbücher, [n.d.] 187 p. (88 K)
Contents: Scan. - Bosc. - Blue. - Five. -
Twis. - Nobl. - Spec. - Copp.

1207. *Sherlock Holmes Abschied*. Übers. von
Beatrice Schott und Tanja Terek. Hamburg:
Mosaik Verlag, 1966. 189 p. (Gesammelte
Werke in Einzelausgaben, 15. Hrsg. von
Nino Erné)

1208. *Sherlock Holmes als Einbrecher*.

[Sherlock Holmes as a Burglar.] *Neue Sherlock Holmes-Geschichten.* Übers. von Rudolf Lautenbach. Stuttgart: Robert Lutz, [1911]. 178 p. (Lutz' Kriminal-und Detektiv-Romane, 52)
Contents: Chas. - 3Stu. - Miss.

1209. *Sherlock Holmes' Kombinationen.* [Übers. von Rudolf Rocholl.] Hamburg: Blüchert Verlag, 1963. 187 p. (Gesammelte Werke in Einzelausgaben, 9. Hrsg. von Nino Erné)
Contents: Iden. - Engr. - RedH. - Croo. - Resi. - Nava. - Fina.

1210. *Sherlock Holmes' Kriminalfälle.* [Übers. von Beatrice Schott.] Hamburg: Blüchert Verlag, 1963. 187 p. (Gesammelte Werke in Einzelausgaben, 8. Hrsg. von Nino Erné)
Contents: Glor. - Musg. - Yell. - Silv. - Gree. - Reig.

1211. *Sherlock Holmes' Kriminalfälle 1: Kriminalstories.* [Übers. von Beatrice Schott.] München: Wilhelm Heyne Verlag, [1965]. 159 p. (Heyne-Bücher, 1163)
Contents: Glor. - Musg. - Yell. - Silv. - Gree. - Reig.

1212. *Sherlock Holmes' Kriminalfälle 2: Kriminalstories.* [Übers. von Rudolf Rocholl.] München: Wilhelm Heyne Verlag, [1965]. 158 p. (Heyne-Bücher, 1169)
Contents: Iden. - Engr. - RedH. - Croo. - Resi. - Nava. - Fina.

1213. *Sherlock Holmes' Kriminalfälle 3: Kriminalstories.* [Übers. von Tanja Terek.] München: Wilhelm Heyne Verlag, [1965]. 157 p. (Heyne-Bücher, 1182)
Contents: Empt. - Norw. - Stoc. - Soli. - Danc. - Blac.

1214. *Sherlock Holmes' Kriminalfälle 4: Kriminalstories.* [Übers. von Beatrice Schott.] München: Wilhelm Heyne Verlag, [1966]. 171 p. (Heyne-Bücher, 1206)
Contents: Chas. - SixN. - 3Stu. - Gold. - Miss. - Abbe. - Seco.

1215. *Sherlock Holmes' Kriminalfälle 5: Kriminalstories.* [Übers. von Tanja Terek.] München: Wilhelm Heyne Verlag, [1966] 175 p. (Heyne-Bücher, 1232)
Contents: Suss. - Prio. - RedC. - 3Gab. - Card. - Bruc. - Dyin.

1216. *Sherlock Holmes' Kriminalfälle 6: Kriminalstories.* [Übers. von Beatrice Schott.] München: Wilhelm Heyne Verlag, [1967]. 188 p. (Heyne-Bücher, 1269)
Contents: Thor. - 3Gar. - Wist. - Bery. - Lady. - Veil. - Devi.

1217. *Sherlock Holmes' Kriminalfälle 7: Kriminalstories.* [Übers. von Beatrice Schott

und Tanja Terek.] München: Wilhelm Heyne Verlag, [1968]. 174 p. (Heyne-Bücher, 1289)
Contents: Shos. - Illu. - Blan. - Cree. - Maza. - Reti. - Lion. - Last.

1218. *Sherlock Holmes' Methoden.* [Übers. von Beatrice Schott.] Hamburg: Blüchert Verlag, 1964. 198 p. (Gesammelte Werke in Einzelausgaben, 11. Hrsg. von Nino Erné)
Contents: Chas. - SixN. - 3Stu. - Gold. - Miss. - Abbe. - Seco.

1219. *Sherlock Holmes' Ritterlichkeit.* [Übers. von Beatrice Schott.] Hamburg: Blüchert Verlag, 1965. 184 p. (Gesammelte Werke in Einzelausgaben, 14. Hrsg. von Nino Erné)
Contents: Thor. - 3Gar. - Wist. - Bery. - Lady. - Veil. - Devi.

1220. *Sherlock Holmes' Rückkehr.* [Übers. von Tanja Terek.] Hamburg: Blüchert Verlag, 1964. 189 p. (Gesammelte Werke in Einzelausgaben, 10. Hrsg. von Nino Erné)
Contents: Empt. - Norw. - Stoc. - Soli. - Danc. - Blac.

1221. *Sherlock Holmes und die Ohren nebst anderen Geschichten.* Übers. von Rudolf Lautenbach und Adolf Gleiner. Illustriert von Richard Gutschmidt. Stuttgart: Robert Lutz, [1908]. 294 p. (Sherlock Holmes-Serie, 9)
Partial contents: Card. - Chas. - 3Stu. - Miss.

1222. *Sherlock Holmes' Verbrecheralbum.* Übers. von Tanja Terek. Hamburg: Blüchert Verlag, 1965. 189 p. (Gesammelte Werke in Einzelausgaben, 12. Hrsg. von Nino Erné)

1223. "Sherlock Holmes," *Volksblatt und Freiheits-Freund* [Neeb-Hirsch Pub. Co., Pittsburgh] (February 9-March 4, 1903). Newspaper in German script.
Contents: Stud.

1224. *Späte Rache.* [Übertragen von George Meyer.] Milwaukee, Wis.: The Herald Co., 1904. 134 p. illus. (Sherlock Holmes Serie) (Herald Bibliothek, 5)
Contents: Stud. - Bosc. - Der Doppelgänger, von L.M.W.
A complete description of the book is given by H. B. Williams in "Spate Rache" (item 2781).

1225. ———. Übers. von Margarete Jacobi. Illustriert von Richard Gutschmidt. Stuttgart: Robert Lutz, [1906]. 232 p. (Sherlock Holmes-Serie, 1)

1226. ———. Übers. von Margarete Jacobi. Stuttgart: Robert Lutz, [1911]. 261 p. (Lutz' Kriminal-und Detektiv-Romane, 10)

1227. *Späte Rache: Roman.* Stuttgart:

Franckh'sche Verlagshandlung, [1938]. 154 p.

1228. *Späte Rache.* [Übertragen von Karl Bach.] Bern: Alfred Scherz Verlag, [1950]. 180 p. (Die schwarzen Kriminalromane, 31)

1229. *Spuren im Moor und andere Sherlock Holmes Stories.* Hrsg. von Nino Erné. Aus d. Engl. Dt. von Beatrice Schott und Tanja Terek. Mit Zeichnungen von Stefan Lemke und Marie-Luise Pricken. [Gütersloh]: Bertelsmann; Stuttgart: Europ. Buch-u. Phonoklub; Wien: Buchgemeinschaft Donauland, [1968]. 745 p.

1230. *Der sterbende Sherlock Holmes: 6 neue Detektivgeschichten.* Übers. von Johannes Hartmann. Illustriert von Georg Hoffmann. Stuttgart: Robert Lutz, [1924]. 256 p. (Sherlock Holmes-Serie, 10)

1231. *Der sterbende Sherlock Holmes nebst 2 anderen Detektiv-Erzählgn.* Übers. von Johannes Hartmann. Stuttgart; Berlin: Nuefeld & Henius, [1927]. 126 p. (Lutz' Kriminal-und Detektiv-Romane, 132)

1232. *Der sterbende Sherlock Holmes nebst zwei anderen Detektiv-Erzählungen.* Übers. von Johannes Hartmann. Stuttgart: Robert Lutz, [n.d.] 125 p. (Lutz' Kriminal-und Detektiv-Romane, 132)
  Contents: Dyin. - Nava. - Devi.

1233. *Der sterbende Sherlock Holmes und andere Detektivgeschichten.* [Übers. von Johannes Hartmann.] Stuttgart: Franckh'sche Verlagshandlung, [1937]. 231 p.
  Contents: Dyin. - Wist. - RedC. - Lady. - Bruc. - Devi. - Iden.

1234. *Studie in Scharlachrot.* [Übers. von Beatrice Schott.] Hamburg: Blüchert Verlag, 1961. 194 p. (Gesammelte Werke in Einzelausgaben, 5. Hrsg. von Nino Erné)

1235. *Das Tal des Grauens: Roman.* Übers. von H. O. Herzog. Berlin: Dom-Verlag, [1926]. 238 p. (Bücher d. Sensation)
  Contents: Vall.

1236. *Das Tal des Grauens.* [Übertragen von Karl Bach.] Bern: Alfred Scherz Verlag, [1948]. 196 p. (Die schwarzen Kriminalromane, 13)

1237. *Das Tal der Furcht.* Übers. von Heinz Kotthaus. Hamburg: Blüchert Verlag, 1960. 196 p. (Gesammelte Werke in Einzelausgaben, 3. Hrsg. von Nino Erné)

1238. ———. Übers. von Heinz Kotthaus. Gütersloh: Signum Verlag, 1962. 190 p.

1239. *Das Tal der Furcht: Kriminalroman.* [Deutsch von Heinz Kotthaus.] [Hamburg]: SM Signum Taschenbücher, [n.d.] 190 p. (129 K)

1240. *Die tanzenden Männchen und andere Detektivgeschichten.* Übers. von Rudolf Lautenbach. Illustriert von Richard Gutschmidt. Stuttgart: Robert Lutz, [1906]. 311 p. (Sherlock Holmes-Serie, 8)
  Contents: Danc. - Prio. - Blac. - SixN. - Abbe. - Seco.

1241. ———. Stuttgart: Franckh'sche Verlagshandlung, [1936]. 197 p.

1242. *Die verschleierte Mieterin: Neue Sherlock Holmes-Abenteuer.* [Übers. von Eva Fritsche.] Berlin: Aufwärts-Verlag, [1939]. 96 p. (Der Dreissig-Pfennig-Roman, 141)
  Contents: Veil.

1243. "Das Zeichen der Vier," *Volksblatt und Freiheits-Freund* [Neeb-Hirsch Pub. Co., Pittsburgh] (August 14-September 1903). Newspaper in German script.
  Contents: Sign.

1244. *Das Zeichen der Vier.* [Übertragen von George Meyer.] Milwaukee, Wis.: The Herald Co., [1904?] illus. (Sherlock Holmes Serie) (Herald Bibliothek)

1245. ———. Übers. von Margarete Jacobi. Illustriert von Richard Gutschmidt. Stuttgart: Robert Lutz, [1906]. 239 p. (Sherlock Holmes-Serie, 2)

1246. ———. Bern: Alfred Scherz Verlag, [1948]. 184 p. (Sherlock Holmes, 2) (Die schwarzen Kriminalromane, 9)

1247. ———. Übers. von Tatjana Wlassow. Hamburg: Blüchert Verlag, 1961. 188 p. (Gesammelte Werke in Einzelausgaben, 4. Hrsg. von Nino Erné)

English Readers

1248. *The Adventure of the Three Garridebs.* Herausgegeben von T[heodor] Schumacher. Anm.-München: Hueber, [1957]. 21 p. (Huebers fremdsprachliche Texte, 88)

1249. *The Hound of the Baskervilles.* Berne; Paris: Phoenix Pub. Co. Ltd.; Scherz & Hallwag, [1947]. 219 p. (Scherz Phoenix Books, 97)

1250. ———. Simplified by Wilhelm Grünewald. Braunschweig; Berlin; Hamburg; München; Kiel; Darmstadt: Westermann, 1954. 54 p. (Fundamental English Readers, 7)

1251. *The Naval Treaty: A Sherlock Holmes-Story.* Simplified by Kurt Zeidler. Braunschweig; Berlin; Hamburg: Westermann, 1948. 27 p. (Fundamental English Readers, 2)

1252. ———. Adapted for school reading by

Mary Hottinger. In collaboration with F[riedrich] L[eopold] Sack. Bern: Francke, [1958]. 39 p. (Coll. of English Texts, 80)

Parodies and Pastiches

1253. *Detektiv Sherlock Holmes und seine weltberühmten Abenteuer.* Berlin: Verlagshaus für Volksliteratur und Kunst, [1907]. 10 v. (32 p. ea.) (F. Butsch, editor)
The original Sherlock Holmes and Harry Taxon pastiches, mentioned by Anthony Boucher in "Holmesiana Hispanica" (item 3705). These stories appeared soon after in Spanish, Portuguese, and Swedish.
Contents: Vol. 1-10: [Unknown].

1254. *Aus den Geheimakten des Weltdetektivs: Kriminal-Wochenschrift.* Berlin: Verlagshaus für Volksliteratur und Kunst, [1907-1910]. 147 v. (32 p. ea.) (F. Butsch, editor)
A continuation of the above series under a different title.
Contents: Vol. 11-157: [Unknown].

1255. *Der Welt-Detektiv.* Berlin: Verlagshaus für Volksliteratur und Kunst, [1909]. 8 v. (96 p. ea.) (Salon-Ausgabe)
Each volume contains three stories from the above series, beginning with vol. 108.
Contents: Vol. 1-8: [Unknown].

1256. Stemmle, R. A. *Der Mann der Sherlock Holmes war: Ein heiterer Kriminalroman.* [The Man Who Was Sherlock Holmes: An Amusing Detective Story.] Berlin-Schöneberg: Gebrüder Weiss Verlag, [1963]. 199 p.

GREEK

1257. [*To chryso phasamen.* Athens: A. Soygantzh, n.d.] 31 p. (Serlok Holms, 4)
Contents: Gold.

1258. [*E exi Napoleontes.* Athens: A. Soygantzh, n.d.] 32 p. (Serlok Holms, 2)
Contents: SixN.

1259. [*Melete sto kokino.* Metaphrasis epo A. F. Zala. Athens: Ekdotikos Oikos Letpoy Dimitrakou A. E., n.d.] 80 p. (10)
Contents: Stud.

1260. [*E peripeteles tou Serlok Holms.* Athens: Pechlivanides, n.d.] 48 p. illus.

1261. [*Serlok Holms.* Athens: B. Damianakou & Cie., n.d.] 479 p.
Contents: Lady. - Card. - Blan. - 3Gab. - Suss. - Shos. - Thor. - Bruc. - Cree. - Copp. - Veil. - Reti. - Iden. - Bosc. - Illu. - Lion. - RedH. - Scan. - Maza. - Spec. - Bery. - Five.

1262. [*Serlok Holms: E billa me tes halkines oxues kai alla diegemata.* Metaphrasis epo

Kaite Strimenea. Athens: Atlantis, 1960.] 128 p.
Partial contents: Copp.

1263. [*To sima ton tessaron.* Metaphrasis epo A. Chalas. Athens: P. Dimitraeos, n.d.] 76 p.
Contents: Sign.

1264. [*To skyli ton Baskervil.* Metaphrasis epo Hatjegregores. Athens: Galaxias, 1965.] 144 p.
Contents: Houn.

GUJARATI

1265. [*Chamat-kārika khuna.* Tr. by Chandulāla Jethālāla Vyāsa. 2nd ed. Vadhavana, 1929.] ii, 254 p.
Contents: Stud.

1266. [*Kal ke kutaro.* Tr. by Jethālāl Somaiyā. Bombay: Vora & Co., 1957.] 280 p.
Contents: Houn.

1267. [*Lal Mandal.* Tr. by M. G. Patel. Bombay: Vora & Co.]

1268. [*Śerlok Homs nām parākramo.* Tr. by Jethālāl Somaiyā. Bombay: Vora & Co., 1959-1960.] 6 v.
Contents: Adventures.

1269. [*Śerlok Homs nām sāhaso.* Tr. by Jethālāl Somaiyā. Bombay: Vora & Co., 1964.] 6 v.

1270. [*Śerlok Homs ni vato.* Tr. by M. G. Patel. Bombay: Vora & Co.]

HEBREW

1271. [*Emek ha-pahad.* Tr. by Nehemya Porat. Tel-Aviv: Tevel, 1953.] 211 p.
Contents: Vall.

1272. [*Hotan ha-arbaa.* Tr. by Shelomo Arav. Tel-Aviv: J. Čečik, 1951.] 31 p.
Contents: Sign.

1273. [*Kalvam shel bney Baskerwille.* Tr. by Uriel Halperin. Tel-Aviv: Omanut, 1954.] 254 p.
Contents: Houn.

1274. [*Shaaruriya be-Bohemiya, ve odd sipurim.* Tr. by Yizhak Levanon. Tel-Aviv: El ha-maayan, 1953.] 142 p.
Partial contents: Scan.

1275. [*Sherlock Holmes.* Tr. by Pinhas Sapirhen. Tel-Aviv: Josef Sreberk, 1952.] 214 p.
Contents: Adventures.

1276. [————. Tel-Aviv: "Shlomo Srebrek" Publishing House Ltd., 1952.] 215 p.

Contents: SixN. - Reig. - Norw. - Seco. - Twis. - Bosc. - Stoc.

1277. [————. Tel-Aviv.] 146 p.
Contents: Engr. - Five. - Stoc. - Musg. - Gold. - Fina.

1278. [*Sherlock Holmes, aluf hapesha.* Tr. by Yehuda Harel. Tel-Aviv: Sifrey Mistorin, 1960.] 238 p.
Contents: Case Book.

1279. [*Sherlock Holmes: Hakira ba-shani.* Tr. by A. Ben-Dan. Tel-Aviv: Sifrei Maariv, 1960.] 126 p.
Contents: Stud.

HINDI

1280. [*Afim ka adda.* Tr. by Vrishabcharan Jain. Delhi: Dnan Prakashan, 1956.] 115 p.
Contents: 3Stu. - Scan. - Twis.

1281. [*Badalā.* Abridged and tr. by Prakās Pandit. Delhi : Hind Pocket Books, n.d.] 127 p.
Contents: Houn.

1282. [*Maut ki chāya.* Abridged and tr. by Prakas Pandit. Delhi: Hind Pocket Books, 1965.] 107 p.
Contents: Vall.

1283. [*Saralak Homja ki jāsūsi.* Tr. by Devendrakumār. Delhi: Hind Pocket Books, n.d.] 117 p.
Contents: Adventures.

1284. [*Sikari Kutta.* Tr. by Anand Prakasah. Lucknow: Asoka Prakashan, 1955.] iii, 277 p.
Contents: Houn.

HUNGARIAN

1285. *A nábob kincse: Regény.* Forditotta Fái J. Béla. Budapest: Singer és Wolfner kiádasa, 1895. 161 p. (Egyetemes Regénytar, X.11)
Contents: Sign.

1286. *A sátán kutyája.* Budapest: AZ Erdekes Ujsàg Kiadôhivatala,[n.d.] 2 v. (216, 213 p.)
Contents: Houn. - SixN. - Danc.

1287. *A sátán kutyája: Regény.* [Forditotta, Árkos Antal; Szecskó Tamás, rajzaival.] Budapest: Móra Ferenc Könyvkiado, 1966. 212 p. illus. (Delfin Könyvek)
Contents: Houn.

1288. *A sátán kutyája.* [Forditotta Arkos Antal.] Bukarest: Ifjúsági Könyvkiado, 1967. 232 p.
Contents: Houn.

ICELANDIC

1289. *Baskerville-hundurinn.* Kristmundur Bjarnason pýddi. Reykjavík:Idunnar, 1965. 157 p. (Sigildar Sögur, 8)

1290. *Raudi hringurinn: Sherlock Holmes leynilögreglusögur.* Reykjavík: Leiftur h. f., 1958. 148 p.
Contents: Adventures.

1291. *Sherlock Holmes.* II. [Loftur Gudmundsson, islenzkadi.] Reykjavík: Skemmtiritautgafan, Prentsmidjan Holar h. f., 1945. 299 p.
Contents: Vall.

1292. *Tígrisdýrid fra San Pedro: Sherlock Holmes leynilögreglusögur.* Reykjavík: Leiftur h. f., 1958. 172 p.
Contents: Adventures.

IRISH

1293. *Cú na mBaskerville .i. The Hound of the Baskervilles.* [Tr. by] Nioclás Tóibin. [Dublin]: Oifig Diolta Foillseacháin Rialtais [Irish Government Publications], 1934. 219 p.

1294. *Eachtrai Sherlock Holmes.* [Memoirs of Sherlock Holmes.] [Tr. by] Proinnsias O Brogain. [Dublin]: Oifig Diolta Foillseachain Rialtais, 1936. 509 p.

ITALIAN

1295. *Un'avventura di Sherlock Holmes.* Versione italiana di Attilio Leproux. Milano: Società Editoriale Milanese, 1909. 91 p. (Biblioteca per Tutti, 26)

1296. *Le avventure di Sherlock Holmes.* [Unica traduzione autorizzata di Maria Gallone.] Milano: Rizzoli Editore, [1950]. 329 p.
Contents: Adventures.

1297. ————. [Unica traduzione autorizzata dall'inglese di Maria Gallone.] [Milano; Verona]: Arnoldo Mondadori Editore, [1958]. 2 v. (184, 190 p.) (Il girasole. Biblioteca economica Mondadori, 84, 92)
————. [Milano; Verona]: Arnoldo Mondadori Editore, [1961]. 2 v. (184, 190 p.) (Opere di Sir A. Conan Doyle, 1, 3)
Contents: Vol. 1. Scan. - RedH. - Iden. - Bosc. - Five. - Twis. - Vol. 2. Blue. - Spec. - Engr. - Nobl. - Bery. - Copp.

1298. *Le avventure di Sherlock Holmes: Romanzo.* Milano: Tipografia Editrice Verri, 1895. 159 p. (Biblioteca Azzurra)

1299. *Il cane dei Baskerville.* Milano: C. Del Duca, 1965. 244 p. (Anni verdi)

1300. *Il mastino dei Baskerville.* [Unica

traduzione autorizzata dall'inglese di Maria Gallone.] [Milano; Verona]: Arnoldo Mondadori Editore, [1957]. (Il girasole. Biblioteca economica Mondadori, 69)

1301. *Il mastino dei Baskerville: Un'altra avventura di Sherlock Holmes.* Unica traduzione autorizzata di Maria Gallone. Milano: Rizzoli Editore, [1950]. 203 p.

1302. *Le memorie di Sherlock Holmes.* Traduzione [dall'inglese] di Maria Gallone. Milano: Rizzoli Editore, [1950]. 285 p.
Contents: Memoirs.

1303. ———. [Unica traduzione autorizzata dall'inglese di Maria Gallone.] [Milano; Verona]: Arnoldo Mondadori Editore, [1960]. 2 v. (176, 194 p.) (Il girasole. Biblioteca economica Mondadori, 136, 137)
———. [Milano; Verona]: Arnoldo Mondadori Editore, [1960]. 2 v. (176, 194 p.) (Opere di Sir A. Conan Doyle, 10, 11)
Title of vol. 2: *I signori di Reigate: Le memorie de Sherlock Holmes.*
Contents: Vol. 1. Silv. - Yell. - Stoc. - Glor. - Musg. - Vol. 2. Reig. - Croo. - Resi. - Gree. - Nava. - Fina.

1304. *Novissime avventure di Sherlock Holmes.* Traduzione di Giacomo Prampolini. Milano: Arnoldo Mondadori Editore, 1920.
Contains six adventures from Case Book.

1305. *Le nuove imprese di Sherlock Holmes.* [I faggi rossi, Il pollice dell'ingegnere, ed altri racconti.] Firenze: Casa Editrice Nerbini [A. Vallecchi], 1918. 88 p. illus. (Il romanzo mensile del soldato, 9)
Contents: Copp. - Engr.

1306. *Il ritorno di Sherlock Holmes.* [Unica traduzione autorizzata di Maria Gallone.] Milano: Rizzoli Editore, [1950]. 362 p.
Contents: Return.

1307. ———. [Unica traduzione autorizzata dall'inglese di Maria Gallone.] [Milano; Verona]: Arnoldo Mondadori Editore, [1959]. 2 v. (208, 207 p.) (Il girasole. Biblioteca economica Mondadori, 123, 127)
———. [Milano; Verona]: Arnoldo Mondadori Editore, [1962]. 2 v. (198, 203 p.) (Opere di Sir A. Conan Doyle, 7, 8)
Contents: Vol. 1. Empt. - Norw. - Danc. - Soli. - Prio. - Blac. - Vol. 2. Chas. - SixN. - 3Stu. - Gold. - Miss. - Abbe. - Seco.

1308. *Lo scritto rosso: Un'avventura di Sherlock Holmes.* Firenze: Adriano Salani, 1950. 102 p. (L'ulivo. Biblioteca Salani, 13)
Contents: Stud.

1309. ———. [Firenze]: Salani Editore, [1960]. 211 p. (I romanzi della rosa, 47)

1310. *Il segno dei quattro.* [Unica traduzione

autorizzata dall'inglese di Maria Gallone.] Milano: Rizzoli Editore, [1949]. 189 p.
Contents: Sign.

1311. ———. [Unica traduzione autorizzata dall'inglese di Maria Gallone.] [Milano; Verona]: Arnoldo Mondadori Editore, [1958]. 187 p. (Il girasole. Biblioteca economica Mondadori, 102)
———. [Milano; Verona]: Arnoldo Mondadori Editore, [1962]. 187 p. (Opere di Sir A. Conan Doyle, 5)

1312. ———. [Versione di Carla Faraglia.] [Roma]: Gherardo Casini Editore, [1966]. 185 p. (I libri del sabato, 40)

1313. *Il segno dei quattro: Un'avventura di Sherlock Holmes.* Firenze: Adriano Salani, 1951. 116 p. (L'ulivo. Biblioteca Salani, 33)

1314. *Sherlock Holmes e uno studio in rosso.* [Versione di O. Vavra e P. Castelli.] [Roma]: Gherardo Casini Editore, [1966]. 186 p.
Contents: Stud.

1315. *Sherlock Holmes,* [*il poliziotto dilettante*]. Nuova traduzione di Cino Liviah, e nuovi disegni di L. Fornari. Milano: Società Editoriale Milanese [Pagani E. C.], 1909. 229 p. illus.

1316. *Sherlock Holmes, il poliziotto dilettante: Il regno dei quattro.* Firenze: Adriano Salanti, 1908. 244 p. (Biblioteca Salani illustrata, 346)
Contents: Sign.

1317. *Sherlock Holmes, il poliziotto dilettante: Lo scritto rosso.* Firenze: Adriano Salani, 1908. 210 p. (Biblioteca Salani illustrata, 347)
Contents: Stud.

1318. *Sherlock Holmes, il poliziotto dilettante: Uno strano delitto.* Nuova traduzione di Cino Liviah. Milano: Sesto S. Giovanni; Società Editoriale Milanese, 1911. 229 p. illus.
Contents: Stud.

1319. *Sherlock Holmes in quattro romanzi e ventiquattro racconti.* A cura di Alberto Tedeschi. Traduzione di Maria Gallone. [Milano; Verona]: Arnoldo Mondadori Editore, [1964]. ix, 1214 p.
Contents: Stud. - Sign. - Vall. - Houn. - Adventures. - Case Book.

1320. *Uno strano delitto: Romanzo.* Prima versione italiana. Milano: Società Editoriale Milanese, 1907. 284 p. (Libro Popolare, 6)
Contents: Stud.

1321. *Uno studio in rosso.* [Traduzione dall'inglese di Alberto Tedeschi.] [Milano; Verona]: Arnoldo Mondadori Editore, [1958]. 188 p. (Il girasole. Biblioteca economica Mondadori, 82)

———. [Milano; Verona]: Arnoldo Mondadori Editore, [1962]. 188 p. (Opere di Sir A. Conan Doyle, 2)
Contents: Stud.

1322. *Uno studio in rosso: Primo libro di Sherlock Holmes.* Unica traduzione autorizzata di Alberto Tedeschi. Milano: Rizzoli Editore, 1949. 191 p.

1323. *Il taccuino di Sherlock Holmes.* [Unica traduzione autorizzata di Maria Gallone.] Milano: Rizzoli Editore, [1951]. 285 p.
Contents: Case Book.

1324. ———. [Unica traduzione autorizzata dall'inglese di Maria Gallone.] [Milano; Verona]: Arnoldo Mondadori Editore, [1958 -1959]. 2 v. (184, 187 p.) (Il girasole. Biblioteca economica Mondadori, 97, 114)
———. [Milano; Verona]: Arnoldo Mondadori Editore, [1962]. 2 v. (184, 187 p.) (Opere di Sir A. Conan Doyle, 4, 6)
Title of vol. 1: *La criniera del leone: Taccuino di Sherlock Holmes.*
Contents: Vol. 1. Illu. - Maza. - 3Gab. - Suss. - 3Gar. - Veil. - Shos. - Vol. 2. Lion. - Blan. - Thor. - Gree. - Reti.

1325. *Tre romanzi di Sherlock Holmes: Uno studio in rosso. Il segno dei quattro. La valle della paura.* Traduzione di Maria Gallone. [Milano; Verona]: Arnoldo Mondadori Editore, [1965]. 441 p.
Contents: Stud. - Sign. - Vall.

1326. *L'ultimo saluto di Sherlock Holmes.* [Unica traduzione autorizzata di Maria Gallone.] Milano: Rizzoli Editore, [1951]. 226 p. (Tutte le opere di Conan Doyle)
Contents: His Last Bow.

1327. ———. [Traduttrice Maria Gallone.] [Milano; Verona]: Arnoldo Mondadori Editore, [1960-1961]. 2 v. (177, 165 p.) (Il girasole. Biblioteca economica Mondadori, 138, 139)
———. [Milano; Verona]: Arnoldo Mondadori Editore, [1962]. 2 v. (177, 165 p.) (Opere di Sir A. Conan Doyle, 138, 139)
Title of vol. 2: *L'avventura del poliziotto morente: L'ultimo saluto di Sherlock Holmes.*
Contents: Vol. 1. Wist. - Card. - RedC. - Bruc. Vol. - 2. Dyin. - Lady. - Devi. - Last.

1328. *La valle della paura.* [Unica traduzione autorizzata di Maria Gallone.] Milano: Rizzoli Editore, [1950]. 200 p.
Contents: Vall.

1329. ———. [Unica traduzione autorizzata dall'inglese di Maria Gallone.] [Milano; Verona]: Arnoldo Mondadori Editore, [1960]. 205 p. (Il girasole. Biblioteca economica Mondadori, 133)
———. [Milano; Verona]: Arnoldo

Mondadori Editore, [1962]. 205 p. (Opere di Sir A. Conan Doyle, 9)

English Readers

1330. *The Adventures of Sherlock Holmes: The Blue Carbuncle. The Three Students.* Introduzione e note di A. Franzinetti e J. M. J. Rees. Torino; Milano; Padova: G. B. Paravia e C., 1960. xiv, 66 p.

JAPANESE

1331. [*Akage kumiai.* Tr. by Seijirô Tanaka. Tôkyô: Chûô kôron-sha, 1963.] 276 p.
Partial contents: RedH.

1332. [*Baskervilles-ke no inu.* Tr. by Ken Nobuhara. Tôkyô: Shinchô-sha, 1954.] 266 p.

1333. [———. Tr. by Suzuki. Tôkyô: Kadokawa-shoten, 1956.] 250 p. (1122)

1334. [———. Tr. by Ken Nobuhara. Tôkyô: Tôkyô sôgen-sha, 1956.] 196 p. (Sekai suiri shôsetsu zenshû, 3)

1335. [———. Tr. by Tomoji Abe. Tôkyô: Sôgen-sha, 1960.] 254 p. (207)

1336. [———. Tr. by Seijirô Tanaka. Tôkyô: Chûô kôron-sha,1963.] 191 p.

1337. [*Hiiro no kenkyû.* Tr. by Ken Nobuhara. Tôkyô: Shinchô-sha, 1953.] 197 p.
Contents: Stud.

1338. [———. Tr. by Shûhei Asano. Tôkyô: Geijutsu-sha, 1956.] 189 p.

1339. [———. Tr. by Tomoji Abe. Tôkyô: Kadokawa-shoten, 1959.] 178 p. (1830)

1340. [———. Tr. by Tomoji Abe. Tôkyô: Tôkyô Sôgen-sha, 1960.] 184 p. (Sôgen Suiri Bunko, 205)

1341. [*Hiiro no kenkyû: Sherlock Holmes saigo no aisatsu.* Tr. by Ken Nobuhara. Tôkyô: Shinchô-sha, 1956.] 276 p. (Sherlock Holmes zenshû, 1)
Contents: Stud. - His Last Bow.

1342. [*Hiiro no kenkyû. Yonin no shomei. Baskervilles-ke no inu. Kyôfu no tani.* Tr. by Tomoji Abe. Tôkyô: Kawade-shobô Shinsha, 1959.] 366 p. illus.
Contents: Stud. - Sign. - Houn. - Vall.

1343. [*Kyôfu no tani.* Tr. by Ken Nobuhara. Tôkyô: Shinchô-sha, 1953.] 254 p. (550)
Contents: Vall.

1344. [——— Tr. by Gen'ichi Kume. Tôkyô: Kôdan-sha, 1957.] 244 p. illus.

1345. ———. Tr. by Tomoji Abe. Tôkyô:

Tôkyô Sôgen-sha, 1960.] 251 p. (Sôgen Suiri Bunko, 208)

1346. [————. Tr. by Kaisaku Noda. Tôkyô: Kaisei-sha, 1967.] 226 p.

1347. [*Kyôfu no tani. Baskervilles-ke no inu.* Tr. by Rampo Edogawa. Tôkyô: Heibon-sha, 1930.] 407 p. (1)
Contents: Vall. - Houn.

1348. [————. Tr. by Ken Nobuhara. Tôkyô: Shinchô-sha, 1956.] 292 p. (Sherlock Holmes zenshû, 2)

1349. [*Kyuketsuki.* Tr. by Chikashi Uchida. Tôkyô: Kaisei-sha, 1967.] 230 p.
Contents: Suss. - 3Gab. - Lion.

1350. [*Mei tantei Holmes.* Adapted by Gen'ichi Kume. Illustrated by Asom Koga. Tôkyô: Kôdan-sha, 1957.] 340 p. (World Famous stories, 54)
Contents: Houn. - RedH.

1351. [————. Tr. by Shigeru Shiraki. Tôkyô: Akane-shobô, 1965.] 211 p. (Shônen shôjo sekai suiri bungaku zenshû, 17)

1352. [*Mei tantei Holmes. Baskervilles-ke no inu.* Tr. by Yûzô Chiyo. Tôkyô: Kaisei-sha, 1966.] 308 p.

1353. [*Sherlock Holmes.* Tôkyô: Kaizo-sha, 1928.] 618 p.

1354. [*Sherlock Holmes no bôken.* Tr. by Takanobu Ito. Tôkyô: Kobun-dô, 1946.] 195 p.

1355. [————. Tr. by Rampo Edogawa. Tôkyô: Heibon-sha, 1946.] 280 p.

1356. [————. Tr. by Takekazu Kikuchi. Tôkyô: Iwanami-shoten, 1952.] 260 p. (608)
Contents: Nobl. - Blue. - Bosc. - RedH. - Scan.

1357. [————. Tr. by Ken Nobuhara. Tôkyô: Shinchô-sha, 1953.] 353 p. (512)
Contents: Adventures.

1358. [————. Tr. by Katsumi Hayashi. Tokyo: Iwanami-shoten, 1955.] 318 p.
Contents: Adventures.

1359. [————. Tr. by Ken Nobuhara. Tôkyô: Shinchô-sha, 1956.] 247 p. (Sherlock Holmes zenshû, 5)

1360. [————. Tr. by Yukio Suzuki. Tôkyô: Kadokawa-shoten, 1957.] 2 v. (204, 207 p.) (1642, 1643)

1361. [————. Tr. by Tomoji Abe. Tôkyô: Tôkyô Sôgen-sha, 1960.] 439 p. (Sogen Suiri Bunko, 201)

1362. [————. Tr. by Takekazu Kikuchi. Tôkyô: Iwanami-shoten, 1962.] 276 p.
Contents: Blue. - Spec. - RedH. - Bosc. - Scan. - Nobl.

1363. [————. Tr. by Yukio Suzuki. Tôkyô: Kadokawa-shoten, 1963.] 407 p.
Contents: Adventures.

1364. [————. Tr. by Tomoji Abe. Tôkyô: Kawade-shobô, 1967.] 326 p.
Contents: Adventures.

1365. [*Sherlock Holmes no bôken. Kaisô no Sherlock Holmes.* Tr. by Tomoji Abe. Tôkyô: Kawade-shobô Shinsha, 1958.] 357 p. illus. (Sekai Bungaku zenshû, 3)
Contents: Adventures. - Memoirs.

1366. [*Sherlock Holmes no funkkatsu.* Tr. by Yasuo Ôkubo. Tôkyô: Hayakawa-shobô, 1963.] 386 p.
Contents: Return.

1367. [*Sherlock Holmes no jikenbo.* Tr. by Ken Nobuhara. Tôkyô: Shinchô-sha, 1953.] 296 p.
Contents: Case Book.

1368. [————. Tr. by Yasuo Ôkubo. Tôkyô: Hayakawa-shobô, 1958.] 330 p. (Hayakawa Pocket Mystery Books, 451)

1369. [————. Tr. by Ken Nobuhara. Tôkyô: Shinchô-sha, 1959.] 317 p. (574)

1370. [*Sherlock Holmes no kaisô.* Tr. by Takekazu Kikuchi. Tôkyô: Iwanami-shoten, 1952.] 248 p. (609)
Contents: Silv. - Croo. - Musg. - Nava. - Fina.

1371. [————. Tr. by Yukio Suzuki. Tôkyô: Kadokawa-shoten, 1955.] 328 p. (1115)
Contents: Memoirs.

1372. [————. Tr. by Tomoji Abe. Tôkyô: Tôkyô Sôgen-sha, 1960.] 355 p. (Sôgen Suiri Bunko, 202)

1373. [————. Tr. by Takekazu Kikuchi. Tôkyô: Iwanami-shoten, 1963.] 210 p.

1374. [*Sherlock Holmes no kikan.* Tôkyô: Kogyokudo shoten, 1926.] 496 p.
Contents: Return.

1375. [————. Tr. by Otokichi Mikami. Tôkyô: Heibon-sha, 1929.] 382 p. (4)

1376. [————. Tr. by Ken Nobuhara. Tôkyô: Shinchô-sha, 1953.] 350 p. (513)

1377. [————. Tr. by Ken Nobuhara. Tôkyô: Shinchô-sha, 1956.] 261 p. (Sherlock Holmes zenshû, 6)

1378. [———. Tr. by Takekazu Kikuchi. Tôkyô: Iwanami-shoten, 1963.] 202 p.
Contents: Empt. - Danc. - Chas. - Blac. - Gold.

1379. [*Sherlock Holmes no kioku.* Tr. by Otokichi Mikami. Tôkyô: Heibon-sha, 1930.] 371 p. (3)
Contents: Memoirs.

1380. [*Sherlock Holmes no omoide.* Tr. by Ken Nobuhara. Tôkyô: Shinchô-sha, 1953.] 320 p. (511)
Contents: Memoirs.

1381. [———. Tr. by Ken Nobuhara. Tôkyô: Shinchô-sha, 1956.] 211 p. (Sherlock Holmes zenshû, 3)

1382. [*Sherlock Holmes saigo no aisatsu.* Tr. by Ken Nobuhara. Tôkyô: Shinchô-sha, 1955.] 278 p. (777)
Contents: His Last Bow.

1383. [———. Tr. by Yasuo Okubo. Tôkyô: Hayakawa-shobô., 1959.] 251 p. (Hayakawa Pocket Mystery Books, 452)

1384. [———. Tr. by Tomoji Abe. Tôkyô: Tôkyô Sôgen-sha, 1960]. 291 p. (Sôgen Suiri Bunko, 204)

1385. [*Sherlock Holmes no seikan.* Tr. by Tomoji Abe. Tôkyô: Tôkyô Sôgen-sha, 1960.] 480 p. (Sôgen Suiri Bunko, 203)
Contents: Return.

1386. [———. Tr. by Yukio Suzuki. Tôkyô: Kadokawa-shoten, 1962.] 446 p.

1387. [*Sherlock Holmes no seikan. Sherlock Holmes no saigo no aisatsu.* Tr. by Tomoji Abe. Tôkyô: Kawade-shobô Shinsha, 1958.] 327 p. illus. (Sekai Bungaku zenshû, 4)
Contents: Return. - His Last Bow.

1388. [*Sherlock Holmes zenshû.* (Sherlock Holmes Series.) Tôkyô: Getsuyô-shobô, 1951-1952.] 13 v.
Contents: Vol. 1. Stud. - Vol. 2. Sign. - Vol. 3-4. Adventures. - Vol. 5-6. Memoirs. - Vol. 7-8. Return. - Vol. 9. Houn. - Vol. 10. Vall. - Vol. 11. His Last Bow. - Vol. 12-13. Case Book.

1389. [*Shinku no isshi.* Tr. by Sakichi Kuroda. Tôkyô: Kôgyoku-dô, 1923.] 254 p.
Contents: Stud.

1390. [*Shinya no kyôfu.* Tr. by Gen'ichi Kume. Tôkyô: Kaisei-sha, 1966.] 232 p.
Contents: Stud.

1391. [*Yonin no sain.* Tr. by Gen'ichi Kume. Tôkyô: Kôdan-sha, 1967.] 276 p.
Contents: Sign.

1392. [———. Tr. by Tomoji Abe. Tôkyô: Kadokawa-shoten, 1960.] 170 p. (1831)

1393. [———. Tr. by Tomoji Abe. Tôkyô: Tôkyô Sôgen-sha, 1960.] 184 p. (Sôgen Suiri Bunko, 206)

1394. [*Yottsu no sain.* Tr. by Shûhei Asano. Tôkyô: Geijutsu-sha, 1956.] 175 p.
Contents: Sign.

1395. [*Yottsu no sain. Sherlock Holmes no jikenbo.* Tr. by Ken Nobuhara. Tôkyô: Shinchô-sha, 1956.] 309 p. (Sherlock Holmes zenshû, 4)
Contents: Sign. - Case Book.

1396. [*Yottsu no shomei.* Tr. by Ken Nobuhara. Tôkyô: Shinchô-sha, 1953.] 182 p.
Contents: Sign.

1397. [*Yottsu no shomei. Hiiro no kenkyû.* Tr. by Gen'ichi Kume. Tôkyô: Kaisei-sha, 1966.] 308 p.
Contents: Sign. - Stud.

English Readers

1398. *The Adventure of the Beryl Coronet, and A Question of Diplomacy.* With introduction and notes by T. Sawamura. Tôkyô: Kenkyû-sha, [1935]. vii, 77 p. (Conan Doyle Series, 6) (Kenkyû-sha Pocket English Series)

1399. *The Beryl Coronet, and The Red-Headed League.* Edited, with notes, by Masao Hirai. Tôkyô: Kenkyû-sha Ltd., 1951. v, 95 p. (Sherlock Holmes Series, 3) (Kenkyû-sha Pocket English Series, 107)

1400. *The Adventure of the Blue Carbuncle, and The Dealings of Captain Sharkey with Stephen Craddock.* With introduction and notes by T. Sawamura. Tôkyô: Kenkyû-sha, [1932]. vii, 69 p. (Conan Doyle Series, 12) (Kenkyû-sha Pocket English Series)

1401. *The Boscombe Valley Mystery, and The Five Orange Pips.* Edited, with notes, by Natsuo Shumata. Tôkyô: Kenkyû-sha Ltd., 1951. v, 89 p. (Sherlock Holmes Series, 2) (Kenkyû-sha Pocket English Series, 106)

1402. *The Adventure of the Cardboard Box.* Edited, with notes, by Kenji Miki. Tokyo: Gakusei-sha Atom Mysteries, by Ready Vocabulary Method, [n.d.] 122 p. (310)

1403. *The Adventure of the Dancing Men, and Captain Sharkey.* With introduction and notes by T. Sawamura. Tôkyô: Kenkyû-sha, [n.d.] (Conan Doyle Series, 3) (Kenkyû-sha Pocket English Series)

1404. *The Empty House, and The Missing*

Three-Quarter. Edited, with notes, by Yûzô Aoki. Tôkyô: Kenkyû-sha Ltd., [1953]. v, 104 p. (Sherlock Holmes Series, 8) (Kenkyû-sha Pocket English Series, 114)

1405. *The Naval Treaty, and The Three Students.* Edited, with notes, by Torao Uyeda. Tôkyo: Kenkyû-sha Ltd., 1951. v, 105 p. (Sherlock Holmes Series, 4) (Kenkyû-sha Pocket English Series, 4)

1406. *The Norwood Builder.* [Notes by] Yuzo Aoki. Tôkyô: Nan'un-dô, [n.d.] 66 p. (Nan'un-do's Modern Readings)

1407. *The Norwood Builder, and Other Stories.* [Tôkyô]: Nan'un-dô, 1959, ii, 185 p. (Sherlock Holmes Series, 3)
Text in English and Japanese.
Contents: Norw. - Musg. - Yell.

1408. *The Red-Headed League, and Other Stories.* [Tôkyô]: Nan'un-dô, 1958. iv, 275 p. (Sherlock Holmes Series, 1)
Text in English and Japanese.
Contents: RedH. - Danc. - 3Stu. - Silv.

1409. *The Red-Headed League, and The Dancing Men.* Tokyo: Nan'un-dô, 1959. ii, 147 p. (Sherlock Holmes Series) (Nan'un-do's Pocket Phoenix Library)
Text in English and Japanese.

1410. *A Scandal in Bohemia, and The Greek Interpreter.* Edited, with notes, by Torao Uyeda. Tôkyô: Kenkyû-sha Ltd., [1955]. v, 103 p. (Sherlock Holmes Series, 5) (Kenkyû-sha Pocket English Series, 111)

1411. *Silver Blaze, and The Crooked Man.* Edited, with notes, by Kazuo Yamada. Tôkyô: Kenkyû-sha Ltd., [1953]. v, 102 p. (Sherlock Holmes Series, 6) (Kenkyû-sha Pocket English Series, 112)

1412. *The Six Napoleons, and The Dancing Men.* Edited, with notes, by Yoshiaki Fuhara. Tokyo: Kenkyû-sha Ltd., [1953]. v, 105 p. (Sherlock Holmes Series, 7) (Kenkyû-sha Pocket English Series, 113)

1413. *The Adventure of the Speckled Band.* Ogawa: Shôyei-dô, [n.d.] 59, 28 p. (The Friend of English, 6)
Text in English and Japanese.

1414. *The Speckled Band, and Other Stories.* Tôkyô: Kenkyû-sha, 1958. iv, 229 p. (61)
Contents: Spec. - Bery. - Danc.

1415. *The Speckled Band, and The Blue Carbuncle.* Edited, with notes, by Masami Nishikawa. Tôkyô: Kenkyû-sha Ltd., 1951. v, 90 p. (Sherlock Holmes Series, 1) (Kenkyû-sha Pocket English Series, 105)

1416. *The Adventure of the Speckled Band,*

and The Los Amigos Fiasco. With introduction and notes by T. Sawamura. Tôkyô: Kenkyû-sha, [1942]. vii, 65 p. (Conan Doyle Series, 5) (Kenkyû-sha Pocket English Series)

1417. *The Adventure of the Man with the Twisted Lip.* Tr. by Yu Tezuka. Tokyo: Tôzai-sha, 1909. 79, 60 p.
Title from cover.
Japanese text with notes in English and Japanese.

1418. *The Man with the Twisted Lip.* Tr. by Itazu Yukisato. Tôkyô: Nan'un-dô, 1960. ii, 78 p. (Nan'un-dô's Pocket Phoenix Library, 48)
Text in English and Japanese.

1419. *The Man with the Twisted Lip.* Notes by Yûzô Aoki. Tôkyô: Nan'un-dô, [n.d.] 65 p. (Nan'un-dô's Modern Readings)

1420. *The Man with the Twisted Lip, and Other Stories.* [Tôkyô]: Nan'un-dô, 1959. ii, 177 p. (Sherlock Holmes Series, 2)
Text in English and Japanese.
Contents: Twis. - Chas. - Fina.

1421. *Adventures of Sherlock Holmes.* With translation and notes by T. Yamazaki. [Tôkyô: Eibun Sekai Meicho Zenshû Kankosho], 1927. 257 p. (World's Classics in English, 1)
Text in English and Japanese.
Contents: Musg. - Bosc. - Five.

1422. *The Adventures of Sherlock Holmes.* Edited with introduction and notes by Toshio Kikkawa. Ôsaka: Ôsaka Kyôiku Tosho Co., 1957. iii, 136 p. (Contemporary English Series, 21)
Contents: Iden. - Engr. - Copp.

1423. *The Memoirs of Sherlock Holmes (Selected).* [Tokyo]: The Hokusei-dô Press, [1932]. 187 p.
Contents: Silv. - Croo. - Nava. - Fina.

1424. *New Selections from Conan Doyle.* No. 1. Tôkyô: The Sansei-dô Co., [1944]. 97 p.
Contents: Danc. - Twis.

1425. *New Sherlock Holmes Tales.* Revised and annotated by Frank H. Lee. Selected by Minoru Matsumoto. Tôkyô: Kôbun-sha Ltd., [1927]. 125 p. illus. (The Prince of Wales Series, 4)
Contents: Veil. - Shos. - Reti.

1426. *Selected Readings from Conan Doyle.* First Series. Edited with introduction and notes by Torajirô Sawamura. Tôkyô: Kenkyû-sha, [1924]. iv, 220 p. (Kenkyû-sha English Texts)
Partial contents: Blue. - Spec. - Danc.

1427. *Selected Readings from Conan Doyle.*

Second Series. Edited with introduction and notes by Torjirô Sawamura. Tôkyô: Kenkyû-sha, 1935. iv, 238 p. (Kenkyû-sha English Texts)
Partial contents: Bery. - Soli. - RedH.

1428. *Three Adventures of Sherlock Holmes.* Edited and annotated by Kagetomi Ueno. Tôkyô: Kinsei-dô Ltd., [n.d.] 122 p. (Modern English Series)
Contents: Nobl. - Soli. - Gold.

KANARESE

1429. [*Bayalāgada rahasya.* Tr. by C. K. Mūrti. Bangalore: Indira, 1963.] 78 p.
Contents: Bosc.

KOREAN

1430. [*Yeo'seod'gae eui Napoleon oe sa'pyeon.* Tr. by Jo Yong-man. Seoul: Yang'mun'sa, 1959.]

LETTISH

1431. *Baskervilas suns: Šerloka Holmsa dēka.* Tulkojis E[mils] Feldmanis. Riga: Izdevieciba "Grāmatu draugs," 1930. 175 p.

1432. *Bāskervilu suns: Stāsts.* Tulkojis Anna Bauga. Riga: Latgosizdat, 1957. 161 p.

LITHUANIAN

1433. [*Antroji deme:* Iš užrašu apie Šerloka Holmsa. Tr. by P. Plungé and B. Žegunis. Vilnjus: Izd-vo CK LKSM Litvy, 1957.] 62 p.
Contents: Seco.

1434. [*Juodasis Piteris:* Iš užrašu apie Šerloka Holmsa. Tr. by B. Žegunis. and P. Plungé. Vilnjus: Izd-vo CK LKSM Litvy, 1957.] 56 p.
Contents: Blac.

1435. [*Užrašai apie Šerloka Holmsa.* Tr. by R. Zagorskiené and K. Ambrasas. Vilnjus: Vaga, 1965.] 428 p.
Contents: Memoirs.

MACEDONIAN

1436. [*Avanturite na Šerlok Holms.* Tr. by Tome Momirovski. Skopje: Kočo Racin, 1961.] 296 p.
Contents: Adventures. - Memoirs. - Return.

MALAY

1437. [*Bhitiyute tālvara.* Tr. by Mathew Luke. Kozhikode: P. K. Brothers, 1964.] 290 p.
Contents: Vall.

1438. [*Chĕrita-Chĕrita Sherlakk Hōmes.* Di-Tĕrjĕmahkan oleh Ahmad Murad bin Nasru'd-din. Tanjong Malin: 1938.]

1439. [―――. Di-Tĕrjĕmahkan oleh Norma Sjahrudin. Kuala Lumpur: Oxford University Press, 1962.] ix, 156 p.
Contents: Sa-Patah Kata (Foreword). - Spec. - RedH. - Blue. - Silv. - Daftar Kata (Vocabulary)

1440. [*Manja mukham* (*Detective Stories*). De-Tĕrjĕmahkan oleh Malāyattūr Rāmakrishnan. Konni, Kerala: Venus Press & Book Depot, n.d.] 147 p.
Partial contents: Five. - Lady.

1441. [*Mannamukham.* Di-Tĕrjĕmahkan oleh Malāyattūr Ramakrishnan. Konni: Venus Press & Book Depot, 1959.] 147 p. illus.

1442. [*Serlakk Hōmes.* London: Macmillan & Co. Ltd., 1951.] 102 p. illus. (The Malay Home Library Series, 17)

1443. [―――. Di-Tĕrjĕmahkan oleh Malayāttūr Rāmakrishnan. Madras: Janata, 1956.] vi, 198 p.

1444. [*Serlakk Hōmes kathakal.* De-Tĕrjĕmahkan oleh ,Malāyattūr] Rāmakrishnan. Kozhikode: P. K. Brothers, 1958.] 219 p.

MARATHI

1445. [*Chandrašekhar.* Tr. by Madhv Manohar. Poona: Asimita Prakašan, 1963.] 116 p.

1446. [*Vātā chaughānchā.* Tr. by V. S. Modak. Poona: Nilkantha Prakašan, 1963.] iv, 141 p.
Contents: Sign.

NORWEGIAN

1447. *Af Dr. Watsons optegnelser.* Autoriseret oversaettelse af Elisabeth Brochmann. Kristiania: H. Aschehoug & Co. (W. Nygaard), 1905. 254 p. (Sherlock Holmes i arbeide igjen, 2)
Contents: Chas. - SixN. - 3Stu. - Gold. - Miss. - Seco. - Abbe.

1448. *Dr. Watsons optegnelser.* Autoriseret oversaettelse av Elisabeth Brochmann. Kristiania: Forlagt av H. Aschehoug & Co. (W. Nygaard), 1918. 190 p.
―――. Oslo: 1941. 198 p.
Contents: Chas. - SixN. - 3Stu. - Gold. - Miss. - Seco.

1449. *De fires tegn: Detektivhistorie.* Christiania: "Morgenbladets" Foljeton, 1891. 172 p.
Contents: Sign.

1450. *De fires tegn.* Oversat av Arvid Skappel. Kristiania: Helge Erichsen & Co., 1915. 120 p.

1451. ———. Oversatt av Nils Lie. Oslo: Gyldendal Norsk Forlag, 1941. 221 p.
Contents: Sign. - RedH (oversatt av Colbjorn Helander).

1452. ———. Oversatt av Nils Lie. Innledning og merknader ved Nils Nordberg. Oslo: Gyldendal Norsk Forlag, [1971]. 124 p. (Den svarte serie, 37)

1453. *Forfulgt.* Uddrag av nogle optegnelser ved dr. John Watson. Kristiania: "Skandinavisk Bibliotheks" Forlag (Nik. Olsen), 1893. 126 p. illus.
Contents: Stud.

1454. "Gullorgnetten," [Oversat av Fridtjof Knudsen]. *10 fantastiske detektiv historier.* Redigert av Tage la Cour. Oslo: A / S Helge Erichsens Forlag, [n.d.] p. 134-158.
Contents: Gold.

1455. "Hans siste bukk," *10 fantastiske spion historier.* Redigert av Tage la Cour. Oslo: A / S Helge Erichsens Forlag, [n.d.] p. 46-63.
Contents: Last.

1456. *Hunden fra Baskerville: En ny fortaelling om Sherlock Holmes.* Autoriseret oversaettelse ved Elisabeth Brochmann. Kristiania: Forlagt af H. Aschehoug & Co. (W. Nygaard), 1902. 263 p.
———. 2nd ed. 1911. 246 p.
———. The same ed. Oslo: 1941. 185 p.

1457. *Hunden fra Baskerville: En beretning om Sherlock Holmes.* Oversettelse, innledning og merknader ved Nils Nordberg. [Oslo]: Gyldendal Norsk Forlag, [1971]. 159 p. (Den svarte serie, 32)

1458. *Sherlock Holmes i arbeide igjen.* Autoriseret oversaettelse af Elisabeth Brochmann. Kristiania: Forlagt af H. Aschehoug & Co. (W. Nygaard), 1904. 249 p.
Contents: Empt. - Norw. - Danc. - Soli. - Prio. - Blac.

1459. *Sherlock Holmes i Stoke Moran.* "Avisens" foljeton. Kristiania: Nicolai Olsens Bogtrykkeri, 1899. 30 p.
———, Fortaellinger af Conan Doyle med flere. p. 3-39.
Contents: Spec.

1460. *Sherlock Holmes og Lauristone Garden Mysteriet: Detektivfortelling.* Kristiania: P. Omtvedts Forlag, 1907. 80 p.
A very bad and incomplete translation of Stud.

1461. *Sherlock Holmes: Syv hendelser fra hans liv og virke.* Utvalg, oversettelse, innledning og merknader ved Nils Nordberg. [Oslo]: Gyldendal Norsk Forlag, [1969]. 159 p. (Den svarte serie, 22)

Contents: Stud (chap. 1-2). - Spec. - Silv. - Musg. - Scan. - Twis. - Fina.

1462. *Sherlock Holmes vender tilbake: Syv mysterier fra hans saksarkiver.* Utvalg, oversettelse, innledning og merknader bed Nils Nordberg. [Oslo]: Gyldendal Norsk Forlag, [1970]. 156 p. (Den svarte serie, 27)
Contents: Innledning: Myten om Sherlock Holmes. - Empt. - Bruc. - Chas. - Blue. - RedH. - Thor. - Last. - Merknader [Summaries of the seven stories].

1463. *Spioncentralen og andre Sherlock Holmes-fortaellinger.* Autoriseret oversaettelse av Chr. S. Brochmann. Kristiania: Forlagt av H. Aschehoug & Co. (W. Nygaard), 1919. 156 p.
Contents: RedC. - Bruc. - Devi. - Last.

1464. *Ein studie i raudt (Sherlock Holmes).* Bergen: Gula Tidend Boksamling, 1936. 124 p.
Contents: Stud.

1465. *En studie i rödt.* Oversat av Arvid Skappel. Kristiania: Helge Erichsen & Co., 1914. 135 p.
Contents: Stud.

1466. "En udvalgt samling af Sherlock Holmes' eventyr." (Oversat av P. Jerndorff-Jessen.] *I ledige timer.* Kristiania: Aktieselskabet "Allers Familie-Journals" Trykkeri, 1902. Vol. 29, p. 1-476.
Contents: Adventures. - Sign.
The Adventures are illustrated with all the illustrations of Sidney Paget.

1467. "Vår fornemme klient," Oversat av Lotte Holmboe. *Verdens beste kriminalfortellinger.* Oslo: Helge Erichsens Forlag, [n.d.]
Contents: Illus.

ORIYA

1468. [*Kālāntaka.* Tr. by Laksmīnārāyan Mahānti. Berhampur: Das Brothers, 1965.] iv, 359 p.
Contents: Houn.

1469. [*Marana duāre.* Tr. by Udayanāth Sadangi. Berhampur: Das Brothers, 1958.] 2 v.
[———. Berhampur: Das Brothers, 1958.] iv, 120 p.
Contents: Vall.

PERSIAN

1470. [*A Case of Identity.* Tehran: Privately Printed, n.d.] [22] p.

POLISH

1471. *Dr. Watson opowiada.* Tłumaczenie zbiorowe. [Okładkę projecktował Zbigniew

Zaja. Poznań: Wydawnictwo Poznańskie, 1960.] 234 p.
Contents: Shos. - Cree. - Croo. - 3Gab. - SixN. - Veil. - Blan. - Copp. - Lion. - Gold.

1472. *Dolina trwogi.* Przełożył Tadeusz Evert. Warszawa: Iskry, 1961. 189 p.
Contents: Vall.

1473. *Pies Baskerville'ów.* Z 12-oma ilustracjami z pierwszego wydania londyńskiego. Rzym: Polski Dom Wydawniczy K. Brieter & Co., 1946. 192 p.

1474. ———. [Posłowie Maciej Żurowski. Przekład anonimowy przejrzała i uzupełniła Eleonora Romanowicz.] Warszawa: Iskry, 1954. 204 p.
———. Warszawa: Iskry, 1955. 172 p.
———. Warszawa: Iskry, 1958. 236 p.

1475. *Późna Zemsta.* [Przełożyla z angielskiego E. S. Okładkę proj. art. mal Jerzy Młodnicki.] Rzym: Polski Dom Wydawniczy, 1947. 159 p.
Contents: Stud.

1476. *Przygody Sherlocka Holmesa.* [Przełożył Tadeusz Evert, Jan Meysztowicz, Jerzy Dzialak, Irena Doleżal-Nowicka, Kazimierz Kwaśniewski.] Warszawa: Iskry, 1955. 465 p.
———. Warszawa: Iskry, 1956. 411 p.
———. Warszawa: Iskry, 1963. 435 p.
Contents: Musg. - Chas. - Silv. - Bery. - Reig. - Stoc. - Nava. - Scan. - Iden. - Five. - Blue. - Dyin. - Fina. - Empt. - 3Stu. - Maza. - Norw. - Soli. - Yell. - Thor. - RedH.

1477. *Sherlock Holmes niepokonany.* Przełożył Jan Skalny, Jerzy Regawski. Poznań: Wydawnictwo Poznańskie, 1960. 231 p.

1478. *Studium w szkarłacie.* [Przełożył Tadeusz Evert.] Warszawa: Iskry, 1956. 145 p.
———. Warszawa: Iskry, 1957. 168 p.
Contents: Stud.

1479. *Tańcujace figurki.* Chicago, Ill.: Polish-American Pub. Co., [192-?] 54 p. illus.
At head of title: Z Przygód Sherlocka Holmesa.
Contents: Danc.

1480. *Tańczace sylwetki.* Tłumaczenie Zbiorowe. [Prełożył z angielskiego: Tadeusz Evert, Jan Meysztowicz, Jerzy Regawski, Jan Skalny, Irena Szeligowa, Jan Stanislaw Zaus.] [Poznań]: Wydawnictwo Poznańskie, 1967. 373 p.
Contents: Glor. - Resi. - Danc. - Prio. - Blac. - Shos. - SixN. - Copp. - Gold. - Gree. - Wist. - Croo. - Engr. - Blan. - Lion.

1481. *Znak czterech.* Prezełożyła Krystyna Jurasz-Dambska. Warszawa: Iskry, 1957. 173 p.
Contents: Sign.

1482. *Znamie czterech: Powieść.* Z angielskiego przełożyła E. Zmijewska. Dod. do Słowa. Warszawa: druk. Noskowskiego, 1898. 116 p.
Contents: Sign.

English Readers

1483. *Short Stories.* Adapted by Wanda Krajewska. Warszawa: Państwowe Zakłady Wydawnictw Szkolnych, [1965]. 99 p.
Contents: Danc. - Dyin. - 3Stu. - Fina. - Empt. - Blac. - Resi. - Stownik (Vocabulary). - Stownik imion wtasnych.

Parodies and Pastiches

1484. Golembowicz, Wacław. *Przygody chemiczne Sherlocka Holmesa.* [Chemical Adventures of Sherlock Holmes.] Warszawa: Nasza Księgarnia, 1959.
———. *Chemické príhody Sherlocka Holmesa.* Přeložil Karol Dubecký. [Ilustroval Ever Pucek.] [Košice]: Mladé Letá, [1965]. 207 p.
Contents (in Czech): Brilianty lorda Sandwicha. - Tajomstvo cerveného pudru. - Pohl'adnica z Brightonu. - Opity pavuk. - Cervena nevädza. - Deviaty den. - Elektrické kreslo. - Posledny suboj.

1485. Romanski, Marek. *Koniec Sherlocka Holmesa: Opowiesc melancholijna.* [The End of Sherlock Holmes: A Melancholy Tale.] [Rysunki, uklad graficzny i okladka St(anislaw) Metelski.] Rzym: Polski Dom Wydawniczy, 1946. 64 p. illus.

PORTUGUESE

1486. *A alliança de casamento.* Versão de Henrique Lopes de Mendonca. Lisboa: Livraria Ferreira & Oliveira, Limitada, 1907. 161 p. (Memorias de um policia amador)
Contents: Stud.

1487. *Aventuras de Sherlock Holmes.* Versão de Manuel de Macedo. [Ilustrado de Sidney Paget.] Lisboa: Livraria Ferreira & Oliveira, Limitada, 1907. 186 p. (Memorias de um policia amador)
Contents: Bery. - Nobl. - Spec. - Five. - Iden. - Copp.

1488. ———. Tradução de Carlos Chaves. [São Paulo]: Edições Melhoramentos, [1954]. 290 p. (Série Sherlock Holmes, 3)
———. 2. ed. [São Paulo]: Edições Melhoramentos, [1955]. 290 p. (Obras de Conan Doyle, 3)
———. Revista por Gina de Freitas. Lisboa: Livraria Bertrand, [n.d.] [270] p. (Série Sherlock Holmes, 3)
Contents: Adventures.

1489. *O carbunculo azul.* [Lisboa]: Edições

"Phenix," [n.d.] 204 p. (Aventuras extraordinárias de Sherlock Holmes, 1)
Contents: Blue. - Iden. - 12, P. W. [a pastiche with Sherlock Holmes and Harry Taxon]. - Spec. - O caso de hotel de Paris [a pastiche with Sherlock Holmes and Harry Taxon].

1490. *O cão dos Baskervilles.* Tradução de Lígia Junqueira. [São Paulo]: Edições Melhoramentos, [1954]. 177 p. (Série Sherlock Holmes, 6)
———. 2. ed. [São Paulo]: Edições Melhoramentos, [1955]. 177 p. (Obras de Conan Doyle, 6)
———. Revista por Gina de Freitas. Lisboa: Livraria Bertrand, [n.d.] [192] p. (Série Sherlock Holmes, 6)
Contents: Houn.

1491. *Em estudo vermelho.* Tradução de Branca de Villa-Flor. Nova edição. Rio de Janeiro; Paris: H. Garnier, Livreiro-Editor, [1908]. 164 p.
Contents: Stud.

1492. *Um estudo em vermelho.* Tradução de Hamilcar de Garcia. [São Paulo]: Edições Melhoramentos, [1954]. 147 p. (Série Sherlock Holmes, 1)
———. 2. ed. [São Paulo]: Edições Melhoramentos, [1955]. 147 p. (Obras de Conan Doyle, 1)
———. Revista por Gina de Freitas. Lisboa: Livraria Bertrand, [n.d.] [158] p. (Série Sherlock Holmes, 1)
Contents: Stud.

1493. *A firma dos quatro.* Versão de Manuel de Macedo. [Ilustrado de F. W. Townsend.] Lisboa: Livraria Ferreira, 1908. 180 p. (Memorias de um policia amador)
Contents: Sign.

1494. *Histórias de Sherlock Holmes.* Tradução de Agenor Soares de Moura. [São Paulo]: Edições Melhoramentos, [1954]. 276 p. (Série Sherlock Holmes, 9)
———. 2. ed. [São Paulo]: Ediões Melhoramentos, [1955]. 276 p. (Obras de Conan Doyle, 9)
———. Revista por Gina de Freitas. Lisboa: Livraria Bertrand, [n.d.] [252] p. (Série Sherlock Holmes, 9)
Contents: Case Book.

1495. *A lenda do cão phantasma.* Versão de Manuel de Macedo. [Ilustrado de Sidney Paget.] Lisboa: Livraria Ferreira, 1908. 215 p. (Memorias de um policia amador)
Contents: Houn.

1496. *As melhores novelas de Conan Doyle.* [Selecção, tradução do original e nota sobre o autor de Elysio Correia Ribeiro.] Lisboa: Editorial Hélio, 1947. 209 p. (Colecção "Antologia," 10)

Contents: Nota sobre o autor. - SixN. - Scan. - Iden. - RedH. - 3Gar. - Cree. - Maza.

1497. *Memórias de Sherlock Holmes.* Tradução de Joaquim Machado. [São Paulo]: Edições Melhoramentos, [1954]. 267 p. (Série Sherlock Holmes, 4)
———. 2. ed. [São Paulo]: Edições Melhoramentos, [1955]. 267 p. (Obras de Conan Doyle, 4)
———. Revista por Gina de Freitas. Lisboa: Livraria Bertrand, [n.d.] [242] p. (Série Sherlock Holmes, 4)
Contents: Memoirs.

1498. *Memórias do Dr. Watson.* Tradução de Romeu Avellar. Rio de Janeiro: Emiel Editora, [n.d.] 196 p.
Contents: Stud.

1499. *Morte de Sherlock Holmes.* Versão de Christovam Ayres (filho). Lisboa: Livraria Ferreira, 1909. 162 p. (Memorias de um policia amador)
Contents: Gree. - Croo. - Nava. - Fina. - Bruc.

1500. *Novas aventuras de Sherlock Holmes.* Versão de Manuel de Macedo. [Ilustrado de Sidney Paget.] Lisboa: Livraria Ferreira, 1909. 196 p. (Memorias de um policia amador)
Contents: Scan. - Blue. - Twis. - Bosc. - RedH. - 3Stu.

1501. ———. [Lisboa: Edição Romano Torres, n.d.] 111 p. (Colecção 'Aventuras Policiais," 1)
Contents: Nava. - Soli. - Bery.

1502. *Recordações de Sherlock Holmes.* Versão de Christovam Ayres (filho). [Ilustrado de Sidney Paget.] Lisboa: Livraria Ferreira, 1908. 189 p. (Memorias de um policia amador)
Contents: Silv. - Yell. - Glor. - Musg. - Stoc. - Resi. - Reig.

1503. *A ressurreição de Sherlock Holmes.* Versão de Elias Borges. Lisboa: Livraria Ferreira, 1909. 191 p. (Memorias de um policia amador)
Contents: Empt. - Norw. - Danc. - Soli. - Prio. - Blac.

1504. *Sherlock Holmes e a lenda do cão fantasma: Novela policial.* [Lisboa: João Romano Torres, n.d.] 96 p. (Colecção "Aventuras Policiais e Misteriosas," 3)
Contents: Houn.

1505. *Sherlock Holmes triumphante.* Versão de Augusto Gil. [Ilustrado de Sidney Paget.] Lisboa: Livraria Ferreira, 1908. 205 p. (Memorias de um policia amador)
Contents: Chas. - SixN. - 3Stu. - Miss. - Abbe. - Seco.

1506. *O signo dos quatro.* Tradução de Hamílcar de Garcia. [São Paulo]: Edições Melhoramentos, [1954]. 139 p. (Série Sherlock Holmes, 2)
———. 2. ed. [São Paulo]: Edições Melhoramentos, [1955]. 137 p. (Obras de Conan Doyle, 2)
———. Revista por Gina de Freitas. Lisboa: Livraria Bertrand, [n.d.] [204] p. (Série Sherlock Holmes, 2)
Contents: Sign.

1507. *O último adeus de Sherlock Holmes.* Tradução de Alvaro Pinto de Aguiar. [São Paulo]: Edições Melhoramentos, [1954]. 221 p. (Série Sherlock Holmes, 8)
———. 2. ed. [São Paulo]: Edições Melhoramentos, [1955]. 221 p. (Obras de Conan Doyle, 8)
———. Revista por Gina de Freitas. Lisboa: Livraria Bertrand, [n.d.] [204] p. (Série Sherlock Holmes, 8)
Contents: His Last Bow.

1508. *O vale do terror.* Tradução de Álvaro Pinto de Aguiar. [São Paulo]: Edições Melhoramentos, [1954]. 204 p. (Série Sherlock Holmes, 7)
———.2. ed. [São Paulo]: Edições Melhoramentos, [1955]. 204 p. (Obras de Conan Doyle), 7)
———. Revista por Gina de Freitas. Lisboa: Livraria Bertrand, [n.d.] [188] p. (Série Sherlock Holmes, 7)
Contents: Vall.

1509. *A volta de Sherlock Holmes.* Tradução de Lígia Junqueira. [São Paulo]: Edições Melhoramentos, [1954]. 315 p. (Série Sherlock Holmes, 5)
———. 2. ed. [São Paulo]: Edições Melhoramentos, [1955]. 315 p. (Obras de Conan Doyle, 5)
———. Revista por Gina de Freitas. Lisboa: Livraria Bertrand, [n.d.] [288] p. (Série Sherlock Holmes, 5)
Contents: Return.

1510. *Aventuras extraordinarias d'um policia secreta.* Lisboa: Empresa Literária Universal, [n.d.] 66 v. (24 p. each)
Contents: 1. O mercador de cadaveres, por Fernand Laven. - 2. A filha do usuario, por Fernand Laven. - 3. O crime de um jogador, por Fernand Laven. - 4. A mala sangrenta. - 5. O Noivo desparecido. - 6. O roubo do diamante azul. - 7. Blackwel, pirata do Tamisa [Anonymous]. - 8. O faro de Sherlock Holmes [Anonymous]. - 9. Os moedeiros falsos. - 10. O outro eu. - 11. O tesouro do negreiro. - 12. O kodak traiçoeiro. - 13. As rendas da rainha. - 14. Sombra e luz. - 15. O testamento falso. - 16. Génio e loucura. - 17. As joias sangrentas. - 18. O fantasma de Milster. - 19. Jack, o estripador. - 20. A caveira de bronze. - 21. O judeu polaco. - 22. O morto ressuscitado. -

23. A maquina infernal. - 24. O ladrão fidalgo. - 25. O trapeiro de Paris. - 26. Os ciumes do lord. - 27. A rainha do ar. - 28. A linda irmã da caridade. - 29. O quadro revalador. - 30. O punhal do Negus. - 31. No país da espionagem. - 32. O rei dos contrabandistas. - 33. Os Pirilampos de Nova York. - 34. Envenenadora Castle Rock. - 35. O tumulo no farol. - 36. A torre misteriosa. - 37. Paixão fatal. - 38. O rapto do Morgadinho. - 39. A vingança da Camorra. - 40. O terror de Boston. - 41. Um êrro da Justiça. - 42. Uma vitima da inocencia. - 43. Misterios d'um crime. - 44. A' porta da morte. - 45. A caça ao homem. - 46. O medico criminoso. - 47. Uma familia tragica. - 48. Um drama na India. - 49. O segredo do pantano. - 50. A encarcerada. - 51. O filho natural. - 52. A praga maldita. - 53. Os companheiros do crime. - 54. A loucura do ciume. - 55. O rei da India. - 56. O testamento do presidiario. - 57. Alma negra. - 58. O homem macaco. - 59. [Unknown]. - 60. Drama n'um balão. - 61-63. [Unknown]. - 64. O carnaval em colonna. - 65-66. [Unknown].

These stories, with Sherlock Holmes and Harry Taxon, are by Conan Doyle [sic] unless otherwise noted. The stories are the same as those in item 1512, but are numbered in a different sequence.

1511. *Aventuras extraordinarias d'um policia secreta,* [por] Conan Doyle [sic]. Lisboa: Empresa Literária Universal, [1909]. 25 v. (47 to 64 p. each)
Contents: 1. O barbeiro assassino. - 2. O bandido negro. - 3. Um roubo no fundo do mar. - 4. Automato misterioso. - 5. A espia Florença. - 6. A herança invejada. - 7. O homem da máscara. - 8. A morte do urso. - 9. O drama no atelier. - 10. Cinco milhões de brilhantes. - 11. Sherlock Holmes na ratoeira. - 12. Os pêssegos envenenados. - 13. Na taberna de Bob Bull. - 14. Un crime no teatro. - 15. O estrangulador de Praga. - 16. Um combate sôbre o gêlo. - 17. A sociedade dos 13. - 18. A escola do crime. - 19. A casa misteriosa. - 20. O crime do castelo. - 21. O judeo polaco [dated Oct. 1909]. - 22. O testamento do presidiário. - 23. Os companheiros do crime. - 24. Uma familia trágica. - 25. O trapeiro de Paris.

1512. *Aventuras extraordinarias d'um policia secreta.* Lisboa: A Novella Popular — Empresa Lusitana Editora, [Janeiro 1909-Julho 1913]. 218 (?) v. (24 p. each)
Contents: 1. O mercador de cadaveres, por Fernand Laven. - 2. A filho do usurario, por Fernand Laven. - 3. O crime d'um jogador, por Fernand Laven. - 4. O incendio do polo*. - 5. Rocabol, o bandido*. - 6. A mala sangrenta. - 7. O noivo desapparecido. - 8. A virgem da Floresta*. - 9. O roubo do diamante azul. - 10. Blackwel, o pirata do Tamisa [Anonymous]. - 11. Os voluntarios

de Guise*. - 12. O faro de Sherlock Holmes [Anonymous]. - 13. Os moedeiros falsos. - 14. O outro eu. - 15. O thesouro do negreiro. - 16. O Kodac Triçoeiro. - 17. As Rendas da Rainha. - 18. Sombra e Luz. - 19. O crime da porta Saint-Martin*. - 20. O testamento falso. - 21. Genio e loucura. - 22. O assassinio mysterioso*. - 23. As joias sangrentas. - 24. O phantasma do castello de milster. - 25. Um prego n'um craneo*. - 26. Jack, o estripador. - 27. A caveira de Bronze. - 28. O assassinio das creancas*. - 29. O judeu polaco. - 30. O morto ressussitado. - 31. O capitão vermelho - 32. A machina infernal. - 33. O ladrão fidalgo. - 34. 600:000 frs. de diamantes*. - 35. O trapeiro de Paris. - 36. Os ciumes do lord. - 37. As façanhas de Piedde-Boeuf*. - 38. A rainha do ar. - 39. A linda Irmã da caridade. - 40. A morte pelo correio*. - 41. O quadro revelador. - 42. O punhal do negus. - 43. No paiz da espionagem. - 44. O rei dos contrabandistas. - 45. A casa tragica*. - 46. Os pyrilampos de Nova-York. - 47. A envenenadora de Castle Rock. - 48. O forçado martyr*. - 49. O tumulo no pharol. - 50. Paixão fatal. - 51. A torre mysteriosa. - 52. Os treze Apaches. - 53. O rapto do morgadinho. - 54. A vingança de camorra. - 55. O segredo do sepulchro*. - 56. O terror de Boston. - 57. Um erro da justiça. - 58. Uma victima da inocencia. - 59. O segredo da Somnambula*. - 60. Mysterios d'um crime, por Julio Lermina. - 60. (Suppl.) O homem invisivel. - 61. A'porta da morte. - 62. A caça ao homem. - 63. O medico criminoso. 64. Uma familia tragica. - 65. Um drama na India. - 66. O segredo do pantano. - 67. A encarcerada. - 68. O filho natural. - 68. (Suppl.) A mulher dos olhosverdes. - 69. A praga maldita. - 70. Os companheiros do crime. - 71. O loucura do ciume. - 72. O rei da India. - 73. O testamento do presidiario. - 73. (Suppl.) Elixir magico. - 74. Alma négra. - 75. O homem macaco. - 76. A dama velada. - 77. Em volta d'um throno. - 77. (Suppl.) Odio de mulher. - 78. O contrabandista de opio. - 79. Drama n'um balão. - 80. Os bastidores do crime. - 81. O carnaval em Colonna. - 81. (Suppl.) O crime de Grosvenor Place. - 82. A'caça da fortuna. - 83. A prisioneira do campanario. - 84. O naufragio do corfú. - 85. Escola dos criminosos. - 86. A tatuagem azul. - 86. (Suppl.) A mão cortada. - 87. A sociedade dos 13. - 88. Cacada nas trevas. - 89. O mercador de escravas. - 90. O thesouro do indio. - 91. Nupcias tragicas. - 91. (Suppl.) O rapido do Aryzona. - 92. Os subterraneos do Vienna. - 93. O atleta desapparecido. - 94. A ilha da peste. - 94. (Suppl.) As cabeças embalsamadas. - 95. O falsario. - 96. A viuva sanguinaria. - 97. O quarto maravilhoso. - 98. A dama verde. - 98. (Suppl.) A quadrilha dos carabineiros. - 99. O vampiro de Londres. - 100. A mulher do véu branco. - 101. O barbeiro do lord. - 102. O demonio do Circo Angelo. - 103. O adorador do diabo. - 104. O forçado. - 105. Uma noite de terror. - 106. O carrasco de Londres. - 107. O roubo do collar. - 108. Os bandidos de Palermo. - 109. A estalagem dos mortos. - 110. Amor e odio. - 111. Duplo assassinio. - 112. O crucificado. - 113. A vontade alheia. - 114. Os assassinios de Middlesworth. - 115. O rei dos bandidos. - 116. Os doze corações. - 117. Quem é o morto*. - 118. O Mastim de Soho. - 119. Mortal Angustia. - 120. O drama da morte*. - 121. O thesouro mexicano. - 122. A Condessa Gatuna. - 123. A mulher das quatro cabeças. - 124. Um ladrão de luva branca*. - 125. Professor Flax. - 126. O negro mysterioso. - 127. Os pêcegos malditos. - 128. A filha do morto*. - 129. Uma sessão d'animatographo. - 130. A amante do Principe. - 131. O crime do castello Saavedra. - 132. O mysterio da Avenida Madison*. - 133. As ruinas de Pompeia. - 134. Os segredos do Jiu-Jitsu. - 135. O bahu mysterioso. - 136. Enterrados vivos*. - 137. Os ultimos dias de Messina. - 138. A mão occulta. - 139. O segredo da tabaqueira. - 140. Rehabilitação d'um pae*. - 141. A drogaria mysteriosa. - 142. O falso general. - 143. O estrangulador de Praga. - 144. O alfinete de brilhantes*. - 145. A caveira medalhão. - 146. Um roubo no Vaticano. - 147. Os signaes da morte. - 148. Qual das duas?* - 149. A filha do Radjah. - 150. O Idolo Hindu. - 151. Um veneno subtil. - 152. Um drama no comboio. - 153. Os homens fataes. - 154. Os fogos fatuos. - 155. Um busca de uma herança. - 156. Boda interrompida. - 157. O Castello de Falford. - 158. Os treze tiros. - 159. O mysterio do Palacio. - 160. Quinze dias de vida. - 161. O terror de Londres. - 162. O ladrão de mulheres. - 163. A Paixão d'um bandido. - 164. A sede do oiro. - 165. A creoula millionaria. - 166. Os filhos de Siva. - 167. No Harem do Sultão. - 168. O Manequim de cèra. - 169. O diario da morte. - 170. A experiencia do esculptor. - 171. Drama de ciumes. - 172. Cinco milhões de brilhantes. - 173. Os bandidos da Fronteira. - 174. A morte-viva. - 175. O Engenheiro do Schah. - 176. Uma herança tragica. - 177. Justo Castigo. - 178. O certificado no. 209. - 179. O homem da mão decepada. - 180. A maldição de uma perola. - 181. Uma infamia legal. - 182. A ultima victima do idolo. - 183. As joias da favorita. - 184. Os envenenadores do opio. - 185. O jogo da vida. - 186. O homem automatico. - 287. Lady Florencia. - 188. Os herdeiros de lord Randolf. - 189. Odio de Mulher. - 190. A Estalagem de Avinhão. - 191. Os Charlataes de mumias. - 192. O cão da policia. - 193. Annuncio C. S. 8517. - 194. O Thesouro mysterioso. - 195. O roubo mysterioso. - 196. A escravatura branca. - 197. O demonio de Stamford Hill. - 198. O morto-vivo. - 199.

Um casamento de conveniencia. - 200. O diamante da Rainha. - 201. O Louco assassino. - 202. Um novo barba azul. - 203. O segredo da morta. - 204. O Chinó da Princeza. - 205. Os mysterios da guilhotina. - 206. A voz do outro mundo. - 207. A ultima proeza de Scherlock-Holmes. - 208. Ressurreição de Scherlock-Holmes. - 209. Scherlock Holmes em Lisboa.

Except for Nos. 1, 2, 3, 10, 12, 60 and the twenty-five numbers followed by an asterisk which are not a part of the Sherlock Holmes-Harry Taxon adventures, Conan Doyle's name appears on the title pages of the first 125 (Nos. 1-116) adventures; the remainder are anonymous. It should also be noted that the names of all characters, except Sherlock Holmes, have been changed (Dr. Watson has become Harry Taxon!), and the stories bear little if any resemblance to the original stories.

1513. *O falsificador da morte.* Lisboa: Imprensa Beleza, [n.d.] 95 p. ("Aventuras," 1)
Also contains: As joias da favorita.

1514. *Genio e loucura.* Nova edicão cuidadosamente revista. Lisboa: Empresa Lusitana Editora, [n.d.] 92 p. (Aventuras extraordinarias d'um policia secreta, 2)

1515. *Memorias íntimas de Sherlock Holmes: El tesoro del negrero.* Buenos Aires: Novelas de Aventuras, [n.d.] 64 p. (Sherlock Holmes, 5)

1516. *Romance policiel,* [por] Conan Doyle [sic]. Lisboa: Livraria Editora - Guimarães & C. a, 1934. 15 (?) v. (approx. 80 p. each)
Contents: 1. O roubo do brilhante azul. Traducção de Henrique Marques Junior. - 2. O banqueiro assassinado.- 3. O crime d'um jogador. - 4. Um prego no craneo. - 5. A filha do usurario. - 6. A prisioneira do subterraneo. - 7. O homem da mão decepada. - 8. 500:000 francos roubados. - 9. A sociedade dos 13. - 10. O atleta desparecido. - 11. O rei dos bandidos. - 12. O crucificado. - 13. O ladrão de mulheres. - 14. A estalagem dos mortos. - 15. O segrêdo do medalhão.

1517. *O roubo do brilhante azul.* Traducção de Henrique Marques Junior. Lisboa: Guimarães & C. a, Editores, 1917. 153 p. (Colecção Horas de Leitura, 131)
Also contains: O banqueiro assassinado.

1518. *O terror de Londres.* Lisboa: Henrique Torres Editor, 1952. 32 p. (Aventuras de Sherlock Holmes)

RUMANIAN

1519. *Aventurile lui Sherlock Holmes.* [In romîneste de Marius Măgureanu.]

[Bucuresti]: Editura Tineretului, 1958. 280 p. (3253)
Contents: Twis. - Five. - Spec. - Devi. - Bruc. - Lady. - Dyin. - Maza. - Wist.

1520. *Cîinele din Baskerville.* [Traducere de Mircea Alexandrescu Costache Popa.] Bucuresti: Editura Tineretului, 1957. 215 p.

1521. *Coama leului.* [Traducere de Andrei Bantas.] Bucuresti: Editura Tineretului, 1966. 231 p.
Contents: Adventures.

1522. *Două aventuri ale lui Sherlock Holmes.* [Traducere de Andrei Bantas.] Bucuresti: Editată de revista Stiinta si tehnică, 1957. 32 p.

1523. *Sherlock Holmes két kalandja.* [Traducere de Anna Bácski.] Bucuresti: A Stiintă si tehnică Folyóirat Kiadása. 32 p.

RUSSIAN

1524. [*The Adventures of Detective Sherlock Holmes.* Tr. by G. A. Charsky. St. Petersburg: Gubinsky Pub. House, 1903.]

1525. [———. Tr. by A. B. Golovin. St. Petersburg: "Capitol Pub. House," 1905.] 37-64 p. (General Library)
Contents: Norw.

1526. [———. Tr. by N. N. Mazurenko. St. Petersburg: "The Police Herald," 1909.] 127, 160 p.
Contents: Sign. - Houn.

1527. [*The Adventures of Sherlock Holmes.* Moscow: Sytin, 1904.] 101, 95, 112 p.
Contents: Stud. - Sign. - Scan. - RedH. - Iden. - Bosc. - Five. - Twis.

1528. [———. Moscow: Sytin, 1908.] 80 p.
Contents: Empt. - Danc. - Blac.

1529. [———. Moscow: Sytin, 1908.] 112 p.
Partial contents: Gree.

1530. [———. Moscow: Sytin, 1908.] 119 p.
Partial contents: Silv.

1531. [———. Moscow: Sytin, 1908.] 112 p.
Partial contents: Spec.

1532. [———. Moscow: Sytin, 1908.] 103 p.
Contents: Vengeance (Stud).

1533. [———. Moscow: Sytin, 1909.] 112 p.
Partial contents: Miss Irene Adler (Scan.)

1534. [———. Moscow: Sytin, 1909.] 112 p.
Partial contents: Soli.

1535. [———. Leningrad: Krasnaja Gazeta, 1929.] 221 p.

1536. [*The Adventures of Sherlock Holmes, A Famous Detective.* Tr. and with a foreword by L. Chersky. St. Petersburg, 1910.] 190 p.

1537. [*The Adventures of Sherlock Holmes: From Dr. Watson's Memoirs.* 1st ed. Kiev: "The Southern Star," 1909.] 32 p.
Contents: Resi. - Musg.

1538. [*The Aristocrat Bachelor: From the Adventures of Sherlock Holmes.* Tr. by A. Repina. Moscow: Chicherin, 1905.] 334 p.
Contents: Nobl. - Bery. - Copp. - Silv. - Musg. - Reig. - Gree. - Nava. - Fina.

1539. [*The Blue Carbuncle.* Tr. by V. Stenichav. Introduction by M. Gershenzon. Moscow; Leningrad: "Detizdat," 1937.] 31 p. illus.

1540. [*Collected Works.* Moscow: Sytin, 1904.] illus.
Partial contents: Vol. 1 Vengeance (Stud). - Sign. 95 p. - Vol. 3. Silv. - Yell. - Stoc. - Glor. - Musg. - Reig. 119 p. - Vol. 6. Gree. - Croo. - Resi. - Nava. - Fina. 111 p. - Vol. 7. Empt. - Danc. - Blac. 80 p. - Vol. 8. Soli. - SixN. - Prio. - Norw. 112 p.
Issued as free supplements to the magazine *Around the World.*

1541. [———. St. Petersburg: Sojkin, 1909-1911.]
Partial contents: Vol. 1. Red on White (Stud), Tr. by N. Obleukov. - Sign. 131, 108 p. - Vol. 13, Houn, Tr. by E. N. Lomikovska. 159 p. - Vols. 19-20. New Works. 287 p. - Vol. 22. The Marvelous Discovery. - New Memoirs of Sherlock Holmes (Devi. - RedC). - The Silver Mirror and Other Tales. 318 p.
Issued as free supplements to the magazine *Nature and People.*

1542. [*A Collection of Works in Eight Volumes.* Illustrated by N. Ushakov. Moscow: Pravda Pub. House, 1966.] 8 v. (Ogonyok Library)
Partial contents: Vol. 1. Arthur Conan Doyle: His Life and Books, by M. Urnov. - Stud, Tr. by N. Treneva. - Sign, Tr. by M. Litvinova. - Scan, Tr. by N. Vojtinska. - RedH, Tr. by M. and N. Chukovsky. - Iden, Tr. by N. Vojtinska. - Bosc, Tr. by M. Bessarab. - Five, Tr. by N. Vojtinska. - Twis, Tr. by M. and N. Chukovsky. - Blue, Tr. by M. and N. Chukovsky. - Spec, Tr. by M. and N. Chukovsky. - Engr, Tr. by N. Emelyanikova. - Nobl, Tr. by D. Livshchits. - Bery, Tr. by V. Shtengel. - Copp, Tr. by N. Emelyanikova. - Conan Doyle and Sherlock Holmes, by A. Narkevich. 548 p. - Vol. 2. Silv, Tr. by U. Zhukova. - Yell, Tr. by N. Volpin. - Stoc, Tr. by N. Kolpakova. - Glor, Tr. by G. Lubimova. - Musg, Tr. by D. Livshchits. - Reig, Tr. by T. Ruzska. - Croo. Tr. by D. Zhukov. - Resi, Tr. by D. Zhukov. - Gree, Tr. by N. Volpin. - Nava, Tr. by D. Zhukov. - Fina, Tr. by D. Livshchits. - Empt, Tr. by D. Livshchits. - Norw, Tr. by U. Zhukova. - Danc, Tr. by M. and N. Chukovsky. - Soli, Tr. by N. Sannikov. - Prio, Tr. by N. Volzhina. - Blac, Tr. by N. Emelyanikova. - Chas, Tr. by M. Litvinova. - SixN, Tr. by M. and N. Chukovsky. - 3Stu, Tr. by N. Yavno. - Gold, Tr. by N. Sannikov. - Miss, Tr. by U. Levchenko. - Abbe, Tr. by L. Borovog. - Seco, Tr. by N. Emelyanikova. 548 p. - Vol. 3. Houn, Tr. by N. Volzhina. - Wist, Tr. by N. Volpin. - Card, Tr. by V. Ashkenazi. - RedC, Tr. by E. Ber. - Bruc, Tr. by N. Dechterova. - Dyin, Tr. by Shtengel. - Lady, Tr. by U. Zhukova. - Devi, Tr. by A. Ilf. - Last, Tr. by N. Dechterova. - Maza, Tr. by A. Polivanova. - Suss, Tr. by N. Dechterova. - 3Gar, Tr. by N. Dechterova. - Cree, Tr. by M. Kan. - Lion, Tr. by M. Baranovich. - Reti, Tr. by M. Kan. 480 p.

1543. [*The Dancing Men: Tales.* Abridged. Tr. by M. and N. Chukovsky. Illustrated by G. Balashova. The Military Pub. House, The Ministry of Armed Forces of the USSR, 1946.] 64 p. (The Little Library of the Journal of the Red Army Soldier, No. 9 [54])
Also contains: Twis.

1544. [*A Drama in Woolwich's Arsenal. A Christmas Story.* St. Petersburg: Stasulevich Pub. House, 1909.] 73 p.
Contents: Bruc. - Blue.

1545. [*The Famous Detective Sherlock Holmes: The Adventure of the Christmas Goose.* Moscow: Konovalov Pub. House, 1908.] 24 p.
Contents: Blue.

1546. [*The Famous Detective Sherlock Holmes: The Adventure of the Red-Headed Man.* Moscow: Konovalov Pub. House, 1908.] 24 p.
Contents: RedH.

1547. [*The Famous Detective Sherlock Holmes: Secret Signs.* Moscow: Konovalov Pub. House, 1908.] 24 p.
Contents: Danc.

1548. [*The Famous English Detective Sherlock Holmes.* Moscow: Beltsov Pub. House, 1908.] 415 p.
Contents: Pills of Life and Death. - The Society of Red-Headed Thieves (RedH). - A Riot Witness on the Boat for Criminals.
"Fearful, secret, bloody crimes. Complete description of amazing, improbable adventures of Sherlock Holmes during the solving of these crimes and arrest of criminals." (Subtitle)

1549. [*The Famous English Detective Sherlock Holmes: Collection of Tales and His Adventures.* St. Petersburg: "Gramotnost" Pub. House, 1916.] 192 p.

1550. [*The Final Problem: From the Secret Documents of the Detective Sherlock Holmes: A Drama of the Alps.* With a supplement to the 10th issue of Heinz von Bergen's novel "Irma, the Criminal's Daughter." St. Petersburg: Gaupt, 1908.] 31 p.

1551. [*The Greek Interpreter: From the Adventures of Sherlock Holmes.* Moscow: "Alpha," 1921.] 30 p. ("Inexpensive Books")

1552. [*The Hound of the Baskervilles: New Adventures of Sherlock Holmes.* Tr. by E. N. Lomikovska. St. Petersburg: "New Journal of Foreign Literature," 1902.] 96 p.

1553. [————. St. Petersburg: Panteleev Pub. House, 1902.] 120 p.

1554. [*The Hound of the Baskervilles: The Last Novel.* Moscow: Efimov, 1903.] 238 p.

1555. [*The Hound of the Baskervilles: Adventures of Sherlock Holmes.* Moscow: Sytin, 1908.] 165 p.

1556. [*The Hound of the Baskervilles.* Tr. by A. Chudnovsky. Exc. Society, Dela Pub. House, 1915.] 164 p.

1557. [————. Tr. by E. N. Lomikovska. Leningrad: "Priboj," 1927.] 232 p.

1558. [————. Leningrad: "The Red Newspaper," 1928.] 187 p. illus.

1559. [————. Tr. by N. S. Vojtinska. Illustrated by M. A. Taranova. Leningrad: "Leninzdat," 1947.] 379 p.

1560. [————. Tr. by N. Volzhina. Moscow; Leningrad: Detgiz, 1948.] 168 p.

1561. [————. Tr. by N. Volzhina. Moscow: Goslitizdat, 1955.] 160 p.

1562. [————. Vladimir: Vladimir Book Publisher, 1956.] 160 p.

1563. [*The Inscription in Blood.* Tr. by F. Laterner. St. Petersburg: "Poucheniye," 1904.] 224 p. (The Adventures of Sherlock Holmes, Vol. 1)
   Contents: Stud.

1564. [*The Knife of the Dancer: The Last Adventures of Sherlock Holmes. (The Devil's Rock)* St. Petersburg: "Herald," 1908.] 96 p.

1565. [*The Lady with the Revolver: Four Tales of Sherlock Holmes.* Tr. by N. D. Obleukhov. Moscow: Efimov, 1905.] 155 p.
   Contents: Chas. - Which of the Three? (3Stu). - Blac. - The Incident in School (Prio).

1566. [*The Last Adventures of Sherlock Holmes, A Famous English Detective.* Foreword and tr. by L. Chersky. St. Petersburg: 1910.] 190 p.

1567. [*The Man with the Twisted Lip.* Tr. by M. and N. Chukovsky. The Military Pub. House, The Ministry of Armed Forces of the USSR, 1945.] (The Little Library of the Journal of the Red Army Soldier)

1568. [*Memoirs of Sherlock Holmes, A Famous Detective.* Tr. by V. A. Magskoj. St. Petersburg: Trud, 1903.] 255 p.
   Contents: Silv. - Yell. - Stoc. - Glor. - Musg. - Reig.

1569. [————. Tr. by N. D. Obleukhov. Moscow: Efimov, 1904.] 175 p.

1570. [————. Tr. by A. Tufanov. Leningrad: Krasnaja Zvezda, 1928.] 192 p.

1571. [————. Tr. by A. Tufanov. Illustrated by R. Fitingov. Leningrad: "The Red Newspaper," 1928.] 192 p.
   Additional supplement to the magazine *Around the World.*

1572. [*Mysterious Adventures of the English Detective Sherlock Holmes.* Compiled according to Dr. Watson's Memoirs. St. Petersburg: 1908.] 319 p.

1573. [————. Kholmushin: 1916.] 160 p.

1574. [*Mysterious Adventures of the Famous Detective Sherlock Holmes: The Mysterious Theft.* No. 2. Moscow: Konovalov Pub. House, 1908.] 14 p.

1575. [*Mysterious Adventures of the Famous Detective Sherlock Holmes: The Mysterious Drama.* No. 3. Moscow: Konovalov Pub. House, 1908.] 14 p.

1576. [*Mysterious Adventures of the Famous Detective Sherlock Holmes: The Mysterious Man.* No. 4. Moscow: Konovalov Pub. House, 1908.] 14 p.

1577. [*Mysterious Adventures of the Famous English Detective Sherlock Holmes: A Collection of Secret Notes.* St. Petersburg: Vilde Pub. House, 1908.] 319 p.

1578. [*New Adventures of Sherlock Holmes.* Tr. by N. D. Obleukhov. Moscow: Efimov, 1904.] 203 p.

1579. [————. Tr. by N. D. Obleukhov. 2nd ed. Moscow: Vilde Pub. House, 1907.] 207 p.

1580. [————. Tr. by A. Bondi. Leningrad, GIZ, 1928.] 178 p.

1581. [*New Tales of Sherlock Holmes.* Tr. by Pigelou. Moscow: Sablin, 1909.] 145 p.

1582. [*Notes About a Famous Detective.* Tr. by N. d'André. St. Petersburg: Mitjurnikova, 1902.] 252 p.
Partial contents: Croo. - Resi. - Yell. - Stoc. - Glor.

1583. [————. Tr. by N. d'André. Moscow: Klukin Pub. House, 1903.] 160 p.
Contents: Croo. - Resi. - The Naval Drama. - The Yellow Mask. - Unsuccessful Mystification. - The Fatal Secret.

1584. [————. Tr. by N. d'André. N. Novgorod: Breev Pub. House, 1905.] 252 p.

1585. [————. Tr. by N. Vojtinska. Introduction by P. Gronrov and B. Kostelanec. Leningrad: Molodaya Gvardija, 1946.] 468 p.

1586. [————. Tr. and introduction by K. Chukovsky. Moscow: Detizdat, 1956.] 623 p. illus.

1587. [————. Tr. by N. Vojtinska. Kujbyshev: Kn. izd., 1956.] 428 p. illus.

1588. [————. Tr. by Korney Chukovsky *et al.* Illustrated by N. Tsejtlina. Compiled by S. M. Pozharsky. Moscow: State Pub. House of Children's Literature, 1956.] 621 p.
Contents: About Sherlock Holmes, by Korney Chukovsky. - RedH. - Bosc. - Scan. - Five. - Twis. - Blue. - Spec. - Nobl. - Yell. - Musg. - Fina. - Empt. - Danc. - Prio. - Blac. - SixN. - Seco. - Houn.

1589. [————. Tr. by N. Chukovsky *et al.* Kishinev: Gosizdat Moldavii, 1957.] 627 p. illus.

1590. [————. Tr. by N. Vojtinska. Frunze: Kirgizuzhpedgiz, 1957.] xvi, 468 p. illus.

1591. [————. Tr. by N. Chukovsky *et al.* Kiev: Molod, 1957.] 564 p. illus.

1592. [————. Tr. by N. Vojtinska *et al.* Introduction by P. Bejsov. Uljanovsk: Uljan Pravda, 1957.] 420 p. illus.

1593. [————. Introduction by K. Chukovsky. Erevan: "Ajpetrat," 1958.] 536 p. illus. (Adventure Library)

1594. [————. Alma-Ata: "Zhazishy," 1969.] 368 p.

1595. [*Notes About Sherlock Holmes. The Maracot Deep.* Tr. by N. Chukovsky *et al.* Alma-Ata: Kaz. Uchpedgiz, 1957.] 696 p. illus.

1596. [*One of the Three: A Tale.* Moscow: Klukin Pub. House, 1905.] 31 p.
Contents: 3Stu.

1597. [*The Recent Adventures of Sherlock Holmes: Crime Under the Shade of the Oak.* 1st ed. Moscow: Klukin Pub. House, 1908.] 24 p.

1598. [*The Red-Headed League.* Tr. by M. and N. Chukovsky. The Military Pub. House, The Ministry of Armed Forces of the USSR, 1945.] (The Little Library of the Journal of the Red Army Soldier)

1599. [*The Red-Headed League and Other Tales.* Tr. by F. Laterner. St. Petersburg: "Poucheniye," 1905.] 226 p. (The Adventures of Sherlock Holmes, Vol. 2)

1600. [————. Tr. by M. and N. Chukovsky. Under the general editorship of Korney Chukovsky. Moscow; Leningrad: "Detgiz," 1945.] 135 p. illus.
Contents: About Sherlock Holmes, by Korney Chukovsky - RedH. - Blue. - Twis. - Spec. - Danc.

1601. [————. Tr. by Korney Chukovsky. Illustrated by A. Ermolajeva. Moscow: State Pub. House of Children's Literature, 1945.] 133 p.
Contents same as above.

1602. [*Red on White: A Novel.* Tr. by N. D. Obleukhov. Compiled according to the personal memoirs of John Watson, the old retired doctor in the English Army. 2nd ed. Moscow: Efimov, 1907.] 208 p.
Contents: Stud.

1603. [*Red on White: Tales of Sherlock Holmes.* Afterword by M. Tugusheva. Moscow: "Children's Literature," 1968.] 495 p. illus.
Contents: Stud. - Nava. - Bruc. - 3Stu. - Glor. - Reig. - Silv. - Lion. - Norw. - Stoc.

1604. [*The Resurrected Sherlock Holmes: New Memoirs of a Famous Detective.* Tr. by V. A. Magska. St. Petersburg: "Trud," 1904-1905.] 2 v. (258, 320 p.)

1605. [*The Resurrected Sherlock Holmes: The Latest Adventures of a Famous Detective.* Moscow: Chicherin Pub. House, 1905.] 272 p.

1606. [*The Return of Sherlock Holmes: New Tales.* Tr. by E. N. Lomikovska. St. Petersburg: Bulgakov, 1904.] 507 p.

1607. [————. Tr. by N. D. Obleukhov. Moscow: Efimov, 1904.] 172 p.

1608. [————. Tr. by E. N. Lomikovska. St. Petersburg: Sojkin, 1909.] 301 p.

1609. [*The Secrets of the Grimpensky Swamp: A Tale.* Moscow: "Mosc. Publication," 1915.] 64 p. (Library of Novels)
Contents: Houn.

1610. [*The Sign of the Four.* Tr. by N. D. Obleukhov. Moscow: Efimov, 1903.] 202 p. (Collected Works of A. Conan Doyle)

1611. [*The Sign of the Four: The Adventures of Sherlock Holmes.* Moscow: Sytin, 1908.] 95 p.

1612. [*The Sign of the Four: A Novel.* Leningrad: Krasnaya Zvezda, 1928.] 292 p.

1613. [*The Sign of the Four.* Moscow: Klukin Pub. House.] 172 p.

1614. [*The Six Napoleons.* Tr. by M. and N. Chukovsky. The Military Pub. House, The Ministry of Armed Forces of the USSR, 1945] (The Little Library of the Journal of the Red Army Soldier, No. 20 [45])

1615. [*The Six Napoleons: A Tale.* Tr. by P. Petrov. Sofiia: Naroden Strazh, 1949.] 59 p. illus. (No. 9)

1616. [*The Six Napoleons: Five Tales About Sherlock Holmes.* Moscow: Efimov, 1905.] 192 p.
    Contents: SixN. - Gold. - Miss. - Abbe. - Seco.

1617. [———. 2nd ed. Moscow: Poplavsky Pub. House, 1907.] 190 p.
    Contents same as above.

1618. ["The Speckled Band," *Zvezda* (St. Petersburg) (December 1893).]
    The first Russian translation of a Sherlock Holmes adventure.

1619. [*The Speckled Band and The Blue Carbuncle: From the Adventures of Sherlock Holmes.* Tr. by V. Voskhodov Moscow: "The Universal Library," 1917.] 74 p.

1620. [———. Tr. by N. Chukovsky. Moscow: Military Pub. House of the Armed Forces of the USSR, 1945.] 65 p.

1621. [*The Swamp Mystery.* Tr. by N. d'André. Moscow: Klukin Pub. House, 1904.] 224 p.
    Contents: Houn.

1622. [*Tales of Sherlock Holmes.* Tr. by N. D. Obleukhov. Moscow: Efimov, 1904.] 234 p.
    Contents: Return.

1623. [———. Tr. by N. D. Obleukhov. 2nd ed. Moscow: Vilde Pub. House, 1907.] 224 p.
    Contents same as above.

1624. [———. Vladikavkaz: Kazarov, 1910.] 219 p.
    Contents same as above.

1625. [*The Theft of the Submarine Plans: Memoirs of Sherlock Holmes.* Moscow: 1910.] 136 p.
    Contents: Bruc.

1626. [*The Tiger of San Pedro and Other Tales: From the Memoirs of Sherlock Holmes.* Moscow: Poplavsky Pub. House, 1909.] 144 p.
    Contents: Wist. - The Crime Under the Shade of the Oak. - The Silver Mirror. - The Little Barrel with the Caviar.

English Readers

1627. *The Blue Carbuncle and Other Stories.* [Adaptation, notes and vocabulary by S. I. Petrushin. Moscow: Government Published Literature in a Foreign Language, 1956.] 110 p.

1628. *The Boscombe Valley Mystery.* [Moscow: Government Published Literature in a Foreign Language, 1958.] 125 p.
    Contents: Bosc. - Twis. - Nobl. - Bery. - Copp. - SixN.

1629. *The Hound of the Baskervilles.* [Leningrad: Uchpedgiz, 1936.] 109 p.

1630. ———. Adapted for the 8th form of secondary school by N. Diakonova and M. Rickman. 2nd ed. Leningrad: State Text-Book Pub. House of the Ministry of Education of the RSFSR Leningrad Branch, 1960. 124 p.
    Introduction in Russian.

1631. *The Lion's Mane and Other Stories.* [Adaptation, notes and vocabulary by E. L. Majskoj. Leningrad: Uchpedgiz, 1962.] 135 p. illus.
    A book in the English language for 8th and 9th grades of the middle school.
    The pictorial title page and introduction are in Russian; the footnotes and vocabulary at the end in Russian and English.
    Contents: Lion. - 3Stu. - SixN. - Nava. - Silv. - Bery.

1632. *The Red-Headed League.* Slightly abridged and annotated with (1) explanations in simple English, as well as translations, where necessary, into Russian, French, and German, of the more difficult words and phrases and (2) numerous questions for the purposes of conversation, by Wm. Sharpe Wilson. [St. Petersburg: "Petersburg Educational Magazine"], 1904. x, 86 p. (Modern English Stories for Students of the English Language and for Use in School, No. 1)

1633. *The Sign of the Four.* [Leningrad; Moscow: Uchpedgiz, 1948.] 115 p.

1634. ———. [Moscow: 1967.] 125 p.
    Also contains: Spec. - Twis.

1635. *A Study in Scarlet.* Based on Conan Doyle's Tale. Adaptation, notes and vocabulary by Ju. A. Markov. Moscow, "Progress," 1964. 119 p.

Parodies and Pastiches

1636. [Semenov, M. "Sherlock Holmes's Defeat," *Izvestia* (Moscow) (April 13, 1958).] ———. ———, Tr. in part by Edward Hurwitz. *BSJ*, 8, No. 3 (July 1958), 158-160.

SERBO-CROATIAN

1637. *Avanture Šerloka Holmsa.* [Preveli Ružica i Aleksandar Vlaškalin. Opremio: Zdenko Balabanić.] Rijeka: Otokar Keršovani, 1963. 187 p. (Odabrana djela Conana Doyle-a)
Contents: Scan. - RedH. - Iden. - Bosc. - Blue. - Spec. - Engr. - Nobl.

1638. ———. Aptyp Kohah, [n.d.] 295 p.
Contents: Yell. - Miss. - Soli. - Reig. - 3Stu. - Twis. - Spec. - Danc. - Norw. - Copp. - RedH. - Nobl.

1639. *Baskervilski pas: Roman.* [Preložil Zoran Kostić.] [Beograd]: Kosmos, [1960]. 204 p.

1640. *Baskervilski pas.* [Preveli Ružica i Aleksandar Vlaškalin. Opremio: Zdenko Balabanić.] Rijeka: Otokar Keršovani, 1963. 205 p. (Odabrana djela Conana Doyle-a)
Contents: Predgovor [Introduction]. - Houn. - Shos. - Maza.

1641. *Dolina straha.* [Preložil Slavica Foht.] Sarajevo: Svjetlost, 1961. 193 p.
Contents: Vall.

1642. *Doživljaji Šerloka Holmsa.* [Preložil Ljubivoje Stefanović a Jovan Mesarović.] Beograd: Novo Pokolenje, 1951. 331 p.
Contents: Adventures. - Memoirs. - Return.

1643. *Nenastanjena kuća.* [Preveli Ružica i Aleksandar Vlaškalin. Opremio: Zdenko Balabanić.] Rijeka: Otokar Keršovani, 1963. 201 p. (Odabrana djela Conana Doyle-a)
Half title: Povratak Šerloka Holmsa.
Contents: Empt. - Norw. - Danc. - Soli. - Prio. - Blac. - Chas. - Cree.

1644. *Njegov zadnji podvig. Crveni krug. I druge priče.* [Preveli Ružica i Aleksandar Vlaškalin. Opremio: Zdenko Balabanić.] Rijeka: Otokar Keršovani, 1963. 223 p. (Odabrana djela Conana Doyle-a)
Contents: Card. - RedC. - Dyin. - Last. - Illu. - Blan. - 3Gab. - Suss. - 3Gar. - Thor.

1645. *Pjegava vrpca.* [Preložil Vesna Grbin.] Zagreb: Sportska Štampa, 1952. 32 p.
Contents: Spec.

1646. *Zagonetna smrt: Kriminalna pripoviest.* Zagreb: Tisak i Naklada Knjižare L. Hartmana (St. Kugli), [191-?] 53 p. (Hrvatska biblioteka. Svezka 237-238)
Contents: Silv.

1647. *Znak četvorice.* [Preveli Ružica i Aleksandar Vlaškalin. Opremio: Zdenko Balabanić.] Rijeka: Otokar Keršovani, 1963. 228 p. (Odabrana djela Conana Doyle-a)
Contents: Sign. - Stud.

1648. *Žuto lice.* [Preveli Ružica i Aleksandar Vlaškalin. Opremio: Zdenko Balabanić.] Rijeka: Otokar Keršovani, 1963. 249 p. (Odabrana djela Conana Doyle-a)
Half title: Sjećanja na Šerloka Holmsa.
Contents: Yell. - Silv. - Stoc. - Glor. - Musg. - Reig. - Croo. - Resi. - Gree. - Nava. - Fina.

SINDHI

1649. [*Sharlak Homes jo.* Hyderabad: R. H. Ahmad & Brothers, 1962.] 167 p.

SINHALESE

1650. [*The Adventures of Sherlock Holmes.* Colombo: M. D. Gunasena & Co., Ltd., 1961.] 424 p.

1651. [*Baskavilhi ruduru baluva.* Tr. by R. N. H. Perera. Colombo: M. D. Gunasena & Co., Ltd.] iii, 151 p.
Contents: Houn.

1652. [*Siv salakuna.* Tr. by M. D. N. Austin. Colombo: M. D. Gunasena & Co., Ltd., 1966.] v, 187 p.
Contents: Sign.

SLOVAK

1653. *Dobrodružstvá Sherlocka Holmesa. 1. Zväzok. Studia v červenom. Podpis štyroch. Dobrodružstvá Sherlocka Holmesa.* [Preložil Alfonz Bednár.] Bratislava: Slovenský Spisovateľ, 1965. 506 p.
Contents: Stud. - Sign. - Adventures.

1654. ———. *2. Zväzok. Spomienky na Sherlocka Holmesa. Návrat Sherlocka Holmesa.* [Preložil Alfonz Bednár.] Bratislava: Slovenský Spisovateľ, 1965. 532 p.
Contents: Memoirs. - Return.

1655. *Dobrodružstvi čierneho Petra.* Z angl. preložil Gustáv Mandelík. Trenč: Gansel, 1921. 47 p. (Z dobrodražstvi detektiva Sherlocka Holmesa)
Contents: Blac.

1656. *Návrat Sherlocka Holmesa.* [Preložil Alfonz Bednár.] Bratislava: Slovenský Spisovateľ, 1966. 446 p.
Contents: His Last Bow. - Case Book.

1657. *Pes Baskervillský: Výber z noviel.* [Preložil Alfonz Bednár.] [Bratislava]: Spoločnosť Priateľov Krásnych Kníh [Slovenský Spisovateľ], 1957. 495 p.
Contents: Stud. - Adventures. - Houn. - O Sherlockovi Holmesovi, A. Bednár.

1658. *Poklad z Agry: Výber z noviel.* [Preložil Alfonz Bednár.] [Bratislava]: Spoločnosť Priatelov Krásnych Kníh [Slovenský Spisovatel], 1958. 456 p.
Contents: Sign. - Memoirs. - Vall.

1659. *Príhody Sherlocka Holmesa.* [Preložil Jakub Žbodák.] Bratislava: Mladé Letá, 1958. 137 p.
Contents: Memoirs.

1660. *Zmiznutý beryllov diadém.* [Preložil Alexander Trstenský.] Nitra: Pallas, [1948]. 80 p.
Contents: Bery.

SLOVENIAN

1661. *Baskervillski Pas. Dolina Strahu.* [Prevedla Stanko Klinar in Marko Jakše.] Ljubljana: Državna Založba Slovenije, 1963. 331 p.
Contents: Houn. - Vall.

1662. *Mojster Sherlock Holmes.* [Prevedla Ivan Herga in Mirko Napast.] Ljubljana: Državna Založba Slovenije, 1963. 226 p.
Contents: Case Book.

1663. *Prigode Sherlocka Holmesa.* [Prevedla Natalija Hujs.] Ljubljana: Državna Založba Slovenije, 1963. 212 p.
Contents: Scan. - Iden. - Twis. - Blue. - Spec. - Nobl. - Bery. - Stoc. - Croo. - Resi.

1664. *Sherlock Holmes.* [Prevedla Daša Komac.] Ljubljana: Mladinska Knjiga, 1963. 2 v. (116, 104 p.)
Contents: Adventures.

1665. *Sherlock Holmes in Baskervillske Pes.* [Prevedel Ivan Dolenc.] Maribor: Obzorja, 1953. 158 p.

1666. *Sherlock Holmes kot vlomilec in Pogrešani Nogometaš.* [Prevedel Ivan Dolenc.] Maribor: Obzorja, 1952. 33 p.
Contents: Chas. - Miss.

1667. *Slovo Sherlocka Holmesa.* [Prevedel Boris Verbič.] Ljubljana: Državna Založba Slovenije, 1963. 195 p.
Contents: His Last Bow.

1668. *Spomini Sherlocka Holmesa.* [Prevedla Berta Assejev.] Ljubljana: Prešernova Družba, 1962. 128 p.
Contents: Memoirs.

1669. *Študija v Škrletnem. Znamenje Štirih.* [Prevedel Marko Jakše.] Ljubljana: Državna Založba Slovenije, 1963. 220 p.
Contents: Stud. - Sign.

1670. *Vrnitev Sherlocka Holmesa.* [Prevedla Dana Drašler.] Ljubljana: Državna Založba Slovenije, 1963. 181 p.

Contents: Blac. - Danc. - Prio. - Chas. - 3Stu. - Gold. - Miss. - Abbe.

SPANISH

1671. *El archivo de Sherlock Holmes.* [Traducción de Amando Lázaro Ros.] [Barcelona]: Editorial Molino, [1967]. 200 p. (Selecciones de Biblioteca Oro) (245)
Contents: Preface. - Thor. - Cree. - Lion. - Veil. - Shos. - Reti.

1672. *La aventura del cliente ilustre.* Traducción: Andrés Maria Mateo. México, D. F.: Editorial Diana, S.A., 1961. 163 p. (Colección Caiman, 155)
Contents: Illus. - Blan. - Maza. - 3Gab. - Suss. - 3Gar. - Thor.

1673. *Aventuras de Sherlock Holmes.* Traducción por José Francés. [Los dos últimos traducción por Julio y Ceferino Palencia.] Madrid: La Editorial Española-Americana, [1907-1908]. 8 v.
Contents: Vol. 1. Policía fina. 252 p. - Vol. 2. El problema final. 207 p. - Vol.3. El sabueso de los Basquerville. 252 p. - Vol. 4. Triunfos de Sherlock Holmes. 215 p. - Vol. 5. Nuevos triunfos de Sherlock Holmes. 208 p. - Vol. 6. La resurrección de Sherlock Holmes. 238 p. - Vol. 7. Un crimen extraño. 224 p. - Vol. 8. La marca de los cuatro. 252 p.

1674. ———. Traducción por J. Bonet, J. Zamacois, y Arturo Costa Alvarez. Barcelona: Editorial Sopena, [1907-1908?] 7 v.
Contents: Vol. 1. Aventuras de Sherlock Holmes. 255 p. - Vol. 2. La marca de los cuatro. 224 p. - Vol. 3. Nuevas hazañas. 272 p. - Vol. 4. Triunfos. 239 p. - Vol. 5. Nuevos triunfos. 208 p. - Vol. 6. El sabueso de los Basquerville. 253 p. - Vol. 7. Un crimen extraño. 224 p.

1675. ———. Traducción por Emilio María Martínez. Edición ilustrada. Barcelona: Gassó Hermanos, Editores, [1909?] 203 p.
Contents: Blue. - Spec. - Engr. - Nobl. - Bery. - Copp. - Iden.

1676. ———. Traducción por Emilio María Martínez. [Ilustrado por V. Buil.] México, D.F.: Editora Nacional Edinal, S. de R. L., 1957. 217 p. (Colección Económica, 358)
Contents same as above.

1677. ———. [Portada de Claudio di Girolamo.] [Santiago de Chile]: Zig-Zag, [1961]. 204 p.
Contents: Stud. - Five. - Twis. - Spec. - Stoc. - Glor. - Reig. - Seco. - Fina. - Empt. - Danc. - Soli. - Blac. - SixN. - Gold. - Suss.

1678. ———. Primera Serie. [Versión española de J. Tejero Corretcher y Baldomero Porta.] Barcelona: Editorial Bruguera, S.A., [1963] [192] p. (Colección "Marabu," 56)

Contents: Scan. - RedH. - Bosc. - Five. - Twis. - Blue. - Spec.

1679. ———. Selección y prólogo de Oscar Hurtado. La Habana: Editorial Nacional de Cuba, 1964. xv, 277 p. (Biblioteca del Pueblo)
Contents: Stud. - Vall. - Scan. - Fina.

1680. *Aventuras de un tesoro.* México, D.F.: Editora Nacional Edinal, S. de R. L., 1960. 220 p. (Colección Económica, 869)
Contents: Sign.

1681. *La banda moteada.* Madrid: Dédalo, 1964. 40 p.
Contents: Spec.

1682. *La casa vacía.* Santiago de Chile: Empresa Editora Zig-Zag, S.A., 1948. 149 p. (Colección "La Linterna," Serie Escarlata, 73)
Contents: Empt. - Norw. - Danc.

1683. ———. Madrid: Dédalo, 1960. 44 p.
Contents: Empt.

1684. *Cinco pepitas de naranja.* Santiago de Chile: Empresa Editora Zig-Zag, S.A., 1945. 155 p. (Colección "La Linterna," Serie Escarlata, 33)
Contents: Five. - Twis. - Blue. - Spec.

1685. *El círculo de la muerte.* Madrid: Cid, 1954. 80 p.
Contents: Spec.

1686. *Un crimen extraño.* Traducción de J. y C. Palencia. Buenos Aires: Colección "Luciérnaga," [1944]. 189 p. (Serie "Amarilla Policial," 7)
Contents: Stud.

1687. ———. [Traducción de Julio Castro Barreiro.] Buenos Aires: Editorial Fénix, [1947]. 159 p. (Colección El Gato Diabólico, 2)

1688. ———. Madrid: Diana, 1952. 58 p. (Aventuras de Sherlock Holmes)

1689. ———. México, D.F.: Ediciones Estrella, [n.d.] 123 p.

1690. ———. México, D.F.: Editorial Victoria, [n.d.] [146] p.

1691. *La dama del brillante azul.* Traducción de Arturo Costa Alvarez. Barcelona: Editorial Sopena, 1912. 223 p.

1692. *La diadema de berilos.* Traducción de Juan Maldonado. México, D.F.: Editorial Castillo, S. R. L., [1944]. 141 p.
Contents: Bery. - Blue. - Silv. - Stoc. - Musg. - Glor.

1693. *Un escándalo en Bohemia.* Traducción por Emilio María Martínez. Barcelona: Editorial Gassó Hermanos, [1909?] 202 p.

1694. *Estrella de plata.* Santiago de Chile: Empresa Editora Zig-Zag, S.A., 1947. 166 p. (Colección "La Linterna," Serie Escarlata, 49)
Contents: Estrella de plata. - Yell. - El corredor de cambios. - Glor.

1695. *Estudio en escarlata.* Traducción de Joel R. Aramburo. México, D.F.: Editorial Novaro-México, S. A., [1956]. 178 p. (Colección Nova-Mex, 61)
Contents: Stud.

1696. ———. Traducción de Luz Maria T. de Ojeda. México, D. F.: Editorial Diana, S.A., 1961. 172 p. (Colección Caimán, 156)
Contents: Stud. - Scan. - Bosc.

1697. ———. Barcelona: Bruguera, 1963. 190 p.

1698. *Estudio en rojo.* Traducción por José Menéndez Novella. Madrid: Editorial Rivadeneyra, 1906. 255 p.
Contents: Stud.

1699. ———. Traducción por José Menéndez Novella. Madrid: Editorial Calleja, 1908. 245 p.

1700. ———. Versión castellana directa del inglés de José Menéndez Novella. Ilustraciones de Picolo y Ortega Hernandez. Madrid: La Novela de Ahora - Saturnino Calleja Fernández, [1922]. 75 p. (La Novela de Ahora, Segunda Epoca, 36)

1701. ———. Traducción de Pedro Arganda. La Plata (R. A.): Editorial Calomino, [1945]. 176 p. (Ediciones Populares Calomino)

1702. ———. Santiago de Chile: Empresa Editora Zig-Zag, S.A., 1945. 198 p. (Colección "La Linterna," Serie Escarlata, 1)

1703. ———. [Ilustrado por P. Hernández.] México, D.F.: Editora Nacional Edinal, S. de R. L., 1961. 244 p. (Colección Económica, 867)

1704. ———. Versión castellana. [Ilustraciones de Pícolo y Ortega Hernández.] Madrid: Saturnino Calleja Fernandez, [n.d.] 243 p. (Biblioteca Calleja. Obras Literarias de Autores Celebres, 105)

1705. *El intérprete griego.* Santiago de Chile: Empresa Editora Zig-Zag, S.A., 194-? (Colección "La Linterna," Serie Escarlata, 65)

1706. *La liga de los belirrojos.* Santiago de Chile: Empresa Editora Zig-Zag, S.A., 1945.

150 p. (Colección "La Linterna," Serie Escarlata, 23)

1707. "La liga de los Cabezas Rojas," *Los mejores cuentos policiales*. Selección y traducción de Adolfo Bioy Casares y Jorge Luis Borges. Buenos Aires: Emecé Editores, S.A., [1943]. p. 47-69.
———, *BSJ* [OS], 2, No. 3 (July 1947), 291-306.

1708. ———. *Los más famosos cuentos policiacos*. Introducción por Mariano Sánchez Roca. La Habana: Ediciones Faro, 1961.

1709. *La marca de los cuatro*. Madrid: Diana, [n.d.] 58 p.
Contents: Sign.

1710. ———. Traducción de Julio y Ceferino Palencia. Germanías; Valencia: Editorial Prometeo, [n.d.] [208] p. (Aventuras de Sherlock Holmes)
Contents: Sign. - Engr. - Spec.

1711. ———. Traducción de J. Bonet. Barcelona: Editorial Sopena, [n.d.] 224 p.

1712. *Lo mejor de Sherlock Holmes*. [Traducción de Luz María T. de Ojeda.] México, D.F.: Editorial Diana, S. A., [1953]. 332 p. illus.
Contents: Stud. - Sign. - Scan. - Houn. - Bosc.

1713. *Memorias de Sherlock Holmes*. [Traducción de Amando Lázaro Ros.] [Barcelona]: Editorial Molino, [1967]. 256 p.
Contents: Memoirs.

1714. *Nuevas y últimas aventuras de Sherlock Holmes*. Versión de Adela Grego. Valencia: Editorial Promoteo, [1930?] 267 p.
Contents: Case Book.

1715. *Nuevos triunfos de Sherlock Holmes*. Traducción de J. Zamacois. Barcelona: Ramón Sopena, Editor, [n.d.] 237 p. illus.
Contents: SixN. - Abbe. - Reig. - Seco. - Twis. - Blue. - Fina.

1716. *Once aventuras de Sherlock Holmes*. [Traducción de E. Gual.] [México, D.F.]: Editorial "Olimpo," [1952]. [352] p. (Sherlock Holmes Publication Quincenal) Title and publisher from cover.
Contents: 2. RedH. - 3. Five. - 4. Bosc. - 5. Iden. - 6. Twis. - 7. Blue. - 10. Nobl. - 13. Silv. - 16. Glor. - 17. Musg. - 18. Reig.

1717. *El perro de Baskerville*. México, D.F.: Editorial Victoria, [n.d.] 178 p.

1718. ———. [Versión española de Baldomero Porta.] Barcelona: Editorial Bruguera, S.A., [1963]. [188] p. (Colección "Marabu," 40)

1719. *Policía fina*. Traduccion de José Francés. Ilustraciones de Saul Tolmo. Madrid: La Novella Ilustrada, [n.d.] 269 p. (Aventuras de Sherlock Holmes)
Contents: Nobl. - Bery. - Blue. - Silv. - Stoc. - Musg. - Glor. - Nava.

1720. *El pulgar del ingeniero*. Santiago de Chile: Empresa Editora Zig-Zag, S.A., 1946. 165 p. (Colección "La Linterna," Serie Escarlata, 41)
Contents: Engr. - Nobl. - Bery. - Copp.

1721. *Reaparece Sherlock Holmes*. [Traducción de Amando Lázaro Ros.] [Barcelona]: Editorial Molino, [1967]. 224 p.
Contents: Return.

1722. *Resurrección de Sherlock Holmes*. República de Chile; México, D.F.: Editorial Arco, 1946. 148 p. (Colección Scotland Yard)
Contents: Empt. - Norw. - Danc.

1723. *El ritual de los Musgraves*. Santiago de Chile: Empresa Editora Zig-Zag, S.A., 194-? (Colección "La Linterna," Serie Escarlata, 57)

1724. "El ritual de los Musgraye," *Antología de las mejores novelas policiacas* (*Primera selección*). Barcelona: Ediciones Acervo, 1958. p. 79-99.

1725. *El sabueso de los Baskerville*. Traducción de Arturo Costa Alvarez. Rio de Janeiro; Buenos Aires: Editorial Tor, S. R. L., [1949]. 187 p. (Serie "Amarilla Policial," 10)

1726. ———. Traducción de Arturo Costa Alvarez. México, D.F.: Editora Nacional Edinal, S. de R. L., 1957. 253 p. illus. (Colección Económica, 362)

1727. *La señal de los cuatro*. La Plata: Editorial Calomino, [1943]. 186 p.
Contents: Sign.

1728. ———. Traducción de L. N. Buenos Aires: Colección "Luciérnaga," [1943]. 190 p. (Serie Amarilla de Aventura y Misterio, 4)

1729. ———. Traducción de L. N. Buenos Aires: Editorial Tor, S. R. L., [1948]. 190 p. (Serie "Amarilla Policial," 4)

1730. ———. Santiago de Chile: Empresa Editora Zig-Zag, S. A., 194-? (Colección "La Linterna," Serie Escarlata, 13)

1731. "La señal de los cuatro," *Selecciones Sherlock Holmes* [Buenos Aires], 1, No. 2 (Noviembre de 1953), 3-82.

1732. "Los señores de Reigate," *Historias de detectives*. Selección, prólogo y notas de Luis

Enrique Délano. Santiago de Chile: Zig-Zag, 1939. p. 46-64.

1733. *Sherlock Holmes.* Traducción del inglés, prólogo y notas de Amando Lázaro Ros. Madrid: Aguilar, 1953. 2 v. (1215, 1193 p.) (Obras completas)
Gilt-edged with a red limp morocco binding.
Contents: Vol. 1. Stud. - Sign. - Adventures. - Memoris, - Houn. - 2. Return. - Vall. - His Last Bow. - Case Book.

1734. ———. Traducción del inglés, prólogo y notas de Amando Lázaro Ros. [Madrid]: Aguilar, [1964]. 2 v. (1015, 1105 p.)
Plastic binding.
Contents same as above.

1735. ———. Especialmente editado y condensado para los Libros Clásicos de Oro Ilustrados por Charles Verral. Ilustraciones de Tom Gill. Traducción de Dolores B. de Robles. México, D.F.: Editorial Novaro, 1965. 96 p. (Clásicos de Oro Ilustrados, 12)
Contents: Mr. Sherlock Holmes (from Stud). - Spec. - Nava. - Iden. - Blue. - RedH. - Fina. - Epílogo.

1736. *Sherlock Holmes no ha muerto.* [Traducción de Amando Lázaro Ros.] [Barcelona]: Editorial Molino, [1967]. 208 p. (Selecciones de Biblioteca Oro, 242)
Contents: Chas. - SixN. - 3Stu. - Gold. - Miss. - Abbe. - Seco.

1737. *Sherlock Holmes publicación quincenal.* [Traducción de E. Gual.] [Uruguay: Editado por Editorial Albatros, S. A.] México, D.F., Distribuidor en la Rep. Mexicana: Distribuidora de Periódicos Libros y Revistas, S.A., Ave. Instituto Técnico 269, México, D. F. En el extranjero: Editorial Albatros, S. A., [1952-1953]. 26 v. (32 p. each)
Some of the covers are illustrated with scenes from the Basil Rathbone films.
Contents: 1. Scan. - 2. RedH. - 3. Five. - 4. Bosc. - 5. Iden. - 6. Twis. - 7. Blue. - 8. Spec. - 9. Engr. - 10. Nobl. - 11. Bery. - 12. Copp. - 13. Silv. - 14. Yell. - 15. Stoc. - 16. Glor. - 17. Musg. - 18. Reig. - 19. Croo. - 20. Resi. - 21. Gree. - 22. Nava. - 23. Fina. - 24. Empt. - 25. Norw. - 26. Danc.

1738. *Sherlock Holmes sigue en pie.* [Traducción de Amando Lázaro Ros.] [Barcelona]: Editorial Molino, [1967]. 215 p. (Selecciones de Biblioteca Oro) (244)
Contents: Preface. - Illu. - Blan. - Maza. - 3Gab. - Suss. - 3Gar.

1739. *El signo de los cuatro.* [Versión española de Baldomero Porta.] Barcelona: Editorial Bruguera, S.A., [1963]. [153] p. (Colección "Marabu," 88)
Contents: Sign.

1740. "El tratado naval," *Detectives y bandidos,* 1, No. 3 (Diciembre 10 de 1951), 4-31.
Contents: Nava.

1741. *Les tres estudiantes.* La Plata: Editorial Calomino, [1944, c.1943]. 190 p.
Contents: 3Stu. - Gree. - Five. - Resi. - Soli. - Gold. - Fina.

1742. *Triunfos de Sherlock Holmes.* Traducción de José Francés. Madrid: La Editorial Española-Americana, 1907. 213 p. (Aventuras de Sherlock Holmes)
Contents: 3Stu. - Twis. - Five. - Croo. - Resi. - RedH. - Soli. - Bosc.

1743. ———. México: Editorial Victoria, [n.d.] 138 p.
Contents: 3Stu. - Twis. - Five. - Resi. - Iden. - Soli. - Bosc.

1744. *El último saludo de Sherlock Holmes.* [Traduccíon de Amando Lázaro Ros.] [Barcelona]: Editorial Molino, [1967]. 240 p.
Contents: His Last Bow.

1745. *Los últimos casos de Sherlock Holmes.* [Traducción: Andrés María Mateo.] México, D.F.: Editorial Diana, S. A., [1957]. viii, 259 p.
Contents: His Last Bow.

1746. *El valle del terror.* Traducción de M. Vallvé. Barcelona: Edc. y Publ. Iberia (Imp. Sabaté), 1928. 250 p.
Contents: Vall.

1747. ———. [Versión española de Baldomero Porta.] Barcelona: Editorial Bruguera, S.A., [1964]. [191] p. (Colección "Marabu," 112)

1748. "El valle del terror," *Revolucion* [Habana, Cuba] (Junio-Agosto 1965).

1749. *¡Vuelve Sherlock Holmes!* [Traducción de Leonor Tejada.] [México, D.F.]: Organización Editorial Novaro, S.A., [1966]. 315 p. (Nova Dell, 40)
Translated from *Great Stories of Sherlock Holmes* (item 690).
Contents: Thor. - Reig. - Danc. - Silv. - Stoc. - Gree. - Abbe. - Blac. - Chas. - SixN. - Devi. - Shos.

Parodies and Pastiches

1750. Edwards, Alberto. *Román Calvo: El Sherlock Holmes Chileno,* by "Miguel de Fuenzalida" (pseudonym of Alberto Edwards). Edited, with introduction, notes and vocabulary, by Raymond L. Grismer and Mary B. MacDonald. New York: The Macmillan Co., 1946. x, 154 p. illus.
Contents: Sobre la pista del corsario. - La catástrofe de la punta del diablo. - El hombre misterioso de la calle de Santa Rosa.

1751. Jardiel Poncela, Enrique. "Novísimas aventuras de Sherlock Holmes," *El libro del convaleciente: Inyecciones de alegría para hospitales y sanatorios.* [The Convalescent's Book: Hypos of Fun for Hospitals and Sanatoria.] Zaragoza: Colección Hispania, 1939. p. 83-136. illus.
———. ———, ———. [Madrid: Biblioteca Nueva, n.d.] p. 83-136.
———. ———, ———. [Segunda edición.] Buenos Aires: Editorial Juventud Argentina, S.A., [1945]. p. 52-95. illus.
———. *7 Novísimas aventuras de Sherlock Holmes.* Barcelona: Ediciones G. P., [n.d.] 96 p. (Enciclopedia Pulga, 95)
   Contents: Prólogo: Mi encuentro con Sherlock Holmes. - La serpiente amaestrada de Whitechapel. - El hombre de barba azul marino. - La momia analfabeta de "Craig Museum." - El Anarquista incomprensible de Piccadilly Circus. - La misa negra del barrio de Soho. - El frío del Polo. - Los Asesinatos incongruentes del castillo de Rock.

1752. ———. "Los treinta y ocho asesinatos y medio del castillo de Hull (Novísimas aventuras de Sherlock Holmes), "*Exceso de Equipaje.* Madrid: Biblioteca Nueva, 1943. p. 291-318.
———. ———, Precedido de "Enrique Jardiel Poncela," por José López Rubio. [Madrid: 1953.] 63 p. (La Novela del sabado, 1, No. 4)

1753. Martyn, John L. *Sherlock Holmes.* Madrid: Editorial Dólar, [n.d.] 156 p. (Colección Celebridades, 65)

1754. *Los amores de un bandido.* México, D. F.: Editora Nacional Edinal, S. de R. L., 1956. 224 p. illus. (Memorias íntimas de Sherlock Holmes) (Colección Económica, 612)
   Also contains: Los ladrones de mujeres de Chinatown. - El novio sospechoso. - El asesinato en el harén.

1755. *Blackwell, el pirata del Támesis.* Granada: Editorial Atlante, [n.d.] 221 p. (Memorias íntimas de Sherlock Holmes, 4)
   Also contains: Una gota de tinta sólamente. - El castigo en el crimen. - Sherlock Holmes "maître d'hôtel."

1756. *En el circo de Dresde.* México, D.F.: Editora Nacional Edinal, S. de R. L., 1962. 219 p. illus. (Memorias íntimas de Sherlock Holmes) (Colección Económica, 895)
   Also contains: Un viaje a San Gotardo. - El capitan desaparecido. - Los asesinatos del profesor Flax.

1757. *La dama del velo.* México, D.F.: Editora Nacional Edinal, S. de R. L., 1956. 304 p. illus. (Memorias íntimas de Sherlock Holmes) (Colección Económica, 609)
   Also contains: Un aparecido de la tumba. - El almirante Nelson, detective. - El castigo de una mala acción.

1758. *El fabricante de diamantes.* Barcelona: F. Granada y C. a, Editores, [n.d.] 222 p. illus. (Memorias íntimas de Sherlock Holmes)
   Also contains: La chapa número 209. - El diario de una muerta. - De la muerte a la vida.

1759. *La hija del usurero.* México, D.F.: Editora Nacional Edinal, S. de R. L., 1962. 262 p. illus. (Memorias íntimas de Sherlock Holmes) (Colección Económica, 868)
   Also contains: El codak traidor. - El enigma de la mesa de juego. - El vestido de la reina.

1760. ———. Granada; Barcelona: Editorial Atlante, [n.d.] 204 p. illus. (Memorias íntimas de Sherlock Holmes, 3)
   Contents same as above.

1761. ———. Barcelona: F. Granada y C. a, [n.d.] 255 p. illus.
   Contents same as above.

1762. *Jack, el destripador.* Granada; Barcelona: Editorial Atlante, [n.d.] 224 p. illus. (Memorias íntimas de Sherlock Holmes, 5)
   Also contains: En la tumba, junto a la máquina infernal. - Muerto resucitado. - El trapero de Paris.

1763. ———. Barcelona: F. Granada y C. a, [n.d.] 280 p. illus.
   Contents same as above.

1764. "Jack El Destripador," Tr. by Anthony Boucher. *The Harlot Killer: The Story of Jack the Ripper in Fact and Fiction.* Edited by Allan Barnard. New York: Dodd, Mead & Co., 1953. p. 211-214.

1765. *La ladrona del hotel.* México, D.F.: Editora Nacional Edinal, S. de R. L., 1956. 222 p. illus. (Memorias íntimas de Sherlock Holmes) (Colección Económica, 611)
   Also contains: Clavado en cruz. - La misa negra en Nápoles. - El sabueso de Soho.

1766. ———. Barcelona: F. Granada y C. a, Editores, [n.d.] 222 p. illus. (Memorias íntimas de Sherlock Holmes)
   Contents same as above.

1767. *La maleta sangrienta.* México, D.F.: Editora Nacional Edinal, S. de R. L., 1956. 224 p. illus. (Memorias íntimas de Sherlock Holmes) (Colección Económica, 539)
   Also contains: El puñal del Negus. - La sepultura del faro. - Alrededor de un trono.

1768. *Una noche de terror.* México, D.F.: Editora Nacional Edinal, S. de R. L., 1956.

240 p. (Memorias íntimas de Sherlock Holmes) (Colección Económica, 606)

Also contains: El barbero de lord Sullivans. - El demonio del Circo Angelo. - Los doce corazones.

1769. *El rey de los bandidos.* México, D.F.: Editora Nacional Edinal, S. de R. L., 1956. 255 p. (Memorias íntimas de Sherlock Holmes) (Colección Económica, 608)

Also contains: El drama en el Circo Angelo. - El carnaval de Colonia. - La voluntad ajena.

1770. *El robo del collar de perlas.* México, D.F.: Editora Nacional Edinal, S. de R. L., 1957. 223 p. illus. (Memorias íntimas de Sherlock Holmes) (Colección Económica, 607)

Also contains: El galeote. - El destino de la familia Walpole. - El terrible fantasma.

1771. *El secreto del escultor.* México, D.F.: Editora Nacional Edinal, S. de R. L., 1956. 224 p. illus. (Memorias íntimas de Sherlock Holmes) (Colección Económica, 613)

Also contains: Cinco millones en brillantes. - Un drama de celos. - Un mechón de cabellos.

1772. *Las señas de la muerta.* México, D.F.: Editora Nacional Edinal, S. de R. L., 1962. 247 p. illus. (Memorias íntimas de Sherlock Holmes) (Colección Económica, 896)

Also contains: La fuerza de las sospechas. - El veneno de Robur Hall. - Una apuesta extraordinaria.

1773. *Sherlock Holmes y el contrabandista de opio.* México, D.F.: Editora Nacional Edinal, S. de R. L., 1956. 246 p. illus. (Memorias íntimas de Sherlock Holmes) (Colección Económica, 605)

Also contains: Una corrida de torros en Granada. - Tibo-Tib. - El adorador del diablo.

1774. *El testamento del director.* México, D.F.: Editora Nacional Edinal, S. de R. L., 1957. 208 p. illus. (Memorias íntimas de Sherlock Holmes) (Colección Económica, 604)

Also contains: Atentado en un velódromo de hamburgo. - La logia anarquista.

1775. *El vendedor de cadáveres,* [por] Arturo Conan Doyle [sic]. Buenos Aires: Novelas de Aventuras, [n.d.] 64 p. (Memorias íntimas de Sherlock Holmes)

1776. ———. Barcelona: F. Granada y C. a, [n.d.] 256 p. illus. (Memorias íntimas de Sherlock Holmes)

Also contains: La desaparición de un novio. - La trampa del viejo edificio. - El tesoro del negrero.

1777. *Las víctimas de la codicia.* México, D.F.:

Editora Nacional Edinal, S. de R. L., 1956. 292 p. illus. (Memorias íntimas de Sherlock Holmes) (Colección Económica, 610)

Also contains: Un regalo de bodas macabro. - La modelo del fasificador de billetes de Banco. - El doble crimen de los Alpes bávaros.

1778. *La viuda roja de París.* México, D.F.: Editora Nacional Edinal, S. de R. L., 1960. 256 p. (Memorias íntimas de Sherlock Holmes) (Colección Económica, 870)

Also contains: El criminal en el Ejército de Salvación. - La habitación número 13. - En las manos de la Maffia.

1779. *La voluntad ajena,* [por] Arturo Conán Doyle [sic] . Buenos Aires: Novelas de Aventuras, [n.d.] 58 p. (Memorias íntimas de Sherlock Holmes, 9)

The pastiches in the above incomplete list, with Sherlock Holmes and Harry Taxon, in the series *Memorias íntimas de Sherlock Holmes* have also been published in German, Portuguese, and Swedish and are listed under those languages.

SWAHILI

Parodies and Pastiches

1780. Abdulla, Muhammed Said. *Mzimu wa Watu wa Kale.* [The Spirits of the Ancestors.] [Illustrated by Margaret E. Gregg.] Dar es Salaam: The Eagle Press; East African Literature Bureau, 1960. 86 p.

First-prize winner in the Swahili story-writing competition of 1957-1958.

Review: BSJ, 15, No. 2 (June 1965), 70-74 (Bernth Lindfors).

1781. Katalambula, Faraji H. H. *Simu ya Kifo.* [Trail of Death.] Dar es Salaam: East African Literature Bureau, [1965]. [76] p. illus.

Review: BSJ, 17, No. 1 (March 1967), 42-44 (Bernth Lindfors).

SWEDISH

1782. *Äfventyret med djäfvulsfotroten, jämte andra Sherlock Holmes historier.* Bemyndigad öfversättning från engelskan af H. Flygare. Stockholm: Hugo Gebers Förlag, [1915]. 172 p. (Min vän privat-detektivens äfventyr, 8)

Contents: Devi. - RedC. - Lady. - Dyin.

1783. *Agra-skatten.* Öfversättning från engelskan. Stockholm: Ejnar Cohns Förlag, [1891]. 196 p.

Contents: Sign.

1784. "Agra-skatten," *Guldets makt. Agra-skatten.* Autoriserad öfversättning från engelskan. Stockholm: P. A. Huldbergs Bokförlagsaktiebolag, [1905]. p. 145-304.

———, ———. Stockholm: Adolf Johnsons Förlag, [1905]. p. 145-304. (Ungdomens bibliotek, 103)

1785. *Den återuppståndne Sherlock Holmes.* Helsingfors: Frenckellska Tryckeri-Aktiebolaget, 1903. 9 v. (Helsingfors-Postens Terracottabibliotek)
Contents: Vol. 1. Empt. - Vol. 2. Norw. - Vol. 3. Danc. - Vol. 4. Soli. - Vol. 5 Prio. - Vol. 6. Blac. - Chas. - Vol. 7. SixN. - 3Stu. - Vol. 8. Gold. - Miss. - Vol. 9. Abbe. - Seco.

1786. ———. Öfversättning från engelskan [af H. Flygare]. Stockholm: Hugo Gebers Förlag, [1904]. 2 v. (1-96, 97-232 p.) (Min vän privatdetektivens äfventyr, 4)
———. Same ed., with identical title page, in one volume.
———. Andra upplagan. [1908] 232 p.
Contents: Empt. - Norw. - Danc. - Soli. - Prio. - Blac. - Chas. - SixN. - 3Stu.

1787. ———. Oavkortad översättning från engelska originalet av Alfred Wingren. Malmö: Världslitteraturens Förlag, [1930]. 191 p.
Contents: Empt. - Norw. - Danc. - SixN. - Abbe. - Seco.

1788. *Baskervilles hund.* Översättning från engelskan av H. Flygare. Stockholm: Hugo Gebers Förlag, [1911]. (Hugo Gebers Enkronasbibliotek, 37)

1789. ———. Översättning från engelskan av H. Flygare. Stockholm: B. Wahlströms Förlag, 1912. 159 p. (B. Wahlströms 25 öresböcker, 11)

1790. ———. Översättning från engelskan av H. Flygare. Fjärde upplagan [sic 5th ed.] Stockholm: Hugo Gebers Förlag, 1924. 176 p. (Min vän privatdetektivens äventyr, 3)

1791. ———. Översättning från engelska av H. Flygare. Stockholm: B. Wahlström Bok-förlag, [1936]. 190 p.

1792. ———. Översättning av Ragnhild Hallén. Stockholm: Lindqvist, [1947]. 200 p.

1793. ———. Översättning av Ragnhild Hallén. Helsingfors: Söderström & Co., 1947. 200 p. (Berömda romaner, 6)

1794. ———. [Till svenska av Ingrid Ekman Nordgaard.] Illustrerad av Stig Södersten. Stockholm: Natur och Kultur, 1954. 175 p. (Skattkammarbiblioteket)

1795. ———. Översättning från engelskan av Anders Eje. [Illustrerad av Gunnar Lindvall.] Stockholm: Saxon & Lindström [Seelig], 1955. 221 p. (Sherlock Holmes' största äventyr)

1796. ———. Stockholm: Lindqvist, 1958. 187 p. (Tigerböckerna, 13)

1797. *Baskervilles hund, jämte ännu några af Sherlock Holmes äfventyr.* Översättning från engelskan af H. Flygare. Stockholm: Hugo Gebers Förlag, [1902]. 308 p. (Min vän privatdetektivens äfventyr, 3)
———. Andra upplagan. [1902] 308 p.
———. Tredje upplagan. [1907] 312 p.
Contents: Houn. - Nava. - Fina.

1798. *Baskervilles hund, och andra berättelser.* [Översättning av Nils Holmberg. Illustrationer av Georg Lagerstedt och Sidney Paget. Omslag av Georg Lagerstedt.] Stockholm: Albert Bonniers Förlag, [1957]. 204 p. (De odödliga ungdomsböckerna, 33)
Contents: Houn. - Five. - Gree.

1799. *Berättelser om Sherlock Holmes: Vald samling.* [Illustrerad av Sidney Paget.] [Helsingborg: Allers Familj-Journals Förlag, 1902.] 14 v. (331 p.) (På lediga stunder, 27-41)
Contents: Introduction. - RedH. - Bosc. - Twis. - Blue. - Five. - Engr. - Nobl. - Copp. - Iden. - Bery. - Scan.

1800. *Beryllkronan: Detektivberättelse. Andra samlingen av Sherlock Holmes äventyr.* Stockholm: Nordiska Förlaget, [1918]. 222 p. (19)
Contents: Bery. - Twis. - Blue. - Spec. - Engr. - Nobl.

1801. *Brons gåta, jämte andra Sherlock Holmes-historier.* Bemyndigad översättning från engelskan av H. Flygare och M. Lindqvist. Stockholm: Hugo Gebers Förlag, [1923]. 164 p. (Min vän privatdetektivens äventyr, 9)
Contents: Thor. - Maza. - Gree. - Gamla brev om Sherlock Holmes [Old Letters About Sherlock Holmes]. - Last.

1802. *De dansande figurerna: Detektivberattelser.* [Översättning från engelskan af H. Flygare.] Stockholm: B. Wahlströms Förlag, [1914]. 127 p. (B. Wahlströms 25 öresböcker, 139)
Contents: Danc. - Soli. - SixN. - Empt.

1803. *De dansande figurerna och andra berättelser.* [Översättning av Nils Holmberg. Omslag av Ola Ericson.] Stockholm: Albert Bonniers Förlag, [1970]. 105 p. (Röda Ramen)
At head of title: Sherlock Holmes' äventyr.
Contents: Danc. - Norw. - Devi.

1804. *En diplomatisk hemlighet.* Bemyndigad öfversättning af H. Flygare. Stockholm: Hugo Gebers Förlag, [1905]. 48 p. (Min vän privatdetektivens äfventyr, 6)
Contents: Seco.
The cover is reproduced in *Sherlock Holmes, 1891-1916,* by Ted Bergman (item 3701).

91

1805. *En diplomatisk hemlighet, jämte andra detektivhistorier.* Översättning från engelskan [af H. Flygare]. Stockholm: B. Wahlströms Förlag, 1914. 128 p. (B. Wahlströms 25 öresböcker, 136)
Contents: Seco. - Norw. - 3Stu.

1806. "Dramat i Reigate," *Sherlock Holmes Detektiv-Historier.* Stockholm: Skandias Bokförlag, [1909]. Vol. 32, p. 1-9.
Contents: Reig.

1807. *Fasans dal: En ny Sherlock Holmes historia.* Bemyndigad översättning från engelskan av H. Flygare. Stockholm: Hugo Gebers Förlag, [1916]. 223 p. (Min vän privatdetektivens äventyr, 9)
Contents: Vall.

1808. *Förföljd: Roman.* Förf. till "De fyras tecken." Öfversättning från engelska orig. "A Study in Scarlet" af B. F. Stockholm: Nordin & Josephson, [1893]. 182 p.

1809. ———. Förf. till "De fyras tecken." Öfversättning från engelska originalet "A Study in Scarlet" [af B. F.] Stockholm: Fenix, Bok-& Konstförlag (f.d. Ferdinand Hey'ls Förlag), [1904]. 191 p.

1810. ———. Förf. till "De fyras tecken." Öfversättning från engelska originalet "A Study in Scarlet" [af B. F.] Stockholm: Svenska Romanförlaget, [1906]. 191 p.

1811. ———. Förf. till "De fyras tecken." Översättning från engelska originalet "A Study in Scarlet" [af B. F.] Malmö: Andersson & Claussons bokförlag, 1914. 4 v. (32, 32, 32, 24 p.) (Vårt bibliotek, samling I, häften 27, 28, 29, 30)

1812. *Det försvunna barnet.* [Typografi och illustr. av Torstein Landström.] Göteborg: Konstindustriskolan, 1966. 48 p. (Ur Sherlock Holmes' bragder)
Contents: Prio.

1813. *Det försvunna barnet, m. fl. detektivhistorier.* Översättning från engelskan [af H. Flygare]. Stockholm: B. Wahlströms Förlag, 1914. 127 p. (B. Wahlströms 25 öres-böcker, 155)
Contents: Prio. - Blac. - Chas.

1814. *De fyras tecken.* Öfversättning från engelskan af Walborg Hedberg. Stockholm: Nordin & Josephson, [1891]. 194 p.
Contents: Sign.

1815. ———. Andra upplagan. Stockholm: Fenix, Bok-& Konstförlag (f.d. Ferdinand Hey'ls Förlag), [1904]. 194 p.

1816. ———. Tredje upplagan. Stockholm: Fenix, Bok-& Konstförlag (f.d. Ferdinand Hey'ls Förlag), [1904]. 194 p.

The cover is reproduced in *Sherlock Holmes, 1891-1916,* by Ted Bergman (item 3701).

1817. ———. Fjärde upplagan. Stockholm: Svenska Romanförlaget, [1907]. 198 p.

1818. ———. Översättning från engelska originalet av Ellen Ryding. Stockholm: Nordiska Förlaget, [1911]. 160 p. (Nordiska Förlagets 25-öresböcker, 41)

1819. *De fyras tecken: Detektiv-roman.* Öfversättning från engelskan [af Walborg Hedberg]. Stockholm: Björck & Börjesson, [1913]. 120 p. (B. & B:s Romanbibliotek, Ny serie 4)

1820. *De fyras tecken.* Översättning från engelskan av Ellen Ryding. Stockholm: Nordiska Förlaget, [1918]. 192 p. (9)

1821. ———. Oavkortad översättning från det engelska originalet av fil. mag. Viktor Olsson. Malmö: Världslitteraturens Förlag, [1930]. 182 p.

1822. ———. Stockholm: Lindqvist, 1948. 173 p. (Triangelböckerna, 10)

1823. ———. Helsingfors: Söderström & Co., 1948. 173 p. (Triangelböckerna, 10)

1824. ———. [Till svenska av Eva Håkanson.] Illustrerad av Per Silfverhjelm. Stockholm: Natur och Kultur, [1955]. 153 p. (Skattkammarbiblioteket)

1825. *De fyras tecken, och andra berättelser.* ["De fyras tecken" är översatt av Curt Berg. Ovriga berättelser av Nils Holmberg. Illustrationer av F. H. Townsend och Sidney Paget. Omslag av Georg Lagerstedt.] Stockholm: Albert Bonniers Förlag, [1956]. 207 p. (De odödliga ungdomsböckerna, 32)
Contents: Sign. - Twis. - Bery. - Silv.

1826. *Det gula ansiktet: Detektivberättelser. Tredje samlingen av Sherlock Holmes äventyr.* Stockholm: Nordiska Förlaget, [1918]. 192 p. (21)
Contents: Yell. - Copp. - Silv. - Glor. - Musg. - Stoc.

1827. *Den guldbågade pincenezen, jämte andra detektivhistorier.* Öfversättning från engelskan [af H. Flygare]. Stockholm: Hugo Gebers Förlag, [1904]. 101 p. (Min vän privatdetektivens äfventyr, 5)
Contents: Gold. - Miss. - Abbe.

1828. ———. Översättning från engelskan [af H. Flygare]. Stockholm: B. Wahlströms Förlag, [1914]. 128 p. (B. Wahlströms 25 öresböcker, 134)
Contents same as above.

1829. "Historien om Svarte Peter," *Mörka slottet.* Översättning av A. Berg. Andra upplagan. Stockholm: Holmquists Boktryckeris Förlag, [1925]. p. 133-160.
Contents: Blac.

1830. *Huset vid Caulfield Gardens.* Översättning av O. Nachman. Stockholm: Holmquists Boktryckeris Förlag, [1924]. 156 p.
Contents: Bruc. - Wist. - Prio.

1831. ———. Från engelskan av O. Nachman. Stockholm: Holmquists Boktryckeris Förlag, [1928]. 176 p.
Contents: Bruc. - Wist. - Prio. - ManW.

1832. *Ingenjörens tumme och andra berättelser.* [Översättning av Nils Holmberg. Omslag av Ola Ericson.] Stockholm: Albert Bonniers Förlag, [1970]. 123 p. (Röda Ramen)

1833. *Mannen med ärret och andra berättelser.* [Översättning av Nils Holmberg. Omslag av Ola Ericson.] Stockholm: Albert Bonniers Förlag, [1970]. 123 p. (Röda Ramen)
At head of title: Sherlock Holmes' äventyr.
Contents: ManW. - Bery. - Silv. - Dyin.

1834. *Mästerdetektiven Sherlock Holmes.* [De två förstnämnda är översätta av Curt Berg, de senare av Nils Holmberg.] Stockholm: Albert Bonniers Förlag, [1964]. 481 p.
Contents: Stud. - Sign. - Houn. - Vall.

1835. *Min vän privatdetektiven Sherlock Holmes: Glimtar ur en stor mans liv.* [My Friend, the Private Detective Sherlock Holmes: Glimpses of a Great Man's Life.] Förord av Ellery Queen. [Omslag av Svenolov Ehrén. Illustrationer av Sidney Paget. Förordet som är hämtat ur *In the Queens' Parlour,* är översatt av Margareta Suber. Ovriga svenska texter valda från tidiga översättningar av Sherlock Holmes' Äventyr.] Stockholm: Bokförlaget Fabel AB [Seelig], [1964]. 63 p. (Fabels rariteter)
A book of quotations.

1836. *Min vän privatdetektivens äfventyr.* Ofversättning af O. S. Stockholm: Hugo Gebers Förlag, [1893]. 2 v. (300, 259 p.)
Contents: Vol. 1. Spec. - RedH. - Iden. - Bosc. - Twis. - Scan. - Five. - Bery. - Engr. - Blue. - Copp. - Vol. 2. Silv. - Card. - Yell. - Stoc. - Glor. - Musg. - Nobl. - Reig. - Croo. - Resi. - Gree.

1837. *Nagra Sherlock Holmes-minnen.* Bemyndigad öfversättning [af H. Flygare]. Stockholm: Hugo Gebers Förlag, [1909]. 102 p. (Min vän privatdetektivens äfventyr, 7)
Contents: Wist. - Bruc.

1838. ———. Oavkortad översättning direkt från originalet av Viktor Olsson. Malmö: Världslitteraturens Förlag, [1928]. 194 p.
Contents: His Last Bow.

1839. *Den odödlige Sherlock Holmes.* Med inledning av Curt Berg. [Översättning av Nils Holmberg.] Stockholm: Albert Bonniers Förlag, [1954]. 459 p.
Contents: Conan Doyle, Sherlock Holmes och Doktor Watson, av Curt Berg. - Adventures. - Silv. - Yell. - Stoc. - Glor. - Musg. - Reig. - Croo. - Resi. - Gree. - Prio. - Chas. - SixN. - Card. - Nava. - Fina.

1840. *Det prickiga bandet.* [Helsingborg: Allers Familj-Journals Forlag, 1900.] 27 p. (På lediga stunder, 257, 258)
Contents: Spec.

1841. *Privatdetektiven Sherlock Holmes äfventyr.* Första serien. Öfversättning från engelskan af Tom Wilson. Stockholm: Björk & Börjesson, [1907]. 2 v. (275, 232 p.)
Contents: Vol. 1. Scan. - Red. - Iden. - Bosc. - Five. - Twis. - Blue. - Spec. - Engr. - Nobl. - Vol. 2. Bery. - Copp. - Silv. - Yell. - Stoc. - Glor. - Musg. - Reig. - Croo. - Resi. - Gree.

1842. ———. Första serien. Öfversättning från engelskan af Tom Wilson. Andra upplagan. Stockholm: Björck & Börjesson, [1910]. 2 v. (249, 279 p.) (Berömda böcker, 15, 16)
Contents same as above except Iden is omitted.
The cover of vol. 2 is reproduced in *Sherlock Holmes, 1891-1916,* by Ted Bergman (item 3701), and in *SHJ,* 7, No. 2 (Spring 1965), 60.

1843. *Privatdetektiven Sherlock Holmes' äventyr.* Tva serier i en volym. Översättning från engelskan av Tom Wilson. Ny upplaga. Stockholm: Björck & Börjessons Bokförlag, [1947]. 479 p.
Contents same as item 1841.

1844. *Privatdetektiven Sherlock Holmes bragder.* Öfversättning af Bob [K. B.] [Illustrerad av Sidney Paget.] Stockholm: Const. Olofsons Förlag, [1899]. 319 p.
Contents: Silv. - Scan. - RedH. - Iden. - Blue. - Bosc. - Twis. - Spec. - Engr. - Nobl.

1845. ———. Öfversättning af Bob [K. B.] Stockholm: Const. Olofsons Förlag, [1901]. 639 p.
Contents: Silv. - Scan. - RedH. - Iden. - Blue. - Bosc. - Twis. - Spec. - Engr. - Nobl. - Bery. - Copp. - Card. - Yell. - Stoc. - Glor. - Musg. - Reig. - Croo. - Resi. - Gree. - Nava. - Fina.
The first 319 pages are printed from the same plates as the item above.

1846. *Problemet: Detektivberättelser. Fjärde*

samlingen av Sherlock Holmes äventyr. Stockholm: Nordiska Förlaget, [1918]. 192 p. (23)
Contents: Fina. - Reig. - Croo. - Resi. - Gree. - Nava.

1847. Röda ligan: Detektivberättelser. Första samlingen av Sherlock Holmes äventyr. Stockholm: Nordiska Förlaget, [1918]. 190 p. (17)
Contents: RedH. - Scan. - Iden. - Bosc. - Five.

1848. "Sen hämnd," På lediga stunder: En utvald roman- och novellsamling afsedd för familjekretsen. Tolfte bandet. Helsingborg: Allers Familj-Journals Förlag, 1898. p. 1-106.
Contents: Stud.

1849. Sherlock Holmes' äfventyr. Öfversättning från engelskan [af O. S.] Andra upplagan af "Min vän privatdetektivens äfventyr." Första serien. Stockholm: Hugo Gebers Förlag, [1902]. 3 v. (1-96, 97-192, 193-313 p.) (Min vän privatdetektivens äfventyr, 1)
Contents: Spec. - RedH. - Iden. - Bosc. - Twis. - Scan. - Five. - Bery. - Engr. - Blue. - Copp.

1850. ———. Öfversättning från engelskan [af O. S.] Andra upplagan af "Min vän privatdetektivens äfventyr." Andra serien. Stockholm: Hugo Gebers Förlag, [1902]. 2 v. (1-128, 129-264 p.) (Min vän privatdetektivens äfventyr, 2)
Contents: Silv. - Card. - Yell. - Stoc. - Glor. - Musg. - Nobl. - Reig. - Croo. - Resi. - Gree.

1851. ———. Öfversättning från engelskan [af O. S.] Tredje upplagan af "Min vän privatdetektivens äfventyr." Stockholm: Hugo Gebers Förlag, [1905]. 2 v. (313, 264 p.) (Min vän privatdetektivens äfventyr, 1, 2)
Contents: Vol. 1. Spec. - RedH. - Iden. - Bosc. - Twis. - Scan. - Five. - Bery. - Engr. - Blue. - Copp. - Vol. 2. Silv. - Card. - Yell. - Stoc. - Glor. - Musg. - Nobl. - Reig. - Croo. - Resi. - Gree.

1852. Sherlock Holmes äventyr. Översättning från engelska originalet av Ellen Ryding. Stockholm: Nordiska Förlaget, [1911]. 4 v. (158, 189, 178, 181 p.) (Nordiska Förlagets 25-öresböcker, 7, 23, 33, 51)
Contents: Vol. 1. Scan. - RedH. - Iden. - Bosc. - Five. - Vol. 2. Twis. - Blue. - Spec. - Engr. - Nobl. - Bery. - Vol. 3. Copp. - Silv. - Yell. - Stoc. - Glor. - Musg. - Vol. 4. Reig. - Croo. - Resi. - Gree. - Nava. - Fina.
The cover of vol. 3 is reproduced in Sherlock Holmes, 1891-1916, by Ted Bergman (item 3701).

1853. ———. Fran engelskan av Oscar Nachman. Stockholm: B. Wahlströms Förlag, [1923-1924]. 4 v. (48 p. each) (Ungdomsbiblioteket, 158, 160, 162, 164)
Contents: Vol. 1. Empt. - Danc. - Soli. - Vol. 2. Gold. - Abbe. - SixN. - Vol. 3. Bery. - Norw. - Miss.

1854. ———. Oversatt av Oscar Nachman. Stockholm: Nutidens Förlags AB, [1926]. 271 p.
Contents: Stud. - Wist. - Bruc. - Resi. - Soli. - Gree.

1855. ———. Oavkortad översättning från engelska originalet av fil. mag. E. Knutsson. Malmö: Världslitteraturens Förlag, [1930]. 180 p.
Contents: Scan. - RedH. - Bosc. - Twis. - Spec. - Copp.

1856. ———. Första delen. Från engelskan av Nils Holmberg. Illustrationer av Sidney Paget och Georg Lagerstedt. Stockholm: Albert Bonniers Förlag, [1945]. 294 p. (De odödliga ungdomsböckerna, 32)
Contents: Scan. - RedH. - Bosc. - Houn.

1857. ———. Andra delen. Från engelskan av Nils Holmberg. Illustrationer av Sidney Paget. Stockholm: Albert Bonniers Förlag, [1945]. 338 p. (De odödliga ungdomsböckerna, 33)
Contents: Five. - Twis. - Spec. - Engr. - Bery. - Silv. - Glor. - Musg. - Gree. - Nava. - Last.

1858. ———. Tredje delen. Från engelskan av Nils Holmberg. Illustrationer av Georg Lagerstedt. Stockholm: Albert Bonniers Förlag, [1946]. 368 p. (De odödliga ungdomsböckerna, 34)
Contents: Empt. - Norw. - Danc. - SixN. - Gold. - Seco. - 3Gar. - Bruc. - Reti. - Dyin. - Devi. - Fina.

1859. ———. Stockholm: Lindqvist, [1953]. 190 p.
Contents: RedH. - Bosc. - Twis. - Spec. - Engr. - Reig.

1860. ———. Helsingfors: Söderström & Co., [1953]. 190 p. (Berömda romaner, 9)
Contents same as above.

1861. ———. Översättning från engelskan. Stockholm: Lindqvist, [1961]. 220 p.
Contents same as above.

1862. "Sherlock Holmes äventyr," Illustrationer Guy Deel. Oversättning Nils Holmberg. Ungdomens bästa böcker. I urval och sammandrag av Reader's Digest. Stockholm: Reader's Digest Aktiebolag, [1967]. p. 353-510.
Contents: Prologue (from Stud). - Copp. -

Danc. - Silv. - Spec. - Reig. - Blue. - Twis. - RedH.

1863. *Sherlock Holmes' bragder.* Aukoriserad översättning från engelskan [af H. Flygare]. Stockholm: Hugo Gebers Förlag, [1929]. 4 v. (286, 291, 313, 294 p.)
Contents: Vol. 1. Spec. - RedH. - Bosc. - Twis. - Scan. - Five. - Bery. - Engr. - Blue. - Copp. - Vol. 2. Iden. - Silv. - Card. - Yell. - Stoc. - Glor. - Musg. - Nobl. - Reig. - Croo. - Resi. - Gree. - Vol. 3. Gold. - Empt. - Norw. - Danc. - Soli. - Prio. - Blac. - Chas. - SixN. - 3Stu. - Miss. - Abbe. - Vol. 4. RedC. - Seco. - Wist. - Bruc. - Devi. - Lady. - Thor. - Maza. - Cree. - Last.

1864. ———. Oavkortad översättning fran engelska originalet av kand. Ragnar Malmberg. Malmö: Världslitteraturens Förlag, [1930]. 186 p.
Contents: Five. - Blue. - Iden. - Bery. - Nobl.

1865. *Sherlock Holmes i Baskervilles hund.* Stockholm: Förl. Fickboken, [1943]. 128 p.

1866. *Sherlock Holmes och Dr. Watson.* [Oversättning av Nils Holmberg.] Stockholm: Albert Bonniers Förlag, [1955]. 452 p.
Contents: Empt. - Norw. - Soli. - Blac. - 3Stu. - Gold. - Miss. - Abbe. - His Last Bow (except Card). - Case Book.

1867. *Sherlock Holmes' upptäckter: Detektivberättelser.* Innehall: Den bla karbunkeln, Silver Blaze, Musgrave Ritualen, Dubbelgangaren. Med 12 illustrationer. Cedar Rapids, Iowa: N. Fr. Hansen's Boktryckeri, [ca. 1930]. 160 p.
Cover title: Den bla karbunkeln.
Contents: Blue. - Silv. - Musg. - Stoc.

1868. "En skandal i Böhmen," *Sherlock Holmes Detektiv-historier.* Stockholm: Skandias Bokförlag, [1909]. Vol. 33, p. 1-?
Contents: Scan.

1869. *En skandal i Böhmen och andra berättelser.* [Översättning av Nils Holmberg. Illustrationer av Sidney Paget. Omslag av Georg Lagerstedt.] Stockholm: Albert Bonniers Förlag, [1957]. 217 p. (De odödliga ungdomsböckerna, 34)
Contents: Scan. - RedH. - Bosc. - Engr. - Danc. - SixN. - Nava. - Fina.

1870. *Det spräckliga bandet och andra berättelser.* [Översättning av Nils Holmberg. Omslag av Ola Ericson.] Stockholm: Albert Bonniers Förlag, [1970]. 112 p. (Röda Ramen)
At head of title: Sherlock Holmes' äventyr.
Contents: Spec. - RedH. - Nava.

1871. *En studie i rött.* Översättning från engelska originalet av Ellen Ryding. Stockholm: Nordiska Förlaget, [1910]. 156 p. (Nordiska Förlagets 25-öresböcker, 2)
Contents: Stud.

1872. ———. Översättning från engelska originalet av Ellen Ryding. Stockholm: Nordiska Förlaget, [1918]. 192 p.

1873. ———. Översättning från engelska originalet av Ellen Ryding. Stockholm: Åhlén & Åkerlunds Förlag, [1927]. 221 p.

1874. ———. Oavkortad översättning direkt från engelska originalet av Viktor Olsson. Malmö: Världslitteraturens Förlag, [1928]. 123 p.

1875. ———. [Till svenska av Eva Håkanson. Illustrerad av Niels-Christian Hald.] Stockholm: Natur och Kultur, [1962]. 166 p. (Skattkammarbiblioteket)

1876. *En studie i rött. De fyras tecken.* Från engelskan av Curt Berg. [Illustrationer av Georg Lagerstedt och F. H. Townsend.] Stockholm: Albert Bonniers Förlag, [1944]. 305 p. (De odödliga ungdomsböckerna, 31)
At head of title: Sherlock Holmes.
Contents: Stud. - Sign.

1877. *En studie i rött, och andra berättelser.* ["En studie i rött" är översatt av Curt Berg. Ovriga berättelser av Nils Holmberg. Illustrationer av Georg Lagerstedt och Sidney Paget. Omslag av Georg Lagerstedt.] Stockholm: Albert Bonniers Förlag, [1956]. 198 p. (De odödliga ungdomsböckerna, 31)
At head of title: Sherlock Holmes äventyr.
Contents: Stud. - Glor. - Musg. - Spec.

1878. [*En studie i rött,* är översatt av Curt Berg. *Ovriga berättelser,* av Nils Holmberg.] Stockholm: Albert Bonniers Förlag, [1964]. 454 p. (Bonniers Folkbibliotek)
Title: *Sherlock Holmes.*
Contents: Stud. - Scan. - RedH. - Five. - Twis. - Blue. - Spec. - Engr. - Silv. - Yell. - Musg. - Gree. - Danc. - SixN. - Glor. - Fina.

1879. *Det tomma huset, och andra berättelser.* [Översättning av Nils Holmberg. Omslag och illustrationer av Georg Lagerstedt.] Stockholm: Albert Bonniers Förlag, [1958]. 247 p. (De odödliga ungdomsböckerna, 35)
At head of title: Sherlock Holmes äventyr.
Contents: Empt. - Norw. - Gold. - Seco. - 3Gar. - Reti. - Bruc. - Dyin. - Devi. - Last.

1880. *Tragedien på Birlstones herrgård: En ny Sherlock Holmes historia.* Bemyndigad översättning från engelskan av H. Flygare. Stockholm: Stockholmstidningens Tryckeri, 1915. 2 v. (129, 138 p.)
Title of vol. 2: *Fasans dal.*
Part 1 was serialized in the daily newspaper *Stockholmstidningen* from April

10-27, 1915, and Part 2 from September 11-October 1, 1915.
Contents: Vall.

English Readers

1881. *The Hound of the Baskervilles.* Abbreviated and simplified for use in schools. Stockholm (tr. i Danmark): Sv. Bokförl. (Bonnier), [1953]. 64 p. illus. (Easy Readers, 15)
————. New ed. Köpenhamn: Grafisk Forlag; Stockholm: Sv. Bokförlag (Bonnier), [1967]. 96 p. illus. (Easy Readers, C)
Based on a vocabulary of 1,800 words.

1882. *Selected Adventures and Memoirs of Sherlock Holmes.* Med förklarande anmärkningar utgifna af C. A. Ringenson, fil. dr., lektor vid Ostermalms högra allm. läroverk. Stockholm: Beijers Bokförlagsaktiebolag, [1904]. 130 p.
————. 2nd ed. Stockholm: Svenska Bokförlaget Bonniers, 1929. 133 p.
————. 3rd ed. 1954. 128 p.
Contents: RedH. - Iden. - Blue. - Stoc. - Gree.

1883. *The Speckled Band: A Sherlock Holmes Story.* Simplified for use in schools. Stockholm: Svenska Bokförlaget (Bonniers), [1958]. 16 p. illus. (Beginners' Books, 4)

1884. *The Speckled Band.* Simplified for use in schools. New ed. Köpenhamn: Grafisk Forlag; Stockholm: Sv. Bokförlag (Bonnier), 1967. 48 p. illus. (Easy Readers, A)
————. Simplified for use in schools and for private study. New ed. Köpenhamn: Grafisk Forlag; Stockholm: Sv. Bokförlag (Bonnier), 1968. 48 p. illus. (Easy Readers, A)
Based on a vocabulary of 500 words.

1885. *A Study in Scarlet.* Med anmärkningar av Hugo Hultenberg, lektor vid högre realläroverket på Norrmalm. Uppsala: Askerbergs Bokförlagsaktiebolag, [1914]. 139 p.
————. New ed. Stockholm: Fritzes Bokförlag, [1925]. 135 p. (Modern English Authors, 3)

1886. Levin, Erik. *Ordlista till Adventures and Memoirs of Sherlock Holmes by Conan Doyle.* [Word List to . . .] Utgivna av C. A. Ringenson. Stockholm: Beijer, [1907]. 33 p.
————. ————. 3rd ed. Stockholm: Albert Bonniers Forlag, [1952]. 30 p.

Parodies and Pastiches

1887. [Ekelöf, Tage.] *Nya Sherlock Holmes äventyr.* Stockholm: Internationell Litteratur, 1951. 156 p.

1888. Hellberg, Eira. *Gwendoline Carrs sällsamma protokoll: Sherlock Holmes tillägnad.* Stockholm: Svenska Andelsförlaget, 1919. 164 p.
"The detective-heroine's grandfather's mother was nurse to the young Sherlock, and the Carr family's negro-servant, Sam, had a maternal aunt who served as cook for Dr. Watson's father — then a gold-digger in California. No wonder the book is dedicated to the Master!" (Tage la Cour)

1889. [Serner, Martin Gunnar.] "Branden i Breuil Superieur," *D:r Zimmertürs bisarra möten,* av Frank Heller [pseud.] Stockholm: Albert Bonniers Förlag, [1929]. p. 151-181.
"A brilliant travesty of 'The Adventure of the Norwood Builder'—and a *tour de force.*" (Tage la Cour)

1890. [————.] "De ödesdigra skorna," *De ödesdigra skorna: Kriminalnoveller,* [av] Frank Heller [pseud.] Stockholm: Albert Bonniers Förlag, [1944]. p. 213-241.

1891. [Wagman, Oskar.] *Nya Sherlock Holmes historier,* av Sture Stig [pseud.] Stockholm: Wahlström & Widstrand, [1910]. 225 p.
"Very talented pastiches, especially of Dr. Watson, by a Swedish vicar." (Ted Bergman)

1892. [————.] *Sherlock Holmes i ny belysning,* av Sture Stig [psued.] Stockholm: Wahlström & Widstrand, [1908]. 232 p.
Six pastiches.

1893. *Sherlock Holmes detektiv-historier.* Stockholm: Skandias Bokförlag, [1908]. 28 v. (32 p. each)
Contents: 1. Den unga änkans hemlighet. - 2. Gåtan vid spelbordet. - 3. Procentarens dotter. - 4. De blodiga juvelerna. - 5. Människofällan i det gamla huset. - 6. Den försvunne brudgummen. - 7. Overkyparens goda väderkorn. - 8. Advokatens älskade. - 9. Ladyn med kanariebriljanten. - 10. Mannen med de sju hustrurna. - 11. Blackwell, Themsensjörövaren. - 12. Falskmyntarna i London. - 13. Drottningens spetsklädning. - 14. Guldgrävarehyddans hemlighet. - 15. Slavhandlarnas skatt. - 16. Blott en droppe bläck. - 17. Snille och vansinne. - 18. Huru Jack Uppskäraren blev tillfangatagen. - 19. Den förädiske Kodak. - 20. På Kafé National. - 21. Den polske juden. - 22. En adlig långfingrad person. - 23. Spöket i Milster Castle. - 24. I kistan bredvid helvetesmaskinen. - 25. Den återuppstandne. - 26. Lumpsamlaren i Paris. - 27. Lady Ruths äktenskapsosämja. - 28. Oceana, luftens drottning.
A series of pastiches dealing with the adventures of Sherlock Holmes and his associate Harry Taxon. These stories have also appeared in German, Portuguese, and Spanish and are listed under those languages.

TELUGU

1894. [*Neraparisodhana.* Madras: Chandamama Publications, 1955.] 95 p.
Contents: Stud.

Parodies and Pastiches

1895. [Appala Narasimha Prasad, Tholeti, and Kōrāda Venkata Subbārāvu. *Nammunammakapō!*] 1963. iii, 73 p.
Based on Houn.

TURKISH

1896. *Baskerviller'in Köpegi.* Ceviren Selâmi İzzet Sedes. Istanbul: Hâdise Yayinevi, 1958. 223 p.

1897. ———. Ceviren Ender Gürol. Istanbul: Varik Yayinevi, 1963. 162 p.

1898. *Dörtlerin Esrari.* Ceviren Selâmi İzzet Sedes. Istanbul: Hâdise Yayinevi, 1958.] 124 p.
Contents: Sign.

1899. *Serlok Holmes.* İstanbul: Cocuk Yayinlari Müessesesi Matbaasi, 1959. 96 p. illus.

1900. *Sherlock Holmes: Calinan Vasiyetname.* İstanbul: Nebioglu Yayinevi, 1964. 65 p.

1901. *Zümrütlü Tac.* [Ankara: Kemal Uzcan, n.d.] 16 p. (Sherlock Holmes Serisiden, 22)
A very free translation of Bery.
No. 22 of a series that includes many pastiches.

Parodies and Pastiches

1902. *Sherlock Holmes: Karin Desen Jak.* İstanbul: Nebioglu Yayinevi, 1964. 64 p.

UKRAINIAN

1903. [*Pes Baskerviliv.* Roman perekl. z anglijs' koi. Kiiv. L. (z. beziehen: Berlin W 62, Kurfürstenstr. 83): Ukrain. Verlag, 1920.] 278 p. (Biblioteka Kriminal'nich romaniv, 1, 2)

1904. [*A Study in Scarlet.*] Edmonton, Alta.: Ukrainska Knyharnia, [n.d.] 112 p.

1905. [*Znak čotir'och.* Kiiv. L. (z. beziehen: Berlin W 62, Kurfürstenstr. 83): Ukrain. Verlag, 1920.] 179 p. (Biblioteka Kriminal'nich romaniv, 3)
Contents: Sign.

URDU

1906. [*Khali makan.* Tr. by Tirth Ram Firozpuri. Delhi: Narayan Dutta Sahgal & Sons, n.d.] 144 p.
Contents: Return.

1907. [*Vadi-i-Khauf.* Tr. by Tirth Ram Firozpuri. Delhi: Narayan Dutta Sahgal & Sons, n.d.] 364 p.
Contents: Vall.

UZBEK

1908. [*Čipor lenta.* Tr. by Mirziëd Mirzoidov. Taskent: Goslitizdat UzSSR, n.d.] 39 p.
Contents: Spec.

1909. [*Šerlok Holms qhaquida quikojalar.* Tr. by Vaqhob Rŭzimatov. Taškent: Ëš Gvardija, n.d.] 312 p. illus.
Contents: Case Book.

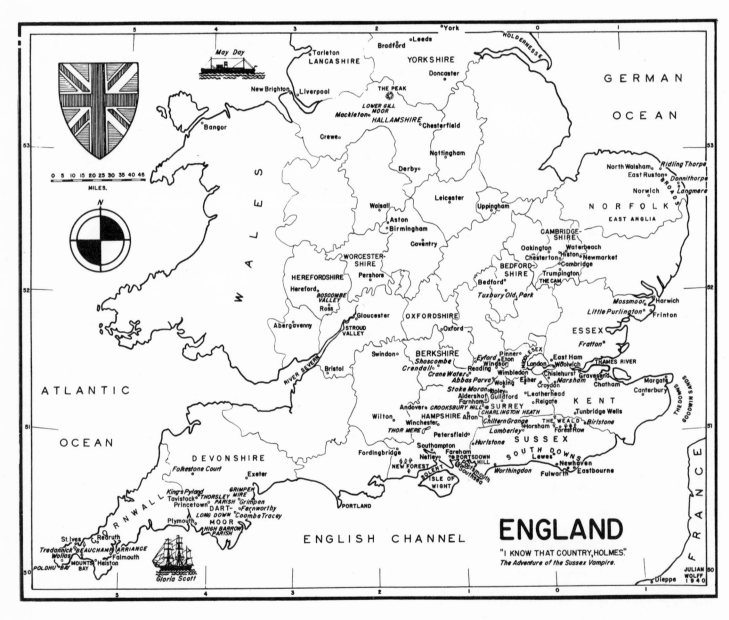

Sherlock Holmes's England. Map by Julian Wolff (4110).

98

V | The Writings about the Writings

Like the Sacred Writings, the writings about them are divided into three sections. The first section includes writings that cover several facets of the Canon; the second, writings that concern a particular tale; and the third, writings that deal with a specific subject not related to any single tale. In the third section, for example, the writings devoted primarily to Sherlock Holmes are listed under his name and then under various subheadings, such as *Education, Limits of Knowledge,* and *Retirement;* those concerned mainly with Dr. Watson appear under his name, and so on. Writings in which two or more subjects are discussed are listed under the most prominent subject if there is one, or in the *General and Miscellaneous* section.

It has not been possible to list the countless letters and *brief* items about the Canonical tales published in periodicals and newspapers. Only the more important and interesting ones have been included. Nor has it been possible to provide a minute subject breakdown comparable to that in Don Redmond's *Cumulative Index to the Baker Street Journal* and the annual supplements thereto (item 4186). Although the subject classification is rather broad, it should still be possible to locate the desired information. Since most personal names and titles appear in the two Indexes, they can also be used as a subject approach to the items in the bibliography.

Information about the content of the writings has been provided by quoting a summarizing statement by the author, by another Sherlockian, or by the compiler. In the case of most verses and songs (listed with the verses), a few quoted lines have been used in place of summaries. Bibliographies, chronologies, verses (including the tales in verse), etc., having to do with a particular tale or subject appear under the name of the tale or subject. Otherwise, they are listed under general headings such as *Bibliographies, Chronologies,* and *Verses.* An exception are the quizzes, which are all listed under one heading.

A General and Miscellaneous

1910. Ahlgren, Stig. "Hur och varför privatdetektiven med Sherlock Holmes blivit en nutidslegend," *Vecko-Journalen* [Stockholm] (January 2, 1969).
————. ————, *BSCL*, No. 7 (1969), 15-16.
"How and why the private detective Sherlock Holmes has become a present legend."

1911. Almqvist, Josef. "Vem var Sherlock Holmes?" ["Who Was Sherlock Holmes?"] *Aftonbladet* [Stockholm] (July 10, 1950).
————. ————, *BSCL*, No. 3 (1964), 12-16.
A retrospective look at the Canon in the year 6950.

1912. Amis, Kingsley. "My Favorite Sleuths: A Highly Personal Dossier on Fiction's Most Famous Detectives," *Playboy,* 13, No. 12 (December 1966), 145, 343-344, 346-349.
A discussion of the Master and his prodigies.

1913. Anderson, Sir Robert. "Sherlock Holmes, Detective, As Seen by Scotland Yard," *T. P.'s Weekly,* 2, No. 47 (October 2, 1903), 557-558.
————. ————, *VH*, 4, No. 2 (April 1970), 2-4.
Contents: Story interest and logic. - Some exaggeration and absurdity. - Sherlock Holmes and Scotland Yard. - Sir Conan Doyle's real aim. - Sherlock Holmes and the police. - Scotland Yard's real problem. - Holmes's contempt for law. - Felony-compounding.

1914. Andrew, C. R., and Page Heldenbrand. *Two Baker Street Akronisms.* Summit, N.J.: The Pamphlet House for the Sherlock Holmes Society of Akron, Ohio, 1945. 11 p.
Contents: The Strange Case of Colonel

99

General and Miscellaneous

Moran, by C. R. Andrew. - The Duplicity of Sherlock Holmes, by Page Heldenbrand.

1915. Atholl, Justin. "The Immortal Detective: A Contribution to Holmesology," *Chambers's Journal,* 18 (September 1949), 541-543.

1916. Attorps, Gösta. "Ansiktet på duken" ["The Face on the Canvas"], *Ungdomsskeppen.* Stockholm: Wahlström & Widstrand, [1944]. p. 20-30.

1917. Baring-Gould, William S. " 'I . . . Have Even Contributed to the Literature of the Subject,' " *The Annotated Sherlock Holmes.* New York: Clarkson N. Potter, [1967]. Vol. 1, chap. 3, p. 23-26.
A review of the critical milestones in the writings about the Writings.

1918. ———. " 'I Hear of Sherlock Everywhere Since You Became His Chronicler,' " *The Annotated Sherlock Holmes.* New York: Clarkson N. Potter, [1967] . Vol. 1, chap. 1, p. 3-18.
A beautifully illustrated introductory chapter on the literary agent and the first appearances of the tales.

1919. ———. *Sherlock Holmes of Baker Street: A Life of the World's First Consulting Detective.* New York: Clarkson N. Potter, Inc., [1962]. 336 p.
———. ———. New York: Bramhall House, [c.1962]. 336 p.
———. ———. New York: Popular Library, 1963. ix, 300 p.
———. *Sherlock Holmes: A Biography of the World's First Consulting Detective.* With 9 portraits, a facsimile of the alleged will, and 21 other illustrations. London: Rupert Hart-Davis, 1962. 284 p.
———. *Moi, Sherlock Holmes.* Traduit de l'anglais par Claude Frégnac. Paris: Buchet / Chastel, [1964]. 302 p.
———. *Er, Sherlock Holmes, Und Seine Denkwürdigsten Fälle Die erste Biographie des ersten Detektivs der Welt.* [Ins Deutsche übertragen von Elisabeth und Hans Herlin. Hamburg: Nannen-Verlag GmbH, 1965.] 198 p.
Reviews: BSG, 1, No. 3 (1961), 4 (Peter A. Ruber); *BSP,* No. 4 (October 1965), 3-4 (Chris Redmond); *Edmonton Journal* (October 28, 1962) (Hugh MacLennan); *Garroter,* 1, No. 1 (March 1972), 9-10 (Glenn Shea); *Grue,* No. 30 (August 1962), 3 (Dean Grennell), and reprinted in *The SHsf Fanthology One* (The Professor Challenger Society, 1967), 27-28; *Guardian* (September 21, 1962), 6; *Library Journal,* 87 (May 1, 1962), 1780 (J. F. Harvey); *National Review,* 13 (November 6, 1962), 357-358 (Guy Davenport); *New Statesman,* 64 (September 28, 1962), 420 (G. W. Stonier); *New York Herald Tribune Books* (April 8, 1962), 12 (Richard Martin Stern), and reprinted in *CPBook,* No. 19 (June 1969), 375; *New York Times Book Review* (May 13, 1962), 13 (Anthony Boucher); *SHJ,* 6, No. 1 (Winter 1962), 29 (Lord Donegall); *Spectator,* 209 (October 12, 1962), 569 (Rosalie Packard); *Springfield Republican* (May 27, 1962), 4D (R. F. Husband); *Time & Tide,* 43 (September 20-27, 1962), 25-26 (Miles Melrose); *Times Literary Supplement* (October 26, 1962), 829, and reprinted in *BSJ,* 12, No. 2 (June 1962), 123.

1920. ———. "Side-Lights on *Sherlock Holmes of Baker Street*: An Adventure in the Higher (?) Criticism," *BSJ,* 13, No. 2 (June 1963), 74-76.
Excerpts from reviews of the author's book.

1921. Barzun, Jacques. "Five Thousand Orange Pips, or the Seeds of Pedantry," *The American Scholar,* 37, No. 4 (Autumn 1968), 680, 682, 684.
———. ———, *CPBook,* 4, No. 16 (Fall 1968), 312-314.
A long and scholarly review of *The Annotated Sherlock Holmes.*

1922. ———. "Not 'Whodunit?' But 'How?' First Aid for Critics of the Detective Story," *The Saturday Review of Literature,* 27, No. 45 (November 4, 1944), 9-11.
———. [Revised and enlarged with title]: "From *Phèdre* to Sherlock Holmes," *The Energies of Art: Studies of Authors Classic and Modern,* [by] Jacques Barzun. New York: Harper & Brothers, [1956]. p. 303-323.
"How to tell Holmes from Hawkshaw: the true detective story as distinguished from stories merely of murder, mystery and detectives." (Edgar W. Smith)

1923. Baxter, Frank Condie. "A Reminiscence of Sherlock Holmes," *The Hound of the Baskervilles.* Garden City, N.Y.: Doubleday, Page & Co., 1926.
———. "Introduction to *The Hound of the Baskervilles, " BSJ,* 12, No. 2 (June 1962), 106-112. (Incunabulum)
———. "The Hound of the Baskervilles," *West by One and by One.* San Francisco: Privately Printed, 1965. p. 27-33.
The author visits 221B Baker Street and chats with Watson about Holmes's retirement, Sir Arthur, and the part he played when, as a youth, he was employed by Holmes to trace a mutilated copy of *The Times* in Houn.

1924. Bell, H. W., ed. *Baker-Street Studies.* [London]: Constable & Co. Ltd., 1934. x, 223 p.
Limited to 500 copies.
———. ———. [Foreword by Edgar W. Smith.] Morristown, N.J.: The Baker Street

Irregulars, 1955. x, 223 p. (BSI Incunabula, No. 3)

Limited and facsimile edition of 350 copies.

Contents: Introductory Note, by H. W. Bell. - Explanation. - Holmes' College Career, by Dorothy L. Sayers. - Medical Career and Capacities of Dr. J. H. Watson, by Helen Simpson. - The Limitations of Sherlock Holmes, by Vernon Rendall. - The Singular Adventures of Martha Hudson, by Vincent Starrett. - The Mystery of Mycroft, by Ronald A. Knox. - Mr. Moriarty, by A. G. Macdonell. - Sherlock Holmes and the Fair Sex, by S. C. Roberts. - The Date of 'The Sign of Four,' by H. W. Bell. - Note on Doctor Watson's Wound, by H. W. Bell.

1925. Bell, Joseph. "The Adventures of Sherlock Holmes," *The Bookman* [London], 3 (December 1892), 79-81.

————. " 'Mr. Sherlock Holmes,' " *A Study in Scarlet.* London: Ward, Lock & Bowden, Ltd., 1893. p. xiii-xx.

————. ————, *BSJ* [OS], 2, No. 1 (January 1947), 45-49. (Incunabulum)

A review in which Holmes's prototype pays tribute to his favorite student and discusses the method of deductive reasoning.

1926. Bengtsson, Frans G. "Conan Doyle och anden i flasken" ["Conan Doyle and the Bottle Imp"], *Folk som sjöng, och andra essayer.* Illustrationer av Gunnar Brusewitz. Stockholm: Albert Bonniers Förlag, 1955.

————. ————, ————. Andra upplagan. Stockholm: P. A. Norstedt & Söners Förlag, [1955]. p. 115-123.

1927. Bentley, E. C. "Trent's Last Case," *Those Days.* London: Constable & Co., 1940. Chap. 9, p. 249-251.

————. Part of the section on Sherlock Holmes was quoted in a letter from James M. Sandoe and published in *BSJ* [OS], 1, No. 2 (April 1946), 207-208.

The author is critical of the exaggerated unreality of the character of Holmes and the extreme seriousness of Holmes and his imitators.

1928. Berman, Ruth, ed. *The SHsf Fanthology One.* The Professor Challenger Society, 1967. 32 p. (McArdle Press Publication, No. 3)

Contents: Preface. - The Dynamics of an Asteroid, by Robert Bloch. - Matter in Motion, by John Boardman. - Three (Sherlock Holmes at Camelot, The Case of the Incomplete Concept, Design Proposal: Sherlockian Playing Cards: Preliminary), by Dean Dickensheet. - Fundamental, My Dear Watson, by Dick Eney. - Review of *Sherlock Holmes of Baker Street,* by Dean Grennell. - Lupoff's Book Week, by Dick Lupoff. - Petrie Letter, by Bruce Pelz.

1929. ————. *The SHsf Fanthology 2.* Minneapolis, Minn.: The Professor Challenger Society, September 1971. 21 p. illus.

Contents: The Martian Who Hated People, by Edward Ludwig. - A Letter (Mycroft to S.), by Jon White. - Moriarty and the Binomial Theorem, by Doug Hoylman. - The Irregular Reviewer: "The Private Life of Sherlock Holmes," by Dean Dickensheet.

1930. ————. *The SHsf Fanthology 3.* Minneapolis, Minn.: The Professor Challenger Society, February 1972. 37 p. illus.

Contents: The Case of the Doctor Who Had No Business, or The Adventure of the Second Anonymous Narrator, by Richard A. Lupoff. - Annotations in Afghanistan, a discussion by members of Apa-L. - Holmes Was a Vulcan, by Priscilla Pollner. - A Limerick, by Mary Ellen Rabogliatti. - Sherlock Holmes in Oz, by Ruth Berman.

1931. Blakeney, T. S. *Sherlock Holmes: Fact or Fiction?* London: John Murray, [1932]. ix, 133 p.

————. ————. [Foreword by Edgar W. Smith.] Morristown, N.J.: The Baker Street Irregulars, 1954. ix, 133 p. (BSI Incunabula, No. 2)

Limited and facsimile edition of 350 copies.

Contents: Preface. - Mr. Sherlock Holmes. - Holmes and Scotland Yard. - The Literature Relating to Sherlock Holmes. - The Career of Sherlock Holmes: Chronological Survey. - Appendix I: 1. Watson's Second Marriage. - 2. Bibliography of Sherlock Holmes, As Revealed in Some Characteristic *Obiter Dicta.* - Appendix II: The Holmes-Moriarty Hypothesis.

1932. ————. "Some Disjecta Membra," *SHJ,* 4, No. 3 (Winter 1959), 101-103.

Contents: The Blue Carbuncle. - The Final Problem. - The Dutch Steamship "Friesland". - Maiwand and After.

1933. ————. "More Disjecta Membra," *SHJ,* 5, No. 2 (Spring 1961), 55-56.

Contents: The Gloria Scott. - Dead Sea Scrolls. - 221B.

1934. ————. "Disjecta Membra (Second Series)," *SHJ,* 8, No. 1 (Winter 1966), 16-17.

Contents: Copper Beeches. - Spats. - The Royal Mallows. - The Case Book. - R. F. May's "Botanical Enquiry". - Location of The Hound.

1935. Blegen, Theodore C. *The Crowded Box-Room: Sherlock Holmes As Poet.* La Crosse: Sumac Press, 1951. 49 p.

Limited to 300 copies.

Contents: Spotlight on 221B. - Sports and

General and Miscellaneous

General and Miscellaneous

Games. - Chains, Webs, Threads, Trains. - Animals and Nature. - Medicine, Mathematics, Music. - Industry and Business. - Buildings and Appurtenances. - History and Literature. - "And what is left . . .?" - Portrait of a Poet.

1936. ———, and E. W. McDiarmid. "Salute to Sherlock Holmes," *Sherlock Holmes: Master Detective.* Edited by Theodore C. Blegen & E. W. McDiarmid. La Crosse: Printed for the Norwegian Explorers, St. Paul & Minneapolis, 1952. p. 7-20.

Several reasons are given as to why the Sherlock Holmes adventures are among the most enjoyable of the world's literature.

1937. ———, ———, eds. *Sherlock Holmes: Master Detective.* La Crosse: Printed for the Norwegian Explorers, St. Paul & Minneapolis, 1952. 86 p.

Limited to 500 copies.

Contents: Salute to Sherlock Holmes, by Theodore C. Blegen & E. W. McDiarmid. - Along Comes Charles - or Was Sherlock Holmes a Sportsman? by Theodore C. Blegen. - Sherlock Holmes and the Law, by Stephen G. Palmer, III. - Did Sherlock Holmes Return? by E. W. McDiarmid. - The Adventure of the Tired Housewife, by Anne Oakins Rosso. - An East Wind Coming, by Willard Wilson.

1938. Boothroyd, J. B. "Baker Street Revisited, or The Case of the Unexplodable Myth," *Punch,* 220 (June 20, 1951), 738-739.

"A thoughtful analysis of the implications of the mythos; with commentary upon the Exhibition and quotations from Harvey Officer's *Baker Street Song Book.*" (Edgar W. Smith)

1939. Boucher, Anthony. "Baker Street Immortal," *The New York Times Book Review* (January 21, 1968), 1, 32-33.

———. ———, *CPBook,* 4, No. 14 (Winter 1968), 266-268.

A review of *The Annotated Sherlock Holmes* which also contains information on Holmes and Watson and Sherlockian scholarship.

1940. Bouvet, G. "Introduction," *Four Adventures of Sherlock Holmes.* Paris: Didier, 1958. p. 3-14.

Contents: 1. L'Homme. - 2. L'Oeuvre. - 3. Sherlock Holmes. - 4. Les Dernières Années. - Popularity of Sherlock Holmes. - Bibliographie. - Périodiques. - Sir Arthur Conan Doyle et Son Oeuvre.

1941. Brend, Barbara. " 'You Have Been in Afghanistan, I Perceive,' " *SHJ,* 9, No. 4 (Summer 1970), 131-132. illus.

A brief account of the author's trip, in August 1969, to Afghanistan, where she visited the teahouses and the Maiwand memorial for some trace of Holmes and Watson.

1942. Brend, Gavin. *My Dear Holmes: A Study in Sherlock.* London: George Allen & Unwin Ltd., [1951]. 183 p. illus.

Contents: Preface. - 1. Master Sherlock. - 2. Oxford or Cambridge. - 3. Before Baker Street. - 4. My Dear Watson. - 5. The Home of Holmes. - 6. The Early Eighties. - 7. Snow and Stains. - 8. My Dear Miss Morstan. - 9. My Dear Mrs. Watson. - 10. Marriage and Its Problems. - 11. Mainly Moriarty. - 12. Back to Baker Street. - 13. What Happened in '96. - 14. Back Again to Baker Street. - 15. My Dear Mrs. Watson the Second. - 16. His Last Bow. - Appendix: 1. Chronological Table. - 2. The Bibliography of Sherlock Holmes.

Reviews: BSJ, 1, No. 4 (October 1951), 138-139 (Christopher Morley); *SOS,* 4, No. 2 (July 1970), 2-3 (Thomas Drucker).

1943. Bristowe, W. S. "Sherlock Holmes Reaches His Century," Illustrations from the original drawings by Sidney Paget. *ICI Magazine* [London] (January 1954), 29-31.

"A pleasant and scholarly look at the Baker Street scene, with arguments for Oxford as the Master's college and for January, 1854, as the date of his birth." (Edgar W. Smith)

1944. Broun, Heywood. "Sherlock Holmes and the Pygmies," *The Woman's Home Companion,* 57 (November 1930), 21.

———. ———, *Profile by Gaslight.* Edited by Edgar W. Smith. New York: Simon and Schuster, 1944. p. 3-11.

———. ———, *Encore,* 7, No. 38 (April 1945), 468-474.

"No modern mystery writer known to me has succeeded in shaking off the influence of Holmes and Conan Doyle. Each of the popular detectives has assumed some of his attributes."

1945. Brown, Ivor. "The Immortal Shadow," *The Scotsman* (January 25, 1954).

———. ———, *CPBook,* 2, No. 5-6 (Summer-Fall 1965), 96.

"Sherlock Holmes the centenarian an absorbing study." (Subtitle)

1946. Burnett, Vivian. "The Shelving of Sherlock," *The Reader* (August 1905), 344-346.

"Few will deny that Sherlock Holmes is greater than Doyle. The name of the character is known in many a place where the author's name would scarcely be recognized."

1947. [Canby, Henry Seidel.] "Sherlock Holmes and After," *The Saturday Review of Literature,* 6, No. 52 (July 19, 1930), 1201.

An appraisal of the Canonical tales and other detective stories.

1948. Carr, John Dickson. "Hail, Holmes!" *The New York Times* (February 14, 1965), II, 1, 5.

———. ———, *CPBook*, 1, No. 3 (Winter 1965), 42-43.

"An excellent discussion of the Sherlock Holmes saga, obviously inspired by the opening of *Baker Street*." (Julian Wolff)

1949. Carter, John. "Detective Fiction," *New Paths in Book Collecting: Essays by Various Hands*. Edited with an introduction by John Carter. London: Constable & Co., 1934. p. 31-63.

———. ———, ———. New York: Charles Scribner's Sons, 1934. p. 31-63.

———. Published separately with title: *Collecting Detective Fiction*. London: Constable, [1939]. [31] p.

———. "Collecting Detective Fiction," *The Art of the Mystery Story*. Edited and with a commentary by Howard Haycraft. New York: Simon and Schuster, 1946. p. 453-475.

———. Reprint of 1st edition. Freeport, N.Y.: Books for Libraries Press, 1967. p. 31-63.

A brief summary of the history of the detective story, including the Sherlock Holmes period.

1950. Carvalho, Elysio de. *Sherlock Holmes no Brasil*. [Sherlock Holmes in Brazil.] Rio de Janeiro: Casa A. Moura, [1921]. 226 p.

Partial contents: Sherlock Holmes no Brasil. - A sciencia ao servico do crime. - Bertillon. - Sherlock Holmes nao é uma ficcao.

1951. Čechura, Rudolf. "Sherlock Holmes' Story," *Věda a technika mládeži* [Prague], No. 5 (1968), 166, 202-203, 240, 274, 315, 351, 387, 419, 441, 530, 567.

———. ———. *Nikdo nemá alibi*, [by] Rudolf Čechura. Praha: Práce, 1969. p. 88--109.

A treatise on Holmes, the Canon, the Sherlockian literature, the societies, etc.

1952. Chandler, Frank Wadleigh. "The Literature of Crime-Detection," *The Literature of Roguery*. In two volumes. Boston and New York: Houghton, Mifflin and Co., 1907. Vol. 2, chap. 13, p. 524-548. (The Types of English Literature. Edited by William Allan Neilson)

———. ———, ———. [One volume reprint edition.] New York: Burt Franklin, [1958].

Contains frequent references to the Sherlockian literature, in the chapter under this heading, for its outstanding place in the field.

1953. Chesterton, G. K. "Sherlock Holmes," *A Handful of Authors: Essays on Books and Writers*, by G. K. Chesterton. Edited by Dorothy Collins. London and New York: Sheed and Ward, 1953. p. 168-174.

———. ———, ———. New York: Kraus Reprint Co., 1969. p. 168-174.

Two critical essays that first appeared in *The Daily News* [London] in 1901 and 1907.

1954. ———. "Sherlock Holmes and God," *G. K.'s Weekly* (February 21, 1935), 403-404.

———. ———, *BSJ*, 15, No. 4 (December 1965), 216-217.

"Not once is there a glance at the human and hasty way in which the stories were written; not once even an admission that they ever were written. The real inference is that Sherlock Holmes really existed and that Conan Doyle never existed. If posterity only reads these latter books, it will certainly suppose them to be serious. It will imagine that Sherlock Holmes was a man. But he was not; he was only a god."

1955. [Christ, Jay Finley.] *Finch's Final Fling: Being the Last in the Series of Profound, If Not Startling Observations on the Sherlockian Scene*, by J. A. Finch, retired, and collected for posterity by J. Finley Christ, editor. New York; Copenhagen: The Candlelight Press, 1963. [22] p.

Limited to 200 copies.

Contents: Editorial Preface. - Testament of J. A. Finch. - Baby Sitter in Brass Buttons. - A Boo for the London *Times*. - Sherlock Was an Irishman. - Sherlock at a Wedding. - "It Won't Do," Said Sherlock. - Sherlock Holmes as Author. - Sherlock Holmes, Scientist. - Dogging the Footprints. - Sherlock's Slip of the Tongue. - The Case of the Chinaman's Chance. - Sherlock Comes to Grand Rapids. - Henry Baker's Old Hat. - How Are the Crops?

Reprints of Sherlockian sketches that appeared in "A Line o' Type or Two" in the *Chicago Tribune* from 1945 to 1947.

Review: SHJ, 6, No. 2 (Spring 1963), 61 (Lord Donegall).

1956. [———.] *Flashes by Fanlight*, by J. A. Finch [pseud.] Edited by Jay Finley Christ. [Chicago]: The Fanlight Press, 1946. [24] p.

Limited to 250 copies.

Contents: Editor's Foreword. - Sherlock Holmes Is Everywhere. - A Rare Fit of Laughter. - Names in Holmesian Tales. - Keeping Score on Sherlock Holmes. - Sherlock at the Phone. - Sherlock's Hangover. - Such Language, Dr. Watson! - Sherlock and the *Bible*. - Sherlock Pulls a Fast One. - Machinery of Detection. - In Defense of Sherlock. - Mme. Tussaud's Neighbor. - A House Facing East. - That House in Baker Street.

Contributions of "J. A. Finch" to "A Line o' Type or Two" in the *Chicago Tribune*.

1957. [———.] *Gleanings by Gaslight*, by J. A. Finch [pseud.] Edited by Jay Finley Christ.

[Chicago]: The Fanlight House, 1947. vi, 15 p.

Contents: Editor's Foreword. - The Portmans of Baker Street (November 9, 1946). - Baker Streets to Spare (August 31, 1946). - A Tree Grew in London (September 5, 1946). - Sherlock's Domicile: The Rooms (February 26, 1947). - Sherlock's Domicile: The Furnishings (March 1, 1947). - "B" Culture on Baker St. (January 14, 1947). - Irregular Scout on Baker Av. (January 25, 1947). - Sherlock as Pinup Man (December 13, 1946). - Profile with Pipe (September 6, 1946). - The Moon and Dr. Watson - I (March 22, 1947). - The Moon and Dr. Watson - II (April 8, 1947). - Sherlock's Friend Charlie (October 14, 1946).

Reprints from "A Line o' Type or Two" in the *Chicago Tribune* with a few additions and alterations.

1958. ———. *Soundings in the Saga.* [Chicago]: The Fanlight House, 1948. vi, 13 p.

Limited to 100 copies.

Contents: Explanatory. - "I am Sherlock Holmes". - Watson and Marriage. - An M.P. Writes to Baker Street. - Dr. Watson's Literary Agent. - Watson Reads the *Strand*. - Dr. Watson and Mr. Pickwick. - Sherlock and Pickwick. - The Sign of the Missing Four. - Sherlock Borrowed Something Blue. - A Case of Arrested Development. - A Baskerville Goes to the Dogs. - A Fast Man with a Sixpence (*Chicago Tribune*, July 21, 1948).

Eleven of the twelve notes were published for the first time.

1959. Clark, Henry C. "The Best Introduction to Holmes," *The Third Cab.* [Boston: The Speckled Band, 1960] p. 1-4.

The author tells how Samuel S. Drury, a Master of English at Pomfret School in Connecticut, introduced the boys in his dormitory to the Master Detective, and then Clark questions Holmes's judgment in protecting some of his clients and Watson's claim to being a swift runner.

1960. Clendening, Logan. "My Personal Recollections of Sherlock Holmes," *The University Review* [University of Kansas City], 4, No. 2 (Winter 1937), 80-87.

Firsthand observations by one who knew and loved his subject well.

1961. Cumings, Thayer. *Seven on Sherlock: Some Trifling Observations on the Greatest of All Private Consulting Detectives.* Privately Printed for The Five Orange Pips of Westchester County and Other Friends at Christmas, 1968. [39] p. illus.

Limited to 221 copies.

Contents: 1. Sherlock Holmes and Advertising. - 2. A Sheaf of Weird Telegrams. - 3. The Great Holmes Sale. - 4. A Check on Lady Frances. - 5. Concerning Holmes' Fees. - 6. Holmes and the U.S.A. - Constitution and Buy-Laws of The Baker Street Irregulars, by Elmer Davis. - 7. On an Unheralded Hero.

Review: BSP, No. 46 (April 1969), 2-3.

1962. Cutter, Robert A., ed. *Sherlockian Studies: Seven Pieces of Sherlockiana.* [Jackson Heights, N.Y.: The Baker Street Press, 1947.] 39 p.

Limited to 200 copies.

Contents: Foreword, by Edgar W. Smith. - The Sage of Baker Street, by Jay Finley Christ. - The Mystery of the 10-20 Thirt, by E. Tudor Gross. - The Eyes Have It - A Quiz, by Mycroft Holmes. - Sherlock Backs a Turkey, by Jay Finley Christ. - A Pair o' Mystery Reviews, by Howard Haycraft. - A Tall Adventure of Sherlock Holmes, by Robert A. Cutter. - Doctor Watson Speaks. - Sherlock Explains, by Robert A. Cutter. - Answers to the Quiz. - Envoy.

1963. *The Daily Californian Weekly Magazine,* 4, No. 9 (January 14, 1969), 7-14.

Partial contents: Sonnet: San Francisco to Sherlock, by Anthony Boucher. - Sherlock and His Friends: An Irregular Memoir, by Vincent Starrett. - Two 'New' Holmes Tales: The Field Bazaar; How Watson Learned the Trick, [with an introduction by Edgar W. Smith]. - The Case of the Acephalous Agronomist, [by Vincent Starrett]. - Speculations on The Hound, by T. S. Eliot. - Sherlock and Starrett: An Investigation of Sources, by Tom Collins.

1964. ———, 4, No. 18 (April 4, 1969), 11-18.

Partial contents: A Baker Street Folio: Five Letters from FDR, [with the original introduction by Edgar W. Smith]. - Sherlockian Sonnets, by Vincent Starrett.

1965. Daish, W. G. "Ponderings on Pitfalls, " *SHJ,* 5, No. 4 (Summer 1962), 118-119.

"Being originally a letter to the Editor of the *New Strand* Magazine."

1966. Dakin, D. Martin. *"Ten Literary Studies:* A Criticism," *SHJ,* 9, No. 4 (Summer 1970), 120-122; 10, No. 2 (Summer 1971), 67-68.

A critical and detailed commentary on the topics discussed by Trevor Hall in his book (item 2014).

1967. Davis, Elmer. "Introduction," *The Later Adventures of Sherlock Holmes.* New York: The Limited Editions Club, 1952. Vol. 1, p. v-xxi.

———. ———, *Introducing Mr. Sherlock Holmes.* Edited by Edgar W. Smith. Morristown, N.J.: The Baker Street Irregulars, 1959. [unpaged]

1968. De Blois, Frank. "Is Sherlock Holmes Alive?" *Parade* (April 20, 1952), 24-25.

"Londoners insist they see the sleuth after violent crimes are committed . . . ."

1969. DeCasseres, Benjamin. ["Holmes in the News"], *Sherlock Holmes Is in the News,* by Charles Honce. Mount Vernon, N.Y.: The Golden Eagle Press, 1944. p. 1.

————. ————, *For Loving a Book,* by Charles Honce. Mount Vernon, N.Y.: The Golden Eagle Press, 1945. p. 35-38.

————. ————, *CPBook,* 1, No. 4 (Spring 1965), 77.

A nostalgic divertissement on the Sacred Writings.

1970. Depken, Friedrich. *Sherlock Holmes, Raffles und ihre Vorbilder: Ein Beitrag zur Entwicklungsgeschichte und Technik der Kriminalerzählung.* Heidelberg: Carl Winter's Universitätbuchhandlung, 1914. xi, 105 p. (Anglistische Forschungen, Heft 41)

————. *Sherlock Holmes, Raffles, and Their Prototypes.* Translated and digested by Jay Finley Christ. [Chicago]: The Fanlight House, 1949. xii, 89 p.

This paper was developed from a seminar at Heidelberg in 1912-1914. The study is limited to the crime story as an offshoot of the criminal novel, tracing the history of the former in the 19th and 20th centuries. It begins with the questions: (1) How much did Poe influence Gaboriau? (2) How much did Conan Doyle adopt from these two? and (3) To what extent did Hornung depend on Doyle?

1971. Dettman, Bruce. "Gilchrist's Corner," *SOS,* 1-3, No. 2 (October 1966-July 1969).

Book and film reviews and notes of interest on Sherlockiana.

1972. Ditzel, Paul. "Sherlock Holmes Is Alive and Well!" *The Lion,* 52, No. 7 (January 1970), 14-16.

An informative article on the Holmes mystique and the reasons for its continued growth. Illustrated with sketches and a photograph of Basil Rathbone and Nigel Bruce.

1973. Donegall, Lord. *"The Blanched Soldier, The Devil's Foot* and *The Solitary Cyclist,"* *SHJ,* 7, No. 1 (Winter 1964), 13-16. (Baker Street and Beyond, No. 18)

A synopsis and discussion of these three adventures.

1974. ————. *"The Cardboard Box, The Five Orange Pips, The Copper Beeches,"* *SHJ,* 7, No. 3 (Winter 1965), 78-81. (Baker Street and Beyond, No. 19)

1975. [————.] "The Corollarogical Holmes," *SHJ,* 4, No. 1 (Winter 1958), 1-2. (Editorial)

A commentary on and a few verbal samples of Michael Harrison's research for his book *In the Footsteps of Sherlock Holmes* (item 2017).

1976. [————.] "Editorial Notes," *SHJ,* 3, No. 3- (Autumn 1957-).

Informative commentaries on current happenings in the Holmesian world. *SHJ's* counterpart to *BSJ's* "From the Editor's Commonplace Book" (items 2199 and 2262).

1977. ————. " 'Europe Was Ringing with His Name,' " *The New Strand,* 1, No. 3 (February 1962), 302-304. (Baker Street and Beyond, No. 3)

A word or two about the January cases (Vall, Chas, Abbe, Blan, RedC) and Julian Wolff's map of Europe.

1978. [————.] "For the Commonplace Book," *SHJ,* 3, No. 1- (Summer 1956-).

A regular department of the *Journal* in which newspaper and magazine articles, letters, and new items concerning Holmes and Watson are quoted. The column is comparable to W. T. Rabe's *CPBook* (item 4190).

1979. ————. "Fortryllelsen ved Sherlock Holmes sagaen" ["The Fascination of the Sherlock Holmes Saga"], Oversat af A. D. Henriksen. *Sherlock Holmes Årbog* II (1966), 7-14.

1980. ———— "Holmes Face-Saves—Unnoticed Bigamy—Red-Headed Problems —Fake Murders," *The New Strand,* 1, No. 12 (November 1962), 1441-1443. (Baker Street and Beyond, No. 12)

A discussion of Resi, Nobl, RedH, and Thor.

1981. ————. "Lunatic Banker's Royal Client—Dr. Watson Tries Semi-Fiction," *SHJ,* 6, No. 2 (Spring 1963), 46-49. (Baker Street and Beyond, No. 16)

A discussion of Bery, 3Stu, and the Oxford-Cambridge problem.

1982. ————. *"A Scandal in Bohemia* and *Wisteria Lodge,"* *SHJ,* 6, No. 3 (Winter 1963), 81-84. (Baker Street and Beyond, No. 17)

A synopsis and commentary on these two adventures.

1983. ————. "The Spectral Hound," *The New Strand,* 1, No. 11 (October 1962), 1300-1302. (Baker Street and Beyond, No. 11)

A discussion of Glor, Sign, and Houn.

1984. ————. "A Study in Ignorance," *SHJ,* 3, No. 1 (Summer 1956), 1.

The first editorial by the "new editor and his Violet Hunter."

General and Miscellaneous

General and Miscellaneous

1985. ———. "Too Hot to Mollies?—Those Phoney Ciphers—Bank for Blan," *The New Strand*, 2, No. 2 (February 1963), 1717-1720. (Baker Street and Beyond, No. 15)

A discussion of Vall, Abbe, RedC, and Blan.

1986. ———. "A Treaty for Breakfast—Pig-sticking in London—The Twist-Again Men," *The New Strand*, 1, No. 9 (August 1962), 1048-1050. (Baker Street and Beyond, No. 9)

A discussion of Nava, Blac, and Danc.

1987. ———. "Tsutsugamushi—The Biblical Holmes—Tie-Pin from Vic. R. I.—Wot, No Vampires?" *The New Strand*, 1, No. 13 (December 1962), 1569-1572. (Baker Street and Beyond, No. 13)

A commentary on Dyin, Gold, and Bruc.

1988. ———. "Wives Galore—A Tragi-Comedy—Multiple Blood Stains," *The New Strand*, 2, No. 1 (January 1963), 1623-1625. (Baker Street and Beyond, No. 14)

A discussion of Sign, Miss, and Seco.

1989. Doyle, Adrian Conan. ["Letter"], *The Daily Telegraph* [London] (October 8, 1955), 6.

———. ———, *SHJ*, 2, No. 4 (Winter 1955), 19-20.

A reply to E. P. Greenwood's letter to the *Telegraph* (October 1, p. 6) in which Mr. Greenwood suggests that the Holmes stories are read only by "middle-aged and old-fashioned people."

1990. Dunbar, Robin. *The Detective Business.* Chicago: Charles H. Kerr & Co., 1909. 29 p.

Contents: The Detective Business. - Sherlock Holmes Up-To-Date. - A Detective Among Philosophers. - Is Sherlock Holmes True to Life?

1991. Eliot, T. S. *"The Complete Sherlock Holmes Short Stories,"* *The Criterion*, 8, No. 32 (April 1929), 552-556.

———. ———, *SHJ*, 7, No. 3 (Winter 1965), 82-83.

A review, in the form of an essay, of the John Murray short story omnibus in which Mr. Eliot states that "every writer owes something to Holmes. And every critic of The Novel who has a theory about the reality of characters in fiction would do well to consider Holmes."

1992. Elkins Park Junior High School. Section 68. *Baker Street Gazette.* Edited by Richard Gerber. November 15, 1967. 17 p. illus.

"The Baker Street Gazette with its magazine supplement, *The Londoner,* were projects of an 8th grade English class at Elkins Park Junior High School in Elkins Park, Pennsylvania. The students read *The Adventures of Sherlock Holmes* by Sir Arthur Conan Doyle and created this newspaper based on these stories and other works of Doyle." (Jacqueline M. Larkin)

1993. ———. *The Londoner.* Edited by Richard Fox. November 15, 1967. 18 p. illus.

1994. ———. Section 78. *Better Holmes & Guardians.* Edited by Cindy Kauffman and Dale Armstrong. November 13, 1967. 53 p. illus.

1995. Elwin, Malcolm. "The Romantics," *Old Gods Falling.* London: Collins, 1939. Chap. 8, pt. 1, p. 264-267.

———. ———, ———. New York: The Macmillan Co., 1939. p. 264-267.

Partial contents: Schoolboys' favourites. - Conan Doyle, Sherlock Holmes, and the *Strand Magazine.* - Doyle's career as a novelist.

1996. Engholm, Kaj. " 'Which Detective Novel Do You Like Best of All?' " *IR*, 5, No. 11 (November 1965), 1-3.

A laudatory discussion by a Danish Sherlockian of the Canonical tales and their common denominator—the introduction or opening to each of them.

1997. Evans, Laurence. "The Detective in Fiction," *Coming Events in Britain* (December 1958), 16-19, 52.

A beautifully illustrated article on the great detectives: Sherlock Holmes, Sergeant Cuff, Father Brown, Lord Peter Wimsey, and Hercule Poirot.

1998. Evans, Wainwright. "Was There a Real Sherlock Holmes?" Illustrated by Paul Calle. *Saga*, 8, No. 3 (June 1954), 51-53, 78-79.

———. Condensed with title: "Is Sherlock Holmes Alive?" *The Reader's Digest*, 65, No. 388 (August 1954), 87-89.

"Generations of loyal admirers have spent money, time and effort to breathe life into the greatest sleuth in fiction—and they've succeeded."

1999. Fernández, Carlos Cuenca. "La verdadera historia de Sherlock Holmes" ["The True Story of Sherlock Holmes"] *Misterio* [México, D. F.], 74 (August 1940), 104-108.

A careless but well-intentioned account of Drs. Doyle and Bell, the *Strand,* etc.; first published in Spain about 1930.

2000. Finer, Cherry. "Three Holmesian Problems," *Illustrious Client's Third Case-Book.* Edited by J. N. Williamson and H. B. Williams. [Indianapolis, Ind.: The Illustrious Clients, 1953.] p. 133-134.

"Once, at least, in every ardent Sherlockian's life, he puzzles over three problems—in order of importance, the question of the compass in 'The Musgrave

Ritual,' the question of the Jezail bullet in Watson's arm or leg, and the time at which Holmes decided to become a detective."

2001. The Five Orange Pips. *The Best of the Pips: A Collection of the Writings About the Writings,* by members of The Five Orange Pips, Scion Society of The Baker Street Irregulars. Westchester County, N.Y.: The Five Orange Pips, 1955. x, 114 p.
Contents: Introduction, by Richard Warner Clarke. - A Trilogy, by Richard Warner Clarke. - The Rooms in Baker Street, by Frank A. Waters. - Upon the Probable Number of Cases of Mr. Sherlock Holmes, by Frank A. Waters. - The Old Shikari: Prolegomena to a Memoir of Colonel Sebastian Moran, by Edgar W. Smith. - The Crown Diamond, by James Montgomery. - Meditations of Martha, by Owen P. Frisbie. - On the Origin of the Hound of the Baskervilles, by Owen P. Frisbie. - Sherlock to Mycroft, by Owen P. Frisbie. - Colonel Warburton's Madness, by Norman W. Ward. - Report of a Recent Conversation in a Remote Cottage on the South Downs, by Norman W. Ward. - Sherlock Holmes and Advertising, by Thayer Cumings. - Don't Write - Telegraph! by Thayer Cumings. - Dr. Mortimer Before the Bar, by Benjamin S. Clark. - The Pathological Holmes, by Benjamin S. Clark.
Reviews: SOS, 2, No. 1 (October 1967), 2-3 (Bruce Dettman); *SHJ,* 2, No. 4 (Winter 1955), 35 (Colin Prestige).

2002. Fredman, L. E. "Prolegomena to a Literary Science," *Carnival* [Tulane University], 1, No. 2 (Winter 1959).
————. ————, *Quadrant* [Sydney, Australia], 6, No. 4 (1962), 67-72.
————. Reprinted in part with title: "A Note on Watson's Youth," *SHJ,* 5, No. 3 (Winter 1961), 87.
A scholarly survey of the Sherlockian scene and the dating of Watson's marriage to Mary Morstan as a sample problem.

2003. Furneaux, Rupert. "Doubtful Identities," *The World's Strangest Mysteries: Happenings That Have Intrigued and Baffled Millions.* London: Odhams Press Ltd., [1961]. p. 235-247.

2004. Gardner, Erle Stanley. " 'Come Right In, Mr. Doyle,' " *The Atlantic Monthly,* 180, No. 3 (September 1947), 102-104.
"Mr. Doyle, in Hollywood, learns from a cinemagnate what the Sherlock Holmes tales really need to pep them up and give them box-office appeal." (Edgar W. Smith)

2005. Gardner, Ralph. "Baker Street and the Bible," *The Hibbert Journal,* 50 (April 1952), 283-286.
A pragmatic view of the "reality" of Sherlock Holmes and Jesus Christ.

2006. Gerteis, Walter. "Sherlock Holmes kann nicht sterben" ["Sherlock Holmes Cannot Die"], *Detektive, ihre Geschichte im Leben und in der Literatur.* [München]: Heimeran Verlag, [1953]. p. 111-130.
Contents: The Rare Myth of a Whole Century. - Holmes Returns from the Dead. - "I am the last court of appeals for all doubtful cases." - The Unattainable Master of Deduction. - Nick Carter, the Sherlock Holmes of the "Small Readers."

2007. Gore-Booth, Sir Paul. "My Cup of Tea—Sherlock Holmes," *BSJ,* 12, No. 3 (September 1962), 157-161.
"The text of a radio broadcast given by the High Commissioner for the United Kingdom [over the Indian Radio, New Delhi, on June 5, 1962]. Although not addressed primarily to advanced Sherlockians, its delightful style makes it of interest to all." (Julian Wolff)

2008. ————. "Sherlock Holmes," *SHJ,* 5, No. 3 (Winter 1961), 70-73.
Contents: Oxford or Cambridge? - Holmes's Life. - Watson: Army and Marriages. - Conan Doyle Problem. - The New Detection. - Never Dull. - Fact or Fiction?
An address delivered at St. Stephens College, Delhi, India, on August 8, 1961, by a distinguished member of the Sherlock Holmes Society of London that is "in the highest Sherlockian tradition" (Julian Wolff) and is "the perfect novice's introduction to the study of the Holmes-Watson Saga" (Lord Donegall).

2009. Grazebrook, O. F. *Studies in Sherlock Holmes.* [London: Privately Printed, ca. 1949.] 7 v.
Contents: Vol. 1. Oxford or Cambridge. - Vol. 2. Politics and Premiers. - Vol. 3. Royalty. - Vol. 4. Dr. Watson and Rudyard Kipling. - Vol. 5. The Author of the Case Book. - Vol. 6. Something of Dr. Watson. - Vol. 7. The Bohemian Marriage.

2010. "The Greatest Gumshoe," *Newsweek,* 54, No. 7 (August 24, 1959), 86-87.
An illustrated commentary on the centennial of Sir Arthur Conan Doyle.

2011. Green, Roger Lancelyn. "Dr. Watson's First Critic, or 'The Adventure of the Hoaxed Detective,' " *SHJ,* 3, No. 4 (Summer 1958), 8-9.
A brief discussion, with extensive quotations, of three articles by Andrew Lang, "the first critic ever to take the cases of Mr. Sherlock Holmes as the actual reports of Dr. Watson rather than the fictional flings of Dr. Doyle."

2012. Haines, Helen E. "The Lure of Crime,"

What's in a Novel. New York: Columbia University Press, 1942. Chap. 10, p. 226-228.

"The Sherlock Holmes volumes are classics in their originality, skill of workmanship, their sustained interest and plausibility. Doyle still remains the master of the field."

2013. Hall, Trevor H. *The Late Mr. Sherlock Holmes & Other Literary Studies.* London: Gerald Duckworth & Co. Ltd., [1971]. x, 142 p. illus.

————. ————. New York: St. Martin's Press, [1971]. x, 142 p. illus.

Contents: List of Illustrations [by Sidney Paget]. - List of Abbreviated References. - Introduction. - 1. Sherlock Holmes: Ascetic or Gourmet? - 2. The Book-Collector. - 3. Dr. Watson's Marriages. - 4. Sherlock Holmes and Andrew Lang. - 5. Dr. Watson and the English Counties. - 6. The Problem of the Unpublished Cases. - 7. The Late Mr. Sherlock Holmes. - Appendix. Mea Culpa. - Index of Cases. - Index of Names, Places, and Publications.

Reviews: Mystery Reader's Newsletter, 5 (November - December 1971), 39 - 40 (Stanley Carlin); *SHJ,* 10, No. 2 (Summer 1971), 66 (Lord Donegall).

2014. ————. *Sherlock Holmes: Ten Literary Studies.* London: Gerald Duckworth & Co. Ltd., [1969]. xii, 157 p. illus.

————. ————. New York: St. Martin's Press, [1970]. xii, 157 p. illus.

Contents: Preface. - Introduction. - 1. The Reminiscences of John H. Watson, M.D. - 2. The Early Years of Sherlock Holmes. - 3. A Note on Sherlock Holmes's Schooling. - 4. The Erudition of Sherlock Holmes. - 5. Sherlock Holmes's University and College. - 6. Sherlock Holmes, Madness and Music. - 7. A College Friendship? - 8. The Documents in the Case. - 9. A Note on *The Priory School.* - 10. The Love Life of Sherlock Holmes. - Indexes.

"The first major addition to the Higher Criticism since Baring-Gould's monumental *The Annotated S.H.*" (Lord Donegall)

Reviews: New York Times Book Review (January 10, 1971), 22 (Allen J. Hubin); *SOS,* 5, No. 1 (January 1971), 3-7 (Thomas Drucker); *SHJ,* 9, No. 3 (Winter 1969), 105-106 (Lord Donegall); 9, No. 4 (Summer 1970), 120-122 (Martin Dakin); 10, No. 1 (Winter 1970), 22-24 (Trevor H. Hall); 10, No. 2 (Summer 1971), 67-68 (Martin Dakin); 10, No. 2 (Summer 1971), 68 (Trevor H. Hall); *Sherlockiana,* 14, Nr. 3 (1969), 9.

2015. [Hansen, Robert.] *Kriminalromaner,* af Jens Anker [pseud.] København: Forlaget Forum, 1948. p. 55-77.

Twenty-three pages of the author's book on mystery and detective stories are devoted to the Canonical tales.

2016. Harrison, Michael. "America Discovers Sherlock Holmes," *The Queen* (January 27, 1954), 26, 45.

————. ————, *CPBook,* 3, No. 10 (Fall 1966), 201-202.

An article on the Great Detective's centenary explaining why this country has taken up the Holmes Cult.

2017. ————. *In the Footsteps of Sherlock Holmes.* London: Cassell & Co., 1958. xii, 292 p. illus.

————. ————. New York: Frederick Fell, Inc., [1960]. xii, 292 p. illus.

Contents: A Foreword Which Is Also an Explanation. - 1. Introducing Mr. Sherlock Holmes's London. - 2. Mr. Sherlock Holmes Strolls Along the Strand. - 3. As Famous as Baker Street. - 4. London After 1878. - 5. Travel in Victorian London. - 6. We Meet Dr. Watson. - 7. Holborn in the Eighties. - 8. Where Holmes and Watson Met. - 9. Baker Street in the Eighties. - 10. '221B,' Baker Street. - 11. Keeping Up Appearances. - 12. How London Lived in the Eighties. - 13. Out Together. - 14. Their First Case Together. - 15. A Study in Suburbia. - 16. A Respectable Suburb. - 17. More Suburbia. - 18. A Look at Southwark and Beyond. - 19. Safer in a Hansom. - 20. Old Scotland Yard and Whitehall. - 21. Back to the West End. - 22. North-West Passage. - 23. Out of London. - 24. The County of Surrey. - 25. Beyond the Surrey Border. - 26. Again Surrey. - 27. Affairs of State. - 28. Methods of Approach. - 29. Back to London. - 30. Holmes the Musician. - 31. Harrovian Interlude. - 32. Due North. - 33. The Garden of England. - 34. Towards the Setting Sun. - Source Material. - Index.

"Sherlock Holmes is studied by an admirer who views Holmes and his colleague Dr. Watson against the background of Victorian England. Places and people mentioned in the stories are discussed, the contemporary scene described in detail, and Holmes's origins and career dissected." (*Booklist*)

Reviews: Booklist, 56 (June 15, 1960), 622; *Christian Science Monitor* (June 2, 1960), 11 (S. B. Bellows); *DCC,* 8, No. 2 (February 1972), 11 (Robert W. Hahn); *IR,* 1, No. 4 (September 1961), 5 (Poul Arenfalk); *Library Journal,* 85 (July 1960), 2593 (E. F. Walbridge); *Manchester Guardian* (January 9, 1959), 6 (Roger Fulford); *New York Times* (July 12, 1960), 33 (Charles Poore), and reprinted in *CPBook,* 3, No. 11 (Winter 1967), 210; *New York Times Book Review* (September 4, 1960), 13 (Anthony Boucher); *San Francisco Chronicle* (July 21, 1960), 31; *SHJ,* 4, No. 1 (Winter 1958), 1-2 (Lord Donegall); *Sherlockiana,* 14, Nr. 4 (1969), 14-15; *Wisconsin Library Bulletin,* 56 (July 1960), 220; *World - Herald Magazine* [Omaha] (April 9, 1972), 34 (Victor P. Hass).

2018. ——. ——. [Revised ed.] Newton Abbot: David & Charles, [1971]. 292 p.

——. ——. New York: Drake Publishers, 1972. 292 p.

Contents same as in item 2017, but includes an additional foreword and several new photographs.

2019. Hartman, Harry. *The Holy Quire.* [Illustrated by William Dixon. Culver City, Calif.: Luther Norris, December 1970.] 48 p.

Limited to 300 copies.

Contents: This Land, This England. - Sacred Litany. - I Met Holmes in London. - Holmes Revisited (or The Saga of the Unrecorded Cycle). - Afghan A'Gley. - Watson Pleads the Fifth Amendment. - Leave Us Face It. - The Adventure of the Pickled Hand. - The Beaune of Contention. - Five Pillows of Wisdom. - Holmes and Automation. - The Valley of Cheer.

2020. Haycraft, Howard, ed. *The Art of the Mystery Story: A Collection of Critical Essays.* New York: Simon and Schuster, 1946. ix, 545 p.

——. ——. New York: Grosset & Dunlap, [1961]. ix, 565 p. (The Universal Library, UL91)

Contains numerous references to Holmes, including: Sherlock Holmes and His Influence, by Dorothy L. Sayers. - The Private Life of Sherlock Holmes, by Vincent Starrett. - Watson Was a Woman, by Rex Stout.

2021. ——. "Introduction: The Time, the Place, and the Man," *Sherlock Holmes' Greatest Cases.* New York: Franklin Watts, [1966]. p. 1-16.

——. ——. Published separately and presented by the author to the Irregulars at their annual dinner on January 5, 1968. 16 p.

——. ——, *Sherlock Holmes' Greatest Cases.* New York: Bantam Books, [September 1968]. p. 1-10.

2022. ——. "Introduction: The True Story of Sherlock Holmes," *The Boys' Sherlock Holmes.* New York and London: Harper & Brothers, 1936. p. ix-xix.

——. ——, *Introducing Mr. Sherlock Holmes.* Edited by Edgar W. Smith. Morristown, N.J.: The Baker Street Irregulars, 1959. [unpaged]

——. ——, *The Boys' Sherlock Holmes.* New and enlarged ed. New York and Evanston: Harper & Row, [1961]. p. ix-xix.

2023. ——. "Mr. Holmes of Baker Street: Three New Volumes Pay Varied Homage to London's Greatest Bloodhound," *The New York Times Book Review* (April 2, 1944), 1, 15.

A review of the 1944 Sherlock Holmes trilogy: *Profile by Gaslight, The Misadventures of Sherlock Holmes,* and *Sherlock Holmes and Dr. Watson: A Textbook of Friendship.*

2024. ——. "A Pair o' Mystery Reviews," *Sherlockian Studies.* Edited by Robert A. Cutter. [Jackson Heights, N.Y.: The Baker Street Press, 1947.] p. 24.

A review of Stud and Sign that first appeared, in a slightly different form, in *The Art of the Mystery Story.*

2025. ——. "Profile by Gaslight," *Murder for Pleasure: The Life and Times of the Detective Story.* New York; London: D. Appleton-Century Co., [1941]. Chap. 3, p. 45-61. illus.

——. ——, ——. With an introduction by Nicholas Blake. London: Peter Davies, [1942]. Chap. 3, p. 45-61.

——. Condensed with title: "The Profile Emerges," *Profile by Gaslight.* Edited by Edgar W. Smith. New York: Simon and Schuster, 1944. p. 12-22.

"If Holmes-worship has become something of a cult in late years, it is certainly defensible as the most innocent and least harmful of all its kind. Its unashamed insistence that what-never-was always-will-be stands in oddly human fashion for a Higher Sanity in a too-real world."

2026. Hedgegrove, Quentin. " 'The House Regrets . . . ,' " *SHJ,* 3, No. 4 (Summer 1958), 19.

A brief account of a debate held February 20, 1958, between the Kingston Debating Society and members of the Sherlock Holmes Society on the motion "This House regrets the Return of Sherlock Holmes."

2027. [Heldenbrand, Page.] *Heldenbrand's Christmas Perennial.* Cover illustration by Hugh Connolly. New York: Appledore Towers Letter Press, 1954. [11] p.

Limited to 100 copies.

Contents: Foreword. - A Letter from Uffa. - The Man with the Monogrammed Middle.

2028. Helling, Cornelis. "Kille vlijmscherpe denker Sherlock Holmes bij knappend haardvuur" ["Cold, Sharp Thinker Sherlock Holmes at the Crackling Fireplace"], *Vara-Gids* [Amsterdam] (January 27, 1970), 6-7.

A knowledgeable article on the Saga by the Dutch Sherlockian authority.

2029. ——. "What Is the Most Dramatic Incident in the Canon?" *BSJ,* 14, No. 3 (September 1964), 156-157.

Some dramatic occurrences in the tales, including the author's favorite.

The Writings About the Writings

General and Miscellaneous

The Writings About the Writings

General and Miscellaneous

2030. Hellman, Arthur D. "The Man from 221B: A New Look at the Saga of Sherlock Holmes," *Ivory Tower* [University of Minneapolis], 15, No. 5 (March 1968), 18-22.
Excerpts from chapters 3, 10, 13, and the conclusion of the author's book manuscript, *The Saga of Sherlock: Requiem for a Dying Era.*

2031. Henriksen, A. D. " 'A Case of Identity'—Hvem var Sherlock Holmes?" ["Who Was Sherlock Holmes?"], *Sherlock Holmes Årbog* I (1965), 75-85.

2032. ———. "Jeg hører om Sherlock overalt" ["I Hear of Sherlock Everywhere"] *Kronik* (September 17, 1954).
———. ———, *CPBook*, 1, No. 1 (Summer 1964), 3.

2033. ———. ———, *Sherlock Holmes Årbog* III (1967), 77-84.

2034. ———. "Den legendariske Baker Street" ["The Legendary Baker Street"], *Sherlock Holmes Årbog* II (1966), 40-52.

2035. ———. "Sherlock Holmes: En Englaender, der erobrede Verden" ["Sherlock Holmes: An Englishman Who Conquered the World"], *Philobiblon* [København], Nr. 4 (February 1946), 63-68.

2036. ———. "Sherlock Holmes Still Going Strong—," *Dagbladet Fyn* (May 8, 1963).
———. ———, *Sherlockiana*, 8, Nr. 1-2 (1963), 1-3.
Text in Danish.

2037. ———. *221B Baker Street: Sherlock Holmes' Privatliv.* [København]: Privattryk, 1949. 57 p. illus.
Limited to 442 copies, of which 221 are numbered.
Contents: 221 B. - 221 B, 1. sal. - Dagligt liv i 221 B. - "Data, data, data!" - Bogerne i 221 B. - Holmes' vaabenskjold og exlibris. - En dansk "irregulaer". - Det "rigtige" 221 B--og "Sherlocks smøge". - "Elementaert, min kaere Watson--". - 221 B--endnu en gang.
A beautifully illustrated study of the Master's home life.

2038. ———. "Vor tids saga" ["The Saga of Our Times"], *Sherlock Holmes Årbog* II (1966), 85-88.
Comments, in Danish, by G. K. Chesterton, Hannen Swaffer, Howard Spring, Otto Gelsted, and Knud Hannestad.

2039. The Heritage Club. *Sandglass.* No. I:17. New York: [1952]. 4 p.
———. ———. No. IR:17. New York: [1952]. 4 p.
A reprint of the Limited Editions Club's monthly letter (item 2093), included with *The Adventures of Sherlock Holmes,* volume 1 of a three-volume set published by the Heritage Club (item 702).

2040. ———. ———. No. III and IV:22. New York: [1957]. 4 p.
A second monthly letter, included with volumes 2 and 3: *The Later Adventures of Sherlock Holmes* and *The Final Adventures of Sherlock Holmes.*

2041. Hill, Edwin C. "Sherlock Holmes Is Not Dead," *The Human Side of the News.* New York City: Walter J. Black, Inc., 1934. p. 127-133.

2042. ———. "221-B, Baker Street," *Scribner's Magazine,* 100, No. 5 (November 1936), 68.
A brief commentary on Holmes, his prototype Dr. Joseph Bell, and the untold tales.

2043. Hill, Pope R., Sr. *Part One.* [Athens, Ga.: Privately Printed], 1947. v, 29 p.
"A pamphlet, deriving from Mr. Hill's book manuscript *Dating Sherlock Holmes,* in which the theory of 'a vast hidden substructure to the Sherlock Holmes stories' is adumbrated." (Edgar W. Smith)

2044. ———. *The Sherlock Holmes Hoax.* [Athens, Ga.: Privately Printed], 1952. 28 p.
"A further development of Prof. Hill's 'substructure' thesis, holding that all 60 tales carry a hidden plot and solution; with an exposition and demonstration of this thesis in the instance of *Silver Blaze.*" (Edgar W. Smith)

2045. Hogan, John V. L. "An Unsolved Puzzle in the Writings," *BSJ*, 3, No. 3 (July 1953), 173-174.
A paper delivered on the occasion of the author's induction into the BSI on January 9, 1953.

2046. Holroyd, James Edward. *Baker Street By-ways: A Book About Sherlock Holmes.* London: George Allen & Unwin Ltd., [1959]. 158 p. illus.
Contents: Profile. - One Man's Pilgrimage. - How It All Began. - Sidney Paget's Drawings. - Dorr Steele and Some Others. - Where Was 221B? - Solutions by Numbers. - Fanciful Furnishings. - 'Our Sanctum'. - The Shaggiest Dog. - Sherlock Holmes in Regent Street. - Pistol Packing Partners. - Dr. Watson and Mr. Wilde. - A Baker Street Portrait Gallery.
Review: SHJ, 4, No. 2 (Spring 1959), 31-32 (Lord Donegall).

2047. ———. "The Egg-Spoon," *SHJ*, 1, No. 1- (May 1952-   ).
A counterpart to *BSJ's* "From the Editor's Commonplace Book" department,

featuring "delightful dippings into the Sherlockian shell of knowledge by a commentator whose yolk of wisdom is encased in an albumen of wit" (Edgar W. Smith). Some of the material was used in the author's *Baker Street By-ways*.

2048. ———. "Homage to Holmes," *The New Statesman and Nation* (NS), 47, No. 1194 (January 23, 1954), 92, 94.

———. Revised with title: "How It All Began," *Baker Street By-ways*, [by] James Edward Holroyd. London: George Allen & Unwin Ltd., [1959]. p. 28-37.

2049. [———.] " 'Other People's News,' " by Horace Harker [pseud.] *SHJ*, 1, No. 3 (June 1953), 22-23.

Ten news items about the Sherlockian scene.

2050. ———, ed. *Seventeen Steps to 221B: A Collection of Sherlockian Pieces by English Writers*. With an introduction by James Edward Holroyd. Illustrated. London: George Allen & Unwin Ltd., [1967]. 181 p.

Contents: 1. From the Diary of Sherlock Holmes, by Maurice Baring. - 2. Dr. Watson Speaks Out, by A. A. Milne. - 3. Studies in the Literature of Sherlock Holmes, by Ronald Knox. - 4. The Chronological Problem, by S. C. Roberts. - 5. Dr. Watson, by Desmond MacCarthy. - 6. The Dates in The Red-Headed League, by Dorothy L. Sayers. - 7. 'Ring for Our Boots,' by Arthur Marshall. - 8. Sherlockiana: The Faith of a Fundamentalist, by Bernard Darwin. - 9. The Passing of Sherlock Holmes, by E. V. Knox. - 10. The Case of the Gifted Amateur, by J. C. Masterman. - 11. The Route of the Blue Carbuncle, by Gavin Brend. - 12. The Adventure of the Deptford Horror, by Adrian Conan Doyle. - 13. 'Another Glass, Watson!' by John Dickson Carr. - 14. 'Our Client's Foot Upon the Stair,' by James Edward Holroyd. - 15. The Truth About Moriarty, by W. C. Bristowe. - 16. April 1891-April 1894, by Lord Donegall. - 17. Back Yards of Baker Street, by Bernard Davies. - Annex: Examination Paper, by R. Ivar Gunn.

Reviews: BSC, 1, No. 2 (March 1968), 4 (Benjamin Small); *SOS*. 2, No. 4 (April 1968), 2-3 (Bruce Dettman); *SHJ*, 8, No. 2 (Spring 1967), 64 (Lord Donegall); *Yorkshire Post* (June 8, 1967) (Trevor H. Hall).

2051. Homén, Olaf. "Rymmare och fasttagare" ["Hide-and-Seek"], *I marginalen*. Helsingfors: Holger Schildt; Stockholm: Albert Bonnier, [1917]. p. 165-173.

A discussion of Herr Depken's booklet (item 1970).

2052. Honce, Charles. *Books and Ghosts: A Fresh Unveiling of a Newspaperman's Literary Preferences and Friendships*. Mount Vernon: S. A. Jacobs; The Golden Eagle Press, 1948. xiv, 102 p.

Limited to 111 copies.

Partial contents: The Mystery of the Cardboard Hat Box. - A Baker Street View of Europe. - My First Meeting with Sherlock Holmes. - Going, Going, Gone!

2053. ———. *For Loving a Book: Further News Adventures Among Bins and Bibliophiles*. With an overture by H. L. Mencken. Mount Vernon, N.Y.: The Golden Eagle Press, 1945. xxiv, 114 p. illus.

Limited to 111 copies.

Partial contents: Sherlock Holmes in Sharps and Flats. - Sherlockiana. - A Lady Sherlock. - Holmes in the News. - Sherlock Spends a Day in the Country. - A Note on Freddy Steele. - The Lowdown on Edgar W. Smith. - A Holmes Collection and What Became of It. - Was Holmes a Crook? - Baker Street on the Potomac. - A Salvage Operation. - The Baker Street Twins. - A Footnote on the Same Gents. - Thieves' Kitchen, by Vincent Starrett.

"Scattered throughout these Sherlockian numbers are pieces by or quotations from Harry Hansen, Benjamin De Casseres, Kenneth Fearing, Christopher Morley, Vivian Brown, David Randall, Vincent Starrett, Jacob Blanck, Edgar W. Smith and Franklin D. Roosevelt."

2054. ———. *Mark Twain's Associated Press Speech and Other News Stories on Murder, Modes, Mysteries, Music and Makers of Books*. New York: Privately Printed at Christmas Time, 1940. xxi, [128] p.

Limited to 100 copies.

Partial contents: The Man Who Launched Sherlock Holmes. - The Baker Street Irregulars. - The Bibliography of Sherlock Holmes. - Ballade of Baker Street, by Carolyn Wells.

2055. ———. *The Public Papers of a Bibliomaniac, Together with Some Private Leaves from a Collector's Scrapbook*. Prelude by Ellery Queen. Mount Vernon: The Golden Eagle Press, 1942. xviii, 170 p.

Limited to 100 copies.

Partial contents: Postscript on Sherlock Holmes. - "The Creeping Man," by Edgar W. Smith. - A New Sherlock Holmes Adventure ["The Man Who Was Wanted"].

2056. ———. *Sherlock Holmes Still Is in the News: The Singular Facts Concerning Some Newspaper Yarns About an Immortal*. With a Nostalgic Divertissement on the Sacred Writings, by Benjamin De Casseres. Mount Vernon, N.Y.: The Golden Eagle Press, 1944. [4] p.

Printed on the outside of a double leaf uncut at top.

General and Miscellaneous

The Writings About the Writings

General and Miscellaneous

———. ———, *CPBook*, 1, No. 4 (Spring 1965), 77-80.

———. Condensed with title: "Sherlock Holmes in the News," *Profile by Gaslight*. Edited by Edgar W. Smith. New York: Simon and Schuster, 1944. p. 71-84.

Inside stories on the facts and circumstances behind some noteworthy headlines.

Review: For Loving a Book, by Charles Honce. p. 35-38 (footnote) (John Selby).

2057. ———. *Tales from a Beekman Hill Library and Other News Stories on Tunes, Travels, Tribulations and Trenchering*. Drawings by Joe Cunningham and Milt Morris. Mount Vernon, N.Y.: Uttered by S.A. Jacobs at the Golden Eagle Press, 1952. 125 p.

Limited to 100 copies.

Partial contents: Sherlock Holmes — In Person (April 5, 1952). - Sensation in Baker Street (June 27, 1952).

2058. ———. *To Talk of Many Things*. Mount Vernon: Imprinted by S. A. Jacobs at his Golden Eagle Press, 1950. 58 p. illus.

Limited to 88 copies.

Partial contents: "Come Up and See My Etchings". - Heresy on the Sherlock Holmes Front.

2059. Hoveyda, Fereydoun. "Sherlock Holmes chevalier de la légion d'honneur!" *Histoire du roman policier*. [Paris: Les Editions du Pavillon, 1965.] p. 58-65.

An introduction to the Sacred Writings, with interesting commentaries on the "Chevalier of the Legion of Honor."

2060. Invitation to Learning (*Radio Program*). "The Adventures of Sherlock Holmes," *The New Invitation to Learning*. Edited by Mark Van Doren. New York: Random House, [1942]. p. 236-251.

———. ———, ———. New York: The New Home Library, [1944]. p. 236-251.

Transcript of a CBS radio forum in which Mark Van Doren, Elmer Davis, Rex Stout, and Jacques Barzun dissect the writings of John H. Watson.

2061. ———. "Conan Doyle: Adventures of Sherlock Holmes," *Invitation to Learning: Discussions of Great Books and Significant Ideas*, 2, No. 3 (Fall 1952), 251-257.

Transcript of a CBS radio broadcast of July 27, 1952, during which Adrian Conan Doyle, Gilbert Highet, and Lyman Bryson discuss the Sacred Writings.

2062. Isherwood, Christopher. *"The Speckled Band* by Arthur Conan Doyle," *Exhumations: Stories, Articles, Verses*. New York: Simon and Schuster, [1966]. p. 16, 88-90.

A short essay in which the author discusses his favorite "escape reading": the adventures of Sherlock Holmes; and selects Spec as his favorite story.

2063. Jaffee, Irving L. *Elementary My Dear Watson: A Series of Articles on the Great Detective and Some Others*. Brooklyn, N.Y.: Theo. Gaus' Sons, Inc., [1965]. 82 p. illus.

Contents: Foreword. - Pt. 1. The Sage of Baker Street. - "The Final Problem". - Sherlock Holmes' Last Case. - Sherlock Holmes — Ancestor. - Famous Detectives of Fiction. - "The Man with the Twisted Lip". - Sherlock Holmes Calling. - "The Naval Treaty". - "The Boscombe Valley Mystery". - "The Sign of Four". - The Strange Story of Jonathan Small. - Pt. 2. Some Other Detectives, Real and Imaginary. - He Finds Them. - Eleven Days. - So That Was Mike's Secret.

An admirably written and readable collection of essays reprinted from *Famous Detective Stories* and *Double-Action Detective Magazine* in which Holmes and Watson are discussed from a contemporary point of view.

2064. [Jeffs, Bernard.] "After You, Sherlock!" *Medical Pocket Quarterly*, 25, No. 3 (December 1, 1944), 10.

The part played by medical men in the development of detective stories, including Drs. Watson, Bell, and Doyle.

2065. Joffroy, Pierre. "Sherlock Holmes," Photos: Izis. *Paris Match*, No. 539 (August 8, 1959), 36-45, 64.

A profusely and beautifully illustrated account of the Master and his followers, "Les Irréguliers de Baker Street."

2066. "John H. Watson, M.D.," *Medical Pocket Quarterly*, 25, No. 4 (March 1, 1945), 10-14.

Mainly about the Writings and the higher criticism.

2067. [Kennedy, Bruce.] "Editorial," *SOS*, 1- (October 1966-   ).

Interesting commentaries on the Sherlockian scene by the Bannister.

2068. ———, ed. *Four Wheels to Baker Street: An Anthology of Sherlockiana*. With an introduction by T. S. Blakeney. Illustrated by Jon V. Wilmunen. [Fulton, Mo.]: The Three Students Plus, 1968. [viii], 21 p. (Rockford Illustrated Publications)

Contents: Preface, by Bruce Kennedy. - Introduction, by T. S. Blakeney. - On My Knees! by H. W. Starr. - If We Have to Be Whimsical, by S. Tupper Bigelow. - "Got Any Beeton's Today?" or The Byways of the Sherlockian Game, by Nathan L. Bengis. - The American Encyclopedia, by Chris Redmond.

Reviews: BSP, No. 41 (November 1968), 5 (Chris Redmond); *SOS*, 3, No. 1 (January 1969), 3-4 (Bruce Dettman).

2069. ———. "The Meaning of Holmes," *SOS*, 2, No. 2 (December 1967), 6.
"Holmes is something more than a hobby; he is a way of life."

2070. ———. *Some Trifling Monographs: Studies in Sherlock Holmes.* Rockford Illustrated Publications, 1968. 14 p.
Limited to 35 copies.
Contents: The Giant Rat. - Chronicles in Cocaine. - "No characters in this book are fictional, although the author should very much like to meet any who claim to be". - The Adventure of the Broken Home.

2071. Kimball, Elliot. *Injecta Membra.* Clinton, Conn.: [Unpublished typescript], 1963. [42] p.
Contents: Prolegomenon. - 1. Multiple Mention of Murray. - 2. Of Oysters and Grouse. - 3. Latrineal Latitudes. - 4. Topographia Watsoniana. - 5. Seeing Without Observing. - 6. Holmesian Penury. - 7. Concerning Retirement Age. - 8. A Policeman of Parts. - 9. Canonical Dactyloscopy. - 10. The Bradstreet Problem. - 11. Breakfast at 221B Baker Street. - 12. Mrs. Joseph Turner. - 13. Orontes. - 14. An Honorable Man.
Location: Toronto Central Library.

2072. Klinefelter, Walter. *Ex Libris A. Conan Doyle: Sherlock Holmes.* Decorations by Dale Nichols. Chicago: Black Cat Press, 1938. 58 p. illus.
Limited to 250 copies.
Contents: His Genesis and Make-up. - The Sources of His History. - His Writings. - Epilogue. - Notes.

2073. Knox, Ronald. "Studies in the Literature of Sherlock Holmes," *The Blue Book* (Conducted by Oxford Undergraduates), 1, No. 2 (July 1912), 111-132.
———. ———, *Blackfriars* [Oxford], 1, No. 3 (June 1920), 154-172.
———. ———, *Essays in Satire*, by Ronald A. Knox. London: Sheed and Ward, [1928]. Chap. 5, p. 145-175.
———. ———, ———. New York: E. P. Dutton & Co., [1930]. Chap. 5, p. 145-175.
———. ———, *The Incunabular Sherlock Holmes.* Edited by Edgar W. Smith. Morristown, N. J.: The Baker Street Irregulars, 1958. p. 37-59.
———. ———, *Seventeen Steps to 221B.* [Edited by] James Edward Holroyd. London: George Allen & Unwin Ltd., [1967]. p. 30-45.
"A mock-solemn enquiry into the inconsistencies in the Holmes legend; in fact a satire on the Higher Criticism. It . . . [quotes] imaginary foreign professors

on 'the Watson-narrative,' making the French scholar call him Vatson and the Italian refer to him as Guatson." (Gilbert K. Chesterton)

2074. Kottmeyer, William. "Something About the Author," *Cases of Sherlock Holmes.* Adapted by William Kottmeyer. St. Louis: Webster Division, McGraw-Hill Book Co., [1947]. p. 105-118.
An introduction to Sir Arthur and the Sherlock Holmes stories for elementary-school children.

2075. Kupferberg, Herbert. "Baker Street Dialogue," *The New York Herald Tribune* (May 22, 1959), 12.
———. ———, *CPBook*, 2, No. 5-6 (Summer-Fall 1965), 118; 121.
Holmes and Watson discuss Sir Arthur's centennial and the continued appeal of their adventures.

2076. La Cour, Tage. *Mord i biblioteket.* [Murder in the Library.] Stockholm: Sällskapet Bokvännera, [1953]. 82 p. illus. (Bokvännens Småskrifter, Nr. 9)
Limited to 600 copies.
———. ———, *Studier i rødt*, af Tage la Cour. København: Carit Andersens Forlag, 1956. p. 7-96.
Pages 20-28, 67-68, and 70-71 of this history of the "whodunit" deal with the Sherlock Holmes stories.

2077. ———. "Sherlock Holmes og Hans Gengangere," *Den Forsvundne Hamlet: Sherlock Holmes løser et bibliofilt problem, af Vincent Starrett.* København: Rosenkilde og Bagger, 1952. p. 7-12.

2078. ———. "Sherlockiana," *Rejsen til månen, og andre udflugter i den lettere bogverden.* I udvalg ved Tom Kristensen. København: [Strubes Forlag], 1965. p. 108-116.
Limited to 1000 copies.

2079. ———. *Studier i rødt: Causerier om kriminalliteratur.* [Studies in Red: Essays About Crime Literature.] København: Carit Andersens Forlag, 1956. 134 p. illus.
Limited to 1500 numbered copies.
Contents: Forord. - Mord i biblioteket. - Skandinaviske kriminalfortaellinger. - Mysteriet om en hansom cab.

2080. ———, and Harald Mogensen. *Mordbogen: Kriminal-og detektivhistorien i billeder og tekst.* [Grafisk tilrettelaegning: Freddy Pedersen. Produktion: Sture Jensen. Omslagsfotografi: Lennart Larsen. Printed in Czechoslovakia.] [København]: Lademann, [1969]. 191 p.
———. *The Murder Book: An Illustrated History of the Detective Story.* [Tr. by Roy

Duffell.] London: George Allen & Unwin Ltd., [1971]. 191 p.

———. ———. [New York]: Herder and Herder, [1971]. 191 p.

A very handsome and lavishly illustrated book on the history of the detective story in all media. It contains many references to and illustrations of the Sherlock Holmes stories, including the following partial contents: Arthur Conan Doyle and Sherlock Holmes. - Sherlock Holmes and Dr. Watson at 221B Baker Street—Victorian London. - What Did Sherlock Holmes Look Like? - Sherlock Holmes on the Stage and Screen and in Ballet and Operetta. - Sherlock Holmes Solves the Mystery of Jack the Ripper. - *The Hound of the Baskervilles.* - Picturesque Master Criminals.

Reviews: SHJ, 9, No. 4 (Summer 1970), 140 (Lord Donegall); *Sherlockiana,* 14, Nr. 3 (1969), 10.

2081. ———, Åke Runnquist, and Jörgen Elgström. "Om Sherlock Holmes" ["About Sherlock Holmes"], *Mord i biblioteket: Detektivromanens maerkvaerdige historie.* København: Rosenkilde og Bagger, 1965. p. 33-40.

2082. Langenfelt, Gösta. "Saken är klar, käre Watson!" ["We Have Got Our Case, My Dear Watson!"] *Dagens Nyheter* (February 19, 1933).

———. ———, *BSCL,* No. 1 (January 1963), 4-9.

On the identification of the King of Scandinavia and the books of Bell and Blakeney.

2083. Lauritzen, Henry. "Fra Laeseren til Sherlock Holmes" ["From the Reader to Sherlock Holmes"], *Sherlock Holmes Årbog* I (1965), 48-70.

2084. ———. "Hvorfor dyrker man Sherlock Holmes?" ["Why Do We Study Sherlock Holmes?"] *Sherlockiana,* 7, Nr. 3-4 (1962), 12-16.

2085. ———. *Mesterdetektiver under Lup.* [Master Detectives Under a Magnifying Glass.] [Aalborg: 1970.] 65 p. illus.

Limited to 1013 copies.

Review: Sherlockiana, 15, Nr. 3-4 (1970), 11.

2086. ———. *Mr. Sherlock Holmes.* Aalborg: Aksel Schølins Bogtrykkeri, [1968]. [15] p. illus.

Limited to 500 copies.

An exquisitely illustrated and printed booklet, in Danish, on the Sherlockian Saga.

2087. ———. "Den udødelige Sherlock Holmes" ["The Immortal Sherlock Holmes"], *Stolpen, Stolpedalsskolens Elevblad* [Aalborg] (February 1964), 2-3.

2088. LaVallo, Frank. "The Case of the Deathless Detective," *The Texas Quarterly,* 11, No. 2 (Summer 1968), 180-199.

An outstanding essay on Doyle and the Canonical tales.

2089. Leblanc, Maurice. "A propos de Conan Doyle," *Les Annales Politiques et Littéraires,* 95 (August 1, 1930), 111.

———. "Apropos of Conan Doyle," Tr. by Dr. Kai-Ho Mah. *BSJ,* 21, No. 2 (June 1971), 100-103.

A fine tribute to the "creator" of Sherlock Holmes by the author of three delightful parody-pastiches with Arsène Lupin and Herlock Sholmes.

2090. Lejeune, Anthony. "Age of the Great Detective," *The Times Literary Supplement: Crime, Detection and Society* (June 23, 1961), vii.

———. "De eeuw van de Grote Detectives," *Elseviers Weekblad* [Netherlands], 17, No. 28 (July 15, 1961), 15.

An illustrated article on Holmes and his successors.

2091. "Letters to Baker Street," *BSJ* [OS], 1-4, No. 1 (April 1946-January 1949); (NS), 11, No. 2 (June 1961); 11, No. 4- (December 1961-).

A department of *The Baker Street Journal* in which the editor quotes letters from readers. Excerpts from other letters are also quoted in "From the Editor's Commonplace Book" (items 2199 and 2262). Many contain important contributions to the literature and should not be overlooked in any serious study of the Canon.

2092. Lichtenstein, Alfred. *Der Kriminal-roman. Eine literarische und forensisch-medizinische Studie mit Anhang: Sherlock Holmes zum Fall Hau.* [The Detective Novel. A Literary and Forensic Medical Study with Appendix: Sherlock Holmes to the Hau Case.] München: Ernst Reinhardt, 1908. 61 p. (Grenzfragen der Literatur und Medizin in Einzeldarstellungen von Dr. S. Rahmer, 7. Heft)

2093. The Limited Editions Club. *Monthly Letter.* No. 215. New York: June 1950. 4 p.

The story behind the Club's monumental eight-volume edition of *Sherlock Holmes* (item 701).

2094. The Literary Guild. *Wings.* Vol. 10, No. 9. New York: September 1936. 26 p. illus.

Partial contents: The September Selection: "The Complete Sherlock Holmes," introduced by Burton Rascoe. - Conan Doyle. - Too Real to be Fiction, by Christopher Morley. - Mr. Sherlock Holmes.

2095. Livingston, Guy. "Holmes of Baker

Street," *Britannia and Eve*, 42, No. 5 (May 1951), 14-15, 55. illus.

"Fiction's greatest detective in whose honour an exhibition is being held in connection with the Festival of Britain." (Subtitle)

2096. [Lowndes, Robert A. W.] "The Editor's Page," *Startling Mystery Stories*, 2, No. 4 (Fall 1968), 4-5, 123-127.

A long and informative review of *The Annotated Sherlock Holmes*, with additional information on the tales and the writings about them.

2097. Lundin, Bo. "Sherlock Holmes som forskningsobjekt," *Studiekamraten*, 51, No. 7 (October 24, 1969), 100-112.

2098. MacArthur, James. "The Creator of Sherlock Holmes," *A Study in Scarlet and The Sign of the Four*. New York and London: Harper & Brothers, 1904. p. vii-xv.

A fine introduction, dealing mainly with the Sherlock Holmes stories, in which Mr. MacArthur prophetically states, "It is doubtful whether Dr. Doyle will ever surpass himself in the stories which are gathered in these three volumes. They represent not only the best of his work but the most masterly detective stories which have ever been written."

2099. Mackay, Ian. *The Real Mackay: Being Essays by Ian Mackay*. Edited by Stanley Baron. With illustrations by Vicky and a profile by R. F. Cruikshank. London: "News Chronicle" Publications Department, 1953. xiv, 146 p.

Partial contents: I Become a Regular Irregular (January 15, 1952). - Haunted by Holmes (March 4, 1952).

2100. Males, U. Harold. "Introduction," *Adventures of Sherlock Holmes*. New York: Harper & Row, 1966. p. vii-xvii.

Contents: The Victorian Age. - The Character of Sherlock Holmes. - The Man Behind the Mask. - The Themes and Characteristics of the Stories. - A Final Appreciation.

2101. Mansfield, Vincent M. "Re: Sherlock Holmes," *Thuria*, 1, No. 1 (1964), 33.

2102. Martell, Edward. "The World Honours the Man Who Never Was—And Argues About His Life and Home," *The Recorder* [London] (January 11, 1954), 4.
————. ————, *CPBook*, 2, No. 5-6 (Summer-Fall 1965), 99.

2103. Maurice, Arthur Bartlett. "The Detective in Fiction," *The Bookman*, 15, No. 3 (May 1902), 231-236.

"The name of Sherlock Holmes, with that of Dupin, will in the end be found very near the apex; but in the realm of material achievement Lecoq must stand alone."

2104. ————. "Forty Years of Sherlock," *The Bookman*, 66, No. 2 (October 1927), 160-162.

An anniversary review and tribute.

2105. [————.] "The Genesis of Sherlock Holmes," *The Bookman*, 12, No. 6 (February 1901), 550-553.

A commentary on the literary agent's article in *Tit-Bits* (item 3922).

2106. [————.] "The Reappearance of Sherlock Holmes," *The Bookman*, 13, No. 5 (July 1901), 409.

2107. [————.] "Señor Sherlock Holmes; The New Doyle Story; Sherlock in Russia; Sherlock and the Ku Klux Klan," *The Bookman*, 41, No. 2 (April 1915), 118-121 illus.

2108. [————.] "Sherlock Holmes," *The Bookman*, 31, No. 6 (February 1911), 562-563.

Notes on "the most widely known character in all fiction" and the quality of the post-Reichenbach adventures.

2109. [————.] "Some Inconsistencies of Sherlock Holmes," *The Bookman*, 14, No. 5 (January 1902), 446-447.
————. ————, *The Incunabular Sherlock Holmes*. Edited by Edgar W. Smith. Morristown, N.J.: The Baker Street Irregulars, 1958. p. 1-2.

A commentary on points now long familiar.

2110. May, John. "Sherlock Holmes," *Men Only* [London], 47 (May 1951), 88.

A slight piece but worth noting because of the interesting caricature of Holmes by Hynes on the magazine's cover.

2111. McCleary, G. F. "The Cult of Sherlock Holmes," *The Fortnightly* (NS), 170, No. 1015 (July 1951), 485-488.
————. ————, *CPBook*, 5, No. 18 (Spring 1969), 357-360.

"Historical and topical commentary on the doings of those, in England and in America, who strive to 'keep green the memory of Sherlock Holmes.' " (Edgar W. Smith)

2112. ————. *On Detective Fiction and Other Things*. London: Hollis & Carter, 1960. 161 p.

Partial contents: The Apotheosis of Sherlock Holmes. - The Original of Sherlock Holmes. - An Examination Paper on the Exploits of Sherlock Holmes.

2113. McDade, Thomas M. "Baker Street and

General and Miscellaneous

Canon Lore," *The American Book Collector*, 19, No. 1 (September 1968), 17-18.

A review of *The Annotated Sherlock Holmes*, including a commentary on Sherlockian lore.

2114. McDiarmid, E. W., and Theodore C. Blegen, eds. *Exploring Sherlock Holmes*. Edited by E. W. McDiarmid & Theodore C. Blegen for the Norwegian Explorers of Minneapolis and Saint Paul. La Crosse: Sumac Press, 1957. 123 p.

Limited to 400 copies.

Contents: These Were Hidden Fires, Indeed! by Theodore C. Blegen. - Professor Sherlock Holmes, Ph.D., by E. W. McDiarmid. - The Master and the Mass Media, by E. W. Ziebarth. - Another Incubus in the Saddle, by John B. Wolf. - The Final Problem — Where? by Bryce Crawford, Jr., and R. C. Moore. - The Battered Tin Dispatch Box, by Thomas L. Daniels. - Of Violence at Meiringen, by Philip S. Hench. - A Note About Contributors.

2115. [McLauchlin, Russell.] "Mrs. Hudson Speaks," *BSJ* [OS], 2, No. 3 (July 1947), 328-331.

"A recording made by Miss ZaSu Pitts for the meeting of the Amateur Mendicant Society of Detroit on March 14, 1947, and for Baker Street Irregulars everywhere."

2116. Merriman, Charles O. "Mr. Sherlock Holmes in the City of London," *BSJ*, 15, No. 1 (March 1965), 18-21.

A general discussion of Watson's table of limitations, Mycroft Holmes, the income at 221B, and some Sherlockian sites associated with London.

2117. Messac, Régis. "Les déductions de Sherlock Holmes," *Le "detective novel" et l'influence de la pensée scientifique*. Paris: Librairie Ancienne Honoré Champion, 1929. Chap. 3, p. 580-620.

A long and impressive chapter in this work of enormous scholarship is devoted to the Canonical tales.

2118. Milne, A. A. "Dr. Watson Speaks Out," *The Nation and Athenaeum*, 44, No. 7 (November 17, 1928), 254-255.

————. ————, *By Way of Introduction*, by A. A. Milne. New York: E. P. Dutton & Co., 1929. p. 95-101.

Also published in a limited deluxe autographed edition.

————. ————, ————. London: Methuen & Co. Ltd., 1929. p. 91-98.

Reprinted in 1931 (Gateway Library).

————. ————, *The Incunabular Sherlock Holmes*. Edited by Edgar W. Smith. Morristown, N.J.: The Baker Street Irregulars, 1958. p. 101-108.

————. ————, *Seventeen Steps to 221B*. [Edited by] James Edward Holroyd. London:

George Allen & Unwin Ltd., [1967]. p. 25-29.

————. "Dr. Watson taler ud—," Oversat af A. D. Henriksen. *Sherlockiana*, 7, Nr. 1-2 (1962), 8-10.

————. ————, *Sherlock Holmes Årbog* I (1965), 17-24.

A review of the omnibus *Sherlock Holmes* (London: John Murray, 1927) as it might have been done by Dr. Watson.

2119. ————. "New Explorations in Baker Street," *The New York Times Magazine* (March 9, 1952), 10, 20.

An illustrated article dealing mainly with Watson's *head* wound which affected both his memory and writing, and the dates of Holmes's birth (unknown) and death (May 4, 1891).

2120. ————. "The Watson Touch," *If I May*. London: Methuen & Co. Ltd., [1920]. p. 141-144.

————. ————, ————. New York: E. P. Dutton & Co., [1921]. p. 179-183.

————. ————, ————. New popular edition. New York: E. P. Dutton & Co., 1925. p. ————. "The Watson Touch," *If I May*. London: Methuen & Co. Ltd., [1920]. p. 141-144.

————. ————, ————. New York: E. P. Dutton & Co., [1921]. p. 179-183.

————. ————, ————. New popular edition. New York: E. P. Dutton & Co., 1925. p. 179-183.

————. ————, *BSJ* [OS], 3, No. 1 (January 1948), 67-69. (Incunabulum)

————. ————, *The Incunabular Sherlock Holmes*. Edited by Edgar W. Smith. Morristown, N. J.: The Baker Street Irregulars, 1958. p. 93-96.

"Inspiration in the matter of how detective stories should be written." (Edgar W. Smith)

2121. "Miscellany from 221B Baker Street," *The London Mystery Magazine*, No. 8 (February-March 1951), 82-83; No. 9 (April-May 1951), 66-67; No. 10 (June-July 1951), 58-59.

Commentaries on the London of Sherlock Holmes's day, the whereabouts of 221B, etc.

2122. Monte, Alberto del. "L'eredità di Sherlock Holmes," *Breve storia del romanzo poliziesco*. Bari: Editori Laterza, 1962. Chap. 12, p. 144-158. (Biblioteca di cultura moderna, 568)

2123. Montgomery, James. *Art in the Blood, and What Is This Thing Called Music?* (or *Body and Soul*). [Philadelphia: Privately Printed, 1950.] [9] p. (Montgomery's Christmas Annual, No. 1)

Includes a photograph of "Irene Adler and the King of Bohemia."

2124. ———. *Shots from the Canon.* [Philadelphia: Privately Printed, 1953.] 26 p. illus. (Montgomery's Christmas Annual, No. 4)

Cover design by Bruce Montgomery.

Contents: Foreword. - "I have a Song to Sing, O!" - "Sherlock Holmes" (Words and music by Claude Ralston. - Shangri-La Revisited? - Man or Mountain. - It Pays to Advertise. - Survival of the Fittest. - How Green Was the Yard. - Meiringen Musings. - Meiringen in 1890 (Engraving). - Dear Me, Mr. Expert! Dear Me! - A Case of Identity? - Gilbert and the Detectives. - A Sensational Exception. - Paging Birdy Edwards. - Chronologically Speaking. - A Comedy of Errors. - More Victims for the Hound? - "A Taste for Honey". - The Mystery of the Downs. - A Canonical Toast to Rachel Howells. - A Hearty Sea-Story. - Hair-Trigger Embroidery. - Sherlock Holmes and the Sleepless Watchman.

2125. ———. *Sidelights on Sherlock.* [Philadelphia: Privately Printed, 1951.] [14] p. illus. (Montgomery's Christmas Annual, No. 2)

Contents: An Irregular Song. - Chopin in Baker Street. - Notes from My Dispatch-Box. - Apocryphal Hallamshire? - Honi soit qui mal y pense. - To the fore in love and war. - Simon called Peter? - Crime makes a triple play? - It's a wise dog that knows his own lama. - Affinity? - Slip showing? - Better never than late. - He never told a lie? - Veiled nomenclature? - The Adventure of the Irene Adler Recording.

2126. ———. *Three Trifling Monographs.* Illustrations by Bruce Montgomery. [Philadelphia: Privately Printed, 1952.] [18] p. (Montgomery's Christmas Annual, No. 3)

Contents: Four Birds in a Gilded Age. - Those Gorgeous Magazines. - Speculation in Diamonds.

2127. Morley, Christopher. "Clinical Notes by a Resident Patient," *Profile by Gaslight.* Edited by Edgar W. Smith. New York: Simon and Schuster, 1944. p. 48-59.

The author made it a practice to set down random thoughts as they came to him out of his cogitations upon the life and times of the Master. What he called his "clinical notes," written in his happily-assumed capacity as one of Dr. Watson's resident patients in the house on Baker Street, are a veritable quarry of reminiscences and speculations.

2128. ———. ———, *BSJ* [OS], 1-4, No. 1 (April 1946-January 1949); (NS), 1-4, No. 3 (January 1951-July 1954).

In twenty-four of the above twenty-eight issues, Mr. Morley contributed, with the assistance of Stanley Hopkins and Jane Nightwork, further observations of the Baker Street scene.

2129. ———. "In Memoriam: Sherlock Holmes," *The Saturday Review of Literature,* 7, No. 2 (August 2, 1930), 21. (The Bowling Green)

———. ———, *The Complete Sherlock Holmes.* Garden City, N.Y.: Doubleday, Doran and Co., 1930. Vol. 1, p. vii-xiv.

———. ———, *Internal Revenue,* [by] Christopher Morley. Garden City, N.Y.: Doubleday, Doran & Co., 1933. p. 70-80.

———. ———, *Introducing Mr. Sherlock Holmes.* Edited by Edgar W. Smith. Morristown, N.J.: The Baker Street Irregulars, 1959. [unpaged]

———. ———, *The Stories of Sherlock Holmes.* Vol. 2. *The Redheaded League.* New York: Caedmon Records, 1966. Printed on album.

———. ———, *Prefaces Without Books: Prefaces and Introductions to Thirty Books,* by Christopher Morley. Selected by Herman Abromson with an Introduction by Jerome Weidman. [Austin]: The University of Texas, Humanities Research Center, [1970]. p. 22-27.

"A critical analysis of the spirit of the tales. By its use as the introduction to the Doubleday omnibus (both the two-volume and the one-volume editions) it is undoubtedly the most widely published of all essays in Sherlockiana." (Edgar W. Smith)

2130. ———. "Introduction," *The Final Adventures of Sherlock Holmes.* New York: The Limited Editions Club, 1952. Vol. 2, p. v-viii.

———. ———, *Introducing Mr. Sherlock Holmes.* Edited by Edgar W. Smith. Morristown, N.J.: The Baker Street Irregulars, 1959. [unpaged]

2131. ———. "Introduction," *Sherlock Holmes and Dr. Watson: A Textbook of Friendship.* Edited by Christopher Morley. New York: Harcourt, Brace and Co., [1944]. p. 1-22.

———. "A Textbook of Friendship." *The Incunabular Sherlock Holmes.* Edited by Edgar W. Smith. Morristown, N.J.: The Baker Street Irregulars, 1958. p. 171-180.

"The detective and the doctor move with all the other great pairs of masculine good humor: with Don Quixote and Sancho, with Crusoe and Friday, with Jim Hawkins and John Silver, with Huck and Tom. Their adventures are a textbook of friendship."

2132. ———. *The Ironing Board.* Garden City, N.Y.: Doubleday & Co., 1949. 255 p.

———. ———. London: Faber and Faber Ltd., [1950]. 263 p.

———. ———. Freeport, N.Y.: Books for Libraries Press, [1968]. 255 p. (Essay Index Reprint Series)

Partial contents: A Christmas Story Without Slush. - Codeine (7 Per Cent). - Watson à la Mode.

2133. ——. "Some Hitherto Unpublished Notes," *BSJ Christmas Annual*, No. 2 (1957), 31-33.

Written in 1950 and published in *BSJ* as a memorial to the founder of the Baker Street Irregulars.

2134. ——. *Streamlines*. Garden City, N.Y.: Doubleday, Doran & Co., 1936. x, 290 p.
——. ——. London: Faber & Faber Ltd., [1937]. x, 290 p.

Partial contents: Was Sherlock Holmes an American? - Doctor Watson's Secret. - Two Suppressed Holmes Episodes. - Studies on Baker Street.

2135. Mott, Frank Luther. "The Case of the Best Seller Mystery," *Golden Multitudes: The Story of Best Sellers in the United States*. New York: The Macmillan Co., 1947. p. 264-265.

"A full page is devoted to the Master, and the scholarship of his disciples is commended." (Edgar W. Smith)

2136. Murch, A. E. *The Development of the Detective Novel*. London: Peter Owen Ltd., [1958]. 272 p.
——. ——. New York: Philosophical Library, [1958]. 272 p.
——. ——, [Excerpt] *The London Mystery Selection*, No. 41 (April 1959), 108-117.
——. ——. [Revised edition.] Port Washington, N.Y.: Kennikat Press, [1968]. 272 p.

A scholarly and fascinating study of the genre from its beginnings, with numerous references to and a chapter (10, p. 167-191) on Sherlock Holmes.

Review: SHJ, 4, No. 1 (Winter 1958), 22-23 (Colin Prestige).

2137. Murray, David. "The Detectives: 1. Sherlock Holmes," *New York Post Daily Magazine* (March 2, 1964), 21.

Part 1 of an article in six parts on the great detectives.

2138. Naganuma, Kohki. [*Greetings from Sherlock Holmes*. Tokyo: Bungei Shunju Ltd., 1970.] 258 p. illus.

Text in Japanese.

Contents: 1. Holmes Is Still Alive in Our Hearts. - 2. A Certain Period in Enigma. - 3. Enviable Life of a Pilgrim [about the Swiss Tour]. - 4. A Glimpse of the Room at Baker Street. - 5. The Case That Shouldn't Have Happened. - 6. The Man in Exile. - 7. Basic Patterns for Solving Problems. - 8. Japan Broadcasting Company's Reproduction of Sherlock Holmes Series of BBC Production.

Review: SHJ, 9, No. 4 (Summer 1970), 141 (Lord Donegall).

2139. ——. [*Sherlock Holmes and His Bluish Smoke*. Tokyo: Bungei Shunju Ltd., 1966.] 221 p. illus.

Text in Japanese.

Contents: 1. Holmes and His University. - 2. Holmes and Cocaine. - 3. Holmes and Tobacco. - 4. A Study in Tires. - 5. Holmes and His Retirement.

Review: SHJ, 8, No. 1 (Winter 1966), 28-29 (Lord Donegall).

2140. ——. [*Sherlock Holmes in the Mist*. With introduction by Lord Donegall and Julian Wolff. Tokyo: Bungei Shunju Ltd., 1968.] 249 p. illus.

Text in Japanese.

Contents: Pt. I. 1. On Tobacco, Again. - 2. The Scowrers. - 3. Another Profile of Doyle. - 4. Again on Professor Bell. - Pt. II. 1. Ellery Queen Versus Jack the Ripper. - 2. Miscellaneous Opinions on Jack the Ripper.

Review: SHJ, 9, No. 1 (Winter 1968), 29 (Lord Donegall).

2141. ——. [*The Sherlock Holmes-Moriarty Duel*. Tokyo: Bungei Shunju Ltd., 1967.] 242 p. illus.

Text in Japanese.

Contents: Pt. I. Miscellaneous Notes (five chapters dealing respectively with Houn, Prio, Stud, Glor, and Musg). - Pt. II. The Marriage of Dr. Watson. - Pt. III. The Sherlock Holmes-Moriarty Duel.

Review: SHJ, 8, No. 4 (Summer 1968), 135 (Lord Donegall).

2142. ——. [*The Study on Sherlock Holmes: A Miscellany*. Tokyo: Asahi Shimbun-sha, 1961.] 215 p. illus.

Text in Japanese.

Contents: 1. Sherlock Holmes Is Still Alive. - 2. A Country Doctor in Southsea. - 3. Doyle's Murder Case. - 4. Return of Sherlock Holmes. - 5. Construction of the Works. - 6. On Dr. Bell. - 7. Contributors to the Birth of Sherlock Holmes. - 8. Holmes and Watson. - 9. Holmes and the Science of Deduction. - 10. Holmes and His Reward. - 11. Alma Mater of Sherlock Holmes. - 12. Holmes and the Fair Sex. - 13. Baker Street 221B. - 14. The Baker Street Irregulars.

According to Dr. Naganuma, this is the most complete study of Sherlock Holmes ever to appear in the Orient. It was a best seller in Japan at the time of its publication.

Review: SHJ, 5, No. 3 (Winter 1961), 90 (Lord Donegall).

2143. ——. [*The World of Sherlock Holmes*. Tokyo: Bungei Shunju Ltd., 1962.] 237 p. illus.

Text in Japanese.

Contents: 1. Holmes and His Favorite Tactics of Displaying. - 2. Holmes and Cocaine. - 3. Holmes and His Disguises. - 4. Holmes and Communications. - 5. Holmes and Pistols. - 6. John H. Watson, M.D. - 7. Watson As Practitioner. - 8. Mrs. Hudson. - 9. Holmes the Barman.

Review: SHJ, 5, No. 4 (Summer 1962), 122-123 (Lord Donegall).

2144. Narkevich, A. ["Conan Doyle and Sherlock Holmes," *A Collection of Works in Eight Volumes,* by Sir Arthur Conan Doyle. Moskva: Pravda Pub. House, 1966.] Vol. 1, p. 543-546.
———. ———, Tr. by Ted Schulz. *VH,* 4, No. 2 (April 1970), 8-10; 4, No. 3 (September 1970), 7.

2145. "A New Holmes Mystery," *Fourth Leaders from The Times, 1952: A Selection from the Past Twelve Months.* London: The Times Pub. Co. Ltd., [1953]. p. 7-8.
An attempt to identify the Sherlock Holmes story Conan Doyle said he thought out while at St. Alkmund's Church in Shrewsbury.

2146. Nielsen, Bjarne. "—*I Hear of Sherlock Everywhere*—" [Danmark]: Spredte Betragtninger over et kaert emne, 1964. 20 p.
Limited to 221 copies.
———. ———, *Kolophon* [København], Nr. 1 (1965), 8-14.
Text in Danish.

2147. Nielsen, K. Møller. "Sherlock Holmes og Dr. Watson tager imod" ["Sherlock Holmes and Dr. Watson Receive a Guest"], *Sherlockiana,* 13, Nr. 3 (1968), 7-8.

2148. Nordberg, Nils. "Innledning: Dr. Conan Doyle, Dr. Watson og Sherlock Holmes," *Sherlock Holmes: Syv hendelser fra hans liv og virke.* [Oslo]: Gyldendal Norsk Forlag, [1969]. p. 7-15.

2149. Opdycke, John B. "Introduction," *Adventures of Sherlock Holmes.* New York and London: Harper & Brothers, [1930]. p. ix-liii.
———. ———, *Introducing Mr. Sherlock Holmes.* Edited by Edgar W. Smith. Morristown, N.J.: The Baker Street Irregulars, 1959. [unpaged]
"Why detective fiction should be read in high schools, and why Sherlock Holmes is *the* detective to be read." (Edgar W. Smith)

2150. Oursler, Will. "Sherlock Holmes—Dead or Alive?" *Bluebook,* 97, No. 1 (May 1953), 6-12.
Edgar Smith considered this to be one of the best articles ever written about Holmes, Watson, Doyle, and the Irregulars.

2151. Page, Andrew, ed. *A Case of Bishops-gate Jewels, or Lovers of Sherlock Holmes Speak Their Pieces.* Edited, revised and enlarged for the Baker Street Pageboys & the Priory School of New York. New York: [Privately Produced], 1971. [34] p.
A revision of the monograph edited by Chris Redmond (item 2162).

2152. Pattrick, Robert R. "Ponderings by the Politician," *West by One and by One.* San Francisco: Privately Printed, 1965. p. 107-112.
Contents: Two Holmeses at Home. - "I Hear of Sherlock Everywhere" Dept. - Very Little Danger. - "Holmes . . . sent off several wires". - Some Gleanings from Baedeker. - The London Library.

2153. Pearson, Edmund. "Ave atque Vale, Sherlock!" ["Hail and Farewell, Sherlock!"] *The Outlook,* 146, No. 12 (July 20, 1927), 386-387. (The Book Table)
———. ———, *CPBook,* 4, No. 16 (Fall 1968), 315.

2154. Peck, Harry Thurston. "A Chat About Sherlock Holmes," *The Independent,* 53 (November 21, 1901), 2757-2760.
A high and discerning tribute, at this early day, to the genius of the creator and the created.

2155. ———. "The Detective Story," *Studies in Several Literatures.* New York: Dodd, Mead and Co., 1909. Chap. 14, p. 257-278.
———. ———, ———. Freeport, N.Y.: Books for Libraries Press, [1968]. Chap. 14, p. 257-278.
Contains considerable commentary on the Sherlock Holmes stories.

2156. Petersen, Svend. *The Testamentary Capacity of Sherlock Holmes. Parallel Cases. The Unwritten Canon Lore.* [N.p.: Privately Produced, n.d.] [16] p.
Three papers read on January 6, 1950, June 15, 1951, and April 19, 1952.

2157. Pina, Luís de. "Sherlock Holmes no Porto: Contribuiçao portuguesa para a história do romance policial cientifico," *Revista de Gvimaraes,* 71, No. 1-2 (January-June 1961), 65-107. illus.
"Sherlock Holmes in Porto: Portuguese contribution to the history of the scientific police novel."

2158. Portuondo, José Antonio. "Holmes y Lupin de América" ["Holmes and Lupin of America"], *Américas,* 6, Nr. 9 (September 1954), 13-16, 26-27.

2159. Queen, Ellery. "The Doyle Decade," *Twentieth Century Detective Stories.* Edited by Ellery Queen. Illustrated by Seymour Nydorf. Cleveland and New York: The World Pub. Co., [1948]. p. 240-249.
———. ———, *Ellery Queen's Mystery Magazine,* 14, No. 69 (August 1949), 88-94. (Queen's Quorum: Part Three)
———. ———, *Queen's Quorum: A History of the Detective-Crime Short Story as Revealed by the 106 Most Important Books Published in This Field Since 1845,* by Ellery Queen. Boston: Little, Brown and Co., 1951. Chap. 4, p. 29-45.
———. ———, *Queen's Quorum. . . .*

The Writings About the Writings

General and Miscellaneous

Supplements Through 1967. New York: Biblo and Tannen, 1969. p. 29-45.

A discussion of some of the most important detective stories, including *The Adventures of Sherlock Holmes,* to appear during the 1890's.

2160. ———. *In the Queens' Parlor and Other Leaves from the Editors' Notebook.* New York: Simon and Schuster, 1957. ix, 195 p.
———. ———. London: Victor Gollancz Ltd., 1957. ix, 195 p.

There are several references to Sherlock Holmes in this collection of introductions from *EQMM,* including "The Great O-E Theory" and "High Sherloctane."

2161. R., J. N. B. "The Case Against Watson," *Desiderata,* 4, No. 44 (November 2, 1951), 1-3. (Editorial)

Primarily a discussion, with quotations, of S. C. Roberts's introduction to *Sherlock Holmes: Selected Stories* (item 736).

2162. Redmond, Chris, ed. *A Case of Bishopsgate Jewels, or Levers of Sherlock Holmes Speak Their Pieces.* Kingston, Ontario: The Baker Street Pageboys, 1966. [20] p.

Eighteen selected paragraphs that express the authors' praises of the Master. See also item 2151.

2163. ———, ed. *The Jerker Street Banal: A Sherlockian Quarterly (?) of Irregularity.* Vol. 1, No. 1. Kingston, Ontario: The Baker Street Pageboys, October 1966. 1 issue.

"A parody of *The Baker Street Journal,* including three worthy items of Sherlockian scholarship (though from a strange point of view) and burlesques of the *BSJ's* features and departments."

2164. Redmond, Don. " 'I Hear of Sherlock Everywhere,' " *The Gamut: The Bulletin of the University of Kansas Library Staff Association,* 11, No. 3 (February 1965), 4-6.
———. ———, *Books and Libraries at the University of Kansas,* 2, No. 6 (March 1965), 5-7.

2165. Rennie, I. Drummond. "Is Holmes Watson?" *The Lancet,* No. 7686 (December 19, 1970), 1304-1305.

Conclusive arguments supporting the cerebral superiority of Dr. Watson over Sherlock Holmes are presented. Recent evidence is brought forward to show that Holmes and Watson are separate individuals, neither of them female, and that though both are still alive, both have, with the passage of time, suffered intellectual dilapidation to the point of dementia.

2166. ["Review of *The Adventures of Sherlock Holmes*"], *The New York Times* (October 16, 1892), 19, and reprinted in *BSJ,* 9, No. 3 (July 1959), 189.

2167. ["Reviews of *The Case-Book of Sherlock Holmes*"], *Booklist,* 24 (November 1927), 67; *The Bookman,* 66 (September 1927), 91 (Gilbert Seldes); *Boston Transcript* (June 25, 1927), 4 (E. F. Edgett); *Independent,* 119 (July 16, 1927), 68; *Nation and Athenaeum,* 41 (July 16, 1927), 520 (Edwin Muir); 44 (November 17, 1928), 254-255 (A. A. Milne); *New York Evening Post* (June 26, 1927), 9 (H. E. Dounce); *New York Herald Tribune Books* (June 26, 1927), 9; *New York Times Book Review* (June 26, 1927), 9; *Outlook,* 146 (July 20, 1927), 386; *Pittsburgh Monthly Bulletin,* 32 (October 1927), 440; *Saturday Review,* 144 (July 16, 1927), 101; *Spectator,* 139 (July 2, 1927), 25; *Times Literary Supplement* (June 23, 1927), 438; *World* [New York] (August 21, 1927), 7m (Vincent Starrett).

2168. ["Reviews of *His Last Bow*"], *Athenaeum* (December 1917), 680; *Boston Transcript* (October 27, 1917), 8; *Dial,* 64 (January 17, 1918), 77-78; *Independent,* 92 (November 24, 1917), 385; *Nation,* 105 (December 20, 1917), 694; *New York Times Book Review* (October 28, 1917), 433; *Publishers' Weekly,* 92 (December 8, 1917), 2026 (Fremont Rider); *Reedy's Mirror* (February 22, 1918) (Vincent Starrett); *Spectator,* 119 (December 15, 1917), 718; *Springfield Republican* (November 11, 1917), 17; *Times Literary Supplement* (October 25, 1917), 516.

2169. ["Reviews of *The Memoirs of Sherlock Holmes*"], *Athenaeum,* No. 3455 (January 13, 1894), 47, and reprinted in *CPBook,* 4, No. 14 (Winter 1968), 275; *The Hundred Best Crime Stories,* Edited by Julian Symons (London: The Sunday Times, [n.d.]), 3.

2170. Rexroth, Kenneth. "Sherlock Holmes," *Saturday Review,* 51, No. 17 (April 27, 1968), 53, 58. (Classics Revisited, 64)
———. ———, *CPBook,* 4, No. 15 (August 1968), 281-282.

"There are no better records of the profoundly normal oddity of Victorian England and early twentieth-century France, nor more humane ones, than the detective tales of Conan Doyle ... . They are possessions like unto pearls of great price, for, alas, we will never be as odd again."

2171. Richards, Bob. "Elementary But Fascinating," *The Territorial Enterprise and Virginia City News* (February 4, 1966), 2, 14.

"A bit of reminiscing concerning one of the greatest character creations of all time."

2172. Ridley, M. R. "Sherlock Holmes and the Detective Story," *The Listener,* 51, No. 1298 (January 14, 1954), 65-66.

2173. Ringsted, Henrik V. "Sherlock Holmes

lever endnu" ["Sherlock Holmes Is Still Alive"], *London i lup*. København: Thanning og Appels Forlag, 1953. p. 51-76.

2174. Roberts, R. Ellis. "The Undying Detective," *The Saturday Review of Literature*, 21, No. 17 (February 17, 1940), 10-11.

A long review of Vincent Starrett's *221B: Studies in Sherlock Holmes* (item 2230) in which Mr. Roberts argues that Holmes was a Durham not a Cambridge man and that he was of British rather than American origin.

2175. Roberts, S. C. "Baker Street Cult," *Time and Tide*, 40, No. 22 (May 30, 1959), 628-629.

A survey of Doyle's story-writing ability, versatility, basic passions, and the genesis of Sherlock Holmes.

2176. ———. "The Cult of Sherlock," *John O'London's Weekly*, 63, No. 1545 (February 19, 1954), 162.

"In this 'leader' in the *Weekly's* Sherlock Holmes Centenary issue, the Master of Pembroke defends his fellow devotees against the gibes of the Gentiles." (Edgar W. Smith)

2177. ———. *Holmes and Watson: A Miscellany*. London: Oxford University Press, 1953. 137 p.

Contents: Sherlock Holmes: 1. His Creation. - 2. His Life. - 3. His Temperament. - 4. His Attitude to Women. - 5. His Music. - 6. His Kinship with Dr. Johnson. - *Dr. Watson:* 1. The Chronological Problem. - 2. His Life. - *The Baker Street Scene:* 1. 221B in Retrospect. - 2. Last Words. - *Two Unrecorded Adventures:* 1. Christmas Eve. - 2. The Strange Case of the Magatherium Thefts.

Reviews: Booklist, 50 (November 1, 1953), 95; *Nation*, 177 (October 31, 1953), 356; *New York Herald Tribune Book Review* (December 27, 1953), 8 (James Sandoe), and reprinted in *CPBook*, 2, No. 5-6 (Summer-Fall 1965), 107; *Punch*, 225 (November 4, 1953), 558-559 (Anthony Powell); *Saturday Review*, 36 (October 24, 1953), 36 (Sergeant Cuff); *SHJ*, 1, No. 4 (December 1953), 20, 19 (Ivar R. Gunn); *Springfield Republican* (December 6, 1953), 9C; *Times Literary Supplement* (November 20, 1953), 752.

2178. ———. "Introduction," *Sherlock Holmes: Selected Stories*. London: Oxford University Press, 1951. p. vii-xxiii.

———. ———, *Introducing Mr. Sherlock Holmes*. Edited by Edgar W. Smith. Morristown, N.J.: The Baker Street Irregulars, 1959. [unpaged]

A penetrating examination of several Canonical problems.

2179. Routley, Erik. *The Puritan Pleasures of the Detective Story: A Personal Monograph*. London: Victor Gollancz Ltd., 1972. 253 p.

The first five chapters of this highly enjoyable and stimulating book are devoted to the Sherlock Holmes stories—"the Bach of detective fiction." Appendix I includes a valuable analysis and chart of Holmes's cases.

2180. Santori, Daniela. *Conan Doyle and Sherlock Holmes*. Relatore Prof. Claudio Gorlier. Sessione straordinaria 1967-68. 196 p. (Tesi N. 3634)

Thesis—Milano: Universita' Commerciale Luigi Bocconi.

2181. Sayers, Dorothy L. "Introduction," *The Great Short Stories of Detection, Mystery and Horror*. London: Victor Gollancz Ltd., 1928. p. 9-47.

———. ———, *The Omnibus of Crime*. Edited by Dorothy L. Sayers. New York: Payson and Clarke Ltd., 1929. p. 9-47.

Reissued in 1961.

———. "Detective Fiction: Origins and Development," *Writing Detective and Mystery Fiction*. Edited by A. S. Burack. Boston: The Writer, 1945. Chap. 1, p. 3-48.

Second edition published in 1967.

———. ———, *The Art of the Mystery Story*. Edited and with a commentary by Howard Haycraft. New York: Simon and Schuster, 1946. p. 71-109.

———. ———, *Tales of Detection and Mystery from "The Omnibus of Crime."* New York: Macfadden-Bartell Corp., 1962. p. 7-40.

A long and important historical introduction, with a section on "Sherlock Holmes and His Influence."

"Conan Doyle took up the Poe formula and galvanised it into life and popularity. He cut out the elaborate psychological introductions, or restated them in crisp dialogue. He brought into prominence what Poe had only lightly touched upon—the deduction of staggering conclusions from trifling indications in the Dumas-Cooper-Gaboriau manner. He was sparkling, surprising, and short. It was the triumph of the epigram."

2182. ———. *Unpopular Opinions*. London: Victor Gollancz Ltd., 1946. 190 p.

———. ———. New York: Harcourt, Brace & Co., [1947]. vii, 236 p.

Partial contents: Holmes' College Career. - Note on Reginald Musgrave. - Dr. Watson's Christian Name: A Brief Contribution to the Exegetical Literature of Sherlock Holmes. - Dr. Watson, Widower. - Note on the Date of "The Sussex Vampire". - The Dates in "The Red-Headed League". - Note on Dr. Watson's Handwriting.

2183. "The Schoolboys' Holmes," *Fourth Leaders from The Times, 1950: A Selection*

The Writings About the Writings

General and Miscellaneous

General and Miscellaneous

from the Past Twelve Months. London: The Times Pub. Co. Ltd., [1950]. p. 82-83.

"It is pleasant to think of him [the boy] setting out on this joyous adventure on the long, long trail from the Scandal in Bohemia to the Retired Colourman."

2184. Scott, Byron. "The Doctor Did It," [Illustrated by Siculan]. *Today's Health*, 48, No. 10 (October 1970), 57-59, 70-72.

The story of Dr. Doyle and the Sherlock Holmes tales interestingly retold.

2185. The Scowrers and Molly Maguires of San Francisco and The Trained Cormorants of Los Angeles County. *West by One and by One: An Anthology of Irregular Writings.* San Francisco: Privately Printed, 1965. 157 p.

Contents: Introduction, by Poul Anderson. - On "Scowrer," by Anthony Boucher. - A Song for The Scowrers, by Worthen Bradley. - On the Later Tales, by Edgar W. Smith. - The Case of the Illustrious Predecessor, by Armine D. Mackenzie. - The Adventure of the Yellow House, by Gratia Jones. - The Hound of the Baskervilles, by Frank C. Baxter. - The Giant Rat of Sumatra, by John M. Nill. - The Sky-Pilot, by C. E. Lauterbach. - Who Was Isadora Persano? by Joel Hedgpeth. - The Case of the Sunburned Peer, by Don Douglass. - Skipping Stones at Reichenbach, by Ruth Berman. - A Case of Lost Identity, by Lenore Glen Offord. - The Professor and *The Valley of Fear*, by B. M. Castner. - Two Partial Pastiches, by Paula Salo. - The Camberwell Poisoning Case, by Stillman Drake. - Another Bird in a Gilded Cage, by Don Hardenbrook. - Ponderings by the Politician, by Robert R. Pattrick. - A Sherlockian Zoo, by Adelaide P. Ewing and Robert R. Pattrick. - In the Island of Uffa, by Poul Anderson. - The Moriarty Gambit, by Fritz Leiber. - "Two Good Men," by Dean W. Dickensheet. - An Introduction to Filk Singing, by Karen K. Anderson.

Reviews: BSP, No. 12 (June 1966), 3 (Bruce Dettman); *SHJ*, 7, No. 3 (Winter 1965), 91 (Lord Donegall).

2186. Sewell, Gordon. "Holmes and Watson in the South Country: Wessex Notebook—A Regional Miscellany," *The Southern Daily Echo* (October 2, 1957).

————. ————, *SHJ*, 3, No. 3 (Autumn 1957), 10-12.

————. ————, *CPBook*, 2, No. 5-6 (Summer-Fall 1965), 93.

Contents: Watson at Netley. - Familiar with Winchester. - Rural Dangers. - Forest Crime. - Von Bork's Hideout.

2187. ————. "Sherlock Holmes Is Now 100 Years Old: Wessex Notebook—A Regional Miscellany," *The Southern Daily Echo* (January 7, 1954).

————. ————, *CPBook*, 2, No. 5-6 (Summer-Fall 1965), 95-96.

Contents: Hampshire Man? - Near Winchester. - West Country Case. - The Original Watson. - An Immortal.

2188. Shanks, Edward. " 'You Know My Methods, Watson,' " *John O'London's Weekly*, 20, No. 500 (November 17, 1928), 222.

"*The Complete Sherlock Holmes*; Characters who walk out of the written page; The lovableness of Watson" (Subtitle)

2189. Sherbrooke-Walker, Ronald. "Sherlock Holmes," *The Cadet Journal and Gazette*, 25 (November 1963), 254-255.

"The article is slight, but is designed to introduce the young reader to Mr. Holmes, and (more important) it defends the Canon against the charge of having no appeal to the youth of today." (Colin Prestige)

2190. "Sherlock Holmes: A Case-Book of Sherlockiana to Celebrate the Centenary of Holmes's Creator, Sir Arthur Conan Doyle (Born May 22, 1859)," BBC Home Service, Thursday, May 28, 1959, 10:30-11:00 p.m.

Introduced by Leonard Maguire. Linking script by Eddie Boyd. Compiled and produced by W. Gordon Smith.

2191. "Sherlock Holmes, el más vivo de los héroes de ficción' ["Sherlock Holmes, the Most Alive of the Heroes of Fiction"], - *Cruzeiro internacional edición en castellano* [Rio de Janeiro: La Empressa Grafica o Cruzeiro S.A.], 9, Nr. 12 (June 16, 1965), 66-71.

A profusely illustrated article on the birth of Holmes and his subsequent career; with information on the Baker Street Irregulars and the Sherlock Holmes Society of London.

2192. "Sherlock Holmes: The Great Detective Takes a New Lease on Life," *Life*, 16, No. 18 (May 1, 1944), 77-82.

Text and pictures on the illustrators, the stage and screen portrayals, and the BSI.

2193. "Sherlockholmitos," *The Times Literary Supplement*, 31 (October 27, 1932), 782.

An examination of some preliminary textual problems in the Canon.

2194. Simmons, Walter. "Sherlock Holmes Lives On," *Facts*, 5, No. 1 (July 1944), 45-49.

An essay on "the most thoroughly alive character of literature."

2195. Simpson, A. Carson. *Simpson's Sherlockian Studies.* Philadelphia: Privately Printed by International Printing Co., 1953-1960. 8 v. illus.

Limited to 221B copies.

Contents: Vol. 1-4. Sherlock Holmes's Wanderjahre. - Vol. 5-7. Numismatics in the

Canon. - Vol. 8. I'm off for Philadelphia in the Morning.

Note: Vol. 9 entitled *Canonical Philately* was never printed but the manuscript was reproduced and issued by William R. Smith in 1971.

2196. Smith, Edgar W. *Baker Street and Beyond: Together with Some Trifling Monographs.* Morristown, N.J.: The Baker Street Irregulars, 1957. 53, [153] p. illus. maps. (BSI Incunabula, No. 5)

Limited to 350 copies.

A reissue of the *Sherlockian Gazetteer* (item 4268), with five of Dr. Julian Wolff's definitive maps; and also including a selection of the author's essays and verses.

Contents: Baker Street and Beyond: A Sherlockian Gazetteer. - Sonnet: John H. Watson to Sherlock Holmes. - A Scandal in Identity. - Sonnet: Sherlock Holmes to John H. Watson. - Dr. Watson and the Great Censorship. - Sonnet: Sherlock Holmes to Irene Adler. - "Good Night, Mister Sherlock Holmes". - Sonnet: Sherlock Holmes to James Moriarty, Sc.D. - The Napoleon of Crime. - The Old Shikari. - The Suppressed Adventure of the Worst Man in London. - Sherlock Holmes and the Great Hiatus. - Sonnet: Sherlock Holmes to Mycroft Holmes. - The Adventure of the Veiled Author. - Sonnet: Mary Morstan to J. H. Watson. - Sonnet: Sherlock Holmes to Mrs. Hudson. - Sonnet: To Violet de Merville. - Ballade of the Bright Stair-Rods. - The Disappearance of Mr. James Phillimore. - Sonnet: To the Old Lady of Murray Hill. - Up from the Needle. - God Rest You, Mary Sutherland! - The Solitary Cyclist Rides Again. - The Quasi-Final Problem. - "He Stoppeth One of Three . . ." - Saved by the Bell-Rope. - The Long Road from Maiwand. - Triolet: On the Immortality of Sherlock Holmes and Dr. Watson. - An Unrecorded Incident. - A Ghost in Baker Street. - "You Have Not Been in Afghanistan, I Perceive".- To Sherlock Holmes: Born January 6, 1854.

2197. ———, ed. *A Baker Street Four-Wheeler: Sixteen Pieces of Sherlockiana.* [Maplewood, N.J., and New York: The Pamphlet House, 1944.] 77 p.

Limited to 200 numbered copies (first ed.)

Contents: Foreword. - The Man Who Was Wanted: A Fragment, by Sir Arthur Conan Doyle [sic]. - A Plot for a Sherlock Holmes Story, by Sir Arthur Conan Doyle. - Sherlock Holmes's Prayer, by Christopher Morley. - Mr. Holmes: A New Judgment, by J. P. Jackson. - Behind the Abbey Door, by Rev. Leslie Marshall. - To Sherlock Holmes, by P. M. Stone. - Sherlock and Son, by Marion Prince. - To William Gillette, by Vincent Starrett. - The Sartorial Sherlock Holmes, by Humfrey Michell. - Sonnet: San Francisco to Sherlock, by Anthony Boucher. - Sherlock Holmes on the Turf, by C. R.

Andrew. - What Son Was Watson? by Bliss Austin. - Billy, by James Keddie, Jr. - Ballade of the Bright Stair-Rods, by Helene Yuhasova. - The Disappearance of Mr. James Phillimore, by Edgar W. Smith. - Sherlock Holmes Speaks.

2198. [———.] "The Editor's Gas-Lamp," *BSJ* [OS], 1-4 (April 1946-January 1949); (NS), 1-10 (January 1951-October 1960).

A regular feature of *The Baker Street Journal* in which the late Buttons-cum-Commissionaire illuminated a number of Sherlockian subjects. Each editorial is listed separately under an appropriate subject.

2199. [———.] "From the Editor's Commonplace Book," *BSJ* [OS], 1-4 (April 1946-January 1949); (NS), 1-10 (January 1951-October 1960).

News of and cogent commentaries on the Sherlockian world, including excerpts from letters to the editor.

2200. [———.] "I Heard of Sherlock Everywhere . . . ," *BSJ*, 5, No. 4 (October 1955), 195-196. (The Editor's Gas-Lamp)

A description of Mr. Smith's trip to Europe.

2201. [———.] "The Implicit Holmes," *BSJ* [OS], 1, No. 2 (April 1946), 111-112. (The Editor's Gas-Lamp)

———. ———, *The Final Adventures of Sherlock Holmes.* New York: The Limited Editions Club, 1952. Vol. 2, p. 1775-1777.

———. ———, *BSJ*, 10, No. 4 (October 1960), 195-196. (The Editor's Gas-Lamp)

———. "What Is It That We Love in Sherlock Holmes?" *The Annotated Sherlock Holmes.* New York: Clarkson N. Potter, [1967]. Vol. 1, chap. 12, p. 103-104.

———. "Hvad er det, vi elsker hos Sherlock Holmes?" [Oversat af A. D. Henriksen.] Illustrationerne af Henry Lauritzen. *Sherlockia,* 1, Nr. 3-4 (1956), 10-12.

———. The same translation with title: "Den evige Holmes i os selv," *Sherlock Holmes Årbog* I (1965), 25-28.

"It is not Sherlock Holmes who sits in Baker Street comfortable, competent and self-assured; it is we ourselves who are there, full of a tremendous capacity for wisdom, complacent in the presence of our humble Watson, conscious of a warm well-being and a timeless imperishable content. . . . That is the Sherlock Holmes we love—the Holmes implicit and eternal in ourselves."

2202. ———, ed. *The Incunabular Sherlock Holmes.* Morristown, N.J.: The Baker Street Irregulars, 1958. 186 p. illus. (BSI Incunabula, No. 6)

Limited to 350 copies.

Contents: Foreword, by Edgar W. Smith (1958). - Some Inconsistencies of Sherlock Holmes, by Arthur Bartlett Maurice (1902).

General and Miscellaneous

General and Miscellaneous

- More Sherlock Holmes Theories, by Arthur Bartlett Maurice (1902). - "The Hound of the Baskervilles" At Fault, by Frank Sidgwick (1902). - The Resources of Mycroft Holmes, by Charlton Andrews (1903). - The Unmasking of Sherlock Holmes, by Arthur Chapman (1905). - Sherlock Holmes, by Harry Graham (1905). - Studies in the Literature of Sherlock Holmes, by Ronald A. Knox (1912). - Sherlock Holmes and the Drood Mystery, by Edmund L. Pearson (1914). - Belsize as a Commentator: Sherlock Holmes, by Vernon Rendall (1917). - The Watson Touch, by A. A. Milne (1920). - How Watson Learned the Trick, by A. Conan Doyle (1924). - Dr. Watson Speaks Out, by A. A. Milne (1928). - A Note on the Watson Problem, by S. C. Roberts (1929). - The Truth About Professor Moriarty, by A. G. Macdonell (1929). - Prolegomena to the Life of Dr. Watson, by S. C. Roberts (1930). - Dr. Watson, Widower, by Dorothy L. Sayers (c. 1935). - Sherlock Holmes Is Mr. Pickwick, by Wilbur K. McKee (1941). - A Textbook of Friendship, by Christopher Morley (1944). - Sherlock Holmes's Prayer, by Christopher Morley (1944).

Review: SHJ, 4, No. 1 (Winter 1958), 3 (Lord Donegall).

2203. ———, ed. *Introducing Mr. Sherlock Holmes.* Morristown, N.J.: The Baker Street Irregulars, 1959. 1 v. (unpaged) illus. (BSI Incunabula, No. 7)

Limited and facsimile edition of 350 copies.

A collection of introductory essays by Vincent Starrett, S. C. Roberts, Dr. Joseph Bell, Howard Haycraft, Dr. John H. Watson, Rex Stout, Fletcher Pratt, Anthony Boucher, John B. Opdycke, Elmer Davis, Dr. A. C. Doyle, Christopher Morley, Edgar W. Smith, and Louis Untermeyer.

2204. ———, ed. *Profile by Gaslight: An Irregular Reader About the Private Life of Sherlock Holmes.* [Illustrations by Julian Brazelton and Frederic Dorr Steele. Endpaper maps by Julian Wolff.] New York: Simon and Schuster, 1944. xv, 312 p.

Also published in an unspecified number of numbered copies for friends and admirers of Sherlock Holmes who attended the BSI dinner at the Murray Hill Hotel on March 31, 1944.

Contents: Foreword, by E. W. S. - Introduction, by Louis Untermeyer. - 1. *Sherlock Holmes the Legend.* To a Very Literary Lady, by Vincent Starrett. - Sherlock Holmes and the Pygmies, by Heywood Broun. - The Profile Emerges, by Howard Haycraft. - To an Undiscerning Critic, by A. Conan Doyle. - 2. *Sherlock Holmes the Man.* Ex Libris Sherlock Holmes, by Howard Collins. - Was Sherlock Holmes a Drug Addict? by George F. McCleary. - Triolet on the Immortality of Sherlock Holmes and Dr. Watson, by "Buttons". - Clinical Notes by a Resident Patient, by Christopher Morley. - Was the Later Holmes an Impostor? by Anthony Boucher. - Sherlock Holmes in the News, by Charles Honce. - The Dental Holmes, by Charles Goodman. - The Other Friendship: A Speculation, by P. M. Stone. - The Coat of Arms of Sherlock Holmes, by Belden Wigglesworth. - The True and Proper Coat of Arms, by W. S. Hall. - Genealogical Notes on Holmes, by Rufus S. Tucker. - The Case of the Missing Patriarchs, by Logan Clendening. - Monody on the Death of Sherlock Holmes, by E. E. Kellett. - 3. *About Dr. Watson.* A Belated Eulogy, by Reginald Fitz. - Dr. Watson, by Stephen Vincent Benét. - Watson Was a Woman, by Rex Stout. - That Was No Lady, by Julian Wolff. - The Mystery of the Second Wound, by James Keddie, Sr. - Ballade of Watson in the Morning, by Belden Wigglesworth. - Dr. Watson's Christian Name, by Dorothy L. Sayers. - Sonnet: Mary Morstan to J. H. Watson, by Helene Yuhasova. - Thoughts on Seeing "The Hound of the Baskervilles" at the Cinema, by "Evoe". - 4. *The Baker Street Scene.* Sonnet on Baker Street, by Christopher Morley. - The Long Road to Maiwand, by Edgar W. Smith. - The Singular Adventures of Martha Hudson, by Vincent Starrett. - Annie Oakley in Baker Street, by Robert Keith Leavitt. - The Significance of the Second Stain, by Felix Morley. - Ballade of Baker Street, by Carolyn Wells. - A Scandal in Identity, by Edgar W. Smith. - The Secret Message of the Dancing Men, by Fletcher Pratt. - Three Identifications, by H. W. Bell. - 221B, by Vincent Starrett. - 5. *The Baker Street Irregulars.* The Constitution and Buy-Laws of the Baker Street Irregulars, by Elmer Davis. - The Baker Street Irregulars, by Alexander Woollcott. - An Unrecorded Incident. - Anthem: The Road to Baker Street, by Harvey Officer. - L'Envoi. - A Sherlockian Bibliography.

Reviews: Chicago Sun Book Week (April 9, 1944), 4 (Elizabeth Bullock); *Chicago Tribune* (April 9, 1944), VII, 10 (Vincent Starrett); *Kirkus,* 12 (February 1, 1944), 56; *New York Herald Tribune Weekly Book Review* (April 9, 1944), 4 (M. L. Becker); *New York Times Book Review* (April 2, 1944), 1 (Howard Haycraft); *New Yorker,* 20 (April 8, 1944), 92; *Springfield Republican* (April 9, 1944), 4.

2205. [———.] "Sherlock Holmes *Is* an American," *BSJ* [OS], 1, No. 1 (January 1946), 66-68. (From the Editor's Commonplace Book)

Mr. Smith tells of his unsuccessful attempts to locate Sherlock Witherington Holmes, whose two verses, "Procession" and "Sacrifice," were published in *Some University of Alabama Poets* (Birmingham: The Studio Book Shop, 1927). The latter verse was reprinted in *BSJ* [OS], 2, No. 2 (April 1947), 144.

2206. [———.] ["Sherlock Holmes: The Hunt Goes On"], *BSJ* [OS], 1, No. 2 (April 1946), 193-194. (From the Editor's Commonplace Book)

Three persons bearing the Master's name have been discovered: Sherlock W. Holmes, of Birmingham, Ala.; Sherlock Holmes, ex-soldier, of Tacoma, Wash.; and Sherlock Holmes, sailor, of Norman, Okla. Edgar Smith offered a year's subscription to *BSJ* to the first person who furnished "authentic information leading to the capture, dead or alive, of a Sherlock Holmes."

2207. [———.] "Sherlock Holmes Has Been Found! Not One of the Ilk, But *Two!*" *BSJ* [OS], 1, No. 4 (October 1946), 464-465.

A letter to Nathan Bengis from Sherlock Holmes in Olympia, Wash.; and another from Walter P. Armstrong relating his discovery of a second Sherlock Holmes in Memphis, Tenn.

Postscript: In an article entitled "No, Watson, It Isn't the Needle! Sherlock Holmes Lives Now!" (Chicago [AP]) (*The Denver Post* [May 18, 1969], 24), William J. Conway reports that an examiner for the state auditor of Washington is named Sherlock Holmes! To avoid problems, he is listed in the Olympia telephone directory under "Holmes, S. G." The article is accompanied by a photograph of Mr. Holmes that also appears in *BSJ*, 19, No. 3 (September 1969), 185. This is the same Holmes discovered by Mr. Bengis in 1946.

2208. ———. " 'You Have Not Been in Afghanistan, I Perceive,' " *BSJ Christmas Annual*, No. 1 (1956), 21-23.

———. ———, *Baker Street and Beyond: Together with Some Trifling Monographs*. Morristown, N.J.: The Baker Street Irregulars, 1957. [unpaged]

A report on what the author did *not* see of Sherlockian interest during his visit to the Middle and Far East.

2209. Somerset G. S. Intermediate School. *Baker Street Bulletin, Jan. 30, 1892*. Edited by Wendy Judge and John Carlano. Somerset, N.J.: [1969]. [11] p. illus.

Several entertaining items by members of a seventh-grade English class.

2210. Sommar, Carl Olov. "Sherlock Holmes och litteraturen," *Boken i vårt hjärta*. En skrift till Thure Nyman. [Stockholm]: Bok-vännerna, [1969]. p. 141-149.

2211. Sons of the Copper Beeches. *Leaves from the Copper Beeches*. [Edited by Ames Johnston, Thomas Hart, Henry A. Shalet, and H. W. Starr. Illustrated by H. W. Starr.] Narberth, Pa.: Livingston Pub. Co., 1959. viii, 134 p.

Limited to 500 numbered copies.

Second issue published in a paperbound edition in 1972.

Contents: Jim Montgomery, by Robert Aucott. - A Word to the Sons of the Copper Beeches, by Thomas Hart. - The Location of "The Three Students," by T. S. Blakeney. - De Re Pharmaca, by J. Raymond Hendrickson. - A Challenge from Baker Street, by Charles Fisher. - The Adventures of the Dead Detective, by Page Heldenbrand. - Sherlock Meets the Analyst, by Frank J. Eustace, Jr. - It Must Have Been Two Other Fellows, by A. Carson Simpson. - An Apology Ode, by Henry A. Shalet. - Murder at the Murray Hill, by Edgar W. Smith. - The London of the Canon, by Ames Johnston. - Some Reflections on That Little Thing of Chopin's, by Winifred M. Christie. - The Poisons of the Canon, by George B. Koelle. - A Submersible Subterfuge, by H. W. Starr. - The Princes of the Tower, by Wilton Marion Krogman. - The Jezail Bullet, by John Ball, Jr. - Appendix: Excerpt from the Condensed Version of the By-Laws.

2212. The Speckled Band. *The Second Cab: Fifteen Sherlockian Essays, One Sonnet and a Quiz*. Edited by James Keddie, Jr. [Boston: Privately Printed at Stoke Moran, 1947.] 93 p.

Limited to 300 numbered copies.

Contents: Foreword, by Vincent Starrett. - Gasogene, Coal Box, Persian Slipper, by James Keddie, Sr. - John H. Watson to Sherlock Holmes: A Sonnet, by Helene Yuhasova. - The Fascination of Sherlock Holmes, by Herbert F. West. - Clients in Jeopardy, by Henry C. Clark. - The Surgeon Probes Doctor Watson's Wound, by Roland Hammond. - 9 K-9's — A Cur's Quiz, by Douglas Lawson. - The Curious Problem of the Railway Timetables, by Roger T. Clapp. - The French Background of Sherlock Holmes: Aspects and Possibilities, by Belden Wigglesworth. - What Sherlock Didn't Know, by Stuart C. Rand. - London at the Turn of the Century, by P. M. Stone. - Prolegomena to a Memoir of Professor Moriarty, by Edgar W. Smith. - Holmes and the Royal Navy, by Fletcher Pratt. - The Case of the Neophyte and the Motet, by Richard Wait. - The Historicity of Sherlock Holmes, by Dirk J. Struik. - Sherlock in Kansas, by Willis B. Wood. - Letter from Porlock, by Herbert T. Hand, Jr. - Sherlock's Big Brother, by Mandel E. Cohen. - Answers to the Quiz.- The Line-Up.

2213. ———. *The Third Cab: A Collection of Sherlockiana from the Files of the Speckled Band*. [Boston: Privately Printed at Stoke Moran, 1960.] 84 p.

Limited to 500 numbered copies.

Contents: The Best Introduction to Holmes, by Henry C. Clark. - The Speckled Band — What Is It? by Douglas Lawson. -

The Speckled Band, by Cyrus Durgin. - The Battle of Charing Cross, by Rudolph Elie. - Watson Medicus, by Samuel R. Meaker. - In Defense of Sherlock Holmes, by E. Timothy-Howe Buxton. - On the Authorship of the Tales-Within-the-Tales, by Edgar W. Smith. - Top Secret, by Norman Ballou. - Holmes and Thorndyke—A Real Friendship, by Francis M. Currier. - Where Did you Get That Hat . . . Band? by Herbert T. Hand, Jr. - The Yellow Birds, by Roger T. Clapp. - L'Envoie, by P. M. Stone.

2214. Spring, Howard, "Conversation in Baker Street," *The Saturday Book*. Fifth year. Edited by Leonard Russell. [London]: Hutchinson, [1945]. p. 109-112.
———. ———, *Ellery Queen's Mystery Magazine*, 15, No. 74 (February 1950), 111-115.
———. "Samtale i Baker Street," [Oversat af A. D. Henriksen]. *Sherlock Holmes Årbog* II (1966), 18-24.
"The author of *My Son, My Son!* chats familiarly with Mrs. Hudson in warm and reminiscent mood." (Edgar W. Smith)

2215. Stark, Beverly. "How Old Is Sherlock Holmes?" *The Bookman*, 51, No. 5 (July 1920), 579-581.
A commentary on the Master's date of birth and his popularity in Spain, Latin America, and Russia.

2216. Starrett, Vincent. *Book Column.* [Introduction by Harry J. Owens.] Chicago: The Caxton Club, 1958. xiii, 242 p.
Limited to 350 copies.
Partial contents: Mystery in Baker Street. - The Adventure of the Lost Pants. - Of Codes and Ciphers. - A Second Note on Baker Street. - Sherlock and the Immortals. - Who Wrote "Sherlock Holmes"? - Sherlockian Scholarship in Excelsis. - Christmas in Baker Street.
Most of the essays and paragraphs in this collection first appeared in the author's "Books Alive" column of the *Chicago Sunday Tribune*.

2217. ———. *Books and Bipeds.* New York: Argus Books, Inc., [1947]. 268 p.
Partial contents: 1942. Nova 57 Minor. - The Man Who Was Wanted. - Art in the Blood. - *1943.* Woollcott and the Baker Street Irregulars. - Sherlock Holmes in China. - New Light on Irene Adler. - The Ten Best Detective Stories(?). - Dr. Doyle and Dr. Watson. - *1944.* A Valentine for Irene Adler. - A Sherlockian Anniversary. - Six Detectives in Miniature. - Frederic Dorr Steele. - Sherlock Holmes: Bachelor or Widower? - Sherlock Holmes, Booklover. - *1945.* Baker Street Inventory. - The Adventures of Sheerluck Hums. - Sherlockholmitos. - The Island of Uffa. - More (or Less) About Uffa. - Six Watson Cryptograms. - The Adventure of the Masked Ball.
A selection of essays and paragraphs from Mr. Starrett's weekly book column in the *Chicago Sunday Tribune*.

2218. ———. "Calix Meus Inebrians Quam Praeclarus Est," *BSJ* [OS], 1, No. 1 (January 1946), 7-8.
"I will myself take Mr. Sherlock Holmes of Baker Street. I will take him, if need be—in two handsome volumes—to a desert island, and do without the Bible, the Iliad, and Shakespeare."

2219. ———. "Enter Mr. Sherlock Holmes," *Atlantic Monthly*, 150, No. 1 (July 1932), 81-87.
———. ———, *The Private Life of Sherlock Holmes*, [by] Vincent Starrett. New York: The Macmillan Co., 1933. p. 1-18.
———. ———, ———. Revised and enlarged. The University of Chicago Press, [1960]. p. 1-12.
"A figure of incredible popularity, who exists in history more surely than the warriors and statesmen in whose time he lived and had his being. An illusion so real, as Father Ronald Knox has happily suggested, that one might some day look about for him in Heaven, forgetting that he was only a character in a book."

2220. ———. "From Poe to Poirot," *Books Alive: A Profane Chronicle of Literary Endeavor and Literary Misdemeanor.* With an Informal Index by Christopher Morley. New York: Random House, 1940. Chap. 9, p. 184-210.
———. ———, ———. Freeport, N.Y.: Books for Libraries Press, [1969]. Chap. 9, p. 184-210.
"For the inspiration that led Conan Doyle to write the tales of Sherlock Holmes we have to thank, first, his unemployment; second, his acquaintance with the works of Poe and Emile Gaboriau; and, third, his intimate knowledge of the methods and mannerisms of his old teacher, Dr. Joseph Bell of Edinburgh, who was the prototype of Holmes."

2221. ———. "In Praise of Sherlock Holmes," *Reedy's Mirror* [St. Louis] (February 22, 1918), 106-107.
———. ———, *BSJ*, 18, No. 1 (March 1968), 15-21.
The first piece ever written by this Sherlockian scholar *par excellence* about "the transcendental detective *par excellence*."

2222. ———. "Introduction," *The Adventures of Sherlock Holmes.* New York: The Limited Editions Club, 1950. Vol. 1, p. v-xviii.

———. ———, ———. New York: The Heritage Press, [1952]. p. v-xviii.

———. ———, *Introducing Mr. Sherlock Holmes.* Edited by Edgar W. Smith. Morristown, N.J.: The Baker Street Irregulars, 1959. [unpaged]

"More than any other form of fiction except the children's fairy tale, of which it is the successor, the detective story is an allegory or parable of wickedness overcome by virtue, of evil confounded and put to flight by truth and justice. 'Sherlock Holmes is what every man desires to be,' in the words of Hesketh Pearson, 'the knight-errant who rescues the unfortunate and fights single-handed against the powers of darkness.' "

2223. ———. "Introduction," *Appointment in Baker Street,* [by] Edgar W. Smith. [New York: The Pamphlet House, 1938.] p. 9-11.

———. "Explanation," *221B: Studies in Sherlock Holmes.* Edited by Vincent Starrett. New York: The Macmillan Co., 1940. p. xi-xvi.

"Let us be done with all this talk of—anything you may happen to dislike in the daily headlines. Let us talk rather of those things that are permanent and secure, of high matters about which there can be no gibbering division of opinion. Let us talk of the realities that do not change, of that higher realism which is the only true romance. Let us talk again of Sherlock Holmes."

2224. ———. "A Note on Mr. Sherlock Holmes," *Esquire,* 1 (May 1934), 59, 96, 98.

"A speculation, for students of the whole art of detection, on the whereabouts of their idol." (Subtitle)

2225. ———. "Portrayers of Sherlock Holmes," *The Private Life of Sherlock Holmes.* Revised and enlarged. The University of Chicago Press, [1960]. p. 115-127

A combined revision of "Impersonators of Mr. Sherlock Holmes," "Sherlock Holmes in Parody and Burlesque," and "The Evolution of a Profile."

2226. ———. "The Private Life of Sherlock Holmes," *The Bookman,* 75, No. 8 (December 1932), 812-818.

———. ———, *The Private Life of Sherlock Holmes.* New York: The Macmillan Co., 1933. p. 77-93.

———. ———, ———. Revised and enlarged. The University of Chicago Press, [1960]. p. 51-62.

———. ———, ———. *The Art of the Mystery Story.* Edited and with a commentary by Howard Haycraft. New York: Simon and Schuster, 1946. p. 146-157.

"When the melancholy Holmes was not a-sleuthing, and Watson was not occupied with crime, they engaged in the most refined of diversions, as Mr. Starrett shows, by bringing together passages which refer to the great detective's leisure hours." (*The Bookman*)

2227. ———. *The Private Life of Sherlock Holmes.* New York: The Macmillan Co., 1933. viii, 214 p.

———. ———. London: Ivor Nicholson & Watson Ltd., 1934. xi, 199 p. illus.

———. ———. New York, N.Y.: Haskell House Publishers Ltd., 1971. 199 p. illus.

Contents: Enter Mr. Sherlock Holmes. - The Methods of Mr. Sherlock Holmes. - The Return of Mr. Sherlock Holmes. - No. 221-B Baker Street. - The Private Life of Mr. Sherlock Holmes. - The Untold Tales of Dr. Watson. - Ave Sherlock Morituri et Cetera. - The Real Sherlock Holmes. - Impersonators of Mr. Sherlock Holmes. - Sherlock Holmes in Parody and Burlesque. - The Evolution of a Profile. - Epilogue. - Appendix: An Examination Paper on Sherlock Holmes, by Desmond MacCarthy [sic]. - A Final Examination Paper on the Life and Work of Sherlock Holmes, by E. V. Knox. - Bibliography.

Reviews: BSJ, 22, No. 3 (September 1972), 189 (Michael Murphy); *Booklist,* 30 (January 1934), 147; *Christian Century,* 50 (November 15, 1933), 1442; *London Mercury,* 30 (August 1934), 381 (Clennell Wilkinson); *New York Herald Tribune Books* (October 22, 1933), 17 (M. L. Becker); *New York Times Book Review* (October 29, 1933), 4 (Isaac Anderson); *Saturday Review of Literature,* 10 (December 2, 1933), 307 (Elmer Davis), and reprinted in *BSG,* 1, No. 4 (April 1962), 65-73; *Springfield Republican* (November 5, 1933), 7.

2228. ———. ———. Revised and enlarged. The University of Chicago Press, [1960]. vii, 155 p. illus.

———. ———. London: George Allen & Unwin Ltd., [1961]. 155 p.

Contents: 1. Enter Mr. Sherlock Holmes. - 2. The Methods of Sherlock Holmes. - 3. The Return of Sherlock Holmes. - 4. No. 221B Baker Street. - 5. The Private Life of Sherlock Holmes. - 6. The Singular Adventures of Martha Hudson. - 7. The Untold Tales of Dr. Watson. - 8. Ave Sherlock Morituri et Cetera. - 9. The Real Sherlock Holmes. - 10. Portrayers of Sherlock Holmes. - 11. The Baker Street Irregulars. - 12. The Adventure of the Unique Hamlet. - Epilogue.

Reviews: Chicago Sunday Tribune (May 1, 1960), 7 (Charles Collins); *CR* 1, No. 4 (September 1960), 17 (Dean Dickensheet); *Library Journal,* 85 (May 1, 1960), 1796 (E. F. Walbridge); *New Republic,* 142 (May 9, 1960), 15 (Rex Stout); *New York Herald Tribune Book Review* (May 1, 1960), 11 (James Sandoe); *New York Times Book Review* (September 4, 1960), 13 (Anthony

General and Miscellaneous

Boucher); *San Francisco Chronicle* (June 5, 1960), 29 (L. G. Offord); *SHJ*, 4, No. 4 (Spring 1960), 132-133 (James Edward Holroyd); 5, No. 3 (Winter 1961), 90 (Lord Donegall).

2229. ———. "Sherlock Holmes and After," *Persons from Porlock and Other Interruptions*, Chicago: Normandie House, 1938. p. 61-64.

Limited autographed edition of 399 copies printed by the Black Cat Press.

"I happen to prefer allegory to realism, and the romantic Sherlock Holmes (with all he symbolizes) to the contemporaneous bad manners of a Sam Spade."

2230. ———, ed. *221B: Studies in Sherlock Holmes*, by Various Hands. New York: The Macmillan Co., 1940. xvi, 247 p. illus.

———. ———. [Foreword by Edgar W. Smith.] Morristown, N.J.: The Baker Street Irregulars, 1956. xvi, 247 p. illus. (BSI Incunabula, No. 4)

Limited and facsimile edition of 350 copies.

———. ———. Foreword by Edgar W. Smith and a new introduction by the Editor. New York: Biblo and Tannen, 1969. xxii, 247 p. illus.

Contents: Explanation, by Vincent Starrett. - The Memoirs of Sherlock Holmes: The Field Bazaar, by A. Conan Doyle. - Was Sherlock Holmes an American? by Christopher Morley. - Nummi in Arca, by R. K. Leavitt. - On the Emotional Geology of Baker Street, by Elmer Davis. - Dr. Watson's Secret, by Jane Nightwork. - The Care and Feeding of Sherlock Holmes, by Earle F. Walbridge. - Three Identifications, by H. W. Bell. - The Other Boarder, by James Keddie. - Sherlock Holmes and Music, by Harvey Officer. - Sussex Interview, by P. M. Stone. - The Adventure of the Unique Hamlet, by Vincent Starrett. - Mr. Sherlock Holmes and Dr. Samuel Johnson, by Richard D. Altick. - Sherlock Holmes in Pictures, by Frederic Dorr Steele. - The Creator of Holmes in the Flesh, by Henry James Forman. - Appointment in Baker Street, by Edgar W. Smith. - A Sherlock Holmes Crossword, by F. V. Morley.

Reviews: Atlantic Monthly (April 1940); *Boston Transcript* (February 24, 1940), 3 (Marian Wiggin); *New York Herald Tribune Books* (March 31, 1940), 18 (M. L. Becker); *New York Times Book Review* (February 18, 1940), 3; *Saturday Review of Literature*, 21 (February 17, 1940), 10-11 (R. Ellis Roberts).

2231. Steele, Frederic Dorr. "Sherlock Holmes," *Sherlock Holmes: Farewell Appearances of William Gillette, 1929-1930*. [Souvenir Booklet, November 22, 1929.] p. 3-7.

———. "Reminiscent Notes," *Sherlock*

Holmes: A Play, by William Gillette. Garden City, N.Y.: Doubleday, Doran & Co., 1935. p. xxi-xxx.

"A little history of the world's most famous fictional character." (Subtitle)

2232. Stewart-Gordon, James. "The Real Sherlock Holmes," *The Ottawa Journal*, 80, No. 31 (January 16, 1965), 35.

———. Condensed with title: "The Case of the Durable Detective," *The Reader's Digest*, 86, No. 514 (February 1965), 207-210.

———. Condensed with title: "The Case of the Immortal Detective," *The Reader's Digest* [U.K. Edition] (October 1966).

———. ———, *CPBook*, 3, No. 11 (Winter 1967), 211-214. (Reprinted from its first condensed appearance in *The Reader's Digest*)

One of the best general discussions of Holmes, Watson, and Doyle ever written.

2233. Stone, P. M. "In Memoriam: *Collier's Weekly*," *BSJ*, 7, No. 3(July 1957), 165-172.

An essay on the Collier's series of Sherlock Holmes stories, Freddie Steele's illustrations, and *The Sherlock Holmes Number*.

2234. Storr, Anthony. "A Black-and-White World," *The Times Literary Supplement* (June 23, 1961), ii.

"A discussion of the detective story with considerable mention of Holmes. (In a special section of the *TLS*, 'Crime, Detection and Society.')" (Julian Wolff)

2235. Stout, Rex. "Introduction," *The Later Adventures of Sherlock Holmes*. New York: The Limited Editions Club, 1952. Vol. 3, p. v-xi.

———. ———, *Introducing Mr. Sherlock Holmes*. Edited by Edgar W. Smith. Morristown, N.J.: The Baker Street Irregulars, 1959. [unpaged]

2236. Struik, Dirk J. "The Historicity of Sherlock Holmes," *The Second Cab*. Edited by James Keddie. [Boston: The Speckled Band, 1947.] p. 73-77.

"This mania for so-called historical criticism has also affected the person of Sherlock Holmes, despite the obvious fact that his influence is apparent throughout the whole world of crime detection. It therefore behooves us to sum up, for our own benefit and that of later generations, the reasons for our certainty that Holmes actually lived, and why we know that Doyle's relation to Holmes was at most comparable to that of Parson Weems to George Washington or that of Homer to the fleet-footed Achilles."

2237. Suter, Peter. "Sherlock Holmes and the Reichenbach Falls: The Fatal Plunge That

Did Not Take Place," *Schweiz Suisse Svizzera Switzerland* [Swiss National Tourist Office], No. 1 (1968), 1.

————. ————, *CPBook,* 5, No. 18 (Spring 1969), 345-347.

An illustrated article about Holmes's method of deduction, the Reichenbach incident, and the 1968 Swiss Tour.

2238. Swanson, Martin J. "And He Endureth Forever," *BSG,* 1, No. 4 (April 1962), 62-64.

A fine tribute by this sixteen-year-old author to Holmes, Watson, and the Sherlockian gentlemen.

2239. Swinnerton, Frank. "Holmes—World Figure," *John O'London's Weekly,* 63 (February 19, 1954), 165, 169.

"A warm appraisal of the Master and his 'creator'; diminished, unfortunately, by a quotation from 'The Case of the Man Who Was Wanted' (by Arthur Whitaker) in support of Dr. Doyle's 'creativeness.' " (Edgar W. Smith)

2240. Symons, Julian. *The Detective Story in Britain.* [London]: Published for the British Council by Longmans, Green & Co., [1962]. 48 p. illus. (Writers and Their Work, No. 145)

————. ————, *Books and Bookmen,* 7, No. 12 (September 1962), 22-33.

A valuable monograph with a chapter devoted to Sherlock Holmes.

2241. Tarvin, James. "Sherlock Holmes as a Classic," *SIS,* 1, No. 2 (December 1965), 21-23.

An attempt by a non-Sherlockian to analyze the lure of Holmes and the Canon while determining the real nature of a literary classic.

2242. Taylor, Matt. "Holmes Still Lives at Night," *The Miami Herald* (March 24, 1970).

————. ————, *DCC,* 6, No. 5 (August 1970), 4.

"So at night, I read again of Sherlock Holmes, the detective who will never die, and who still pricks the social conscience."

2243. Thomas, Gilbert. *How to Enjoy Detective Fiction.* London: Rockliff, 1947. 108 p. (The How to Enjoy Series)

As might be expected, this delightful little book contains considerable commentary on the Sacred Writings.

2244. Thomson, H. Douglas. *Masters of Mystery: A Study of the Detective Story.* London: Wm. Collins Sons & Co. Ltd., [1931]. 288 p.

————. ————. [Folcroft, Pa.]: The Folcroft Press, Inc., [1969]. 288 p.

A work replete with references to the tales, including a chapter entitled "Sherlock Holmes" (p. 122-143).

2245. ————, ed. "A Sherlock Holmes Miscellany," *The Sherlock Holmes.* [Compiled and prepared by Richard Lonsdale-Hands Associates.] London: Whitbread & Co. Ltd., [1957]. p. 11-43.

An introductory commentary and selections from the writings of Sir Arthur Conan Doyle, E. M. Wrong, Ronald A. Knox, Dorothy L. Sayers, H. Douglas Thomson, T. S. Blakeney, Vincent Starrett, Howard Haycraft, John Dickson Carr, Gavin Brend, S. C. Roberts, E. V. Knox, and "Sagittarius."

2246. [Traz, Georges de.] *Les romans policiers,* [par] François Fosca [pseud.] Paris: Wesmael-Charlier, [1964]. 124 p.

Pages 69-76 are devoted to the Sherlock Holmes saga.

2247. Untermeyer, Louis. "Introduction," *Profile by Gaslight.* Edited by Edgar W. Smith. New York: Simon and Schuster, 1944. p. xix-xx

————. ————, *Introducing Mr. Sherlock Holmes.* Edited by Edgar W. Smith. Morristown, N.J.: The Baker Street Irregulars, 1959. [unpaged]

"We know little concerning the origins of King Arthur and Robin Hood and Roland and Paul Bunyan—once living men, now they are legends. Sherlock Holmes is a glorious example to the contrary. He is . . . a legend that has come to life."

2248. Van Liere, Edward J. *A Doctor Enjoys Sherlock Holmes.* New York: Vantage Press, [1959]. 141 p.

Contents: Doctor Watson and the Weather. - The Anatomical Sherlock Holmes. - "Brain Fever" and Sherlock Holmes. - Curare and Sherlock Holmes. - Sherlock Holmes and the Portuguese Man-of-War. - Doctor Watson and Nervous Maladies. - Dogs and Sherlock Holmes. - The Botanical Doctor Watson - The Surgical Doctor Watson. - Sherlock Holmes, the Chemist. - Doctor Watson's Universal Specific. - Doctor Watson, Endocrinologist. - Genetics and Sherlock Holmes. - The Zoological Doctor Watson. - Doctor Watson, Cardiologist. - The Physiologic Doctor Watson. - Sherlock Holmes and Doctor Watson, Perennial Athletes. - The Therapeutic Doctor Watson. - Doctor Watson, General Practitioner.

2249. ————. "Essays on Sherlock Holmes," *West Virginia Medical Journal,* 55 (October 1959), 371.

————. ————, *100 Editorials,* Medical Center, West Virginia University, and Executive Office, West Virginia State Medical Association, 1963. p. 44.

2250. Wallace, H. Frank. "Sherlock Holmes,"

General and Miscellaneous

Please Ring the Bell. London: Eyre & Spottiswoode, [1952]. Chap. 9, p. 121-133.

In a beautifully written book of memoirs, the author devotes a chapter to two of his oldest and dearest friends—Sherlock Holmes and Dr. Watson.

2251. Walsh, William J., ed. *A Curious Collection.* Illustrated by Jon V. Wilmunen. [Suffern, N.Y.]: The Musgrave Ritualists Beta, 1971. 31 p.

Contents: No Real Treasure — Just the Butler's Body! by Lord Donegall. - The Clubable Watson, by Dean W. Dickensheet. - The Cask of Amontillado: Chapter Two, by Susan Elizabeth Dahlinger. - Cherchez la Femme, by Bruce D. Kennedy. - The Case of the Restless Rocks, by Kathryn E. Karlson. - What Was the Source? That Is the Question, by Nathan L. Bengis.

2252. Weber, William C. "Introduction," *Famous Tales of Sherlock Holmes.* New York: Dodd, Mead & Co., [1958]. p. v-viii.

"Holmes and Watson and all the immortal crew are as *alive* today as they were in the 1880's. And they will live as long as books are read."

2253. Wells, Carolyn. *The Technique of the Mystery Story.* Introduction by J. Berg Esenwein. Springfield, Mass.: The Home Correspondence School, [1913]. xiv, 336 p. (The Writer's Library. Edited by J. Berg Esenwein)

——. ——. New and revised edition. Springfield, Mass.: The Home Correspondence School, [1929]. xiv, 435 p.

An exhaustive and notable study of the mystery story, with many illuminating glimpses of Sherlock Holmes.

2254. West, Herbert F. "The Fascination of Sherlock Holmes," *The Second Cab.* Edited by James Keddie. [Boston: The Speckled Band, 1947.] p. 19-24.

——. ——. [Hanover, N.H.]: Privately Printed [Sumac Press], 1971. [7] p.

Limited to 100 copies.

A testimonial on the lure of the Sacred Writings.

2255. "Wigmore Street Post-Bag," *SHJ,* 1, No. 1- (May 1952-).

Letters to the editor from both sides of the Atlantic. Many contain valuable observations and commentaries on articles in the *Journal.*

2256. Williamson, J. N. *A Critical History and Analysis of the "Whodunit."* [Indianapolis, Ind.: Privately Printed, 1951.] [26] p.

Spiral binding.

"A concise and interestingly presented treatment of the detective story through the years, with the emphasis, of course, on Sherlock Holmes." (Edgar W. Smith)

2257. ——, and H. B. Williams, eds. *Illustrious Client's Case-Book.* With a foreword by Vincent Starrett. [Indianapolis, Ind.: The Illustrious Clients, 1948.] 67 p. illus.

Cover title: Client's Case-Book.

Contents: In Lieu of a Foreword, by Vincent Starrett. - Editors' Preface. - A Non-Sherlockian's Poem, by Maryesther Williamson. - "H." Stands for ——? by Jane Throckmorton. - My First Meeting with Sherlock Holmes, by Ben Abramson. - Lament to Youth and Sherlock Holmes, by H. B. Williams. - Musgrave Mathematics, by Jay Finley Christ. - Banquet Song, by H. B. Williams. - The Wiles of Mary Morstan, by J. N. Williamson. - "A Most Dark and Sinister Business," by Helen Howard. - In Defense of Scotland Yard — A Communication from Inspector Athelney Jones, reported by J. N. Williamson. - Who Is Who, and When, in *The Gloria Scott,* by C. R. Andrew. - I Always Smoke Ships Myself, by H. B. Williams. - Sherlock vs. Elliott, by Irvin C. Cole. - Hymn to Him, by Chris Hamilton. - Sherlock Holmes: An Illustration, by J. N. Williamson. - The Curious Incident of the *Tour de Force,* by Edgar W. Smith. - Mr. Sherlock Holmes: Misogamist or Misogynist? by J. N. Williamson. - Sherlock Holmes, the Chemist, by Bernard L. Doll. - Then Falls Thy Shadow, by the Sub-Librarian [H. B. Williams]. - Sonnet: To Violet De Merville, by Helene Yuhasova. - Sherlock Holmes and Boxing, by the Northumberland [J. N. Williamson]. - The Very Good Doctor: An Illustration, by J. N. Williamson. - The Terrible Death of Crosby, the Banker, by J. N. Williamson. - Frustration, by Dorothy Gray.

2258. ——, ed. *Illustrious Client's Second Case-Book: Nine Sherlockian Essays, Four Pastiches, Three Poems, Two Quizes, A Letter, A Song.* Edited . . . illustrated and designed by J. N. Williamson. With an introduction by Ellery Queen. [Indianapolis, Ind.: The Illustrious Clients, 1949.] 96 p.

Cover title: Client's 2nd Case-Book.

Contents: Introduction, by Ellery Queen. - Editor's Introduction. - Another Non-Sherlockian's Poem, by Maryesther Williamson. - A Sherlockian Crossword Puzzle, by Jane Throckmorton. - The Adventure of the Double Santa Claus, by B. L. T. - Sherlock and Two Impostors, by Jay Finley Christ. - That New Jersey Miss, by J. N. Williamson. - Notes from Northumberland Avenue, by J. N. Williamson. - Holmes and Watson Slept Here, by Helen Howard. - The Ageless Holmes — Another Communication from Inspector Athelney Jones, reported by J. N. Williamson. - That Scotland Yarder, Gregson — What a Help (?) He Was, by Clifton R. Andrew. - H. & W., Colorists, Textilests Ltd., by Irvin C. Cole. -

God Rest You, Mary Sutherland! By Edgar W. Smith. - Has Anybody Here Seen Moriarty? by Bernard Doll. - Curses Canonical, by the Sub-Librarian. - The Adventure of the Politician, the Lighthouse, and the Trained Cormorant, by J. N. Williamson. - Brain Storms, by Dorothy Gray. - Illustration, by Jerry N. Williamson. - The Case of the Crazy Americans, by Stanley McComas. - Sherlock Stays After School, by Nathan Bengis. - In Memoriam — Baron Adelbert Gruner, by Judith Fielder. - The Underground, by Robert A. Cutter. - The Adventure of the Bogle-Wolf, by Anthony Boucher. - Answer Page.

2259. ———, and H. B. Williams, eds. *Illustrious Client's Third Case-Book: Eighteen Sherlockian Essays, Four Quizzes, Three Tales-in-Verse, Three Poems, Two Limericks, Two Pastiches, a Parody.* With an introduction by Christopher Morley. [Indianapolis, Ind.: The Illustrious Clients, 1953.] 200 p.
    Spiral binding.
    Contents: Introduction, by Christopher Morley. - Editors' Introduction. - Sherlock Saga, by Vincent Starrett. - Thanks to Dr. Watson, by Nathan L. Bengis. - Sherlock Stays After School (An Addendum), by Nathan L. Bengis. - "He Stoppeth One of Three. . . ," by Edgar W. Smith. - Heresy on the Sherlock Holmes Front, by Charles Honce. - Royalty, by Owen F. Grazebrook. - Watson's Glamour Girls, by James P. Gleason. - My First Meeting with Sherlock Holmes, by G. T. Fleming-Roberts. - Doctor Watson, I Presume? by R. P. Graham. - The Greatest Tertian, by Anthony Boucher. - *The* Woman, by Isaac S. George. - Sherlock Holmes and Jack the Ripper, by Gordon Neitzke. - Sherlock's Murder Bag, by J. N. Williamson. - Three Footnotes to The Adventure of the Illustrious Client, by Bliss Austin. - Sonnet on Devonshire, by Robert A. Cutter. - A Non-Canonical Clue, by H. B. Williams. - An Illustrious Quiz, compiled by the Illustrious Clients. - Mycroft the Mighty, by Isaac S. George. - What Did Sherlock Holmes Drink? by Jorgen Cold. - The Horatian Spirit in Holmes, by Morris Rosenblum. - The Adventure of the Vial Climax, by J. N. Williamson. - Three Holmesian Problems, by Cherry Finer. - Valuable Sherlockian Hunting-Ground, by Doyle W. Beckemeyer. - Was It July or September, in "The Sign of the Four"? by C. R. Andrew. - Sub-Librarian's Quiz, by the Sub-Librarian. - His Last Bow, or The Final Final Problem, by Isaac S. George. - Notes from Northumberland Avenue, by J. N. Williamson. - Who Wore That Hat? by James P. Gleason. - The Adventure of the Perfect Husband, by August Derleth. - Solution of the Second Wound, by J. N. Williamson. - The Grate Fur Koat Mystery, by Albert J. Bromley. - Sherlock Stands

Supreme, by Isaac S. George. - Answer Page. - Afterword, by H. B. Williams. - An Afterword to the Afterword, by J. N. Williamson.

2260. Wölchen, Fritz. *Der Literarische Mord. Eine Untersuchung über die englische und amerikanische Detektivliteratur.* Nürnberg: Nest Verlag, [1953]. [348] p.
    Contains numerous references to Doyle, including a chapter entitled "In Baker Street" (p. 97-173).

2261. Wolf, Ben. "Zero Wolf Meets Sherlock Holmes," *BSJ*, 14, No. 2 (June 1964), 108-117.
    A cleverly written paper on the Canonical subjects of dogs, romance, tobacco, art, and the esthetic ancestry of Holmes.

2262. [Wolff, Julian.] "From the Editor's Commonplace Book," *BSJ*, 11- (March 1961-).
    A continuation of a department begun by the late Edgar Smith (item 2199) relating newsworthy items to the reader. The department is somewhat comparable to *SHJ's* "For the Commonplace Book" (item 1978) and W. T. Rabe's *CPBook* (item 4190).

2263. Woolsey, F. W. "Sherlock Holmes Is Still Alive!" *The Courier-Journal & Times Magazine* [Louisville] (December 31, 1967), 18-20.
    An illustrated article on the Master with mention of Doyle, the Irregulars, Morley, Gillette, and Rathbone.

2264. Yew, Elizabeth. "The Best and Wisest Man," *SIS*, 1, No. 3 (1966), 7-15.
    A discussion of Holmes, Watson, and the Baker Street scene.

B *Tales*

THE ADVENTURE OF THE ABBEY GRANGE

2265. Starr, H. W. "*The Abbey Grange,* or Who Used Eustace?" *BSJ*, 21, No. 4 (December 1971), 215-220, 223.
    Mary Fraser deliberately married Sir Eustace Brackenstall for his money and then, with the connivance of her maid Theresa, decided to get rid of him and keep the money. For the killing, they protected themselves by working the love-sick Crocker into such a rage and into such a situation that he killed Eustace himself without the slightest notion that he was merely a tool. Holmes was at first taken in, then realized he could never convict the women, but by

prosecution would merely ruin the fundamentally innocent Crocker. Thus he had been outwitted for the second time by a woman.

THE ADVENTURE OF THE BERYL CORONET

2266. Shalet, Henry A. "An Apology Ode," *Leaves from the Copper Beeches.* Narberth, Pa.: Livingston Pub. Co., 1959. p. 55-56.
A tale in verse.

2267. Simpson, A. Carson. "Whose Was It? Conjectures on a Coronet," *BSJ Christmas Annual,* No. 2 (1957), 9-17.
The borrower of the Beryl Coronet is identified as H. R. H. Albert Edward, Prince of Wales.

THE ADVENTURE OF BLACK PETER

2268. Daniels, Thomas L. "A Follow-Up Report on Black Peter," *BSJ,* 11, No. 3 (September 1961), 167.
During a trip to Norway the author hired a crew to operate three small whaling ships. Among the seamen was the grandson of the harpooner Patrick Cairns!

2269. Swanson, Martin J. "Daniel Defoe, Deptford, and Doctor Watson," *BSJ,* 15, No. 4 (December 1965), 206-207.
Watson's literary style in this tale may have been influenced by Defoe's *Journal of the Plague Year.*

THE ADVENTURE OF THE BLANCHED SOLDIER

2270. Clum, Florence. "Prithee Why So Pale?" *BSJ,* 5, No. 4 (October 1955), 226-229.
A tale in verse.

THE ADVENTURE OF THE BLUE CARBUNCLE

See also *Holmes — Eyesight* (Items 2973-2974)

2271. Arenfalk, Poul. " '. . . The Second Morning After Christmas. . . ,' " *IR,* 2, No. 6 (December 1962), 1-3.
An explanation of why Watson delayed wishing his old friend "the compliments of the season" until after Christmas.

2272. Beckemeyer, Doyle W. "Valuable Sherlockian Hunting-Ground," *Illustrious Client's Third Case-Book.* Edited by J. N. Williamson and H. B. Williams. [Indianapolis, Ind.: The Illustrious Clients, 1953.] p. 135-140.
"By the process of elimination, the only blue gem that can qualify is a sapphire, which miraculously satisfies the 'blue carbuncle' on all accounts."

2273. Bergman, Ted. "A Most Valuable Institution," *BSCL,* No. 6 (1968), 17-22.
"Which daily paper did Henry Baker read?"

2274. Bigelow, S. Tupper. "Barred-Tailed Geese," *SHJ,* 6, No. 4 (Spring 1964), 108-109.
A report on the author's correspondence with the Research Staff of *Encyclopaedia Britannica* and with Peter Scott, a world renouned ornithologist, concerning the existence of this species of geese.

2275. ———. "The Blue Enigma," *BSJ,* 11, No. 4 (December 1961), 203-214.
A detailed examination of the errors committed by Watson and Holmes in "one of the best stories in the Sherlockian Saga."

2276. Brend, Gavin. "The Route of the Blue Carbuncle," *SHJ,* 2, No. 4 (Winter 1955), 2-6.
———. ———, *Seventeen Steps to 221B.* [Edited by] James Edward Holroyd. London: George Allen & Unwin Ltd., [1967]. p. 100-105.

2277 Christ, Jay Finley. "Henry Baker's Scotch Bonnet," *BSJ,* 13, No. 2 (June 1963), 86.

2278. ———. "Sherlock Backs a Turkey," *Sherlockian Studies.* Edited by Robert A. Cutter. [Jackson Heights, N.Y.: The Baker Street Press, 1947.] p. 23.
"There was something askew with the carbuncle, blue, / Found in the crop of a goose!"

2279. Dickensheet, Dean and Shirley. "The Profession of Henry Baker: A Minor Exercise in Application of Method," Illustrated by William Dixon. *PD Annual,* 1, No. 1 (1970), 36-40. (The Master's Corner)
A meticulous analysis of Henry Baker and his attire reveals that he was a uniformed guard or attendant at the British Museum and that Holmes did not bother to speculate on Baker's occupation because he had already seen him in the Libraries or Reading Room of the Museum.

2280. Donegall, Lord. " '. . . The Compliments of the Season,' " *The New Strand,* 1, No. 2 (January 1962), 155-158. (Baker Street and Beyond, No. 2)
A summary and discussion of the Holmesian Christmas story.

2281. Iraldi, James C. "The Other Geese," *BSJ,* 4, No. 3 (July 1954), 156-159.
An accusing finger is pointed at Holmes for his failure to share the thousand-pound reward, offered for the return of the Blue Carbuncle, with Henry Baker and Peterson, who contributed to its recovery.

2282. Judson, Ralph. "The Chemistry of 'The Blue Carbuncle,' " *BSJ*, 9, No. 4 (October 1959), 243-244. (Two Critiques)

"Our famous detective appears to trip badly in his dissertation upon the nature of the Carbuncle."

2283. Kasson, Philip. "The True Blue: A Case of Identification," *BSJ*, 11, No. 4 (December 1961), 200-202.

The precious stone Holmes referred to was not a blue carbuncle but the famous Hope Diamond.

2284. Kimball, Elliot. "Chronology of *The Blue Carbuncle*," *BSJ*, 11, No. 4 (December 1961), 215-217.

Even though five scholars have dated this adventure 1889, the author insists it occurred on December 27, 1890.

2285. Morley, Christopher. "The Blue Carbuncle, or The Season of Forgiveness," *The Adventure of the Blue Carbuncle*. New York: The Baker Street Irregulars, 1948. p. 9-16.

―――. "A Christmas Story Without Slush," *The Ironing Board*. Garden City, N.Y.: Doubleday & Co., 1949. p. 95-101.

2286. Robertson, Allen, and E. J. C. " 'Commuting a Felony': An Opinion from British Counsel," by E. J. C. "An Opinion from American Counsel," by Allen Robertson. *BSJ* [OS], 3, No. 3 (July 1948), 309-316.

Legal opinions on Holmes's intended meaning of "commuting," "committing," or "compounding" a felony in this tale.

2287. Rosenberger, Edgar S. " 'Twas the Second Morning After Christmas," *BSJ*, 21, No. 4 (December 1971), 196-199.

A tale in verse.

2288. Smith, Edgar W. "The Story of the Blue Carbuncle," *The Adventure of the Blue Carbuncle*. New York: The Baker Street Irregulars, 1948. p. 59-64.

"A chronology of the seventh short story, in the light of secular and canonical history."

2289. Stix, Thomas L. "Un-Christmaslike Thoughts on *The Blue Carbuncle*," *BSJ*, 11, No. 4 (December 1961), 218-221.

The author takes issue with Christopher Morley and Edgar Smith for maintaining that this is the best of all Christmas stories.

2290. Wells, Arlene S. "Christmas in Baker Street," *BSJ Christmas Annual*, No. 3 (1958), 6.

"So, on this festive gala Day, / I hope your Christmas goose will lay, / As did that one so long ago, / A bright blue gem for you."

2291. Zeisler, Ernest Bloomfield. "A Pigment of the Imagination," *SHJ*, 5, No. 2 (Spring 1961), 50-52.

A delightful article on the controversy which developed over a statement by "Mildred Sammons" in "A Line o' Type or Two" (*Chicago Tribune* [December 26, 1946], 10) that the blue carbuncle could not have been found in the goose's crop because a goose has no crop.

THE BOSCOMBE VALLEY MYSTERY

2292. Baxter, Alfred W. "The Incident of the Grey Cloth," *VH*, 3, No. 2 (April 1969), 2-7.

The grey object James McCarthy reported seeing in the ground as he ran toward his dying father was not a coat but the giant rat of Sumatra; and Charles McCarthy died, not by the hand of his son, but from the head wounds he received when leaping back against a tree at the sight of this huge grey rat.

2293. Bigelow, S. Tupper. "Was It Baxter?" *SHJ*, 7, No. 4 (Spring 1966), 125-126.

An attempt to identify the Baxter whom Holmes was thinking of when he uttered his famous sentence, "There, but for the grace of God, goes Sherlock Holmes." (A commentary by Nathan Bengis appears in Vol. 8, p. 67.)

2294. Jaffee, Irving L. " 'The Boscombe Valley Mystery,' " *Elementary My Dear Watson*. Brooklyn, N.Y.: Theo. Gaus' Sons, [1965]. p. 55-56.

THE ADVENTURE OF THE BRUCE-PARTINGTON PLANS

2295. Arenfalk, Poul. "Where Is the Key of the Key-Mystery of 'The Bruce-Partington Plans?' " *IR*, 1, No. 4 (September 1961), 1-4.

2296. Brend, Gavin. "The Man from Campden Mansions," *BSJ*, 2, No. 3 (July 1952), 136-137. (Baker Street Doggerel)

"O gone are the days when I used to dine / With Eduardo Lucas and Oberstein." Monsieur Louis La Rothière.

2297. "The Bruce-Partington Keys," *SHJ*, 2, No. 2 (December 1954), 14-15.

An exchange of letters between R. Kelf-Cohen and Paul Gore-Booth and a comment from Felix Morley on the mystery of the keys.

2298. Callaway, J. S. "An Enquiry into the Identity of the Bruce-Partington Submarine," *BSJ*, 21, No. 3 (September 1971), 151-153. illus.

2299. Crump, Norman. "Inner or Outer Rail?" *SHJ*, 1, No. 1 (May 1952), 16-23.

A consideration of whether the body of Arthur Cadogan West was placed on the roof of an inner- or outer-rail circle train.

2300. Morrow, Daniel. "What Were the Technical Papers, Mycroft?" *SS*, 1, No. 1 (January 1971), 2-4.
A discussion of the B-P plans and the state of submarine development in England during the 1880's and 1890's.

THE ADVENTURE OF THE CARDBOARD BOX

2301. Bell, H. W. "On the Variant Readings of 'The Resident Patient,' " *Sherlock Holmes and Dr. Watson*. London: Constable & Co., 1932. p. 40-45.
———. ———, *BSJ* [OS], 1, No. 3 (July 1946), 312-314, 317. (Incunabulum)
The first study devoted to the problem of the duplicate mind-reading episode in Card and Resi.

2302. Clum, Florence. "So He Boxed Their Ears," *BSJ*, 2, No. 4 (October 1952), 210-213.
A tale in verse.

2303. Dardess, John. " 'It Will Just Cover That Bare Space on the Wall,' " *BSJ*, 20, No. 2 (June 1970), 103-109.
Based on the supposition that in 1887 mention of the American clergyman would be more apt to recall the Tilton-Beecher trial of 1874 than Beecher's trip to England on behalf of the North at the time of the Civil War, the mind-reading scene which opens Resi is given a different interpretation. A reason is offered for the duplication of this passage in Card.

2304. Hall, Trevor H. "The Documents in the Case," *Sherlock Holmes: Ten Literary Studies*. London: Gerald Duckworth & Co., [1969]. Chap. 8, p. 109-122.
A scholarly reexamination of the suppression of Card from *The Memoirs* and the transposition of the mind-reading incident from this adventure to Resi.

2305. Leavitt, Robert Keith. "The Preposterously Paired Performances of the Preacher's Portrait," *BSJ* [OS], 3, No. 4 (October 1948), 404-417.
A careful examination of the mind-reading passages concerning the portrait of Henry Ward Beecher in Card and Watson's watch in Resi, together with the records of the Tilton-Beecher trial of 1874, reveals that Watson was the natural son of the Reverend Beecher—a truly remarkable discovery!

2306. Potter, H. C. "The Case of the Blatant Duplication," *BSJ*, 20, No. 2 (June 1970), 86-90.
"In which of the cases does the anecdote

rightfully belong? Why? What precedents and reasons had Baring-Gould for including it in *Box* and excising it from *Patient*? [*The Annotated Sherlock Holmes*] How could his editing run counter to that of the A. Conan Doyle Memorial . . . Edition?"

2307. Smith, Edgar W. "The Curious Incident of the *Tour de Force*," *The Saturday Review of Literature*, 18, No. 17 (August 20, 1938), 11-12.
———. ———, *Illustrious Client's Case-Book*. Edited by J. N. Williamson and H. B. Williams. [Indianapolis, Ind.: The Illustrious Clients, 1948.] p. 40-44.
A further commentary on the duplicate passage in Card and Resi in which Holmes deduces Watson's train of thought.

THE ADVENTURE OF CHARLES AUGUSTUS MILVERTON

2308. Bailey, L. W. "The Dark Lady of Appledore Towers," *SHJ*, 4, No. 4 (Spring 1960), 113-115.
The unnamed lady may have been of Jewish extraction and her correspondent was the Prince of Wales, later King Edward VII.

2309. Brend, Gavin. "*Charles Augustus Milverton:* The Date," *SHJ*, 6, No. 3 (Winter 1963), 74-76.
An unfinished article in which the late author attempts to establish that this adventure belongs in the post-Reichenbach period.

2310. Dakin, D. Martin. "Some Milvertonian Doubts," *SHJ*, 7, No. 2 (Spring 1965), 46-48.
Mr. Dakin calls attention to certain problems in this case and suggests that Holmes's engagement to Agatha, Milverton's housemaid, was a hoax.

2311. Donegall, Lord. " 'The Worst Man in London,' " *The New Strand*, 1, No. 4 (March 1962), 424-426. (Baker Street and Beyond, No. 4)
After dating the adventure February 1899, the author is somewhat critical of Holmes and Watson for their housebreaking activities during the Milverton episode.

2312. Fenton, Irving M. "An Analysis of the Crimes and Near-Crimes at Appledore Towers in the Light of the English Criminal Law," *BSJ*, 6, No. 2 (April 1956), 69-74.
A calendar of crimes chargeable to both Holmes and Watson.

2313. Holstein, Leon S. " 'But Be Very Careful. . . ,' " *BSJ*, 14, No. 1 (March 1964), 22-23.
A tale in verse.

2314. Kimball, Elliot. "The Milverton Mess," *SHJ*, 5, No. 4 (Summer 1962), 100-102.

"Recourse to factual evidence in the Canonical Text, and to sound analysis of *all* circumstances, establishes the Milverton case as an adventure occurring in January of the year 1886."

2315. Lauterbach, Charles E. "The Plumber and His Fiancée," *BSJ*, 6, No. 4 (October 1956), 201-202.
———. ———, *Baker Street Ballads.* [Culver City, Calif.: Luther Norris, March 1971.] p. 9-10.
"A plumber and his love were strolling / A-down a moonlit lane. . . ."
"The plumber was Sherlock Holmes in disguise, alias Gerald Escott. . . . His companion was the charming Miss Agatha Fizzlewit."

2316. Merritt, Russell L. "Re: The Adventure of the Worst Man in London," *BSJ Christmas Annual,* No. 4 (1959), 296-301.
Holmes commits three acts which seem either stupid, crude, or outrageous: drawing a gun on Milverton, engaging himself to Milverton's maid, and safebreaking. His actions are entirely justified, however, when it is understood that he anticipated Milverton's murder—probably through recognizing the coat-of-arms on the blackmail note shown to him by Milverton, the most objectionable of Holmes's opponents.

2317. Morton, Humphrey. " 'A Long Drive to Hampstead,' " *SHJ*, 5, No. 1 (Winter 1960), 22-23.
A detailed tracing of the probable route taken by Holmes and Watson from Oxford Street to Heath Row.

2318. ———. "A Milvertonian Identification," *SHJ*, 6, No. 1 (Winter 1962), 14-15.
"Milverton moved to The Logs in 1896, changed its name to Appledore Towers, and was in residence until his timely and unlamented death a year or two later."

2319. [Richard, Peter, comp.] *The Milverton Manuscript: An Analysis Together with Other Milvertoniana.* London: The Milvertonians of Hampstead, 1963. [24] p.
Contents: Introduction, by Peter Richard. - The Milverton Manuscript: An Analysis. - Stories by Other Authors with Plots That Resemble "Charles Augustus Milverton." - A Note on Dust-Jackets. - Notes on the Milverton Evening of the Sherlock Holmes Society. - A Note on the Original Illustrations. - The Catalogue of a Milvertonian Collection: Some Additional Items. - A Note on the Milvertonians of Hampstead.

2320. [———.] *A Milvertonian Miscellany.* London: The Milvertonians of Hampstead, 1962. [18] p.

Contents: Introduction, by Peter Richard. - The Catalogue of a Milvertonian Collection. - Occasionally They Were Milverton. - Milverton — Stage Productions in America and Holland. - Re: C. A. Milverton, by T. S. Blakeney. - "Give Me Data" — The Milverton Extracts, by Alan Wilson.

2321. [———.] *Some Notes for the Information of the Milvertonians of Hampstead.* [London: The Milvertonians of Hampstead, March 1959.] 4 p.
Contents: The Manuscript. - Original Appearance. - First Book Appearance. - The Illustrators. - The People of the Drama. - At the Cinema. - On the Stage. - Wireless Broadcasts. - Gramophone Records. - The Place: An Identification. - The Date.

2322. Rosenberger, Edgar S. "A Study in Blackmail," *BSJ* [OS], 3, No. 3 (July 1948), 361-364.
A tale in verse.

2323. Von Krebs, Maria. "Agatha Is Her Name," *SHJ*, 4, No. 2 (Spring 1959), 41-42.
———. ———, *The Saint Mystery Magazine,* 12, No. 2 (August 1959), 126-128.
"Irene" of the Briony Lodgers suggests that the exalted title of "*The* Woman" does not belong to Irene Adler but to Holmes's ex-fiancée, Agatha.

2324. Wilson, Alan. " 'Son of Escott': A Milverton Story for Which the World Will Never Be Prepared," *BSJ*, 10, No. 3 (July 1960), 161-163.
A truly remarkable discovery that Escott (Sherlock Holmes) fathered a son while engaged to Agatha!

THE ADVENTURE OF THE COPPER BEECHES

2325. George, Isaac S. "Violet the Hunter," *BSJ*, [OS], 4, No. 1 (January 1949), 29-37.
"Purporting to be the tale of a hoax perpetrated on a persistent lover which ends in success for the lover but tragedy for others, the story within the story, written with tongue very much in cheek, tells of the deliberate, studied and persistent effort of one Violet Hunter to attract Holmes sentimentally with the purpose of reducing him to a state of matrimonial bliss. It is the story of a woman who was out to get her man."

2326. Schutz, Robert. "Half Sister; No Mystery," *BSG,* 1, No. 2 (1961), 14-15.
The author agrees with H. B. Williams's conclusion that Violet Hunter was Sherlock's half sister, but does not agree that she had changed her name from Thulio Vernet or that Watson was aware of the relationship of Violet to Sherlock.

2327. Williams, H. B. "Half Sister; Half Mystery," *BSJ*, 8, No. 2 (April 1958), 100-103.

"Thulio Vernet [Violet Hunter] and Sherlock Holmes chose to become as strangers and deny the ties of family relationship."

'THE ADVENTURE OF THE CREEPING MAN

2328. Egan, Joseph J. "Conan Doyle's *The Adventure of the Creeping Man* as Stevensonian Analogue," *Studies in Scottish Literature*, 7, No. 3 (January 1970), 180-183. (Notes and Documents)

It is suggested that in writing this tale Doyle was influenced by Robert Louis Stevenson's *The Strange Case of Dr. Jekyll and Mr. Hyde* (1886).

2329. Levine, Arthur L. "Lowenstein's Other Creeper," *BSJ*, 6, No. 1 (January 1956), 30-33.

"The whole picture of the Creeping Man smacks so of the picture of the Abominable Snowman that there is a strong probability that they are of the same origin—that Lowenstein's other creeper is the Abominable Snowman of the Himalayas!"

2330. Simms, Bartlett D. "Dr. Watson: An Adventure in Orthopedics," *The ACA Journal of Chiropractic*, 7, No. 2 (February 1970), 44-45.

A discussion of Professor Presbury's back syndrome and Watson's wound.

2331. Van Liere, Edward J. "Doctor Watson, Endocrinologist," *A Doctor Enjoys Sherlock Holmes*. New York: Vantage Press, [1959]. p. 83-87.

"It is possible that people who are not familiar with the science of endocrinology might gain the impression that the administration of ape serum could produce the effects so vividly described in *The Adventure of the Creeping Man*. The concept that such a serum exists is, of course, rank nonsense."

2332. Wellman, Manly Wade. "The Professor Was a Creep," *BSJ*, 3, No. 1 (January 1953), 29-30.

A tale in verse.

THE CROOKED MAN

2333. Foss, Thomas Frederick. "Colonel James Barclay," *BSJ*, 20, No. 4 (December 1970), 231-233.

Lt. Col. Foss, who has been awarded the Irregular Shilling with the Titular Investiture of "Colonel James Barclay," attempts to show that Barclay's character has been much maligned: that he was an unusually able, just, and honest soldier who

had risen from the ranks to command his regiment; that Corporal Wood's story of the Colonel's being responsible for his betrayal into the insurgent's hands was based on such flimsy evidence as to be quite unreliable; that the row he observed through the window between Col. and Mrs. Barclay was a husband-and-wife quarrel, which inevitably occur from time to time, even in the best regulated households. The sudden appearance of Wood's horribly deformed figure caused Barclay to have a heart attack, fall and crack his skull on the fender.

2334. Hinrich, D. "The Royal Mallows 1854-1888," *SHJ*, 6, No. 1(Winter 1962), 20-22.

The first battalion of the Royal Mallows (the old 117th) is identified as the second battalion of the Royal Irish Fusiliers (late 89th Foot).

2335. Stix, Thomas L. "Casual Comments on *The Crooked Man*," *BSJ*, 12, No. 2 (June 1962), 99-100.

In spite of the defects in this tale, it is quite possibly the most important of the sixty tales because it explains the whole theory on which the detective story is based.

2336. Wilkinson-Latham, C. "Royal Mallows (Princess Victoria's, Royal Irish Fusiliers) 1888," *SHJ*, 9, No. 4 (Summer 1970), 137. illus.

Additional information on the famous Irish regiment whose first battalion was commanded by Col. Barclay.

THE ADVENTURE OF THE DANCING MEN

2337. Andrew, Clifton R. "The Closed Window Mystery in *The Dancing Men*," *BSJ*, 11, No. 3 (September 1961), 178-179.

An examination of "the odd incident of Mrs. Cubitt (née Elsie Patrick) closing and fastening the window in the study through which her husband had just been shot and killed."

2338. Christ, Jay Finley. "The Dancing Men," *SHJ*, 1, No. 4 (December 1953), 24-25.

Similarities are noted between G. J. Cubitt's "Restless Imps" and Doyle's "Dancing Men."

2339. Davis, Norman M. "The Case of the Finished Alphabet," *BSJ*, 19, No. 2 (June 1969), 85-90.

Holmes and Watson discuss the dancing men cipher.

2340. Hearn, Otis. "Some Further Speculations Upon the Dancing Men," *BSJ*, 19, No. 4 (December 1969), 196-202.

Abe Slaney and Elsie are unmasked as Chicago Anarchists (Nihilists) sending messages in symbols adapted from the

Union Army's *Manual of Signals* (1865) and using the Nihilist Transposition method of concealing one enciphered message inside another. Behind them lurks the real wire-puller, Moriarty, who has infiltrated the Anarchist organization to use it for his own ends.

2341. Helling, Cornelis. "Thurston, the Billiard-Player (-Maker)," *BSJ*, 13, No. 1 (March 1963), 48-49.

An advertisement in *The Strand Magazine* for December 1910 concerning home billiard tables made by Thurston & Co. Ltd., is proof enough that Watson's friend was both a billiard-player and a billiard-maker.

2342. ———. "The True Story of the Dancing Men," *BSJ*, 4, No. 3 (July 1954), 160-163.

The author quotes a letter from G. J. Cubitt denying that he invented the dancing men cipher, as reported by Gavin Brend (item 4224), According to Mr. Helling it was most likely worked out jointly by Drs. Watson and Doyle.

2343. Kahn, David. ["The Codebreaking Holmes"], *The Codebreakers: The Story of Secret Writing*. New York: The Macmillan Co., 1967. Chap. 21, p. 794-798.
———. ———, *SHJ*, 8, No. 4 (Summer 1968), 128-131.

A penetrating analysis of Holmes's method of solving the dancing men cryptograms.

2344. Kasner, Edward, and James Newman. "Chance and Chanceability," *Mathematics and the Imagination*. With drawings and diagrams by Rufus Isaacs. New York: Simon and Schuster, 1940. Chap. 9, p. 223-235.

The introductory part of Danc is quoted and then the cryptogram is presented as an excellent example of "reasoning by probable inference."

2345. Koelle, John B. "Random Thoughts on *The Dancing Men*," *BSJ*, 16, No. 1 (March 1966), 18-20.

"The sad fact emerges that while Sherlock was dividing his energies between chemical endeavours and a rather casual approach to cryptographic analysis, Abe Slaney, 'the most dangerous crook in Chicago,' was quietly erasing the Cubitt family."

2346. Link, Gordden. "On Watson's Discovery of the Words 'ETAOIN SHRDL' on a Study-Table in Baker Street," *BSJ*, 2, No. 1 (January 1952), 30.

"These were the magic words I found—/ Hear how their Celtic letters sound— / ETAOIN SHRDL!"

2347. Mather, Philip R. "The Dance of Death," *BSJ*, 5, No. 3 (July 1955), 157-159.
A tale in verse.

2348. Orr, Lyndon. "A Case of Coincidence," *The Bookman*, 31, No. 2 (April 1910), 178-180.
———. ———, *BSJ*, 19, No. 4 (December 1969), 203-205.

A suggestion (denied by Doyle) that the dancing men cryptogram was borrowed from a puzzle entitled "The Language of the Restless Imps" (*St. Nicholas* [May 1874], 439).

2349. Pattrick, Robert R. "A Study in Crypto-Choreography," *BSJ*, 5, No. 4 (October 1955), 205-209.

"Messrs. Pratt and Schenck speak of both leg 'positions' *and* leg 'combinations.' This is a completely unwarranted supposition. There are *no* leg 'combinations.' There are leg 'positions' only. . . ." Includes three charts: Family Groupings; Known Figures, with Five New Mirror Images; and Complete Alphabet with Numerals.

2350. ———. ["Letter"], *BSJ*, 6, No. 4 (October 1956), 245-246. (From the Editor's Commonplace Book)

An answer to Prof. Schenck's comments on the author's Dancing Men Code.

2351. Pratt, Fletcher. "The Secret Message of the Dancing Men," *Profile by Gaslight*. Edited by Edgar W. Smith. New York: Simon and Schuster, 1944. p. 274-282.

A parallel is drawn between the cipher of the Dancing Men and the Great Cipher of Rossignol— coincidentally each employs 1,568 different symbols!

2352. Prestige, Colin. "Agents to Evil," *BSJ*, 5, No. 3 (July 1955), 144-147.

A catalog of thirty words, with commentary, that are additional possibilities to the three five-letter words *sever, lever,* and *never* which were mentioned by Holmes.

2353. Sanderson, Shirley. "Another Case of Identity," *SHJ*, 6, No. 3 (Winter 1963), 86-87.

The author and her brother visit what their research leads them to believe is Ridling Thorpe Manor in Norfolk—Walcott House, the main house in the village of Walcott.

2354. Schenck, Remsen Ten Eyck. "Holmes, Cryptanalysis and the Dancing Men," *BSJ*, 5, No. 2 (April 1955), 80-91.

Includes two tables on the leg and arm positions and one on the symbol equivalents for the complete alphabet.

2355. ———. ["Letter"], *BSJ*, 6, No. 2 (April

1956), 123-125. (From the Editor's Commonplace Book)

A rejoinder to Robert Pattrick's "A Study in Crypto-Choreography."

2356. Smith, William. "Studies on the Dancing Men: Being a Survey of the Subject as Treated by Many and Diverse Hands," *BSJ*, 19, No. 2 (June 1969), 79-84.

Contents: 1. A Brief History of Cryptography. - 2. Textual Variants of the Cipher. - 3. The Cipher Analysed — the Master Criticised — the Cipher Completed. - 4. Possible Origins of the Cipher.

THE ADVENTURE OF THE DEVIL'S FOOT

2357. Andersen, Verner. "Alrunes Rod: Radix pedix diabolis," *Medicinsk Forum* [København] 23, Nr. 1 (1970), 7-12.

———. ———, *Sherlockiana*, 15, Nr. 1-2 (1970), 5-7.

2358. Bonn, Ronald S. *"Radix Pedis Diaboli,"* *BSJ*, 18, No. 2 (June 1968), 90-93.

"Concerning the chemical identification of the Devil's Foot Root, with some remarks upon certain common slurs against Watson's credibility, and one proposal for an alteration in the generally accepted body of scholarship surrounding the Canon."

2359. Clum, Florence. "The Blame's a Foot," *BSJ*, 4, No. 4 (October 1954), 214-217.

A tale in verse.

2360. Cooper, Peter. "The Devil's Foot: An Excursion into Holmesian Toxicology," *The Pharmaceutical Journal*, 197 (December 24, 1966), 657-658.

———. ———, *SHJ*, 8, No. 2 (Spring 1967), 59-61.

———. ———, *BSJ*, 18, No. 2 (June 1968), 94-96.

The "reddish-brown, snuff-like powder" that killed or drove insane the Tregennis family is identified as muavi (erythropleum guineense), an ordeal drug of the Congo region.

2361. Redmond, Chris. "Moore Mystery," *BSP*, No. 43 (January 1969), 2.

On the mystery and fate of Dr. Moore Agar, who advised Holmes to rest or suffer the consequences of a complete breakdown.

THE ADVENTURE OF THE DYING DETECTIVE

2362. Asher, Richard. "Malingering," *SHJ*, 4, No. 2 (Spring 1959), 54-58. illus.

In this interesting paper on the methods and techniques employed in feigning an illness, Dr. Asher briefly discusses Holmes's malingering in Dyin.

2363. Jenkins, Walter S. "Tsutsugamushi to You, Dr. Ober," *BSJ*, 18, No. 2 (June 1968), 84.

The author disagrees with Dr. Ober on the tsutsugamushi fever theory.

2364. L'Etang, Hugh. "Some Observations on the Black Formosa Corruption and Tapanuli Fever," *SHJ*, 4, No. 2 (Spring 1959), 58-60.

Contents: Tsutsugamushi Disease or Scrub Typhus. - Tapanuli Fever. - The Black and White Ivory Box.

2365. Ober, William B. "Conan Doyle's Dying Detective: Problem in Differential Diagnosis," *New York State Journal of Medicine*, 67, No. 15 (August 1, 1967), 2141-2145.

———. ———, *CPBook*, 3, No. 12 (Spring 1967), 232-235.

The Director of Laboratories at Knickerbocker Hospital believes that Holmes was feigning a rickettsial infection called tsutsugamushi disease.

2366. Rosenberger, Edgar S. "Half-Crowns and Oysters," *BSJ*, 1, No. 4 (October 1951), 132-135.

A tale in verse.

THE ADVENTURE OF THE EMPTY HOUSE

See also *Colonel Sebastian Moran* (items 3532-3537)

2367. Ashton, Ralph A. "Colonel Moran's Infamous Air Rifles," *BSJ*, 10, No. 3 (July 1960), 155-159.

Contents: Biographical Note [on von Herder]. - The Specifications. - The Bolzenbüchse. - Development. - The Illustrations. - Post Hoc.

The Colonel's weapon was designed by modifying the 18th-century Bolzenbüchse air rifle.

2368. Bigelow, S. Tupper. "Was It Attempted Murder?" *BSJ*, 14, No. 2 (June 1964), 99-107.

"The law of England in 1894, even as it has been construed since then, was of such a nebulous and uncertain character that no one, whether barrister, solicitor or legal textbook writer, can say with perfect assurance whether Sebastian Moran would have been convicted of the attempted murder of Sherlock Holmes in 1894 or someone else who tried the same thing today would be convicted."

2369. Davies, Bernard. "The Mews of Marylebone," *SHJ*, 6, No. 1 (Winter 1962), 6-10.

The author retraces the route Holmes and Watson took to the Empty House.

2370. Earle, Ralph. "The Curious Incident of the Avoidance of Probate, With Some Reflections on the Premature Senility of Colonel Sebastian Moran," *BSJ*, 17, No. 3 (September 1967), 144-147.

2371. Elie, Rudolph. "The Battle of Charing Cross," *The Third Cab*. [Boston: The Speckled Band, 1960.] p. 17-25.
 The author examines the fight Holmes had with Thomas Mathews, the ruffian who knocked out Holmes's left canine in the waiting room at Charing Cross, and concludes that Mathews and Moriarty were the same person.

2372. Helling, Cornelis. "Parker's Jew's-Harp," *BSJ*, 19, No. 3 (September 1969), 178.
 A note on Col. Moran's sentinel Parker and his harp, mentioned by Holmes in Empt.

2373. Kimball, Elliot. "The Pseudo-Crucial Crocus," *BSJ*, 16, No. 1 (March 1966), 3-5.
 Mr. Kimball sharply disagrees with Gavin Brend (*My Dear Holmes*, p. 129) for assuming the events in this case took place in February rather than in early April of 1894 as stated by Watson.

2374. McLauchlin, Russell. "Ballade on a Daring Theme," *BSJ* [OS], 2, No. 1 (January 1947), 16-17.
 "Great benefactor of the race, / This question troubles me a lot. / From Sussex send the word apace. / Where was the Colonel when he shot?"

2375. Rosenberger, Edgar S. "Welcome Holmes!" *BSJ*, 3, No. 4 (October 1953), 236-240.
 A tale in verse.

2376. Schultz, Robert S. "The Ballistics of the Empty House," *BSJ* [OS], 2, No. 4 (October 1947), 373-379.
 A detailed study of the attempted murder of Holmes by Moran reveals the fallaciousness of Percival Wilde's contention (*Design for Murder*, chap. 4) that the events as described by Watson could not have happened.

2377. Stix, Thomas L. "A Little Dirt on *The Empty House*," *BSJ*, 14, No. 2 (June 1964), 93-95.

2378. Wallace, Vincent. "How Adair Met Moran," *BSJ*, 19, No. 4 (December 1969), 240.
 The bibliography in Col. A. E. Stewart's *Tiger and Other Game: The Practical Experiences of a Soldier Shikari in India* (London: 1927) lists *A Summer in High Asia*, by F. E. S. Adair—possibly a relative of Ronald Adair, through whom the latter met Col. Moran.

2379. Wilde, Percival. "The Bust in the Window," *BSJ* [OS], 3, No. 3 (July 1948), 300-305.
 A rebuttal of Mr. Schultz's article in which the author ends by challenging Schultz to "a duel to the death" with slide rules as the weapons.

2380. Williams, H. B. "A Non-Canonical Clue," *Illustrious Client's Third Case-Book*. Edited by J. N. Williamson and H. B. Williams. [Indianapolis, Ind.: The Illustrious Clients, 1953.] p. 94-99.
 "It may well be that much future light on certain obscurities of the Canon must come from without its pages as has this non-canonical clue of 'The Adventure of the Empty House' come from the 'Gourmet's Guide to London.' "

The Great Hiatus

2381. Armstrong, Walter P. "The Truth About Sherlock Holmes," *BSJ* [OS], 1, No. 4 (October 1946), 391-401.
 "Holmes did not return. He did not return because he had never been away.... Not only was Holmes in London, but he was living in the same house with Watson all the time. Watson has deceived us. But we cannot blame him, for the deception was necessary in order to trap the wily members of the Moriarty gang who remained."

2382. Ball, John. "The Path of the Master," *BSJ*, 21, No. 1 (March 1971), 26-32.
 In the company of his Sherlockian son, the author revisits certain historical locations in London, makes a pilgrimage to the Reichenbach Falls in Switzerland, and then breaks what he believes to be new Irregular ground by being granted an extraordinary private audience (in Northern India) with His Holiness, the Dalai Lama of Tibet. From this rare and privileged visit, new evidence concerning Holmes's sojourn in the Land of Snows is uncovered.

2383. Baring-Gould, William S. " 'You May Have Heard of the Remarkable Explorations of a Norwegian Named Sigerson. . . ,' " *BSJ*, 17, No. 3 (September 1967), 152-160.
 ———. ———, *The Annotated Sherlock Holmes*. New York: Clarkson N. Potter, [1967]. Vol. 2, chap. 48, p. 320-328.
 A critical examination of the three schools of Sherlockian commentary (the Apologistic or Fundamental School, the Interpretive School, and the Sensationalist School) on the Great Hiatus—the three years between May 1891 and May 1894 when "all the world, except his brother Mycroft, thought Sherlock Holmes dead."

2384. Boucher, Anthony. "Ballade of the Later Holmes," *BSJ* [OS], 1, No. 1 (January 1946), 44.

The Writings About the Writings

A reply in verse to Jay F. Christ's denial that the Holmes who returned was, as Mr. Boucher contends, an imposter. "A master did return indeed!"

2385. ———. "Was the Later Holmes an Impostor?" *Profile by Gaslight.* Edited by Edgar W. Smith. New York: Simon and Schuster, 1944. p. 60-70.

The author argues that Holmes did, in fact, fall over the cliff at the Reichenbach and that the man who in 1894 returned to London was in reality his cousin Sherrinford.

2386. Christ, Jay Finley. "The Later Holmes an Imposter: A Sequel," *BSG,* 1, No. 1 (1961), 21-33.

A refutation of Anthony Boucher's dualistic hypothesis that there were "two Holmeses."

2387. Christie, Winifred M. "On the Remarkable Explorations of Sigerson," *SHJ,* 1, No. 2 (September 1952), 39-44.

Mrs. Christie believes the Master's visit to the chief lama had far more behind it than simple curiosity.

2388. Donegall, Lord. "April 1891-April 1894," *The New Strand;* 1, No. 6 (May 1962), 678-680. (Baker Street and Beyond, No. 6)

———. ———, *Seventeen Steps to 221B.* [Edited by] James Edward Holroyd. London: George Allen & Unwin Ltd., [1967]. p. 161-166.

The author traces Holmes's activities during the Great Hiatus.

2389. Fage-Pedersen, Anders. *A Case of Identity.* Bilag til [Supplement to] *Sherlockiana,* 8, Nr. 1-2 (1963). 7 p.

Text in Danish.

An attempt to show that Sherlock Holmes and Dr. Nikola, a mystical doctor who traveled in Tibet during the Hiatus, are the same person.

2390. Foss, T. F. "The Missing Years," *SHJ,* 9, No. 3 (Winter 1969), 86-87.

Holmes did not spend two years in Tibet posing as a Norwegian explorer named Sigerson, but instead assisted his country by ferreting out information on Russian intrigues in India.

2391. Grosbayne, Benjamin. "Sherlock Holmes's Honeymoon," *BSJ,* 21, No. 3 (September 1971), 143-150.

"The most famous consulting detective of his age was not the stranger to the grand passion that he was made out to be; he married and left a son to carry on his own contribution to the world; and, most intriguing of all, he became a distinguished operatic conductor and toured the musical centres of the world with his wife, the famous contralto, Irene Adler."

2392. King, Martin J. "Holmes in Hoboken?" *SS,* 1, No. 2 (September 1971), 3-5.

The Meyers Hotel is identified as the place where Sherlock and Irene were reunited for the birth of their son, Nero Wolfe.

2393. M., J. "Notes of a Bookman," *Harper's Weekly,* 45 (August 31, 1901), 881.

Documents and correspondence from various sources, including Holmes, Watson, and Doyle, on the resuscitation of Sherlock Holmes.

2394. Martin, Alastair. "Finding the Better Half," *BSJ,* 20, No. 2 (June 1970), 74-78.

A clever but farfetched attempt to identify Moriarty as a woman (namely the widow of Count Dracula) whom Holmes encountered at the Reichenbach, wed, and spent three years with during the Great Hiatus.

2395. McComas, Stanley. "Lhove at Lhassa," *BSJ,* 1, No. 2 (April 1951), 43-51.

Evidence is presented to support the contention that after the Reichenbach affair, Holmes and Irene Adler (by then divorced from Godfrey Norton) were married in Florence and then spent the next three years traveling about Asia.

2396. McDiarmid, E. W. "Reichenbach and Beyond," *BSJ Christmas Annual,* No. 2 (1957), 34-43.

A detailed examination of the theories advanced by Sherlockian scholars on the Reichenbach Incident and the Great Hiatus.

2397. Nelson, James. "Sherlock and the Sherpas," *BSJ,* 7, No. 3 (July 1957), 161-164.

The author suggests that "while Holmes was on absence without leave, in the 1890's, he met in those Himalayan peaks a woman who was more of a challenge than Irene Adler—that he met the Abominable Snow*woman*. Natural law and common sense assume that it is their descendants who are today making Holmesian footprints in the snows of time." This takes the prize for the most fanciful of all Sherlockian conjectures!

2398. Robertson, Allen. "Baker Street, Beecher and Borden," *BSJ,* 3, No. 1 (January 1953), 44-47.

"Perhaps, as a souvenir of his experience in Fall River, Holmes wanted to have a little reminder, for his room in Baker Street. Hence the unframed picture of Henry Ward Beecher, who was responsible for his grandfather [the Rev. S. Holmes] being in New Bedford, and therefore for his own opportunity to work on the Lizzie Borden case."

2399. Shields, Gilbert. "The Mysterious Return of Sherlock Holmes," *The*

Marquette Journal [Marquette University] (Winter 1951), 9-13.

Another refutation of Mr. Boucher's theory that the later Holmes was an imposter.

2400. Simpson, A. Carson. *Sherlock Holmes's Wanderjahre.* Philadelphia: Privately Printed by International Printing Co., 1953-1956. 4 v. (20, 27, 23, 25 p.) maps. (Simpson's Sherlockian Studies, Vol. 1-4)

Limited to 221B copies.

Contents: Pt. 1. Fanget An! - Pt. 2. Post Huc nec ergo Propter Huc Gabetque. - Pt. 3. In fernem Land, unnahbar euren Schritten. - The Himalayan Leech. - On to Lhasa. - The Abominable Snowman. - Buddhistic Studies. - Sigerson's Explorations. - Mount Everest. - Appendix. - Pt. 4. Auf der Erde Rücken rührt' ich mich viel. - His Homeward Trip. - His Trip Eastward. - Preparations for the Trip. - From Florence to Tibet.

2401. Sisson, Jon. Borden. "Dr. Handy's Wild-Eyed Man," *BSJ,* 20, No. 3 (September 1970), 170-179.

A document purportedly written in 1892 by Dr. Benjamin Handy of Fall River, Massachusetts, describes Holmes's acquaintance with Lizzie Borden and his investigation of the murders of her father and stepmother. Handy concludes that Holmes may have committed the murders himself. An introduction to Handy's document summarizes the theory that Holmes was the father of the detective Nero Wolfe, and an addendum offers evidence that Wolfe's mother was Lizzie Borden.

2402. Smith, Edgar W. "Sherlock Holmes and the Great Hiatus," *BSJ* [OS], 1, No. 3 (July 1946), 277-285.

————. ————, *Baker Street and Beyond: Together with Some Trifling Monographs.* Morristown, N.J.: The Baker Street Irregulars, 1957. [unpaged]

A whimsy dealing with the good fortune enjoyed by the murderer of Andrew J. Borden and Abby Durfee Borden in consequence of the Master's fettering.

2403. Wilson, Evan M. "The Trip That Was, or Sherlock Holmes in the Middle East," *BSJ,* 20, No. 2 (June 1970), 67-73.

The author's association, extending over thirty years, with the Middle East has led him to conclude that it would have been impossible for Holmes to have made the journey he described to Watson. Mr. Wilson does believe, however, that Holmes could have visited Persia and the Holy Land.

2404. Wincor, Richard. *Sherlock Holmes in Tibet.* New York: Weybright and Talley, [1968]. 137 p.

"Being an astonishing account of Holmes' hitherto unknown years, now revealed in a most extraordinary narrative from his own notebook." (Dust jacket)

Also contains extracts from the works of Bishop Berkeley and *The Tibetan Book of the Dead.*

Reviews: BSP, No. 52-53 (October-November 1969), 5 (Glenn S. Holland); *SOS,* 4, No. 1 (January 1970), 4-6 (Thomas Drucker); *Startling Mystery Stories,* 2, No. 5 (Winter 1968 / 69), 124-127 (Robert A. W. Lowndes).

THE ADVENTURE OF THE ENGINEER'S THUMB

2405. Austin, Bliss. "Furor Teutonicus," *BSJ,* 5, No. 1 (January 1955), 19-24.

A tale in verse.

2406. ————. "Thumbing His Way to Fame," *BSJ* [OS], 1, No. 4 (October 1946), 424-432. illus.

Although a great case when compared with the work of other detective-author teams, it cannot be ranked as one of Holmes's and Watson's best efforts.

2407. Christ, Jay Finley. "Thumbs Up: Thumbs Down?" *SHJ,* 2, No. 1 (July 1954), 41-42.

An observation on Victor Hatherley's missing thumb.

2408. Clark, Benjamin S. "Was There More to Watson Than Met the Private Eye?" *BSJ,* 19, No. 4 (December 1969), 216-219.

The patent absurdities in this adventure are found to be Watson's revenge and examples of his pawky vein of humor.

2409. "The Engineer's Thumb Symposium," *SHJ,* 5, No. 4 (Summer 1962), 107-112.

Contents: Introduction, by Lord Donegall. - An Engineer's Thoughts on "The Engineer's Thumb," by Ian McNeil. - The Case of the Engineer's Hand, by Frank Allen.

2410. Gillies, Joseph H. "Where Is Eyford? (Of *The Adventure of the Engineer's Thumb*)," *BSJ,* 19, No. 4 (December 1969), 213-215. illus.

The adventure took place in Twyford, Berks, which Watson disguised as Eyford. The evidence in Bradshaw is elementary and conclusive.

2411. Rabe, W. T. "An Engineer's Tom Thumb," *BSJ,* 19, No. 4 (December 1969), 220-221.

The dimensions of the hydraulic-press room show that Victor Hatherley was only three-and-a-half feet tall!

THE FINAL PROBLEM

See also *The Great Hiatus* (items 2381-2404) and *Professor Moriarty* (items 3538-3592)

The Writings About the Writings

Tales

2412. Addlestone, Alan. "Some Notes About Meiringen, Reichenbach, and the Château de Lucens," *VH*, 3, No. 1 (January 1968), 9-11.

The author describes his pilgrimage to the Shrine at Reichenbach and visit to the Sir Arthur Conan Doyle Museum.

2413. Andrew, Clifton R. "A Rejoinder to Professor Hill," *BSJ*, 5, No. 3 (July 1955), 154-156.

A rebuttal of Pope R. Hill's substructure theory as it applies to the plot of this tale.

2414. Austin, Bliss, ed. *Holmes and the Theory of Games.* Westfield, N.J.: The Hydraulic Press, September 1953. 8 p.

Limited to 100 numbered copies.

Three extracts from advanced textbooks by Oskar Morgenstern and a retrospection by the editor on the Master's "flight" from Moriarty.

2415. Ball, John. "The Practical Art of Baritsu, the Japanese Wrestling System; With Some Observations on Its Use by Mr. Sherlock Holmes," *BSJ*, 14, No. 1 (March 1964), 31-36.

The author, who holds a Japanese-awarded black belt, examines Holmes's knowledge of Baritsu, describes the art, identifies the Master's sensei (teacher), and determines his rank as a *Baritsudoka*. After examining in detail the site of the celebrated combat at the Reichenbach Falls, he provides data on the techniques which the Master utilized in overcoming the Napoleon of Crime without being dragged to his own death in the process.

2416. Bengis, Nathan L. "Plot Against Holmes," *SHJ*, 1, No. 1 (May 1952), 15, 14.

Mr. Bengis relates his discovery of how Silas K. Hocking planted the idea in Doyle's mind as to how he might put an end to Holmes.

2417. Berman, Ruth. "Skipping Stones at Reichenbach," *West by One and by One.* San Francisco: Privately Printed, 1965. p. 61-63.

It was the Swiss youth, not Moran, who gave Holmes "that evil five minutes on the Reichenbach ledge."

2418. Boswell, Rolfe. "The Haunting of the Nark," *BSJ* [OS], 1, No. 4 (October 1946), 462-463.

"Adapted from *Fit the Eighth* (The Vanishing), 'The Hunting of the Snark,' by *Lewis Carroll,* alias Charles Lutwidge Dodgson, alias 'Professor Moriarty.' "

"He had softly and suddenly vanished away— / For the Prof was a *Carroll,* you see."

2419. "By the Reichenbach Falls," *The Times* (August 31, 1966), 9.

———, *BSCL*, No. 5 (1966), 4-5.

" 'The Final Problem,' which brought Holmes and Moriarty to their fatal confrontation, was so apparently conclusive that to this day there are many who find Holmes's explanation of how he escaped unsatisfactory."

2420. Clark, Benjamin S. *"The Final Problem,"* *BSJ*, 16, No. 2 (June 1966), 68-69.

A blasphemous suggestion that Holmes staged the Reichenbach Incident with a nonexistent Moriarty to obtain a three-year rest cure for his addiction to dope.

2421. Crawford, Bryce, and R. C. Moore. "The Final Problem—Where?" *Exploring Sherlock Holmes.* Edited by E. W. McDiarmid & Theodore C. Blegen. La Crosse: Sumac Press, 1957. p. 82-87.

An account of the authors' visit to the Fall of Reichenbach where a careful examination of the terrain and interviews with several local inhabitants reveal the exact site of the epochal struggle.

2422. Davies, Bernard. "Canonical Connections," *SHJ*, 5, No. 2 (Spring 1961), 37-41.

"Viewed in retrospect, Holmes's scheme must stand for all time as his most amazing feat of creative reasoning, as opposed to pure analysis. . . . The double bluff of the Ostend train and the luggage marked 'Paris' was pure genius."

2423. Giasullo, Frank. "Baritsu at the Reichenbach," *BSJ*, 15, No. 2 (June 1965), 96.

"A more logical throw to use on that ledge in Switzerland would have been the hip throw (Ogoshi)."

2424. Gibson, Theodore W. "You're Matching Me," *BSJ Christmas Annual*, No. 1 (1956), 15-18.

A discussion of the example from the Canon used by John Von Neumann and Oskar Morgenstern (item 2449) and by Edward Kasner and James Newman (item 2344) to illustrate the theory of probability.

2425. Grasse, Marvin. "Who Killed Holmes?" *The Atlantic Monthly*, 195, No. 6 (June 1955), 88-90.

An astonishing disclosure of how Watson and Mycroft were able to rid themselves of Sherlock on that fateful day at the Falls. The later Holmes has yet to be identified.

2426. Hall, W. S. "A Visit to the Reichenbach Falls," *BSJ*, 1, No. 4 (October 1951), 123-127.

An interesting account of the author's visit to Meiringen and the "turned-off" Falls.

2427. Hardenbrook, Don and Margaret. "The

Moriart," by Gaston Huret III. Tr. by Don and Margaret Hardenbrook. *BSJ*, 9, No. 2 (April 1959), 88-89.

———. ———, *BSJ*, 12, No. 4 (December 1962), 198-199.

"They frappled on the huddy brink / In dortal combat, hand to hand; / Then with a brist, a subtle flink, / The Moriart unplanned."

2428. Hench, Philip S. "Of Violence at Meiringen," *Exploring Sherlock Holmes*. Edited by E. W. McDiarmid & Theodore C. Blegen. La Crosse: Sumac Press, 1957. p. 97-120.

A vivid account of the author's visit to the Reichenbach Falls in pursuit of the Norwegian Explorers' objective of erecting a plaque (item 4856) at this "fixed point in a changing world."

2429. Hill, Pope R. *"The Final Problem:* An Exemplification of the Substructure Theory," *BSJ*, 5, No. 3 (July 1955), 149-153.

Doyle put clues in this adventure to show that Holmes was not dead.

2430. Hughes, Richard. ["Letter"], *Sports Illustrated*, 18, No. 23 (June 10, 1963), 91-92.

———. ———, *BSJ*, 14, No. 1 (March 1964), 36.

A footnote to Baring-Gould's essay (item 3165) in which the Chief Banto of the Baritsu Chapter of BSI offers an explanation of Holmes's baffling reference to *baritsu.*

2431. Hulbert, William C. "Echoes from Reichenbach," *BSJ* [OS], 3, No. 2 (April 1948), 183-187.

During a visit to the renowned Reichenbach gorge, the author and Aubrey Pershouse heard "two human sounds that rose miraculously above that hellish cacophony."

2432. Jaffee, Irving L. " 'The Final Problem,' " *Elementary My Dear Watson*. Brooklyn, N.Y.: Theo. Gaus' Sons, [1965]. p. 13-15.

"If . . . we believe that Holmes was suffering from some deep-rooted psychotic trauma and that Moriarty, 'he of mathematical celebrity,' was merely the product of Holmes' own disturbed mind, we are led inescapably to the next conclusion that the great detective was bent on nothing else than suicide in his wild flight into Switzerland. Many of the events unfolded in the narrative in question would seem to support this notion."

2433. Judson, Ralph. "The Mystery of Baritsu: A Sidelight Upon Sherlock Holmes's Accomplishments," *BSJ Christmas Annual,* No. 3 (1958), 10-16.

The Master's knowledge of Baritsu, the name given by Mr. Barton-Wright to his method of Ju-Jutsu, enabled him to overcome Moriarty during their death struggle on the path above the Reichenbach Falls.

2434. ———. "Sidney Paget and the Reichenbach Falls Fight," *BSJ*, 9, No. 4 (October 1959), 243. (Two Critiques)

"If Paget's imaginary picture was right, Sherlock Holmes could not possibly have disengaged himself and avoided falling over the brink together with his maddened enemy."

2435. Karlson, Kathy. "May 4, 1891," *BSP*, No. 48 (June 1969), 1.

"I'm the only one who'd seen that murder done. / No one else knows this in Meiringen town. / So you, silent friend, will be the only one."

2436. Kellett, E. E. "Monody on the Death of Sherlock Holmes," *Jetsam: Occasional Verses*. E. Johnson, Cambridge University, 1897.

———. ———. [With a note by Vincent Starrett.] Ysleta: Edwin B. Hill, 1934. [4] p. (Sherlockiana)

———. ———, *Profile by Gaslight*. Edited by Edgar W. Smith. New York: Simon and Schuster, 1944. p. 137.

"Let scoundrels all rejoice / Throughout our mourning land, / For Sherlock Holmes is gone, / Gone to a better Strand."

2437. Kennedy, Bruce. "By the Falls," *SOS Annual*, No. 2 (January 1968), 15.

"Thus the villains face their doom, / While Watson lives three years in gloom."

2438. McLauchlin, Russell. "The Case of the Fallible Falls-Finder," *BSJ*, 12, No. 4 (December 1962), 223-227.

While on a trip to Meiringen, the author mistakes the Alpbachfall for the Reichenbach. Illustrated with a double-page reproduction of Meiringen as it appeared in 1890.

2439. Michaelsson, Georg. "Vem dödade Sherlock Holmes?" ["Who Killed Sherlock Holmes?"] *Svenska Dagbladet* (November 25, 1956).

———. ———, *BSCL*, No. 4 (1965), 11-16.

A further argument that Watson and Mycroft were responsible for the Master's death at the Reichenbach.

2440. Montgomery, James. "Meiringen Musings," *Shots from the Canon*. [Philadelphia: Privately Printed, 1953.] p. 9-11.

An observation on the fire that destroyed the village of Meiringen soon after "that fateful fourth of May, 1891." Illustrated with the same steel engraving as in item 2438.

Tales

2441. Portugal, Eustace. "The Holmes-Moriarty Duel," *The Bookman* [London], 86, No. 512 (May 1934), 97-99.
———. ———, CPBook, 4, No. 16 (Fall 1968), 310-312.
A contention that the Master died in the struggle at the Reichenbach Falls and that the Professor survived and took his place.

2442. Rabe, W. T. "Reichenbach Visited '05," *BSJ*, 10, No. 3 (July 1960), 167-169.
Quotations, with brief comments, from the *Guide Through Europe 1905*.

2443. Reeler, Kenneth Clark. " 'Well Then, About That Chasm . . . ,' " *HO*, 1, No. 5 (July 1971), 3-6; 1, No. 6 (August 1971), 5-7; 1, No. 7 (September 1971), 3-4.
"Those missing three years of Holmes' life were not spent embarking on improbable adventures . . . he was engaged in a grand deception to entrap Moriarty, who hadn't died at all . . . *The Valley of Fear* did not occur on a January 7-8 which happened to occur in April that year of 1891; but in some year following the Great Hiatus. In short, that Professor Moriarty, had Watson occasion to ask, might also have said: *'Well then, about that chasm. I had no serious difficulty in getting out of it, for the very simple reason that I never was in it. . . .' "*

2444. Rouby, Jason. "A Confidential Communication," Received by Jason Rouby. *BSJ*, 15, No. 4 (December 1965), 224-226.
An epistle from "the quondam Professor Moriarty," explaining the mystery of the "struggle" on the brink of the Reichenbach Falls, his disappearance, his spiritual and moral rehabilitation, and his subsequent career in the U.S. under the assumed name of J. Edgar Hoover.

2445. Silverstein, Albert and Myrna. "Concerning the Extraordinary Events at the Reichenbach Falls," *BSJ*, 20, No. 1 (March 1970), 21-29.
The Canonical account of the confrontation between Holmes and Moriarty found in Fina and Empt contains a total of sixteen major implausibilities. These implausibilities, some of them never before enumerated, are analyzed with an eye toward a reconstruction that will, at last, give Sherlockians the *truth* about all the events leading up to, during, and following that historical meeting. The reconstruction consists of two major premises: Holmes worked out and executed an ingenious trap for Moriarty using himself as bait; and Holmes's motive for disappearing subsequent to the confrontation was decided upon long before the meeting with Moriarty, was indeed to make the world not know what had become of him, and was still the most reasonable strategy despite Moran's knowledge that Holmes had not perished.

2446. Smith, Edgar W. "The Quasi-Final Problem," *BSJ* [OS], 2, No. 3 (July 1947), 307-310.
———. ———, *Baker Street and Beyond: Together with Some Trifling Monographs.* Morristown, N.J.: The Baker Street Irregulars, 1957. [unpaged]
———. ———, CPBook, 3, No. 13 (Summer 1967), 249-251.
———. "The Cliff-Hanger," *A Baker Street Quartette.* New York: The Baker Street Irregulars, [1950]. p. 37-44.
A tale in verse.

2447. Thorington, J. Monroe. ["Letter to Alex Carson Simpson"], *Sherlock Holmes's Wanderjahre.* Pt. 2, p. 23-27. (Simpson's Sherlockian Studies, Vol. 2)
Dr. Thorington describes a fragment of an alpenstock he discovered below the Reichenbach with the initials "S.H." and the figures '91 at the top of the staff!

2448. Utechin, Nicholas. "A Day of Danger," *SOS*, 3, No. 1 (January 1969), 10-14.
Holmes exaggerated his story to Watson about the day he narrowly escaped death—first by the hand of Moriarty, then by a two-horse van, and finally by a falling brick.

2449. Von Neumann, John, and Oskar Morgenstern. "Some Elementary Games," *Theory of Games and Economic Behavior.* Princeton University Press, 1944. Chap. 4, Sec. 18.4.4, p. 176-178.
———. ———, ———. [3rd ed.] New York: John Wiley & Sons, [1964]. p. 176-178. (Science Editions)
Holmes's flight from Moriarty is used as an example of the game of Matching Pennies.

THE FIVE ORANGE PIPS

2450. Brend, Gavin. "The Five Orange Pips," *SHJ*, 2, No. 3 (Summer 1955), 2.
"It takes me some time to get to grips / With this sinister business of orange pips."

2451. Clark, Benjamin. "The Horsham Fiasco," *BSJ*, 1, No. 1 (January 1951), 4-8.
An inquiry into some of the extraordinary features of this tale.

2452. Clarke, Richard W. "The Story I Like Best," *BSJ* [OS], 3, No. 2 (April 1948), 188-190.
———. "On 'The Five Orange Pips,' " *The Best of the Pips.* Westchester County, N.Y.: The Five Orange Pips, 1955. p. 3-6.
The author believes this adventure is one of the best and that the first scion society is well named.

2453. Morley, Felix. "How the Child Got into the Chimney," *BSJ Christmas Annual*, No. 3 (1958), 7-9.

Watson metamorphized the chimney contents from heavy ordnance, as used by Clark Russell in *A Sea Queen*, into a sobbing child.

2454. Russell, W. Clark. "Three in Charge," *The Strand Magazine*, 2 (October 1891), 372-382.
————. ————, *BSJ* [OS], 3, No. 3 (July 1948), 341-357. (Incunabulum)
Edgar Smith tentatively identified this fine sea story as the one Watson was reading while Holmes sat cross-indexing his records of crime.

2455. Wellman, Manly Wade Hampton. "A Ku Klux Report," *BSJ* [OS], 2, No. 4 (October 1947), 425-426.
Part B of an essay entitled "Two Southern Exposures of Sherlock Holmes."

2456. ————. "Pip-Pip Colonel Openshaw!" *BSJ* [OS], 3, No. 1 (January 1948), 21-23.
A tale in verse.

THE "GLORIA SCOTT"

2457. Andrew, C. R. "Who Is Who, and When, in *The Gloria Scott*," *Illustrious Client's Case-Book*. Edited by J. N. Williamson and H. B. Williams. [Indianapolis, Ind.: The Illustrious Clients, 1948.] p. 30-32.
Victor Trever was not a natural son of Old Man Trever but a stepson.

2458. Lauterbach, Charles E. "Mutiny on the *Gloria Scott*," *Baker Street Ballads*. [Culver City, Calif.: Luther Norris, March 1971.] p. 2-3.
"The *Gloria Scott* her anchor hove, / Her sails flung to the breeze; / With pennants snapping, halyards taut, / She sought the seven seas."

2459. Welch, George W. "The Terai Planter," *BSJ*, 6, No. 1 (January 1956), 35-39.
A clever but fantastic interpretation of the events at Donnithorpe.

THE ADVENTURE OF THE GOLDEN PINCE-NEZ

2460. Andrew, C. R. "The Story I Like Best," *BSJ* [OS], 2, No. 1 (January 1947), 43-44.
"*The Golden Pince-Nez* has everything to make it the composite Sherlock Holmes tale."

2461. Crocker, Stephen F. "Pseudepigraphical Matter in the Holmesian Canon," *BSJ*, 2, No. 3 (July 1952), 158-164.
Holmes's "short cut" in solving this case is compared with the first episode of *The History of the Destruction of Bel and the Dragon* as recorded in the Old Testament Apocrypha.

THE GREEK INTERPRETER

2462. Symonds, R. F. *The Greek* (?) *Interpreter*. [Marblehead, Mass.: Privately Produced], April 30, 1948. 7 p.

THE HOUND OF THE BASKERVILLES

2463. Austin, Bliss. *Dartmoor Revisited, or Discoveries in Devonshire*. Pittsburgh, Pa.: The Hydraulic Press, 1964. [10] p. (A Baker Street Christmas Stocking, No. 10)
————. "Dartmoor Revisited," *Kalki*, 3, No. 4 (Fall 1969), 131-134. illus.
About James Branch Cabell, Sir Richard Cabell (the original Sir Hugo Baskerville?), and Conan Doyle.

2464. Baring-Gould, William S. " 'Dr. Watson Has Gone to Widecombe,' " *BSJ*, 15, No. 1 (March 1965), 8-15.
The village of the Coombe Tracy is identified as a hamlet called Widecombe-in-the-Moor, Baskerville Hall as Lew House, Grimpen Mire as Grimspound Bog, Cleft Tor as Cleft Rock, and Foulmire as Fox Tor Mire. Illustrated with three of Julian Wolff's maps.

2465. ————. "Introduction: But Hark! The Hound!" *The Hound of the Baskervilles*. [New York]: The New American Library, [June 1967]. p. ix-xx.
"Here you will find Holmes and Watson and Sir Arthur Conan Doyle at their best."

2466. *Baskerville Hall*. [Privately reproduced by Owen P. Frisbie.] [4] p.
————. Page 1 reprinted in *BSJ*, 3, No. 1 (January 1953), 61.
A reproduction of the holograph manuscript, dated 1742, recounting the legend of the Baskervilles.

2467. Bedford, Michael, and Bruce Dettman. " 'A Cunning Preparation,' " *BSJ*, 16, No. 4 (December 1966), 231-233.
An illuminating discussion of the phosphorescent hound of the Baskervilles.

2468. Bengis, Nathan L. "Variety Is the Spice of Sherlockiana," *BSG*, 1, No. 4 (April 1962), 37-46.
"A prolegomenon to a compendium of the various states of the 1902 American edition of *The Hound of the Baskervilles*, published by McClure, Phillips & Co." (Subtitle)

2469. Bigelow, S. Tupper. "The Singular Case of Fletcher Robinson," *BSG*, 1, No. 2 (1961), 19-21.
"Fletcher Robinson was not only the inspiration of *The Hound*; he was a co-plotter and the co-fabricator of its details."

2470. Boucher, Anthony. "Footnote to a

The Writings About the Writings

Tales

Footnote," *BSJ*, 18, No. 2 (June 1968), 100-101.

The only two years in which Holmes could have had a box at Covent Garden for *Les Huguenots* during October were 1890 and 1891; and as 1891 was impossible, the probable date for this tale is 1890.

2471. Campbell, Maurice. "The First Sherlockian Critic—1902," *SHJ*, 1, No. 2 (September 1952), 3-5, 24.

A commentary on Frank Sidgwick's letter (item 2504), part of which is quoted, concerning the various dates in Houn.

2472. ———. *"The Hound of the Baskervilles*: Dartmoor or Herefordshire?" *Guy's Hospital Gazette*, 67 (May 30, 1953), 196-204.

Evidence that the events in this adventure may have taken place in Herefordshire.

2473. Christ, Jay Finley. "A Very Large Scale Map," *SHJ*, 6, No. 3 (Winter 1963), 72-74.

The author describes how he and Langdale Pike (his alternate Sherlockian ego) constructed a diagram of the Baskerville environs—within a five mile radius of the Hall.

2474. Clark, Benjamin. "Dr. Mortimer Before the Bar," *BSJ* [OS], 3, No. 3 (July 1948), 269-277.

———. ———, *The Best of the Pips.* Westchester County, N.Y.: The Five Orange Pips, 1955. p. 97-106.

"The only way in the least degree likely that the spaniel could have penetrated the bog was, of course, in the company of his master, Dr. James Mortimer. If this contention is valid, it necessarily follows that Dr. Mortimer must have been in league with Stapleton."

2475. Ellis, John Blunden. "The Chemistry of the Hound," *SHJ*, 7, No. 4 (Spring 1966), 132. (Wigmore Street Post-Bag)

2476. Frisbie, Owen P. "On the Origin of the Hound of the Baskervilles," *The Chronicle* [Middleburg, Va.], 17, No. 3 (September 11, 1953).

———. ———, *The Best of the Pips.* Westchester County, N.Y.: The Five Orange Pips, 1955. p. 51-55.

"On the origin of the Hound, nothing is known of blood lines. One can, however, form a reasonably accurate opinion as to what breeding would be necessary to produce a hound of his stamp."

2477. Gordon, Richard M. "Sherlock Homage," *Ellery Queen's Mystery Magazine*, 51, No. 6 (June 1968), 130. (Crhymes)

———. ———, *CPBook*, 4, No. 15 (August 1968), 302.

"A Hound of Hell was sent to kill / The bad Sir Hugo Baskerville, / And then, at least so it appears, / It hung around for years and years / To dine on old Sir Hugo's heirs. / It was a sad state of affairs, / But it was fixed up nice and neat / By Sherlock Holmes of Baker Street."

2478. Green, Roger Lancelyn. "Baskerville Hall," *SHJ*, 8, No. 2 (Spring 1967), 61.

A suggestion that Lustleigh, three miles north of Bovey Tracey, is the original Baskerville Hall.

2479. Hayes, Frederic, Harvey Barcus, and Ray King. "They Were the Footprints of *What* Hound?" *Voices from Baker Street*, 2. Ferndale, Mich.: The Old Soldiers of Baker Street, 1965. Side 2, Band 4.

"Members of the Amateur Mendicant Society and the Oakland County Kennel Club debate the breed of the Hound of the Baskervilles. AMS Frederic Hayes speaks for the Dachshund, AMS-OCKC Harvey Barcus argues the mastiff, and Ray King puts forward the points in favor of his beagle, Pierre, 'who sweeps the morning dew.' Mr. King and Pierre carried the evening. Recorded, the Detroit Press Club, 1964." (Record album)

2480. Hoerr, Willmer A. "The Case of the Disturbing Double," *BSJ*, 18, No. 4 (December 1968), 220-221.

Certain similarities between *Vanity Fair* and Houn suggest that Watson may have been guilty of a bit of plagiarism.

2481. Holland, Glenn S. "On the Origin of the Hound," *BSJ*, 19, No. 1 (March 1969), 34-37.

The ancient legend of the Baskervilles is skillfully reconstructed.

2482. Holroyd, James Edward. "The Shaggiest Dog," *Baker Street By-ways.* London: George Allen & Unwin Ltd., [1959]. p. 87-91.

2483. Howard, Alan. "A New Year for the Hound," *SHJ*, 2, No. 3 (Summer 1955), 3-6.

An argument in favor of the year 1894.

2484. Jenkins, William D. "Elementary, My Dear Cabell," *Kalki*, 3, No. 4 (Fall 1969), 134-135. illus.

Considers another possible point of contact between Cabell and Doyle in addition to the one in Houn.

2485. Jones, G. Basil. "The Dog and the Date," *SHJ*, 2, No. 2 (December 1954), 11-13.

The adventure took place in 1899, after *The Return*, but was deliberately antedated to conceal the fact that Holmes was still alive.

2486. Jones, Kelvin. "The Geography of *The*

146

Hound of the Baskervilles," *SHJ*, 7, No. 3 (Winter 1965), 84-86, 96.

An essay on Baskerville Hall and its environs in which Wooder Manor, near Hedge Barton, is identified as the Hall.

2487. Kissane, James and John M. "Sherlock Holmes and the Ritual of Reason," *Nineteenth Century Fiction*, 17, No. 4 (March 1963), 353-362.

Houn almost uniquely shows the hero-detective specifically championing empirical science against the challenge of the supernatural. Essential to the story's ritualistic design, the supernatural alternative is presented but is never really insistent.

2488. [Knox, E. V.] "A Ramble on Dartmoor," by Evoe. *Punch*, 214 (January 21, 1948), 46.
———. ———, [Extracts] *BSCL*, No. 7 (1969), 7-8.

The thesis is advanced that the tale was originally written in verse and may even have been intended for grand opera.

2489. Krogman, W. M. "Anthropology in *The Hound of the Baskervilles*," *BSJ*, 20, No. 3 (September 1970), 132-136.

In this adventure the Master showed a good working knowledge of anthropology. His knowledge of archeology is shown by repeated reference to prehistoric burial tumuli or barrows. In racial matters he referred to problems of ethnic background, even going so far as to equate behavior patterns with ethnic type. In a purely biological sense he and Sir Henry discussed the "anatomical peculiarities" of the peoples of South Africa (probably the Bushman specifically). The Master's use of anthropological lore mirrored the knowledge and ideas of his day.

2490. Lauterbach, C. E. "The Hound of the Baskervilles," *BSJ*, 4, No. 3 (July 1954), 164.
———. ———, *Baker Street Ballads*. [Culver City, Calif.: Luther Norris, March 1971.] p. 1.

A tale in verse set to the meter of "The Night Before Christmas."

2491. [Maurice, Arthur Bartlett.] "More Sherlock Holmes Theories," *The Bookman*, 15, No. 3 (May 1902), 215-218.
———. ———, *The Incunabular Sherlock Holmes*. Edited by Edgar W. Smith. Morristown, N.J.: The Baker Street Irregulars, 1958. p. 3-11.

A review of the story in its serialized form.

2492. May, R. F. *"The Hound of the Baskervilles*: A Botanical Enquiry," *SHJ*, 6, No. 1 (Winter 1962), 26.

Speculation about some rare orchids that may have been growing on the moor.

2493. McLauchlin, Russell. "Name That

Hound!" *BSJ*, 9, No. 2 (April 1959), 83-84.
It is suggested that his name was Tray.

2494. Merriman, Charles O. "Random Baskerville Jottings," *SHJ*, 9, No. 2 (Summer 1969), 48-50.

An illustrated description of several sites of Sherlockian interest that the author visited during a West County holiday.

2495. Metcalfe, Percy. "In Search of Baskerville Hall," *SHJ*, 7, No. 1 (Winter 1964), 6-8.

The author's visits to Dartmoor have led him to conclude that Manaton is the site of the Hall.

2496. Morley, Felix. "An Addendum to 'Dr. Watson Has Gone to Widecombe,' " *BSJ*, 15, No. 1 (March 1965), 16-17.

Watson did not go to Widecombe (Coombe Tracy) as suggested by Baring-Gould (item 2464) to interview Mrs. Laura Lyons but to Bovey Tracey.

2497. Pattrick, Robert R. "Watson Writes from Baskerville Hall," *BSJ Christmas Annual*, No. 5 (1960), 293-298.

"The last two of the seven reports Watson sent Holmes at Dartmoor never reached him, because Holmes only learned by other means of Watson's observing him in disguise, of the relationship between Selden and Mrs. Barrymore, and of the 'L. L.' note to Sir Charles." (Mark Purcell)

2498. Pickard, Charles M. "The Reticence of Doctor Mortimer," *BSJ*, 7, No. 3 (July 1957), 153-155.

Dr. James Mortimer noticed the resemblance between Stapleton and the portrait of Hugo Baskerville and related his suspicions to Holmes, but Holmes admonished him to remain silent.

2499. Pratt, Fletcher. "Introduction," *The Later Adventures of Sherlock Holmes*. New York: The Limited Editions Club, 1952. Vol. 2, p. v-xi.
———. ———, *Introducing Mr. Sherlock Holmes*. Edited by Edgar W. Smith. Morristown, N.J.: The Baker Street Irregulars, 1959. [unpaged]

"*The Hound of the Baskervilles* . . . possesses an extraordinary degree of interest, as being not only the single case in which Conan Doyle transcended the limitations and produced an absolutely pure detective story in the long form, but one of the few cases in which any one ever did."

2500. [Rabe, W. T.] *Footprint of the Hound Found in the Yew Alley of Baskerville Hall*. [Ferndale, Mich.: Privately Printed, 1964.] 1 sheet (20 x 14 in.)

"Reproduction courtesy [of the] Criminal Investigation Division, New Scotland Yard.

The Writings About the Writings

Tales

Tales

Case assignment: Inspector Lestrade, ret. Aug. 3, 1964."

Enclosed with a letter dated October 22, 1964, to W. T. Rabe from G. Lestrade in which he discusses the footprint of the gigantic hound.

2501. Ruber, P. A. "On a Defense of H. W. Bell," *BSG*, 1, No. 3 (1961), 15-17.

". . . [the] evidence is enough to prove *The Hound* took place before April, 1891, the date of *The Final Problem*. Then, taking into account that Watson was married to Mary Morstan in late fall of 1887, and that he did not have any wife at the time of *The Hound*, plus the other reasoning outlined in Mr. Bell's work, . . . would definitely prove that September, 1886, is as logical as all the other dates offered by the remaining chronologists."

2502. ———. "Sir Arthur Conan Doyle & Fletcher Robinson: An Epitaph," *BSG*, 1, No. 2 (1961), 22-28.

"We shall always be grateful to both Sir Arthur and Fletcher Robinson for their *Hound* story. It shall always be considered a collaboration, for one without the other would not have given us the greatest of the Tales. Here live eternally the two renowned—they live—though we may pass away."

2503. San Juan, E. "Reflections on *The Hound of the Baskervilles*," *BSJ*, 20, No. 3 (September 1970), 137-139.

2504. S[idgwick], F[rank]. " 'The Hound of the Baskervilles' at Fault (An Open Letter to Dr. Watson)," *The Cambridge Review*, 23, No. 574 (January 23, 1902), 137.

———. ———, *The Incunabular Sherlock Holmes*. Edited by Edgar W. Smith. Morristown, N.J.: The Baker Street Irregulars, 1958. p. 13-16.

———. ———, *BSCL*, No. 7 (1969), 4-6.

Identified by A. A. Milne and, later, by Maurice Campbell (item 2471) as being the first study in Sherlockian higher criticism.

2505. Simms, Bartlett Dale. "Devonshire Again," *BSJ*, 21, No. 2 (June 1971), 107-109.

Newton Tracey and the area south of Okehampton and the village of Merrymeet should be considered as a possible locale for Houn. This environment seems to be verified by Herbert Carey in "Down Devon Lanes," where the lonely moors, the Dartmoor bogs, the ponies, etc., are mentioned. Chagford, a resort area, was the focal point of the tale and legend.

2506. Solovay, Jacob C. "The Hound," *BSJ*, 14, No. 3 (September 1964), 161.

"Savage and gaunt, with jaws of bluish flame, / Huge as a lioness, with fire-ringed eyes, / Creature of fear and horror to despise, / Too weird for thought, too wicked for a name."

2507. Spectorsky, Fannie. "My Experience with Jean de Reszke," *BSJ*, 13, No. 3 (September 1963), 148-149.

A brief account of Mrs. Spectorsky's singing lessons with *le maître*, de Reszke, a name mentioned by Holmes in Houn.

2508. Starrett, Vincent. *"The Hound of the Baskervilles," Best Loved Books of the Twentieth Century*. New York: Bantam Books, [1955]. p. 4-6.

"There are sixty recorded adventures in the Holmes canon. Of these *The Hound of the Baskervilles* is probably the masterpiece, in Christopher Morley's opinion and mine."

2509. Welch, George W. "A Study in Moonlight," *BSG*, 1, No. 3 (1961), 18-25.

"This article is an attempt to prove that this case took place, not in 1889, nor in 1886 (as suggested by Mr. H. W. Bell), nor yet in 1899 (the year favoured by Mr. Gavin Brend), but in that 'annus mirabilis,' 1894."

A CASE OF IDENTITY

2510. Brend, Gavin. "The Lady from Camberwell," *BSJ*, 2, No. 4 (October 1952), 198. (Baker Street Doggerel)

"O Mary Sutherland, tell me that / My eyes may feast upon your hat."

2511. Smith, Edgar W. "God Rest You, Mary Sutherland!" *Illustrious Client's Second Case-Book*. Edited by J. N. Williamson. [Indianapolis, Ind.: The Illustrious Clients, 1949.] p. 42-46.

———. ———, *A Baker Street Quartette*. New York: The Baker Street Irregulars, [1950]. p. 13-20.

———. ———, *Baker Street and Beyond: Together with Some Trifling Monographs*. Morristown, N.J.: The Baker Street Irregulars, 1957. [unpaged]

———. ———, *CPBook*, 3, No. 13 (Summer 1967), 244-246.

A tale in verse.

2512. Walsh, William J. "Upon the Identity of Bisulphate of Baryta," *BSJ*, 20, No. 2 (June 1970), 110-111.

The compound mentioned by Holmes is identified as chloride of barium.

THE ADVENTURE OF THE ILLUSTRIOUS CLIENT

2513. Andrew, Clifton R. "My Old Friend Charlie Peace," *SHJ*, 4, No. 4 (Spring 1960), 118-119.

The author comments briefly on the "violin virtuoso" before quoting from an article entitled "Burglars and Burgling" (*The Strand Magazine* [March 1894], 283-

284) in which Charlie Peace, the "crowned king of all burglars, housebreakers and scoundrels," is discussed.

2514. Austin, Bliss. "Three Footnotes to *The Adventure of the Illustrious Client,*" *Illustrious Client's Third Case-Book.* Edited by J. N. Williamson and H. B. Williams. [Indianapolis, Ind.: The Illustrious Clients, 1953.] p. 89-92.

2515. ———. *A Toast to the Confreres of the Illustrious Client.* Westfield, N.J.: The Hydraulic Press, June 2, 1953. [8] p.
Limited to 60 copies.
An attribution of the origins of Col. Sir James Damery and General de Merville to the literary agent's subconscious memories of World War I battlefields. Illustrated with two maps.

2516. Chorley, Jennifer. " 'Goodly Volumes . . . ,' " *SHJ,* 7, No. 4 (Spring 1966), 118-119.
Mrs. Chorley's research in the London Library has enabled her to identify Lomax, the Sub-Librarian, as a certain James A. S. Barrett and the volume chosen by Lomax for Watson as *A History of Chinese Porcelain,* by Cosmo Monkhouse. She also comments briefly on another "goodly volume": Winwood Reade's *The Martyrdom of Man.*

2517. Fenton, Irving. "On Friendship," *BSJ,* 9, No. 1 (January 1959), 23-25.
A biographical sketch of the Master's old friend, Charlie Peace.

2518. Fiedler, Judith. "In Memoriam—Baron Adelbert Gruner, 1860-1913," *Illustrious Client's Second Case-Book.* Edited by J. N. Williamson. [Indianapolis, Ind.: The Illustrious Clients, 1949.] p. 79-82.

2519. Fredman, L. E. "The Not-So-Illustrious Client," *BSJ,* 20, No. 4 (December 1970), 239-241.
Claims Violet de Merville was the illegitimate daughter of the Prince of Wales, adding another scandal to his long list, and reflecting the tension between Victorian myth and reality.

2520. Rhode, Franklin. " 'My Old Friend Charlie Peace,' " *BSJ,* 16, No. 2 (June 1966), 77-80.
"Exceedingly delightful it is to speculate on the thoughts of Mr. Sherlock Holmes when he uttered the above remark about the burglar and assassin of whom one of his mistresses said, 'He was a demon beyond the power of a Shakespeare to paint.' "

2521. [———.] "Some Sidelights on the Illustrious Client," by Langdale Pike [pseud.] *DCC,* 3, No. 1 (November 1966), 2-3. (The World of Sherlock Holmes)
A brief discussion of Albert Ed-ward—Prince of Wales and, later, Edward VII.

2522. Schutz, Robert H. "My Old Friend . . . ?" *BSJ Christmas Annual,* No. 5 (1960), 286-288.
The author offers three descriptions from a catalog of Madame Tussaud's Exhibition at Baker Street Station to support his belief that Charlie Peace and Holmes were not actually friends.

2523. [Smith, Edgar W.] "Sonnet: To Violet de Merville," by Helene Yuhasova [pseud.] *Illustrious Client's Case-Book.* Edited by J. N. Williamson and H. B. Williams. [Indianapolis, Ind.: The Illustrious Clients, 1948.] p. 54.
———. ———, *Baker Street and Beyond: Together with Some Trifling Monographs.* Morristown, N.J.: The Baker Street Irregulars, 1957. [unpaged]
"I wonder what Adelbert really knew? / I wonder what his diary said of *you?*"

2524. Williamson, J. N. "The Adventure of the Vial Climax," *Illustrious Client's Third Case-Book.* Edited by J. N. Williamson and H. B. Williams. [Indianapolis, Ind.: The Illustrious Clients, 1953.] p. 127-132.
A tale in verse.

THE DISAPPEARANCE OF LADY FRANCES CARFAX

2525. Clark, Benjamin. "Holmes on the Range," *BSJ,* 3, No. 2 (April 1953), 91-97.
An analysis of the Master's illogical and bizarre conduct of this case.

2526. Cumings, Thayer. "A Check on Lady Frances," *BSJ,* 5, No. 3 (July 1955), 133-138.
———. ———, *Seven on Sherlock.* [New York]: Privately Printed, 1968. p. 23-26.
A remarkable visit with the brother of Jules Vibart and Marie Devine, formerly personal maid to Lady Frances Carfax, during which the author sees a replica of the check on Silvester's Bank for fifty pounds.

2527. Dorian, N. Currier. "Busy Bodies," *BSJ,* 4, No. 1 (January 1954), 38-40.
A tale in verse.

2528. Kaser, Michael C. "The Dating of 'Lady Frances Carfax,' " *BSJ,* 7, No. 2 (April 1957), 87-91.
The author shows that the exact dating of this tale cannot be more precisely narrowed than between 1896, the date selected by himself, and July 1902, the date assigned by Baring-Gould.

2529. ———. "A Solution to 'Lady Frances Carfax,' " *BSJ,* 9, No. 2 (April 1959), 85-87.
A reexamination of the evidence has convinced Mr. Kaser that the adventure

actually took place during the summer of 1898.

2530. Lauterbach, C. E. "The Sky-Pilot," *West by One and by One.* San Francisco: Privately Printed, 1965. p. 42-43.

"The Reverend Doctor Schlessinger [sic] / Was a mighty man of God."

2531. [Rhode, Franklin.] "A Very Large Clock," by Langdale Pike [pseud.] *DCC,* 4, No. 2 (February 1968), 2. (The World of Sherlock Holmes)

A commentary on Big Ben and Watson's reference to it in this story.

HIS LAST BOW

2532. Cox, J. Randolph. "Thwarting at the Channel," *BSJ,* 15, No. 4 (December 1965), 208-212.

A comparison between this tale and *The Thirty-Nine Steps,* by John Buchan.

2533. Donegall, Lord. " 'His Last Bow,' " *The New Strand,* 1, No. 10 (September 1962), 1162-1164. (Baker Street and Beyond, No. 10)

Contents: Holmes' War Service. - Great Passages. - The Authorship.

2534. George, Isaac S. "His Last Bow, or The Final Final Problem," *Illustrious Client's Third Case-Book.* Edited by J. N. Williamson and H. B. Williams. [Indianapolis, Ind.: The Illustrious Clients, 1953.] p. 152-154.

A tale in verse.

2535. Jaffee, Irving L. "Sherlock Holmes Calling," *Double-Action Detective and Mystery Stories,* No. 11 (July 1958), 82-86.
————. ————, *Elementary My Dear Watson.* Brooklyn, N.Y.: Theo. Gaus' Sons, [1965]. p. 47-51.

Primarily an excursion into the Master's activities at the time of his war service in 1914.

2536. Rosenberger, Edgar S. " 'There's an East Wind Coming, Watson,' " *BSJ,* 17, No. 2 (June 1967), 67-69.

A tale in verse.

2537. Sellars, Crighton. "Altamont," *BSJ* [OS], 3, No. 1 (January 1948), 59.

"Working for England and German disgrace, / Flaunted his subterfuge right in their face, / Called himself ALTAMONT—little they guessed / Why Holmes picked that name from among all the rest."

2538. Smith, Edgar W. "The Adventure of the Veiled Author," *BSJ* [OS], 1, No. 2 (April 1946), 129-135.
————. ————, *Baker Street and Beyond: Together with Some Trifling Monographs.* Morristown, N.J.: The Baker Street Irregulars, 1957. [unpaged]

After eliminating both Watson and the literary agent as possible authors of "His Last Bow," Mr. Smith concludes that Mycroft was the veiled author of this tale.

2539. Van Liere, Edward J. "The Story I Like Best," *BSJ,* 3, No. 1 (January 1953), 39-42.
————. "The Sherlock Holmes Story I Like Best," *Medical and Other Essays.* Morgantown: West Virginia University Library, 1966. p. 152-155.

"The most satisfying of all the tales is *His Last Bow: An Epilogue of Sherlock Holmes.* . . . The plot is simple; it is historical; it is interesting and entertaining; it has suspense; it is plausible; it ends happily and on a high note."

2540. Wigglesworth, Belden. "The Road from Skibbareen," *BSJ,* 7, No. 4 (October 1957), 236-239.

"It was not to England that Sherlock Holmes went—it was to Russia; and the doom of Von Bork was sealed."

THE ADVENTURE OF THE LION'S MANE

2541. Hedgpeth, Joel W. "Re-Examination of *The Adventure of the Lion's Mane,*" *The Scientific Monthly,* 60, No. 3 (March 1945), 227-232.
————. ————, *BSJ* [OS], 3, No. 3 (July 1948), 285-294.

A review of the pathology of jellyfish stings and a discussion of the case investigated by Holmes.

2542. Van Liere, Edward J. "Sherlock Holmes and the Portuguese Man-of-War," *West Virginia Medical Journal,* 48 (January 1952), 10-12.
————. ————, *A Doctor Enjoys Sherlock Holmes.* New York: Vantage Press, [1959]. p. 35-40.

"Since it is generally believed that *Cyanea capillata* cannot cause the death of an individual, and since the symptoms described in *The Adventure of the Lion's Mane* were so grave, the coelenterate which Holmes had in mind probably was no other than *Physalia,* commonly known as the Portuguese man-of-war. Exposure to the tentacles of this creature is apt to produce a chain of alarming symptoms."

2543. Wolff, Julian. "Remember the Mane?" *BSJ* [OS], 3, No. 4 (October 1948), 471-475.

An investigation into the bibliographical aspects of the adventure, including a quotation on the "scourge of the ocean, the VENOMOUS CYANAEA," from *The New Illustrated Natural History,* by John George Wood.

2544. Zahl, Paul A. "Glass Menageries of the

Sea," With illustrations from photographs by the author. *The National Geographic Magazine*, 107, No. 6 (June 1955), 797-822.

The opening pages of this article on *Cyanea capillata* and other jellyfish stem straight from "The Lion's Mane."

THE ADVENTURE OF
THE MAZARIN STONE

2545. Baring-Gould, William S. " '. . . It Is Undoubtedly Queer . . . ,' " *The Annotated Sherlock Holmes*. New York: Clarkson N. Potter, [1967]. Vol. 2, chap. 75, p. 748-750.

A review of the literature on this tale.

2546. Dickensheet, Dean W. and Shirley J. "A Remarkable Invention," *BSJ*, 14, No. 4 (December 1964), 208-215.

The authors deny that Holmes could have used or invented the Neophone long-playing disc as suggested by Herbert Kupferberg and propose instead that the Master used a Poulsen Telegraphone to record and play his violin rendition of Offenbach's *Barcarolle*.

2547. Kupferberg, Herbert. "The Adventure of the Bodiless Virtuoso," *High Fidelity*, 8, No. 5 (May 1958), 34-35, 122-124.

———. ———, *BSJ*, 14, No. 4 (December 1964), 201-207.

An astonishing deduction that Holmes not only used but may have invented the Neophone long-playing record which deceived Count Negretto Sylvius and Sam Merton.

2548. Montgomery, James. "Speculation in Diamonds," *Three Trifling Monographs*. [Philadelphia: Privately Printed, 1952.] p. 16-21.

———. ———, *SHJ*, 1, No. 4 (December 1953), 30-36.

———. ———, *The Best of the Pips*. Westchester County, N.Y.: The Five Orange Pips, 1955. p. 35-43.

An analysis of Maza and *The Crown Diamond* confirms that the story is based on the play and not the other way around.

2549. Newton, G. B. "Concerning the Authorship of 'The Mazarin Stone,' " *SHJ*, 4, No. 2 (Spring 1959), 52-54.

An interesting speculation that Billy the page was the author of this tale. (For a divergent opinion, see Edgar Smith's letter on p. 107 of the same volume.)

2550. R[hode], F[ranklin] W. "The Uncrowned Queen of Horror," by Langdale Pike. *DCC*, 5, No. 1 (October 1968), 2-3. (The World of Sherlock Holmes)

A brief paper on Madame Tussaud and her wax museum.

2551. Shea, Glenn J. "An Analysis of 'The Mazarin Stone,' " *HO*, 1, No. 4 (June 1971), 4-6.

2552. Shreffler, Philip A. "The Problem of the Twelve Mazarin Stones," *DCC*, 6, No. 2 (March 1970), 2-3.

Evidence that the Mazarin stone was one of twelve diamonds owned by the Cardinal Mazarin, State Minister of France from 1642 to 1661.

THE ADVENTURE OF
THE MISSING THREE-QUARTER

2553. Prestige, Colin. " 'Stand by Us for God's Sake,' " *SHJ*, 1, No. 4 (December 1953), 8-9.

An analysis of Godfrey Staunton's hieroglyphic message to Dr. Leslie Armstrong.

THE MUSGRAVE RITUAL

See also *T.S. Eliot* (items 3991-4003)

2554. Anderson, Poul and Karen. "The Curious Behaviour of the Ritual in the Daytime," *BSJ Christmas Annual*, No. 5 (1960), 304-311.

"The Canon leaves us . . . with a Ritual made valueless by its ambiguity as to time, a setting sun which will not touch the horizon for two or more hours, an absurdly small manor, and sunlight somehow shining through stone walls." The editor explains that American editions omit a couplet.

2555. Bengis, Nathan L. " 'Rache' for Rachel," *BSJ*, 2, No. 3 (July 1952), 152-157.

A tale in verse.

2556. ———. "What Was the Source? That Is the Question," *A Curious Collection*. Edited by William J. Walsh. [Suffern, N.Y.]: The Musgrave Ritualists Beta, 1971. p. 28-31.

The Musgrave Ritual may have been inspired by an account of the Apulian treasure story published in *The Wonders of the Little World, or A General History of Man*, by Nathaniel Wanley (London: T. Basset, 1678).

2557. ———. "Whose Was It? An Examination into the Crowning Lapse of Sherlockian Scholarship," *BSJ*, 3, No. 2 (April 1953), 69-76.

The crown discovered at Hurlstone Manor was the St. Edward's Crown used at the coronations of English kings prior to the time of the Commonwealth.

2558. Brend, Gavin. "The Black Boy's Visit to Hurlstone," *BSJ*, 3, No. 4 (October 1953), 217-224.

After refuting the reconstructions of Nathan Bengis and H. D. W. Sitwell, the author advances his own theory that "The Black Boy" (one of Prince Charles's nicknames) actually visited West Sussex to retrieve a cache of money.

2559. Christ, Jay Finley. "Musgrave

Mathematics," *Illustrious Client's Case-Book*. Edited by J. N. Williamson and H. B. Williams. [Indianapolis, Ind.: The Illustrious Clients, 1948.] p. 14-19.

A study of Holmes's methods in solving the problems of the Musgrave Ritual.

2560. [Dalton, Philip.] "The Musgrave Ritual Discussed," *SHJ*, 1, No. 3 (June 1953), 45-46.

A report on a discussion of this tale at the Sherlock Holmes Society's meeting of March 10, 1953.

2561. Donegall, Lord. "No Real Treasure—Just the Butler's Body!" *The New Strand*, 1, No. 8 (July 1962), 938-940. (Baker Street and Beyond, No. 8)
———. ———, *HO Annual*, No. 1 (1971), 29-32.

A synopsis and discussion of the story.

2562. Goslin, Vernon. "The Gormansboro' Ritual," *SHJ*, 9, No. 3 (Winter 1969), 85-86.

Similarities between "The Four-Leaved Shamrock" (retitled "The Gormansboro' Ritual" by Mr. Goslin), a drawing-room comedietta in three acts by C. J. Hamilton which appeared in *Beeton's Christmas Annual* (1887), and "The Musgrave Ritual" suggest that the literary agent may have recalled the play when he wrote his story.

2563. Green, Roger Lancelyn. "Illicit Treasure Seekers: Another Literary Osmosis," *SHJ*, 4, No. 2 (Spring 1959), 72-73.

Stanley Weyman's "Sefton's Servant" and H. Rider Haggard's *Colonel Quaritch, V.C.* are compared with Musg.

2564. Hardenbrook, Don. "Infinitely Stranger," *BSJ Christmas Annual*, No. 1 (1956), 47-51.

While browsing in a Los Angeles antique shop, the author and Dean Dickensheet discover a hunting crop which they identify as the one Reginald Musgrave must have presented to the Master as a token of his gratitude. The date "1878" stamped on the crop is irrefutable proof that the adventure occurred during that year.

2565. Merriam, Joseph E. "Holmes at Hurlstone, or The Royal Diadem Recovered," *BSJ*, 21, No. 3 (September 1971), 131.

A tale in verse.

2566. Merrill, Edward A. "The Case of the Missing Calendar," *BSJ*, 21, No. 3 (September 1971), 132-139; [Addendum] 22, No. 1 (March 1972), 46-48. illus.

An extension of the debate on whether the cryptic clue in the Musgrave Ritual, "What was the Month? The sixth from the First," applies to July under the Gregorian Calendar or to October under the Old Style common in England during the first half of the 17th century. Less ambiguous statements in Holmes's narrative relative to such circumstances as: At what hour did Holmes arrive at Hurlstone? What did he find when he reached the Oak Tree? When did he enter the Old Door? and What did he see there? are analyzed with respect to the different conditions of the direction of the sun, and the hour in the afternoon when it has descended to an angle of 2 vertical to 3 horizontal, as prevail in each of the two months under consideration. The weight of the evidence establishes a strong probability for the summer month, but it is not confirmed by eliminating the impossible until it is shown that the conformation of the Manor House could not have appeared as Holmes described it in the autumn month.

2567. ———. "Holmes and Brunton: Civil Engineers," *BSJ*, 20, No. 1 (March 1970), 39-47; [Addendum] 20, No. 4 (December 1970), 243. illus.

Winner of the 13th annual Morley-Montgomery Memorial Award for the best contribution to *BSJ* in 1970.

An engineering analysis of the helioastrometric, trigonometric, and topographic problems of the Musgrave Ritual. Ambiguities which have concerned Sherlockian scholars in the past are clarified but the demonstration that, if a rod of 6 feet throws a shadow of 9 feet, an *elm tree* of 64 feet will *not* throw one of 96 feet, presents a new one not previously recognized. It is resolved by the deduction that both Holmes and Brunton, solving the riddle of the ritual with incredible precision, must have used more modern techniques than Holmes admitted in his narrative to Watson.

2568. Montgomery, James. "A Canonical Toast to Rachel Howells," *Shots from the Canon*. [Philadelphia: Privately Printed, 1953.] p. 23.

"So here's a toast to Rachel, / Torn with passion though she be, / Avenger to dishonored love— / And lost virginity."

2569. "Musgrave Ritual," *BSJ*, 8, No. 3 (July 1958), 183.

Translated into Greek by Dr. Raymond Hendrickson.

2570. Prestige, Colin, and Guy Warrack. "Oratio Recta Twice Removed," *SHJ*, 6, No. 2 (Spring 1963), 55-56.

An exchange of letters between these two eminent Sherlockians concerning Watson's use of inverted commas in relating what Richard Brunton, the butler at Hurlstone Manor, said to Reginald Musgrave, Musgrave later repeated to Holmes, and Holmes subsequently stated to Watson. A "comical" problem!

2571. "Ritualia Musgraviensia," *BSJ* [OS], 4, No. 1 (January 1949), 114.

Copied from the original Latin by Morris Rosenblum in collaboration with Dr. Thorneycroft Huxtable.

2572. Simpson, A. Carson. "The Curious Matter of the Anonymous Latin Epitaph," *BSJ*, 11, No. 4 (December 1961), 235-237.
"Both Epitaph and Ritual are anonymous and undated, and both contain the same question, 'Where was the sun?' "

2573. Sitwell, H. D. W. "Some Notes on St. Edward's Crown and the Musgrave Ritual," *BSJ*, 3, No. 2 (April 1953), 77-82.
Ralph Musgrave was at first the right-hand man of Charles the Second in his wanderings and then became a close confidant of Prince Charles.

2574. Utechin, Nicholas. "Hurlstone and the Ritual," *BSJ*, 21, No. 3 (September 1971), 140-142. illus.
An attempt to establish Hurlstone Hall's orientation, using the evidence of Musg and the directions in the Ritual itself. Eight possible positions for the L-shaped house are postulated: five are eliminated immediately, failing to fulfill the data's requirements. A sixth is unlikely; a seventh (Baring-Gould's choice) is possible. The author's choice ("ancient nucleus" running NS, new wing WE at southern end) fits the story's data, the Ritual's directions, and is esthetically pleasing.

THE NAVAL TREATY

2575. Arenfalk, Poul. "Is 'The Naval Treaty' Really the Best Sherlock Holmes Story?" *IR*, 1, No. 3 (March 1961), 1-5.
Several discrepancies are pointed out to show that it is not, as claimed by Paul V. Rubow in his Ph.D. dissertation, the best of the sixty tales.

2576. Chorley, Jennifer. " 'Briarbrae' Revisited: A Photographic Pilgrimage," *SHJ*, 6, No. 2 (Spring 1963), 56-57.
A report on the trip to Inchcape House, Woking, considered to be the model for Percy Phelps's house.

2577. Chujoy, Anatole. "The Only Second Stain," *BSJ*, 4, No. 3 (July 1954), 165-168.
An explanation of the apparent discrepancy between Watson's reference to Seco in Nava and the actual story.

2578. Jaffee, Irving L. " 'The Naval Treaty,' " *Double-Action Detective Magazine*, No. 22 (May 1960), 101-104.
————. ————, *Elementary My Dear Watson*. Brooklyn, N.Y.: Theo. Gaus' Sons, [1965]. p. 51-54.

2579. McLauchlin, Russell. "I Am Contemplating My Naval . . . Treaty," *BSJ*, 1, No. 2 (April 1951), 52-54.
A tale in verse.

2580. Redmond, Chris. "An Identification of Colonel Warburton," *SOS*, No. 3 (February 1967), 5-6.
Col. Warburton (Engr) and Percy Phelps are identified as being the same person.

2581. Stix, Thomas L. "We Ask the Questions!" *BSJ*, 17, No. 3 (September 1967), 149-151.
Questions primarily concerned with this adventure.

THE ADVENTURE OF THE NOBLE BACHELOR

2582. Girand, John. "Frank Moulton's Arizona Adventures," *BSJ*, 19, No. 4 (December 1969), 206-212.
One of the central characters in this tale is an American girl, Hattie Doran, who is married to Francis Hay Moulton. The essay, based on extensive research of Arizona historical records, traces his adventures while prospecting near Tombstone, his capture by the Apache Indians, his discovery of the secret Apache gold mine, and his escape with a fortune in gold.

2583. Jenkins, William D. "A Purloined Letter: Conan Doyle from Bret Harte," *BSJ*, 22, No. 2 (June 1972), 81-83.
A plot analogy between Harte's ballad "Her Letter" (*The Poetical Works of Bret Harte*, 1880) and Nobl (1892).

2584. Jones, Gratia. "The Adventure of the Yellow House, or What Became of Hattie Doran?" *West by One and by One*. San Francisco: Privately Printed, 1965. p. 19-26.
Mrs. Jones visits Mrs. Francis H. Moulton in an effort to settle a chronological discrepancy.

2585. Shaw, John Bennett. "An Adventure Within 'The Adventure of the Noble Bachelor,' " *SHJ*, 9, No. 1 (Winter 1968), 21-23.
The author's research enables him to substantiate Francis and Hatty Doran Moulton's story, as remembered and *accurately* recorded by Watson.

THE ADVENTURE OF THE NORWOOD BUILDER

2586. Aronson, Marvin E. "The Case of the Norwood Builder," *BSJ*, 15, No. 1 (March 1965), 22-25.
The Coroner of London during the late 19th century reports his findings that Jonas Oldacre actually perished in the fire and that Mr. Cornelius then impersonated the retired builder, deceiving even the Master of disguises!

2587. Brend, Gavin. "Mr. J. Oldacre," *SHJ*, 1, No. 3 (June 1953), 2. (Baker Street Doggerel)
"This brave new world does indeed

Tales

bewilder / Your humble servant, The Norwood Builder.''

THE ADVENTURE OF THE PRIORY SCHOOL

2588. Bigelow, S. Tupper. "Hallamshire Revisited," *BSJ*, 13, No. 2 (June 1963), 87-90.

A review of the literature on the location of the county of Hallamshire where the action of this story takes place.

2589. ———. "The Hoof-Marks in *The Priory School*," *BSJ*, 12, No. 3 (September 1962), 169-174.

———. *Klöv-sparen i The Priory School*. Oversättning av Ted Bergman. Stockholm: The Baker Street Cab Lantern, 1965. [12] p.

Limited to 21 copies.

Winner of the 5th annual Morley-Montgomery Memorial Award for the best contribution to *BSJ* in 1962.

A demonstration of Watson's error in depicting the walk and canter of the horse.

2590. Clarkson, Steve. " 'Sir Huxtable's' Sidelights on Prio," *HO*, 1, No. 2 (April 1971), 4-5.

In this "somewhat disjointed series of remarks which are intended solely to illuminate or emphasize facets of Prio," the author discusses such major items as the chronology, the character of the personalities involved, the bicycle tires, the horse's (cow's) foottracks, and the faults of Holmes.

2591. Donegall, Lord. "Kidnapping, Murder, Cycle Tracks, A Duke and His Cheque!" *The New Strand*, 1, No. 7 (June 1962), 810-812. (Baker Street and Beyond, No. 7)

———. "Thoughts on 'The Adventure of the Priory School,' " *HO*, 1, No. 1 (March 1971), 10-14.

A discussion of an adventure "which owes its importance to the still remaining doubt: did Holmes take a £6,000 bribe from the Duke of Holdernesse to cover up murder—Misprision of Felony, in fact."

2592. Gardner, George K. " 'What Sherlock Did Know,' " *The Atlantic Monthly*, 177, No. 1 (January 1946), 31-32.

———. ———, *BSJ*, 1, No. 3 (July 1951), 89-90.

"Sir Henry Hawkins, as Mr. Stuart Rand contends [item 2902], was indeed a great lawyer; but as far as the *Priory School* case is concerned, had he cross-examined the bicycle instead of Sherlock Holmes, the bicycle, instead of fading, would have thrown him off."

2593. Hall, Trevor H. "A Note on *The Priory School*," *Sherlock Holmes: Ten Literary Studies*. London: Gerald Duckworth & Co., [1969]. Chap. 9, p. 123-131.

"Of ducal matters concerning Holdernesse and Greyminster and of scholastic matters concerning the Abbey and Priory Schools, with surprising undertones of Oberstein and Von Bork. 'Deep waters,' indeed!" (Lord Donegall)

2594. Hyslop, James T. "A Priori," *BSJ* [OS], 3, No. 4 (October 1948), 452-457.

A tale in verse.

2595. Morley, Christopher. "Tail Light on Horace," *BSJ* [OS], 4, No. 1 (January 1949), 39-41.

"From Dr. Thorneycroft Huxtable's projected new edition. Translated from *Orbilius Pupillus*. Endorsed by him 'This Xmas, B.C. 22.' "

2596. Naganuma, Kohki. ["A Study in Tires," *Sherlock Holmes and His Bluish Smoke*. Tokyo: Bungei Shunju Ltd., 1966.] Chap. 4.

———. "On Tires in *The Priory School*," *BSJ*, 16, No. 2 (June 1966), 94-100.

"Regarding the impressions of the tires, Doyle cannot be considered infallible in every respect. For he could not run his own bicycle skillfully enough in *The Priory School!*"

2597. Stowe, Thomas D. "More About Tires in *The Priory School*," *BSJ*, 16, No. 4 (December 1966), 219-221.

"A bicycle's direction *can* be told from its track. However, both Doyle and Dr. Naganuma failed to indicate the method. In general, however, Doyle comes out of all this bicycle business with flying colours."

2598. Symons, T. H. B. "Some Notes on the Sixth Duke of Holdernesse," *BSJ*, 9, No. 1 (January 1959), 5-9.

"A number of considerations suggest that the person disguised as the Sixth Duke of Holderenesse by Watson was in fact the Eighth Duke of Devonshire."

THE ADVENTURE OF THE RED CIRCLE

2599. Blake, S. F. "Sherlock Holmes and the Italian Cipher," *BSJ*, 9, No. 1 (January 1959), 14-20.

Gennaro Lucca's code was based on the English rather than the Italian alphabet.

2600. Boswell, Rolfe. "Squaring the Red Circle," *BSJ*, 1, No. 3 (July 1951), 113-114.

The evidence suggests this undated case took place in 1902.

2601. Griffin, Daniel. "Emilia Lucca's Story," *BSJ*, 15, No. 2 (June 1965), 97-102.

A consideration of the tale told by the wife of Gennaro, with the startling conclusion that "besides being a congenital liar, she was an opportunist and a dissembler, guilty of duplicity at very best, and at worst—well, our minds can only guess at the fathomless depths of evil."

2602. Pachter, Josh. "Come Now, Gentlemen!" *BSJ*, 20, No. 3 (September 1970), 168-169.

Lucca showed his wife how to insert the letter *K* between *J* and *L* so that he could send his messages in the English alphabet. Louis E. Lord, S. F. Blake, and D. A. Yates (all quoted in vol. 2, p. 698, of *The Annotated Sherlock Holmes*) erred in their analysis of the problem.

2603. Reed, John Shelton. "A Note on 'The Long Island Cave Mystery' Mystery," *BSJ*, 19, No. 2 (June 1969), 112-113.

The island of Mr. Leverton's adventure, referred to by Holmes in RedC, is not the Long Island of New York but of Tennessee.

2604. Yates, Donald A. "A Final Illumination on the Lucca Code," *EL*, 3, No. 1 (March 1955), 5-9.
———. ———, *BSJ*, 6, No. 3 (July 1956), 146-151.

An explanation of how Holmes was able to intercept and interpret the coded messages between Gennaro and Emilia Lucca.

THE RED-HEADED LEAGUE

2605. Barnes, W. J. "Saxe-Coburg Square—A New Identification," *SHJ*, 2, No. 3 (Summer 1955), 31-34.

The location of the premises where the principal action took place is fixed in the easterly block on Goswell Road adjacent to Northampton Square.

2606. Bengis, Nathan L. ["Letter"], *SHJ*, 2, No. 2 (December 1954), 43.

The question is asked: "What did John Clay do with the earth excavated in digging the tunnel?" An answer by Samuel F. Howard appears in *BSJ*, 7, No. 4 (October 1957), 251.

2607. Bergman, Ted. "Fallet City and Suburban Bank" ["The Case of the City and Suburban Bank"], *BSCL*, No. 2 (July 1963), 27.

Text in Danish.
The "Red-Headed League Bank Branch" is identified as Barclay's Old Street / Pittsfield Street Branch (formerly the London and Provincial Bank).

2608. Bigelow, S. Tupper. *"The Red-Headed League* Revisited," *BSP*, No. 25 (July 1967), 3-4.

A further possibility of how Clay removed the earth from his tunnel.

2609. Brandreth, Dale A. "The Sherlock Holmes Story I Like Best—and Why," *BSJ* [OS], 1, No. 4 (October 1946), 460-461.

The choice of this thirteen-year-old member of the Scandalous Bohemians of Akron is RedH.

2610. Brend, Gavin. "Jabez Muses," *BSJ*, 3, No. 3 (July 1953), 169.

" 'Copy out letter "A," ' he said— / And all because my hair is red!"

2611. Burnham, Ernest C. "The Tattooed Fish in *The Red-Headed League*," *BSJ*, 12, No. 4 (December 1962), 219-222.

"It could be assumed that Wilson's tattoo was probably done in Japan and that it was never a delicate pink originally, and that Holmes took a shot in the dark and came up with an extremely lucky guess, obviously not based on knowledge."

2612. Christ, Jay Finley. "The Story I Like Best," *BSJ* [OS], 2, No. 4 (October 1947), 427-428.
———. *My Favorite Sherlockian Adventure.* [Chicago: Privately Printed, December 1947.] [4] p.

"Good Sherlock took full many a crook / In Adventures beyond compare; / And the best of the lot is the crafty plot / of the man with the flaming hair."

2613. De Groat, Raymond A. "The Guilty Pawnbroker, or The Lost Summer of 1890," *BSJ*, 14, No. 1 (March 1964), 27-30.

"This paper could have been entitled 'The Adventure of the Missing Red-Head and All of the Multitudinous Concatenations Related Thereto,' for it is really an investigation of the guilt of Jabez Wilson."

2614. Erickson, Carl T. "Royal Blood and Feet of Clay," *BSJ*, 4, No. 2 (April 1954), 98-99.

John Clay, instigator of the League of Red-Headed Men, is the third cousin twice removed to Queen Elizabeth II.

2615. Foster, Richard W. "John Clay and Lebanon, Pennsylvania, U.S.A.," *BSJ*, 21, No. 2 (June 1971), 97-99.

John Clay, the forger, was young but already a capable thief. Despite his skill in eluding Scotland Yard, it can be surmised that his vanity could mar his otherwise ingenious schemes: his dissolution of the Red-Headed League prematurely, for example. Where did this young Englishman, educated at Eton and Oxford, ever hear of Lebanon, Pa.? A visit to the locality and extended research failed to turn up any claim to fame for that town whatsoever. Surely Clay learned of its existence from Ted Baldwin, whom he no doubt met in England when Baldwin had come in search of Birdy Edwards. Perhaps it was Baldwin's native city. Later Clay, in his contempt for the not overbright pawnbroker, seized on the most absurd place-name he could think of: Lebanon, Pennsylvania, U.S.A.

Tales

Tales

2616. McPharlin, Paul. "Sweet Auburn," *BSJ* [OS], 4, No. 1 (January 1949), 24-27.
A tale in verse.

2617. Morley, Frank V. "I Am Puzzled About Saxe-Coburg Square," *BSJ*, 5, No. 3 (July 1955), 139-141.

2618. Pattrick, Robert R. "October 9, 1890," *SHJ*, 3, No. 1 (Summer 1956), 16-17.
The author argues that the sign "The Red-Headed League Is Dissolved, October 9, 1890" was dated correctly but that it was intended, deliberately and confusingly, to refer to a Thursday, whereas the events of the tale occurred on a Saturday.

2619. "*The Red-Headed League* Reviewed," *SHJ*, 2, No. 1 (July 1954), 29-34.
A summary of a discussion that took place at a meeting of the Sherlock Holmes Society on March 16, 1954. Includes two footnotes by James Edward Holroyd and Clifton R. Andrew.

2620. Roberts, Daisy Mae. " 'The Red-Headed League' and 'The Rue Morgue,' " *Scholastic Magazine,* 32 (February 26, 1938), 19E-20E.
A comparison between the literary formulas of these two classic detective stories, and between Holmes and Dupin.

2621. Sayers, Dorothy L. "The Dates in 'The Red-Headed League,' " *The Colophon,* 5, Pt. 17 (January 1934), [8] p.
————. ————, *Unpopular Opinions.* London: Victor Gollancz Ltd., 1946. p. 168-178.
————. ————, ————. New York: Harcourt, Brace & Co., [1947]. p. 189-209.
————. ————, *BSJ* [OS], 2, No. 3 (July 1947), 279-290. (Incunabulum)
————. ————, *MacKill's Mystery Magazine,* 3, No. 4 (February 1954), 72-80.
————. ————, *The Incunabular Sherlock Holmes.* Edited by Edgar W. Smith. Morristown, N.J.: The Baker Street Irregulars, 1958. p. 143-159.
————. ————, *Seventeen Steps to 221B.* [Edited by] James Edward Holroyd. London: George Allen & Unwin Ltd., [1967]. p. 57-67.
"An examination and explanation of the anachronisms, with proposals for their reconciliation." (Edgar W. Smith)

2622. Scholefield, C. E. "Red-Headed Clients' Conundrums," *SHJ*, 10, No. 3 (Winter 1971), 74-76.
Advances the thesis that one of the tunnel's terminals was located at McFarlane's carriage-building depot rather than on Jabez Wilson's premises. Other problems concerning John Clay are also discussed. (A refutation by Paul D. Herbert of the McFarlane tunnel theory appears in the following issue on p. 137-138.)

2623. Stix, Thomas L. "Concerning *The Red-Headed League*," *BSJ*, 4, No. 2 (April 1954), 93-96.
————. Enlarged with title: "The 7 Errors in *The Red-Headed League*," *Ellery Queen's Mystery Magazine,* 39, No. 1 (January 1962), 79-82.
A master critic points out "*seven* mistakes, misstatements, and foolish and erroneous deductions" in this great tale.

THE REIGATE PUZZLE

2624. Ball, John. "The Twenty-Three Deductions," *BSJ*, 8, No. 4 (October 1958), 234-237.
In solving the problem presented by the death of William Kirwan, Holmes examined a scrap of paper and gave certain conclusions which he drew from it. He then stated that there were twenty-three additional deductions from the same source, but did not cite them. This paper, employing Holmes's methods as described by himself, defines these deductions and presents the list.

2625. Holstein, L. S. "The Puzzle of Reigate," *BSJ*, 2, No. 4 (October 1952), 221-225.
"Watson had, innocently, become involved with persons of dire purposes, the Cunninghams, Kirwan, and probably Hayter, and was the cat's-paw for them in writing the note, or part of it at least."

2626. Kallis, Stephen A. "Reigate Revisited," *BSJ*, 14, No. 1 (March 1964), 37-38.
A defense of Holmes and Watson against the accusations of Mr. Stix.

2627. Stix, Thomas L. "The Reigate Puzzler," *BSJ*, 13, No. 2 (June 1963), 93-95.
A critical examination of a case the author thinks was unworthy of the Master.

THE RESIDENT PATIENT

See also *Card* (items 2301-2307)

2628. Heldenbrand, Page. "On an Obscure Nervous Page," *BSJ*, 4, No. 3 (July 1954), 154-155.
One Page comes to the defense of another page who served Dr. Percy Trevelyan.

2629. Pachter, Josh. *The Brook Street Mystery Unraveled: Being Certain Revelations Regarding Dr. Percy Trevelyan and Mr. Sherlock Holmes.* Ann Arbor, Mich.: The 0.06976 Press, [1972]. 33 p.
Limited to 200 numbered copies.
A monograph in five parts: 1. Proof that Holmes's solution to Blessington's murder was incorrect; 2. A reconstruction of the actual solution; 3. Proof that Holmes and Trevelyan were fraternal twins; 4. A fictionalized presentation of the events leading up to Holmes's birth; and 5. A tongue-in-

cheek appendix discussing the addresses of Holmes and Trevelyan.

THE ADVENTURE OF THE RETIRED COLOURMAN

2630. Bengis, Nathan L. "Smothered Mate," *BSJ*, 10, No. 4 (October 1960), 213-220. illus.
Valentine Qualtrough's *Chess Strategy* (Manchester: Mallinson and Parkman, 1936) includes two chess games played during June 1898 between Joseph Amberley and Dr. Raymond Earnest, besides two other games by William Wallace of the famous murder trial. Both the Amberley-Earnest games prophesy the July tragedy, because the latter was subconsciously warning Amberley, who gives his unconscious cooperation. In the second game, Amberley sacrifices his queen to defeat the king.

2631. Bigelow, S. Tupper. "Chess and Sherlock Holmes," *SHJ*, 4, No. 1 (Winter 1958), 12-14.
The reason why the jurors returned a verdict of "guilty" in the William Wallace case of 1931 was because they had read and remembered the words of the Master in Reti: "Amberley excelled at chess—one mark, Watson, of a scheming mind." Wallace was a member of the Liverpool Central Chess Club.

2632. Dahlinger, Susan. "The Adventures of a Hated Rival," *SOS*, 4, No. 2 (July 1970), 4-5.
About amateur detective Barker whom Holmes jokingly described as his hated rival on the Surrey shore.

2633. Miller, William G. "The Mystery of the Indelible Pencil," *BSJ*, 21, No. 1 (September 1971), 175-176.

A SCANDAL IN BOHEMIA

2634. Anderson, Poul. " 'The King of Scandinavia,' " [Oversat af A. D. Henriksen]. *Sherlock Holmes Årbog* I (1965), 42-47.
Text in Danish.

2635. Andrew, C. R. "What Kind of Shenanigans Went on at St. Monica's?" *BSJ Christmas Annual*, No. 1 (1956), 42-45.
"The 'difficulties' in *A Scandal in Bohemia* were brought about by a combination of Holmes's and Watson's understandable lack of knowledge of the rules and regulations of the marriage contract in 1888, together with the unknown quantity of Mr. Godfrey Norton's status."

2636. Arenfalk, Poul, and Erik Hall. *When Was Sherlock Holmes in Copenhagen? Who Are the Characters in "A Scandal in Bohemia"? A Work of Research.* [Illustrations by Erik Hall.] Copenhagen: The Danish Baker Street Irregulars, 1960. 95 p.

2637. Ashton, Ralph A. "Forget St. Monica's . . . What Happened at Briony Lodge?" *BSJ*, 8, No. 3 (July 1958), 163-168.
Holmes, not Godfrey Norton, and Irene Adler were married at St. Monica's. Mr. Norton, the alleged bridegroom, was "either a figment the well-matched pair invented, or Irene Adler's counsellor, and a witness at the marriage."

2638. Bailey, L. W. "The Scandal Behind the 'Scandal,' " *SHJ*, 9, No. 3 (Winter 1969), 82-85.
The author believes that the hereditary King of Bohemia who visited Holmes on March 20, 1888, was the Crown Prince Rudolf and that it was Viktor Adler, not the *fictitious* Irene Adler, who was in possession of a document compromising to Rudolf.

2639. Bigelow, S. Tupper. "If We Have to be Whimsical," *Four Wheels to Baker Street.* Edited by Bruce Kennedy. [Fulton, Mo.]: The Three Students Plus, 1968. p. 4-6.
Judge Bigelow ridicules the whimsical school of writing in his treatment of the wedding problems of Irene Adler.

2640. Blackburn, Julian. "The Identity of the King of Bohemia," *BSJ*, 21, No. 2 (June 1971), 114-116.
The King of Bohemia was Prince Alexander of Battenberg (1857-1893), Monarch of Bulgaria. He had an affair with the opera singer Johanna Loisinger. He sent her his photograph with a mirror attached so that she could look at the "lovely and enchanting features" of the "most beautiful singer I know"—a gift she was very likely unwilling to part with. The Crown Princess of Germany was determined that Alexander should marry her daughter Victoria at this time and, after Alexander's abdication, the Great Powers were struggling over his future. It was therefore essential for him to retrieve the photograph.

2641. Blakeney, T. S. "A Case for Identification—In Bohemia," *SHJ*, 3, No. 2 (Winter 1956), 15-16.
"One cannot claim certainty, but on the whole the case for the Archduke Franz Ferdinand being the so-called King of Bohemia appears to be plausible."

2642. Christ, Jay Finley. "Problems in *A Scandal in Bohemia,*" *BSG*, 1, No. 2 (1961), 5-13. illus.

2643. Clark, John D. "The King of Bohemia?" *BSJ*, 15, No. 3 (September 1965), 142-146.
A persuasive argument in which the "King of Bohemia" is identified as Kaiser Wilhelm II, who was crowned King of Prussia and Emperor of Germany upon the death of Emperor Friedrich III on June 15, 1888.

Tales

2644. Clarkson, Paul S. "A Scandalous Case of Identity," *BSJ*, 19, No. 4 (December 1969), 230-234.

The author finds a probable original for Irene Adler—Pauline Lucca, an Italian-Irish-Viennese opera singer (born April 25, 1841) who was a good friend of Bismarck.

2645. Dickensheet, Dean. "A Last Word for Irene Adler," *SOS*, 2, No. 2 (December 1967), 5.

Irene saw Holmes for the last time, not at her wedding but on the steps of Briony Lodge, disguised as "an elderly woman."

2646. Eaton, Herbert. "The King of Bohemia Unmasked," *VH*, 3, No. 1 (January 1969), 2-6.

——. "Kungen av Böhmen demaskerad," Tr. by Ted Bergman. *BSCL*, No. 8 (1970), 19-25.

"That disguised monarch was Milan Obrenovich IV, first King of Serbia."

2647. Fox, Lyttleton. "A Case of Identity: Is Irene Adler at 107 a Practising Psychiatrist?" *BSJ*, 16, No. 1 (March 1966), 21-22.

A review in *The Times Literary Supplement* for July 19, 1963, of Irene Adler's *Freud for the Jung*, a humorous farce about psychiatry, prompted this speculation on the whereabouts of *the* woman. "Wherever Irene Adler is and whatever she's doing, that youthful and brave spirit is marching on—Jung in heart and a Freud of no one!"

2648. George, Isaac S. "*The* Woman," *Illustrious Client's Third Case-Book.* Edited by J. N. Williamson and H. B. Williams. [Indianapolis, Ind.: The Illustrious Clients, 1953.] p. 79.

"There once was '*The* Woman' Irene / Whose mind was most active and keen. / With good-natured pleasure / She quite took his measure / And stole from the Master the scene."

2649. Grazebrook, O. F. *The Bohemian Marriage: Being an Extract from a Hitherto Unpublished History 'The Kingdom of Scandinavia,'* by H-l-e B-ll-c. [London: Privately Printed, ca. 1949.] 32 p. (Studies in Sherlock Holmes, No. 7)

2650. Hoff, Ebbe C. and Phebe M. "The Affair at St. Monica's," *BSJ*, 13, No. 1 (March 1963), 5-15.

The authors quote the complete text of a document entrusted to Dr. Norberg from the Queen of Bohemia revealing the full story of the part her husband Wilhelm Gottsreich Sigismond had in contributing to the peace of Europe.

2651. Holstein, Leon S. "A Scandal in St. Monica," *BSJ*, 2, No. 1 (January 1952), 49-52.

A description of what really happened at Godfrey's and Irene's wedding at the Church of St. Monica.

2652. Lauterbach, C. E. "That Voice," *BSJ*, 9, No. 3 (July 1959), 153.

——. ——, *Baker Street Ballads.* [Culver City, Calif.: Luther Norris, March 1971.] p. 7.

"That voice, ah yes! you'll hear it oft / In tender mockery, and soft, / 'Good night, Mr. Sherlock Holmes!' "

2653. [Lochhead, Marion.] " 'Dear Sherlock Holmes Died in My Arms,' " by Irene Adler. *The Scotsman* (May 23, 1959), 7.

——. ——, *BSJ*, 13, No. 1 (March 1963), 40-42.

Irene's intimate memories of Godfrey and Sherlock. The story reminds one of Roxane who lost first her husband, Christian de Neuvillette, and then her friend and real love, Cyrano de Bergerac.

2654. Longfellow, Esther. "And Did You Once See Sherlock Plain? (I. A. to S. H.)," *BSJ* [OS], 1, No. 3 (July 1946), 260.

"So ended, ere it had begun, / The game we played, that neither won; / Well—check or stalemate—it was fun. / 'Good night, Mr. Sherlock Holmes!' "

2655. McLauchlin, Russell. "I Can't Endorse This Czech," *BSJ* [OS], 1, No. 3 (July 1946), 292-295.

A rhymed version of Scan that has the distinction of being the first in a series of tales in verse.

2656. ——. "A Re-Examination of the 'Scandal' Problem," *BSJ*, 6, No. 1 (January 1956), 18.

" 'It's actually just a plumber's rocket, / This curious cigar-shaped little toy.' "

2657. Michell, Humfrey. "The Wonderful Wedding," *BSJ*, 4, No. 1 (January 1954), 22-23.

To account for the difficulties inherent in the marriage ceremony of Irene and Godfrey, the author suggests Holmes invented the entire affair to persuade Wilhelm Gottsreich that he had nothing more to fear from Miss Adler.

2658. Osborn, Steven. "Irene," *BSP*, No. 44 (February 1969), 1.

"Did fellow Norton fill the bill? / Was it heartbreak, and disaster?"

2659. Patterson, Linda. "Hum! Ha! Quite So," by Irene Adler (as told to Linda Patterson), *BSJ*, 17, No. 4 (December 1967), 209-213.

"When a woman conquers a famed misogynist and also pulls the wool over the eyes of royalty, well, a little boasting is only natural."

2660. Rosenblum, Morris. "Anticipating Sherlock Holmes, or A Grecian Irene Adler and the Fire Trick," *BSJ*, 2, No. 3 (July 1952), 135.

"Sherlock Holmes's trick of using a false alarm of fire to disclose the hiding place of a precious picture was anticipated in ancient times."

2661. Smith, Edgar W. " 'Good Night, Mister Sherlock Holmes,' " *BSJ* [OS], 2, No. 4 (October 1947), 415-419.

———. ———, *Baker Street and Beyond: Together with Some Trifling Monographs.* Morristown, N.J.: The Baker Street Irregulars, 1957. [unpaged]

From her deathbed in Hoboken, New Jersey, Irene recalls and reflects on some of the events in her short life, especially her entanglements with Gottsreich and Godfrey. A lovingly and beautifully written essay.

2662. ———. "A Scandal in Identity," *Profile by Gaslight.* Edited by Edgar W. Smith. New York: Simon and Schuster, 1944. p. 262-273.

———. ———, *Baker Street and Beyond: Together with Some Trifling Monographs.* Morristown, N.J.: The Baker Street Irregulars, 1957. [unpaged]

"An essay seeking to establish the common identity of Watson's King and Stevenson's Prince Florizel of Bohemia; and their joint identity, in turn, with 'one of the highest, noblest, most exalted personages in England.' "

2663. [———.] "Sonnet: Sherlock Holmes to Irene Adler," by Helene Yuhasova [pseud.] *BSJ* [OS], 1, No. 2 (April 1946), 118.

———. ———, *A Lauriston Garden of Verses,* by Helene Yuhasova. Summit, N.J.: The Pamphlet House, 1946. p. [15].

———. ———, *Baker Street and Beyond: Together with Some Trifling Monographs.* Morristown, N.J.: The Baker Street Irregulars, 1957. [unpaged]

"This mind in petticoat confusion whirled."

2664. Sundholm, Göran. "Vem var Kungen av Böhmen?" *BSCL*, No. 7 (1969), 17-20.

———. "Who Was the King of Bohemia?" Tr. by the author; revised and edited by Herbert A. Eaton. *VH*, 4, No. 3 (September 1970), 2-4.

"Albert Wilhelm Heinrich von Hobenzollern, the hereditary Prince of Prussia."

2665. Taylor, Phillipa. "A Valentine to Sherlock," *BSJ*, 6, No. 2 (April 1956), 82.

"But my most sincere regards / I send, and with them sign / This Valentine. / In admiration and esteem, / Irene. / February 14, 1889."

2666. Welblund, Erling. "Hvem var Kongen af Skandinavien?" ["Who Was the King of Scandinavia?"] *The Daily Fyn* (1961).

———. ———, *Sherlockiana*, 7, Nr. 1-2 (1962), 7.

"Holmes, instead of the completely meaningless words 'The King of Scandinavia' (there was no such king), for instance, could have said 'The King of Diamonds.' What Holmes meant was: that is no business of yours. He had no intention of exposing the identity of a client and therefore made a joke, too highbrow, it seems for the poor Lord St. Simon." (Ted Bergman)

2667. Wellman, Manly Wade. "Scoundrels in Bohemia," *BSJ*, 4, No. 4 (October 1954), 232-238.

A retelling and reinterpretation of the Irene Adler adventure.

2668. Wigglesworth, Belden. "Rondeau to Irene Adler," *BSJ* [OS], 1, No. 4 (October 1946), 403.

"Did Baker Street *quite* lack a Queen?"

2669. [Williams, Howard B.] "Then Falls Thy Shadow," by the Sub-Librarian. *Illustrious Client's Case-Book.* Edited by J. N. Williamson and H. B. Williams. [Indianapolis, Ind.: The Illustrious Clients, 1948.] p. 50-53.

An examination of a few of the things that betray the inner feeling of the Master toward *the* woman.

2670. Williamson, J. N. "A Scandal in 'A Scandal in Bohemia,' " *BSJ*, 1, No. 4 (October 1951), 141-143.

"The solution of Watson's reference to Irene as 'the late,' heretofore one for conjecture, is simple. Wilhelm, not trusting to Holmes's ability, and using the detective for an alibi, murdered *the* woman."

2671. ———. "That New Jersey Miss," Lyrics by J. N. Williamson. *Illustrious Client's Second Case-Book.* Edited by J. N. Williamson. [Indianapolis, Ind.: The Illustrious Clients, 1949.] p. 25-26.

"To be sung to the tune of *Irene.*"

2672. Wolff, Julian. "The Adventures of Sherlock Holmes: Some Observations Upon the Identification of Irene," *BSJ*, 7, No. 1 (January 1957), 29-31.

———. ———, *HO Annual*, No. 1 (1971), 27-28.

"Dr. Watson came closest to revealing her true identity when he wrote that she was born in New Jersey. For, while to Sherlock Holmes and to a host of other admirers, Irregular as well as Bohemian, she is always *the* woman, our heroine, distinguished from all other lilies of the field, is known to the world as the Jersey Lily."

Tales

2673. ———. "The King of Bohemia," *Practical Handbook of Sherlockian Heraldry.* Compiled by Julian Wolff. New York: [Privately Printed], 1955. p. 22-23.

———. "The Arms of the King of Bohemia," *BSJ*, 15, No. 3 (September 1965), 147-149.

It was the Grand Duke Rudolf, the only son of Franz Josef, Emperor of Austria-Hungary, who appeared before Holmes and Watson and used one of his father's lesser titles.

THE ADVENTURE OF THE SECOND STAIN

2674. Andrew, C. R. "Don't Sell Holmes's Memory Short," *BSJ*, 4, No. 4 (October 1954), 219-222.

The author quotes from Felix Morley (item 2678) and from Bruc to show that 1894, not 1887, was the logical year for this adventure.

2675. Hoffmann, Banesh. "A Reverent Comment on *The Second Stain,*" *BSJ*, 13, No. 2 (June 1963), 91-92.

A defense of Trelawney Hope's actions in leaving an important document unguarded in his bedroom.

2676. Holmes, Marcella. "Sherlock Holmes and the Prime Minister," *BSJ*, 5, No. 1 (January 1955), 34-39.

"(1) Lord Beaconsfield was Lord Bellinger; (2) *The Adventure of the Second Stain* took place in 1878 or 1879; (3) Watson had no part in the affair beyond taking down a verbatim account some years after the event, but introduced himself into the story as part of his policy of concealing the year and decade."

2677. Kernish, Robert. "The Curious Case of the Second Stain," *BSJ*, 16, No. 3 (September 1966), 173-174.

The inconsistencies between the published version of this case and Watson's reference to it in Nava suggest that the good Doctor fabricated a case involving a "second stain" and presented it as an authentic account in order to lay damaging rumors to rest.

2678. Morley, Felix. "The Significance of the Second Stain," *Profile by Gaslight.* Edited by Edgar W. Smith. New York: Simon and Schuster, 1944. p. 243-259.

"In endeavoring to prove that there were three different cases 'which Watson associated with a second stain,' Mr. Bell charges that this expression 'obsessed' Watson. Very probable, since the fact if not its definition obsesses everyone today. For what the good doctor was trying to tell us in the oft-repeated phrase was that a second stain of continental war would settle down upon Europe at a time when an umbrella-carrying British Prime Minister and an irresponsible German dictator would be the chief protagonists on that Continent. And even Sherlock Holmes could not foresee or avert what was involved."

2679. Stix, Thomas L. "A Few Irreverent Remarks on 'The Second Stain,' " *SHJ*, 6, No. 1 (Winter 1962), 19-20.

One of the criticisms is directed at Trelawney Hope for the seemingly careless way he safeguarded the important document entrusted to him.

THE ADVENTURE OF SHOSCOMBE OLD PLACE

2680. Andrew, C. R. "Sherlock Holmes on the Turf," *A Baker Street Four-Wheeler.* Edited by Edgar W. Smith. [Maplewood, N.J., and New York: The Pamphlet House, 1944.] p. 38-42.

An argument for the re-dating of this adventure.

2681. Clum, Florence H. "Shenanigans at Shoscombe (or, a Spaniel Come to Judgment)," *BSJ* [OS], 3, No. 2 (April 1948), 202-205.

A tale in verse.

THE SIGN OF THE FOUR

See also *Dr. Watson — Wives*
(items 3407-3435)

2682. Andrew, Clifton R. "On the Dating of *The Sign of the Four,*" *BSJ*, 1, No. 2 (April 1951), 66-69.

———. Revised with title: "Was It July or September, in *The Sign of the Four?*" *Illustrious Client's Third Case-Book.* Edited by J. N. Williamson and H. B. Williams. [Indianapolis, Ind.: The Illustrious Clients, 1953.] p. 141-149.

From weather reports of 1888, the year of the story, the author has found that July was an unusually cold month of that year; and since Holmes and Watson were discussing a newly arrived letter dated July 7, Watson must have meant by "a September evening" an evening as cold as one in September.

2683. Bell, H. W. "The Date of 'The Sign of Four,' " *Baker Street Studies.* Edited by H. W. Bell. London: Constable & Co., [1934]. p. 201-219.

An attempt to show that the adventure took place September 27-30, 1887, rather than September 7-8, as first suggested by the author (*Sherlock Holmes and Dr. Watson*, p. 38).

2684. Bengis, Nathan L. " 'Signs' of a Bookman," *The Bookworm*, 1, No. 8 (December 1967), 10-12.

A discussion of the more than 200 variant copies, in English, of Sign acquired by Mr.

Bengis during a lifetime of collecting Sherlockiana. (These books are now a part of the Sir Arthur Conan Doyle collection at the Toronto Central Library.)

2685. ———. *The "Signs" of Our Times: An Irregular Bibliography.* New York: [Privately Produced], June 1956. 29 p.
———. ———. Errata and Emendations. 1963. 24 p.
"A compilation of the first, early, and later editions of *The Sign of (the) Four,* including piracies, with associational data." This is not a mere listing but a complete description of more than 150 known variants, with a long and informative introduction. A brilliant and important contribution to the literature.

2686. Blakeney, T. S. "Thoughts on *The Sign of Four,*" *SHJ,* 3, No. 4 (Summer 1958), 6-8.
"Observations or deductions on minor topics, not necessarily connected closely with the main story."

2687. Christ, Jay F. *A New Chronology of The Sign of the Four.* Chicago: [Privately Produced], Nov. 1944. 18 p.
"A scholarly examination of the internal evidence, buttressed by meteorological and astronomical data, to establish the dates as September 25-27, 1888." (Edgar W. Smith)

2688. [———.] *Song of Hi-Aurora,* [by] Langdale Pike [pseud.] [Michigan City, Ind.: Privately Printed, 1957.] [4] p.
"Swift Aurora! Gone? Forever? / Gone? Perhaps; but we remember. / Trim Aurora! *We remember!*"

2689. Crocker, Stephen F. "The Barometric Dr. Watson: A Study of 'The Sign of the Four,' " *The Quarterly of the Phi Beta Pi Medical Fraternity* [Menasha, Wis.], 43, No. 3 (November 1946), 157-159.
———. ———, *BSJ* [OS], 3, No. 2 (April 1948), 196-201.
An application of Dr. Van Liere's contentions (item 4527) to this tale.

2690. ———. "Louder, Holmes! And Stop Muttering! or The Route to Thaddeus Sholto's," *SHJ,* 1, No. 2 (September 1952), 14-21.
"The route to Thaddeus Sholto's carefully retraced and mapped, with corrections noted where Watson's ear deceived him." (Edgar W. Smith)

2691. Drake, Stillman. "A Letter to *The Times,*" *VH,* 1, No. 2 (April 1967), 4-8.
The grandson of Dr. Watson makes public a letter dated January 6, 1916, in which Watson explains how he acquired (stole!) the Agra treasure in order to win Mary Morstan as his bride.

2692. Foss, T. F. "Regina *v.* Holmes and Another," *BSJ,* 18, No. 1 (March 1968), 22-31.
Holmes and Watson are arraigned on a charge of deliberately misleading the reading public. The prosecution's case rests on the fact that Watson (ex-Medical Department with the Army in India) blindly accepted Jonathan Small's statement that his companions in crime at Agra were Sikhs when their names plainly showed that they could not possibly have been. The prosecution's case is ably rebutted by the defense's demonstrating that Holmes was a modest man to whom self-aggrandizement was anathema and that Watson, as a medical man, was uninterested in the sect or tribe of his patients, only in their cure. Additionally, when Watson wrote Sign he had other things on his mind (Miss Morstan).

2693. Hearn, Otis. "Thoughts on the Bust of Miss Mary Morstan," *BSJ,* 20, No. 4 (December 1970), 210-214.
Psychological analysis shows that the apparent story of Sign is not the real one. The real *treasure* is Mary Morstan's maidenly bosom; the real detection and pursuit are Watson's effort to verify this bosom's size and shape and to gain some proprietary authority over it. From characteristics of the pearls which Mary hid in this *treasure chest,* it appears that she had a size 32 to 34 bust.

2694. [Hendrickson, J. Raymond.] "A Letter to the Sons of the Copper Beeches," *BSJ,* 16, No. 3 (September 1966), 158-159.
Frederick Featherstonehaugh ffinch-ffarrington, a Deputy under-under-under Secretary to the British Postal Service, London Division, protests a libelous charge that a letter posted by Thaddeus Sholto on July 7 was not delivered until September.

2695. Jaffee, Irving L. " 'The Sign of Four' " and "The Strange Story of Jonathan Small," *Elementary My Dear Watson.* Brooklyn, N.Y.: Theo. Gaus' Sons, [1965]. p. 57-67.
An excellent summary of the novel and the story that forms the closing chapter.

2696. Kimball, Elliot. "Oreamnosis," *SHJ,* 7, No. 4 (Spring 1966), 115-118.
The author discusses the various chronological pronouncements on Sign to show how Sherlockian chronology has not been based on a strict scientific methodology.

2697. Knox, Ronald A. "The Mathematics of Mrs. Watson," *New Statesman and Nation* [Literary Supplement] (NS), 4, No. 90 (November 12, 1932), 588, 590.
A review of H. W. Bell's *Sherlock Holmes and Dr. Watson* and Thomas Blakeney's *Sherlock Holmes: Fact or Fiction* in which

161

Msgr. Knox discusses at length the problem in dating Sign.

2698. Leavitt, Robert Keith. "Who Was Cecil Forrester," *BSJ* [OS], 1, No. 2 (April 1946), 201-204.

"So there we have him—at least in outline: Colonel Cecil Forrester-Farintosh-Woodhouse-Upwood, former friend of Captain Morstan and probably of the none-too-scrupulous Major Sholto, sometime husband of Mary Morstan's employer, party hanger-on, card-sharp and all-too-dubious hero of the strange adventure of the politician, the lighthouse, and the trained cormorant."

2699. [McCleary, George F.] "The Apotheosis of Sherlock Holmes," by the "Londoner." *The National Review*, 127 (December 1946), 504-508.

On the dating of Sign, with a commentary on the Irregulars.

2700. Metcalfe, Percy. "Reflections on *The Sign of Four*, or Oreamnosis Once Removed. Pt. 1. The Date," *SHJ*, 8, No. 4 (Summer 1968), 114-118; "Postscript," 9, No. 1 (Winter 1968), 20.

The author quotes the divergent opinions of the main chronologists on the dating of this case and then presents his own conclusions. In short, it took place in September 1888.

2701. ——. "——. Pt. 2. The Journeys Through London," *SHJ*, 9, No. 1 (Winter 1968), 14-20.

Contents: The Journey to Thaddeus Sholto's. - Where Is Pondicherry Lodge? - From Pondicherry Lodge to Lower Camberwell. - From Mrs. Forrester's to Pinchin Lodge and Back to Pondicherry Lodge. - From Pondicherry Lodge to Smith's Wharf. - The Agra Treasure.

2702. Pattrick, Robert R. "The Oasis in the Howling Desert," *SHJ*, 4, No. 4 (Spring 1960), 126-128.

Another tracing of the cab route to Sholto's home on Binfield Road.

2703. Rawley, James McKee. "Rondeau by Watson," *BSJ*, 9, No. 4 (October 1959), 230.

"I hoped *I* had not killed him, but / For one mad moment in that night, / I felt I had."

2704. *"The Sign of Four," Cyclopedia of Literary Characters.* Edited by Frank N. Magill. New York: Harper & Row, [1963]. p. 1037.

A brief note on each of the principal characters.

2705. ——, *Masterpieces of World Literature in Digest Form.* Second Series. Edited by Frank N. Magill. New York: Harper & Row, [1955]. p. 964-966.

——, *Masterplots.* Combined Edition. Edited by Frank N. Magill. New York: Salem Press, [1960]. Vol. 5, p. 2870-2872.

——, ——. English Fiction Series. New York: Salem Press, [1964]. p. 796-797.

——, ——. Comprehensive Library Edition. New York: Salem Press, [1968]. Vol. 7, p. 4819-4820.

A critique and synopsis of the story.

2706. Smith, Edgar W. *"The Sign of the Four,"* *BSJ* [OS], 1, No. 4 (October 1946), 495; (NS), 4, No. 2 (April 1954), 125-126.

The Sign of the Four, not *The Sign of Four*, is the correct title of Watson's second published adventure.

2707. Stephens, Charles B. "Holmes's Longest Shot?" *BSJ* [OS], 3, No. 1 (January 1948), 44-46.

On the advertisement he placed in the *Standard* concerning the missing steam launch *Aurora*.

2708. Watson, Harold F. "An Old Sea Dog in Baker Street," *BSJ*, 18, No. 1 (March 1968), 32-38.

Parallels between Robert Louis Stevenson's *Treasure Island* and John H. Watson's *The Sign of the Four*.

2709. Zeisler, Ernest B. "Some Points Concerning *The Sign of the Four*," *SHJ*, 4, No. 2 (Spring 1959), 70-71.

An erratum to section 1 of the author's *Baker Street Chronology* (item 3780) in which he now places the opening day of the case after December 1887 and the action from April 17 to 20, 1888.

SILVER BLAZE

2710. Arenfalk, Poul. " 'Silver Blaze,' " *IR*, 3, No. 7 (May 1963), 1-2.

Some discrepancies are noted on the contents of John Straker's pockets and hands at the time of his death.

2711. Bigelow, S. Tupper. *"Silver Blaze*: The Master Vindicated," *BSJ*, 15, No. 2 (June 1965), 79-82.

"There is no evidence of any illegal, improper, unethical or even venial conduct on the part of the Master in the entire story."

2712. Brend, Gavin. ["A Horse! A Horse!"] *BSJ*, 2, No. 2 (April 1952), 72. (Two Verses)
——. ——, *SHJ*, 2, No. 2 (December 1954), 20. (Baker Street Doggerel, No. 3)

"I'm Shoscombe Prince and I'd have you know / That I won the Derby long ago. / So I can't understand this ridiculous craze / For that fatuous animal, Silver Blaze."

2713. [Buxton, Edward Timothy-Howe.] "He

Solved the Case and Won the Race," by Timothy Howe. *The Third Cab.* [Boston: The Speckled Band, 1960.] p. 39-41.

A refutation of Red Smith's attack (item 3064) attributing dishonest motives to some of the Master's actions.

2714. Christ, Jay Finley. "Silver Blaze: An Identification (as of 1893 A.D.)," *BSJ* [OS], 4, No. 1 (January 1949), 12-15.

"It is upon the horse Common that our nomination falls for prototype of Silver Blaze."

2715. Frisbie, Owen P. "But There Goes the Bell . . . ," *BSJ*, 7, No. 2 (April 1957), 74-77.

The *Racing Calendar* for 1881 reveals the names of the jockeys who had mounts in the Wessex Cup.

2716. Hammond, Roland. "The Attempted Mayhem of 'Silver Blaze,'" *BSJ* [OS], 1, No. 2 (April 1946), 157-161.

An investigation by Dr. Hammond, including an actual experiment duplicating the operation performed on Silver Blaze to render him lame, demonstrates that it requires more than the mere jab of a knife, as Holmes claimed, to injure the tendons of a horse's ham sufficiently to cripple him.

2717. Lauritzen, Henry. " 'Den mest bemaerkelsesvaerdige Hest' " [" 'The Most Remarkable Horse' "], *Sherlock Holmes Arbog* II (1966), 53-61. illus.

2718. Lauterbach, Charles E. "King's Pyland Derby," *BSJ Christmas Annual*, No. 2 (1957), 18-19.

———. ———, *Baker Street Ballads.* [Culver City, Calif.: Luther Norris, March 1971.] p. 31-33.

"The sun rose in a cloudless sky, / 'Twas Pyland's day of days; / The multitude by thousands came— / But where was Silver Blaze? / Hop! Hop! Hop! Das Pferdchen geht gallop!"

2719. Rennie, Rud. "Sherlock Holmes Outmoded at Tracks, Watson," *New York Herald Tribune* (September 11, 1955), III, 6.

———. ———, *CPBook*, 2, No. 5-6 (Summer-Fall 1965), 114.

A retelling of the Wessex Cup race, with a note on how Dr. J. G. Catlett of the Horse Identification Bureau uses a more efficient method of identifying horses than the one used by Holmes.

2720. Schutz, Robert H. *A Common Sherlockian Monograph.* [Pittsburgh, Pa.]: Plane Tree Press, 1969. [2] p.

A privately printed folder on the line of descent, from Darley Arabian to Common, the horse identified by Christ and Baring-Gould as Silver Blaze.

2721. Small, C. Russell. " 'The Curious In-cident,' or From Homer to Holmes," *BSJ*, 2, No. 4 (October 1952), 229-230.

" 'As Telemachus drew near, the dogs that love to bark began to wag their tails, but did not bark.' [*The Odyssey*] . . . So short the path from Homer to Holmes!"

2722. Smith, Edgar W. "A Long Shot—A Very Long Shot," *BSJ*, 1, No. 3 (July 1951), 91-94.

A tale in verse.

2723. Stephens, Charles B. "Silas Brown, or Who Shot Desborough's Bolt?" *BSJ* [OS], 2, No. 3 (July 1947), 257-261.

"Silver Blaze appeared at Winchester in the pink of running condition, Desborough's bolt was conveniently shot shortly past the halfway mark to assure the victory of his rival, and we can only hope that Silas Brown came in for enough of a share of Holmes's winnings on the race to offset the loss of his wagers on his own entry."

2724. Stern, Allison. "To Silver Blaze," *BSJ*, 10, No. 2 (April 1960), 90.

"All Europe knows that I'm the hoss / That brought renown to Colonel Ross."

2725. Stix, Thomas L. "Sherlock Holmes Impeached. II. *Silver Blaze,*" *BSJ*, 15, No. 2 (June 1965), 76-78.

"Mr. Holmes made a killing, and a very questionable one at that."

2726. W[elch], G. W. "The 'Silver Blaze' Formula," *SHJ*, 3, No. 1 (Summer 1956), 19.

———. ———, *In the Footsteps of Sherlock Holmes*, by Michael Harrison. London: Cassell & Co., 1958. p. 129.

Two methods are suggested by which Holmes could have calculated the speed of the train to Exeter.

2727. Wilson, Evan M. "*Silver Blaze*: Some Identifications with Respect to Dartmoor," *BSJ*, 21, No. 2 (June 1971), 103-106.

The identification of King's Pyland with Princetown cannot be accepted, as the text of Silv, unlike Houn, makes no reference to the convict prison there and as the location of King's Pyland is described as isolated and lonely. Capleton must be two miles east, not west, of Tavistock. The latter is on a branch line, not the main railway line, from London.

2728. [Wolff, Julian.] "The Dynamics of the Binomial Theorem," *BSJ*, 13, No. 4 (December 1963), 199-200. (The Editor's Gas-Lamp)

A further examination of the calculation used by Holmes to determine the train's speed.

2729. Zeisler, Ernest B. "Some Observations Upon *Silver Blaze,*" *BSJ*, 11, No. 4 (December 1961), 238-240.

Tales

The author insists that Holmes did *not* bet on Silver Blaze and that the month of the Wessex Cup Race was definitely July.

THE ADVENTURE OF
THE SIX NAPOLEONS

2730. Frisbie, Owen P. "The Story I Like Best," *BSJ* [OS], 2, No. 2 (April 1947), 205-207.

The author tells why he has chosen this tale as the one he favors most.

THE ADVENTURE OF
THE SOLITARY CYCLIST

2731. Lauterbach, Charles E. "The Abduction of Lady Violet Smith," *BSJ*, 7, No. 1 (January 1957), 18-19.
————. ————, *Baker Street Ballads.* [Culver City, Calif.: Luther Norris, March 1971.] p. 12-13.
" 'You say this lassie is your wyffe, / That's not the way I figger; / By Cristes blood, your widow shee—' / And then he pu'd the trigger!"

2732. [Smith, Edgar W.] "The Solitary Cyclist Rides Again," by Helene Yuhasova [pseud.] *BSJ* [OS], 2, No. 4 (October 1947), 412-414.
————. ————, *A Baker Street Quartette.* New York: The Baker Street Irregulars, [1950]. p. 29-36.
————. ————, *Baker Street and Beyond: Together with Some Trifling Monographs.* Morristown, N.J.: The Baker Street Irregulars, 1957. [unpaged]
————. ————, *CPBook*, 3, No. 13 (Summer 1967), 248-249.
A tale in verse.

THE ADVENTURE OF
THE SPECKLED BAND

2733. Baring-Gould, William S. "The Problem of the Speckled Band," *BSJ*, 15, No. 3 (September 1965), 167-173.
————. " 'It Is . . . the Deadliest Snake in India,' " *The Annotated Sherlock Holmes.* New York: Clarkson N. Potter, [1967]. Vol. 1, chap. 18, p. 263-266.
A review of the literature on Dr. Roylott's messenger of death.

2734. Bengis, Nathan L. "A Scandal in Baker Street," *BSJ* [OS], 2, No. 2 (April 1947), 145-157; 2, No. 3 (July 1947), 311-321.
Contents: 1. A Case of Mistaken Identity. - 2. The Curious Affair of the First Stain.
"Being an exegesis upon the *langue d'oyle* of the apocryphal play entitled *The Speckled Band* as compared with the *langue d'oc* of the canonical story of the same name, with a consideration of a new angle on the private life of Dr. John H. Watson."

2735. Boswell, Rolfe. "Dr. Roylott's Wily Fillip: With a Proem on Veneration of Vipers," [Illustrated by W. S. Hall]. *BSJ* [OS], 1, No. 3 (July 1946), 307-311.

2736. Bryan-Brown, F. D. "Some Thoughts on 'The Speckled Band,' " *SHJ*, 10, No. 3 (Winter 1971), 89-92.
Contents: The chronology of the story. - A few notes on India in Roylott's time. - The ages of the Dramatis Personae. - A few problems about Grimesby Roylott. - The strange story of Helen Stoner. - The strange conduct of Sherlock Holmes.

2737. Chorley, Jennifer. "An Amazing Epistle—Fact or Forgery?" *BSJ*, 15, No. 3 (September 1965), 165-166.
A remarkable discovery of a letter to Sherlock Holmes, dated June 1889, in which Helen Stoner Armitage confesses to a triple killing—her Mama, twin sister Julia, and stepfather Dr. Grimesby Roylott. If true, the Master was outwitted by a second woman!

2738. Klauber, Lawrence M. "The Truth About the Speckled Band," *BSJ* [OS], 3, No. 2 (April 1948), 149-157.
The causative agent in the deaths of Julia Stoner and Dr. Roylott was not a snake, as reported by the fallible Watson, but a skink, a smooth-scaled lizard of the family Scincidae.

2739. Lawson, Douglas. "The Speckled Band—What Is It?" *BSJ*, 4, No. 1 (January 1954), 12-20.
————. ————, *The Third Cab.* [Boston: The Speckled Band, 1960.] p. 5-11.
"The Speckled Band, which supposedly brought about the deaths of Julia Stoner and Dr. Grimesby Roylott, was truly a *Tic Polonga* or Russell's Viper."

2740. Nash, Ogden. "Just Holmes and Me, and Mnemosyne, Makes Three," *The New Yorker*, 41, No. 9 (April 17, 1965), 42.
————. ————, *There's Always Another Windmill.* With Decorations by John Alcorn. Boston; Toronto: Little, Brown and Co. [1968]. p. 15-16.
"Well, whatever caused Holmes' error and Miss Stoner's overlooking it, / I have this reflection to cheer me . . . / Great minds forget alike."

2741. Rhode, Franklin. " 'Palmer and Pritchard Were Among the Heads of Their Profession,' " *BSJ*, 17, No. 2 (June 1967), 70-74; 18, No. 1 (March 1968), 39-43.
Contents: Pt. 1. William Palmer, the Sporting Surgeon of Rugeley. - Pt. 2. Edward Pritchard, the Satyr of Sauchiehall Street.

2742. Smith, Edgar W. "Saved by the Bell-Rope," *A Baker Street Quartette.* New York: The Baker Street Irregulars, [1950]. p. 21-28.
————. ————, *Baker Street and Beyond:*

Together with Some Trifling Monographs. Morristown, N.J.: The Baker Street Irregulars, 1957. [unpaged]
————. ————, *CPBook*, 3, No. 13 (Summer 1967), 246-248.
A tale in verse.

2743. "De Vergissing van Sherlock Holmes" ["Sherlock Holmes's Error"], *Panorama* [Amsterdam], Nr. 51 (December 12-18, 1970), 52-53. illus.
A detailed discussion of Carl Gans's discovery (*Scientific American*, 222 [June 1970], 93) that a morass adder or Russell's viper is incapable of concertina movement and therefore could not have climbed the bell rope in Julia Stoner's bedroom. Only members of the species of constrictors or choke snakes could have done that, but they are not poisonous!

THE STOCKBROKER'S CLERK

2744. Goslin, Vernon. "The Singular Stockbroker's Clerk," *SHJ*, 8, No. 3 (Winter 1967), 90-93.
An examination of this singular case shows that Holmes, not Hall Pycroft, was the "confounded fool."

A STUDY IN SCARLET

2745. Andrew, C. R. "A Difficulty in *A Study in Scarlet*," *BSJ* [OS], 3, No. 1 (January 1948), 13-14.
"A close analysis of Sherlock Holmes's technique in trapping the killer, Jefferson Hope, as set forth in *A Study in Scarlet*, leads one to believe that Holmes either put a great deal of faith in his luck or else that he had mentally catalogued Hope as being a downright idiot."

2746. Arenfalk, Poul. "Mormon-Mysteriet og andre mysterier i *En Studie i rødt*," *Sherlockiana*, 3, Nr. 1-2 (1958), 2-5.
————. "The Mormon Mystery and Other Mysteries in *A Study in Scarlet*," *SHJ*, 4, No. 4 (Spring 1960), 128-132.

2747. Bengis, Nathan L. "*The* Woman," *VH*, 3, No. 2 (April 1969), 8-9.
A tribute to Mrs. Mary Jean Hickling (Gwynne) Bettany Kernahan who recommended Stud to Ward, Lock & Company for publication in *Beeton's Christmas Annual*.

2748. Cameron, Mary S. "Mr. and Mrs. Beeton's Christmas Annual," *BSJ Christmas Annual*, No. 2 (1957), 5-8.
Information on the Beetons, their Christmas Annual, and the publishing firm of Ward, Lock & Company.

2749. Christ, Jay Finley. "Sherlock and the Canons," *BSJ*, 3, No. 1 (January 1953), 5-12.
"*A Study in Scarlet* violates the principles of the canons of the detective story, as

widely accepted. In spite of this, it is an amusing and absorbing tale."

2750. Clarkson, Steve. "Another Case of Identity," *BSJ*, 22, No. 2 (June 1972), 84-86.
The unnamed accomplice who recovered the gold wedding band for Jefferson Hope is identified as Irene Adler, "the only member of the fair sex who ever got the best of Sherlock Holmes—twice."

2751. Donegall, Lord. " ' "I Should Like to Meet Him," I said,'—Dr. J. H. Watson," *The New Strand*, 1, No. 5 (April 1962), 548-550. (Baker Street and Beyond, No. 5)
A summary and discussion of the adventure "from which all blessings flow."

2752. Fusco, Andrew G. "The Final Outrage of Enoch J. Drebber," *BSJ*, 20, No. 3 (September 1970), 150-153.
The author has built a substantial case against Enoch Drebber, alleging that he was even more of a rogue than Watson painted him. Simply, Mr. Fusco reasons from the excessive emotion displayed by the Charpentier women that Drebber had attempted illicit advances toward young Alice—and probably succeeded. This, coupled with Inspector Gregson's reference to "the babe unborn," appears to support a contention that Alice was, in fact, pregnant as a result of the former Mormon's advances, and this would seem a more credible cause of the extreme discomfiture which had overcome the women.

2753. Griffith, Adrian. "Some Observations on Sherlock Holmes and Dr. Watson at Barts," *St. Bartholomew's Hospital Journal*, 55, No. 12 (December 1951), 270-275.
————. ————, *CPBook*, 2, No. 7-8 (Winter-Spring 1966), 142-147.
"Intimate and fascinating speculations on the associations of both partners with this place of their meeting." (Edgar W. Smith)

2754. Hall, Trevor H. "*The Reminiscences of John H. Watson, M.D.*," *Sherlock Holmes: Ten Literary Studies*. London: Gerald Duckworth & Co., [1969]. Chap. 1, p. 11-17.
"New light on the Ur-Watson, of which Stud in *Beeton's* (1887) was a 'reprint': —evidence for the existence of a *Strand Magazine* prior to 1887 and, therefore, some 14 years before the 1st issue of Messrs. Newnes' *The Strand Magazine*, on January 1st, 1891." (Lord Donegall)

2755. Hall, William S. "An Enquiry Into the Nature of a Certain Nineteenth Century *Beeton's Christmas Annual*," *BSJ*, 13, No. 2 (June 1963), 112-114.
Points of difference between the BSI facsimile of *Beeton's* (item 448) and the original (item 416).

2756. Hammersgaard, Erik. *Mormon-*

Tales

Mysteriet—endnu en gang. [The Mormon Mystery—Once Again.] Bilag til [Supplement to] *Sherlockiana*, 6, Nr. 4 (1961). 3 p.

2757. Harrison, Michael. "Conan Doyle and the St. Luke's Mystery," Illustrated by Buster. *The London Mystery Selection*, No. 38 (September 1958), 76-82.
———. Revised and enlarged with title: "A Study in Surmise," *Ellery Queen's Mystery Magazine*, 57, No. 2 (February 1971), 58-79.
A major contribution to Sherlockian documentation showing how Stud was inspired by events arising from the disappearance on November 12, 1881, of Urban Napoleon Stanger, a case referred to in the newspapers as "The St. Luke's Mystery." Mr. Harrison also traces the origin of Sherlock Holmes to Wendel Scherer, the private consulting detective who was called in to help locate the missing Stanger, and points out possible sources for "Baker" in Baker Street, and the inspiration for the names of Dr. Watson and the Baker Street Irregulars.

2758. ———. "A Study in Suburbia," *In the Footsteps of Sherlock Holmes.* London: Cassell & Co., 1958. p. 112-115.

2759. Henrickson, J. Raymond. "De Re Pharmaca," *Leaves from the Copper Beeches.* Narberth, Pa.: Livingston Pub. Co., 1959. p. 11-14.
The pill used by Jefferson Hope to kill Joseph Stangerson contained nicotine, one of the swiftest and most deadly poisons known.

2760. H[olroyd], J[ames] E. "Dr. Watson at the Criterion," *SHJ*, 2, No. 2 (December 1954), 26.
He frequented this establishment because it was a center for horse-racing men.

2761. Koelle, John B. "Go *West*, Young Man," *BSJ*, 19, No. 4 (December 1969), 222-223.
A brief examination of one of Watson's more glaring errors—placing the Wasatch Mountains to the west of Salt Lake City rather than to the east.

2762. Marshall, Margaret. "Alkali Dust in Your Eyes," *The American Scholar*, 37, No. 4 (Autumn 1968), 650-654. (Reappraisals: I)
———. ———, *CPBook*, 5, No. 18 (Spring 1969), 352-356.
An excellent summary of the great alkali plain episode in which the author, a former Utahan and ex-Mormon, takes Sir Arthur to task for his erroneous topographic descriptions of the area.

2763. McCluskey, Judy. "The Cleveland Cop Who Saved Sherlock: Holmesian Detective Here Traces Down Supt. Schmitt's Great Deed Despite Rampant Local Crime," *The Plain Dealer Sunday Magazine* [Cleveland] (December 7, 1969), 16-17.
A review and discussion of the following article; with a photograph of Schmitt and a full-page photograph of Ralph R. Mendelson by Andrew Cifranic.

2764. Mendelson, Ralph. "Hero Neglected: A True Account," *BSJ*, 19, No. 3 (September 1969), 166-171.
A fine tribute to Jacob W. Schmitt, Superintendent of Police in Cleveland from 1871 to 1893, who was not only an outstanding police chief, but is credited with having helped Holmes by sending him information on Enoch J. Drebber, a former Clevelander who was found dead at No. 3 Lauriston Gardens.

2765. Morgan, Robert S. *Spotlight on a Simple Case, or Wiggins, Who Was That Horse I Saw with You Last Night.* Decorations by Edgar W. Smith. Frontispiece by Arthur Josephson. Illustrations of presidential campaign items from the author's collection of Political Americana. Wilmington, Del.: Privately Printed by The Cedar Tree Press, [1959]. 51 p.
Limited to 500 numbered copies.
An interesting assessment of Holmes's first recorded case and visit to the U.S. in 1876.

2766. Pattrick, Robert R. "Genesis," *BSJ*, 2, No. 4 (October 1952), 196-197.
An additional clue overlooked by Edgar Smith (item 2806) helps confirm the true date of the beginning as 1882.

2767. Randall, David A. "Bibliographical Notes," *BSJ* [OS], 2, No. 1 (January 1947), 104-105.
Comments on the first and later editions of Stud.

2768. ———. "A Study of *A Study in Scarlet*, London: Ward, Lock & Co., 1888; or, A Scandal in Bibliography," *BSJ* [OS], 1, No. 1 (January 1946), 102-106. (Bibliographical Notes)
An illuminating discussion and description of the two issues (or editions) of a book that is not only much rarer than the *Beeton's Christmas Annual* for 1887, but is also one of the rarest books of modern times.

2769. Redmond, D. A. "The Masons and the Mormons," *BSJ*, 18, No. 4 (December 1968), 229-231.
Enoch J. Drebber was a member of a secret or irregular lodge and wore a gold Masonic ring as a cover "to lend respectability dend possibly to provide an entrée to genuine lodges in his travels."

2770. Ritunnano, Jeanne. "Mark Twain vs. Arthur Conan Doyle on Detective Fiction,"

The Mark Twain Journal, 16, No. 1 (Winter 1971-72), 10-14.

An analysis and comparison of *A Double-Barreled Detective Story* with Stud.

2771. Schutz, Robert H. *A List of References to Date of A Study in Scarlet.* Pittsburgh, Pa.: The Arnsworth Castle Business Index, February 1964. 1 p.

2772. [Smith, Edgar W.] "Christmas in 1887," *BSJ Christmas Annual,* No. 5 (1960), 315-316. (The Editor's Gas-Lamp)

It is fitting that Mr. Smith's last editorial should be concerned with Watson's *A Study in Scarlet* which first appeared in his *Reminiscences* (a book that is regrettably lost to the world) and was then reprinted in *Beeton's.*

2773. ———. "Publishers' Note," *Beeton's Christmas Annual,* No. 28 (1887). [Morristown, N.J.: The Baker Street Irregulars, 1960.] p. [169-172].

A bibliographical commentary on *Beeton's* and the facsimile edition.

2774. [———.] "To Mrs. Beeton," *BSJ Christmas Annual,* No. 1 (1956), 3-4. (The Editor's Gas-Lamp)

"It was she, or whoever she stood for, who had the courage and the vision to give to mankind *A Study in Scarlet*—and with it Sherlock Holmes."

2775. Solovay, Jacob C. "Watson Searches for Quarters," *BSJ,* 1, No. 1 (January 1951), 3.
———. ———, Last stanza tr. into Danish by A. D. Henriksen. *Sagen om Baker Street.* København: [Grafisk Cirkel], 1958. p. 10. Reprinted in *Sherlockiana,* 3, Nr. 3-4 (1958), 10.

"Yes, Stamford, I could use a partner now / To share some lodgings at a modest price."

2776. Stone, Ridley. "What's Yours?" A commentary by Ridley Stone, with verse by Carolyn Stone. *VH,* 5, No. 1 (January 1971), 2-6.

A consideration of the circumstances surrounding that fateful day at the Criterion Bar leads to the questions: "What did Watson and Stamford drink at the Criterion that put them in such a mellow mood that they had lunch together—at Watson's expense? Not only how much but, primarily, WHAT?"

2777. *"A Study in Scarlet,"* Cyclopedia of *Literary Characters.* Edited by Frank N. Magill. New York: Harper & Row, [1963]. p. 1092-1093.

A brief note on each of the principal characters.

2778. ———, *Masterpieces of World Literature in Digest Form.* First Series.

Edited by Frank N. Magill. New York: Harper & Row, [1952]. p. 938-941.
———, *Masterplots.* Combined Edition. Edited by Frank N. Magill. New York: Salem Press, [1960]. Vol. 6, p. 3005-3007.
———, ———. English Fiction Series. New York: Salem Press, [1964]. p. 813-815.
———, ———. Comprehensive Library Edition. New York: Salem Press, [1968]. Vol. 7, p. 5036-5038.

A critique and synopsis of the story.

2779. Tracy, Jack. *Conan Doyle and the Latter-Day Saints.* [Frankfort, Ind.: Privately Produced, 1971.] 27 p. illus.

The author compares the Mormon culture in Utah 1846-1860 with the descriptions in "The Country of the Saints," and concludes (members of the LDS Church will be happy to know) that the Mormon section of Stud is a wholly fictional work written by Doyle.

2780. Von Krebs, Maria. " 'Rache' Is the German for 'Revenge,' " *BSJ,* 10, No. 1 (January 1960), 12-14.

A scene in Stud is based on one in Mark Twain's *A Tramp Abroad,* published seven years earlier. The common device, *Rache* marked on a wall, is illustrated in both books.

2781. Williams, H. B. *"Späte Rache,"* *BSJ,* 14, No. 3 (September 1964), 158-160.

A bibliographic description of a paperback entitled *Späte Rache* (item 1224). Includes a reproduction of the cover and two illustrations.

2782. Williamson, J. N. "The Sad Case of Young Stamford," *BSJ* [OS], 3, No. 4 (October 1948), 449-451.

The "Young Stamford" who is remembered for having introduced Watson to Holmes may also have been "Archie Stamford, the forger" in Soli, a helper of John Clay known as "Archie" in RedH, and the Stamford in Houn.

2783. Wood, Cal. "Stamford: A Closer Look," *BSP,* No. 32 (February 1968), 1-2.

Young Stamford knew too much about Holmes to have acquired such knowledge from an occasional encounter with him in the chemical laboratory at Bart's. He was his roommate!

2784. Wrigley, Robert L. "Geographical and Historical *Errata* in *A Study in Scarlet,"* *BSJ,* 15, No. 3 (September 1965), 159-164.

An examination of some questionable statements in Jefferson Hope's narrative.

2785. Zeisler, Ernest Bloomfield. "A Chronological Study in Scarlet," *BSJ,* 7, No. 3 (July 1957), 133-140.

"All in all, we can conclude that there is no essential inconsistency in Watson's chronicle, and that, as in the case of the

The Writings About the Writings

Tales

work of another great writer [William Shakespeare], all apparent difficulties can be resolved."

*Battle of Maiwand and
Dr. Watson's Wound(s)*

2786. Ball, John. "The Jezail Bullet," *Leaves from the Copper Beeches.* Narberth, Pa.: Livingston Pub. Co., 1959. p. 121-126.

A tightly reasoned essay in which the author examines the statements in the Canon and the various theories advanced by students as to the location of Watson's wound; and arrives, by a process of elimination, at the "definitive" conclusion that he was wounded on the left buttock but relocated his wound in a more satisfactory and mentionable region.

2787. Baring-Gould, William S. " 'Your Hand Stole Towards Your Old Wound . . . ,' " *BSJ*, 16, No. 3 (September 1966), 131-134.
————. ————, *The Annotated Sherlock Holmes.* New York: Clarkson N. Potter, [1967]. Vol. 1, chap. 34, p. 606-609.

A review of the literature on Watson's wound(s)—*two*, according to the author.

2788. Bell, H. W. "Note on Dr. Watson's Wound," *Baker Street Studies.* Edited by H. W. Bell. London: Constable & Co., [1934]. p. 220-223.

"Watson was wounded both in the heel and in the left shoulder; and it is evident that the inaccuracy, or worse, with which, in this connection, he has been charged, is due to his native reticence."

2789. Brain, Peter. "Dr. Watson's War Wounds," *The Lancet*, No. 7634 (December 20, 1969), 1354-1355.

An explanation of how his leg and shoulder wounds could have been caused by the same bullet.

2790. Brend, Gavin. "From Maiwand to Marylebone," *SHJ*, 1, No. 3 (June 1953), 40-44.

Another tracing of Watson's activities between July 27 and March 4 suggests that Stud took place in 1881 rather than 1882, the year assigned by Edgar Smith (item 2806).

2791. Chorley, Jennifer. "No Bar for Maiwand," *SHJ*, 7, No. 2 (Spring 1965), 54.

Describes a specimen of an old campaign medal that may have been awarded to Asst. Surgeon J. H. Watson for his part in the Maiwand battle.

2792. Cumings, Thayer. "On an Unheralded Hero," *Seven on Sherlock.* [New York]: Privately Printed, 1968. p. 39.

"Had Murray not heard his master's moans / We might never have ever heard of Holmes. / For the murderous Ghazis would have gored him for sure / And Watson would never have reached Peshawur."

2793. Dardess, John. "The Maiwand-Criterion Hiatus," *BSJ* [OS], 4, No. 1 (January 1949), 115-117.

A further argument in favor of Edgar Smith's position that Watson was wounded *twice* at Maiwand.

2794. Donegall, Lord. "Dr. Watson's Picture-Story," *SHJ*, 8, No. 2 (Spring 1967), 63.

Six photographs, with captions, of the Battle of Maiwand.

2795. Folsom, Henry T. "Seventeen Out of Twenty-Three," *BSJ*, 14, No. 1 (March 1964), 24-26.

Watson acquired his other wound during a *second* hitch in the Army, from the summer of 1881 to early 1883. "At that time, while apparently encountering some Ghazi guerilla in a border incident, he caught a *second* Jezail, this time in the leg."

2796. Hammond, Roland. "The Surgeon Probes Doctor Watson's Wound," *The Second Cab.* Edited by James Keddie. [Boston: The Speckled Band, 1947.] p. 28-31.

"Watson's wound may have been located nearer to the base of the neck than in the shoulder region."

2797. Hartman, Harry. "Afghan A'Gley," *BSJ*, 13, No. 1 (March 1963), 50-52, 54.
————. ————, *The Holy Quire.* [Culver City, Calif.: Luther Norris, December 1970.] p. 20-23.

One man's story of Watson at the Battle of Maiwand, with speculations on what might have been if Orderly Murray had not been on the job.

2798. Hepburn, W. B. "The Jezail Bullet," *The Practitioner*, 197 (July 1966), 100-101.
————. ————, *SHJ*, 8, No. 1 (Winter 1966), 18-19.

Contents: A Mediocre General Practitioner. - Intracranial Injury Theory. - The 'Two Bullet Theory'. - The Real Explanation.

2799. Howard, Samuel F. "More About Maiwand," *BSJ*, 7, No. 1 (January 1957), 20-25.

Watson was not wounded at the Battle of Maiwand on July 27, 1880, but in the campaign of Maiwand earlier in the month and did not, as Dr. Zeisler contends, remain at Kandahar until September 10.

2800. Keddie, James, Sr. "The Mystery of the Second Wound," *Profile by Gaslight.* Edited by Edgar W. Smith. New York: Simon and Schuster, 1944. p. 173-177.

"The hinterlands of the Assistant-

Surgeon Watson was the billet for the second jezail bullet."

2801. Lesh, Richard D. "Watson, Come Here; I Want You: In Afghanistan," *BSJ*, 14, No. 3 (September 1964), 136-138.
"On the Afghan travels of the biographer of Mr. Sherlock Holmes."

2802. Metcalfe, N. Percy. "The Date of *The Study in Scarlet*," *SHJ*, 4, No. 2 (Spring 1959), 37-40.
Another argument supporting the English view that this case took place in 1881 and not in 1882 as the Americans contend.

2803. Schutz, Robert H. *A Bibliography of the Writings on Watson's Wound(s)*. Pittsburgh, Pa.: The Arnsworth Castle Business Index, June 1960. 1 p.
———. Revised with title: "Dr. Watson's Wound(s): A Selected Bibliography," *BSJ*, 16, No. 3 (September 1966), 136-137.

2804. Sellars, Crighton. "Ballistics," *BSJ* [OS], 1, No. 2 (April 1946), 162.
———. ———, *BSP*, No. 26 (August 1967), 1.
"Surely no Afghan slug from a jezail / Ever hit male / More queerly!"

2805. Slovak, Richard. "Re-Dating *A Study in Scarlet*, or The Very Long Road from Maiwand," *HO*, 1, No. 1 (March 1971), 19-28.
A careful study of the entire Canonical chronology shows that this adventure occurred between March 4 and 7, 1884.

2806. Smith, Edgar W. *The Long Road from Maiwand*. [New York: The Pamphlet House], 1940. [4] p.
———. ———, *Profile by Gaslight*. Edited by Edgar W. Smith. New York: Simon and Schuster, 1944. p. 195-201.
———. ———, *Baker Street and Beyond: Together with Some Trifling Monographs*. Morristown, N.J.: The Baker Street Irregulars, 1957. [unpaged]
"An examination of the evidence bearing upon the dating of a certain encounter in the chemical laboratory at St. Bartholomew's Hospital in London." (Subtitle)
Mr. Smith argues that too much had occurred after the Battle of Maiwand for Watson to have sailed from Bombay before April 1880, which would place Stud in March 1882 instead of March 1881.

2807. Smith, William. " 'You Have Been in Gettysburg, I Perceive,' " *BSJ*, 13, No. 2 (June 1963), 77-85.
Watson was wounded both at the Battle of Gettysburg in 1863 and the Battle of Maiwand in 1880.

2808. [Sovine, J. W.] "The Singular Bullet," by Dr. Hill Barton [pseud.] *BSJ*, 9, No. 1 (January 1959), 28-32.

"Dr. Watson was struck in the left shoulder by a jezail bullet, and this was his one and only military wound. All the commotion and puzzlement among the many commentators followed simply because that jezail bullet, after entering Watson's body, took an Irregular course."

2809. Van Liere, Edward J. "Dr. John H. Watson and the Subclavian Steal," *Archives of Internal Medicine*, 118, No. 3 (September 1966), 245-248.
———. ———, *Medical and Other Essays*. Morgantown: West Virginia University Library, 1966. p. 160-166.
His forgetfulness or slight mental confusion can be attributed to an impaired blood supply to the brain, the result of a circulatory disturbance caused by an obstruction in the injured subclavian artery.

2810. Welch, G. W. " 'No Mention of That Local Hunt, Watson,' " *SHJ*, 5, No. 3 (Winter 1961), 82-83.
Watson gave up hunting because of the wound he received at the Battle of Maiwand.

2811. Williamson, J. N. "Solution of the Second Wound," *Illustrious Client's Third Case-Book*. Edited by J. N. Williamson and H. B. Williams. [Indianapolis, Ind.: The Illustrious Clients, 1953.] p. 191.
———. ———, *BSJ*, 16, No. 3 (September 1966), 135.
"We take our cue, we're not to blame; / Holmes simply missed a 'V. R.' aim / And hit poor Watson (what a shame!), / Which made the doctor slightly lame."

2812. Zeisler, Ernest Bloomfield. "A Final Word About Maiwand," *BSJ*, 9, No. 2 (April 1959), 103-110.
A critical examination of the literature on the Battle of Maiwand.

2813. ———. "The Road from Maiwand," *BSJ*, 5, No. 4 (October 1955), 220-225.
A further substantiation of the position held by Edgar Smith, John Dardess, and Gavin Brend that the meeting between Holmes and Watson took place in March 1882 and not March 1881.

THE ADVENTURE OF THE SUSSEX VAMPIRE

2814. Baker, Kate. "Re: Vampires," *BSP*, No. 41 (November 1968), 1-2.
"Though seldom as colourful as their fictional counterparts, living vampires do exist and can be cured. The suspected Sussex vampire proved to be nothing of the sort; still, had it been otherwise, Sherlock Holmes would have found a highly intriguing case."

THE PROBLEM OF THOR BRIDGE

2815. De La Torre, Lillian. "The Problem of

Tales

A. M. on Thor Bridge," *BSJ* [OS], 3, No. 4 (October 1948), 497-500.

An account of this case was first written up not by Watson but by Dr. Hans Gross in his *System der Kriminalistik*, published in 1893. Dr. Gross's distorted version of the story is included in Miss de la Torre's article.

2816. Tinning, Herbert P. "A Reassessment of the Dating of 'The Problem of Thor Bridge,' " *DCC*, 6, No. 4 (June 1970), 3-4.
————. Revised and enlarged with title: "On the Dating of 'The Problem of Thor Bridge,' " *HO*, 1, No. 1 (March 1971), 15-17.

An analysis of the chronology for this tale suggests that it began on Monday, October 4, 1886.

THE ADVENTURE OF
THE THREE GABLES

2817. Holland, Glenn. "A Left-Handed Defence of 'The Three Gables,' " *BSP*, No. 45 (March 1969), 2-4.

An incredible suggestion that Holmes's uncharacteristic behavior in this story can be attributed to an inebriated condition.

2818. Rhode, Franklin. "Langdale Pike and Steve Dixie: Two Cases of Identity," *BSJ*, 20, No. 1 (March 1970), 17-20.

Langdale Pike, a journalistic friend and confidant of Holmes, is identified as George R. Sims, and Steve Dixie, the Negro bruiser, as an acquaintance of Sims.

THE ADVENTURE OF
THE THREE GARRIDEBS

2819. McLauchlin, Russell. "Apocryphal?" *BSJ* [OS], 1, No. 4 (October 1946), 475-476.

3Gar is primarily a rewriting of RedH and, therefore, should be included in the Apocrypha rather than the Canon.

2820. Redmond, Chris. "Thoughts on *The Three Garridebs*," *BSP*, No. 24 (June 1967), 4.

" 'It may have been a comedy, it may have been a tragedy.' "

2821. Rosenberger, Edgar S. "Bats in His Belfry," *BSJ*, 9, No. 1 (January 1959), 38-40.
A tale in verse.

THE ADVENTURE OF
THE THREE STUDENTS

2822. Bristowe, W. S. "The Three Students in Limelight, Electric Light and Daylight," *SHJ*, 3, No. 2 (Winter 1956), 2-5.

An examination of some unsolved problems in this tale, including recollections of the author's bit part in the 1923 film version.

2823. Hall, Trevor H. "Sherlock Holmes and

Andrew Lang," *The Late Mr. Sherlock Holmes & Other Literary Studies*. London: Gerald Duckworth & Co., [1971]. Chap. 4, p. 64-79.

On the Lang-Rendall controversy re Lang's essay in 1904 and Rendall's almost identical arguments in 1917 concerning "The Three Students."

2824. Lang, Andrew. "At the Sign of the Ship," *Longman's Magazine*, 44 (July 1904), 269-271.

Holmes and Watson were the victims of an elaborate hoax perpetrated by Hilton Soames and Gilchrist.

2825. Rendall, Vernon. "Belsize as a Commentator: Sherlock Holmes," *The London Nights of Belsize*. London: John Lane; New York: John Lane Co., 1917. Chap. 8, p. 135-157.
————. ————, *The Incunabular Sherlock Holmes*. Edited by Edgar W. Smith. Morristown, N.J.: The Baker Street Irregulars, 1958. p. 75-92.

A commentary dealing with some of the alleged flaws in this adventure.

2826. Schwartz, Richard S. "Three Students in Search of a Scholar," *BSJ Christmas Annual*, No. 2 (1957), 45-49.

An essay on some Greek scholars, with special attention to Thucydides, who played an important role in 3Stu.

2827. Smith, Edgar W. " 'He Stoppeth One of Three . . . ,' " *BSJ*, 1, No. 1 (January 1951), 15-17.
————. ————, *Illustrious Client's Third Case-Book*. Edited by J. N. Williamson and H. B. Williams. [Indianapolis, Ind.: The Illustrious Clients, 1953.] p. 16-19.
————. ————, *Baker Street and Beyond: Together with Some Trifling Monographs*. Morristown, N.J.: The Baker Street Irregulars, 1957. [unpaged]
A tale in verse.

THE MAN WITH THE TWISTED LIP

2828. Arenfalk, Poul. "Mysteries in 'The Man with the Twisted Lip,' " *IR*, 2, No. 5 (March 1962), 1-4.

After drawing attention to all the improbable events and contradictory explanations in this adventure, the author concludes that it is an imaginative story concocted by Watson.

2829. Beierle, John D. "The Curious Incident of the Drive Through Middlesex and Surrey," *BSJ*, 7, No. 4 (October 1957), 216-219.

Because of certain curious features in the text, Mr. Beierle believes that the literary agent, not Watson, was the author of this "work of pure fiction."

2830. Davies, Bernard. "Holmes and the

Halls," *SHJ*, 7, No. 3 (Winter 1965), 68-73.

The author advances the interesting thesis that Holmes and Neville St. Clair were old friends and first became acquainted while performing as protean actors in the London music halls.

2831. Harris, Robert G. "It's Not Always 1957," *BSJ*, 8, No. 1 (January 1958), 29-32.

"Far from involving a lengthy circumnavigation of the Home Counties as Mr. Beierle would have it, the text details succinctly an accurate itinerary barely seven miles in length commencing in Stepney in Middlesex, continuing through Surrey and concluding at the Cedars in Kent precisely as Mr. Holmes described it."

2832. Jaffee, Irving L. " 'The Man with the Twisted Lip,' " *Double-Action Detective and Mystery Stories*, No. 9 (Winter 1957-1958), 99-104.

————. ————, *Elementary My Dear Watson*. Brooklyn, N.Y.: Theo. Gaus' Sons, [1965]. p. 39-46.

A consideration of this tale from the standpoint of the three classic criteria of all good mystery stories—plot, atmosphere, and character delineation.

2833. Mather, Philip. *"The Man with the Twisted Lip," BSJ*, 19, No. 3 (September 1969), 131.

A tale in verse.

2834. Moore, John Robert. "Sherlock Holmes Borrows a Plot," *Modern Language Quarterly*, 8, No. 1 (March 1947), 85-90.

A commentary on the similarities in plot between Thackeray's "Miss Shum's Husband" in *The Yellowplush Papers* and Twis.

2835. Playfair, Giles. "John and James," *BSJ* [OS], 1, No. 3 (July 1946), 271-276.

In order to protect himself against a libel suit in his account of the tale, Watson attempted to disguise the authorship by changing his Christian name from John to James. Perhaps out of vanity, he then committed the unpardonable offense of attaching his real name to another character, thus falsifying the name of the actual hero.

2836. Townsend, C. E. C. "The Bar of Gold," *SHJ*, 2, No. 1 (July 1954), 25-28.

"The vilest murder-trap on the whole riverside" was located on Wapping High Street rather than in Upper Swandam Lane.

2837. Wilson, Alan. "Where Was the 'Bar of Gold?' " *SHJ*, 6, No. 3 (Winter 1963), 84-85.

An argument in support of No. 22 Upper Thames Street at the corner of the block bounded by Paul's Pier Wharf and Castle Baynard Wharf.

THE VALLEY OF FEAR

2838. Austin, Bliss. [*The Valley of Fear.*] Pittsburgh, Pa.: Hydraulic Press, 1970. [3] p. (A Baker Street Christmas Stocking)

Remarks on the serialization of this story in the Associated Sunday Magazines from September 20 to November 22, 1914. Includes a colored photoprint of the cover design depicting the characters in Vall by M. C. Perly for the September 13 issue of the *Boston Sunday Post Sunday Magazine*.

2839. Benjamin, Philip. "They Never Sleep: Pinkerton's 'Private Eyes' Have Been on Duty for More Than a Hundred Years," *The New York Times Magazine* (August 27, 1961), 40-44.

————. ————, *BSJ*, 14, No. 1 (March 1964), 8-13.

An article on Pinkerton's National Detective Agency, the oldest agency of its kind in the world.

2840. Boucher, Anthony. "Introduction," *The Final Adventures of Sherlock Holmes*. New York: The Limited Editions Club, 1952. Vol. 1, p. v-xviii.

————. ————, *Introducing Mr. Sherlock Holmes*. Edited by Edgar W. Smith. Morristown, N.J.: The Baker Street Irregulars, 1959. [unpaged]

"If the resultant fusion is not quite satisfactory novelistically, it at least provides us with plentiful opportunity within one volume to observe Sherlock Holmes at his best. . . . Like the superb episodes from the memoirs of Etienne Gerard, the story manages at once to be deftly amusing and intensely exciting; and, whatever our feelings concerning the dates or the intrusion of Moriarty, we can only be deeply grateful to Dr. Watson for having served it up so magnificently."

2841. ————. "A Note on Scowrers," *VH* [OS], 1, No. 1 (Spring 1962), 3-4.

————. "On 'Scowrer,' " *West by One and by One*. San Francisco: Privately Printed, 1965. p. 3-4.

A brief essay on the etymology of the word *scowrer*.

2842. Broehl, Wayne G. *The Molly Maguires*. Cambridge, Mass.: Harvard University Press, 1964. vi, 409 p.

"Doyle met William Pinkerton during a transatlantic crossing shortly after the turn of the century, became intrigued with Allan Pinkerton's account of the Mollies, and constructed the American portion of *Valley of Fear* as almost a paraphrase of the actual story."

2843. Dardess, John. "On the Dating of *The Valley of Fear*," *BSJ* [OS], 3, No. 4 (October 1948), 481-482. (Letters to Baker Street)

"No—Watson did not forget that he once

Tales

Tales

knew Moriarty; he simply forgot that he once denied knowing him."

2844. Dickensheet, Dean W. "The Molly Maguires," *VH* [OS], 1, No. 2 (Fall 1962), 4-5.

A discussion and quotation of an account of the Maguires, as printed in the *Chicago Tribune* in 1876.

2845. ———. " 'Two Good Men,' " *West by One and by One.* San Francisco: Privately Printed, 1965. p. 145-151.

"Being an analysis of the chronology of *The Valley of Fear* based on recently discovered collateral evidence combined with heretofore unconsidered Canonical data." (Subtitle)

2846. Gibson, Theodore W. "The Birlstone Masquerade," *BSJ*, 6, No. 3 (July 1956), 168-169.

"What Watson could not appreciate, with his intensely British outlook, is the fact that 'Pinkerton's American Agency' simply could not afford to overlook one, let alone two, murderous attacks on one of its operatives because of his actions while on a case."

2847. Liljegren, S. B. *The Irish Element in The Valley of Fear.* Uppsala: A.-B. Lundequistska; Copenhagen: Ejnar Munksgaard, 1964. 47 p. (Irish Essays and Studies, No. 7)

2848. Merriman, C. O. "A Case of Identity—No. 2," *SHJ*, 5, No. 3 (Winter 1961), 83-86.

The author endeavors to show that Groombridge House is actually Birlstone Manor, and not just a model as claimed by Mr. Montgomery in the following monograph.

2849. Montgomery, James. *A Case of Identity.* Philadelphia: International Printing Co., 1955. 12 p., 31 plates. (Montgomery's Christmas Annual, No. 6)

Limited to 300 copies.

"The fictional Birlstone Manor is not an accurate reproduction of the factual Groombridge Place. Therefore, Groombridge Place was the *inspiration*—not the *model*—for Birlstone Manor."

2850. ———. "Dear Me, Mr. Expert! Dear Me!" *Shots from the Canon.* [Philadelphia: Privately Printed, 1953.] p. 12-13.

Mr. Montgomery reports his discovery of the serialization in the U.S. of Vall by the Associated Sunday Magazines.

2851. Newton, G. B. "The Date of *The Valley of Fear,*" *SHJ*, 2, No. 4 (Winter 1955), 38-42.

Evidence that the story took place in January 1890.

2852. Parker, Hyman. "Birdy Edwards and the

Scowrers Reconsidered," *BSJ*, 14, No. 1 (March 1964), 3-7.

"It is the purpose of this trifling monograph to examine the validity of the charges and conclusions contained in Watson's discussion of the Scowrers and their relationship to the mine and railroad owners as well as the Pinkertons."

2853. Peck, Andrew Jay. *"The Valley of Fear* Revisited," *BSJ*, 20, No. 3 (September 1970), 142-149.

While the Scowrers and Molly Maguires engaged in unlawful deeds, they were not as bad as Doyle and other historians have depicted them. The Mollies arose because there was no union to fight for the rights of the Irish miners. Conditions in the mines were terrible, and the living conditions of the miners were just as bad. Although early historians castigated the Mollies for their excessive acts of violence, it has been shown that there were also acts of violence on the part of the mine owners. While this does not exonerate the Molly Maguires, modern historians have come to the conclusion they were not the gang of cutthroats that Doyle and others have portrayed them to be.

2854. Prestige, Colin. "A Study in Fear or the Scarlet Valley," *SHJ*, 9, No. 2 (Summer 1969), 63-64; [Addendum], 9, No. 4 (Summer 1970), 142-143.

A brief discussion of Part 2 of Vall, written, according to Mr. Prestige, by Birdy Edwards himself.

2855. Randall, David A. *"The Valley of Fear* Bibliographically Considered: With a Few Notes on Its Sources and Some Textual Problems," *BSJ* [OS], 1, No. 2 (April 1946), 232-237. (Bibliographical Notes)

2856. Stephens, Charles B. "The Birlstone Hoax," *BSJ* [OS], 4, No. 1 (January 1949), 5-11.

"Whatever the reasons for its apparent lack of popularity, particularly among American readers, the fact remains that *The Valley of Fear* is a principal source of data on Fred Porlock, Professor Moriarty, and Jean-Baptiste Greuze; it gives Holmes his best opportunity to display his powers as a cryptanalyst; Billy the page makes one of his rare appearances; and it contains the classic exchange in which Holmes had to admit that his biographer had scored 'A touch! A distinct touch!' "

2857. [Wolff, Julian.] *"Re Greuze,"* *BSJ*, 12, No. 4 (December 1962), 195-197. (The Editor's Gas-Lamp)

A possible identification of the two paintings by Jean-Baptiste Greuze mentioned in Vall. The first painting, *Girl with Arms Folded*, is reproduced on p. 197; the second, L'Amitié (*La Jeune Fille à l'Agneau?*) on p. 9 of the March 1966 issue.

2858. Zeisler, Ernest B. "Concerning *The Valley of Fear*," BSJ, 4, No. 3 (July 1954), 144-147.

An argument favoring the year 1888 rather than 1897, the date proposed by Anthony Boucher (item 2840).

THE ADVENTURE OF THE VEILED LODGER

2859. Potter, H. C. "The Veiled Lodger Revisited," *BSJ*, 22, No. 3 (September 1972), 158-165.

This tale has been castigated as no adventure at all, merely an overly delayed confession of a mystery in which Holmes played no part. The author blames these allegations on Watson's Victorian reticence and scrupulous care to project "the honor . . . of illustrious personages"—in this case Holmes himself. He maintains that a careful restudy of Veil, in terms of his hypothesis, sheds revealing light on the long standing enigma of Holmes's misogyny.

THE ADVENTURE OF WISTERIA LODGE

No items

THE YELLOW FACE

2860. Schutz, Robert H. *A Discussion of Some Problems Encountered in The Yellow Face.* [Pittsburgh, Pa.]: The Arnsworth Castle Business Index, 1961. [4] p.

Limited to 12 copies.

———. "Some Problems in *The Yellow Face*," BSJ, 12, No. 1 (March 1962), 31.

About John Hebron, a Negro lawyer from Atlanta and first husband of Effie.

2861. Wellman, Manly Wade Hampton. "The Hebron Marriage," *BSJ* [OS], 2, No. 4 (October 1947), 422-424.

Part A of an essay entitled "Two Southern Exposures of Sherlock Holmes."

C *Sherlock Holmes*

GENERAL AND MISCELLANEOUS

2862. Ball, John. "Early Days in Baker Street," BSJ, 5, No. 4 (October 1955), 211-219.

By examination of Canonical evidence in many of Watson's narratives, the author proposes the theory that Holmes was not the private individual he claimed to be, but was in actuality a Queen's Messenger with the extraordinary authority that this status included. Many instances are cited where the Master was granted privileges that no ordinary citizen, no matter how distinguished, could possibly have received. Dr. Watson's role is reexamined in this light.

2863. Baring-Gould, William S. " 'The Best and Wisest Man Whom I Have Ever Known,' " *The Annotated Sherlock Holmes.* New York: Clarkson N. Potter, [1967]. Vol. 1, chap. 8, p. 47-66. illus.

A discussion of the literature on the Master's birth date, birthplace, ancestry, and education.

2864. Barzun, Jacques. "Sherlock Holmes's Will—A Forgery," BSJ, 6, No. 2 (April 1956), 75-81.

A textual analysis of the document (reproduced in facsimile) discovered by Mr. Bengis reveals it to be fraudulent!

2865. [Bengis, Nathan L.] *Baker Street Legacy: The Will of Sherlock Holmes.* New York: The Musgrave Ritualists, 1951. [4] p.

Limited to 221 copies.

———. ———, *London Mystery Magazine*, No. 25 (June 1955), 14-17.

———. ———, *BSJ*, 6, No. 2 (April 1956), 80-81.

———. ———, *SOS*, 1, No. 5 (June 1967), 5-7; Addendum, 3, No. 2 (July 1969), 15-16.

A facsimile of the Master's will and testament, dated April 16, 1891. The document was found among the effects of the late Mycroft Holmes by Mr. Bengis.

2866. ———. "Where There's a Will, There's a Pay," BSJ, 6, No. 4 (October 1956), 226-232.

The author defends the authenticity of the Will of Sherlock Holmes against Professor Barzun's allegations that it is a forgery.

2867. Berg, Curt. *Fallet Baker Street 111.* [The Case of 111 Baker Street.] Stockholm: Albert Bonniers Förlag, [1951]. 56 p. illus.

Limited to 50 copies.

Contents: [Sherlock Holmes in Private and Public Life. - Sherlock Holmes and Music. - Sherlock Holmes and the Game of Chance.]

2868. Bigelow, S. Tupper. "A Counterfeit of the Sage of Baker Street," *The Globe Magazine* [Toronto] (January 16, 1965), 10-12.

———. ———, *CPBook*, 1, No. 3 (Winter 1965), 52-54.

"In an article illustrated with scenes from *Baker Street*, the author takes off from the musical to discuss Sherlock Holmes in general and correct some misconceptions." (Julian Wolff)

2869. Christ, Jay Finley. " 'What Sherlock Didn't Know,' " *The Atlantic Monthly*, 177, No. 1 (January 1946), 30-31. (Letters to and from the Editor)

A commentary on Stuart C. Rand's article by the same title (item 2902).

2870. Clark, Benjamin S. "Sherlock Holmes" (A Guest Editorial), *BSJ*, 12, No. 2 (June 1962), 67-69. (The Editor's Gas-Lamp)
An attempt to explain the unexplainable—the Master's universal popularity.

2871. Davies, Bernard. "Was Holmes a Londoner?" *SHJ*, 4, No. 2 (Spring 1959), 42-47.
"Wherever he was born and wherever he may have travelled, Mr. Sherlock Holmes became a Londoner at a very early age."

2872. De Groat, Ray. "Sherlock Holmes: Humanitarian," *VH*, 3, No. 3 (September 1969), 6-7.
"Sherlock shows himself to be more than master of those human qualities which all gentle men (in the most Victorian meaning) possess. Furthermore, he extends them to all."

2873. Dorian, N. Currier. "The Berkeley Letters," *BSJ*, 3, No. 3 (July 1953), 164-168.
Excerpts of letters to Lady Ester Berkeley from Mrs. Holmes concerning her young sons Sherlock and Mycroft.

2874. Ebblewhite, John. "Sir Sherlock Holmes," *SHJ*, 6, No. 2 (Spring 1963), 54.
Speculation on why he refused a knighthood while accepting lesser rewards from England and other countries.

2875. [Felts Jack L.] ["The Occult Holmes"], *Individualist Society Bulletin* [Tahlequah, Okla.] (February 1965), 3.
———. ———, *BSJ*, 15, No. 1 (March 1965), 32-33.
"Doyle's study of the occult was based on what he perceived functioning through Sherlock Holmes."

2876. Goodman, Charles. "The Dental Holmes," *BSJ* [OS], 2, No. 4 (October 1947), 381-393.
Further intimate details of the Master's life as revealed by his dentist, Dr. Charles S. Wilson, in a second letter to Dr. Goodman.

2877. ———. "Dr. Wilson Writes Again," *BSJ*, 10, No. 4 (October 1960), 197-206.
After a lapse of thirteen years, Holmes's dental surgeon has written another letter—this one from his Retreat near the Sussex Bee Farm!

2878. Gordon, Irwin L., ed. *Who Was Who, 5000 B.C. to Date: Biographical Dictionary of the Famous and Those Who Wanted to Be.* Cover by A. J. Frueh. Illustrated by C. H. Sykes. Philadelphia: David McKay, [1914]. 121 p.

Contains a humorous biography, with an illustration, of Holmes on p. 54-57.

2879. "The Greatest Detective of Them All—He's 100," *The Irish Times* (January 9, 1954).
———, *CPBook*, 2, No. 5-6 (Summer-Fall 1965), 94.
An Irish tribute to the Master on this momentous occasion.

2880. Hall, Trevor H. "A College Friendship?" *Sherlock Holmes: Ten Literary Studies.* London: Gerald Duckworth & Co., [1969]. Chap. 7, p. 93-108.
"The case for a Trinity College friendship between Edmund Gurney, later Hon. Secretary of the Society for Psychical Research, and Holmes. And much interesting information." (Lord Donegall)

2881. ———. "The Late Mr. Sherlock Holmes," *The Late Mr. Sherlock Holmes & Other Literary Studies.* London: Gerald Duckworth & Co., [1971]. Chap. 7, p. 108-129.
A progressive and permanent impairment of his eyesight resulting from a disease known as tobacco-amblyopia may have led him to commit suicide in 1914.

2882. Hardenbrook, Don. "Another Bird in a Gilded Cage," by Gaston Huret III. Tr. by Don Hardenbrook. *West by One and by One.* San Francisco: Privately Printed, 1965. p. 102-106.
———. "Sherlock Holmes' ven: Toulouse-Lautrec," [Oversat af A. D. Henriksen]. *Sherlock Holmes Arbog* II (1966), 26-30.
"Sherlock Holmes, if not Dr. Watson, must have known and been a good friend of the great painter, Henri de Toulouse-Lautrec."

2883. Harrison, Michael. "Face to Face: Sherlock Holmes Interviewed," *Courier*, 41, No. 4 (October 1963), 41-43.
———. ———, *BSJ*, 16, No. 2 (June 1966), 88-93.
During a televised interview the great detective discusses the scandals of Victorian times, the great train robbery, the Anglo-American alliance, the police, and his brain.

2884. Hartman, Harry. "Holmes and Automation," *BSJ*, 17, No. 4 (December 1967), 233-238.
———. ———, *The Holy Quire.* [Culver City, Calif.: Luther Norris, December 1970.] p. 39-45.
Verbal speculation on the effects of automation, had it been known in 1895, with pessimistic prognostication on the probable future.

2885. ———. "The Valley of Cheer," *The Holy Quire.* [Culver City, Calif.: Luther Norris, December 1970.] p. 46-48.

A fantasy centering on Holmes's entry into Heaven, and his meeting with Christopher Morley, Marlowe, Sam Johnson, and others. Also includes a brief discussion of religion between Holmes and St. Peter.

2886. Holmes, David M. "Sherlock Holmes Was a Creature of Decadence," *BSJ*, 15, No. 2 (June 1965), 103-113.

A scholarly examination of the manifestations of Holbrook Jackson's four chief characteristics (Perversity, Artificiality, Egoism, and Curiosity) of the Victorian Decadence in Holmes.

2887. Jackson, J. P. "Mr. Holmes: A New Judgment," *The Manchester Guardian* (April 10, 1944), 4.
————. ————, *A Baker Street Four-Wheeler.* Edited by Edgar W. Smith. [Maplewood, N.J., and New York: The Pamphlet House, 1944.] p. 18-19.

An estimate of his psychological makeup and impulses.

2888. Jones, Gratia. "Interview with Mrs. Hudson," *BSJ*, 8, No. 1 (January 1958), 11-15.

A loving tribute to Mr. Sherlock Holmes by the lady who knew him best.

2889. Kallis, Stephen A. "Morte de Sherlock," *BSJ*, 14, No. 3 (September 1964), 166-171.

An alternate and pleasanter speculation on his death to the one offered by Baring-Gould in the epilogue to his biography of the World's First Consulting Detective. . . . The Master waits with King Arthur and other great Englishmen on the Isle of Avalon to come forth again—waits "with his friends in that isle of eternal youth until the day that England will need them all."

2890. Kennedy, Bruce D. "Cherchez la Femme," *A Curious Collection.* Edited by William J. Walsh. [Suffern, N.Y.]: The Musgrave Ritualists Beta, 1971. p. 12-18.

A takeoff on Rex Stout's "Watson Was a Woman" to show that it was Holmes, not Watson, who was the female! Another slanderous attack upon the Master's sexual makeup—and, one hopes, the last!

2891. Kjellberg, Lennart. "Letter to Gösta Rybrant," from Sherlock Holmes; transmitted by Lennart Kjellberg. *BSCL*, No. 4 (1965), 22-24.

In a letter dated November 8, 1954, the Master defends himself against the accusations leveled at him by Gösta Rybrant (item 2906).

2892. Knox, E. V. "The Passing of Sherlock Holmes," Illustrated by Wyndham Robinson. *The Strand*, 116 (December 1948), 76-82.
————. ————, *Seventeen Steps to 221B.*

[Edited by] James Edward Holroyd. London: George Allen & Unwin Ltd., [1967]. p. 82-89.

"Almost everything has been written about Sherlock Holmes—except his obituary notice. Here is an attempt to record what the London 'Times' might have said about Holmes (if he had really lived) when he died." (*The Strand*)

2893. [Levine, Arthur L.] "Sherlock Holmes in Space," by Alicia Cutter [pseud.] *BSJ*, 13, No. 3 (September 1963), 166-168.

He would not only have been interested in the great adventure of space exploration, but would have been selected as an astronaut because of his unique qualifications.

2894. [MacCarthy, Desmond.] "The Advantages of Sherlock Holmes," *Life and Letters*, 5, No. 27 (August 1930), 123-127.
————. ————, [first part] *A Baker Street Christmas Stocking,* [by] Bliss Austin. Pittsburgh, Pa.: Hydraulic Press, 1969. [unpaged]

In spite of imperfections in the Saga, the Master remains unaffected by them and without rival or successor.

2895. Macgowan, Kenneth. "Sherlock Holmes," *Sleuths: Twenty-Three Great Detectives of Fiction and Their Best Stories.* Edited by Kenneth Macgowan. New York: Harcourt, Brace and Co., 1931. p. 36.
————. ————, *The Misadventures of Sherlock Holmes.* Edited by Ellery Queen. Boston: Little, Brown and Co., 1944. p. [xxiii].

A biography in the style of "Who's Who."

2896. Marshall, Leslie. "A Trifle Trying," *BSJ*, 21, No. 1 (March 1971), 38-39.

Incidents in which Holmes tried the seemingly endless patience of his fellow lodger.

2897. McDiarmid, E. W. "Epithets in the Canon," *BSJ*, 19, No. 3 (September 1969), 144-148.

"An attempt to enumerate and characterize the names by which Holmes was called and the circumstances, where relevant, relating to the occasion."

2898. McLuhan, Marshall. "Sherlock Holmes vs. the Bureaucrat," *Explorations*, No. 8 (October 1957), 10-11.

"Every facet, every item of a situation, for Holmes, has total relevance. There are no irrelevant details for him." The bureaucrat, on the other hand, is "devoid of simultaneous modes of awareness or observation."

2899. [Morley, Christopher.] *Sherlock Holmes's Prayer,* [by] S. H. Note by J. H. W.

[New York]: Harcourt, Brace and Co., 1944. [4] p.

"Specially printed for the Sherlock Holmes dinner of the Baker Street Irregulars, March 31, 1944."

———. ———, *A Baker Street Four-Wheeler.* Edited by Edgar W. Smith. [Maplewood, N.J., and New York: The Pamphlet House, 1944.] p. 16-17.

———. ———, *The Incunabular Sherlock Holmes.* Edited by Edgar W. Smith. Morristown, N.J.: The Baker Street Irregulars, 1958. p. 181-182.

2900. Pearson, Hesketh. "Sherlock Holmes," *G.K.'s Weekly,* 10, No. 238 (October 5, 1929), 59.

———. ———, *CPBook,* 1, No. 4 (Spring 1965), 74-75.

"Sherlock Holmes is a very great creation, and will outlive every character in every 'serious' novel of his period."

2901. Rand, Stuart C. "Holmes the Absolute," *BSJ,* 3, No. 4 (October 1953), 211-214.

"Holmes is fundamentally an Absolute, with a capital 'A.' He is always right . . . right with the rightness of a sledge-hammer when it drives a spike or a tack. When and where his Truth struck, there was no escape."

2902. ———. "What Sherlock Didn't Know," *The Atlantic Monthly,* 176, No. 5 (November 1945), 122, 125, 127.

———. ———, *The Second Cab.* Edited by James Keddie. [Boston: The Speckled Band, 1947.] p. 46-50.

———. ———, *BSJ,* 1, No. 3 (July 1951), 83-88.

Holmes is cross-examined by Sir Henry Hawkins, a prominent member of the British bar, on the conduct of some of his cases.

2903. Redmond, Chris. "From Yorkshire to Montague Street," *VH,* 1, No. 3 (September 1967), 3-5.

A biographical sketch of the Master's early years.

2904. Rendall, Vernon. "The Limitations of Sherlock Holmes," *Baker-Street Studies.* Edited by H. W. Bell. London: Constable & Co., [1934]. p. 63-84.

"If he sacrificed everything, Watson included, to his work, he may have been justified by the results he obtained. He should be compared not with Socrates, but with a masterly egotist like Gibbon the historian, who concentrated his life and energy on work he could do better than anyone else."

2905. Roberts, S. C. "The Personality of Sherlock Holmes," *SHJ,* 1, No. 1 (May 1952), 2-7.

A study of his background and characteristics.

2906. Rybrant, Gösta. "Öppet brev till Sherlock Holmes" ["Open Letter to Sherlock Holmes"], *Aftonbladet* (October 31, 1954).

———. ———, *BSCL,* No. 4 (1965), 17-20.

Accuses him of some incorrectness and snobbishness.

2907. S[chrandt], J[ack]. "A Friend of John Watson," *DCC,* 4, No. 3 (May 1968), 2.

A tribute to "the greatest man who ever lived."

2908. Siegel, Jack M. "The First Citizen of Baker Street," *The Chicago Review,* 2, No. 2 (Spring 1947), 49-55.

"In all the annals of detection, fact and fiction alike, the name of Sherlock Holmes stands unchallenged; a paragon of logic, a literary masterpiece that has stood and will stand the ravages of time. For Holmes is immortal; his contemporaries, knowing only the fleeting mantle of flesh and blood, have long since passed from the scene, yet he remains, a deathless legend."

2909. Simmons, George. "Sherlock Holmes—The Inner Man," *BSJ* [OS], 2, No. 2 (April 1947), 129-135.

"It is the mind, the character, and the philosophy of Sherlock Holmes that have made him one of the landmarks in English literature, and in his own day made him a world figure."

2910. [Smith, Edgar W.] "Christmas with Sherlock Holmes," *BSJ Christmas Annual,* No. 4 (1959), 259-260. (The Editor's Gas-Lamp)

A pleasant speculation on how he spent this festive day.

2911. [———.] "On Fictional Characters," *BSJ,* 6, No. 1 (January 1956), 3-4. (The Editor's Gas-Lamp)

A brief commentary on "the best-known character in all fiction"—Robinson Crusoe (*or* Sherlock Holmes!).

2912. [———.] "Sherlock Holmes and the Literati," *BSJ* [OS], 3, No. 3 (July 1948), 267-268. (The Editor's Gas-Lamp)

"There are few figures in the world of letters who have not been touched, since the Master came to greatness, by the magic of his being."

2913. ———. ["Sherlock Holmes Was a Real Person"], *BSJ* [OS], 1, No. 2 (April 1946), 187-188. (From the Editor's Commonplace Book)

Proof exists in the Index volume of the *Encyclopaedia Britannica* (14th ed.) that he was a *real* person. His name appears in roman type which is used to distinguish real persons from fictional characters, whose names are in italics.

2914. Spears, Fred W. "Swifter Than the Years," *BSJ*, 18, No. 4 (December 1968), 232-239.

The author presents a "four-fold array of facts from which it may be inferred that the rate of diminution of Holmes's powers was swifter than the passage of his years as a man. If this be true, it follows that his post-retirement activities must have been relatively limited."

2915. Starrett, Vincent. "Sherlock Holmes: Notes for a Biography," *The Bookman*, 76, No. 2 (February 1933), 166-171.
―――. "Ave Sherlock Morituri et Cetera," *The Private Life of Sherlock Holmes*. New York: The Macmillan Co., 1933. p. 103-117.
―――. ―――, ―――. Revised and enlarged. The University of Chicago Press, [1960]. p. 93-101.

A biographical sketch, with an annotated bibliography of his writings.

2916. Walsh, Michael. "Why Sherlock Holmes?" *BSP*, No. 27 (September 1967), 5.

He remains the greatest detective in literature because he alone possesses a personality as well as a great mind.

2917. Wigglesworth, Belden. "The French Background of Sherlock Holmes: Aspects and Possibilities," *The Second Cab*. Edited by James Keddie. [Boston: The Speckled Band, 1947.] p. 39-45.

"The reality of the French background of Sherlock Holmes becomes more evident when we consider his comings and goings on the Continent, both official and unofficial, his dealings with persons both in and out of authority, and various activities of one sort and another."

2918. Wilson, Willard. "An East Wind Coming," *Sherlock Holmes: Master Detective*. Edited by Theodore C. Blegen & E. W. McDiarmid. La Crosse: Printed for the Norwegian Explorers, St. Paul & Minneapolis, 1952. p. 62-86.

The author advances the thesis that Holmes had a subconscious concern, an obsession even, with the East, and then relates a story in which he witnessed Holmes's performance as a Chinese magician at the Hotel de Pekin during the summer of 1931.

2919. [Wolff, Julian.] " 'Yes, Virginia, There Is a Sherlock Holmes,' " *BSJ*, 11, No. 4 (December 1961), 195-196. (The Editor's Gas-Lamp)
―――. ―――, *The Book Club of Detroit Newsletter*. Fifth Meeting, 1961-62 Season.
―――. " 'Ja, Virginia, der er en Sherlock Holmes,' " [Oversat af A. D. Henriksen]. *Sherlock Holmes Årbog* II (1966), 81-84.

His existence is just as real and just as important as the existence of Abraham Lincoln, King Arthur, Robin Hood, and Santa Claus.

2920. Wright, Lee. "Mrs. Hudson Speaks," *BSJ* [OS], 1, No. 2 (April 1946), 219-223.

Further reflections on the Master and his friendships.

ANCESTRY, FAMILY, AND NAME

See also *Mycroft Holmes*
(items 3500-3522) and
Heraldry (items 3868-3873)

2921. Anderson, Poul. "Art in the Blood," *BSJ*, 6, No. 3 (July 1956), 133-137.

The close resemblance between Leonardo da Vinci and Holmes would seem to indicate a common ancestry.

2922. Arenfalk, Poul, and Erik Hall. "Who Were the Parents of Sherlock Holmes?" *IR*, 3, No. 8 (November 1963), 1-5.

They were Edward Holmes, an English musician and author, and Louisa Sarah Webbe.

2923. Bengis, Nathan L. "The Graft I Refused to Take," *BSG*, 1, No. 1 (1961), 5-9.

Holmes invented his Vernet pedigree to hide the fact that he was a foundling and did not know his parents.

2924. Boswell, Rolfe. "A Connecticut Yankee in Support of Sir Arthur," *BSJ* [OS], 2, No. 2 (April 1947), 119-127.

The statement by the literary agent that Sherlock was distantly related to Oliver Wendell Holmes has prompted this study of the Holmes genealogy, including the correct Holmes coat of arms.

2925. Brockway, Wallace. "France's Share in Sherlock Holmes," *Tricolor*, 1, No. 2 (May 1944), 111-115.

The Vernet influence on the Master.

2926. Galerstein, David. "The Abkhasians," *HO*, 2, No. 2 (April 1972), 12-13, 11.

To account for the Master's longevity (118 years), the theory is advanced that he may have descended from a group famous for long life spans, that lived in the Soviet Republic of Abkhasia.

2927. Gilleo, Constance. "The Adventure of the French Sideshow," *VH*, 2, No. 3 (September 1968), 2-6.

A paper questioning the widely-held view that Holmes's artistic ancestors were members of the French Vernet family.

2928. Hall, Trevor H. "The Early Years of Sherlock Holmes," *Sherlock Holmes: Ten*

Literary Studies. London: Gerald Duckworth & Co., [1969]. Chap. 2, p. 18-35.

New evidence suggesting a Sussex origin and a parental tragedy.

2929. Harrison, Michael. "The Blue Blood of the Holmeses: A Genealogical Note, as an Appendix to the Saga," *BSJ*, 14, No. 2 (June 1964), 81-83.

"Holmes . . . was connected with the Peerage of Great Britain and the Peerage of Ireland, not only as of the past, but of the present. This consciousness of noble blood it was which made Holmes so very 'difficult'—not diffident—in the presence of those who, too often, treated him as of a lower social grade."

2930. ———. "Why Didn't I Check Montague Street? (Especially No. 24)," *BSJ*, 20, No. 4 (December 1970), 196-199.

The *Post Office London Directory* for 1881 lists a Mrs. Holmes as residing at 24 Montague Street. Because Holmes took rooms on that street in 1887, it is assumed he was living at this address with his mother or a relative.

2931. Redmond, Chris. "Art in the Blood: Two Canonical Relatives. I. 'I Shall Be the Hans Sloane of My Age,' " *BSJ*, 15, No. 2 (June 1965), 86-89.

Sir Hans Sloane, founder of the British Museum, was an ancestor of and an influence on Holmes.

2932. Redmond, D. A. "On the Name of Sherlock," *SHJ*, 8, No. 3 (Winter 1967), 86-88.

2933. Rosenberger, Edgar S. " 'My Ancestors Were Country Squires,' " *BSJ*, 9, No. 4 (October 1959), 197-204.

"Birth of middleaged parents, an upperclass, conventional childhood in the Yorkshire countryside, and their heredity explain the Holmes sons' traits: their celibacy and professional success, Sherlock's amazing integration of personality, and Mycroft's lethargy and / or serenity. The artistic genius of the Vernet family of Paris was transplanted to Yorkshire by marriage to Sherlock's father, a hypothetical member of the British civil service." (Mark Purcell)

2934. Ruber, P. A. "Sherlock Holmes' Christian Name," *BSG*, 1, No. 3 (1961), 36-38.

The Master was of English rather than French descent and his full name is Sherringford Sherlock Holmes.

2935. Sauvage, Leo. "Sherlock Holmes and the French," *BSJ*, 8, No. 4 (October 1958), 215-217.

On his ties and contacts with France; i.e., the Vernets, the Legion of Honor, cities, and wines.

2936. Tucker, Ruflus S. "Genealogical Notes on Holmes," *Profile by Gaslight.* Edited by Edgar W. Smith. New York: Simon and Schuster, 1944. p. 125-134.

His father's name was Sigurd or Siger; his grandfather's, Sherringford. He was distantly related to Oliver Wendell Holmes and to Doyle by marriage. Other contributors to his ancestral strain were Micah Clarke, Orlande de Lassus, Sir Nigel Loring, Etienne Gerald, Charles de Baatz, Daniel, and Zadig.

2937. Wigglesworth, Belden. "The Coat of Arms of Sherlock Holmes," *Profile by Gaslight.* Edited by Edgar W. Smith. New York: Simon and Schuster, 1944. p. 104-113.

A studied conception of an appropriate heraldry for the Master.

2938. Willis, Reg. "Your Family Origin: Holmes," *The Boston Traveler* (February 19, 1958).

———. ———, *Oakland Tribune* (April 14, 1960), 34.

———. ———, *BSJ*, 17, No. 4 (December 1967), 224.

The family lineage of Holmes (of York), with an illustration of its coat of arms.

BIRTH DATE

2939. Bengis, Nathan L. "What Was the Month?" *BSJ*, 7, No. 4 (October 1957), 204-214. illus.

A substantiation of January 6 as the birthday of Sherlock Holmes.

2940. Boswell, Rolfe. "A Rare Day in June," *BSJ*, 7, No. 1 (January 1957), 13-17.

A chronological inquiry into the date of the Master's nativity suggests he was born on Saturday, June 17, 1854.

2941. Henriksen, A. D. "On the Year of Sherlock Holmes's Birth," *SHJ*, 1, No. 1 (May 1952), 39-40.

A summary of the views of Sherlockians on this profound question.

2942. Hoffecker, Douglas M. "Forgive Us, Oh Lord!" *BSJ*, 5, No. 1 (January 1955), 40-42.

The Baker Street Irregulars and their British cousins are accused of having erred in dubbing Holmes a centenarian in 1954. He was born in 1867!

2943. McLauchlin, Russell. "On the Dating of the Master's Birth," *BSJ*, 6, No. 3 (July 1956), 138-142.

"No, there is no doubt about it: the birthmonth of Sherlock Holmes is either May or June. The field has been narrowed by five-sixths. And the January date is exposed as pure, superstitious folly."

2944. Meili, Philip C. "A Light to Enlighten: A Theological Reflection," *BSJ*, 19, No. 2 (June 1969), 109-111.

A theological basis for the January 6 date.

2945. Vander Rhin, William. "Upon the Dating of the Master's Birth," *Bulletin* [The Unknowns of Buffalo, New York], 2, No. 2 (January-February 1964), 10-13.

———. ———, *BSJ*, 15, No. 2 (June 1965), 114-117.

"We can no longer assume Mr. McLauchlin's theory to be anything but an incredible fantasy, a ridiculous conjecture. . . . *Vive, vive* January 6—long may it endure."

DRUG ADDICTION

2946. Berman, Ruth. "On an Irregular Needle," *BSJ*, 11, No. 3 (September 1961), 158.

"Irregulars explode in wrath, / They do not stop to wheedle, / When folks who think they're quoting Holmes / Cry, 'Quick, Watson! the needle.' "

2947. Carey, Eugene F. "Holmes, Watson and Cocaine," *BSJ*, 13, No. 3 (September 1963), 176-181, 195.

The author agrees with Dr. McCleary that "Holmes had none of the attributes of the injudicious drug user or of the addict" but insists that "he was, for a time at least, a judicious user of cocaine."

2948. Kaplan, Robyn. "Holmes as an Addict," *BSP*, No. 30 (December 1967), 3.

Proof that he could not have been addicted to either cocaine or morphine.

2949. [McCleary, George F.] "Was Sherlock Holmes a Drug Addict?" by An Occasional Correspondent. *The Lancet*, 2 (December 26, 1936), 1555-1556.

———. ———, *Profile by Gaslight*. Edited by Edgar W. Smith. New York: Simon and Schuster, 1944. p. 40-45.

———. ———, *Encore*, 7, No. 35 (January 1945), 90-93.

"All we know of Holmes's alleged addiction can be explained if we assume that he did not actually take the drug, but mystified Watson into believing that he did. The facts can be explained on no other hypothesis."

2950. Miller, William H. "Some Observations on the Alleged Use of Cocaine by Mr. Sherlock Holmes," *BSJ*, 19, No. 3 (September 1969), 161-165.

Winner of the 12th annual Morley-Montgomery Memorial Award for the best contribution to *BSJ* in 1969.

"There can be no doubt that Sherlock Holmes was not addicted to narcotic drugs. There is very little evidence to support such a belief, and the facts are all against it. A knowledge of the man himself and his abilities, as well as the few drugs available for hypodermic injection during the time of Holmes's experimentation, has made possible the elementary deductions that lead us to the true contents of his syringe."

2951. Morrow, Lorents A. "The Hoax That Raised (Co)caine," *BSJ*, 17, No. 3 (September 1967), 164-167.

Watson was goaded by Holmes into fabricating incidents about the detective's use of narcotics.

2952. Musto, David F. "A Study in Cocaine: Sherlock Holmes and Sigmund Freud," *The Journal of the American Medical Association*, 204, No. 1 (April 1, 1968), 27-32.

———. ———, *CPBook*, 4, No. 15 (August 1968), 297-302.

"Cocaine stimulated the early careers of two brilliant investigators, Sigmund Freud and Sherlock Holmes. In fact, their common attraction to the euphoric properties of the leaf may be more than a coincidence."

2953. Naganuma, Kohki. ["Sherlock Holmes and Cocaine," *The World of Sherlock Holmes*. Tokyo: Bungei-Shunju Shin-sha, 1962.] Chap. 2, p. 31-51.

———. ———, *BSJ*, 13, No. 3 (September 1963), 170-175.

"Historical discrepancies concerning the use of cocaine injections between the facts and Watson's records."

2954. "Sherlock Holmes var ej kokainist" ["Sherlock Holmes Was No Cocaine Addict"], *Svenska Dagbladet* (August 22, 1937).

———, *BSCL*, No. 1 (January 1963), 10-14.

2955. [Solovay, Jacob C.] "Holmes and Watson Converse on the Drug Habit," *BSJ*, 13, No. 3 (September 1963), 169.

"I crave the mental lift that makes me soar; / Morphine, cocaine, even your words of praise, / Or, better still, some dark and lovely crime." (Holmes)

"Forget your foolish drugs. Don't fret, don't fear, / There's ample wickedness to serve your ends." (Watson)

2956. [Wolff, Julian.] "A Narcotic Monograph," *BSJ*, 13, No. 3 (September 1963), 182-184. (The Editor's Gas-Lamp)

A review of the literature, with a bibliography on Holmes and cocaine.

EDUCATION

2957. Adams, Stephen. "Holmes: A Student of

London?" *SHJ*, 2, No. 4 (Winter 1955), 17-18.

The difficulties surrounding the Cambridge / Oxford problem can be easily solved by assigning him to London University.

2958. Blakeney, T. S. "The Location of 'The Three Students,' " *SHJ*, 4, No. 1 (Winter 1958), 14.

"Being a footnote to N. P. Metcalfe's 'Oxford or Cambridge or Both?' "

2959. Brend, Gavin. "Oxford or Cambridge," *My Dear Holmes*. London: George Allen & Unwin Ltd., [1951]. Chap. 2, p. 18-28.

An examination of the five cases (Glor, Musg, Miss, 3Stu, and Cree) which refer to university affairs suggests that Holmes attended Oxford.

2960. ———. "Was Sherlock Holmes at Westminster?" *The Trifler* [London] (July 1953), 6.

———. ———, *SHJ*, 2, No. 1 (July 1954), 39-41.

New signposts point to Westminster.

2961. Bristowe, W. S. "Oxford or Cambridge?" *SHJ*, 4, No. 2 (Spring 1959), 75-76.

The author agrees with both R. L. Green and F. J. M. Stratton that Holmes was an Oxford man.

2962. Cochran, Leonard. "Sherlock Holmes and Logic: The Education of a Genius," *BSJ*, 17, No. 1 (March 1967), 15-19.

"Siger Holmes, at the request of his younger son, sought out Professor Moriarty to serve as logic tutor to Sherlock Holmes during the summer which immediately followed upon Holmes's year at Oxford with Charles Lutwidge Dodgson."

2963. Grazebrook, O. F. *Oxford or Cambridge.* [London: Privately Printed, 1949.] 58 p. (Studies in Sherlock Holmes, No. 1)

"We can be absolutely certain, after a detailed analysis of the evidence, that it was not Cambridge; and as Mr. Hilaire Belloc has written quite often, 'of two things one,'—to Oxford the glory."

2964. Green, Roger Lancelyn. " 'At the University': Some Thoughts on the Academic Experiences of Mr. Sherlock Holmes," *SHJ*, 9, No. 4 (Summer 1970), 123-125.

A refutation of Mr. Hall's claim for Cambridge, with a counter-claim supporting Oxford.

2965. Hall, Trevor H. "A Note on Sherlock Holmes's Schooling," *Sherlock Holmes: Ten Literary Studies*. London: Gerald Duckworth & Co., [1969]. Chap. 3, p. 36-43.

"A subject about which the extreme significance of the lack of positive in-formation failed to be appreciated by Brend, Roberts, Blakeney and other Higher Critics." (Lord Donegall)

2966. ———. "Sherlock Holmes's University and College," *Sherlock Holmes: Ten Literary Studies*. London: Gerald Duckworth & Co., [1969]. Chap. 5, p. 56-85.

After an extensive review of the literature on the Oxford / Cambridge dispute, the author presents his own "conclusive" evidence that Holmes's undergraduate years were spent at Trinity College, Cambridge.

2967. Kennedy, Bruce. "Alma Mater, or Two Unexplained Years," *BSJ*, 19, No. 3 (September 1969), 158-160.

"Holmes found the formal educational system at Sidney Sussex [College at Cambridge] not to his liking and left to pursue his education independently and take more subjects of his own choosing."

2968. McDiarmid, E. W. "Professor Sherlock Holmes, Ph.D.," *Exploring Sherlock Holmes*. Edited by E. W. McDiarmid & Theodore C. Blegen. La Crosse: Sumac Press, 1957. p. 27-41.

Contents: Sherlock Holmes's educational career. - Sherlock Holmes and research. - The publications of Holmes. - Holmes as teacher. - Holmes and the accoutrements of higher education. - Holmes and higher education.

2969. Metcalfe, N. P. "Oxford or Cambridge or Both?" *BSJ Christmas Annual*, No. 1 (1956), 7-14.

———. Revised with title: "Holmes's University Career—A Reassessment," *SHJ*, 9, No. 4 (Summer 1970), 125-130. illus.

Glor points to Cambridge, Musg and 3Stu to Oxford, Miss to Cambridge, and Cree to Oxford.

2970. Morley, Christopher. "Sherlock Holmes Revisits Cambridge," *The Courier*, 9, No. 6 (December 1947), 87-89.

———. ———, *BSJ* [OS], 3, No. 3 (July 1948), 295-299. (Clinical Notes by a Resident Patient)

"Perhaps now more accessible to the softer emotions, Holmes always goes to Cambridge in autumn, to stroll those paths of golden litter under the beech avenues."

2971. Sayers, Dorothy L. "Holmes' College Career," *Baker-Street Studies*. Edited by H. W. Bell. London: Constable & Co., 1934. p. 1-34.

———. ———, *Unpopular Opinions*. London: Victor Gollancz Ltd., 1946. p. 134-147.

———. ———, ———. New York: Harcourt, Brace & Co., [1947]. p. 167-183.

———. ———, *MacKill's Mystery Magazine*, 3, No. 2 (December 1953), 57-69.

"An exhaustive analysis of the evidence

establishing a case for Sidney Sussex, Cambridge; with a chronology from Holmes's birth to the date of 'The Musgrave Ritual.' " (Edgar W. Smith)

2972. Schutz, Robert H. *A Bibliography of the Identification of Holmes's College and University.* Pittsburgh, Pa.: The Arnsworth Castle Business Index, June 1961. 1 p.

EYESIGHT

2973. Dorwart, Thomas H. "Thoughts Concerning Certain Infamous Conclusions: Being a Reply to Mr. Jason Rouby," *BSJ*, 16, No. 4 (December 1966), 216-218.
References to colors by Holmes prove that he could distinguish red from blue and therefore was not a "congenital dichromatic deuteranope" as suggested by Jason Rouby.

2974. Rouby, Jason. "The Adventure of the Bluish Carbuncle," *BSJ*, 16, No. 2 (June 1966), 70-73.
An analysis of the Blue Carbuncle from clues in the Canon and other writings, plus a clinical dissertation on Holmes's physical condition, advancing the theory that he was color-blind and that the Blue Carbuncle was actually a pigeon-blood ruby.

2975. Williamson, Jerry N. " 'And Especially Your Eyes,' " *SHJ*, 3, No. 3 (Autumn 1957), 17-19.
The author discusses the question: "Why did Sherlock Holmes time and again request Watson to read newspapers, commonplace books, etc., aloud when the normal inclination should be to read them himself?" and then concludes that he must have been hypermetropic, or farsighted.

HEALTH

2976. Goodman, Charles. "The Dental Holmes," *Profile by Gaslight.* Edited by Edgar W. Smith. New York: Simon and Schuster, 1944. p. 85-96.
Inside information on the oral hygiene of Sherlock Holmes by his personal dentist, Dr. Charles S. Wilson.

2977. Weiss, Jay. "Holmes as a Patient; With Special Emphasis on His Dental Status," *BSJ*, 13, No. 2 (June 1963), 96-98.
Astute observations on his health by a practicing dentist.

HUMOR

2978. Cooper, A. G. "Holmesian Humour," *SHJ*, 6, No. 4 (Spring 1964), 109-113.
The author cites a number of examples of humor from the 292 examples that he has unearthed in the Canon.

2979. Lauterbach, Charles E. and Edward S. "The Man Who Seldom Laughed," *BSJ Christmas Annual*, No. 5 (1960), 265-271.

Holmes was jovial and exhibited mirth 316 times in his sixty adventures. Watson was too deaf to notice his laughter.

INCOME

2980. Brown, Ivor. "Holmes and His Money," *John O'London's Weekly*, 2, No. 25 (March 24, 1960), 332.
————. ————, *CPBook*, No. 19 (June 1969), 383.
Although Holmes claimed to charge for his services on a fixed scale, except when he remitted altogether, the scale is never made clear, and the few references to money, together with considerations of his living costs, raise interesting questions.

2981. Cumings, Thayer. "Concerning Mr. Holmes's Fees," *BSJ*, 8, No. 4 (October 1958), 210-213.
————. ————, *Seven on Sherlock.* [New York]: Privately Printed, 1968. p. 27-30.
"It was these fascinating day-to-day *unrecorded* adventures which provided Holmes with the wherewithal to live—and live to the hilt—the wonderful, wonderful life he lived. Sorry—*lives!*"

2982. Gilbert, T. R. "In Account with Sherlock Holmes, Esquire," *The Dark Horse* [London], 36, No. 1 (December 1954), 21-23.
————. ————, *BSJ*, 16, No. 3 (September 1966), 147-149.
Some notes on "cheques drawn" and "credits paid in" from the page of an old passbook of Holmes that was revealed to the author by a retired messenger at the Capital and Counties Bank.

2983. Harbottle, S. T. L. " 'My Charges Are on a Fixed Scale . . . ?' " *SHJ*, 2, No. 1 (July 1954), 22-25.
An argument casting doubt on the reputed statement by Holmes that his professional fees were based on a fixed scale.

2984. Kennedy, Bruce. "Sherlockian Richness," *SIS*, 1, No. 3 (1966), 17-18.
Holmes must have inherited some money from his mother in order to live so comfortably.

2985. King, Martin J. "The Capitalistic Holmes," *BSJ*, 20, No. 2 (June 1970), 91-97.
A detailed examination of his earnings and savings by a knowledgeable Sherlockian and stockbroker.

2986. Leavitt, R. K. "Nummi in Arca, or The Fiscal Holmes," *221B: Studies in Sherlock Holmes.* Edited by Vincent Starrett. New York: The Macmillan Co., 1940. p. 16-36.
An analysis of Holmes's fiscal transactions with his clients.

2987. Mitchell, R. C. "The Stipend of Mr.

Holmes," *SHJ*, 9, No. 2 (Summer 1969), 50-52.

Evidence that his "steady source of income" resulted from an official position he held with the Government.

2988. Robertson, A. M. "Baker Street Finance," *SHJ*, 5, No. 3 (Winter 1961), 74-77; 5, No. 4 (Spring 1962), 117-118.

An examination of the Canon reveals that Holmes never once received a payment based on his "fixed scale" or ever remitted a fee.

2989. Serow, William J. "Some Thoughts on the Cost of Living in Sherlockian Days, or Sic Transit Glorious Money," *BSJ*, 20, No. 2 (June 1970), 98-102.

A discussion of twenty-seven Canonical references and comments by Baring-Gould on the principal monetary references, which give some indication of the living costs in the 1880's and 1890's.

2990. [Smith, Edgar W.] "Sherlock Holmes & Co.," *BSJ*, 6, No. 4 (October 1956), 195-196. (The Editor's Gas-Lamp)

"It may well be that his business card, if he had one, did not read simply SHERLOCK HOLMES, CONSULTING DETECTIVE, but HOLMES, WATSON, MERCER, JOHNSON, WIGGINS & CO. The 'co.' would, of course, be the Baker Street Irregulars *en masse*."

2991. Wodehouse, P. G. "From a Detective's Notebook," *Punch*, 236 (May 20, 1959), 677-679.

————. ————, *CPBook*, 3, No. 12 (Spring 1967), 226-227.

Private investigator Adrian Mulliner converses on Holmes's casualness about his income as a consulting detective and concludes that such indifference can be explained by recognizing that he was, in reality, Professor Moriarty and had an income from another source.

LIMITS OF KNOWLEDGE

GENERAL

2992. Bengis, Nathan. "Sherlock Stays After School," *Illustrious Client's Second Case-Book.* Edited by J. N. Williamson. [Indianapolis, Ind.: The Illustrious Clients, 1949.] p. 72-78.

————. "————: An Addendum," *Illustrious Client's Third Case-Book.* Edited by J. N. Williamson and H. B. Williams. [Indianapolis, Ind.: The Illustrious Clients, 1953.] p. 15.

An enumeration of some of his "more glaring oversights, inconsistencies, and outright blunders."

2993. Bennett, Edwin G. "The Anatomy of the Canon," *BSJ*, 6, No. 2 (April 1956), 83-86.

Watson bore such an aversion to spiritualism and its related pursuits that he chose Doyle as his literary agent, and then emphasized Holmes's use of the logical method of deduction to discredit Sir Arthur's illogical claims for spiritualism.

2994. Berg, Stanton O. "Sherlock Holmes: Father of Scientific Crime Detection," *The Journal of Criminal Law, Criminology and Police Science*, 61, No. 3 (September 1970), 446-452.

————. ————, *The Armchair Detective*, 5, No. 2 (January 1972), 81-87, 98.

————. "Trackin' Over Sherlock's Shoulder," *The Montana Lawman's Gunsmoke Gazette* [The Governor's Crime Control Commission], 1, No. 3 (January-February 1972), 4-5; 1, No. 4 (March-April 1972), 14, 17. illus.

The article establishes and thoroughly analyzes the concept that Doyle through Holmes acted as a catalyst in the evolving of the modern investigative, identification, and forensic sciences. It reviews what other authors have said on the subject as well as the credit given to Holmes by his contemporaries in the police science field. The impact on each of the important sciences (fingerprints, ballistics, questioned documents, forensic chemistry, etc.) is considered and the evidence carefully documented. In the process of documentation, much historical data on the forensic and police sciences are outlined.

2995. Christ, Jay Finley. ["Review of *The Unknown Murderer*, by Theodor Reik"], *American Journal of Police Science*, 36, No. 4 (November-December 1945), 301-304.

A commentary on Dr. Reik's "frivolous discussion of certain references to the detective methods of one Sherlock Holmes."

2996. Corrington, Julian D. "Adventuring with Sherlock Holmes," *Exploring with Your Microscope.* New York; Toronto; London: McGraw-Hill Book Co., 1957. Chap. 13, p. 197-216.

His use of the low-power microscope is briefly noted.

2997. ————. "Famous Lost Slides Discovered: Sherlock Holmes's Mounts Unearthed, Good As New," *Nature Magazine*, 46, No. 8 (October 1953), 446-447.

"They bore labels in his own well-known script. One was designated 'St. Pancras police murder,' and the other carried the legend 'Charing Cross coiner.'"

2998. ————. "Sherlock Holmes Buys a Microscope," *Adventures with the Microscope.* Rochester, N.Y.: Bausch & Lomb Optical Co., [1934]. Chap. 26, p. 404-429.

A dialogue between Holmes and Watson on the value of the microscope in crime detection.

2999. Hall, Trevor H. "The Erudition of Sherlock Holmes," *Sherlock Holmes: Ten Literary Studies.* London: Gerald Duckworth & Co., [1969]. Chap. 4, p. 44-55.

The importance of its profound appraisal in determining his alma mater.

3000. Hitchings, J. L. "Sherlock Holmes the Logician," *BSJ* [OS], 1, No. 2 (April 1946), 113-117.

"By one of the greatest strokes of genius in history, a character has been brought into being whose fame as a logician rivals that of the world's greatest thinkers."

3001. Hogan, John C. "A Short Manual on Holmesian (Sherlock, That Is) Methodology for Criminologists, Criminals and T.V. Lawyers," *The Brief* [Phi Delta Phi Quarterly], 58, No. 1 (Fall 1962), 38-47.

"No man lives or has ever lived who has brought the same amount of study and of natural talent to the detection of crime as Mr. Sherlock Holmes. . . . Although none of Mr. Holmes' writings on crime are available today, they are recommended and would be valuable reading for anyone who contemplates a career in criminal work."

3002. ———, and Mortimer D. Schwartz. "The Manly Art of Observation and Deduction," *The Journal of Criminal Law, Criminology and Police Science*, 55, No. 1 (March 1964), 157-164.

———. ———, *Malayan Police Magazine*, 30, No. 2 (June-July 1964).

An examination of Holmes's power of observation and method of deduction.

3003. Holmes, Roger W. "The Detective and His Art," *The Rhyme of Reason: A Guide to Accurate and Mature Thinking.* Student's edition. New York: Appleton-Century-Crofts, Inc., [1939]. Chap. 5, p. 147-168. (The Century Philosophy Series)

Partial contents: Sherlock Holmes and the Prediction Technique. - The Psychology and Logic of Prediction Are Quite Different. - Don't Look Now, but the Argument from Prediction Is Mighty Suspicious. - Our Hero and the Local Constabulary: The Method of *Reductio Ad Absurdum.*

3004. Kosloske, Ann M. "Sherlock Holmes: Spectacular Diagnostician," *Marquette Medical Review*, 29, No. 1 (January 1963), 29-31.

An interesting discussion of the Master and his methods by a senior medical student.

3005. Krejci-Graf, Karl. "Sherlock Holmes, Scientist, Including Some Unpopular Opinions," *SHJ*, 8, No. 3 (Winter 1967), 72-78.

Contents: Introduction. - What Constitutes a Scientist? - Single Properties of Scientists. - Hypotheses and Theories. - Appreciation of Others. - Limits of Knowledge. - Watson As Biographer. - Holmes's Knowledge of Special Sciences. - Conclusion.

3006. Kubicek, Earl C. "Mr. Sherlock Holmes: Scholar and Scientist," *The Saint Mystery Magazine*, 13, No. 6 (June 1960), 47-53.

3007. Mackenzie, J. B. "Sherlock Holmes' Plots and Strategy," *The Green Bag*, 14 (September 1902), 407-411.

———. ———, *BSJ Christmas Annual*, No. 1 (1956), 56-61. (Incunabulum)

An unfavorable examination of his deductive process and legal transgressions.

3008. [Maurice, Arthur Bartlett.] "The Ultimate Sources of Sherlock Holmes," *The Bookman*, 27 (April 1908), 113-114. (Chronicle and Comment)

The author briefly traces the evolution of the method of deductive reasoning which reached its pinnacle with Holmes.

3009. McDade, Thomas M. "Sherlock Holmes and the F.B.I.," *Ellery Queen's Mystery Magazine*, 29, No. 2 (February 1957), 96-103.

A former G-man compares the methods of the Master Detective with those of the Bureau.

3010. Polak, A. Laurence. "Baker Street Reflections," *Puffs, Balloons and Smokeballs.* Illustrated by Leslie Starke. Little London, Chichester, Sussex: Justice of the Peace, Ltd., 1952. p. 59-65.

"For the ordinary lawyer, who fortunately spends little of his professional life in close contact with violent crime, the fascination of Sherlock Holmes lies in the intellectual mastery of his deductive methods."

3011. Post, Melville Davisson. *The Man Hunters.* Illustrations by William D. I. Arnold. London: Hutchinson & Co., [1926]. ix, 348 p.

This book has several references to Holmes, and upholds him on the value of ashes, footprints, etc.

3012. Prestige, Colin. "Sherlock Holmes—Detective," *SHJ*, 2, No. 3 (Summer 1955), 26-30.

The sixty chronicles are divided into three groups according to the detective work involved, and examples from each group are discussed to illustrate the Master's ability in his chosen profession.

3013. Rhinelander, Philip H. "Patter Song:

The Writings About the Writings

Sherlock Holmes

Sherlock Holmes," *BSJ* [OS], 1, No. 2 (April 1946), 152-153.

"The science of deduction / If you follow my instruction, / Must be based on observation. . . ."

3014. Scarlett, E. P. "The Method of Zadig," *Archives of Internal Medicine*, 117 (June 1966), 832-835.

A noted Canadian physician, author, and Sherlockian scholar discusses the methods of Voltaire's Zadig, Dr. Joseph Bell, and Holmes.

3015. Schenck, Remsen Ten Eyck. "Baker Street Fables," *BSJ*, 2, No. 2 (April 1952), 85-92.

"Viewed dispassionately, on the evidence instead of purely through emotion, Holmes emerges not as a great loss to physical science but as a dabbler in chemistry on the small-boy level . . . ; not as a potentially renowned concert violinist but as an ordinary music-lover with the added ability to play simple airs on the violin."

3016. Silverstein, Albert. "Sherlock Holmes and the Interference Theory of Forgetting," *BSJ*, 14, No. 4 (December 1964), 216-218.

Holmes demonstrates his psychological acumen in Stud by propounding a theory of how people forget that is very contemporary. The theory states that we forget what we know as a result of the interference from new material (retroactive interference) or from previously learned materials (proactive interference). While the most recent versions of this theory emphasize the forgetting from prior materials, Holmes seemed to emphasize the forgetting produced by subsequently learned materials. However, considering that his statement appeared thirteen years prior to the first experimental evidence for any interference theory, it is a remarkable feat. The statement of Holmes's theory may be found in the passage in which he proudly announces his ignorance of the Copernican theory.

3017. ———. "Sherlock Holmes, Psychology, and Phrenology; or, Sailing Full Steam Ahead Requires a Full Head of Steam," *BSJ*, 22, No. 1 (March 1972), 18-23.

An analysis is made of the Master's techniques of psychological deductions and examples given of each. These techniques include deductions of a person's prior circumstances from their effects upon his anatomy and / or upon the condition of his possessions, deductions of a person's prior behavior from the effects of such behavior on his clothing or visage, deductions of a person's actions from a motivational analysis of that person, and deductions about a person's inner behavior from observations of outer behavior. These techniques are totally irrelevant to the practice of phrenology, which Holmes has been alleged to have engaged in, and it can be shown that his entire attitude toward science and practical affairs is antithetical to phrenology. More likely, Holmes's psychological acumen is related to the theories and techniques of Francis Galton, the father of the study of individual differences in psychology. (See also items 3160-3161.)

3018. Starrett, Vincent. "The Methods of Mr. Sherlock Holmes," *The Private Life of Sherlock Holmes*. New York: The Macmillan Co., 1933. p. 19-38.

———. ———, ———. Revised and enlarged. The University of Chicago Press, [1960]. p. 13-26.

3019. Thorwald, Jürgen. "Spuren im Staub; oder *Etappen der forensischen Chemie und Biologie*," *Die Stunde der Detektive: Werden und Welten der Kriminalistik*. [Zürich]: Droemer, [1966]. II, 1, p. 286-295.

———. "Clues in the Dust: Forensic Chemistry and Biology," *Crime and Science: The New Frontier in Criminology*. Tr. by Richard and Clara Winston. New York: Harcourt, Brace & World, Inc., [1967]. II, 1, p. 233-235.

Unfortunately, the translation of the section on Holmes and Watson has been considerably condensed.

3020. Wernette, J. Philip. "Holmes and Watson Were Wrong," *The Michigan Quarterly Review*, 10, No. 2 (Spring 1971), 119-124.

"Professor Wernette shows that Holmes's knowledge in all fields was much greater than Watson indicated in that famous tabulation in *A Study in Scarlet*; Holmes did not ignore information that might crowd out other data but acted on the principle that 'All knowledge comes useful to the detective.' " (Julian Wolff)

3021. Williamson, J. N. "Sherlock's Murder Bag," *Illustrious Client's Third Case-Book*. Edited by J. N. Williamson and H. B. Williams. [Indianapolis, Ind.: The Illustrious Clients, 1953.] p. 84-88.

About some of the articles he used to aid him in his investigations.

Knowledge of Acting and Disguises

3022. Haynes, George C. " 'What the Law Had Gained the Stage Had Lost,' " *BSJ Christmas Annual*, No. 5 (1960), 301-303.

A fourteen-year-old student of the Canon opens the "clues closet" to Holmes's former career as an actor.

3023. Heldenbrand, Page. "Sherlock Holmes in Disguise," *BSJ* [OS], 1, No. 3 (July 1946), 318-322.

"Sherlock Holmes certainly did not miss his calling. As a detective he stands alone. But from our glimpses of 'Sherlock Holmes in Disguise,' it is not unlikely that—as Athelney Jones put it—he would indeed 'have made an actor and a rare one.' "

3024. Kaye, Marvin. *The Histrionic Holmes: An Analysis and Dissertation on the Impersonatory Genius of Sherlock Holmes.* With technical notes and a compendium of his performances by Marvin Kaye. With illustrations by Tom Walker. [Culver City, Calif.: Luther Norris, November 1971.] 52 p.
  Limited to 300 copies.
  The first comprehensive study of one of the least explored areas of Sherlockian scholarship: the Master's skill as an actor and Napoleon of Disguise!

3025. Kennedy, Bruce. "1899—Where Was Holmes?" *BSP*, No. 26 (August 1967), 4.
  "William Gillette" was a pseudonym used by Holmes when he played the part in *Sherlock Holmes.*

3026. Lauterbach, Charles E. "The Folks I Sometimes Meet," *Baker Street Ballads.* [Culver City, Calif.: Luther Norris, March 1971.] p. 30-31.
  "Gadzounds! it's Sherlock in disguise!"

3027. Rea, Roy. "Sherlock Holmes: Master Dramatist," *BSJ*, 4, No. 1 (January 1954), 5-11.
  "Holmes is more than a great detective, and deserves some consideration for his theatrical abilities. . . . There are those who, with Vincent Starrett, would prefer a day with Mr. Holmes even to one with Master Shakespeare."

3028. Skottowe, Philip F. "Sherlock Holmes and the Stage," *SHJ*, 7, No. 3 (Winter 1965), 73-77.
  On the Master's dramatic impersonations and his earlier career as a competent and successful actor.

3029. Solovay, Jacob C. "Watson Comments on Holmes's Acting," *BSJ Christmas Annual*, No. 5 (1960), 299.
  "You change your person as you change your part. / Never a vestige of the amateur." (Watson)
  "I could have rivaled Bernhardt, Mansfield, Irving— / But what detective could have filled my place?" (Holmes)

3030. Warrack, Guy. "Disguises in Baker Street," *SHJ*, 9, No. 3 (Winter 1969), 74-78.
  An excellent treatment of Holmes's genius in the art of disguise. The disguises of a few other characters are also discussed.

3031. Wilson, Alan. "Holmes the Histrionic," *SHJ*, 5, No. 4 (Summer 1962), 103-105.

An intriguing article in which the author refers to Sir Henry Irving and the Lyceum Theatre and to the possibility that Holmes might have been a minor member of his company.

Knowledge of Advertising

3032. Cumings, Thayer. "Sherlock Holmes and Advertising," *BSJ* [OS], 1, No. 4 (October 1946), 385-390.
  ———. ———, *The Best of the Pips.* Westchester County, N.Y.: The Five Orange Pips, 1955. p. 79-86.
  ———. ———, *Seven on Sherlock.* [New York]: Privately Printed, 1968. p. 1-8.
  "Unquestionably, Sherlock Holmes was advertising minded. One of the rituals he observed meticulously was a regular matinal perusal of the advertising columns."

3033. Gilham, A. A. "Holmes in Advertising," *SHJ*, 6, No. 1 (Winter 1962), 18-19.
  A consideration of his advertising ability and the part he is playing in the advertising world of today.

3034. Lauritzen, Henry. "Sherlock Holmes ser paa annoncer" ["Sherlock Holmes Looks at Advertisements"], *Stiftsnyt* [Aalborg] (October 1960), 3-7.
  ———. ———, *BSCL*, No. 5 (1966), 19-24.

3035. Lofstedt, Nelson. "221B Madison Avenue," *BSJ*, 17, No. 4 (December 1967), 202-208.
  "The most impressive thing about Holmes as an advertising man is his knowledge of so much of the field. He is well equipped to handle most of the key functions of an advertising agent—as copywriter, media adviser, production supervisor."

3036. Ziebarth, E. W. "The Master and the Mass Media," *Exploring Sherlock Holmes.* Edited by E. W. McDiarmid & Theodore C. Blegen. La Crosse: Sumac Press, 1957. p. 42-65.
  Examples of how he used advertising in his day and how the mass media use him in our day.

Knowledge of Anatomy

3037. Fabricant, Noah D. "Sherlock Holmes as an Eye, Ear, Nose, and Throat Diagnostician," *The Eye, Ear, Nose & Throat Monthly*, 36, No. 9 (September 1957), 523-526.
  An appraisal of his abilities in the field of the author's specialty, with a word on his knowledge of teeth.

3038. Hart, Archibald. "The Effects of Trades Upon Hands," *BSJ* [OS], 3, No. 4 (October 1948), 418-420.
  A brief commentary on Holmes's

The Writings About the Writings

Sherlock Holmes

proficiency in deducing a person's trade from the characteristic marks his occupation has left on his hands.

3039. Klauder, Joseph V. "Sherlock Holmes as a Dermatologist: With Remarks on the Life of Dr. Joseph Bell and the Sherlockian Method of Teaching," *A.M.A. Archives of Dermatology and Syphilogy*, 68, No. 4 (October 1953), 363-377.
———. Revised with title: "Sherlock Holmes and Dermatology," *Skin: Dermatology in General Practice*, 1, No. 2 (March 1962), 45-54.
———. ———, *CPBook*, 2, No. 7-8 (Winter-Spring, 1966), 131-140.
The late Clinical Professor of Dermatology, Graduate School of Medicine, University of Pennsylvania, reports on a dermatological clinic as it might have been conducted by Holmes.

3040. Perlman, David. "Pitting a Famous Sleuth Against Heart Disease," *San Francisco Chronicle* (March 1, 1968), 4.
———. ———, *CPBook*, 4, No. 15 (August 1968), 283.
A report on how Dr. Mark C. Silverman is using Holmes's method of examining hands to detect heart disease.

3041. Rouby, Jason. "On Identification by Comparison of Ears," *BSJ*, 15, No. 1 (March 1965), 26-27.
A discussion of the observation on the shapes of babies' ears and their alleged fathers as a contemporary method for deciding bastardy cases, by a former Arkansas county judge, using the same techniques employed by Holmes in Card.

3042. Schenck, Remsen Ten Eyck. "The Effect of Trades Upon the Body," *BSJ*, 3, No. 1 (January 1953), 31-36.
An examination of occupational marks on teeth, hands, etc., including those of Holmes and Watson.

3043. Van Liere, Edward J. "The Anatomical Sherlock Holmes," *A Doctor Enjoys Sherlock Holmes*. New York: Vantage Press, [1959]. p. 19-24.
The many pertinent allusions to anatomical science in the tales indicate that "Holmes was much more interested in gross structures of the body, especially osteology, than in microscopic structures."

Knowledge of Anthropology and Archaeology

See also *Houn* (item 2489)

3044. Boswell, Rolfe. "Skull-Diggery at Piltdown: A Baker Street Irregularity," *BSJ*, 13, No. 3 (September 1963), 150-155.
Clues in the Canon suggest the Master had a hand in the Piltdown forgery.

3045. Compton, Carl B. "Sherlock Holmes, Archaeologist," *Pennsylvania Archaeologist*, 27 (December 1957), 138-140.
"Holmes was a forerunner of scientific detection and, in a way, of scientific archaeology."

3046. Durrenberger, E. Paul. "More About Holmes and the Piltdown Problem," *BSJ*, 15, No. 1 (March 1965), 28-31.
After correcting some apparent misinterpretations by Rolfe Boswell, the author advances his own hypothesis that Holmes discovered Charles Dawson's Piltdown man was a fake and reported his findings to the Royal Anthropological Institute.

3047. Eney, Dick. "Fundamental, My Dear Watson," *Spy Ray*, Operation Crifanac 229 (July 1963), 1-4.
———. ———, *SHsf Fanthology One*. Edited by Ruth Berman. The Professor Challenger Society, 1967. p. 21-26.
Holmes subscribed in large part to the theory of Criminal Anthropology and either derived his theories of criminology from the writings of Lombroso or developed them independently.

3048. Krogman, Wilton Marion. "Sherlock Holmes as an Anthropologist," *The Scientific Monthly*, 80, No. 3 (March 1955), 155-162.
———. ———, *CPBook*, 2, No. 7-8 (Winter-Spring 1966), 149-156.
"Among the fields in which he showed considerable knowledge was anthropology. Primarily, his interests were concerned with what we today classify as physical anthropology, but he knew archaeology and ethnography as well."

Knowledge of British Law
(Including His Legal Transgressions)

See also *Blue* (items 2271-2291),
Chas (items 2308-2324),
Prio (items 2588-2598),
and *Silv* (items 2710-2729)

3049. Beckemeyer, Doyle W. "The Irregular Holmes," *BSJ*, 2, No. 1 (January 1952), 18-20.
"It was undoubtedly Scotland Yard's restraints and lackadaisical methods that led Holmes to feel justified in putting his knowledge of housebreaking and burglary, however irregular it might be, to practical use in his own capacity as a private detective."

3050. Bigelow, S. Tupper. "Misprision of Felony and Sherlock Holmes," *SHJ*, 5, No. 3 (Winter 1961), 68-70.
A vindication of the "totally unjustified charges" made against Holmes by the author in the following article.

3051. ———. "Sherlock Holmes and Misprision of Felony," *BSJ*, 8, No. 3 (July 1958), 139-146.

Judge Bigelow accuses him of having committed the heinous offense of misprision of felony no less than seventeen times in twelve of his cases.

3052. ———. "Sherlock Holmes Was No Burglar," *BSJ Christmas Annual*, No. 3 (1958), 26-37.

A defense of Holmes's and Watson's burglarious activities.

3053. Blaustein, Albert P. "Sherlock Holmes: Was Conan Doyle's Famed Detective a Lawyer?" *American Bar Association Journal*, 34, No. 6 (June 1948), 473-474.
———. "Sherlock Holmes as a Lawyer," *BSJ* [OS], 3, No. 3 (July 1948), 306-308.

A portrait of him as a lawyer, judge, and legal philosopher.

3054. Fenton, Irving. "Holmes and the Law," *BSJ*, 7, No. 2 (April 1957), 79-83.

"In general, Holmes exhibits no greater knowledge of the British law than does the intelligent layman who reads *The Times* of London and the crime literature of the day."

3055. Harbottle, S. T. L. "Sherlock Holmes and the Law," *SHJ*, 1, No. 3 (June 1953), 7-10.

An examination of the gaps in his knowledge of British criminal law.

3056. H[olmgren], R. B. "Sherlock Holmes and Justice," *DCC*, 2, No. 5 (July 1966), 2.

A brief appraisal of his actions against the perspective of British police traditions.

3057. Honce, Charles. "Was Holmes a Crook?" *For Loving a Book*. Mount Vernon, N.Y.: The Golden Eagle Press, 1945. p. 51-52.

A short piece in which are quoted a letter from Jacob Blanck and a reply from Edgar Smith theorizing about his criminal and American background.

3058. Jensen, Jens. "Sherlock Holmes og retfaerdigheden" ["Sherlock Holmes and Justice"], *Sherlockiana*, 6, Nr. 2-3 (1961), 8-10.

A justification of his decisions on cases that did not go through the ordinary legal channels, and his assumption of this role.

3059. Johnson, Frederic A. "Sherlock Holmes, the Criminal?" *BSJ*, 10, No. 3 (July 1960), 172-174.

"Whatever the circumstance, Sherlock Holmes adhered firmly to the accredited policies of law enforcement and to the eternal triumph of righteousness."

3060. Levy, Mark. "On the Morality of One Mr. Sherlock Holmes," *BSJ*, 21, No. 1 (March 1971), 40-43.

He could easily have been a master criminal but refrained from engaging in a life of crime, proving that he *was* moral.

3061. Mallalieu, J. P. W. "Shady Mr. Holmes," *The Spectator*, 190 (February 27, 1953), 247.
———. ———, *CPBook*, 2, No. 5-6 (Summer-Fall 1965), 89.

A corroboration of Red Smith's indictment of Holmes and Watson for their alleged illegal sporting activities.

3062. Page, Andrew. "On the Reasoning of One Mark Levy: A Rebuttal on the 'Morality' of Sherlock Holmes," *HO*, 1, No. 3 (May 1971), 5-7.

3063. Palmer, Stephen G. "Sherlock Holmes and the Law," *Sherlock Holmes: Master Detective*. Edited by Theodore C. Blegen & E. W. McDiarmid. La Crosse: Printed for the Norwegian Explorers, St. Paul & Minneapolis, 1952. p. 36-44.

The author reviews and answers Mr. Blaustein's arguments, and then provides his own argument to prove that "Holmes was not a legal man by training, and further, that he had very little regard for the law except when it suited his own purposes."

3064. Smith, Red. "The Nefarious Holmes," and "Dear Me Mr. Holmes," *New York Herald Tribune* (January 13, 1953; January 14, 1953), 24; 26. (Views of Sport)
———. ———, *Views of Sport*. Illustrations by Marc Simont. New York: Alfred A. Knopf, 1954. p. 185-191.
———. ———, *CPBook*, 1, No. 1 (Summer 1964), 10-11.

3065. ———. "What! Sherlock Holmes a Crook?" *The Sign: A National Catholic Monthly Magazine*, 43, No. 1 (August 1963), 54-55.

Evidence of his willingness to use inside information to his own advantage in connection with sporting events.

3066. Stix, Thomas L. "Sherlock Holmes Impeached. I.," *BSJ*, 15, No. 2 (June 1965), 75-76.

"Through bribery, *suppressio veri, suggestio falsi*, burglary, helping murderers to escape, commuting a felony, withholding information which kept an innocent man in duress (more or less vile), by encouraging the rich and subjugating the poor, by bluff, by subterfuge, by rigged gambling, by disguise, by laziness, this opium-drugged anti-Robin Hood has much to answer for."

Knowledge of Chemistry

3067. Clark, John D. "A Chemist's View of

Canonical Chemistry," *BSJ*, 14, No. 3 (September 1964), 153-155.

"Holmes was a distinguished forensic chemist. But it is only fair to remind the world that as a chemist he was something more. From Baker Street to the Ecole Polytechnique to the Rutherford Laboratories at Cambridge, and on to Alamogordo—the trace is there for anyone to see."

3068. Doll, Bernard L. "Sherlock Holmes, the Chemist," *Illustrious Client's Case-Book.* Edited by J. N. Williamson and H. B. Williams. [Indianapolis, Ind.: The Illustrious Clients, 1948.] p. 48-49.

"If Sherlock had not decided to become the world's only unofficial consulting detective, he would most probably have turned to chemistry as the means of earning his bread and cheese."

3069. Glock, M. F. V. "The Chemist Holmes," *Investigations*, 1, No. 3 (May 1971), 4-6.

3070. Graham, R. P. "Sherlock Holmes: Analytical Chemist," *Journal of Chemical Education*, 22, No. 10 (October 1945), 508-510.

"Holmes chemical interests . . . were largely centered in the organic branch of chemistry. His forte was analytical organic chemistry."

3071. Holstein, Leon S. " '7. Knowledge of Chemistry—Profound,' " *BSJ*, 4, No. 1 (January 1954), 44-49.

" 'Knowledge of Chemistry—Profound' [the seventh of the Master's 'limits' as defined by Watson in his famous list] is an appraisal that stands the test of time, and it is as true on January 6, 1954, as it was in March of 1882."

3072. Michell, J. H. and Humfrey. "Sherlock Holmes the Chemist," *BSJ* [OS], 1, No. 3 (July 1946), 245-252.

Discusses several areas of his life but emphasizes his chemical experiments and research in coal tar derivatives.

3073. Price, A. Whigham. "Holmes and Chemistry," *BSJ*, 3, No. 1 (January 1953), 20-24.

To cover the alarming facts unearthed by Mr. Schenck in "Baker Street Fables" (item 3015), the author advances the theory that Watson may have tried to discredit Holmes in a mild sort of way by recording some minor inaccuracies his companion uttered about chemistry.

3074. Redmond, D. A. "Some Chemical Problems in the Canon," *BSJ*, 14, No. 3 (September 1964), 145-152.

A detailed and fully documented study of the subject, under the headings: 1. The Acetones. 2. The Test for Haemoglobin. 3.

The Deal-Topped Table. 4. The Bunsen Burner. - The Bisulphate of Baryta. 6. The Blue Carbuncle.

3075. Schenck, Remsen T. "Knowledge of Chemistry—Not So Profound," *BSJ*, 4, No. 4 (October 1954), 229-231.

A disputation of Mr. Holstein's endeavor to establish that Holmes was a competent chemist.

3076. Van Liere, Edward J. "Sherlock Holmes, the Chemist," *A Doctor Enjoys Sherlock Holmes.* New York: Vantage Press [1959]. p. 69-76.

"The casual reader naturally takes it for granted that Holmes' love for chemistry was due to his interest in crime detection; that is, he intended to use the knowledge he gained from his experiments for practical purposes. We recognize this today as applied research. . . . Holmes was interested in pure or basic research, too—in other words, research which has no immediate practical value."

Knowledge of Cryptography

See also *Danc* (items 2337-2356),
Miss (item 2553),
and *RedC* (items 2599-2604)

3077. Schorin, Howard R. "Cryptography in the Canon," *BSJ*, 13, No. 4 (December 1963), 214-216.

A critical analysis of the cryptographic messages used in Glor, Danc, Vall, and RedC.

3078. Schulman, David. "Sherlock Holmes: Cryptanalyst," *BSJ* [OS], 3, No. 2 (April 1948), 233-237.

Evidence of his outstanding ability as a cipher expert.

Knowledge of Fingerprints

3079. Bigelow, S. Tupper. "Fingerprints and Sherlock Holmes," *BSJ*, 17, No. 3 (September 1967), 131-135.

A discussion of the literature on the subject, followed by references to fingerprints in the Canon which prove that Holmes fully realized the importance of this method of identification.

3080. Hogan, John C. "The Fine Art of Finger-Print Detection," *BSJ*, 13, No. 2 (June 1963), 99-107.

An illustrated article describing a simple method for developing latent fingerprints by means of powders, with some commentary on Holmes's expertise in the art of fingerprinting.

Knowledge of Food and Alcoholic Beverages

3081. Bellairs, George. "Sherlock Holmes,

Epicure," *Wine and Food: A Gastronomical Quarterly* [London: The Wine and Food Society], No. 82 (Summer 1954), 86-90.

A pleasant look at the things he ate and drank, with a bow to his incomparable taste and discernment.

3082. Brodie, Robert N. "Clues *à la Carte*," *SHJ*, 9, No. 4 (Summer 1970), 130-131.

A discussion of the eleven cases in which food, drink, or their services "serve either as the focal point of the adventure, as its dramatic climax, or as the clue that begins or reinforces the reasoning that leads Holmes to his conclusion."

3083. Carr, John Dickson. " 'Another Glass, Watson!' " *The Sherlock Holmes.* [Compiled and prepared by Richard Lonsdale-Hands Associates.] London: Whitbread & Co. Ltd., [1957]. p. 5-10.
————. ————, *Seventeen Steps to 221B.* [Edited by] James Edward Holroyd. London: George Allen & Unwin Ltd., [1967]. p. 126-131.

On the eating and drinking habits of Holmes and Watson.

3084. Cold, Jørgen. "What Did Sherlock Holmes Drink?" *Illustrious Client's Third Case-Book.* Edited by J. N. Williamson and H. B. Williams. [Indianapolis, Ind.: The Illustrious Clients, 1953.] p. 110-118.
————. "Snak om, hvad de drak i Baker Street" ["What Did They Drink in Baker Street"], *Sherlockiana*, 6, Nr. 2-3 (1961), 5-8.
————. ————, *Sherlock Holmes Årbog* III (1967), 52-58.

An investigation concerning the liquids, particularly the liquor, consumed by Holmes and Watson.

3085. Durgin, Cyrus. "The Speckled Band," *The Third Cab.* [Boston: The Speckled Band, 1960.] p. 12-16.

"Some questions upon the subject: 'How reliable were Dr. Watson's remarks upon the Master's knowledge of wines and music?' " (Subtitle)

3086. Hall, Trevor H. "Sherlock Holmes: Ascetic or Gourmet?" *The Late Mr. Sherlock Holmes & Other Literary Studies.* London: Gerald Duckworth & Co., [1971]. Chap. 1, p. 13-22.

3087. Hartman, Harry. "The Beaune of Contention," *BSG*, 1, No. 3 (1961), 11-14.
————. ————, *The Holy Quire.* [Culver City, Calif.: Luther Norris, December 1970.] p. 33-35.

A defense of drinking and drinkers, with corroborating evidence adduced from the Canon; including a brief return visit to the Alpha Inn in Bloomsbury.

3088. Liebe, Poul Ib. " 'Sherlock's Delights,' " *BSJ*, 8, No. 2 (April 1958), 104-106.

The recipes for his favorite dishes: Oyster Special, Grouse à la Holmes, and Apricot Pie.

3089. Lotinga, Aage. "Nogle gastronomiske studier over Baker Street 221 B" ["Some Gastronomic Studies at 221B Baker Street"], *Sherlockiana*, 2, Nr. 1-2 (1957), 2-4.

3090. Lyall, Gavin. "Drinking for Thrills," *The Compleat Imbiber 7: An Entertainment.* Edited by Cyril Ray and designed by Charles Hasler. London: Studio Vista Ltd., 1964. p. 17-29.
————. ————, ————. New York: Paul S. Eriksson, 1964. p. 17-29.

In the first part of this article on the drinking habits of the "thriller heroes," the author explains that Holmes was not much of a drinker because of his addiction to cocaine. This would also account for his lack of interest in sex, his minginess, and his not being recruited by M.I.6 during World War I.

3091. Monberg, Claus. "Epikuraeeren Sherlock Holmes," *Ekstrabladets kronik* (June 22, 1954).
————. ————, *Sherlockiana*, 15, Nr. 1-2 (1970), 1-3.

3092. Munkebo, Sven V. "Man skal ikke blande sig i Sherlock Holmes' sager" ["Don't Meddle in Sherlock Holmes's Affairs"], *Aalborg Stiftstidende* (April 20, 1969), 21.
————. ————, *Sherlockiana*, 14, Nr. 2 (1969), 5-7.

While on a trip to France the author investigates to see how far Mr. Pratt was right when he assumed that the white wines which Holmes, in chap. 9 of Sign, invites his guest, Athelney Jones, to partake of must have been Montrachet.

3093. Pratt, Fletcher. "The Gastronomic Holmes," *BSJ*, 2, No. 2 (April 1952), 94-99.
————. "Gastronomen Sherlock Holmes," [Oversat af Peter Jerndorff-Jessen]. *Sherlock Holmes Årbog* III (1967), 44-51.

An examination of the record reveals that he "was one of the true epicures of history. . . . A genuine gourmet, both in food and wine."

3094. Rodell, Marie F. "Living on Baker Street," *BSJ* [OS], 2, No. 1 (January 1947), 35-37.

"Perhaps, in spite of his apparent lack of interest in gastronomy, it was Watson himself who invented *pâté-de-foie-gras* pie."

3095. Shaw, John Bennett. " 'Alimentary, My Dear Watson,' " *BSJ*, 17, No. 2 (June 1967), 98-100.
————. " 'Alimentaert, min kaere Watson!' " [Oversat af Peter Jerndorff-Jessen]. *Sherlock Holmes Årbog* III (1967), 59-63.

"Dr. Watson was the typical Britisher in his eating and drinking habits and, as in all else, Holmes was the exception."

3096. [Smith, Edgar W.] "Holmes the Epicure," *BSJ*, 10, No. 3 (July 1960), 131-132. (The Editor's Gas-Lamp)
"It is good to know that this 'reasoning machine' was also a man with a hearty appetite and a discriminating choice in appeasing it."

3097. ———. "Up from the Needle," *The Saturday Review of Literature*, 19, No. 14 (January 28, 1939), 13-14.
———. ———, *BSJ* [OS], 2, No. 1 (January 1947), 85-88.
———. ———, *Baker Street and Beyond: Together with Some Trifling Monographs.* Morristown, N.J.: The Baker Street Irregulars, 1957. [unpaged]
"The reputation attributed to Sherlock Holmes for addiction to cocaine and morphine has served, unfortunately, to obscure the name he more justly deserves for a sound and civilized attitude toward the venial narcotic alcohol."

3098. Walbridge, Earl F. "The Care and Feeding of Sherlock Holmes," *221B: Studies in Sherlock Holmes.* Edited by Vincent Starrett. New York: The Macmillan Co., 1940. p. 54-58.
"Breakfast was Sherlock Holmes's best meal. There are at least two dozen references to it in the saga. Breakfast was frequently the only meal he permitted himself when the game was afoot. . . . Food was renounced altogether when he was keen on a case."

Knowledge of Geology

3099. Blank, E. W. "Was Sherlock Holmes a Mineralogist?" *Rocks and Minerals* [Peekskill, N.Y.], 22 (March 1947), 237.
A brief look at his capacities as an expert on rocks and minerals.

3100. Redmond, Chris. "Holmes and Holmium," *BSP Christmas Annual*, No. 1 (1966), 14-15.
Sherlock Holmes, along with Per T. Cleve, was involved in the early research on a rare earth named Holmium (Ho165).

Knowledge of Graphology

3101. Christie, Winifred. "Sherlock Holmes and Graphology," *SHJ*, 2, No. 4 (Winter 1955), 28-31.
About his contribution to graphology. "He was as proficient in handwritings as he was in tobacco ash."

3102. Swanson, Martin J. "Graphologists in the Canon," *BSJ*, 12, No. 2 (June 1962), 73-80.

A study of graphology as employed by Holmes, Mrs. St. Clair, Mycroft, Birdy Edwards, and Watson, including an analysis of the Master's own handwriting.

Knowledge of Heredity

3103. Musto, David F. "Sherlock Holmes and Heredity," *The Journal of the American Medical Association*, 196, No. 1 (April 4, 1966), 45-49.
———. ———, *CPBook*, 2, No. 7-8 (Winter-Spring 1966), 125-129.
Contents: Nineteenth Century Theories of Inheritance. - Darwin, Galton, and Mendel. - Holmes's Contribution. - Inheritance of Personality. - Particulate Inheritance. - Holmes and Moriarty. - Holmes's Ancestry.

3104. Van Liere, Edward J. "Genetics and Sherlock Holmes," *A Doctor Enjoys Sherlock Holmes.* New York: Vantage Press, [1959]. p. 88-95.
"Allusions are made in several of the tales to the subject of genetics—that is, the science of heredity. Many of the observations set forth, although perhaps not entirely acceptable today, are nevertheless intellectually stimulating."

Knowledge of History

3105. Bell, Whitfield, J. "Holmes and History," *BSJ* [OS], 2, No. 4 (October 1947), 447-456.
"Certainly to have judged Holmes's knowledge of history as 'nil' would have been as undiscerning as Watson's estimation of Holmes's literary attainments. The fact simply is that in history Holmes was a student and a scholar who might have honored the faculty of arts at any university."

Knowledge of Languages and Literature

3106. [Bengis, Nathan L.] *Baker Street Rubáiyát*, by Sherlock Holmes (With apologies to Edward FitzGerald). New York: [Privately Printed], 1949. [4] p.
Limited to 100 numbered copies.
———. ———, *SHJ*, 4, No. 2 (Spring 1959), 69.
A parody of the *Rubáiyát* verses, in eight quatrains, as by Sherlock Holmes, in apostrophe to John H. Watson. In *SHJ* there is an introduction citing evidence from *Houn* that Holmes was well acquainted with the FitzGerald translation.

3107. Boyer, Sharon R. "Sherlock Holmes and the Classics," *BSJ*, 12, No. 1 (March 1962), 23-30.
"Of all the scholars who have been attracted and devoted to the Classics, none has ever been as illustrious, and yet, paradoxically, more little known than the

world's greatest detective, Sherlock Holmes." This paper is an attempt to show "the breadth and depth of that interest as it has been recorded in the Canon of Conan."

3108. Dickensheet, Dean W. "Sherlock Holmes—Linguist," *BSJ*, 10, No. 3 (July 1960), 133-142.

"To summarize, Holmes is fluent in English, Idiomatic American, French, German, Italian, Norwegian, and, of necessity, Gaelic. His professional activity shows the necessity for a knowledge of Russian, Swedish, Dutch, and probably Chinese. His travels after Reichenbach required a knowledge of Arabic, but the languages of the Tibeto-Burman group, as well as any other Asian or African tongues, were probably spoken through interpreters. He had a superior knowledge of Latin, and was capable of making comparative studies of ancient Cornish and Chaldean. Without any direct evidence, we may assume that he knew some Greek, some Persian, and had at least some knowledge of the philological antecedents of English, French, and German."

3109. Goslin, Vernon. "Sherlock Holmes and the Shakespearean Canon," *SHJ*, 8, No. 1 (Winter 1966), 12-14.

The Master is revealed as a Shakespearean scholar whose magnum opus might well have been *A Study of the Influence of a German University Education Upon the Behaviour of a Crown Prince of Scandinavia*, with its subtitle: *Some Practical Observations Upon the Crime of Fratricide*.

3110. McLauchlin, Russell. "Sherlock Holmes Was Mr. W. H.," *BSJ*, 9, No. 1 (January 1959), 10-13.

The true author of the Shakespearean plays and sonnets was William (Sherlock) Holmes; written during his hiatus.

3111. Olney, Clarke. "The Literacy of Sherlock Holmes," *SHJ*, 2, No. 4 (Winter 1955), 9-15.

———. ———, *The University of Kansas City Review*, 22, No. 3 (March 1956), 176-180.

Professor Olney adds substantially to the findings of Vernon Rendall (item 2904) and others that Watson seriously undervalued Holmes's knowledge of literature.

3112. Rabe, W. T. "Once More, Watson, into the Breach!" *BSG*, 1, No. 1 (1961), 10-13.

Watson deduces that Holmes is the author of *Henry V!*

3113. Rosenkjar, Patrick R. "Holmes, the Man of Letters," *BSJ*, 15, No. 2 (June 1965), 95, 102.

———. ———, *SIS*, 1, No. 1 (June 1965), 19-21.

"It is absolutely certain that Holmes acquired the varied knowledge of literature, which he demonstrated so often in later years, before he met Watson."

3114. [Vander Rhin, William.] " 'Knowledge of Literature—Nil?' " by J. R. Stefanie [pseud.] *SHJ*, 6, No. 4 (Spring 1964), 120-122.

Contents: 1. Examples of Holmes's Literary Background. - 2. Holmes's Use of the Vernacular in Regard to Literature. - 3. Arguments Against Holmes's Literary Knowledge. - 4. Summary.

3115. Von Krebs, Maria. " 'Knowledge of Literature—Nil.' Indeed?" *BSJ*, 8, No. 3 (July 1958), 149-157.

Passages from the Canon are quoted to show that Holmes had "from at least fair to widely extensive knowledge" of foreign languages, literature, music, and art.

Knowledge of Music

See also *Maza* (items 2546-2547) and *Gilbert and Sullivan* (items 4011-4016)

3116. Barzun, Jacques. "How Holmes Came to Play the Violin," *BSJ*, 1, No. 3 (July 1951), 108-112.

"Holmes played the violin with uncommon skill. Indeed, his technique was so uncommon that he frequently played with the instrument 'thrown across his knee.' . . . At those moments, I submit, Holmes was thinking of his childhood and his mother; he was reproducing something of the atmosphere he had known when he first began to show an interest in music—childish scrapings across the strings of his mother's fiddle, doubtless when she herself had finished practicing."

3117. Berg, Curt. "Sherlock Holmes och musiken" ["Sherlock Holmes and Music"], *Dagens Nyheter* (August 17, 1947).
———. ———, *Fallet Baker Street 111.* Stockholm: Albert Bonniers Forlag, [1951].
———. ———, *BSCL*, No. 2 (July 1963), 5-10.

A discussion of Guy Warrack's book (item 3140) and Holmes's monograph on Lassus.

3118. Boswell, Rolfe. "The Affair of Sherlock's Fiddle—Was Conan Doyle's Holmes a Violinist or Violist?" *The Musical Digest*, 30, No. 7 (August-September 1948), 6-7, 25.
———. "Quick, Watson, the Fiddle," *BSJ* [OS], 3, No. 4 (October 1948), 435-440.

"Writers who deal in musical terminology often complain that printers and proofreaders appear to be unaware that the violin's darkling congener is spelt 'viola.' There, then, is the solution to the problem of the unorthodox fiddling position. Holmes played the viola!"

3119. Boucher, Anthony. "The Records of Baker Street," *BSJ* [OS], 4, No. 1 (January 1949), 97-104.

An exhaustive study of the recordings that might have been acquired by Holmes and Watson.

3120. Christie, Winifred M. "Some Reflections on That Little Thing of Chopin's," *Leaves from the Copper Beeches*. Narberth, Pa.: Livingston Pub. Co., 1959. p. 81-89.

A careful search through the works of Chopin reveals that the melody in question is the A-minor Etude, Op. 25, No. 11.

3121. Clarkson, Paul S. " 'In the Beginning . . . ,' " *BSJ*, 8, No. 4 (October 1958), 197-209.

An attempt to prove by the recorded musical history of the period that Stud began on Saturday, March 5, 1881.

3122. Grosbayne, Benjamin. "Sherlock Holmes—Musician," *BSJ* [OS], 3, No. 1 (January 1948), 47-57.

"This side of his nature, the artistic, which he always kept carefully concealed, is best understood when we consider him as a musician."

3123. ——. "To Sherlock Holmes —Violinist," *BSJ* [OS], 2, No. 1 (January 1947), 26-27.

"So here's an artless triolin / To Sherlock Holmes's violin!"

3124. Grudeff, Marian, and Raymond Jessel. "The Avant-Garde on Baker Street," *New York Herald Tribune Magazine* (May 9, 1965), 43.

"The fact that the great sleuth was a composer of genius is a matter that seems to have escaped the attention of most students of Holmesian lore."

3125. Hall, Trevor H. "Sherlock Holmes, Madness and Music," *Sherlock Holmes: Ten Literary Studies*. London: Gerald Duckworth & Co., [1969]. Chap. 6, p. 86-92.

The author is critical of Guy Warrack (item 3140) for suggesting that Holmes was a schizophrenic (an opinion based on his behavior while listening to a Sarasate violin sonata in RedH) and that he did not write a monograph on the Polyphonic Motets of Lassus.

3126. Kennedy, Bruce. "The Sound of Music," *SOS*, 1, No. 6 (August 1967), 4.

Holmes played both the violin and the debro guitar—the latter instrument is played over the knee!

3127. Kjell, Bradley. "How Holmes Helped Select a Stradivarius," *SOS*, 2, No. 3 (February 1968), 4-5.

The author tells how he purchased a violin

modeled after the Stradivarius owned by Sarasate!

3128. McMahon, Thomas P. ["Fiddle Riddle"], *The New York Times* (March 28, 1965), II, 15.

——. ——, *BSJ*, 15, No. 2 (June 1965), 126.

An addendum to "Tra-la-la-lira-lira-lay," by Harold Schonberg.

3129. Montgomery, James. "What Is This Thing Called Music? (or Body and Soul)," *Art in the Blood, and What Is This Thing Called Music? (or Body and Soul)*. [Philadelphia: Privately Printed, 1950.] [unpaged]

——. ——, *BSJ*, 1, No. 4 (October 1951), 144-145.

——. ——, First stanza tr. into Danish by A. D. Henriksen. *Sangen om Baker Street*. København: [Grafisk Cirkel], 1958. p. 11. Reprinted in *Sherlockiana*, 3, Nr. 3-4 (1958), 10.

"When Sherlock Holmes began to brood, / And things were getting dreary, / His violin revealed his mood / (The chords were weird and eerie)."

3130. Officer, Harvey. "Sherlock Holmes and Music," *221B: Studies in Baker Street*. Edited by Vincent Starrett. New York: The Macmillan Co., 1940. p. 71-73.

"Diligent search has failed to unearth a copy of that precious monograph [on the Polyphonic Motets of Orlando di Lasso]. The name of Sherlock Holmes does not occur in *Grove's Dictionary of Music*. In spite of these facts we are clearly justified in ranking Holmes among the great musicologists of our time."

3131. Ohman, Anders R. "Violinisten på 221 Baker Street" ["The Violin Player of 221 Baker Street"], *Svenska Dagbladet* (July 28, 1957).

——. ——, *BSCL*, No. 2 (July 1963), 21-26.

A discussion of Holmes's Lassus monograph and Decca's LP record *Doctor Watson Meets Sherlock Holmes* (item 5560).

3132. Roberts, S. C. "The Music of Baker Street," *The Oxford Magazine*, 65, No. 15 (May 1, 1947), 273-275.

——. ——, *BSJ* [OS], 2, No. 4 (October 1947), 429-432.

——. "Sherlock Holmes: His Music," *Holmes and Watson: A Miscellany*. London: Oxford University Press, 1953. p. 45-50.

A review of Guy Warrack's *Sherlock Holmes and Music*.

3133. Rosenkjar, Pat. "Holmes and Tchaikovsky," *SIS*, 1, No. 3 (1966), 21-23, 26.

"Holmes not only enjoyed good music,

but also the friendship of the greatest musical genius of the later nineteenth century, Peter Ilyich Tchaikovsky."

3134. Rybrant, Gösta. "Fallet tra-la-la-lira-lira-lay" ["The Case of . . ."], *Aftonbladet* (December 26, 1953).
———. ———, *BSCL*, No. 2 (July 1963), 13-20.
"That little thing of Chopin's" is identified as Sarasate's E-major transcription of Chopin's Nocturne in E-flat major.

3135. Schonberg, Harold C. "Tra-la-la-lira-lira-lay," *The New York Times* (March 7, 1965), II, 11.
———. ———, *BSJ*, 15, No. 2 (June 1965), 83-85.
The senior music critic of *The New York Times* identifies the instrument Holmes played across his knees as the vielle, and the piece by Chopin as the first of the Polish Songs—"The Maiden's Wish."

3136. Smith, William. " 'That Little Thing of Chopin's:' The Laying of the Ghost," *BSJ*, 13, No. 1 (March 1963), 24-30.
Primarily a discussion of Mrs. Christie's article in which the author concludes that the "little thing of Chopin's" was not the A-minor Etude but the Fourth Polonaise, in C minor.

3137. Starr, Herbert W. "Sherlock Holmes, Violin-Player," *BSJ*, 13, No. 1 (March 1963), 37-38.
"If we assume that Holmes possessed an opporable big toe—that is, a prehensile foot—he could indeed have held and played the violin in the manner which Watson described."

3138. Svensson, Sven E. "Brev till Curt Berg" ["Letter to Curt Berg"], *BSCL*, No. 2 (July 1963), 11-12.
A commentary on Berg's article and the Motets of Lassus.

3139. Wait, Richard. "The Case of the Neophyte and the Motet," *The Second Cab*. Edited by James Keddie. [Boston: The Speckled Band, 1947.] p. 70-72.
The author tells of his search for a meaningful definition of the polyphonic motets that Holmes wrote about in his learned monograph.

3140. Warrack, Guy. *Sherlock Holmes and Music*. London: Faber and Faber Ltd., [1947]. 56 p.
———. ———, *SHJ*, 9, No. 4 (Summer 1970), 114-117; 10, No. 1 (Winter 1970), 7-12; 10, No. 2 (Summer 1971), 39-44.
A penetrating study of the Master as a concertgoer, composer, and violinist by a conductor, composer, and past chairman of the Sherlock Holmes Society.

3141. White, William Braid. "Sherlock Holmes and the Equal Temperament," *BSJ* [OS], 1, No. 1 (January 1946), 39-43.
A scholarly analysis of the Master's musical capacities that explains his choice of the violin as his medium of expression.

3142. [Wolff, Julian.] "Just What Was That Thing of Chopin's?" *BSJ*, 13, No. 1 (March 1963), 3-4. (The Editor's Gas-Lamp)
After listing seven items on the subject and the conclusions reached by each author, Dr. Wolff offers his own non-musical suggestion that "when Watson wrote 'Tra-la-la-lira-lira-lay,' he was not quoting Holmes (or Chopin) at all, but was merely misquoting Tennyson."

3143. Zeisler, Ernest B. "Tra-la-la-lira-lira-lay," *SHJ*, 4, No. 1 (Winter 1958), 11-12.
A refutation of Paul Clarkson's position (item 3121) that Stud began a day later than Friday, March 4, 1881—the date assigned by Dr. Zeisler. He also identifies the tune Holmes sang in the cab as Chopin's Waltz in E minor. (A discussion of the article appears in letters to the editor from Eric H. Thiman, Ernest B. Zeisler, and Bernard Davies on p. 78-80 and 105-106 of the same volume.)

Knowledge of Nature

See also *Sherlock Holmes — Retirement* (items 3220-3238)

3144. Crocker, Stephen F. "Sherlock Holmes's Appreciation of Nature," *Philological Papers*, 6 [*West Virginia University Bulletin*, Series 49, No. 12-V, June 1949], 86-99.
"Appreciation of nature found a definite place among Holmes's many gifts. The evidence—revealed by Watson, attested by Mycroft, and confirmed by Holmes—is conclusive. If some doubting Thomas objects by taking the anti-sleuthistic view that the trio never existed and that the Writings are mere fiction, let him be spared from such heresy by heeding the testimony of Basil Rathbone [item 3230]. He visited Holmes in the summer of 1946, and found him living close to nature in a thatched cottage on the Sussex Downs."

3145. McGaw, Lisa. "Some Trifling Notes on Sherlock Holmes and Ornithology," *BSJ*, 10, No. 4 (October 1960), 231-234.
"It is my own belief that Holmes has a keen interest in birds—aren't the birds and the bees a natural combination?—and the lack of reference in the Canon to this interest does not surprise me. How much evidence is there of Holmes's bee-keeping proclivities before his retirement?"

Knowledge of Philosophy
[Including His Religious and Philosophical Beliefs]

3146. Crocker, Stephen F. "Sherlock Holmes Recommends Winwood Reade," *BSJ*, 14, No. 3 (September 1964), 142-144.

Passages from Reade's *The Martyrdom of Man* are quoted and compared with some of Holmes's philosophical pronouncements in order to show how the book helped confirm the Master's own agnostic beliefs.

3147. Folsom, Henry T. " 'My Biblical Knowledge Is a Trifle Rusty . . . ,' " *BSJ*, 15, No. 3 (September 1965), 174-182.

Winner of the 8th annual Morley-Montgomery Memorial Award for the best contribution to *BSJ* in 1965.

"Is it really possible to define Holmes's religious beliefs at all? To a limited degree it is; at least, working at it negatively, we can discover several things which he was not. Holmes was not a Buddhist or even greatly influenced by Buddhism in any of its three major forms: Mahayana, Hinayana, or Lamanism. Nor was he a Roman Catholic—at least certainly not a practicing one. But beyond these two observations we tread on very uncertain ground. Still, it does not seem that Holmes was a freethinker; that would imply atheism."

3148. Harris, A. Francis. ["Letter"], *BSJ*, 15, No. 4 (December 1965), 246-247.

An argument favoring Holmes's Buddhist leanings; but still denied by Rev. Folsom in a letter on p. 247 of the same issue.

3149. Hertzberg, Francis. " 'There Is Nothing in Which Deduction Is So Necessary as in Religion,' " *The Liberal Catholic*, 37, No. 2 (June 1968), 56-58.

3150. Jones, Kelvin. "That Deep Romantic Chasm," *SHJ*, 9, No. 2 (Summer 1969), 57-59.

Similarities between the Master's philosophical beliefs and those of Samuel Taylor Coleridge and Thomas Carlyle.

3151. Lauterbach, Charles E. "In Pessimistic Mood," *BSJ*, 11, No. 4 (December 1961), 241.

" 'But is not all life pathetic and futile?' " (Holmes)

"We reach, we strive; we strain so hard / To grasp some shining prize / To find at last that we have seized / A bauble in disguise."

3152. Marshall, Leslie. "Behind the Abbey Door: A Meditation Upon the Religious and Philosophical Beliefs of Sherlock Holmes," *A Baker Street Four-Wheeler*. Edited by Edgar W. Smith. [Maplewood, N.J., and New York: The Pamphlet House, 1944.] p. 20-24.

"An account, with some marginalia, of the Master's Sunday school upbringing, his devoutness in the face of disbelief, and his manifest familiarity with both the Old and New Testaments."

3153. ————. "Sherlock Holmes, Philosopher," *BSJ*, 19, No. 1 (March 1969), 38-40.

An analysis of some philosophical statements made by a great detective and a potentially great philosopher.

3154. [Morley, Christopher.] "Sherlock Holmes's Religion," [by] Horace Reynolds Stahl [pseud.] *The Saturday Review of Literature*, 10, No. 35 (March 17, 1934), 559. (The Bowling Green)

Instances of his religious tendencies.

3155. Rosenberger, Edgar S. "The Religious Sherlock Holmes," *BSJ* [OS], 3, No. 2 (April 1948), 138-147.

"It is in the field of homiletics that we perceive the truly religious nature of Sherlock Holmes. Again and again throughout the tales we see Holmes the philosopher, Holmes the theologian, Holmes the humble minister of the gospel. Even as the prophets of old, he pondered the infinite mysteries of life, and sought an answer."

3156. Rosenblum, Morris. "The Horatian Spirit in Holmes," *Illustrious Client's Third Case-Book*. Edited by J. N. Williamson and H. B. Williams. [Indianapolis, Ind.: The Illustrious Clients, 1953.] p. 119-126.

"The Horatian influence strongly affected Holmes' thinking and way of life."

3157. Schutz, Robert H. *"Do You Know the Young Lady?"* [Pittsburgh]: The Arnsworth Castle Business Index, 1961. [2] p.

Limited to 12 copies.

"Since *The Martyrdom of Man* was first published in 1872, it would have been available to Holmes during that critical period of 1878 to 1880. It may have been the deciding factor in his drawing away from the Church, and his separation from home and family."

3158. Watson, John Gillard. "The Religion of Sherlock Holmes," *The Literary Guide*, 70, No. 12 (December 1955), 12-14.

"The evidence is clear that before *The Final Problem*, Holmes was a rationalist; the evidence for a religious outlook comes *after* that adventure. Perhaps this was the effect of Tibet, not to mention Mecca; or merely a decline in his critical faculties. Whatever his later opinions, Holmes was undoubtedly not religious until after his travels abroad, following the Moriarty adventure."

3159. Williams, Anthony L. "Sherlock Holmes and Religion: With a Note on His Early Life and Eccentricities," *SHJ*, 8, No. 2 (Spring 1967), 44-46.

"Sherlock Holmes embraced a number of religions, and, ever willing to learn ('Education never ends, Watson'), a person such as he would require almost a complete life-time to come to a satisfactory conclusion based on the consideration of all the data." (A criticism of the article appears in a letter to the editor by John Gillard Watson on p. 67 of vol. 9 and a reply by A. L. Williams on p. 109-110 of vol. 9.)

Knowledge of Phrenology and Physiognomy

3160. McDade, Thomas M. "Heads and Holmes," *BSJ*, 11, No. 3 (September 1961), 162-166.

Holmes, an apparent believer in the principles of phrenology, is the subject of a phrenological analysis. The article is illustrated with a phrenological head of the Master by Edward Turner.

3161. Stern, Madeleine B. "The Game's a Head, or Holmes's Curious Faculties (Skullduggery and the Great Hiatus)," *BSJ*, 20, No. 3 (September 1970), 157-165.

Sherlock Holmes's phrenological studies are considered as the whetstone for his science of detection and as the logical outgrowth of his interest in physiognomy, temperament and craniology. His relations with the well-known phrenologists, Lorenzo Fowler and the latter's daugher Jessie, are discussed, as well as his self-analysis. It is indicated that Holmes practiced phrenology during the period of the Great Hiatus. The article concludes with Jessie Fowler's phrenological analysis of Doyle, reprinted from *The Phrenological Journal* of April 1897.

Knowledge of Politics

3162. Mackay, Ian. " 'Knowledge of Politics—Feeble?' " *SHJ*, 1, No. 2 (September 1952), 25-30.

Evidence that this appraisal of Watson's was wrong. Holmes is identified as a Liberal with socialist leanings, a pacifist, a Union-Now advocate, and a "League of Nations man when Woodrow Wilson was in rompers."

3163. Metcalfe, N. Percy. "Holmes and Politics—A Retrospection," *SHJ*, 1, No. 4 (December 1953), 11-19.

A reconsideration of his interest, if any, in politics, in light of Mr. Mackay's article.

3164. Williamson, J. N. "Sherlock Holmes: Patriot," *SHJ*, 3. No. 2 (Winter 1956), 19.

Speculation on the virtues of patriotism "as exemplified by one of England's foremost citizens."

Knowledge of Sports and Games

See also *Fina* (items 2412-2449)

3165. Baring-Gould, William S. "Sherlock Holmes, Sportsman," *Sports Illustrated*, 18, No. 21 (May 27, 1963), 34-46.

"The definitive article on the subject and a major contribution to the literature; in elegant format, illustrated with some very original etchings by T. B. Allen." (Julian Wolff)

3166. Blegen, Theodore C. "Along Comes Charles—or Was Sherlock Holmes a Sportsman?" *Sherlock Holmes: Master Detective*. Edited by Theodore C. Blegen & E. W. McDiarmid. La Crosse: Printed for the Norwegian Explorers, St. Paul & Minneapolis, 1952. p. 21-35.

A cursory review, and refutation in the person of Charles, of Holmes's sportsmanship and his prowess in boxing, fencing, card playing, and hunting and marksmanship.

3167. Evans, Webster. "Sherlock Holmes and Sport," *SHJ*, 2, No. 3 (Summer 1955), 35-42.

A discussion of his known and theoretical sports, games and pastimes, including one of the author's pet theories—"that Holmes is now a keen golfer and was always a secret one."

3168. Fage-Pedersen, Anders. *Sportsmanden Sherlock Holmes eller Afhang Englands skaebne af de tyrkiske bade?* [The Sportsman Sherlock Holmes, or Did the Fate of England Depend on the Turkish Baths?] Bilag til [Supplement to] *Sherlockiana*, 8, Nr. 3-4 (1963). 6 p.

3169. Hand, Herbert T. "Where Did You Get That Hat . . . Band?" *BSJ* [OS], 4, No. 1 (January 1949), 18-23.

————. ————, *The Third Cab*. [Boston: The Speckled Band, 1960.] p. 59-63.

"Holmes a boxing Blue, Mr. Morley? . . . indeed yes, but a jumping Blue, a running Blue and a fencing Blue also! A 'four letter' man without benefit of consonants or vowels."

3170. Holroyd, James Edward. "Holmes, Man of Action," *The Observer* [London] (June 16, 1968).

————. ————, *Sherlockiana*, 15, Nr. 1-2 (1970), 4.

3171. Johnson, Edward R. "Did Sherlock Holmes Practice Yoga?" *BSJ*, 17, No. 1 (March 1967), 13-14.

A question answered in the affirmative, of course.

3172. Morrow, L. A. "The Game Is . . . ," *BSJ*, 7, No. 1 (January 1957), 32-38.

"Without a doubt Holmes's game was whist, and his devotion to it must have been exceedingly great."

3173. Olin, Ola. "Hommage to the Sherlock Muse," *BSCL*, No. 6 (1968), 29-30.
Text in Swedish.
A commentary on the Master's ability as a swordsman.

3174. Petersen, Svend. "When the Game Was Not Afoot," *BSJ* [OS], 4, No. 1 (January 1949), 59-71.
After citing several references to support his thesis that Holmes was a master chess player, the author fabricates a set of chessmen from the pages of the Conanical Writings.

3175. Schonberg, Harold. "Yet Another Case of Identity," *SHJ*, 6, No. 4 (Spring 1964), 115-118.
Watson avoided any mention of Holmes's ability as a chess player in order to cover up the fact that in 1895 Holmes impersonated the American chess player Harry Nelson Pillsbury at the Hastings Tournament.

3176. Scott, Henry D. "Missing Three-Quarter One-Third Discovered," *BSJ* [OS], 2, No. 1 (January 1947), 13-15.
The story of how Holmes made quarterback on the All-time, All-literary football team.

3177. Sturm, Claes. "Var Sherlock Holmes framstaende idrottsman?" ["Was Sherlock Holmes an Outstanding Sportsman?"] *All Sport* (April 15, 1956).
————. ————, *BSCL*, No. 3 (1964), 4-6.
A discussion of his sports activities, with the question left unanswered.

3178. Van Liere, Edward J. "Sherlock Holmes and Doctor Watson, Perennial Athletes," *BSJ*, 6, No. 3 (July 1956), 155-164.
————. ————, *A Doctor Enjoys Sherlock Holmes*. New York: Vantage Press, [1959]. p. 117-126.
Dr. Van Liere cites several examples to show that Holmes and Watson were men of superior strength and exceptional stamina, and then deliberates on the question, left unanswered, of how these two men were able to keep themselves in such good physical condition when neither engaged in any form of regular exercise.

3179. Webster, H. T. "Observations on Sherlock Holmes as an Athlete and Sportsman," *BSJ* [OS], 3, No. 1 (January 1948), 24-31. illus.
"No reader of the Sacred Writings can fail to note, as did Dr. Watson, that Sherlock Holmes possessed a considerable degree of natural athleticism, and that he was an adept at several athletic skills. Very early in the canon Watson puts on record his illustrious friend's ability as a singlestick player, a boxer, and swordsman."

3180. [Williamson, J. N.] "Sherlock Holmes and Boxing," by the Northumberland. *Illustrious Client's Case-Book*. Edited by J. N. Williamson and H. B. Williams. [Indianapolis, Ind.: The Illustrious Clients, 1948.] p. 55-56.
Quotations from the Canon testifying to the Master's pugilistic ability.

3181. Wincor, Richard. "The Sherlock Holmes Opening," *BSJ*, 15, No. 2 (June 1965), 92-94.
An article on the opening devised by the Master chess player to defeat Vigor, the Hammersmith wonder, mentioned in Suss, and identified as Anton Vigorsky, a five-year-old chess prodigy residing in Hammersmith.

PERSONALITY

See also *Psychological and Sexual Interpretations* (items 4236-4241)

3182. Astrachan, Boris M., and Sandra Boltax. "The Cyclical Disorder of Sherlock Holmes," *The Journal of the American Medical Association*, 196, No. 12 (June 20, 1966), 1094.
————. ————, *CPBook*, 2, No. 7-8 (Winter-Spring 1966), 130.
In a letter to the editor, Drs. Astrachan and Boltax advance the hypothesis that Holmes suffered from a manic-depressive disorder. This would account for his alternating periods of lethargy and activity.

3183. Blegen, Theodore C. "These Were Hidden Fires, Indeed!" *Exploring Sherlock Holmes*. Edited by E. W. McDiarmid & Theodore C. Blegen. La Crosse: Sumac Press, 1957. p. 9-26.
A delightful essay on the emotional, unmachinelike traits of Holmes.

3184. Chieco, Lorenzo J. "The Signature of Sherlock Holmes," *BSJ*, 3, No. 3 (July 1953), 157-159.
This "Certified Grapho-Analytical Psychologist" has been able to reconstruct the Master's signature from an analysis of his character and personality traits.

3185. Delblanc, Sven. "Baker Street 221 B—Sodom and Gomorrah!" *BSCL*, No. 4 (1965), 25-26.
A Freudian look at the "dark regions of Mr. Holmes' life."

3186. Fage-Pedersen, Anders. "Neurotikeren Sherlock Holmes: Nogle betragtninger over Mesterens sjaeleliv" ["The Neurotic Sherlock Holmes: Some Considerations on the Master's Life of the Soul"],

Sherlockiana, 3, Nr. 3-4 (1958), 14-15.

———. ———, *Sherlock Holmes Årbog* III (1967), 71-76.

Dr. Fage-Pedersen believes that Holmes suffered from an inferiority complex which he overcame through the mechanism of overcompensation.

3187. Hartman, Harry. "Sacred Litany," *BSG*, 1, No. 4 (April 1962), 27-32.

———. ———, *The Holy Quire.* [Culver City, Calif.: Luther Norris, December 1970.] p. 9-13.

An essay on his character and personality in the form of a political nominating speech.

3188. Johnson, E. Randolph. "The Human Mr. Holmes," *BSP*, No. 36 (June 1968), 2-3; No. 37 (July 1968), 5-6.

3189. Kallis, Stephen A. "The Secret of Sherlock Holmes," Illustrated by Donna Wilson. *BSJ*, 17, No. 4 (December 1967), 214-218.

He was able to change into a cat—a werecat!

3190. Leiber, Fritz. "Scoundrel and Meddler," *PD*, 2, No. 3 (August 1969), 1, 3-4.

A scathing depth analysis of "the first modern Englishman to drop out and turn on."

3191. [Smith, Edgar W.] "The Softer Holmes," *BSJ*, 7, No. 1 (January 1957), 3-4. (The Editor's Gas-Lamp)

"Sherlock Holmes was, underneath, a soft and poetic man. The mask did not slip often, but when it did, it showed a real worth that even Watson could not conceal."

3192. Vash, George. "The States of Exhaustion of Mr. Sherlock Holmes," *The Journal of the American Medical Association*, 197, No. 8 (August 22, 1966), 664-665.

Dr. Vash points out in contradiction to the hypothesis set forth by Drs. Astrachan and Boltax that occasional inertia in a man of creativity is not so unusual and in Holmes's case is far less than would occur in a manic-depressive.

3193. Wallace, David A. "Sherlock Holmes, the First Hippie," *BSJ*, 19, No. 1 (March 1969), 46-47.

A convincing argument that he was a hip Bohemian, or, in current parlance, a "hippie."

3194. Williamson, J. N. *Sherlock Holmes: A New Kind of Analysis.* Lawrence, Ind.: The Mary Neal Co., 1969. [16] p.

Limited to 94 numbered copies.

A monograph that could have been entitled *From Sherlock Holmes to Astrology and Back Again.* The author's interest in and writings about the Master Sleuth have resulted in his becoming a professional writer specializing in astrology. Mr. Williamson contributed an article on Holmes and astrology in 1962, and it is only natural that he should return to make another and major contribution in which he demonstrates that "the astrological natal chart of Sherlock Holmes, born January 6, 1854, *fits* him perfectly."

3195. ———. "The Star-Crossed Personality of Sherlock Holmes," *BSJ*, 12, No. 3 (September 1962), 163-168.

"So it is that Sherlock Holmes . . . has the vast majority of characteristics, positive and negative, of an astrological native of the birth of Capricorn."

PROTOTYPE — DR. JOSEPH BELL

See also *The Literary Agent*
(items 3906-3984) and
Literary Parallels and Comparisons
(items 3985-4092)

3196. Bigelow, S. Tupper. "In Defense of Joseph Bell," *BSJ*, 10, No. 4 (October 1960), 207-212.

A criticism of Adrian Conan Doyle's "ridiculous hypothesis" that his father was the prototype of Sherlock Holmes.

3197. Donegall, [Lord]. "Filial Three-Pipe Dream," *SHJ*, 3, No. 2 (Winter 1956), 1, 11.

An editorial on Irving Wallace's essay (item 3209) and the exchange of letters, quoted therein, that followed between Adrian Conan Doyle, Irving Wallace, and J. L. H. Stisted.

Dr. Joseph Bell, of Edinburgh, often considered to have been the model for Sherlock Holmes. (3196-3209).

3198. Doyle, Adrian Conan. "Apropos Dr. Bell," *Saturday Review of Literature,* 31, No. 32 (August 7, 1948), 23.

In a letter to the editor, Sir Arthur's son calls attention to "the old and exploded fable that Dr. Bell was the originator of Sherlock Holmes."

3199. Guthrie, Douglas. "Dr. Bell of Edinburgh," *The Scotsman* (May 23, 1959).
————. ————, *BSJ,* 13, No. 4 (December 1963), 202-204.

"Sherlock Holmes was indeed fortunate in being depicted from a model of such nobility and merit, and it is only fitting that, in paying a centenary tribute to Sir Arthur Conan Doyle, we should remember and honour the teacher who inspired much of his creative work." (A full-page photograph of Dr. Bell appears on p. 201 of *BSJ.*)

3200. Handasyde. "The Real Sherlock Holmes," *Good Words and Sunday Magazine* [London] (1902), 159-163. illus.

"Dr. Joseph Bell, with his public and private reputation, occupies a unique position; and it is matter for lively conjecture which he values most, the fame of the kind Scottish surgeon that has given him so firm a place in the hearts of Midlothian, or the more world-wide reputation achieved by the cosmopolitan detective, Sherlock Holmes."

3201. Harnagel, Edward F. "Doctors Afield: Joseph Bell, M.D.—The Real Sherlock Holmes," *The New England Journal of Medicine,* 258, No. 23 (June 5, 1958), 1158-1159.

A critique on the life of Dr. Bell, including a bibliography with clinical and biographical sources.

3202. Jones, Harold Emery. "The Original of Sherlock Holmes," *Collier's,* 32, No. 15 (January 9, 1904), 14-15, 20.
————. ————, *Conan Doyle's Best Books.* New York: P. F. Collier & Son, [n. d.] Vol. 1, p. i-xii.
————.————, *The Boys' Sherlock Holmes.* New York: Harper & Brothers, 1936. p. 85-90.
————. ————, ————. New and enlarged edition. New York and Evanston: Harper & Row, [1961]. p. 85-90.
————. ————, *A Cavalcade of Collier's.* Edited by Kenneth McArdle. New York: A. S. Barnes & Co., [1959] p. 74-78.
"The writer was a fellow-student of Conan Doyle. Together they attended the surgical demonstrations of Joseph Bell, at the Edinburgh Royal Infirmary. This man exhibited incredibly acute and sure deductive powers in diagnosis and in guessing the vocation of patients from external signs. Sir Henry Little-John, another medical lecturer heard by the two students, was remarkable for his sagacious expert testimony, leading to the conviction of many a criminal. Thus is the character of Sherlock Holmes easily and naturally accounted for, and the absurd fiction that Conan Doyle drew upon Poe for his ideas is silenced forever."

3203. "The Original of Sherlock Holmes," *The Book Buyer,* 11, No. 2 (March 1894), 61-64.

A well-illustrated article reciting many of the familiar facts and parallels.

3204. Saxby, Jessie M. E. *Joseph Bell, M.D., F.R.C.S., J.P., D.L., Etc.* An appreciation by an old friend. With eleven illustrations. Edinburgh and London: Oliphant, Anderson & Ferrier, 1913. 92 p.

"When first Conan Doyle's remarkable creation brought its author fame he informed the public that (when a student at Edinburgh) he found the prototype of Sherlock Holmes in his admired professional 'chief,' Dr. Joseph Bell. . . . Rather unfortunately the world was led to understand that the two personalities were identical in every respect, and since Dr. Bell's death in October 1911 the Press has unwittingly given more and more weight to the mistaken representation of a good man's personality, and that must be the excuse of one who knew him intimately for now venturing to recall some reminiscences which will show his absolute *un*likeness, save in one respect, to Conan Doyle's masterpiece."
Review: SHJ, 8, No. 4 (Summer 1968), 119-120 (Nathan L. Bengis).

3205. Scarlett, E. P. "The Genesis of a Legend," *Historical Bulletin* [Calgary Associate Clinic], 9, No. 4 (February 1945), 79-82.

"A further note on Dr. Joseph Bell and Sherlock Holmes." (Subtitle)

3206. ————. "The Old Original," *Historical Bulletin* [Calgary Associate Clinic], 8, No. 3. (November 1943), 5-10.
————. ————, *BSJ,* 13, No. 4 (December 1963), 205-209.

"Notes on Dr. Joseph Bell whose personality and peculiar abilities suggested the creation of Sherlock Holmes." (Subtitle) Includes some personal recollections of Dr. Bell by Z. M. Hamilton, as set forth in two letters, and by Robert Louis Stevenson in a letter dated April 5, 1893.

3207. Smith, Sir Sydney. "Dr. Bell and Sherlock Holmes," *Mostly Murder.* With a foreword by The Hon. Lord Cameron. London: George G. Harrap & Co. Ltd., [1959]. Chap. 2, p. 28-39.
————. ————, ————. With a foreword by Erle Stanley Gardner. New York: David McKay Co., [1959]. Chap. 2, p. 28-39.

Part of this chapter deals with the method of deductive reasoning used by these two men.

3208. Starrett, Vincent. "Dr. Bell and Dr. Black," *BSJ*, 7, No. 4 (October 1957), 197-203.

A commentary on "the accepted prototype of Sherlock Holmes," together with five letters from Dr. Bell to his friend Dr. Hugh Black.

3209. Wallace, Irving. "The Incredible Dr. Bell." *The Saturday Review of Literature*, 31, No. 18 (May 1, 1948), 7-8, 28.

————. ————, [Condensed] *The Reader's Digest*, 52, No. 314 (June 1948), 119-121.

————. ————, *The Saturday Review Gallery*. Selected from the complete files by Jerome Beatty, Jr., and the Editors of The Saturday Review. New York: Simon and Schuster, 1959. p. 107-113.

————. Revised and enlarged with title: "The Real Sherlock Holmes," *The Fabulous Originals: Lives of Extraordinary People Who Inspired Memorable Characters in Fiction*. New York: Alfred A. Knopf. 1955. p. 22-45.

————. ————, ————. London: Longmans, Green and Co., [1956]. Chap. 2, p. 18-39.

————. ————, *The Sunday Gentleman*. New York: Simon and Schuster, 1965. p. 392-415.

The Sunday Gentleman includes a ten-page afterword entitled "What Has Happened Since . . ." in which the author relates the literary controversy that raged between him and Adrian Conan Doyle as to who was actually the prototype of Sherlock Holmes—Dr. Joseph Bell or Sir Arthur Conan Doyle. A further refutation by Adrian Conan Doyle of Mr. Wallace's claim appears in *SHJ*, 7, No. 4 (Spring 1966), 130-131.

QUOTATIONS

3210. Rosenblum, Morris. "The Quotable Holmes," *BSJ* [OS], 2, No. 3 (July 1947), 263-268.

Except for *The Oxford Dictionary of Quotations* (item 3218), the books of quotations have failed to include the wise sayings of Sherlock Holmes.

3211. "Doctor Watson Speaks," *Sherlockian Studies*. Edited by Robert A. Cutter. [Jackson Heights, N.Y.: The Baker Street Press, 1947.] p. 32-34.

Twenty-five quotations about Watson and Holmes.

3212. *Holmes.* [Compiled by Mo Lebowitz. North Bellmore, N.Y.: The Antique Press, 1964.] [8] p.

Limited to 90 copies.

A beautifully printed and illustrated brochure containing "a few terse observations and philosophies of Mr. Sherlock Holmes."

3213. *My Life with Sherlock Holmes: Conversations in Baker Street,* by John H. Watson, M.D. Edited by J. R. Hamilton. London: John Murray, [1968]. 105 p. illus.

Contents: Editor's Foreword. - Our First Meeting. - The Man Holmes. - His Interests and Tastes. - The Detective. - On Human Nature. - Holmes and Myself. - Epilogue. - Index.

The editor has skillfully woven the confidential conversations between Holmes and Watson into a continuous narrative so that a self-portrait of Holmes is revealed as well as the complete character of Watson.

Reviews: BSP, No. 54 (July 1970), 4 (Glen Holland); *SHJ*, 9, No. 1 (Winter 1968), 28 (Lord Donegall); *Sherlockiana*, 13, Nr. 4 (1968), 16.

3214. "The Opinions of Mr. Sherlock Holmes," [Compiled] by Fred Walter. *BSJ*, 9, No. 4 (October 1959), 223-225.

Quotations from the Sacred Writings on what he thought about some of his more famous cases.

3215. "The Science of Deduction," *101 Years' Entertainment: The Great Detective Stories, 1841-1941*. Edited by Ellery Queen. Boston: Little, Brown and Co., 1941. p. 22-44.

"A cento of the four most famous Holmesian deductions, distilling the very essence of the Master: (1) The Episode of Dr. Watson's Watch; (2) Holmes the Mind Reader; (3) The Secrets of Dr. Mortimer's Walking-Stick; and (4) The Affair of the Porlock Letter."

3216. "Sherlock Holmes Speaks," *A Baker Street Four-Wheeler*. Edited by Edgar W. Smith. [Maplewood, N.J., and New York: The Pamphlet House, 1944.] p. 71-75.

Fifty-two quotations from the Master.

3217. "Sidelights on Sherlock Holmes, as Revealed in Some Characteristic *Obiter Dicta,*" *Sherlock Holmes: Fact or Fiction?* by T. S. Blakeney. London: John Murray, [1932]. p. 116-129.

A comparison of his remarks on the art of deduction, life, women, etc.

3218. "Sir Arthur Conan Doyle, 1859-1930," *The Oxford Dictionary of Quotations.* Second edition. London; New York: Oxford University Press, 1959. p. 187-188.

Forty-six quotations from the Canonical tales.

3219. *The Whole Art of Detection,* by Sherlock Holmes. Compiled by John Bennett Shaw. Introduction by Vincent Starrett. [Design & topography by Norman W. Forgue.] Chicago: Black Cat Press, [1968]. [51] p.

Limited miniature edition with a profile in relief of Holmes on the cover.

Contents: Preface. - Introduction. - Book 1. Sherlock Holmes on the Art of Detection. - Book 2. Sherlock Holmes and the Practical Application of the Art. - Appendix.

"This little book is a small attempt, indeed, to fill the gap left by Holmes's unpublished reference work. The entire canon, the sixty published stories recounting the cases of Mr. Holmes, was carefully combed for directions, explications and musings upon his art, which *was* The Whole Art of Detection. In all but a very few instances these are direct statements by Sherlock Holmes himself." (Preface)

RETIREMENT

3220. Ball, John. "The Case of the Elderly Actor," *BSJ*, 9, No. 4. (October 1959), 209-222.

Teddy Fairchild, a young American reporter on his first assignment, is sent to England to interview Holmes on his one hundred and fifth birthday. An actor is hired for the occasion to impersonate Holmes. Teddy is in on the gag, and is asked to interview him as though he were actually the detective. The reporter returns to New York only to discover that he missed interviewing the actor and interviewed the real Sherlock Holmes.

3221. Ballou, Norman V. "Top Secret," *The Third Cab.* [Boston: The Speckled Band, 1960.] p. 48-51.

Speculations on the activities of Holmes since his supposed retirement.

3222. Baring-Gould, William S. " 'The Friends of Mr. Sherlock Holmes Will Be Glad to Learn That He Is Still Alive and Well . . . ,' " *SOS*, 1, No. 4 (April 1967), 5-12.

———. ———, *The Annotated Sherlock Holmes.* New York: Clarkson N. Potter, [1967]. Vol 2, chap. 77, p. 769-775.

A review of the literature on his retirement.

3223. Chenhall, W. H. "The Retirement of Sherlock Holmes," *SHJ*, 5, No. 1 (Winter 1960), 19-22.

An explanation of where and why he retired.

3224. Dorian, N. Currier. "The Bee-Keeper of Sussex," *BSJ*, 2, No. 4 (October 1952), 205-209.

"Some of the keenest memories of my childhood on the Sussex Downs are those of an abrupt but kindly old gentleman who let me call him 'Uncle Sherlock.' "

3225. Graham, R. P. "Sherlock Holmes in Retirement," *BSJ* [OS], 1, No. 4 (October 1946), 469-472.

"Sherlock Holmes retired to devote himself to chemistry—specifically to research in organic and analytical chemistry."

3226. Hill, Pope R., Sr. "Sherlock Holmes Meets Jean Henri Fabre," *BSJ* [OS], 2, No. 1 (January 1947), 63-64, 66.

Fabre, one of the greatest entomologists of all time, may have been responsible for Holmes's decision to retire in order to devote himself to the study of insects.

3227. Lauterbach, Charles E. "What Doth the Bee?" *BSJ*, 12, No. 2 (June 1962), 101.

———. ———, *Baker Street Ballads.* [Culver City, Calif.: Luther Norris, March 1971.] p. 25.

"Who is the keeper of the bees? / I think you know the chappie; / He's tall and thin, and has a pal / Who's just a little sappy."

3228. Merriman, Charles O. "The Game Is Afoot," *SHJ*, 5, No. 4. (Summer 1962), 105-106.

The Master's bee farm is traced to the Birling Manor Farm.

3229. Morley, Christopher. "A Southdown Christmas," *The Saturday Review*, 36, No. 52 (December 26, 1953), 5-7, 39-40.

While vacationing in Eastbourne the author attempts to identify the cottage to which, some fifty years before, Holmes retired to keep bees.

3230. Rathbone, Basil. " 'Daydream,' " *BSJ* [OS], 2, No. 4 (October 1947), 442-446.

———. ———. *Esquire*, 46, No. 6 (December 1956), 168.

———. ———, *In and Out of Character.* Garden City, N.Y.: Doubleday & Co., [1962]. p. 184-188.

———. ———, *SOS*, 2, No. 1 (October 1967), 5-8.

———. "Dagdrøm," [Oversat af A. D. Henriksen]. *Sherlockiana*, 12, Nr. 3 (1967), 7-9.

A memorable visit with the Master on his bee farm in Sussex.

3231. Redmond, Chris. "A Kiplingian Requiem on Holmes," *BSP*, No. 27 (September 1967), 3.

"For Sherlock long ago betook / Himself to—Sussex, so they say. / But merely open up your book: / 'Lo, all our pomp of yesterday!' "

3232. ———. "Retirement," *BSP*, No. 29 (November 1967), 4.

"The mystique is gone or broken—the detective has retired / To keep bees and write along the Sussex shore. / But his deeds are still recorded in the Doctor's sixty tales: / Take the book down; Sherlock Holmes can live once more."

3233. Schenck, Remsen T. "Holmes in Hymettus," *BSJ*, 10, No. 3 (July 1960), 147-150.

His main beekeeping interest concerned selective breeding. His innovation consisted in swapping queen cells from queenless hives, while the new queens were still segregated from the workers.

3234. Sellars, Crighton. "A Visit to Sherlock Holmes," *BSJ*, 2, No. 1 (January 1952), 5-17.

Among the infrequent reports we have on him since his retirement, none is more revealing or interesting than Mrs. Sellars'. Some of the subjects discussed during her visit to Holmescroft in Sussex are the Sherlock Holmes Exhibition in the Borough of Marylebone, the part he played in World Wars I *and* II, and his recent work on a secret reversible magnetic system that will repel foreign or enemy objects. It is also illuminating, and reassuring, to find that the Holmes household consists of not only the Master but his wife Irene, the former widow of Godfrey Norton; his secretary Mary Sutherland; Mrs. Watson, the housekeeper; and the servant Buttons who, though not identified, is "Buttons-cum-Commissionaire" Edgar Smith.

3235. Stone, P. M. "Sussex Interview," *221B: Studies in Sherlock Holmes*. Edited by Vincent Starrett. New York: The Macmillan Co., 1940. p. 74-87.

3236. Watson, John H. "Preface," *His Last Bow: Some Reminiscences of Sherlock Holmes*. London: John Murray, 1917. p. v.
———. ———, *Introducing Mr. Sherlock Holmes*. Edited by Edgar W. Smith. Morristown, N.J.: The Baker Street Irregulars, 1959. [unpaged]

"The friends of Mr. Sherlock Holmes will be glad to learn that he is still alive and well, though somewhat crippled by occasional attacks of rheumatism. He has, for many years, lived in a small farm upon the Downs five miles from Eastbourne, where his time is divided between philosophy and agriculture."

3237. Williams, H. B. "So Bee It," *BSJ Christmas Annual*, No. 3 (1958), 58-60.

While visiting with Mr. Hoag, the author discovers a letter written to Mr. Hoag's father from Holmes in which he discusses his bees and Watson.

3238. Williamson, J. N. "The Ageless Holmes: Another Communication from Inspector Athelney Jones," Reported by J. N. Williamson. *Illustrious Client's Second Case-Book*. Edited by J. N. Williamson. [Indianapolis, Ind.: The Illustrious Clients, 1949.] p. 34.

"The last time I saw Holmes was at his Sussex bee-farm a year ago: he was playing cricket with some guests!"

SMOKING AND TOBACCO

3239. Brook, Geoffrey. "Sherlock Holmes's Pipe," *BSJ*, 10, No. 3 (July 1960), 152-154.

The traditional curved pipe appears neither in the tales nor in Paget's illustrations. It seems to have been introduced by William Gillette in his impersonation of Holmes.

3240. Clum, Florence. "On the Ashes of the Various Tobaccos (A Dim View, by a Non-Smoker)," *BSJ* [OS], 3, No. 3 (July 1948), 338-339.
———. ———, *The Pipe Smoker's Ephemeris* (Winter 1967-68), 3-4.
———. ———, Last two stanzas tr. into Danish by A. D. Henriksen. *Sangen om Baker Street*. København: [Grafisk Cirkel], 1958. p. 12. Reprinted in *Sherlockiana*, 3, Nr. 3-4 (1958), 11.

"And yet this human chimney-pot, whose pall / Of fumes beclouded home, street, park, and pleasance, / Had the consummate hardihood to call / The air of London sweeter for his presence!"

3241. Fladeland, Edwin. "Holmes and Tobacco," *BSP*, No. 31 (January 1968), 1.

3242. "He Is Fiction's Most Noted Smoker," *The Tobacco News* [Washington, D.C.], 4, No. 4 (December 1962), 2.
———, *CPBook*, 1, No. 1 (Summer 1964), 5.
A brief article about "the most celebrated smoker in the world of letters."

3243. Henriksen, A. D. "Piberygeren Sherlock Holmes" ["The Pipe-Smoking Sherlock Holmes"], Vignetter: Henry Lauritzen. *Sherlockiana*, 13, Nr. 4 (1968), 13-14.

3244. ———. "Snak om tobak i Baker Street: Af dr. John H. Watsons optegnelser," *Sherlockiana*, 6, Nr. 1 (1961), 1-3.
———. ———, *Stop* [København], Nr. 12 (February 1967), 17-19.
———. "Tobacco Talk in Baker Street: Extract from the Saga," *BSJ*, 17, No. 2 (June 1967), 86-89.
A compilation of important sayings about pipes and tobacco in the Canonical tales.

3245. Hicks, John L. "No Fire Without Some Smoke," *BSJ*, 5, No. 1 (January 1955), 27-33.

"A close study of the Sacred Writings reveals that Sherlock Holmes's powers as a logician were due largely to his pipe—and primarily to his briar pipe."

3246. La Cour, Tage. "Storm P., Pipes and Sherlock Holmes," *Tobacco Talk in Baker Street*, by Robert Storm Petersen and Tage la Cour. New York: The Baker Street Irregulars, 1952. p. 17-26.
———. "Storm P. og Piberne," *Stop* [København], 2, Nr. 6 (1965), 18, 21.

3247. Lauterbach, Charles E. "Tobacco Smoke," *BSJ*, 8, No. 3 (July 1958), 178.

———. ———, *Baker Street Ballads*. [Culver City, Calif.: Luther Norris, March 1971.] p. 29.

"When care has got me on the hook / And life begins to drag / I like to seek a quiet nook / And fill my pipe with shag."

3248. Löffler, Henner. *Über die Rauchgewohnheiten Sherlock Holmes'*. [The Smoking Habits of Sherlock Holmes.] Köln: [Privately Produced], 1970. 18 p.

Limited to 120 numbered copies.

This treatise attempts to prove that he was not only a confirmed pipe smoker and a casual cigar smoker, but a connoisseur of tobacco in all its forms, depending on the situation: for work he preferred the pipe; in his leisure, the cigar. It also tries to prove that there was a very definite principle for the way he kept his pipes, tobacco, cigars, and cigarettes.

3249. Naganuma, Kohki. ["Sherlock Holmes and Pipes"], *The Sun* [Tokyo], No. 33 (March 1966), 120-124.

(Further discussions of Holmes's smoking habits by Dr. Naganuma appear in *Sherlock Holmes and His Bluish Smoke* and *Sherlock Holmes in the Mist* [items 2139-2140].)

3250. Petersen, Robert Storm, and Tage la Cour. *Tobacco Talk in Baker Street*. New York: The Baker Street Irregulars, 1952. 25 p. illus.

A booklet containing an illustrated Holmes burlesque, "A Pipe of Tobacco," by the Danish cartoonist and founder of the Danish Sherlock Holmes Society, Robert Storm Petersen, and an essay by Tage la Cour on "Storm P., Pipes and Sherlock Holmes."

3251. Redmond, Chris. "The Mysterious Coal-Tars," *SIS*, 1, No. 1 (June 1965), 6-9.

About Holmes's research on coal-tar derivatives and his smoking habits.

3252. Sherbrooke-Walter, R. D. "Holmes, Watson and Tobacco," *SHJ*, 1, No. 2 (September 1952), 7-12.

"Holmes knew everything about tobacco—except how really to enjoy it. He possessed neither palate nor restraint and yet he criticised what he deemed Watson's excesses. Watson knew nothing of tobacco scientifically and smoked heavily but retained at least his olfactory sense. He censured Holmes as a self-poisoner by tobacco. The pot and the kettle, with Watson, for once, a little brighter than Holmes!"

3253. Williams, H. B. "I Always Smoke Ships Myself," *Illustrious Client's Case-Book*. Edited by J. N. Williamson and H. B. Williams. [Indianapolis, Ind.: The Illustrious Clients, 1948.] p. 33-36.

"Sherlock Holmes was an inveterate smoker, a user of the sovereign weed in all its forms. The pages of the recorded adventures are replete with allusions to this."

TRAVEL

See also *The Great Hiatus* (items 2381-2404) and *Railways* (items 4354-4362)

3254. Bergman, Ted. "Sherlock Holmes besök i sverige 1895" ["Sherlock Holmes's Visit to Sweden in 1895"], *BSCL*, No. 1 (January 1963), 15-20.

"Deals with references in Soli, Blac, Musg, Nobl, Fina, Gold and Bruc to the Master's visit to Sweden in July 1895; at the same time as the visit of the German Kaiser Wilhelm II."

3255. Cumings, Thayer. "Holmes and the U.S.A.," *Seven on Sherlock*. [New York]: Privately Printed, 1968. p. 31-35.

"The fact that Sherlock Holmes not only was a great student of American customs and language but also had traveled extensively in the States cannot be challenged."

3256. Girdler, Allan. "Visit by Sherlock Holmes to Kansas City Disclosed," *Tulsa Daily World* (January 1, 1967).

A report on the results of Milton Perry's research, as presented at a meeting of the Great Alkali Plainsmen (and Plainswomen), into the Master's activities in Kansas City, Mo., during 1879-1880.

3257. Kaser, Michael C. "Sherlock Holmes on the Continent," *BSJ*, 6, No. 1 (January 1956), 19-24.

Detailed information on his journeys to France and Switzerland.

3258. Morley, Christopher. "Was Sherlock Holmes an American?" *The Saturday Review of Literature*, 11, No. 1 (July 21, 1934), 6; 11, No. 2 (July 28, 1934), 23. (The Bowling Green)

———. ———, *Streamlines*. Garden City, N. Y.: Doubleday, Doran & Co., 1936. p. 54-65.

———. ———, ———. London: Faber & Faber Ltd., [1937]. p. 54-65.

———. ———, *221B: Studies in Sherlock Holmes*. Edited by Vincent Starrett. New York: The Macmillan Co., 1940. p. 5-15.

"That Holmes was reared in the States, or had some schooling here before going up to Cambridge, seems at least arguable."

3259. Redmond, Chris. "Sherlock Holmes and Canada," *BSP*, No. 25 (July 1967), 1. (Editorial)

The author takes note of the few

references to Canada in the Saga and considers the possibility of Holmes having visited this country.

3260. Simpson, A. Carson. *I'm Off for Philadelphia in the Morning.* Philadelphia: Privately Printed by International Printing Co., 1960. 38 p. (Simpson's Sherlockian Studies, Vol. 8)

Limited to 221B copies.

Contents: Pt. 1. Preliminary. - Pt. 2. Progenitorial Pondering. - (A) Before Montague Street. - (B) Before Irene. - (C) Another Hypothesis. - (D) What Happened in France. - (E) Further Light from the Past. - (F) College Years. - (G) Further Considerations of Age. - (H) The Verdict. (I) Like Father, Like Son? - (J) Holmes and Philadelphia.

3261. Wood, Willis B. "Sherlock in Kansas," *The Second Cab.* Edited by James Keddie. [Boston: The Speckled Band, 1947.] p. 78-81.

"The evidence is *prima facie* that Sherlock, or more probably Altamont, was sometime actually in Kansas. He saw our 'moors'—hence Moorville."

VOICE

3262. Brodie, Robert N. "The Voice of Sherlock Holmes," *The Stories of Sherlock Holmes.* Vol. 4 *Silver Blaze.* Read by Basil Rathbone. New York: Caedmon Records, [1968]. Printed on back of album.

————. Slightly changed with title: "The Sound of Sherlock," *SHJ,* 9, No. 1 (Winter 1968), 24-25.

"The Canon provides a wealth of clues from which we can deduce the tone, timbre, diction and expression of the voice of Sherlock Holmes."

WOMEN AND OFFSPRING(?)

See also *Chas* (items 2308-2324),
Copp (items 2325-2327),
The Great Hiatus (items 2381-2404),
Scan (items 2634-2673), and
Rex Stout (items 4040-4046)

3263. Asher, Richard. "Holmes and the Fair Sex," *SHJ,* 2, No. 3 (Summer 1955), 15-22.

An interesting essay dealing with the questions: "Did Holmes attract women? Did women attract Holmes? Was there ever any serious romance in Holmes's life?"—all answered in the affirmative, of course.

3264. Coopersmith, Jerome. "The Strange Case of Sherlock Holmes, the Lover," *Life International,* 38, No. 6 (March 22, 1965), 73.

The author of the libretto for *Baker Street* explains why he dared to present Holmes as a romantic admirer of Irene Adler.

3265. Goldfield, Barbara Anne. "Sherlock Holmes Versus the Fair Sex," *BSP,* No. 9-10 (March-April 1966), 1-2.

What the ladies thought of the world's first consulting detective.

3266. Halbach, Helan. "The Other Woman: A Romantic Conjecture," *BSJ,* 20, No. 3 (September 1970), 179

"If Holmes had known our Miss Borden, / he might first have reasoned, then guessed: / Unconvinced by the corpses and motive / but keen on her manner of dress."

3267. Hall, Trevor H. "The Love Life of Sherlock Holmes," *Sherlock Holmes: Ten Literary Studies.* London: Gerald Duckworth & Co., [1969]. Chap. 10, p. 132-147.

"In which Holmes's son (born 1892), the author believes, far from being Rex Stout's detective, Nero Wolfe (see Baring-Gould [item 1919]), was born as the result of a brief, but idyllic, interlude—rudely interrupted by Colonel Sebastian Moran—in Montenegro, and was named Sherlock John Hamish Mycroft Vernet Holmes-Adler." (Lord Donegall)

3268. Kimball, Elliot. "A Multiclarificient," *SHJ,* 7, No. 2 (Spring 1965), 48-50.

A scholarly study of the genetic constitutions of Sherlock and Mycroft in which the author concludes that they were intersexes of the XXY type—that is to say, "there is no evidence that either felt the erotic urgency so common in garden-variety XY males."

3269. Longfellow, Esther. "The Distaff Side of Baker Street," *BSJ* [OS], 1, No. 1 (January 1946), 9-13.

"Certainly Sherlock Holmes understood women, and surely the only explanation of it lies in this theory: that he was once married—at a very early age—emerging shortly as a widower and that slightly cynical but undisillusioned man we know."

3270. Prince, Marion. "Sherlock and Son," *A Baker Street Four-Wheeler.* Edited by Edgar W. Smith. [Maplewood, N.J., and New York: The Pamphlet House, 1944.] p. 27-29.

Stanley Hopkins is identified as the son of Holmes, the widower.

3271. Roberts, S. C. "Sherlock Holmes and the Fair Sex," *Baker Street Studies.* Edited by H. W. Bell. London: Constable & Co., [1934]. p. 177-199.

————. "Sherlock Holmes: His Attitude to Women," *Holmes and Watson: A Miscellany.* London: Oxford University Press, 1953. p. 28-44.

"Holmes cannot, on a proper examination of the evidence, be any longer regarded as the embodiment of asexual ratiocination. . . . Evidences of the affectionate feelings which Holmes entertained from time to time towards his lady clients peep out from Watson's narrative."

3272. Starrett, Vincent. "Sherlock Holmes, Widower," *American Notes and Queries*, 2 (April 1942), 11-12.

A negative answer to a reader's important query.

3273. Stern, Allison. "Romance in Baker Street," *BSJ*, 6, No. 3 (July 1956), 170.

"I like to see him sitting with his fiddle on his knee, / A lovely lady opposite, the table set for tea, / While, as the shadows lengthen, an amorous alliance? / . . . In the best and wisest man on earth, I have complete reliance!"

3274. Warner, Edith. "Holmes a Libertine?" *BSJ*, 19, No. 2 (June 1969), 67.

"Holmes the seducer" and "Irene the producer" were the parents of the late poet Dame Edith Sitwell.

3275. Wellman, Manly Wade. "The Great Man's Great Son: An Inquiry into the Most Private Life of Mr. Sherlock Holmes," *BSJ* [OS], 1, No. 3 (July 1946), 326-336.

The author states that neither Lord Peter Death Brendon Wimsey nor Police Inspector Stanley Hopkins was the son of Sherlock Holmes. He then presents an elaborate argument to show that the offspring of the great detective was none other than Bertie Wooster's valet Jeeves, born to the Master and his landlady in 1891.

3276. Williamson, J. N. "Mr. Sherlock Holmes: Misogamist or Misogynist?" *Illustrious Client's Case-Book.* Edited by J. N. Williamson and H. B. Williams. [Indianapolis, Ind.: The Illustrious Clients, 1948.] p. 45-47.

A look at what he had to say about the feminine sex.

WRITINGS, LIBRARY, AND INDEX

3277. Austin, Bliss. "Two Bibliographical Footnotes. I," *BSJ*, 4, No. 1 (January 1954), 41-42.

A further discussion (item 3297) of the books carried by Holmes in Empt.

3278. Bengis, Nathan L. "An Irregular Club Sandwich," *DCC*, 5, No. 2 (January 1969), 2-3.

An identification of the Hebrew rabbi and the deep-sea fish expert, along with a commentary on other out-of-the-way information in Holmes's Index.

3279. Berman, Ruth. "On Docketing a Hebrew Rabbi," *BSJ*, 10, No. 2 (April 1960), 80-82.

An analysis of Holmes's system of in-

dexing reveals that the rabbi was Hermann Adler, Chief Rabbi of the United Congregations of the British Empire from 1891 to 1911.

3280. Bigelow, S. Tupper. "Those Five Volumes," *BSJ*, 11, No. 1 (March 1961), 31-37.

The books Holmes thought would fill that gap on the second shelf (Empt) are identified as the Grant Allen translation of Catullus's *Attis*, Bunyan's *Holy War*, and William Yarrell's *A History of British Birds* (in three volumes).

3281. Blakeney, T. S. "Bibliography of Sherlock Holmes," *Sherlock Holmes: Fact or Fiction?* London: John Murray, [1932]. p. 114-115.

A supplement to S. C. Roberts's list of published and projected works by Holmes.

3282. Collins, Howard. "Ex Libris Sherlock Holmes," *The Saturday Review of Literature*, 25, No. 1 (January 3, 1942), 13-15.

————. ————, *Profile by Gaslight.* Edited by Edgar W. Smith. New York: Simon and Schuster, 1944. p. 26-39.

"What Sherlock Holmes read and wrote is highly important for the influence it must have had upon the development and refinement of his innate faculties, and, hence, upon his capacity to do the great deeds he did. Mr. Howard Collins has explored and given critical appraisal to the whole gamut of the Master's accomplishments in the literary field, and his study has great value both for its historical accuracy and for its inspirational suggestion." (Edgar W. Smith)

3283. Cumings, Thayer. "The Great Holmes Sale," *Seven on Sherlock.* [New York]: Privately Printed, 1968. p. 18-22.

A descriptive catalog of seventeen items recently "offered" at an auction in Baskerville Hall, Grimpen Moor, Devonshire.

3284. Dobson, A. W. *"Whitaker's* and Beyond," *SHJ*, 8, No. 3 (Winter 1967), 79-81.

On the use Holmes made of this almanac and the use that can be made of it now to fill in background information about the Saga.

3285. Hall, Trevor H. "The Book-Collector," *The Late Mr. Sherlock Holmes & Other Literary Studies.* London: Gerald Duckworth & Co., [1971]. Chap. 2, p. 23-39.

"Holmes was not quite the distinguished book-collector that Miss Madeleine B. Stern, of New York, and other experts have wishfully built him up to be. Indeed, a learned *exposé*." (Lord Donegall)

3286. Hertzberg, A. Francis. "His Scrap-

Books . . . and His Homely Untidiness," *SOS Annual*, No. 2 (January 1968), 15-19.

3287. Holroyd, James Edward. "Baedeker and Baker Street," *The Cornhill Magazine*, 173 (Winter 1962-63), 139-145.
Baedeker's handbook, *London and Its Environs* for 1881, provides a key to the private lives of Holmes and Watson and to many vanished London landmarks.

3288. Klinefelter, Walter. "The Writings of Mr. Sherlock Holmes," *BSJ* [OS], 1, No. 4 (October 1946), 409-416.
From several scattered references in the Canon, the author has compiled a descriptive list of all the literary works that can be identified as having come from the Master's pen.

3289. La Cour, Tage. "Sherlock Holmes som forfatter" ["Sherlock Holmes as an Author"], *Varia: Essays om Bøger*. København: Carit Andersens Forlag, 1951. p. 58-75.
————. *Ex Bibliotheca Holmesiana: The First Editions of the Writings of Sherlock Holmes*. With six title-pages designed by Viggo Naae. Copenhagen: The Danish Baker Street Irregulars (Sherlock Holmes Klubben i Danmark), 1951. 27 p.
Limited to 300 copies.
————. ————, *The Amateur Book Collector* [now called *The American Book Collector*], 5, No. 6 (February 1955), 3-6.
————. ————, *The American Book Collector*, 20, No. 2 (October 1969), 19-22.
A bibliography, with commentary, on fifteen of his published monographs.

3290. Mackenzie, Armine D. "The Case of the Illustrious Predecessor," *Wilson Library Bulletin*, 19, No. 4 (December 1944), 278-279.
————. ————, *BSG*, 1, No. 2 (1961), 29-31.
————. ————, *West by One and by One*. San Francisco: Privately Printed, 1965. p. 15-18.
Contents: Sherlock Holmes Was a Special Librarian. - His Special Library. - Librarian or Detective. - Professional Shortcomings.

3291. Redmond, Chris. "The American Encyclopedia," *Four Wheels to Baker Street*. Edited by Bruce Kennedy. [Fulton, Mo.]: The Three Students Plus, 1968. p. 19-21.
Johnson's New Universal Cyclopedia of 1881 is identified as the American encyclopedia Holmes turned to in Five for information about the Ku Klux Klan.

3292. Roberts, S. C. "A Bibliography of Sherlock Holmes," *Doctor Watson*. London: Faber & Faber Ltd., [1931]. p. 31-32.
Contents: Published Works. - Printed for Private Circulation. - Reminiscenses. - Projected or Unfinished Works.

3293. Rudberg, Gösta. "Holmesiana," *Bokvännen* [Stockholm], No. 7 (1965).
————. ————, *BSCL*, No. 5 (1966), 12-16.
A discussion in Swedish of Holmes, the writer, his library and his favorite books.

3294. Schutz. Robert H. "An Empty Space Monograph," *SOS*, 4, No. 2 (July 1970), 11-12.
Additional information on *Catullus*, one of the books mentioned by Holmes in Empt.

3295. [Smith, Edgar W.] " 'Let Me Recommend This Book . . . ,' " *BSJ* [OS], 2, No. 2 (April 1947), 111-112. (The Editor's Gas-Lamp)
A commentary on some of the authors and books recommended in the Sacred Writings.

3296. Starrett, Vincent. "The Writings of Mr. Sherlock Holmes," *The Bookman*, 76, No. 2 (February 1933), 170-171.
————. ————, *The Private Life of Sherlock Holmes*. New York: The Macmillan Co., 1933. p. 113-117.
————. ————, ————. Revised and enlarged. The University of Chicago Press, [1960]. p. 98-101.
An annotated list of his literary works.

3297. Stern, Madeleine B. "Sherlock Holmes: Rare-Book Collector (A Study in Book Detection)," *The Papers of the Bibliographical Society of America*, 47, No. 2 (Spring 1953), 133-155.
————. ————. New York: Schulte Pub. Co., [1953]. 23 p.
————. ————, *BSJ, 3, No. 3 [July 1953], 133-155*.
The Master's book collections are described: 1. the working library related to his specific interests (tobacco and soil analysis, toxicology and secret writing, fencing and boxing, bee culture, etc.; 2. his small, elegant, and very private assemblage of treasures (including the first Aldine Catullus, a Bodoni Horace, firsts of Baxter, Fuller's *Holy Warre*. Poe, etc.). Holmes's methods of acquisition and his secretiveness about his rarities are discussed and his suppliers are identified.

3298. Utechin, Nicholas. *"Upon the Distinction Between the Ashes of the Various Tobaccos,"* *SOS*, 2, No. 4 (April 1968), 7-9.
The author relates his astonishing discovery of what may be the introduction to Holmes's famous monograph on tobaccos.

3299. Wolff, Julian. "A Catalogue of 221B Culture," *To Doctor R.: Essays Here Collected and Published in Honor of the Seventieth Birthday of Dr. A. S. W.*

Rosenbach, July 22, 1946. Philadelphia: [Privately Printed], 1946. p. 253-262.

An impressive catalog of sixty-six items in the Sherlock Holmes Library, with an informative introduction.

3300. Wynne-Jones, Patricia. "New Light on the Early English Charters," *SHJ,* 1, No. 3 (June 1953), 38-39.

The author's studies take her to "a small and seldom frequented library" where she discovers that it was in this very library (the name unfortunately is not given) that the Master pursued his researches into Early English charters (3Stu).

D Dr. Watson

GENERAL AND MISCELLANEOUS

3301. Almqvist, Josef. "Dr. Watson avslöjad" ["Dr. Watson Unmasked"], *Aftonbladet* (July 17, 1950).
———. ———, *BSCL,* No. 4 (1965), 6-10.

"Describes Watson as a war-injured mystic with serious periods of excesses and loss of memory, abandoned by his wife and deeply in trouble." (Ted Bergman)

3302. Austin, Bliss. *The Biography of a Biography.* Pittsburgh, Pa.: Hydraulic Press, 1966. [2] p. (A Baker Street Christmas Stocking, No. 12)

A tribute to Sir Sydney Roberts in the form of a scholarly analysis of the development of his famous biography of Dr. Watson (item 3352). Includes photocopies of the title page and two manuscript sheets. (The manuscript is owned by Carl Anderson.)

3303. Baker, Kate G. "Watson," *BSP,* No. 28 (October 1967), 1.

"Watson was . . ./ Boobus Britannicus? Seeming so, but yet / Loyal as the typically British bull pup."

3304. Baring-Gould, William S. " 'Good Old Watson!' " *The Annotated Sherlock Holmes.* New York: Clarkson N. Potter, [1967]. Vol. 1, chap. 9, p. 67-80. illus.

An examination of the literature on his middle name, ancestry, youth, education, and military career.

3305. Benét, Stephen Vincent. "My Favorite Fiction Character," *The Bookman,* 62, No. 6 (February 1926), 672-673.
———. [With a note by Vincent Starrett.] Ysleta: Edwin B. Hill, 1938. [4] p. (Sherlockiana)
———. "Dr. Watson," *Profile by Gaslight.* Edited by Edgar W. Smith. New York: Simon and Schuster, 1944. p. 154-155.

"As far as professional skill goes, one cannot rank him with the leaders, I fear—his practice was too subject to continual interruption. But his bedside manner must have been ideal. I would rather die some pleasantly fictional death with Watson in attendance than recover under the aseptic hands of a modern practitioner."

3306. Bengis, Nathan L. "Take a Bow, Dr. Watson," *BSJ,* 8, No. 4 (October 1958), 218-229.

An essay, in two parts, defending his intellectual prowess and writing ingenuity.

3307. Bonn, Ronald S. "The Problem of the Postulated Doctor," *BSJ,* 14, No. 1 (March 1964), 14-21.

Winner of the 7th annual Morley-Montgomery Memorial Award for the best contribution to *BSJ* in 1964.

"What if, once, we were to treat Watson as a piece [rather than as a player]? What if we should re-examine the entire fabric of the Holmes biography as a case—the Problem of the Postulated Doctor? . . . we are left to conclude in sorrow and terror that what we thought to be merely the biography of the greatest detective of modern times is in fact the autobiography of the greatest non-governmental criminal who ever lived."

3308. Boyd, Andrew. "Dr. Watson's Dupe," *Encounter,* 14, No. 3 (March 1960), 64-66.
———. ———, *SHJ,* 5, No. 2 (Spring 1961), 42-44.

"Watson was an imposter with a shady past, who controlled Holmes. His ignorance of Indian personal names, in *The Sign of the Four,* shows that his career in the Indian Army was a fraud. He was driven from England on the brink of a promising medical career, because of money troubles and dubious school-day personal relations, as shown by his references to and actions with Percy Phelps. He then both successfully blackmailed Holmes, who obtained money questionably, and took advantage of Holmes's addiction to narcotics." (Lawrence R. Dawson)

3309. Brend, Gavin. "The Trusty Servant," *BSJ,* 6, No. 1 (January 1956), 25-27.

"Conan Doyle now rests near those same glades and in the shadow of that truly Watsonian character, the Trusty Servant."

3310. Bristowe, W. S. "The Mystery of the Third Continent, or Was Dr. John H. Watson a Philanderer?" *SHJ,* 2, No. 2 (December 1954), 27-39.

A search for the third continent reveals that Watson travelled to the U.S. in 1885 to see his dying brother and that after his brother's death, he fell in love with an American girl who eventually jilted him. He then returned to England in the spring of 1887 to join Holmes.

3311. Campbell, Maurice. "Sherlock Holmes and Dr. Watson," *Guy's Hospital Gazette* (December 22, 1934), 524-530; (January 5, 1935), 2-7; (January 19, 1935), 27-33.

————. *Sherlock Holmes and Dr. Watson: A Medical Digression.* London: Printed by Ash & Co. Ltd. for Guy's Hospital Gazette Committee, [1935]. 56 p.

————. ————. [Revised.] London: Printed by Ash & Co. Ltd. for Guy's Hospital Gazette Committee, 1951. 28 p.

Contents: 1. The Medical Knowledge of Dr. Watson. - 2. Their Chemistry, Anatomy, and Pharmacology. - Watson's Practice; His Service in the South African War; and His Second Marriage.

3312. Christ, Jay Finley. "The Height o' Watson," *BSG*, 1, No. 4 (April 1962), 55-60.

An examination of the Canon suggests that he was about five feet seven inches tall, stout, and had a thick neck.

3313. ————. *John H. Watson Never Went to China.* [Privately Produced]: March 1949. 4 p.

An argument against John Dickson Carr's conclusion (*Life of Sir Arthur Conan Doyle,* p. 46) that Dr. James Watson was the original of John H. Watson. The honor was more likely bestowed upon another of Doyle's contemporaries—Patrick Heron Watson.

3314. Coltart, J. S. "The Watsons," *The Fortnightly Review,* 129 (May 1931), 650-657.

Random observations on some of Watson's characteristics and the nature of his home life.

3315. "The Curious Case of Dr. Watson," *The Journal of the American Medical Association,* 150, No. 14 (December 6, 1952), 24-25.

An inquiry into the life of John H. Watson.

3316. Davidson, Avram. "The Case of the Doped-Up Doctor," *Cry* [Seattle], No. 149 (April 1961), 9.

————. ————, [With an added note by the author and by the editor]. *BSJ,* 11, No. 3 (September 1961), 175-177.

Watson was the cocaine addict—not Holmes!

3317. Davies, Bernard. " 'Doctor Boyd's Bleat,' " *SHJ,* 5, No. 3 (Winter 1961), 88-89.

A refutation of Dr. Boyd's allegation that "Watson invented his Army service in India in order to hide an unsavoury period in his past."

3318. Dickensheet, Dean W. "The Clubable Watson," *A Curious Collection.* Edited by William J. Walsh. [Suffern, N. Y.]: The Musgrave Ritualists Beta, 1971. p. 6-11.

From the two brief references to Watson's club in Houn and Danc, the author, with the help of *Whitaker's Almanack* for 1889, makes out a strong case in favor of a literary club named The Savage Club. Watson's *second* club was The Author's.

3319. Fitz, Reginald. "A Belated Eulogy: To John H. Watson, M.D.," *The American Journal of Surgery,* 31, No. 3 (March 1936), 584-589.

————. ————, *Profile by Gaslight.* Edited by Edgar W. Smith. New York: Simon and Schuster, 1944. p. 141-153.

Professional testimony that he was both a great man and a good doctor.

3320. Foster, Alan H. "On the Selection of John H. Watson, M.D.," *BSJ,* 14, No. 3 (September 1964), 139-141.

"Holmes's selection of Watson was not chance. With his instinctive knowledge he knew Watson would ask for explanations, would bring his powers to a keener edge, and would record faithfully most of his cases."

3321. Fry, Michael. "Elementary Dr. Watson," *MD Medical News Magazine,* 1, No. 7 (July 1957), 59-61.

An excellent illustrated capsule biography of "the medical world's most unorthodox general practitioner."

3322. Galerstein, David. "Doctor Watson: An Overdue Evaluation," *BSJ,* 17, No. 3 (September 1967), 139-143.

"While Holmes is the greatest detective—no one can compare to him in that respect—and a good violinist, that is all. Watson, on the other hand, is a great writer, excellent doctor, man of letters and adventurer. He was a better all-around man, by far, than Sherlock Holmes."

3323. Grove, Janet L. "Dr. Watson and the Vice," *VH,* 3, No. 3 (September 1969), 2-5.

A discussion of seven common denominators between Watson and the conventional vice (defined herein as a stock comic character).

3324. Hall, Trevor H. "Dr. Watson and the English Counties," *The Late Mr. Sherlock Holmes & Other Literary Studies.* London: Gerald Duckworth & Co., [1971]. Chap. 5, p. 80-85.

3325. Hartman, Harry. "Dr. Watson Pleads the Fifth Amendment," *BSJ,* 15, No. 3 (September 1965), 150-153.

————. "Watson Pleads the Fifth Amendment," *The Holy Quire.* [Culver City, Calif.: Luther Norris, December 1970.] p. 24-27.

An enumeration of how he cut corners to help Holmes, and what an American Congressional Committee might have done to a fellow like him.

Dr. Watson

3326. Hobson, Joan. " 'Elementary, My Dear Doctor,' " *Private Practice*, 1, No. 8 (September 1969), 20-22, 40, 46.

"How Dr. Conan Doyle helped Dr. Watson help Sherlock Holmes through thick and thin." (Subtitle)

An interesting account of the life of Dr. John Hamish Watson.

3327. Holland, Glenn. "Holmes Speaks," *BSP*, No. 52-53 (October-November 1969), 5-6.

"In conclusion, I can only show my friend as a competent doctor, an excellent writer, and the rarest gem in all of God's world, a true friend."

3328. Howard, Helen. " 'A Most Dark and Sinister Business,' " *Illustrious Client's Case-Book*. Edited by J. N. Williamson and H. B. Williams. [Indianapolis, Ind.: The Illustrious Clients, 1948.] p. 26-27.

A devilish campaign has been started by Mr. Struik (item 3362) to discredit Holmes by "the innocent appearing device of building up little-by-little the naive and lovable Dr. Watson into an appalling superman."

3329. Johnson, Virginia P. "The Adventure of the Misguided Males," *BSJ* [OS], 3, No. 4 (October 1948), 501-505.

Further evidence that not only was Watson a woman, but also that he was the *wife* of Sherlock Holmes!

3330. Jones, Gratia. "The Puzzle of the Indispensable Man," *BSJ*, 16, No. 3 (September 1966), 160-162.

"And so it is that we have the indispensable man—to Sherlock Holmes, to the Agent, and to us—John H. Watson, M.D."

3331. Kaplan, Jonathan. "Doctor Watson: A Profile of the Long-Suffering Companion of Sherlock Holmes," *BSJ*, 19, No. 4 (December 1969). 227-229.

This article is the beginning of what the author hopes will be a reevaluation of Watson in light of his strengths and admirable qualities.

3332. Karlson, Katherine. "Why Watson Wasn't a Woman," *BSP* (NS), 1, No. 2 (August-September 1971), 2.

An argument based upon the premise that it would have taken a female Watson longer than ten minutes to dress when summoned by Holmes in the opening scene of Abbe.

3333. Kennedy, Bruce. "Never," *SOS*, 2, No. 4 (April 1968), 9-10.

A speculation on Watson's connection with the Ku Klux Klan.

3334. Kimball, Elliot. *Dr. John H. Watson at Netley*. [N. p.: n. p., 1962.] 8 p.

An investigation of his army medical course reveals that he left for India in 1880.

3335. ———. "A Retort Courteous," *BSG*, 1, No. 4 (April 1962), 60-61.

A rebuttal to Professor Christ's contention that Watson was "a short, stout man."

3336. [———.] "The Stature of John H. Watson," [by] Llabmik Toille [pseud.] *BSG*, 1, No. 3 (1961), 5-10.

"In epitome, the ingenious and accurate Swillens Method has been adapted to demonstrate stature of Sherlockian personages. It has been shown that Watson was five feet and ten inches *tall*. Watson may not be deemed 'short' without embarking upon egregious and stultifying error."

3337. ———. *Watsoniana*. First Series. [Clinton, Conn.: The Toille Press], 1962. 56 p.

Contents: Preface. - Introduction, by S. Tupper Bigelow. - The Watsons of Northumberland. - The Admirable Murray. - Watson's Neurosis. - The Missing Year. - Watson's Parentage. - Watson's Career. - Catalogue.

Review: *SHJ*, 6, No. 1 (Winter 1962), 30 (Lord Donegall).

3338. [Knox, E. V.] "Thoughts on Seeing 'The Hound of the Baskervilles' at the Cinema," by Evoe. *Punch*, 197 (July 29, 1939), 60.

———. ———, *Profile by Gaslight*. Edited by Edgar W. Smith. New York: Simon and Schuster, 1944. p. 188-189.

"What imbecile production, what madness of the moon / Has screened my glorious Watson as well nigh a buffoon?"

3339. Lauritzen, Henry. *Min kaere Watson*. [My Dear Watson.] Aalborg: Frede og L. C. Lauritzen's Forlag, 1954. 31 p. illus.

Limited to 413 numbered copies.

An attempt to give Watson rehabilitation—unfortunately by diminishing Holmes.

Review: *BSJ*, 5, No. 2 (April 1955), 117-118 (Edgar W. Smith)

3340. Lauterbach, Charles E. "Diogenes Gets His Man," *BSJ*, 9, No. 1 (January 1959), 21-22.

". . . Doc Watson is your MAN, sir!"

3341. ———. "The Fountain of Youth," *BSJ*, 10, No. 3 (July 1960), 175-176.

"Come, Watson, come! Reveal the charm / That wrought this priceless joy— / Why try to hide transparent truth? / . . . You've been in Prague, my boy!"

3342. Lewis, D. B. Wyndham. "The Case for Watson," *Time and Tide*, 38, No. 11 (March 16, 1957), 312-313.

3343. Lewis, Seymour. "The Duplicity of Watson," Illustrated by Buster. *The London Mystery Selection,* No. 37 (June 1958), 83-88.

A discussion of his wound(s), medical practice, and marriages.

3344. MacCarthy, Desmond. "Dr. Watson," BBC, Wednesday, December 4, 1929, 9:20-9:40 p.m. (Miniature Biographies, No. 3)

———. ———, *The Listener,* 2 (December 11, 1929), 775-777.

———. ———, *Memories.* New York: Oxford University Press, 1953. p. 165-171.

———. ———, ———. London: Macgibbon & Kee, 1953. p. 165-171.

———. ———, *Seventeen Steps to 221B.* [Edited by] James Edward Holroyd. London: George Allen & Unwin Ltd., [1967]. p. 50-56.

An excellent short biography of the friend and chronicler of Sherlock Holmes.

3345. Marshall, Arthur. " 'Ring for Our Boots,' " *The New Statesman and Nation,* 36, No. 916 (September 25, 1948), 256-257.

———. ———, *Seventeen Steps to 221B.* [Edited by] James Edward Holroyd. London: George Allen & Unwin Ltd., [1967]. p. 68-73.

An admirable essay on how Watson's marital and professional obligations were affected by his obedient service to Holmes.

3346. Mende, Fred. "Will the Real Watson Please Stand, or The Case for Surgeon-Major Preston," *BSJ,* 21, No. 1 (March 1971), 33-37. illus.

Attention is called to the career of a medical officer in the British Army who conceivably could have been the original of Dr. Watson. The salient facts supporting this theory are that Alexander Francis Preston participated in the Afghan Campaign of 1878-80 and was twice wounded with at least one (and possibly both) of the wounds being received in the Battle of Maiwand while serving with the Berkshire Regiment.

3347. Morrison, Kathleen I. "John H. Watson, M.D.," *Historical Bulletin* [Calgary Associate Clinic], 8, No. 1 (May 1943), 1-10.

"In a Bulletin which deals with medical history it is only proper that physicians of fiction should have a place, and of this company of literary immortals Dr. Watson is unquestionably the greatest."

3348. Parsons, Alan. "A Word, My Dear Watson, in Your Defence," *Brittania & Eve* [London] (December 1932), 18-19, 114, 116.

"A reasoned plea for the famous foil who played Boswell to Sherlock Holmes's Johnson." (Subtitle)

3349. Queen, Ellery. "High Sherloctane, or Having Fun with Words," *In the Queens' Parlor and Other Leaves from the Editors'* *Notebook.* New York: Simon and Schuster, 1957. p. 169-170.

———. ———, ———. London: Victor Gollancz Ltd., 1957. p. 169-170.

"Watson Was a Woman [item 3360] was the work of a sly and sinister Sherloctopus. . . . His 'monstrous perpetration' was the most irreverent irregularity ever to irrupt among the blushing members of that canonical and conanical conclave, the B.S.I."

3350. Redmond, D. A. "Is the Real Watson Number One, Two, Or —?" *BSJ,* 21, No. 3 (September 1971), 158-162.

He is identified as Surgeon George Watson, M. B., of the Bengal Medical Dept. Illustrated with a center-spread sketch of the action at Maiwand, July 26, 1880.

3351. ———. "The Prosthesis Fixation, or Stop! You're Pulling My Wooden Leg," *DCC,* 4, No. 5 (September 1968), 4-6.

Watson's fixation about the artifical devices used by Jonathan Small, Josiah Amberley, and Jabez Wilson may have resulted from a subconscious fear of being mutilated.

3352. Roberts, S. C. "Prolegomena to the Life of Doctor Watson: I. Watson's Early Life," *Life and Letters,* 4, No. 21 (February 1930), 119-132.

———. ———, *Essays of the Year (1929-1930).* [Compiled by Frederick Joseph Harvey Darton.] London: Argonaut Press, [1930]. p. 113-132.

———. Revised and enlarged with title: *Doctor Watson: Prolegomena to the Study of a Biographical Problem, with a Bibliography of Sherlock Holmes.* London: Faber & Faber Ltd., [1931]. 32 p. (Criterion Miscellany, No. 28)

———. "Dr. Watson: His Life," *Holmes and Watson: A Miscellany.* London: Oxford University Press, 1953. p. 60-92.

———. ———, Pt. I reprinted in *The Incunabular Sherlock Holmes.* Edited by Edgar W. Smith. Morristown, N.J.: The Baker Street Irregulars, 1958. p. 123-142.

———. *Doctor Watson.* With an introduction by Bruce Kennedy. The Three Students Plus, 1971. 32 p. [Reprint of Faber & Faber edition.]

"More than prolegomena: the biography is as complete, perhaps, as any ever will be." (Edgar W. Smith)

Review: SOS, 6, No. 1 (January 6, 1972), 3-6 (Thomas Drucker).

3353. Rosenkjar, Patrick R. "There Are Hardly Any Data,' " *BSJ,* 16, No. 3 (September 1966), 163-166.

"The early life of John H. Watson, with some observations upon continents." (Subtitle)

3354. [Smith, Edgar W.] "A Friend Indeed,"

BSJ, 5, No. 3 (July 1955), 131-132. (The Editor's Gas-Lamp)

"Let any who will have their other personages, high or low, whose intimate presence, day after day, would be too much or too little for us to bear. We, for all he is and for all he could give us, will take Watson."

3355. [————.] "John H. Watson, B. 1852," *BSJ*, 2, No. 1 (January 1952), 3-4. (The Editor's Gas-Lamp)

"We see him now, in the retrospect of his centennial, as the symbol of a day and age long gone and much beloved: a better symbol, we may come to think, than Sherlock Holmes himself."

3356. [————.] "Sonnet: Sherlock Holmes to John H. Watson," *A Lauriston Garden of Verses*, by Helene Yuhasova [pseud.] Summit, N.J.: The Pamphlet House, 1946. p. [11].

————. ————, *Baker Street and Beyond: Together with Some Trifling Monographs*. Morristown, N.J.: The Baker Street Irregulars, 1957. [unpaged]

"*My* wisdom lay, perhaps, in choosing you / To stand beside me as my foil and shield."

3357. Solovay, Jacob C. "Dr. Watson," *BSJ* [OS], 3, No. 3 (July 1948), 283.

"You shine with grace, though with reflected glory. . . ."

3358. Sovine, J. W. "The Three Watsons," *SHJ*, 4, No. 2 (Spring 1959), 66-68.

A view of the cinematic Watson, the biographic Watson, and the actual Watson.

3359. Steel, Kurt, "The Truth About Watson," *Ellery Queen's Mystery Magazine*, 7, No. 29 (April 1946), 79-83.

"Another reply to Rex Stout's obscene heresy, this time suggesting a female Watson before June, 1887, and a male one thereafter." (Edgar W. Smith)

3360. Stout, Rex. "Watson Was a Woman," *The Saturday Review of Literature*, 23, No. 19 (March 1, 1941), 3-4, 16.

————. ————, *The Pocket Mystery Reader*. Edited by Lee Wright. New York: Pocket Books, [August 1942]. p. 220-228.

————. ————, *Profile by Gaslight*. Edited by Edgar W. Smith. New York: Simon and Schuster, 1944. p. 156-165.

————. ————, *Ellery Queen's Mystery Magazine*, 7, No. 29 (April 1946), 72-78.

————. ————, *The Art of the Mystery Story*. Edited and with a commentary by Howard Haycraft. New York: Simon and Schuster, 1946. p. 311-318.

————. ————, ————. New York: Grosset & Dunlap, [1961]. p. 311-318.

————. ————, *The Saturday Review*

Gallery. Selected from the complete files by Jerome Beatty, Jr., and the Editors of The Saturday Review. New York: Simon and Schuster, 1959. p. 114-120.

A monstrous suggestion that Watson was really Mrs. Sherlock Holmes—Irene Adler Watson Holmes! ". . . [her] whole purpose, from beginning to end, was to confuse and bewilder us regarding her identity."

3361. ————. "What to Do About a Watson," *The Mystery Writer's Handbook*, by the Mystery Writers of America. Edited by Herbert Brean. New York: Harper & Brothers, [1956]. Chap. 22, p. 161-163.

The author who gave Archie Goodwin to Nero Wolfe discusses the value of a Watson to the fictional detective.

3362. Struik, Dirk J. "The Real Watson," *BSJ* [OS], 2, No. 1 (January 1947), 29-33.

"Watson emerges in final analysis as a much better man than he seems to give himself credit for being."

3363. Tinning, Herbert P. *The Singular Exploits of John H. Watson, M. D., in the Antarctic Regions, 1892-1893.* [Chicago, Ill.: Privately Produced, Michaelmas 1970.] 16 p.

Limited to 222 numbered copies.

A monograph that relates his exploits during the Great Hiatus. It takes the reader from Kensington to the Antarctic Regions aboard the Dundee Whaling Expedition of 1892 to 1893. Included is an explanation of the mysterious relocation of Watson's practice and also a proposal for the origin of the Canonical Toasts.

3364. Titus, Eve. "Message from the Mouster," *BSJ*, 10, No. 2 (April 1960), 91-95.

Proof from Basil of Baker Street (items 6172-6174) that Watson does have a mind!

3365. Vaill, C. B. H. "A Study in Intellects," *BSJ* [OS], 3, No. 3 (July 1948), 278-282.

Watson is virtually an intellectual giant when compared with some other characters in the Sacred Writings.

3366. Walsh, Michael. "What Was Watson Like?" *BSP*, No. 20 (February 1967), 3.

An unfavorable comparison between the cinematic Watson, as portrayed by Nigel Bruce, and the Canonical Watson.

3367. Weeks, A. L. "The Adventure of Lady Diana and the Bees," *BSG*, 1, No. 3 (1961), 26-27.

A humorous anecdote about an unruffled Col. Watson and the bees in a titled lady's pants.

3368. Wetherbee, Winthrop. "The Third Continent: Further Light on Dr. Watson," *BSJ*, 2, No. 3 (July 1952), 124-134.

A sound demonstration that he spent his youth in the U.S., not in Australia, despite his "babblings of Ballarat."

3369. Wigglesworth, Belden. "Ballade of Watson in the Morning," *Profile by Gaslight.* Edited by Edgar W. Smith. New York: Simon and Schuster, 1944. p. 178-179.

"With Baker Street's master no mystery's seen, / Because Sherlock Holmes had no set routine. / I ask, though reply dies ever a-borning: / '*When* did Watson get up in the morning?' "

3370. Wolff, Julian. "That Was No Lady," *The American Journal of Surgery,* 58, No. 2 (November 1942), 310-312.

———. ———, *Profile by Gaslight.* Edited by Edgar W. Smith. New York: Simon and Schuster, 1944. p. 166-172.

"Reply to Mr. Stout in which are included some observations upon the nature of Dr. Watson's wound." (Subtitle)

3371. Woodhead, Ed S. "In Defense of Dr. Watson," *BSJ* [OS], 1, No. 4 (October 1946), 417-422.

There is abundant evidence in the Canon to show that he was not only a great historian, but a brilliant and modest man.

ANCESTRY, FAMILY, AND NAME

See also *Card* (items 2301-2307)
and *Heraldry* (items 3868-3873)

3372. Austin, Bliss. "What Son Was Watson? A Case of Identity," *A Baker Street Four-Wheeler.* Edited by Edgar W. Smith. [Maplewood, N.J., and New York: The Pamphlet House, 1944.] p. 43-53.

It is suggested that there were two Watsons, John and James; that John died prematurely, and that James, seizing a good opportunity, thereupon masqueraded as his elder brother, even to the extent of trying, though evidently failing, to deceive Holmes himself.

3373. Blakeney, T. S. "The Apocryphal Ancestry of Dr. Watson," *BSJ,* 7, No. 2 (April 1957), 69-73.

A letter from an Emma Henrietta Redgauntlet, quoted therein, has induced the author to construct a tentative pedigree for Dr. John *Henry* Watson.

3374. Coltart, J. S. "This Watson," *The Cornhill Magazine,* 77 (November 1934), 513-526.

A highly original and scholarly paper expounding the theory that there were two brothers Watson—John and James—which would account for the apparent inconsistencies in *their* Writings.

3375. Oursler, Will. "His French Cousin," *BSJ Christmas Annual,* No. 1 (1956), 32-34.

Evidence that Dr. John *Holmes* Watson was the Master's first cousin.

3376. [Puhl], Gayle Lange. " 'I Never Even Knew That You Had a Brother,' " *BSC,* 1, No. 2 (March 1968), 2.

"It is quite evident that whatever Watson did during that time [April 1883-October 1886], he did *not* spend it nursing his sick brother."

3377. Redmond, Chris. "Art in the Blood: Two Canonical Relatives. II. 'The History of My Unhappy Brother,' " *BSJ,* 15, No. 2 (June 1965), 87-89.

"The life story of one H. Watson, the elder brother of our worthy doctor, who lost his money in England and emigrated to Ballarat; but having no luck in the gold fields there, he took to drink and died."

3378. Sayers, Dorothy L. "Dr. Watson's Christian Name," *Profile by Gaslight.* Edited by Edgar W. Smith. New York: Simon and Schuster, 1944. p. 180-186.

———. ———, With subtitle: "A Brief Contribution to Exegetical Literature of Sherlock Holmes," *Unpopular Opinions.* London: Victor Gollancz Ltd., 1946. p. 148-151.

———. ———, ———. New York: Harcourt, Brace & Co., [1947]. p. 184-188.

"There can be no possible doubt that Watson's first Christian name was 'John'. . . . Yet, in 1891, we find Watson publishing the story of *The Man with the Twisted Lip,* in the course of which Mrs. Watson refers to him as 'James'. . . . There is only one plain conclusion to be drawn from the facts. Only one name will reconcile the appellation 'James' with the initial letter 'H'. The doctor's full name was 'John Hamish Watson'. 'Hamish' is, of course, the Scottish form of 'James'."

3379. Simpson, A. Carson. "A Chronometric Excogitation," *BSJ Christmas Annual,* No. 4 (1959), 273-279.

It may be deduced from the watch of Watson's father that the senior Watson was an experienced railway engineer from England who went to Australia during the railroad boom of the 1850's. This hypothesis is corroborated by the fact (Engr and Stoc) that Watson could build up a depleted practice within six months of 1889 among the officials at Paddington Station.

3380. Throckmorton, Jane. " 'H.' Stands For———?" *Illustrious Client's Case-Book.* Edited by J. N. Williamson and H. B. Williams. [Indianapolis, Ind.: The Illustrious Clients, 1948.] p. 7-8.

Watson's middle name was *Huffham,* after Charles John Huffham Dickens.

3381. Watson, Harold F. "A Note on Watsonian Heraldry," *BSJ*, 17, No. 3 (September 1967), 176-177.

"If Dr. John H. Watson was of Scottish ancestry, his arms almost certainly were *Argent* (or perhaps *or*) issuing from a mount in base *vert* on oak tree proper surmounted by a fesse *sable* (or *azure*)."

3382. Willis, Reg. "Your Family Origin: Watson," *The Boston Traveler* (October 30, 1959).

————. ————, *BSJ*, 17, No. 4 (December 1967), 225.

The family lineage of Watson (of Clan Buchanan), with an illustration of its coat of arms.

BATTLE OF MAIWAND AND WOUNDS

See *Stud* (items 2786-2813)

BULL PUP

3383. Ashton, Ralph A. "The Fourth Occupant, or The Room with the Twisted Tongue," *BSJ*, 11, No. 1 (March 1961), 38-40.

"Being an explanation of the apparent mistake of Mary Morstan Watson in calling her husband 'James' in *The Man with the Twisted Lip*." (Subtitle)

Mary was not referring to Watson when she used the name "James," but to his bull pup. (The controversial dog was mentioned by Watson during his first meeting with Holmes at Bart's.)

3384. Curjel, Harald. "Dr. Watson's Bull Pup," *SHJ*, 10, No. 2 (Summer 1971), 49-50.

3385. Fletcher, George. "Sighting-in on Watson's Bull Pup," *BSJ*, 21, No. 3 (September 1971), 156-157.

The "bull pup" was a military rifle.

3386. Holstein, L. S. "Bull Pups and Literary Agents," *BSJ Christmas Annual*, No. 3 (1958), 54-57.

"It's a fair speculation that the bull pup was a phony contrived by the literary agent to build up (in his judgment) the adventure."

3387. Kennedy, Bruce. "What Bull Pup?" *SIS*, 1, No. 3 (1966), 19-20.

————. ————, *BSJ*, 16, No. 4 (December 1966), 215.

Watson fabricated the ferocious little dog (he was listed as a "shortcoming") to warn Holmes to watch his step.

3388. Lauterbach, Charles E. "Mrs. Hudson Puts Her Foot Down," *BSJ Christmas Annual*, No. 1 (1956), 41.

————. ————, *Baker Street Ballads*.

[Culver City, Calif.: Luther Norris, March 1971.] p. 21-22.

"When she regained her underpinning, / The lady vengeance swore - / She banished Shag and he was seen / In Baker Street no more."

3389. Mingey, Edward J. "The Bull Pup's Disappearance, or Who Paid Watson's Rent?" *BSJ*, 7, No. 3 (July 1957), 141-146.

"Watson's pressing financial necessities left him with but one choice, when forced to decide between the bull pup's welfare and the preservation of Holmes's anatomy."

3390. Morgan, Robert S. "The Puzzle of the Bull Pup," *BSJ Christmas Annual*, No. 1 (1956), 35-40.

The author suggests that the bull pup met with a fatal accident when Watson moved to 221B. The resultant shock to Watson's nervous system produced a permanent defection of his memory, which may explain his "outrageous lapses in chronology."

3391. Stockler, J. R., and R. N. Brodie. "The Problem of the Dog That Wasn't," *SHJ*, 9, No. 2 (Summer 1969), 61-62.

The "bull pup" was not a dog at all but a small calibre revolver which, in the military slang of the day, was referred to as a "Bull Pup."

3392. Tracy, Jack. "A Lot of Bull Pup," *BSJ*, 21, No. 3 (September 1971), 154-155.

Watson's famous bull-pup remark was an indication of his habit of keeping a dog when circumstances permitted, but the pup had no real existence when the statement was made.

INCOME

3393. Brodie, Robert N. and Janet B. "Dr. Watson's Finances—An Enquiry," *BSJ*, 18, No. 2 (June 1968), 104-106.

"His pension, his practice and his writing, combined with a modest capital, seem to comprise the financial framework of Watson's life. Apparently they permitted him considerable latitude, and no serious crises intervened to drain his resources."

3394. McLaren, R. M. "Doctor Watson—Punter or Speculator?" *SHJ*, 1, No. 1 (May 1952), 8-10.

"He spent half his wound pension on gambling—not on the Turf but on the Stock Exchange."

3395. Williams, H. B. "The Unknown Watson," *BSJ*, 13, No. 1 (March 1963), 43-45.

Speculation on his private life and source of income up to the time he met Holmes.

MEDICAL PRACTICE

See also *Medicine* (items 4111-4127)

3396. Allen, John F. "Min käre Watson" ["My Dear Watson"], *Puls* (1965).
———. ———, *BSCL*, No. 5 (1966), 6-11.
An analysis of Watson, the medical man.

3397. Graham, R. P. "Doctor Watson, I Presume?" *The American Journal of Surgery*, 71, No. 4 (April 1946), 574.
———. ———, *Illustrious Client's Third Case-Book*. Edited by J. N. Williamson and H. B. Williams. [Indianapolis, Ind.: The Illustrious Clients, 1953.] p. 72-73.
"Even if Watson's medical degree was not what it might have been, he earned, many times over, a doctorate of letters."

3398. [Katzen, Olga.] "Doctor . . . ?" by Sagittarius [pseud.] *The London Mystery Magazine* (April-May 1950), 4-5.
"But there's something queer in his medical career, / For he never had a single case."

3399. Meaker, Samuel R. "Watson Medicus," *The Third Cab*. [Boston: The Speckled Band, 1960.] p. 26-37.
"Being a survey of the practice of medicine by gaslight, together with some reflections upon the professional capacities of Dr. John H. Watson." (Subtitle)

3400. "Medicine Has a Vital Role in Armchair Adventure," *The Medical Tribune* [New York], 5, No. 102 (September 26-27, 1964).
———, *CPBook*, 1, No. 2 (Fall 1964), 38-39.
An interesting account of Watson and his medical practice.

3401. [Pelz, Bruce.] "Petrie Letter," *Nyet Vremia* 68 (February 3, 1966), 1.
———. ———, *The SHsf Fanthology One*. Edited by Ruth Berman. The Professor Challenger Society, 1967. p. 31-32.
———. ———, *The Rohmer Review*, No. 3 (August 1969), 16-17.
A letter dated April 1, 1898, from Dr. Flinders Petrie of Fu-Manchu fame criticizing his predecessor, Dr. Watson, for letting his practice deteriorate in order to keep company with a strange detective.

3402. Pennell, Vernon. "A Resumé of the Medical Life of John H. Watson, M. D., Late of the Army Medical Department, with an Appendix of the London University Regulations for Medical Degrees for the Year 1875," *SHJ*, 3, No. 2 (Winter 1956), 6-11.

3403. Simpson, Helen. "Medical Career and Capacities of Dr. J. H. Watson," *Baker-Street Studies*. Edited by H. W. Bell. London: Constable & Co., [1934]. p. 35-61.

"Watson the medical man could, despite his brilliant beginnings, never have aspired to any position of world-wide consequence; Watson the biographer is second only to the greatest names."

3404. Van Liere, Edward J. "Doctor Watson, General Practitioner." *West Virginia Medical Journal*, 55 (October 1959), 364-367.
———. ———, *A Doctor Enjoys Sherlock Holmes*. New York: Vantage Press, [1959]. p. 135-141.
"We may think of the faithful Dr. Watson answering a call, perhaps late at night, his stethoscope concealed in his hat, and his trusty medical bag filled with the acceptable drugs. We can picture him further, riding along in his hansom—the lights of which shine dimly through the fog—rattling over the cobblestones of the old London streets, carrying on the tradition of his noble profession."

SMOKING AND TOBACCO

3405. Keen, Sherry. "Ship's or 'ship's'? That Is the Question," *BSJ*, 3, No. 4 (October 1953), 234-235.
A search for the tobacco Watson referred to when he told Holmes, "I always smoke 'ship's' myself."

3406. Wimbush, J. C. "Watson's Tobacconist," *SHJ*, 1, No. 2 (September 1952), 35-36.
R. H. Hoar & Co. Ltd. is identified as the Bradley of Oxford Street where Watson procured his tobacco.

WIVES

3407. Akers, Arthur K. "Who Was Mrs. Watson's First Husband?" *BSJ*, 10, No. 1 (January 1960), 35-36.
"Since Watson's name was indisputably John, why should his wife refer to him as 'James'? In reason and in logic, this could only have been the Freudian inadvertence ascribable to there once having been a James."

3408. Andrew, Clifton R. "What Happened to Dr. Watson's Married Life After June 14, 1889?" *BSJ Christmas Annual*, No. 3 (1958), 42-44.
A commentary on the treatment accorded Mrs. Watson by her husband in deference to Holmes's cajolery in Twis.

3409. Austin, Bliss. "Sonnet: On the Second Mrs. Watson at Her Needle Work," *BSJ*, 3, No. 2 (April 1953), 98.
"Yet Sherlock is the one you did belie, / So, if he doesn't care—no more do I."

Dr. Watson

3410. Baring-Gould, William S. " 'Now, Watson, the Fair Sex Is Your Department,' " *The Annotated Sherlock Holmes.* New York: Clarkson N. Potter, [1967]. Vol. 1, chap. 22, p. 325-330.

A discussion of his *three* marriages and wives.

3411. Blakeney, T. S. "Watson's Second Marriage," *Sherlock Holmes: Fact or Fiction?* London: John Murray, [1932]. p. 113-114.

A refutation of S. C. Roberts's claim that Miss Violet de Merville was the second Mrs. Watson.

3412. Douglass, Ruth. "The Camberwell Poisoner," *Ellery Queen's Mystery Magazine,* 9, No. 39 (February 1947), 57-63.

The author offers her own explanation of the Mrs. Watson problem, in reply to Rex Stout and Kurt Steel.

3413. Hall, Trevor H. "Dr. Watson's Marriages," *The Late Mr. Sherlock Holmes & Other Literary Studies.* London: Gerald Duckworth & Co., [1971]. Chap. 3, p. 40-63.

"Watson was married five times: to Constance Adams in 1884 or 1885, to a Miss X, with both a mother and aunt in 1886, to the mother-less and aunt-less Mary Morstan in 1888 or 1889, to a Miss Y in 1896 and to a Miss Z in 1902."

3414. Haynes, George. "The Last Mrs. Watson," *SHJ,* 6, No. 2 (Spring 1963), 53-54.

A confirmation of Christopher Morley's contention that Lady Frances Carfax was the third and last Mrs. Watson.

3415. Hoff, Ebbe Curtis. "The Adventure of John and Mary," *BSJ,* 9, No. 3 (July 1959), 136-152.

An excellent article on the wedded life of John and Mary Watson in which the author discusses Watson's early life and talents, his first meeting with Mary, the date of their marriage, the wedding, their married life, and Mary's illness and death.

3416. Hunt, T. B., and H. W. Starr. "What Happened to Mary Morstan," *BSJ* [OS], 2, No. 3 (July 1947), 237-246.

"Mary Morstan did not cast off her husband [as first suggested by H. W. Starr (item 3431)]; she fought courageously—and with the Doctor's self-sacrificing help—against the inroads of insanity. Again and again his love and medical skill pulled her back from the shadows of the asylum: to her he gave the closing years of his life, attending her in seclusion, saving her from the final horror of institutional care."

3417. Lauterbach, Charles E. "The Bachelor," by John Habakkuk Watson. *Baker Street Ballads.* [Culver City, Calif.: Luther Norris, March 1971.] p. 14.

"I'd not exchange for bachelorhood / My own domestic blister; / I'm glad when Mary looked demure / I up and kister!"

3418. Leavitt, Robert Keith. "The Fourth Conanical Toast: Proposed at the B.S.I. Dinner on January 9, 1953," *BSJ,* 3, No. 2 (April 1953), 83.

"I give you that mysterious daisy—/ Dr. Watson's Second Wife!"

3419. MacGregor, Marilyn. "Moriarty, the Apaches, and the First Mrs. Watson," *VH,* 2, No. 2 (April 1968), 2-3.

"The young woman Watson met and courted in San Francisco, Alice Whiting, became the Alice Watson in London on November 1, 1886." See also item 885.

3420. McCleary, George F. "When Did Watson First Meet His First Wife?" *BSJ* [OS], 2, No. 2 (January 1947), 50-53.

The author believes that July, not September as claimed by H. W. Bell, was the month when Watson and Mary Morstan were married. They agree the event took place in 1887.

3421. Moriarty, Daniel L. "The Woman Who Beat Sherlock Holmes," *BSJ,* 9, No. 2 (April 1959), 69-82.

Winner of the 2nd annual Morley-Montgomery Award for the best contribution to *BSJ* in 1959.

"When Sherlock Holmes made the statement to John Openshaw that he had been beaten once by a woman, most observers believed that he was speaking of Miss Irene Adler. There can be no doubt that Holmes had in mind the woman who took Watson away from him. However, as cunning and as resourceful as Mary Watson was, it took her sixteen years to beat him decisively."

3422. Morley, Christopher. "Dr. Watson's Secret," *The Saturday Review of Literature,* 11, No. 22 (December 15, 1934), 371. (The Bowling Green)

———. ———, *Streamlines.* Garden City, N.Y.: Doubleday, Doran & Co., 1936. p. 66-74.

———. ———, ———. London: Faber & Faber Ltd., [1937]. p. 66-74.

———. ———, by Jane Nightwork [pseud.] *221B: Studies in Sherlock Holmes.* Edited by Vincent Starrett. New York: The Macmillan Co., 1940. p. 46-53.

By accepting the hypothesis that Watson and Mary Morstan were secretly married in the spring of 1887 but pretended it did not happen until autumn, other chronological reconciliations are possible.

3423. [———.] "Watson à la Mode," by Jane Nightwork. *BSJ* [OS], 1, No. 1 (January 1946), 15-20.

———. ———, *The Ironing Board.* Garden

City, N.Y.: Doubleday & Co., 1949. p. 159-165.

————. ————, ————. London: Faber and Faber Ltd., [1950]. p. 159-165.

"Watson's so called second marriage was when he and Mary decided to resume mutual bed and board. So Watson's second wife was actually his first; and there never was a third."

3424. Rabe, W. T. "Variations on a Casual Remark," *BSJ Christmas Annual*, No. 3 (1958), 61-62.

"From Baker Street to church, he went, / A groom at any cost. / *Watson deserted me for a wife.*"

3425. Sayers, Dorothy L. "Dr. Watson, Widower," *Unpopular Opinions*. London: Victor Gollancz Ltd., 1946. p. 152-168.

————. ————, ————. New York: Harcourt, Brace & Co., [1947]. p. 189-209.

————. ————, *MacKill's Mystery Magazine*, 3, No. 5 (January 1954), 77-92.

————. ————, *The Incunabular Sherlock Holmes.* Edited by Edgar W. Smith. Morristown, N.J.: The Baker Street Irregulars, 1958. p. 143-159.

"Is it not perhaps less extravagant to suppose a trifling *lapsus calami* on the part of a man like Watson, who in so many instances has been proved guilty of similar inaccuracies, than to drag in a wholly hypothetical marriage, unrecorded, and lasting less than twelve months, with the sole purpose of explaining Watson's temporary absence from Baker Street?"

3426. Seemann, Verner. "Dr. Watson udi AEgteskab" ["Dr. Watson in Marriage"], *Sherlock Holmes Årbog* II (1966), 31-38.

3427. Simpson, A. Carson. "It Must Have Been Two Other Fellows," *Leaves from the Copper Beeches.* Narberth, Pa.: Livingston Pub. Co., 1959. p. 41-53.

"Who, then, was James? If Elmer Davis could evoke a *daughter* of Mrs. Forrester to provide a third wife for Watson, may we not suggest that there was a Forrester *son*? . . . It was James *Forrester,* then, and not James Watson, of whom his mother spoke. In the light of this, the problem of 'John or James' vanishes."

3428. [Smith, Edgar W.] "Sonnet: Mary Morstan to J. H. Watson," by Helene Yuhasova [pseud.] *Profile by Gaslight.* Edited by Edgar W. Smith. New York: Simon and Schuster, 1944. p. 187.

————. ————, *A Lauriston Garden of Verses,* by Helene Yuhasova. Summit, N. J.: The Pamplet House, 1946. p. [17].

————. ————, *Baker Street and Beyond: Together with Some Trifling Monographs.* Morristown, N.J.: The Baker Street Irregulars, 1957. [unpaged]

"I'll hold you, John, / Or James, as close and fondly disciplined / As ever woman held the man upon / Whose faith her hopes are fixed."

3429. Smith, Francis. " 'The Only Selfish Action I Can Recall,' " *SHJ,* 9, No. 4 (Summer 1970), 134-135.

A close examination of Holmes's telling remark to Watson reveals that "the Casanova of many nations and three continents" did not marry a second time, as many commentators believe, but, instead, was having an *affaire* with a married woman!

3430. Solovay, Jacob C. "Watson Takes a Wife," *BSJ Christmas Annual*, No. 2 (1957), 44.

"So, Watson, you are shortly taking leave / You much prefer the husband to the sleuth."

3431. Starr, H. W. "Some New Light on Watson," *BSJ* [OS], 1, No. 1 (January 1946), 55-63.

His marriages did not involve new brides, but were reconciliations with Mary, who had been driven into separation by the doctor's extra-professional engagements.

3432. Wigglesworth, Belden. " 'Many Nations and Three Separate Continents': An Inquiry into One Aspect of the Life of John H. Watson, M.D.," *BSJ* [OS], 2, No. 3 (July 1947), 273-278.

A discussion of his *three* marriages and *two* wounds.

3433. Williams, Stephen. "An Unsung Heroine," *Punch,* 226 (January 6, 1954), 68-69.

"Tribute to Mrs. Watson on the occasion of Sherlock Holmes's hundredth anniversary." (Subtitle)

3434. Williamson, J. N. " 'The Latest Treatise Upon Pathology,' " *BSJ,* 6, No. 4 (October 1956), 208-214.

"Mary Watson, tired of her husband's disinterest, his frequent journeys with Holmes, and his admitted visits to the widow Norton, divorced Watson in 1901 and, in the summer of 1902, Watson took Irene as his lawful wife, much to the chagrin of Sherlock Holmes who was fond of Mary and still rather irked by Watson's betrayal of their friendship."

3435. ————. "The Wiles of Mary Morstan," *Illustrious Client's Case-Book.* Edited by J. N. Williamson and H. B. Williams. [Indianapolis, Ind.: The Illustrious Clients, 1948.] p. 21-25.

"To Doctor Watson, she is always *the* woman."

WRITINGS

3436. Balfour, R. E. "New Light on Dr.

The Writings About the Writings

Dr. Watson

Watson's Early Works," *The Cambridge Review*, 56 (November 2, 1934), 65-67.

The many discrepancies in Sign and Scan have convinced Mr. Balfour that these two tales are spurious episodes—the first having been written by some unknown journalist and the second by Mrs. Hudson—and are not part of the "genuine Saga" as recorded by Watson.

3437. Ball, John. "The Second Collaboration," *BSJ*, 4, No. 2 (April 1954), 69-74.

"Of the many mysteries of the Canon, perhaps the most perplexing is the exact role played by the Literary Agent in making Watson's priceless manuscripts available to a profoundly grateful posterity."

3438. Bengis, Nathan L. "Thanks to Dr. Watson: A Study in Conanical Plagiarism," *Illustrious Client's Third Case-Book*. Edited by J. N. Williamson and H. B. Williams. [Indianapolis, Ind.: The Illustrious Clients, 1953.] p. 5-14.

Similarities between nine tales by Watson and five short stories by Doyle.

3439. Bristowe, W. S. "A Note on the Watson-Doyle Partnership," *BSJ*, 3, No. 3 (Autumn 1957), 4-5.

Speculations on the literary partnership between the two doctors.

3440. C[ochran], G. L. "A Note on the Authenticity of the Writings of John H. Watson, M. D.," *DCC*, 2, No. 2 (December 1965), 2-3.

"An attempt to introduce a probable argument showing that the position of Sherlockian scholars regarding the authenticity of the tales and the authorship of John H. Watson is not only reasonable, but eminently tenable."

3441. Dakin, D. Martin. "The Problem of the *Case-Book*," *SHJ*, 1, No. 3 (June 1953), 29-34.

An inquiry into the claims of the stories in the *Case Book* to inclusion in the Watsonian canon reveals that some are undoubtedly genuine but that others are forgeries, either in whole or in part.

3442. ———. "Second Thoughts on the *Case-Book*," *SHJ*, 3, No. 1 (Summer 1956), 8-9.

An elaboration of the theory advanced by the author in his previous article on the *Case Book*.

3443. Doyle, Adrian Conan. "Dr. Watson's Creator," *New York Herald Tribune* (April 12, 1952).

———. ———, *CPBook*, 1, No. 1 (Summer 1964), 8.

A letter to Art Buchwald (see also item 4711) in which the son of Sir Arthur tries to set the record straight as to who was the actual author of the Sherlock Holmes stories. Was there ever any doubt?

3444. Gibson, Theodore W. "Notes on Dr. Watson's Notes," *BSJ*, 7, No. 2 (April 1957), 105-108.

The chronicler of the Canon is taken to task for relying too heavily on his memory and for supplying details he had not accurately observed.

3445. Grazebrook, O. F. *The Author of the Case Book.* [London: Privately Printed, 1949.] 32 p. (Studies in Sherlock Holmes, No. 4)

"A strong case is advanced for a deteriorated, or even a deutero Watson, with chapter and verse cited." (Edgar W. Smith)

3446. Hall, W. S. "Don't Blame Watson," *BSJ*, 3, No. 2 (April 1953), 84-86.

While acting as Watson's literary agent, Sir Arthur deliberately touched up each new adventure in order to puzzle the more avid readers.

3447. Hand, Herbert T. "Letter from Porlock," *The Second Cab*. Edited by James Keddie. [Boston: The Speckled Band, 1947.] p. 82-85.

Holmes urges Watson to be even more obscure in his writings to avoid international complications and personal libel suits.

3448. Harbottle, S. T. L. "The Case-Book Cipher Unveiled," *SHJ*, 3, No. 4 (Summer 1958), 9-10.

By an ingenious method of treating certain key sentences in the *Case Book* as anagrams, Mr. Harbottle has made the incredible discovery that Inspector Lestrade is the real author of this work.

3449. Heldenbrand, Page. "The Adventures of the Dead Detective," *Leaves from the Copper Beeches*. Narberth, Pa.: Livingston Pub. Co., 1959. p. 33-34.

"It can only be that the needy Watson, equipped with battered tin dispatch-box, sought out once more his astute editor and fiscal alchemist, and it was decided that Holmes should resume business at the same old stand—dealing in updated cases—with Conan Doyle fabricating the story of his rebirth."

3450. Helling, Cornelis. "About a Much-Despised Book—*The Case-Book of Sherlock Holmes*," *SHJ*, 6, No. 1 (Winter 1962), 24-26.

The author takes exception to those scholars who maintain that the *Case Book* contains only apocryphal stories, and explains why he thinks they are "all well-written and thrilling narratives" and "that some are equal to the best of the others, in varying degrees."

3451. ——. "The Third Person," *BSJ*, 6, No. 4 (October 1956), 203.

Watson actually wrote Last and Maza, but in the third person.

3452. ——. "The True Author of Last and Maza," *SHJ*, 7, No. 4 (Spring 1966), 123-124.

An examination of a facsimile of the opening words to Vall adds even more proof that these two tales could only have been written by Watson.

3453. Kennedy, Bruce. "The Watson Myth," *VH*, 1, No. 3 (September 1967), 6-7.

Mr. Kennedy has arrived at the startling conclusion that Holmes was the true author of the Sacred Writings and that Watson was merely a figment of Holmes's imagination.

3454. ——. "Why Doyle?" *SOS*, 1, No. 4 (April 1967), 12.

He agreed to act as the literary agent and to take credit for the authorship of the sixty tales so that Watson's medical practice would not be adversely affected.

3455. Ketcham, George G. "The Case of the Mendacious Medico," *BSJ*, 15, No. 4 (December 1965), 227-228.

Watson is not a "bumbling boob" but only seems to be because of his gallant effort to confuse fact with fiction in order to deceive Moriarty. (If the Professor is still alive, as some writers maintain, then Sherlockians could be doing Holmes a great disservice in their endless attempts to correct Watson's *intentional* errors and misstatements!)

3456. Kirtz, Frank Groom. "The Strange Case of John H. Watson, M.D., Late Indian Army—A Study of the Reliability of Witnesses," *The St. Louis Bar Journal*, 9, No. 5 (March 1961), 13-24.

A discussion of some discrepancies and inaccuracies in the reminiscences of "one of history's greatest witnesses, Dr. John H. Watson."

3457. Mingey, Edward J. "A Case of Mistaken Identity," *BSJ*, 12, No. 3 (September 1962), 146-149.

An unsuccessful attempt to prove that the literary agent, not Watson, was the chronicler of Holmes's adventures.

3458. Montgomery, James. "It Pays to Advertise," *Shots from the Canon*. [Philadelphia: Privately Printed, 1953.] p. 6.

An advertisement of "The Doyle Literary Agency" that appears on p. 31 of *Collier's Weekly* for October 31, 1903, should settle for all time the Doyle-Watson controversy!

3459. Sellars, Crighton. "When, How and Why?" *BSJ*, 1, No. 3 (July 1951), 104-105.

"But where appeared the Agent? Tell me that! / And why did Watson seek him for the job?"

3460. Smith, Edgar W. "On the Authorship of the Tales-Within-the-Tales," *The Third Cab*. [Boston: The Speckled Band, 1960.] p. 42-47.

"It seems that we must enlarge our roster of those who contributed to the Canon from the four who have until now held that high distinction [Watson, Holmes, Mycroft, and Doyle] to a considerably greater number. They all did their best—the Pinkertons and the Armitages and the Fergusons and the rest—and what they did was sometimes good."

3461. [——.] "The Other Giant," *BSJ*, 1, No. 3 (July 1951), 81-82. (The Editor's Gas-Lamp)

"Dr. John H. Watson was fortunate in having as his literary agent so fast a friend and so fine a writer as Dr. A. Conan Doyle."

3462. Tomashefsky, Steven. "Canon and Conan," *BSJ*, 18, No. 4 (December 1968), 224-228.

A number of inconsistencies in certain of the tales are cited to show that such errors came from the pen of Doyle who, in addition to acting as Watson's literary agent, collaborated with him whenever Watson's practice made it necessary for him to devote more time to his patients and less to his chronicles.

E *Other Characters*

GENERAL AND MISCELLANEOUS

3463. Adams, Robert Winthrop. "John H. Watson, M. D., Characterologist," *BSJ*, 4, No. 2 (April 1954), 81-92.

An excellent discussion of Watson's mastery of characterization, with examples, and the books he must have consulted to assist him in his descriptions of people. Holmes's traits are also described and enumerated.

3464. Clark, Henry C. "Clients in Jeopardy," *The Second Cab*. Edited by James Keddie. [Boston: The Speckled Band, 1947.] p. 25-27.

An examination of four of the most famous cases (Copp, Five, Gree, and Houn) in which the Master neglected the safety of his clients; or, "How some of those who placed themselves under the protective arm of Mr. Sherlock Holmes came through by the skin of their teeth." (Edgar W. Smith)

3465. Eaton, Herbert. "The Clients Observed," *VH*, 4, No. 2 (April 1970), 5-7.

A discussion and listing of the clients Holmes represented in both the published and unpublished cases.

3466. ———. "The Moral Effect of Life in the Colonies," *VH*, 5, No. 1 (January 1971), 7-8.
A look at several persons who were influenced by the British Colonies.

3467. Holland, Glenn S. "The 'Small, But Very Efficient, Organization' and Other Small Problems," *BSJ*, 21 No. 2 (June 1971), 84-89, 96.
An analysis of the following fourteen members of the Holmes organization who aided the Master in many of his cases: Wiggins, Simpson, Cartwright, Sherman, Fred Porlock, Mercer, Langdale Pike, Shinwell (Porky) Johnson, Billy, Pompey, Mycroft, Lomax, Wilson Hargreave, and Merivale.

3468. Holroyd, James Edward. "A Baker Street Portrait Gallery," *Baker Street By-ways*. London: George Allen & Unwin Ltd., [1959]. p. 114-158.
Contents: Dr. John H. Watson. - Mrs. Hudson. - Mycroft Holmes. - The Yard. - Colonel Moran. - Horace Harker. - Irene Adler. - Henry Baker. - Dr. Lysander Starr *et al.* - The 'Exploits'.
"Random reflections on some of the author's favorites in the Baker Street Gallery."

3469. [———.] "The Case of Dr. Lysander Starr," by Horace Harker [pseud.] *SHJ*, 4, No. 1 (Winter 1958), 18-19.
———. "Dr. Lysander Starr *et al,*" *Baker Street By-ways*. London: George Allen & Unwin Ltd., [1959]. p. 147-153.
On the duplicity and multiplicity of names in the Saga.

3470. Lauritzen, Henry. "Alkoholikere i Conanen" ["Alcoholics in the Canon"], *Sherlockiana*, 10, Nr. 3 (1965), 9-12.

3471. MacDougald, Duncan. "Some Onomatological Notes on 'Sherlock Holmes' and Other Names in the Sacred Writings," *BSJ*, 12, No. 4 (December 1962), 213-218.

3472. Morrisson, Douglas. "Observations of Criminal Ineptitude in the Canon," *SOS*, 1, No. 6 (August 1967), 5.
The "bungling episode of the nefarious Jefferson Hope" and the "episode of the delayed thumb print of Jonas Oldacre" are cited as examples of the many acts of inept criminal reasoning.

3473. Pascoe, James. "So Many Enemies," *SHJ*, 7, No. 2 (Spring 1965), 50-51.
A brief essay on some of the Master's adversaries by the winner of the "Intermediate Examination Paper."

3474. Petersen, Svend. "Art Jargon in the Canon," *BSJ*, 2, No. 2 (April 1952), 101-102.
Eight instances where the literary agent substituted his first name for the true first name.

3475. Starr, H. W. "A Case of Identity, or The Adventure of the Seven Claytons," *BSJ*, 10, No. 1 (January 1960), 5-11.
———. ———, *Escape!* [Santa Ana, Calif.], 1, No. 1 (January 1961), 19-23.
———. ———, *Tarzan Alive*, by Philip José Farmer. Garden City, N.Y.: Doubleday & Co., 1972. p. 208-214.
"John Clayton, cab driver [Houn] is John Clayton, fifth Duke of Greyminster, father of the 'sixth Duke of Holdernesse' and of John Clayton, 'Lord Greystoke.' The kidnapped 'Lord Saltire' [Prio] is William Cecil Clayton, first cousin of John Clayton III, 'Lord Greystoke,' seventh Duke of Greyminster—popularly known as Tarzan of the Apes."

3476. Swanson, Martin J. "Collectors in the Canon," *BSJ*, 13, No. 3 (September 1963), 136-141.
An illustrated listing and discussion of the multitude of objects amassed by the hobbyist collectors who parade through the Sacred Writings.

3477. Van Dieren, Bernard J. "What Has Become of Them?" *BSJ*, 4, No. 4 (October 1954), 197-204.
The lives of twenty-seven characters are traced since they left the pages of the Canonical tales.

3478. [Williams, H. B.] "Curses Canonical," by the Sub-Librarian. *Illustrious Client's Second Case-Book*. Edited by J. N. Williamson. [Indianapolis, Ind.: The Illustrious Clients, 1949.] p. 50-54.
How some of the characters expressed themselves in times of stress and emotion.

BAKER STREET IRREGULARS

3479. Fiske, Richard. "Wiggins-V.C.," *BSJ* [OS], 3, No. 4 (October 1948), 474-476.
" 'Wot for, me lads, is one of them there military secrets—'tween me, His Majesty the King, and Mr. Sherlock Holmes.' "

3480. Harrison, Michael. "The Ballad of the Queen's Shilling," *BSJ*, 15, No. 4 (December 1965), 195-198.
" 'Yes . . . I done my stretch with the B. S. I.— / and a raggedy corps we were. / But we took our bob for a well-done job, / when we might have ate skilly in stir. . . .' "

BUTLERS

3481. Jones, G. Basil. "Butlers in the Canon," *BSJ*, 1, No. 1 (January 1951), 18-24.

"If, as is abundantly clear, one of the chief values of the whole chronicle is as a social document crystallizing the institutions of an irrecoverable past, its butlers cannot be overlooked. For who more than they symbolize the security, the prosperity, the ordered graciousness, and withal, perhaps, the self-complacency of Victorian living?"

CHILDREN

3482. Holland, Glenn S. "Sherlock Holmes and Children," *BSJ*, 17, No. 4 (December 1967), 239-240.

Incidents are cited to show that the Master was found of children.

3483. Quayle, Edward. "Suffer the Little Children . . . ," *BSJ* [OS], 3, No. 4 (October 1948), 463-470.

Some facts about the boys and girls who figured as victims or vanquished in the solution to some of Holmes's cases, and an evaluation of the place they had in his life.

CLERGYMEN

3484. Kerby, Frederick M. "The Forgotten Clergymen in the Canon," *BSJ*, 4, No. 4 (October 1954), 223-228.

3485. Rice, Otis R. "Clergymen in the Canon," *BSJ*, 4, No. 3 (July 1954), 133-143.

NOBILITY

3486. Grazebrook, O. F. *Royalty*. [London: Privately Printed, 1949.] 38 p. (Studies in Sherlock Holmes, No. 3)
————. ————, *Illustrious Client's Third Case-Book*. Edited by J. N. Williamson and H. B. Williams. [Indianapolis, Ind.: The Illustrious Clients, 1953.] p. 27-59.

The author traces some of the great figures in Victorian history who found themselves at 221B Baker Street.

3487. White, William Braid. "Dr. Watson and the Peerage," *BSJ* [OS], 2, No. 1 (January 1947), 18-23.

A discussion of British peerage and the mistakes Watson made when using the titles bestowed upon members of the nobility.

POLITICIANS

3488. Grazebrook, O. F. *Politics and Premiers*. [London: Privately Printed, 1949.] 38 p. (Studies in Sherlock Holmes, No. 2)

"The high political figures in the Canon march in review—and are identified convincingly with their secular prototypes." (Edgar W. Smith)

SCHOOLMASTERS

3489. Bryan-Brown, Frederick. "Sherlockian Schools and Schoolmasters," *SHJ*, 3, No. 1 (Summer 1956), 2-7.

A paper on Holmes's and Watson's education and the minor characters who were concerned with the teaching profession.

WOMEN (GENERAL)

3490. Clarke, Richard W. "Certain Ladies of Baker Street," *BSJ*, 2, No. 1 (January 1952), 34-38.
————. "On Certain Ladies of Baker Street," *The Best of the Pips*. Westchester County, N.Y.: The Five Orange Pips, 1955. p. 9-13.

"In the saga of Holmes and Watson, the ladies are, for the most part, sadly neglected. Usually we are given but a brief description of these creatures, and then they are summarily dismissed."

3491. Dalton, Pat. "Women of the Canon. 2. The Working Girls," *SHJ*, 10, No. 2 (Summer 1971), 44-47; "3. The Ladies of Title," 10, No. 3 (Winter 1971), 86-89. illus.

3492. Davis, Elmer. "On the Emotional Geology of Baker Street," *221B: Studies in Sherlock Holmes*. Edited by Vincent Starrett. New York: The Macmillan Co., 1940. p. 37-40.

Speculations on the love life of Holmes and Watson.

3493. De Groat, Ray. "Les Belles Dames Holmesienne, or Dr. Watson's Weakness," *VH*, 2, No. 1 (January 1968), 5.

"But the ones I love best are Holmesienne names, / The feminine ones that never grow cold."

3494. Hardwick, Mollie. "Women of the Canon. 1. The Women of Influence," *SHJ*, 10, No. 1 (Winter 1970), 2-6; "4. The Victims," 10, No. 4 (Summer 1972), 115-119. illus.

3495. Rouby, Jason. " 'Dear Lady Abigail . . . ,' " Edited by Jason Rouby, "Vanderbilt and the Yeggman." *BSJ*, 20, No. 4 (December 1970), 206-209.

Four letters to the purported editor-counselor of the London *Times*, 188- to 190-, asking for advice on matters of the heart. These letters from "Bohemian," "M. S.," "Brewer's Daughter," and "Mrs. J. N. G." may have come from the "agony column."

3496. West, Katharine. *Chapter of Governesses: A Study of the Governess in English Fiction, 1800-1949*. London: Cohen & West Ltd., [1949]. p. 153-159.

Six pages of this portrait gallery of governesses are devoted to Mary Morstan and Violet Hunter.

BILLY

3497. Keddie, James. "Billy," *A Baker Street Four-Wheeler*. Edited by Edgar W. Smith. [Maplewood, N.J., and New York: The Pamphlet House, 1944.) p. 54-56.

————. ————. Supplement to *Sherlockiana* (1959). [2] p.

A word of praise for the lad who served his Master so well.

3498. Newton, G. B. "Billy the Page," *SHJ*, 2, No. 3 (Summer 1955), 7-10.

"There were at least three if not more page-boys employed at various times at 221B. The question is, which of them was the authentic Billy of whom we are so fond?"

3499. Page, Andrew. " 'A Canonical Question,' " *HO*, 1, No. 4 (June 1971), 7.

A further query concerning Holmes's page(s).

MYCROFT HOLMES
(INCLUDING THE DIOGENES CLUB)

3500. Andrews, Charlton. "The Resources of Mycroft Holmes," *The Bookman*, 18, No. 3 (December 1903), 365-372.

————. ————, Pt. 1 reprinted in *The Incunabular Sherlock Holmes* Edited by Edgar W. Smith. Morristown, N.J.: The Baker Street Irregulars, 1958. p. 17-23.

————. ————, *CPBook*, 4, No. 15 (August 1968), 292-296.

Contents: 1. He Repudiates Sherlock. - 2. He Solves the Mystery of the Shakespearian Authorship. - 3. He Solves the Mystery of the Man in the Iron Mask.

A satire in which the great detective's brother, during the course of an interview, performs a few *tours de force*.

3501. Barrett, William G. "The Diogenes Club," *SHJ*, 9, No. 2 (Summer 1969), 53-55.

A history and an identification of the London club that was founded by Mycroft and quite possibly Sherlock.

3502. Bigelow, S. Tupper. "Identifying the Diogenes Club: An Armchair Exercise," *BSJ*, 18, No. 2 (June 1968), 67-73.

A thorough study of the clubs in Pall Mall lends support to Dr. Wolff's identification of the Diogenes Club as the Travellers'. "The chief tradition of The Travellers' is that members do not speak to each other." Includes a map of eighty London clubs.

3503. Clark, Benjamin S. "Mycroft Come Back; All Is Forgiven," *BSJ*, 21, No. 3 (September 1971), 169-174.

3504. Cohen, Mandel E. "Sherlock's Big Brother," *The Second Cab*. Edited by James Keddie. [Boston: The Speckled Band, 1947.] p. 86-90.

Answers to the questions: "What do we know about this brother? How did he fit into Sherlock's life? What did Sherlock think about him, and what does this tell us about the great detective?"

3505. Cox, J. Randolph. "Mycroft Holmes: Private Detective," *BSJ*, 6, No. 4 (October 1956), 197-200.

The early episodes in his career as a private consultant are in the guise of a series of short stories about a former law clerk named *Martin Hewitt*.

3506. Fox, Lyttleton. "Mycroft Recomputed," *BSJ*, 19, No. 1 (March 1969), 4-11.

A highly original and provocative paper attempting to show that Mycroft was an anthropomorphic analog computer.

3507. Frisbie, Owen P. "Sherlock to Mycroft," *The Best of the Pips*. Westchester County, N.Y.: The Five Orange Pips, 1955. p. 57.

"Why is it you refuse to use your powers?"

3508. George, Isaac S. "Mycroft the Mighty," *Illustrious Client's Third Case-Book*. Edited by J. N. Williamson and H. B. Williams. [Indianapolis, Ind.: The Illustrious Clients, 1953.] p. 108-109.

"His brain was well-ordered and tidy, / And stored up with facts like a file—/ And never for great reward sighed he / While serving the crown with a smile."

3509. Hogan, John C. "Sherlock Holmes—Was He a 'Playboy'?" *BSJ*, 16, No. 2 (June 1966), 101-107.

————. "Was Sherlock Holmes a Playboy?" *VIP, The Playboy Club Magazine*, No. 12 (Winter 1966), 20, 30, 70.

————. ————, *CPBook*, 3, No. 11 (Winter 1967), 218-220.

Holmes not only had a key to the Playboy Club of London, but was a charter member. His brother Mycroft was a co-founder of the Club. It was then located in Pall Mall and operating under the disguised name "The Diogenes Club."

3510. Jenkins, William D. "The Adventure of the Misplaced Armchair," *BSJ*, 19, No. 1 (March 1969), 12-16.

On Mycroft's government post and membership in the Unionist ("Diogenes Club").

3511. Kennedy, Bruce. *Mycroft: A Study into the Life of the Brother of Sherlock Holmes.* With an introduction by Bruce Dettman; illustrations by Jon V. Wilmunen. Rockford, Ill.: The Three Students Plus, 1969. 24 p. (Rockford Illustrated Publications)

Contents: Introduction. - Mycroft - 1. The Man. - 2. In the Family. - 3. What was Mycroft Holmes? - 4. The Queerest

Club . . . - 5. The Fiscal Mess. - 6. Et Fin. *Review: SHJ*, 9, No. 3 (Winter 1969), 106 (Lord Donegall).

3512. Knox, Ronald A. "The Mystery of Mycroft," *Baker Street Studies*. Edited by H. W. Bell. London: Constable & Co., 1934. p. 131-158.

Accuses Sherlock's brother of having been a member of the Moriarty organization and of supplying both Holmes and Moriarty with information about the other.

3513. Levine, Arthur L. "The Books Are in Need of an Audit," *BSJ*, 8, No. 1 (January 1958), 36-40.

About the man who *was* the British Government and regrettably is not still.

3514. McKee, Wilbur K. "The Son of a Certain Gracious Lady," *BSJ*, 8, No. 3 (July 1958), 133-138.

Mycroft was not the brother of Sherlock but the son of the "gracious lady" whom Holmes visited at Windsor (Bruc).

3515. *Meeting Brother Mycroft.* London: The Times Pub. Co., [n. d.] 1 p. (The Times Broadsheets, Set 4, No. 30)

————. Reissued in 1944. 2 p.

One of 144 broadsheets, issued in 18 sets, first produced by *The Times* during World War I in order to meet a demand from the trenches for literature in convenient form. Extract from Gree.

3516. Merriman, C. O. "In Clubland," *SHJ*, 7, No. 1 (Winter 1964), 29-30. (Wigmore Street Post-Bag)

An identification of the Athenaeum with the Diogenes Club, based mainly on the fact that Doyle became a member in 1901.

3517. ————. "The Toast Is 'Mycroft Holmes,' " *SHJ*, 2, No. 2 (December 1954), 2-3.

————. ————, *The Accountant*, 135 (December 22, 1956), 645.

A commentary on Mycroft and his career as a government auditor.

3518. Mitchell, R. C. "A Portrait of Mycroft," *SHJ*, 9, No. 3 (Winter 1969), 96-99.

A valuable study of the similarities and differences between the two brothers.

3519. Narunsky, Harry. "Big Brother Is Watching," *BSJ*, 17, No. 1 (March 1967), 9-12.

"We know Mycroft was born in 1847, died in 1903, worked for (or was) the British government, as well as the fact that he could drive a hansom, and the few facts given in our two glimpses of him. We can only agree that '. . . we would gladly have heard more of him. . . .' "

3520. Nathanson, Philip. "Mycroft as a Computer: Some Further Input," *BSJ*, 19, No. 2 (June 1969), 96-100.

An ingenious theory, in support of Professor Fox's, that MYCROFT is an acronym for a computer which Charles Babbage supposedly developed for the British Government between 1834 and 1849, the latter date approximating the "birth" of Sherlock's "brother."

3521. Redmond, D. A. "The Armchair Still Misplaced," *BSJ*, 22, No. 2 (June 1972), 78-80.

A corroboration of J. Randolph Cox's theory that Mycroft was Martin Hewitt.

3522. Weiss, Jeffrey N. "Mycroft Recomputed?" *BSJ*, 19, No. 2 (June 1969), 94-95.

A refutation of the thesis advanced by Littleton Fox in which Mr. Weiss concludes that "Mycroft was Holmes's flesh-and-blood brother, and not a collection of nuts and bolts."

MRS. HUDSON

See also *Baker Street, 221B*
(items 3637-3693)

3523. Eaton, Herbert. "Some Facts Concerning the Early Life of Mrs. Hudson," *VH*, 1, No. 1 (January 1967), 2-3.

The story of how the landlady and her son "Billy the page" came into enough money to pay for a twenty-nine-year lease on the house at 221 Baker Street.

3524. Kalt, Bryson R. "A Toast to Mrs. Hudson," *BSJ*, 15, No. 4 (December 1965), 221.

"So now we toast that martyred soul, / Who toiled with all her might / For that eccentric lodger / We honour here tonight."

3525. Kennedy, Bruce. "Mrs. Turner of Baker Street," *BSP*, No. 21 (March 1967), 2.

"The true landlady at 221 (or 111) was Mrs. Turner, with Hudson merely being her name in Watson's chronicles of Holmes."

3526. Offord, Lenore Glen. "The Brief Adventure of Mr. Turner," *BSJ* [OS], 1, No. 3 (July 1946), 253-259.

When Holmes addressed Mrs. Hudson as "Mrs. Turner," it was neither a slip of his tongue nor of Watson's pen. She had been married for a short time, Mr. Turner turned out to be a bigamist, and she hastily took back her original name.

3527. Pattrick, Robert R. "The Case of the Superfluous Landlady," *BSJ*, 3, No. 4 (October 1953), 241-243.

Mrs. Turner was not the "other" landlady but the maid.

3528. Shaw, John Bennett. *Mrs. Martha*

Other Characters

Hudson. [Tulsa: Privately Printed, 1967.] [4] p. illus.

Limited to 30 numbered copies.

"A keepsake from the Martha Hudson Memorial Breakfast, Algonquin Hotel, New York City, January 5, 1968."

"She was not THE woman, but she *was* THE Lady of the house."

3529. [Smith, Edgar W.] "Sonnet: Sherlock Holmes to Mrs. Hudson," by Helene Yuhasova [pseud.] *BSJ* [OS], 4, No. 1 (January 1949), 58.

———. ———, *Baker Street and Beyond: Together with Some Trifling Monographs.* Morristown, N.J.: The Baker Street Irregulars, 1957. [unpaged]

"We see you, Martha—calm, austere and wise—/ Britannia herself, in stern Victorian guise."

3530. [———.] "To Mrs. Hudson," *BSJ*, 7, No. 4 (October 1957), 195-196. (The Editor's Gas-Lamp)

"This estimable woman came closer than anyone else, save only Dr. Watson, to sharing the life and living of Sherlock Holmes."

3531. Starrett, Vincent. "The Singular Adventures of Martha Hudson," *Baker Street Studies.* Edited by H. W. Bell. London: Constable & Co., 1934. p. 85-130.

———. ———, *Bookman's Holiday: The Private Satisfactions of an Incurable Collector.* New York: Random House, [1942]. p. 47-81.

———. ———, ———. Freeport, N. Y.: Books for Libraries, [1971]. p. 47-81. (Essay Index Reprint Series)

———. ———, *Profile by Gaslight.* Edited by Edgar W. Smith. New York: Simon and Schuster, 1944. p. 202-229.

———. ———, *The Private Life of Sherlock Holmes.* Revised and enlarged. The University of Chicago Press, [1960]. p. 63-86.

"Of all the men and women who walked and talked with Holmes and Watson, none had an intimate and continuing relationship to compare with that enjoyed by Mrs. Hudson, the faithful and long-suffering landlady of 221B. Mr. Vincent Starrett, who surely must have lodged for many moons himself in Baker Street, gives us this feeling picture of a devoted woman who served the master not only in the heyday of his fame, but also in the later and less eventful years of his retirement on the Sussex Downs." (Edgar W. Smith)

COLONEL SEBASTIAN MORAN

See also *Empt* (items 2367-2380) and *Fina* (items 2412-2449)

3532. Andrew, C. R. "The Strange Case of Colonel Moran," *Two Baker Street Akronisms.* Summitt, N.J.: The Pamphlet House, 1945. p. 3-6.

"An explanation of the circumstances which enabled the big-game hunter to escape the toils." (Edgar W. Smith)

3533. Bigelow, S. Tupper. "Two Canonical Problems Solved," *BSJ Christmas Annual,* No. 4 (1959), 261-271.

Patience Moran, the niece of Jabez Wilson and Col. Moran, witnessed the killing in Bosc but remained silent to protect her father's post as lodgekeeper. As Wilson's maid she ignored the regular disposal of earth from his house, having been told that she was to be surprised with a new billiard room built in the basement. Moran was still alive in Illu for lack of any real evidence to convict him of Adair's murder or of the attempted murder of Holmes.

3534. Clarkson, Stephen. *The Man-Eater of Jahlreel, or The Adventure of a Heavy-Game Hunter in India.* Baltimore, Md.: The American Press, Inc., February 1970. 7 p.

Limited to 250 numbered copies.

"Being a transcription of an original manuscript found in a portmanteau said to have belonged to the famous *Shikari,* author, and military officer, Colonel Sebastian Moran, formerly of the First Bangalore Pioneers."

3535. Jopson, I. "Someday," *SOS,* 4, No. 1 (January 1970), 7-8.

A startling revelation by Moran that the Master was "a two-faced devil"—his friend, Professor Moriarty, and his worst enemy, Sherlock Holmes.

3536. Kogan, Richard. ". . . An Honourable Soldier," *BSJ,* 9, No. 4 (October 1959), 226.

A denial of Pete Williams's suggestion (*BSJ,* 9, No. 2 [April 1959], 123) that "powerful pressures" saved Moran from the gallows.

3537. Smith, Edgar W. "Old Shikari: Prolegomena to a Memoir of Colonel Sebastian Moran," *The Best of the Pips.* Westchester County, N.Y.: The Five Orange Pips, 1955. p. 25-34.

———. ———, *Baker Street and Beyond: Together with Some Trifling Monographs.* Morristown, N.J.: The Baker Street Irregulars, 1957. [unpaged]

"The career of such an evil giant warrants, in all conscience, a more detailed and a more definitive exposition than these prolegomena can afford; yet it may be hoped that enough evidence has been adduced, from the fragmentary data we possess, to suggest the solid place he merits in the world's hierarchy of crime."

PROFESSOR MORIARTY

See also *Empt* (items 2367-2380)
and *Fina* (items 2412-2449)

3538. Anderson, Poul. "A Treatise on the Binomial Theorem," *BSJ*, 5, No. 1 (January 1955), 13-18.

"It seems probable . . . that Moriarty was working on the basic idea of number itself, and that he developed a general binomial theorem applicable to other algebras than the one we know."

3539. Arenfalk, Poul. "The Mystery of Sherlock Holmes Versus Moriarty and The Secret Behind the Fight at the Falls of Reichenbach: A Work of Research," Tr. into English by Peter Jerndorff-Jessen. *Sherlockiana*, 4, No. 2-3 (1959), 5-15. (Special Number of *Sherlockiana* printed in English)

3540. Ashton, E. G. "International Investigators, Inc.," *Ellery Queen's Mystery Magazine*, 19, No. 99 (February 1952), 68-80.
————. "Sociedade Internacional de Detectives," *Misterio-Magazine* [Edicao Brasileira do *EQMM*], No. 41 (December 1952), 41-53.

Received a special award for the Best Sherlockiana in *EQMM's* 6th annual detective short-story contest.

The Examining Body of The Three Eyes (International Investigators, Inc.), a club of eight famous sleuths, considers a communication from a certain acrostical T. A. LaMont advancing the vicious theory that Moriarty was Watson.

3541. Austin, J. Bliss, Gloria H. Schutz, and Robert H. Schutz. *A Bibliography of the Writings About Professor Moriarty.* Pittsburgh, Pa.: The Arnsworth Castle Business Index, December 1962. 3 p.
————. Reprinted in part with title: "A Moriarty Symposium," *BSJ*, 12, No. 4 (December 1962), 240-241. (Bibliographical Notes)

3542. Baring-Gould, William S. " 'He Is the Napoleon of Crime, Watson,' " *Show*, 5, No. 2 (March 1965), 65-69. illus.
————. ————, The first half of this essay is reprinted in *The Annotated Sherlock Holmes.* New York: Clarkson N. Potter, [1967]. Vol. 1, chap. 10, p. 81-84.

3543. Berman, Ruth. "Moriarty - MC2," *BSJ*, 9, No. 1 (January 1959), 46-47.

"Professor Moriarty was more than forty years in advance of the discovery of the quantum theory (which appeared in its true form in 1926)."

3544. Blakeney, T. S. "The Holmes-Moriarty Hypothesis," *Sherlock Holmes: Fact or Fiction?* London: John Murray, [1932]. Appendix 3, p. 130-134.

Objections to theory that the Master and Professor were the same man.

3545. Bloch, Robert. "The Dynamics of an Asteroid," *BSJ*, 3, No. 4 (October 1953), 225-233.
————. ————, *SHsf Fanthology One.* Edited by Ruth Berman. The Professor Challenger Society, 1967. p. 5-12.

Moriarty tells on his deathbed how he survived the Reichenbach fall—even though the accident left him partly paralyzed and confined to a wheelchair for sixty years —and then atoned for his former criminal life (and in so doing was triumphant over a certain Detective) through his anonymous research to help scientists build rocket launchers and satellites. (According to David Wallace, Moriarty actually invented a spacecraft which enabled him to escape to the moon where he is still carrying on his criminal activities. We can only hope that Mr. Bloch is right and not Mr. Wallace!)

3546. Boucher, Anthony. *On the Nomenclature of the Brothers Moriarty.* [With a note by Vincent Starrett.] Ysleta: Edwin B. Hill, 1941. [4] p. (Sherlockiana)
Limited to 25 copies.
————. ————. San Francisco: The Beaune Press, 1966. [4] p. (Especiality No. 2)
Limited to 225 copies.

"A plausible theory as to the circumstances which may have led Dr. Watson to believe that both (or all three) of the Moriarty ilk were named James." (Edgar W. Smith)
Review: SHJ, 8, No. 2 (Spring 1967), 66 (Lord Donegall).

3547. Bristowe, W. S. "Sherlock Holmes Unmasked! He Was a Murderer, Alleges Moriarty's Nephew," *The Times*, Magazine Section (November 13, 1960), 24.
————. ————, *CPBook*, 2, No. 5-6 (Summer-Fall 1965), 100-102; 3, No. 12 (Spring 1967), 236-238.
————. Enlarged with title: " 'What a Terrible Criminal He Would Have Made,' " *SHJ*, 5, No. 1 (Winter 1960), 6-14.
————. "The Truth About Moriarty," *Seventeen Steps to 221B.* [Edited by] James Edward Holroyd. London: George Allen & Unwin Ltd., [1967]. p. 144-160.

Dr. Bristowe quotes a letter he received from Mr. James Moriarty, the son of Colonel James Moriarty and nephew of Professor James Moriarty, giving "the Moriarty family's version of what happened on May 4, 1891, at the Reichenbach Falls, together with an account of the events leading up to that final encounter between Sherlock Holmes and Professor Moriarty, and the long drawn out aftermath."

The Writings About the Writings

Other Characters

3548. Buchholtz, James. "A Tremor at the Edge of the Web," *BSJ*, 8, No. 1 (January 1958), 5-9.

Interesting speculations on the nefarious career of Professor James Moriarty, Sc. D.

3549. Castner, B. M. "The Professor and *The Valley of Fear,*" *West by One and by One.* San Francisco: Privately Printed, 1965. p. 67-81.

"Professor Moriarty—not, indeed, the original Professor, but the man who was playing that role during the months immediately preceding the date of *The Final Problem*—was Sherlock Holmes himself."

3550. Durrenberger, E. Paul. "Holmes and Moriarty," *BSJ*, 15, No. 4 (December 1965), 222-223.

"The professor simply outwitted Holmes. Holmes never had an interview with Moriarty; never saw him at Victoria Station; never pushed him over Reichenbach Falls."

3551. Eliot, T. S. "Macavity: The Mystery Cat," *Old Possum's Book of Practical Cats.* New York: Harcourt, Brace and Co., 1939. p. 32-34.

———. ———, ———. Nicolas Bentley drew the pictures. London: Faber and Faber, 1945. p. 32-34.

———. ———, ———. Read by T. S. Eliot. London: Argo Record Co. (No. 116); New Rochelle, N.Y.: Spoken Arts (No. 758).

———. ———, *Ellery Queen's Mystery Magazine,* 24 (July 1954), 108-109.

———. ———, *BSJ*, 4, No. 4 (October 1954), 208-210.

———. ———, *SOS*, 4, No. 1 (January 1970). Printed on back cover.

This verse has also appeared in several anthologies.

"Macavity's a Mystery Cat: he's called the Hidden Paw—/ For he's the master criminal who can defy the Law. / He's the bafflement of Scotland Yard, the Flying Squad's despair: / For when they reach the scene of crime—Macavity's not there!"

3552. Foss, T. F. "The Case of the Professor's Ineptitude," *SHJ*, 8, No. 4 (Summer 1968), 125-126.

An examination of Moriarty's activities reveals him to be "a slap-happy, irresponsible criminal practitioner."

3553. Galbraith, A. S. "The Real Moriarty," *BSJ Christmas Annual,* No. 2 (1957), 55-62.

A study of the use Holmes and Moriarty made of mathematics, with a conclusion that the real Moriarty was a mathematician.

3554. Heldenbrand, Page. "The Duplicity of Sherlock Holmes," *Two Baker Street Akronisms.* Summit, N.J.: The Pamphlet House, 1945. p. 7-11.

"Sherlock Holmes and Doctor Watson have perpetrated a great fraud against their public, theretofore unrevealed. For it is this writer's conviction that the villainous Professor Moriarty and his criminal organization did not exist, and that the mysterious events in which 'Moriarty' figured are pure fiction."

3555. Henderson, David. " 'No Sich Person!' " *SHJ*, 7, No. 3 (Winter 1965), 93-94. (Wigmore Street Post-Bag)

A denial that Colonel James Moriarty ever existed.

3556. Hinrich, D. "The Professor, the Colonel and the Station Master," *SHJ*, 7, No. 2 (Spring 1965), 52-54.

An examination and resolution of some contradictions concerning the three brothers.

3557. Hoffmann, Banesh. "Annotations Can Have Sinister Connotations," *BSJ*, 18, No. 2 (June 1968), 102-103.

There is evidence in *The Annotated Sherlock Holmes* that Moriarty is still alive and as ruthless as ever.

3558. Hogan, John C. "Opportunities for Asteroidal Crime," *Air Force Magazine and Space Digest,* 45, No. 6 (June 1962), 70-71.

———. ———, *BSJ*, 12, No. 4 (December 1962), 210-212.

A review of Professor Moriarty's great work, *The Dynamics of an Asteroid,* suggesting that the Soviet space program may have benefited from Moriarty's mathematical theories.

3559. ———. "Sherlock Holmes and Outer Space," *BSJ*, 11, No. 3 (September 1961), 159-161.

An incredible hypothesis that *The Dynamics of an Asteroid* is actually a master blueprint for the establishment of a criminal "upper world" in outer space corresponding to the "underworld" on earth.

3560. Hoylman, Doug. "Moriarty and the Binomial Theorem," *Proper Boskonian* [New England Science Fiction Association], No. 6 (1970).

———. ———, *The SHsf Fanthology 2.* Edited by Ruth Berman. Minneapolis, Minn.: The Professor Challenger Society, September 1971. p. 14-19.

"The author believes that Holmes was ignorant of higher mathematics and really didn't understand what that famous treatise was all about." (Julian Wolff)

3561. Jopson. I. "The Moriarty Organisation and the Beginners of T.H.R.U.S.H.," *SHJ*, 9, No. 1 (Winter 1968), 25-26.

The unnamed Professor whose key men formed the Technological Hierarchy for the Removal of Undesirables and the Subjugation of Humanity, better known as T.H.R.U.S.H., is identified as Holmes's archenemy. The reference is on p. 79 of *The Dagger Affair*, one of the "Man from U.N.C.L.E." series.

3562. Krejci-Graf, Karl. "The Binomial Theorem," *SHJ*, 9, No. 2 (1969), 62.

The Professor's treatise on the Binomial Theorem may have been written as a solution to the Fermat Problem.

3563. ["Letter to Baker Street"], from "A Student of Professor Moriarty's," *BSJ*, 11, No. 4 (December 1961), 242, 244.

A refutation of Mr. Hogan's hypothesis that Moriarty's book has something to do with interplanetary space bodies.

3564. Macdonell, A. G. "The Truth About Professor Moriarty," *The New Statesman* [London], 33 (October 5, 1929), 776-778.

———. "Mr. Moriarty," *Baker Street Studies*. Edited by H. W. Bell. London: Constable and Co., 1934. p. 159-175.

———. ———, *The Spanish Pistol and Other Stories*. London: Macmillan and Co., 1939. p. 208-220.

———. ———, *The Incunabular Sherlock Holmes*. Edited by Edgar W. Smith. Morristown, N.J.: The Baker Street Irregulars, 1958.. p. 115-121.

Only one explanation will account for Moriarty's death at the Reichenbach Falls in May 1891 and reappearance in 1899. The Professor never existed. He was invented by Holmes to cover up some of his failures.

3565. Mather, Philip R. "Moriarty's Here Tonight," *BSJ*, 12, No. 4 (December 1962), 209.

"Friends of Sherlock, on your guard; / Evil forces wield their might! / No help will come from Scotland Yard; / And Moriarty's here tonight."

3566. Meyer, Karl E. "Dr. Mo and 007: A Scandal in Identity," *SHJ*, 8, No. 2 (Spring 1967), 55-57.

The true identities of James Bond, Dr. Mo, and "M" are made known for the first time—James Moriarty, Professor Moriarty, and Colonel Moriarty!

3567. ———. "Elementary, Sir—Moriarty Is Back," *The Washington Post* (August 13, 1963), A18.

Holmes is consulted by the son of Inspector Lestrade concerning the recent activities of Professor Moriarty.

3568. Moriarty, Daniel L. "The Peculiar Persecution of Professor Moriarty," *BSJ*, 10, No. 1 (January 1960), 15-34.

3569. Morrow, L. A. "Letters from Somewhere," *BSJ*, 16, No. 1 (March 1966), 6-8.

Three letters from the brother of Moriarty warning him that a certain doctor-writer is planning to make him the villain in his stories.

3570. ———. "More Letters from Somewhere," *BSJ*, 18, No. 3 (September 1968), 144-147.

A fourth letter concerning the family reputation—this one from Moriarty's sister—and a fifth from the brother of young Stamford telling of his and John Clay's scheme to "turn his red hair into real gold."

3571. Officer, Harvey. "The Song of Professor Moriarty," *A Baker Street Song Book*. New York: The Pamphlet House, 1943. p. 14.

———. ———, *BSJ* [OS], 1, No. 3 (July 1946), 300.

"Moriarty was a villain, / Out for arson, theft or killin'; London was pervaded by him, / Only Sherlock dared defy him."

3572. Pattrick, Robert R. "Moriarty Was There," *BSJ Christmas Annual*, No. 3 (1958), 45-53.

Holmes and Moriarty began their separate careers in 1877; and the Professor was responsible for some of the early cases in which the Master was not completely successful.

3573. Puhl, Gayle Lange. "Odd Clippings . . . Re Witchcraft," *BSC*, 2, No. 2 (September 1969), 8-10.

"Professor James Moriarty is a warlock!"

3574. Redmond, Chris. "Moriarty," *BSP*, No. 22 (April 1967), 3.

"Yes, the foulest of the villains to whom Sherlock Holmes gave chase, / Till that most dramatic meeting on a cliff-edge, face to face, / Is, according to Sherlockians, still lurking every place: / They will cry, with righteous anger, 'Moriarty.' "

3575. Shreffler, Philip A. "The Dark Dynasty: A Djinn Genealogy," *BSJ*, 21, No. 1 (March 1971), 22-25.

Barnardo Eagle, a famous 19th-century conjurer known also as "The Napoleon of Wizards," is identified as the father of "The Napoleon of Crime" who, according to both Baring-Gould and the author, was born on Halloween 1846. It is further suggested in a "sinister postscript" that Eagle's daughter Georgiana, the young witch, may have been Irene Adler.

3576. Siegel, Norman. "Letter Addressed to a Mister Sherlock Holmes," *BSJ*, 18, No. 3 (September 1968), 148-149.

"Most honoured, most hated, most habitual foe, / Now well past one hundred and five: / I thought I would write you so I'd let you know / That I am very much alive!"

Other Characters

3577. Simmons, George. "Some Moriarty-Poincaré Correspondence," *BSJ* [OS], 2, No. 3 (July 1947), 246-255.

A series of letters between the Professor and the French mathematician Henri Poincaré about the mathematical physics of heavenly bodies.

3578. Simpson, A. Carson. "The Curious Incident of the Missing Corpse," *BSJ*, 4, No. 1 (January 1954), 24-34.

Moriarty's body was never recovered because his extraordinary intellect and mathematical capacity enabled him to invent a small, self-powered atomic accelerator which he turned on himself as he began his plunge into the Reichenbach gorge.

3579. Skene Melvin, David. "Some Notes on the Name of the Brothers Moriarty," *BSJ*, 21, No. 2 (June 1971), 90-96.

One of the great Sherlockian puzzles has been why Watson gave the brothers Moriarty the same first name. A careful analysis, however, of the manner in which the Moriartys are spoken of and to, and a realization of the plentitude of compound names in Victorian England and in the Canon, leads inescapably to the solution that they do not have the same first name but rather have the compound surname of James Moriarty.

3580. [Smith, Edgar W.] "On the Dynamics of a Sputnik," *BSJ*, 8, No. 1 (January 1958), 3-4. (The Editor's Gas-Lamp)

"It was Professor Moriarty who ordained the dynamics of the sputnik."

3581. ———. "Professor Moriarty Muses," *BSJ*, 7, No. 4 (October 1957), 229.

"If I could beat that man, if I could free / Society of *him*, then I should feel / My own career had reached its apogee. . . ."

3582. ———. "Prolegomena to a Memoir of Professor Moriarty," *The Second Cab*. Edited by James Keddie. [Boston: The Speckled Band, 1947.] p. 57-64.

———. *The Napoleon of Crime: Prolegomena to a Memoir of Professor James Moriarty, Sc. D.* Summit, N.J.: The Pamphlet House, 1953. [23] p. illus.

Limited to 221 copies.

———. ———, *Baker Street and Beyond: Together with Some Trifling Monographs.* Morristown, N.J.: The Baker Street Irregulars, 1957. [unpaged]

"A reluctant tribute to a great mind, with especial emphasis on the part Moriarty played in atomic physics."

3583. [———.] "Sonnet: Sherlock Holmes to James Moriarty, Sc. D. (May 4, 1891)," by Helene Yuhasova [pseud.] *The Saturday Review of Literature*, 28, No. 40 (October 6, 1945), 13.

———. ———, *A Lauriston Garden of Verses*, by Helene Yuhasova. Summit, N.J.: The Pamphlet House, 1946. p. [13].

———. ———, *Baker Street and Beyond: Together with Some Trifling Monographs.* Morristown, N.J.: The Baker Street Irregulars, 1957. [unpaged]

"Today our cosmic meeting we'll adjourn— / Today you'll go — tomorrow I'll return!"

3584. Starr, H. W. "A Submersible Subterfuge, or Proof Impositive," *Leaves from the Copper Beeches*. Narberth, Pa.: Livingston Pub. Co., 1959. p. 97-108.

Captain Nemo of *Twenty Thousand Leagues Under the Sea* is identified as Professor Moriarty. "Here we have the first major step up in a spectacular criminal career whose final step down was a long one to the bottom of Reichenbach Falls."

3585. Starrett, Vincent. "The Two Moriarties," *The Saturday Review of Literature*, 10, No. 3 (February 17, 1934), 491. (The Bowling Green)

———. ———, *BSJ*, 12, No. 4 (December 1962), 241.

———. ———, *BSP*, No. 23 (May 1967), 5-6.

The author's famous letter on the first names of Professor and Colonel Moriarty.

3586. Stix, Thomas L. "Who's Afraid of the Big Bad Moriarty?" *BSJ*, 12, No. 4 (December 1962), 200, 243.

The Professor was not so sinister at all, and the person most afraid of him was Holmes!

3587. Wallace, David. "Reichenbach Revisited, or Moriarty Again!!" *BSJ*, 19, No. 3 (September 1969), 172-175.

A terrifying announcement that the arch-criminal somehow survived his fall into the Reichenbach and escaped to the moon where, with his fiendish apparatus, he is still able to corrupt the minds of men—and on an even larger scale than before. Earthlings beware!

3588. White, Amelia M. "The Problem of the Three Moriartys," *BSJ*, 7, No. 4 (October 1957), 225-228.

The stationmaster in Fina was the Professor's brother but his name was not James, and Col. James Moriarty was their uncle.

3589. White, Paul. "The Case of the Men Named James," *BSJ*, 6, No. 1 (July 1956), 46-50.

There were two Moriartys and they were both known as James.

3590. Williamson, Jerry Neal. " 'There Was Something Very Strange,' " *BSJ*, 12, No. 4 (December 1962), 201-209.

Moriarty was the *brother* of Sherlock and Mycroft!

3591. Wilson, Alan. " 'You Crossed My Path,' " *SHJ*, 4, No. 3 (Winter 1959), 89-90.
A chronological reconciliation between Moriarty's death at the Reichenbach and his alleged reappearance in the Birlstone case.

3592. Wodehouse, P. G. "Onwards and Upwards with the Fiends," *Punch*, 228 (February 16, 1955), 222-223.
An analysis of Moriarty as the inferior of Fu Manchu among Fiends in Human Shape.

F *Other Subjects*

AFRICA

3593. Kirby, Percival R. "Sherlock Holmes and South Africa," *SHJ*, 9, No. 1 (Winter 1968), 6-10.
Occasions on which this country plays a part in the tales.

3594. Lindfors, Bernth. "Sherlock Holmes in Africa. Part I. Kenya," *BSJ*, 15, No. 2 (June 1965), 67-70.
A teacher introduces the Sacred Writings to African secondary school boys in Kenya.

ANIMALS

See also *Houn* (items 2436 - 2509),
Silv (items 2710 - 2729),
and *Bull Pup* (items 3383-3392)

3595. Bridgeman, Roger. "Horses and Hounds," *SHJ*, 9, No. 2 (Summer 1969), 59-61.
An examination of Holmes's knowledge of horses and dogs suggests that he spent his early years in the country and not in London as Bernard Davies has proposed (item 2871).

3596. Cole, Eleanor S. "Holmes, Watson and the K-9's," *BSJ*, 1, No. 1 (January 1951), 25-29.
A discussion of the dogs contacted by Holmes and Watson.

3597. Ewing, Adelaide P., and Robert R. Pattrick. "A Sherlockian Zoo," *West by One and by One*. San Francisco: Privately Printed, 1965. p. 113-124.
A complete listing of all the creatures appearing in the pages of the Canon.

3598. "Grimesby Roylott Rides Again?" *The Times* (October 14, 1960), 15.
———, *CPBook*, 2, No. 5-6 (Summer-Fall 1965), 90.
On the use of animals as accomplices, including Roylott's swamp adder and Stapleton's hound.

3599. Holstein, L. S. "Holmes and *Equus Caballus*," *BSJ*, 20, No. 2 (June 1970), 112-116.
After reviewing his equestrian feats, attainments, and associations, the author advances the opinion that the Master's interest in horses "far exceeded and was broader and more profound than the generally accepted views amongst most devotees."

3600. "I Am a Dog-Fancier Myself (Shos)," *BSCL*, No. 8 (1970), 9-11; No. 9 (1971), 24.
Contents: Toby (Sign). - Pompey (Miss).
Quotations "for the lovers of our four-legged Sherlockian friends."

3601. Jenkins, William D. "A Humiliation of Lions," *BSJ*, 12, No. 4 (December 1962), 228-235.
An investigation of the Canon reveals mostly negative references to cats, suggesting that Watson was an ailurophobe.

3602. Lauritzen, Henry. *Holmes og Heste.* [Holmes and Horses.] Aalborg, [Danmark: Silkeborg Bogtrykker], 1959. 29 p. illus.
Limited to 313 numbered copies.
Published in the centenary year of Conan Doyle and the Danish Jockey Club, this booklet deals with all kinds of horses in the Canon, especially the thoroughbreds Silver Blaze (identified with Common) and Shoscombe Prince.

3603. Lauterbach, Charles E. "His Last Bow-Wow," *Baker Street Ballads*. [Culver City, Calif.: Luther Norris, March 1971.] p. 15-16.
"Now there's a galaxy of pooches / As strange as one could name; / They crossed the path of Sherlock Holmes / And made the Hall of Fame."

3604. Palmer, Stuart. "Notes on Certain Evidences of Caniphobia in Mr. Sherlock Holmes and His Associates," *BSJ*, 5, No. 4 (October 1955), 197-204.
An essay on the psychological implications of Holmes's relations with the canine species.

3605. "Sherlock Holmes' Animals," *DVM Newsmagazine of Veterinary Medicine*, 2, No. 2 (February 1970), 6-8, 11. illus.
Excerpts from Houn, Stud, Silv, Veil, and Spec; with brief commentaries.

3606. Solovay, Ethel F. "Holmes Goes to the Dogs!" *BSJ* [OS], 3, No. 4 (October 1948), 493-496.
A study of the Master's four-footed aides.

3607. Van Liere, Edward J. "Dogs and Sherlock Holmes," *Harvard Medical Alumni Bulletin*, 22, No. 4 (June 1948), 114-116.
———. ———, *A Doctor Enjoys Sherlock*

Holmes. New York: Vantage Press, [1959]. p. 48-53.

"To those interested in animals, it is gratifying to know that two of the most popular heroes of detective fiction —Sherlock Holmes and Dr. Watson—both loved dogs. They did not like them in a sickly, sentimental sense, but rather with a genuine, masculine affection. They regarded them as dogs, not as human beings, and emphasized and respected their canine personalities. I am sure every self-respecting dog would want to be so regarded."

3608. ———. "The Zoological Doctor Watson," *A Doctor Enjoys Sherlock Holmes.* New York: Vantage Press, [1959]. p. 96-101.
Frequent allusions to animal life in the tales are noted.

3609. Willson, Robert F. "The Veterinary Holmes," *BSJ,* 8, No. 1 (January 1958), 33-35.
A contention that the education he received in veterinary medicine "started him on the road to becoming the world's greatest criminal investigator."

THE APOCRYPHA

3610. Blakeney, T. S. "Widening the Canon," *SHJ,* 8, No. 4 (Summer 1968), 108-111; 9, No. 1 (Winter 1968), 10-13.
A scholarly discussion of "those Doylian writings that appear to have *some* Holmesian association."

3611. Christ, Jay Finley. "Sherlock and Two Impostors," *Illustrious Client's Second Case-Book.* Edited by J. N. Williamson. [Indianapolis, Ind.: The Illustrious Clients, 1949.] p. 19-25.
A critical essay on Lost and ManW.

3612. Christopher, J. R. "The Case of the Vanishing Locomotives, or A Hell of a Way to Run a Railroad," *The Armchair Detective,* 1, No. 2 (January 1968), 56-58.
A discussion of the following three tales that involve the disappearance of a moving train from its tracks: "The Lost Special" by Arthur Conan Doyle, "The Adventure of the Lost Locomotive" by August Derleth, and "Snowball in July" by Ellery Queen.

3613. Donegall, Lord. "Introduction, Including Summaries of the Perplexing Literary Problems About the Two Stories," *The Sherlockian Doyle.* [Culver City, Calif.: Luther Norris, October 1968.] p. 1-13.
———. An adaptation with title: "Lost and ManW," *SHJ,* 9, No. 3 (Winter 1969), 89-94.
"A review of the evidence in favour of and in opposition to the Canonisation of 'The Lost Special' and 'The Man with the Watches.' "

3614. Folsom, Henry T. " 'It Is My Business to Follow the Details of Continental Crime,' " *BSJ,* 19, No. 3 (September 1969), 132-136.
An explanation of why Holmes was unwilling to solve the mystery of the disappearing train in Lost.

3615. Green, Roger Lancelyn. "The Case of Two Literary Doctors," *SHJ,* 9, No. 3 (Winter 1969), 95-96.
Watson furnished Doyle with material from several of Holmes's unpublished cases. The cases were then disguised and made into stories by the two doctors and published in *Round the Fire Stories.*

3616. ———. "Sherlock Holmes Writes to the Papers," *SHJ,* 3, No. 1 (Summer 1956), 11, 14.
"In neither case [Lost, ManW] is Mr. Holmes mentioned by name, but the accounts of each contain letters to the public press which could not possibly come from any other hand."

3617. Hedgegrove, Quentin. "The Case Against," *SHJ,* 3, No. 1 (Summer 1956), 15-16.
A denial that Holmes was the correspondent in Lost and ManW.

3618. Helling, Cornelis. "A Sequel to Completing the Canon," *SHJ,* 6, No. 2 (Spring 1963), 55.
Two items are suggested in addition to those recommended by Mr. Richard.

3619. Jenkins, William D. "A la Recherche du Train Perdu," *BSJ,* 19, No. 3 (September 1969), 137-143, 189.
"The Lost Special" constitutes the prologue in a Canonical trilogy: the substantive case being "The Matter of Supreme Importance to the French Government"; the epilogue, "The Case of the Papers of ex-President Murillo." Interestingly enough, the authorship of the famous letter to *The Times,* quoted in Lost, is ascribed to Watson, "an *amateur* reasoner," rather than to Holmes, "a *professional* reasoner."

3620. McLauchlin, Russell. "A Grim Fairy Tale," *BSJ,* 3, No. 3 (July 1953), 160-161.
An apocryphal tale in verse of ManW.

3621. Missal, Ruth R. "A Case of Identities," *BSJ,* 6, No. 4 (October 1956), 216-222.
The results of the author's preliminary research into the true identities of the Rochesterians in ManW.

3622. Montgomery, James. "The Crown Diamond," *The Best of the Pips.* Westchester County, N.Y.: The Five Orange Pips, 1955. p. 35-48.
"A full and authoritative account of the origin and later adaptation of this pure corn

from which 'The Mazarin Stone' sprang full-panoplied." (Edgar W. Smith)

3623. [Morley, Christopher.] "A Letter from Yoxley, Kent," *Letters from Baker Street.* Edited by Edgar W. Smith. [New York: The Pamphlet House, 1942.] p. 17-19.

A communication from Stanley Hopkins, O.B.E., shedding light on the proposal to subsume Lost and ManW into the Canon.

3624. ———. "Studies on Baker Street," *Streamlines.* Garden City, N.Y.: Doubleday, Doran & Co., 1936. p. 261-263.

The suggestion is offered that no research in the Sherlockian lore is complete without reference to the apocryphal play *The Speckled Band.*

3625. ———. "Two Suppressed Holmes Episodes," *The Saturday Review of Literature,* 10, No. 33 (March 3, 1934), 523. (The Bowling Green)
———. ———, *Streamlines.* Garden City, N.Y.: Doubleday, Doran & Co., 1936. p. 259-261.
———. ———, *BSP,* No. 23 (May 1967), 6.

A note on the anonymous letters in Lost and ManW.

3626. Richard Peter. "Completing the Canon," *SHJ,* 6, No. 1 (Winter 1962), 10-14; 6, No. 3 (Winter 1963), 76-81; 6, No. 4 (Spring 1964), 114-115.

A listing of and commentary on what the author considers to be twelve additions to the accepted sixty adventures.

3627. Schutz, Robert H. "The Further Writings of Dr. John H. Watson," *BSJ* [OS], 10, No. 4 (October 1960), 241-243.

Support is given to Jane Nightwork's assumption that Watson was also the author of *Round the Red Lamp.*

3628. Smith, Edgar W. "By Way of Introduction," *The Field Bazaar: A Sherlock Holmes Pastiche,* by Sir Arthur Conan Doyle. Summit, N.J.: The Pamphlet House, 1947. p. 7-10.
———. ———, *The Daily Californian Weekly Magazine,* 4, No. 9 (January 14, 1969), 11.

On the Apocrypha, and particularly "The Field Bazaar."

3629. ———, ed. *Letters from Baker Street.* [New York: The Pamphlet House, 1942.] 60 p.

Limited to 400 numbered copies, of which the first 200 are in a deluxe binding.

"A communication appearing in the London *Times* of July 3, 1890, from an amateur reasoner of some celebrity; and a communication appearing in the *Daily Gazette* in March or April, 1892, over the signature of a well-known criminal investigator. Together with the stories in

which these letters are quoted: *The Lost Special* and *The Man with the Watches* by Sir Arthur Conan Doyle. Illuminated by a noteworthy communication from Stanley Hopkins, O.B.E., Chief Inspector C.I.D. (Retired), written and received through the good offices of Christopher Morley and further illuminated by a communication from the eminent Holmesian scholar Vincent Starrett." (Subtitle)

3630. Starrett, Vincent. "A Letter from Chicago, Illinois," *Letters from Baker Street.* Edited by Edgar W. Smith. [New York: The Pamphlet House, 1942.] p. 57-58.

On the authorship of the letters written to the *Times* and the *Daily Gazette.*

ARCHITECTURE

3631. Gill, William H. "Some Notable Sherlockian Buildings," *SHJ,* 4, No. 4 (Spring 1960), 124-126.

3632. Van Liere, Edward J. "The Architectural Sherlock Holmes," *BSJ,* 13, No. 3 (September 1963), 156-163.
———. ———, *Medical and Other Essays.* Morgantown: West Virginia University Library, 1966. p. 143-152.

"Many interesting references to architecture may be found in the novels. This indicates that Dr. Watson and Sherlock Holmes both had more than a passing interest in architecture. The references are especially pleasing, because they are seldom detailed or technical, and as a consequence may be enjoyed by all."

ARMY

3633. Layng, Charles. "Watson's War with the Army," *BSJ,* 2, No. 2 (April 1952), 73-80.

"Are you perchance interested in the foulest sort of traitors, fiendish murderers, cheats at cards, vicious martinets or just plain all-around blackguards? If so, you'll find them among Doctor Watson's colonels, who were all of these things and worse."

3634. Sellars, Crighton. "Dr. Watson and the British Army," *BSJ* [OS], 2, No. 3 (July 1947), 332-341.

"In Watson's stories collected in the Canon we find, upon investigation, that he is so jealous of the good reputation of certain Army regiments that, though he is only too quick to note a real regiment when a member of it is of good reputation, he resorts to the subterfuge of inventing a regimental name or number if the individual of whom he is writing is of low repute or has done anything reprehensible."

AUSTRALIA

3635. Chorley, Jennifer. "Some Diggings

Down Under," *SHJ*, 6, No. 2 (Spring 1963), 49-51.

Speculations on some "ex-Australians" and others, with special reference to Glor, Sign, Bosc, and Abbe; with a few allusions from Nava, etc.

3636. Fredman, L. E. "About Down Under," *SHJ*, 6, No. 3 (Winter 1963), 96-97. (Wigmore Street Post-Bag)

A clarification of points raised by Mrs. Chorley regarding Australia.

BAKER STREET, 221B

3637. Abbey National Building Society. *The Immortal Sherlock Holmes.* London: [1968]. [8] p.

An illustrated advertising booklet issued by a firm whose head office is considered by many to be located on the site of the original 221B.

3638. Aronson, Marvin E. "The Case of the Unhappy Landlord," by Isaac Hudson (as told to Marvin Aronson, M.D.). *BSJ*, 15, No. 4 (December 1965), 218-220.

A justified complaint by the husband of Martha Hudson for not being mentioned in the Saga, after his many long years of patient service to the illustrious tenants.

3639. Frisbie, Owen P. "Meditations of Dr. Watson: Baker Street," *BSJ*, 12, No. 1 (March 1962), 22.

"Of all the numbers that our mem'ries see / Is that best loved of all: 2-2-1B."

3640. Galerstein, David. "Sidelights on Baker Street," *BSJ*, 17, No. 1 (March 1967), 25-27.

"Holmes found it necessary to rent other rooms in the same building—and probably ended up leasing the entire house."

3641. Honce, Charles. "Sensation in Baker Street," *Tales from a Beekman Hill Library.* Mount Vernon, N.Y.: Uttered by S. A. Jacobs at the Golden Eagle Press, 1952. p. 67-73.

The author tells of the attention he attracted while strolling along Baker Street in a deerstalker!

3642. Hopkirk, Peter. "When Only Holmes Can Help," *The Times* (December 16, 1967), 1.

————. ————, *Sherlockiana*, 13, Nr. 1-2 (1968), 4.

"Letters addressed to him continue to arrive at Baker Street, many of them with requests for the great detective's help."

3643. Husted, Ellery. "Baker Street from Guam," *BSJ* [OS], 4, No. 1 (January 1949), 118-122.

————. Condensed with title: "The Case of the Baker Street Plans," *The Reader's Digest*, 56 (March 1950), 49-50.

————. "Sherlock Holmes misstänkt," *Det Bästa ur Reader's Digest* [Stockholm] (May 1950), 61-62.

An amusing story about how the author's floor plans of 221B were held up by Cincpac's censors.

3644. Jacobs, Leonard. "Baker Street," *BSJ*, 6, No. 2 (April 1956), 101-105.

An interesting history of a thoroughfare that has become inseparably linked with the name of Sherlock Holmes.

3645. Keddie, James [Sr.] "The Other Boarder," *The Saturday Review of Literature*, 15, No. 20 (March 13, 1937), 12, 14.

————. ————, *221B: Studies in Sherlock Holmes.* Edited by Vincent Starrett. New York: The Macmillan Co., 1940. p. 68-70.

Speculation on the activities behind the scenes at 221B.

3646. Kennedy, Bruce. "The Untidy Holmes?" *SOS*, No. 2 (November 1966), 2-4.

"It was Watson, not Holmes, who gave the rooms at 221B Baker Street their familiar untidiness."

3647. Lindsley, Mary F. "By Hansom to Baker Street," *PD*, 1, No. 3 (March 1968), 2. (The Master's Corner)

"We leave / Temple Bar, / Westminster, Soho, our daily sightseeing done, / To turn into an ordinary street / Where an invisible house outwatched / the Blitz, / Armored in non-existence."

3648. Morley, Christopher. "Report from Baker Street," *The New York Times Book Review* (November 27, 1949), 45.

————. ————, *CPBook*, 3, No. 9 (Summer 1966), 182.

A discussion of the author's visit to the site of Holmes's apartment.

3649. Oliver, Merle. "Sherlock Holmes Lives!—And Answers His Mail," *The Detroit News Magazine* (May 4, 1969), 33-37. illus.

————. ————, *CPBook*, 5, No. 18 (Spring 1969), 343-344.

Extracts of letters from persons who still seek the Master's help. As Holmes no longer resides at 221B, the letters are answered by Janet Hall, an advertising assistant for the Abbey National Building Society at No. 221. In an earlier article entitled "Quick, Watson, the Stamps," ' (*New York Sunday News*, Magazine Section [April 21, 1968], 16), publicity manager R. Rendel is shown answering Holmes's mail. Sherlockians everywhere salute you Miss Hall and Mr. Rendel!

3650. Russell, Audrey. "Baker Street, W.1," *London Calling*, No. 913 (May 2, 1957), 8-9.

An illustrated history of this world-famous street, with emphasis on its two most famous residents.

3651. Shearn, A. L. "The Street and the Detective," *BSJ Christmas Annual,* No. 2 (1957), 50-54.

"A critical analysis of the relationship between Baker Street and Sherlock Holmes." (Subtitle)

3652. [Smith, Edgar W.] "Ballade of the Bright Stair-Rods," by Helene Yuhasova [pseud.] *A Baker Street Four-Wheeler.* Edited by Edgar W. Smith. [Maplewood, N.J., and New York: The Pamphlet House, 1944.] p. 57.
————. ————, *A Lauriston Garden of Verses,* by Helene Yuhasova. Summit, N.J.: The Pamphlet House, 1946. p. [21-22].
————. ————, *Baker Street and Beyond: Together with Some Trifling Monographs.* Morristown, N.J.: The Baker Street Irregulars, 1957. [unpaged]

"The bright rods climbing by the stair: / Half-opened door and sweet night air, / And peace within, against the odds / Of wild, dark business everywhere—/ Thank Watson for the bright stair-rods!"

3653. Starrett, Vincent. "Introduction," *Baker Street and Beyond: A Sherlockian Gazetteer,* by Edgar W. Smith. New York: The Pamphlet House, 1940. p. 9-10.

A note on some other eminent persons who have lived on Baker Street.

3654. ————. "Mr. Holmes of Baker Street," *Real Detective Tales* (December 1932).
————. "No. 221-B Baker Street," *The Private Life of Sherlock Holmes.* New York: The Macmillan Co., 1933. p. 56-76.
————. ————, ————. Revised and enlarged. The University of Chicago Press, [1960]. p. 38-50.

The Baker Street scene, with an account of Dr. Briggs's identification of the house—at No. 111.

3655. W., F. "Sherlock Doesn't Live Here Any More," *The Abbey Road Journal,* 1, No. 12 (Autumn 1935), 14-18.

"How mail still comes to 221B Baker Street, where, allegedly, the offices of the Abbey Road Building Society are now located." (Edgar W. Smith)

3656. Wells, Carolyn. "Ballade of Baker Street," *Collier's,* 41, No. 21 (August 15, 1908), 14.
————. ————, *Two Ballads in Praise of Sherlock Holmes.* Ysleta: Edwin B. Hill, 1937. p. [2].
————. ————, *Mark Twain's Associated Press Speech and Other News Stories,* by Charles Honce. New York: Privately Printed, 1940. p. 94-95.
————. ————, *Profile by Gaslight.* Edited by Edgar W. Smith. New York: Simon and Schuster, 1944. p. 260-261.

"Sherlock! My fondest wishes are / That on a day I yet may greet, / Haply in some far avatar, / Those hallowed rooms in Baker Street."

3657. Wright, Lee. "Mrs. Hudson Speaks," *BSJ* [OS], 1, No. 1 (January 1946), 45-50.

The landlady explains how she happened to rent the second or top storey of her house to Holmes and Watson.

3658. Yates, Donald A. "Baker Street—The Quiet Years," *BSJ,* 8, No. 1 (January 1958), 10.

" 'For three long years that window shade's been / drawn. . . .' "

221B, Description of

3659. Baring-Gould, William S. "Mrs. Hudson's Inheritance," *BSJ,* 17, No. 1 (March 1967), 28-36.
————. Reprinted as the second half (p. 92-102) of " 'I Have My Eye on a Suite in Baker Street,' " *The Annotated Sherlock Holmes.* New York: Clarkson N. Potter, [1967]. Vol. 1, chap. 11, p. 85-102. illus.

Winner of the 10th annual Morley-Montgomery Memorial Award for the best contribution to *BSJ* in 1967.

A detailed description of the physical features and furnishings. "For Holmes and Watson, in every way, it was indeed 'a most desirable residence.' "

3660. Galerstein, David. "Watson's Room or a Spare Room?" *BSJ,* 19, No. 3 (September 1969), 176-177.

An argument in support of a third bedroom.

3661. "Holmesiana," *The Strand,* 118, No. 711 (March 1950), 98-99.

"Plans and a map, based on data in the stories, prepared by an enthusiast."

3662. Holroyd, James Edward. " 'Our Sanctum,' " *Baker Street By-ways.* London: George Allen & Unwin Ltd., [1959]. p. 81-86.

3663. Keddie. James, Sr. "Gasogene, Coal Box, Persian Slipper," *The Saturday Review of Literature,* 15, No. 9 (June 27, 1936), 12-13.
————. ————, *The Second Cab.* Edited by James Keddie, Jr. [Boston: The Speckled Band, 1947.] p. 15-17.

A letter to Christopher Morley concerning the above-mentioned items.

3664. McCullam, William. "The Problem of the Veiled Lodgings," *BSJ,* 19, No. 2 (June 1969), 101-108.

An architect's view of the location and interior.

Other Subjects

3665. McPharlin, Paul. "221B Baker Street: Certain Physical Details," With plans by R. Spearman Myers. *BSJ* [OS], 2, No. 2 (April 1947), 180-194.

A detailed description of the interior, including floor plans, a photograph of the sitting room by Dr. Briggs, and drawings of the furnishings.

3666. Newton, G. B. "This Desirable Residence," *SHJ*, 3, No. 2 (Winter 1956), 12-14.

Contents: A Waiting-Room? - Nine Rooms. - The Ground Floor. - The First Floor. - The Top Floor. - Holmes's Bedroom. - Watson's Bedroom. - Domestic Staff.

3667. Schutz, Robert H. *A Modest Sherlockian Monograph.* Pittsburgh, Pa.: Plane Tree Press, 1970. [2] p. illus.

A privately printed folder on the sanitary facilities.

3668. Waters, Frank A. "The Rooms in Baker Street," *The Best of the Pips.* Westchester County, N.Y.: The Five Orange Pips, 1955. p. 15-20.

A description of the rooms and furnishings.

3669. Weaver, Ronald R. "Bow Window in Baker Street," *BSJ*, 5, No. 2 (April 1955), 93-95.

Because the bow window came to be altered, the absence of such a window should not be a fatal objection in identifying the true location.

3670. Wilmunen, Jon V. "A Diagram of the Rooms at 221B," *The Gamebag*, No. 2 (1966), 16.

3671. Wolff, Julian. "I Have My Eye on a Suite in Baker Street," *BSJ* [OS], 1, No. 3 (July 1946), 296-299.

————. ————, *SOS Annual,* No. 2 (January 1968), 9-11.

A description and detailed floor plan by the chief Sherlockian cartographer.

3672. ————. "The Un-curious Incident of the Baker Street Bathroom," *BSJ*, 17, No. 1 (March 1967), 37-41.

"Since bathrooms were used not only in ancient times, but also by contemporaries of Holmes and Watson, it does not seem illogical to believe that 221B possessed one." Includes a photograph of a Victorian bathroom, a letter to Capt. Julian Wolff from Edgar Smith, dated May 31, 1944, and Dr. Wolff's floor plan.

221B, Location of

3673. Arenfalk, Poul. "Is 221B Baker Street No. 21 or No. 31?" *IR*, 1, No. 1 (April 1960), 1-2.

A refutation of Harold Morris's identification and confirmation of Bernard Davies's.

3674. Baring-Gould, William S. "The Problem of No. 221," *BSJ*, 8, No. 2 (April 1958), 69-77.

————. Reprinted as the first half (p. 86-89) of " 'I Have My Eye on a Suite in Baker Street,' " *The Annotated Sherlock Holmes.* New York: Clarkson N. Potter, [1967]. Vol. 1, chap. 11, p. 85-102. illus.

A review of the various theories on the location of 221 Baker Street, with the suggestion that the house was located "on the west (or left going north) side of Baker Street, *below* Dorset Street." In an additional commentary in *The Annotated Sherlock Holmes* (p. 90-92), the author concurs with Mr. Davies's choice of No. 31.

3675. Brend, Gavin. "The Home of Holmes," *My Dear Holmes.* London: George Allen & Unwin Ltd., [1951]. Chap. 5, p. 46-53.

It was located at No. 61 Baker Street in the block between Blanford Street and Dorset Street.

3676. Davies, Bernard. "The Back Yards of Baker Street," *SHJ*, 4, No. 3 (Winter 1959), 83-88.

————. ————, *Seventeen Steps to 221B.* [Edited by] James Edward Holroyd. London: George Allen & Unwin Ltd., [1967]. p. 167-178.

An argument in favor of No. 31.

3677. [Donegall, Lord.] "221B," *SHJ*, 4, No. 4 (Spring 1960), 109-110. (Editorial)

————. "221 B Baker Street — Et forfriskende syn på det evige spørgsmål," [Oversat af A. D. Henriksen]. *Sherlockiana*, 5, Nr. 3-4 (1960), 10-11.

"In all this, we refrain from pronouncing judgment. Nor do we share a burning desire that the precise position of 221B should be located. On the contrary, long live Nos. 111, 221, 27, 19, 59-63, 56, 57, 58, 108, 109, 31, 21 and any other numbers that were not thought of first."

3678. Donohue, Michael. "I've Got Your Number," *BSJ Christmas Annual*, No. 1 (1956), 52-55.

The numerology for 221B is worked out according to Helena Davis's theory as set forth in her article "Your Address, Please," *The American Home* (April 1952).

3679. Harris, Robert G. "A Confirmation of Mr. McLauchlin's Thesis Independently Arrived At," *BSJ*, 2, No. 2 (April 1952), 71.

Includes a photograph of "221B" Gloucester Place.

3680. Harrison, Michael. "Why '221B'?" *BSJ*, 14, No. 4 (December 1964), 219-222.

"A Sherlockian suggests a reason for

Watson's choice of that particular imaginary number." (Subtitle)

3681. Holroyd, James Edward. "Solutions by Numbers," *Baker Street By-ways*. London: George Allen & Unwin Ltd., [1959]. p. 68-74.

An ingenious manipulation of numbers in Musg, RedH, and Sign reconfirms No. 109 as the true original.

3682. ———. "221B Baker Street?" *The Cornhill Magazine*, No. 987 (Summer 1951), 244-254.

———. "Where Was 221B?" *Baker Street By-ways*. London: George Allen & Unwin Ltd., [1959]. p. 53-67.

A careful examination of the different claims regarding the exact location of 221 in which the author supports Mr. Short's claim for No. 109.

3683. Hyslop, James T. "The Master Adds a Postscript (An Extract from the Files of John H. Watson, M.D.)." Transcribed by James T. Hyslop. *BSJ* [OS], 2, No. 2 (April 1947), 113-118.

A dialogue between Holmes and Watson during which they place the location of their old rooms at No. 19, in south Baker Street, rather than at No. 111, in north Baker Street, as maintained by Dr. Briggs and concurred in by Vincent Starrett. (Holmes and Watson should know!)

3684. Kennedy, Bruce. "The Mystery of 221B," *BSP*, No. 2 (August 1965), 2.

Some of the theories about its location are briefly summarized.

3685. Maun, Ian. "Remarkable Sign," *SHJ*, 9, No. 2 (Summer 1969), 69. (Wigmore Street Post-Bag)

The author has discovered a photograph (reproduced therein) taken around 1910 showing the corner of Upper Baker Street. Outside No. 44 is a sign that reads "Holmes, 44."

3686. McLauchlin, Russell. "What Price Baker Street?" *BSJ*, 2, No. 2 (April 1952), 65-70.

"The partners lived in Gloucester Place; which is one street west of Baker Street and also runs from Portman Square to the Marylebone Road. That is where Mrs. Hudson's house stood—and still stands."

3687. Morris, Sir Harold. "Sherlock Holmes," *Back View*. London: Peter Davies, [1960]. Chap 7, p. 48-56.

"In his autobiography he tells us that No. 21 Baker Street, five doors down the street, was at one time his great-grandfather's residence and that it was on the suggestion of his father, Malcolm Morris, to his colleague, Dr. Arthur Conan Doyle, that the figures '21' formed the basis of the editorial disguise for the famous rooms." (Bernard Davies) (A further discussion of this identification appears in letters to the editor of *SHJ* by A. Lloyd-Taylor, Bernard Davies, W. G. B. Maitland, and Harold Morris on p. 137-138 of vol. 4, p. 29-30 of vol. 5, and p. 64-65 and 97 of vol. 6.)

3688. Pattrick, Robert R. "No. 221: Confirming the Location," *BSJ*, 8, No. 3 (July 1958), 161-162.

Evidence corroborating Baring-Gould's location.

3689. Ringsted, Henrik V. "21 Baker Street Is the Real 221B," *Sherlockiana*, 5, Nr. 1-2 (1960). 1. (Nyt fra Baker Street)

Text in Danish.

3690. Roberts, Sir Sydney. "221B," *SHJ*, 5, No. 2 (Spring 1961), 54-55.

A defense of Sir Harold's statement that Watson substituted "221B" for "21" Baker Street.

3691. Schutz, Robert H. *A Bibliography of the Location of 221B*. Pittsburgh, Pa.: The Arnsworth Castle Business Index, December 1960. 2 p.

———. ———. Addenda. Pittsburgh, Pa.: The Arnsworth Castle Business Index, June 1961. 1 p.

3692. Short, Ernest H. "221B Baker Street: Where Sherlock Holmes Lived," *BSJ* [OS], 4, No. 1 (January 1949), 48, 50-52. (From the Editor's Commonplace Book)

A paper, partially quoted and paraphrased by Edgar Smith, designating 109 as the true location.

3693. Utechlin, Nicholas. "A Mathematical Interlude," *SHJ*, 8, No. 4 (Summer 1968), 123-124.

Mr. Holroyd's numerical methods for obtaining the figure 109 has prompted Mr. Utechlin to a similar mathematical manipulation of the Agra Treasure numbers in order to achieve other Baker Street addresses which researchers have advanced as the site. (The author was unable to produce No. 59 but Mr. Holroyd did on p. 23-24 of vol. 9.)

BIBLIOGRAPHIES (GENERAL)

See also *Collecting Sherlockiana* (items 3791-3816)

3694. Baring-Gould, William S. "The Bibliographical Holmes: A Selective Compilation," *Sherlock Holmes of Baker Street*. New York: Clarkson N. Potter, [1962]. Appendix 2, p. 321-336.

Contents: The Writings of John H. Watson, M.D. - The Writings of Mr. Sherlock Holmes. - The Writings of Dr. Conan Doyle. - The Higher Criticism. - Parodies, Pastiches, and the Tales-in-Verse.

The Writings About the Writings

Other Subjects

- Books, Articles, and Short Stories of Related Interest.

A well-organized bibliography that is especially valuable because of its annotations.

3695. ———. "Some of 'The Writings About the Writings,'" *The Annotated Sherlock Holmes*. New York: Clarkson N. Potter, [1967]. Vol. 2, p. 807-824.

A comprehensive listing of 834 books and articles, with annotations for many of them appearing throughout the author's monumental study of the Sacred Writings.

3696. Barzun, Jacques, and Wendell Hertiz Taylor. *A Catalogue of Crime.* New York: Harper & Row, [1971]. xxxi, 831 p.

A critical inventory of the genre, including the Sherlock Holmes novels, collected short stories, and selected writings (p. 165-166, 488-492, and 685-698). The book is appropriately dedicated "to Poe's progeny who purloined the letter and disseminated the spirit."

Review: BSJ, 21, No. 1 (March 1971), 44-48 (Julian Wolff).

3697. Bengis, Nathan L. "Bibliographical Notes," *BSJ* [OS], 4, No. 1 (January 1949), 128-129; (NS), 2, No. 1 (January 1952), 40-43.

Definitive information on seven volumes in the "Souvenir Edition" published by George Newnes between 1901 and 1906.

3698. Bergman, Ted. "Bibliografiska noteringar" ["Bibliographical Notes"], *BSCL,* No. 3 (1964), 7-10.

A description of some little-known Swedish editions of the stories.

3699. [———.] "Good Old Index," *BSCL,* No. 2- (July 1963-).

The Swedish counterpart to the "Baker Street Inventory."

3700. [———.] *Index.* The Solitary Cyclists of Stockholm, 1965. 1 leaf (laid in *BSCL,* No. 4).

———. ———. 1968. 1 leaf (laid in *BSCL,* No. 6).

Briefly annotated listings of articles published in *The Baker Street Cab Lantern.*

3701. ———. *Sherlock Holmes, 1891-1916.* [Stockholm]: The Baker Street Cab Lantern, 1964. [40] p. illus.

Limited to 75 numbered copies.

"A bibliography enumerating and describing eighty-three original and variant editions of the Swedish translations of Dr. John H. Watson's Sherlock Holmes stories."

Review: SHJ 7, No. 2 (Spring 1965), 60-61 (Lord Donegall).

3702. Berner, William A. *Sherlock Holmes &*

Related Detective Fiction. No. 1-12; Winter 1968-Summer 1972. San Francisco, Calif. (4712 17th St.). 12 issues. Quarterly.

Title of List No. 1-3: *Holmesiana.*

Annotated lists of Sherlockiana and associated items for sale by Mr. Berner.

3703. Blau, Peter E. *A Sherlockian Discography.* [Pittsfield, Mass.: The Spermaceti Press, 1972.] [7] p.

"Published for the Annual Dinner of the Baker Street Irregulars, 7 January 1972."

3704. ———. "The Sherlockian *EQMM,*" *The Queen Canon Bibliophile,* 2, No. 1 (February 1970), 15-16.

A chronological list of seventy-one items published in *Ellery Queen's Mystery Magazine* between March 1943 and February 1969.

3705. Boucher, Anthony. "Holmesiana Hispanica," *BSJ* [OS], 2, No. 3 (July 1947), 360-365. (Bibliographical Notes)

Contents: Introduction - Translations. - Anthology Appearances. - Critique. - Dramatization. - Pastiches. - Dramatic Pastiches. - Film Pastiche. - Parodies. - References.

3706. Cameron, Mary S. "Bibliographical Notes," *BSJ,* 8, No. 3 (July 1958), 169-173.

Bibliographical details on a hitherto unknown edition of the *Adventures and Memoirs of Sherlock Holmes and Sign of Four,* published by James Askew and Son (item 646).

3707. Christ, Jay Finley. *The Fiction of Sir Arthur Conan Doyle: Arranged Alphabetically and Chronologically.* [Harbert, Mich.]: Privately Printed, 1959. 34 p.

Primarily a non-Sherlockian bibliography, but included because of its importance to the Conan Doyle researcher.

Review: SHJ, 4, No. 4 (Spring 1960), 132 (James Edward Holroyd).

3708. ———. *Sherlock Comes to America.* [Michigan City, Ind.: Privately Printed], 1952. [4] p.

A discussion of the earliest periodical appearances of the tales in the U.S.

3709. Dalliba, W. Swift. *First Editions and Issues of the Sherlock Holmes Stories of Sir Arthur Conan Doyle.* New York: [Privately Produced], March 9, 1956. 2 p.

3710. ———. *A List of Sir Arthur Conan Doyle's Sherlock Holmes Books (with Bibliographical Notes). Part I. English Firsts, Sets, Omnibus and Variant Editions; Continental and Foreign Editions.* New York: [Privately Produced], March 13, 1953. 5 p.

3711. ———. *The Return of Sherlock Holmes, 1903-04-05: Bibliographical and Miscellaneous Notes.* New York: [Privately Produced], March 12, 1954. 7 p.

3712. De Waal, Ronald Burt. "A Bibliography of Sherlockian Bibliographies," *The American Book Collector,* 20, No. 2 (October 1969), 13-18.
———. Revised and enlarged with title: "A Bibliography of Sherlockian Bibliographies and Periodicals," *The Papers of the Bibliographical Society of America,* 64, Third Quarter (1970), 339-354.
An annotated listing of bibliographies compiled by some of the foremost Holmes scholars. The list contains bibliographies of English and foreign language editions and periodical appearances of the tales, parodies and pastiches, articles, books, manuscripts, films and plays, exhibition and archival materials, and other miscellany, including the literary works of Sherlock Holmes. The enlarged version lists twenty-eight Sherlockian serial publications. (The same bibliographies appear in *The World Bibliography,* but are listed by subject, with the general bibliographies appearing here.)

3713. Dickensheet, Dean W. *Sherlockiana in "The Saint Detective Magazine" (Spring 1953-October 1958), and "The Saint Mystery Magazine" (November 1958-August 1960, September 1961-).* Pittsburgh, Pa.: The Arnsworth Castle Business Index, March 1963. 1 p.

3714. ———, and J. R. Christopher. "The Sherlockiana of Anthony Boucher: A Bibliographic Study," *VH,* 5, No. 2 (April 1971), 2-4; 5, No. 3 (September 1971), 8-10.
An annotated listing of Mr. Boucher's many contributions to the literature.

3715. ———, and William Goodrich. *A List of Sherlockiana Appearing in The Ellery Queen Mystery Magazine.* Pittsburgh, Pa.: The Arnsworth Castle Business Index, November 1963. 1 p.

3716. Donegall, Lord. " 'I Am an Omnivorous Reader,' " *SHJ,* 5, No. 3-(Winter 1961-).
The British counterpart to the "Baker Street Inventory." While not as comprehensive as the "Inventory," it provides excellent reviews of the monographic publications.

3717. Feldman, Lew David. *Doyle-ia Est Omnis Divisa in Partes Tres: A Catalogue of the Opera.* Jamaica, N.Y.: House of El Dieff, 1955. 56 p.
Contents: That Which Was in the Library of A. Conan Doyle. - That Which Was Written by A. Conan Doyle. - That Which Was Recorded by John H. Watson, M.D. Concerning His Friend Sherlock Holmes. -

Supplement: Books from the Library of Vincent Starrett.

3718. ———. "Hitherto Unrecorded First Separate Editions," *BSG,* 1, No. 1 (1961), 17-20. (Bibliography)
A brief note on and illustrations of five booklets by A. Conan Doyle in *The Handy Classic Series,* two of which are Iden and Scan (items 132 and 234).

3719. [———.] *103rd Birthday of Sherlock Holmes, Baker Street Irregulars, Annual Dinner, New York City.* Jamaica, N.Y.: House of El Dieff, January 11, 1957. [4] p.
A brochure describing the author's adventures with first editions of the Canon, including his possession of copies of the George Newnes *Adventures* and *Memoirs* in dust jackets.

3720. Halbach, Helan. *A Study in Black and White.* Catalog No. 1-4, and two supplements; Christmas 1968-Spring 1972. Santa Barbara, Calif. (P. O. Box 613). 6 issues.
An excellent catalog series listing Sherlockiana for sale by Mrs. Halbach. The items are described in considerable detail and many are briefly annotated.

3721. Iraldi, James C. *The James C. Iraldi S. Holmes Collection Being Offered for Sale.* Long Island City, N.Y.: [Privately Produced, 1969]. [14] p.
A valuable descriptive list, in five parts, of Mr. Iraldi's fine collection of Sherlockiana representing an accumulation over thirty-five years.

3722. Ivanov, Christine. *Sir Arthur Conan Doyle and Sherlock Holmes.* Milwaukee: [Writer's Bibliographic Service], 1947. 8 p.
"A bibliography selected and arranged for feature writers, newspaper reporters, and librarians." (Subtitle)

3723. Kondratieve, Yu. ["Checklist"], *1961 S'ian Who's Who and What's What.* Edited by W. T. Rabe. Ferndale, Mich.: Old Soldiers of Baker Street, 1961. p. 122.
A list of some Sherlock Holmes stories published in the USSR in Russian and English, including articles by Soviet authors on the subject.

3724. La Cour, Tage. "Sherlock Holmes i Skandinavien," *Studier i rødt.* København: Carit Andersens Forlag, 1956. p. 103-105.
———. "Sherlock Holmes in Scandinavia," Tr. by Poul Ib Liebe. *Sherlock Holmes at Elsinore,* by Carl Muusmann. New York: The Baker Street Irregulars, 1956. p. 5-6.
———. ———, *The American Book Collector,* 9, No. 9 (May 1959), 22-23.
A discussion of the various translations and imitations of the Canonical tales in Scandinavia.

3725. ———. "Some Scandinavian Items to the Baker Street Inventory," *SHJ*, 3, No. 3 (Autumn 1957), 8-10.

A brief history of Sherlockian publications in Scandinavia, including a list of thiry-one items.

3726. Locke, Harold. *A Bibliographical Catalogue of the Writings of Sir Arthur Conan Doyle, M.D., LL.D., 1879-1928.* Tunbridge Wells: D. Webster, 1928. 84 p.

Contents: Introductory Note. - Contributions to Magazines. - Pamphlets. - Plays. - Prefaces. - Published Works. - Uniform Editions. - Index.

Incomplete and occasionally not quite accurate, but a valuable bibliography nonetheless, containing much of interest on the appearance of the tales.

3727. [Mortlake, Harold.] *Sherlock Holmes.* London: Harold Mortlake & Co., [1969]. 86 p. illus. (Catalog No. 133)

An extremely valuable catalog of a collection containing 877 items, 627 of which are Sherlockiana and the remainder other works by Doyle. The collection is particularly noteworthy because it includes a large number of translations and plagiarisms. It was purchased by the Metropolitan Toronto Central Library.

3728. [———.] *Conan Doyle / Sherlock Holmes.* Supplementary list 2. London: Harold Mortlake & Co., [1972]. 7 p.

Ninety-seven items listed under the headings: A. Conan Doyle, Sherlock Holmes in Translation, Holmes—iana Plagiarisms, and Conan Doyle's Other Works. A supplement to and laid in Mortlake's Catalog No. 137.

3729. Nordon, Pierre. "Bibliographie," *Sir Arthur Conan Doyle: l'Homme et l'Oeuvre.* [Paris]: Didier, [1964]. p. 439-456.

———. "Bibliography," *Conan Doyle.* Tr. by Frances Partridge. [London]: John Murray, [1966]. p. 347-360.

———. ———, ———. New York: Holt, Rinehart and Winston, [1967]. p. 347-360.

The bibliography is divided into three sections: Bibliography: Works by Sir Arthur Conan Doyle; Biographical Archives; and General Sources. The first section is a supplement to Harold Locke's *Bibliographical Catalogue;* the second, a brief list of some archival material in the family estate; and the third, a checklist of 145 publications, 37 of which are concerned with Sherlock Holmes.

3730. Queen, Ellery. *The Detective Short Story: A Bibliography.* Boston: Little, Brown and Co., 1942. 146 p.

An impressive listing, partly annotated, with twenty-seven Sherlockian items, mostly parodies and pastiches, as well as several anthologies in which some of the Canonical tales appear.

3731. ———. "Introduction," *Illustrious Client's Second Case-Book.* Edited by J. N. Williamson. [Indianapolis, Ind.: The Illustrious Clients, 1949.] p. 1-9.

———. "Sherlock Holmes First Editions: A New and Revised Catalogue of the Queen Collection," *Ellery Queen's Mystery Magazine,* 23, No. 123 (February 1954), 65-73.

———. ———, *Antiquarian Bookman,* 14, No. 7 (August 14, 1954), 387-390.

A listing and discussion of seventeen "keystone" books in this remarkable collection.

3732. [Randall, David A.] *A Catalogue of Original Manuscripts, and First and Other Important Editions of the Tales of Sherlock Holmes, as Written by Sir Arthur Conan Doyle, Together with Important Biographies, Pastiches, Articles, etc., and a Few Extraordinary Association and Unique Items.* New York: The Scribner Book Store, [1943]. 52 p.

An annotated list of 156 items from Vincent Starrett's collection.

3733. ———. "A Tentative Enquiry into the Earliest Printings, in Book Form, of the First Four Sherlock Holmes Short Stories: A Scandal in Bohemia, The Red-Headed League, A Case of Identity, and The Boscombe Valley Mystery; With a Conclusion Tending to Prove That in the Case of Two of Them Certainly, and Two of Them Possibly—America First!" *BSJ* [OS], 2, No. 4 (October 1947), 491-496. (Bibliographical Notes)

3734. Schutz, Robert H. *A List of Bibliographical References to Editions of the Sherlock Holmes Canon.* Pittsburgh, Pa.: The Arnsworth Castle Business Index, August 1963-February 1964. 13 p.

A checklist, in nine parts, covering the Canon from *A Study in Scarlet* to *The Case Book of Sherlock Holmes.*

3735. Shaw, John Bennett. [*Checklist.* Tulsa, Okla.; Santa Fe, N.M.] 1 v. (loose-leaf)

The dean of Sherlockian collectors has compiled and maintains a list of Sherlockiana, from 1890 to date, arranged under the headings: Books and Pamphlets, Reviews, Scion Material, and Periodical Material.

3736. "Sir Arthur Conan Doyle," *Abstracts of English Studies.* Vol. 13, No. 7- (March 1970-).

A University of Colorado publication in which Thomas W. Ross of Colorado College contributes excellent summaries of articles in *BSJ.*

3737. ——, *The National Union Catalog, Pre-1956 Imprints: A Cumulative Author List Representing Library of Congress Printed Cards and Titles Reported by Other American Libraries.* [London]: Mansell, 1971. Vol. 148, p. 237-286.

——, *The National Union Catalog, 1956 through 1967.* Totowa, N.J.: Rowman and Littlefield, [1971]. Vol. 31, p. 44-46.

The longest and most valuable catalog of books by Doyle published to date. There are 1341 items in vol. 148 and 71 in vol. 31, many in other languages, with location symbols for the various libraries. This is a catalog that all Sherlockian collectors and scholars will find extremely useful. A photocopy of the 53 folio pages can be obtained from most large academic and public libraries. The catalog is kept up to date with monthly, quarterly, and annual supplements.

3738. ——, *The New Cambridge Bibliography of English Literature.* Edited by George Watson. Cambridge at the University Press, 1969. Vol. 3, p. 1046-1048.

A modest listing of 132 items; about half of them are concerned with Sherlock Holmes.

3739. ——, *Victorian Studies,* 1, No. 4- (June 1958-).

In the annual "Victorian Bibliography," edited by Ronald E. Freeman and published in the June issue, Professor Lauterbach of Purdue University has been, since 1965, responsible for several briefly annotated items on Sherlock Holmes.

3740. Skeppstedt, Ingvar. "Jämforelse mellan några svenska Holmes-översättare," *BSCL,* No. 8 (1970), 12-18; two appendixes laid in.

A comparison of five Swedish translations.

3741. Smith, Edgar W. *Baker Street Inventory: An Elementary Bibliography.* New York: The Pamphlet House, 1944. 34 p.

A preliminary bibliography to the one listed below.

3742. ——. *Baker Street Inventory: A Sherlockian Bibliography.* Summit, N.J.: The Pamphlet House, 1945. 81 p.

Limited to 300 numbered copies.

Contents: Introduction. - The Sacred Writings: First Editions and Other Book Appearances; Omnibus Editions. - The Apocrypha. - The Higher Criticism: Biographies; Collected Essays and Criticism; Reference Works and Miscellaneous.

The first and most comprehensive annotated bibliography published up to the appearance of the *World Bibliography.* All the items in Edgar Smith's *Inventory,* as well as those in the *BSJ* "Inventory," are now included in this compilation.

3743. ——. "Baker Street Inventory," *BSJ* [OS], 1-4 (January 1946-January 1949); (NS), 1-10 (January 1951-December 1960).

Of the fifty-eight issues, including five *Christmas Annuals,* of the *Journal* that were edited by Edgar Smith, forty-one contain a supplement to his *Inventory.*

3744. ——. *Sherlock Holmes: The Writings of John H. Watson, M.D., Late of the Army Medical Department (Pseud. A. Conan Doyle): A Bibliography of the Sixty Tales Comprising the Canon.* [Morristown, N.J.: The Baker Street Irregulars, 1962.] 119 p. illus.

Contents: Preface. - Introduction, by Vincent Starrett. - Bibliography: A. Book Editions. The Sixty Tales Comprising the Canon: 1. *A Study in Scarlet* 1887. - 2. *The Sign of the Four* 1890. - 3. *The Adventures of Sherlock Holmes* 1892. - 4. *The Memoirs of Sherlock Holmes* 1894. - 5. *The Hound of the Baskervilles* 1902. - 6. *The Return of Sherlock Holmes* 1905. - 7. *His Last Bow* 1917. - 8. *The Valley of Fear* 1915. - 9. *The Case-Book of Sherlock Holmes* 1927. - "Pastiches": 10. *The Field Bazaar* 1947. - 11. *How Watson Learned the Trick* 1947. - Plays: 12. *The Speckled Band* 1912. - 13. *The Crown Diamond* 1958. - B. Collected Editions. - C. Periodical Contributions.

This is a revision and extension of the bibliography serialized under the title "Bibliographical Notes" in *BSJ* during 1955, 1956, and 1957. As stated in the compiler's preface, it is "a comprehensive and definitive listing of all the first and other important book editions of the Sherlockian Tales, of the collections embracing them, of their first periodical appearances, and of the plays, pastiches, and miscellanea by Dr. Doyle having to do with Sherlock Holmes."

3745. "Some Press Cuttings on the Centenary, 1954," *SHJ,* 2, No. 1 (July 1954), 10.

Twenty-three items, arranged chronologically from January 6 to March 5, about the 100th birthday of Doyle.

3746. Starrett, Vincent. "A Selected Bibliography," *The Private Life of Sherlock Holmes.* New York: The Macmillan Co., 1933. p. 199-214.

——. ——, ——. London: Ivor Nicholson & Watson Ltd., 1934. p. 185-199.

A selection of the more interesting and most important items, some briefly annotated, in the author's collection.

3747. Williams, H. B. "Bibliographical Notes," *BSJ Christmas Annual,* No. 4 (1959), 293-295.

Contents: An Unlisted "Study in Scarlet"? - The Case of the Golden Blonde.

3748. Wolff, Julian. "Baker Street Inventory," *BSJ,* 11- (March 1961-).

The Writings About the Writings

Other Subjects

When Dr. Wolff succeeded Edgar Smith as editor of *BSJ*, he also assumed responsibility for maintaining this invaluable section of the *Journal*.

BIOLOGY AND BOTANY

3749. Van Liere, Edward J. "The Biologic Doctor Watson," *The Quarterly of the Phi Beta Pi Medical Fraternity*, 45, No. 1 (March 1948), 16-21.

The many references to plant and animal life in the tales show that he was a keen student of the biological sciences.

3750. ———. "The Botanical Doctor Watson," *BSJ*, 7, No. 2 (April 1957), 96-104.

———. ———, *A Doctor Enjoys Sherlock Holmes.* New York: Vantage Press, [1959]. p. 54-61.

CHRONOLOGIES (GENERAL)

3751. Baring-Gould, William S. " 'As to Your Dates, That Is the Biggest Mystification of All,' " *The Annotated Sherlock Holmes.* New York: Clarkson N. Potter, [1967]. Vol. 1, chap. 16, p. 235-241.

An explanation of three chronological breaks in the Holmes-Watson partnership: 1. April 1883 (Spec)-October 1886 (Resi), during which Watson may have visited America (identified as the third continent). 2. November 1895 (Bruc)-October 1896 (Veil). 3. May 1901 (Prio)-May 1902 (Shos).

3752. ———. *The Chronological Holmes: A Complete Dating of the Adventures of Mr. Sherlock Holmes of Baker Street, as Recorded by His Friend John H. Watson, M.D., Late of the Army Medical Department.* Expanded, corrected, and revised. [New York: Privately Produced], 1955. iii, 178 p.

Limited to 300 copies.

Contents: Introduction. - 1. "The Date Being — ?" - 2. ". . . One Would Wish to Tidy It Up." - 3. The Chronological Holmes.

"Much more than the new, exact dating of the Tales which its name implies: its manifold discursions and commentary provide a veritable concordance of the writings about the Writings." (Edgar W. Smith)

3753. ———. "A New Chronology of Sherlock Holmes and Dr. Watson," *BSJ* [OS], 3. No. 1 (January 1948), 107-125; 3, No. 2 (April 1948), 238-251.

———. "The Chronological Holmes," *The Chronological Holmes.* Expanded, corrected, and revised. [New York: Privately Produced], 1955. Pt. 3, p. 153-178.

———. ———, *Sherlock Holmes of Baker Street.* New York: Clarkson N. Potter, [1962]. Appendix 1, p. 293-319.

Contents: I. The Early Period: 1844-Early

January 1881. - II. The Partnership, to Dr. Watson's First Marriage: Early January 1881-Monday, November 1, 1886. - III. From Dr. Watson's First Marriage to the Death of the First Mrs. Watson: Monday, November 1, 1886-Late December 1887. - IV. From Dr. Watson's Return to Baker Street to His Marriage to Mary Morstan: Late December 1887-Wednesday, May 1, 1889. - V. From Dr. Watson's Second Marriage to the Disappearance of Sherlock Holmes: Wednesday, May 1, 1889-Monday, May 4, 1891. - VI. The Great Hiatus: Monday, May 4, 1891. - Thursday, April 5, 1894. - VII. From Holmes's Return on Thursday, April 5, 1894 to Dr. Watson's Third Marriage on Saturday, October 4, 1902. - VIII. The Partnership's Last Period: January-October 1903. - IX. The Later Cases: 1909, 1912-14, 1920, 1939-45.

3754. Bell, H. W. *Sherlock Holmes and Dr. Watson: The Chronology of Their Adventures.* London: Constable & Co., 1932. xix, 131 p.

Limited to 500 copies.

———. ———. [With a foreword by Edgar W. Smith.] New York: The Baker Street Irregulars, 1953. xix, 131 p. (BSI Incunabula, No. 1)

Limited and facsimile edition of 350 numbered copies.

Contents: Introduction. - Acknowledgement. - Explanation. - Chronological Outline. - On the Period of Holmes's Active Practice. - I. The Early Period: Summer, 1875-4 March 1881. - II. The Partnership, to Dr. Watson's First Marriage: 4 March 1881-c. 1 November 1887. - On the Variant Readings of *The Resident Patient.* - III. From Dr. Watson's First Marriage to the Disappearance of Sherlock Holmes: c. 1 November 1887-4 May 1891. - IV. From Holmes's Return to Dr. Watson's Second Marriage: April 1894-c. January 1896. - V. The Period of Dr. Watson's Second Marriage: 1896. - VI. From Dr. Watson's Return to Baker Street to His Third Marriage: c. January 1897-Summer 1902. - VII. The Last Period: Summer 1902-Autumn 1903. - VIII. The Two Later Cases: 1907, 1912-14. - Appendix: The Undatable Cases.

3755. Blakeney, T. S. "The Career of Sherlock Holmes: Chronological Survey," *Sherlock Holmes: Fact or Fiction?* London: John Murray, [1932]. p. 47-111.

———. ———, ———. [With a foreword by Edgar W. Smith.] Morristown, N.J.: The Baker Street Irregulars, 1954. ix, 133 p. (BSI Incunabula, No. 2)

A well worked-out and comprehensive chronology.

3756. Brend, Gavin. "A Hint to the Next Chronologist," *BSJ*, 8, No. 2 (April 1958),

123-125. (From the Editor's Commonplace Book)

"His best prospect will be to try to upset all previous notions on the date of Watson's first marriage."

3757. Chorley, Jennifer. "1896-1963: 'The Wheel Has Come Full Circle,' " *SHJ*, 6, No. 3 (Winter 1963), 89-90.

A diary of Sherlockian events in that "great year" of 1895.

3758. Christ, Jay Finley. "An Adventure in the Lower Criticism," *BSG*, 1, No. 3 (1961), 28-35; 1, No. 4 (April 1962), 13-19.

Contents: Pt. 1. Doctor Watson and the Calendar. - Pt. 2. Dr. Watson and the Moon.

An exhaustive analysis of the chronological discrepancies in Watson's narratives.

3759. ———. *Irregular Chronology of Baker Street. I. Fragments.* [Chicago]: The Fanlight House, 1947. vi, 23 p.

Limited to 250 copies.

Contents: Author's Preface. - The Canons of This Research. - *A Study in Scarlet. - The Sign of the Four. - Silver Blaze. - The Cardboard Box. - The Final Problem.*

3760. ———. *An Irregular Chronology of Sherlock Holmes of Baker Street.* [Chicago]: The Fanlight House, 1947. x, 81 p.

Limited to 175 copies.

Contents: Alphabetical List of the Cases. - Author's Preface. - Canons of This Research. - 1. *A Study in Scarlet.* - 2. *The Sign of The Four.* - 3. *The Adventures.* - 4. *The Memoirs.* - 5. *The Hound of the Baskervilles.* - 6. *The Return.* - 7. *The Valley of Fear* and *His Last Bow.* - 8. *The Casebook.* - 9. Chronological Table. - 10. Unsolved Problems.

———. ———. A Chronological Supplement. [n.d.] [4] p.

The supplement is a chronological note on "The Case of the Man Who Was Wanted."

3761. [———.] *Sherlock's Anniversaries,* [by] Langdale Pike. Edited by Jay Finley Christ. New York: Crowborough Private Press, [1961]. [22] p.

Limited to 500 numbered copies.

Reprints of twelve monthly columns published in *The Chicago Tribune* in 1947 detailing the month in which each of the adventures occurred.

3762. Christensen, Flemming. *Chronologica Watsonensis. I. Resultaterne.* [Lemvig, Danmark: Privattryk], 1965. [10] p.

Limited to 52 copies.

3763. Donegall, Lord. "Do-It-Yourself Chronology," *SHJ*, 7, No. 4 (Spring 1966), 114-115.

The author has devised a system for working out a perpetual calendar as an aid to chronologists.

3764. Erné, Nino. "Sherlock Holmes chronologisch: Ein Wort zum Geleit" ["The Chronological Sherlock Holmes: A Guide"], *Sämtliche Sherlock Holmes Stories.* Hamburg: Mosaik-Verlag, [1967]. Vol. 1, p. 9-16.

———. ———, ———. [Gütersloh]: C. Bertelsmann Verlag, [n.d.] Vol. 1, p. 9-16.

3765. Folsom, Henry T. *Through the Years at Baker Street: A Chronology of Sherlock Holmes.* [Washington, N.J.: Privately Produced, 1962.] 37 p.

———. ———. Revised edition. [Washington, N.J.: Privately Produced, 1964.] 60 p.

Review: SHJ, 7, No. 1 (Winter 1964), 28 (Lord Donegall).

3766. Heldenbrand, Page. *Holy Days from the Sacred Writings.* [New York: Appledore Towers Letter Press, 1958.] [4] p.

"A pocket reminder for the devout Sherlockian," from "You have been in Afghanistan, I perceive," to "Oxford wins by a goal and two tries."

3767. Krejci-Graf, Karl. "Astronomical Dates," *SHJ,* 7, No. 4 (Spring 1966), 109-113.

The tales have been dated according to Watson's descriptions of meteorological and astronomical phenomena.

3768. ———. "Contracted Stories," *BSJ,* 16, No. 3 (September 1966), 150-157.

A reconstruction of the original sequence of events in Sign, RedH, Wist, and Vall. The discordances in these stories came about because Watson "condensed what took place over a long time, omitting the intervals when nothing happened and sometimes inserting earlier events later when it suited the coherence of the narration."

3769. Montgomery, James. "Chronologically Speaking," *Shots from the Canon.* [Philadelphia: Privately Printed, 1953.] p. 18

About the Sherlockian chronologies, especially the chronology of T. S. Blakeney.

3770. Moore, R. Peter. *An Apocryphal Chronology of the Cases of Mr. Sherlock Holmes, Late of 221B, Baker Street, N.W.1. Mentioned But Unreported in the Memoirs of John H. Watson, M.D., Late of the Army Medical Department, Edited by Sir Arthur Conan Doyle. Unto Which Is Added Divers Heretical Oscillations, and Other Coruscations Both Curious and Profitable.* London: Imprimatur Round the Corner from The British Museum, 1954. 18 p. Unpublished typescript.

3771. Newton, G. B. "The Chronological Holmes," *SHJ,* 3, No. 1 (Summer 1956), 10-11.

The Writings About the Writings

Other Subjects

A critical evaluation of Baring-Gould's scholarly book by the same title.

3772. Pattrick, Robert R. "A Sherlock Holmes Chronology," *BSJ*, 13, No. 1 (March 1963), 62.

A handy reference table listing the sixty tales in chronological order, with the date each tale took place and the name of the Sherlockian who established the date.

3773. Peck, Andrew Jay. *"The Date Being—?" A Compendium of Chronological Data.* [Bronx, N.Y.]: Privately Printed, 1970. [33] p. (spiral binding)

Limited to 200 numbered copies.

The long introduction containing a discussion of the more important chronologists, their methods and conclusions is followed by valuable chronological data arranged in tables.

Reviews: HO, 1, No. 1 (March 1971), 32 (Richard Slovak); *Mystery Reader's Newsletter*, 4, No. 4 (May 1971), 40 (Stanley Carlin); *SHJ*, 10, No. 2 (Summer 1971), 66-67 (Lord Donegall); *VH*, 5, No. 2 (April 1971), 7 (Thomas Drucker).

3774. Robbins, Frank E. *Annals of Sherlock Holmes.* [N.p.: Privately Printed, Christmas 1934.] [4] p.

A chronological record of the lives and cases of Holmes and Watson.

3775. Roberts, S. C. *A Note on the Watson Problem.* Cambridge University Press, 1929. [8] p.

Limited to 100 copies.

——. ——, *BSJ* [OS], 1, No. 1 (January 1946), 29-32.

——. "The Chronological Problem," *Holmes and Watson: A Miscellany.* London: Oxford University Press, 1953. p. 55-60.

——. "A Note on the Watson Problem," *The Incunabular Sherlock Holmes.* Edited by Edgar W. Smith. Morristown, N.J.: The Baker Street Irregulars, 1958. p. 109-113.

——. "The Chronological Problem," *Seventeen Steps to 221B.* [Edited by] James Edward Holroyd. London: George Allen & Unwin Ltd., [1967]. p. 46-49.

A critical examination of the chronological problem as presented by Ronald Knox (item 2073).

3776. Schutz, Robert H. *What Was the Month?* Volume One. Pittsburgh, Pa.: The Plane Tree Press, [December 1965]. 14 p.

Limited to 34 copies.

3777. Smith, Edgar W. "Dr. Watson and the Great Censorship," *BSJ*, 2, No. 3 (July 1952), 138-151.

——. ——, *Baker Street and Beyond: Together with Some Trifling Monographs.* Edited by Edgar W. Smith. Morristown, N.J.: The Baker Street Irregulars, 1957. [unpaged]

The chronicler wrote and published the tales only when he thought Holmes was dead or safely in retirement. Includes a tabulation of the dates the adventures occurred and their first appearance in print, together with a chart showing schematically the impact of the Great Censorship.

3778. Starr, Herbert W. "The Present State of Sherlockian Chronology: A Proposal Submitted to The Baker Street Irregulars," *BSJ*, 11, No. 3 (September 1961), 151-157.

"The only possible explanation is that these inconsistencies and inaccuracies are usually intentional, and that Holmes approved of them."

3779. Walter, Fred. "Re-dating the Reichenbach Incident (by Way of 'The Red-Headed League')," *BSJ*, 8, No. 4 (October 1958), 230-233.

"All cases previously dated 1894 and some of those dated 1895 will have to be moved up a year."

3780. Zeisler, Ernest Bloomfield. *Baker Street Chronology: Commentaries on the Sacred Writings of Dr. John H. Watson.* Chicago: Alexander J. Isaacs, [1953]. x, 168 p.

Limited to 200 copies.

Contents: Preface, by Vincent Starrett. - Introduction. - 1. Chronological Landmarks. - 2. Before Reichenbach. - 3. After the Return. - 4. Summary. - Index.

A brilliant and exhaustive analysis of the evidence on the datings of the tales, with a new and challenging chronology.

CLOTHING

3781. Blake, S. F. "Sherlock Holmes's Dressing Gown(s)," *BSJ*, 10, No. 2 (April 1960), 86-89.

His dressing gown is described by Watson as having different colors because he owned two in 1889, both damaged in a fire and replaced by a third.

3782. Christ, Jay Finley. "The Pipe and the Cap," *BSJ*, 9, No. 1 (January 1959), 43-45.

Conjectures on the curved pipe and the fore-and-aft cap.

3783. Clayton, J. K. "The Hat Trick," *SHJ*, 2, No. 1 (July 1954), 19-21.

A brief essay on the various kinds of hats worn by Holmes.

3784. Helling, Cornelis. "About Deerstalkers and Inverness Capes," *BSJ*, 2, No. 4 (October 1952), 202-204.

"It is well known that Dr. Watson, throughout his Writings, mentions neither a deerstalker cap as such nor an inverness cape. . . . So inverness cape and deerstalker cap seem decidedly to be *trouvailles* on the part of Sidney Paget."

3785. Michell, Humfrey. "The Sartorial Sherlock Holmes," *A Baker Street Four-Wheeler*. Edited by Edgar W. Smith. [Maplewood, N.J., and New York: The Pamphlet House, 1944.] p. 31-36.

A discussion of Holmes's and Watson's wardrobes, with a footnote on dressing gowns by Christopher Morley.

3786. Morley, Christopher. ["The Sherlock Holmes Dressing Gown"], *BSJ*, 2, No. 2 (April 1952), 83-84. (Clinical Notes from a Resident Patient)

An announcement of the dressing gown "Jane Nightwork" proposed that the BSI Inc. should design, license, and sell to a few high-class outlets.

3787. R[hode], F[ranklin] W. "Some Random Notes on Canonical Headgear," by Langdale Pike. *DCC*, 4, No. 1 (December 1967), 2-3. (The World of Sherlock Holmes)

3788. Sherbrooke-Walter, Ronald. "Clothes Canonical," *SHJ*, 6, No. 4 (Spring 1964), 104-108.

A review of the raiment that people wore in the days when Holmes and Watson strode down Regent Street.

3789. "Sherlock Holmes and the Adventure of the Extraordinary Discoveries," *Gentlemen's Quarterly*, 34, No. 1 (February 1965), 58-67.

"Some remarkable fashion ideas for the current year hunted down by the greatest detective of them all—here played by the star of the new musical *Baker Street*—Fritz Weaver."

3790. Staedler, Bernhard. "Sherlock Holmes nyttjade ej lösmanschetter," *BSCL*, No. 5 (1966), 17-18.

An explanation of why he could not possibly have worn loose cuffs.

COLLECTING SHERLOCKIANA

See also Appendix II

3791. Austin, Bliss. "A Fine Collection," *SHJ*, 5, No. 3 (Winter 1961), 92-93. (Wigmore Street Post-Bag)

A letter to the editor in which Dr. Austin mentions some rarities in his magnificent collection of Sherlockiana.

3792. Bengis, Diana U. "My Rival," *SHJ*, 3, No. 3 (Autumn 1957), 21.

Mrs. Bengis discusses her husband's hobby, and concludes with the following admonition: "I don't mind the rivalry of Sherlock Holmes as long as my husband tells me that for him I'll always be *the* woman."

3793. Bengis, Nathan L. " 'Got Any Beeton's Today?' or, The Byways of the Sherlockian Game," *Four Wheels to Baker Street*. Edited by Bruce Kennedy. [Fulton, Mo.]: The Three Students Plus, 1968. p. 7-18.

An excellent essay on the variety of material awaiting the potential or beginning collector.

3794. ————. "Happy Hunting," *BSJ*, 13, No. 4 (December 1963), 242-250.

Interesting experiences about running down some Sherlockian rarities, including early newspaper appearances of Sign.

3795. ————. "Why I Collect Sherlockiana," *Hobbies*, 59, No. 1 (March 1954), 126-130.
————. ————, [Revised and enlarged] *The American Book Collector*, 9, No. 9 (May 1959), 15-19.

The whys and wherefores of collecting Sherlockiana, with valuable information on important editions of the stories, books about Holmes, pastiches, and association items.

3796. Boucher, Anthony. "Prolegomena to a Holmesian Discography," *BSJ* [OS], 1, No. 2 (April 1946), 229-231.

A listing and discussion of a few Sherlockian discs for the record collector.

3797. De Waal, Ronald Burt. "Libraries and Sherlockiana," *BSJ*, 19, No. 1 (March 1969), 44-45.

The author urges a greater effort to see that more Sherlockiana is acquired by libraries.

3798. [Donegall, Lord.] "Holmesian Photographs," *SHJ*, 7, No. 1 (Winter 1964), 2.

An editorial note on the Society's newly formed collection of photographs "taken during the period 1880-1914, showing London street scenes, etc., and illustrating many places mentioned in the Saga exactly as they appeared at the time of the stories."

3799. [————.] "Rarer-Avises," *SHJ*, 5, No. 2 (Spring 1961), 33-34. (Editorial)

Morsels of information about Canonical rarities. Other rare items are described in letters from Bliss Austin (item 3791), Stanley MacKenzie, A. H. Goldstone, and Lord Donegall on p. 92-94 of the same volume.

3800. Greenwood, E. P. "Archives and Records," *SHJ*, 2, No. 4 (Winter 1955), 16.

A request for references and material on Holmes and the Sherlock Holmes Society for the Society's library.

3801. Hall, Joseph E. ["Letter"], *BSJ*, 2, No. 1 (January 1952), 54-55. (From the Editor's Commonplace Book)

On the establishment of a Sherlock Holmes Collection in the Rare Books Division of the Library of Congress. Unfortunately, the collection seems to have been short-lived.

3802. ———. "Signposts to Baker Street," *The Bookworm*, 1, No. 5 (October 1944), 16-19.

Advice and encouragement for the collector and prospective collector.

3803. Hertzberg, Francis. "The Case of the Missing Memorial," *The Mystery Reader's Newsletter*, 3, No. 5 (June 1970), 15-16.

As the number of public and commercial memorials honoring Holmes seems to be diminishing, the author suggests that the Master can still be honored and enjoyed by having a Sherlock Holmes Room in one's own home or, on a more modest scale, by keeping a Holmes scrapbook.

3804. ———. " 'He Had a Horror of Destroying Documents,' " *BSJ*, 18, No. 2 (June 1968), 97-99.

Following the examples of both James Edward Holroyd (item 3806) and Sherlock Holmes, Rev. Hertzberg describes how he is docketing his collection of pictures and cuttings related to the Sacred Writings.

3805. Holland, Glenn S. "A Word from Nathan Garrideb on Collecting," *BSP*, No. 51 (September 1969), 3.

A guide for the junior Sherlockian.

3806. Holroyd, James Edward. "Fanciful Furnishings," *Baker Street By-ways*. London: George Allen & Unwin Ltd., [1959]. p. 75-80.

A chapter about the author's imaginary purchases and collection of miniature association items for his own 221B.

3807. Honce, Charles. " 'Come Up and See My Etchings,' " *To Talk of Many Things*. Mount Vernon, N.Y.: Imprinted by S. A. Jacobs at his Golden Eagle Press, 1950. p. 19-20.

The author discusses his Sherlockian memorabilia and where he keeps them.

3808. ———. "A Holmes Collection and What Became of It," *For Loving a Book*. Mount Vernon, N.Y.: The Golden Eagle Press, 1945. p. 47-50.

A commentary on the Vincent Starrett collection sold to The Scribner Book Store (item 3732), including quotations from Harry Hansen and Vincent Starrett.

3809. [Kennedy, Bruce.] "Editorial," *SOS*, 3, No. 2 (July 1969), 1-2.

Mr. Kennedy believes that private collections of Sherlockiana should be left to the Baker Street Irregulars so that a coast-to-coast library can be established for interested Sherlockians. (The compiler has been pleasantly surprised to find just how much material, either monographic publications or photocopies of articles, can be acquired through the interlibrary loan service of a local library. He has obtained well over a thousand items in such a manner for the *World Bibliography*.)

3810. Klinefelter, Walter. *A Packet of Sherlockian Bookplates*. Nappanee, Ind.: Private Press of the Indiana Kid, 1964. [13] p.

Limited to 150 copies.

A scholarly discussion, with reproductions, of eight bookplates that adorn the books of well-known Sherlockians.

3811. Montgomery, James. "Those Gorgeous Magazines," *The Trifling Monographs*. [Philadelphia: Privately Printed, 1952.] p. 10-15.

On the joys of collecting the first magazine appearances of the stories in England and the U.S.

3812. Randall, David A. "Sherlock, Tobacco, and a Gold-Headed Cane," *The Last Bookman*, [by Peter Ruber]. New York City: The Candlelight Press, 1968. p. 77-79.

Primarily a discussion of Vincent Starrett's collection, as listed in Mr. Randall's *Catalogue* (item 3732), including Harry Hansen's laudatory commentary published in the New York *World-Telegram* on February 7, 1940.

3813. Shaw, John Bennett. "A Little Child Shall Lead," *SOS*, 3, No. 1 (January 1969), 8-9.

A brief report on the author's collecting activities, including ninth-grader Raymond Funk's "discovery" of a pastiche entitled "Sherlock Holmes Buys a Microscope" (item 2998).

3814. [Smith, Edgar W.] "A Bibliographical Note," *BSJ*, 9, No. 1 (January 1959), 3-4. (The Editor's Gas-Lamp)

"There is much profit to be gained from the reading of the Tales of Sherlock Holmes in the format of their original appearances: it seems, if we may admit to be possible, that something extra is added in this way to the charm and meaning the stories hold."

3815. [———.] "Something Can Be Added," *BSJ*, 1, No. 4 (October 1951), 121-122. (The Editor's Gas-Lamp)

On the enjoyment of reading the Canonical first editions.

3816. Tyler, Desmond. "S. H. Tape Archive," *SHJ*, 9, No. 4 (Summer 1970), 142. (Wigmore Street Post-Bag)

Mr. Tyler asks for help in developing a "Sherlock Holmes Sound Archive" which he plans eventually to turn over to the Sherlock Holmes Society.

COMMUNICATION

3817. Berl, E. Ennalls. "Sherlock Holmes and

the Telephone," *BSJ*, 3, No. 4 (October 1953), 197-210.

"So why the telephone blind-spot in the Master for so many years I leave to a keener intelligence than mine. My purpose is simply to point out its existence in certain cases, and to show the manner in which it might have simplified the Master's detection, and how, even, it might have averted tragedy."

3818. Cumings, Thayer. "Don't Write —Telegraph!" *The Best of the Pips.* Westchester County, N.Y.: The Five Orange Pips, 1955. p. 87-95.

————. "A Sheaf of Weird Telegrams," *Seven on Sherlock.* [New York]: Privately Printed, 1968. p. 9-17.

A catalog and discussion of twenty-three telegraphic messages in the Canon.

3819. [Donegall, Lord.] "Why No Telephone? (1890 to 1898)," *SHJ*, 10, No. 2 (Summer 1971), 37-38. (Editorial)

3820. Naganuma, Kohki. ["Holmes and Communication," *The World of Sherlock Holmes.* Tokyo: Bungei-Shunju Shin-sha, 1962.] Chap. 4, p. 85-120.

————. ————, *BSJ*, 21, No. 1 (March 1971), 14-21.

An examination of twenty-five cases involving the use or misuse of telegrams, letters, packages, and the telephone.

3821. Thornton, A. G. "The Bell That Didn't Ring," *John O'London's,* 1, No. 9 (December 3, 1959), 275.

————. ————, *CPBook,* No. 19 (June 1969), 280.

"Sherlock Holmes knew of the existence of the telephone but he never used it." (Letters of response to this article are reprinted on p. 281-282 of *CPBook.*)

3822. Waters, F. A. " 'Holmes or Watson Here,' " *SHJ*, 3, No. 2 (Winter 1956), 21-22.

On the introduction of the telephone to England and its installation in the Baker Street residence.

COMMUNIST COUNTRIES

3823. Armour, Richard. "Ban: Hungary Has Banned Sherlock Holmes—News Item," *BSJ*, 4, No. 1 (January 1954), 21.

"For there is fear of such a sleuth / In lands where they have murdered Truth."

3824. Čechura, Rudolf. "The Canon in Eastern Europe," *SHJ*, 8, No. 4 (Summer 1968), 124.

A brief report on the availability of Czech, Polish, and Slovak translations.

3825. "Chinese Assail Sherlock Holmes as Bourgeois British Watchdog," *The New York Times* (July 11, 1968), 7.

————, *CPBook,* No. 19 (June 1969), 384.

A commentary on an article printed in the Shanghai newspaper *Wen Wei Pao* excoriating Lo Jui-ching, a former Minister of Public Security in Communist China, for urging security agents to emulate the Master.

3826. Chujoy, Anatole. "Sherlock Holmes in Russia," *BSJ*, 3, No. 3 (July 1953), 170-172.

Information about some pre-revolutionary translations.

3827. Fisher, Charles. "Baker Street Banned!" *Forum* [Philadelphia], 106 (November 1946), 420-421.

Holmes chats with Watson on the significance of Moscow's denunciation of his accomplishments.

3828. [Henriksen, A. D.] "Sherlock i Sovjet," *Sherlockiana,* 1, Nr. 2 (1956), 7; 2, Nr. 1-2 (1957), 6.

————. "Sherlock Holmes in the Soviet Union," *SHJ*, 3, No. 2 (Winter 1956), 16-18.

————. "Sherlock Holmes i Sovjetunionen," *Sherlock Holmes Arbog* I (1965), 71-74.

An interesting discussion about M. and N. Chukovsky's translations of and prefatory remarks to four Canonical tales published in "The Red Soldiers' Library" during World War II. Includes reproductions of two of the covers and two of the illustrated pages.

3829. ————, and Gustav P. "Sherlock Holmes i Sovjet: Afsluttende bemaerkninger," *Sygekassen,* Nr. 3 (1952), 22-23.

————. ————, *CPBook,* 1, No. 4 (Spring 1965), 70-71.

3830. Hurwitz, Edward. ["Letter"], *BSJ*, 7, No. 1 (January 1957), 58-59. (From the Editor's Commonplace Book)

"While there may have been attacks on Holmes as representative of that tranquil era which the Soviet government professes to hate, nevertheless he generally has been held in high regard both officially and unofficially."

3831. [Knox, E. V.] "The Immortal Sleuth of 221B Baku Street," by Evoe. *The Pick of Punch 1959: An Annual Selection.* Edited by Nicolas Bentley. New York: E. P. Dutton and Co., [1959]. p. 23-24.

About the "bloodthirsty agent of capitalist intrigues" and the Soviet Union.

3832. "No Sherlock for Red China," *The Philadelphia Inquirer* (July 14, 1968).

————, *CPBook,* No. 19 (June 1969), 384.

————, *HO,* 1, No. 7 (September 1971), 7.

Another commentary on Lo Jui-ching, with the speculation that he could have been a secret member of the BSI!

3833. Olyunin, Rostislav. "Sherlock Holmes in Russia," *Sputnik* [London], No. 1 (January 1968), 62-63.

An informative article on the translations and imitations, from Spec in 1893 to the eight-volume edition in 1966.

3834. Rabe, W. T. "How Red Was Holmes' Circle? or, There Are Commies in the Bottom of My Garden. Mother!" *EI*, 1, No. 1 (August 1953), 11-14.

On "that nasty old capitalist, Sherlock Holmes," and the Communists.

3835. Redmond, Chris. "Nihilism, NKVD, and the Napoleon of Crime," *SHJ*, 7, No. 4 (Spring 1966), 104-107.

A study of the Master's lifelong fight against Nihilism and Communism. "Not only did he eternally oppose Moriarty, but also the social system he and his descendants stand for—Communism."

3836. Redmond, D. A. "The Countess, the Master, and the Tsar," *SHJ*, 7, No. 4 (Spring 1966), 108.

Interesting speculations on Holmes's post-retirement activities with the Tsarist entourage and his fight against Communism.

3837. "Sherlock Holmes Incurs Wrath of a Soviet Critic," *The New York Times* (September 25, 1946), 8.

A brief notice on the denunciation of Holmes by S. Chernov in the *Moscow Evening News*.

COPYRIGHT

3838. Berman, Harold J. "Rights of Foreign Authors Under Soviet Law," *Bulletin of the Copyright Society of the U.S.A.*, 7, No. 2 (December 1959), 67-81.

"A slightly condensed English translation of the oral argument presented by the author in Russian to the Supreme Court of the RSFSR in Moscow, August 17, 1959, in behalf of The Sir Arthur Conan Doyle Estates against four Soviet state publishing houses and the Ministry of Culture of the USSR."

3839. ———. "Sherlock Holmes in Moscow," *The Oxford Lawyer*, 2, No. 2 (Michaelmas 1959), 29-37.

———. ———, [Abridged] *Harvard Law School Bulletin*, 11, No. 4 (February 1960), 3-5.

———. ———, [Abridged] *SHJ*, 4, No. 4 (Spring 1960), 119-121.

———. ———, *The Lawyer*, 8, No. 2-3 (Trinity & Michaelmas 1965), 53-58.

"The attorney who sought, to collect royalties on the Tales published in the U.S.S.R. tells of his defeat, in this 'Second Adventure of the Red Circle.'" (Edgar W. Smith)

3840. "The Case of the Pig in the Poke," *Forbes*, 107, No. 11 (June 1, 1971), 36.

"In which Forbes' own Sherlock Holmes deciphers a mysterious advertisement." (Subtitle)

3841. "Heir of Conan Doyle in Court to Bar a Copyright Sale Now," *The New York Times* (April 8, 1971), 36.

Mrs. Nina Harwood, widow of Sir Arthur's son Denis and beneficiary of the Doyle estate, started legal proceedings in London to prevent the sale of the author's copyrights by the estate trustees, Fides Union Fiduciaire of Geneva.

3842. "Move to Halt Conan Doyle Estate Sale," *The Times* (April 8, 1971), 2.

Further commentary on Mrs. Harwood's actions to delay the sale of the literary, film, and television copyrights. An advertisement by Fides announcing the intended sale appeared in the previous day's paper on p. 25.

3843. "Sherlock Holmes Up for Auction," *Los Angeles Times* (April 8, 1971), I, 4.

3844. Wincor, Richard. "Who Owns Sherlock Holmes?" *From Ritual to Royalties: An Anatomy of Literary Property*. New York: Walker and Co., [1962]. Chap. 3, p. 61-84.

"A discussion of property rights in fictional [sic] characters, using the Master as the archetype of a character who exists beyond the works in which he appears." (Julian Wolff)

3845. Yew, Elizabeth. "A Slight Case of Literary Piracy," *Thuria*, 1, No. 1 (1964), 29-32.

A review of and commentary on the feud between Baker Street Irregulars and the son of Dr. Watson's literary agent.

CRIMES

3846. Pratt, Fletcher. "Very Little Murder," *BSJ*, 5, No. 2 (April 1955), 69-76.

A careful and definitive analysis of the crimes investigated by Holmes. Includes the following tables: (1) A Legal Summary of the Cases; (2) Disposition of the Cases in Which Action Was Required; and (3) A Case-by-Case Analysis.

DEATHS AND BURIALS

3847. Shaw, John Bennett. "Doctor Watson Didn't Write About Taxes, Either," *BSJ*, 19, No. 4 (December 1969), 235-239.

A highly interesting study of Canonical deaths and burials in which the author, former director of a Tulsa funeral parlor, estimates that of the 263 persons who lose their lives, a mere six are given any kind of service or burial. He attributes such gaps to

Watson's and the literary agent's aversion to death and the disposal of bodies.

ENGLAND

See also *Place Identifications* (*General*) (items 4221-4231)

3848. Baring-Gould, William S. "The London of Holmes and Watson," *BSJ*, 9, No. 3 (July 1959), 165-170.
Contents: 1. The Strand. - 2. Barts. - 3. The Langham Hotel. - 4. The Lyceum Theatre.

3849. Brooks, Collin. "The Right Wrong Thing: Conan Doyle and the Spirit of the Nineties," *The Bookman* [London], 79 (December 1930), 174-175.
———. ———. [San Francisco: The Beaune Press, December 1966.] [9] p. (Vintage No. 2)
Limited to 222 numbered copies.
"Hand set and printed, in Baskerville type, by Shirley & Dean Dickensheet."
A comparison of social life as portrayed by Conan Doyle and Jane Austen.

3850. Campbell, Maurice. "The Worlds of Conan Doyle and Dorothy Sayers," *SHJ*, 7, No. 2 (Spring 1965), 36-41.
Contents: England in 1881-1903. - England: 1904-1921. - England: 1921-1935. - Comparisons of Conan Doyle and Dorothy Sayers.

3851. Harrison, Michael. *The London of Sherlock Holmes.* Newton Abbot: David & Charles, [1972]. 232 p.
———. ———. New York: Drake Publishers, 1972. 232 p.
The author vividly depicts late Victorian London as he acts as guide for the tour of the neighborhoods and houses that the Master and his contemporaries, real and fictional, inhabited. Handsomely illustrated with close to a hundred photographs and drawings, it is a unique guide to the London of the past, filled with curious bits of information and gossip.
Review: *Times Literary Supplement* (April 7, 1972), 391.

3852. Hertzberg, A. Francis. "He Was Walking by My Side: Holmesian London," *BSJ*, 17, No. 2 (June 1967), 96-97.
The Master's presence is not to be felt primarily in places like The Sherlock Holmes or the Criterion Bar but while walking along that magical thoroughfare called Baker Street.

3853. Johnston, Ames. "The London of the Canon," *Leaves from the Copper Beeches.* Narberth, Pa.: Livingston Pub. Co., 1959. p. 75-79.
The London of Holmes's day is compared with the London of today.

3854. Merriman, Charles O. "A Tourist Guide to the London of Sherlock Holmes: Walk I," *SHJ*, 10, No. 1 (Winter 1970), 19-22; "Walk II," 10, No. 2 (Summer 1971), 54-56; "Walk III," 10, No. 3 (Winter 1971), 92-94; "Walk IV," 10, No. 4 (Summer 1972), 129-131. illus.
"The purpose of this Guide is to enable the visitor to London to view this Great Metropolis through the eyes of Holmes and Watson and to acquire some of the atmosphere of 1895 in the process."

3855. Olsson, Jan Olof. "London," *BSCL*, No. 6 (1968), 31-32.
Extracts, in Swedish, from *Dagens Nyheter* (January 20, 1968).

3856. Ostermeyer, C. W. "Sherlock Holmes as a Social Document of the Nineteenth Century," *Argus* [Melbourne] (1945).
———. ———, *BSJ* [OS], 1, No. 2 (April 1946), 154-156.
"To most of us Sherlock Holmes recalls exercises in deduction and the solving of mysteries, but also the records of his exploits afford us valuable evidence of the social structure of English life in the closing years of the nineteenth century."

3857. [Schutz, Robert H.] *Scenes from Sherlock Holmes' London.* [Pittsburgh, Pa.: Privately Printed, December 1968.]
Limited to 17 numbered copies.
A set of five envelopes containing an illustration and descriptive note of the following: 1. A London Pub on Saturday Night. - 2. Bottle-Selling Outside St. Bartholomew's Hospital. - 3. Roll Call: Corps of Commissionaires. - 4. London Library Reading Room. - 5. Night Mail (Paddington).

3858. [Smith, Edgar W.] "The Days We Envy," *BSJ*, 4, No. 3 (July 1954), 131-132. (The Editor's Gas-Lamp)
"One of the things we envy Mr. Sherlock Holmes is the fact that he lived in the days he did. We envy him for it, and we take him to our hearts as we do because he is a symbol of those days — and because the days themselves are days we envy."

3859. [———.] "The World That Was," *BSJ*, 7, No. 2 (April 1957), 67-68. (The Editor's Gas-Lamp)
"To look back upon that world of the 1880's and the 1890's . . . is to realize, from our own perspective today, that it must have been a world with much to commend it—for it was this world, after all, that gave us Sherlock Holmes."

3860. Stone, P. M. "London at the Turn of the Century," *The Second Cab.* Edited by James Keddie. [Boston: The Speckled Band, 1947.] p. 51-56.
Delightful recollections of a youthful visit to Sherlockian London in 1904.

3861. Wolf, John B. "Another Incubus in the Saddle," *Exploring Sherlock Holmes.* Edited by E. W. McDiarmid & Theodore C. Blegen. La Crosse: Sumac Press, 1957. p. 66-81.

Professor Wolf deals with the question: "The adventures are the stuff of great literature, but did Dr. Watson embellish them with enough textual richness to make them also a source for the history of the era?"

FORMS OF ADDRESS

3862. Browne, P. A. "Some Notes on Forms of Address," *SHJ,* 5, No. 1 (Winter 1960), 14-15.

Forms of address used by Holmes and Watson and by the inspectors of Scotland Yard.

3863. [Smith, Edgar W.] "On the Forms of Address," *BSJ,* 9, No. 3 (July 1959), 131-132. (The Editor's Gas-Lamp)

"The use of the simple, unadorned 'Holmes' and 'Watson' has something solid and respectful and respectable about it; something that is lacking in the easy and almost immediate resort to Christian names that besets us today."

GASOGENES AND LANTERNS

3864. Christ, Jay Finley. "The Gasogene," *BSJ* [OS], 1, No. 1 (January 1946), 69.

———. ———, *BSJ,* 14, No. 3 (September 1964), 135.

A scientific diagram and description of this noble instrument.

3865. Clum, Florence H. "To Jay Finley Christ (Upon Seeing His Diagram of a Gasogene in the Journal)," *BSJ* [OS], 1, No. 2 (April 1946), 224.

———. ———, *BSJ,* 14, No. 3 (September 1964), 135.

"Thy gasogene is nothing but a Silex!"

3866. Cross, Melvin. "The Lantern of Sherlock Holmes," *BSJ* [OS], 1, No. 4 (October 1946), 433-442.

A discussion, with photographs, of the various types of dark lanterns mentioned in the Saga.

3867. Harrison, Michael. "In Praise of the Baker Street Gasogene," *BSJ,* 18, No. 4 (December 1968), 222-223.

A verse in eight stanzas, as by Dr. Watson, on the indispensable gasogene, with a note concerning an 1878 advertisement about the Appareil Gazogène-Briet.

HERALDRY

See also *Ancestry, Family, and Name* (items 2921-2938 and 3372-3382)

3868. Dobson, A. W. "Arms and the Man," *SHJ,* 8, No. 1 (Winter 1966), 20-23.

Inaccuracies and inconsistencies in the use of armorials and titles in the Canon.

3869. Hall, W. S. "The True and Proper Coat of Arms of Mr. Sherlock Holmes: With Also the Coats of Arms of John H. Watson, M.D., and James Moriarty, Sc.D.," *Profile by Gaslight.* Edited by Edgar W. Smith. New York: Simon and Schuster, 1944. p. 114-124.

"The bearings proposed for the Master by Mr. Wigglesworth [item 2937] find no sympathetic response in the mind of Mr. W. S. Hall, whose long and painstaking research in the authorities has convinced him that the suggestions advanced are superfluous because Sherlock Holmes actually had a coat of arms—as did also Dr. Watson and Professor Moriarty. Mr. Hall (as is his vicarious right) offers a new motto: *Justum et tenacem propositi* [just and firm of purpose]." (Edgar W. Smith)

3870. Redmond, Chris. "A Revisitation of Canonical Arms," *BSJ,* 17, No. 2 (June 1967), 84-85.

"The three buglehorns of Holmes and the ermine of Watson bore upturned crescents upon them. If their fathers were not, in turn, eldest sons, the differencing might even be the second-generation symbol of a crescent upon a crescent."

3871. Whitfield, B. G. "Heraldry in Sherlock Holmes," *The Coat of Arms: An Heraldic Quarterly Magazine,* 2, No. 16 (October 1953), 283-286.

"A searching examination of Dr. Watson's knowledge of heraldry, if any, as revealed in his Writings." (Edgar W. Smith)

3872. Wolff, Julian. *Practical Handbook of Sherlockian Heraldry, with Some Observations upon the Identification of the Screened and with Illustrations from Various Sources.* New York: [Privately Printed], 1955. viii, 27 p.

Contents: Introduction. - A Sherlockian Roll of Arms: Sir Arthur Conan Doyle. - Sherlock Holmes. - John H. Watson, M. D. - Baskerville. - The Duke of Holdernesse. - Lord Robert St. Simon. - Some Remarks upon an Azure Field. - A Note on the Quartering of the Union Jack with the Stars and Stripes. - Grice Paterson. - The Head Lama. - Lady Beatrice Falder. - His Holiness the Pope. - Lord Cantlemere. - Hilton Cubitt. - The Royal Family of Scandinavia. - The French Republic. - Oxford University. - Cambridge University. - Alexander Holder. - Hugo de Capus. - Professor Moriarty. - The Illustrious Client. - Lord Bellinger and Trelawney Hope. - The King of Proosia. - Reginald Musgrave. - Dundas. - Charles I. - Napoleon Bonaparte. - General de Merville. - Colonel Sebastian Moran. - Sholto. - The

Sultan of Turkey. - The Reigning Family of Holland. - Sir Charles Chandos. - Colonel Sir James Damery. - Colonel Upwood. - John Clay. - George III. - The King of Bohemia. - Don Murillo of San Pedro. - Bibliography and References.

3873. ———. *A Visitation of Conanical Arms: Being an Annexe to the Practical Handbook of Sherlockian Heraldry.* New York: [Privately Printed], 1956. [8] p.

HOROLOGY

3874. Donegall, Lord. "The Horological Holmes," *SHJ*, 8, No. 4 (Summer 1968), 120-123.

Contents: Silver Blaze. - The Sign of Four. - The Camberwell Poisoning Case. - The Man with the Watches. - Marine Chronometers.

ILLUSTRATORS AND ILLUSTRATIONS

3875. Baring-Gould, William S. " 'Your Pictures Are Not Unlike You, Sir, If I May Say So,' " *The Annotated Sherlock Holmes.* New York: Clarkson N. Potter, [1967]. Vol. 1, chap. 5, p. 33-36. illus.

A brief discussion of the lives and illustrations of Sidney Paget and Frederick Dorr Steele, with a note on Sherlock Holmes in comic strips and advertising.

3876. Christ, Jay Finley. "Who Spilled the Beans?" *BSJ*, 13, No. 4 (December 1963), 230-231.

A commentary on some editorial errors in the illustrations to the Heritage Press edition of *Sherlock Holmes* (item 702).

3877. Helling, Cornelis. "About Some Remarkable Holmesian Jackets and Covers," *SHJ*, 5, No. 2 (Spring 1961), 53-54; 5, No. 3 (Winter 1961), 91.

A discerning look at the illustrations that decorate the covers and dust jackets of books in England and the U.S.

3878. Henriksen, A. D. "Sherlock Holmes og hans Illustratorer" ["Sherlock Holmes and His Illustrators"], *Philobiblon* [København] (February 1952), 60-67.

3879. Holroyd, James Edward. "Dorr Steele and Some Others," *Baker Street By-ways.* London: George Allen & Unwin Ltd., [1959]. p. 44-52.

3880. Hunt, Roy. *The Something Hunt: A Sherlockian Portfolio of 10 Prints.* Introduction by Nathan L. Bengis. [Culver City, Calif.]: Privately Printed by Luther Norris, 1967. 10 prints.

Limited to 221 numbered copies.

Contents: Sherlock Holmes—Street Scene. - Sherlock Holmes and the Empty House. - An Evening with Sherlock Holmes.

- Hound of the Baskervilles. - Hound of the Baskervilles. - Clive Brook as Sherlock Holmes. - William Gillette as Sherlock Holmes. - Arthur Wontner as Sherlock Holmes. - Basil Rathbone as Sherlock Holmes. - Gustave von Seffertitz as Professor Moriarty.

Reviews: Armchair Detective, 1, No. 2 (January 1968), 62 (Allen J. Hubin); *BSP,* No. 33 (March 1968), 4; *New York Times Book Review* (October 22, 1967), 46 (Anthony Boucher); *SHJ,* 8, No. 3 (Winter 1967), 102 (Lord Donegall).

3881. Klinefelter, Walter. *Sherlock Holmes in Portrait and Profile.* With an introduction by Vincent Starrett. Syracuse University Press, 1963. ix, 104 p. illus.

"Currently, no doubt, the picture of Sherlock Holmes in most minds is that of Basil Rathbone; but it was not always so—once it was the portrait of William Gillette. The evolution of that famous profile is a story in itself, the story of the detective's illustrators no less than his impersonators. It is that story Walter Klinefelter tells in his delightful book." (Introduction)

Reviews: BSC, 1, No. 3 (June 1968), 4 (Benjamin Small); *Courier* [Syracuse, N.Y.] (September 1963); *English Literature in Transition,* 7, No. 1 (1964), 48 (E. S. Lauterbach); *Library Journal,* 88 (December 15, 1963), 4761 (James Sandoe); *New York Times Book Review* (January 26, 1964), 20 (Anthony Boucher); *SHJ,* 6, No. 4 (Spring 1964), 128 (Lord Donegall); *Sherlockiana,* 9, Nr. 3 (1964), 10.

3882. Lauritzen, Henry. "Tegnernes Sherlock Holmes" ["Sherlock Holmes Illustrators"], *Sherlock Holmes Årbog* III (1967), 36-43.

3883. Montgomery, James. *A Study in Pictures.* Philadelphia: International Printing Co., 1954. 64 p. illus. (Montgomery's Christmas Annual, No. 5)

Limited to 300 copies.

"Cover design after *Beeton's* by Bruce Montgomery."

"Being a 'trifling monograph' on the iconography of Sherlock Holmes. Containing also two reference tables and an index, as well as thirty-two illustrations from the Canon." (Subtitle)

The two tables (p. 53-62) list "the first and other important illustrators of the Canon," along with "the total number of different pictures drawn by the artist for each story, including magazine appearances, book editions, and reprints."

Review: SHJ, 2, No. 2 (December 1954), 4.

3884. Pearson, Edmund. "Sherlock Holmes Among the Illustrators," *The Bookman,* 75, No. 4 (August 1932), 354-359.

An illustrated account of the pictorial Holmes.

*An illustration by Sidney Paget (**3891-3898**) for the tale "Silver Blaze," which first appeared in* The Strand Magazine *for December 1892 (**357**).*

3885. [Richard, Peter, comp.] *Charles Augustus Milverton Among the Illustrators.* With a frontispiece by Sidney Paget. London: The Milvertonians of Hampstead, 1961. [8] p.

Contents: Introduction. - Sidney Paget. - Frederic Dorr Steele. - Charles Raymond Macauley. - A Listing of the C.A.M. Illustrations. - Milverton in Caricature.

3886. Smith, Edgar W. "A Note on the Illustrators," *Baker Street Inventory: A Sherlockian Bibliography.* Summit, N.J.: The Pamphlet House, 1945. p. 77-81.

A listing of twenty-two artists and the number of drawings each has contributed to the magazine and book appearances of the tales mentioned therein.

3887. Starrett, Vincent. "The Evolution of a Profile," *The Private Life of Sherlock Holmes.* New York: The Macmillan Co., 1933. p. 176-186.

3888. Steele, Frederic Dorr. "Sherlock Holmes in Pictures," *The New Yorker,* 13, No. 14 (May 22, 1937), 35-42.

————. ————, *221B: Studies in Sherlock Holmes.* Edited by Vincent Starrett. New York: The Macmillan Co., 1940. p. 129-137.

"An account of the work of various ar-

tists, including the author himself, whose drawings have embellished the tales. In *The New Yorker,* several typical illustrations are reproduced." (Edgar W. Smith)

3889. Williams, H. B. "Pleasure in Pictures," *BSJ,* 13, No. 4 (December 1963), 232-235.

Additional remarks on the discrepancies in the Heritage Press illustrations (item 702).

3890. Wilmunen, Jon. "Illustration of the Canon," *BSP,* No. 54 (July 1970), 2-4.

The author and illustrator of *The Gamebag* presents his theory of how Holmes, Watson, and their surroundings should be depicted.

Sidney Paget

3891. Butler, Maida. "Genesis of a Watson," *SHJ,* 1, No. 2 (September 1952), 22-24.

Just as the illustrator's brother "Wal" Paget served as his model for Holmes, so did he take as his model for Watson the noted architect Alfred Morris Butler.

3892. Holroyd, James Edward. " 'Our Client's Foot Upon the Stair,' " *The Cornhill Magazine,* No. 1030 (Winter 1961-62), 239-250. illus.

————. ————, *Seventeen Steps to 221B.*

[Edited by] James Edward Holroyd. London: George Allen & Unwin Ltd., [1967]. p. 132-143.

A discussion of the sitting room and visitors at 221B as depicted by Paget in *The Strand Magazine*.

3893. ———. "The Return of Sherlock Holmes," *Picture Post* [London], 49, No. 8 (November 25, 1950), 41.

———. Revised and enlarged with title: "Sidney Paget's Drawings," *Baker Street By-ways*. London: George Allen & Unwin Ltd., [1959]. p. 38-43.

"An account of the part Sidney Paget played in giving the Master substance, with commentary on the beloved artist's life and ways." (Edgar W. Smith)

3894. ———. "Sherlock Holmes in Regent Street," *Baker Street By-ways*. London: George Allen & Unwin Ltd., [1959]. p. 92-97.

About the reversed printing of Paget's Regent Street drawing in *The Strand Magazine* and in the English book editions of Houn.

3895. [Paget, Sidney.] "Holmes Revisited," *MD Medical Newsmagazine*, 7, No. 10 (October 1963), 193-196.

Eleven Paget drawings, with captions, from *The Strand Magazine*.

3896. [———.] "I Perceive, Watson, That Someone Has Been Tampering with the Words," *Mayfair*, 5, No. 10 (October 1970).

———. ———, *Sherlockiana*, 15, Nr. 3-4 (1970), 14-16.

———. ———, *SHJ*, 10, No. 1 (Winter 1970), 17-18.

Nine Paget illustrations with new captions. Five are reproduced in *SHJ*, with the original captions on p. 36.

3897. Paget, Winifred. "Full Circle," *SHJ*, 1, No. 1 (May 1952), 27-28.

———. Revised with title: "He Made Holmes Real," *John O'London's Weekly*, 63 (February 19, 1954), 177.

"Miss Paget recalls with charm and nostalgia the early days of her father's association with Sherlock Holmes." (Edgar W. Smith)

3898. "The Sidney Paget Centenary," *SHJ*, 5, No. 1 (Winter 1960), 5.

A tribute to *the* illustrator on the occasion of his hundredth birthday. Includes twelve of his illustrations, reduced in size, from *The Strand Magazine*.

Frederic Dorr Steele

3899. Austin, Bliss. "Triolet on Frederic Dorr Steele (1874-1944)," *BSJ* [OS], 1, No. 2 (April 1946), 137.

"With joyful skill he breathed life / Into a name, a street, an age."

3900. Honce, Charles. "A Note on Freddy Steele," *For Loving a Book*. Mount Vernon, N.Y.: The Golden Eagle Press, 1945. p. 43-44.

———. ———, *BSJ*, 12, No. 2 (June 1962), 70-72.

A tribute to the most distinguished American illustrator of the Canonical tales. Includes a reproduction of the famous self-portrait of Steele with the Master.

3901. ———. "A Sherlock Holmes Birthday," *A Sherlock Holmes Birthday and Other Bookish Stories Conceived in the Form of News*. New York: Privately Printed, 1938. p. 15-19.

An article, dated April 17, 1937, about Doyle and Steele on the occasion of the semicentennial.

3902. Morton Galleries, New York. *Memorial Exhibition: Frederic Dorr Steele, March 26 to April 7, 1945*. 1 leaf.

3903. Steele, Frederic Dorr. "My First Meeting with Sherlock Holmes," *BSJ* [OS], 4, No. 1 (January 1949), 86-89.

A letter to Allen Robertson, dated March 3, 1940, concerning the artist's illustrations and introduction to the Master.

3904. ———. "Veteran Illustrator Goes Reminiscent," *The Colophon* (New Graphic Series), 1, No. 3 (September 1939), 1-12.

"Notable among the illustrations under reminiscence are, of course, the standard representations of Sherlock Holmes which this beloved artist gave the world." (Edgar W. Smith)

INDIANS

3905. Shaw, John Bennett. *Sherlock and the American Indian*. Tulsa, Okla.: [Privately Printed, December 1967]. [4] p.

Fifteen quotations from the Canon about the Red Indian, with a comment on each in Cherokee and English.

THE LITERARY AGENT

3906. Adcock, A. St. John. "Sir Arthur Conan Doyle," *The Bookman* [London], 43 (November 1912), 95-110.

———. ———, [Condensed] *Gods of Modern Grub Street: Impressions of Contemporary Authors*. New York: Frederick A. Stokes Co., 1923. p. 83-89.

An excellent biographical sketch which in *The Bookman* includes twenty-nine illustrations.

3907. Arnstein, Felix. "The 'Adventures' of Arthur Conan Doyle," *The Armchair Detective*, 3, No. 3 (April 1970), 166-169.

Frederic Dorr Steele (3899-3904) imagines Sherlock Holmes at home at 221B Baker Street.

An interesting and informative article on his many and diverse activities.

3908. Baumgarth, Ernest A. "The Adventure of the Literary Agent," *SHJ*, 4, No. 2 (Spring 1959), 34-37.

A memorable recollection of the author's interview in May 1922 with Dr. Doyle concerning his lecture in Detroit on spiritualism.

3909. Brean, Herbert. "Rejecto ad Absurdum," *BSJ*, 14, No. 2 (June 1964), 73-76.
———. "Are You There, Arthur?" Read by Herbert Brean. *Voices from Baker Street*, 2. Ferndale, Mich.: The Old Soldiers of Baker Street, 1965. Side 1, band 4.

During an imaginary phone conversation with the literary agent, an American magazine editor rejects *A Study in Scarlet* and recommends that the doctor try "the Beeton people in London."

3910. Brown Ivor. *Conan Doyle: A Biography of the Creator of Sherlock Holmes.* London: Hamish Hamilton, [1972]. xi, 145 p.
Review: Times Literary Supplement (July 14, 1972), 812.

3911. Calheiros, Francisco Osório de. "Sir Arthur Conan Doyle, D.L., L.L.D., M.D.," *Boletim da Academia Portuguesa de Ex-Libris*, No. 13 (1960), 17-22. illus.
———. ———. Academia Portuguesa de Ex-Libris, 1960. 28 p. illus.
An offprint limited to 200 numbered and signed copies.

3912. Carr, John Dickson. *The Life of Sir Arthur Conan Doyle.* New York: Harper & Brothers, [1949]. x, 304 p. illus.
———. ———. Garden City, N.Y.: Doubleday & Co., 1949. 359 p. (Dolphin Books, C117)
———. ———. London: John Murray, [1949]. 361 p. illus.
———. ———. London: Pan Books Ltd., [1953]. 285 p. (GP20)

———. *Conan Doyle.* [Översättning av Nils Holmberg.] Stockholm: Albert Bonnier, 1950. 350 p.

———. *La vida de Sir Arthur Conan Doyle.* [Traducción de José Donoso Yánez.] [Santiago de Chile]: Zig-Zag, [1951]. 390 p.

———. *La vie de Sir Arthur Conan Doyle.* Traduit de l'anglais par André Algarron. Paris: Robert Laffont, [1958]. 468 p.

———. *Sir Arturo Conan Doyle: Creador de Sherlock Holmes.* Traducción de Félix Blanco. México: Editorial Renacimento, S.A., [1960]. 376 p. illus.

"Mr. Carr has told the story of this many-sided man—for whom, be it said, no group has a higher admiration that the Irregulars themselves—better than anyone has told it before. . . . There will be, surely, no readers of the Sherlock Holmes tales who will not wish also to read this life of a man who walked and talked with Sherlock Holmes." (Edgar W. Smith)

Reviews: Atlantic Monthly, 183 (April 1949), 82-83 (Charles J. Rolo); *BSJ* [OS], 4, No. 1 (January 1949), 3-4 (Edgar W. Smith); *Catholic World,* 169 (June 1949), 236 (Robert Wilberforce); *Chicago Sun-Times* (February 18, 1949), (James Sandoe); *Christian Science Monitor* (May 19, 1949), 14 (Henry Sowerby); *Commonweal,* 49 (March 4, 1949), 525-526 (Elizabeth Johnson); *Ellery Queen's Mystery Magazine,* 12 (December 1948), 4-6; *Kirkus,* 16 (December 15, 1948), 653; *Library Journal,* 74 (January 1, 1949), 55 (Earle F. Walbridge); *Manchester Guardian* (February 4, 1949), 3 (R. G. J.); *New Republic,* 120 (February 14, 1949), 23-24 (Anne L. Goodman); *New Statesman and Nation,* 37 (March 19, 1949), 279 (Arthur Marshall); *New York Herald Tribune Weekly Book Review* (February 6, 1949), 3 (Edgar W. Smith); *New York Times Book Review* (February 6, 1949), 5 (Howard Haycraft); *San Francisco Chronicle, This World* (January 30, 1949), 20 (Joseph Henry Jackson); *Saturday Review of Literature,* 32 (March 5, 1949), 19, 31-32 (Elmer Davis).

3913. ———. "When Conan Doyle Was Sherlock Holmes: The Case of George Edalji," *Harper's Magazine,* 198 (January 1949), 31-40.

3914. Cromie, Robert. "Conan Doyle's Place in Modern Literature," *The Twentieth Century* [London], 2, No. 5 (May 1901), 187-205.

An admirable essay on Doyle's writings in which Mr. Cromie rates him as "a representative of our first rank in British fiction." The Canonical tales are but briefly mentioned because they "have been so exhaustively discussed around the world there is little to say about them" (and this written in 1901!).

3915. [Donegall, Lord.] "Centenary Digression," *SHJ,* 4, No. 3 (Winter 1959), 81.

An editorial commentary on some of the literary agent's own writings.

3916. Dorsenne, Jean. "Sir Arthur Conan Doyle," *Les Nouvelles Littéraires* [Paris], 4, No. 152 (September 12, 1925), 1.

———. "A French View of Conan Doyle," *The Living Age,* 327 (November 28, 1925), 567-469.

"More about Doyle than about Holmes, but nevertheless a tribute which proves that a prophet is not without honor even in his grandmother's country." (Edgar W. Smith)

3917. Doyle, Adrian Conan. "Conan Doyle Was Sherlock Holmes," *John O'London's Weekly,* 50 (November 5, 1943), 46.

"For the mental prototype of Sherlock Holmes, we need search no further than his creator."

3918. ———. "Secret Life of Master Detective: Doyle Himself Was Model for Super Sleuth Sherlock Holmes Says Son," *The Detroit News* (May 12, 1960), 8C.

———. ———, *CPBook,* 1, No. 2 (Fall 1964), 29-30.

An explanation of why the author believed there was only one "real" Sherlock Holmes, along with details of his father's personality.

3919. [———, ed.] *Sir Arthur Conan Doyle Centenary, 1859-1959.* [London: John Murray, April 1959.] 135 p.

Limited to 100 numbered copies.

Bound in red morocco, gilt, with arms of Conan Doyle.

———. ———. London: John Murray, [November 1959]. 135 p.

———. ———. Garden City, N.Y.: Doubleday & Co., [n.d.] 135 p.

Contains a foreword by Adrian Conan Doyle; "Some Aspects of Sir Arthur Conan Doyle's Works and Personality," by P. Weil-Nordon; and many illustrations, appreciations, etc., from the Doyle archives.

Reviews: SHJ, 5, No. 1 (Winter 1960), (Lord Donegall); [Source unknown] (February 26, 1960), and reprinted in *CPBook,* 2, No. 5-6 (Summer-Fall 1965), 115.

3920. ———. "Some Family Facts," *BSJ,* 12, No. 3 (September 1962), 139-141.

A description and an illustration of Doyle's coat of arms.

3921. ———. *The True Conan Doyle.* With a preface by General Sir Hubert Gough. London: John Murray, [1945]. 24 p. illus.

———. ———. New York, N. Y.: Coward-McCann, Inc., [1946]. 30 p. illus.

"A short biography of Sir Arthur by his son, with frequent and illuminating references to the subject's friend, Mr. Sherlock Holmes." (Edgar W. Smith)

3922. [Doyle, Sir Arthur Conan.] "Conan Doyle Tells the True Story of Sherlock Holmes," *Tit-Bits,* 39 (December 15, 1900), 287.

An interview during which Doyle is quoted at length on how he came to write the first twenty-six tales.

3923. ———. "Memories and Adventures," *The Strand Magazine,* 66, No. 394 (October 1923), 323-336; 66, No. 395 (November 1923), 445-455; 66, No. 396 (December 1923), 557-566; 67, No. 397 (January 1924), 84-96; 67, No. 398 (February 1924), 121-131; 67, No. 399 (March 1924), 234-246; 67, No. 400 (April 1924), 334-344; 67, No. 401 (May 1924), 441-451; 67, No. 402 (June 1924), 563-574; 68, No. 403 (July 1924), 16-24.

———. ———. London: Hodder and Stoughton Ltd., [1924]. 408 p. illus.

———. ———. With illustrations. Boston: Little, Brown and Co., 1924. ix, 410 p.

———. ———. [Second edition.] London: John Murray, [1930]. 460 p. illus.

———. ———. [*The Works of Sir Arthur Conan Doyle.*] The Crowborough Edition. Garden City, N.Y.: Doubleday, Doran & Co., 1930. Vol. 24 (xiv, 467 p.)

———. *Avventure e ricordi.* Traduzione autorizzata. Milano: L. F. Cogliati de G. Martinelli, 1925. 446 p.

———. *Ma Vie Aventureuse.* Traduction de Louis Labat. Paris: Albin Michel, Editeur, [1932]. 349 p. (Collection des Maîtres de la Littérature Etrangère)

———. [*Waga omoide to bôken: Conan Doyle jiden.* Tr. by Ken Nobuhara. Tôkyô: Shinchô-sha, 1965.] 415 p.

———. *Souvenirs et Aventures.* Préface et notes de Gilbert Sigaux. [Traduction française de Gilbert Sigaux.] Lausanne: Editions Recontre, [1968]. 484 p. (Oeuvres littéraires complètes, tome 20)

Contents: Preface. - 1. Early Recollections. - 2. Under the Jesuits. - 3. Recollections of a Student. - 4. Whaling in the Arctic Ocean. - 5. The Voyage to West Africa. - 6. My First Experiences in Practice. - 7. My Start at Southsea. - 8. My First Literary Success. - 9. Pulling Up the Anchor. - 10. The Great Break. - 11. Sidelights on Sherlock Holmes. - 12. Norwood and Switzerland. - 13. Egypt in 1896. - 14. On the Edge of a Storm. - 15. An Interlude of Peace. - 16. The Start for South Africa. - 17. Days with the Army. - 18. Final Experiences in South Africa. - 19. An Appeal to World's Opinion. - 20. My Political Adventures. - 21. The Years Between the Wars. - 22. The Years Between the Wars (cont'd). - 23. Some Notable People. - 24. Some Recollections of Sport. - 25. To the Rocky Mountains in 1914. - 26. The Eve of War. - 27. A

Sir Arthur Conan Doyle [1859-1930], affectionately referred to as "the literary agent" (3906-3984).

Remembrance of the Dark Years. - 28. Experiences on the British Front. - 29. Experiences on the Italian Front. - 30. Experiences on the French Front. - 31. Breaking the Hindenburg Line. - 32. The Psychic Quest. - Index.

In the second edition chapter 25 has been omitted, and the last chapter, retitled "Up to Date," has been rewritten.

Reviews: Bookman, 60 (December 1924), 493-494 (Louis Bromfield); *Boston Transcript* (September 27, 1924), 1 (E. F. Edgett); *Cargoes for Crusoes* (New York: D. Appleton & Co., 1924), 201-202 (Grant Overton); *Independent,* 113 (November 15, 1924), 402; *Literary Digest International Book Review* (November 1924), 877 (A. B. Maurice); *Nation,* 119 (December 17, 1924), 682-683 (R. F. Dibble); *New York Evening Post, Literary Review* (October 18, 1924), 1 (M. E. Stone); *New York Herald and Tribune* (October 26, 1924), 4 (Llewelyn Powys); *New York Times Book Review* (September 28, 1924), 1, 24 (J. Donald Adams); *Outlook,* 138 (October 15, 1924), 256 (Edmund Lester Pearson); *Saturday Review of Literature,* 1 (October 18, 1924), 199-200 (Arthur W. Colton); *Springfield Republican* (October 12, 1924), (Lilian Whiting); *Times Literary Supplement* (September 25, 1924), 591.

3924. ———. "Mr. Sherlock Holmes to His

Readers," *The Strand Magazine,* 73, No. 425 (March 1927), 281-284.

————. Slightly abridged and used as the "Preface" to *The Case-Book of Sherlock Holmes.* London: John Murray, [1927]. p. 5-7.

————. ————, *Introducing Mr. Sherlock Holmes.* Edited by Edgar W. Smith. Morristown, N.J.: The Baker Street Irregulars, 1959. [unpaged]

"And so, reader, farewell to Sherlock Holmes! I thank you for your past constancy, and can but hope that some return has been made in the shape of that distraction from the worries of life and stimulating change of thought which can only be found in the fairy kingdom of romance."

3925. ————. "Some Personalia About Mr. Sherlock Holmes," *The Strand Magazine,* 54, No. 324 (December 1917), 531-535.

————. Enlarged with title: "Sidelights on Holmes," *Memories and Adventures.* London: Hodder and Stoughton Ltd., [1924]. Chap. 11, p. 96-110.

Contents: 1. "The Speckled Band". - 2. Barrie's Parody on Holmes. - 3. Holmes on the Films. - 4. Methods of Construction. - 5. Problems. - 6. Curious Letters. - 7. Some Personal Cases. - 8. Strange Happenings.

Sections 1-4 are not included in *The Strand Magazine.*

3926. ————. "To an Undiscerning Critic," *Some Piquant People,* by Lincoln Springfield. London: T. Fisher Unwin Ltd., [1924]. p. 107.

————. ————. [With a note by Vincent Starrett.] Ysleta: Edwin B. Hill, 1937. [4] p. (Sherlockiana)

————. ————, *Profile by Gaslight.* Edited by Edgar W. Smith. New York: Simon and Schuster, 1944. p. 23-24.

————. ————, *BSJ,* 10, No. 4 (October 1960), 211.

————. ————, *An 'Undiscerning Critic' Discerned.* [San Francisco: The Beaune Press, December 1968.] p. [6].

Sir Arthur's reply, in verse, to Mr. Guiterman's satirical verse (item 3933) in which he defends himself against the charge of ingratitude for his reference in Stud to Poe's Dupin as "a very inferior fellow" and to Gaboriau's Lecoq as "a miserable bungler."

3927. ————. "The Truth About Sherlock Holmes," *Collier's,* 72, No. 26 (December 29, 1923), 9-10, 28.

Nearly everything he wrote about Holmes in *Memories and Adventures* has been brought together in this one article.

3928. Doyle, Lady Conan. "Conan Doyle *Was* Sherlock Holmes," *Pearson's Magazine,* 78 (December 1934), 574-577. (Great Authors, No. 1)

"How my husband solved police mysteries in private: The conception and vivifying of Sherlock Holmes and Dr. Watson."

3929. Engholm, Kaj. "Conan Doyle," *Ti Kriminelle Minutter.* [København]: Spektrum, 1966. p. 9-12.

3930. Goldwyn, Robert M. "The Birth of Sherlock Holmes," *Harvard Medical Alumni Bulletin,* 31, No. 1 (October 1956), 21-23.

A paper presented as the subject of the author's Boylston Medical Society dissertation in March 1956.

The early life of Doyle, with emphasis on his medical career, Dr. Joseph Bell, and the Canonical tales.

3931. Gordon, Harold. "Some Recollections of Sir Arthur Conan Doyle," [With an Introductory Note and Diverse Surmises by William R. Smith]. *BSJ,* 12, No. 3 (September 1962), 137-138.

Two brief anecdotes demonstrating Doyle's "knack for quick and accurate deductions similar to those of his mentor, Dr. Joseph Bell."

3932. Green, Roger Lancelyn. " 'In the Steps of the Master,' " *SHJ,* 10, No. 2 (Summer 1971), 61-62.

A review of a documentary play entitled *Conan Doyle Investigates: A Reconstruction of the Edalji Case,* by Roger Woddis; performed at the Victoria Theatre, Stoke-on-Trent, in April 1971.

3933. Guiterman, Arthur. "To Sir Arthur Conan Doyle," *The Laughing Muse.* New York and London: Harper & Brothers, [1915]. p. 218-220.

————. ————, *An 'Undiscerning Critic' Discerned.* [San Francisco: The Beaune Press, December 1968.] p. [4-5].

In an otherwise admiring letter in verse, the author is critical of Doyle for allowing the Master, in shameless ingratitude, to sneer at Poe's Dupin as "very inferior," and to label Gaboriau's clever Lecoq "a bungler."

3934. [————, and Sir Arthur Conan Doyle.] *An 'Undiscerning Critic' Discerned.* [San Francisco: The Beaune Press, December 1968.] [8] p. (Vintage No. 4)

Limited to 222 numbered copies.

"Hand set and printed, in Baskerville type, by Shirley & Dean Dickensheet."

Contents: Introduction, by Dean W. Dickensheet. - To Sir Arthur Conan Doyle, by Arthur Guiterman. - To an Undiscerning Critic, by A. Conan Doyle. - A Mercifully Short History of The Beaune Press.

3935. Hamilton, Cosmo. "A. Conan Doyle: There Is Only Change," *People Worth Talking About.* New York: Robert M. McBride & Co., 1933. Chap. 17, p. 157-164.
————. ————, ————. Freeport, N.Y.: Books for Libraries Press, [1970]. Chap. 17, p. 157-164. (Essay Index Reprint Series)

3936. Hardwick, Michael and Mollie. "The Man Who Was Sherlock Holmes: An Investigation into the Relationship Between the Famous Detective and His Creator, Sir Arthur Conan Doyle," BBC Home Service, Thursday, December 19, 1963, 7:30-8:15 p.m.
Credits: Producer, Joe Burroughs.
Cast: Alan Wheatley (Sherlock Holmes), James McKechnie (Dr. Watson), Marius Goring (Sir Arthur Conan Doyle), Richard Hurndall (Narrator), Shirley Cooklin, Olga Lindo, Moira Mannion, Peter Bartlett, John Broster, Humphrey Morton, Lewis Stringer, Cyril Luckham, and Godfrey Kenton.

3937. ————. *The Man Who Was Sherlock Holmes.* London: John Murray, 1964. 92 p. illus.
————. ————. [Paperback edition.] London: John Murray, 1964. 92 p.
————. ————. Garden City, N.Y.: Doubleday & Co., 1964. 92 p. illus.
"The idea of this book is to show that the brilliance of Holmes is the reflected light of his creator's many sided character and of a life lived to the full. It has been asserted that if Music could have composed itself, the result would have been Bach. Is it too fanciful of us to suggest that if Sherlock Holmes could have written himself, the result might have been Arthur Conan Doyle?" (Foreword)
Review: SHJ, 6, No. 4 (Spring 1964), 128 (Lord Donegall).

3938. Hatch, Robert. "The Real Conan Doyle," *The Idler* [Oxford], 1, No. 2 (February 1967), 3.
A biographical sketch, illustrated with a Sidney Paget drawing.

3939. Helling, Cornelis. "Dr. Arthur Conan Doyle: Was He Dr. John H. Watson?" *BSJ,* 22, No. 1 (March 1972), 10-11. illus.
A sketch-map of the first printing of Prio is signed "John H. Watson," while the map itself is in the hand of Doyle, proving that the two doctors were the same person.

3940. Henriksen, A. D. "Arthur Conan Doyle: 100 år," *Sherlockiana,* 4, No. 1 (1959), 2.
————. "En engelsk Gentleman," *Kronik* [København] (May 22, 1959).

3941. Hoehling, Mary. *The Real Sherlock Holmes: Arthur Conan Doyle.* New York: Julian Messner, [1965]. 191 p.
For ages 12 to 16.

"An excitingly 'whole' portrait of Conan Doyle as man and writer. . . . Though the use of fictional dialogue may be criticized, it is based on fact and the inferences drawn are legitimate." (Clayton E. Kilpatrick)
Reviews: Best Sellers, 25 (May 15, 1965), 102; *Christian Science Monitor* (May 6, 1965), 8 (P. M. D.); *Horn Book,* 41 (August 1965), 396 (Jane Manthorne); *Library Journal,* 90 (June 15, 1965), 2894 (Clayton E. Kilpatrick); *New York Times Book Review* (July 4, 1965), 12 (Anthony Boucher); *New Yorker,* 41 (December 4, 1965), 244, 246 (Emily Maxwell).

3942. How, Harry. "A Day with Dr. Conan Doyle," *The Strand Magazine,* 4, No. 20 (August 1892), 182-188. illus.
An interview with Sir Arthur in which he discusses his life, Holmes, and Joseph Bell ("the gentleman whose ingenious personality suggested Sherlock Holmes to his old pupil"). Includes a letter dated June 16, 1892, from Dr. Bell to Dr. Doyle.

3943. Hynd, Alan. "When Conan Doyle Played Sherlock Holmes," *Liberty* [Toronto], 39, No. 11 (February 1963), 29, 40-41. illus.
"Discusses Sir Arthur's alleged connection with some real-life crimes. Interesting, if true—but not mentioned previously by Sir Arthur or his biographers." (Julian Wolff)

3944. "Immortal Romantic," *MD Medical Newsmagazine,* 3, No. 10 (October 1959), 130-134.
Contents: Beginnings. - Student Days. - The Physician. - The Writer. - The Soldier. - Crusader. - Spiritualist.

3945. Johnson, Allen S. "Doctors Afield: Arthur Conan Doyle," *The New England Journal of Medicine,* 249, No. 14 (October 1, 1953), 567-569.

3946. Kernahan, Coulson. "Personal Memories of Sherlock Holmes," *The London Quarterly and Holborn Review,* 159 (October 1934), 449-460.
The author reveals that Stud was published in *Beeton's Christmas Annual* on the strength of his wife's recommendation. At the time she was married to G. T. Bettany, chief editor to Ward, Lock & Co. The remainder of this fine article is devoted to recollections of Doyle, "the Headland of Honesty and of Helpfulness to others."

3947. Kittle, C. Frederick. "Arthur Conan Doyle: Doctor and Writer (1859-1930)," *Journal of the Kansas Medical Society,* 61, No. 1 (January 1960), 13-18.
————. Revised and enlarged with title: "Arthur Conan Doyle, Detective-Doctor," *University of Minnesota Medical Bulletin,* 36, No. 8 (April 1965), 278-292.

———. Slightly changed with title: "The Case of the Versatile A. Conan Doyle," *The University of Chicago Magazine,* 42, No. 2-3 (September-December 1969), 8-14.

3948. Klinefelter, Walter. "The Case of the Conan Doyle Crime Library," *BSJ,* 12, No. 1 (March 1962), 43-47.

———. ———. [With *The Books in the Criminological Library,* as catalogued by Mr. Lew D. Feldman.] La Crosse, Wis.: Sumac Press, 1968. 28 p.

Limited to 300 copies.

A refutation of Dr. Rosenbach's claim (item 3960) that Doyle used his crime library as a source of reference when writing the Sherlock Holmes stories. Except for Vall, they were all written before Doyle had such a library.

3949. Lamond, John. *Arthur Conan Doyle: A Memoir.* With an epilogue by Lady Conan Doyle. London: John Murray, [1931]. xiv, 310 p. illus.

———. ———. Port Washington, N. Y.: Kennikat Press, [1972]. xiv, 310 p. illus.

Partial contents: First Appearance of Sherlock Holmes (p. 25-29). - Sherlock Holmes and *The Strand Magazine* (p. 43-45). - The Adventure of Two Collaborators, by Sir James M. Barrie (p. 46-50).

"Those who are primarily interested in Sir Arthur Conan Doyle as the romantic novelist, the vivid descriptive writer, the user of clean, strong prose, and above all the infinitely ingenious creator of Sherlock Holmes, will be disappointed in this book. But those who are mainly attracted to him as the indefatigable apostle of Spiritualism will find that his life has provided an admirable text for a readable and generally reasonable discourse." (*Times Literary Supplement*)

Review: Times Literary Supplement (October 8, 1931), 767.

3950. [Lang, Andrew.] "The Novels of Sir Arthur Conan Doyle," *The Quarterly Review,* 200 (July 1904), Art. 8, p. 158-179.

Part of this article (p. 175-179) is devoted to "the adventures of Dr. Watson with Mr. Sherlock Holmes."

3951. Mackenzie, Sir Compton. "The Man Behind Sherlock Holmes," *Certain Aspects of Moral Courage.* Garden City, N.Y.: Doubleday & Co., 1962. Chap. 10, p. 164-186.

The Adventures of Conan Doyle by Sherlock Holmes in which Sir Arthur attempts to right the wrong done to George Edalji and Oscar Slater.

3952. Mannion, Rodney A. "The Humor of Doyle—An Appreciation," *BSJ,* 18, No. 3 (September 1968), 152-153, 155.

Instances of comical situations in his other writings.

3953. Maurice, Arthur Bartlett. "Sherlock Holmes and His Creator," *Collier's,* 41, No. 21 (August 15, 1908), 11-14, 24-27.

Contents: Sir Arthur Conan Doyle: His Career and Personality. - Concerning Mr. Sherlock Holmes: Where the Detective Idea Came From. - Concerning Conan Doyle: As a Literary Workman — Some Impressions of His Work.

3954. Nichols, Beverley. "Sir Arthur Conan Doyle, or An Ungrateful Father," *Are They the Same at Home? Being a Series of Bouquets Diffidently Distributed.* New York: George H. Doran Co., [1927]. Chap. 16, p. 86-90.

After an imaginary interview with Sir Arthur, Mr. Nichols exclaims, "I would prefer to have recalled Conan Doyle as a calm agnostic, smoking a pipe and dreaming of fresh crimes in the flames of his blazing fire. . . . I would rather have one story of Sherlock Holmes than a whole volume of spirit messages from the faintly ridiculous shade of Mr. W. T. Stead."

3955. Nordon, Pierre. *Sir Arthur Conan Doyle: l'Homme et l'Oeuvre.* Paris-Bruxelles: Didier, 1964. 482 p. illus. (Coll. Etudes Anglaises, 17)

———. ———. [Paris]: Didier, [1964]. viii, 481 p. illus. (Etudes Anglaises, 17)

———. *Conan Doyle.* Translated from the French by Frances Partridge. [London]: John Murray, [1966]. xi, 370 p. illus.

———. ———. New York: Holt, Rinehart and Winston, [1967]. 370 p. illus.

Awarded the Prix Guizot by the Académie Française.

Reviews: BSP, No. 25 (July 1967), 4; *Book Week* (July 9, 1967), 4 (Alan Pryce-Jones); *Christian Science Monitor* (February 8, 1967), 9 (Eric Forbes-Boyd); *Detroit Free Press* (July 16, 1967) (Bill Rabe), and reprinted in *CPBook,* 3, No. 13 (Summer 1967), 243; *Economist,* 221 (November 12, 1966), 695; *Harper's Magazine,* 235 (December 1967), 112-113 (Justin Kaplan); *Independent-Journal* (August 26, 1967), M13, and reprinted in *CPBook,* 3, No. 12 (Spring 1967), 240; *Library Journal,* 92 (June 15, 1967), 2396 (Katherine Tappert Willis); *Minneapolis Star* (July 24, 1967), 11A (Theodore C. Blegen), and reprinted in *CPBook,* 3, No. 13 (Summer 1967), 251-252; *Minneapolis Tribune* (July 16, 1967) (Robert Sorensen), and reprinted in *CPBook,* 3, No. 13 (Summer 1967), 254; *National Review,* 19 (August 22, 1967), 915 (Shane Leslie); *New Statesman,* 72 (December 23, 1966), 941 (Maruice Richardson); *New York Times* (July 18, 1967), 35 (Thomas Lask), and reprinted in *CPBook,* 4, No. 14 (Winter 1968), 276; *New York Times Book Review* (July

23, 1967), 5 (Ivor Brown), and reprinted in *CPBook*, 3, No. 13 (Summer 1967), 253; *Newsweek*, 70 (July 17, 1967), 91A-93 (S. K. Oberbeck); *SHJ*, 7, No. 2 (Spring 1965), 60; 7, No. 3 (Winter 1965), 90; 8, No. 1 (Winter 1966), 28 (Lord Donegall); *Sherlockiana*, 11, Nr. 3 (1966), 9; *Sun* [Paris] (May 27, 1965), and reprinted in *SHJ*, 7, No. 3 (Winter 1965), 95; *Times Educational Supplement* (November 25, 1966), 1312, and reprinted in *CPBook*, 3, No. 11 (Winter 1967), 222; *Times Literary Supplement* (March 18, 1965), 216; *Wall Street Journal* (August 1, 1967), 14 (Edmund Fuller), and reprinted in *CPBook*, 3, No. 12 (Spring 1967), 240.

3956. Pearson, Hesketh. *Conan Doyle: His Life and Art.* London: Methuen & Co., [1943]. vii, 193 p. illus.

————. ————. London: Published for the British Publishers Guild by Methuen and Co., [1946]. vii, 207 p. (Guild Books, No. 224)

————. *Conan Doyle.* New York: Walker & Co., [1961]. 256 p.

"Pearson's work is a popular biography with few footnotes and no bibliography. His main contention is that the simplicity of Conan Doyle enabled him to write exactly what the public wanted to read. ... By repeatedly stressing Doyle's naivete, simplicity, and faults as a writer, Pearson, though undoubtedly correct, often gives an uncomplimentary tone to his portrait of Doyle." (Edward S. Lauterbach)

Reviews: English Fiction in Transition, 5 (1962), 48-49 (E. S. Lauterbach); *John O'London's Weekly*, 50 (October 8, 1943), 1-2 (Norman Collins); *New York Herald Tribune Books* (July 10, 1962), 10; *San Francisco Chronicle* (December 3, 1961), 39 (L. G. Offord); *Saturday Review*, 44 (October 28, 1961), 24-25 (John T. Winterich).

3957. ————. "Sherlock Holmes and 'The Strand,' " *The Strand*, 105 (August 1943), 44-47.

"Commentary on a relationship which spanned more than a generation." (Edgar W. Smith)

3958. Rawson, Mitchell. "A Case for Sherlock," *Sports Illustrated* [Eastern edition], 14 (March 13, 1961), 9-10.

"The Jeffries-Johnson title prize fight nearly had Arthur Conan Doyle as its referee." (Subtitle)

3959. Raymond, E. T. "Sir Arthur Conan Doyle as Dr. Watson," *The Living Age*, 300 (March 22, 1919), 730-733.

"An identification to be preferred to the several others which make him one with Holmes." (Edgar W. Smith)

3960. Rosenbach, A. S. W. "The Trail of Scarlet," *The Saturday Evening Post*, 205, No. 14 (October 1, 1932), 8-9, 32, 34, 36.

————. ————, *A Book Hunter's Holiday: Adventures with Books and Manuscripts.* Boston; New York: Houghton Mifflin Co., 1936. Chap. 3, p. 37-94.

Contains information about detective fiction and Doyle's crime library which the author believed was "the actual reference library used by Conan Doyle in the creation of his immortal detective, Sherlock Holmes."

3961. Rosenblum, Morris. "11 Picardy Place, Edinburgh: The Birthplace of Sir Arthur Conan Doyle," *BSJ*, 13, No. 4 (December 1963), 211-213.

A description of Dr. and Mrs. Rosenblum's visit to this literary landmark and their suggestion that the house be turned into a "Sherlock Holmes-John H. Watson-Sir Arthur Conan Doyle Museum."

3962. Rubow, Paul V. "A. Conan Doyle," *Epigonerne: Afhandlinger og portraetter.* København: Ejnar Munksgaard, 1956. p. 124-130.

3963. "Sherlock Holmes in Real Life," by a Barrister and ex-Official of New Scotland Yard. [Illustrations by Howard K. Elcock.] *The Strand Magazine*, 64 (September 1922), 282-289.

3964. "Sir Arthur Conan Doyle," *Cyclopedia of World Authors.* Edited by Frank N. Magill. New York: Harper & Brothers, [1958]. p. 312-314.

3965. ————, *A Library of Literary Criticism: Modern British Literature.* Compiled and edited by Ruth Z. Temple and Martin Tucker. New York: Ungar, [1966]. Vol. 1, p. 234-236.

Four critical excerpts on the literary agent and the Canonical tales.

3966. ————, *Twentieth Century Authors.* Edited by Stanley J. Kunitz and Howard Haycraft. New York: H. W. Wilson Co., 1942. p. 396-397.

3967. "Sir Arthur Conan Doyle, M.D.," *St. Bartholomew's Hospital Journal*, 56, No. 3 (March 1952), 333-334.

"A plea for a little more attention to Sherlock Holmes's great and good friend but with no diminution of attention to Holmes himself or to Watson." (Edgar W. Smith)

3968. "Sir Arthur Conan Doyle: Physician, Historical Novelist, Creator of Sherlock Holmes," *Clinical Excerpts* [New York: Winthrop Chemical Co.], 19, No. 8 (1945), 227-234.

————, *CPBook*, 2, No. 7-8 (Winter-Spring 1966), 157-164.

3969. [Smith Edgar W.] "A. C. D. — 1859-1930," *BSJ*, 9, No. 4 (October 1959), 195-196. (The Editor's Gas-Lamp)
An Irregular's tribute to the memory of a great man on his centennial.

3970. [———.] "On Certain Literary Hoaxes," *BSJ*, 3, No. 2 (April 1953), 67-68. (The Editor's Gas-Lamp)
A criticism of Adrian Conan Doyle for seeking to identify his father with Holmes.

3971. [Smith, Greenhough.] "The Passing of Conan Doyle," *The Strand Magazine*, 80 (September 1930), 227-230.

3972. Snyder, Charles. "There's Money in Ears, But the Eye Is a Gold Mine: Sir Arthur Conan Doyle's Brief Career in Ophthalmology," *Archives of Ophthalmology*, 85 (March 1971), 359-365.

3973. Starrett, Vincent. "The Real Sherlock Holmes," *The Golden Book Magazine*, 12, No. 72 (December 1930), 81-84.
———. ———, *The Private Life of Sherlock Holmes*. New York: The Macmillan Co., 1933. p. 118-138.
———. ———, ———. Revised and enlarged. The University of Chicago Press, [1960]. p. 102-114.
———. ———, *Midway* [University of Chicago Press], No. 2 (1960), 70-84.
———. [Condensed] "Hvem var Sherlock Holmes?" ["Who Was Sherlock Holmes?"] *Det Bedste fra Reader's Digest* [Danish edition] (March 1964), 141-144, 147.
———. *Hvem var Sherlock Holmes?* København: Dansk Bogforlag, 1965. 8 p.
An account of Doyle's sleuthing in the George Edalji and Oscar Slater cases.

3974. "True Tales of 'Sherlock Holmes,' " *The Literary Digest*, 107, No. 13 (December 27, 1930), 26, 28. illus.
A "personal glimpse" at the Edalji-Slater cases, with quotations from Mr. Starrett's *Golden Book* article.

3975. Van Der Plas, Michel. "Conan Doyle: Schepper van een traditie" ["Conan Doyle: Creator of a Tradition"], *Elsevier* (August 12, 1967), 54-56.

3976. Voorhis, Harold V. B. "Sherlock Holmes Was a Mason," *The Royal Arch Mason*, 8, No. 8 (Winter 1965), 248.
"In a short article, the author mentions three references to Freemasonry in the tales (not including the reference to a masonic device in *A Study in Scarlet*) and considers Holmes was a Mason by identifying him with Sir Arthur Conan Doyle, who was a member of the order." (Julian Wolff)

3977. Wallace, Vincent. "Holmes and Houdini," *BSJ*, 19, No. 2 (June 1969), 91-93.

The effect Doyle's friendship with the Master Magician and his interest in spiritualism had on the Master Detective; with a note on Houdini and Doyle by Julian Wolff.

3978. Welch, George W. "Some Fragmentary Notes on 'Undershaw' To-day," *SHJ*, 4, No. 2 (Spring 1959), 40, 65.
Comments on the house Doyle lived in from 1897 to 1907.

3979. Williams, J. E. Hodder. "Arthur Conan Doyle," *The Bookman* [London], 22, No. 127 (April 1902), 6-13. illus.
———. ———, *The Bookman* [New York], 17 (August 1903), 647-651.

3980. [Wolff, Julian.] "Deus Ex Machina," *BSJ*, 12, No. 3 (September 1962), 131-132. (The Editor's Gas-Lamp)
In a special Sir Arthur Conan Doyle issue of the *Journal*, the editor pays a long-delayed tribute to a man who was not only Watson's literary agent but a great author in his own right. A full-page photograph of Doyle appears on p. 133.

3981. Wood, James Playsted. *The Man Who Hated Sherlock Holmes: A Life of Sir Arthur Conan Doyle*. Illustrated by Richard M. Powers. [New York: Pantheon Books, 1965.] 180 p.
For ages 12 to 16.
"He has built his story around the true if paradoxical fact that Doyle resented the success of Sherlock Holmes, feeling that it took both his own creative time and the eye of the critics away from more worthy endeavors. This is an entertaining theme; and Wood develops it straightforwardly and interestingly, with a nice understanding of both the man and his work." (Anthony Boucher)
Reviews: Best Sellers, 25 (May 15, 1965), 102; *Book Week* (May 9, 1965), 22 (M. S. Libby); *Horn Book*, 41 (August 1965), 396; *Library Journal*, 90 (June 15, 1965), 2894 (Clayton E. Kilpatrick); *New York Times Book Review* (July 4, 1965), 12 (Anthony Boucher); *Saturday Review*, 48 (May 15, 1965), 56 (Alice Dalgliesh).

3982. Wright, Thomas. "Dr. Conan Doyle," *Hind Head, or the English Switzerland and Its Literary and Historical Associations*. London: Simpkin, Marshall, Hamilton, Kent & Co., Ltd., 1898. p. 11-12.
———. "Sir A. Conan Doyle," *Hindhead, or the English Switzerland and Its Literary and Historical Associations*. Second edition. [Olney, Bucks: The Cowper Press], 1907. p. 14-15.
———. ———, *BSJ*, 12, No. 3 (September 1962), 136.
A brief but interesting tribute to Doyle and Holmes.

3983. Yellen, Sherman. "Sir Arthur Conan Doyle: Sherlock Holmes in Spiritland," *International Journal of Parapsychology*, 7, No. 1 (Winter 1965), 33-63.

An examination of Doyle's conversion to spiritualism from the biographical and literary viewpoints, with some interesting observations on the Sacred Writings. Includes a summary in English, French, German, Italian, and Spanish.

3984. Young, Filson. "Sir Arthur Conan Doyle," *Boston Sunday Post, Magazine Section* (September 6, 1914), 3-4. illus.

"The English author's intimate friend gives an intimate pen picture of Sir Arthur as a man."

LITERARY PARALLELS AND COMPARISONS

James Boswell and Dr. Samuel Johnson

3985. Altick, Richard D. "Mr. Sherlock Holmes and Dr. Samuel Johnson," *221B: Studies in Sherlock Holmes*. Edited by Vincent Starrett. New York: The Macmillan Co., 1940. p. 109-128.

" 'I am lost without my Boswell!' [Scan] . . . By those six words Holmes shows us that he recognized how closely the relationship between him and his companion followed the distinguished literary model. He knew he was playing Dr. Johnson to Watson's Boswell, and he accepted the role good-humoredly."

3986. Christ, Jay Finley. "James Boswell and the Island of Uffa," *BSJ* [OS], 1, No. 1 (January 1946), 24-27.

Some twenty personal and place names used by Watson may have been derived from Boswell.

3987. Roberts, S. C. "Sherlock Holmes: His Kinship with Dr. Johnson," *Holmes and Watson: A Miscellany*. London: Oxford University Press, 1953. p. 50-54.

A comparison between the Holmes-Watson and Johnson-Boswell associations.

Thomas Carlyle

3988. Crocker, Stephen F. "Watson Doctors the Venerable Bede," *BSJ*, 9, No. 3 (July 1959), 157-164.

"By a juxtaposition of sources, a metamorphosis of images, and a conglutination of ideas, Watson comes up with what is perhaps his weightiest metaphysical utterance, by doctoring the Venerable Bede with Carlyle."

3989. Jenkins, William D. "Who Might Thomas Carlyle Be?" *BSJ*, 16, No. 4 (December 1966), 222-230.

"Holmes's personality and mode of life were probably derived from Carlyle's *Sartor Resartus*. The prototype is Diogenes Teufelsdröckh, Professor of *Allerly-Wissenschaft* at the University of Weissnichtwo."

Charles Dickens

See also *The Mystery of Edwin Drood* (items 4135-4141)

3990. McKee, Wilbur K. *Sherlock Holmes Is Mr. Pickwick.* Brattleboro, Vt.: Privately Printed, The Vermont Printing Co., 1941. 13 p.

Limited to 300 copies.

———. ———, *The Incunabular Sherlock Holmes.* Edited by Edgar W. Smith. Morristown, N.J.: The Baker Street Irregulars, 1958. p. 161-169.

Several indications are given as to why the author thinks Samuel Pickwick and Holmes are the same person.

T. S. Eliot

3991. Clutton-Brock, Alan. "T. S. Eliot and Conan Doyle," *The Times Literary Supplement* (January 19, 1951), 37. (Letters to the Editor)

Attention is drawn to Eliot's use in *Murder in the Cathedral* of the first two questions and answers in the Musgrave Ritual.

3992. Cole, Irvin C. "Sherlock vs. Eliot," *Illustrious Client's Case-Book.* Edited by J. N. Williamson and H. B. Williams. [Indianapolis, Ind.: The Illustrious Clients, 1948.] p. 36.

"Fly the sea / Pet of a Brigadier be, / Not a Baskerville hound, this Blaze— / Just a dogofasonofafather, nothing fazed."

3993. Fleissner, Robert F. " 'The Bafflement of Scotland Yard': T. S. Eliot's Mystery Cat and Dostoevsky's Raskolnikov," *BSJ*, 18, No. 3 (September 1968), 150-151.

Eliot's use of the expression "the Napoleon of Crime" is evidence that he was influenced by both Doyle and Dostoevsky.

3994. Hardenbrook, Don. "T. S. Eliot and the Great Grimpen Mire," by Gaston Huret III. Tr. from the French by Don Hardenbrook. *BSJ*, 6, No. 2 (April 1956), 88-93.

———. "T. S. Eliot og den store Grimpen mose," [Oversat af A. D. Henriksen]. *Sherlockiana*, 10, Nr. 1-2 (1965), 3-6.

A careful comparison of his "East Coker" (*Four Quartets*, 1943) with the description of the Mire in Houn.

3995. Henriksen, A. D. "T. S. Eliot on

Sherlock Holmes," *SHJ*, 7, No. 3 (Winter 1965), 81-83.

A summary and discussion of his writings about the Sherlock Holmes stories, with a note on his use of the Musgrave Ritual and description of the great Grimpen Mire.

3996. Herzog, Evelyn. "Mr. Holmes and Mr. Eliot: A Trifling Monograph," *Albertinum* [New Haven, Conn.: Albertus Magnus College], 30 (1967), 14-20.

———. ———, *SOS*, 4, No. 1 (January 1970), 9-14.

Connections between Eliot and the Sacred Writings, especially as demonstrated in "Macavity: The Mystery Cat" (item 3551).

3997. Jenkins, William D. "The Sherlockian Eliot," *BSJ*, 12, No. 2 (June 1962), 81-83.

Citations of Canonical references in his poetry.

3998. Jensen, Aage. "T. S. Eliot om Sherlock Holmes (i *Criterion*, 1928 [sic 1929])," Uddraget og oversat af Aage Jensen. *Sherlockiana*, 10, Nr. 1-2 (1965), 2-3.

A commentary on and extracts from his review (item 1991) of *The Complete Sherlock Holmes Short Stories*.

3999. Loesch, Katharine. "A Dangerous Criminal Still at Large," *Notes and Queries*, 6, No. 1 (January 1959), 8-9.

Parallel ideas and one exact parallel of phrase suggest that Macavity was based on the character of Professor Moriarty.

4000. Nicholas, Constance. "The Murders of Doyle and Eliot," *Modern Language Notes*, 70, No. 4 (April 1955), 269-271.

The ten-line stichomythy in *Murder in the Cathedral* was taken from the Musgrave Ritual.

4001. Preston, Priscilla. "A Note on T. S. Eliot and Sherlock Holmes," *The Modern Language Review*, 54, No. 3 (July 1959), 397-399.

Instances where Eliot's imagination was stimulated by the Canonical tales.

4002. Smith, Grover. "T. S. Eliot and Sherlock Holmes," *Notes and Queries*, 193, No. 20 (October 2, 1948), 431-432.

———. ———, *BSJ*, 12, No. 2 (June 1962), 84, 128.

Further commentary on Eliot's use of the Musgrave Ritual in his play *Murder in the Cathedral.*

4003. Webster, H. T., and H. W. Starr. "Macavity: An Attempt to Unravel His Mystery," *BSJ*, 4, No. 4 (October 1954), 205-210.

Eliot may have wished to suggest that "the soul of Professor Moriarty transmogrified into a cat has achieved the final

arrogance of breaking natural as well as human law."

Richard Austin Freeman

4004. Currier, Francis M. "Holmes and Thorndyke: A Real Friendship," *BSJ* [OS], 3, No. 2 (April 1948), 176-182.

———. ———, *The Third Cab.* [Boston: The Speckled Band, 1960.] p. 52-58.

Evidence supporting P. M. Stone's argument that Dr. John Evelyn Thorndyke, the eminent medico-legal expert and consulting detective, and the Master were actually acquainted.

4005. Stone. P. M. "The Other Friendship: A Speculation," *Profile by Gaslight.* Edited by Edgar W. Smith. New York: Simon and Schuster, 1944. p. 97-103.

"Sherlock Holmes and John Evelyn Thorndyke during the course of their contemporary careers were not wholly unaware of one another's professional activities. . . . these eminent foes of the London criminal world of a half century ago actually met upon certain occasions and even exchanged views upon celebrated cases which were, plainly, beyond the resources of Scotland Yard."

Emile Gaboriau

4006. [Lieck, Albert.] "Monsieur Lecoq—A Comparison," *Justice of the Peace and Local Government Review, Literary Supplement*, 102, No. 50 (December 10, 1938), i-ii.

Similarities between Lecoq and Holmes in which the author defends Lecoq against Holmes.

John Galsworthy

4007. Bailey, L. W. "Holmes and Soames," *BSJ*, 18, No. 4 (December 1968), 195-200.

An attempt to match the literary styles of Galsworthy and Doyle on the occasion of the former's centenary in 1967.

4008. Herzog, Evelyn. "Irene! (gasp!) Irene!" *BSJ*, 18, No. 4 (December 1968), 201-207.

Irene Adler and Irene Heron Forsyte (*The Forsyte Saga*) are the same woman.

4009. Holroyd, James Edward. "Holmes (Sherlock) and Soames (Forsyte)," *SHJ*, 9, No. 3 (Winter 1969), 78-82.

Comparisons between these two characters and the Holmesian-Forsyte sagas. Illustrated with five pictures of the London scene.

4010. Redmond, D. A. "Another Gasp *in re* Irene," *BSJ*, 19, No. 1 (March 1969), 41.

Further evidence on behalf of Miss

The Writings About the Writings

Other Subjects

Herzog's identification of Irene Heron with Irene Adler.

Gilbert and Sullivan

4011. Berg, Emanuel. "For It's Greatly to Their Credit," *BSJ*, 9, No. 2 (April 1959), 90-98.

Similarities between Holmes and Gilbert and Watson and Sullivan.

4012. Hoerr, W. A. "The Case of the Curious Slight," *BSJ*, 16, No. 1 (March 1966), 26-27.

Possible answers to why Holmes never took notice of Gilbert and Sullivan, even though their operas were the leading musical productions during his most active period.

4013. Montgomery, James. "Four Birds in a Gilded Age," Ilustrated by Bruce Montgomery. *BSJ*, 2, No. 4 (October 1952), 186-195.

———. ———, *Three Trifling Monographs*. [Philadelphia: Privately Printed, 1952.] p. 3-9.

"These two pairs of men *were* very near to each other, they *were* great admirers and close followers of the others' work, they *were* intimate personal friends, drawn still more irresistibly together by the joint public adulation which both pairs received."

4014. ———. "Gilbert and the Detectives," *Shots from the Canon*. [Philadelphia: Privately Printed, 1953.] p. 15.

———. ———, *BSJ*, 18, No. 1 (March 1968), 13.

A commentary on Reginald Allen's suggestion that Gilbert and Sullivan would have used Sherlock Holmes's name rather than Paddington Pollaky's in their song "Patience" had it been written ten years later.

4015. ———. "A Sensational Exception," *Shots from the Canon*. [Philadelphia: Privately Printed, 1953.] p. 16.

———. ———, *BSJ*, 18, No. 1 (March 1968), 14.

An account and explanation of John K. Clayton's discovery of an allusion to Holmes in the Gilbertian libretto of the operetta *A Sensational Novel*.

4016. Peck, Andrew J. " 'And Gripper Shall Turn Out to be Sherlock Holmes in Disguise,' " *BSP*, No. 35 (May 1968), 1-2.

A different interpretation is given to the appearance of the Master's name in *A Sensational Novel*.

James Joyce

4017. Jenkins, William D. "It Seems There Were Two Irishmen . . . ," *Modern Fiction Studies*, 15, No. 1 (Spring 1969), 63-71.

Evidence that Joyce occasionally used Doyle's (and Watson's) writings as source material.

4018. Kenner, Hugh. "Baker Street to Eccles Street: The Odyssey of a Myth," *The Hudson Review*, 1, No. 4 (Winter 1949), 481-499.

———. ———, [Revised] *Dublin's Joyce*. London: Chatto & Windus, 1955. Chap. 10, p. 158-178.

———. ———, ———. Bloomington: Indiana University Press, 1956. Chap. 10, p. 158-178.

A scholarly analysis of "the most significant subaesthetic phenomenon of the late nineteenth century," with profound Joycean undertones and analogues.

Rudyard Kipling

4019. Grazebrook, O. F. *Dr. Watson and Rudyard Kipling*. [London: Privately Printed, 1949.] 30 p. (Studies in Sherlock Holmes, No. 5)

Limited to 100 copies.

"The literary links between these two great English writers, and their inevitable meeting, are dealt with at length and in sympathetic detail." (Edgar W. Smith)

4020. Maitland, W. G. B. "Rudyard Kipling and Sherlock Holmes," *SHJ*, 1, No. 4 (December 1953), 37-38.

Points of contact between the Master and Kipling.

Jack London

4021. Walker, Dale L. "Jack London, Sherlock Holmes, and the Agent," *BSJ*, 20, No. 2 (June 1970), 79-85.

An examination of London's interest in and indebtedness to the Canonical Writings.

H. P. Lovecraft

4022. Swanson, Martin J. "Sherlock Holmes and H. P. Lovecraft," *Now* [Fairleigh Dickinson University], 4, No. 1 (Winter 1963), 35-37.

———. ———, *BSJ*, 14, No. 3 (September 1964), 162-165.

"H. P. Lovecraft doubtlessly followed with eager interest the adventures and life of Sherlock Holmes, and many of Lovecraft's assumptions and conclusions closely parallel those of the Great Detective."

Stuart Palmer

4023. Palmer, Stuart. "The I-O-U of Hildegarde Withers," *BSJ* [OS], 3, No. 1 (January 1948), 6-11.

An acknowledgment of debt to the Holmes saga for helping the author to create Miss Hildegarde Withers.

Edgar Allan Poe

4024. Chapman, Arthur. "The Unmasking of Sherlock Holmes," *The Critic*, 46, No. 2 (February 1905), 115-117.

————. ————, *The Incunabular Sherlock Holmes*. Edited by Edgar W. Smith. Morristown, N.J.: The Baker Street Irregulars, 1958. p. 25-29.

————. ————, *CPBook*, 4, No. 15 (August 1968), 290-291.

During a surprise visit to 221B, Monsieur C. Auguste Dupin embarrasses the Master when he accuses him of using some of the methods employed by Poe.

4025. Fischer, Carl. "Deductive Dynamic Duo," *The Young Catholic Messenger*, 82, No. 31 (May 6, 1966), 14.

————. ————, *CPBook*, 3, No. 10 (Fall 1966), 190.

An essay on the two most famous French and English detectives.

4026. Solovay, Jacob C. "Sonnet: Sherlock Holmes to Edgar Allan Poe," *BSJ* [OS], 4, No. 1 (January 1949), 38; (NS), 4, No. 2 (April 1954), 80.

————. ————, *Sherlock Holmes: Two Sonnet Sequences*. [Culver City, Calif.: Luther Norris, November 1969.] [unpaged]

————. "Sherlock Holmes til Edgar Allan Poe," [Oversat af A. D. Henriksen]. *Sangen om Baker Street*. København: [Grafisk Cirkel], 1958. p. 11. Reprinted in *Sherlockiana*, 3, Nr. 3-4 (1958), 10-11; 14, Nr. 4 (1969), 16.

"They'll *always* read what my friend Watson wrote."

Sax Rohmer

4027. Biggers, Julian L. "Letter to Sherlock" and "Annotations," *The Rohmer Review*, No. 6 (February 1971), 7-8.

4028. [Hahn, Robert.] "A Case of Identity," *PD*, 2, No. 5 (March 1970), 1, 3-4.

A letter from Watson to Holmes noting certain similarities between the Fu Manchu and Sherlock Holmes stories and revealing that his friend has been masquerading as Moris Klaw! Illustrated with a drawing of Klaw (Holmes) from Roy Hunt's folio *Fu Manchu and Company* (Culver City, Calif.: Luther Norris, 1970).

4029. Peck, Andrew Jay. "A Case of Identity," *The Rohmer Review*, No. 2 (January 1969), 9-17.

————. ————, *SOS*, 5, No. 1 (January 1971), 8-17.

"Being a trifling monograph upon the similarities between Sir Denis Nayland Smith and Sherlock Holmes." (Subtitle)

4030. R[ush], D[avid] M. "A Few Similarities," *DCC*, 1, No. 4 (May 1965), 3-4.

A brief comparison between the hero of the Fu Manchu stories and Holmes.

George Bernard Shaw

4031. Boswell, Rolfe. "Sarasate, Sherlock and Shaw," *BSJ*, 2, No. 1 (January 1952), 22-29.

"Sarasate is the link between Holmes and the peppery music critic."

4032. Cohen, Allen. "Holmes and Higgins —Were They Friends?" *BSJ*, 14, No. 1 (March 1964), 43-44.

Similarities between the Master and Professor Henry Higgins of *Pygmalion* and *My Fair Lady* suggest that they could easily have been acquainted.

4033. Cross, Leslie. "Sherlock Holmes, Writer: An Unsolved Case," *BSJ*, 14, No. 1 (March 1964), 39-42.

A discussion of his remarkable literary talents, followed by a suggestion that he may have been the anonymous author of "Shaw's" plays.

4034. Enright, Robert. "Holmes and Higgins," *SIS*, 1, No. 1 (June 1965), 14-18.

Another comparison between the Master Sleuth and the master phoneticist and speech teacher.

4035. Shields, Thomas A. "The Relationship Between Holmes and Shaw," *BSJ*, 17, No. 2 (June 1967), 90-91.

Holmes's first encounter with Shaw (at the time Shaw was a reviewer for the *Pall Mall Gazette*) occurred in May 1885 when they assisted the Salvation Army in bringing about England's first true consent law on prostitution.

Bram Stoker

4036. Johnson, E. Randolph. "The Victorian Vampire," *BSJ*, 18, No. 4 (December 1968), 209-211.

"Reflections regarding certain remarkable affinities between *Dracula* and the Sacred Writings, together with some comment upon the possible horrific origins of *The Hound of the Baskervilles*." (Subtitle)

4037. Jones, Kelvin. "The Curious Case of the Sussex Vampire," *SHJ*, 10, No. 2 (Summer 1971), 51-53.

A discussion of Holmes's personality in connection with certain 19th-century ideas on vampirism in which disturbing similarities are noted between the Great Detective and Dracula.

4038. Leonard, William. "Re: Vampires," *BSJ Christmas Annual*, No. 2 (1957), 20-25.

The author supports Professor Christ's

The Writings About the Writings

Other Subjects

261

The Writings About the Writings

Other Subjects

theory that Dracula was Moriarty, and then goes one step further by suggesting that the mysterious Alphonse Van Helsing, the physician who was called in to help track down Count Dracula, was Sherlock Holmes in disguise.

4039. R[ush], D[avid] M. "Holmes and the Dracula Legend," *DCC*, 3, No. 1 (November 1966), 4-5.
Speculation on the Master's knowledge of and attitude toward the Count Dracula legend.

Rex Stout

4040. Clark, John D. "Some Notes Relating to a Preliminary Investigation into the Paternity of Nero Wolfe," *BSJ*, 6, No. 1 (January 1956), 5-11.
Wolfe was the illegitimate offspring of Holmes and Irene!

4041. Kennedy, Bruce. "The Crowning Point," *BSP*, No. 29 (November 1967), 3.
A meeting with Rex Stout in which, among other things, he tells how he happened to write his highly controversial essay "Watson Was a Woman" (item 3360).

4042. ———. "The Truth About Nero Wolfe," *BSJ*, 18, No. 3 (September 1968), 154-155.
The evidence used by Baring-Gould to prove that Wolfe was the son of Holmes was circumstantial and insufficient.

4043. Paul, Barbara. "Holmes, Wolfe, and Women," *BSJ*, 18, No. 4 (December 1968), 208.
Both Sherlock and Nero became disenchanted with women because of an ill-fated marriage.

4044. Peck, Andrew Jay. "Like Father, Like Son?" *BSJ*, 19, No. 1 (March 1969), 42-43.
A refutation of Miss Paul's theory as to the reason for Wolfe's aversion to women, and a denial that he was Holmes's son.

4045. Queen, Ellery. "The Great O-E Theory," *In the Queens' Parlor and Other Leaves from the Editors' Notebook*. New York: Simon and Schuster, 1957. p. 4-5.
———. ———, ———. London: Victor Gollancz Ltd., 1957. p. 4-5.
A consideration of the similarities between the names "Nero Wolfe" and "Sherlock Holmes."

4046. Stix, Thomas L. "Six Characters in Search of an Author," *BSJ*, 16, No. 1 (March 1966), 28-29.
Similarities and differences between Watson and Archie Goodwin, Holmes and Wolfe, and Conan Doyle and Rex Stout.

Henry David Thoreau

4047. Blau, Peter E. "In Memoriam: Henry David Thoreau," *BSJ*, 19, No. 3 (September 1969), 152-153.
The "trout in the milk" comment by Holmes in Nobl is traced to a sentence of Thoreau's.

4048. Shreffler, Philip A. "Holmes and Thoreau," *BSJ*, 19, No. 3 (September 1969), 145-151.
The Master not only had a deep and lasting love of the natural world, but was intimately acquainted with the works of Thoreau. In an Editor's Note, Dr. Wolff offers further evidence that "the chronicler of Holmes's adventures was familiar with the writings of Thoreau." (Thomas Drucker advances a divergent opinion in *SOS*, 4, No. 1 [January 1970], 3-4.)

Jules Verne

4049. Helling, Cornelis. "Sherlock Holmes and Jules Verne," *SHJ*, 8, No. 2 (Spring 1967), 67-68. (Wigmore Street Post-Bag)
Some points of comparison between the Vernian and the Holmesian worlds.

4050. ———. " 'Sherlock Holmes' retrouvé dans 'Les Enfants du Capitaine Grant'?" *Bulletin de la Société Jules Verne*, No. 8 (September 1937), 109-116.
Doyle modeled his detective, in part at least, on the astute Australian police officer in "The Children of Captain Grant."

Oscar Wilde

4051. Holroyd, James Edward. "Dr. Watson and Mr. Wilde," *SHJ*, 2, No. 2 (December 1954), 5-10.
———. ———, *Baker Street By-ways*. London: George Allen & Unwin Ltd., [1959]. p. 103-113.
Evidence of the affinity between these two litterateurs of Baker Street and Tite Street.

4052. [Rhode, Franklin W.] "Oscariana & Sherlockiana," by Langdale Pike. *DCC*, 5, No. 4 ([May] 1969), 2-4.
A comparison between Wilde and Holmes.

P. G. Wodehouse

4053. Cox, J. Randolph. "Elementary, My Dear Wooster!" *BSJ*, 17, No. 2 (June 1967), 78-83.
Parallels between the tales of Holmes and Watson and those of Jeeves and Bertie Wooster.

4054. "En Studie i Sherlock og Jeeves," *Sherlockiana*, 16, Nr. 2 (1971), 5-6.

4055. Anderson, Poul. "The Archetypical Holmes," *BSJ*, 18, No. 3 (September 1968), 139-143.

Winner of the 11th annual Morley-Montgomery Memorial Award for the best contribution to *BSJ* in 1968.

Traces the evolution of the Holmes figure, beginning in the third century B.C. with Archimedes and ending in our own with Leonard Nimoy as Mr. Spock in the television show *Star Trek.*

4056. Baker, Kate G. "Gandalf Through Spock," *BSP*, No. 35 (May 1968), 3.

A refutation of the Sherlock-Spock and Holmes-Gandalf theories set forth by Barbara Goldfield and Debbie Clark.

4057. Bayer, Robert John. *Some Notes on a Meeting at Chisham.* With an introduction by Vincent Starrett. Chicago: Camden House, 1948. [20] p.

Limited to 60 copies.

The bee-keeping detective Carver in the Father Brown story "The Man with Two Beards" is in reality Sherlock Holmes.

4058. Bengis, Nathan L. "Plots for Sale — Cheap; Apply: 221B," *The Armchair Detective*, 1, No. 4 (July 1968), 116-117.

Resemblances between Headon Hill's *Zamba the Detective* (item 5903) and some of the Canonical tales.

4059. Blakeney, T. S. "Sherlock Holmes and Some Contemporaries," *SHJ*, 7, No. 1 (Winter 1964), 3-6; 7, No. 2 (Spring 1965), 41-45.

"Some of the influences, both positive and negative—i.e., by imitation and the reverse—that Sherlock Holmes has had on his contemporaries and on contemporary detective-story writing."

4060. Boardman, John. "Matter in Motion," *Kipple* 105 (August 1, 1966), 11-13.

————. ————, *The SHsf Fanthology One.* Edited by Ruth Berman. The Professor Challenger Society, 1967. p. 13-15.

Holmes and Lord Peter Wimsey had a common ancestor—namely, C. Auguste Dupin. Includes a family tree also showing Nero Wolfe's relationship to Holmes and James Bond's relationship to the Wimseys. A most remarkable family tree!

4061. Clark, Debbie. "Holmes—A Wizard?" *BSP*, No. 33 (March 1968), 1.

Compares J. R. R. Tolkien's great Wizard, Gandalf the Grey, with the Master.

4062. ————. "Sherlock Holmes and Don Quixote," *BSP*, No. 28 (October 1967), 8.

An analogy between these two great literary characters. (It is interesting to note that the title of Goldman's play and film *They Might Be Giants* refers to Don Quixote's windmills.)

4063. Gleason, James P. "The Sergeant and the Felony Commuter," *BSJ*, 9, No. 3 (July 1959), 173-174.

Commentary on another parallel: "the attitude of leniency when it came to apprehending a felon, proclaimed by the Sergeant in 'The Pirates of Penzance' and displayed at times by Holmes himself."

4064. Goldfield, Barbara. "The Caped Crusader and the World's First Consulting Detective," *BSP*, No. 13 (July 1966), 2-3.

An interesting comparison between Batman and Holmes, Robin and Watson, and the Joker and Moriarty.

4065. ————. "Did Sherlock Holmes Have Pointed Ears?" *BSP*, No. 30 (December 1967), 2-3.

Parallels between Spock and Sherlock.

4066. Greene, Sir Hugh. "The Rivals of Sherlock Holmes," *SHJ*, 10, No. 2 (Summer 1971), 56-57.

The editor of the book by the same title (London: The Bodley Head, 1970; New York: Pantheon Books, 1970) discusses the great detective's views on other practitioners of his profession.

4067. Griffith, Jack. "The Sherlock Holmes of Babylon," *The London Mystery Selection*, 44 (March 1960), 102-104.

"It was a similar method of detection which put the prophet Daniel firmly among the great detectives of all time."

4068. Hardenbrook, Don. "Horatio and Dr. John H. Watson: A Literary Relationship," *BSJ* [OS], 3, No. 3 (July 1948), 358-360.

"Whatever resemblances Holmes and Hamlet may enjoy, both Holmesian and Shakespearean scholars have missed a bet by failing to compare Dr. Watson and Horatio. These 'faithful friends' take after one another to a remarkable degree."

4069. [Henriksen, A. D.] "Midt i en James Bond tid" ["In the Days of James Bond"], *Sherlock Holmes Arbog* I (1965), 92-94.

The Master taught James Bond everything he knows! (Except about women, of course!)

4070. Hoerr, Willmer A. "The Case of the Archetypical Agent," *BSJ*, 18, No. 1 (March 1968), 10-12.

"Because he [Ignatius Paul Pollaky, the second-best private detective in Victorian England] was very close-mouthed and lacked a literary friend, we shall probably

The Writings About the Writings

Other Subjects

The Writings About the Writings

Other Subjects

never know just what his exploits were, but quite possibly he too had his Gorgianos, his Milvertons, and his McFarlanes."

4071. Holroyd, James Edward. "Did Sherlock Holmes Originate in *B. O. P.?*" Illustrated by Jack Matthew. *Boy's Own Paper,* 85, No. 4 (January 1963), 20-22.

Attention is drawn to many striking parallels between Holmes and Watson and Hugh Lawrence and J. H. Thurston of "Uncle Jeremy's Household," a Doyle story that ran in *B. O. P.* several months before the publication of *Beeton's Christmas Annual* for 1887. Further comments by the author appear in *SHJ,* 8, No. 2 (Spring 1967), 58.

4072. Iraldi, James. "That Extraordinary Man," *BSJ,* 3, No. 1 (January 1953), 13-17.

The life of Holmes is compared with that of Nicolò Paganini, the violin virtuoso. Illustrated with a portrait of Paganini attributed to Horace Vernet (No. 4).

4073. Katju, Kailas Nath. *Sherlock Holmes in India.* [Calcutta: Privately Printed, 1951.] 47 p.

Contents: The Story of the Spurious Child. - The Story of the Handcart Wheel Tracks. - The Story of a Dramatic Arrest and the Inevitable Lantern. - The Story of the Knife with a Broken Tip.

True stories of criminal cases that were solved by the application of the Master's methods, by a Hindu Irregular and former Governor of West Bengal.

4074. Lachman, Marvin. "The American Sherlock Holmes: A Study in Scarlet Impersonation," *The Mystery Reader's Newsletter,* 3, No. 2 (December 1969), 2-5.

During a visit with Craig Kennedy and Walter Jameson, Holmes and Watson point out a number of coincidental (?) similarities between Arthur Benjamin Reeve's work and that of their sponsor, Sir Arthur Conan Doyle.

4075. Lang, Milton C. "A Study in Heredity," *BSJ,* 14, No. 2 (June 1964), 89-92.

The traits of Sir Kenelm Digby, an alleged ancestor of Holmes, are compared with those of the Master.

4076. Lauterbach, Charles E. "The Friendship Club," *BSJ Christmas Annual,* No. 3 (1958), 38-41.

The poet laureate of the BSI spins a lovely legend in verse about how on a hilltop he watched while Don Quixote and Sancho Panza, Robinson Crusoe and Friday, Sherlock Holmes and John Watson, Tom Sawyer and Huckleberry Finn,* and other great pairs of masculine good humor met in the name of friendship.

4077. Liljegren, S. B. *The Parentage of*

Sherlock Holmes. Stockholm: Almqvist & Wiksell Periodicals Co., [1971]. 21 p. (Irish Essays and Studies, No. 8)

Doyle's inspiration for the world's superdetective came from Wilkie Collins's Sergeant Cuff in *The Moonstone* (1868).

4078. Lindfors, Bernth. "A Shadow of Sherlock Holmes in Tanzania," *BSJ,* 17, No. 1 (March 1967), 42-44.

A brief account of Taraji H. H. Katalambula's Swahili novel *Simu ya Kifo* (item 1781) in which shades of Sherlock Holmes can be glimpsed.

4079. ———. "Sherlock Holmes in Africa. Part II. Zanzibar," *BSJ,* 15, No. 2 (June 1965), 70-74.

———. "Sherlock's Shade at Work in Zanzibar," *East African Standard* (September 3, 1965).

A comparison between Muhammed Said Abdulla's *Mzimu wa Watu wa Kale* (item 1780) and the Canonical tales.

4080. Linsenmeyer, John. "Holmes and Wimsey: A Study in Similarities," *BSJ,* 21, No. 4 (December 1971), 207-214.

4081. "Literary Osmosis," *SHJ,* 4, No. 4 (Spring 1960), 138-139; 5, No. 1 (Winter 1960), 27-28. (Wigmore Street Post-Bag)

Examples of similarities or parallels between the Sacred Writings and other literary works as reported by Nathan L. Bengis, Colin Prestige, Cornelis Helling, Sydney C. Roberts, A. M. Robertson, James Edward Holroyd, and Lord Donegall.

4082. Lupoff, Richard A. "The Case of the Doctor Who Had No Business, or The Adventure of the Second Anonymous Narrator, *Startling Mystery Stories,* 3, No. 2 (Winter 1969), 66-75.

———. ———, *The SHsf Fanthology 3.* Edited by Ruth Berman. Minneapolis, Minn.: The Professor Challenger Society, February 1972. p. 4-16.

The second anonymous narrator of *Tarzan of the Apes* is identified as John H. Watson; the first, of course, is Edgar Rice Burroughs.

4083. Metcalfe, Percy. "Rivals of Sherlock Holmes—Or Were They?" *SHJ,* 10, No. 4 (Summer 1972), 122-128.

A learned paper dealing with the stories and writers in Sir Hugh Greene's collection of detective stories. See also item 4066.

4084. Rauber, D. F. "The Immortality of Sherlock Holmes," *BSJ,* 21, No. 2 (June 1971), 110-113.

"Holmes has always existed, but he has gone through many metamorphoses, the tracing out of which should be a primary task of Holmesian scholarship. I have proposed the theory and given a *terminus a quo* in Zadig and a *terminus ad quem* in Nero Wolfe, as well as an intermediate example in Daniel. It remains for others to pick up the torch and pursue the quest."

4085. Robbins, Frank E. "Socrates and Sherlock Holmes," *Michigan Alumnus Quarterly Review,* 47, No. 11 (February 22, 1941), 165-171.

———. ———, *BSJ,* 17, No. 3 (September 1967), 168-175.

A comparison between the traits and capacities of these two great men reveals some striking similarities.

4086. Stewart-Gordon, James. "Britain's Amazing Killer Catcher," Illustration by Peter Cross. *Clipper* [Pan American World Airways], 10, No. 6 (December-January 1970-71), 12-14, 16.

———. Condensed with title: "Sherlock Holmes Lives Again," *Reader's Digest,* 50 (February 1971), 203-206, 209-210.

———. ———, *DCC,* 8, No. 3 (April 1972), 7-8.

The author writes about another "real-life" Holmes—Dr. Keith Simpson, a British professor "whose powers of observation and deduction approach the legendary."

4087. ———. "Real-Life Sherlock Holmes," *Reader's Digest,* 79 (November 1961), 281-288.

"Sir Sydney Smith, Britain's great medical detective, has followed in the footsteps of Doyle's hero—often proving that crime is more suspenseful than fiction."

4088. Tomashefsky, Steven. " 'He Has Several Good Cases to His Credit,' " *SIS,* 1, No. 1 (June 1965), 10-13.

Mainly a comparison between Van Dine's Philo Vance and Holmes.

4089. Visiak, E. H. "New Light on Holmes," *SHJ,* 6, No. 4 (Spring 1964), 122-123.

Similarities between "The Restless Fays" in the *Boy's Own Paper* (1881) and "The Dancing Men" and between other Doyle stories and those of Poe and Dickens.

4090. Ward, Alfred C. "The Detective Story: Conan Doyle, Austin Freeman, H. C. Bailey," *Aspects of the Modern Short Story: English and American.* With twenty-two portraits. London: University of London Press, Ltd., 1924. Chap. 16, p. 211-226.

A comparison between Sherlock Holmes, John Thorndyke, and Reginald Fortune.

4091. Wooldridge, Clifton R. *The American Sherlock Holmes: A Whirl of Mystery in Real Life,* by Clifton R. Wooldridge, the world's most famous sleuth. Chicago: Laird & Lee, [c.1908, 1913]. 249 p. illus.

"Actual experiences and hairbreadth escapes that eclipse the greatest detective achievements in modern fiction." (Title page) The frontispiece bears the caption, "The world's great detective and criminologist"—a preposterous claim, to say the least. Everyone knows Sherlock Holmes is not only the greatest detective but that he has no rivals!

4092. Wright, A. B. "Sheridan Le Fanu: Harbinger of the Detective Story," *SHJ,* 6, No. 3 (Winter 1963), 88-89.

Doyle could have obtained some of his ideas for a description of Holmes, including his given name, from Le Fanu's *A Lost Name* in which one of the characters is Carmel Sherlock.

MANUSCRIPTS

4093. Blau, Peter E. *A Brief Census of the Manuscripts of the Canon.* [Pittsfield, Mass.: The Spermaceti Press, 1971.] [6] p.

"Published for the Annual Dinner of the Baker Street Irregulars, 8 January 1971."

The booklet contains a list of the manuscripts, their location (when known), auction record, location of reproductions, and a bibliography.

4094. Brown, Francis C. "A Most Singular Manuscript, Indeed!" *VH,* 1, No. 3 (September 1967), 2.

An account of Lew Feldman's purchase of *The Adventure of the Greek Interpreter* on December 18, 1964, for the Doyle estate.

4095. "Conan Doyle Ms Brings $5,400," *The New York Herald Tribune* (March 23, 1966), 17.

———, *CPBook,* 3, No. 10 (Fall 1966), 191.

A notice of the purchase by Lew Feldman of *The Adventure of the Abbey Grange.*

4096. "Conan Doyle: The Adventure of the Disappearing Documents," *The Times* (April 6, 1969), 1-2.

———, *CPBook,* No. 19 (June 1969), 377-379.

Some irregular goings-on between the "keeper" of a museum, an antiquarian bookman, and a university.

4097. Dalliba, William Swift. "The Manuscripts of the Sherlock Holmes Stories," *BSJ,* 10, No. 3 (July 1960), 164-166. (Bibliographical Notes)

A list of seventeen holographs and their locations.

4098. [Donegall, Lord.] "A Homing Pigeon," *SHJ,* 7, No. 2 (Spring 1965), 34.

An editorial note on the sale of *The Greek Interpreter.*

4099. Feldman, Lew David. *Sir Arthur Conan Doyle Archives.* New York: [House of El Dieff, December 1970]. 1 leaf folded to 4 p.

Other Subjects

The Writings About the Writings

Other Subjects

A description of "the largest and most important selection of material relating to the life and work of Sir Arthur Conan Doyle ever offered at one time." The collection was offered for $362,500!

4100. Honce, Charles. "More Sherlock Holmes Turns Up," *The Washington Post* (August 17, 1947), 5L.
———. ———, *CPBook,* 1, No. 3 (Winter 1965), 62.
An article on Adrian Conan Doyle's discovery in 1942 of *The Man Who Was Wanted* and in 1947 of *The Crown Diamond* and *Some Personalia About Mr. Sherlock Holmes.*

4101. K., M. " 'The Sign of the Four,' " *The Saturday Review of Literature,* 10, No. 38 (April 7, 1934), 609. (The Bowling Green)
Information about this manuscript, listed in a 1909 Anderson catalog, with extracts of four letters from the literary agent to J. M. Stoddart, editor of *Lippincott's.*

4102. McDade, Thomas M. "A Day at the Sale," *BSJ,* 16, No. 4 (December 1966), 202-204.
A firsthand report on the Parke-Bernet sale, March 22, 1966, during which some Doyle manuscripts, including *The Adventure of the Abbey Grange* and a page from *The Hound of the Baskervilles,* were sold.

4103. "Ms of Conan Doyle Is Sold for $12,600," *The New York Times* (December 19, 1964), 26.
———, *BSJ,* 15, No. 1 (March 1965), 60.
An item concerning the successful bid by Lew Feldman for *The Adventure of the Greek Interpreter.*

4104. Nold. "Sherlock Holmes til salg for 14 millioner kr." [Sherlock Holmes for Sale — $2,000, 000"], *Aarhuus Stiftstidende* (April 20, 1969).
"Unfinished mystery story has shaken Sherlock Holmes fans around the world. Conan Doyle's son as villain in financial thriller." (Subtitle tr. from Danish)

4105. Randall, David A. "A Census of the Known Existing Original Manuscripts of the Sacred Writings," *BSJ* [OS], 1, No. 4 (October 1946), 504-508. (Bibliographical Notes)
"Their auction records, present location, etc., chronologically arranged." (Subtitle)

4106. Skeat, T. C. " 'The Case of the Missing Three-Quarter,' " *The British Museum Quarterly,* 22, No. 3-4 (April 1960), 54-56.
———. ———, *SHJ,* 5, No. 1 (Winter 1960), 17-18.
A discussion of Holmes's use of the British Museum and the gift of this manuscript to the Museum.

4107. [Smith, Edgar W.] "The Great Hatbox Mystery," *BSJ* [OS], 2, No. 4 (October 1947), 371-372. (The Editor's Gas-Lamp)
Further commentary on the reported discovery of certain "unpublished writings of Sir Arthur Conan Doyle, including an important new Sherlock Holmes manuscript," in an old hatbox in the vaults of an English village bank.

MAPS

4108. Bodeen, George H. *Sherlock Holmes Illustrated Map of London.* Approximate Date 1890. Rand McNally & Co., [n.d.] Col. map 14 ½ x 21 in.

4109. Honce, Charles. *Europe and the Isles, as Seen from Baker Street.* New York: February 24, 1948. No. 337, for AMS. 1 leaf. (AP Newsfeatures)
———. "A Baker Street View of Europe," *Books and Ghosts.* Mount Vernon: The Golden Eagle Press, 1948. p. 75-81.
A commentary on Dr. Wolff's Sherlock Holmes Map on Europe.

4110. Wolff, Julian. *The Sherlockian Atlas.* New York: [Privately Printed], 1952. [44] p. (13 maps)
Limited to 400 copies.
Contents: Foreword. - 1. London. - 2. England. - 3. Europe. - 4. The Island of Ufa [sic]. - 5. The World. - 6. The Surrey Side. - 7. It Is Full of Old Houses. - 8. His Last Bow Window. - 9. United States. - 10. Dartmoor. - 11. Operation Reichenbach. - 12. Sherlock Holmes in Japan. - 13. The Apocrypha.
These maps have been reproduced in several Sherlockian publications and in color on Lord Donegall's Christmas cards (item 4820).

MEDICINE

See also *Dyin* (items 2362-2366)
and *Dr. Watson — Medical Practice*
(items 3396-3404)

4111. Anderson, Philip C. "Murder in Medical Education," *The Journal of the American Medical Association,* 204, No. 1 (April 1, 1968), 21-25.
An excellent essay on the value of murder-detective stories, including Sherlock Holmes.

4112. Carter, H. S. "Medical Matters in the Sherlock Holmes Stories: From the Records of John H. Watson, M.D.," *Glasgow Medical Journal,* 28, No. 12 (December 1947), 414-426.
"A superb summation of the pathology of Baker Street in all of its ramifications." (Edgar W. Smith)

4113. Clark, Benjamin S. "The Pathological Holmes," *The Best of the Pips.* Westchester

County, N.Y.: The Five Orange Pips, 1955. p. 107-114.

"Disease, dipsomania, mental aberration and physical handicaps mentioned in the Canon, arranged in alphabetical order." (Subtitle)

4114. Gray, Dorothy. "Brain Storms," *Illustrious Client's Second Case-Book.* Edited by J. N. Williamson. [Indianapolis, Ind.: The Illustrious Clients, 1949.] p. 62-63.

"In reading the Cases, please notice this fact; / When danger or trouble was near / The characters often succumbed to a fit, / Brain fever was sure to appear."

4115. Guthrie, Douglas. "Sherlock Holmes and Medicine," *The Canadian Medical Association Journal,* 85, No. 18 (October 28, 1961), 996-1000.

———. ———, *SHJ,* 5, No. 4 (Spring 1962), 112-116.

———. ———, *Janus in the Doorway.* London: Pitman Medical Pub. Co. Ltd., 1963. p. 287-297.

———. ———, ———. Springfield, Ill.: Charles C. Thomas, [1963]. p. 287-297.

Contents: The Author and His Models. - The Influence of Joseph Bell. - The Victorian Scene. - Detection and Diagnosis. - Sherlock Holmes and the Doctors. - Reconstructions and Researches.

4116. ———. "Sherlock Holmes and the Medical Profession," *BSJ* [OS], 2, No. 4 (October 1947), 465-471.

———. "Sherlock Holmes og Laegestanden," Robert Storm Petersen til at illustrere foredraget. *Medicinsk Forum* [København], 1, Nr. 10 (December 1948), 305-317.

After discussing the medical men who appear in the Saga (some twenty in all), Dr. Guthrie concludes that "the Sherlock Holmes stories may be placed alongside *Don Quixote* as an accessory text book of Medicine, and . . . the practitioner of medicine may find much to interest and to assist him in the exploits of Sherlock Holmes and Doctor Watson."

4117. Martland, Harrison S. "Dr. Watson and Mr. Holmes," *Landmarks in Medicine: Laity Lectures of the New York Academy of Medicine.* New York; London: D. Appleton-Century Co., 1939. Chap. 3, p. 83-171.

The Sherlockian influence in forensic medicine.

4118. Scarlett, E. P. "Doctor Out of Zebulun," *Archives of Internal Medicine,* 118, No. 2 (August 1966), 180-186.

"The doctor in detective fiction with an expanded note on Dr. John Thorndyke." (Subtitle) Drs. Bell, Doyle, and Watson are also given their due.

4119. "Sherlockiana Medica," *MD Medical Newsmagazine,* 10, No. 3 (March 1966), 238-242.

———, *CPBook,* 3, No. 9 (Summer 1966), 167-171.

An illustrated article on the following medical men who played a prominent part in the tales: Leslie Armstrong, James Mortimer, Grimesby Roylott, Stamford, and Percy Trevelyan.

4120. Smith, Arthur C. "In the Footsteps of Sherlock Holmes," *Harvard Alumni Bulletin,* 42, No. 24 (April 12, 1940), 814-819.

"The story of the beginnings of legal medicine, against the background of the same in Baker Street." (Edgar W. Smith)

4121. Van Liere, Edward J. " 'Brain Fever' and Sherlock Holmes," *The West Virginia Medical Journal,* 49, No. 3 (March 1953), 77-80.

———. ———, *A Doctor Enjoys Sherlock Holmes.* New York: Vantage Press, [1959]. p. 25-30.

"Dr. Watson has been taken to task by some critics in the medical profession for using the term 'brain fever.' . . . The Holmesian enthusiast will rejoice that the term is again in good repute and is accepted by the medical fraternity."

4122. ———. "Doctor Watson and Nervous Maladies," *BSJ,* 4, No. 2 (April 1954), 100-108.

———. ———, *A Doctor Enjoys Sherlock Holmes.* New York: Vantage Press, [1959]. p. 41-47.

"The harrowing adventures experienced by some of the characters in the stories of Sherlock Holmes, and the great shocks they sustained, often induced in them a state of high nervous tension. References to such individuals are numerous."

4123. ———. "Doctor Watson, Cardiologist," *BSJ,* 9, No. 1 (January 1959), 33-37.

———. ———, *A Doctor Enjoys Sherlock Holmes.* New York: Vantage Press, [1959]. p. 102-107.

"Dr. Watson did not profess to be a cardiologist, but rather a general practitioner of medicine. There are more allusions to minor surgery and to nervous disorders in the tales than there are to diseases of the heart or circulation. There are, however, several references to the latter which are of historical interest to medical students and practicing physicians."

4124. ———. "Doctor Watson's Universal Specific," *BSJ,* 2, No. 4 (October 1952), 215-220.

———. ———, *A Doctor Enjoys Sherlock Holmes.* New York: Vantage Press, [1959]. p. 77-82.

An examination of the conditions under

The Writings About the Writings

Other Subjects

which Watson's favorite remedy, brandy, was used.

4125. ——. "The Physiologic Doctor Watson," *A Doctor Enjoys Sherlock Holmes.* New York: Vantage Press, [1959]. p. 108-116.
    Contents: Physiologists. - Endocrinology. - Digestion. - A Weaker Sex? - Mental Development in the Young. - Curare and Physiology. - Muscle Physiology.

4126. ——. "The Surgical Doctor Watson," *The West Virginia Medical Journal,* 53, No. 5 (May 1957), 186-187.
    —— ——, *A Doctor Enjoys Sherlock Holmes.* New York: Vantage Press, [1959]. p. 62-68.
    "Dr. Watson professed to be a general practitioner of medicine. Such a person is called upon from time to time to do minor, but under ordinary conditions he does not attempt to do major, surgery. . . . there is no particular reference to major surgery in any of the tales. . . . On the other hand, numerous allusions are made to minor surgery."

4127. ——. "The Therapeutic Doctor Watson," *The West Virginia Medical Journal,* 47, No. 5 (May 1951), 148-150.
    ——. ——, *A Doctor Enjoys Sherlock Holmes.* New York: Vantage Press, [1959]. p. 127-134.
    "From what has been related, it appears that Dr. Watson's therapeutic armamentarium, insofar as efficacious drugs are concerned, was sadly limited. But the fact must not be forgotten that he had at his command a number of powerful medicines: morphine, cocaine, belladonna, and strychnine, to name a few."

NAVY

4128. Pratt, Fletcher. "Holmes and the Royal Navy," *The Second Cab.* Edited by James Keddie. [Boston: The Speckled Band, 1947.] p. 65-69.
    An examination of the three cases (Nava, Bruc, and Last) where Holmes "rendered services of the utmost apparent importance to the Royal Navy."

NETHERLANDS

4129. Helling, Cornelis. "Sherlock Holmes in Holland," *BSJ* [OS], 2, No. 4 (October 1947), 409-411.
    Evidence of the Master's popularity in Holland, with comments on the Dutch translations, illustrations, plays, and films.

NEWSPAPERS

See also *Sherlock Holmes — Knowledge of Advertising* (items 3032-3036)

268

4130. Foss, T. F. "The Press and Holmes," *BSJ,* 18, No. 4 (December 1968), 214-219.
    A knowledgeable account of the British press during the Master's day.

4131. Hyslop, John. "Sherlock Holmes and the Press," *SHJ,* 4, No. 1 (Winter 1958), 4-8.
    Concerns his interest in newspapers and their apparent lack of interest in him.

4132. Redmond, Chris. " 'Nothing in the Papers, Watson?' " *SIS,* 1, No. 2 (December 1965), 36-38.
    An inspection of *The Times* for November 21, 1895, bears out Holmes's claim (Bruc) that the paper contained nothing of interest.

4133. R[hode], F[ranklin] W. "Pike's Peek at the Pink 'Un," by Langdale Pike. *DCC,* 1, No. 5 (August 1965), 2, 4. (The World of Sherlock Holmes)
    ——. Revised and enlarged with title: "The 'Pink 'Un': A Short History of *The Sporting Times,*" *BSJ,* 15, No. 4 (December 1965), 213-215.
    A reference to *The Sporting Times,* better known as the "Pink 'Un," in Blue prompted this brief history of a London daily.

4134. Utechin, Nicholas. "A Tedious Morning's Reading," *SHJ,* 10, No. 2 (Summer 1971), 59-61.
    Another examination of *The Times* for November 21, "1891" [sic 1895] containing much the same information as Chris Redmond's article.

NONCANONICAL CASES

See also *The Great Hiatus* (items 2381-2404) and *The Apocrypha* (items 3610-3630)

The Mystery of Edwin Drood

4135. Bengis, Nathan L. "Sherlock Holmes and the Edwin Drood Mystery," *BSJ,* 5, No. 1 (January 1955), 5-12.
    The author describes three Sherlockian solutions to Charles Dickens's famous unfinished mystery and mentions a surmise by Doyle on the subject.

4136. Lang, Andrew. "At the Sign of the Ship," *Longman's Magazine,* 46 (September 1905), 473-480.
    A pastiche in the form of a long conversation between Holmes and Watson in which Holmes arrives at the conclusion that Edwin Drood was not murdered but reappeared disguised as Datchery.

4137. Lauritzen, Henry. *Sherlock Holmes løser Edwin Drood Gaaden.* [Sherlock Holmes Solves the Edwin Drood Riddle.] [Aalborg, Danmark: Privattryk] , 1964. 76 p. illus.
    Limited to 513 copies.
    The book is dedicated to Mr. Hiram

Grewgious who said, "Now you know, *I* never had a play dedicated to *me!*" There is a list of characters in *Edwin Drood*, a summary, and the story of the book and its fate. The main part, however, is the solving by Holmes of the Edwin Drood Mystery. Holmes comes to the conclusion that Edwin was strangled by Jasper and that Hiram Gregious was Dick Datchery. When sober, Jasper might have believed Neville did the murder, but when under the influence of opium he might know the truth and this could be Dickens's "new idea . . . difficult to work."

4138. [Pearson, Edmund.] "Sherlock Holmes Solves the Mystery of Edwin Drood," by the Librarian. *Boston Evening Transcript* (April 2, 1913), 25.

————. "Sherlock Holmes and the Drood Mystery," *The Secret Book.* New York: The Macmillan Co., 1914. Chap. 3, p. 46-49.

————. ————, *BSJ* [OS], 1, No. 2 (April 1946), 138-147. (Incunabulum)

————. ————, *The Incunabular Sherlock Holmes.* Edited by Edgar W. Smith. Morristown, N.J.: The Baker Street Irregulars, 1958. p. 61-74.

4139. [Prestige, Colin.] ["The Master Would Easily Have Solved *The Mystery of Edwin Drood*"], *SHJ*, 9, No. 1 (Winter 1968), 26-27. (Transactions 1967-68)

An account of the Society's second joint meeting with the Dickens Fellowship on March 12, 1968, during which the proposition in the title was debated.

4140. ————. "Sherlock Holmes and Edwin Drood," *BSJ*, 18, No. 3 (September 1968), 131-133.

Three cases (Spec, Engr, and Houn) exemplifying the Master's ability to solve mysteries without leaving Baker Street are cited to show how easily he could have solved this mystery.

4141. Smith, Harry B. "Sherlock Holmes Solves the Mystery of Edwin Drood," *Munsey's Magazine*, 83, No. 3 (December 1924), 385-400.

————. *How Sherlock Holmes Solved the Mystery of Edwin Drood.* Glen Rock, Pa.: Walter Klinefelter, 1934. 57 p.

Limited to 33 copies.

"The famous detective applies his critical method to the most fascinating of all literary puzzles." (*Munsey's*)

Jack the Ripper

4142. Bailey, L. W. "The Case of the Unmentioned Case: A Sherlock Holmes Speculation," Read by John Glen. BBC Home Service, Wednesday, November 10, 1965, 8:44-8:59 p.m.

————. ————, *The Listener*, 74 (December 16, 1965), 998-999.

————. ————, *BSJ*, 16, No. 3 (September 1966), 167-172.

"Since Sherlock Holmes never mentions Jack the Ripper, though Jack's murders took place 1888-1891 when Holmes was at his prime; since Holmes was never consulted on the case; since one victim was seen accompanied by the wearer of a deerstalker's hat; since both men knew thoroughly London's East End, the effective use of disguise, and anatomy; since Jack had an extreme aversion to women and sex and Holmes was at least unattracted to them; and since Holmes was insane and separated from Watson during the time in question, Sherlock Holmes was probably Jack the Ripper." (David G. Osborne)

4143. Christensen, Flemming. "Who's Afraid of Big Bad Jack? or An Attempt to Disclose the Identity of Jack the Ripper," *BSJ*, 15, No. 4 (December 1965), 229-235.

————. An addendum with title: "Who Wasn't Turner?" *BSJ*, 18, No. 2 (June 1968), 110.

A most ingenious but alarming essay establishing "beyond the shadow of a doubt" that this "monster of wickedness, insatiable in his lust for blood," was none other than John (James) H. Watson.

4144. Dettman, Bruce. "Who Wasn't Jack the Ripper," *BSJ*, 17, No. 4 (December 1967), 219-221.

The author states unequivocally that no individual in the Canon was responsible for the Whitechapel murders; and suggests that Holmes failed in his attempt to capture the most sensational criminal of the century.

4145. Fisher, Charles. "A Challenge from Baker Street," *Leaves from the Copper Beeches.* Narberth, Pa.: Livingston Pub. Co., 1959. p. 15-32.

A convincing demonstration that Holmes, with the aid of Toby, not only tracked down Jack the Ripper (identified as Horace Harker [SixN]), but detected the killer's unspeakable employer—Professor James Moriarty!

4146. Grady, Thomas F. "Two Bits from Boston," *BSJ Christmas Annual*, No. 5 (1960), 272-275.

The literary agent was unable to stop Jack, but the Master did!

4147. Heldenbrand, Page. "Another Bohemian Scandal," *BSJ* [OS], 4, No. 1 (January 1949), 72-73.

Holmes was unsuccessful in his attempt to apprehend the Ripper.

4148. Kennedy, Bruce. "Jack in Abyss," *BSJ*, 17, No. 4 (December 1967), 222.

The Napoleon of Crime is identified as Jack the Ripper.

Other Subjects

4149. Lauterbach, Edward S. "Holmes and the Ripper," *BSJ*, 18, No. 2 (June 1968), 111-113.

A verse in thirty-one stanzas relating how Holmes and Watson waylaid and killed Jack the Rip, otherwise known as Professor Moriarty.

4150. ———. "Jack the R.I.P.," Illustrated by William Dixon. *PD Annual*, 1, No. 2 (1971), 79-80.

" 'I'll rip and rip,' the Ripper sang, / 'I'll slash! And hack! And nip! / 'I'll send your bloody soul to hell / 'For I am Jack the R.I.P.' "

4151. Leavitt, Jack. "Mr. Holmes, Please Take the Strand," *BSJ*, 18, No. 3 (September 1968), 170-179.

The verbatim record, as recorded by Anthony Cleaver and transcribed by his son Thomas, of Holmes's cross-examination by the defense attorney for James Calhoun in which he admits to the Ripper slayings.

4152. Neitzke, Gordon. "Sherlock Holmes and Jack the Ripper," *Illustrious Client's Third Case-Book*. Edited by J. N. Williamson and H. B. Williams. [Indianapolis, Ind.: The Illustrious Clients, 1953.] p. 80-83.

John H. Watson is finally revealed as Jack the Ripper.

4153. Salowich, Alex N. "He Could Not Have Sat Idly," *BSJ*, 18, No. 2 (June 1968), 107-109.

After eliminating Athelney Jones, Watson, and Moriarty as suspects in the slayings, the author opts for Sir James Saunders, M.D., who was indebted to Holmes for professional services (Blan). Holmes remained silent to protect the good name of the London medical profession.

4154. Smith, Edgar W. "The Suppressed Adventure of the Worst Man in London," *Baker Street and Beyond: Together with Some Trifling Monographs*. Morristown, N.J.: The Baker Street Irregulars, 1957. [unpaged]

Speculation on the possibility that Holmes may have had a hand in helping to clear up the brutal knife slayings reported in *The Times* between August and November of 1880.

4155. Whitehead, Robert A. ["Letter"], *BSJ*, 18, No. 2 (June 1968), 117-118. (Letters to Baker Street)

"When Sherlock Holmes was tracing Jack the Ripper, as he must have done, he was searching for the murderer of five streetwalkers, not seven. On reading Mr. Cullen's book [*When London Walked in Terror* (Boston: Houghton Mifflin Co., 1965)], however, one learns that Sherlock never caught the Ripper, though he must have come close, for the real Jack the Ripper (not the Professor, the Master, the Doctor, or the Inspector) committed suicide by drowning himself in the Thames on 3 December 1888."

Other Cases

4156. Brodie, Robert N. "Holmes and the British Postal Forgeries," *BSJ*, 19, No. 3 (September 1969), 154-157.

An examination of five unreported cases involving forgeries of British postage stamps which may have been solved by Holmes.

4157. Fleissner, R. F. "The Macomber Case: A Sherlockian Analysis?" *BSJ*, 20, No. 3 (September 1970), 154-156, 169.

Central to the plot of Ernest Hemingway's "The Short Happy Life of Francis Macomber" is the puzzle of whether or not Margaret Macomber was the deliberate slayer of her husband. Invoking the spirit of Holmes, the literary sleuth may come up with the answer that has vexed modern scholars.

4158. Goldfield, Barbara. "Sherlock Holmes Meets the Living Corpse," *BSP Christmas Annual*, No. 1 (1966), 9.

Speculation on what may have been one of the untold tales—"The Singular Adventure of the Phantom of the Paris Opera."

4159. Goslin, Vernon. "Sherlock Holmes and the Cheddington Crimes," *SHJ*, 8, No. 2 (Spring 1967), 53-54.

Had Scotland Yard studied the Master's methods, the gang of British criminals who robbed a Royal Mail train near Cheddington, Buckinghamshire, on August 8, 1963, could have been apprehended much sooner.

4160. Hartman, Harry. "Leave Us Face It," *The Holy Quire*. [Culver City, Calif.: Luther Norris, December 1970.] p. 28-30.

Application of Sherlockian methods to the solution of the mystery of the purloined Walt Whitman manuscript.

4161. Haskell, Henry C. "Unending Speculation About Poor Mozart," *Kansas City Star* (April 1968).

———. ———, *CPBook*, 4, No. 16 (Fall 1968), 305.

A discussion of points raised by Dr. N. C. Louros in a lecture he delivered in Chicago concerning the composer's mysterious death, with an observation by Holmes.

4162. Lane, Richard L. "The Adventure of the 4th Napoleon ('The Service for Lord Backwater'), *BSJ*, 20, No. 1 (March 1970), 30-35.

Holmes's "Service for Lord Backwater" (Nobl) was an undercover role as bodyguard for Napoleon IV when he went to Africa with the British relief troops during the Zulu War (January to July 1879). A coincidence involving the troopship *Orontes* (Stud) is revealed.

4163. Levine, Arthur L. "A Man of 'Formidable Resourcefulness': An Essay in the Manner of a Footnote to History," *BSJ*, 4, No. 3 (July 1954), 169-173.

Holmes was responsible for discovering the famous note from Alfred Zimmerman which proposed an alliance between Germany, Mexico, and Japan against the United States if the U. S. did not remain neutral during World War I.

4164. Levinson, John O. "The Case of the Vanished 3," as it might have been told by John H. Watson, M.D., to John O. Levinson. *The Golf Journal* (June 1968), 20-23.

————. "The Three That Was Four," by John H. Watson. *American Bar Association Journal*, 54 (August 1968), 777-780.

————. ————, *Rx Sports and Travel: The Recreation and Leisure Magazine for Physicians*, 4, No. 2 (March-April 1969), 16-18, 41.

"The nonpareil English sleuth determines the truth in the case of Roberto de Vicenzo and the erroneous score card during the 1968 Masters Golf Tournament." (*Rx Sports and Travel*)

4165. Morrow, L. A. "A Diplomatic Secret," *SHJ*, 2, No. 4 (Winter 1955), 21-25.

How Holmes was called in to protect Guglielmo Marconi during his experiments with wireless telegraphy.

4166. Norman, Barry. "Elementary My Dear Goya!" *The Daily Mail* [London] (November 20, 1965).

————. ————, *CPBook*, 3, No. 13 (Summer 1967), 259.

Holmes discusses the famous case of the stolen Goya painting.

4167. Pedley, Katharine Greenleaf. *Moriarty in the Stacks: The Nefarious Adventures of Thomas J. Wise*. Berkeley, Calif.: Peacock Press, 1966. 27 p.

A fascinating study of the career of the world's most successful forger, in which the author advances the opinion that Doyle and Wise may have been acquainted and that the Great Detective's exposition of the possibilities of scientific detection was responsible for Wise's giving up his more overt criminal activities.

4168. Randall, David A. "The Adventure of the Notorious Forger," *BSJ* [OS], 1, No. 3 (July 1946), 371-377. (Bibliographical Notes)

An elaboration of the part Holmes played in exposing Wise, with the conclusion that Moriarty, Moran, and Wise were all *Mycroft!*

4169. Redmond, Chris. "More Ballistics," *BSP*, No. 26 (August 1967), 2. (Editorial)

Speculation on the kind of investigation Holmes would have conducted into the murder of President Kennedy.

4170. R[ush], D[avid] M. "Holmes and the Opera Ghost," *DCC*, 1, No. 3 (April 1965), 3.

A conjecture about the Master's knowledge of the phantom at the Paris Opera House.

4171. [Smith, Edgar W.] "The Adventures That Might Have Been," *BSJ*, 6, No. 2 (April 1956), 67-68. (The Editor's Gas-Lamp)

"It is instructive to speculate upon the unhappier fate that might have attended a number of very bloody criminals if only Sherlock Holmes had been invited, or permitted, to put himself upon their trail."

NUMISMATICS

4172. Christ, Jay Finley. "Glittering Golden Guineas," *The Numismatist*, 64, No. 10 (October 1951), 1103-1105.

A brief discussion of the numismatic references in the Saga.

4173. Davis, Norman M. "Here Are Your Wages," *BSJ*, 21, No. 2 (June 1971), 77-79.

A history and valuation of Victorian shillings, the coins Holmes gave to the original Baker Street Irregulars and the coins that are now awarded to members of BSI.

4174. Dudley, W. E. "A Coming Plague," *BSJ*, 21, No. 2 (June 1971), 80-83.

An article dealing with the horrors of Decimalisation. "This most idiotic thing since Prohibition is especially painful to all good Sherlockians. The Canon rests solidly on good old Victorian tradition and that includes the Coin of the Realm. To us the Irregular Shilling will never become the Irregular Five Pence. We refuse to change the Master's miles and acres into metric terms. The old British coinage is as much a part of the Canon as is the London fog. Most of all we refuse to give up the Guinea, that 'gaseous vertebrate' of the financial kingdom. For you see, to us the fictional is truly more real than the transitory fact."

4175. Marsh, Leslie. "It Is Quite a Three Pipe Problem," *Punch*, 236 (May 20, 1959), 680-681.

————. ————, *CPBook*, 3, No. 12 (Spring 1967), 228-229.

"A comparison of some of the £sd prices paid in the Canon with those that prevail today—and a confession that no common denominator can be found, except for the item of blackmail." (Edgar W. Smith)

4176. Merritt, Russell L. "Finances in Baker Street," *BSJ*, 8, No. 4 (October 1958), 238-240.

A discussion of currency in the Writings, including two charts comparing the currency of Holmes's time with its modern-day American and English equivalents.

4177. Simpson, A. Carson. *Numismatics in the Canon.* Philadelphia: Privately Printed by International Printing Co., 1957-1959. 3 v. (40, 43, 38 p.) illus. (Simpson's Sherlockian Studies, Vol. 5-7)

Limited to 221B numbered copies.

Contents: Pt. I. Full Thirty Thousand Marks of English Coin. - (1) British Coins. - Pt. II. A Very Treasury of Coin of Divers Realms. - (1) British Coins (Concluded). - (2) United States Coins. - (3) Other Modern Coins. - (4) Ancient Coins. - Pt. III. Small Titles and Orders. - (5) Paper Money. - (6) Counterfeiting. - (7) Medals. - (8) Decorations. - (9) Orders.

PERIODICALS AND ANNUALS

4178. *The Arnsworth Castle Business Index.* June 1960-February 1964. Pittsburgh, Pa.: Arnsworth Castle, a Scion Society of the Baker Street Irregulars. 16 issues. frequency varied.

A bibliographical series prepared by Robert H. Schutz.

4179. *The Baker Street Cab Lantern.* No. 1-9; 1963-1971. Stockholm: The Solitary Cyclists of Sweden. 9 issues. illus. annual.

Text in Swedish and English.

Edited by Ted Bergman.

4180. *Baker Street Collecting.* Vol. 1-2, No. 1-2; February 1968-September 1969. Hebron, Ill.: Puhl Hall Press. 6 issues. illus. frequency varied.

Edited by Gayle Lange Puhl, February 1968-January 1969; by Ray Funk, September 1969.

4181. *The Baker Street Gasogene: A Sherlockian Quarterly.* Vol. 1, No. 1-4; 1961-1962. New York: Peter A. Ruber. 4 issues. illus.

Edited by Peter A. Ruber.

4182. *The Baker Street Journal: An Irregular Quarterly of Sherlockiana* [Old Series]. Vol. 1-4, No. 1; January 1946-January 1949. New York: Ben Abramson (for the Baker Street Irregulars). 13 issues. illus.

Edited by Edgar W. Smith.

4183. *The Baker Street Journal: An Irregular Quarterly of Sherlockiana* (New Series). Vol. 1-21, No. 1-4; January 1951-December 1971. Morristown, N.J.; New York, N.Y.: The Baker Street Irregulars. 84 issues. illus.

Edited by Edgar W. Smith, 1951-1960; by Julian Wolff, 1961- .

Subscriptions: Julian Wolff, M.D., 33 Riverside Drive, New York, N. Y. 10023 ($4 a year).

4184. *The Baker Street Journal Christmas Annual.* No. 1-5; 1956-1960. Morristown, N.J.: The Baker Street Irregulars. 5 issues. illus.

Edited by Edgar W. Smith.

4185. *The Baker Street Journal: An Irregular Quarterly of Sherlockiana* (Old and New Series). 1946-1969. New York: AMS Press, Inc., [1971]. 23 v. ($365 paperbound; $435 library bound)

4186. *B.S.J. 1946-69: A Cumulated Index to The Baker Street Journal.* Dedicated to the study of Mr. Sherlock Holmes. Compiled by D. A. Redmond. New York: The Baker Street Irregulars, 1970. iv, 104 p.

An indispensable subject and author-title index. The latter index was compiled from the annual *BSJ* indexes. It is kept up to date with an annual subject index laid in the March issue of *BSJ*.

4187. *Baker Street Pages.* No. 1-54; July 1965-July 1970. Lawrence, Kansas; Kingston, Ontario: The Baker Street Pageboys. 51 issues. illus. monthly (3 double nos.)

Also issued a *Christmas Annual* in December 1966.

Edited by Chris Redmond.

4188. *The Baker Street Pages* (New Series). Vol. 1, No. 7; June-July 1972. Los Angeles: The Baker Street Pageboys. 7 issues. bimonthly.

Edited by Glenn S. Holland.

4189. *Bulletin.* Vol. 1-2, No. 1-6; July 1963-July 1964. The Unknowns of Buffalo, New York. [?] issues. illus. monthly.

Also issued an *Annual* in December 1963, a *Jubilee Edition* in July 1964, and an *Almanak* in July 1964.

Edited by James R. Stefanie.

4190. *The Commonplace Book.* Vol. 1-5; Summer 1964-June 1969. Ferndale, Mich.: Old Soldiers of Baker Street. 19 issues (384 p.) illus. frequency varied.

Edited by W. T. Rabe.

Contains reproductions of newspaper and magazine articles and reviews, old and new, of Sherlockian interest.

4191. *The Cormorants' Ring.* Vol. 1, No. 1-4; September 1958-September 1960. The Trained Cormorants of Los Angeles County. 4 issues. illus. frequency varied.

Edited by Dean W. Dickensheet.

4192. *The Devon County Chronicle: Serving the Parishes of Grimpen, Thorsley and High Barrow.* Vol. 1-7, No. 1-6; December 1964-August 1971. The Chicago BSI. 38 issues. bimonthly.

Edited by Robert W. Hahn.

Subscriptions: Robert W. Hahn, 509 S. Ahrens Ave., Lombard, Ill. 60148 ($2 a year).

4193. *Encyclical Letter.* Vol. 1-[?]; April 1953-[?]. Detroit, Mich.: Amateur Mendicant Society. [?] issues.

Edited by Russell McLauchlin and W. T. Rabe.

4194. *The Growler.* Vol. 1, No. 1-2; 1950, November 1958. The Diogenes Club of Brooklyn. 2 issues.

Edited by R. Cogan Clyne and George J. McCormack.

4195. *The Holmesian Observer.* Vol. 1, No. 1-9; March-November 1971. Bronx, N.Y.: The Priory School of New York. 9 issues. frequency varies.

Also issued an *Annual* in December 1971.

Edited by Andrew Page.

Subscriptions: Andrew Page, 3130 Irwin Ave., Bronx, N.Y. 10463 ($1.25 a year; $1.80 overseas).

4196. *Investigations: An Irregular Journal of Atlanta-Area Sherlockiana.* Vol. 1, No. 1-3; January-May 1971. Atlanta, Ga.: The Confederates of Wisteria Lodge. 3 issues. illus. bimonthly.

Edited by Mrs. E. M. Hughes.

4197. *Irregular Report.* No. 1-11; April 1960-November 1965. Copenhagen: The Literary League, The King of Scandinavia's Own Sherlockians. 11 issues. frequency varied.

Text in English.

Edited by Poul Arenfalk.

4198. *The Pontine Dossier.* Vol. 1-2; February 1967-February 1970. Culver City, Calif.: Luther Norris. 9 issues. illus. quarterly.

4199. *The Pontine Dossier Annual* (New Series). Vol. 1, No. 1-2; 1970-1971. Culver City, Calif.: Luther Norris. 2 issues (80 p.) illus.

The official publication of the Praed Street Irregulars. Includes articles on both the Pontine and Sherlockian tales. Correspondence about the journal and the PSI should be addressed to Luther Norris, 3844 Watseka Ave., Culver City, Calif. 90230.

4200. *The Scandal Sheet.* Vol. 1, No. 1-2; January-September 1971. The Scandalous Bohemians of New Jersey. 2 issues. frequency varies.

Edited by Robert A. W. Lowndes.

Subscriptions: Norman S. Nolan, 68 Crest Road, Middletown, N. J. 07748) (free to members; $2 a vol. to non-members).

4201. *Shades of Sherlock.* Vol. 1-5, No. 2; October 1966-August 1971. Fulton, Mo.;

Chappaqua, N.Y.: The Three Students Plus. 18 issues. illus. semiannual.

Also issued an *Annual* in January 1967 and January 1968.

Edited by Bruce Kennedy. Illustrated by Howard Diehl. Printed by Bradley Kjell.

4202. *Sherlock Holmes Årbog.* Vol. 1-3; 1965-1967. København: Martins Forlag. 3 issues (94, 94, 82 p.) illus. annual.

Text in Danish.

Edited by A. D. Henriksen. Illustrated by Henry Lauritzen *et al.* Translated by A. D. Henriksen *et al.*

4203. *The Sherlock Holmes Journal.* Vol. 1-10, No. 1-4; May 1952-Summer 1972. The Sherlock Holmes Society of London. 40 issues. illus. semiannual.

Edited by the Marquis of Donegall.

Subscriptions: The Sherlock Holmes Society of London, The Studio, 39 Clabon Mews, London, S.W.1 American subscriptions: Cecil A. Ryder, Jr., 118 Carr Dr., Glendale, Calif. 91205 ($9 a year).

4204. *Sherlockiana.* Vol. 1-16. No. 3-4; 1956-1971. Bagsvaerd: Sherlock Holmes Klubben i Danmark (The Danish Baker Street Irregulars). 46 issues. illus. quarterly.

Text in Danish and English.

Edited by A. D. Henriksen, 1956-1970; by Henry Lauritzen, 1971- .

Subscriptions: Henry Lauritzen, Vesterbro 60, 9000 Aalborg, Denmark ($2 a year).

4205. *Sidelights on Holmes.* Vol. 1-3, No. 1-2; 1966-1969. Oak Park, Ill.: The Priory Scholars of Fenwick High School. 10 issues. quarterly.

Edited by John Sikorski.

4206. *Studies in Scarlet.* No. 1-3; June 1965-1966. Pearl River, N.Y. 3 issues.

Title of first issue: *Some Studies in Scarlet.*

Edited by Steven Thomashefsky and Robert Enright.

4207. *Three Pipe Problems.* Vol. 1, No. 1-2; September 1970-October 1971. Rockford, Ill.: The Baker Street Irrationals. 2 issues.

Title of first issue: *Astounding Deductions.*

Edited by John Jacobson, 1970; by Bradley Kjell, 1971- .

Subscriptions: Bradley Kjell, 1732 Sexton Dr., Rockford, Ill. 61108

4208. *Vermissa Herald* [Old Series]. Vol. 1-2, No. 1; Spring 1962-Fall 1963. Orinda, Calif.: The Scowrers and Molly Maguires. 3 issues. frequency varied.

Other Subjects

Edited by Paula Salo. Printed by Karen Anderson.

4209. *The Vermissa Herald: A Journal of Sherlockian Affairs.* Vol. 1-5, No. 1-3; January 1967-September 1971. San Francisco: The Scowrers and Molly Maguires. 15 issues. illus. triannual.

Edited by William A. Berner and Herbert A. Eaton.

Subscriptions: William A. Berner, 4712 17th St., San Francisco, Calif. 94117 ($1.50 a year; $2 overseas).

4210. *The Victorian Journal.* Vol. 1, No. 1-4; 1970-December 1971. Tacoma, Wash.: The Victorian Gentlemen, 4 issues. quarterly.

Edited by Tom Mengert.

4211. Austin, Bliss. *A Baker Street Christmas Stocking.* Westfield, N.J.; Pittsburgh, Pa.: The Hydraulic Press, 1953-1956, 1958-1959, 1961-1971. 17 issues. illus. (Christmas Annual)

"Being a miscellany of Holmesian trivia contrived to convey Irregular Greetings at Christmas." (Subtitle)

4212. Montgomery, James. *Montgomery's Christmas Annual.* [Philadelphia: Privately Printed, 1950-1955.] 6 issues. illus.

Contents: 1. Art in the Blood, and What Is This Thing Called Music? (or Body and Soul). - 2. Sidelights on Sherlock. - 3. Three Trifling Monographs. - 4. Shots from the Canon. - 5. A Study in Pictures. - 6. A Case of Identity.

4213. Pattrick, Robert R. *Ponderings by the Politician.* [Los Angeles: Privately Produced, 1951-1956.] 6 issues. (Christmas Annual)

4214. Williams, H. B. *Notes by the Sub-Librarian.* Indianapolis, Ind.: [Privately Produced], January 1959-1968. 12 issues. triannually, January 1959-February 1960; annually, 1961-1968. (Christmas Annual) Limited to 75 copies.

4215. Wilmunen, Jon V. *The Gamebag.* Buhl, Minn.: The Gamekeepers of Northern Minnesota, 1965-1969. 5 issues. illus. (Christmas Annual) Limited to 50 copies.

PHILATELY

4216. Blau, Peter E. "In Memoriam: Dr. Leander Starr Jameson," *BSJ,* 18, No. 2 (June 1968), 88-89. illus.

"The lack of philatelic recognition of Sherlock Holmes, Irregularly remedied by Julian Wolff's 1957 discovery of a Bohemian commemorative, has been further rectified by a 1967 Rhodesian issue honouring Dr. Leander Starr Jameson. Although Dr. Jameson does not appear in the Canon in his own person, he is doubly represented—by Colonel Lysander Stark [Engr] and Dr. Lysander Starr [3Gar]."

4217. Pierce, Arthur. "Was Sherlock Holmes a Stamp Collector?" *The Philatelist,* 13, No. 12 (September 1947), 340-342.

———. ———, *Approaches to Philately.* Compiled by G. B. Erskine. [London]: Blandford Press Ltd., [1950]. Chap. 8, p. 71-77.

———. ———. Issued separately "for private distribution at a meeting of The Sons of the Copper Beeches at the Union League, Philadelphia, February 20, 1953." 7 p.

Evidence of his interest in philately.

4218. Shaw, John Bennett, comp. [*The Philatelic Holmes.*] Tulsa, Okla.: [Privately Printed, Christmas 1966]. [4] p.

———. ———, *SHJ,* 8, No. 2 (Spring 1967), 50-51.

A collection of postmarks in which the names of the towns are similar or identical to Canonical characters, places, and Sherlockians.

4219. Simpson, A. Carson. *Canonical Philately.* [Philadelphia: Privately reproduced by William R. Smith, 1971.] [29] p. (Simpson's Sherlockian Studies, Vol. 9)

Contents: Author's Foreword. - 1. Stamps, Postmarks and Postoffices. - 2. Philatelic Iconography. - A Chronological Addendum. - Footnotes.

The last of the author's *Sherlockian Studies,* dated December 25, 1961, was intended for a limited edition of 221B copies. Unfortunately, it was never printed.

4220. Wolff, Julian. *A Ramble in Bohemia.* New York: United Nations Philatelic Chronicle, April 1, 1957. [8] p. illus.

———. ———, *BSJ,* 18, No. 2 (June 1968), 85-87.

A summary of the available data on the Sherlock Holmes memorial stamp issued in 1988 by the Republic of Bohemia. A reproduction of the stamp also appears in *BSJ,* 8, No. 3 (July 1958), 184.

PLACE IDENTIFICATIONS (GENERAL)

4221. Baring-Gould, William S. "Three Canonical Churches," *BSJ,* 16, No. 1 (March 1966), 24-25.

A brief commentary on St. Saviour's (Iden), St. George's (Nobl), and the Church of St. Monica (Scan).

4222. Bell, H. W. "Three Identifications: Lauriston Gardens, Upper Swandam Lane, Saxe-Coburg Square," *221B: Studies in Sherlock Holmes.* Edited by Vincent Starrett. New York: The Macmillan Co., 1940. p. 59-67.

The locations are placed, respectively, at

No. 318, Brixton Road; Stoney Lane; and No. 5, Bridgewater Square.

4223. ———. "Three Identifications: Two Localities in 'The Six Napoleons,' the Drive to Thaddeus Sholto's House, Birlstone Manor," *Profile by Gaslight*. Edited by Edgar W. Smith. New York: Simon and Schuster, 1944. p. 283-289.

The two localities are identified as No. 14, Pitt Street and No. 51, Campden Hill Road; the course of the blind ride is traced; and the manor is located at Brambletye in Sussex.

4224. Brend, Gavin. "The Haunts of Sherlock Holmes," *Coming Events in Britain* [British Travel and Holiday Association] (October 1952), 16-17; (December 1952), 24-26.

———. Pt. 2 reprinted with title: "Through Sherlock Holmes Country," *San Francisco Examiner* (March 8, 1953), II, 8.

A discussion of several places in and outside of London that are marked by some Sherlockian adventure. The article is accompanied by some well-chosen photographs.

4225. Gore-Booth, Paul H. "The Journeys of Sherlock Holmes: A Topographical Monograph," *BSJ* [OS], 3, No. 2 (April 1948), 159-168.

A classification and analysis of the places to which the various recorded cases took Holmes and Watson.

4226. Goslin, Vernon. "Further Identifications," *SHJ*, 9, No. 4 (Summer 1970), 143-144. (Wigmore Street Post-Bag)

Answers to the questions: "Where was 'The Bar of Gold'? Where was Holmes's College? Why did Windibank choose the surname 'Angel' in Iden?"

4227. Howard, Helen. "Holmes and Watson Slept Here," *Illustrious Client's Second Case-Book*. Edited by J. N. Williamson. [Indianapolis, Ind.: The Illustrious Clients, 1949.] p. 29-33.

A survey of the ten inns where Holmes and Watson spent one or more nights while working on problems away from London.

4228. Jones, Kelvin. "Sherlock Holmes in Lee," *SHJ*, 8, No. 3 (Winter 1967), 93-96.

Place identifications in Twis and Reti.

4229. Merriman, Charles O. "In Search of Sherlock Holmes," *SHJ*, 8, No. 1 (Winter 1966), 7-12.

Contents: Meiringen and The Final Problem. - Pinkertons and The Valley of Fear. - Montpelier and "The Disappearance of Lady Frances Carfax". - The Devil's Foot. - The Case of the Dancing Men. - The Valley of Fear. - The Lion's Mane.

4230. Norton, Sir Charles. "Holmes and Westminster," *SHJ*, 7, No. 4 (Spring 1966), 102-104.

A paper by the Lord Mayor of Westminster on "the associations which Holmes and those friends and foes who shared his adventures had with this City, bearing in mind that Westminster now includes the old Boroughs of Paddington and St. Marylebone."

4231. Prestige, Colin. "South London Adventures," *SHJ*, 3, No. 3 (Autumn 1957), 5-8.

Contents: Mary Morstan's Journey. - Lauriston Gardens. - Tavern Search.

An analysis of the findings of the Norwegian Explorers' tour of Holmesian London on June 18, 1957.

POISONS

See also *Devi* (items 2357-2361),
Lion (items 2541-2544),
Spec (items 2733-2743),
and *Stud* (item 2759)

4232. Allen, F. A. "Devilish Drugs," *May and Baker Pharmaceutical Bulletin*, 5, No. 12 (December 1956), 118-121; 6, No. 1 (January 1957), 9-12.

———. ———, *SHJ*, 3, No. 3 (Autumn 1957), 12-14; 3, No. 4 (Summer 1958), 11-12.

"The examples dealt with in these two articles are a small representative selection from a large number and it is said from time to time that all common, and uncommon, objects of the fiction poisons' sea-shore have now come to collection. The collection will, however, never be finally completed; modern fictional poisoners keep well up with the recent advances."

4233. Koelle, George B. "The Poisons of the Canon," *Leaves from the Copper Beeches*. Narberth, Pa.: Livingston Pub. Co., 1959. p. 91-96.

"A cursory examination reveals that poisons figure with more or less prominence in over a dozen chronicles of the Canon. Their variety is remarkable. They include synthetic and natural products, and the origins of the latter embrace the animal, vegetable, and even bacteriological kingdoms. While some are fairly commonplace and can be dismissed with a passing reference, several are bizarre in the extreme; a few apparently have never been recorded elsewhere."

4234. Sovine, J. W. "The Toxicanon," *BSJ*, 8, No. 2 (April 1958), 107-112.

An enumeration and discussion of the twenty poisons which appear in twenty-two of the cases.

4235. Van Liere, Edward J. "Curare and

Sherlock Holmes," *Harvard Medical Alumni Bulletin*, 27, No. 2 (January 1953), 15-17.

————. ————, *A Doctor Enjoys Sherlock Holmes*. New York: Vantage Press, [1959]. p. 31-34.

Scientific commentary contrasting Watson's unscientific treatment of the "arrow poison" in Stud to his sound handling of the same drug in Suss.

PSYCHOLOGICAL AND SEXUAL INTERPRETATIONS

See also *Sherlock Holmes — Personality* (items 3182-3195)

4236. Adelman, Kenneth L. "The Relationship of a Physician and a Master," *BSJ*, 20, No. 4 (December 1970), 215-222.

A consideration of the personalities of Holmes and Watson and the areas of conflict between the two men.

4237. Bailey, L. W. "The Psychology of Holmes and Watson," *SHJ*, 4, No. 2 (Spring 1959), 73-75.

"Watson's emotions towards Holmes are basically those of a son towards his father . . . psychologically, in short, it might be said that Holmes is Watson's father!"

4238. Lieberman, Herman. "The Mysterious Characters of Sherlock Holmes and Dr. Watson," *BSJ*, 20, No. 4 (December 1970), 223-230.

The author attacks a new cult—that of the Watsonians who romanticize the characters of Watson and Holmes. Arguing that a true Sherlockian would use Holmes's methods but amplify his techniques to include those available today, he makes use of psychoanalytic techniques to probe the mystery of the true characters of this twosome. He analyzes Watson's frenzied adoration of Holmes as well as Holmes's foibles, including his sexual orientation, to provide Sherlockians with a more realistic foundation for their admiration of the Master.

4239. Shaw, John Bennett. "To Shelve or to Censor," *SOS*, 5, No. 2 (August 14, 1971), 4-12.

"Some disturbing thoughts about the disgusting evidence from the Sherlock Holmes Canon." (Subtitle)

4240. Starr, H. W. "On My Knees!" *Four Wheels to Baker Street*. Edited by Bruce Kennedy. [Fulton, Mo.]: The Three Students Plus, 1968. p. 1-3.

Professor Starr comments on certain allegedly suggestive passages in the Writings that lend themselves to a psychoerotic or Freudian interpretation.

4241. Van der Sterren, H. A. "Een Kind-

scheidsfantasie van Sir Arthur Conan Doyle en de Heldenbaden van Sherlock Holmes" ["Childhood Memory of Sir Arthur Conan Doyle and the Heroic Deeds of Sherlock Holmes"], *Psychologische und Neurologische Blätter*, 49 (1946), 304-330.

A Freudian analysis of Doyle and the Sherlock Holmes stories, with a summary in English and French.

RATINGS OF THE TALES

4242. Doyle, A. Conan. "A Sherlock Holmes Competition," Set by A. Conan Doyle. *The Strand Magazine*, 73, No. 425 (March 1927), 281.

An invitation to readers to guess the twelve short stories that the author considered the best. The results of the contest (the first prize of £100 and an autographed copy of *Memories and Adventures* was won by R. T. Norman), along with an explanation of how Doyle made his selection, appear on p. 611-612 of the June issue.

4243. Eustace, Frank J. "Sherlock Meets the Analyst," *Leaves from the Copper Beeches*. Narberth, Pa.: Livingston Pub. Co., 1959. p. 35-40.

A valuable analysis and classification of the cases as they appear to the Master, to Inspector Lestrade or Scotland Yard, to Watson, to Doyle, and to the author; with an added table of the composite preferences expressed by the Sons of the Copper Beeches.

4244. Morton, Humphrey, and William Swift Dalliba. "*Strand Magazine* Prizewinners of 1927," *SHJ*, 2, No. 4 (Winter 1955), 7-8.

An account of the 1927 Sherlock Holmes Competition by two Sherlockians who entered and won a prize.

4245. [Smith, Edgar W.] "The Least of These . . . ," *BSJ*, 3, No. 3 (July 1953), 131-132. (The Editor's Gas-Lamp)

An editorial commentary on how the tales have been rated, from the twelve best by Doyle in 1927 and the BSI in 1944, to the twelve least significant—still to be determined.

4246. ————. "On the Later Tales," *West by One and by One*. San Francisco: Privately Printed, 1965. p. 7-14.

The author believes the test of *familiarity* is the best criterion that can be used to appraise the post-Reichenbach stories.

4247. [————.] *"The 'Ten Best' and the 'Ten Least,' "* *BSJ*, 4, No. 2 (April 1954), 117-119.

The tabulated results of a 1954 poll among Sherlockians to determine the consensus as to the "ten best" and the "ten least" of the short stories. For purposes of comparison, the ratings by Doyle and by the

Irregulars in 1944 of the "twelve best" are also given.

4248. [———.] *"The 'Ten Best' Contest,"* BSJ, 9, No. 4 (October 1959), 237-240.

The results of a contest announced in the April *Journal* (p. 125), declaring S. Tupper Bigelow of Toronto the winner.

4249. [———.] "The 'Twelve Best,' " *BSJ* [OS] , 1, No. 4 (October 1946), 457-460. (The Story I Like Best)

A list of the twelve best short stories, plus the seven runners-up, chosen by Doyle in his contest, together with a list of thirty-six stories in the order rated by members of BSI.

4250. "The Solitary Cyclists' Popularity Voting," *BSCL*, No. 5 (1966), 3.

Text in Swedish.

Results of the voting: 1. Houn (58 points). - 2. Spec (34). - 3. Sign (24). - 4. Vall (22). - 5. Twis (20). - 6. Silv (18). - 7. Musg (18). - 8. Soli (17). - 9. RedH (13). - 10. Bruc (11).

REFERENCE WORKS

4251. Bigelow, S. Tupper, ed. *An Irregular Anglo-American Glossary of More or Less Unfamiliar Words, Terms and Phrases in the Sherlock Holmes Saga.* [Toronto: Castalotte & Zamba, 1959.] [47] p. (spiral binding)

"For the earnest Holmesian scholar, this little book will offer little, but for all those outside that erudite and esoteric class who nevertheless worship at the feet of the Master, and their name is legion, it is humbly thought that it might fill a need in helping them to understand what Watson was really talking about when he referred to such things as gasogenes, wideawake and billycock hats, commonplace books, growlers, a penang-lawyer . . . a Cockford or a Bradshaw."

4252. Christ, Jay Finley. "A Complete Concordance?" *SHJ*, 4, No. 3 (Winter 1959), 97-98.

A consideration of some problems that would be encountered in compiling a concordance to the Sacred Writings.

4253. ———. *An Irregular Guide to Sherlock Holmes of Baker Street.* [Introduction by Edgar W. Smith.] New York: Argus Books; Summit, N.J.: The Pamphlet House, 1947. 118 p.

———. ———. A Supplement. [Chicago]: The Fanlight House, 1947. [12] p.

———. ———. Second Supplement. Chicago: The Fanlight House, 1948. [8] p.

An indispensable index to words, ideas, personal names, etc., with page references to the Garden City omnibus edition of *The Complete Sherlock Holmes.*

4254. Cole, Irvin C. "H. & W., Colorists, Textilests Ltd.," *Illustrious Client's Second Case-Book.* Edited by J. N. Williamson. [Indianapolis, Ind.: The Illustrious Clients, 1949.] p. 40-41.

A tally of colors, textiles, and fabrics found in the Canon.

4255. Dakin, D. Martin. *A Sherlock Holmes Commentary.* Newton Abbot: David & Charles, [1972]. 320 p.

———. ———. New York: Drake Publishers, 1972. 320 p.

An encyclopedic treatise on the sixty tales with copious notes on all debatable points; arranged by story and subject. It supplements *The Annotated Sherlock Holmes.*

Reviews: DCC, 8, No. 4-5 (September 1972), 15 (D. Martin Dakin); *SHJ*, 10, No. 4 (Summer 1972), 135-136 (Lord Donegall); *Times Literary Supplement* (April 7, 1972), 391.

4256. Hardwick, Michael and Mollie. *The Sherlock Holmes Companion.* Illustrations by Sidney Paget. London: John Murray, [1962]. ix, 232 p.

———. ———. Garden City, N.Y.: Doubleday & Co., [1963]. ix, 232 p.

Contents: Who's Who. - Plots of the Stories. - A Sampler of Quotations. - Mr. Holmes and Dr. Watson. - Sir Arthur Conan Doyle.

Reviews: Library Journal, 88 (May 1, 1963), 1906 (James Sandoe); *Manchester Guardian Weekly* (September 27, 1962); *MD Medical Newsmagazine,* 7, (October 1963), 193-196; *New York Times Book Review* (May 5, 1963), 16 (Anthony Boucher); *SHJ,* 6, No. 1 (Winter 1962), 29-30 (Lord Donegall); *Times Literary Supplement* (October 26, 1962), 829.

4257. Lauterbach, Charles E. "A Modest Proposal," *BSJ,* 12, No. 1 (March 1962), 34-41.

"Being a small treatise in which a brief plea is made for a more accurate and intelligent method of making references in divers articles concerning the numerous adventures of The Great London Detective at 221B Baker Street, Sherlock Holmes, with his good friend John H. Watson, M.D., and all other Baker Street Regulars and Irregulars." (Subtitle)

As an aid to interested scholars, Dr. Lauterbach has included Professor Christ's key to the story titles and a guide "giving the introductory words of every fiftieth paragraph in *The Complete Sherlock Holmes.*"

4258. ———. "The Word Length of the Adventures of Sherlock Holmes," *BSJ,* 10, No. 2 (April 1960), 101-104.

"This study concerns itself with the word length of the adventures of Sherlock Holmes as recorded in *The Complete Sherlock*

Holmes. The statistics are based on an actual count, made with the assistance of an electric counter."

4259. Morley, Christopher. "A Guide to the Complete Sherlock Holmes," *Sherlock Holmes and Dr. Watson: A Textbook of Friendship.* Edited by Christopher Morley. New York: Harcourt, Brace and Co., [1944]. p. 351-364.
———. "Vejledning til Sherlock Holmes sagaen," [Oversat ₒaf A. D. Henriksen]. *Sherlock Holmes Arbog* II (1966), 62-80.
Plots of the sixty tales in a textbook intended for high-school students.

4260. Page, Andrew. *A Canonical Handbook.* Owings Mills, Md.: [Privately Produced], June 1971. [5]. 28 p.
———. ———. [2nd ed..] Owings Mills, Md.: [Privately Produced], June 1971 [June 1972]. [7], 34, [2] p.
A valuable guide to people, places, seasons, and things in the Sacred Writings; with a preface by Steve Clarkson, an author's introduction, a foreword by D. A. Redmond, and an afterword by John Bennett Shaw.

4261. Park, Orlando, *Sherlock Holmes, Esq., and John H. Watson, M. D.: An Encyclopaedia of Their Affairs.* [Evanston, Ill.]: Northwestern University Press, 1962. viii, 205 p.
An extremely useful guide to the towns, estates, railroad stations, persons, and objects in the Canon. It attributes each reference (Abbas Parva to Zoo) to the proper story. Twenty pages are devoted to Holmes and ten to Watson.
Reviews: Archives of Dermatology, 88 (August 1963), 176-177 (William Blake Gibson), and reprinted in *CPBook,* 2, No. 7-8 (Winter-Spring 1966), 140; *BSP,* No. 31 (January 1968), 6 (B. H.); *SHJ,* 6, No. 2 (Spring 1963), 61 (Lord Donegall).

4262. Petersen, Svend. *A Sherlock Holmes Almanac.* [Washington, D.C.: Privately Produced], 1956. [132] p.
Contents: Almanac. - Index by Persons. - Index by Cases. - Comparison of Authorities. - Dates Unknown.

4263. Pickard, Charles M. "Holmes and Watson in America," *BSJ,* 6, No. 4 (October 1956), 205-207.
An interesting compilation of the counties, towns and cities "named" after the Master and his Boswell.

4264. Rabe, W. T., ed. *1961 S'ian Who's Who and What's What.* Introduction by Russell McLauchlin. With illustrations by Thurston, Minge, Montgomery, Lauritzen and many others, known and unknown. Ferndale, Mich.: Old Soldiers of Baker Street, 1961. xiv, 122 p.

"For the first time anywhere everything about everybody who is anybody S'ian and anything that is even remotely H'ian, however far removed." (Dust jacket)
Reviews: SHJ, 5, No. 4 (Summer 1962), 97-98 (Lord Donegall); *Toronto Evening Telegram* (September 8, 1962), and reprinted in *CPBook,* 1, No. 4 (Spring 1965), 76.

4265. ———, ed. *Who's Who and What's What.* Ferndale, Mich.: Old Soldiers of Baker Street, 1962. xiv, 122 p.
Cover title: 1962 Sherlockian Who's Who & What's What, Including an All-New Who's Where.
Contents: Dedicatory Introduction: To E. W. S. - Special Abbreviations. - Foreword. - I. Plaques *et al.* - II. The Societies. - III. The Followers. - Assorted Appendices.
———. ———. First Supplement: To Part III. Summer 1965. [12] p.
Review: SHJ, 6, No. 2 (Spring 1963), 62 (Lord Donegall).

4266. Redmond, Chris, ed. *The Sherlockian ABC.* Kingston, Ontario: The Remarkable Invention Press, 1967. [29] p.
"For each letter of the alphabet, the book offers a Sherlockian name or phrase and a few pertinent and Conanical comments."

4267. Smith, Edgar W. *Appointment in Baker Street: A Repertory of the Characters, One and All, Who Walked and Talked with Sherlock Holmes.* [New York: The Pamphlet House, 1938.] 75 p.
Limited to 250 numbered copies.
———. ———, *221B: Studies in Sherlock Holmes.* Edited by Vincent Starrett. New York: The Macmillan Co., 1940. p. 142-243.
Contents: Introduction, by Vincent Starrett. - The Master Attends. - The Appointments Are Kept. - The Chase Is Done. - Envoy.
A sentence or two about the host of minor characters—870 in all—who stroll through the pages of the Saga.

4268. ———. *Baker Street and Beyond: A Sherlockian Gazetteer.* With five detailed and illustrated maps from the pen of Julian Wolff. [New York: The Pamphlet House, 1940.] 53 p.
Limited to 300 numbered copies of which the first 100 are in a deluxe binding.
———. ———, *Baker Street and Beyond: Together with Some Trifling Monographs.* Morristown, N.J.: The Baker Street Irregulars, 1957. p. 1-53.
Contents: Foreword, by Christopher Morley. - Introduction, by Vincent Starrett. - Urbi et Orbi. - A Sherlockian Gazetteer. - Envoy.

RESEARCH AND SCHOLARSHIP

4269. Anderson, Poul. "The James Quotient,"

BSJ, 15, No. 3 (September 1965), 154-158.

Three problems are presented as examples of pseudo-scholarship: the Christian name of Sherlock's and Mycroft's father, the Paradol Chamber, and the two James Moriartys.

4270. Bigelow, S. Tupper. " 'Good Old Index!' " *SHJ*, 7, No. 1 (Winter 1964), 20-21.

A discussion of the card index, consisting of some 7,000 cards, that this eminent Canadian Sherlockian and collector prepared on the writings about the Writings. The index must be second only to the Master's!

4271. ———. "A Fertile Field," *SOS*, 2, No. 5-6 (June-August 1968), 5-7.

More about Sherlockian scholarship and the author's card-index file, which numbers over 100,000 entires. (The file is now housed and maintained in the Toronto Central Library.)

4272. Brend, Gavin. "The Key to the Story Titles," *SHJ*, 1, No. 2 (September 1952), 6.

A poetic thanks to Dr. Christ "for giving us this helpful list."

4273. Darwin, Bernard. "The Great Holmes Joke," *John O'London's Weekly*, 63 (February 19, 1954), 169.

"A plea for a return to the fundamentals: less speculation on dates and the location of wounds, and more devotion to the 'atmosphere' of the Tales as tales—and especially the earlier ones." (Edgar W. Smith)

4274. ———. "Sherlockiana: The Faith of a Fundamentalist," *Every Idle Dream*. With illustrations by Elinor Darwin. London: Collins, 1948. p. 87-96.

———. ———, *Seventeen Steps to 221B*. [Edited by] James Edward Holroyd. London: George Allen & Unwin Ltd., [1967]. p. 74-81.

An explanation of the author's attachment to Sherlock Holmes and his reasons for resisting the validity of most of the writings on the Sacred Writings.

4275. Dettman, Bruce. "Junior Sherlockiana: Is It Doomed?" *VH*, 2, No. 3 (September 1968), 8-9.

A criticism of the high percentage of inferior material published in junior periodicals, with some sound suggestions for bringing about an improvement.

4276. Dickensheet, Dean. ["Letter"], *BSP*, No. 35 (May 1968), 4-5.

A critical commentary on Chris Redmond's letter (item 4289) regarding the current status of Sherlockian scholarship.

4277. [Donegall, Lord.] "Canonical Curiosa," *SHJ*, 6, No. 2 (Spring 1963), 37-38.

Most of this editorial is devoted to the reference problem John Murray created when the pagination was changed in the 11th impression (1962) of *The Complete Sherlock Holmes Long Stories*.

4278. ———. " 'Overture . . . and Beginners!' " *The New Strand*, 1, No. 1 (December 1961), 37-40. (Baker Street and Beyond, No. 1)

———. ———, *SHJ*, 5, No. 3 (Winter 1961), 65-66. (Editorial)

An introduction for the potential Holmesian researcher.

4279. Foss, T. F. " 'Nothing Could Be More Inexplicable,' " *BSJ*, 19, No. 4 (December 1969), 195.

"The pundit's pen widely it roams / O'er the exploits of Watson and Holmes / In prodigious profusion: / Yet it causes confusion / To study those scholarly tomes."

4280. Gray, Dorothy. "Frustration," *Illustrious Client's Case-Book*. Edited by J. N. Williamson and H. B. Williams. [Indianapolis, Ind.: The Illustrious Clients, 1948.] p. 67.

"Originality about / The Master of Whodunit / Seems hopeless, for no matter what / You want to write, THEY'VE DONE IT!"

4281. Hiebert, Gareth. "Bringing Holmes into the Classroom: St. Olaf to Pioneer in Teaching of the Detective Story," *St. Paul Pioneer Press, Living and Lesiure Section* (December 14, 1969), 1.

An announcement of a new course in detective fiction to be taught by Randolph J. Cox, Reference Librarian at St. Olaf College. The article is illustrated with a photograph of Mr. Cox in his finest Sherlockian attire—and he plans to dress the same while teaching the class!

4282. H[ogan], J[ohn] C. "Who's Who in Crime," *DCC*, 2, No. 4 (March 1966), 2-3.

The author describes his system for maintaining an index card file of personal names, places, and dates of criminal activities. Includes a reproduction of a sample card.

4283. Honce, Charles. "Heresy on the Sherlock Holmes Front," *To Talk of Many Things*. Mount Vernon, N.Y.: Imprinted by S. A. Jacobs at his Golden Eagle Press, 1950. p. 21-24.

———. ———, *Illustrious Client's Third Case-Book*. Edited by J. N. Williamson and H. B. Williams. [Indianapolis, Ind.: The Illustrious Clients, 1953.] p. 20-26.

An appeal for less fantasy and more personal, historical, and bibliographical material. Mr. Honce quotes a story by Alvin Steinkopf about Holmes and *The Strand*

Other Subjects

Magazine (item 4326) as an example of writing that fits his specifications.

4284. Jenkins, William D. "Dendroscandology (Go-Climb-a-Tree Department)," *BSJ*, 18, No. 1 (March 1968), 44-45.

A refutation of Dr. Ober's ridiculous and unwarranted comments (item 2365) concerning the "cult of Sherlockolatry" and the "nihilipilification" of Doyle by "such sects in this cult as 'The Baker Street Irregulars.' "

4285. Osborn, Steven. "Thoughts on Juniorism," *BSP*, No. 40 (October 1968), 4-5.

An important and legitimate distinction is made between "junior" and "senior" Sherlockian scholarship.

4286. Peck, Andrew. "In Defense of Juniorism," *BSP*, No. 39 (September 1968), 3.

An affirmation of the contribution that young Sherlockians can make to the study of the Canonical tales.

4287. Redmond, Chris. "Editorial," *BSP*, No. 7 (January 1966), 1-2.
————. "Back to the Canon" (A Guest Editorial), *BSJ*, 16, No. 4 (December 1966), 195-196. (The Editor's Gas-Lamp)

"I am not advocating the Sherlockian equivalent of the 'Back to the Bible Movement.' I am not—perish the thought!—condemning outside scholarship. I am simply objecting to the perversion of the great name of Sherlockian scholarship for things which transparently are not."

4288. ————, ed. *An Introduction to Sherlock Holmes.* Kingston, Ontario: The Baker Street Pageboys, 1968. [9] p.

"With information about Sherlockian activities and the Constitution of the Baker Street Pageboys." (Subtitle)

4289. ————. ["Letter"], *SOS*, 2, No. 3 (February 1968), 9-10.
————. ————, *BSP*, No. 33 (March 1968), 2-3.

A criticism of present-day Sherlockian scholarship, with suggestions for "restoring" it to its former high standards.

4290. ————. "*The Pooh Perplex:* Review," *BSP*, No. 17 (November 1966), 4-5.

The author discusses two principal kinds of scholarship—the laudatory and the analytical—and recommends Frederick C. Crew's book for its insights into Sherlockian scholarship.

4291. ————. "Studies in the Philosophy of Sherlock Holmes," *BSP*, No. 47 (May 1969), 1-5.

A critical reexamination and evaluation of the scholarship.

4292. Rosenberger, Edgar S. "An Irregular's Life" (With Apologies to Gilbert and Sullivan), *BSJ Christmas Annual*, No. 1 (1956), 19-20.

"An Irregular's life is a bedlam of strife / As he tries, in a manner of speaking, / To conduct many bouts, to resolve many doubts, / And discover the truth he is seeking."

4293. [Smith, Edgar W.] "A Perspective on Scholarship," *BSJ*, 3, No. 1 (January 1953), 3-4. (The Editor's Gas-Lamp)

An admonition to those who "resort to the facetious or the half-baked" in writing about the Writings.

4294. Tomashefsky, Steve. "Response to Mr. Dickensheet," *BSP*, No. 37 (July 1968), 2-3.

A rejoinder to Dean Dickensheet's response to the letter by Chris Redmond, with a criticism of the junior societies.

4295. Toronto Central Library. *A Weekend with Sherlock, December 4 & 5, 1971.* Presented by the Metropolitan Toronto Library Board.

Program for the first conference ever held on the Sacred Writings. The speakers and panel leaders were Ronald De Waal, Cameron Hollyer, Jay Macpherson, David Skene Melvin, Derrick Murdoch, Donald Redmond, Rupert Schieder, and John Bennett Shaw.

SCIENCE FICTION

4296. Boucher, Anthony. "Sherlock Holmes and Science Fiction," *BSJ*, 10, No. 3 (July 1960), 143-146.
————. ————, *New Frontiers*, 1, No. 3 (August 1960), 10-14.
————. ————, *The Science-Fictional Sherlock Holmes.* Denver: The Council of Four, 1960. p. 9-13.

Watson narrated cases with sober solutions and only referred to those with science-fictional situations, except for Cree. The literary agent also published the five Professor Challenger tales and two other s-f stories.

4297. Dickensheet, Dean W. "Strange and Fantastic Business," *Shangri-L'Affairs* [Los Angeles], No. 49 (February-March 1960), 7-9.

"Prolegomenon to a study of the science fiction and fantasy adventures of Sherlock Holmes." (Subtitle)

4298. Dickson, Gordon R. "Half a Hoka —Poul Anderson: An Appreciation," *17th World Science Fiction Convention.* Program booklet.
————. ————, *The Science-Fictional Sherlock Holmes.* Denver: The Council of Four, 1960. p. 32-34.

A giant Holmes and Watson examine the

normal size s-f author Poul Anderson and discuss his qualifications and talents.

SCOTLAND YARD

4299. Andrew, Clifton R. "That Scotland Yarder, Gregson—What a Help (?) He Was," *Illustrious Client's Second Case-Book.* Edited by J. N. Williamson. [Indianapolis, Ind.: The Illustrious Clients, 1949.] p. 35-39.

"Opinions and theories re what effect, if any, the participation of Gregson, *et al* of the Yard had upon the career of Holmes and, conversely, the careers of two or three Scotland Yarders."

4300. "The Black Museum at Scotland Yard,' *BSJ*, 16, No. 2 (June 1966), 81. illus.

Quotations concerning the Yard's museum of crime.

4301. Blakeney, T. S. "Holmes and Scotland Yard," *Sherlock Holmes: Fact or Fiction?* London: John Murray, [1932]. p. 24-35.

"Sherlock Holmes is nothing if not a contrast to Scotland Yard. His reputation, indeed, has largely been built up by the regularity of his successes over the official force, successes due to his entirely different attitude towards methods adopted in their solution."

4302. Brend, Gavin. ["The Man from the Yard"], *BSJ*, 2, No. 2 (April 1952), 72. (Two Verses)

———. ———, *SHJ*, 1, No. 1 (May 1952), 14. (Baker Street Doggerel, No. 1)

"A life of ease I am much afraid / Was denied to Inspector G. Lestrade."

4303. Carr, John Dickson. "Holmes Wouldn't Recognize It," *The New York Times Magazine* (February 21, 1954), 10, 35-37.

"Scotland Yard, so long derided in fiction and fact, today basks in the admiration of whodunit cultists and the public, too." (Subtitle)

4304. Dorian, N. Currier. " 'A Bad Lot,' " *BSJ*, 6, No. 1 (January 1956), 51-57.

"The prevalent idea that Holmes had no use for Scotland Yard or any of the professional forces is not in keeping with the facts, and a misunderstanding of the Master's attitude toward Lestrade, who was the object of the great majority of all his sarcasms and criticisms, has been a large contributor to the growth of this erroneous idea."

4305. " 'Dupin and Sherlock Holmes: The New Detective,' " (from a correspondent). *The Times* (May 18, 1921), 5.

Innovations that have taken place in British detective work, including the introduction of the motor-vehicle, are briefly noted. (A commentary about the article

appears on p. 8 of James Montgomery's *Christmas Annual* for 1953.)

4306. Frisbie, Owen P. "Sonnet: Sherlock Holmes to Stanley Hopkins," *BSJ* [OS], 3, No. 2 (April 1948), 232.

"A full fifteenth of all recorded cases / You handled at the start, then called on me / To ask advice."

4307. Holstein, L. S. "Inspector G. Lestrade," *BSJ*, 8, No. 2 (April 1958), 78-84.

"Of all characters, excepting perhaps Watson and Mrs. Hudson, none seems to have had a more intimate or longer-lasting contact with Holmes than Inspector G. Lestrade of Scotland Yard. He was associated with Holmes in more of the recorded cases than any other member of the Metropolitan Police."

4308. Kennedy, Bruce. "A Concise Concordance of Abuse in the Canon," *VH*, 4, No. 1 (January 1970), 4-8.

A list of forty-nine quotations in which the Master is critical of the official police force.

4309. Kimball, Elliot. "Origin and Evolution of G. Lestrade," *SHJ*, 6, No. 1 (Winter 1962), 4-5; 6, No. 2 (Spring 1963), 43-45.

Contents: 1. Onomatological Considerations. - 2. A Matter of Mancinism.

4310. Montgomery, James. "A Visit to Scotland Yard," *BSJ* [OS], 1, No. 3 (July 1946), 323-325.

———. "The Adventure of the Irene Adler Recording," *Songs of Baker Street.* Read and sung by James Montgomery. Morristown, N.J.: The Baker Street Irregulars, 1959. Side 1, band 1, 4.

Inspired by his visit to the Museum of Crime where he sees mementos of Sherlock Holmes, the author wrote an ode entitled "An Irregular Song" (item 4459).

4311. Pratt, Fletcher. "Sherlock Holmes vs. Arsène Lupin," *The American Mercury,* 37 (January 1936), 86-93.

Differences are noted between plodding Scotland Yard and the brilliant French Sûreté.

4312. Pulling, Christopher. "Amateurs of Crime: Scotland Yard Angle on Fictional Detectives," *The Times* (November 10, 1956), 7.

———. ———, Reprinted in part in *BSJ*, 7, No. 2 (April 1957), 117-118. (From the Editor's Commonplace Book)

The author, who served for thirty-five years on the Senior Headquarters Staff of New Scotland Yard, defends Gregson and Lestrade against the impertinences of Holmes.

4313. ———. "Sherlock Holmes and Scotland

Yard," *The Police College Magazine,* 2, No. 4 (March 1953), 291-294.

————. ————, *SHJ,* 1, No. 3 (June 1953), 12-17.

Extracts from a paper read to the Sherlock Holmes Society on September 23, 1952.

4314. ————. ————, *SHJ,* 8, No. 2 (Spring 1967), 39-43.

In his second published talk to the Society on October 6, 1966, Mr. Pulling outlines the main points of contention between Holmes and the Yard and then tells about the various repercussions that resulted from his original talk.

4315. Redmond, D. A. "The Yard, Volume After Volume of Its Story," *SHJ,* 8, No. 1 (Winter 1966), 19-20.

A commentary on the books that have been written about Scotland Yard.

4316. Solovay, Jacob C. "Holmes Reflects on Two Colleagues," *BSJ,* 9, No. 3 (July 1959), 171.

"Gregson and Lestrade—oh, what a handsome pair!"

4317. Starrett, Vincent. "Before Sherlock Holmes," *BSJ* [OS], 2, No. 1 (January 1947), 5-11.

A capsule history of Scotland Yard up to the time of Holmes.

4318. Williamson, J. N. "In Defense of Scotland Yard," A communication from Inspector Athelney Jones. Reported by J. N. Williamson. *Illustrious Client's Case-Book.* Edited by J. N. Williamson and H. B. Williams. [Indianapolis, Ind.: The Illustrious Clients, 1948.] p. 28-29.

"We are not and never have been a group of idiots, despite what Mr. High-and-Mighty may have said."

THE STRAND MAGAZINE

4319. [Hastings, MacDonald.] "Conan Doyle and His Creator Hated Sherlock Holmes," *John O'London's Weekly,* 58 (February 4, 1949), 57-58.

"Conan Doyle and *The Strand Magazine* are associated with each other as inseparably as Diogenes with his tub or D'Artagnan with his sword."

4320. Hertzberg, A. Francis. "Holmes, Reichenbach and 'The Strand,'" *SHJ,* 8, No. 2 (Spring 1967), 46-49; 8, No. 3 (Winter 1967), 82-86.

Contents: 1. January 1891-December 1893. - 2. January-June 1894, Including Three Most Tentative Identifications.

"Being the striking results of some laborious research in early issues of *The Strand Magazine.*" (Subtitle)

4321. ————. "The Strand," The Mystery Reader's Newsletter, 4, No. 5 (July-August 1971), 23-24. illus.

4322. Honce, Charles. "The Man Who Launched Sherlock Holmes," *Mark Twain's Associated Press Speech and Other News Stories.* New York: Privately Printed, 1940. p. 58-59.

A tribute, dated February 2, 1935, to Greenhough Smith, the *Strand's* first editor.

4323. Morley, Christopher. "Notes on Baker Street," *The Saturday Review of Literature,* 19, No. 14 (January 28, 1939), 12-13.

Illuminating sidelights, with appropriate and grateful tribute to Greenhough Smith.

4324. Pound, Reginald. *The Strand Magazine, 1891-1950.* London: Heinemann, 1966. 200 p. illus.

————. *Mirror of the Century: The Strand Magazine, 1891-1950.* South Brunswick, N.J.: A. S. Barnes, 1967. 200 p. illus.

A work replete with references to Doyle and Holmes, including three chapters entitled "Enter Sherlock Holmes," "Conan Doyle and the Fairies," and "Farewell to Sherlock Holmes."

Extracts from chap. 5 reprinted with title: "Birth of Sherlock Holmes," *The Times* (January 14, 1966), 11; *The Third Degree* [Mystery Writers of America], 22, No. 1 (January 1966), 14-15.

4325. "Sherlock of the 'Strand,'" [by] Old Fag. *John O'London's Weekly,* 43 (June 21, 1940), 341.

Old enthusiasms renewed by a rediscovery of the original volumes with the complete Paget illustrations.

4326. Steinkopf, Alvin. [*"The Strand Magazine"*], *To Talk of Many Things,* by Charles Honce. Mount Vernon, N.Y.: Imprinted by S. A. Jacobs at his Golden Eagle Press, 1950. p. 22-24.

————. ————, *Illustrious Client's Third Case-Book.* Edited by J. N. Williamson and H. B. Williams. [Indianapolis, Ind.: The Illustrious Clients, 1953.] p. 22-26.

"Nearly every crime that Sherlock Holmes ever solved was solved first in *The Strand Magazine.* For a dozen years and more the famous detective invented by Sir Arthur Conan Doyle and the pale blue monthly seemed to merge their personalities. Holmes and *The Strand* were one."

THE SUPERNATURAL

See also *Suss* (item 2814) and *Bram Stoker* (items 4036-4039)

4327. Osborn, Steven R. "Mr. Sherlock Holmes and the Devil," *BSJ,* 18, No. 4 (December 1968), 212-213.

A brief discussion of the supernatural in the Sacred Writings.

TEXTUAL CRITICISM

4328. Austin, Bliss. "Two Bibliographical Footnotes. II," *BSJ*, 4, No. 1 (January 1954), 43.

Further light upon some of the foreign language quotations discussed by Morris Rosenblum (item 4338).

4329. Blake, S. F. " 'The Game Is Afoot,' " *BSJ*, 9, No. 4 (October 1959), 205-207.

The "game" (Abbe) must be a carnivorous beast—murderous and afoot. The tiger not only provides Watson's favorite animal simile or metaphor, but is also always a symbol of vigor, audacity, or violence.

4330. Buchholtz, Ruth. "Seventy-Seven Canonical Sevens," *BSJ*, 8, No. 1 (January 1968), 41-44.

An interesting compilation of seventy-seven sevens that appear in the tales (e.g., "SEVEN years older than Sherlock Holmes is his brother Mycroft. SEVEN percent solution of cocaine Holmes used.").

4331. Byrnes, Garrett D. "The Adventure of the Four Measuring-Sticks," *BSJ*, 7, No. 1 (January 1957), 5-12.

A preliminary study to determine the readability of the Sacred Writings.

4332. "An Elementary Attribution," *The Times* (May 12, 1953), 7.
———, *CPBook*, 2, No. 5-6 (Summer-Fall 1965), 90.
———, *BSP*, No. 29 (November 1967), 1.
On the cherished misquotation, "Elementary, my dear Watson."

4333. Helling, Cornelis. "About Some Very Effective Introductory Sentences in the Saga," *BSJ*, 13, No. 4 (December 1963), 236-237.

4334. Hill, Pope R. "The Substructure Theory," *BSJ*, 4, No. 1 (January 1954), 52-53.

"Sir Arthur Conan Doyle did not publish the Sherlock Holmes stories as originally conceived and written. He wrote each story twice, and published his second version, which is not the real story."

4335. Nelson, James. "Beginning Revisions of the Sacred Writings," *BSJ*, 20, No. 3 (September 1970), 166-167.

An absurd suggestion that the Canon be revised and simplified. (Some of the stories already have been—for children!)

4336. Parker, Robert G. "Out!—Damned Preposition," *VH*, 1, No. 1 (January 1967), 6-8.

A search of the Canon reveals 13-½ sentences ending with the preposition "with."

4337. Robinson, Ernest F. "Comparative Zoology of Baker Street," *BSJ* [OS], 2, No. 4 (October 1947), 401-408.

A study of the zoological similes used in describing some of the characters.

4338. Rosenblum, Morris. "Foreign Language Quotations in the Canon," *BSJ* [OS], 3, No. 4 (October 1948), 425-434.

A scholarly discussion and catalog of the foreign language quotations and the works in which they first appeared.

4339. ———. "The Greek Interprets Sherlock Holmes," *BSJ*, 4, No. 4 (October 1954), 211-213.

The author notes a few passages that have been translated into classical Greek.

4340. ———. "Hafiz and Horace, Huxtable and Holmes," *BSJ* [OS], 1, No. 3 (July 1946), 261-269.

"Dr. Thorneycroft Huxtable" discusses Watson's use of a quotation from Horace at the end of Stud.

4341. ———. "Reflections on 'a Hebrew Rabbi,' " *BSJ*, 20, No. 1 (March 1970), 38.

In Scan, Watson uses the pleonasm "Hebrew rabbi." There are many precedents for this solecism, however, and "the fault of style, if any, is venial."

4342. ———. "Some Latin Byways in the Canon," *BSJ* [OS], 3, No. 1 (January 1948), 15-20.

"Reminders of the fact that Watson and Holmes received their education at a time when Latin was the chief subject in the curriculum are found in many places in the Sacred Writings."

4343. Smith, Edgar W. "Notes on the Collation," *The Adventures of Sherlock Holmes*. New York: The Limited Editions Club, 1950. Vol. 1, p. xix-xxiii.
———. ———, ———. New York: The Heritage Press, [1952]. Vol. 1, p. xix-xxiii.
———. ———, *Introducing Mr. Sherlock Holmes*. Edited by Edgar W. Smith. Morristown, N.J.: The Baker Street Irregulars, 1959. [unpaged]

"Commentary on the textual arrangement and emendations distinguishing this definitive edition of the tales."

4344. [———.] "On the Canonical Titlings," *BSJ*, 1, No. 2 (April 1951), 41-42. (The Editor's Gas-Lamp)

"By his titles alone would we know him. For here is Watson at his best—not only a great artist, a great employer of words, a faithful *raconteur*, but a great imaginer as well."

4345. [————.] "The Sudden Death of the Cardinal Numbers," *BSJ*, 9, No. 2 (April 1959), 67-68. (The Editor's Gas-Lamp)

"The high incidence of numbers in the titling of the Canon leads one to speculate upon the confusion that might prevail in this area . . . if the practice were to spread."

4346. ————. "Bibliographical Notes," *BSJ*, 10, No. 1 (January 1960), 39-41; 10, No. 2 (April 1960), 97-99.

A discussion of textual variants in the Canon.

4347. ————. ————, *BSJ*, 10, No. 4 (October 1960), 227-230.

Further commentary on the Canonical titles.

4348. Vaill, C. B. H. "Quick, Watson, the Needle!" *BSJ* [OS], 1, No. 4 (October 1946), 445-448.

This phrase "is a cheap and vulgar attempt at characterization which has no basis in fact." Abundant evidence exists to show that Holmes was not addicted to the use of the word "quick"; consequently he never could have uttered such a revolting bleat.

TRANSPORTATION

4349. Potter, Henry C. "Reflections on Canonical Vehicles and Something of the Horse," *BSJ*, 21, No. 4 (December 1971), 200-206.

Winner of the 14th annual Morley-Montgomery Memorial Award for the best contribution to *BSJ* in 1971.

An affectionate survey of the horsedrawn conveyances appearing in the Saga, the horses and the men who drove them, by an author who is well acquainted with such vehicles. A corollary deduction: while Holmes knew his way about this fascinating, bygone world, very probably Watson was the equiphobe.

4350. Springer, Harry W., with David A. Wallace. "The Rôle of Public Transportation in the Solution of Capital Crime," *BSJ*, 21, No. 1 (March 1971), 10-13.

An examination of Silv, Glor, Soli, and Bruc to show how public transportation was of inestimable help in solving these cases.

Hansom Cabs

4351. Cameron, Mary S. "Joseph Aloysius Hansom and His 'Patent Safety Cab,' " *BSG*, 1, No. 4 (April 1962), 51-54.

A brief history of the Hansom cab up to Sherlock Holmes's day.

4352. Dorian, N. Currier. "The Game Is Afoot," *BSJ*, 3, No. 1 (January 1953), 18-19.

"Not wot you'd call a sweet business, / Drivin' this 'ansom cab."

4353. Iraldi, James C. "The Victorian Gondola," *BSJ*, 1, No. 3 (July 1951), 99-103.

"Of all the types of vehicles plying for hire in London streets at the time Sherlock Holmes and Dr. Watson made their debut upon the scene, the most popular was undoubtedly the dashing and picturesque hansom cab."

Railways

4354. Clapp, Roger T. "The Curious Problem of the Railway Timetables," *The Second Cab*. Edited by James Keddie. [Boston: The Speckled Band, 1947.] p. 34-38.

"With one possible exception, *no train in fact left the station stated for the specified destination at or (in most cases) anywhere near the time recorded in any of the Writings.*" Includes an annotated table of train times mentioned in the Canon.

4355. Cutter, Robert A. "The Underground," *Illustrious Client's Second Case-Book*. Edited by J. N. Williamson. [Indianapolis, Ind.: The Illustrious Clients, 1949.] p. 83-87.

A history of the Metropolitan Railway (the Underground) as a background to the four cases in which it is mentioned.

4356. Greenwood, E. P. "Some Random Thoughts on Railway Journeys by Holmes and Watson," *SHJ*, 1, No. 3 (June 1953), 19-21.

4357. Rannie, J. Alan. "The Railway Journeys of Mr. Sherlock Holmes," *The Railway Magazine* [London], 76 (May 1935), 316-321.

Examples of the good use to which the Master put his railway lore. "Sherlock Holmes was indeed more than a casual traveller; he had all the makings of a railwayist."

4358. Redmond, Derek. "Sherlock Holmes' Trains," *BSP*, No. 1 (July 1965), 2.

————. ————, *BSP Christmas Annual*, No. 1 (1966), 13.

A brief discussion of the trains that were in use during Holmes's career.

4359. Robertshaw, Wilfrid. "Bradshaw: The Story of a Time Table," *The Dalesman*, 23, No. 2 (May 1961), 97-98.

————. ————, *BSJ*, 12, No. 2 (June 1962), 102-105.

The history of this famous and once indispensable timetable established by George Bradshaw in 1839.

4360. Robertson, A. M. " 'Railway Cases Were Seldom Trivial,' " *Railway World*, 26 (June 1965), 227-228.

An informative article on the train journeys of Holmes and Watson.

4361. Rosenberger, Edgar S.. "On the Railway Journeys of Sherlock Holmes," *BSJ* [OS], 2, No. 2 (April 1947), 175-179.

"The railways of Victorian England are as much a part of the Sherlock Holmes saga as hansom cabs, gaslights, and the telegraph."

4362. Walsh, B. D. J. "Sherlock Holmes and Railways," *SHJ*, 9, No. 2 (Summer 1969), 40-48.

The most detailed study yet published on the railway journeys chronicled in the Sacred Writings.

Ships

4363. Clarke, Richard W. "On the Nomenclature of Watson's Ships," *BSJ* [OS], 1, No. 2 (April 1946), 119-121.
———. ———, *The Best of the Pips.* Westchester County, N.Y.: The Five Orange Pips, 1955. p. 6-9.

The author traces the names given by Watson to the sailing and steamships, and establishes the identity of the second *Irs.* Watson as the former Alicia Cutter, the name being derived from the cutter *Alicia* in Thor.

4364. Cumings, Thayer, "A Lloyd's Register for Baker Street Irregulars," *BSJ*, 2, No. 3 (July 1952), 178-179.

A tabulation of the ships that sailed the Canonical seas; with their types, masters, home ports, distinguishing marks, source, and a word about their fame.

4365. Fay, Arthur D. "The Ships in the Canon," *BSJ*, 17, No. 1 (March 1967), 3-8.

A chronological listing and discussion of the ships and shipping lines.

4366. Rosenberger, Edgar S. "Seven Sea Chanteys," *BSJ*, 5, No. 3 (July 1955), 148.

"Black Peter Carey, full of drink, / Got in a nasty brawl. / His adversary, in a wink, / Harpooned him to the wall."

4367. Walbridge, Earle F. "At Sea with Sherlock Holmes," *BSJ* [OS], 1, No. 2 (April 1946), 149-151.

"Holmes took to the ocean as naturally as a duck to water, if one may coin a phrase, and Watson's literary style, consciously or otherwise, also assumed a nautical flavor."

4368. Weeks, A. L. "Ships That Pass in the Canon," *BSJ*, 10, No. 1 (January 1960), 49-50.

"Though never seen on sea or land, / These ships were moored on London's Strand."

UNTOLD TALES AND DR. WATSON'S TIN DISPATCH-BOX

4369. Christ, Jay Finley. *The Old Tin Box.* [Chicago: Privately Produced, 1946.] [4] p.
———. ———, *BSJ* [OS], 2, No. 3 (July 1947), 262.
———. ———, *The Tin Dispatch-Box.* Compiled by Chris Redmond. Second edition. Lawrence, Kansas: [Privately Produced], 1965. p. ii.

"In the vaults of Cox was an old tin box / With Watson's name on its lid. / What wouldn't we pay for that box today / And the secret notes there hid?"

4370. Clarkson, P. Stephen. "The Case of the Disappearing Dispatch-Box," *BSJ*, 20, No. 4 (December 1970), 200-203.

This is an attempt to link Holmes's will and probate to the tin box kept under his bed (Musg) and the dispatch-box in the vaults of Cox's Bank at Charing Cross (Gold). The two boxes were, in reality, the same; and Watson spirited Holmes's tin box out of 221B from under the watchful eyes of Mrs. Hudson by the expedient of painting "John H. Watson, M.D., Late Indian Army" on the lid.

4371. Codman, Charles R. *The Unrecorded Adventures of Sherlock Holmes in Their Relation to the Mental Processes of Dr. John H. Watson, Late of the Army Medical Dept.* [Boston: Privately Printed, 1932.] [12] p.

A short monograph on the significance of some of the untold tales, with an amusingly whimsical bibliography.

4372. Daniels, Thomas L. "The Battered Tin Dispatch Box," *Exploring Sherlock Holmes.* Edited by E. W. McDiarmid & Theodore C. Blegen. La Crosse: Sumac Press, 1957. p. 88-96.

A report on the author's search for the missing adventures.

4373. Foster, Alan H. "On the Location of Dr. John H. Watson's Tin Dispatch-Box," *BSJ*, 16, No. 3 (September 1966), 138-146.

Winner of the 9th annual Morley-Montgomery Memorial Award for the best contribution to *BSJ* in 1966.

The dispatch-box was never in the vaults of Cox and Co. but in the Oxford Street Branch of the Capital and Counties Bank, the agents for Holmes, Watson, and Doyle. The unpublished cases are in the literary agent's rather than in Watson's handwriting because of the precaution Sir Arthur took in recopying them. "Armed with this knowledge, perhaps those having the right of access to the vaults at 125 Oxford Street will make public its contents so that the world might experience a combined 'Age of Enlightenment' and 'Age of Reason' once again."

4374. Hall, Trevor H. "The Problem of the Unpublished Cases," *The Late Mr. Sherlock Holmes & Other Literary Studies.* London:

Gerald Duckworth & Co., [1971]. Chap. 6, p. 86-107.

The author discusses twelve of the untold tales as reconstructed in *The Exploits*, theorizes that the dispatch-box was destroyed by Watson's *fifth* wife, and reconstructs the Isadora Persano case.

4375. Hartman, Harry. "Holmes Revisited (or The Saga of the Unrecorded Cycle)," *BSG*, 1, No. 1 (1961), 14-16.

———. ———, *The Holy Quire.* [Culver City, Calif.: Luther Norris, December 1970.] p. 17-19.

The untold adventures are described, with a deciphering of the titles as mentioned by Watson, and the reason why the stories were never released.

4376. McLauchlin, Russell. "Reverie at Cox and Co., Charing Cross," *BSJ* [OS], 2, No. 2 (April 1957), 136-137.

A verse in five stanzas on the unrecorded cases.

4377. Narunsky, Harry. "Concerning the Whereabouts of the Box at Cox," *BSJ*, 20, No. 4 (December 1970), 204-205.

Watson entrusted his tin dispatch-box to Sir Winston Churchill, and it still resides among the Churchill papers.

4378. Redmond, Chris, comp. *The Tin Dispatch-Box: A Compendium of the Unpublished Cases of Mr. Sherlock Holmes.* Second edition. Lawrence, Kansas: [Privately Produced], 1965. iv, 25 p. illus.

Limited to 100 numbered copies.

An invaluable reference work listing and dating 111 cases, with brief comments and a five-letter abbreviation for each case.

Reviews: BSP, No. 6 (December 1965), 4 (Michael Walsh); *SHJ*, 7, No. 3 (Winter 1965), 92 (Lord Donegall).

4379. Starrett, Vincent. "The Untold Tales of Dr. Watson," *The Private Life of Sherlock Holmes.* New York: The Macmillan Co., 1933. p. 94-102.

———. ———, ———. Revised and enlarged. The University of Chicago Press, [1960]. p. 87-92.

"Fragments of mystery, they exist complete in memory—or in anticipation—like tales read long ago and years forgotten; their outlines blur and waver just beyond the edge of thought. It is part of Watson's magic that some of these lost adventures, never set down in print, seem to inhabit the chambers of the mind as memorably as those sixty others that make up the saga."

4380. Uhlin, Åke. "Dr. Watsons nötta blecklåda," *Röster i Radio* [Stockholm], No. 36 (1966).

———. ———, *BSCL*, No. 6 (1968), 23-28.

An article on the tin dispatch-box cases.

4381. Waters, Frank. "Upon the Probable Number of Cases of Mr. Sherlock Holmes," *BSJ*, 3, No. 1 (January 1953), 25-28.

———. ———, *The Best of the Pips.* Westchester County, N.Y.: The Five Orange Pips, 1955. p. 21-24.

An examination of the Canon reveals that he handled some 1,700 cases!

Atkinson Brothers

4382. Redmond, D. A. "Some Notes on the Ceylon Problem," *SHJ*, 7, No. 1 (Winter 1964), 16-18.

A report on the author's research while in Ceylon concerning "the singular tragedy of the Atkinson brothers at Trincomalee" (Scan).

The Camberwell Poisoning Case

4383. Drake, Stillman. "The Camberwell Poisoning Case," *West by One and by One.* San Francisco: Privately Printed, 1965. p. 88-101.

A brilliant reconstruction identifying the victim, murderer, and motive.

French Government

4384. Clark, Edward F. "Study of an Untold Tale," *BSJ*, 13, No. 4 (December 1963), 217-228.

Winner of the 6th annual Morley-Montgomery Memorial Award for the best contribution to *BSJ* in 1963.

"Holmes recovered the stolen art treasure in the south of France from Moriarty's international ring on or about *February 15* . . . and by March 30 had presented his evidence of the thieves' identity to the French authorities in so convincing a manner that the official forces were closing in. With the evidence now at his disposal, Holmes returned to London (pursued by Moriarty or his agents), informed the British authorities, and the stage was set for the tragedy of Meiringen."

Friesland

4385. Jones, Kelvin. "The Professor and the Pterodactyl: An Untold Tale of Dr. Watson," *SHJ*, 8, No. 1 (Winter 1966), 14-16.

An identical theory to the one set forth by Mr. Kierman; namely, that "the shocking affair of the Dutch steamship *Friesland*" (Norw) was the same occasion as that on which Professor Challenger's pterodactyl was lost.

4386. Kierman, Ray. "A Shocking Affair," *BSJ*, 2, No. 2 (April 1952), 103-107.

———. " 'It Is a Curious Little Problem,' " *BSJ Christmas Annual*, No. 2 (1957), 26-30.

The "shocking affair" of this Dutch ship, when Holmes and Watson nearly lost their lives, was the occasion of the pterodactyl brought to England by Professor Challenger from *The Lost World*, being sighted off Start Point by people aboard the *Friesland*. Holmes had chartered the vessel to pursue the creature in its attempt to return to South America.

John Vincent Harden

4387. Jenkins, William D. "A Peculiar Persecution," *BSJ*, 14, No. 1 (March 1964), 45-53.

John Vincent Harden (also sic), the well-known tobacco millionaire whose "peculiar persecution" was occupying Holmes at the time he took up the case of Miss Violet Smith (Soli), is identified as the cousin of the notorious Western outlaw, John Wesley Hardin. Watson occupied the better part of 1893 (the "missing year") in the U.S. editing and arranging for the publication of Wes Hardin's autobiography—omitting, of course, all references to cousin Jack.

Huret

4388. Fleischauer, William E. "Who Was Huret?" *BSJ*, 21, No. 3 (September 1971), 163-168.

Identifies the unpublished case ". . . the tracking and arrest of Huret, the Boulevard assassin" (Gold) as "The Empty House" and Huret as Col. Moran. Huret's victim was President Sadi-Carnot of France. Morgan was captured but Carnot was later killed by Moran's agent. Watson omits the Carnot incident from Empt, replacing it with the fictitious, and impossible, conversation about the Great Hiatus.

Matilda Briggs

4389. Nill, John M. "The Giant Rat of Sumatra," *West by One and by One*. San Francisco: Privately Printed, 1965. p. 34-41.

A reconstruction of a tale "for which the world is not yet prepared . . . [the] Matilda Briggs . . . a ship which is associated with the giant rat of Sumatra" (Suss).

Baron Maupertuis

4390. Redmond, D. A. "The Colossal Schemes of Baron Who?" *BSJ*, 20, No. 1 (March 1970), 14-16.

The fradulent Baron of Arizona, James Addison Reavis, is revealed as Baron Maupertuis (Reig).

President Murillo

4391. ———. "The Problem of the President's Papers," *SHJ*, 8, No. 4 (Summer 1968), 112-113, 126.

Ex-President Murillo (Norw) was Manuel Murillo Toro, President of Colombia in 1864-1866 and 1872-1874.

The Grice Patersons

4392. Anderson, Poul. "In the Island of Uffa," *West by One and by One*. San Francisco: Privately Printed, 1965. p. 125-132.

A reconstruction of "the singular adventures of the Grice Patersons in the island of Uffa" (Five).

4393. Boswell, Rolfe. " 'In Uffish Thought,' " *BSJ* [OS], 1, No. 1 (January 1946), 21-24.

The island is identified as that "great mound" on which Norwich Castle stands, and Professor Moriarty as that noted mathematician Charles Lutwidge Dodgson (Lewis Carroll).

4394. Heldenbrand, Page. "A Letter from Uffa," *Heldenbrand's Christmas Perennial*. New York: Appledore Towers Letter Press, 1954. [unpaged]

The island is actually "Ufa" and was simply misspelled by Watson. Illustrated with Julian Wolff's map of Ufa from *The Sherlockian Atlas*.

4395. Morley, Christopher. ["In the Island of Uffa"], *BSJ*, 1, No. 2 (April 1951), 56-58. (Clinical Notes by a Resident Patient)

Uffa was an enclave of land within land in East Anglia; hence Watson's use of "in" rather than "on."

4396. Price, Edmund T. "The Singular Adventure of the Grice Patersons in the Island of Uffa and the Loss of the British Barque 'Sophy Anderson,' " *BSJ Christmas Annual*, No. 4 (1959), 302-310.

Uffa is actually Ophir, an 1887 dictation slip. Moran knew the area both as a big-game specialist and a student. Kelly's Directories trace the careers of a traveling draper, Paterson, and a Miss Grice, owner of a draper's shop, who must have married. They met Moran, who persuaded them to take their savings on a treasure hunt from which he ascended with sacks of gold dust from the barque *Sophy Anderson* (Five).

4397. Redmond, D. A. "A Charter for Uffa's Ritual," *BSJ*, 10, No. 1 (Winter 1970), 15-16.

A clever attempt to fit together three untold adventures: "the singular adventures of the Grice Patersons in the island of Uffa" (Five), "the singular contents of the ancient British barrow" (Gold), and Holmes's "laborious researches in early English charters" (3Stu).

Isadora Persano

4398. Hedgpeth, Joel. "Who Was Isadora Persano? or A Poet's (?) Revenge," *West by One and by One*. San Francisco: Privately Printed, 1965. p. 44-50.

An identification of the remarkable worm as *Luminodesmus sequoiae*, located in Sequoia National Park, California; and

The Writings About the Writings

Other Subjects

Persano, the journalist-Duellist who was found insane with the worm in a matchbox before him (Thor), as the American author and columnist Ambrose Gwinnett Bierce.

James Phillimore

4399. Dettman, Bruce. "A Long Step," *BSJ*, 18, No. 3 (September 1968), 164-165.

Ambrose Bierce is now identified as Mr. James Phillimore, who stepped back into his house to get an umbrella and was never seen again (Thor).

Russian Woman

4400. Offord, Lenore Glen. "A Case of Lost Identity" (Addressed to the Noble Gentlemen who Invested me with a Title), *West by One and by One*. San Francisco: Privately Printed, 1965. p. 64-66.

"I'm the Old Russian Woman, I haven't a doubt. / As such, on the roster engrave me. / But my untold Adventure—what was it about?" (Musg)

Cardinal Tosca

4401. Young, Francis Albert. "Upon the Identification of Cardinal Tosca," *BSJ*, 14, No. 2 (June 1964), 80.

Cardinal "Tosca," whose sudden death was investigated by Holmes at the express desire of His Holiness the Pope (Blac), was cardinal Ruffo-Scilla.

Sultan of Turkey

4402. Redmond, Chris. "The Commission from the Sultan," *BSJ*, 15, No. 4 (December 1965), 199-201.

Holmes's "commission" (Blan) was connected with the mild reforms he helped to bring about in the corrupt Turkish government of Macedonia.

Colonel Warburton

4403. Fesus, Marilyn. "Once Upon a Time," *BSP*, No. 42 (December 1968), 1.

A verse in six stanzas as by Col. Warburton on his madness (Engr).

Wilson, the Notorious Canary-Trainer

4404. Schonberg, Harold C. "Sherlock and— Malocchio!" *The New York Times* (May 12, 1968), II, 17.

———. ———, *CPBook*, 4, No. 15 (August 1968), 288.

This case (Blac) may have been connected with threats against the life of the famous soprano Adelina Patti.

VERSES (GENERAL)*

4405. Anderson, Karen K. "An Introduction to Filk Singing," *West by One and by One*. San Francisco: Privately Printed, 1965. p. 152-157.

On constructing some Baker Street filk songs (topical parodies of folk songs).

4406. Anderson, Poul. "Irregular Poetics," *BSJ Christmas Annual*, No. 3 (1958), 17-22.

Winner of the 1st annual Morley-Montgomery Memorial Award for the best contribution to *BSJ* in 1958.

The author laments the lack of poetry in the Sacred Writings, and then tries his hand at casting them in poetic form.

4407. Andrew, Clifton R. "Songs for a Sherlock Holmes Melody-Session," *CR*, 1, No. 2 (December 1958), 5; 1, No. 3 (April 1960), 16; 1, No. 4 (September 1960), 19.

4408. Armour, Richard. "On Last Looking into Watson's Holmes," *BSJ* [OS], 1, No. 2 (April 1946), 200.

"Be it ever so humble / There's no place like Holmes'."

4409. [Austin, Bliss.] "Acrostic Sonnet," *Two Irregular Sonnets*, by Goodrich Soyle. [N.p.: Privately Printed, n.d.] [unpaged]

———. "Cum Laude: Sherlock Holmes," *BSJ* [OS], 1, No. 1 (January 1946), 6.

"Once I have been in Baker Street by night, / Looking upon his profile by gaslight, / My sight's too strained such lesser lights to see. / Excuse me, Sir! To me no substitute / Serves half so well as: 'Come, the game's afoot.' "

4410. ———. "Triolet: J. H. W. to S. H." (Apologies to Robert Bridges), *BSJ*, 1, No. 4 (October 1951), 140.

———. ———, [Oversat af A. D. Henriksen]. *Sangen om Baker Street*. København: [Grafisk Cirkel], 1958. p. 16. Reprinted in *Sherlockiana*, 3, Nr. 3-4 (1958), 12.

"When first we met, I did not guess / That someday you would be The Master."

4411. [———.] *Two Irregular Sonnets*, by Goodrich Soyle [pseud.] [N.p.: Privately Printed, n.d.] [4] p.

Limited to 75 numbered copies.

Contents: Acrostic Sonnet. - Sonetto (Quasi una fantasia).

4412. Baker, Kate G. "The Game's Afoot," *BSP*, No. 21 (March 1967), 3.

"Something slipping by / In the grey, fog-ridden streets."

4413. Bartlett, Edward H. "The Reading Chair," *BSJ* [OS], 1, No. 2 (April 1946), 148.

"An appeal, in verse, for the improvement of certain moving hours." (Edgar W. Smith)

4414. Berman, Ruth, and Ron Whyte. *A Sherlockian Christmas Carroll*, sung by

Ruth Berman and Ron Whyte; and *The Case of the Minnesota Authors,* by Robert Pattrick. [Minneapolis, Minn.: The McArdle Press, December 1960.] 11 p.
Limited to 200 numbered copies.

4415. Bloch, Don. "Dashed Off in a Dither," *BSJ,* 14, No. 4 (December 1964), 199.
"No thanks, if you please, to IBM, / For stealing the glamour away from Them. / . . . No mess of cogs and power tubes ever can / Take the place of Our Great Man."

4416. Boucher, Anthony. "Sonnet: San Francisco to Sherlock," *A Baker Street Four-Wheeler.* Edited by Edgar W. Smith. [Maplewood, N.J., and New York: The Pamphlet House, 1944.] p. 37.
———. ———, *The Daily Californian Weekly Magazine,* 4, No. 9 (January 14, 1969), 7.
"Let it be here, where fog curls in the night, / Where cobbled streets and curious Chinese / Bring back the dying days of your delight, / And where the very foghorns proudly hoot, / 'Here, Sherlock! Here the game is still afoot!' "

4417. Brodie, Robert N. "Geoffrey Chaucer Describes Sherlock Holmes," *BSJ,* 20, No. 4 (December 1970), 195.
"In London, so the tales by Watson tell, / There lived a wight named Holmes, to whom befell / Adventures all grotesque, bizarre and strange / From Mackleton in the North to Abbey Grange."

4418. Carlyle, Tess. "Neither Hafiz nor Horace," *SOS Annual,* No. 2 (January 1968), 2.
A verse in seven stanzas on Last, Scan, Lady, Houn, Illu, and Chas.

4419. Cassard, G. C. "Quick, Watson, a Rymbel!" *Promenade,* 7, No. 9 (March 1947), 81.
———. ———, *BSJ* [OS], 2, No. 4 (October 1947), 394.
"Quick, Watson, quick—the needle, *now,* / Before I lose the thread!"

4420. Christ, Jay Finley. "The Sage of Baker Street," *Sherlockian Studies.* Edited by Robert A. Cutter. [Jackson Heights, N.Y.: The Baker Street Press, 1947.] p. 13-14.
"In a gaslight age there lived a sage / In foggy London town. / He dwelt discreet in Baker Street / With pipe and dressing gown."

4421. ———. "The Song of Hiawatson," *BSJ,* 6, No. 3 (July 1956), 143-145.
———. *Song of Dr. Watson,* [by] Langdale Pike [pseud.] [Michigan City, Ind.: Privately Printed, December 1956.] [4] p.
"Thus he left them for our pleasure; / Left a record of a lifetime, / Record of enduring friendship, / Left us Sherlock, left us Watson, / Left them both to us, who love them, / In our hearts to dwell forever."

4422. Clarke, Richard W. "The In-Verse Canon," *BSJ,* 21, No. 1 (March 1971), 3-9.
A retelling of the tales in sixty stanzas.

4423. Craig, Edw. F. "Sherlock Holmes Ain't Got a Thing on Me," *Laff It Off: A Musical Farce in Two Acts.* Book by J. C. Murphy '25 and W. S. Martin '26. Boston, Mass.: C. W. Homeyer & Co., [1925] p. 5-7.

4424. Cutter, Robert A. "Sonnet on Dovenshire," *Illustrious Client's Third Case-Book.* Edited by J. N. Williamson and H. B. Williams. [Indianapolis, Ind.: The Illustrious Clients, 1953.] p. 93.
"There dwells a timeless man of repute / Who unlike mortals can never pass."

4425. Dorian, N. Currier. "In Song as Well as Story," *BSJ,* 6, No. 3 (July 1956), 165-167.
An analysis of the Scottish ballad "Superintendent Barratt" (item 4506).

4426. Fearing, Kenneth. "Sherlock Spends a Day in the Country," *The New Yorker,* 20, No. 4 (March 11, 1944), 32.
———. ———. Ysleta: Edwin B. Hill, June 1944. [4] p. (Sherlockiana)
Limited to 30 copies.
———. ———, *For Loving a Book,* by Charles Honce. Mount Vernon, N.Y.: The Golden Eagle Press, 1945. p. 39-40.
———. ———, *Stranger at Coney Island and Other Poems.* New York: Harcourt, Brace and Co., 1948. p. 22-23.
"Poetic fantasy of the signs that await a reading." (Edgar W. Smith)

4427. Fesus, Marilyn. "Itinerary," *BSJ,* 19, No. 1 (March 1969), 3.
"These several lines brief tribute are / to Arthur Conan Doyle, / to Stamford, the Criterion Bar, / to time's most faithful foil."

4428. Fladeland, Edwin. "Come, Holmes, the Game's Afoot!" *BSP,* No. 28 (October 1967), 7.
"Arise from your cocaine-filled dreams. / Listen to those pitiful screams!"

4429. Frisbie, Owen P. "Meditations of Martha," *The Best of the Pips.* Westchester County, N.Y.: The Five Orange Pips, 1955. p. 49.
"I never 'ad no boarders like them two."

4430. ———. ["Sonnet"], *BSJ* [OS], 2, No. 1 (January 1947), 102-103.
"Oh! Mem'ry's flask holds dreams / for man and boy. / Pour out! Adventure sits with him / who tips / The cup, with Holmes and Watson, / and THE PIPS."

4431. George, Isaac S. "Sherlock Stands Supreme," *Illustrious Client's Third Case-Book.* Edited by J. N. Williamson and H. B. Williams. [Indianapolis, Ind.: The Illustrious Clients, 1953.] p. 195.

"When seeking the outstanding name / Of all who in fiction made fame / I'll take for my journey / The grandson of Vernet / Who shone when 'afoot was the game.' "

4432. Graham, Harry. "Sherlock Holmes," *More Misrepresentative Men.* Pictures by Malcolm Strauss. New York: Fox, Duffield & Co., 1905. p. 98-108.

———. ———, *Misrepresentative Men.* New and enlarged edition. Illustrated by F. Strothmann. London: Gay and Hancock Ltd., 1910. p. 85-92.

———. ———, *BSJ* [OS], 1, No. 4 (October 1946), 449-453. (Incunabulum)

———. ———, *The Incunabular Sherlock Holmes.* Edited by Edgar W. Smith. Morristown, N.J.: The Baker Street Irregulars, 1958. p. 31-35.

"Uplift your teeming tankards to / The great Professor of Deduction!"

4433. Gross, Michael. "Ballade of the Old Love," *New York Herald Tribune* (October 9, 1933), 13.

———. ———, *Two Ballads in Praise of Sherlock Holmes,* by Carolyn Wells [and] Michael Gross. Ysleta: Edwin B. Hill, 1937. [unpaged]

". . . I still like Sherlock Holmes the best."

4434. Hägg, Gösta. "A Sherlockian Sonnet," *BSCL,* No. 7 (1969), 2.

"I take my LANTERN and at once I feel / Its gentle light may something new reveal / Of the great sleuth, I know and love so well."

4435. Hahn, Robert W. "The Irregulars' Room," *BSJ,* 14, No. 2 (June 1964), 122.

"For in that land of eighteen ninety-five, / We, your faithful Watsons, best survive."

4436. Hamilton, Chris. "Hymn to Him," *Illustrious Client's Case-Book.* Edited by J. N. Williamson and H. B. Williams. [Indianapolis, Ind.: The Illustrious Clients, 1948.] p. 37-38.

"It concerns a man named Sherlock / And J. Watson (who's a friend): / Stalwart symbols of an era, / Of a world that has no end."

4437. Hardenbrook, Don. "Miniver Cheevy III," *BSJ* [OS], 4, No. 1 (January 1949), 17.

"He placed the Canon on his knee / And turned the pages."

4438. Hardwick, Mollie. ["Sonnet], *PD,* 1, No. 2 (December 1967), 2. (The Master's Corner)

"Could we, with an eye clairvoyant, / Find the oft-debated door, / Which, in trembling, many a client / (Fair, or famous) stood before?"

4439. Harmand, Betsy. "Deadly Fogs Indeed!" *BSC,* 1, No. 2 (March 1968), 3.

"The two that trod the pavements, / And knew the fogs so well, / Wouldn't miss them, for they have them yet, / From King's Cross to Pall Mall."

4440. Harrison, Michael. "Poem," *SOS,* 1, No. 4 (April 1967), 4.

"Before the fire he's sitting, / looking at the flames; / recalling many a Problem / involving Famous Names."

4441. Henriksen, A. D. *Sangen om Baker Street i dansk gendigtning.* [The Song About Baker Street Recomposed in the Danish Language.] København: [Grafisk Cirkel], 1958. 21 p. illus.

Limited to 200 copies.

———. ———, *Sherlockiana,* 3, Nr. 3-4 (1958), 9-13.

A long and delightful essay dealing with the Irregular poets, and giving translations of typical verses.

4442. Higgins, Pam. "The Game Is Afoot!" *BSP,* No. 24 (June 1967), 3.

" 'The game is afoot!' / This cry rings loudly in my ears / As a thin hand plucks the warm covers off me."

4443. Hilliard, John Northern. "Sherlock Holmes," *The Bookman,* 55, No. 2 (April 1922), 219.

"Although in time his victories monotonous became, / We must confess since he quit work life's never been the same."

4444. Hodan, Barbara. "Seventeen Steps," *BSJ,* 21, No. 2 (June 1971), 69.

———. "Sjutton trappsteg," [Tr. by Ted Bergman]. *BSCL,* No. 9 (1971), 3.

"I have often tread these steps to spend / an evening among friends / And to share for a time the light of familiar faces."

4445. Hyslop, James T. "Sonnet for a 'Six Napoleons' Dinner," *BSJ* [OS], 2, No. 3 (July 1947), 355.

"We have two honored guests with / us tonight: / Each in our hearts reserves for / them a chair."

4446. [Katzen, Olga.] "Hedunit," by Sagittarius [pseud.] *The London Mystery Magazine,* 1, No. 1 (May 1949), 4-5.

———. ———, *The Sherlock Holmes.* [Compiled and prepared by Richard Lonsdale-Hands Associates.] London: Whitbread & Co. Ltd., [1957]. p. 42-43.

———. ———, *CPBook,* No. 19 (June 1969), 364.

"All still follow with Sherlock leading! / Over the edge of time's abyss / Wave a hand to those wheels receding, / Settle down to an hour of bliss!"

4447. Kjell, Bradley. "Apology for His Ignorance," *BSP*, No. 23 (May 1967), 3.
"Skimming through the Sacred Writ / Searching for a fact."

4448. Kredens, Diane. "The Ballad of Sherlock Holmes," *BSP*, No. 30 (December 1967), 1.
"And to this day we read of them / Their ventures have no end."

4449. Larson, Robert C. "The Immortality of Sherlock Holmes, *The Stars and Stripes* (March 18, 1956).
———. ———, *BSJ*, 7, No. 1 (January 1957), 26-27.
"Our realistic age can never spoil / The web of magic by Conan Doyle."

4450. Lauterbach, Charles E. *Baker Street Ballads*. Illustrated by Henry Lauritzen. Edited, with an Introduction by Edward S. Lauterbach. [Culver City, Calif.: Luther Norris, March 1971.] [vi], 34 p.
Limited to 300 numbered copies.
Contents: The Hound of the Baskervilles. - Mutiny on the *Gloria Scott*. - Ballade of the Wily Fox. - That Voice! - Dirge. - The Plumber and His Fiancee. - Woman? Bah! - The Abduction of Lady Violet Smith. - The Bachelor. - His Last Bow-Wow. - What a Man! - Mrs. Hudson Puts Her Foot Down. - The Commission of Abdul Aziz Khan, Sultan of Turkey. - What Doth the Bee? - A Close Shave. - Tonga's Opinion of Sherlock Holmes. - Tobacco Smoke. - The Folks I Sometimes Meet. - King's Pyland Derby. - Vale.
Review: Mystery Reader's Newsletter, 4, No. 4 (May 1971), 40-41 (Stanley Carlin).

4451. ———. "Ballad of the Dancing Men," *BSJ*, 7, No. 3 (July 1957), 147-148.
A tale in eight stanzas using dancing men figures in place of some of the letters.

4452. ———. "Dirge," *Baker Street Ballads*. [Culver City, Calif.: Luther Norris, March 1971.] p. 8.
"The old purple gown still hangs by the door, / His slippers stand under the bed, / But the presence I loved I shall see no more, / For my friend is dead."

4453. ———. "How Lovely Is a Rose!" *BSJ*, 14, No. 2 (June 1964), 88.
A four-stanza verse in response to Holmes's comment, "What a lovely thing a rose is!" (Nava)

4454. ———. "Song of the Lark," *BSJ Christmas Annual*, No. 4 (1959), 280.
"Oh, love, how could I love thee more! / You've jezailed my poor heart. / Come, let us fly to Uffa's shore, / Full never more to part! / Tra-la-la-lira-lira-lay."

4455. ———. "Up in the Attic," *BSJ*, 13, No. 3 (September 1963), 135.
"Come, let us climb these creaky stairs, / And take a curious look / To see what's underneath the eaves / Or in some hidden nook—."

4456. ———. "Whist Ye Not the Game's Afoot?" *BSJ*, 13, No. 1 (March 1963), 39.
A verse in seven stanzas identifying the Queen of Hearts as Irene Adler, the Jack of Diamonds as Watson, the King of Spades as John Clay, the Ace of Clubs as James Browner, the Joker as Moriarty, and the trump as Holmes.

4457. MacGregor, Marilyn. "Happy Birthday, Sherlock Holmes!" *SOH*, 1, No. 2 (1966), 4.
———. ———, *BSJ*, 16, No. 4 (December 1966), 197.
"On the . . . day of Christmas, / Dr. Watson gave to me. . . ."

4458. Mallett, Richard. "Lowbrow's Lament," *Punch*, 188 (January 2, 1935), 26.
———. ———, *BSJ*, 8, No. 2 (April 1958), 85-86.
Mourn for the methods of *Watson*, brothers; / Mourn for his clear unmistakable style; / Though he is gone and his place is another's, / No one can rival him. Not by a mile."

4459. Montgomery, James. "An Irregular Song" (With apologies to Thomas Moore, Sir Arthur Conan Doyle, and an anonymous Irish composer), *BSJ* [OS], 1, No. 3 (July 1946), 325.
———. ———, *Sidelights on Sherlock*. [Philadelphia: Privately Printed, 1951.] [unpaged]
———. ———, *Songs of Baker Street*. Sung by James Montgomery. Morristown, N.J.: The Baker Street Irregulars, 1959. Side 1, band 4.
———. ———, *Voices from Baker Street*, 1. Ferndale, Mich.: The Old Soldiers of Baker Street, December 1961. Side 1, band 3.
Sung to the tune of "Believe Me, If All Those Endearing Young Charms," the ode is a tribute to the Master and to the typical Baker Street Irregular: ". . . the boy who, adoring, is now half a man, or the man who is yet half a boy."

4460. Morley, Christopher. "Morning After," *BSJ*, 2, No. 2 (April 1952), 81. (Clinical Notes from a Resident Patient)
———. ———, *BSJ*, 5, No. 3 (July 1955), 142.
———. ———, *Gentlemen's Relish*. New York: W. W. Norton & Co., [1955]. p. 51.
" 'What would you most enjoy?' / . . . One of the adventures of Sherlock Holmes."

4461. ———. "The New Housemaid (Christmas 1894)," *BSJ*, 5, No. 3 (July 1955), 142-143.

———. ———, *Gentlemen's Relish*. New York: W. W. Norton & Co., [1955]. p. 69.
"This 'ere's a blinkin' place, 221-B. . . ."

4462. ———. "Sonnet on Baker Street," *Two Sonnets*. Ysleta: Edwin B. Hill, 1942. [unpaged]

———. ———, *Profile by Gaslight*. Edited by Edgar W. Smith. New York: Simon and Schuster, 1944. p. 194.
"If this is fancy, history's debarred: / If this is fiction, let fact be ashamed."

4463. ———. "Three Poems," *BSJ*, 11, No. 3 (September 1961), 150.
"My only drug is a good long slug / Of Tincture of Conan Doyle."

4464. ———, and Vincent Starrett. *Two Sonnets*. Ysleta: Edwin B. Hill, 1942. [4] p. (Sherlockiana)
Contents: Sonnet on Baker Street, by Christopher Morley. - 221B (for Edgar W. Smith), by Vincent Starrett.

4465. Nash, Ogden. "Each June I Made a Promise Sober," *The New York Times Book Review* (June 7, 1953), 1.
———. ———, *BSJ*, 3, No. 4 (October 1953), 215-216.
"So every summer I truly intend / My intellectual sloth to end, / And every summer for years and years / I've read Sherlock Holmes and The Three Musketeers."

4466. Norman, Charles. "A Study in Mauve," *BSJ*, 6, No. 1 (January 1956), 28-29.
———. ———, [Oversat af A. D. Henriksen]. *Sangen om Baker Street*. København:[Grafisk Cirkel], 1958. p. 16-18. Reprinted in *Sherlockiana*, 3, Nr. 3-4 (1958), 12. First and last stanzas reprinted in *Sherlock Holmes Årbog* II (1966), 50.
"Oh, why is everything so drab? / And will I never, never ride / Through London in a hansom cab / With a woman heavily-veiled at my side, / Bound—to be sure—for Baker Street?"

4467. Officer, Harvey. *A Baker Street Song Book*. Words and music by Harvey Officer. [New York: The Pamphlet House, 1943.] 31, 21 p.
Contents: 1. The Song of Gregson and Lestrade. - 2. The Song of Doctor Watson. - 3. The Song of Irene Adler. - 4. The Song of Moriarty. - 7. The Chant of the Musgrave Ritual. - 8. The Song of the Polyphonic Motets of Orlando di Lasso. - 9. A Toast to Holmes. - 10. The Song of Toby. - 11. The Song of The Speckled Band. - 12. The Song of the Other Stories. - 13. Sussex Downs. - 14. The Road to Baker Street.

Also contains *The Baker Street Suite for Violin and Piano*, Founded on the Sherlock Holmes stories: 1. A Study in Scarlet. - 2. The Irene Adler Waltz. - 3. The Dancing Men. - 4. Finale.

4468. Osborn, Steven. "The Curtain Goes Up," *BSP*, No. 52-53 (October-November 1969), 4.
"The fog settles down on Baker Street; / A hansom pulls up to the curb."

4469. Oursler, Will. "Baker Street Fever" (With apologies to John Masefield), *BSJ*, 5, No. 2 (April 1955), 77.
———. ———, Last Stanza tr. by A. D. Henriksen. *Sangen om Baker Street*. København: [Grafisk Cirkel], 1958. p. 12. Reprinted in *Sherlockiana*, 3, Nr. 3-4 (1958), 11; *Sherlock Holmes Årbog* II (1966), 49.
"I must go down to the Street again, to the world of / Sherlock Holmes—."

4470. Palmer, Stuart. "To S. H.," *PD*, 1, No. 4 (September 1968), 2. (The Master's Corner)
"Some fragments after the Haiku form."

4471. Parker, Robert G. "A Primer for Americans, Annexe Number One," *BSJ*, 11, No. 4 (December 1961), 197.
Couplets illustrating the "correct" pronunciation of Holmes ("polmes"), Lestrade ("sad" *or* "made"), and Johnnie Rance ("dawnce").

4472. Ralston, Claude. "Sherlock Holmes," Words and Music by Claude Ralston. *The Scottish Students' Song Book*. [Sixth edition.] Published for the Scottish Students' Song Book Committee Ltd. London & Glasgow: Bayley & Ferguson, [December 1897]. p. 240-241.
———. ———, *Shots from the Canon*, by James Montgomery. [Philadelphia: Privately Printed, 1953.] p. 2-3.
———. ———, *VH*, 6, No. 1 (January 1972), 9-10.
"I would indite this ditty to a man who's very cute, / He's the terror of Bill Sloggins and them who'd do a scoot; / He can tell you where you've been to just by looking at your boot, / And you'll know him by the name of Sherlock Holmes!"

4473. Rawley, James McKee. "A Problem in Pastiche," *BSJ*, 11, No. 1 (March 1961), 27-30.
Holmes is eulogized in the styles of Pope, Byron, Shelley, Tennyson, Browning, and Benét.

4474. Redmond, Chris. "A Legend," *BSJ*, 16, No. 2 (June 1966), 67.
"It's fiction, or else legend—but forsooth! / Since we believe it, isn't it the truth?"

4475. ———, ed. *The Lonely Hansom: An*

Anthology of Sherlockian Poetry. Edited by Chris Redmond for The Baker Street Page-boys. Kingston, Ontario: The Remarkable Invention Press, 1967. [22] p.

Contents: O Bit of Whimsey, by Edith B. Warner. - To a Very Literary Lady, by Vincent Starrett. - To Sherlock, by Morris Schreiber. - Limerick, by G. W. Welch. - Sonnet: Sherlock Holmes to Irene Adler, by Helene Yuhasova. - Triolet: On the Immortality of Sherlock Holmes and Doctor Watson, by Edgar W. Smith. - The Hound, by Jacob C. Solovay. - An Irregular Song, by James Montgomery. - Moriarty's Here Tonight, by Philip R. Mather. - That Voice, by C. E. Lauterbach. - The Irregulars' Room, by Robert W. Hahn. - Clerihew, by R. Ivar Gunn. - Sonnet: John H. Watson to Sherlock Holmes, by Helene Yuhasova. - Meditations of Dr. Watson: Baker Street, by Owen P. Frisbie. - Clerihew, by Gavin Brend. - Ballade of the Later Holmes, by Anthony Boucher. - Marvelous, Holmes, Marvelous! by Delos Avery. - Cum Laude: Sherlock Holmes, by Bliss Austin. - 221B, by Vincent Starrett.

Review: SHJ, 8, No. 2 (Spring 1967), 65 (Lord Donegall).

4476. ———. "The Victorian Age," *BSP Christmas Annual,* No. 1 (1966), 8.

". . . And one great figure whom we call our own. / Commemorated in books and poems, / He is our hero, Mr. Sherlock Holmes."

4477. [Redmond, D. A.] *A Song for Sub-Librarians.* [Kingston, Ontario: Privately Produced, 1971.] [2] p.

"To be chanted joyfully over catalogue cards, cocktails or the Canon to the melody of the *Battle Hymn of the Republic.*"

4478. Rhinelander, Philip H. "It's Very Unwise to Kill the Goose (Sherlock Holmes)," *What Cheer.* With an introduction by David McCord. New York: Coward-McCann, 1945. p. 224-225.

———. ———, *The Pocket Book of Humorous Verse.* Gathered, Sifted, and Salted, with an Introduction by David McCord. New York: Pocket Books, Inc., [August 1946]. p. 224-225.

———. ———, *BSJ,* 5, No. 4 (October 1955), 210.

"I want to put an end to crime — but not, I pray, too / soon."

4479. Rosenberger, Edgar S. "Hail, Sherlock Holmes!" *BSJ,* 6, No. 3 (July 1956), 152-153.

"Hail, Sherlock Holmes! Here's to a life / Of individuality: / A lighthouse in an age that's rife / With colorless conformity."

4480. ———. "I Remember, I Remember" (With apologies to Thomas Hood), *BSJ* [OS], 3, No. 4 (October 1948), 421-423.

———. ———, Stanzas 9 and 11 tr. by A. D. Henriksen. *Sangen om Baker Street.* København: [Grafisk Cirkel], 1958. p. 13. Reprinted in *Sherlockiana,* 3, Nr. 3-4 (1958), 11; *Sherlock Holmes Årbog* II (1966), 48.

"Oh happy, blessed Baker Street, / In London long ago; / I think I must have lived there once, / And thither I shall go / To visit Doctor Watson / And Sherlock Holmes, my friends, / In that bright country of the mind, / Where romance never ends."

4481. ———. "Whodunit?" *BSJ,* 2, No. 2 (April 1952), 100.

———. ———, Last stanza tr. by A. D. Henriksen. *Sangen om Baker Street.* København: [Grafisk Cirkel], 1958. p. 9. Reprinted in *Sherlockiana,* 3, Nr. 3-4 (1958), 10.

"In England and America—in fact, the wide world o'er— / In Sherlock Holmes they glory, and pay homage at his / door."

4482. S., C. H. "Lest A. C. Doyle Be Remembered," *The Harvard Lampoon,* 152, No. 6-7 (November 14, 1962), 3.

"So handsome, yet gruesome, / So winsome this twosome."

4483. Schreiber, Morris. "To Sherlock," *BSJ,* 10, No. 2 (April 1960), 96.

Dauntless tracker of lost and trackless men. . . ."

4484. [The Sherlock Holmes Society of London.] "The Clerihew Competition," *SHJ,* 1, No. 4 (December 1953), 26-29.

Examples of the verses in Clerihew form that were entered in this contest, including R. Ivar Gunn's winning epitaph for Moriarty.

4485. [———.] "The Limerick Competition," *SHJ,* 3, No. 1 (Summer 1956), 20-21.

Limericks from members of the Society in this "Sherlimerock" contest that was won by Robert Pattrick.

4486. Smith, Edgar W. *A Baker Street Quartette: Four Sherlockian Tales in Verse.* New York: The Baker Street Irregulars, [1950]. 44 p. illus.

Limited to 221 numbered copies.

———. ———, *CPBook,* 3, No. 13 (Summer 1967), 244-251.

Contents: 1. God Rest You, Mary Sutherland! - 2. Saved by the Bell-Rope. - 3. The Solitary Cyclist Rides Again. - 4. The Cliff-Hanger.

4487. ———. "A Ghost in Baker Street," *BSJ,* 3, No. 1 (January 1953), 37-38.

———. ———, *Baker Street and Beyond: Together with Some Trifling Monographs.* Morristown, N.J.: The Baker Street Irregulars, 1957. [unpaged]

————. ————, First three stanzas tr. by A. D. Henriksen. *Sherlockiana*, 1, Nr. 3-4 (1956), 12; 3, Nr. 3-4 (1958), 11; *Sangen om Baker Street*. København: [Grafisk Cirkel], 1958. p. 14. *Sherlock Holmes Arbog* II (1966), 48-49.

"I turned to speak, but he was gone, / Yet, going, still remained: / A symbol, a phenomenon, / Of all we've lost—and gained."

4488. [————.] *A Lauriston Garden of Verses: Six Sherlockian Sonnets and a Ballade,* by Helene Yuhasova [pseud.] Summit, N.J.: The Pamphlet House, 1946. [24] p. illus.
Limited to 250 numbered copies.
Contents: A Greeting in Arduis: To the Baker Street Irregulars. - Sonnet: John H. Watson to Sherlock Holmes. - Sonnet: Sherlock Holmes to John H. Watson. - Sonnet: Sherlock Holmes to James Moriarty, Sc. D. - Sonnet: Sherlock Holmes to Irene Adler. - Sonnet: Mary Morstan to Dr. Watson. - Sonnet: Sherlock Holmes to Mycroft Holmes. - Ballade of the Bright Stair-Rods.

4489. ————. "A Primer for Americans," *BSJ Christmas Annual*, No. 5 (1960), 276.
Couplets illustrating differences between American and British pronunciation. "We take a word, and sometimes bounce it— / But hark how Sherlock would pronounce it!"

4490. ————. "Sherlock Holmes: Fact or Fiction" (With apologies to Mr. Thomas S. Blakeney), *BSJ*, 8, No. 4 (October 1958), 214.
"If I were one of Moriarty's men, / . . . I'd hate to think that Sherlock Holmes was fact— / I'd much prefer the fiction that he's fiction."

4491. [————.] ["Sherlocution"], *BSJ*, 7, No. 4 (October 1957), 244. (From the Editor's Commonplace Book)
Characteristics and examples of the *Clerihew* (*Sherlockew* or *Sherlocution*).

4492. [————.] "Sonnet: John H. Watson to Sherlock Holmes," *A Lauriston Garden of Verses,* by Helen Yuhasova. Summit, N.J.: The Pamphlet House, 1946. p. [9].
————. ————, *The Second Cab*. Edited by James Keddie. [Boston: The Speckled Band, 1947.] p. 18.
————. ————, *Baker Street and Beyond: Together with Some Trifling Monographs*. Morristown, N.J.: The Baker Street Irregulars, 1957. [unpaged]
"You are a benefactor of the race; / Warrant and symbol of our land's content."

4493. [————.] "To Sherlock Holmes: Born January 6, 1854," *BSJ*, 4, No. 1 (January 1954), 3. (The Editor's Gas-Lamp)
————. ————, *SHJ*, 2, No. 1 (July 1954), 2.
————. ————, *Baker Street and Beyond:*

Together with Some Trifling Monographs. Morristown, N.J.: The Baker Street Irregulars, 1957. [unpaged]
————. "Til Sherlock Holmes: Født 6. januar 1954," [Oversat af A. D. Henriksen]. *BSJ*, 6, No. 3 (July 1956), 186. Reprinted in *Sangen om Baker Street*. København: [Grafisk Cirkel], 1958. p. 18-19. *Sherlockiana*, 3, Nr. 3-4 (1958), 13.
"All, all is change; and change, it seems, is all: / But you are constant, though the heavens fall."

4494. [————.] "Triolet on the Immortality of Sherlock Holmes and Dr. Watson," by "Buttons." *Profile by Gaslight*. Edited by Edgar W. Smith. New York: Simon and Schuster, 1944. p. 47.
————. ————, *Baker Street and Beyond: Together with Some Trifling Monographs*. Morristown, N.J.: The Baker Street Irregulars, 1957. [unpaged]
"They cannot die, because they live / Within the minds and hearts of men."

4495. Solovay, Jacob C. "Holmes to Watson (20 Years After)," *Sherlock Holmes: Two Sonnet Sequences*. [Culver City, Calif.: Luther Norris, November 1969.] [unpaged]
————. ————, *Sherlockiana*, 14, Nr. 4 (1969), 16.
"My good friend Watson, you and I are old, / And time has laid his hand upon our heads."

4496. ————. "Sherlock Holmes (an acrostic)," *BSJ* [OS], 3, No. 2 (April 1948), 158.
"Stop, reader, and admit there was a man!"

4497. ————. *Sherlock Holmes: Two Sonnet Sequences*. With an introduction by August Derleth. With illustrations by Frank Utpatel. [Culver City, Calif.: Luther Norris, November 1969.] [48] p.
Limited to 300 numbered copies.
Contents: PART FIRST — A BAKER STREET DOZEN. Sherlock Holmes (an acrostic. - Watson. - To Stamford. - Irene Adler. - Moriarty. - The Chambers. - Martha Hudson. - To the Irregulars. - The Hound. - Sebastian Moran. - To the Scotland Yarders. - Mycroft Holmes. - Holmes to Watson (20 years after). - PART SECOND—CONVERSATIONS IN BAKER STREET. Holmes Discourses on Crime. - Watson Searches for Quarters. - Holmes and Watson Discuss Lodgings. - Holmes Reflects on Two Colleagues. - Holmes Reminisces to Watson. - Holmes and Watson Converse on the Drug Habit. - Athelney Jones Arrives on the Scene. - Holmes Expounds on Detective Fiction. - Watson Surrenders to Romance. - Holmes Extols Tobacco for Sleuthing. - Watson Takes a Wife. - Sherlock Holmes to Edgar Allan Poe. - Holmes Justifies His Existence.

- Holmes Rebukes the Chronicler. - Watson Examines a Hat. - Watson Reproaches Himself. - Holmes Misjudges a Case. - Watson Appreciates Fine Acting. - Holmes Muses Over the Blue Carbuncle. - Watson Meditates While Writing. - Watson Deplores Holmes's Untidiness. - Holmes Again Lectures Watson on His Literary Shortcomings. - Holmes Expounds on Mycroft. - Watson Mourns the Death of His Master.

Reviews: DCC, 6, No. 1 (December 1969), 6; *New York Times Book Review* (January 11, 1970), 34 (Allen J. Hubin); *SOS,* 4, No. 1 (January 1970), 6 (Thomas Drucker); *SHJ,* 9, No. 3 (Winter 1969), 107 (Lord Donegall); *Sherlockiana,* 14, Nr. 4 (1969), 16; *Startling Mystery Stories,* 3, No. 6 (March 1971), 39 (Robert A. W. Lowndes).

4498. Starrett, Vincent. "The Adventure of the Baffled Detective," *BSJ,* 2, No. 4 (October 1952), 185.

"But this is once your medical recorder / Will chalk a miss for Sherlock, I'm afraid, / As sure as I'm yours truly, G. Lestrade."

4499. ———. "The Adventure of the Cat and the Fiddle," *BSJ* [OS], 3, No. 1 (January 1948), 5.

———. ———, *Sonnets and Other Verse.* Chicago: Dierkes Press, 1949. p. 31.

———. ———, *Ellery Queen's Mystery Magazine,* 38, No. 4 (October 1961), 113.

———. ———, *The Daily Californian Weekly Magazine,* 4, No. 18 (April 4, 1969), 17.

"One curious incident remains to mention: / *The dog did nothing to attract attention!*"

4500. ———. "The Adventure of the Empty Cupboard," *BSJ* [OS], 3, No. 2 (April 1948), 137.

———. ———, *Sonnets and Other Verse.* Chicago: Dierkes Press, 1949. p. 32.

———. ———, *Ellery Queen's Mystery Magazine,* 38, No. 3 (September 1961), 64.

———. ———, *The Daily Californian Weekly Magazine,* 4, No. 18 (April 4, 1969), 17.

"In the bare cupboard certain prints were found: / *They were the footprints of a gigantic hound!*"

4501. ———. *Dupin and Another.* Ysleta: Edwin B. Hill, 1941. [4] p.

———. ———, *Autolycus in Limbo.* New York: E.P. Dutton & Co., 1943. No. 35.

" 'Here is the dusk again, the friendly night! / Unbar the shutters, Edgar, and look down. . . .' "

4502. ———. *Three Poems.* Ysleta: Edwin B. Hill, 1934. [4] p. (Sherlockiana)

Contents: To a Very Literary Lady. - To William Gillette (on his return to the stage in "Sherlock Holmes"). - Scotland Yard.

4503. ———. "To a Very Literary Lady," *Three Poems.* Ysleta: Edwin B. Hill, 1934. [unpaged]

———. ———, *Autolycus in Limbo.* New York: E. P. Dutton & Co., 1943. No. 41.

———. ———, *Profile by Gaslight.* Edited by Edgar W. Smith. New York: Simon and Schuster, 1944. p. 2.

"Since I have heard a door in London slam / And seen great Sherlock issue."

4504. ———. "221B," *Two Sonnets.* Ysleta: Edwin B. Hill, 1942. [unpaged]

———. ———, *Autolycus in Limbo.* New York: E. P. Dutton & Co., 1943. No. 32.

———. ———, *Profile by Gaslight.* Edited by Edgar W. Smith. New York: Simon and Schuster, 1944. p. 290.

———. ———, *BSJ,* 2, No. 1 (January 1952), 4.

———. ———, *In and Out of Character,* by Basil Rathbone. Garden City, N.Y.: Doubleday & Co., 1956. p. 182-183.

———. ———, [Oversat af A. D. Henriksen]. *Sherlockiana,* 2, Nr. 1-2 (1957), 3; 3, Nr. 3-4 (1958), 13. Reprinted in *Sangen om Baker Street.* København: [Grafisk Cirkel], 1958. p. 21. *Sherlock Holmes Årbog* II (1966), 52.

———. ———, Read by Basil Rathbone. *The Stories of Sherlock Holmes.* New York: Caedmon Records, 1963. Vol. 1, side 2.

"Here dwell together still two men of note / Who never lived and so can never die."

4505. Stone, P. M. "To Sherlock Holmes," *A Baker Street Four-Wheeler.* Edited by Edgar W. Smith. [Maplewood, N.J., and New York: The Pamphlet House, 1944.] p. 25-26.

———. ———, [Oversat af A. D. Henriksen]. *Sangen om Baker Street.* København: [Grafisk Cirkel], 1958. p. 15. Reprinted in *Sherlockiana,* 3, Nr. 3-4 (1958), 12; *Sherlock Holmes Årbog* II (1966), 47.

———. "L'Envoie," *The Third Cab.* [Boston: Privately Printed at Stoke Moran, 1960.] p. 83-84.

"For come what may, Life never can bestow / Upon us richer gifts than Sherlock Holmes / —And Baker Street."

4506. "Superintendent Barratt," *Personal Choice of Scottish Folksongs and Ballads,* by Ewan MacColl. [London: Workers' Music Association Ltd., 195-?] p. 15.

———, *BSJ,* 6, No. 3 (July 1956), 166.

"O, Sherlock Holmes is died lang syne / In some forgotten garret, / But that's guid luck, for Holmes wad boke / To hear the name o' Barratt."

4507. Sutherland, Edwin. "Sonnet: To Helene Yuhasova on Reading 'A Lauriston Garden of Verses,' " *BSJ* [OS], 2, No. 1 (January 1947), 34.

"A song of homely things—the things of Holmes."

Other Subjects

4508. Warner, Edith B. "O Bit of Whimsey," *BSJ*, 14, No. 4 (December 1964), 195.
"Reflection on the Master Mind's / Esteemed ubiquity / Indicates Sherlockian kinds / Of vast supremacy."

4509. Wells, Carolyn. "A Ballade of Detection," *The Bookman*, 15, No. 3 (May 1902), 231.
————. ————, *BSJ*, 1, No. 2 (April 1951), 60.
"Sherlock, thy subtle powers I know, / Spirit of search, incarnate quest, / To thee the laurel wreath I throw—."

4510. ————, and Michael Gross. *Two Ballads in Praise of Sherlock Holmes.* [With a note by Vincent Starrett.] Ysleta: Edwin B. Hill, 1937. [4] p. (Sherlockiana)
Contents: Ballade of Baker Street, by Carolyn Wells. - Ballade of the Old Love, by Michael Gross.

4511. Whittemore, Reed. "The Strange Case in Baker Street," *Harper's Bazaar*, 80 (October 1946), 292.
————. ————, *Heroes & Heroines.* Poems by Reed Whittemore. Drawings by Irwin Touster. New York: Reynal & Hitchcock, 1946. p. 3-5.
————. ————, *BSJ*, 5, No. 2 (April 1955), 112-113.
————. ————, *An American Takes a Walk and Other Poems.* Minneapolis: The University of Minnesota Press, [1956]. p. 65-66.
This poem was included for analysis and discussion in the sophomore curriculum, English 201, at Princeton University.

4512. Wigglesworth, Belden. "Rondeau to the Dancing Men on the Occasion of Their First Cotillion," *BSJ* [OS], 2, No. 4 (October 1947), 480-481.

4513. Williams, H. B. "Banquet Song," *Illustrious Client's Case-Book.* Edited by J. N. Williamson and H. B. Williams. [Indianapolis, Ind.: The Illustrious Clients, 1948.] p. 20.
"As Truth and Justice will prevail— / Holmes and Watson are on their trail."

4514. ————. "Lament to Youth and Sherlock Holmes," *Illustrious Client's Case-Book.* Edited by J. N. Williamson and H. B. Williams. [Indianapolis, Ind.: The Illustrious Clients, 1948.] p. 13.
". . . As he who walked with Holmes the God / Forgot the vision, became man the clod."

4515. Williamson, Maryesther. "Another Non-Sherlockian's Poem," *Illustrious Client's Second Case-Book.* Edited by J. N. Williamson. [Indianapolis, Ind.: The Illustrious Clients, 1949.] p. 11.
"Eventually, perhaps, they will realize all: / Sherlock was real, not a character by Doyle!"

4516. ————. "A Non-Sherlockian's Poem," *Illustrious Client's Case-Book.* Edited by J. N. Williamson and H. B. Williams. [Indianapolis, Ind.: The Illustrious Clients, 1948.] p. 6.
"What is this power he has over all? / Why, he was [is!] the greatest detective of all."

WEAPONS

4517. Ashton, Ralph A. "The Secret Weapons of 221B Baker Street," *BSJ*, 9, No. 2 (April 1959), 99-102.
Holmes's secret weapon was a sword concealed in a hunting crop.

4518. Dettman, Bruce, and Michael Bedford, comp. *A Compendium of Canonical Weaponry: Being a Catalogue and Description of the Implements of Foul Play and Justice in the Writings of John H. Watson, M.D.* Compiled, with an Introduction and Notes, by Bruce Dettman and Michael Bedford. With a Foreword by Dean Dickensheet and a Final Word by John Bennett Shaw. Illustrated by Tom Walker. [Culver City, Calif.: Luther Norris, April 1969.] 33 p.
Limited to 300 numbered copies.
Contents: Foreword. - Introduction. - Firearms. - Cutlery. - Blunt Instruments. - Toxins. - Human Agents. - Animals. - Weapons of Extortion, Blackmail and Deceit. - Miscellaneous. - A Final Word. - Chart of Canonical Weaponry.
The introduction first appeared in *VH*, 1, No. 2 (April 1967), 2-3.
Reviews: BSP, No. 48 (June 1969), 5; *Startling Mystery Stories*, 3, No. 3 (Spring 1970), 69-70 (Robert A. W. Lowndes).

4519. Holroyd, James Edward. "Pistol Packing Partners," *Baker Street By-ways.* London: George Allen & Unwin Ltd., [1959]. p. 98-102.

4520. Leavitt, Robert Keith. "Annie Oakley in Baker Street: A Note on the Lamentable Limitations of Mr. Sherlock Holmes's Pistol Marksmanship," *Profile by Gaslight.* Edited by Edgar W. Smith. New York: Simon and Schuster, 1944. p. 230-242.
"All evidence . . . goes to show that Mr. Sherlock Holmes was the most indifferent of marksmen with the handgun, that he showed his contempt for it by the atrocious performance of the V.R. on a brick wall, that he did not trust himself with the arm of the detective force, that Watson, not Holmes, was the reliable shot when it came to gunplay, and finally that Holmes was a rifleman."

4521. Linsenmeyer, John M. "Sherlock Holmes: His Arsenal and the Law," *BSJ*, 18, No. 2 (June 1968), 74-77.

"Holmes and Watson had, in spite of frequent statements to the contrary, some official or quasi-official position exempting them from the firearms control laws."

4522. Percival, William. "Sherlock Holmes and Air-Guns," *SHJ*, 6, No. 1 (Winter 1962), 15-16.

The historical development of air-guns, including a consideration of the walking-stick air rifle used by Moran (Empt) and the Straubenzee air-gun of Count Negretto Sylvius (Maza).

4523. "Some Firearms," *Sherlock Holmes: Catalogue of an Exhibition Held at Abbey House, Baker Street, London, May-September 1951.* Chap. 6, p. 33-37.

————, *The Sherlock Holmes Exhibition: Catalogue [of an Exhibition Held at Plaza Art Galleries, New York, July 1952].* Chap. 5, p. 42-44.

A discussion of the revolvers and air rifle exhibited and arranged by Major Hugh Pollard.

4524. Stanley, John. "Powdersmoke at 221B Baker St.," *Black Mask* (July 1948), 125-126.

An essay on the weapons in the Holmes-Watson arsenal, with a concluding statement that "Sherlock Holmes was one of the world's most famous and well-informed gun fans."

WEATHER

4525. Corrington, J. D. "Baker Street Weather," *The Saint Detective Magazine,* 8, No. 5 (November 1957), 33-53.

The importance of weather in Holmes's solutions to crimes.

4526. Henriksen, A. D. "Vi blader i *Strand Magazine,*" *Sherlockiana,* 7, Nr. 1-2 (1962), 1-6.

————. "We Turn the Pages of *The Strand,*" Tr. by Charles C. Bigelow. *BSJ*, 13, No. 2 (June 1963), 115-121.

A consideration of some passages in this magazine concerning the Canonical weather.

4527. Van Liere, Edward J. "Doctor Watson and the Weather," *The Quarterly of the Phi Beta Pi Medical Fraternity,* 42, No. 3 (November 1945), 144-146, 159.

————. ————, *BSJ* [OS], 3, No. 2 (April 1948), 191-195.

————. ————, *A Doctor Enjoys Sherlock Holmes.* New York: Vantage Press, [1959]. p. 11-18.

Reasons for his frequent allusions to the weather.

The Château de Lucens in the Swiss canton of Vaud. (**4836-4845**).

VI | Sherlockians and The Societies

A Sherlockians (Biographies, Reminiscences, and Tributes)

This section lists tributes to and personal reminiscences of many of the individuals who have contributed to the writings about the Writings. Brief obituary notices and tributes have been omitted. Additional information on these and other Sherlockians will be found in the 1962 edition of *Who's Who and What's What* and its first supplement, and in the "Whodunit" section of *The Baker Street Journal*.

GENERAL

4528. Campbell, Maurice. "Some Early Holmesians," *SHJ*, 8, No. 2 (Spring 1967), 37-38.

This eminent Holmesian (Sherlockian) recalls the activities of other Holmesians during the first three decades.

4529. Honce, Charles. "The Baker Street Twins," *For Loving a Book.* Mount Vernon, N.Y.: The Golden Eagle Press, 1945. p. 59-63.

A commentary on Christopher Morley and Vincent Starrett.

4530. "How It All Began," by S. C. Roberts, Sir Gerald Kelly, Vincent Starrett, and E. V. Knox. *SHJ*, 2, No. 1 (July 1954), 3-6.

Four distinguished Sherlockians write about their first encounter with the great detective.

4531. [Sovine, J. W.] "The Rubáiyát of Baker Street. Part 1. The Terrace," by Dr. Hill Barton [pseud.] *BSJ*, 11, No. 2 (June 1961), 89-92.

A lovingly and beautifully written poetic tribute to the late and great Sherlockians. "These Friends of mine I've never met, they *populate* / the Street, / And in the Bright Hereafter they're the Friends I / want to meet."

BEN ABRAMSON

4532. Abramson, Ben. "My First Meeting with Sherlock Holmes," *Illustrious Client's Case-Book.* Edited by J. N. Williamson and H. B. Williams. [Indianapolis, Ind.: The Illustrious Clients, 1948.] p. 9-12.

——. ——, *BSJ* [OS], 3, No. 3 (July 1948), 365-367.

"To the young, the very young, he came on a magic carpet, transporting the inexperienced, the unawakened, to scenes of Arabian Night splendor and opium-dream fantasia. . . . I was on that magic carpet with Holmes, meeting the most fascinating people, witnessing the goriest murders, experiencing kaleidoscopic emotions. My imagination was ignited with explosive brilliance akin to the atomic bomb over Hiroshima. I haven't been the same since."

4533. [Smith, Edgar W. "Ben Abramson, ?-1955"], *BSJ*, 5, No. 4 (October 1955), 251.

A tribute to the founder and former publisher of the first journal devoted to the writings of Dr. John H. Watson.

WILLIAM S. BARING-GOULD

4534. Kennedy, Bruce. "From Two Points of View: A Study on the Late William S. Baring-Gould," *BSP*, No. 28 (October 1967), 2.

"With Bill's death, 'I feel the Master slipping away . . . and Sherlock Holmes slips a bit further into the fog.' "

4535. ——. "William Stuart Baring-Gould: A Eulogy," *VH*, 1, No. 3 (September 1967), 8.

William S. Baring-Gould (4534-4539).

4536. Morse, Flo. "Sherlock Holmes Comes to Town," *The Reporter Dispatch* [White Plains, N.Y.] (February 9, 1965), 9.

4537. [Prestige, Colin.] "Mr. William S. Baring-Gould [1913-1967], *SHJ*, 8, No. 3 (Winter 1967), 101.

4538. "William Baring-Gould, 54, Dies: Sherlock Holmes 'Biographer,' " *The New York Times* (August 12, 1967), 25.
———, *CPBook*, 4, No. 14 (Winter 1968), 264.

4539. [Wolff, Julian.] "William S. Baring-Gould," *BSJ*, 17, No. 4 (December 1967), 195.
"In the true Irregular tradition, and in accordance with the precepts of Christopher Morley, he was always ready to encourage young Sherlockians, many of whom owe much to his valuable assistance."

RUTH BERMAN

4540. Berman, Ruth. "My First Meeting with Sherlock Holmes," *BSJ*, 13, No. 1 (March 1963), 46-47.
The author credits her brother David with having introduced her to the Master.

ANTHONY BOUCHER

4541. Offord, Lenore Glen, comp. "A Boucher Portrait: Anthony Boucher as Seen by His Friends and Colleagues," *The Armchair Detective*, 2, No. 2 (January 1969), 69-76.
Among the several contributions to this article is a commentary by Robert Frier on "Boucher as a Sherlockian."

4542. "William Anthony Parker White, 1911-1968," *VH*, 2, No. 2 (April 1968), 9.

GAVIN BREND

4543. "Gavin Brend [1904-1958]," *SHJ*, 3, No. 4 (Summer 1958), 3.
A eulogy to the author of *My Dear Holmes* and former Chairman of the Sherlock Holmes Society of London.

JAY FINLEY CHRIST

4544. [Holroyd, James Edward.] "Jay Finley Christ [1884-1963]," *SHJ*, 6, No. 4 (Spring 1964), 127. illus.
A tribute to one of the most distinguished Sherlockian scholars, whose major contributions include the *Irregular Chronology* and the *Irregular Guide.*

4545. Mannion, Rodney. "On Becoming a Sherlockian," *BSJ*, 14, No. 3 (September 1964), 131-134.
An expression of gratitude to Jay Finley Christ, a recipient of the BSI Two-Shilling Award, for introducing Dr. Mannion to the Sacred Writings. Illustrated with a full-page photograph of Professor Christ and a photograph of his Sherlock Holmes study where, according to his wife, "he spent the happiest hours of his life."

DAVID MARTIN DAKIN

4546. Dakin, D. Martin. "Reminiscences of an Old Sherlockian," *SHJ*, 5, No. 1 (Winter 1960), 15-17.
The author recalls his introduction at "about 7 or 8" to the Holmes stories, and then comments on the films and plays and the Sherlock Holmes Society of London.

VIRGINIA DANIEL

4547. Daniel, Virginia. "A Capital Mistake," *BSJ*, 16, No. 2 (June 1966), 108-109. (My First Meeting with Sherlock Holmes)
"The only kindly thought that I will ever have of my freshman English teacher will be that she introduced me, somewhat reluctantly on my part, to the Master."

MICHAEL WILLOUGHBY DEWAR

4548. Dewar, Michael Willoughby. "My First Meeting with Sherlock Holmes," *BSJ*, 3, No. 2 (April 1953), 99-101.
"And from that day to this it has been and will be 'always 1895.' "

DEAN W. DICKENSHEET

4549. Dettman, Bruce. "I Meet Dean Dickensheet," *BSP*, No. 22 (April 1967), 1-2.
The author describes his visit with "Vamberry, the wine merchant."

G. T. FLEMING-ROBERTS

4550. Fleming-Roberts, G. T. "My First Meeting with Sherlock Holmes," *Illustrious Client's Third Case-Book.* Edited by J. N. Williamson and H. B. Williams. [Indianapolis, Ind.: The Illustrious Clients, 1953.] p. 66-71.

A letter dated August 25, 1949, in which the author acknowledges his gratitude to Dr. Watson and to "Northumberland" for introducing him to the world of Sherlock Holmes.

HENRY JAMES FORMAN

4551. Forman, Henry James. "The Creator of Holmes in the Flesh," *221B: Studies in Sherlock Holmes.* Edited by Vincent Starrett. New York: The Macmillan Co., 1940, p. 138-141.

A discussion of the author's introduction to the tales and to Conan Doyle.

SIR PAUL GORE-BOOTH

4552. [Prestige, Colin.] "Sir Paul Gore-Booth," *SHJ,* 8, No. 2 (Spring 1967), 61-62.

A tribute to the new President of the Sherlock Holmes Society of London.

MARGARET GUNN

4553. "Margaret Gunn," *SHJ,* 9, No. 3 (Winter 1969), 102-104; 9, No. 4 (Summer 1970), 142.

Personal tributes from Philip Dalton, Colin Prestige, Humphrey Morton, and Nathan L. Bengis to the lady who served as the Society's Joint Honorary Secretary for eighteen years.

R. IVAR GUNN

4554. Holroyd, James Edward, and Philip Dalton. "R. Ivar Gunn [1891-1953]," *SHJ,* 1, No. 4 (December 1953), 1.

A eulogy to the Society's first Chairman and compiler of the classic "Examination Paper on Sherlock Holmes."

WILLIAM S. HALL

4555. Hall, W. S. "My First Meeting with Sherlock Holmes," *BSJ* [OS], 1, No. 3 (July 1946), 337-339.

The author discovered the Master in his Sunday School Library.

ROLAND HAMMOND

4556. ["Dr. Roland Hammond, 1876-1957"], *BSJ,* 7, No. 4 (October 1957), 247-248.

Tributes to the founder of the Dancing Men of Providence, R.I., and active member of BSI.

HARRY HARTMAN

4557. Hartman, Harry. "I Met Holmes in London," *The Holy Quire.* [Culver City, Calif.: Luther Norris, December 1970.] p. 14-16.

Recollections of a boyhood in London, Ontario, where the author first read the Canonical tales.

CORNELIS HELLING

4558. Helling, Cornelis. "My First Meeting with Sherlock Holmes," *BSJ,* 1, No. 2 (April 1951), 61-62.

The author first met Holmes and Watson in the back room of an Amsterdam butcher's shop.

EDWIN B. HILL

4559. [Berner, William A.] "Edwin B. Hill, 1866-1949: An Appreciation," *VH,* 2, No. 2 (April 1968), 4-5.

A tribute to a pioneer private printer of the Southwest who issued several Sherlockian leaflets and brochures. Two additional articles on Mr. Hill and a checklist of his publications appear in *The American Book Collector,* 18, No. 2 (October 1967), 19-27.

CHARLES HONCE

4560. Honce, Charles. "Going, Going Gone!" *Books and Ghosts.* Mount Vernon, N.Y.: The Golden Eagle Press, 1948. p. 87-89.
————. ————, *BSJ,* 17, No. 3 (September 1967), 161-163.

The author discovered Holmes in the August 15, 1908, issue of *Collier's,* located in his father's barber shop.

4561. ————. "My First Meeting with Sherlock Holmes." *BSJ* [OS], 1 No. 1 (January 1946), 51-54.
————. ————, *Books and Ghosts.* Mount Vernon, N.Y.: The Golden Eagle Press, 1948. p. 83-86.

"I'll continue to like the Sherlock Holmes tales just as they are — minus the modern gadgets."

JAMES KEDDIE

4562. Keddie, James. "My First Meeting with Sherlock Holmes," *BSJ* [OS], 2, No. 4 (October 1947), 420-421.

"As Irene Adler was always *the* woman to Sherlock Holmes, so to me Sherlock Holmes will always be *the* man."

SIR DESMOND MACCARTHY

4563. [Gunn, R. Ivar.] "Sir Desmond Mac-Carthy, 1877-1952," *SHJ,* 1, No. 2 (September 1952), 2.

Sherlockians and The Societies

Sherlockians

A farewell salute to "a gifted and imaginative amateur of the Sherlock Holmes saga."

DUNCAN MACDOUGALD

4564. MacDougald, Duncan. "The Extraordinary Case of the Six Unknown Stories," *BSJ*, 1, No. 4 (October 1951), 128-131.

"Of the 60 stories, I have now read 54 of them from fifteen to fifty times each. But six of these priceless tales I have never even begun! And so there awaits me the indescribable joy of reading for the first time—if some unutterable misfortune should befall me—one of six virginal adventures of the Master."

THE REV. LESLIE MARSHALL

4565. Marshall, Leslie. "My First Meeting with Sherlock Holmes," *BSJ* [OS], 1, No. 4 (October 1946), 454-456.

RUTH MISSAL

4566. Converse, Margaret. "The Curious Case of the Brighton Woman with the Thing About . . . Sherlock Holmes," *Upstate New York* [magazine section of the *Rochester Democrat & Chronicle*] (April 12, 1970), 9-11, 13. illus.

An interesting article about Mrs. Morris E. (Ruth) Missal's (the Solitary Cyclist of Rochester, N.Y.) lifelong devotion to the Sacred Writings and her splendid collection of Sherlockiana.

ENRIQUE MOCELO

4567. Mocelo, Enrique. "How I Became a Sherlockian," *BSJ*, 18, No. 1 (March 1968), 46-47.

This young Cuban refugee relates his Sherlockian experiences behind the "Sugar Curtain."

JAMES MONTGOMERY

4568. Aucott, Robert. "Jim Montgomery," *Leaves from the Copper Beeches*. Narberth, Pa.: Livingston Pub. Co., 1959. p. viii.

"His was, for us, the voice of no defeat— / The Voice of Sherlock Holmes and Baker Street."

4569. "James Montgomery [1898-1955]," *SHJ*, 2, No. 4 (Winter 1955), 36-37.

"James, or Jim as he preferred to be known, was one of the truest and most ardent Sherlockians of our day. He really lived for the saga. Possessing one of the finest libraries of Holmesiana in the world, he was indefatigable in his search for new items."

4570. Montgomery, Bruce. "The Return of Aunt Clara," *Voices from Baker Street*, 2. Ferndale, Mich.: The Old Soldiers of Baker Street, 1965. Side 2, band 6.

———. "Father's Folly, or Great-Aunt Clara Revisited," *BSJ*, 18, No. 1 (March 1968), 8-9.

"We always mention Aunt Clara; / She's held in esteem by us all. / Since my father shed light on her picture, / It now faces front on the wall."

4571. Montgomery, James. "We Never Mention Aunt Clara," *Art in the Blood, and What Is This Thing Called Music? (or Body and Soul)*. [Philadelphia: Privately Printed, 1950.] [unpaged]

———. ———, *BSJ*, 18, No. 1 (March 1968), 6-7.

"We never mention Aunt Clara, / Her picture is turned to the wall, / Though she lives on the French Riviera / Mother says that she's dead to us all."

"It was Jim Montgomery who discovered that his Aunt Clara was really Irene Adler, *the* woman, and added an entirely new annexe to the Canon. As a result, he undoubtedly contributed more to our enjoyment than any other Sherlockian has ever done." (Julian Wolff)

4572. [Smith, Edgar W.] "In Memory of James Montgomery," *BSJ*, 6, No. 1 (January 1956), 60-62.

———. ———, *BSJ*, 18, No. 1 (March 1968), 4.

"There was no man among us more deeply respected, more warmly admired, more dearly loved."

4573. Worthington, William Chesley. "A Memorial to James Montgomery," *BSJ*, 18, No. 1 (March 1968), 3.

"He was the perfect, the complete Sherlockian." A full-page photograph of Jim Montgomery appears on page 5.

CHRISTOPHER MORLEY

4574. [Austin, Bliss.] "Sonetto (Quasi una fantasia)," *Two Irregular Sonnets*, by Goodrich Soyle [pseud.] [N.p.: Privately Printed, n.d.] [unpaged]

———. ———, *A Baker Street Christmas Stocking*. Pittsburgh, Pa.: Hydraulic Press, 1958. [unpaged]

A poetic tribute to the Irregulars' Gasogene—Chris Morley.

4575. Hall, William S. "O Rare Chris Morley," *BSJ*, 11, No. 3 (September 1961), 131-133. (The Editor's Gas-Lamp)

A guest editorial on the founder of BSI and author of "The Bowling Green" column in *The Saturday Review* where the world first heard of this curious society. A full-page drawing of Chris Morley by Wathena E. Slaughter appears on page 134.

4576. Hoffmann, Richard H. "To Christopher Morley," *BSJ*, 13, No. 1 (March 1963), 23.

"Though he has left the earthly scene / He'll *always* be our Gasogene."

4577. [Smith, Edgar W.] "A Great Man Dies," *BSJ*, 7, No. 3 (July 1957), 131-132. (The Editor's Gas-Lamp)

"He stood as one of the literary giants of his time, but for a few of us he was, in particular, the Gasogene of the Baker Street Irregulars—the founder and the inspiration of that little group of which he was so much a part and which became so much a part of him."

4578. Starrett, Vincent. "On the Death of Christopher Morley," *BSG*, 1, No. 4 (April 1962), 8-10.

A moving tribute by one bookman to another.

KATHLEEN I. MORRISON

4579. Honce, Charles. "World's Only 'Lady Sherlock' Carries Baker Street Torch," Illustrated by Jim Bresnan. Distributed by AP News-features, January 29, 1945.

————. "A Lady Sherlock," *For Loving a Book*. Mount Vernon, N.Y.: The Golden Eagle Press, 1945. p. 33-34.

"Miss Kathleen I. Morrison, assistant public librarian at Calgary, Alberta, might be termed the world's only 'Lady Sherlock'; at least she is the only active woman member of the many societies devoted to the lore of Sherlock Holmes."

HUMPHREY MORTON

4580. [Howlett, Anthony D.] "Humphrey Morton [1908-1969]," *SHJ*, 9, No. 3 (Winter 1969), 104. illus.

A personal tribute to the late Chairman of the Milvertonians of Hampstead.

HARVEY OFFICER

4581. Honce, Charles. "Sherlock Holmes in Sharps and Flats," *For Loving a Book*. Mount Vernon, N.Y.: The Golden Eagle Press, 1945. p. 25-28.

A commentary on Harvey Officer's contribution to Sherlockiana.

4582. Officer, Harvey. "My First Meeting with Sherlock Holmes," *BSJ* [OS], 2, No. 2 (April 1947), 224-225.

FULTON OURSLER

4583. [Oursler, Fulton.] "Introduction: Footprints of the Damned," *These Are Strange Tales*, by Anthony Abbot [pseud.] Philadelphia: John C. Winston Co., [1948]. p. 1-4.

————. "The I-O-U of Anthony Abbot," *BSJ* [OS], 3, No. 4 (October 1948), 401-403.

"For the rest of my life I have followed the cloven hoofprints of mischief in life and literature. And it all goes back to Sherlock Holmes and Dr. Watson."

ROBERT STORM PETERSEN

4584. Henriksen, A. D. "En dansk 'irregulaer,' " *221 B Baker Street*. [København]: Privattryk, 1949. p. 41-49.

————. "A Danish Irregular: In Memory of Robert Storm Petersen 10 Years After His Death," Adapted and tr. into English by Jay Finley Christ. *Sherlockiana*, 5, Nr. 1-2 (1960), 6-7.

A tribute to the President of the first Sherlock Holmes Society of Copenhagen.

ELLERY QUEEN

4585. Queen, Ellery. ["My First Meeting with Sherlock Holmes"], *The Misadventures of Sherlock Holmes*. Edited by Ellery Queen. Boston: Little, Brown and Co., 1944. p. v-ix.

————. ————, *BSJ* [OS], 1, No. 2 (April 1946), 195-199.

————. ————, [Revised] *Bibliophile in the Nursery: A Bookman's Treasury of Collectors' Lore on Old and Rare Children's Books*. Edited, with an introduction & notes, by William Targ. Cleveland and New York: The World Pub. Co., [1957]. p. 452-456.

————. ————, ————. Metuchen, N. J.: Scarecrow Reprint Corp., 1969. p. 452-456.

The lifework of one of the Queens was born with the reading, at the age of twelve, of *The Adventures of Sherlock Holmes*.

SIR SYDNEY CASTLE ROBERTS

4586. [Prestige, Colin.] "Sir Sydney Roberts [1887-1966]," *SHJ*, 8, No. 1 (Winter 1966), 26-27.

A eulogy to "The Dean of Sherlockians."

4587. Roberts, S. C. "Sherlock Holmes," *Adventures with Authors*. Cambridge at the University Press, 1966. Chap. 17, p. 227-233.

————. ————, *SHJ*, 8, No. 1 (Winter 1966), 5-7.

————. ————, Tr. in part into Danish in *Sherlockiana*, 12, Nr. 1-2 (1967), 1.

The late President of the Sherlock Holmes Society of London recalls his lifelong interest in Holmesian scholarship.

Adventures with Authors is reviewed by Lord Donegall in *SHJ*, 8, No. 1 (Winter 1966), 27-28.

FRANKLIN DELANO ROOSEVELT

4588. Blau, Peter E. *The Adventure of the F. W. L. by Christopher Morley and A Correspondence with F. D. R.* [Pittsfield, Mass.: The Spermaceti Press, 1970.] [8] p.

A booklet "published for the Annual Dinner of the Baker Street Irregulars, 9

Sherlockians

January 1970," containing an introduction, Christopher Morley's parody (item 6039), and an exchange of letters between Mr. Morley and President Roosevelt about the parody and the BSI.

4589. Honce, Charles. "Baker Street on the Potomac," *For Loving a Book.* Mount Vernon, N.Y.: The Golden Eagle Press, 1945. p. 53-58.

A commentary on Roosevelt's interest in Sherlock Holmes, with quotations from the President's letters concerning matters Sherlockian.

4590. Roosevelt, Franklin Delano. *A Baker Street Folio: Five Letters About Sherlock Holmes from Franklin Delano Roosevelt.* [Compiled and with a prefatory note by Edgar W. Smith.] Summit, N.J.: The Pamphlet House, 1945. [8] p.

Limited to 150 copies.

————. ————, *The Daily California Weekly Magazine,* 4, No. 18 (April 4, 1969), 12, 17.

————. Reprinted in part with title: "Sherlock Holmes in the White House," *BSJ,* 5, No. 2 (April 1955), 78-79.

The late President of the U.S. and former member of BSI maintained an active correspondence with the Buttons-cum-Commissionaire of the Irregulars during the term of his membership, from 1942 to 1945. Four of the letters are addressed to Edgar Smith and one to Belden Wigglesworth. Also reprinted is a map of Roosevelt's "Shangri-La," drawn by members of the *Potomac*'s crew and first published in *Life,* 19 (October 15, 1945), 102, and reprinted in *BSJ* [OS], 1, No. 2 (April 1946), 186. In the upper left-hand corner of the map is "221 B Baker Street," inhabited, as indicated, by the Baker Street Urchins.

JAMES SAUNDERS

4591. "A Metropolitan 'Irregular,' " *Home Office* [Metropolitan Life Insurance Co.] (October 1965), 20-21.

An interview with James Saunders, including two photographs of the "Priory Scholar," in which he tells of his many Sherlockian activities.

EDEN SEARLES

4592. Searles, Eden. "The Master and I," *BSJ,* 10, No. 4 (October 1960), 221B-226.

"I have lived now almost a quarter century, and, for more than half of this long period, the figure of Sherlock Holmes has occupied a large place in my life."

JOHN BENNETT SHAW

4593. Baker, Jack. " 'Sherlock Holmes Still Lives' and Is Well in Baker Street, True

Believer Tells LR Fans," *Arkansas Gazette* [Little Rock] (October 24, 1967).

An account of the talk given by John Bennett Shaw at a luncheon meeting of the 45th annual conference of the Arkansas Library Association.

4594. Cheairs, Jane Feagin. "Booklore Leads to Baker Street," *Tulsalite,* 3, No. 13 (May 16, 1966), 13, 16.

————. ————, *CPBook,* 3, No. 10 (Fall 1966), 189.

A biographical sketch of Mr. Shaw and his Sherlockian activities.

4595. Hatch, Katherine. "Detective Isn't Dead: He Dwells in Fan's Heart," *The Daily Oklahoman* [Oklahoma City] (April 20, 1968), 11.

————. ————, *CPBook,* 4, No. 15 (August 1968), 296.

A report on the talk given by Mr. Shaw at a luncheon of the southwestern chapter of the American Association of Law Libraries on April 18, 1968.

4596. Robinson, Gretchen. "Excitement Surrounds Arrival of Shaw, Collector of Holmesiana," *Greenville Piedmont* (November 29, 1966).

An interview with John Bennett Shaw in advance of his talk to Friends of the Library at the Augusta Circle School in Greenville, South Carolina.

4597. Shaw, John Bennett. ["A Sherlockian Biography"], *SOS,* 2, No. 2 (December 1967), 1-2. (Editorial)

In this short autobiographical sketch, the Acting Hilton Soames of the Three Students Plus tells about his Canonical pursuits.

4598. "Sherlock Holmes Fans Plan to Form Club Here," *The New Mexican* [Santa Fe] (February 28, 1971), D5.

More about Mr. Shaw and his efforts to establish a new scion society in Santa Fe.

CARSON A. SIMPSON

4599. Wise, Robert A. "Bee-Keeping, Indeed!" *BSJ,* 9, No. 1 (January 1959), 41-42.

"The unprecedented retention of the minute details of the Master's life and experiences can now be understood. Deak Simpson is Holmes himself!"

EDGAR W. SMITH

4600. Alexander, Miriam. "My First Meeting with Sherlock Holmes," *BSJ* [OS], 3, No. 1 (January 1948), 70-72.

"Not only have I *met* Sherlock Holmes—I work for him!" These words from Edgar Smith's secretary.

4601. Ball, John. "Summit Meeting," *BSJ,* 16, No. 4 (December 1966), 205-208.

The author describes his reunion with Edgar Smith in the bliss of the hereafter and then, in the company of the master Sherlockian, takes a short trip to visit two other immortals who reside on Baker Street.

4602. [Donegall, Lord.] "Edgar W. Smith," *SHJ*, 5, No. 1 (Winter 1960), 1-2. (Editorial)

"It is certain that no greater blow than the death of E. W. S. has ever been sustained by Sherlockians throughout the world."

4603. "Edgar Smith Dies; Trade Official, 66," *The New York Times* (September 18, 1960), 86.

———, *CPBook*, 1, No. 1 (Summer 1964), 14.

"Head of G.M.'s International Research was authority on Sherlock Holmes." (Subtitle)

4604. Hall, Joseph E. "In Memoriam—Edgar W. Smith," *BSJ*, 12, No. 3 (September 1962), 156.

"Surely there must be some well-hidden dale / Deep in the Sussex Downs, where amid the hives / Of humming bees, the Master, Watson and / Our Edgar stroll forever with their pipes / Talking of motets and the weight of parsley, / Day-dreaming all the time of Baker Street."

4605. Hall, W. S. "How I First Met Edgar W. Smith," *BSJ*, 11, No. 2 (June 1961), 72.

"Holmes and Watson were a large part of Edgar Smith's life, a life that ended too soon and too suddenly, to the despair of all of us devoted to the same delightful study of a unique pair of human beings."

4606. Lauterbach, Charles E. "Vale," *BSJ*, 11, No. 2 (June 1961), 70.

———. ———, To Edgar W. Smith. *Baker Street Ballads*. [Culver City, Calif.: Luther Norris, March 1971.] p. 34.

"While we who linger on the terrace, / Linger brokenhearted."

4607. Marshall, Leslie. "My Last Bow—To E. W. S.," *BSJ*, 11, No. 2 (June 1961), 97.

"The memory of Edgar will be an ever living thing and a happy one."

4608. Mather, Philip R. "The Last Conanical Toast," *SHJ*, 4, No. 4 (Spring 1960), 112.

———. ———, *BSJ*, 10, No. 3 (July 1960), 180; 11, No. 2 (June 1961), 69.

———. ———, Oversat af A. D. Henriksen. *Sherlockiana*, 5, Nr. 3-4 (1960), 15.

"Now, could he be a natural son? / (I've heard it said that Holmes had one.) / No, it's not blood, but mind and heart / That makes him really such a part / Of that great man beyond compare: / Truly in spirit he's the Heir."

4609. McCormack, George J. "Toast Given in Honour of Edgar W. Smith at the Annual Meeting of the Baker Street Irregulars, 10 January 1969," *BSJ*, 19, No. 2 (June 1969), 118.

"Death hath not withered nor custom staled the infinite variety of his friendship."

4610. McLauchlin, Russell. "Dedicatory Introduction: To E. W. S.," *1961 S'ian Who's Who and What's What*. Edited by W. T. Rabe. Ferndale, Mich.: Old Soldiers of Baker Street, 1961. p. vii-ix.

———. ———, *Who's Who and What's What*. Edited by W. T. Rabe. Ferndale, Mich.: Old Soldiers of Baker Street, 1962. p. vii-ix.

"What shall a lonesome friend say about a man who, with a matchless pen in his hand and an unquestionable joy in his bosom, did more to make sound and perpetual our S'ian fellowship than all the members of that fellowship, gathered and combined?"

4611. Morris, James A. "Memoirs of Edgar W. Smith: Gentleman, Scholar and Businessman," *BSJ*, 11, No. 2 (June 1961), 93-96.

A biographical sketch of Edgar's business career in which his lifelong friend and business associate concludes: "To those of us who knew him socially and in business . . . Edgar Smith was truly 'the best and wisest man we have ever known.' "

4612. Prestige, Colin. "It Is Always a Joy," *BSJ*, 11, No. 2 (June 1961), 84-88.

The author describes his visit to 221B Baker Street, Morristown, N.J., on the last Sunday of Edgar Smith's life.

Edgar W. Smith (**4600-4620**).

Sherlockians and The Societies

Sherlockians

Sherlockians and The Societies

Sherlockians

4613. "Sherlock Holmes Center Here: Morris Township Man High Official in 'Baker St.' Group," *Morristown Daily Record* (August 29, 1955), 5.

An illustrated article on Edgar Smith and the Irregulars.

4614. Starrett, Vincent. "Edgar," *BSJ*, 11, No. 2 (June 1961), 73.

One great Sherlockian's tribute to another.

4615. Stix, Thomas L. "Sidelights on Smith," *BSJ*, 11, No. 2 (June 1961), 98-100.

"He was hopelessly and irretrievably in love with a man. . . . And, although the object of Edgar's passion was possibly a fictional character (as some foolish librarians maintain), there was nothing fictional about Edgar's feeling for Mr. Holmes."

4616. Stone, P. M. "Just the Other Day (In Fond Tribute to E. W. S.)," *BSJ*, 11, No. 2 (June 1961), 74-81.

"We think of him now with deep affection and proud remembrance, for he stood foremost among those eminent Sherlockians who have conducted us through the inviting byways of 'Baker Street and Beyond.' "

4617. Stout, Rex. "The Case of the Politician . . . ," *BSJ*, 11, No. 2 (June 1961), 82-83.

"But I doubt if any of them loved him better or were more impressed by his quiet force, his controlled warmth, his perceptive great good sense, his talent for true friendship, his understanding of what a man has a right to expect of another man."

4618. Walbridge, Earle F. "Edgar Wadsworth Smith, 1894-1960: A Bibliography," *BSJ*, 11, No. 2 (June 1961), 105-111. (Bibliographical Notes)

An impressive list of some sixty Sherlockian contributions by the former chief representative for Sherlock Holmes and the Baker Street Irregulars.

4619. [Wolff, Julian.] "In Memoriam: Edgar Wadsworth Smith, 1 April 1894-17 September 1960," *BSJ Christmas Annual* (1960), 259.

4620. [————.] "The Man Who Is Wanted," *BSJ*, 11, No. 2 (June 1961), 67-68. (The Editor's Gas-Lamp)

In an Edgar W. Smith Memorial issue of the *Journal,* Dr. Wolff pays fond tribute to a great Sherlockian and a man who was a personal friend to all. A full-page photograph of Mr. Smith appears on page 71.

VINCENT STARRETT

4621. Buchholtz, James. "Let's Talk About Our Town," *The Delphos Herald* (October 4, 1960).

————. Reprinted in part with title: "Let's Talk About Vincent Starrett," *BSJ*, 13, No. 1 (March 1963), 33-34. (Vincent Starrett Supplement)

A tribute to an author who "will be forever remembered as the definitive biographer of Sherlock Holmes."

4622. *The Devon County Chronicle.* Vincent Starrett Edition. Vol. 2, No. 1 (October 1965), 1-7.

Tributes to the dean of Sherlockians from twenty-five admirers on the occasion of the twentieth anniversary of his titular investiture, *A Study in Scarlet.*

4623. Keddie, James. "Some Random Thoughts on a Great Man and His Art," *BSJ*, 13, No. 1 (March 1963), 35-36. (Vincent Starrett Supplement)

An appreciation of "a gentleman of the highest order," with a brief discussion of some of his more important literary works.

4624. Rathbone, Basil. "Goodbye, My Friend," *BSJ*, 4, No. 2 (April 1954), 75-79.

————. ————, *In and Out of Character.* Garden City, N.Y.: Doubleday & Co., [1962]. p. 214-218.

The late actor describes a memorable visit with Vincent Starrett in Central Park on an autumn day in 1953.

4625. [Ruber, Peter A.] *The Last Bookman.* New York, N.Y.: The Candlelight Press, Inc., 1968. 115 p.

Limited to 2500 copies.

A beautifully illustrated and printed quarto book that contains many tributes by famous writers, including the author's "A Journey into the Life & Times of Vincent Starrett: Author, Journalist, Bibliophile." Items of Sherlockian interest are: *"The Private Life of Sherlock Holmes"*, by Peter Ruber (p. 53-54); "Sherlock, Tobacco, and a Gold-Headed Cane," by David A. Randall; "Holmesian," by Jacob C. Solovay; "Vincent Starrett, B.S.I.," by Henry Dierkes; and "Vincenzio from Chris," by Christopher Morley.

4626. Starrett, Vincent. *Born in a Bookshop: Chapters from the Chicago Renascence.* Norman: University of Oklahoma Press, [1965]. ix, 325 p. illus.

A well-written and fascinating autobiography of a great literary man and the world's foremost Sherlockian, containing much about Sherlock Holmes and the Baker Street Irregulars. A full-page reproduction of the author's Sherlock Holmes bookplate appears facing page 247.

Vincent Starrett (**4621-4629**).

4627. ———. "A Fragment of Autobiography," *Mystery Writers' Annual* (April 1965), 22.

Includes a short parody entitled "The Adventure of the Acephalous Agronomist," by A. Conan Watson.

"I can scarcely write a paragraph on any subject without bringing Holmes into the argument."

4628. ———. "The Last Bookman Meets Sherlock Holmes," *The Chicago Tribune Magazine* (August 10, 1969), 55-70. illus.
———. ———, *DCC*, 5, No. 6 (September 1969), 4-7.

A notable account of the author's visit with Basil Rathbone in 1951 and one with T. S. Eliot in 1956.

4629. ———. "Portrait of the Artist as an Old Dog," *The Chicago Tribune Magazine* (February 28, 1971), 34-36, 40.

THOMAS L. STIX

4630. Stix, Thomas L. "My First Meeting with Sherlock Holmes," *BSJ*, 1, No. 3 (July 1951), 106-107.

HARRY S. TRUMAN

4631. Crocker, Stephen F. "A Declaration from Independence, Mo., or The Affair of the Politician," *BSJ* [OS], 3, No. 4 (April 1946), 477-478.

"Harry S. Truman was born not on May 8, 1884, as usually stated, but on May 8, 1915. He was twelve years old, not in 1896, as might be inferred from the *Journal's* account [1, No. 2 (April 1946), 217], but in 1927, when the 'S' in his name came to stand for *Sherlock.*" Like his illustrious predecessor, President Truman was an honorary member of the Baker Street Irregulars.

RICHARD W. VAN FOSSEN

4632. Van Fossen, Richard W. "My First Meeting with Sherlock Holmes," *BSJ* [OS], 3, No. 2 (April 1948), 206-207.

"Sherlock Holmes completely filled the void of my young imagination, entrenched himself firmly in the position of hero in my young dreams."

STEPHEN DANIEL WILLIAMS

4633. Williams, Stephen Daniel. "Why I Enjoy Reading Sherlock Holmes," *VH*, 2, No. 1 (January 1968), 4.

The author of *The Adventures of Shylar Holmes* recalls his first encounter with "the greatest detective that the world has ever known."

JULIAN WOLFF

4634. Nelson, James. "Irregular Succession," *BSJ*, 13, No. 2 (June 1963), 72-73.

A laudable attempt to prove that Dr. Wolff, Commissionaire of the Baker Street Irregulars, is hereditarily linked to the Canon.

4635. ———. "*Pravda* Accuses C.I.A. and B.S.I.," *BSJ*, 17, No. 2 (June 1967), 77.

"Moscow, April 1—*Pravda* said today that the Central Intelligence Agency has subsidized a certain Doctor Julian Wolff, of 33 Riverside Drive, New York City. He is alleged to be a drop for large sums of CIA money which he passes along to a magazine called *The Baker Street Journal.*"

B The Societies

This section contains items about the societies, their activities, and their publications. The periodicals issued by some of these societies appear in Part V, Section F. Other items of the societies, such as Christmas cards and mementos, are listed in Part VII under *Miscellany*. Numerous accounts of the activities of these societies are published in local newspapers, but only a limited number of these were available to the compiler for listing.

Since the Baker Street Irregulars (also referred to as BSI or the Irregulars) was founded in 1934, some 150 scion societies have flourished from time to time. These societies, together with their addresses, are listed in Appendix III. Two other societies comparable to the BSI are the Sherlock Holmes Society of London and the Sherlock Holmes Klubben i Danmark.

Sherlockians and The Societies

The Societies

Many of the societies sponsor exhibits, tours, commemorative excursions, and annual horse races in honor of "Silver Blaze." They also hold meetings and dinners, including an annual dinner to commemorate the Master's birthday on January 6.

The number of individuals belonging to these societies ranges from approximately 175 for the Irregulars to none for the fictitious Solitary Cyclist of Washington, D.C., founded by "Helene Yuhasova." Their journals are subscribed to not only by the individual members but also by many other Sherlockians and by public and academic libraries.

THE BAKER STREET IRREGULARS

4636. [Anderson, James L.] "The Visiting Fireman Among the Baker Street Irregulars," *Newsletter*, Class of 1924, Columbia College (May 1962), 5-7.

"The Sheriff of Brooklyn, President of the Class of 1924 [of which the editor of *BSJ* is a member], writes most understandingly of the Irregulars, the Journal, the 1961 Silver Blaze and the 1962 dinner—both of which he attended." (Julian Wolff)

4637. [Avery, Delos.] "Marvelous, Holmes, Marvelous!" by Halifax Gadley II [pseud.] *The Chicago Tribune* (July 7, 1944).

———. ———, *BSJ* [OS], 1, No. 1 (January 1946), 28.

"Irregulars of Baker Street / Do you do *anything* but eat? / Once a year you congregate / Around a savoury dinner plate; / But did you ever solve a crime? / If so, please name the place and time. / Instead of catching wanted crooks / You merely make more work for cooks. / I know what Sherlock Holmes will say / If he discovers you some day: / 'The things you concentrate your thoughts on / Are alimentary, my dear Watson.' "

4638. Baring-Gould, William S. "Re: The Baker Street Irregulars," *The American Book Collector*, 9, No. 9 (May 1959), 20-21.

"Chatty and pointed commentary for the initiated and uninitiated alike." (Edgar W. Smith)

4639. ———. " 'A Singular Set of People, Watson . . . ,' " *Esquire*, 65, No. 1 (January 1966), 92-95, 112.

———. ———, *CPBook*, 3, No. 10 (Fall 1966), 196-200.

"The most knowledgeable article about the Baker Street Irregulars that has ever appeared in a non-Sherlockian publication. Illustrated with a photograph of the 1965 dinner and reproductions of the crossword and its solution." (Julian Wolff)

4640. ———. ———, *The Annotated Sherlock Holmes.* New York: Clarkson N. Potter, [1967]. Vol. 1, chap. 6, p. 37-42. illus.

Primarily a new article on the Irregulars, but contains much the same information as the above.

4641. Bengis, Nathan L. "Marked Down—Irregular," *BSJ*, 14, No. 4 (December 1964), 230-238, 245.

An account of BSI's annual proceedings on January 10, 1964. "The story is altogether fictional, but any resemblance to real characters is entirely intentional." (Julian Wolff)

4642. Booth, John E. "Annals of a Sleuth," *The New York Times Magazine* (May 11, 1947), 30-31.

"In *The Baker Street Journal*, inveterate Sherlockians keep alive the Holmes myth." (Subtitle)

4643. Brown, Vivian. "Sherlock Holmes Carries On," Distributed by AP Newsfeatures, March 21, 1945.

———. "The Lowdown on Edgar W. Smith," *For Loving a Book*, by Charles Honce. Mount Vernon, N.Y.: The Golden Eagle Press, 1945, p. 45-46.

Information on the Irregulars and Edgar Smith's contribution to Sherlockiana.

4644. Bylin, Jim. "Sherlock Holmes Still Alive, Club Contends," *Valley Times* (July 15, 1959), 3.

An interview with John Ball, Jr., in which he discusses the Irregulars. Includes a photograph of Mr. Ball.

4645. Cerf, Bennett. ["The Baker Street Irregulars"], *The Saturday Review of Literature*, 31, No. 7 (February 14, 1948), 4. (Trade Winds)

———. ———, *CPBook*, 2, No. 7-8 (Winter-Spring 1966), 161-162.

An account of the author's attendance at the 1948 dinner.

4646. Davis, Douglas M. "Sipping and Supping with the Baker Street Irregulars," *The National Observer* (January 17, 1966), 24.

A four-column article on the Irregulars' annual dinners.

4647. Davis, Elmer. "Constitution and Buy-Laws of the Baker Street Irregulars," *The Saturday Review of Literature*, 10, No. 31 (February 17, 1934), 491. (The Bowling Green)

———. ———, *The Case of the Baker Street Irregulars*, by Anthony Boucher. New York: Simon and Schuster, 1940. p. 3-4.

———. ———. [With a note by Vincent Starrett.] Ysleta, [Texas]: Edwin B. Hill, 1940. [4] p. (Sherlockiana)

———. ———, *Profile by Gaslight.* Edited

308

Some publications of Sherlockian societies (**4178-4215**).

by Edgar W. Smith. New York: Simon and Schuster, 1944. p. 292-293.

————. ————, *BSJ*, 11, No. 3 (September 1961), 149.

————. ————, Read by Frank Waters, January 1965. *Voices from Baker Street*, 2. Ferndale, Mich.: The Old Soldiers of Baker Street, 1965. Side 1, band 1.

————. ————, *Esquire*, 65, No. 1 (January 1966), 95.

————. ————, *BSP*, No. 23 (May 1967), 6.

————. ————, *Seven on Sherlock*, by Thayer Cumings. [New York]: Privately Printed, 1968. p. 37-38.

4648. Donegall, Lord. ["The Two-Shilling Award"], *SHJ*, 10, No. 2 (Summer 1971), 38.
    An acknowledgment of the Marquis of

Donegall's receipt of BSI's highest honor—the Two-Shilling Award. The other recipients have been Rex Stout, William S. Baring-Gould, Vincent Starrett, Jay Finley Christ, William S. Hall, Thomas L. Stix, Julian Wolff, S. Tupper Bigelow, Charles Honce, Lord Gore-Booth, Allen Robertson, and Howard Haycraft.

4649. Dresser, Ivan C. "The Baker Street Widow's Lament," *BSJ*, 4, No. 1 (January 1954), 50-51.
    "Wives young and old all cry out 'Shame!' / Sherlock Holmes is all to blame— / I'm a Baker Street Widow to his name."

4650. Gallico, Paul. "Sherlock Holmes *Must*

The Societies

Live On," *The American Weekly* (August 12, 1945), 10.

"Kept alive by the fertile minds of the Baker Street Irregulars, the Old Gentleman has attained immortality in the hearts of his millions of worshippers throughout the civilized world."

4651. Gibbs, Wolcott. "The Curious Incident of the Dogs in the Night-Time," *The New Yorker*, 24, No. 30 (September 18, 1948), 26-29.

———. ———, *CPBook*, 3, No. 9 (Summer 1966), 179-181.

Over several martinis, Goetz and Harrington discuss the Canonical tales and then crash a meeting of a group they mistakenly believe to be the Irregulars.

4652. Gore-Booth, Paul. "Sherlock Holmes in America," *The Strand*, 116, No. 699 (March 1949), 101, 103. (Some Things Worth Knowing)

A commentary on the Irregulars and their Journal.

4653. Greenfield, Louis. ["The Baker Street Irregulars"], *The Saturday Review of Literature*, 25, No. 3 (January 17, 1942), 21-22. (Trade Winds)

A report on the activities of the BSI annual dinner.

4654. Hartman, Harry. "Five Pillows of Wisdom," *BSG*, 1, No. 2 (1961), 16-18.

———. ———, *The Holy Quire*. [Culver City, Calif.: Luther Norris, December 1970.] p. 36-38.

An exhortation to the President of the U.S. to choose a member of BSI as the next Ambassador to the Court of St. James's, giving cogent reasons, with appropriate allusions from the Canon.

4655. [Henriksen, A. D.] "Hvem er the Baker Street Irregulars?" ["Who Are the Baker Street Irregulars?"], *Sherlock Holmes Årbog* I (1965), 86-91.

4656. Hoagland, Marjorie. "Baker Street Irregulars," *The Christian Science Monitor* (April 29, 1965), 8. (The Home Forum)

———. ———, *CPBook*, 1, No. 4 (Spring 1965), 72-73.

A discussion of the Irregulars, the scion societies, and the Holmes saga.

4657. Honce, Charles. "The Baker Street Irregulars," *Mark Twain's Associated Press Speech and Other News Stories*. New York: Privately Printed, 1940. p. 90-95.

An essay dated December 15, 1934, on the Irregulars and the writings about the Writings.

4658. ———. "Postscript on Sherlock Holmes," *The Public Papers of a Bibliomaniac*. Mount Vernon: The Golden Eagle Press, 1942. p. 155-158.

A brief commentary on BSI and the Speckled Band of Boston, together with a letter from Edgar Smith to Vincent Starrett which Mr. Honce has entitled "The Creeping Man."

4659. ———. "Sherlockiana," *For Loving a Book*. Mount Vernon, N.Y.: The Golden Eagle Press, 1945, p. 29-32.

Includes reprints of two stories by Charles Honce and Harry Hansen about the dinner that was staged by three publishers at the Murray Hill Hotel on March 31, 1944, to commemorate the Master and the publication of *Profile by Gaslight, The Misadventures of Sherlock Holmes,* and *Sherlock Holmes and Dr. Watson.*

4660. Hornfelt, Dorothy. " 'Baker Street Irregulars' Honor the Living Sherlock Holmes," *Saturday Night: The Canadian Illustrated Weekly* [Toronto], 60, No. 49 (August 11, 1945), 33.

A summary and appraisal of the Irregulars and their background.

4661. "In Memoriam: Baker Street," *Time*, 43, No. 16 (April 17, 1944), 98.

A tribute to the Irregulars and their intellectual sponsorship of the 1944 Sherlockian trilogy.

4662. Kaplan, Morris. "Sherlock Holmes Takes Interest in Baffling Murray Hill Case," *The New York Times* (October 24, 1946), 29.

———. ———, *CPBook*, 2, No. 7-8 (Winter-Spring 1966), 163.

"Mystery of the disappearing lawyer and who leaves hotel, and when, may be solved Jan. 2 for Baker St. devotees." (Subtitle)

4663. [Leavitt, Robert Keith.] "The Origin of 221B Worship," by an Old Bibliophile. *BSJ*, 11, No. 3 (September 1961), 135-149; 11, No. 4 (December 1961), 225-234.

Winner of the 4th annual Morley-Montgomery Memorial Award for the best contribution to *BSJ* in 1961.

Contents: Pt. 1. The Chaldean Roots. - Pt. 2. Our Own Dear Little Girlie Becomes a) Legitimate, b) The Subject of Unmitigated Bleat.

"Some notes on the conception, gestation, parturition, and legitimization of the Baker Street Irregulars," (Subtitle)

4664. Mahoney, Tom. "Baker Street Irregulars," *'47: The Magazine of the Year*, 1, No. 6 (August 1947), 98-103.

"An intelligent and illuminating account of the origin and doings of the parent society and its scions." (Edgar W. Smith) The article is illustrated in the margins with a pictorial quiz by Jan Balet.

4665. McDade, Thomas M. "The First Conanical Toast: To 'the Woman'—Pola (Mrs. Rex) Stout," *BSJ*, 16, No. 1 (March 1966), 23.

Delivered at the annual dinner on January 7, 1966.

"I give you *The* Woman of Sherlock's own day, / Irene Adler the beauty, capricious and gay."

4666. McFadden, William J. "Sherlockian Irregulars," *Newark Sunday News* (May 5, 1957), 7-9.

An illustrated article on Edgar Smith and the Irregulars.

4667. McLauchlin, Russell. "The Stately Holmes of England," *Among Friends* [Detroit Public Library], 3, No. 3 (January-March 1949), 1, 3.

4668. Meyer, Karl E. "Irregulars Celebrate Holmes's 110th Birthday," *The Washington Post* (January 12, 1964), Al.
———. ———, *CPBook*, 1, No. 1 (Summer 1964), 15.

4669. [Morley, Christopher.] ["The Baker Street Irregulars"], *The Saturday Review of Literature*, 10, No. 25 (January 6, 1934), 395; 10, No. 27 (January 20, 1934), 423; 10, No. 28 (January 27, 1934), 439; 10, No. 29 (February 3, 1934), 451; 10, No. 31 (February 17, 1934), 491. (The Bowling Green)
———. ———, *BSP*, No. 23 (May 1967), 5-6.

Shows the development of the first Sherlockian society, from the original idea advanced by "Charing Cross" on January 6, 1934, to the BSI Constitution drawn up by Elmer Davis and published in "The Bowling Green" column on February 17, 1934.

4670. ———. ["The Baker Street Irregulars"], *BSJ* [OS], 1, No. 3 (July 1946), 288-291. (Clinical Notes by a Resident Patient)
———. ———, *BSJ*, 13, No. 1 (March 1963), 17-22.
———. Reprinted in part with title: "A Note on the Baker Street Irregulars," *The Adventure of the Blue Carbuncle.* [Deluxe ed.] New York: The Baker Street Irregulars, 1948. p. 67-70.

The beginnings of the BSI by its founder; with a tribute to *the* Man, Edgar W. Smith.

4671. ———. "Codeine (7 Per Cent)," *Ellery Queen's Mystery Magazine*, 6, No. 25 (November 1945), 42-45.
———. ———, *To the Queen's Taste.* The first supplement to *101 Years' Entertainment.* . . . Edited by Ellery Queen. Boston: Little, Brown and Co., 1946. p. 136-141.
———. ———, *The Ironing Board.* Garden City, N.Y.: Doubleday & Co., 1949. p. 110-115.

Dove Dulcet attends a BSI dinner and discusses Holmes's sister and niece Violet Hargreave, and spies and codes.

4672. ———. ["A Membership Directory of the Baker Street Irregulars for 1935"], *BSJ*, 10, No. 3 (July 1960), 178. (From the Editor's Commonplace Book)

4673. ["The Morley-Montgomery Memorial Award"], *BSJ*, 8, No. 2 (April 1958), 121. (From the Editor's Commonplace Book)

An announcement of the establishment by Lew D. Feldman of an annual award of $100 for the best contribution to *The Baker Street Journal.* The award is in honor of Christopher Morley, founder of the Irregulars and its Gasogene-cum-Tantalus, and James Montgomery, the Irregulars' songster extraordinary.

Recipients of the awards are as follows: 1958. Poul Anderson. - 1959. Daniel L. Moriarty. - 1960. Jerry Neal Williamson. - 1961. Robert Keith Leavitt. - 1962. S. Tupper Bigelow. - 1963. Edward F. Clark, Jr. - 1964. Ronald S. Bonn. - 1965. Henry T. Folsom. - 1966. Alan H. Foster. - 1967. William S. Baring-Gould. - 1968. Poul Anderson - 1969. William H. Miller. - 1970. Edward A. Merrill. - 1971. Henry C. Potter.

4674. Nolan, Norman S. *A Case of Identities* (*sic*). Middletown, N.J.: [Privately Printed], May 29, 1971. 1 folded leaf.

"An identification key to the official photograph of the B.S.I. dinner—Jan. 8, 1971, the Players Club, N.Y." (Subtitle)

4675. Officer, Harvey. "The Road to Baker Street," *The Saturday Review of Literature*, 25, No. 3 (January 17, 1942), 21.
———. ———, *A Baker Street Song Book.* New York: The Pamphlet House, 1943, p. 30.
———. ———, *Profile by Gaslight.* Edited by Edgar W. Smith. New York: Simon and Schuster, 1944. p. 301-303.
———. ———, Last stanza tr. into Danish by A. D. Henriksen. *Sangen om Baker Street.* København: [Grafisk Cirkel], 1958. p. 19. Reprinted in *Sherlockiana*, 3, Nr. 3-4 (1958), 13; *Sherlock Holmes Årbog* II (1966), 50-51.
———. ———, First verse and chorus sung by the Cavanagh Choraleers, January 1962. *Voices from Baker Street*, 2. Ferndale, Mich.: The Old Soldiers of Baker Street, 1965. Side 1, band 2.

The Irregulars' anthem sung antiphonally, to the tune of "The Road to Mandalay," at all gatherings.

4676. Parker, Robert G. "I Located the B.S.I.," *BSJ*, 11, No. 1 (March 1961), 58-62.
The author tells of his laborious efforts to

Sherlockians and The Societies

The Societies

311

The Societies

find the address of the Baker Street Irregulars.

4677. Parry, Henry T. "The Baker Street Irregulars Murder Case," *Ellery Queen's Mystery Magazine,* 51, No. 2 (February 1968), 67-73.

"This has to do with a murder at one of our dinners and is written by one who has first-hand knowledge of the proceedings." (Julian Wolff)

4678. Porzio, Ralph. ["The Irregulars of Baker Street"], *BSJ,* 7, No. 3 (July 1957), 188. (From the Editor's Commonplace Book)

"Join, if you will, the bold fraternity / Which dares to deny the Holmes paternity."

4679. Robinson, Henry Morton. "Baker Street Irregularities: The Sacred Cult of Philosherlosophism," *The Saturday Review of Literature,* 26, No. 49 (December 4, 1943), 10-11.

"A mad brotherhood, these Irregulars, bending elbow and knee to the memory of a man who never existed! Within the circle of their quaint fellowship, they practise the cult of 'philo-sherlosophism'—which means 'love and knowledge of Sherlock Holmes.' "

4680. [Scott, Kenneth W.] *The Baker Street Irregulars.* [Washington, Ind.: Privately Produced, 1957.] [7] p.

4681. Shaw, John Bennett. "The Cult of Sherlock Holmes," *The Armchair Detective,* 1, No. 2 (January 1968), 53-55.

An informative discussion of the Sherlockian societies, emphasizing BSI and the scion societies.

4682. "Sherlock Holmes Dinner Held in New York," *Publishers' Weekly,* 145, No. 15 (April 8, 1944), 1459, 1462.

"The dinner in honor of Sherlock Holmes and the three books about him which were published in March was held at the Murray Hill Hotel on March 31 and was a great success."

4683. Silvian, Lee. "That Urge to Merge: A Guide to Serious, Pseudo-Serious and Kooky Clubs," *Signature: The Diners Club Magazine,* 2, Issue 7W / C (July 1967), 38.

Six paragraphs are devoted to the Irregulars.

4684. [Smith, Edgar W.] "An Age Passes," *BSJ* [OS], 1, No. 4 (October 1946), 383-384. (The Editor's Gas-Lamp)

A note on the passing of the Murray Hill Hotel where the Irregulars met each year from 1936 to 1945 in Parlors F and G. The hotel was closed down in 1945.

4685. ———. "The Baker Street Irregulars," *Courier,* 22, No. 1 (January 1954), 81-84.

———. ———, *BSJ,* 12, No. 3 (September 1962), 151-156.

An account of the Society's activities for the benefit and enlightenment of the British public.

4686. [———.] [*"The Baker Street Journal"*], *BSJ* [OS], 1, No. 1 (January 1946), 3-5; 2, No. 1 (January 1947), 3-4; 3, No. 1 (January 1948), 3-4; (NS), 1, No. 1 (January 1951), 1-2; 2, No. 2 (April 1952), 63-64; 4, No. 2 (April 1954), 67-68; 4, No. 4 (October 1954), 195-196; 5, No. 1 (January 1955), 3-4; 5, No. 2 (April 1955), 67-68; *Christmas Annual,* No. 2 (1957), 3-4; 8, No. 3 (July 1958), 131-132; *Christmas Annual,* No. 3 (1958), 3-4; 10, No. 1 (January 1960), 3-4; 10, No. 2 (April 1960), 67-68. (The Editor's Gas-Lamp)

Editorial commentaries on a journal devoted to critical analyses of the Sacred Writings, and which continues its sturdy adherence to the motto given to it by Christopher Morley: "Never has so much been written by so many for so few."

4687. ———. "The Creeping Man," *The Public Papers of a Bibliomaniac,* by Charles Honce. Mount Vernon: The Golden Eagle Press, 1942. p. 156-158.

———. "An Unrecorded Incident," *Profile by Gaslight.* Edited by Edgar W. Smith. New York: Simon and Schuster, 1944. p. 298-300.

———. ———, *Baker Street and Beyond: Together with Some Trifling Monographs.* Morristown, N.J.: The Baker Street Irregulars, 1957. [unpaged]

In a letter dated September 22, 1941, to Vincent Starrett, the author relates the episode of a creeping man in the corridor of the Murray Hill Hotel during the 1941 dinner meeting of the Irregulars.

4688. [———.] "A Greeting in Arduis," by Helene Yuasova [pseud.] *BSJ* [OS], 1, No. 1 (January 1946), 64.

———. ———, *A Lauriston Garden of Verses,* by Helene Yuhasova. Summit, N.J.: The Pamphlet House, 1946. p. [5].

"To the Baker Street Irregulars on the occasion of their Annual Dinner, 1945."

"Despite my prayers to Zeus and great Jehovah / I'm not, alas, a Baker Street Irregular."

4689. [———.] "Investitured Irregular," *BSJ,* 8, No. 3 (July 1958), 192.

A reproduction of the certificate that denotes membership in the BSI.

4690. [———.] "The Kindred Souls," *BSJ,* 2, No. 4 (October 1952), 183-184. (The Editor's Gas-Lamp)

"For it is characteristic of the well-rounded, earthly, generously-sophisticated man, somehow, to be interested in Sherlock Holmes; to see eye-to-eye with the Baker

Street Irregulars in their strength-giving foibles."

4691. ———. "Murder at the Murray Hill," *Leaves from the Copper Beeches*. Narberth, Pa.: Livingston Pub. Co., 1959. p. 57-73.

A short story in which Holmes executes the son of Moriarty during an Irregulars' dinner at the Murray Hill Hotel.

4692. [———.] "Sonnet: To the Old Lady of Murray Hill," by Helene Yuhasova [pseud.] *BSJ* [OS], 2, No. 2 (April 1947), 172.
———. ———, *Baker Street and Beyond: Together with Some Trifling Monographs.* Morristown, N.J.: The Baker Street Irregulars, 1957. [unpaged]

A tribute in verse to the hotel where the Irregulars held several of their annual dinner meetings (the first took place on December 7, 1934, at Christ Cella's). On page 173 in *BSJ* are two photographs of the final BSI gathering at the Murray Hill Hotel on January 3, 1947.

4693. [———.] "Who Is a Baker Street Irregular?" *BSJ* [OS], 3, No. 2 (April 1948), 135-136. (The Editor's Gas-Lamp)
———. ———, *BSJ*, 22, No. 1 (March 1972), 3.

"An Irregular is any kindred soul who gives spontaneously and abundantly of his time and thought in devotion to the Sacred Writings and to the writings about the Writings; who feels his pulse quicken and his steps seem lighter whenever, in a darkling world, he turns the corner of reality into the most magic of all streets."

4694. Snyder, Edward D. "Job for the Irregulars," *The Saturday Review of Literature*, 28, No. 19 (May 12, 1945), 15.

4695. Starrett, Vincent. "The Baker Street Irregulars," *The Private Life of Sherlock Holmes*. Revised and enlarged. The University of Chicago Press, [1960]. p. 128-136.
———. ———, [Revised] *Born in a Bookshop.* Norman: University of Oklahoma Press, [1965]. Chap. 20, p. 276-284.
———. "Sherlock and His Friends: An Irregular Memoir," *The Daily Californian Weekly Magazine*, 4, No. 9 (January 14, 1969), 9-10.

4696. Van Fossen, Richard. "The Magic of Baker Street," *The Archive* [The Students of Duke University, Durham, N.C.], 63, No. 1 (October 1949), 7-9.

4697. Van Gelder, Lawrence. "Sherlock Holmes in 115th Year: Baker St. Irregulars and Others Mark Birthday Here," *The New York Times* (January 7, 1968), 72.

———. ———, *CPBook*, 4, No. 14 (Winter 1968), 263A.
———. ———, *Sherlockiana*, 13, Nr. 1-2 (1968), 4.

An informative discussion of Holmes and the Irregulars by a member of the *Times* staff.

4698. Walbridge, Earle F. "Bibliographical Notes," *BSJ* [OS], 2, No. 2 (April 1947), 226-228.

Comments on the BSI meeting of January 3, 1947, and some Canonical tales owned by Mr. Walbridge.

4699. Wigglesworth, Belden. "Cum Laude: *The Baker Street Journal*," *BSJ* [OS], 1, No. 1 (January 1946), 6.

An acrostic sonnet saluting the *Journal* on the occasion of its first issue.

4700. Wolff, Ezra A. "Ruminations on a First Attendance at the Annual Dinner of the Baker Street Irregulars," *BSJ*, 19, No. 1 (March 1969), 48.

"Irregulars all are egg domes / Who pore through Conanical tomes / Then go to a party / And hiss Moriarty / And drink 'til they think they are Holmes."

4701. ———. "Second Thoughts After the Annual Dinner, 1970," *BSJ*, 20, No. 1 (March 1970), 37.

"Attendance at B.S.I. teaches / That honeyed and erudite speeches / Still drip from the lips. . . ."

4702. ———. "1971 B.S.I. Annual Dinner—Post Mortems," *BSJ*, 21, No. 1 (March 1971), 49.

"Once again we've come to the season / When B.S.I.'s, parting from reason, / Derive from their tomes / About Sherlock Holmes / Conclusions that Doyle would call treason."

4703. [Wolff, Julian.] *"The Baker Street Journal,"* *BSJ*, 11, No. 1 (March 1961), 3-4. (The Editor's Gas-Lamp)

In his first editorial Dr. Wolff, successor to the late Edgar Smith, has written a brief history of the *Journal*.

4704. [———.] "Irregular Commissionaire," *BSJ*, 13, No. 2 (June 1963), 71. (The Editor's Gas-Lamp)

A clarification of the titles used by Irregular officers.

4705. [———.] "One Hundred Issues," *BSJ*, 21, No. 2 (June 1971), 67-68. (The Editor's Gas-Lamp)

A commemorative editorial on the *Journal.*

4706. Woollcott, Alexander. "The Baker Street Irregulars," *The New Yorker*, 10, No.

The Societies

46 (December 29, 1934), 64. (Shouts & Murmurs)

——. ——, *Long, Long Ago*. New York: Viking Press, 1943. p. 172-175.

——. ——, *Profile by Gaslight*. Edited by Edgar W. Smith. New York: Simon and Schuster, 1944. p. 294-297.

——. ——, *The Portable Woollcott*. Selected by Joseph Hennessey, with an introduction by John Mason Brown. New York: Viking Press, 1946. p. 626-629.

A tribute to the Irregulars and to the source of their inspiration.

The Scion Societies

4707. The Baker Street Pageboys. "Constitution," *BSP* (NS), 1, No. 1 (June-July 1971), 5-6.

4708. Belanger, Terry. "Travels with a Pumpkin," *BSJ*, 17, No. 1 (March 1967), 45-47.

The youngest member of the Sons of the Copper Beeches relates his experience of showing up at a meeting with a Sherlock Holmes jack o'lantern.

4709. [Bowe, Edwina.] "The Baker St. Irregulars," *San Francisco Examiner / People, The California Weekly* (February 9, 1964), 2-3.

Information on the Irregulars and the Scowrers.

4710. Bradley, Worthen. "A Song for the Scowrers," *West by One and by One*. San Francisco: Privately Printed, 1965. p. 5-6.

"Brush up your Sherlock, / Start quoting him now. . . ."

4711. Buchwald, Art. "Old Soldiers of Baker Street," *New York Herald Tribune* (March 30, 1952).

——. ——, *CPBook*, 1, No. 1 (Summer 1964), 8.

An interview with Lt. Rabe in which he discusses the military branch of BSI and its research on the writings of Dr. Watson.

4712. Clarke, Richard W. "The Five Orange Pips," *BSJ*, 11, No. 2 (June 1961), 101-102.

A brief history of the oldest Sherlockian scion society, established in 1935.

4713. Clarkson, Paul S., Jr. *The Six Napoleons, Scion Society of the Baker Street Irregulars*. [Introduction by Paul S. Clarkson (Sr.)] [Baltimore, Md.: Privately Printed, December 1969.] [20] p.

Limited to 250 copies.

The history, terminology, and traditions of one of the largest (numbering over 120 members) and most active scion societies.

4714. [Cutter, Robert A.] "Sherlock Explains," *Sherlockian Studies*. Edited by Robert A.

Cutter. [Jackson Heights, N.Y.: The Baker Street Press, 1947.] p. 35-36.

A conversation between Holmes and Watson concerning the Hounds of the Baskerville (sic).

4715. Dame, William M. "The Baltimore Legend of Sherlock Holmes," *The Baltimore Sun Magazine* (March 30, 1947), 9, 20.

An article about the Six Napoleons.

4716. Dickensheet, Shirley. "A Short Resume of Cormorant Activities," *CR*, 1, No. 3 (April 1960), 4-5, 18.

4717. Enright, Robert. "The Murderous Ghazis," *BSP*, No. 15 (September 1966), 1-2.

A sympathetic article on a scion society, subsequently disbanded, that opposes the Establishment—Sherlockian and otherwise. For more up-to-date information—and straight from the "Hippie's" mouth—see Elizabeth Yew's letter in *BSP*, No. 17 (November 1966), 2; and Robert Enright's critical reply in *BSP*, No. 18 (December 1966), 3-4.

4718. Eustace, Frank J. "The Sherlockian Adventures of the Philadelphia Lawyers," *The Shingle* [Philadelphia Bar Association], 28, No. 4 (April 1965), 93-94.

An article on Holmes and members of the Sons of the Copper Beeches, especially their legal lights.

4719. Goldman, Ivan G. "Sherlock Holmes Case Probed: Baker Street Irregulars, Fans of Renowned Detective, Hear Account of His Work on Murder Here," *The Kansas City Star* (June 26, 1968), 5F.

A report on the second annual luncheon of the Sub-Librarians Scion in ALA, Kansas City, Mo., during which Milton Perry, Dean Dickensheet, and Ronald De Waal presented papers on various aspects of the Writings.

4720. Grady, T. Franklin. "Of Julia Stoner, the Spartans, and Us," *BSJ* 19, No. 3 (September 1969), 182.

A tribute to the Speckled Band at its annual meeting on May 9, 1969.

4721. Granger, William. "Eternal Sleuth Serves Up Still Another Solution," *Chicago Sun-Times* (January 8, 1970).

——. ——, *DCC*, 6, No. 2 (March 1970), 5.

An account of the joint birthday party on January 6 of Hugo's Companions and the Hounds of the Baskerville (sic) during which Hans Conreid discussed his portrayal of Professor Moriarty in a Sherlock Holmes radio series.

4722. [Hahn, Robert W.] ["The Hounds of the

Baskerville (sic) and Hugo's Companions''],
DCC, 1, No. 1- (December 1964-).

The proceedings of these two scion societies' annual dinners and meetings in Chicago are reported in various issues of *The Devon County Chronicle.*

4723. [———.] "Tec Fete Boffo in Chi," *DCC*, 6, No. 2 (March 1970), 1, 4, 8.

An interesting account of the Chicago BSI's first *public* observance of the Master's birthday. Vincent Starrett was cited as "Sherlockian of the Year" and Franklin W. Rhode received the Horace Harker Award as the outstanding contributor to the *Chronicle.*

4724. Hart, Thomas. "A Word to the Sons of the Copper Beeches, 1947-1957 (and a Few Trifling Memories After Ten Years)," *Leaves from the Copper Beeches.* Narberth, Pa.: Livingston Pub. Co., 1959. p. 1-8.

4725. Hawkins, Barbara M. "Waggish Sherlockians Toast Master Detective with Tongue in Cheek," *The Journal and Courier, Vista Magazine* [Lafayette, Ind.] (May 8, 1965), 4-5.

An illustrated article on Holmes, the scion societies, and Professor Edward S. Lauterbach.

4726. Hugo's Companions. *In the Footsteps of Sherlock Holmes: A Tour to Switzerland and England Sponsored by Hugo's Companions, September 1971.* [Oak Park, Ill.: Privately Produced, 1970.] 4 p.

The itinerary and application form for this tour, from September 16 to October 2, 1971, arranged by Rex Travel Organization, Inc.

4727. Koelle, John B. "The Singular Experience of J. Forsythe Follansbee," *BSJ*, 13, No. 3 (September 1963), 142-147.

An amusing story in which Follansbee tells how he and a client named "Holmes" attend a dinner of the Sons of the Copper Beeches, after which they visit the Rigoletto Coffee House where the overexuberant and inebriated "Holmes" tries to apprehend the proprietor "Ricoletti" and his abominable wife (an unrecorded case referred to by Holmes in Musg). The evening ends with "Holmes" and "Watson" (Follansbee) being booked on a disorderly conduct charge by one T. Gregory ("Tobias Gregson").

4728. Marranzino, Pasquale. "Icy Sculpture Proved a Bust," *Rocky Mountain News* [Denver] (August 23, 1972), 51.

A member of BSI's Vail Chapter tells how he, along with William K. Whiteford, Marquis Antonio Guadnagni, and Robert Flanigan, erected a bust of the Master on a mountain above the Vail ski resort. The bust

was gone by morning, though, as it had been sculpt out of a block of ice!

4729. McLauchlin, Russell. "On First Looking in on the Chicago Baskervilles (September 30, 1947)," *BSJ* [OS], 3, No. 1 (January 1948), 83.

"Keeping a joyous, long-awaited tryst, / One autumn evening, at the Palmer House, / With Charlie Collins and Jay Finley Christ."

4730. Page, Andrew. "The Baker Street Pageboys and Junior Sherlockiana," *BSP* (NS), 1, No. 1 (June-July 1971), 2-3.

4731. [———.] " 'Gentlemen, Let Me Introduce You to . . . ,' " *HO*, 1, No. 1 (March 1971), 2-5.

An introduction to the first issue of *The Holmesian Observer* explaining the procedures of the Priory School of New York, and giving information on its official publication, officers, and requirements for membership.

4732. ———, ed. *An Introduction to Sherlock Holmes.* Bronx, N.Y.: The Priory School of New York and The Baker Street Pageboys, May 17, 1971. [8] p.

"With information about all Sherlockian activities and the Constitution of the Priory School of New York." (Subtitle)

4733. [———.] ' "A Scion for All Seasons,' " [by] Wiggins. *BSP*(NS), 1, No. 4 (December-January 1971-72), 1-2.

An editorial recommending the merger of junior scions into *"one solid junior organization."* Another view is expressed by "Cartwright" (Glenn Holland) on page 3-4 of the same issue.

4734. Patrick, Ralph K. "The Real Mayor of Topeka in 1890 Was Roswell F. Cofran," *The Times* [North Little Rock, Ark.] (May 8, 1969), 2A (The Reporter's Notebook)

An announcement of the formation and first dinner meeting of the Arkansas Valley Investors, Ltd.

4735. Pratt, Steven. "Vincent Starrett: A Man Who Really Knows Sherlock Holmes," *Chicago Tribune* (October 5, 1969).
———. ———, *DCC*, 6, No. 1 (December 1969), 2.

Mainly about the 25th anniversary meeting of the Hounds of the Baskerville (sic) that was attended by the scion society's founder and most honored member, Mr. Starrett.

4736. Prestige, Colin. "A Small Quartering," *SHJ*, 8, No. 3 (Winter 1967), 99.

A report on this British Holmesian's attendance at the 20th anniversary dinner

The Societies

meeting of the Sons of the Copper Beeches on October 17, 1967.

4737. Redmond, Chris. "Lighthouses, My Boy!" *BSP Christmas Annual*, No. 1 (1966), 2-3.
———. Revised with title: "Lighthouses: A History of the Baker Street Pageboys," *BSP*, No. 49-50 (July-August 1969), 3-5.

4738. Root, Jonathan. "Sherlock Holmes Lives On," *The San Francisco Chronicle* (January 10, 1966), 2.
———. ———, *CPBook*, 3, No. 10 (Fall 1966), 191.
An article about the annual dinner of the Scowrers and Molly Maguires.

4739. The Scandalous Bohemians of New Jersey. "Constitution," *SS*, 1, No. 1 (January 1971). Issued as a separate sheet (2 p.)

4740. "The Scion Societies," *BSJ* [OS], 1-4, No. 1 (April 1946-January 1949); (NS), 1- (January 1951-   ).
A regular department of *The Baker Street Journal* in which Sherlockian societies, usually considered scions or chapters of BSI, report on their meetings and other activities.

4741. ["The Scowrers and Molly Maguires"], *VH*, 1, No. 1-   (January 1967-   ).
The proceedings of this scion society's annual dinners and meetings in San Francisco are regularly reported in *The Vermissa Herald*.

4742. Shepard, Joseph K. "Sherlock Holmes . . . in Indiana," *The Indianapolis Star Magazine* (December 19, 1954), 4, 7. illus.
An interesting account of the activities of the Master Detective as a Hoosier-pro-tem, and of the Sherlockian contributions by Jerry Williamson, "Pete" Williams, *et al*, of the Illustrious Clients.

4743. Smith, Edgar W. "West by One and by One," *BSJ Christmas Annual*, No. 3 (1958), 23-25.
The author relates his visit with the Trained Cormorants and the Scowrers and Molly Maguires.

4744. The Sons of the Copper Beeches. "Excerpt from the Condensed Version of the By-Laws of the Sons of the Copper Beeches," *Leaves from the Copper Beeches*. Narberth, Pa.: Livingston Pub. Co., 1959. p. 127-133.

4745. [Stump, William.] "The Adventure of the 100 Napoleons," *Baltimore Magazine*, 61, No. 3 (March 1968), 30-33. illus.
Holmes and Watson discuss "the world's largest and most flourishing Scion Society"—the Six Napoleons of Baltimore.

THE SHERLOCK HOLMES KLUBBEN I DANMARK

4746. ["The Danish Baker Street Irregulars"], *The Scandinavian Times*.
———. ———, *Sherlockiana*, 4, Nr. 2-3 (1959), 15.
The history and activities of this Danish Society of Sherlockians.

4747. Hansen, Eiler. "Sherlockiana in Denmark: The Club That Honours Sherlock Holmes," *Denmark: A Quarterly Review of Anglo-Danish Relations* [London] (June 1956), 14-15.
An interesting discourse on the reasons-for-being of this society.

4748. Henriksen, A.D. "Københavnsk litterarert klubliv gennem to århundreder" ["Literary Club-Life in Copenhagen During Two Centuries"], *Kolophon* [København], Nr. 2 (1965), 18-22.

4749. Kjelstrup, Olaf. "Alarmerer Sherlock Holmes . . . og et Mord opklares," Fot.: Olaf Kjelstrup. *Billed Bladet*, 14, Nr. 3 (January 16, 1951), 20-21.
———. ———, *CPBook*, 1, No. 2 (Fall 1964), 32-33.
An illustrated article on the activities of the Danish BSI.

THE SHERLOCK HOLMES SOCIETY OF LONDON

4750. "Be at the Third Pillar from the Left Outside the Lyceum Theatre," *SHJ*, 2, No. 4 (Winter 1955), 43-44.
"The Society's tour round select parts of Holmesian London, undertaken on Thursday, July 14, 1955." (Subtitle)

4751. Brend, Gavin. "Our Future Centenaries," *SHJ*, 3, No. 4 (Summer 1958), 4-5.
A discussion and chronology of possible centenary dinners, beginning with "The Musgrave Ritual" in 1978 and ending with "His Last Bow" in 2014.

4752. [Donegall, Lord.] "The Bath Lark," by Colonel Sebastian Moran, etc., etc. *SHJ*, 10, No. 4 (Summer 1972), 105-110.
A delightful version of the Society's weekend frolic, April 28-May 1, 1972, at Bath; organized to aid the YMCA. Includes a list of participants and characters portrayed, as well as photographs of members dressed in their Holmesian regalia.

4753. [———.] "Twenty-First Birthday," *SHJ*, 6, No. 1 (Winter 1962), 1. (Editorial)
A retrospective look at the first twenty-one issues of *The Sherlock Holmes Journal*.

4754. Friendlich, Dick. "With Sherlock on the

River Seeking the Treasure of Agra," *San Francisco Chronicle, This World* (July 23, 1961), 23.

————. ————, *CPBook*, 2, No. 5-6 (Summer-Fall 1965), 92.

Mainly about the cruise undertaken by members of the Society in search of the treasure chest thrown overboard from the launch *Aurora* by Jonathan Small in Sign.

4755. G., M. L. "The River Trip," *SHJ*, 2, No. 2 (December 1954), 40.

A report on the Society's pursuit on July 14, 1954, of the Agra Treasure.

4756. Holroyd, James Edward. "One Man's Pilgrimage," *Baker Street By-ways*. London: George Allen & Unwin Ltd., [1959]. p. 15-27.

The author recalls his many excursions into the byways of Baker Street, including the history and activities of the Society.

4757. [————.] "Verbatim Report of the Chairman's Speech at the Baskervillian Meeting," *SHJ*, 4, No. 2 (Spring 1959), 63-65.

A tour de force in rhyming verse read by the author at the Society's annual dinner on January 8, 1959, and by Lord Donegall at the Irregulars' meeting in New York on the following evening.

4758. Howlett, Anthony. "Aurora Borealis," *SHJ*, 6, No. 1 (Winter 1962), 23-24.

An account of the filming for I.T.V.'s series "Here and Now" of the Society's commemorative excursion down the River Thames in the path of Jonathan Small and the Agra Treasure. The program was written by Rosemary Davies and produced by Michael Ingrams.

4759. ————. "The Royal Empire Music-Hall Evening," *SHJ*, 9, No. 4 (Summer 1970), 132-134.

A report on the Society's "Fest of Melody and Mirth," presented March 12, 1970. Illustrated with a program of the musical and a photograph of Philip Dalton and Michael Pointer singing "The Ghost of Sherlock Holmes." The program has also been reprinted on the back cover of *BSJ*, 20, No. 3 (September 1970).

4760. Krueger, John. "The Wonderful World of Sherlock Holmes," *The Stars and Stripes* [European Edition], 20, No. 76 (July 2, 1961), 9, 12-13.

An article dealing mainly with the Society, and illustrated with scenes from the Holmes films.

4761. "Marylebone Mews Walk 1963," *SHJ*, 6, No. 2 (Spring 1963), 60, 67.

A short account of "an informal tour through some of the mews of Marylebone, following the route to the Empty House, on the evening of Wednesday, March 27."

4762. Merriman, Charles O. "Mr. Sherlock Holmes in the City," *SHJ*, 7, No. 1 (Winter 1964), 8-9.

On the "Holmes and Soames" City of London Walks conducted July 7 and 16, 1964, by the Sherlock Holmes Society and the Victorian Society.

4763. Prestige, Colin. "The Conan Doyle Centenary," *SHJ*, 4, No. 3 (Winter 1959), 99-100.

A discussion of the Society's Centenary Dinner, the manuscript of *The Missing Three-Quarter* presented to the British Museum, and the bookcase given to the St. Marylebone Borough Council to encourage the development of a comprehensive Holmesian collection.

4764. ————. "For a World Now Prepared," *SHJ*, 4, No. 2 (Spring 1959), 61-62.

An interesting account of the Society's formation on February 20, 1951, as an outcome of the Marylebone Borough Council's Sherlock Holmes Exhibit, together with the proceedings of the first three meetings.

4765. [————.] *Itinerary of a Tour Through Holmesian London, 18th June 1957.* The Sherlock Holmes Society of London, 1957. [8] p.

Contents: Foreword, by C. G. P. - Holmesian London: 1. East of Baker Street. - 2. The Route to Scotland Yard. - 3. Mary Morstan's Journey. - 4. The Lauriston Gardens Mystery. - 5. North to the Strand.

4766. ————. "The Sherlock Holmes Society of London," *SHJ*, 1, No. 3- (June 1953-   ).

The proceedings of the Society's annual dinner are reported each year by Colin Prestige in one number of the *Journal*. The dinners held from 1953 to 1972 have had the following Canonical names: 1953. The Blue Carbuncle Dinner. - 1954. The Charing Cross Dinner. - 1955. The Gasfitters' Ball. - 1956. The Bruce-Partington Night. - 1957. Beeton's Christmas Annual. - 1958. The "Gloria Scott" Celebration. - 1959. The Baskerville Banquet. - 1960. The Orange Pip Feast. - 1961. The Garrideb Gathering. - 1962. The Priory School Reunion. - 1963. The Empty House Party. - 1964. The Bohemian Festival. - 1965. The Naval Treat. - 1966. The Speckled Band Commemoration. - 1967. The Red-Headed Evening. - 1968. The Mazarin Stone Setting. - 1969. The Red Circle Conversazione. - 1970. The Silver Blaze Soirée. - 1971. The Copper Beeches Salutation. - 1972. The Sign of the Four Course Repast.

Sherlockians and The Societies

The Societies

The Societies

4767. ——. "Transactions of the Sherlock Holmes Society of London," *SHJ*, 3, No. 3- (Autumn 1957-   ).

An annual record of the Society's meetings and activities, published, except for the first report, in the Winter issue of the *Journal*.

4768. Sherbrooke-Walker, Ronald. "The Why and the Wherefore: A Brief Consideration of Homo Sherlockianus," *SHJ*, 9, No. 1 (Winter 1968), 20-21.

A prolegomenon to a classification of the Society's members according to their particular Holmesian interests and expertise.

4769. Torchia, Andrew. "Elementary, My Dear Watson—'Twas Holmes's Birthday," *Cincinnati Enquirer* (January 8, 1970).

——. ——, *SHJ*, 9, No. 4 (Summer 1970), 113-114. (Editorial)

An account by a reporter from the Associated Press of the Silver Blaze Soirée, the Society's 18th Annual Dinner.

4770. Toth, Robert C. "British Have Bizarre Societies for Anything," *Los Angeles Times* (March 3, 1968), A13.

——. ——, *CPBook*, 4, No. 14 (Winter 1968), 272-273.

——. "Sherlock Holmes Keeps Tight Rein on His Addicts," *Pacific Stars and Stripes* (March 16, 1968), 9-10.

——. ——, *CPBook*, 4, No. 15 (August 1968), 287.

On the activities of the "just-for-fun" society of British Holmesians.

4771. "Twenty Years After," *SHJ*, 10, No. 2 (Summer 1971), 64-65.

Recollections by Jack Thorne, Col. Ronald Sherbrooke-Walker, Colin Prestige, Dr. Maurice Campbell, and Lord Gore-Booth at the Society's 20th anniversary

4772. [Donegall, Lord.] ["The Swiss Pilgrimage"], *SHJ*, 8, No. 1-4 (Winter 1966-Summer 1968), 1-2, 33-34, 69-70, 105. (Editorial)

Preliminary information on the Society's International Sherlock Holmes Tour of Switzerland.

4773. [——, ed.] *Tour of Switzerland in the Footsteps of Sherlock Holmes, 27th April to 5th May, 1968.* Edited by Colonel Sebastian Moran [Lord Donegall]. Drawings by Hans Kuchler. Photographs by Philip Giegel and Lord Donegall. Art work and make-up by Peter Dawson and Lord Donegall. [The Sherlock Holmes Society of London, 1968.] 36 p.

A pictorial supplement to *SHJ*, 8, No. 4, containing a chronological report of the tour in the form of a continuous caption by Lord Donegall to the sixty-five photographs.

4774. Howard, Philip. "Sherlock, Moriarty and All," *The Times* (April 27, 1968), 1.

——. ——, *CPBook*, 5, No. 17 (Winter 1969), 333.

"Members of the Sherlock Holmes Society visit Switzerland dressed as characters in the stories."

4775. Kinnear, Rob. "A Very Peculiar Pilgrimage: Desperate Struggle by Sherlock Holmes," *San Francisco Chronicle, Sunday Punch* (May 12, 1968), 2.

An account of Sir Paul's and Mr. Scholefield's reenactment of the Reichenbach death struggle.

4776. Marshall, William. "The Head of the F.O. Demonstrates the Art of Brinkmanship," Pictures by Kent Gavin. *The Daily Mirror* (May 2, 1968), 15.

——. ——, *CPBook*, 5, No. 17 (Winter 1969), 338-339.

4777. Moynihan, Michael. "Holmes Mania," *The Times* (April 28, 1968), 3.

——. ——, *CPBook*, 5, No. 17 (Winter 1969), 331.

"Or why 40 men and women wore deerstalkers, frock coats and billow skirts and left London Airport's Gate No. 1 for Switzerland." (Subtitle)

4778. Norman, Barry. "A Master of the Middle Temple Locked in Mortal Combat with the Head of the Diplomatic Service," Picture by Ronald Spencer. *The Daily Mail* (May 2, 1968).

——. ——, *CPBook*, 5, No. 17 (Winter 1969), 332.

4779. "Prof. Moriarty Falls to His Fate Again," *The New York Times* (May 2, 1968), 1, 10.

——, *CPBook*, 4, No. 15 (August 1968), 284.

4780. Stix, Thomas L. "Travels of a Donkey," *BSJ*, 18, No. 3 (September 1968), 180.

A brief summary of the tour that was attended by 42 Sherlockians and 50 members of the press, radio, television, and the motion picture industry, representing, in all, 14 nations.

4781. Swiss National Tourist Office. *Tour of Switzerland in the Footsteps of Sherlock Holmes: Programme.* [Illustrations by Hans Kuchler.] [Zurich: 1968.] [24] p.

VII | *Memorials and Mementos*

Under this general heading appear an assortment of items that are primarily tributes to Holmes and Watson. There are two Sherlock Holmes pubs and a hotel, a coffee house named after Watson, a Sir Arthur Conan Doyle museum containing a Sherlock Holmes Room, annual Silver Blaze horse races, exhibits, figurines, commemorative plaques, souvenir menus of the societies' dinners, Christmas cards, bookmatches, a jar of "Holmesmade" honey, tins of tobacco, a Sherlock Holmes tie and medal, a 221B lapel pin, and wallpaper.

It is regrettable that many other items produced by Sherlockians, the societies, and private companies could not be listed and described. Among these items are the numerous greeting cards and advertising materials with Sherlockian motifs, the scion societies' menus and by-laws, Christmas cards, mementos, cocktail coasters and buttons, deerstalkers, Inverness capes, pipes, and cuff links. The list is endless.

An interesting article by Nathan L. Bengis on Sherlockian memorials and ephemera appears in *Four Wheels to Baker Street* (item 3793).

EXHIBITIONS

General

4782. Baring-Gould, William S. " 'Your Merits Should Be Publicly Recognized,' " *The Annotated Sherlock Holmes.* New York: Clarkson N. Potter, [1967]. Vol. 1, chap. 7, p. 43-46. illus.

On the tributes paid to Holmes and Watson in the form of exhibitions, horse races, memorial plaques, figurines, etc.

4783. Bresler, Riva T. "Sherlock's Birthday Celebration," *Library Journal*, 80, No. 3 (February 1, 1955), 262-264.

A charming and authoritative account of the elaborate exhibit at the Los Angeles Public Library, organized by the Trained Cormorants.

4784. Dickensheet, Dean W., and Shirley. *A Catalogue of an Exhibition of Documents and Materials Honouring the Diamond Jubilee of the Literary Career of Sherlock Holmes, Esq.* [San Francisco: The Scowrers and Molly Maguires, January 1963.] [28] p.

"Held during the month of December, 1962, at the San Francisco Public Library; being presented by the Scowrers and Molly Maguires, a scion society of the Baker Street Irregulars, with the most solicitous co-operation of the aforementioned Library and of diverse institutions and individuals." (Subtitle)

4785. Dickensheet, Shirley. "The Hobby Show," *CR*, 1, No. 4 (September 1960), 14-15.

An interesting description of a prize-winning Sherlockian exhibit held at the California Hobby Show in June 1960 by the Trained Cormorants.

4786. [Donegall, Lord.] "Holmes in Holland," *SHJ*, 7, No. 3 (Winter 1965), 67.

An editorial note on and photograph of a Holmesian exhibit at the Hoofdstad Bookshop in Amsterdam. The items were from the collection of Cornelis Helling.

4787. " 'Famous Books' Theme Provides Color," *The Oregonian* (June 12, 1955), B, 4M.

" 'The Adventures of Sherlock Holmes' was amusing story in flowers for float entered by the Portland Bureau of Police. It won first place in government section of entries."

4788. [Kabraji, Christopher.] "Lyon British Week," *SHJ*, 8, No. 1 (Winter 1966), 32.

On the Conan Doyle Exhibition at the Librairie La Proue during October 21-29, 1965.

4789. Lehigh University Library. *Sir Arthur Conan Doyle, 1859-1930: An Exhibition from the Collection of James Bliss Austin, Lehigh '25*[Bethlehem, Pa.], May 1959. [4].

Memorials and Mementos

Contents: Armstrong on Holmes, by Ray L. Armstrong. - In the Exhibition: Manuscript, Printed Works.

4790. Leithead, J. Edward. "Sherlock Holmes Exhibit," *Dime Novel Round-Up*, 37, No. 6 (June 1968), 61-64.

A commentary on Carl Anderson's exhibit of Sherlockiana at the Philadelphia Free Library, together with a discussion of the Holmes influence on the Nick Carter stories.

4791. Metropolitan Toronto Central Library. *The Adventure of the Toronto Exhibit.* [Toronto: Privately Produced, 1970.] 2 p.

An announcement of a Sherlock Holmes Exhibition beginning January 10, 1971, and featuring items purchased from Harold Mortlake and S. Tupper Bigelow. The display was planned by Elizabeth Perry and Cameron Hollyer.

4792. Prestige, Colin. "The Butterdish," *SHJ*, 2, No. 2 (December 1954), 21-25.

A report on the National Crime Book Week held during June 15-19, 1954, including a reprinting of the cards of commentary for thirty-three items which accompanied the exhibit that was arranged by the Sherlock Holmes Society of London.

4793. San Francisco Public Library. *Sherlock Holmes: The Man and the Legend: A Sherlockian Exhibit.* Parkside Branch, 22nd Ave. and Taraval Street, October 2-October 31, 1967.

An illustrated poster.

4794. Schumach, Murray. "Theater to Show Holmes Exhibit: $75,000 Lobby Display on View with 'Baker Street,' " *The New York Times* (February 9, 1965), 42.
————. ————, *CPBook*, 1, No. 3 (Winter 1965), 51.

An exhibit assembled by Lew D. Feldman for the opening of *Baker Street* at the Broadway Theatre.

4795. "Sherlock Holmes Exhibit on Display, CSU Library," *Fort Collins Coloradoan* (March 17, 1968), 26.

A description of items from the collection of Ronald De Waal which were displayed in the Colorado State University Library.

4796. "Sherlock Holmes Exhibit Too Popular to Wind Up," *The Tulsa Daily World* (February 20, 1966), 28-29.
————, *CPBook*, 3, No. 10 (Fall 1966), 192.

An exhibition in the Tulsa Central Library of some 300 items from John Bennett Shaw's collection.

4797. Snyder, Edward D. "Sherlock Holmes at Haverford College," *The Haverford Review*, 4, No. 1 (Spring 1945), 27-30.

Dr. Snyder, who organized an exhibit of Sherlockiana for the Associates of Haverford Library, presents a scholar's observations on the appeal and study of the Canonical tales.

4798. Texas. University. Research Center. *An Exhibition on the Occasion of the Opening of the Ellery Queen Collection.* [Introduction by F. W. Roberts.] [Austin]: January 16, 1959. 27 p.

Limited to 500 copies.
Partial contents: Case I, center: A. Conan Doyle.

4799. Tulsa City-County Central Library. *Sherlockiana—From the Collection of John Bennett Shaw, B.S.I.*, Tulsa, Oklahoma, U.S.A. [4] p.

"An exhibition in the Tulsa City-County Central Library, Tulsa, Oklahoma, January 3 through 31st, 1966, honoring the 112th anniversary of the birth of Sherlock Holmes in the town of Mycroft in the North Riding of Yorkshire, January 6, 1854." (Subtitle)

4800. Walton, Diana. "The Diamond Jubilee of Sherlock Holmes," Photos by Bruce Harlow. *San Francisco Sunday Chronicle, Bonanza* (December 2, 1962), 16-17. illus.

To mark the 75th anniversary of the first published adventure, local members of the Scowrers displayed their Sherlockiana in the San Francisco Public Library.

4801. Woodworth, Betty. "De Waal Exhibit at CSU," *Fort Collins Coloradoan* (January 25, 1970), 9.

An illustrated article on the second Sherlock Holmes display in the CSU Library.

The Sherlock Holmes Exhibition of 1951 and 1952

4802. Borneman, Ernest. "Diggings in Baker Street,". *Harper's Magazine*, 203 (September 1951), 81-83.
————. ————, *CPBook*, 5, No. 18 (Spring 1969), 349-351.

A description of the arrangements for the exhibition at the site of 221B Baker Street.

4803. "Even Dust, Even Fog," *The New Yorker*, 28, No. 14 (May 24, 1952), 19-20. (The Talk of the Town)

4804. "Export Fog in a Bottle? Elementary, Dear Watson," *The New York Times* (January 21, 1953), 11.

Food Minister Gwilym Lloyd-George tells how the Sherlock Holmes Society bottled London fog to send to the exhibition in New York.

4805. Hastings, Peter. "Cho-luk Ho Ma Su of Baker Street," *A.M.* [*The Australian Monthly*] (September 1952), 26-27. illus.

"By transporting 221B Baker Street to America, Sherlock Holmes' disciples have turned the sleuth into an overnight sensation."

4806. Honce, Charles. "A. Conan Doyle's Son Dead Ringer for Detective Sherlock Holmes," *Memphis Commercial Appeal* (April 6, 1952).

———. ———, *CPBook*, 3, No. 10 (Fall 1966), 194.

———. Enlarged with title: "Sherlock Holmes—In Person," *Tales from a Beekman Hill Library*. Mount Vernon, N.Y.: Uttered by S. A. Jacobs at the Golden Eagle Press, 1952. p. 59-66.

Observations on some Holmesian profiles, including Adrian Conan Doyle's, and the London-New York exhibition.

4807. Lloyd-Taylor, A. "The Singular Adventure of the Sherlock Holmes Collection," *The Sherlock Holmes*. [Compiled and prepared by Richard Lonsdale-Hands Associates.] London: Whitbread & Co. Ltd., [1957]. p. 1-3.

An introductory essay on the collection of material exhibited in the Festival of Britain in 1951, in New York the following year, and in The Sherlock Holmes.

4808. Panter-Downes, Mollie. "No. 221B," *The New Yorker*, 27, No. 21 (July 7, 1951), 25-37.

———. ———, *CPBook*, 3, No. 9 (Summer 1966), 172-178.

"A long and true-ringing account from London ('A Reporter at Large') of the Sherlock Holmes Exhibition and the atmosphere in which it was born and has flourished." (Edgar W. Smith)

4809. Roberts, S. C. "Pilgrims at 221B," BBC Third Programme, Sunday, August 19, 1951, 6:40-7:00 p.m.

———. ———, *The Listener*, 46 (August 23, 1951), 303-305. illus.

———. "221B in Retrospect," *Holmes and Watson: A Miscellany*. London: Oxford University Press, 1953. p. 93-104.

A survey of the exhibition.

4810. Prestige, Colin. "Fleet Street on Baker Street," *SHJ*, 1, No. 1 (May 1952), 36-38.

A report on what the London newspapers had to say about the exhibition.

4811. "The Return of Sherlock Holmes," *U.S. Crime*, 1, No. 2 (January 16, 1952), 120-123.

Includes photographs of the London exhibition.

4812. Rickander, Thor. *The Curious Case of the Sherlock Holmes Exhibit*. Stockholm: The Solitary Cyclists of Sweden, 1964. [22] p.

A privately produced brochure containing the lively correspondence that went on in *The Times* during October and November 1950. Among the signers of these letters are such great Canonical persons as John H. Watson, Mycroft Holmes, Kate Whitney, Mrs. Hudson, Oscar Meunier, and G. Lestrade.

4813. "Sherlock Holmes," BBC Home Service, Thursday, June 22, 1951, 7:55-8:30 p.m. Repeated: HS, Thursday, September 14, 1951, 10:25-11:00 p.m.

Cast: Wynford Vaughan Thomas (Guide at 221B), Laidman Browne (Sherlock Holmes), Ivan Samson (Dr. Watson).

"A visit to the rooms of the famous private consulting detective at 221B Baker Street, with scenes from his life and cases dramatised from Dr. Watson's notes as edited by Sir Arthur Conan Doyle." (Subtitle)

4814. *Sherlock Holmes: Catalogue of an Exhibition Held at Abbey House, Baker Street, London, May-September 1951*. [Presented by the Public Libraries Committee of the Borough of St. Marylebone during the Festival of Britain.] [Printed by Wightman and Co. Ltd., 1951.] iv, 59 p. illus.

Contents: Preface, by Bernard Darwin. - 1. Sir Arthur Conan Doyle and the Creation of Sherlock Holmes. - 2. A Selection of Editions and Translations. - 3. Parodies and Cartoons. - 4. Sherlock Holmes at Large. - 5. Some Scientific Problems. - 6. Some Firearms. - 7. "Is there any other point to which you wish to draw my attention?" - 8. Sherlock Holmes on the Stage, by Michael E. Pointer. - 9. Sherlock Holmes on the Screen, by Anthony D. Howlett. - 10. 221B Baker Street. - 11. The Living-Room at 221B.

A souvenir booklet containing a descriptive list of the items exhibited, along with much erudite commentary.

4815. *The Sherlock Holmes Exhibition: Catalogue [of an Exhibition Held at Plaza Art Galleries, New York, July 1952]*. Presented by Adrian M. Conan Doyle. [Printed by L. Middleditch Co., 1952.] iv, 52 p.

Contents like 4814, with the omission of the Preface, Chapters 2, 3, 8, 9, and illustrations.

4816. "The Sherlock Holmes Exposition, or Wot's on in London," *Take It from Here*. Drawings by Meryl Andreas. [London]: Insignia Books, [April 1952]. p. 78-81.

4817. [Smith, Edgar W.] "The Sherlock Holmes Exhibition," *BSJ*, 1, No. 3 (July 1951), [2] p. (Special Supplement: 1, No. 4 (October 1951), 155; 2, No. 3 (July 1952), 123-124.

Information on the exhibit in London and New York.

Memorials and Mementos

MISCELLANY

4818. The Baker Street Irregulars. *Menus.* 1934-
Souvenir menus of their annual dinners.

4819. *Bulldog Pipe Decanter.* Avon Products, Inc., 1972. 6 in.
Shaped in the form of a curved pipe with a removable stem and a bulldog's head, with a deerstalker as the base.
Available in "Wild Country or Oland After Shave," or in "Wild Country or Oland Cologne."

4820. Donegall, Lord, *Mr. Sherlock Holmes.* No. 1-10, 1958-1967.
Lord Donegall's Christmas cards.
Covers: 1958. *The Strand Magazine* cover for December 1913. - 1959. *Beeton's Christmas Annual* cover for 1887. - 1960. *Lippincott's Magazine* cover for February 1890 - 1961. The Sherlock Holmes Map of Europe. - 1962. London. - 1963. The World. - 1964. England. - 1965. Operation Reichenbach. - 1966. The 221B sitting-room at Lucens, plus the Sherlockian map of the United States. - 1967. "It Is Full of Old Houses."
The maps reproduced on the covers for 1961-67 are by Dr. Julian Wolff, and, except for 1965, are accompanied by "An Incomplete Gazetteer." The cards also include an introductory commentary and a greeting.

4821. Hugo's Companions. *221B Lapel Pin.* - Chicago: 1966.
Designed in the form of a miniature doorplate.

4822. The Old Soldiers of Baker Street. *Cards at 221b.* Ferndale, Mich.: [1960]. 50 cards.
"Reproductions of selected items from the silver card tray at 221b Baker Street, London." (Subtitle)

4823. ———. *Holmesmade Honey.* Sussex Apiaries, London Office, 221BEE Baker St. [Ferndale, Mich.: Old SOB's, 1967.] 8 oz. bottle.
Includes an annual report of the Sussex Apiaries.

4824. The Scandalous Bohemians. *Medal.* The Ostlers, 1971. 1-1/ 4 in. (diameter)
A solid silver (.999 fine) Sherlockian medal with a profile of the Master, dated 1895, and the quotation, "The Best and Wisest Man Whom I Have Ever Known," by Watson on the reverse side.
Available from Norman S. Nolan, 68 Crest Rd. , Middleton, N. J. 07748, for $12 or $15 for numbered (to 100) coins.

4825. The Scowrers and Molly Maguires. *Pin.* San Francisco: 1971.
Available to members and collectors from Dean Dickensheet, 2430 Lake St. , Apt. 7, San Francisco, Calif. 94121, at $4.25.

4826. The Sherlock Holmes Society of London. *Calendar for 1895 and 1963.* Designed by Bernard Davies. Christmas 1962. 10 x 8 in.

4827. ———. *Christmas Cards.* 1953-
Covers: 1953. Portrait of Sherlock Holmes, by Sidney Paget. - 1954. The Criterion Bar. - 1955. Lyceum Theatre, by Joseph Pennell. - 1956. [None issued]. - 1957. One-legged news-vendor in "The Illustrious Client," by Howard Elcock. - 1958. The interior of the Lowther Arcade, the Strand, London. - 1959. Northumberland Avenue, by Howard Penton. - 1960. Sherlock Holmes's and Professor Moriarty's death struggle at the Reichenbach, by Arthur Twidle. - 1961. Old Scotland Yard in 1720. - 1962. Piccadilly in the 1880's and 1890's. - 1963. Regent Street entrance to the Café Royal. - 1964. Sherlock Holmes, Dr. Watson, and Stanley Hopkins in "The Adventure of Black Peter," by Sidney Paget. - 1965. Hansom cab, by Tom Eckersley. - 1966. Charing Cross Station and Hotel, by Howard Penton. - 1967. Eastern end of the Strand in the late 1880's, by Joseph Pennell. - 1968. A be-whiskered Victorian merchant offering a Christmas goose across the counter of his market stall, by Gunning King. - 1969. St. James's Hall, Piccadilly, after a concert in 1891, by W. D. Almond. - 1970. The "Gloria Scott." - 1971. Silver Blaze, by Sidney Paget.
Each card includes an explanatory note and a greeting.

4828. ———. *Menus.* 1953-
Souvenir menus, printed in Baskerville type and in various colors, of the Society's annual dinners.

4829. ———. *Sherlock Holmes Tie.*
A dark-blue background with motifs in silver of a deerstalker cap and a curved pipe.

4830. *No. 221B Baker Street.* Denmark: Specially blended for FDB Cigar- og Tobaksfabrikker Esbjerg.
A round tin of tobacco containing "a carefully balanced blend."
Photographs: Sherlockiana, 14, Nr. 3 (1969), 12; 14, Nr. 4 (1969), 16; 15, Nr. 1-2 (1970), 7; 15, Nr. 3-4 (1970), 12.

4831. *Sherlock Holmes Aromatic.* Extremely mild. Philadelphia, Pa.: A. Runge & Co. (1414 S. Penn Square)
A one-pound tin and a 1-1/ 2 ounce plastic packet of tobacco.

4832. *Sherlock Holmes Book-Matches.* Made for the Baker Street Irregulars by the Diamond Match Co., 1959.
A caddy of fifty books of matches in Victorian gaslight color; illustrated with the famous Frederic Dorr Steele profile of Sherlock Holmes on the back and the "B.S.I." insignia on the front.

Photograph: BSJ, 9, No. 2 (April 1959), 126.

4833. *Sherlock Holmes Sign.* Tuckahoe, N.Y.: Alexander Sales, 1968. 4-1 / 4 x 5-1 / 4 in. (Catalog No. D1528)

Hand-screened in black on colored paper and framed in black-finished wrought iron.

Photograph: BSJ, 18, No. 3 (September 1968), 187.

Note: Another miniature replica of the sign adorning The Sherlock Holmes pub was made in 1972 by Brewers Sign Mfg. Co. , St. Albans, Herts, England. The sign is 5-1 / 4 x 4-1 / 4 in., with a swing-type stand 7-1 / 4 in. x 4-3 / 4 in. and hook with a bottle opener.

4834. *Sherlock Holmes Wallpaper.* Chicago: United-DeSoto, 1969. 20 1/ 2 in. wide. (PDQ, 5th ed. , Pattern No. 11594)

Vinyl-coated, prepasted, washable wall covering in one colorway—red, brown, and black on a white background. A sample of the pattern appears in *Sherlockiana*, 14, Nr. 3 (1969), 13; and on the cover of *DCC*, 7, No. 1 (November 1970).

4835. *"Turf" Cigarettes Series of Twenty-Five Conan Doyle Characters.* London: Alexander Boguslavsky, Ltd., [n.d.] 25 cards.

A set of cigarette cards showing, among other Doyle characters, several famous ones from the Canonical tales.

MUSEUM

Château de Lucens

4836. Carvell, Peter. "Mr. Sherlock Holmes, 221b Baker Street, Château de Lucens, Lausanne, Switzerland," Photographs by Michael Hardy. *Weekend Telegraph*, No. 140 (June 9, 1967), 18-22.

———. ———, *CPBook*, 3, No. 12 (Spring 1967), 224-225.

———. "Sherlock Holmes Lives!" *The Canadian* [*Toronto Daily Star*], 3, No. 35 (September 2, 1967), 14-15.

A long and handsomely illustrated article on the late Adrian Conan Doyle's chateau and the Sherlock Holmes Room.

4837. [Donegall, Lord.] "Sir Arthur Conan Doyle Museum," *SHJ*, 7, No. 3 (Winter 1965), 65-66. (Editorial)

———. Reprinted in part in *Sherlockiana*, 11, Nr. 1 (1966), 1.

The author describes his visit to the Museum of the Conan Doyle Foundation.

4838. [———.] "Where It Will Be Always Eighteen-Ninety Seven," *SHJ*, 7, No. 4 (Spring 1966), 97-99. (Editorial)

A description of the 221B room at the chateau, including extracts from Adrian

Conan Doyle's taped commentary played over invisible loud speakers.

4839. Henriksen, A. D. "Conan Doyle museet" ["Conan Doyle Museum"], *Sherlock Holmes Årbog* II (1966), 89-94.

4840. Hesse, Georgia. "Holmes Is Alive and Living in Switzerland," *San Francisco Sunday Examiner and Chronicle, California Living* (October 2, 1966), 34-37. illus.

4841. "Home of Fictitious Sleuth Displayed in Switzerland," *The New York Times* (April 11, 1966), 37. illus.

"Castle solves Sherlock Holmes's problem of where to retire." (Subtitle)

4842. "Sherlock Holmes Gift for Geneva," *The Telegraph* (September 16, 1962).

———, *CPBook*, 3, No. 10 (Fall 1966), 187.

4843. Sir Arthur Conan Doyle Foundation. *Castle of Lucens.* [Lucens: 1966.] 16 p.

Cover title: Château de Lucens.

An illustrated souvenir booklet.

4844. Steel, John A. "A Look at the Sherlock Holmes Museum," *The Scotsman* (June 1, 1966), 10. illus.

4845. [Stettner, Louis.] "Sherlock Château," *MD: Medical Newsmagazine*, 13 (December 1969), 87-90.

Photographs, with brief descriptions, of the Swiss museum.

PLAQUES

General

4846. Andrew, Clifton R. "Memorials to Sherlock Holmes," *BSJ*, 7, No. 4 (October 1957), 240-242.

An informative discussion of the plaques that have been erected to honor Holmes and Watson.

4847. Boothroyd, J. B. "The Air-Gun, Colonel Moran," *Punch*, 226 (February 3, 1954), 173-174.

An unfortunate attempt to find amusement in the fact that several plaques have been put up to commemorate certain incidents in the Canon.

Criterion Bar

4848. Baritsu Chapter of the Baker Street Irregulars, Tokyo. *Plaque.* Erected in Piccadilly on the north wall of the Criterion building, January 3, 1953.

"This plaque commemorates the historic meeting at the original Long Bar at this hotel on January 1st, 1881, of Dr. Stamford and Dr. John H. Watson which led to the

Memorials and Mementos

introduction of Dr. Watson to Mr. Sherlock Holmes."

Photograph: Sherlockian Who's Who and What's What (1962), 14.

4849. Chivers, Lena. "Dr. Watson at Bart's," *The Bedside 'Guardian' 2.* A selection by Ivor Brown from the *Manchester Guardian,* 1952-1953. London: Collins, 1953. p. 56-57.

A brief account of the unveiling of the plaque at the Criterion Restaurant.

4850. Prestige, Colin. "The Criterion Plaque," *SHJ,* 1, No. 3 (June 1953), 10-11.

Maiwand

4851. Lesh, Richard D. "Remarkable, Lesh! Simply Remarkable!" *Voices from Baker Street,* 2. Ferndale, Mich.: The Old Soldiers of Baker Street, 1965. Side 2, band 3.

A report on the Maiwand Jezails' negotiations with the Royal Government of Afghanistan for permission to erect a large stone plaque on the sacred battleground of Maiwand to commemorate the historic occasion when Watson was wounded by a Jezail bullet.

4852. McMorris, Robert. "Sherlockians Score Diplomatic Triumph," *The Omaha World-Herald* (January 19, 1966).
————. ————, *CPBook,* 3, No. 9 (Summer 1966), 181.

The Maiwand Jezails gain approval from the Afghanistan Government for their plan to erect a commemorative marker on the Maiwand Battlefield.

Reichenbach Falls

4853. The Old Soldiers of Baker Street. *Plaque.* Erected at the Rossli Inn in Meiringen, Switzerland, near the Reichenbach Falls, November 1952.

"To this valley in May, 1891, came Dr. Watson and Sherlock Holmes and here Holmes bested the infamous Prof. Moriarty in mortal combat: though Holmes was thought to have perished, he escaped and returned to London in 1894. He has since retired to Sussex and bee-keeping."

Photograph: Sherlockian Who's Who and What's What (1962), 16.

4854. Henriksen, A. D. "Sherlock Holmes fylder 99," *Weekend Social-Demokraten* (January 9, 1953), 1-2.

On the erection of the Rossli plaque and the worldwide celebration of the Master's birthday.

4855. Rabe, W. T. "Sherlock's Alpine Battle Gets Solemn (?) Memorial," *The Philadelphia Inquirer* (December 14, 1952), SO 29.

4856. The Norwegian Explorers of Minnesota and The Sherlock Holmes Society of London. *Plaque.* Erected at the Reichenbach Falls, June 1957.

"Across this 'dreadful cauldron' occurred the culminating event in the career of Sherlock Holmes, the world's greatest detective, when on May 4, 1891, he vanquished Prof. Moriarty, the Napoleon of Crime. Erected by the Norwegian Explorers of Minnesota and the Sherlock Holmes Society of London, 25 June 1957."

Photographs: The Annotated Sherlock Holmes (1967), Vol. 1, p. 46; *BSJ,* 7, No. 4 (October 1957), 231; *Sherlockian Who's Who and What's What* (1962), 17.

St. Bartholomew's Hospital

4857. The Amateur Mendicant Society of Detroit. *Plaque.* Erected at St. Bartholomew's Hospital, January 21, 1954.

"At this place New Year's Day, 1881, were spoken these deathless words: 'You have been in Afghanistan, I perceive' by Mr. Sherlock Holmes in greeting to John H. Watson, M.D., at their first meeting. The Baker Street Irregulars—1953 by the Amateur Mendicants at the Caucus Club."

Photographs: The Annotated Sherlock Holmes (1967), Vol. 1, p. 46; *BSJ,* 4, No. 3 (July 1954), 189; *In the Footsteps of Sherlock Holmes* [Revised ed.] (1971), facing p. 53; *Sherlockian Who's Who and What's What* (1962), 18.

4858. Prestige, Colin, and C. C. Carus Wilson. ["Letters"], *BSJ,* 4, No. 2 (April 1954), 125, 127. (From the Editor's Commonplace Book)

Eyewitness reports on the unveiling of the plaque in Dr. Watson's old hospital.

RAILROAD LOCOMOTIVE

Sherlock Holmes

4859. Day, John R. "S. H. Locomotive," *Sherlockian Who's Who and What's What.* Edited by W. T. Rabe. Ferndale, Mich.: Old Soldiers of Baker Street, 1962. p. 2-6.

A brief history and description, with three photographs, of the No. 8 locomotive named after Sherlock Holmes.

4860. Prestige, Colin. ["Letter"], *BSJ,* 4, No. 2 (April 1954), 122-123. (From the Editor's Commonplace Book)

A description of the ceremonies attendant upon naming the railway engine of Great Britain's Metropolitan Line "Sherlock Holmes."

4861. "The Sherlock Holmes Locomotive," *SHJ,* 1, No. 4 (December 1953), 29; 6, No. 2 (Spring 1963), 60.

RESTAURANTS AND HOTEL

Baker Street Pub

4862. "Baker Street Pub Dedicated," *DCC*, 5, No. 5 ([June] 1969), 1-3.

A report, including Robert Hahn's dedicatory speech, on the formal ceremony for the April 28 opening of this Sherlockian restaurant at 365 West Monro in Chicago.

4863. Francis, Ray. "Who Said Sherlock Holmes Is Dead?" *Chicago Tribune* (December 11, 1969), IIIC, 11.

An illustrated article about three Hartford Plaza Restaurants, one of which is the Baker Street Pub.

My Dear Watson

4864. *My Dear Watson: The Coffee House of Distinction, 113 Baker Street, London, W.1.* Designed by Take 5 and printed by Sydney Lee (Exeter) Ltd., Walter Lane, Exeter.

An attractive menu listing a variety of dishes and beverages, with Holmesian captions and references.

The Sherlock Holmes

4865. "Auf den Spuren von Sherlock Holmes" ["On the Trail of Sherlock Holmes"], *Intercontinental Magazine* [Lufthansa Airlines] (September-October 1964).
———, *CPBook*, 3, No. 12 (Spring 1967), 241-242.

The article is in German, French and English, and is illustrated with a photograph of The Sherlock Holmes pub in London.

4866. "Bei Sherlock Holmes," *Walt Disney's Micky Maus* [Stuttgart], Heft 11 (March 14, 1964), 20-21. illus.

4867. Brennan, Bob. "Tracking Good Eating in Sherlock's Way," *The Cleveland Press* (October 7, 1966), 4.
———. ———, *CPBook*, 4, No. 14 (Winter 1968), 263C.

A memorable evening at The Sherlock Holmes.

4868. Carr, John Dickson. "The Sherlock Holmes," *The House of Whitbread* [London], 18, No. 1 (Spring 1958), 7-11. illus.

"The first public house to be named after the most celebrated detective of fiction was opened by Whitbread last December in London. Formerly 'The Northumberland Arms,' near Trafalgar Square, it is now furnished with a collection of Holmesiana."

4869. [Donegall, Lord.] "House Moving from Baker Street," *SHJ*, 3, No. 4 (Summer 1958), 16-17.

An account of the celebration on December 12, 1957, to mark the completion of moving Holmes's and Watson's household effects from 221B Baker Street to The Sherlock Holmes pub on Northumberland Street.

4870. Douglas, George. "Final Act of a Man Who Never Was," *True*, 45, No. 321 (February 1964), 28-29.

"Sherlock Holmes fans preserve 'his' rooms like a stage set for a play that never ends." (Subtitle)

Colored photographs and a brief description of the pub in the old Northumberland Hotel where Sir Henry Baskerville stayed when he met Holmes.

4871. [Lonsdale-Hands (Richard) Associates.] *The Sherlock Holmes, Northumberland Street, London, W.C.2: Catalogue of the Collection in the Bars and the Grill Room and in the Reconstruction of Part of the Living Room at 221B Baker Street.* With introductory essays by A. Lloyd-Taylor and John Dickson Carr, and a critical miscellany edited by H. Douglas Thomson. London: Whitbread & Co., Ltd., [1957]. ix, 53 p. illus.

4872. Miller, Jay. "How Can You Doubt Holmes' Reality in His Own Pub?" *San Francisco Sunday Chronicle, This World* (August 19, 1962), 35.

4873. Ober, Harry. ["Letter"], *BSJ*, 8, No. 4 (October 1958), 243. (From the Editor's Commonplace Book)

A description of the pub by the first American Irregular to patronize it.

4874. [Smith, Edgar W.] ["The Sherlock Holmes"], *BSJ*, 8, No. 2 (April 1958), 87-89. (From the Editor's Commonplace Book)

4875. Vesey-Fitzgerald, Brian. "The Singular Case of the Classic Detective: After Seventy Years Sherlock Holmes Is Still the Master," *The Sphere*, 232 (February 8, 1958), 220-221.
———. Reprinted in part in *SHJ*, 3, No. 4 (Summer 1958), 22-23.

The background story of the London public house; generously illustrated with photographs.

Sherlock Holmes Hotel

4876. *Sherlock Holmes Hotel, Baker Street, London, W.1.* [1970] [6] p.

An illustrated brochure describing the new hotel and its luxurious accommodations. The hotel has 160 bedrooms, a bar named after Dr. Watson, and a coffee shop called Moriarty's Den.

Memorials and Mementos

THE SILVER BLAZE HORSE RACES

4877. The Baltimore Silver Blaze, Bowie Race Course.
1st. *BSJ*, 21, No. 2 (June 1971), 119. - 2nd. *BSJ*, 22, No. 2 (June 1972), 120.

4878. The Chicago Silver Blaze Purse, Arlington Park.
1st. *BSJ*, 10, No. 4 (October 1960), 252. - 2nd. *BSJ*, 11, No. 3 (September 1961), 183. - 3rd. *BSJ*, 12, No. 4 (December 1962), 236. - 4th. *BSJ*, 13, No. 4 (December 1963), 229. - 5th. *BSJ*, 14, No. 3 (September 1964), 188. - 6th. *DCC*, 1, No. 5 (August 1965), 1, 3-4. - 7th. *DCC*, 2, No. 6 (August 1966), 1-2. - 8th. *DCC*, 3, No. 5 (August 1967), 1, 6, 9. - 9th. *DCC*, 4, No. 5 (September 1968), 1-2. - 10th. *DCC*, 5, No. 6 (September 1969), 1-3. - 11th. *DCC*, 6, No. 5 (August 1970), 1-3. - 12th. *DCC*, 7, No. 6 (August 1971), 1-3. - 13th. *DCC*, 7, No. 4-5 (September 1972), 1, 10.

4879. The Danish Silver Blaze Handicap, Aalborg.
1st. *BSJ*, 13, No. 4 (December 1963), 229. - 2nd. *BSJ*, 14, No. 4 (December 1964), 248. - 3rd. *BSJ*, 15, No. 4 (December 1965), 245. - 4th. *BSJ*, 16, No. 4 (December 1966), 241. - 5th. *BSJ*, 17, No. 4 (December 1967), 241. - 6th. *BSJ*, 18, No. 4 (December 1968), 252. - 7th. *BSJ*, 19, No. 4 (December 1969), 251. - 8th. *BSJ*, 20, No. 4 (December 1970), 246.

4880. The New York Silver Blaze Handicap, Aqueduct Race Track and Belmont Park.
1st. *BSJ*, 2, No. 3 (July 1952), 176. - 2nd. *BSJ*, 3, No. 4 (October 1953), 246. - 3rd. *BSJ*, 5, No. 1 (January 1955), 61-62. - 4th. *BSJ*, 5, No. 4 (October 1955), 251. - 5th. *BSJ*, 7, No. 1 (January 1957), 55-56. - 6th. [Not reported]. - 7th. *BSJ*, 8, No. 3 (July 1958), 181. - 8th. *BSJ*, 10, No. 1 (January 1960), 54-56. - 9th. *BSJ*, 11, No. 1 (March 1961), 41-42. - 10th. *BSJ*, 11, No. 4 (December 1961), 245. - 11th. *BSJ*, 12, No. 4 (December 1962), 236; *New York Herald Tribune* (September 13, 1962), 24. - 12th. *BSJ*, 13, No. 4 (December 1963), 229. - 13th. *BSJ*, 14, No. 4 (December 1964), 248. - 14th. *BSJ*, 15, No. 4 (December 1965), 245. - 15th. *BSJ*, 16, No. 4 (December 1966), 240. - 16th. *BSJ*, 17, No. 4 (December 1967), 241; *Big A*, Seventh Race, The Silver Blaze [Aqueduct Race Track], 1 p., and reprinted in *CPBook*, 3, No. 13 (Summer 1967), 261; *New York Times* (September 16, 1967), 25, and reprinted in *CPBook*, 3, No. 13 (Summer 1967), 260. - 17th. *BSJ*, 18, No. 4 (December 1968), 252. - 18th. *BSJ*, 19, No. 4 (December 1969), 251. - 19th. *BSJ*, 20, No. 4 (December 1970), 246; *The News* [New York] (October 11, 1970), 23M (Gus Dallas). - 20th. *BSJ*, 21, No. 4 (December 1971), 247; *New York Times* (September 12, 1971), V, 9 (Tom Stix).

4881. The Toronto Silver Blaze Handicap, Woodbine Track.
1st. *BSJ*, 11, No. 3 (September 1961), 183. - 2nd. *BSJ*, 12, No. 3 (September 1962), 175. - *BSJ*, 15, No. 3 (September 1965), 185.

STATUARY

4882. Cassin-Scott, Jack. *Figurines of Sherlock Holmes, Dr. Watson, Irene Adler, Mycroft Holmes, and Professor Moriarty.* 1969-1971. 12 in. (Cassin Baker Street Series)
Moulded in latex composition, hand painted, and mounted on a free-standing wooden base. There are at least three variations of Holmes and two of Watson.
Photographs: BSJ, 19, No. 3 (September 1969), 190; 20, No. 1 (March 1970), 60.
Available from Cassin Figures, 108 Melrose Ave., London, NW2 4JX, or Luther Norris, 3844 Watseka Ave., Culver City, Calif. 90230, at $30 ea.

4883. Imrie, Helen. *Figurines of Sherlock Holmes and Dr. Watson.* 1968-1969. 3-1 / 2 in.
Cast in pewter, lightly antiqued, and mounted on a walnut base.
Photograph: CPBook, 4, No. 16 (Fall 1968), 303.
Available from The Soldier Shop, 1013 Madison Ave., New York, N.Y. 10021, at $7.50 ea.

4884. McKellips, Art. *Hand-Carved Wooden Figures of Sherlock Holmes and Dr. Watson.*
Holmes is 24 in. tall, with a removable pipe, magnifying glass, and head that can be turned in any direction. Watson is shorter by about 5 in. and stouter by about 4 in.
Photographs: BSJ, 17, No. 1 (March 1967), 49.
Available from De Ley's Gifts, Loreto Plaza, 3303-C State St., Santa Barbara, Calif. 93105, at $155 ea. (the original price in 1967 was $49.50!).

4885. The Royal London Wax Museum, Chicago. *Wax Figures of Sherlock Holmes and Dr. Watson.*
An illustrated article by Robert W. Hahn about the figures and exhibit appears in *DCC*, 7, No. 5 (June 1971), 4-7; and a letter, with illustration, in *SHJ*, 10, No. 4 (Summer 1972), 136-137.

4886. *Sherlock Holmes Hand Puppet.* Germany: Kersa, [n.d.] 12 in. cloth. (Nr. 302)

4887. Smith, Edgar Pichard. *The Oscar Meunier Bust of Sherlock Holmes.* 7 in.
A reproduction in matte porcelain of the world-famous wax effigy that caused the downfall of Col. Sebastian Moran.

4888. ———. *Statuette of Sherlock Holmes.*

The figure, cast in plaster from the clay model, shows the Master in a reclining position in cap and dressing gown with his pipe and violin.

4889. Whitmore, Luques. *Statuette of Sherlock Holmes.* 17 in. 1963.

Commissioned by Luther Norris.

Cast in unbreakable Durastone, hand finished, and mounted on a wooden base with an individual nameplate.

Photographs: The Annotated Sherlock Holmes (1967), Vol. 1, p. 46; *BSJ*, 13, No. 4 (December 1963), 253; *SHJ*, 6, No. 3 (Winter 1963), 70; *Sherlockiana*, 8, Nr. 3-4 (1963), 7.

Memorials and Mementos

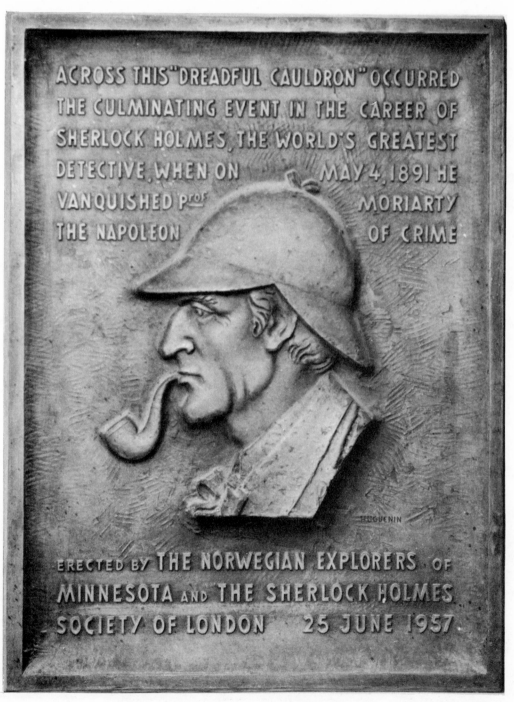

A commemorative plaque at the Reichenbach Falls **(4856).**

A Sherlock Holmes board game (**4913**).

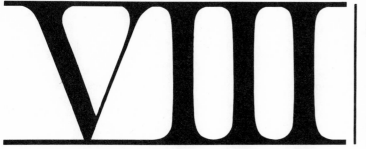

VIII | *Games and Competitions*

See also *Ratings* (items 4242-4250) and *Verses* (items 4484-4485).

BRIDGE

4890. Becker, B. Jay. "Contract Bridge," *The Globe and Mail* [Toronto] (September 8, 1964), and reprinted in *CPBook*, 1, No. 2 (Fall 1964), 25.

4891. Gooden, George S. "Sherlock Holmes Discovers Bridge," *Popular Bridge*, 1, No. 3 (November-December 1967), 39, 41-43.

4892. Sheinwold, Alfred. "Sheinwold on Bridge," Syndicated in U.S. and Canadian newspapers.
   Partial contents: Bridge Detective Must Stay Awake. - Bridge 'Criminals' Could Fill the Nation's Jails. - Careless Play Often Contagious. - The Case of the Missing Ace. - Don't Blame Luck for Playing Crime. - Hand Troubled Sherlock Holmes. - Heedless Player Guilty of Crime. - Losing Trick OK; Contract Was Set. - Safety Play Can Assure Contract. - Sherlock Failed to Detect Crime. - Sherlock Holmes Loses Argument. - Sherlock Holmes Solves a Problem. - Unlosable Finesse Makes Contract. - Want to Win? Learn to Yield. - Watson Stumped by Bridge Crime.

4893. ———. "Sherlock Holmes Revisited," *Popular Bridge*, 2, No. 1 (January-February 1968), 45.

CHESS

4894. Hotspur. "Chess in Fiction," *The British Chess Magazine*, 84, No. 1 (January 1964), 15-16.
   "According to the author all this Baritzu business at the Reichenbach was an invention of Holmes. What he and Moriarty really did was challenge each other at Chess, Moriarty finding himself—as he thought—mate next move after Holmes's 39th move. At this point Moriarty swept himself, board, men, and all into that 'boiling pit of incalculable depth.' " (Lord Donegall)

CROSSWORD PUZZLES

4895. Bernd, Janet. "Crossword Puzzle," *HO*, 1, No. 1 (March 1971), 18.

4896. Bigelow, S. Tupper. "Sherlockian Double-Crostic," *BSJ*, 12, No. 4 (December 1962), 237-239; [Solution] 13, No. 1 (March 1963), 49.

4897. Miller, Wayne, and D. M. Crane. "A Sherlockian Crossword Puzzle," *BSJ* [OS], 1, No. 4 (October 1946), 478-480; [Solution] 2, No. 1 (January 1947), 98.

4898. Morley, Christopher. "The Mycroft Magic Square," *B.S.I. Minutes* (January 9, 1942).
   ———. ———, *Ellery Queen's Mystery Magazine*, 4, No. 2 (March 1943), 124-127.

4899. [Morley, Frank V.] "Sherlock Holmes Crossword," *The Saturday Review of Literature*, 10, No. 44 (May 19, 1934), 703; [Solution and results] 10, No. 46 (June 2, 1934), 727; 10, No. 48 (June 16, 1934), 755. (The Bowling Green)
   ———. *A Sherlock Holmes Cross-Word Puzzle*, by Tobias Gregson, Late of Scotland Yard, and transmitted by him to Christopher Morley. [Privately Printed, 1938.] [8] p.
   Limited to 38 copies.
   ———. "A Sherlock Holmes Cross-Word," *221B: Studies in Sherlock Holmes*. Edited by Vincent Starrett. New York: The Macmillan Co., 1940, p. 244-247.
   ———. ———, *Rex Stout Mystery Quarterly*, No. 2 (August 1945), 130-131.
   ———. ———, *Esquire*, 65, No. 1 (January 1966), 94, [Answer] 112.
   ———. ———, *The Annotated Sherlock*

Holmes. New York: Clarkson N. Potter, [1967]. Vol. 1, p. 38.

The original matriculation test of the Baker Street Irregulars.

4900. Petersen, Svend. "Doctors' Dilemma," *Medical World News*, 9, No. 4 (November 15, 1968), 96, [Answer] 110.

———. ———, *BSJ*, 19, No. 1 (March 1969), 32-33, [Answer] 63.

4901. ———. "A Sherlockian Double-Cross," *BSJ*, 3, No. 3 (July 1953), 182-183.

4902. Robertson, A. M. "A Crude Device," *SHJ*, 4, No. 4 (Spring 1960), [Inset page];[Solution], 5, No. 1 (Winter 1960), 31.

———. ———, *BSP*, No. 31 (January 1968), 3.

4903. Saxe, Stephen. "A Sherlockian Crossword," *BSJ* [OS], 2, No. 2 (April 1947), 208-209; [Solution] 2, No. 3 (July 1947), 346.

4904. Shaw, Dorothy Rowe. *A Sherlock Holmes Crossword Puzzle.* [With an introductory note by John Bennett Shaw.] [Santa Fe, N.M.: Privately Produced, December 1971.] [4] p.

4905. "Sherlockian Crossword," *Manchester Guardian Weekly*, 93, No. 14 (October 7, 1965), 12.

———, *BSJ*, 16, No. 1 (March 1966), 50-51; [Solution], 16, No. 2 (June 1966), 125.

4906. Shreffler, Phil. "Sherlockross-Word," *DCC*, 7, No. 4 (May 1971), 5.

4907. Throckmorton, Jane. "A Sherlockian Crossword Puzzle," *Illustrious Client's Second Case-Book.* Edited by J. N. Williamson. [Indianapolis, Ind.: The Illustrious Clients, 1949.] p. 12-14, [Solution] 96.

4908. Wilmunen, Jon V. "A Sherlockian Crostic," *The Gamebag*, No. 1 (1965), 14-15; No. 2 (1966), 14-15; No. 3 (1967), 19-20 (laid in).

4909. Yates, Donald A. "An Unsolved Baskerville Puzzle," *BSJ*, 7, No. 2 (April 1957), 84-86.

GAMES

4910. *The Adventure of the Disappearing Stars*, by John H. Watson, M.D. [Robert H. Schutz]. Cow-Birling Gap, Sussex: Holmes-Watson Enterprises, Ltd., [1968].

A magic card trick.

4911. *Bringing Sherlock Home*, by Lawrence Treat. Garden City, N.Y.: Heyday House; Doubleday, Doran & Co., 1935.

"7 original picture-clue mystery cases; 6 copies of each for competitive playing."

Contents: Case No. 1. The End of a Wealthy Playboy. - Case No. 2. The Extortion Letter. - Case No. 3. Romantic Interlude. - Case No. 4. The Lunch Room Murder. - Case No. 5. Check Double Check. - Case No. 6. The Episode of the Two Ranneys. - Case No. 7. Merrill's Alibi.

4912. *"Clue," The Great New Sherlock Holmes Game!* Salem, Mass.: Parker Brothers, Inc., 1949. Box: 10-1 / 4 x 20 in.

Contains leaflet of rules for playing, game board, six colored tokens, six miniature weapons, die, pack of twenty-one illustrated cards, and pad of Detective Notes.

"The scene opens in Mr. Boddy's palatial mansion. Mr. Boddy is the victim of foul play and is found in one of the rooms. The object of the game is to discover the answer to these three questions: 1st. Who? Which one of the several suspects did it? 2nd. Where? 3rd. How?"

4913. *Murder on the Orient Express: A Sherlock Holmes Mystery Game.* Hollis, N.Y.: Ideal Toy Corp., 1967. Box: 13-1 / 2 x 19-1 / 2 in. (Famous Mystery Classic Series, No. 2505-6)

Contains instruction booklet, game board, twelve spy figures, Sherlock Holmes figure, Dr. Watson figure, fact sheet pad, report and score sheet pad, and die.

"Object of the game: To gain the most points by logical reasoning and astute observation in determining which spies on the Orient Express have been murdered and which are still alive."

4914. *Sherlock Holmes.* Salem, Mass.: Parker Brothers, Inc., 1904. 56 cards.

"Any number from three to eight can play with one pack. The object is to capture as many burglars, robbers and thieves as possible (counting 1 point each) and to obtain the valuable Sherlock Holmes cards, which count 5 points each."

Review: BSJ, 14, No. 2 (June 1964), 84-87 (Helan G. Halbach).

4915. ———. Playskool Golden Book Classics Picture Puzzles. Puzzle: 11 x 14 in. (120 pieces). (No. 400H)

Taken from cover illustration by Tom Gill of The Golden Picture Classics *Sherlock Holmes* (item 703).

Box also contains *Tom Sawyer*.

4916. ———. Havant, Hants: Minimodels Ltd., [1969]. Box: 8-1 / 4 x 16-1 / 4 in. (Triang Game, TG / 29)

Contains game board depicting a map of London's West End, 48 clue cards, 4 sets of newspaper clippings, 4 Sherlock Holmes figures, 4 Dr. Watson figures, 4 policemen, and instructions.

"For ages 12 to adult. 2-4 players." Each player is both Holmes and Watson. The object is to be the first to present six related clues at 221B Baker Street.

4917. *Sherlock Holmes Detective Kit.* Based on the Billy Wilder film "The Private Life of Sherlock Holmes." [London]: GeminiScan Ltd. for the Publishers, IPC Magazines Ltd., 1970. 11 items in plastic carrying case.

Contents: 1. Portrait of Sir Arthur Conan Doyle and illustrated biography. - 2. Booklet containing Sherlock Holmes tales in fiction and film, with instructions for Cypher Decoder and Detective Game. - 3. Full color cut-out model of Loch Ness Monster for use in detective game. - 4. 'I Spy' pictures. Match your ability to spot detail with that of the great detective. - 5. Sherlock Holmes Cypher Decoder. - 6. Invisible messages for use with detective game. - 7. A picture that 'hangs' upside down on your wall and confuses your friends. - 8. Authentic Baker Street sign with map and description of Holmes's legendary haunts. - 9-10. One Holmes and five Watson identity cards for use in detective game. - 11. Magnifying glass to assist work on item 4.

4918. *Sherlock Holmes 'Follow-the-Clues' Jigsaw.* Based on the Billy Wilder film "The Private Life of Sherlock Holmes." [London]: IPC Magazines Ltd.—Multi Media Promotions, 1970. Box: 10 x 13-1 / 2 in. Puzzle: 19 x 24 in. (850 pieces).

Puzzle from a painting by Alex Jardine.

4919. *The Sherlock Holmes Puzzle.* England: Peter Pan Playthings, [1968]. (Series No. J8034)

This ingenious puzzle consists of seven plastic pieces and a leaflet showing forty designs, including a Sherlock Holmes pipe, that can be made from the pieces.

4920. *Sherlock Holmes: The Game of the Great Detective.* West Springfield, Mass.: National Games, Inc., 1956. Box: 11-1 / 2 x 15-1 / 2 in.

Contains a game board, dice, colored tokens, charts, cards, and instruction booklet.

"Object: To gather all the correct clues describing an imaginary criminal, and the crime—then to get to 221B Baker St. first with the solution."

4921. *Sherlock Holmes Writing Set.* Stuart Hall Co., 1946. Box: 9-1 / 4 x 18-1 / 4 in.

Contains printed and plain sheets and envelopes, instruction booklet, bottle of invisible ink, and bottle of regular ink.

"Four easy-to-learn codes for writing secret notes."

4922. *Silver Blaze—From the Memoirs of Sherlock Holmes.* New York: Springbok Editions, 1966. Box: 14-1 / 4 in. (diameter); Puzzle: 20-1 / 4 in. (diameter). (A Springbok Circular Jigsaw Puzzle, C932)

Also contains two booklets: the story and the solution.

Puzzle from a painting by Barry Evans. *Review: SIS*, 1, No. 3 [1966], 27-28 (Dean Dickensheet).

PHOTOGRAPHIC COMPETITIONS

4923. [Chorley, Jennifer.] "Photographic Competition: 'Holmes's World in 1963,' " *SHJ*, 6, No. 2 (Spring 1963), 60; 6, No. 4 (Spring 1964), 102, 126.

The announcement and results, including reproductions of three prize-winning photographs, of this new competition. The first prize was won by Alan Wilson, who submitted sixteen photographs.

4924. [———.] "Photographic Competition: 'Holmes's World in 1964,' " *SHJ*, 6, No. 4 (Spring 1964), 132; 7, No. 2 (Spring 1965), 34-35, 59.

The announcement and results, including reproductions of five prize-winning photographs, of the second competition. D. Martin Dakin won the first prize in the Color Section and Percy Metcalfe and Humphrey Morton were joint winners of the first prize in the White-and-Black Section.

QUIZZES

4925. The Baker Street Pageboys. *The Pageboys' Composite Quiz.* Kingston, Ontario: [Privately Produced, 1967]. [9] p.

Contents: The Hound of the Baskervilles, by Hugo's Companions (Chicago). - Excerpts from Elliot Kimball's Quiz. - The Irregulars' Quiz, 1946. - The Calculation Is a Simple One. - The Quarterly Quiz, by the Five Orange Pips. - Sherlockript, by Fannie Gross. - The Stockbroker's Clerk, by the Sons of the Copper Beeches. - Real Thoughts, by Ruth Buchholtz.

4926. [———.] "Quizzes," *BSP*, No. 48 (June 1969), 5; No. 51 (September 1969), 2; No. 52-53 (October-November 1969), 3.

Five quizzes in four numbers of the *Baker Street Pages.*

4927. Bedford, Michael. "A Quiz on Smokers in the Canon," *SOS*, 2, No. 3 (February 1968), 8.

Twelve questions in which the reader is asked to identify both the character and the story.

4928. Berg, Emanuel. ["AR"], *BSJ*, 8, No. 3 (July 1958), 187. (From the Editor's Commonplace Book)

A completion puzzle composed of eight questions.

4929. Bergman, Ted. *To Miss Violet Smith.* Privately Produced, January 9, 1964. [9] p. Limited to 21 copies.

4930. Blacker, Carmen. "Christmas Holiday Task: An Intermediate Examination Paper on Sherlock Holmes," *SHJ*, 6, No. 3 (Winter 1963), 92; 6, No. 4 (Spring 1964), 101.

The first prize was awarded to James R. Pascoe (age 12) of Plymouth. Master Pascoe's entry is printed in *SHJ*, 7, No. 1 (Winter 1964), 23-25.

4931. Boucher, Anthony. "A Sherlock Holmes Quiz," *I Knew It All the Time*, by Raymond J. Healy and John V. Cooper. New York: Henry Holt and Co., [1953]. p. 6-10.

Twenty-five multiple-choice questions described by the author as "deliberately simple, and unworthy of the efforts of Irregulars."

4932. Buchholtz, Ruth. ["Quizz"], *BSJ*, 8, No. 4 (October 1958), 246-247. (From the Editor's Commonplace Book)

Ten questions from the lady who competed for the Sherlockian championship on the $64,000 Challenge (item 5005).

4933. Christ, Jay F. *Study Guide for the Adventures of Sherlock Holmes.* [Chicago: American School, 1947.] 23 p.

Based on the Modern Library edition of *The Adventures and Memoirs of Sherlock Holmes*, and prepared for the instruction and training of students of the American School.

4934. Clarke, Richard W. ["Dead Men in the Canon"], *BSJ*, 5, No. 3 (July 1955), 183-186. (From the Editor's Commonplace Book)

The reader is asked to identify the corpse or corpses from each of the twenty-five quotations and to name the tale in which the death occurred.

4935. Collins, Howard. "Upon the Tracing of Footprints by Sherlock Holmes," *BSJ* [OS], 1, No. 4 (October 1946), 443-444, [Answers] 456.

Ten stories to identify from examples of the Master's proficiency in tracing footprints.

4936. Dickensheet, Dean W. *The Adventure of the Blue Carbuncle: An Examination.* Issued as a supplement to *DCC*, 6, No. 2 (March 1970). 2 p.

Twenty questions divided into four groups.

4937. ———. "Death in the Stalls (A Watsonian Fragment)," *VH*, 1, No. 1 (January 1967), 4-5; [Solution] 1, No. 2 (April 1967), 1.

———. ———, *The Ontario Magistrates Quarterly*, 4, No. 3 (July 1967), 9; [Solution], 4 (October 1967). (Q.M.Q. Contest No. 2)

4938. ———. " 'It Is Full of Old Houses,' " *VH*, 4, No. 1 (January 1970), 3.

The reader is asked to match the descriptions of ten Canonical houses to the correct locales and to identify the story in each case.

4939. ———. "Trade Relations," *VH*, 3, No. 3 (September 1969), 9; [Answers] 4, No. 1 (January 1970), 9.

The reader is asked to "pick the individuals in the first and second columns respectively, who share each of the professions in the third column, and to identify the story in each case."

4940. Doll, Bernard. "Has Anybody Here Seen Moriarty?" *Illustrious Client's Second Case-Book.* Edited by J. N. Williamson. [Indianapolis, Ind.: The Illustrious Clients, 1949.] p. 47-49, [Answers] 96.

"This *petit examen* is a not-too-difficult quiz on some of the better known scoundrels and villains which appear in the Sacred Writings. There are ten parts, each of which consists of three clues on one of the miserable curs."

4941. [Donegall, Lord.] "In the Footsteps of Sherlock Holmes Quiz," *SHJ*, 8, No. 4 (Summer 1968), 136, 140.

The original thirty-five questions (five questions a day) that were asked during the Swiss Tour. The contest was won jointly by Roger Lancelyn Green and James Edward Holroyd, who each chalked up 221 points out of a possible 350—and without the use of a Holmes reference library! The *Journal's* contest was won by Vernon Goslin with 350 points; his answers appear in *SHJ*, 9, No. 1 (Winter 1968), 29-33.

4942. [———.] "Our Sixth Competition," *SHJ*, 6, No. 3 (Winter 1963), 69. (Editorial)

A commentary on the first six competitions sponsored by members of the Society, including Miss Carmen Blacker's Examination Paper.

4943. [———.] "Swedish-Norwegian Holmesian Television Quiz," *SHJ*, 8, No. 3 (Winter 1967), 97.

A brief account of the joint quiz program in which the Norwegian winner, Nils Nordberg (item 4992), and the Swedish Holmesian scholar, Ted Bergman, participated. The contest was narrowly won by Mr. Bergman.

4944. "The Eyes Have It—A Quiz," by Mycroft Holmes. *Sherlockian Studies.* Edited by Robert A. Cutter. [Jackson Heights, N.Y.: The Baker Street Press, 1947.]. p. 22, [Answers] 37.

Ten quotations from the Saga in which the reader is asked to identify the person whose eyes are being described and the story in which he appears.

4945. The Five Orange Pips of Westchester County. ["Quiz"] , *BSJ* [OS], 1, No. 3 (July 1946), 369-370.

An identification of the character or case for questions listed under the headings: Violets, Bell-ropes, Lost Week-ends, S.P.C.A., Telegrams, Faces, and Sports.

4946. ———. ["Quiz"] , *BSJ* [OS], 2, No. 2 (April 1947), 219-220.

The reader is asked to identify the type of business engaged in by each of the twenty firms listed.

4947. ———. ["Quiz"], *BSJ*, 3, No. 2 (April 1953), 112.

The annual Five Orange Pips quiz, consisting of ten questions, presented at the 1953 BSI dinner and won by Robert G. Harris.

4948. Gleason, James P. "Watson's Glamour Girls," *Illustrious Client's Third Case-Book.* Edited by J. N. Williamson and H. B. Williams. [Indianapolis, Ind.: The Illustrious Clients, 1953.] p. 60-65, [Answers] 196.

The name of the woman is to be matched with the appropriate descriptive quotation.

4949. ———. "Who Wore That Hat?" *Illustrious Client's Third Case-Book.* p. 157-168, [Answers] 199-200.

The object of this "unreasonable" quiz is to identify a character from a quotation descriptive of his or her headdress.

4950. Gross, Fannie. "Sherlockript," *BSJ*, 7, No. 1 (January 1957), 28; 8, No. 1 (January 1958), 16; 10, No. 2 (April 1960), 100; 10, No. 4 (October 1960), 256.

Four cryptogram quizzes to be decoded and the Sacred Writing named.

4951. ———. "Sherlockwizz," *BSJ*, 7, No. 3 (July 1957), 173-174, [Answers] 186.

The reader is asked to identify ten characters from a brief description of each.

4952. ———. ———, *BSJ*, 7, No. 4 (October 1957), 220, [Answers] 249.

The reader is given excerpts from ten letters and asked to tell who wrote each letter and to whom it was written.

4953. ———. ———, *BSJ*, 8, No. 2 (April 1958), 99; 9, No. 1 (January 1959), 26-27; 9, No. 3 (July 1959), 172.

The missing letters for twenty Sherlockian surnames are to be supplied in the first quiz and twenty pairs of surnames in the second and third quizzes.

4954. ———. ———, *BSJ*, 9, No. 4 (October 1959), 231.

Ten quotations from the Canon, each having a blank space to be filled in with the name of a Sherlockian character.

4955. ———. "Sherlockwizz: 'A Vein of Pawky Humor,' " *BSJ*, 2, No. 2 (April 1952), 93.

Ten questions dealing with bits of Watsonian whimsy. The character and story are to be identified in each case.

4956. ———. "Sherlockwizz: Books and Boats," *BSJ*, 3, No. 4 (October 1953), 244.

Twenty anagrammed names of boats and books to be unscrambled and identified according to the story.

4957. ———. "Sherlockwizz: Business Matters," *BSJ*, 4, No. 4 (October 1954), 218.

Anagrammed names of ten Sherlockian business firms, each containing an extra word representing a commodity or service of special interest to the firm, to be disentangled and the story named in which the reference appears.

4958. ———. "Sherlockwizz: Contuor Kroc tl Rimntle Adrboztor," *BSJ*, 6, No. 1 (January 1956), 34.

The reader is asked to name the Sacred Writings in which ten ciphered items, each with its own code, that belong in the category indicated by the above anagrammed subtitle play an important part.

4959. ———. "Sherlockwizz: Holmes Incognito," *BSJ*, 3, No. 1 (January 1953), 43.

Nine stories in which the Master appears in disguise are to be identified.

4960. ———. "Sherlockwizz: Lithe Patterns Etc.," *BSJ*, 6, No. 3 (July 1956), 154.

Ten anagrammed items belonging in the category designated by the above anagrammed subtitle, to be unscrambled and each put in its proper place.

4961. ———. "Sherlockwizz: The Master of the House," *BSJ*, 1, No. 4 (October 1951), 146-147.

The names of twenty famous Sherlockian homes are to be matched with the men who ruled over them.

4962. ———. "Sherlockwizz: The Master Speaks in Cipher," *BSJ*, 3, No. 2 (April 1953), 113-114.

The reader is asked to decode ten utterances of Sherlock Holmes and to name the story in which each appears.

4963. ———. "Sherlockwizz: Mr. and Mrs.," *BSJ*, 2, No. 4 (October 1952), 214.

Fifteen anagrammed sentences "made up of the letters contained in the names of a

Sherlockian guy and the gal he married for better or for worse." The first correct solution was submitted by Lorents Arnold Morrow.

4964. ———. "Sherlockwizz: Mixed Languages," *BSJ*, 4, No. 1 (January 1954), 54.

Twenty foreign words, phrases, and sentences anagrammed into dubious English, to be unmixed and the story named in which each appears.

4965. ———. "Sherlockwizz: Odd Jobs," *BSJ*, 6, No. 2 (April 1956), 87.

The reader is asked to unscramble ten anagrammed names of Sherlockian characters and the positions they held, and then to identify the tale.

4966. ———. "Sherlockwizz: Odds and Ends," *BSJ*, 10, No. 3 (July 1960), 151.

The character involved in each of ten briefly described oddments and the story are to be identified.

4967. ———. "Sherlockwizz: Physicians and Surgeons," *BSJ*, 5, No. 1 (January 1955), 26.

The reader is asked to name the doctor in each of ten cases.

4968. ———. "Sherlockwizz: The Scene of the Crime," *BSJ*, 5, No. 2 (April 1955), 92.

Anagrammed names of homicide spots and their locations, to be deciphered and the characters named who are the murder victims in these ten cases.

4969. ———. "Sherlockwizz: Scootsach's Cletsar," *BSJ*, 5, No. 3 (July 1955), 160.

Twelve ciphered items that belong in the category of the above ciphered title, to be decoded and the Sacred Writings named in which they appear.

4970. ———. "Sherlockwizz: Spring Summour," *BSJ*, 6, No. 4 (October 1956), 215.

A fifth cryptogram to be decoded and the Sacred Writing named.

4971. ———. "Sherlockwizz: They Brought the Good News to Baker Street," *BSJ*, 2, No. 1 (January 1952), 39.

The reader is asked to unscramble twenty anagrammed titles and names and then to match each case with its good-tidings bearer.

4972. ———. "Sherlockwizz: Twenty Questions," *BSJ*, 4, No. 2 (April 1954), 97.

Questions asked by various characters who are to be identified along with their stories.

4973. [Gunn, R. Ivar.] "An Examination Paper on 'Sherlock Holmes,' " *Life and Letters*, 1, No. 7 (December 1928), 598-600.

———. ———, *The Private Life of Sherlock Holmes*, [by] Vincent Starrett. New York: The Macmillan Co., 1933. p. 189-192.

———. ———, ———. London: Ivor Nicholson & Watson, Ltd., 1934. p. 176-179.

Thirteen multipart questions in this classic examination paper, devised by the first chairman of the Sherlock Holmes Society (the paper was mistakenly attributed to Desmond MacCarthy).

4974. ———. "Examination Paper," *Seventeen Steps to 221B*. [Edited by] James Edward Holroyd. London: George Allen & Unwin Ltd., [1967]. p. 179-182.

Eleven multipart questions in the author's second paper.

4975. ———. "Report on the Christmas Examination Paper," *SHJ*, 1, No. 1 (May 1952), 11-14.

The results of Mr. Gunn's second examination paper, including a list of the twenty-five candidates and their scores. The winner was Noel Percy Metcalf, with a score of 152 out of a possible 160.

4976. Hahn, Robert W. "Villains in the Canon," *DCC*, 6, No. 3 (May 1970), 5, [Answers] 6.

A quiz consisting of thirteen questions, given at the March 18 session of Hugo's Companions and won by John Nieminski.

4977. Halcomb, Robert J. "Quick, Watson, the Answer!" *Saturday Review*, 49, No. 40 (October 1, 1966), 34, [Answers] 64. (Your Literary I.Q.)

———. ———, *BSJ*, 17, No. 1 (March 1967), 24.

The names of ten victims are to be matched with the way in which each met his death and in which story.

4978. Hugo's Companions. "Sherlockian Quiz," *DCC*, 1, No. 1 (December 1964), 4; 1, No. 2 (February 1965), 6; 1, No. 3 (April 1965), 7.

Forty-one questions based on Houn.

4979. ———. ———, *DCC*, 1, No. 4 (May 1965), 7.

Seventeen questions based on the first five chapters of Vall.

4980. The Illustrious Clients. "An Illustrious Quiz," *Illustrious Client's Third Case-Book*. Edited by J. N. Williamson and H. B. Williams. [Indianapolis, Ind.: The Illustrious Clients, 1953.] p. 100-107, [Answers] 196-199.

Contents: The Art of Detection. - Memories. - Sherlockian Sections. - Gosh, What Is It? - Miscellaneous. - Simple, But Instructive. - Illustrious Interrogations. - Foreign Affairs in Baker Street. - Evidence. - Nosing Around. - A Quiz. - Watson's

Zoo—A Quiz. - Behind Closed Doors. - Questions and Answers. - Who Wore That Hat?

4981. Iraldi, James C., and Nathan L. Bengis. "Canonical Boxes," *SHJ*, 1, No. 4 (December 1953), 10, [Answers] 38.

Twenty boxes to be identified by naming the adventure in which each appears and by providing some descriptive detail, such as their contents.

4982. Kimball, Elliot. *Elliot Kimball's Sherlockian Quiz.* [N.p.: Privately Produced, n.d.] 5 p.

One hundred questions on all aspects of the Canon.

4983. King, Martin J. "The Priory School Quiz," *SS*, 1, No. 1 (January 1971), 2, [Answers] 4.

Twenty questions on this tale.

4984. " 'Knights on Baker Street': A Quiz for Sherlockians," *SHJ*, 3, No. 2 (Winter 1956), 11, [Answers] 19.

The reader is asked to give the title of the story in which each of twenty characters appears.

4985. [Knox, E. V.] "A Final Examination-Paper on the Life and Work of Sherlock Holmes," [by] Evoe. *Punch*, 175 (October 31, 1928), 480-481.

———. ———, *The Private Life of Sherlock Holmes*, [by] Vincent Starrett. New York: The Macmillan Co., 1933. p. 193-197.

———. ———, *The Sherlock Holmes.* [Compiled and prepared by Richard Lonsdale-Hands Associates.] London: Whitbread & Co. Ltd., [1957]. p. 39-41.

Seventeen questions to stump the experts.

4986. Lacy, Jack. "For Irregulars Only," *Saturday Review of Literature*, 33, No. 39 (September 30, 1950), 36, [Answers] 38. (Your Literary I.Q.)

Twenty characters whose descriptions are based mostly on the Master's deductions.

4987. Lawson, Douglas. "9 K-9's—A Cur's Quiz," *The Second Cab.* Edited by James Keddie. [Boston: The Speckled Band, 1947.] p. 32-33, [Answers] 91.

From clues provided for nine canines, the reader is asked to identify the story, owner, place, incident, and breed of the dog.

4988. McCleary, G. F. "An Examination Paper on the Exploits of Sherlock Holmes," *On Detective Fiction and Other Things.* London: Hollis & Carter, 1960. p. 60-62.

Thirty questions on the Sherlockian chronicles.

4989. ———. "Three Examination Papers," *The National Review*, 127 (December 1946), 497-503.

A discussion of three quizzes, the second of which is the examination paper by E. V. Knox.

4990. McLauchlin, Russell. "The Problem of the Canonical Couplets," *BSJ* [OS], 2, No. 4 (October 1947), 457-460.

The reader is asked to identify fifty of the tales from an identifying couplet of each.

4991. Morrow, L. A. "Who Was That Lady? A Felicity of Females," *BSJ*, 13, No. 1 (March 1963), 31-32, [Answers] 47.

The lady and the story in each of twenty quoted descriptions from the Canon are to be identified.

4992. Nordberg, Nils. "Sherlock Holmes Norwegian Television Quiz Programme," *SHJ*, 8, No. 2 (Spring 1967), 49, 52.

An account of the author's participation in "Kvitt Eller Dobbelt" ("Double or Quits") during November and December of 1966. Included are the ten questions and answers for the £500 prize won by Mr. Nordberg.

4993. Page, Andrew, ed. *Priory Papers: A Study in Examinations.* [Compiled and edited for The Priory School of New York by Andrew Page. Owings Mills, Md.: Privately Produced, June 1971.] 15 p.

Contents: Introduction, by Steve Clarkson. - 1. Sussex Vampire, by Rosie Vogel. - 2. The Illustrious Clients, by Ken Reeler. - 3. The Bruce-Partington Plans, by Jeff Gross. - 4. Thor Bridge, by Mark Dushey. - 5. Musgrave Ritual, by Andrew Page. - 6. Dying Detective, by Rosie Vogel. - 7. Devil's Foot, by Andrew Page. - 8. Black Peter, by Joe Peralta. - 9. Five Orange Pips, by Dom Corrado. - 10. Three Garridebs, [Anonymous]. - Afterword, by Andrew Page. - Answers.

4994. Pearson, Edmund. "Sherlock Holmes Examination," *Boston Evening Transcript* (191-).

———. ———, *The Outlook*, 146, No. 12 (July 20, 1927), 387. (The Book Table)

———. ———, *CPBook*, 4, No. 16 (Fall 1968), 315.

Nineteen questions "for the amusement of Sherlockians."

4995. [The Priory School of New York.] "Police Officials," *HO*, 1, No. 1 (March 1971), 30; [Answers] 1, No. 3 (May 1971), 3.

Fifteen questions in which the reader is asked to name members of the police force and the cases.

4996. [———.] "Quiz on Clients in the Canon," *HO*, 1, No. 2 (April 1971), 3.

Games and Competitions

4997. [———.] "Quiz on Familiar Quotes in the Canon," *HO*, 1, No. 3 (May 1971), 3; 1, No. 4 (June 1971), 3; [Answers] 1, No. 5 (July 1971), 2.

Twelve quotations to be identified by the story and speaker.

4998. [———.] "Story Quiz on 'The Adventure of the Devil's Foot,' " *HO*, 1, No. 1 (March 1971), 8-9, [Answers] 34.

Forty questions on this tale.

4999. The Red Circle of Washington, D.C. ["Who Got the Shilling(s)"], *BSJ*, 1, No. 4 (October 1951), 154.

5000. Schulz, Ted. "Colonels from the Canon," *BSG*, 1, No. 2 (1961), 32-33.

The reader is asked to identify thirteen colonels, honorable and otherwise, from brief statements.

5001. Schutz, Robert H. *Villains of the Sherlock Holmes Canon.* [Pittsburgh, Pa.: Privately Printed, 1967.]

Limited to 30 sets.

A set of thirty-six cards intended as an educational aid for the Sherlockian student.

5002. Shaw, John Bennett. "Doctor's Special," *BSCL*, No. 7 (1969), 3, [Answers] 24.

"Three specimens of his countless and witty quizzes."

5003. ———. "Quiz on 'The Red Circle,' " *SOS*, No. 3 (February 1967), 4, [Answers] 8.

Nine questions based on animal life in this adventure.

5004. ———. "Twenty Questions on Animals Found in 'The Adventure of the Devil's Foot,' " *VH*, 2, No. 2 (April 1968), 6-7, [Answers] 7.

5005. "The $64,000 Question," New York: WCBS-TV (Ch. 2), Tuesdays, ?-June 12, 1956, 10:00-10:30 p.m.

Capt. Thomas O'Rourke and his wife Bobbye of Baltimore competed separately and each won $32,000 for correctly answering questions on the Sacred Writings. The program was hosted by Hal March. Mrs. O'Rourke was later challenged by Mrs. Ruth Buchholtz of Delphos, Ohio, on "The $64,000 Challenge."

Reviews and Questions: BSJ, 6, No. 3 (July 1956), 186-189 (Edgar W. Smith); 7, No. 1 (January 1957), 58 (Edgar W. Smith); *SHJ*, 3, No. 3 (Autumn 1957), 1 (Lord Donegall).

5006. "The 64,000 Question," ABC Midland, Saturdays, October 12, 19, 1957, 8:00-8:30 p.m.

The contestant was John Hislop, a journalist from Beckenham, Kent. It was the first attempt by a Sherlockian to win £3,200 on A.T.V.'s "64,000 Question."

Review and Questions: SHJ, 3, No. 3 (Autumn 1957), 1-2 (Lord Donegall).

5007. [Smith, Edgar W.] ["Illustrators of the Tales"], *BSJ*, 6, No. 4 (October 1956), 239, [Answers] 240; 7, No. 1 (January 1957), 52.

The reader is asked to identify the illustrators of seven representations of the Master and the medium in which their drawings appeared.

5008. The Sons of the Copper Beeches. ["Quiz"], *BSJ*, 10, No. 1 (January 1960), 46-47.

Eleven questions on "The Adventure of the Stockbroker's Clerk."

5009. Speirs, James. "A Sherlock Holmes Quiz," *BSJ* [OS], 2, No. 3 (July 1947), 351-352.

Twenty-seven questions on the Master and the Sacred Writings.

5010. Stump, William. "The Woman Who Came to Dinner: Being the Case of Mrs. Grace Bluestone and the Stunned Sherlock Holmes Experts," *The Sunday Sun Magazine* [Baltimore] (March 25, 1956), 5, 12.

An illustrated article about one of the leading candidates for the "$64,000 Question" and the Six Napoleons who quizzed her on the Canon.

5011. "The Swedish-Norwegian Sherlock Holmes TV Quiz Programme 1967," *BSCL*, No. 6 (1968), 6-16.

"The Norwegian Holmes Champion, Nils Nordberg, was challenged by the Swede, Ted Bergman, when the Holmes subject was distributed on three successive Saturday evenings, from July 1 to July 15. The presentation of the questions and the answers of the contestants are here stated."

5012. The Three Students Plus. "Quiz on the Canon," *SOS*, 5, No. 1 (January 1971), 7-8; [Answers] 5, No. 2 (August 1971), 13-14.

Fifteen questions "designed for the elite in Sherlockian circles."

5013. [The Trained Cormorants of Los Angeles County.] "The Puzzle Page," *CR*, 1, No. 4 (September 1960), 12-13.

Three quizzes entitled "A Key to Detection," "Faint Recollections," and "Carbo's Railway Carriage Pastimes."

5014. [Williams, Howard B.] "Sub-Librarian's Quiz," by the Sub-Librarian. *Illustrious Client's Third Case-Book.* Edited by J. N. Williamson and H. B. Williams. [Indianapolis, Ind.: The Illustrious Clients, 1953.] p. 150-151, [Answers] 199.

A two-part quiz in which the reader is asked to identify ten members of the Master's "organization" and five senders of telegrams.

IX | *Actors, Performances, and Recordings*

A Criticism

GENERAL

5015. Baring-Gould, William S. " 'You Would Have Made an Actor, and a Rare One,' " *The Annotated Sherlock Holmes.* New York: Clarkson N. Potter, [1967]. Vol. 1, chap. 4, p. 27-32. illus.

A discussion of the stage and film versions of the tales.

5016. Berman, Ruth. " 'The Stage Lost a Fine Actor,' " *BSJ,* 17, No. 3 (September 1967), 136-138.

Links between the Sacred Writings and the actors who have portrayed Sherlock Holmes.

5017. ———. " 'The Stage Lost a Fine Actor When He Became a Specialist in Crime': A Clerihewical Meditation," *VH,* 1, No. 2 (April 1967), 3.

"Did the stage lose? / By now it is no news / That it has often grasped the essence / Of the Holmesian presence."

5018. Cabana, Ray, Jr. "Always Holmes," *Kaleidoscope,* 2, No. 1 (1965), 24-34.

A detailed account of the Sherlock Holmes films featuring Basil Rathbone and Nigel Bruce. Includes thirteen photographs of scenes from the films.

5019. Connor, Edward. "Sherlock Holmes on the Screen Has Never Been Exactly the Man Conan Doyle's Readers Imagined," *Films in Review,* 12, No. 7 (August-September 1961), 409-418.

The author traces the various screen dramatizations of the Master from *Sherlock Holmes Baffled* (1900) to *The Hound of the Baskervilles* (1959). Illustrated with ten photographs.

5020. Daugherty, Frank. "Baker Street Regulars," *The Christian Science Monitor* (August 19, 1944), 7.

An illustrated article on the films and radio programs of "the most regular performers of Sherlock Holmes and Dr. Watson"—Basil Rathbone and Nigel Bruce.

5021. Dickenson, Fred. "Champion Private Eye: Why Sherlock Holmes Has Outlasted Them All," *New York Mirror Magazine* (October 1, 1961), 11.

A tribute explaining why the Master Sleuth has shown more staying power on television than any of his rivals and revealing that he was the first dramatic character to appear on TV (in 1937 Louis Hector portrayed Holmes in "The Three Garridebs" [items 5508 and 5550]).

5022. Garrick, Paul. "Presenting Sherlock Holmes," *High Points* [Board of Education of the City of New York], 37, No. 9 (November 1955), 69-73.

A discussion of the activities in New York schools concerning the analysis and dramatization of the Holmes narratives which Mr. Garrick thinks are ideally suited for the stage.

5023. Gruber, Frank. "Reminiscences. II. On Script-Writing Holmes and Bulldog Drummond," *The Armchair Detective,* 2, No. 1 (October 1968), 56.

Most of this brief but interesting article is concerned with the author's experience of writing the screenplays for *Terror by Night* and *Dressed to Kill* (items 5158-5159).

5024. Hamilton, Cicely. "Elementary, My Dear Watson!" *London Calling* (May 22, 1941), 15, 24.

A look at the film and radio portrayals.

5025. Harmon, Jim. "For Armchair Detectives Only," *The Great Radio Heroes.* Garden City, N.Y.: Doubleday & Co., [1967]. Chap. 8, p. 141-157.

The first part of this chapter is devoted to some of the Canonical tales which have appeared across the airways.

5026. Howlett, Anthony D. *"The Hound of the Baskervilles* on the Screen," *SHJ*, 1, No. 1 (May 1952), 33-35; [Addendum], 1, No. 2 (September 1952), 38.

A history of the filmed version of this adventure from the first production in 1914 by Pathé Frères to the 20th Century-Fox production in 1939.

5027. ———. "Sherlock Holmes on the Screen," *Sherlock Holmes: Catalogue of an Exhibition Held at Abbey House, Baker Street, London, May-September 1951.* Presented for the Festival of Britain by the Public Libraries Committee of the Borough of St. Marylebone. Chap. 9, p. 47-54.

A valuable discussion and listing of several cinematic portrayals of Holmes.

5028. ———. "Shinwell-Johnsoniana," *SHJ*, 4, No. 4 (Spring 1960), 135, 140; 6, No. 1 (Winter 1962), 22-23; 7, No. 1 (Winter 1964), 22-23; 8, No. 4 (Summer 1968), 131-132.

Previews and reviews of Sherlock Holmes radio and television series and motion pictures.

5029. ———. "A Study in Celluloid," *SHJ*, 3, No. 1 (Summer 1956), 12-13.

Seven historic photographs from the collection of Anthony Howlett.

5030. ———, and Michael Pointer. "Holmes on Stage and Screen," *John O'London's Weekly*, 63 (February 19, 1954), 172-173, 171.

A comprehensive and well-illustrated account of the stage, film, and radio impersonations.

5031. Keddie, James. "The Clouded Crystal," *SOS*, 2, No. 4 (April 1968), 5-7.

"A brief look at those who have trod the boards and / or solved problems in the flickers, as the Great Detective."

5032. Maltin, Leonard. "Basil Rathbone as Sherlock Holmes," *Film Fan Monthly* No. 75 (September 1967), 3-5. illus.
———. ———, *The Mystery Lover's Newsletter*, 1, No. 4 (April 1968), 12-13.
"A discussion and review of the famous films." (Subtitle)

5033. Marshall, Jim. "Durable Detective," *Collier's*, 116, No. 9 (September 1, 1945), 26, 66.
———. ———, *The Strand Magazine*, 110 (January 1946), 38-41.
Most of this article deals with the cinematic adaptations of the stories.

5034. Morrow, Daniel. "Tune in Again for Sherlock Holmes," *BSJ*, 22, No. 1 (March 1972), 38-42.

An informative discussion of the Rathbone-Bruce radio programs.

5035. Pickard, Roy. "Sherlock Holmes on the Screen," *BSJ*, 21, No. 2 (June 1971), 70-76.

An interesting review of the films, from *Sherlock Holmes Baffled* in 1900 to *The Private Life of Sherlock Holmes* in 1970.

5036. Pointer, Michael E. "Sherlock Holmes on the Stage," *Sherlock Holmes: Catalogue of an Exhibition Held at Abbey House, Baker Street, London, May-September 1951.* Presented for the Festival of Britain by the Public Libraries Committee of the Borough of St. Marylebone. Chap. 8, p. 44-46.

A brief discussion, followed by a list of items in the exhibit.

5037. ———. " 'Which of You Is Holmes?' A Gallery of Impersonators," *SHJ*, 9, No. 3 (Winter 1969), 87-89; 9, No. 4 (Summer 1970), 118-120; 10, No. 1 (Winter 1970), 13-15; 10, No. 2 (Summer 1971), 47-49; 10, No. 3 (Winter 1971), 94-96; 10, No. 4 (Summer 1972), 131-133.

A series of illustrated articles on the following portrayers of Sherlock Holmes: 1. Charles Brookfield. - 2. Clive Brook. - 3. Hr. Bergendorff. - 4. Hr. Bergvall. - 5. Hr. Knud Nyblom. - 6. Mack Sennett. - 7. Fred Mace. - 8. Henry Oscar. - 9. Carlyle Blackwell. - 10. Alan Moore. - 11. John Barrymore. - 12. Francis Ford. - 13. H. Hamilton Stewart. - 14. Howard Marion Crawford. - 15. Ronald Howard. - 16. Chubb-Lock Holmes. - 17. Shylock Bones. - 18. Sherlocko and Watso. - 19. Julian Royce. - 20. H. A. Saintsbury. - 21. Marcel Myin.

5038. Polites, Constance M. "Sherlock Holmes—On TV," *BSJ*, 6, No. 4 (October 1956), 204.

"The wonder of it, the miracle at last! / The swift, complete return to that dear past!"

5039. The Priory Scholars. *Holmes in the Films of the 30's: Program Notes.* [New York: Privately Produced, February 14, 1958.] 3 p.

An important documentation of the cinematographical history of the period.

5040. ———. *The Priory Scholars of Fordham, a Scion Society of the Baker Street Irregulars, Present The Sleeping Cardinal, the First Sherlock Holmes Sound Film. . . .* [New York: Privately Produced], April 6, 1956. [4] p.

Program notes for the showing of this film and a partly annotated listing of some forty films "which have treated, in great or small fashion, with Sherlock Holmes, his cases, or the intellectual prowess which his very name implies."

5041. ———. *The Universal Holmes: The Twelve Sherlock Holmes Films Made by Basil Rathbone for Universal Pictures: A Portfolio of Poster Art.* [New York: Privately Produced], Christmas 1966. [15] p. illus.

Contains an introductory essay by Chris Steinbrunner, reproductions of the advertising posters, and a synopsis of each film.

5042. Rahill, Frank. "The Murder-Mystery Melodrama: An Inquest," *Theatre Arts*, 25, No. 3 (March 1941), 233-242.

An illustrated article in which pages 235-236 are devoted to reasons why Watson's narratives do not lend themselves to melodramatic treatment—in spite of the fact that Holmes has all the attributes for a melodramatic hero. This opinion is contrary to the one expressed by Paul Garrick in item 5022.

5043. [Richard, Peter, comp.] *Charles Augustus Milverton on Stage, Screen and Radio.* London: The Milvertonians of Hampstead, 1960. [30] p.

A comprehensive survey with credits, cast, and story for *The Speckled Band, Charles Augustus Milverton, The Return of Sherlock Holmes, The Missing Rembrandt,* and *Dr. Watson Meets Sherlock Holmes.*

5044. Rogers, Paul Patrick. "Sherlock Holmes on the Spanish Stage," *The Modern Language Forum*, 16, No. 3 (June 1931), 88-90.

An informative essay about the super-detective as portrayed in the dramatic works of Spanish playwrights.

5045. Rosenberger, Edgar S. "Four Ages," *BSJ*, 2, No. 1 (January 1952), 21.

A verse in four stanzas about Holmes on stage, screen, radio, and television.

5046. Shibuk, Charles. "Dramatizations of the Great Literary Detectives and Criminals. Part IV. Film," *The Armchair Detective*, 2, No. 1 (October 1968), 31-43.

Pages 37-40 of this bibliography contain a chronological list of the films, including the names of the actors who portrayed Holmes and Watson, that have been based upon the Canonical tales or written as original screenplays.

5047. Starrett, Vincent. "Impersonators of Mr. Sherlock Holmes," *The Private Life of Sherlock Holmes.* New York: The Macmillan Co., 1933. p. 139-160.

———. Revised with title: "Portrayers of Sherlock Holmes," *The Private Life of Sherlock Holmes.* Revised and enlarged.

The University of Chicago Press, [1960]. p. 115-127.

The Master on stage and screen.

5048. Stedman, Raymond William. "Sleuth and Shadow," *The Serials: Suspense and Drama by Installment.* Norman: University of Oklahoma, [1971]. Chap. 6, p. 149-152.

A knowledgeable account of the radio dramatizations in the 1930's and 1940's, when William Gillette and Basil Rathbone portrayed Holmes.

5049. Webster, Donald. "Sherlock Holmes on Television," *Investigations*, 1, No. 2 (March 1971), 3-7.

Reviews of the Rathbone-Bruce films via TV and the Howard-Crawford TV series.

CHARLES CHAPLIN

5050. Chaplin, Charles. *My Autobiography.* London: The Bodley Head, [1964]. p. 75-93. illus.

———. ———. New York: Simon and Schuster, 1964. p. 76-93. illus.

———. ———. [Harmondsworth]: Penguin Books, [1966]. p. 76-92. illus.

———. ———. (Illustrated) New York: Pocket Books, [June 1966]. p. 72-90. (No. 78240)

———. *Die Geschichte meines Lebens.* [Übersetzt von Günther Danehl und Hans Jürgen von Koskull.] [Reutlingen]: S. Fischer Verlag, [1964]. p. 74-91.

———. *La mia autobiografia.* Traduzione di Vincenzo Mantovani. [Verona]: Arnoldo Mondadori Editore, [1964]. p. 89-109.

———. *Oma elämä kertani.* [Suomentanut Seere Salminen.] Porvoo; Helsinki: Werner Söderström Osakeyhtiö, [1964]. p. 68-83.

———. *Historia de mi vida.* Traducción de Julio Gómez de la Serna. [Madrid]: Taurus, [1965]. p. 73-88.

Chapter five of this fascinating and important book is devoted to the actor's portrayal of Billy the page boy in William Gillette's plays *The Painful Predicament of Sherlock Holmes* and *Sherlock Holmes* (items 5207 and 5218).

Reviews: BSJ, 14, No. 4 (December 1964), 246 (Cornelis Helling); *SHJ*, 7, No. 1 (Winter 1964), 27-28 (Lord Donegall).

5051. Montgomery, James. "A Comedy of Errors," *Shots from the Canon.* [Philadelphia: Privately Printed, 1953.] p. 19.

The program from the Duke of York's Theatre has been reproduced to show that Chaplin appeared in the play *Sherlock Holmes* in 1905.

5052. Pointer, Michael. " 'Billy, You're a Smart Boy!' " *SHJ*, 8, No. 3 (Winter 1967), 88-90.

Criticism

A history of Master Charles Chaplin's role as Billy, beginning July 27, 1903, at the Pavilion Theatre in London, and ending March 3, 1906, at the Theatre Royle in Rochdale.

WILLIAM GILLETTE

5053. Baldwin, Faith. "My First Meeting with Sherlock Holmes," *BSJ* [OS], 2, No. 1 (January 1947), 54-58.

"I fell in love with Mr. Gillette because I had so long been in love with Holmes. . . . He was entirely S. Holmes with something added."

5054. Bergman, Ted and Ingrid. *Pjasen Sherlock Holmes på Svenska Scener* (*Sherlock Holmes on the Swedish Stage*). [Stockholm: Privately Produced, 1963.] [20] p. illus.

Limited to 50 copies.

In this Christmas offering of 1963 the authors write about some Swedish performances of Gillette's play at the beginning of the 20th century.

Review: SHJ, 6, No. 4 (Spring 1964), 128-129 (Lord Donegall).

5055. Bolitho, William. *The Last Bow.* Privately printed broadside, Wm. Gillette's farewell tour, 1929-30.

———. ———, *The World* [New York] (December 3, 1929), 13.

———. ———, *Camera Obscura*, by William Bolitho. Preface by Noel Coward. New York: Simon and Schuster, 1930. Chap. 47, p. 203-207.

———. ———, ———. London: William Heinemann, [1931]. p. 203-207.

"The return of Sherlock Holmes and the last bow of William Gillette made together at the New Amsterdam a singularly fascinating event."

5056. Booth, J. B. "The London of Sherlock Holmes," *Palmy Days.* London: The Richards Press, [1957]. Chap. 1, p. 17-21.

A delightful account of how Gillette came to write and appear in his highly successful play.

5057. Brock, H. I. "Sherlock Holmes Returns to the Stage," *The New York Times Magazine* (November 10, 1929), 14, 20. illus.

"William Gillette, who nears seventy-five, comes back in the role of the great detective of fiction." (Subtitle)

5058. Cook, Doris E. *Sherlock Holmes and Much More, or Some of the Facts About William Gillette.* [Hartford]: The Connecticut Historical Society, 1970. viii, 112 p. illus.

Contents: Foreword. - 1. Early Years in Hartford, Conn. - 2. Getting Started in the Theatre. - 3. First Successes and Marriage. - 4. Troubled Years. - 5. Acting Again in His Own Plays. - 6. Sherlock Holmes, Etc. - 7. More Acting and a New Play. - 8. "Retirement". - 9. Honors and Last Farewells. - 10. As They Saw Him and As He Was. - Notes.

Reviews: HO, 1, No. 9 (November 1971), 6 (Glenn J. Shea); *SHJ*, 10, No. 2 (Summer 1971), 67 (Lord Donegall).

5059. Hamilton, Clayton. "The Plays of William Gillette," *The Bookman*, 32 (February 1911), 596-597, 601.

A review of his career as a playwright. Includes a photograph of Mr. Gillette as Sherlock Holmes.

5060. Keddie, James. "About a William Gillette Collection," *BSJ*, 12, No. 1 (March 1962), 17-21.

A description of the author's monumental collection on the first great Sherlockian actor. The collection consists of numerous letters, programs, posters, photographs, magazine articles, books by and about the actor as well as those from his library, scrapbook material, and other miscellany.

5061. *Letters of Salutation and Felicitation Received by William Gillette on the Occasion of His Farewell to the Stage in "Sherlock Holmes."* [New York: November 25, 1929.] [61] p.

5062. Lynch, Gertrude. "The Real William Gillette," *The Theatre Magazine*, 13 (April 1911), 122-124. illus.

5063. McLauchlin, Russell. "Alfred Street and Baker Street," *Alfred Street.* Illustrated by Wm. A. Bostick. Detroit: Conjure House, 1946. p. 90-94.

———. "My First Meeting with Sherlock Holmes," *BSJ* [OS], 2, No. 3 (July 1947), 342-344.

A fond memory of William Gillette portraying the Master at the Detroit Opera House. Illustrated with a full-page photograph of the actor on page 345 of *BSJ*.

5064. "Mr. William Gillette in 'Sherlock Holmes,' " *Players of the Day: A Series of Portraits in Colour of Theatrical Celebrities of the Present Time.* London: George Newnes Ltd., [1902]. [unpaged]

5065. Moses, Montrose J. "William Gillette Says Farewell: A Veteran of Three Generations of the American Theatre," *Theatre Guild Magazine*, 7 (January 1930), 30-35, 56. illus.

5066. Shafer, Yvonne. "A Sherlock Holmes of the Past: William Gillette's Later Years," *Players: The Magazine of American Theatre*, 46 No. 5 (June-July 1971), 229-235. illus.

5067. Shepstone, Harold J. "Mr. William Gillette as Sherlock Holmes," *The Strand Magazine* [London], 22 (December 1901), 613-621. illus.

———. ———, *The Strand Magazine* [New York], 22 (January 1902), 613-621. illus.

———. Synopsis of the play (p. 616-618) reprinted in *BSCL*, No. 8 (1970), 5-8.

An admirable review and history of the play.

5068. Sherk, H. Dennis. *William Gillette: His Life and Works.* University Park, Pa., 1961. 232 p.

Dissertation—Pennsylvania State University.

Listed in *Dissertation Abstracts,* 22 (1962), 2513.

Available from University Microfilms, 300 North Zeeb Road, Ann Arbor, Mich. 48106. (Order No. 61-6812)

5069. Starrett, Vincent. "Introduction," *Sherlock Holmes: A Play . . . ,* by William Gillette. Garden City, N.Y.: Doubleday, Doran & Co., 1935. p. v-xiv.

"Unfortunate in their birth years are the babes of today and tomorrow whose first view of Sherlock Holmes upon the stage must be productions lacking the magical presence of Mr. William Gillette. And unhappier still, one thinks, is the destiny of those innocents of a far future who will have no living elders to recall for them that winning personality."

5070. ———. "To William Gillette (on his return to the stage in 'Sherlock Holmes')," *Three Poems,* by Vincent Starrett. Ysleta, [Texas]: Edwin B. Hill, 1934. [unpaged]

———. ———, *A Baker Street Four-Wheeler.* Edited by Edgar W. Smith. [Maplewood, N.J., and New York: The Pamphlet House, 1944.] p. 30.

———. ———, *BSJ*, 7, No. 2 (April 1957), 78; 12, No. 1 (March 1962), 6.

"That you are Holmes himself, and not Gillette, / To voice one's gratitude for your existence!"

5071. Stone, P. M. "Mr. William Gillette," *SHJ*, 4, No. 4 (Spring 1960), 115-118. illus.

A history of the actor's superb role as Sherlock Holmes.

5072. ———. "The Painful Predicament of Sherlock Holmes," *BSJ*, 6, No. 1 (January 1956), 12-17.

An informative discussion of Gillette's one-act skit by the same name.

5073. ———. "William Gillette as Sherlock Holmes," *BSJ*, 10, No. 1 (January 1960), 37-38.

Essentially a condensed version of item 5071.

5074. ———. "William Gillette's Stage Career," *BSJ*, 12, No. 1 (March 1962), 8-16.

"A chronological record of his more important stage productions—apart from his memorable portrayal of Sherlock Holmes—with dates of the first performances." (Subtitle)

5075. ———. *William Hooker Gillette.* Issued as a supplement to *BSJ*, 3, No. 3 (July 1953). [16] p.

"Some notes relating to his distinguished family background, and the circumstances which led to his memorable production of 'Sherlock Holmes'; together with a tribute to his career as actor and playwright."

5076. The Stowe-Day Foundation. *The Curtain Is Up on the William Gillette Exhibit, October 16, 1970, through January 31, 1971, Honoring the Famous Actor-Playwright Who Was Born at Nook Farm, Hartford, Connecticut.* [Preface by Doris E. Cook.] Sponsored by the Stowe-Day Foundation at Nook Farm Visitors' Center, Hartford, Connecticut. 24 p. illus.

Among the many items and photographs in this handsome catalog, seventeen are concerned with Gillette's portrayal of Holmes.

5077. Strang, Lewis C. "William Gillette and 'Sherlock Holmes,' " *Famous Actors of the Day in America.* Second Series. Boston: L. C. Page and Co., 1902. Chap. 6, p. 89-107.

A critical analysis of "a most ridiculously improbable, and, at the same time, a most tremendously absorbing play."

5078. [Van Name, Fred.] *Gillette Castle State Park, Hadlyme, Conn., the Former House of William Gillette, Eminent Actor-Playwright, 1853-1937.* [State Park and Forest Commission, 1956.] [18] p. (Connecticut Vignettes)

A pictorial souvenir booklet.

5079. [Wolff, Julian.] "The Great Profile," *BSJ*, 12, No. 1 (March 1962), 3-4. (The Editor's Gas-Lamp)

"Because he is known to be the image of Sherlock Holmes, to Sherlockians everywhere it is William Gillette who will always be *The* Great Profile." A full-page photograph of the actor appears on page 7.

CARLETON HOBBS

5080. Howlett, Anthony. "Mr. Carleton Hobbs," *SHJ*, 6, No. 4 (Spring 1964), 118-120.

"In all, Carleton Hobbs has been associated with 58 Holmesian radio productions and he has portrayed Sherlock Holmes 54 times over the last eleven years. Every time his portrayal has been impeccable: it is a remarkable achievement."

Actors, Performances, & Recordings

Criticism

EILLE NORWOOD

5081. Morton, Humphrey. "Eille Norwood's Centenary: An Appreciation," *SHJ*, 5, No. 2 (Spring 1961), 59-60.

"Eille Norwood was, indeed, the accepted Sherlock Holmes of the nineteen-twenties, and although both the films and the play were staged in that period—a pity in many ways—it cannot be denied that he made a tremendous impression upon the many thousands who saw him in the part."

BASIL RATHBONE

5082. "Basil Rathbone," *Current Biography: Who's News and Why, 1951*. Edited by Anna Rothe. New York, N.Y.: The H. W. Wilson Co., [1952]. p. 506-508.

5083. "Basil Rathbone, 75, Dies at Home Here," *The New York Times* (July 22, 1967), 1, 25.
————, *CPBook*, 4, No. 14 (Winter 1968), 264-265.

A four-column obituary that includes information on the actor's matchless portrayal of Sherlock Holmes.

5084. Beck, Calvin T. "A Farewell to Basil Rathbone," *Castle of Frankenstein*, 3, No. 4 (1968), 39-41. illus.

5085. [Bergman, Ted.] "Basil Rathbone as Sherlock Holmes: Records and Films," *BSCL*, No. 6 (1968), 3.
Text in Swedish.

5086. Dettman, Bruce. "Basil Rathbone, 1892-1967," *VH*, 2, No. 1 (January 1968), 2-4.

A tribute to "the best Sherlock Holmes of all time."

5087. Goldfield, Barbara. "Basil Rathbone of Baker Street," *BSP*, No. 27 (September 1967), 1-2.

A guest editorial on the late Sherlock Holmes of 135 Central Park West, New York.

5088. Hammond, Thomas. " 'The Adventures of Sherlock Holmes': A Recognition of the Cinematic Holmes," *BSJ*, 17, No. 4 (December 1967), 199-201.
————. ————, *SOS*, 2, No. 2 (December 1967), 7-9.

Primarily a discussion of the second Rathbone-Bruce film, with the following tribute: "It can be said with all honesty that Basil Rathbone *was* Sherlock Holmes. To most of the civilized world he represented a clearer image of the sleuth than did Arthur Wontner, who played Holmes in five English films, or William Gillette in his stage play 'Sherlock Holmes,' or Sir Arthur Conan Doyle, who is said to have played the role his entire life."

5089. Howlett, Anthony. "Mr. Basil Rathbone (1892-1967)," *SHJ*, 8, No. 3 (Winter 1967), 100-101.

A review of the late actor's career as Sherlock Holmes.

5090. Johnson, E. Randolph. "Who Was Basil Rathbone?" *BSJ*, 17, No. 4 (December 1967), 197-198.

"Why he was Sherlock Holmes, of course."

5091. "The Man Who Was Sherlock Holmes," Narrated by Joe Franklin. New York: WOR-TV (Ch. 9), Thursday, September 21, 1967, 10:00-10:30 p.m.

A tribute to Basil Rathbone which featured familiar scenes of Rathbone as Holmes plus scenes from his many other films.

5092. Rathbone, Basil. *In and Out of Character.* Garden City, N.Y.: Doubleday & Co., [1962]. x, 278 p. illus.

Contents: Preface. - 1. War. - 2. The Great Illusion. - 3. Repton School 1906-10. - 4. First Flush of Success. - 5. Ouida. - 6. A Gentleman's Gentleman. - 7. The World Is Not a Stage. - 8. Judas. - 9. Katharine Cornell. - 10. Motion Pictures. - 11. A Home at Last. - 12. The War Years. - 13. "Hi there, Sherlock, how's Dr. Watson?" - 14. The Heiress. - 15. Good-by, My Friend. - 16. J. B. - 17. Last Act, Please. Curtain Going Up. - 18. And So Good Night.

"A fascinating book by one of the best actors of our time, bursting with anecdotes and revealing a private life as attractive, and sometimes as exciting, as the theatrical relationships it describes with such humor and perception." (Vincent Starrett)

Reviews: Chicago Tribune (November 18, 1962) (Vincent Starrett); *Library Journal*, 87 (November 15, 1962), 4181 (G. D. McDonald); *New York Herald Tribune Books* (November 18, 1962), 13 (Judith Crist); *New York Times Book Review* (December 2, 1962), 54 (Lewis Funke).

5093. ————. ["Introduction"], *The Stories of Sherlock Holmes.* Vol. 3. *A Scandal in Bohemia.* Read by Basil Rathbone. New York: Caedmon Records, [1967]. Printed on back of album.
————. ————, [Tr. into Danish by A. D. Henriksen]. *Sherlockiana*, 12, Nr. 3 (1967), 9-10.

". . . those seven years of close association and, I like to think, friendship with Mr. Sherlock Holmes are the most remarkable and gratifying of my career."

5094. Sessa, Jay. "Basil Rathbone," *SOH*, 2, No. 3 (1968), 3.

A brief account of the actor's career and life.

5095. Shipman, David. "Basil Rathbone," *The Great Movie Stars: The Golden Years.* New York: Crown Publishers, Inc., [1970]. p. 454-457. illus.

5096. Warner, Edith. "Cul-de-Sac," *BSJ*, 17, No. 4 (December 1967), 196.

"A. Conan Doyle in Heaven clasped / the new arrival's hand. / Said the former to the latter, / 'Basil Rathbone, you were grand, / depicting Holmes exactly as / I thought my man should be.' "

ARTHUR WONTNER

5097. Helling, Cornelis. "Some Reminiscences of Arthur Wontner," *BSJ*, 11, No. 4 (December 1961), 198.

"The late Arthur Wontner, who was *the* Sherlock Holmes of the Screen, was also one of the most distinguished Honorary Members of the Sherlock Holmes Society of London, and if ever there was a man who deserved this honour it was certainly he."

5098. [Howlett, Anthony D.] "Mr. Arthur Wontner," *SHJ*, 1, No. 2 (September 1952), 13, 12; 5, No. 1 (Winter 1960), 25-26.

A tribute to an honorary member of the Society for his outstanding portrayal of the Master.

B Ballet

5099. *The Great Detective.* London: Sadler's Wells Ballet Theater, January 21-?,1953. 12 performances. British tour, 1953. 11 performances. Queen Elizabeth's coronation, 1953. 5 performances.

Credits: Music, Richard Arnell; Choreography, Margaret Dale; Decor and costumes, Brian Robb; Conductor, John Lanchbery.

Cast: Kenneth Macmillan (The Great Detective), Stanley Holden (His Friend, the Doctor); David Gill, Maurice Metliss, Dudley Davies, Graham McCormack, David Shields, Donald McAlphine (Officers of the Law), Patricia Miller, Margaret Hill, Stella Claire (The Distressed Ladies), Walter Trevor (The Innocent Suspect), Sheilah O'Reilly, Donald Kilgour, Johaar Mosaval, Donald Britton (The Unfortunate Victims), Kenneth Macmillan (The Infamous Professor), Stella Farrance, Joan Blakeney, Madeleine White, Joanne Nisbet, Veronica Vail, Shirley Bishop (His Human Marionettes), David Poole, Donald Britton, Johaar Mosaval, Romayne Austin, Pauline

Scene from the ballet The Great Detective, *1953* (**5099**).

Wadsworth (The Murderous Villains), Stella Farrance, Joan Blakeney, Madeleine White, Joanne Nisbet, Veronica Vail, Shirley Bishop (The Respectable Folk).

Contents: Scene 1. A mistaken arrest and the situation restored. - Scene 2. The Master Criminal spins his evil web. - Scene 3. The Detective's mastery of the art of jujitsu upholds the law, and with the assistance of his disguises, he performs his Dance of Deduction, bringing about the Inevitable Reckoning.

"A Ballet after Sir A. Conan Doyle, introducing typical characters and featuring the struggle for supremacy between the Great Detective and his Arch Enemy, the Infamous Professor."

It is interesting to note that Kenneth Macmillan portrayed both Holmes and Moriarty.

Reviews: BSJ, 4, No. 2 (April 1954), 120-122 (Mrs. Crighton Sellars); *Ballet Annual 1954*, Eighth Issue (London: Adam and Charles Black, 1953), 28 (Arnold L. Haskell); *New York Herald Tribune* (January 22, 1953), 1, 33 (Joseph Newman), and reprinted in *CPBook*, 1, No. 1 (Summer 1964), 15; *New York Herald Tribune* (January 23, 1953), 13, and reprinted in *BSJ*, 3, No. 2 (April 1953), 123; *New York Times Magazine* (February 8, 1953), 44-45; *The Times* (January 22, 1953), 10.

C Films

It has not been possible to determine the exact number of motion pictures about Sherlock Holmes, but over 150 are known. The present list, with credits, casts, reviews, and an occasional summary, is as complete as available resources permit. The films are arranged in approximate chronological order—from 1900 to 1971— and by the names of the actors who portray Holmes and Watson.

A number of films have in their title the name "Sherlock Holmes" or a variation. These, together with some other pseudo-Sherlockian films, usually characterize the detective as a comic figure. Because there is relatively little to connect them with Holmes or with the Canonical tales, or because more complete information is lacking, they are not included in this section. Among these films are: *Miss Sherlock Holmes* (Edison Mfg. Co., 1908); *A Squeedunk Sherlock Holmes* (Edison Mfg. Co., 1909); *El Piccolo Sherlock Holmes* (La Itala Film, 1909); *The Diamond Swindler* (Nordisk Film, 1910)—adapted from the adventures of Harry Taxon; *Arsène Lupin contra Sherlock Holmes* (Berlin: Vitascope GmbH, 1910), with Viggo Larsen and Paul Otto; *Sherlock Holmes contra Professor Moryarty* (Berlin: Vitascope GmbH, 1911), with Viggo

Larsen and Paul Otto; *Sherlock Holmes, Jr.* (Rex Motion Picture Co., 1911), with Helen Anderson; *Sherlock Holmes roulé par Rigadin* (France: 1911); *The Flag of Distress* (Imp Films Co., 1912), with H. S. Mack as Mr. Sherlocko and J. W. Cumpson as Reuben Wilson; *Surelock Jones, Detective* (Thanhouser Co., 1912); *The Robbery at the Railroad Station* (Champion Film Co., 1912)—a short comic film featuring Sherlocko and Watso; *A Midget Sherlock Holmes* (Pathé Frères, 1912); *Baby Sherlock* (Powers, 1912); *Burstup Homes, Detective* (Solax Co., 1913); *Burstup Homes' Murder Case* (Solax Co., 1913); *The Mystery of the Lost Cat* (Solax Co., 1913), featuring Burstup Homes; *The Case of the Missing Girl* (Solax Co., 1913), featuring Burstup Homes; *The Amateur Sleuth* (Gaumont Co., 1913), featuring Herlock Sholmes; *Homlock Shermes* (Crystal Film Co., 1913), with Pearl White; *The Sherlock Holmes Girl* (Thomas A. Edison, 1914), with Bliss Milford; *Sherlock Bonehead* (Kalem Co., 1914), with Marshal Neilan, Ruth Roland, Lloyd Hamilton, and Dick Rosson; *The Amateur Detective* (Thanhouser Film Corp., 1914), with Carey L. Hastings and Ernest C. Ward; *The Champeen Detective* (Superba, 1914), with Charles DeForrest; *Sherlock, the Boob Detective* (Thistle, 1915), with Rena Rogers and Allen Fralick; *A Study in Skarlit* (Comedy Combine-Sunny South, 1915), with Fred Evans as Sherlokz Homz and Will Evans as Professor Moratorium; *A Society Sherlock* (Victor, 1916), with William Garwood and Irma Dawkins; *Sherlock Ambrose* (L-KO, 1918), with Mack Swain; *A Black Sherlock Holmes* (Ebony Film Corp., 1918)—a burlesque on the Sherlock Holmes stories with an all-black cast; *Sherlock Brown* (Metro, 1921)—"a detective yarn not according to Doyle," with Bert Lytell; *Sherlock Jr.* (Metro, 1924), with Buster Keaton; *Sherlock Sleuth* (Pathé Exchange, 1925), with Arthur Stone; *Paramount on Parade* (Paramount, 1930)—a Hollywood frolic containing a satirical sketch on murder mysteries, with Clive Brook as Sherlock Holmes, William Powell as Philo Vance, Warner Oland as Fu Manchu, Eugene Pallette as Sergeant Heath, and Jack Oakie as the victim; *Sherlock's Home* (Vitaphone Corp., 1932); *Leliček ve službách Sherlocka Holmesa* [Lelicek in Sherlock Holmes's Service] (Prague: Elekta, 1932), with Martin Frič as Sherlock Holmes; *The Radio Murder Mystery* (William Rowland-Monte Brice Productions, 1933), with Richard Gordon as Sherlock Holmes; *Crazy House* (Universal Pictures Co., 1943)—an Olsen and Johnson film in which Basil Rathbone and Nigel Bruce appear briefly in the opening scene; *The Big Noise* (20th Century-Fox, 1944)—Laurel and Hardy are shown in deerstalkers and pajamas, with Laurel smoking a calabash pipe; *Arsenio Lupin* (Mexico: Pereda Films, 1945)—includes the final scene from Leblanc's "Herlock Sholmès arrive trop tard" (item 1157); *Abbott*

Bud Abbott and Lou Costello in a 1952 film, "Who Done It? [Universal].

and *Costello Meet the Invisible Man* (Universal-International, 1951)—released in Germany under the title *Auf Sherlock Holmes Spuren* [In the Footsteps of Sherlock Holmes]; *Touha Sherlocka Holmese* [The Longing of Sherlock Holmes] (Prague: Barrandov Studio, 1972), with Radovan Lukavský as Sherlock Holmes and Václav Voska as Dr. Watson.

The Sherlock Holmes Society of London *et al* also have produced several documentary films: *The Sage of Baker Street* (1951); *A Baker Street By-way* (1959); *The World of Sherlock Holmes* (1960); *Return to Hampstead* (1960); *The Life of Sherlock Holmes* (1968); *In the Footsteps of Sherlock Holmes* (1968); *Mr. Sherlock Holmes of London* (1971).

1900

5100. *Sherlock Holmes Baffled.* American Mutoscope and Biograph Co., April 1900, c. February 1903. 1 reel. 18 ft. 16 mm.

"An early trick film, clearly made for viewing on a mutoscope or peepshow machine. Although a tiny, trivial piece, it is historic as being the earliest known use of Sherlock Holmes in moving pictures." (Michael Pointer)

The film was photographed on the roof of the New York studio by Arthur Marvin on April 26, 1900, but was not copyrighted until 1903.

Review: SHJ, 8, No. 4 (Summer 1968), 138, 140 (Michael Pointer).

1905

5101. *Adventures of Sherlock Holmes.* The Vitagraph Co. of America, September 1905. 1 reel.

Alternate title: *Held for a Ransom.*

1908

5102. *Un Rivale di Sherlock Holmes.* Italy: Ambrosio, 1908. 584 ft.

"A pictorial detective story of merit, with many lightning changes of disguise by the detective in his pursuit of the lawbreakers. Exciting scenes and physical encounters are numerous. A sensational subject of superb dramatic effect, without any objectionable features."

Review: Moving Picture World, 2 (May 2, 1908), 401.

5103. *Sherlock Holmes in the Great Murder Mystery.* Crescent Film Mfg. Co., 1908. 1 reel.

A girl is killed by an escaped gorilla, but circumstantial evidence convinces the police that the girl's suitor is responsible for her death. Watson, who has read of the crime, pleads with his old friend and college chum, Sherlock Holmes, to help discover the real culprit which Holmes does and the young man is freed just as he is about to be hanged.

Review: Moving Picture World, 3 (November 28, 1908), 434-435.

345

Actors, Performances, & Recordings

Films

1908-1909 VIGGO LARSEN

5104. *Sherlock Holmes i livsfare.* [Sherlock Holmes in Danger of His Life.] Denmark: Nordisk Film [Great Northern Film Co.] Released November 20, 1908. 348 meters. (Sherlock Holmes I)
Credits: Director and screenplay, Viggo Larsen.
Cast: Viggo Larsen (Sherlock Holmes), Holger-Madsen (Raffles), Aage Brandt, Otto Dethlefsen.
Reviews: Moving Picture World, 3 (December 5, 1908), 450; *New York Dramatic Mirror,* 60 (December 19, 1908), 7.

5105. *Sherlock Holmes II.* Denmark: Nordisk Film, 1908. 210 meters.
Credits: Director and screenplay, Viggo Larsen.
Cast: Viggo Larsen (Sherlock Holmes), Holger-Madsen (Raffles), Poul Gregaard.

5106. *Det hemmelige dokument.* [The Secret Document.] Denmark: Nordisk Film, 1908. 275 meters. (Sherlock Holmes III)
Credits: Director and screenplay, Viggo Larsen.
Cast: Viggo Larsen (Sherlock Holmes), Holger-Madsen, August Blom.

5107. *Sangerindens diamanter.* [The Lady Singer's Diamonds.] Denmark: Nordisk Film. Released January 20, 1909. 180 meters. (Sherlock Holmes IV)
Credits: Director, Viggo Larsen.
Cast: Viggo Larsen (Sherlock Holmes).

5108. *Droske No. 519.* [Cab No. 519.] Denmark: Nordisk Film. Released April 30, 1909. 343 meters. (Sherlock Holmes V)
Credits: Director and screenplay, Viggo Larsen.
Cast: Viggo Larsen (Sherlock Holmes), Elith Pio, August Blom, Gustav Lund.

5109. *Den grå dame.* [The Grey Lady.] Denmark: Nordisk Film. Released August 27, 1909. 307 meters. (Sherlock Holmes VI).
Credits: Director and screenplay, Viggo Larsen.
Cast: Viggo Larsen (Sherlock Holmes), Holger-Madsen, Gustav Lund, Elith Pio.

1910 OTTO LAGONI

5110. *Sherlock Holmes i bondefangerklør.* [Sherlock Holmes in the Claws of Confidence Tricksters.] Denmark: Nordisk Film, 1910. 266 meters.
Cast: Otto Lagoni, Axel Boelsen, Ellen Kornbech.

1911 ALWIN NEUSS

5111. *Millionobligationen.* [The Million Bond.] Denmark: Nordisk Film. Released January 1911. 310 meters.
Cast: Alwin Neuss (Sherlock Holmes), Einar Zangenberg, Mrs. Zangenberg.

1911

5112. *Den forklaedte barnepige.* [The Disguised Nurse.] Denmark: Nordisk Film. Released January 1911. 320 meters.

1911 HOLGER RASMUSSEN

5113. *Medlem af den sorte hånd.* [Member of the Black Hand.] Denmark: Nordisk Film. Released January 1911. 292 meters.
Alternate titles: Den sorte hånd; Mordet i Baker Street [The Murder in Baker Street].
Credits: Director, Holger Rasmussen.
Cast: Holger Rasmussen (Sherlock Holmes), Ingeborg Rasmussen, Erik Crone, Otto Lagoni.

1911

5114. *Hotelmysterierne.* [The Hotel Mysteries.] Denmark: Nordisk Film. Released February 1911. 255 meters. (Sherlock Holmes' sidste bedrift) [Sherlock Holmes's Last Exploit]

1912

5115. *The Hypnotic Detective.* 1912.
Based on Norw but with a detective named Professor Locksley.
Review: Bookman, 36 (October 1912), 120-121.

1911-1913 MACK SENNETT AND FRED MACE

5116. *$500.00 Reward, Their First Kidnapping Case, Trailing the Counterfeiter.* New York: Biograph Co., 1911-1912.
Credits: Director, D. W. Griffith.
Partial cast: Mack Sennett and Fred Mace (Sherlock Holmes).
Three in a series of five slapstick comedies in which both Sennett and Mace impersonate the Master Sleuth.

5117. *At It Again, The Sleuths at the Floral Parade, Their First Execution.* Hollywood: Keystone Studios, November 1912-1913.
Partial cast: Mack Sennett and Fred Mace (Sherlock Holmes).
Three in a new series of eight comedies. The last film (*Their First Execution*) was made without Mace.

5118. *The Tongue Mark.* Majestic Co., 1913.
Partial cast: Fred Mace (Surelock Homes or Sureshock Holmes).

Review of above series: SHJ, 9, No. 4 (Summer 1970), 118 (Michael Pointer).

346

1912 M. TREVILLE

5119. *The Adventures of Sherlock Holmes.* Franco-British Film Co. Released in the U.S. by Universal Features, 1912-1913; in England by Fenning Film Service, 1913.

Cast: M. Treville (Sherlock Holmes), Mr. Moyse (Dr. Watson).

Contents: 1. The Speckled Band. - 2. Silver Blaze. - 3. The Beryl Coronet. - 4. The Musgrave Ritual. - 5. The Reigate Squires. - 6. The Stolen Papers [Nava]. - 7. The Mystery of Boscombe Vale. - 8. The Copper Beeches.

A series of one- and two-reel films with all-English casts except for M. Treville, the French actor who portrayed Sherlock Holmes. The films were produced "with the exclusive permission and under the personal supervision of the author."

Reviews: Moving Picture World (November 23, 1912), 779 (G. F. Blaisdell); (February 8, 1913), 618; (March 1, 1913), 932, 934, (March 8, 1913), 1020.

5120. *Sherlock Holmes Solves "The Sign of the Four."* Thanhouser. Released February 25, 1913.

Partial cast: Harry Benham (Sherlock Holmes).

"This two-reel film gives us a new kind of Sherlock Holmes, a younger and heavier built man than we usually see in the part. But once the story gets into action, with its weird, oriental atmosphere, we forget everything else. The story of the Agra treasure is pictured for us in an intensely fascinating manner. The one-legged man, the East Indian with his blow-pipe, the Sholtos, the Baker Street lodgings, the scenes in India, and the various exciting episodes combine to make this a successful offering. The treasure never comes into the hands of the rightful owner, Mary, as it was cast into the river. A strong production of a famous narrative."

Reviews: Moving Picture World, 15 (February 22, 1913), 822; 15 (March 8, 1913), 998.

1914 ALWIN NEUSS

5121. *Der Hund von Baskervilles.* Germany: Vitaskop GmbH, 1914. Released in the U. S. by Pathe Exchange, March 1915, with title *The Hound of the Baskervilles.* 4 reels. 1,337 meters.

Rated: Jugendverbot (forbidden to children).

Credits: Director, Rudolf Meinert; Screenplay, Richard Oswald; Photography, Karl Freund; Sets, Hermann Warm.

Cast: Alwin Neuss (Sherlock Holmes), Fredrich Kühne, Hanni Weisse, Erwin Fichter, Andreas von Horne.

Review: The Bookman, 39 (August 1914), 602.

1914 JAMES BRAGINGTON

5122. *A Study in Scarlet.* Samuelson Film Mfg. Co. Released December 28, 1914. 6 reels. 5,800 ft. 90 min.

Credits: Producer, George Pearson; Screenplay, Harry Engholm.

Partial cast: James Bragington (Sherlock Holmes), Fred Paul (Jefferson Hope), Agnes Glynne (Lucy Ferrier), Winfred Pearson (Lucy Ferrier as a child), Harry Paulo.

"A drama of revenge and was a detective story only in that Sherlock Holmes was called in towards the end of the film to clear up the mysterious death of two Mormons." (Rachael Low)

Reviews: The Bioscope (1914); *Flashback: The Autobiography of a British Film-maker,* by George Pearson (London: Allen & Unwin Ltd., 1957), 36-38; *Kinematograph Weekly; SHJ,* 7, No. 4 (Spring 1966), 119-123 (Michael Pointer); 8, No. 1 (Winter 1966), 30-31 (Michael Pointer).

1914 FRANCIS FORD AND JACK FRANCIS

5123. *A Study in Scarlet.* Gold Seal-Universal. Released December 29, 1914. 2 reels. 20 min.

Credits: Director, Francis Ford; Scenario, Grace Cunard.

Partial cast: Francis Ford (Sherlock Holmes), Jack Francis (Dr. Watson).

Review: SHJ, 10, No. 1 (Winter 1970), 15 (Michael Pointer).

1916 H. A. SAINTSBURY AND ARTHUR M. CULLIN

5124. *The Valley of Fear.* Samuelson Film Mfg. Co., 1916. 6 reels.

Credits: Director, Alexander Butler: Scenario: Harry Engholm.

Partial Cast: H.A. Saintsbury (Sherlock Holmes), Arthur M. Cullin (Dr. Watson).

1916 WILLIAM GILLETTE AND EDWARD FIELDING

5125. *Sherlock Holmes.* Essanay Film Mfg. Co. Released May 15, 1916. 7 reels.

Credits: Director, Arthur Berthelot; Scenario, H. S. Sheldon.

Cast: William Gillette (Sherlock Holmes), Edward Fielding (Dr. Watson), Marjorie Kay (Alice Faulkner), Ernest Maupain (Prof. Moriarty), Stewart Robbins (Benjamin Forman), Hugh Thompson (Sir Edward Leighton), Ludwig Kreiss (Baron von Stalburg), Mario Majeroni (James Larrabee), William Postance (Sidney Prince), Chester Beery (Craigin), Frank

Actors, Performances, & Recordings

Films

347

348

Hamilton (Tim Leary), Fred Malatesta ("Lightfoot" McTague), Grace Reals (Madge Larrabee), Miss Ball (Therese), Burford Hampden (Billy).

A photoplay, in seven parts, of William Gillette's famous play, with Mr. Gillette, members of his own Company, and several Essanay players in a well-assigned cast.

Reviews: Chicago Tribune (June 19, 1916) (Kitty Kelly); *Detroit Free Press* (August 2, 1916); *Moving Picture World*, 28 (May 27, 1916), 1530-1531 (James S. McQuade); *New York Telegraph* (March 25, 1916) (Gordon Trent).

1921-1923 EILLE NORWOOD AND HUBERT WILLIS

5126. *The Hound of the Baskervilles.* England: Stoll Film Co., 1921. Released in the U.S. by Film Booking Offices of America, September 10, 1922. 5 reels.

Credits: Producer and Director, Maurice Elvey; Screenplay, William J. Elliot.

Cast: Eille Norwood (Sherlock Holmes), Hubert Willis (Dr. Watson), Rex McDougal (Sir Henry Baskerville), Lewis Gilbert (John Stapleton), Frederick Raynham (Osborne), Allen Jeayes (Dr. Mortimer), Betty Campbell.

Review: New York Times (September 11, 1922), 20.

5127. *The Adventures of Sherlock Holmes.* England: Stoll Film Co., 1921. 15 films (2 reels ea.) 35 min. ea.

Credits: Producer and Director, Maurice Elvey; Scenarios, William J. Elliott.

Partial cast: Eille Norwood (Sherlock Holmes), Hubert Willis (Dr. Watson).

Contents: 1. The Dying Detective. - 2. The Devil's Foot. - 3. A Scandal in Bohemia. - 4. The Red-Headed League. - 5. A Case of Identity. - 6. The Man with the Twisted Lip. - 7. The Noble Bachelor. - 8. The Beryl Coronet. - 9. The Yellow Face. - 10. The Resident Patient. - 11. The Tiger of San Pedro [Wist]. - 12. The Priory School. - 13. The Solitary Cyclist. - 14. The Empty House. - 15. The Copper Beeches.

5128. *The Further Adventures of Sherlock Holmes.* England: Stoll Film Co., 1922. 15 films (2 reels ea.) 35 min. ea.

Credits: Producer and Director, George Ridgwell.

Partial cast: Eille Norwood (Sherlock Holmes), Hubert Willis (Dr. Watson).

Contents: 1. The Norwood Builder. - 2. The Boscombe Valley Mystery. - 3. The Musgrave Ritual. - 4. The Reigate Squires. - 5. The Greek Interpreter. - 6. The Naval Treaty. - 7. Black Peter. - 8. Charles Augustus Milverton (with George Foley as Milverton). - 9. The Six Napoleons. - 10. The Abbey Grange. - 11. The Second Stain. - 12. The Red Circle. - 13. The Bruce-Partington Plans. - 14. The Stockbroker's Clerk. - 15. The Engineer's Thumb.

5129. *The Last Adventures of Sherlock Holmes.* England: Stoll Film Co., 1923. 15 films (2 reels ea.)

Credits: Producer and Director, George Ridgwell.

Partial cast: Eille Norwood (Sherlock Holmes), Hubert Willis (Dr. Watson).

Contents: 1. The Speckled Band. - 2. The Blue Carbuncle. - 3. The Three Students. - 4. The Dancing Men. - 5. The Missing Three-Quarter. - 6. The Golden Pince-Nez. - 7. The Last Bow. - 8. The Cardboard Box. - 9. Lady Frances Carfax. - 10. Silver Blaze. - 11. The Gloria Scott. - 12. The Crooked Man. - 13. The Mazarin Stone. - 14. Thor Bridge. - 15. The Final Problem.

1923 EILLE NORWOOD AND ARTHUR CULLIN

5130. *The Sign of Four.* England: Stoll Film Co., 1923. 5 reels.

Credits: Producer, Maurice Elvey.

Partial cast: Eille Norwood (Sherlock Holmes), Arthur Cullin (Dr. Watson), Isobel Elsom (Mary Morstan).

1922 JOHN BARRYMORE AND ROLAND YOUNG

5131. *Sherlock Holmes.* Goldwyn Pictures Corp. Released May 7, 1922. Released in England with title *Moriarty.* 9 reels.

Credits: Producer, F. J. Godsol; Director, Albert Parker; Scenario, Marion Fairfax and Earle Browne; Photography, J. Roy Hunt.

Cast: John Barrymore (Sherlock Holmes), Roland Young (Dr. Watson), Carol Dempster (Alice Faulkner), Hedda Hopper (Madge Larrabee), Peggy Bayfield (Rose Faulkner), Margaret Kemp (Terese), Gustave von Seyffertitz (Professor Moriarty), Anders Randolf (James Larrabee), William H. Powell (Forman Wells), Robert Schable (Alf Bassick), Percy Knight (Sid Jones), Reginald Denny (Prince Alexis), David Torrence (Count Von Stalburg), Robert Fischer (Otto), Lumsden Hare (Dr. Leighton), Louis Wolheim (Craigin), Jerry Devine (Billy), John Willard (Inspector Gregson).

Based on Gillette's stage play, and photographed in England, Switzerland, and the United States.

"Although John Barrymore chose to impersonate the great detective in a farcical manner, he realized the character perfectly. Albert Parker reproduced the thrill of the original stories both in his action and his characterization. The backgrounds, many of which were photographed in England, were exceptionally beautiful." (*Best Moving Pictures*)

Reviews: Best Moving Pictures of 1922-23, Edited by Robert E. Sherwood (Boston: Small, Maynard & Co., 1923), 97; *New York Times* (May 8, 1922), 14; *SHJ*, 10, No. 1 (Winter 1970), 13-14 (Michael Pointer); *Strand Magazine*, 63 (April 1922), 355-360 (Hayden Church).

1929 CARLYLE BLACKWELL AND GEORGES SEROFF

5132. *Der Hund von Baskervilles.* Erda-Film-Produktions-GmbH, 1929.

Credits: Director, Richard Oswald; Screenplay, Herbert Juttke and G. C. Klaren.

Cast: Carlyle Blackwell (Sherlock Holmes), Georges Seroff (Dr. Watson), Alma Taylor (Eliza Barrymore), Fritz Rasp (Jack Stapleton), Betty Bird (Beryl Stapleton), Robert Garrison (Frankland), Alexander Murski, Livio Pavenelli, Valy Arnheim, Carla Bartheel, Jaro Furth.

The last Holmes silent film.

Reviews: Illustrierte Film Kurier; Der Kinematograph; SHJ, 9, No. 4 (Summer 1970), 119-120 (Michael Pointer).

1929 CLIVE BROOK AND H. REEVES-SMITH

5133. *The Return of Sherlock Holmes.* Paramount Famous Players Lasky Corp. Released October 18, 1929. 7,102 ft.

Credits: Director, Basil Dean; Screenplay, Garrett Fort and Basil Dean.

Cast: Clive Brook (Sherlock Holmes), H. Reeves-Smith (Dr. Watson), Harry T. Morey (Professor Moriarty), Donald Crisp (Moran), Betty Lawford, Charles Hay, Phillips Holmes, Hubert Druce, Arthur Mack.

The first Holmes sound film.

Based on "The Dying Detective" and "His Last Bow."

Reviews: New York Times (October 19, 1929), 22 (Mordaunt Hall); *SHJ*, 9, No. 3 (Winter 1969), 88 (Michael Pointer).

1932 CLIVE BROOK AND REGINALD OWEN

5134. *Sherlock Holmes.* Fox Film Corp. Released November 11, 1932. 6,400 ft.

Credits: Director, William K. Howard; Screenplay, Bertram Millhauser; Editor, Margaret Clancy; Camera, George Barnes.

Cast: Clive Brook (Sherlock Holmes), Reginald Owen (Dr. Watson), Miriam Jordan (Alice Faulkner), Ernest Torrence (Professor Moriarty), Howard Leeds (Little Billy), Alan Mowbray (Gore-King), Herbert Mundin (Pub Keeper), Montague Shaw (Judge), Arnold Lucy (Chaplain), Lucien Prival (Hans, the Hun), Roy D'Arcy (Manuel Lopez), Stanley Fields (Tony Ardetti), Edward Dillon (Ardetti's Henchman), Robert Graves, Jr. (Gaston Roux), Brandon Hurst (Secretary to Erskine), Claude King (Sir Albert Hastings).

Reviews: Brooklyn Daily Eagle (November 14, 1932); *New York American* (November 12, 1932) (Regin); *New York Herald* (November 12, 1932) (Lucius Beebe); *New York Times* (November 12, 1932), 20;

Clive Brook and Reginald Owen in Sherlock Holmes (**5134**).

Arthur Wontner and Ian Fleming in The Missing Rembrandt, *1932* (5136).

Picture Show Art Supplement (April 1, 1933), 16; *SHJ*, 9, No. 3 (Winter 1969), 88 (Michael Pointer).

1930-1932 ARTHUR WONTNER AND IAN FLEMING

5135. *The Sleeping Cardinal.* England: Twickenham Film Studios Ltd., 1930. Released in the U.S. by First Division Pictures and the Ameranglo Corp., July 10, 1931, with title *Sherlock Holmes's Fatal Hour.*

Credits: Producer, Julius Hagen; Director, Leslie S. Hiscott; Screenplay, Cyril Twyford; Photography, Sidney Blythe, assisted by William Luff; Art Director, James Carter; Editor, Jack Harris.

Cast: Arthur Wontner (Sherlock Holmes), Ian Fleming (Dr. Watson), Minnie Rayner (Mrs. Hudson), Leslie Perrins (Ronald Adair), Jane Welsh (Kathleen Adair), Norman McKinnell (Colonel Henslowe), William Frazer (Thomas Fisher), Sidney King (Tony Rutherford), Phillip Hewland (Inspector Lestrade), Gordon Begg (Marston), Lewis Goodrich (Colonel Moran), Harry Terry (No. 16), Charles Paton (J. J. Godfrey).

Based on "The Final Problem" and "The Empty House."

Review: New York Times (July 13, 1931), 13 (L. N.)

5136. *The Missing Rembrandt.* England: Twickenham Film Studios Ltd. Released March 21, 1932. Released in the U.S. by First Division Pictures, March 25, 1932. 84 min.

Credits: Producer, Julius Hagen; Director, Leslie S. Hiscott; Photography, Sydney Blythe; Art Director, James Carter; Recording on R.C.A. Photophone, Baynham Honri; Screenplay, Leslie Hiscott and Cyril Twyford; Still photography, Cecil Stanborough.

Cast: Arthur Wontner (Sherlock Holmes), Ian Fleming (Dr. Watson), Francis L. Sullivan (Baron von Guntermann [the name used for Charles Augustus Milverton]), Minnie Rayner (Mrs. Hudson), Dino Galvani (Carlo Ravelli), Miles Mander (Claude Holford), Jane Welsh (Lady Violet Lumsden), Philip Hewland (Inspector Lestrade), Antony Holles (Le Marquis de Chaminade), Herbert Lomas (Manning), Ben Welden (An Agent), Takase (Chang Wu).

Based on "Charles Augustus Milverton."

The story of the film appeared in a booklet published in 1932 by the distributors, P.D.C. Ltd., and has been reprinted in *Charles Augustus Milverton on Stage, Screen and Radio* (London: The Milvertonians of Hampstead, 1960).

Review: New York Times (March 26, 1932), 17 (B. W. N.)

**1932 ARTHUR WONTNER AND
IAN HUNTER**

5137. *The Sign of Four.* England: Associated Radio Pictures, Ltd., 1932. Released in the U.S. by World Wide Pictures, July 22, 1932. 7 reels.
Credits: Producer, Rowland V. Lee; Director, Graham Cutts; Screenplay, W. P. Lipscomb.
Cast: Arthur Wontner (Sherlock Holmes), Ian Hunter (Dr. Watson), Isla Bevan (Mary Morstan), Gilbert Davis (Athelney Jones), Graham Soutten (Jonathan Small), Edgar Norfolk (Captain Morstan), Herbert Lomas (Sholto), Clair Greet (Mrs. Hudson), Miles Malleston (Thaddeus), Roy Emerson (Bailey), Togo (Tonga), Mr. Burnhett (Tattoo Artist), Kynaston Reeves (Bartholomew).
Reviews: New York Sun (August 22, 1932) (M. J.); *New York Times* (August 20, 1932), 7 (A. D. S.).

**1934-1936 ARTHUR WONTNER AND
IAN FLEMING**

5138. *The Triumph of Sherlock Holmes.* England: Real Art Productions Ltd., 1934. Released in the U.S. by Olympia Macri Excelsior Films, May 27, 1935, with title *The Valley of Fear.* 83 min.
Credits: Producer, Julius Hagen; Director, Leslie S. Hiscott; Screenplay, H. Fowler Mear and Cyril Twyford.
Cast: Arthur Wontner (Sherlock Holmes), Ian Fleming (Dr. Watson), Lyn Harding (Professor Moriarty), Leslie Perrins (John Douglas), Jane Carr (Ettie Douglas), Charles Mortimer (Inspector Lestrade), Minnie Rayner (Mrs. Hudson), Michael Shepley (Cecil Barker), Ben Welden (Ted Balding), Roy Emerton (Boss McGinty), Conway Dixon (Ames), Wilfrid Caithness (Colonel Sebastian Moran), Edmund D'Alby (Captain Marvin), Ernest Lynds (Jacob Shafter).
"The film is based on 'The Valley of Fear' and follows the plot of the novel fluently and with considerable ingenuity, except for the now indispensable appearance of Professor Moriarty. Arthur Wontner is the only Sherlock Holmes. His playing throughout is in perfect character and he seems to have walked straight out of the Sidney Paget illustrations which made Sherlock Holmes universally recognisable." (H. D. T.)
Reviews: Another Evening of Sherlock Holmes with the Priory Scholars, [by] Chris Steinbrunner [New York: Privately Produced, January 27, 1967], 1 p.; *Monthly Film Bulletin,* 2, No. 14 (March 1935), 26 (H. D. T.); *New York Herald Tribune* (May 28, 1935) (Marguerite Tazelaar); *New York Times* (May 27, 1935), 20 (F. S. N.); *SOS,* 2,

No. 3 (February 1968), 6-7 (Steve Tomashefsky).

5139. *The Silver Blaze.* England: Twickenham Film Studios Ltd., 1936. Released in the U.S. by Astor, June 10, 1941, with the misleading title *Murder at the Baskervilles.* 6,358 ft. 71 min.
Credits: Producer, Julius Hagen; Director, Thomas Bentley; Screenplay, H. Fowler Mear.
Cast: Arthur Wontner (Sherlock Holmes), Ian Fleming (Dr. Watson), Lyn Harding (Professor Moriarty), John Turnball (Inspector Lestrade), Robert Horton (Colonel Ross), Lawrence Grossmith (Sir Henry Baskerville), Judy Gunn (Diana Baskerville), Arthur Mascre (Jack Trevor), Arthur Goullet (Moran), Martin Walker (Straker), Eve Grey (Mrs. Straker).
Reviews: New York Post (June 11, 1941) (Archer Winsten); *Some Footnotes to a Sherlock Holmes Film Show,* [by] Chris Steinbrunner [New York: The Priory Scholars, May 28, 1965], 2 p.

**1931 RAYMOND MASSEY AND
ATHOLE STEWART**

5140. *The Speckled Band.* British and Dominions Studios, 1931. Released in the U.S. by First Division Pictures and Ameranglo Corp., November 6, 1931. 7 reels.
Credits: Director, Jack Raymond; Screenplay, W. P. Lipscomb; Editor, P. M. Rogers.
Cast: Raymond Massey (Sherlock Holmes), Athole Stewart (Dr. Watson), Lyn Harding (Dr. Rylott), Angela Baddeley (Helen Stonor), Marie Ault (Mrs. Hudson), Nancy Price (Mrs. Staunton).
Review: New York Times (November 7, 1931), 16 (M. H.)

**1932 ROBERT RENDEL AND
FREDERICK LLOYD**

5141. *The Hound of the Baskervilles.* England: Gainsborough Pictures, 1932. Released in the U.S. by First Division Pictures, April 10, 1932. 7 reels. 60 min.
Credits: Director and Scenario, V. Gareth Gundrey; Dialogue, Edgar Wallace.
Cast: Robert Rendel (Sherlock Holmes), Frederick Lloyd (Dr. Watson), Elizabeth Vaughn (Laura Lyons), John Stuart (Sir Henry Baskerville), Reginald Bach (Jack Stapleton), Heather Angel (Beryl Stapleton).
Review: Variety, 106 (April 19, 1932), 15 (Waly).

**1933 REGINALD OWEN AND
WARBURTON GAMBLE**

5142. *A Study in Scarlet.* World-Wide Film,

Athole Stewart as Dr. Watson, Raymond Massey as Sherlock Holmes in The Speckled Band, *1931* **(5140)**.

1933. Released by Fox Film Corp., May 31, 1933. 62 min.

Alternate title: *The Scarlet Ring.*

Credits: Director, Edwin L. Marin; Screenplay, Robert Florey; Continuity and dialog, Reginald Owen.

Cast: Reginald Owen (Sherlock Holmes), Warburton Gamble (Dr. Watson), Allen Dinehart (Thaddeus Merrydew), John Warburton (John Stanford), J. M. Kerrigan (Jabez Wilson), Alan Mowbray (Lestrade), Doris Lloyd (Mrs. Murphy), Billy Bevan (Will Swallow), Leila Bennet (Daffy Dolly), Cecil Reynolds (Baker), Wyndham Standing (Capt. Pyke), Halliwell Hobbs (Malcolm Dearing), Tetsu Komai (Ah Yet), Tempe Piggot (Mrs. Hudson), Anna May Wong (Mrs. Pyke), June Clyde (Eileen Forester).

Reviews: Commonweal, 18 (June 23, 1933), 214; *New York Herald Tribune* (June 1, 1933), 16; *New York Times* (June 1, 1933), 15 (Mordaunt Hall); *New York Times* (June 11, 1933), IX, 3 (Mordaunt Hall); *Newsweek,* 1 (June 10, 1933), 30.

1937 BRUNO GUTTNER AND FRITZ ODEMAR

5143. *Der Hund von Baskervilles.* Ondra-Lamac-Film-GmbH. Released January 12, 1937. Distributed by Bayerische Film GmbH.

Credits: Director, Karl Lamac; Screenplay, Carla von Stackelberg; Photography, Willy Winterstein; Music, Paul Hühn.

Cast: Bruno Güttner (Sherlock Holmes), Fritz Odemar (Dr. Watson), Peter Voss (Lord Henry Baskerville), Friedrich Kayssler (Lord Charles Baskerville), Alice Brandt (Beryl Vendeleure), Fritz Rasp (Barrymore), Lilly Schönborn (Barrymore's Frau), Erich Ponto (Stapleton), Ernst Rotmund (Dr. Mortimer), Gertrud Wolle (Wirtin von Sherlock Holmes), Paul Rehkopf (Sträfling), Hanna Waag (Lady Baskerville), Artur Malkowski (Lord Hugo Baskerville); Klaus Pohl, Ika Thimm, Ernst Schaah, Kurt Lauermann, Horst Birr.

1937 HERMANN SPEELMANS

5144. *Die graue Dame.* [The Grey Lady.] NF.K., Neue Film, KG. Erich Engels. Released February 26, 1937. Distributed by Terra-Filmkunst GmbH.

Credits: Director, Erich Engels; Screenplay, Erich Engels and Hans Heuer; Photography, Edgar Ziesemer; Music, Werner Bochmann.

Cast: Hermann Speelmans (Jimmy Ward), Trude Marlen (Maria Iretzkaja), Elisabeth Wendt (Lola), Edwin Jürgensen (Baranoff), Theo Shall (Harry Morrel) Ernst Karchow (Inspecktor Brown), Werner Finck (John, Diener bei Ward), Werner Scharf (Jack Clark), Hans Halden (James Hewitt), Henry Lorenzen (Archibald Pepperkorn), Reinhold Bernt (Wilson), Eva Tinschmann (Fra Miller), Ursula Herking, Maria Loja, Charles W. Kayser, Paul Schwed.

Based on the play *Die Tat des Unbekannten* (The Deed of the Unknown) by Müller-Puzika.

5145. *Der Mann, der Sherlock Holmes war.*
[The Man Who Was Sherlock Holmes.] Ufa.
Released July 15, 1937. 113 min.

Credits: Producer, Alfred Greven;
Director, Karl Hartl; Screenplay, Robert A.
Stemmle and Karl Hartl; Photography,
Fritz Arno Wagner; Settings, Otto Hunte
and Willy Schüler; Music, Hans Sommer;
Sound, Hermann Fritzsching; Editor,
Gertrud Hinz; Camera, Hans Tost;
Assistant Director, Eduard von Borsody.

Cast: Hans Albers (Sherlock Holmes),
Heinz Rühmann (Dr. Watson), Marieluise
Claudius (Mary Berry), Hansi Knoteck (Jane
Berry), Hilde Weissner (Madame Ganymar),
Siegfried Schürenberg (Monsieur Lapin),
Paul Bildt (Der Mann, der lacht), Franz W.
Schröder-Schrom (Polizei-Direktor), Hans
Junkermann (Exzellenz Vangon), Eduard
von Winterstein (Vorsitzender des Gerichts),
Edwin Jürgensen (Staatsanwalt), Ernst
Legal (Diener Jean), Günther Ballier, Ernst
Behmer, Horst Birr, Gerhard Dammann,
Erich Dunskus, Angelo Ferrari, Lothar
Geist, Aribert Grimmer, Harry Hardt,
Clemens Hasse, Paul Schwed, Willi Schur,
Theo Thony, Ernst Waldow, Erich Walter,
Heinz Wemper, Walter Werner.

"Matinee idol Hans Albers and Heinz
Rühmann play two private detectives
down on their luck who decide to pass
themselves off as Holmes and Watson, and,
in so doing, solve the mystery of a stolen
stamp. Throughout the film the two
principals keep meeting an Englishman who
bursts out laughing at each encounter. In
the denouement he is identified as Conan
Doyle." (Edward Connor) See also item
1256.

Reviews: SHJ, 9, No. 1 (Winter 1968), 35-
36 (Chester R. Collins); *SHJ,* 9, No. 2
(Summer 1969), 67-68 (Michael Pointer);
*Some Incomplete Priory Scholarship on a
Forgotten German Film—"Der Mann, der
Sherlock Holmes war,"* [by] Chris Steinbrunner [New York: The Priory Scholars,
n.d.], [13] p.; *Variety,* 127 (August 18, 1937),
39.

1939-1946 BASIL RATHBONE AND NIGEL BRUCE

5146. *The Hound of the Baskervilles.*
Twentieth Century-Fox Film Corp. Released
March 24, 1939. 7,169 ft. 80 min.

Credits: Producer, Darryl F. Zanuck;
Associate Producer, Gene Markey; Director,
Sidney Lanfield; Screenplay, Ernest Pascal;
Photography, Peverell Marley; Editor,
Robert Simpson; Music Director, Cyril J.
Mockridge.

Cast: Basil Rathbone (Sherlock Holmes),
Nigel Bruce (Dr. Watson), Richard Greene
(Sir Henry Baskerville), Morton Lowry (John

Stapleton), Wendy Barrie (Beryl Stapleton),
Lionel Atwill (Dr. James Mortimer), John
Carradine (Barryman), Barlowe Borland
(Mr. Frankland), Ralph Forbes (Sir Hugo
Baskerville), Mary Gordon (Mrs. Hudson),
Eily Malyon (Mrs. Barryman), Beryl Mercer
(Mrs. Jenifer Mortimer), E. E. Clive (Cabby),
Peter Willes (Roderick), Ivan Simpson
(Shepherd), Ian MacLaren (Sir Charles),
John Burton (Bruce), Dennis Green (Jon),
Evan Thomas (Edwin), Nigel de Brulier
(Convict), Henry Cording.

For the first time in film history the story
is kept correctly in period and follows the
original narrative rather closely. It is often
considered the best Holmes film.

Reviews: Comic Zine, No. 2 (1972), 4-14;
Commonweal, 29 (April 7, 1939), 40;
Hollywood Spectator, 13 (April 1, 1939), 8-
9; *Life,* 6 (April 10, 1939), 50; *Monthly Film
Bulletin,* 6, No. 65 (May 31, 1939), 94 (E. P.);
New Republic, 99 (July 5, 1939), 252 (Otis
Ferguson); *New York Herald Tribune*
(March 25, 1939) (Howard Barnes); *New
York Times* (March 25, 1939), 19 (Frank S.
Nugent); *SHJ,* 4, No. 4 (Spring 1960), 134-
135 (Anthony Howlett); *Spectator,* 163 (July
14, 1939), 52; *Suspense in the Cinema,* by
Gordon Gow (London: A. Zwemmer Ltd.;
New York: A. S. Barnes & Co., 1968), 25-29;
Time, 33 (April 3, 1939), 40; *The Times* (July
10, 1939), 10; *Variety,* 134 (March 29, 1939),
14.

5147. *The Adventures of Sherlock Holmes.*
Twentieth Century-Fox Film Corp. Released
September 1, 1939. 7,349 ft. 81 min.

Credits: Producer, Darryl F. Zanuck;
Associate Producer, Gene Markey; Director,
Alfred Werker; Screenplay, Edwin Blum
and William Drake; Photography, Leon
Shamroy; Editor, Robert Bischoff; Set
decorations, Thomas Little; Music Director,
Cyril J. Mockridge.

Cast: Basil Rathbone (Sherlock Holmes),
Nigel Bruce (Dr. Watson), Ida Lupino (Ann
Brandon), Alan Marshal (Jerold Hunter),
Terry Kilburn (Billy), George Zucco
(Professor Moriarty), Henry Stephenson (Sir
Ronald Ramsgate), E. E. Clive (Inspector
Bristol), Peter Willes (Lloyd Brandon), Mary
Gordon (Mrs. Hudson), George Regas
(Mateo), Mary Forbes (Lady Conynham),
Arthur Hohl (Bassick), May Beatty (Mrs.
Jameson), Holmes Herbert (Justice), Frank
Dawson (Dawes), William Austin (Stranger),
Anthony Kemble Cooper (Tony).

The film is based on Gillette's play, and
relates how Holmes foiled Professor
Moriarty's attempted theft of the Crown
Jewels from the Tower of London. See also
item 6054.

Reviews: Hollywood Spectator, 4 (September 2, 1939), 14 (Bert Harlen); *Monthly
Film Bulletin,* 7, No. 73 (January 31, 1940), 7
(D. E. B.); *New Republic,* 100 (September
20, 1939), 190 (Otis Ferguson); *New York*

Basil Rathbone and Nigel Bruce in one of their celebrated portrayals of Holmes and Watson (**5146-5159**).

Herald Tribune (September 2, 1939); *New York Times* (September 2, 1939), 20 (Frank S. Nugent); *SOS,* 1, No. 6 (August 1967), 2-3 (Bruce Dettman); *SOS,* 2, No. 2 (December 1967), 7-9 (Thomas Hammond); *Spectator,* 164 (March 8, 1940), 328; *Variety,* 135 (September 6, 1939), 14 (Wear).

5148. *Sherlock Holmes and the Voice of Terror.* Universal Pictures. Released September 16, 1942. 7 reels. 65 min.

Credits: Producer, Howard Benedict; Director, John Rawlins; Screenplay, Lynn Riggs and John Bright; Adaptation, Robert D. Andrews; Photography, Woody Bredell; Editor, Russell Schoengarth.

Cast: Basil Rathbone (Sherlock Holmes), Nigel Bruce (Dr. Watson), Evelyn Ankers (Kitty), Thomas Gomez (Meade), Reginald Denny (Sir Evan Barham), Henry Daniell (Anthony Lloyd), Montagu Love (Gen. Jerome Lawford), Olaf Hytten (Fabian Prentiss), Leyland Hodgson (Capt. Roland Shore).

"Summoned by one of Great Britain's administrators, Holmes is asked to aid in putting an end to Nazi saboteurs operating in England as well as uncovering the person or persons behind a series of frightening radio broadcasts in which acts of aggression are foretold by one who identifies himself as 'The Voice of Terror.' " (Ray Cabana, Jr.)

Reviews: BSJ Christmas Annual, No. 1 (1956), 30-31 (Worthen Bradley); *Monthly Film Bulletin,* 10, No. 118 (October 31, 1943), 115 (M. G.); *New York Daily News* (September 19, 1942), 22 (Kate Cameron); *New York Herald Tribune* (September 19,

1942) (Howard Barnes); *New York Post* (September 19, 1942), 10 (Archer Winsten); *New York Times* (September 19, 1942), 9 (Bosley Crowther); *Variety,* 148 (*September 9, 1942*), 14 (*Walt*).

5149. *Sherlock Holmes and the Secret Weapon.* Universal Pictures. Released January 4, 1943. 7 reels. 68 min.

Credits: Associate Producer, Howard Benedict; Director, Roy William Neill; Screenplay, Edward T. Lowe, W. Scott Darling, and Edmund L. Hartmann; Adaptation, W. Scott Darling and Edward T. Lowe; Photography, Les White; Editor, Otto Ludwig; Music, Charles Previn.

Cast: Basil Rathbone (Sherlock Holmes), Nigel Bruce (Dr. Watson), Kaaren Verne (Charlotte Eberti), Lionel Atwill (Professor Moriarty), Dennis Hoey (Inspector Lestrade), Harold DeBecker (Peg Leg), William Post, Jr. (Dr. Franz Tobel), Mary Gordon (Mrs. Hudson), Paul Fix (Mueller), Robert O. Davis (Braun), Holmes Herbert (Sir Reginald), Harry Cording (Brady), Phillip Van Zandt (Kurt).

The "secret weapon" is a new bombsight, whose inventor Holmes tries to protect from the Nazis. See also item 6055.

Reviews: New York Herald Tribune (January 5, 1943) (Joseph Pihodna); *New York Journal-American* (Janary 5, 1943) (G. E. Blackford); *New York Post* (January 5, 1943), 30 (Irene Thirer); *New York Times* (January 5, 1943), 15 (Bosley Crowther); *The Times* (November 23, 1942), 8; *Variety,* 149 (December 30, 1942), 23.

5150. *Sherlock Holmes in Washington.* Universal Pictures. Released March 31, 1943. 7 reels. 6,430 ft. 71 min.

Credits: Producer and Director, Roy William Neill; Associate Producer, Howard Benedict; Screenplay, Bertram Millhauser and Lynn Riggs; Photography, Lester White; Editor, Otto Ludwig.

Cast: Basil Rathbone (Sherlock Holmes), Nigel Bruce (Dr. Watson), Marjorie Lord (Nancy Partridge), George Zucco (Richard Stanley), Thurston Hall (Senator Babcock), Henry Daniell (William Easter), John Archer (Lt. Pete Merriam), Gavin Muir (Bart Lang), Edmund MacDonald (Detective Lt. Grogan), Don Terry (Howe), Bradley Page (Cady), Holmes Herbert (Mr. Ahrens).

The story centers on the microfilm of an important document that has been concealed in a matchbook.

Reviews: Brooklyn Daily Eagle (May 29, 1943); *Monthly Film Bulletin,* 10, No. 109 (January 31, 1943), 6 (E. R.); *New York Post* (May 29, 1943); *Variety,* 150 (March 31, 1943), 8 (Rose).

5151. *Sherlock Holmes Faces Death.* Universal Pictures. Released September 16, 1943. 7 reels. 6,122 ft. 68 min.

Credits: Producer and Director, Roy William Neill; Screenplay, Bertram Millhauser; Photography, Charles Van Enger; Editor, Fred Feitchans; Music Director, H. J. Salter.

Cast: Basil Rathbone (Sherlock Holmes), Nigel Bruce (Dr. Watson), Hillary Brooke (Sally Musgrave), Milburn Stone (Capt. Vickery), Dennis Hoey (Inspector Lestrade), Mary Gordon (Mrs. Hudson), Halliwell Hobbes (Brunton), Frederick Worlock (Geoffrey Musgrave), Gavin Muir (Phillip Musgrave), Arthur Margetson (Dr. Sexton), Olaf Hytten (Capt. MacIntosh), Gerald Hamer (Maj. Langford), Vernon Downing (Lt. Clavering), Minna Phillips (Mrs. Howells).

Based on "The Musgrave Ritual," the plot involves a tower clock that warns of an approaching murder by striking thirteen, a sanitarium with war victims, and a giant chessboard using people as pieces. Holmes finally allows himself to be "murdered" in order to apprehend the villain.

Reviews: New York Daily News (October 8, 1943) (Wanda Hale); *New York Herald Tribune* (October 8, 1943) (Otis L. Guernsey, Jr.); *New York Journal-American* (October 8, 1943); *New York Post* (October 8, 1943) (Irene Thirer); *New York Times* (October 8, 1943), 15 (T. S.); *New York World-Telegram* (October 8, 1943) (Alton Cook); *Variety,* 151 (September 8, 1943), 16 (Kahn).

5152. *Sherlock Holmes and the Spider Woman.* Universal Pictures. Released January 13, 1944. 7 reels. 63 mins.

Credits: Producer and Director, Roy William Neill; Assistant Director, Melville Shyer; Screenplay, Bertram Millhauser; Photography, Charles Van Enger; Editor, James Gibbon.

Cast: Basil Rathbone (Sherlock Holmes), Nigel Bruce (Dr. Watson), Dennis Hoey (Inspector Lestrade), Mary Gordon (Mrs. Hudson), Gale Sondergaard (Adrea Spedding), Arthur Hohl (Adam Gilflower), Alex Craig (Radlik), Vernon Downing (Norman Locke), Teddy Infuhr (Larry).

Holmes attempts to solve what the newspapers call "Pajama Suicides"; and in the guise of an Indian Hindu, eventually learns that the "suicides" are being perpetrated by large spiders whose bite causes madness and a painful agony inducing the victims to suicide.

Reviews: New York Herald Tribune (January 15, 1944) (Howard Barnes); *New York Times* (January 15, 1944), 11 (Bosley Crowther); *Variety,* 153 (January 12, 1944), 24 (Sten).

5153. *The Scarlet Claw.* Universal Pictures. Released May 19, 1944. 74 min.

Credits: Producer and Director, Roy William Neill; Story, Paul Gangelin and Brenda Weisberg; Screenplay, Edmund L. Hartmann; Photography, George Robinson; Editor, Paul Landres; Music Director, Paul Sawtell.

Cast: Basil Rathbone (Sherlock Holmes), Nigel Bruce (Dr. Watson), Kay Harding (Marie Journet), Arthur Hohl (Emile Journet), Gerald Hamer (Potts, Tanner, Ramson), Paul Cavanagh (Lord Penrose), Gertrude Astor (Lady Penrose), Miles Mander (Judge Brisson), David Clyde (Sergeant Thompson), Ian Wolfe (Drake), Victoria Horne (Nora).

"Against the hostilities of a people steeped in beliefs of the supernatural, and with a corpse for their client, Holmes and Watson strive to get at the truth of the monster of the marshes who attacks not only people, but sheep as well. The killer successfully adopts several disguises, and is seen to eerie effect in phosphorescent clothing at night on the moors." (Ray Cabana, Jr.)

Reviews: New York Herald Tribune (May 20, 1944) (Howard Barnes); *New York Times* (May 20, 1944), 12 (Bosley Crowther); *Variety,* 154 (May 24, 1944), 10.

5154. *The Pearl of Death.* Universal Pictures. Released August 25, 1944. 7 reels. 69 min.

Credits: Producer and Director, Roy William Neill; Screenplay, Bertram Millhauser; Photography, Virgil Miller; Editor, Ray Snyder; Music Director, Paul Sawtell.

Cast: Basil Rathbone (Sherlock Holmes), Nigel Bruce (Dr. Watson), Evelyn Ankers (Naomi Drake), Dennis Hoey (Inspector Lestrade), Miles Mander (Giles Conover), Ian Wolfe (Amos Hodder), Charles Francis

(Digby), Holmes Herbert (James Goodram), Mary Gordon (Mrs. Hudson), Rondo Hatton (The Creeper), Richard Nugent (Bates).

"The 'Pearl of Death' refers to the fabulous Borgia pearl which is stolen aboard a ship by Naomi Drake and later placed in one of six wet-plaster busts of Napoleon. The busts are sold to various Londoners who start turning up with their backs broken, as well as their Napoleonic busts." (Ray Cabana, Jr.)

Reviews: New York Herald Tribune (August 26, 1944) (Bert McCord); *New York Times* (August 26, 1944), 15 (P. P. K); *Variety,* 155 (August 30, 1944), 10 (Walt).

5155. *The House of Fear.* Universal Pictures. Released March 16, 1945. 8 reels. 6,241 ft. 69 min.

Credits: Producer and Director, Roy William Neill; Screenplay, Roy Chanslor; Photography, Virgil Miller; Editor, Ray Snyder; Music Director, Don E. George.

Cast: Basil Rathbone (Sherlock Holmes), Nigel Bruce (Dr. Watson), Aubrey Mather (Bruce Alastair), Gavin Muir (Chalmers), Dennis Hoey (Inspector Lestrade), Paul Cavanagh (Simon Merrivale), Holmes Herbert (Alan Cosgrave), Dick Alexander (Ralph King), Cyril Delevanti (Stanley Raeburn), Wilson Benge (Guy Davies), Harry Cording (John Simpson), David Clyde (Alex MacGregor), Florette Hillier (Alison MacGregor), Sally Shepherd (Mrs. Monteith).

"The majority of the action takes place within a dreary Scottish mansion where a unique club of group-insured men known as 'The Good Comrades' resides. One after another the residents of the house disappear as, one after another, decapitated bodies appear. . . . With the disappearance of some pipe tobacco, it is actually Dr. Watson who first discovers the incredible answer to this novel old-house thriller, resulting in *his* disappearance." (Ray Cabana, Jr.)

Reviews: Monthly Film Bulletin, 12, No. 138 (June 30, 1945), 73 (K. F. B.); *New York Herald Tribune* (March 17, 1945) (Otis L. Guernsey, Jr.); *New York Times* (March 17, 1945), 17 (Bosley Crowther); *Variety,* 158 (March 21, 1945), 10 (Sten).

5156. *The Woman in Green.* Universal Pictures. Released June 15, 1945. 7 reels. 6,094 ft. 68 min.

Credits: Producer and Director, Roy William Neill; Screenplay, Bertram Millhauser; Photography, Virgil Miller; Editor, Edward Curtis; Music Director, Mark Levant.

Cast: Basil Rathbone (Sherlock Holmes), Nigel Bruce (Dr. Watson), Hillary Brooke (Lydia Marlowe), Paul Cavanagh (Sir George Fenwick), Henry Daniell (Professor Moriarty), Eve Amber (Maude), Sally Shepherd (Crandon), Tom Bryson (Williams), Matthew Boulton (Inspector Gregson), Mary Gordon (Mrs. Hudson).

London is shocked by a series of ghastly murders, all the victims being young women whose right thumbs have been hacked off. Holmes and Moriarty come to a standoff in the final scenes, when, for a moment, it appears that the Professor may emerge victorious.

Reviews: Monthly Film Bulletin, 12, No. 140 (August 31, 1945), 100 (G. M. D.); *New York Herald Tribune* (June 16, 1945) (Otis L. Guernsey, Jr.); *New York Times* (June 16, 1945), 10 (T. M. P.); *Variety,* 159 (June 20, 1945), 11 (Sten).

5157. *Pursuit to Algiers.* Universal Pictures. Released October 26, 1945. 7 reels. 5,870 ft. 65 min.

Credits: Producer and Director, Roy William Neill; Executive Producer, Howard Benedict; Screenplay, Leonard Lee; Photography, Paul Ivano; Editor, Saul A. Goodkind; Music, Edgar Fairchild; Dialog Director, Raymond Kessler; Assistant Director, Steward Webb.

Cast: Basil Rathbone (Sherlock Holmes), Nigel Bruce (Dr. Watson), Marjorie Riordan (Sheila), John Abbott (Jodri), Martin Kosleck (Mirko), Gerald Hamer (Kingston), Leslie Vincent (Nikolas), Rex Evans (Gregor), Wee Willie Davis (Gubec), Morton Lowry (Sanford), Frederic Worlock (Prime Minister), Tom Dillon (Restaurant Proprietor), Sven Hugo Borg (Johanssen), Wilson Benge (Clergyman), Rosalind Ivan.

Holmes and Watson consent to help protect the heir of Rovenia after the King of that nation is assassinated. Most of the action occurs aboard an ocean liner where Mirko and his henchmen make several attempts on the young man's life.

Reviews: Monthly Film Bulletin, 13, No. 145 (January 31, 1946), 5 (V. M. C. D.); *New York Herald Tribune* (October 27, 1945) (Otis L. Guernsey, Jr.); *New York Times* (October 27, 1945), 12 (Bosley Crowther); *Variety,* 160 (October 31, 1945), 17.

5158. *Terror by Night.* Universal Pictures. Released February 4, 1946. 6 reels. 5,379 ft. 60 min.

Credits: Producer and Director, Roy William Neill; Executive Producer, Howard Benedict; Screenplay, Frank Gruber; Photography, Maury Gertsman; Editor, Saul A. Goodkind; Music Director, Mark Levant.

Cast: Basil Rathbone (Sherlock Holmes), Nigel Bruce (Dr. Watson), Alan Mowbray (Maj. Duncan-Bleek and Col. Sebastian Moran), Renée Godfrey (Vivian Veddar), Dennis Hoey (Inspector Lestrade), Billy Bevan (Train Attendant), Halliwell Hobbes (Train Attendant), Geoffrey Steele (Ronald Carstairs), Boyd Davis (Police Inspector McDonald), Skelton Knaggs (Sands), Mary

Forbes (Lady Margaret), Frederic Worlock (Professor Kilbane), Leyland Hodgson (Conductor), Janet Murdock (Mrs. Shallcross).

A tightly-knit plot involving the apparent theft of a rare diamond ("The Star of Rhodesia") and the mysterious murder of the son of its owner. Except for the opening sequences, the action takes place entirely on a train speeding through the darkness from London to Edinburgh. Holmes, Watson, and Lestrade are all passengers on the train. Ray Cabana, Jr.)

Reviews: Monthly Film Bulletin, 13, No. 149 (May 31, 1946), 67 (G. M. D.); *New York Herald Tribune* (February 9, 1946) (Otis L. Guernsey, Jr.); *New York Times* (February 9, 1946), 9 (Bosley Crowther); *Variety,* 161 (January 30, 1946), 12 (Brog).

5159. *Dressed to Kill.* Universal Pictures. Released May 20, 1946. Released in England with title *Sherlock Holmes and the Secret Code.* 8 reels. 6,477 ft. 72 min.

Credits: Producer and Director, Roy William Neill; Executive Producer, Howard Benedict; Screenplay, Leonard Lee; Adaptation, Frank Gruber; Photography, Maury Gertsman; Editor, Saul A. Goodkind; Music Director, Milton Rosen.

Cast: Basil Rathbone (Sherlock Holmes), Nigel Bruce (Dr. Watson), Patricia Morison (Hilda Courtney), Edmond Breon (Gilbert Emery), Frederic Worlock (Col. Cavanaugh), Harry Cording (Hamid), Mary Gordon (Mrs. Hudson), Carl Harbord (Inspector Hopkins), Patricia Cameron (Evelyn Clifford), Tom P. Dillon (Detective Thompson), Topsy Glyn (Kilgour Child).

The object of Holmes's quest is a set of stolen engraving plates from the Bank of England. Their hiding place is contained in a cipher located in three identical music boxes made at Dartmoor Prison and auctioned in London. Holmes is captured by the thieves and left in a vacant garage, hanging from a beam, his hands bound, while a poisonous gas fills the room. He emerges triumphant for his (Rathbone's) last bow on the screen.

Reviews: Monthly Film Bulletin, 13, No. 151 (July 31, 1946), 99 (G. M. D.); *New York Herald Tribune* (May 25, 1946) (Joe Pihodna); *New York Times* (May 25, 1946), 12 (J. R. L.); *Variety,* 162 (May 22, 1946), 10 (Borg).

Note: The twelve Rathbone-Bruce films released by Universal Pictures can be rented for $50 each from United Films, 1425 South Main, Tulsa, Okla. 74119.

1951 JOHN LONGDEN AND CAMPBELL SINGER

5160. *The Man with the Twisted Lip.* England: Dryer-Weenolsen Production, 1951. 3 reels. 3,214 ft. 35 min.

Alternate title: *The Man Who Disappeared.*

Credits: Producer, Rudolph Cartier; Director, Richard M. Grey.

Cast: John Longden (Sherlock Holmes), Campbell Singer (Dr. Watson), Hector Ross (Neville St. Clair), Ninka Dolega (Mrs. St. Clair), Beryl Baxter (Doreen), Walter Gotell (Luzatto).

"A Sherlock Holmes story in which the detective investigates the disappearance of a missing husband who is traced to an opium-den in Wapping, where the proprietor denies knowledge of him. Holmes finds him upstairs in a pool of blood, is attacked and fights his way out. After various enquiries he solves the mystery." (*Monthly Film Bulletin*)

Review: Monthly Film Bulletin, 18, No. 207 (April 1951), 251.

1959 PETER CUSHING AND ANDRE MORELL

5161. *The Hound of the Baskervilles.* England: Hammer Film Productions Ltd., 1959. Released in the U. S. by United Artists. 7,772 ft. 87 min. color.

Credits: Producer, Anthony Hinds; Director, Terence Fisher; Screenplay, Peter Bryan; Director of photography, Jack Asher; Art Director, Bernard Robinson; Music, James Bernard; Supervising Editor, James Needs; Executive Producer, Michael Carreras; Associate Producer, Anthony Nelson Keyes.

Cast: Peter Cushing (Sherlock Holmes), André Morell (Dr. Watson), Christopher Lee

Peter Cushing in The Hound of the Baskervilles, *1959* (**5161**).

(Sir Henry Baskerville), Ewen Solon (Stapleton), Marla Landi (Cecile Stapleton), Francis De Wolff (Dr. Mortimer), David Oxley (Sir Hugo Baskerville), Miles Malleson (Bishop Frankland), John Le Mesurier (Barrymore), Helen Goss (Mrs. Barrymore), Judi Moyens (Servant Girl), Sam Kydd (Perkins), Michael Mulcaster (Selden), Dave Birks (Servant), Michael Hawkins (Lord Caphill), Ian Hewitson (Lord Kingsblood), Elizabeth Dott (Mrs. Kingsblood).

Reviews: Films and Filming, 5 (May 1959), 22 (Derek Conrad); *Library Journal,* 84 (June 15, 1959), 2054 (Earle F. Walbridge); *Monthly Film Bulletin,* 26, No. 304 (April 1959), 46; *New York Herald Tribune* (July 4, 1959) (Paul V. Beckley), and reprinted in *Filmfacts,* 2 (July 29, 1959), 147; *New York Times* (July 4, 1959), 9 (Bosley Crowther), and reprinted in *Filmfacts,* 2 (July 29, 1959), 147-148; *Newsweek,* 53 (June 8, 1959), 107; *Senior Scholastic,* 74 (May 15, 1959), 47; *SHJ,* 4, No. 1 (Winter 1958), 16-17 (Anthony Howlett), and tr. into Danish by A. D. Henriksen in *Sherlockiana,* 4, Nr. 4 (1959), 17; *SHJ,* 4, No. 4 (Spring 1960), 134-135 (Anthony Howlett); *The Times* (March 30, 1959), 9; *Variety,* 214 (April 1, 1959), 6, and reprinted in *Filmfacts,* 2 (July 29, 1959), 148.

1962 CHRISTOPHER LEE AND THORLEY WALTERS

5162. *Sherlock Holmes und das Halsband des Todes.* Berlin: Constantin Film Verleih, 1962. 7,710 ft. 86 min. German dialogue; English subtitles.

Re-released in February 1968 in an English-dubbed version with title *Sherlock Holmes and the Deadly Necklace.*

Credits: Producer, Artur Brauner; Assistant Director, Frank Winterstein; Director, Terence Fisher; Screenplay, Curt M. Siodmak; Photography, Richard Angst; Art Director, Paul Markwitz; Editor, Ira Oberberg; Costumes, Vera Mügge; Music, Martin Slavin; Sound, Gerhard Müller.

Cast: Christopher Lee (Sherlock Holmes), Thorley Walters (Dr. Watson), Senta Berger (Ellen Blackburn), Hans Söhnker (Professor Moriarty), Hans Nielsen (Inspektor Cooper), Ivan Desny (Paul King), Leon Askin (Chauffeur Charles), Wolfgang Lukschy (Peter Blackburn), Edith Schultze-Westrum (Mrs. Hudson), Bernard Lajarrige (French Polizeiinspektor), Linda Sini (Leichtes Mädchen), Bruno W. Pantel (Williams, Auktionator), Heinrich Gies (Amerikaner), Roland Armontel (Doktor), Max Strassberg (Johnny), Danielle Argence (Bibliothekarin), Corrado Anicelli (Samuels), Franco Giacobini (Jenkins), Waldemar Frahm (Butler), Renate Hütter (Kellnerin), Kurt Hain (Postbeamter), Pierre Gualdi (Wirt).

Holmes and Watson fight for possession of an Egyptian necklace stolen from a Pharaoh's tomb.

Reviews: Monthly Film Bulletin, 35, No. 410 (March 1968), 44; *Some Priory Scholarship on "Sherlock Holmes and the Necklace of Death,"* [[by] Chris Steinbrunner [New York: The Priory Scholars, n.d.], [10] p.; *VH,* 2, No. 3 (September 1968), 7.

1965 JOHN NEVILLE AND DONALD HOUSTON

5163. *A Study in Terror.* England: Compton-Tekli Film Productions Ltd. and Sir Nigel Films Ltd. Released November 9, 1965. Released in the U.S. by Columbia Pictures, April 1966. 8,550 ft. 95 min. color.

Credits: Executive Producer, Herman Cohen; Producer, Henry E. Lester; Director, James Hill; Story and Screenplay, Donald and Derek Ford; Music, John Scott; Director of Photography, Desmond Dickinson; Costumes, Motley; Assistant Director, Barry Langley.

Cast: John Neville (Sherlock Holmes), Donald Houston (Dr. Watson), Robert Morley (Mycroft Holmes), Frank Finlay (Inspector Lestrade), Barbara Leake (Mrs. Hudson), Anthony Quayle (Dr. Murray), John Fraser (Lord Edward Carfax), Barry Jones (Duke of Shires), Cecil Parker (Prime Minister), Dudley Foster (Home Secretary), Barbara Windsor (Annie Chapman), Adrienne Corri (Angela Osborne), Judi Dench (Sally), Kay Walsh (Cathy Eddowes), Edina Ronay (Mary Kelly), Terry Downes (Chunky), Peter Carsten (Max Steiner), Charles Regnier (Joseph Beck), John Cairney (Michael Osborne), Christiane Maybach (Polly Nichols), Avis Bunnage (Landlady), Patrick Newell (P. C. Benson), Liz Stride (Norma Foster), Georgia Brown (Singer).

"Sherlock Holmes has come to the screen in the likes of Basil Rathbone, among others, as has the blood-curdling Jack the Ripper in such frightening items as *The Lodger* and *Hangover Square.* But the twain had never met in the movies until *A Study in Terror.* Sir Arthur Conan Doyle never thought of such a meeting, but the supersleuth and the superkiller are well met now because a sense of humor and an unvarnished, old-fashioned melodrama raise the film several cuts above the normal chiller dreamed up these days. John Neville, Donald Houston, John Fraser, Anthony Quayle, Robert Morley and a covey of comely and brutish denizens of Whitechapel maintain the formal attitudes and authentic Victorian melodramatic flavor that is fictional but fascinating to watch. . . . The entire cast play their roles well enough to make wholesale slaughter a pleasant diversion." (A. J. Weiler) See also items 5881 and 6065.

Donald Houston and John Neville as Watson and Holmes in A
Study in Terror, *1965* **(5163)**.

Reviews: Commonweal, 84 (April 29, 1966), 179, and reprinted in *CPBook,* 3, No. 9 (Summer 1966), 173; *Dagens Nyheter* [Stockholm] (March 13, 1966) (Barbro Hähnel); *DCC,* 2, No. 5 (July 1966), 4; *Films in Review,* 17 (August-September 1966), 453; *Minneapolis Star* (December 8, 1966) (Don Morrison), and reprinted in *CPBook,* 3, No. 10 (Fall 1966), 186; *Minneapolis Tribune* (December 11, 1966) (Ben Kern), and reprinted in *CPBook,* 3, No. 10 (Fall 1966), 186; *Monthly Film Bulletin,* 32, No. 383 (December 1965), 186; *New York Daily News* (November 3, 1966) (K. Carroll); *New York Post* (November 3, 1966) (Archer Winsten); *New York Times* (November 3, 1966), 45 (A. H. Weiler), and reprinted in *Filmfacts,* 9 (January 1, 1967), 315; *New York World Journal Tribune* (November 3, 1966) (William Peper), and reprinted in *Filmfacts,* 9 (January 1, 1967), 315; *Playboy,* 13 (June 1966), 36; *SHJ,* 7, No. 3 (Winter 1965), 88-89 (Anthony Howlett);

Sherlockiana, 12, Nr. 1-2 (1967), 4; *SIS,* 1, No. 3 (1966), 24-26 (Bruce Dettman), and reprinted in *SOS,* 2, No. 2 (December 1967), 3-4; *Svenska Dagbladet* [Stockholm] (March 13, 1966) (Willmar Andersson); *Time,* 88 (November 25, 1966), 125, and reprinted in *CPBook,* 3, No. 10 (Fall 1966), 192, and in *CPBook,* 3, No. 11 (Winter 1967), 210, and in *Filmfacts,* 9 (January 1, 1967), 314-315; *The Times* (November 4, 1965), 17; *Variety,* 241 (November 24, 1965), 6 (Rich.), and reprinted in *Filmfacts,* 9 (January 1, 1967), 315.

1970 ROBERT STEPHENS AND COLIN BLAKELY

5164. *The Private Life of Sherlock Holmes.* England: Mirisch Films. Released by United Artists, October 28, 1970. 11,268 ft. 125 min. color.

World premiere: Stockholm: Riviera, October 28. First showing in the United

Actors, Performances, & Recordings

Films

States: New York: Radio City Music Hall, October 29.

Credits: Producer and Director, Billy Wilder; Associate Producer, I. A. L. Diamond; Screenplay, Billy Wilder and I. A. L. Diamond; Mirisch Production Supervisor, Larry De Waay; Lighting Cameraman, Chris Challis; Camera Operator, Freddy Cooper; Focus Puller, John Palmer; Production Manager, Eric Rattray; Location Manager, Ivo Nightingale: 1st Assistant Director, Tom Pevsner; Production Designer, Alex Trauner; Art Director, Tony Inglis; Assistant Art Director, Frank Willson; Costume Designer, Julie Harris; Wardrobe Mistress, Dorothy Edwards; Wardrobe Master, Johnny Hilling; Chief Make Up, Ernie Gasser; Make Up, Geoff Rodway; Chief Hairdresser, Biddy Chrystal; Hairdresser, Stella Rivers; Editor, Ernie Walter; 1st Assistant Editor, Margaret Miller; Dubbing Editor, Roy Baker; Continuity, Elaine Schreyeck; Production Secretary, Jean Hall; Sound Mixer, Dudley Messenger and J. W. N. Daniel; Boom Operator, J. W. N. Daniel and Charles Mcfadden; Sound Camera, Laurie Read; Set Dresser, Terry Parr; Casting Director, Robert Lennard and Lesley Pettitt; Stillsman, Bob Penn.

Cast: Robert Stephens (Sherlock Holmes), Colin Blakely (Dr. Watson), Irene Handl (Mrs. Hudson), Christopher Lee (Mycroft Holmes), Genevieve Page (Gabrielle Valladon), Clive Revill (Rogozhin), Tamara Toumanova (Petrova), George Benson (Inspector Lestrade), David Kossoff (Mr. Plimsoll), Noel Johnson (Captain of the Boat), Catherine Lacey (Old Lady), Mollie Maureen (Queen Victoria), Peter Madden (Von Tirpitz), Jenny Hanley (Prostitute), Jonathan Cecil (Honeymoon Groom), Nicole Shelby (Honeymoon Bride), Robert Cawdron (Hotel Manager), John Williams (Havelock-Smith), Michael Elwyn (Cassidy), Michael Balfour (Cabby), Frank Thornton (Porter), James Copeland (Guide), Alex McCrindle (Baggageman), Kenneth Benda (Minister), Graham Armitage (Wiggins), Stanley Holloway (1st Gravedigger), Eric Francis (2nd Gravedigger), John Garrie (1st Carter), Godfrey James (2nd Carter), Paul Tann (Chinese Corpse), Ina De La Haye (Petrova's Maid), Dennis Chinnery (1st Mate), Kynaston Reeves (Old Man), Anne Blake (Madame), Marilyn Head (1st Girl), Anna Matisse (2nd Girl), Wendy Lingham (3rd Girl), Penny Brahms (4th Girl), Sheena Hunter (5th Girl), Ismet Hassan, Charle Young Atom, Teddy Kiss Atom, Willie Shearer (Submarine Crew), Daphne Riggs (Lady in Waiting), John Gatrell (Equerry), Martin Carroll (1st Scientist), John Scott (2nd Scientist), Philip Anthony (Lt. Commander), Phillip Ross (McKellar), Annette Kerr (Secretary), Tina and Judy Spooner (Twins).

Based on four unpublished adventures of Holmes and Watson, and filmed over a six-month schedule at Pinewood Studios, London, with locations at Inverness, Scotland; Oxford, and London. See also items 4917, 4918, and 5918.

Reviews: The Advocate [Los Angeles], 4 (December 9-22, 1970), 20-21 (James Moriarty [Tim Kelly]); *Aftonbladet* [Stockholm] (November 3, 1970) (Jurgen Schildt); *Armchair Detective,* 4, (April 1971), 178 (J. Randolph Cox); *BSJ,* 21, No. 2 (June 1971), 75-76 (Roy Pickard); *Billy Wilder's The Private Life of Sherlock Holmes: Final Production Notes* (Iver Heath, Buckinghamshire: Pinewood Studios, 1970), 25 p.; *The Bright Side of Billy Wilder, Primarily,* by Tom Wood (Garden City, N. Y.: Doubleday & Co., 1970), 231-234; *Cashiers du cinéma,* No. 228 (March-April 1971), 62-63 (Pascal Kane); *Chicago Tribune Magazine* (August 22, 1971) (Vincent Starrett); *Cinema,* 6 (Spring 1971), 49-50 (R. M.); *Dagens Nyheter* [Stockholm] (October 30, 1970), 20 (Hanserik Hjertén); *DCC,* 7, No. 2 (January 1971), 3-8 (R. W. Hahn, John Nieminski, Vincent Starrett, Gene Leeb, Herb Tinning, Dave Levinson, Phil Liput); *Expressen* [Stockholm] (September 11, 1969) (Ted Bergman); (January 14, 1970); (February 8, 1970) (Lottie Molund); (October 31, 1970) (Lasse Bergström); *Films and Filming,* 17 (January 1971), 34-35; *Firemans Fund* (1970), and reprinted in *DCC,* 7, No. 1 (November 1970), 5; *HO,* 1, No. 7 (September 1971), 6 (Philip A. Shreffler); *London Daily Express* (July 1, 1969) (Peter Grosvenor); *Los Angeles Herald-Examiner* (July 15, 1969), C5; (July 27, 1969), E3 (James Bacon); *New York Daily News* (October 30, 1970), 64 (Kathleen Carroll); *New York Morning Telegraph* (October 30, 1970), 3 (Joe Rosen); *New York Post* (October 30, 1970), 40 (Frances Herridge); *New York Times* (October 30, 1970), 26 (Vincent Canby), and reprinted in *DCC,* 7, No. 1 (November 1970), 3-4; *New Yorker,* 46 (November 14, 1970), 168; *Newark Evening News* (October 30, 1970), 54 (Joseph Gale); *Newsweek,* 86 (November 2, 1970), 108 (Alex Keneas); *No,* No. 7 (February 1971) (Dean Dickensheet), and reprinted in *SHsf Fanthology,* No. 2 (September 1971), 19-21; *Parade* (May 10, 1970), and reprinted in *DCC,* 6, No. 4 (June 1970), 6; *Paris Match* (January 2, 1971), 58 (Alexandre Astruc); *Saturday Review,* 53 (December 5, 1970), 44 (Arthur Knight); *Screen World,* 22 (1971), 184-185; *SHJ,* 9, No. 2 (Summer 1969), 66 (Anthony Howlett); 10, No. 1 (Winter 1070), 29-30 (Anthony Howlett); *Sherlockiana,* 15, Nr. 3-4 (1970), 10; 16, Nr. 1 (1971), 3 (A. D. Henriksen); *Sight and Sound,* 39 (Winter 1969-1970), 26-27 (John Gillett); 40 (Winter 1970-1971), 47-48 (Peter Ohlin); *Svenska Dagbladet* [Stockholm] (October 30, 1970),

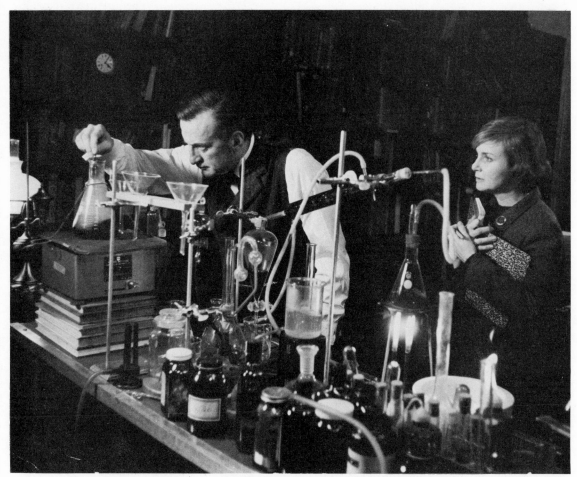

*George C. Scott and Joanne Woodward play Sherlock Holmes and
Dr. [Mildred] Watson in the 1971 film,* They Might Be Giants
(**5165**).

11 (Gunnar Unger); *Time,* 96 (November 9,
1970), 79 (Stefan Kanfer), and reprinted in
DCC, 7, No. 1 (November 1970), 5; *The
Times* (December 4, 1970), 10 (John Russell
Taylor); *Variety,* 260 (October 28, 1970), 17
(Gene); *Vecko-Journalen* [Stockholm]
(August 7, 1969) (Stig Ahlgren); (December
2, 1970) (Marianne Zetterström); *VH,* 3, No.
3 (September 1969), 8-9 (Bruce Dettman); 5,
No. 1 (January 1971), 6; 5, No. 2 (April
1971), 5-6 (Richard Combs and Arlene
Kramborg); *Women's Wear Daily* (October
30, 1970), 12 (Gail Rock).

1971 GEORGE C. SCOTT AND
JOANNE WOODWARD

5165. *They Might Be Giants.* Universal / Newman-Foreman Pictures. Released
March 9, 1971. 88 min. (originally 91 min.)
color.

Credits: Producer, John Foreman;
Director, Anthony Harvey; Screenplay,
James Goldman; Associate Producer, Frank
Caffey; Photography, Victor J. Kemper;
Production designer, John Robert Lloyd;
Music, John Barry; Costumes designer, Ann
Roth; Editor, Gerald Greenberg.

Cast: George C. Scott (Justin
Playfair / Sherlock Holmes), Joanne
Woodward (Dr. Mildred Watson), Jack

Gilford (Wilbur Peabody), Lester Rawlins
(Blevins Playfair), Rue McClanahan (Daisy),
Ron Weyand (Dr. Strauss), Kitty Winn
(Grace), Peter Fredericks (Grace's
Boyfriend), Sudie Bond (Maud), Jenny Egan
(Miss Finch), Theresa Merritt (Peggy—
Telephone Operator No. 1), Al Lewis
(Messenger), Oliver Clark (Mr. Small), Jane
Hoffman (Telephone Operator No. 2),
Dorothy Greener (Telephone Operator No.
3), M. Emmet Walsh (Sanitation Man No.
1), Louis Zorich (Sanitation Man No. 2),
Michael McGuire (Telephone Guard),
Eugene Roche (Policeman), James Tolkan
(Mr. Brown), Jacques Sandulescu (Brown's
Driver), Worthington Miner (Mr. Bagg),
Frances Fuller (Mrs. Bagg), Matthew Cowles
(Teenage Boy), Candy Azzara (Teenage
Girl), John McCurry (Police Lt.), Tony
Capodilupo (Chief), F. Murray Abraham
(Usher), Staats Cotsworth (Winthrop), Paul
Benedict (Chestnut Vendor), Ralph Clanton
(Store Manager), Ted Beniades (Cab
Driver).

Justin Playfair, a brilliant lawyer, suffers
a mental breakdown after the death of his
wife and becomes firmly convinced he is
Sherlock Holmes. He dresses like him, talks
like him, etc. His psychiatrist, Dr. Mildred
Watson, gradually comes to believe in him
and together they go out into the world to
defeat the Moriartys. One of the most

361

refreshing and entertaining Holmes films ever made, with an actor whose performance equals those of Gillette and Rathbone.

The film was based on a play by the same author and title (item 5240). See also item 5902.

Reviews: Chicago Daily News (June 10, 1971), 100-101 (Kathleen Carroll); *Cosmopolitan* (July 1971), 12 (Liz Smith); *Courier-Post* [Camden, N.J.] (March 31, 1971); *Denver Post* (April 26, 1971), 33 (Barry Morrison); *Detroit Free Press* (April 7, 1971) (Susan Stark); *Detroit News* (April 9, 1971), 20-A (A. L. McClain); *DCC,* 7, No. 5 (June 1971), 9 (Robert W. Hahn); *Films and Filming,* 17 (May 1971), 40-41; *Films in Review,* 22 (May 1971), 314 (Gwenneth Britt); *HO,* 1, No. 5 (July 1971), 8; 1, No. 8 (October 1971), 5, 4 (Andrew Page); *Life,* 70 (April 30, 1971), 17 (Richard Schickel); *Los Angeles Times* (March 10, 1971) (Kevin Thomas), and reprinted in *Filmfacts,* 14 (1971), 174-175; *New York Times* (June 10, 1971), C 51 (Vincent Canby), and reprinted in *HO,* 1, No. 8 (October 1971), 6; *Newsday* (June 10, 1971) (Joseph Gelmis), and reprinted in *Filmfacts,* 14 (1971), 174; *Philadelphia Daily News* (April 24, 1971), 12 (Joe Baltake); *Philadelphia Evening Bulletin* (April 18, 1971); *Rocky Mountain News* [Denver] (April 24, 1971), 130 (Pat Hanna); *San Francisco Chronicle* (May 6, 1971), 46 (Paine Knickerbocker); *Saturday Review,* 54 (May 8, 1971), 40 (Hollis Alpert); *Senior Scholastic,* 98 (May 3, 1971), 21; *Time,* 97 (April 26, 1971), 97 (Stefan Kanfer); *TV Guide,* 20 (October 21, 1972), A-6 (Judith Crist); *Variety,* 262 (March 3, 1971; 17 (Gold.), and reprinted in *Filmfacts,* 14 (1971), 174; *VJ,* 1, No. 4 (1971), 4 (Tom Mengert); *Village Voice,* 16 (June 24, 1971), 60 (Molly Haskell), and reprinted in *Film-facts,* 14 (1971), 175.

D *Musicals*

1964-1965 FRITZ WEAVER AND PETER SALLIS

5166. *Baker Street: A Musical Adventure of Sherlock Holmes.* Book by Jerome Coopersmith. Music and lyrics by Marian Grudeff and Raymond Jessel. Boston: Shubert Theatre, December 28, 1964 - January 16, 1965. Toronto: O'Keefe Center, January 20 - February 6, 1965. New York: Broadway Theatre, February 16 - October 31, 1965. New York: Martin Beck Theatre, November 4-14, 1965. 311 performances.

Credits: Producer, Alexander H. Cohen; Director, Harold Prince; Choreography, Lee Becker Theodore; Musical direction, Harold

Hastings; Dance arrangements, John Morris; Orchestrations, Don Walker; Orchestra conductor, Arthur Wagner; Diamond Jubilee Parade, Bil Baird's Marionettes; Production design, Oliver Smith; Lighting, Jean Rosenthal; Costumes, Motley; Production Associate, Hildy Parks; Produced in association with Gabriel Katza.

Cast: Fritz Weaver (Sherlock Holmes), Peter Sallis (Dr. Watson), Martin Gabel (Professor Moriarty), Daniel Keyes (Inspector Lestrade), Inga Swenson (Irene Adler), Patrick Horgan (Captain Gregg), Paddy Edwards (Mrs. Hudson), Virginia Vestoff (Daisy), Martin Wolfson (Baxter), Teddy Green (Wiggins), Bert Michaels (Duckbellows), Sal Pernice (Nipper), George Lee (Perkins), Mark Judge Sheil (Macipper), Jay Norman (Murillo), Avin Harum, Christopher Walken, Tommy Tune (Three Killers), Gwenn Lewis (Tavern Singer).

Contents: Act I. Prologue: Baker Street, London. Scene 1. The Baker Street flat. Scene 2. The stage of the Theatre Royal. Scene 3. Backstage at the Theatre Royal. Scene 4. An alley in Baker Street. Scene 5. Irene's flat. Scene 6. The Baker Street flat. Scene 7. The London underworld. Scene 8. Moriarty's ship. Act II. Scene 1. A street in London. Scene 2. Moriarty's ship. Scene 3. Interior of a carriage. Scene 4. The cliffs of Dover. Scene 5. A part of London. Scene 6. The Baker Street flat. Scene 7. A hall in London. Scene 8. Baker Street

"This mélange was created from *A Scandal in Bohemia, The Final Problem* and

Fritz Weaver in the Broadway show Baker Street: A Musical Adventure of Sherlock Holmes (**5166**).

The Adventure of the Empty House, with a gay disregard for characters, places and time, all of which are adapted to the author's convenience. Holmes and Professor Moriarty do indeed fall over a cliff in supposedly mortal combat, but in the rather contrived and amusing happy ending, the villain escapes to the Continent, and Holmes, that coldly calculating intellectual machine, falling ever so slightly under the spell of Irene Adler, the American actress-adventuress, is about to follow her to America." (William H. Matthews, Jr.)

See also items 5556, 5563, and 5574.

5167. ———, *Playbill* [New York], 2, No. 2 (February 1965), 19-26, 32-38.

———, ———, 2, No. 5 (May 1965), 17-24, 30-36.

———, ———, 2, No. 6 (June 1965), 17-24, 30-36.

———, ———, 2, No. 10 (October 1965), 17-24, 34-40.

Contents: Cast. - The Company. - Understudies. - Scené Synopsis. - Musical Numbers. - Who's Who in the Cast.

5168. ———. Toronto: O'Keefe Center for the Performing Arts, Wednesday, January 20-February 6, 1965. 32 p.

A souvenir program.

5169. ———. New York: Dunetz and Lovett, [1965]. 32 p.

A souvenir program.

5170. Coopersmith, Jerome. *Baker Street: A Musical Adventure of Sherlock Holmes.* Book by Jerome Coopersmith. Music and lyrics by Marian Grudeff and Raymond Jessel. Adapted from the stories by Sir Arthur Conan Doyle. Garden City, N.Y.: Doubleday & Co., 1966. 188 p. illus. (Doubleday Theatre Series)

Also published in a paperback edition.

5171. Grudeff, Marian, and Raymond Jessel. *Baker Street: A Musical Adventure of Sherlock Holmes.* Music and lyrics by Marian Grudeff and Raymond Jessel. New York: Edward B. Marks Music Corp., [1965]. 4 scores.

Contents: [1] I'm in London Again (3 p.) - [2] Cold Clear World (7 p.) - [3] I Shall Miss You Holmes (3 p.) - [4] Buffalo Belle (5 p.)

5172. ———. ———. *Vocal Selections.* Music and lyrics by Marian Grudeff and Raymond Jessel. New York: Edward B. Marks Music Corp., [1964]. Score (20 p.) illus.

Contents: Photographs. - About the Show . . . and Sherlock Holmes. - A Married Man. - Finding Words for Spring. - What a Night This is Going to Be. - I'd Do It Again. - Jewelry.

5173. ———. *Marches from "Baker Street."*

Music and lyrics by Marian Grudeff and Raymond Jessel. Arranged for band by John Cacavas. New York: Edward B. Marks Music Corp., [1965]. Condensed score (11 p.) Duration: approx. 4 1/2 min.

Contents: Jewelry. - Diamond Jubilee Parade. - Scots Guards. - Leave It to Us, Guv! - Roof Space.

Reviews: Boston Globe (December 29, 1964) (Kevin Kelly);* *Boston Herald* (December 29, 1964) (Elinor Hughes);* *Boston Sunday Herald* (Loretta Leone);* *Boston Traveler* (December 29, 1964) (Alta Maloney);* *Christian Science Monitor* (December 29, 1964) (Frederick H. Guidry);* (February 20, 1965), 6 (Louis Chapin); *Dance Magazine,* 39 (April 1965), 18-19 (Doris Hering); *Detroit Free Press* (February 13, 1965), 12-A (Bill Rabe);* *DCC,* 1, No. 3 (April 1965), 3-4 (Nathan L. Bengis); *Library Journal,* 91 (February 15, 1966), 960 (William H. Matthews, Jr.); *Life,* 58 (April 2, 1965), 133-134, 137-138 (Tom Prideaux); *Medical Tribune,* Weekend Edition, 6 (March 20-21, 1965), 20 (Julian Wolff), and reprinted in *BSJ,* 15, No. 2 (June 1965), 90; *National Review,* 17 (June 29, 1965), 561 (Priscilla L. Buckley); *New Complete Book of the American Musical Theater,* [by] David Ewen (New York: Holt, Rinehart and Winston, 1970), 31-32; *New York Daily News* (February 17, 1965), 64 (John Chapman); *New York Herald Tribune* (November 24, 1964), 20 (Stuart W. Little);* (February 17, 1965), 15 (Walter Kerr); *New York Herald Tribune Magazine* (February 14, 1965), 25 (Herbert Kupferberg);* (March 7, 1965), 17 (Walter Kerr);* *New York Journal American* (February 17, 1965) (John McClain); *New York Morning Telegraph* (February 18, 1965) (Whitney Bolton); *New York Post* (February 17, 1965) (Richard Watts, Jr.); (February 28, 1965), 20 (Richard Watts, Jr.); *New York Theatre Critics' Reviews,* 26 (February 17, 1965), 374-377; *New York Times* (February 11, 1965), 42 (Sam Zolotow);* (February 14, 1965), II, 1, 5 (John Dickson Carr);* (February 17, 1965), 36 (Howard Taubman); (February 18, 1965), 28 (Sam Zolotow);* (February 28, 1965), II, 1 (Howard Taubman); (March 7, 1965), II, 3 (John Keating); [Full-page advertisement] (March 7, 1965), II, 2; *New York Times Book Review* (July 17, 1966), 33 (Anthony Boucher); *New York World-Telegram and Sun* (February 17, 1965), 33 (Norman Nadel);* (March 2, 1965), 10 (Norman Nadel); *New Yorker,* 41 (February 20, 1965), 31-33; 41 (February 27, 1965) 94, 96 (John McCarten); *Newark Evening News* (February 17, 1965) (Edward Sothern Hipp); *Newsday* (February 17, 1965) (George Oppenheimer); *Newsweek,* 65 (March 1, 1965), 84; *Record American* [Boston] (December 30, 1964) (Elliot Norton);* *Rogue,* 10 (August 1965), 60-64 (Ralph Luna); 10 (August 1965), 3-5 (Dave

Actors, Performances, & Recordings

Musicals

Stevens); *Saturday Review,* 68 (March 6, 1965), 22 (Henry Hewes); *SHJ,* 7, No. 4 (Spring 1966), 129-130 (Lord Donegall); *Show,* 5 (April 1965), 9, 91 (Otis L. Guernsey, Jr.); *Standard-Times* [New Bedford, Mass.] (December 29, 1964) (J. B.);* *SIS,* 1, No. 2 (1965), 2-3; *Time,* 85 (February 26, 1965), 78; *The Times* (March 15, 1965), 6; *Toronto Daily Star* (January 21, 1965) (Nathan Cohen);* *Toronto Globe and Mail* (January 21, 1965) (Herbert Whittaker);* (January 23, 1965) (Ralph Hicklin);* *Toronto Globe Magazine* (January 16, 1965), 10-12 (S. Tupper Bigelow);* *Variety* (Febuary 24, 1965), 70 (Hobe.); *Wall Street Journal* (February 18, 1965), 14 (Richard P. Cooke); *Women's Wear Daily* (February 17, 1965), 47 (Martin Gottfried).

*Reprinted in *CPBook,* 1, No. 3 (Winter 1965), 41-56.

5174. [Donegall, Lord.] "The Musical Holmes," *SHJ,* 7, No. 2 (Spring 1965), 33-34. (Editorial)

Lord Donegall, James Holroyd, and Anthony Howlett discuss *Baker Street* with Jerome Coopersmith.

5175. Gehman, Richard. "The Case of the Tortured Tunesmiths (or Quick, Watson—the Music!)," *Maclean's,* 78 (April 3, 1965), 14-15, 26, 28. illus.

"Canada's Grudeff and Jessel: how they set 'Baker Street' to music."

5176. [Hahn, Robert W.] "Baker Street: A Summary of the Reviews," *DCC,* 1, No. 2 (February 1965), 3-5; 1, No. 4 (May 1965), 4.

5177. Rosenberger, Edgar S. "On the Street Where He Lives," *BSJ,* 8, No. 3 (July 1958), 147-148.

———. ———, [Oversat af A. D. Henriksen]. *Sherlockiana,* 4, Nr. 4 (1959), 18.

"Oh, what have they done to our Sherlock? Alas, / They've made him a silly buffoon."

5178. Tomashefsky, Steven, and Robert Enright. "Baker Street," *SIS,* 1, No. 1 (June 1965), 3-6. (Editorial)

A review of the reviews written by some major critics about the musical.

5179. Warner, Edith. "No Place Like Ho(l)mes (After Seeing *Baker Street*)," *BSJ,* 15, No. 2 (June 1965), 91.

"But a stunning accolade / came from fans who paid and stayed / yet could have left and shown more common sense."

1971 MICHAEL KEARNS AND
DONALD LIVESAY

5180. *The Marvelous Misadventure of Sherlock Holmes: A Musical Mystery for Children.* Chicago: Goodman Theatre, July 6-August 14, 1971.

Credits: Writer and Director, Thom Racina; Costume Design, Ferrucio Garavaglia; Set Design, Alicia Finkel; Lighting Design, Jerrold Gorrell; Scenic Artist, Robert Moody; Choreography, Mark Ganzel; Original Music and Lyrics, Thom Racina.

Cast: Michael Kearns (Sherlock Holmes), Donald Livesay (Dr. Watson), Linda Taccki (Countess Von Hassenfeffer), Bruce Boxleitner (The Creepy Salami), Judith-Marie Bergan (Helga, the Maid), David Coleman (Frederick), Ruth Hytry (Freida), Patrick Lavery (Franz), Mark Ganzel (Herr Schultz), Janet Austin (Frau Schultz), Mark Burchard (The Innkeeper), Jack Godby (Master of Ceremonies).

Contents: Act I. Scene 1. The Office of Sherlock Holmes on Baker Street. Scene 2. A Road in Bohemia. Scene 3. The Mansion Garden. Scene 4. Somewhere in the Mansion. Scene 5. The Conservatory in the Mansion. - Act II. Scene 1. Outside the Castle Inn. Scene 2. The Castle Inn. Scene 3. Outside the Castle Inn. Scene 4. The Mansion Garden.

Reviews: Chicago Tribune (July 18, 1971) (Lynn Van Matre); *DCC,* 7, No. 6 (August 1971), 9 (Robert W. Hahn).

E *Plays*

This section lists the published plays,* performances of both the published and unpublished plays, promptbooks, typescripts, souvenir programs, and reviews that came out between 1893 and 1972 in English, Czech, Danish, French, German, Norwegian, Russian, Spanish, and Swedish. Some of the plays are serious dramatizations while others, perhaps a majority, are humorous and satirical. The Canonical tales that have been dramatized for the stage are Blac, Blue, Chas, Copp, Dyin, Houn, Maza, Reig, 3Gar, Sign, Spec, and Stud.

Information on the stage dramatizations was gathered mostly from playbills and reviews, many of which are in the theater collection at the Library and Museum of the Performing Arts in New York's Lincoln Center. Information on the Swedish dramatizations came primarily from Ted and Ingrid Bergman's excellent monograph entitled *Sherlock Holmes on the Swedish Stage.* Although there are some 50 plays and over 100 separate productions listed, the section is by no means complete. It is the compiler's hope that additional information

*The two published plays and one unpublished play by Doyle are listed with either the Apocrypha or Manuscripts.

can be made available in a supplement to this bibliography.

William Gillette's play *Sherlock Holmes* is by far the most successful of the Holmes dramatizations. Between its first production in Buffalo, New York, on October 23, 1899, and its latest in Amherst, Massachusetts, on September 20, 1970, the play has been performed thousands of times by many casts in several countries. According to a printed postcard of Gillette, the play had been performed 4,457 times as of June 25, 1904! Thirty-nine separate productions of the play in various cities of the United States, England, France, Germany, Norway, and Sweden are listed here, together with the credits and cast for each production. The play has also been dramatized for screen, radio, and television. It has been the subject of two satirical skits, *The Remarkable Pipe Dream of Mr. Sherlock Holmes* and *Sheerluck Jones, or Why D'Guilette Him Off?* A Dutch novelization of the play (item 1061) was published in Amsterdam twenty years before the English publication appeared in 1922 (item 5237).

Gillette performed the leading role over 1,300 times between 1899 and 1932. He also portrayed Holmes in a film version of his play in 1916, appeared in the first Sherlock Holmes radio dramatization in 1930, and made a recording for Audio Rarities. His performances were enormously successful, and many Sherlockians believe he resembled the Master more closely than any one before or since. William Gillette, a tall, spare figure of a man smoking a curved meerschaum pipe and wearing a deerstalker's cap and long cape, is inextricably connected with the role of the famous detective. Frederic Dorr Steele said of him, "I can think of no more perfect realization of a fictional character on the stage." In a personal note to the actor upon his return to the stage in 1929, Booth Tarkington wrote, "I would rather see you play Sherlock Holmes than be a child again on Christmas morning." To honor the great actor, an annual William Gillette Memorial Luncheon is held in New York on the same day as the annual BSI dinner.

Even though Holmes has been played by numerous actors, it is perhaps fair to say that for the first generation of Sherlockians, William Gillette *was* Sherlock Holmes; for the second, Basil Rathbone *was* and still *is* Sherlock Holmes; for the third—we can only speculate on who will be *the* Sherlock Holmes.

5181. Bridgham, Gladys Ruth. *A Case for Sherlock Holmes: A Comedy in Two Acts.* For female characters only. Boston: Walter H. Baker & Co., 1914. 30 p. (Baker's Edition of Plays)

5182. Brookfield, Charles, and Seymour Hicks. *Under the Clock.* London: Court Theatre, November 25, 1893-March 3, 1894. 92 performances.
Partial cast: Charles Brookfield (Sherlock Holmes), Seymour Hicks (Dr. Watson).
An extravaganza in one act in which Holmes and Watson are portrayed for the very first time.
Reviews: SHJ, 9, No. 3 (Winter 1969), 87-88 (Michael Pointer); *The Times* (November 27, 1893), 7.

5183. [Carr, John Dickson.] "The Adventure of the Conk-Singleton Papers," by Dr. John H. Watson. *The Unicorn Mystery Book Club News,* 1, No. 9 (1949), 8-9, 16.
————. ————, *Ellery Queen's Mystery Magazine,* 52, No. 4 (October 1968), 67-70.
A parody-pastiche in dramatic form, performed in April 1948 at the Mystery Writers of America's annual Edgar Allan Poe Awards Dinner with the following cast: Clayton Rawson (Sherlock Holmes), Lawrence G. Blochman (Dr. Watson), John Dickson Carr (The Mysterious Visitor).

5184. ————. "The Adventure of the Paradol Chamber," *The Unicorn Mystery Book Club News,* 2, No. 3 (1949), 8-9, 14-15.
————. ————, *Ellery Queen's Mystery Magazine,* 15, No. 75 (February 1950), 106-110.
————. ————, *BSJ,* 15, No. 3 (September 1965), 136-138.
————. ————, *Ellery Queen's Minimysteries.* Edited by Ellery Queen. New York and Cleveland: The World Pub. Co., [1969]. p. 189-194.
A dramatic sketch given at the Mystery Writers of America Annual Dinner show, The March of Crime.

5185. [Clapp, Roger T.] "The Adventure of the Yellow Birds," *Providence Sunday Journal Magazine* (December 11, 1949), 3-6, 8.
Contents: The Yellow Birds, story synopsis by Roger T. Clapp; pictures by H. Raymond Ball. - English 23, story by Henry H. Smith; pictures by Edward C. Hanson. - Is Sherlock Holmes Still Alive? by Jeannette Hopkins.
A report on the presentation of Mr. Clapp's melodrama *The Yellow Birds* by members of Professor Ben Brown's English 23 class at Brown University.

5186. ————. "The Yellow Birds: A Sherlock Holmes Adventure in Five Scenes," *The Third Cab.* [Boston: The Speckled Band, 1960.] p. 64-80.
————. ————, *BSJ,* 17, No. 2 (June 1967), 102-112.
A dramatization of the story that won the prize offered by The Speckled Band in 1949 for the best pastiche based on the untold adventure of "Wilson, the Notorious Canary Trainer," mentioned by Watson in Blac.

5187. Crane, Burton. *The Mystery of the*

Plays

Silver-Backed Hairbrush: A Whodunit in One Act. Boston: Baker's Plays, [1950]. 22 p.

"First presented by the Tokyo Women's Club in the auditorium of the Y.M.C.A. in Tokyo, Japan. It was staged by the author."

Two characters—Chesterton and his assistant, Dobson—are comic versions of Holmes and Watson.

5188. Doyle, Sir Arthur Conan. *The Crown Diamond: An Evening with Sherlock Holmes: A Play in One Act.* Bristol: Hippodrome, May 2, 1921. 1 performance. London: Coliseum, May 16-22, August 29-September 4, 1921. 28 performances.

Credits: Producer, Stanley Bell.

Cast: Dennis Neilson-Terry (Sherlock Holmes — the famous Detective), [Unknown] (Dr. Watson — His Friend), [Unknown] (Billy — Page to Mr. Holmes), [Unknown] (Col. Sebastian Moran — an intellectual Criminal), [Unknown] (Sam Merton — a Boxer).

"The Adventure of the Mazarin Stone" (October 1921) was based on this play.

5189. ———. *The Speckled Band: An Adventure of Sherlock Holmes.* London: *Adelphi Theatre,* June 4-August 7, 1910.

Credits: Acting Manager (for George Edwardes), Charlton Mann; Stage Manager, W. W. Keene; Assistant Stage Manager, A. Bachner; Scenery, F. L. Schmitz; Wigs, Clarkson; Miss Silver's Dresses, Mrs. Caleb Porter; Musical Director, Brigata Bucalossi.

Cast: H. A. Saintsbury (Sherlock Holmes), Claude King (Dr. Watson), Lyn Harding (Dr. Grimesby Rylott—a retired Anglo-Indian Surgeon, owner of Stoke Place), Christine Silver (Enid Stoner—Dr. Rylott's Step-daughter), Agnes Thomas (Mrs. Staunton—Housekeeper to Dr. Rylott), A. S. Homewood (Rodger Rogers—Butler to Dr. Rylott), Wilton Ross (Ali, an Indian—Valet to Dr. Rylott), Arthur Burne (Mr. Scott Wilson—engaged to Enid's Sister), Spencer Trevor (Mr. Armitage—the Village Grocer), J. J. Bartlett (Mr. Longbrace—Coroner), Frank Ridley (Mr. Brewer—Foreman of the Jury), Geoffrey Hill (Inspector Downing), George Laundy (Coroner's Office), A. G. Craig (Mr. Holt Loaming—Client of Sherlock Holmes), Gwendolen Floyd (Mrs. Soames—Client of Sherlock Holmes), A. Corney Grain (Mr. James B. Montague—Client of Sherlock Holmes), Frank Ridley (Mr. Milverton—Client of Sherlock Holmes), Cecil F. Lowrie (Billy—Page to Sherlock Holmes), C. Later (Peters—a Butler), Jurors at the Inquest).

Music: Overture - "Egmont" by Beethoven. - 1st Entr'acte. "The Speckled Band" (An Indian Melody in G Minor) by Brigata Bucalossi. - 2nd Entr'acte. "Pagliacci" by Leoncavallo. - 3rd Entr'acte. a. "Hilary" by A. Corney Grain. b.

"L'Amour est Eternel" by Brigata Bucalossi.

Contents: Act I. The Hall of Stoke Place, Stoke Moran. Two years elapse between Acts I and II. - Act II. Scene 1. Dr. Rylott's Study, Stoke Place. Scene 2. Mr. Sherlock Holmes' Rooms, Upper Baker Street, London. - Act III. Scene 1. The Hall of Stoke Place. Scene 2. Enid's Bedroom, Stoke Place.

Based broadly on the Canonical tale by the same name.

5190. ———. ———. London: Globe Theatre, August 8-October 29, 1910.

Credits: Charles Frohman's General Manager, W. Lestocq; Stage Manager, W. W. Keene; Assistant Stage Manager, A. Bachner; Scenery; F. L. Schmitz; Musical Director, Brigata Bucalossi.

Cast: H. A. Saintsbury (Sherlock Holmes), H. Lawrence Leyton (Dr. Watson), Herbert Waring (Dr. Grimesby Rylott), Christine Silver (Enid Stonor), Alice Beet (Mrs. Staunton), Ernest Cosham (Rodgers), Wilton Ross (Ali), Arthur Burne (Scott Wilson), Spencer Trevor (Armitage), J. J. Bartlett (Longbrace), Frank Ridley (Brewer), W. Coats Bush (Inspector Downing), George Laundy (Coroner's Officer), Henry Williams (Holt Loaming), Gwendolen Floyd (Mrs. Soames), Frank G. Bayley (James B. Montague), Frank Ridley (Milverton), Cecil F. Lowrie (Billy), C. Later (Peters), (Jurors at the Inquest).

5191. ———. ———. Boston, Mass.: Boston Theatre, October 24-? 1910. New York: Garrick Theatre, November 21-December 17, 1910. 32 performances.

Credits: Managing Directors, Charles Frohman and William Harris; Stage Director, George A. Highland; Stage Manager, Walter Soderling; Scenery, Homer F. Emmons.

Cast: Charles Millward (Sherlock Holmes), Ivo Dawson (Dr. Watson), Edwin Stevens (Dr. Grimesby Rylott), Irene Fenwick (Enid Stonor), Katherine Brook (Mrs. Staunton), John Findlay (Rodgers), H. H. McCollum (Ali), Cyril Chadwick (Scott Wilson), Ben Field (Armitage), Alexander Frank (Longbrace), Ivan F. Simpson (Brewer), W. Coats Bush (Inspector Downing), John M. Troughton (Coroner's Officer), Frank Shannon (Holt Loaming), W. Soderling (James B. Montague), Ivan F. Simpson (Milverton), Kenneth Meinken (Billy), C. Later (Peters), (Jurors at the Inquest).

5192. ———. ———. Under the management of Mr. Arthur Hardy. London: Strand Theatre, February 6-25, 1911.

Credits: General Manager, Fred Pemberton; Stage Manager, W. W. Keene; Assistant Stage Manager, Oswald Strong;

Scenery, F. L. Schmitz; Musical Director, Brigata Bucalossi.

Cast: O. P. Heggie (Sherlock Holmes), Claude King (Dr. Watson), Lyn Harding (Dr. Grimesby Rylott), Christine Silver (Enid Stonor), Grace Edwin (Mrs. Staunton), A. S. Homewood (Rodgers), Gerald Rogers (Ali), Alfred Beaumont (Scott Wilson), E. H. Brooke (Armitage), Walter Ringham (Longbrace), Frank Ridley (Brewer), Geoffrey Hill (Inspector Downing), George Laundy (Coroner's Officer), A. G. Craig (Holt Loaming), Alfred Beaumont (James B. Montague), Frank Ridley (Milverton), Cecil F. Lowrie (Billy), (Jurors at the Inquest).

5193. ———. ———. Southampton: Grand Theatre, May 8, 1911-?

Partial cast: A. Corney Grain (Sherlock Holmes), Harold S. Standing (Dr. Watson), Walter Ringham (Dr. Grimesby Rylott), Herbert Bradford (Milverton).

5194. ———. ———. Chicago: Studebaker Theatre, February 1914-?

Partial cast: H. Cooper Cliffe (Sherlock Holmes), Lyn Harding (Dr. Grimesby Rylott), Renee Kelly (Enid Stonor), Hylton Allen (Scott Wilson).

5195. ———. ———. London: St. James's Theatre, September 22-December 10, 1921. 92 performances. Royalty Theatre, December 26, 1921-Janaury 14, 1922. 20 performances.

Cast: H. A. Saintsbury (Sherlock Holmes), Kenneth Rivington (Dr. Watson), Victor Pierpoint (Billy), Lyn Harding (Dr. Grimesby Rylott), Mary Merrall (Enid Stonor), Charles Barratt (Ali), George Mallett (Rodgers), Grace Edwin (Mrs. Staunton), Claude Watts (Scott Wilson), J. J. Bartlett (Longbrace), Arthur Cromer (Brewer), Archibald Forbes (Armitage), Ernest Ruston (Holt Loaming), Alan Craven (Milverton), Edward Stirling (James B. Montague), Edward Leader (Coroner's Officer), William Barlot (Inspector Downing), C. Later (Peters).

5196. ———. ———. England and France: The London Players, 1922.

Partial cast: Henry Oscar (Sherlock Holmes), Edward Stirling (Dr. Grimesby Rylott), Margaret Vaughan and Elizabeth Dundas (Enid Stonor).

5197. ———. ———. Pasadena, Calif.: Pasadena Community Playhouse, September 3-12, 1931. 10 performances.

Credits: Director, Gilmor Brown; Associate Director, Morris Ankrum; Art Director, Corliss McGee; General Production Manager, Murray Yeats.

Cast: Ralph Freud (Sherlock Holmes), Thomas Browne Henry (Dr. Watson), Robert Kreisman (Billy), Morris Ankrum (Dr. Grimesby Rylott), Elizabeth Porter

(Enid Stonor), John Waldron (Ali), Franlin Provo (Rodgers), Sharley Simpson (Mrs. Staunton), Jack Rea (Scott Wilson), Frederick Blanchard (Longbrace), Howland Chamberlain (Brewer), Frank Starr (Armitage), Lewis Winslow (Holt Loaming), Robert Chapin (Milverton), John Blagdon (James B. Montague), C. C. Walton (Coroner's Officer), C. Later (Peters), (Coroner's Jury).

5198. ———. ———. Manchester: Library Theatre, September 22-October 10, 1970.

Credits: Director, Paul Webster; Assistant, Gloria Parkinson; Design, Gillian Edwards; Lighting and sound, Martin McCallum.

Cast: Alan Moore (Sherlock Holmes), Michael Keating (Dr. Watson), Mike Savage (Dr. Roylott), Richard Henry (Ali), Alan Luxton (Rodgers), Ian McDiarmid (Armitage and Mr. Montague), Malcolm Storry (Foreman of the Jury and Mr. Milverton), Kevin Williams (Mrs. Scott Wilson and Billy), Paul Seed (Coroner's Officer and Mr. Loaming), Richard Vanstone (Coroner), Diana Lambert (Helen Stoner), Elizabeth Kelly (Mrs. Staunton).

5199. ———. ———. [London: 1910.] 30, 41, 28 leaves. Typescript.

Promptbook. Includes property and light plots for the London production.

Location: Library & Museum of the Performing Arts at Lincoln Center.

5200. ———. ———. [New York: Rosenfield, 1910.] 35, 56, 28 leaves. Typescript.

Promptbook. Includes property and light plots for the New York production.

Location: Library & Museum of the Performing Arts at Lincoln Center.

Reviews of above play: The Bookman, 32 (October 1910), 147 (C. Hamilton); *Columbian Magazine,* 3 (January 1911), 706-707 (A. E. Bergh); *Green Book Album,* 5 (February 1911), 249, 302; *Illustrated London News,* 136 (June 11, 1910), 932; 159 (October 1, 1921), 452; *Life,* 56 (December 8, 1910), 1065 (J. S. Metcalfe); *New Statesman,* 17 (October 1, 1921), 703 (Desmond MacCarthy); *New York Daily Tribune* (November 22, 1910) (A. W.); *New York Dramatic Mirror,* 64 (November 23, 1910), 7; *New York Evening Sun* (November 22, 1910); *New York Herald* (November 22, 1910); *New York Times* (November 22, 1910), 7; *Pearson's Magazine,* 25 (February 1911), 258; *Playgoer and Society Illustrated* (NS), 2 (July-August 1910), 155-172 (Edward Morton), and reprinted in part in *Charles Augustus Milverton on Stage, Screen and Radio* (London: The Milvertons of Hampstead, 1960); *Saturday Review of Literature,* 10 (April 21, 1934), 647 (Christopher Morley); *SHJ,* 9, No. 3 (Winter 1969), 88-89 (Michael Pointer); 9, No. 4 (Summer 1970),

Plays

119 (Michael Pointer); 10, No. 1 (Winter 1970), 13 (Michael Pointer); 10, No. 1 (Winter 1970), 24-26 (Colin Prestige); *Sketch* [Supplement], 70 (June 15, 1910), 6-8; 71 (July 20, 1910), 47; *The Times* (June 6, 1910), 12. Sixteen other reviews of the first performance are listed in an Adelphi advertisement in *The Times* (June 7, 1910), 10.

5201. [Eames, Charles.] "The Case of the Purloined Train," *Esquire*, 60, No. 4 (October 1963), 121. illus.
———. Revised with title: "The Case of the Elusive Train," *BSJ*, 14, No. 4 (December 1964), 196-198.
The script of the Sherlockian puppet show presented in the IBM Pavilion at the New York World's Fair.

5202. Fenisong, Ruth, and Samuel Sayer. *Sherlock Holmes: A Play for Marionettes in Four Scenes.* New York: National Play Bureau, Works Progress Administration, Federal Theatre Project, July 1937. 38 p. (Federal Theatre Playscript, No. 22)
"Adapted for marionettes from Conan Doyle's *Speckled Band* by Ruth Fenisong with the collaboration of Samuel Sayer."

5203. Fenn, John. *Sherlock Holmes and the Affair of the Amorous Regent.* Adapted from stories by Sir Arthur Conan Doyle. Minneapolis: Theatre in the Round, July 13-30, 1972. 10 performances.
Credits: Director, John Fenn; Associate Director, Robert Roedocker; Set Design, Jon Neuse; Lighting Design, Richard Borgen; Costume Design, Karen Gerst; Sound Effects, Bob Friedman; Properties, Lisa Hoffmeister.
Cast: Charters H. Anderson (Sherlock Holmes), John McKay (Dr. Watson), Mark Miller (Billy), David Selberg (His Majesty King Wilhelm von Ormstein), Brian Ann Zoccola (Jenny Bassick), Mark Page (Alf Bassick), Joseph P. Franken (Sid Prince), Ron Pitzerell (Inspector George Lestrade), Barbara Bradshaw (Miss Irene Adler), Ron R. Cherry (Beads), James Naiden (Professor James Moriarty), Midge Semans (Miss Northton), Richard W. Viall (Kraigin), Andy Waggoner (Bell Boy), Ric Stuefer (Room Clerk), Paul Carland, Tim and Todd Cashman, Robert Englund, Paul Letofsky, Katie MacEachern, Nancy and Norman Read, Heather Simon, Mark Swanson, Andy Waggoner (The Baker Street Irregulars).
Reviews: Minneapolis Star (July 14, 1972.) 17A (Peter Altman; (July 25, 1972), II, 16B (Don Morrison); *Minneapolis Tribune* (July 9, 1972), 10D (Mike Steele); (July 14, 1972), 15B (Bob Lundegaard).

5204. George, Charles. *Sherlock*Holmes: A Play in a Prologue and Three Acts.* Founded on "A Study in Scarlet," by A. Conan Doyle. Boston, Mass., and Los Angeles, Calif.: [Walter H. Baker Co., 1936]. 128 p. (Baker's Royalty Plays).

5205. Gillette, William. *The Painful Predicament of Sherlock Holmes.* New York: Metropolitan Opera House, March 24-? 1905.
Cast: William Gillette (Sherlock Holmes), Ethel Barrymore (Gwendolyn Cobb), Henry McArdle (Billy), W. R. Walters and Frank Andrews (Asylum Attendants).

5206. ———. *The Harrowing Predicament of Sherlock Holmes* [alternate title for *The Painful Predicament of Sherlock Holmes*]. New York: Criterion Theatre, April 14-? 1905.
Cast: William Gillette (Sherlock Holmes), Jessie Busley (Gwendolyn Cobb), Henry McArdle (Billy).

5207. ———. *The Painful Predicament of Sherlock Holmes.* London: Duke of York's Theatre, October 3-? 1905.
Cast: William Gillette (Sherlock Holmes), Irene Vanbrugh (Gwendolyn Cobb), Charles Spencer Chaplin (Billy).
The skit (a fantasy "in about one-tenth of an act") was produced at the Duke of York's Theatre as a curtain-raiser to Gillette's play *Clarice.*

5208. ———. *The Painful Predicament of Sherlock Holmes: A Fantasy in One Act.* [Introduction by Vincent Starrett.] Chicago: Ben Abramson, 1955. 25 p.

5209. ———. *Sherlock Holmes: A Drama in Four Acts,* by A. Conan Doyle [sic] and William Gillette. Buffalo, N.Y.: Star Theatre, October 23-25, 1899. 3 performances. Syracuse, N.Y. 1 performance. Rochester, N.Y. 1 performance. New York: Garrick Theatre, November 6, 1899-June 16, 1900. 235 performances.
Credits: Producer, Charles Frohman; Stage Manager, William Postance; Scenery, Ernest Gros; Incidental Music, William Furst.
Cast: William Gillette (Sherlock Holmes), Bruce McRae (Dr. Watson), Ruben Fax (Benjamin Forman), Henry McArdle (Billy), Harold Heaton (Sir Edward Leighton), Thomas McGrath (Count Von Stalburg), George Wessells (Professor Moriarty), Ralph Delmore (James Larrabee), George Honey (Sidney Prince), Henry Harman (Alf Bassick), Thomas McGrath (Craigin), Elwyn Eaton (Tim Leary), Soldene Powell (McTague), William Postance (John), Soldene Powell (Parsons), Katherine Florence (Alice Faulkner), Kate Ten Eyck (Mrs. Faulkner), Judith Berolde (Madge Larrabee), Hilda Englund (Terese), Kate Ten Eyck (Mrs. Smeedley).
Contents: Act I. Drawing Room at the Larrabees'. - Act II. Scene 1. Professor

A theatrical poster for the play written by William Gillette in which he played the title role (5209).

Moriarty's Underground Office. Morning. Scene 2. Sherlock Holmes's Apartments in Baker Street. Evening. - Act III. The Stepney Gas Chamber. Midnight. - Act IV. Doctor Watson's Consulting Room — Kensington. The following evening.

"Being a hitherto unpublished episode in the career of the great detective and showing his connection with the strange case of Miss Faulkner."

5210. ——. ——. Philadelphia: Broad Street Theatre, February 4-? 1901. Boston: Hollis Street Theatre, February 25-March 3, 1901.

Credits: Producer, Charles Frohman; Stage Manager, William Postance; Scenery, Ernest Gros; Incidental Music, William Furst.

Cast: William Gillette (Sherlock Holmes), Fred'k Truesdell (Dr. Watson), Ruben Fax (John Forman), Harold Heaton (Sir Edward Leighton), Alfred S. Howard (Count Von Stahlburg), George Wessels (Professor Moriarty), Ralph Delmore (James Larrabee), George Honey (Sidney Prince), Henry Harmon (Alfred Bassick), Thomas McGrath (Jim Craigin), Elwyn Eaton (Thomas Leary), Julius Weyms ("Lightfoot" McTague), Henry Koerper (John), Soldene Powell (Parsons), Henry McArdle (Billy), Maude Fealy (Alice Faulkner), Jane Thomas (Mrs. Faulkner), Olive Oliver (Madge Larrabee), Louise Collins (Thérèse), Gertrude Dawes (Mrs. Smeedley).

5211. ——. ——. Malden, Mass.: Malden Auditorium, April 17-? 1901.

Credits and cast same as above except

that Cuyler Hastings portrayed Sherlock Holmes.

5212. ——. ——. Liverpool: Shakespeare Theatre, September 2-? 1901. London: Royal Lyceum Theatre, September 9, 1901-April 11, 1902. 216 performances.

Credits: Producer, Charles Frohman.

Cast: William Gillette (Sherlock Holmes), Percy Lyndal (Dr. Watson), Sydney Herbert (John Forman), Harold Heaton (Sir Edward Leighton), Walter Selby (Count Von Stalburg), W. L. Abingdon (Professor Moriarty), Ralph Delmore (James Larrabee), Fuller Mellish (Sidney Prince), Henry Harmon (Alfred Bassick), Griffith Evans (Jim Craigin), Henry J. Hadfield (Thomas Leary), David Campbell ("Lightfoot" McTague), Soldene Powell (John), Frank D. Pengelly (Parsons), Henry McArdle (Billy), Maud Fealy (Alice Faulkner), Ethel Lorrimore (Mrs. Faulkner), Charlotte Granville (Madge Larrabee), Louise Collins (Thérèse), Claire Pauncefort (Mrs. Smeedley).

The performance on February 1, 1902, was attended by King Edward VII and Queen Alexandra.

5213. ——. ——. Boston: Hollis Street Theatre, October 27-November 2, 1902. New York: Knickerbocker Theatre, November 3-29, 1902. 28 performances.

Credits: Producer, Charles Frohman.

Cast: William Gillette (Sherlock Holmes), Herbert Percy (Dr. Watson), Edgar Selwyn (John Forman), Frank Andrews (Sir Edward Leighton), Frank Wilson (Count Von Stahlburg), Griffith Evans (Professsor Moriarty), Ralph Delmore (James Larrabee), Quinton McPherson (Sidney Prince), Ben Graham (Alfred Bassick), Thomas McGrath (Jim Craigin), Sidney Walters (Thomas Leary), Charles Gibson ("Lightfoot" McTague), Harry Kooper (John), Harry McArdle (Billy), Henry J. Hadfield (Parsons), Mabel Howard (Alice Faulkner), Maudé Giroux (Mrs. Faulkner), Alida Cortelyou (Madge Larrabee), Margaret Gordon (Thérèse), Ethel Lorrimore (Mrs. Smeedley).

5214. ——. ——. Boston Theatre, May 18-24, 1903.

Credits: Producer, Charles Frohman; Stage Manager, William Postance.

Cast: Herbert Kelcey (Sherlock Holmes), J. Palmer Collins (Dr. Watson), Frank L. Davis (Benj. Forman), Andrew Williams (Sir Edward Leighton), Arthur Grimwood (Count Von Stahlburg), Charles Canfield (James Larrabee), David Davies (Professor Moriarty), Charles A. Morgan (Sidney Prince), Allen Davenport (Alf. Bassick), W. R. Walters (Jim Craigin), Percy Campbell (Tim Leary), Harry Walters ("Lightfoot" McTague), Frank Adams (John), Walter

Plays

McArdle (Billy), Archie Curtis (Parsons), Effie Shannon (Alice Faulkner), Lorina Atwood (Madge Larrabee), Winona Shannon (Terese), Mrs. Samuel Charles (Mrs. Faulkner), Kate Korrimore (Mrs. Smeedley).

5215. ——. ——. Washington, D.C.: Lafayette, November 14-20, 1904.
Credits: Management, Gus Bothner and Robert Campbell.
Cast: Erroll Dunbar (Sherlock Holmes), John De Gez (Dr. Watson), J. Hay Cossar (James Larrabee), David Davies (Professor Moriarty), Harry Dickeson (Benjamin Forman), G. A. Coutts (Sidney Prince), Irving Williams (Alf. Bassick), Charles Courtnay (Sir Edward Leighton), Thomas Desmond (Count Von Stalburg), James D. Croly (Jim Craigin), Robert Graham (Lein Leary), Charles Weaver ("Lightfoot" McTague), George Odell (Billy), William Betts (Parsons), Jay Shattuck (John), Kate Campbell (Alice Faulkner), Marie Gebhart (Madge Larrabee), Josephine Clairmont (Terese).

5216. ——. ——. New York: Empire Theatre, March 6-April 15, 1905. 41 performances.
Credits: Producer, Charles Frohman.
Cast: William Gillette (Sherlock Holmes), William Courtleigh (Dr. Watson), Sidney Herbert (John Forman), Frank Andrews (Sir Edward Leighton), Alfred S. Howard (Count Von Stahlburg), George W. Wessels (Professor Moriarty), Ralph Delmore (James Larrabee), Quinton McPherson (Sidney Prince), George Sumner (Alfred Bassick), W. R. Walters (Jim Craigin), Julius Weymss (Thomas Leary), Harold Heaton ("Lightfoot" McTague), Henry S. Chandler (John), Harry McArdle (Billy), Soldene Powell (Parsons), Jane Laurel (Alice Faulkner), Julia Thomas (Mrs. Faulkner), Hilda Spong (Madge Larrabee), Sybil Campbell (Thérèse), Maude Giroux (Mrs. Smeedley).
According to an Empire advertisement in *The New York Times*, the performance on April 15 was the 362nd in New York.

5217. ——. ——. Elizabeth, N.J.: Lyceum Theatre, September 28-? 1905.
Cast: Erroll Dunbar (Sherlock Holmes), William Little (Dr. Watson), J. Hay Cossar (James Larrabee), Charles J. Edmonds (Professor Moriarty), Harry Dickeson (Benjamin Forman), Joseph Allenton (Sidney Prince), J. F. Wighaman (Alf Bassick), Charles Courtnay (Sir Edward Leighton), Frederick Rose (Count Von Stahlberg), Wilson Mostyn (Jim Craigin), Jos. Finn (Thomas Leary), Charles Weaver (Light-foot McTague), Owen Martin (Billy), William Betts (Parsons), Jay Shattuck (John), Leora Spellman (Alice Faulkner), Mathilde Weffing (Madge Larrabee), Eda Bothner (Terese).

5218. ——. ——. London: Duke of York's Theatre, October 17-December 2, 1905.
Credits: Producer, Charles Frohman; Scenery, Ernest Gros; Incidental Music, William Furst.
Cast: William Gillette (Sherlock Holmes), Kenneth Rivington (Dr. Watson), Eugene Mayeur (John Forman), Reginald Dance (Sir Edward Leighton), Frederick Morris (Count Van Stalburg), George Sumner (Professor Moriarty), Francis Carlyle (James Larrabee), Quinton McPherson (Sidney Prince), William H. Day (Alfred Bassick), Chris Walker (Jim Craigin), Henry Walters (Thomas Leary), Walter Dison ("Lightfoot" McTague), Thomas Quinton (John), G. Merton (Parsons), Charles Chaplin (Billy), Marie Doro (Alice Faulkner), De Olia Webster (Mrs. Faulkner), Adelaide Prince (Madge Larrabee), Sybil Campbell (Thérèse), Ethel Lorrimore (Mrs. Smeedley).

5219. ——. ——. Boston: Castle Square Theatre, December 24-30, 1906.
Credits: Staged by W. C. Masson.
Cast: Howell Hansel (Sherlock Holmes), Shelley Hull (Dr. Watson), Mark Kent (John Forman), Reginald Simpson (Sir Edward Leighton), Robert A. Thorne (Count Von Stahlburg), Ben Johnson (Professor Moriarty), John Waldron (James Larrabee), Louis Albion (Sidney Prince), Charles Miller (Alfred Bassick), Edward Wade (Jim Craigin), Robert A. Thorne (Thomas Leary), Lawrence Eyre ("Lightfoot" McTague), Henry S. Powell (John—Moriarty's Clerk), Frederick Totten (Parsons—Servant at Dr. Watson's), Louis F. Owen (Billy), Elfrida Lasche (Alice Faulkner), Grace Foote (Mrs. Faulkner), Jane Evans (Madge Larrabee), Frances Brandt (Thérèse), Helen Scott (Mrs. Smeedley).

5220. ——. ——. Lyceum Theatre, October 13-14, 1910. 2 performances.
Credits: Producer, Charles Frohman; Director, Robert Morris; Manager, Robert M. Eberle.
Cast: William Gillette (Sherlock Holmes), Clifford Bruce (Dr. Watson), A. Romaine Callender (Benj. Forman), John F. Hines (Billy), Frank Andrews (Sir Edward Leighton), Griffith Evans (Count Von Stalburg), J. E. Miltern (Professor Moriarty), Wm. Riely Hatch (James Larrabee), Albert Parker (Sidney Prince), Stewart Robbins (Alf Bassick), Griffith Evans (Craigin), Frank Andrews (Tim Leary), H. E. Moray (Lightfoot McTague), Frederick Wallace (John), H. E. Lindsley (Parsons), Louise Rutter (Alice Faulkner), Margaret Greene (Mrs. Faulkner), Marion Abbott (Madge Larrabee), Josephine Brown (Terese), Nellie Robinson (Mrs. Smeedley).

5221. ——. ——. Providence, R.I.: B. F. Keith's Theatre, May 15-? 1911.

Credits: Producer, Charles Frohman.

Cast: Lowell Sherman (Sherlock Holmes), Fred LeDuke (Dr. Watson), Elinor McEwen (Madge Larrabee), Richard Pitman (Benj. Forman), Harry Carlton (James Larrabee), Dorothy Shoemaker (Terese), C. Wilson Hummell (Sidney Prince), Grayce Scott (Alice Faulkner), Berton Churchill (Professor Moriarty), Frank Brady (John), Albert Lando (Alf Bassick), H. Dudley Hawley (Billy), Harry C. Arnold (Tim Leary), Fraak Hopkins ("Lightfoot" McTague), Don Hancock (Parsons, A. C. Henry (Sir Edward Leighton), Everett Newcomb (Count Von Stalburg).

5222. ———. ———. Toledo, Ohio: R. F. Keiths, July 21-? 1913.

Credits: Director, George Farren.

Cast: Sam B. Hardy (Sherlock Holmes), A. S. Byron (Dr. Watson), Harold Hendee (John Forman), H. H. France (Sir Edward Leighton), G. Allyn Zang (Count Von Stahlburg), Edwin B. Bailey (Professor Moriarty), William H. Sullivan (James Larrabee), Royal Tracy (Sidney Prince), H. H. France (Alfred Bassick), G. Allyn Zang (Jim Craigin), William Jacob (Thomas Leary), Neil Pratt (Billy), William Jacob (Parsons), Fay Bainter (Alice Faulkner), Elise Scott (Madge Larrabee), Gilda Leary (Terese).

5223. ———. ———. New York: Empire Theatre, October 11-November 6, 1915.

Credits: Producer, Charles Frohman.

Cast: William Gillette (Sherlock Holmes), Edward Fielding (Dr. Watson), Stewart Robbins (Benj. Forman), Burford Hampden (Billy), Marshall Vincent (Sir Edward Leighton), Wade Hampton, Jr. (Count Von Stalburg), Joseph Brennan (Professor Moriarty), Edwin Mordant (James Larrabee), Stuart Fox (Sidney Prince), Fulton Russell (Alf Bassick), Louis Hendricks (Craigin), H. G. Bates (Tim Leary), H. A. Morey ("Lightfoot" McTague), Philip Sanford (John), Earl Redding (Parsons), Helen Freeman (Alice Faulkner), Evangelyn Blaisdale (Mrs. Faulkner), Marion Abbott (Madge Larrabee), Grace Reals (Terese), Nellie Robinson (Mrs. Smeedley).

5224. ———. ———. Scranton, Pa.: August 7-13, 1916.

Credits: Producer, S. Z. Poli; Director, Augustin Glassmire.

Cast: Walter Richardson (Sherlock Holmes), Stewart E. Wilson (Dr. Watson), Henry Carleton (James Larrabee), Arthur Buchanan (Professor Moriarty), Kerwin Wilkinson (Sidney Prince), Edouard D'Oize (John Forman), Willie Wheeler (Billy), James Brennan (Jim Craigin), Renton Day (Thomas Leary), Wilbur Norman ("Lightfoot" McTague), Tony Hodges (John), Helen Gillingwater (Mrs. Faulkner

and Parsons), Edith Winchester (Madge Larrabee), Bertha Mann (Alice Faulkner).

5225. ———. ———. Pasadena, Calif.: Pasadena Community Playhouse, November 6-22, 1922.

Credits: Director, Gilmor Brown; Assistant, Eloise Sterling; Chairman of Production and Wardrobe Committee, Jerry Jerrems; Stage Settings, F. C. Huxley, H. E. Billheimer, and H. Arden Edwards; Incidental Music, Justin Gilbert.

Cast: Joseph Bell (Sherlock Holmes), Everett McCammon (Dr. Watson), Glenn Balch (Benjamin Forman), Frederic Wright (Billy), Edwin F. Gillette (Sir Edward Leighton), Russell M. Guthridge (Count Von Stalburg), Edward Murphey (Professor Moriarty), Cyrus Kendall (James Larrabee), Merwin Gouldthrite (Sidney Prince), George Sabin (Alf Bassick), Godfrey Mortimer (Craigin), Kent Blanche (Tim Leary), Allan Bartlett ("Lightfoot" McTague), Herbert Sollars (John), Edna Holbrook Bliss (Parsons), Ruth Pollock (Alice Faulkner), Dorothy Hooper (Mrs. Faulkner), Cloyde Duval Dalzell (Madge Larrabee), Estelle Tennis (Terese), Ruth Finnell (Mrs. Smeedley).

5226. ———. ———. Washington, D.C.: National Theatre, January 29-February 4, 1923. Philadelphia: Broad Street Theatre, 1923.

Credits: Producer, Charles Frohman; Manager, Joseph R. Williams; Stage Director, F. Cecil Butler.

Cast: William Gillette (Sherlock Holmes), Edward Fielding (Dr. Watson), Harold West (Benj. Forman), Dorian Anderson (Billy), Thomas A. Braidon (Sir Edward Leighton), Ralph Kirkwood (Count Von Stalburg), Leslie Stowe (Professor Moriarty), E. J. Ratcliffe (James Larrabee), William Podmore (Sidney Prince), Harry M. Cooke (Alf. Bassick), Henry Morey (Craigin), Fred Fulton (Tim Leary), Cyril Ingram ("Lightfoot" McTague), Robert Bert (John), Harry James (Parsons), Nora Swinburne (Alice Faulkner), Zeffie Tilbury (Mrs. Faulkner), Ada Sinclair (Madge Larrabee), Raphaella Ottiano (Terese), Mary Rawlston (Mrs. Smeedley).

5227. ———. ———. New York: Cosmopolitan Theatre, February 20-March 3, 1928.

Credits: Director, Clifford Brooke; Supervisor, Mabel Brownell.

Cast: Robert Warwick (Sherlock Holmes), Stanley Logan (Dr. Watson), Philip Heege (Forman), George Alison (Sir Edward Leighton), J. H. Brewer (Count Von Stalburg), Fred L. Tiden (Jim Larrabee), Frank Keenan (Dr. Moriarty), Horace Braham (Sid Prince), Conway Wingfield (Bassick), Edward Rose (Jim Craigin), John Littell (Tim Leary), Ralph Vincent

Actors, Performances, & Recordings

Plays

William Gillette, actor and playwright (5205-5239).
(The Bettmann Archive)

("Lightfoot" McTague), Robert Linden (John), Raymond Guion (Billy), Edgar Henning (Parsons), Vivian Martin (Alice Faulkner), Julia Hoyt (Madge Larrabee), Fritzi Scheff (Terese), Jennie A. Eustace (Mrs. Faulkner).

Although *Sherlock Holmes* was played in modern dress, the text of the play remained the same as in its original production without any other modernization except that a musical score written for the first production was omitted.

5228. ———. ———. "Farewell Tour," 1929-1930, 1931-1932.
Partial list of performances: Springfield, Mass.: November 15, 1929. Boston: Hollis Street Theatre, November 18-? 1929. New York: New Amsterdam Theatre, November 25, 1929-January 4, 1930. 45 performances. Washington, D.C.: National Theatre, January 6-11, 1930. Baltimore: January 13-? 1930. Newark: Shubert Theatre, January 20-? 1930. Philadelphia: January 27-February ? 1930. Cleveland: Ohio Theatre, April 7-? 1930. Boston: Colonial Theatre, December 28, 1931-? Wilmington, Del.: March 19, 1932. Princeton, N.J.: May 12, 1932.
Cast: William Gillette (Sherlock Holmes), Wallis Clark (Dr. Watson), Brinsley Shaw (John Forman), Byron Russell (Sir Edward Leighton), Alfred Ansel (Count Von Stalburg), John Miltern (Professor Moriarty), Montague Shaw (James Larrabee), William Postance (Sidney Prince), F. Augustus Keough (Alfred Bassick), William H. Barwald (Jim Craigin), Herbert Wilson (Thomas Leary), Henry

Lambert ("Lightfoot" McTague), Fred Tasker (John), Burford Hampden (Billy), Donald Campbell (Parsons), Peg Entwistle (Alice Faulkner), Dorothy Peabody Russell (Mrs. Faulkner), Roberta Beatty (Madge Larrabee), Kate Byron (Thérèse), Rose Kingston (Mrs. Smeedley).

5229. ———. ———. Washington, D.C.: The Roadside Theatre, August 10-? 1936.
Credits: Staged by Harrold A. Weinberger; Settings, Edith I. Allen; Costumes, Dorothy Croissant; Pianist, Jeanne Brayshaw.
Cast: George Farrington (Sherlock Holmes), S. Carlton Ayers (Dr. Watson), Milton Freedman (John Forman), Edward Stevlingson (Sir Edward Leighton), Blake B. Espey (Count Von Stalburg), Fred Haskin, Jr. (Professor Moriarty), Harrold A. Weinberger (James Larrabee), Harrison Libbey (Sidney Prince), John Rappolt (Alfred Bassick), Edward Stevlingson (Jim Craigin), John McKnight (Thomas Leary), Blake B. Espey ("Lightfoot" McTague), Frank S. Koonce (John), Frank S. Koonce (Billy), John McKnight (Parsons), Adele Gusack (Alice Faulkner), Joanne Adams (Mrs. Faulkner), Betty Gray (Madge Larrabee), Jean Smith (Terese), Joanne Adams (Mrs. Smeedley).

5230. ———. ———. Michigan City, Ind.: The Theatre of the Dunes, July 4-6, 1941. 3 performances.
Credits: Staged by L. Newell Tarrant; Settings, Gulielma Daves.
Cast: Robert Claborne (Sherlock Holmes); Leake Bevil (Dr. Watson), John Alnutt (John Forman), Frank Chant (Sir Edward Leighton), Alan Stapleton (Count Von Stalburg), Robert Leser (Professor Moriarty), John Morgan (Jim Larrabee), Gene Gambrill (Jim Craigin), Frank Hopkins (Thomas Leary), Robert Enright ("Lightfoot" McTague), Mark Hipkins (John), David Ogren (Billy), Rosa Neil Reynolds (Parsons), Dolores Crane (Alice Faulkner), Laura Alnutt (Mrs. Faulkner), Phoebe Anne Petersen (Madge Larrabee), Virginia Stevens (Thérèse).

5231. ———. ———. Amherst, Mass.: Kirby Theater, Amherst College, September 18-20, 1970. 3 performances.
Credits: Director and Designer, Walter Boughton; Lighting and Technical Direction, Ralph McGoun; Stage Manager, Timothy Fort.
Cast: Geoffrey Keller (Sherlock Holmes), Morris Bailey (Dr. Watson), Elaine Bromka (Madge Larrabee), Timothy Fort (John Forman), Marie Melaugh (Terese), Robert Brown (James Larrabee), Peter Trencher (Sidney Prince), Deborah Kelly (Alice Faulkner), Robert Murphy (Professor Moriarty), George Spelvin (John), Julian Decyk (Alfred Bassick), Steven Sarafian

(Billy), Graham Brown ("Bull" Craigin), David Rimmer ("Lightfoot" Leary), Oronoco Green ("Dummy" McTague), Kenneth Hoxsie (Parsons), Joshua Karter (Count Von Stalburg), Chauncey Panncefort (Sir Edward Leighton), Paul Jensen (Presiding at the pianoforte).

5232. ———. *Sherlock Holmes: A Drama in Four Acts, Being a Hitherto Unpublished Episode in the Career of the Great Detective and Showing His Connection with the Strange Case of Miss Faulkner.* [New York: Z. & L. Rosenfield, 1900.] 53, 48, 35, 44 leaves. Typescript.
Promptbook for the New York production.
Location: Library & Museum of the Performing Arts at Lincoln Center.

5233. *William Gillette in Sherlock Holmes, as Produced at the Garrick Theatre, New York.* Published with the authorization of Mr. Charles Frohman. New York: R. H. Russell, 1900. [16] p. illus.
A souvenir program.

5234. *Charles Frohman Presents William Gillette in "Sherlock Holmes."* [London: Nassau Press, 1901.] 10 p.
———, *The Playgoer* [New York] (November 1907), 79-86.
———, *CPBook*, 1, No. 3 (Winter 1965), 57-60.
Program for the first performance of this play at the Royal Lyceum Theatre.

5235. *William Gillette in Sherlock Holmes, as Produced at the Garrick Theatre, New York; The Lyceum Theatre, London; Etc.* Published with the authorization of Mr. Charles Frohman. New York: R. H. Russell, 1902. [16] p. illus.
A souvenir program.

5236. *Sherlock Holmes: Farewell Appearances of William Gillette, 1929-1930.* [November 22, 1929.] [16] p. illus.
Contents: The Cast - The Scenes. - Foreword, by William Gillette - Sherlock Holmes: A Little History of the World's Most Famous Fictional Character, by Frederic Dorr Steele. - William Gillette — Hail and Farewell, by Clayton Hamilton. - William Gillette's Return to the Stage, by Walter Prichard Eaton. - The Return of William Gillette.
A souvenir program.

5237. Gillette, William. *Sherlock Holmes: A Drama in Four Acts.* Adapted by Arthur Conan Doyle [sic] and William Gillette from the story by Arthur Conan Doyle entitled "The Strange Case of Miss Faulkner." Revised 1922 by Arthur Conan Doyle [sic] and William Gillette. London: S. French, Ltd.; New York: S. French, 1922. 123 p. (French's Acting Edition, No. 489)

5238. ———. With title: *Sherlock Holmes: A Play, Wherein Is Set Forth The Strange Case of Miss Alice Faulkner,* by William Gillette. Based on Sir Arthur Conan Doyle's Incomparable Stories. With an introduction by Vincent Starrett. Preface to this edition by William Gillette. Reminiscent notes by Frederic Dorr Steele and line drawings by Frederic Dorr Steele. Garden City, N.Y.: Doubleday, Doran & Co., 1935. xxx, 191 p.

5239. ———. With title: "Sherlock Holmes: A Melodrama in Four Acts," *Famous Plays of Crime and Detection: From Sherlock Holmes to Angel Street.* Compiled by Van H. Cartmell and Bennett Cerf. Introduction by John Chapman. Philadelphia: The Blakiston Co., 1946. p. 1-77.
———. ———, ———. Freeport, N. Y.: Books for Libraries Press, [1971]. p. 1-77.

Reviews of above play: Athenaeum, 2 (September 14, 1901), 360; *Boston Advertiser* (February 19, 1901); *Boston Transcript* (November 1, 1910) (K. M.); *Buffalo Express* (October 24, 1899); *Criterion* (November 1899), 21 (J. I. C. Clarke); *Current Literature,* 50 (January 1911), 73-81; *Dramatic Criticism,* Vol. 3, 1900-1901 (London: Greening & Co., 1902), 257-260 (J. T. Grein), and reprinted in *SHJ,* 4, No. 1 (Winter 1958), 21-22; *New York Daily Mirror* (November 27, 1929) (Walter Winchell); *New York Dramatic Mirror* (November 18, 1899); (October 16, 1915), 9; *New York Evening Post* (November 26, 1929) (Wilella Waldorf); *New York Herald Tribune Books* (December 1, 1935), 44 (W. P. Eaton); *New York Telegram* (November 26, 1929) (Samuel Spewach); *New York Telegraph* (December 6, 1910); (October 12, 1915); *New York Times* (October 24, 1899), 5; (November 5, 1899), 18; (November 7, 1899), 5; (November 4, 1902), 9; (March 7, 1905), 9; (October 12, 1915), 11; (October 17, 1915), VI, 8; (February 21, 1928), 18; (November 18, 1929), 20; (November 24, 1929), X, 1, 2; (November 26, 1929), 28; (December 10, 1929), 36; *New York Tribune* (November 7, 1899); *Post Express* [Rochester, N.Y.] (October 14, 1910); *Saturday Review of Literature,* 13 (January 4, 1936), 18 (H. F.); *Stage,* 13 (October 1935), 76 (Earle Walbridge); 14 (August 1937), 90-91; *Tatler,* No. 12 (September 18, 1901), 573 (J. M. B.); *Theatre,* 51 (February 1930), 68; *Theatre Arts Monthly,* 14 (February 1930), 105, 112-113 (John Hutchens); 20 (January 1936), 82; *The Times* (September 10, 1901), 4.

5240. Goldman, James. *They Might Be Giants.* London: Theatre Royal, June 28-July 29, 1961.
Cast: Harry H. Corbett (Sherlock Holmes), Avis Bunnage (Dr. Mildred Watson), Joan Littlewood, John Junkin,

Brian Murphy, Barbara Ferris, Declan Mulholland.

"In *They Might Be Giants* Holmes wears a deerstalker and Inverness cape, but he is actually a rich madman—a 'classic case of paranoia' as he is called by the woman psychiatrist who comes to serve as his amourous Dr. Watson." (Felix Barker)

Reviews: *London Evening News* (June 29, 1961) (Felix Barker), and reprinted in *SHJ*, 5, No. 3 (Winter 1961), 95; *The Times* (June 29, 1961), 5.

5241. Greene, Clay M. *The Remarkable Pipe Dream of Mr. Shylock Holmes*. Brooklyn: Columbia Theatre, February 26-March 4, 1900.

Cast: Alexander Clark (The Remarkable Mr. Holmes), Thos. Leary (Mr. Ditto, Professor Moriarty), Harry Kelly (The Heavy Mr. Larrabee), Ulric B. Collins (The Villainous Mr. Bassick), Horace Thrum (The Assistant Villainous Mr. Leary), William Sellery (The Assistant Villainous Mr. McTague), Edward Begley (The Pugnacious Billy), Amy Ashmore (The Peculiar Miss Faulkner), Mabel Russell (The Wicked Mrs. Larrabee), The Pipe (By Itself).

A one-act skit that appeared with *'Round New York in 80 Minutes*.

5242. Hardwick, Michael and Mollie. *Four Sherlock Holmes Plays: One-Act Plays*, by Michael & Mollie Hardwick from stories by Sir Arthur Conan Doyle. London: John Murray, [1964]. vi, 129 p.

Second impression published in a paperback edition in 1966.

Contents: Foreword. - Notes for Producers. - The Speckled Band. - Charles Augustus Milverton. - The Mazarin Stone. - The Blue Carbuncle.

Review: *SHJ*, 7, No. 1 (Winter 1964), 28 (Lord Donegall).

5243. ———. *The Game's Afoot: Sherlock Holmes Plays*, by Michael & Mollie Hardwick from stories by Sir Arthur Conan Doyle. London: John Murray, [1969]. x, 102 p.

Contents: Foreword. - Notes for Producers. - The Three Garridebs. - The Reigate Squires. - Black Peter. - The Dying Detective.

Review: *SHJ*, 9, No. 3 (Winter 1969), 106 (Lord Donegall).

5244. Hershey, John. *The Sign of the Four: A Sherlock Holmes Adventure in One Act*. Adapted by John Hershey from the story of the same name by Sir Arthur Conan Doyle. New York: Samuel French, 1937. 37 p.

5245. Kelly, Tim. *If Sherlock Holmes Were a Woman: A Comedy in One Act for Seven Girls*. Boston, Mass.: Baker's Plays, [1969]. 30 p.

Shirley Holmes, a young college student with a vivid imagination, lives her life in imitation of the master detective. Her conversation is a continual quoting from the Sacred Writings. Her big moment comes when the housemother in her dorm is found dead under odd circumstances. Shirley promptly locks all the suspects in a communal study and attempts to solve the "murder" as Holmes might have done. A peculiar twist solves the crime in spite of Shirley's deduction, but her faith in Holmes remains unshaken.

5246. ———. *The Last of Sherlock Holmes: A Comedy in One Act*. Boston, Mass.: Baker's Plays, [1970]. 19 p.

During a typical day at 221B Baker Street, Watson brings news that Professor Moriarty, captured by Holmes that very morning despite an ingenious disguise, has escaped once again. Now it is up to Holmes to prove, via the new tool of fingerprinting, the arch-villain's true identity. It turns out to be Watson, who has already prepared a death certificate for his old friend. By the time Holmes reacts to the funny-tasting wine the doctor has served him, Watson is out the door with a lovely new client heading somewhere romantic for a spot of supper.

5247. Knight, Joan. *The Hound of the Baskervilles*. Adapted for the Perth Repertory Company by Joan Knight. Perth, Scotland: Perth Theatre, April 7-17, 1971.

Credits: Director, Mike Ockrent; Design, Shaun Irwin; Lighting, Jonathan Allen.

Cast: Tim Preece (Sherlock Holmes), Richard Simpson (Dr. Watson), Irene Beveridge (Maid), Andrew Burt (Dr. Mortimer), William Corlett (Sir Henry Baskerville), Charles Bentley (John Clayton), Colin Higgins (Barrymore), Gregor Sampson (The Stranger), Virginia Stark (Mrs. Barrymore), Ian Bamforth (Jack Stapleton), Jean Rimmer (Beryl Stapleton), Sam Brown (Convict), Charles Bentley (George Frankland), Virginia Stark (Laura Lyons), David Birch (Inspector Lestrade).

Review: *SHJ*, 10, No. 2 (Summer 1971), 62-63 (Nicholas Utechin).

5248. Mitchell, Basil. *The Holmeses of Baker Street*. London: Lyric Theatre, February 15-?, 1933.

Credits: Producer, Leon M. Lion; Adapters, William J. Rapp and Leonardo Bercovici.

Cast: Felix Aylmer (Sherlock Holmes), Sir Nigel Playfair (Dr. Watson), Rosemary Ames (Shirley Holmes), Alfred Clark (William), Vincent Holman (Detective-Inspector Withers), Martin Walker (Mr. Canning), Eva Moore (Mrs. Watson), Ernest Borrow (Laker), Ewell B. Gessing ("Scrunchy" Malone), Joan Cary (Maid), Henry Hallatt (Sir Joseph Masterman).

Reviews: *Illustrated London News*, 182

(February 25, 1933), 286; *Spectator*, 150 (February 24, 1933), 248; *Theatre World*, 19 (March 1933), 122 (F.J.D.); *The Times* (February 16, 1933), 10; *Week-End Review* (February 25, 1933), 202.

5249. ————. ————. New York: Masque Theatre, December 9, 1936-January 23, 1937. 53 performances.

Credits: Producer, Elizabeth Miele; Adapters, William J. Rapp and Leonardo Bercovici; Staged by Reginald Bach; Settings, Kate Drain Lawson.

Cast: Cyril Scott (Sherlock Holmes), Conway Wingfield (Dr. Watson), Helen Chandler (Shirley Holmes), John Parrish (Williams), Stuart Casey (Inspector Withers), Don Dillaway (Mr. Canning), Cecilia Loftus (Mrs. Watson), Raymond Bramley (Inspector Laker), Beatrice Graham (Maid), Arthur Marlowe (Joe Murray), Jack Lee (Tom Braggs), Murray Stephens (Arthur Singer).

Reviews: *Brooklyn Daily Eagle* (December 10, 1936) (Arthur Pollock); *New York American* (December 10, 1936) (Gilbert W. Gabriel); *New York Daily Mirror* (December 10, 1936) (Robert Coleman); *New York Daily News* (December 10, 1936) (Burns Mantle); *New York Evening Journal* (December 10, 1936) (John Anderson); *New York Herald Tribune* (December 10, 1936) (Richard Watts, Jr.); *New York Post* (December 10, 1936) (John Mason Brown); *New York Sun* (December 10, 1936), (Richard Lockridge); *New York Times* (December 10, 1936), 34 (Brooks Atkinson); *New York World-Telegram* (December 10, 1936) (Douglas Gilbert); *Variety*, 125 (December 10, 1936), 60 (Ibee).

5250. Murray, John. "A Case for Mrs. Hudson," *Plays*, 11, No. 7 (April 1952), 1-14, 85.

————. ————, *Mystery Plays for Young People: A Collection of Royalty-Free One-Act Dramas of Mystery and Suspense.* Boston: Plays, Inc., 1956. p. 148-152.

In the absence of Sherlock Holmes, Mrs. Hudson solves a mystery involving a stolen ring.

5251. Parry, John. *The Hound of the Overspills.* Cambridge University, Trinity Theatre, February 26-March 3, 1969.

Cast: Prince Charles (Sherlock Holmes), [Unknown] (Dr. Watson), [Unknown] (Sir Cummerbund Overspill), [Unknown] (Gipsy Girl), [Unknown] (Inspector Station).

A portion of the collegiate revue *Revolution*, which is produced annually by the Dryden Society of Trinity College, Cambridge University, England. The script for this travesty is reprinted in *CPBook*, No. 19 (June 1969), 367-372.

5252. Piggin, Julia R. "The Case of the Copper Beeches," *Scholastic Teacher* [Practical English edition], 39 (October 14, 1965), 14-16, 23, 27-29, 37.

A dramatization of "The Adventure of the Copper Beeches."

5253. Rathbone, Ouida. *Sherlock Holmes.* Boston: Majestic Theatre, October 10, 1953. 1 performance. New York: New Century Theatre, October 30-31, 1953. 3 performances.

Credits: Producer, Bill Doll; Staged by Reginald Denham; Settings and Costumes, Stewart Chaney; Incidental Music, Alexander Steinert.

Cast: Basil Rathbone (Sherlock Holmes), Jack Raine (Dr. Watson), Elwyn Harvey (Mrs. Hudson), John Dodsworth (Rt. Hon. Trelawney Hope), Richard Wendley (Arthur Cadogan West), Eileen Peel (Lady Hope), Gregory Morton (Eduardo Lucas), Margit Forssgren (Anna), Chester Stratton (Count Louis de Rothière), Jarmila Novotna (Irene Adler), Terence Kilburn (Walker), Bryan Herbert (Lestrade), Mary Orr (Miss Alice Dunbar), Evan Thomas (Andrew), Thomas Gomez (Professor Moriarty), Martin Brandt (Hugo Oberstein), Ludwig Roth (Captain Von Herling), St. John Phillipe (Prince Bulganin), Arthur N. Stenning (Gregson), Alfred A. Hesse (Villard).

Contents: Act I Scene 1. 221B Baker Street, London. An evening, March 1895. Scene 2. 16 Godolphin Square. The same night. - Act II. Scene 1, 221B Baker Street. The same night. Scene 2. 13 Caulfield Gardens. Early the following morning. Scene 3. A chalet overlooking the Reichenbach Falls. Three days later. - Act. III. The chalet overlooking Reichenbach Falls. Two months later.

Mrs. Basil Rathbone adapted her play primarily from Scan, Bruc, and Fina.

5254. ————. *"Sherlock Holmes": A New Play in Three Acts.* [1953] 57, 45, 25 p. Unpublished typescript.

Location: James Bliss Austin, Pittsburgh.

5255. "Sherlock Holmes," *On Stage.* Boston: The Jerome Press, October 1953. [8] p.

Program for the first appearance of this play at the Majestic Theatre.

5256. ————, *The Playbill for the New Century Theatre* [October 1953], 9-24.

Contents: Credits and Cast. - Scenes. Who's Who in the Cast.

5257. ————. New York: Program Pub. Co., [October 1953]. [16] p.

A souvenir program for the New Century Theatre production that includes an article entitled "Life with Sherlock Holmes" in which Ouida Rathbone tells how her play came to be written.

Reviews of above play: Cue (October 24, 1953), 16 (Edgar W. Smith), and reprinted in part in *BSJ*, 4, No. 1 (January 1954), 61-

62, and in *CPBook*, 2, No. 5-6 (Summer-Fall 1965), 108; *New York Daily Mirror* (November 1, 1953) (Robert Coleman), and reprinted in *CPBook*, 1, No. 1 (Summer 1964), 15; *New York Daily News* (October 31, 1953) (John Chapman); *New York Herald Tribune* (October 31, 1953) (Walter F. Kerr); *New York Journal American* (October 31, 1953) (John McClain); *New York Post* (November 1, 1953) (Richard Watts, Jr.), and reprinted in *CPBook*, 2, No. 5-6 (Summer-Fall 1965), 120; *New York Times* (October 31, 1953), 11 (Brooks Atkinson); (November 8, 1953), II, 1 (Brooks Atkinson); (November 15, 1953), II 3 (Reginald Denham); *New York World-Telegram and The Sun* (October 31, 1953) (William Hawkins); *New Yorker*, 29 (November 7, 1953), 75-76 (Wolcott Gibbs); *San Francisco Chronicle, This World* (November 1, 1953), 16 (Herbert Kupferberg); *Theatre Arts*, 38 (January 1954), 17; *Variety*, 192 (November 4, 1953), 61 (Hobe).

5258. Rice, Charles P. *The Sign of the Four.* Adapted from the novel by A. Conan Doyle. New York: West End Theatre, November 9-14, 1903. New York: F. F. Proctor's, January 11-16, 1904.

Credits: Producer, Charles L. Durban.

Cast: Walter Edwards (Sherlock Holmes), Charles D. Coburn (Dr. Watson), Van H. Kinze (Athelney Jones), Frank Tucker (Jonathan Small), Agnes Porter (Wiggins), Robert Lothian (Tonga), Leonard Hoyt (Major John Sholto), William Sheetz (Lal Chowdar), George Willard (Mordicia Smith), William Davis (Jim Smith), Mabel Hazlett (Mary Morstan), Georgine Brandon (Mrs. John Sholto), Mrs. Frank Tucker (Mrs. Hudson), Louise Lander (Bessie Hudson), Jessie Barnes (Mrs. Smith).

Review: New York Dramatic Mirror, 50 (November 21, 1903), 17.

5259. ———. ———. Nashville, Tenn.: Bijou Theater, September 14-?, 1904.

Credits: Producer, Charles L. Durban.

Cast: Walter Edwards (Sherlock Holmes), Frank Sylvester (Dr. Watson), Jane Wheatley (Mrs. John Sholto), Marion Lore (Mary Morstan), Marie Justice (Wiggins), Virginia Kinsley (Mrs. Hudson), Louise Lander (Bessie Hudson), Messrs. Willard, Toy, Tucker and Bennett.

Review: Nashville American (September 15, 1904), 8.

5260. ———. ———. Adapted from the novel by A. Conan Doyle. [New York: 1903.] 110 leaves. Unpublished typescript.

Location: Library & Museum of the Performing Arts at Lincoln Center.

5261. Rogers, Charles. *Sherlock Holmes* Glasgow: May 1894.

Partial cast: John Webb (Sherlock Holmes), St. John Hammond (Dr. Watson). The first Holmes play.

5262. St. Clair, Robert. *Mark Twain's A Double Barrelled Detective Story: A Mystery-Comedy in Three Acts.* Adapted for the stage by Robert St. Clair. Manuscript editing and general revisions by Verne E. Powers. Evanston, Ill.: Row, Peterson and Co., [1954]. 144 p. illus.

Illustrated with scenes from the Clearview High School, Lorain, Ohio (March 25-26, 1954), and the Robbinsdale High School, Robbinsdale, Minn. (May 20-21, 1954) productions.

The following are credits and cast for the Ohio premiere:

Partial credits: Director, Valerie Jenkins; Technical Director, Estes Bonsor.

Cast: Donald Carek (Sherlock Holmes), Joe Wozniak (Arthur ["Archy"] Stillman), Joanne Lucas (Mrs. Stillman), Virginia Rust (Nancy Palmer), Elaine Simko (Amanda Sink), Martha Beck (Rosemary Hillyer), Kenneth Book (Sammy Hillyer), Carole Monos (Mrs. Hogan), Virginia Wozniak (Katy Hogan), Marie Wozniak (Sadie Smith), Jack Mason (Jacob Fuller), Ruth Nore ("Injun" Hattie), Harvey Teaman (Flint Buckner), John Zivic (Fetlock Jones), Steve Moldovan (Pat Riley), Brian Carey (Donovan), Darrell Deitrich (Ham Sandwich), Carolyn Barnes (Millie).

"The time is approximately the year 1900. The visible action of the play is initiated in Mrs. Stillman's house in New England and concluded in the 'Hope Tavern,' a small inn situated in the Western mining town of Hope Canyon, Colorado, about a year later."

5263. Spence, Wall. *The Sign of the Four: A Mystery Play in Three Acts.* Minneapolis, Minn.: The Northwestern Press, 1940. [100] p.

"Suggested by Sir Arthur Conan Doyle's famous Sherlock Holmes story of the same name."

5264. Terry, J. E. Harold, and Arthur Rose. *The Return of Sherlock Holmes.* Cardiff: Playhouse, October 1-? 1923. London: Princes Theatre, October 9, 1923-January 26, 1924. 130 performances.

Credits: Producer, Eille Norwood; Presented by B. A. Meyer; Stage Director, Stafford Hilliard; Stage Manager, Paul Gill; Scenery, Paul Gill and J. Crosbie-Frazer; Musical Director, Edward Mervyn.

Cast: Eille Norwood (Sherlock Holmes), H. G. Stoker (Dr. Watson), Edward Mervyn (Sims—Manservant to Dr. Shlessinger), Hilda Moore (Cecilia—Shlessinger's Sister), Stafford Hilliard (Mortimer Profennis —A Scientist), Molly Kerr (Lady Frances Carfax), Arthur Cullin (The Rev. Dr. Shlessinger—alias "Holy Peters"), Eric Stanley (Charles Augustus Milverton—A

Blackmailer), Ann Desmond (Jenny Saunders), Victor Evans (Billy Cartwright—A Messenger Boy), Lauderdale Maitland (Col. Sebastian Moran—Late of the Indian Army; successor to Prof. Moriarty), Lichfield Owen (Old Meff), C. Lander (Scottie), Harley Merica (John Willie), J. S. Carre (Pat), Jack Minster (Froggie), Edward Mervyn (Ike), Geoffrey Bevan (John Clay—Foreman of Moran's gang), Noel Dainton (The Hon. Philip Green—affianced to Lady Frances), J. S. Carre (Mons. Oscar Meunier—A Modeller in Wax), Paul Gill (Detective-Inspector Lestrade of Scotland Yard), Esme Hubbard (Mrs. Hudson).

Music: Overture - "Sherlock Holmes" by Edward Mervyn. - "Melody in G" and "Berceuse" by Eille Norwood.

Contents: Act I. At Dr. Shlessinger's. - Act II. At Dr. Watson's. - Act III. Scene 1. The Entrance Hall of an Unfurnished House. Scene 2. The Basement of the same. - Act IV. At Sherlock Holmes's.

Reviews: Bystander (November 21, 1923), 578-579 ("Jingle"); *Illustrated Sporting and Dramatic News* (November 24, 1923), 470; *New Statesman,* 35 (August 9, 1930), 567-568 (Desmond MacCarthy), and reprinted in *Essays of the Year, 1930-1931* (London: The Argonaut Press, 1931), 204-210; *New York Times* (October 11, 1923), 23; *Stage* (October 1923), and reprinted in *Charles Augustus Milverton on Stage, Screen and Radio* (London: The Milvertons of Hampstead, 1960).

5265. ———. ———. Regent Theatre, 1930.
Partial cast: Ivan Agabeg (Sherlock Holmes), Mr. Bates (Dr. Watson).

5266. ———. ———. Revised by L. Arthur Rose and Ernest Dudley. Bromley, Kent: New Theatre, January 20-February ? 1953.
Credits: Producer, Stanley Van Beers; Director of Productions, Geoffrey Edwards; Stage Director, Joan Craft; Stage Manager, Don Deuchars; Settings, John Burnard; Scenery, Joseph Stokes and Paul Southey.
Cast: Geoffrey Edwards (Sherlock Holmes), Jack Lambert (Dr. Watson), Yvonne Manners (Cecilia), Henry Soskin (Mortimer Porfennis), Pay Sandys (Lady Frances Carfax), Alan Edwards (The Rev. Dr. Shlessinger), Edward Wheatleigh (Charles Augustus Milverton), Edna Petrie (Jenny Saunders), Frederick Murphy (Billy Cartwright), Willoughby Goddard (Col. Sebastian Moran), Myles Rudge (The Hon. Philip Green), Scott Harrold (Detective-Inspector Lestrade), Barbara Bolton (Mrs. Hudson).
Contents: Act. I. Scene 1. The Lounge Hall at Dr. Shlessinger's. Scene 2. At Sherlock Holmes', Baker Street. - Act. II. Scene 1. The Lounge Hall at Dr. Shlessinger's. Scene 2. At Sherlock Holmes', Baker Street.

5267. Wallace, Edgar. *Sexton Blake.* London: Prince Edward Theatre, September 18-October 11, 1930.
Cast: Arthur Wontner (Sexton Blake), Eve Gray (Muriel Raeburn), John Roderick (Tinker), Wilfred Babbage (Paul Cairns), David Hawthorne (Detective-Inspector Coutts), Arthur Macrae (Leslie Waring), Dora Gregory (Mrs. Bardell), Pauline Loring (Lydia Carrington), Harcourt Brooke (Creeper), Frank Tennant (Selton).
In this play Arthur Wontner appeared in his first Sherlock Holmes role—as Holmes's imitator, Sexton Blake.
Reviews: Illustrated London News, 177 (September 27, 1930), 550, *The Times* (September 19, 1930), 8.

5268. Watson, Malcolm, and Edward La Serre. *Sheerluck Jones, or Why D'Guillette Him Off?* London: Terry's Theatre, October 29, 1901-February 1, 1902.
Cast: Clarence Blakiston (Sheerluck Jones), Carter Pickford (Dr. Rotson), J. Egerton Hubbard (John Toanfroman), J. Willes (Prof. MacGillicuddy), Russell Norrie (James Scarabee), Gunnis Davis (Little Billee), Alice Powell (Madge Scarabee), Gordon Lee (Alice Baulkner).
Contents: 1st Par. A Musical Evening at the Scarabees. - 2nd. Par. Sheerluck Finds His Match and Lights a Pipe with It. - 3rd Par. The Trail of the Cigar. - 4th Par. The Pleasures of Home.
"N. B.—No one arriving after 10 o'clock, and very few seated before that hour, can possibly understand the plot of the piece."
A capital travesty of Gillette's play.
Reviews: The Playgoer [London], 1 (November 1901), 172, 298; *The Times* (October 30, 1901), 4.

5269. Yew, Elizabeth. *The Doomsday Book: A Pastiche in Four Acts.* 82 p. Unpublished typescript.
Performed at the Lowell High School in San Francisco on May 14, 1965.

5270. *You See Too: A Musical Farce in Seven Paroxisms.* Performed on board a British warship in 1915.
Partial cast: G. E. A. Jackson (Sherlock Holmes), E. L. B. Damant (Dr. Watson), P. E. Goldsmith (Professor Moriarty).
Review: The Bookman, 42 (September 1915), 3-4.

CZECH

5271. Skopeček, Jan. *Baskervillský pes.* Na motivy románu sira Arthura Conana Doyla "Pes baskervillský." Praha: DILIA [Czechoslovak Literary Agency], [1965]. 126 p.
A play in three acts based on *The Hound of the Baskervilles.*

377

Plays

DANISH

5272. *Baskervilles Hund: Detektivkomedie i 5 akter (8 afdelinger).* Efter Conan Doyles roman af samme navn. København: Carl Allers Establissement, 1943. 63 p. illus.

DUTCH

5273. Terry, J. E. Harold, and Arthur Rose. *De Terugkeer van Sherlock Holmes.* [The Return of Sherlock Holmes.] Tr. into Dutch by F. Hageman. Amsterdam: Grand Theatre, 1924.

Credits: Producer, Henri de Vries.

Cast: Henri de Vries (Sherlock Holmes), Th. van Schaick (Dr. Watson), Minny de Jong (Billy Cartwright), Mies Versteeg (Lady Frances Carfax), Andre van Dijk (Philip Green), H. Kluizenaar (Lestrade), Anna Sluyters (Mrs. Hudson), Gerard Arbous (Moran), Ch. Laurentius (Domine Shlessinger), Mary Beeckman (Cecilia), J. Apel (Mortimer Porfennis), Piet te Nuyl (Milverton), W. Mols (John Clay), Carel Kuhn (Sims), F. Verhagen (Old Meff), Betty Brouwer (Jenny Saunders).

FRENCH

5274. Decourcelle, Pierre. *Sherlock Holmes: Pièce en cinq actes et six tableaux.* D'après l'original de Sir Arthur Conan Doyle [sic] et William Gillette. Paris: Théâtre Antoine, December 20, 1907-?

Cast: Gémier (Sherlock Holmes), Saillard (le docteur Watson), Harry-Baur (Le professeur Moriarty), Charlier (Orlebar), Maxence (Le comte Stahlberg), G. Flateau (Le baron d'Altenheim), Henry-Houry (Benjamin Forman), Jarrier (Bassik), G. Dalleu (Fletcher), Raoul Terrier (Bribb), Marchal (Jarvis), Marc Gérard (Fitton), Pierre Laurent (Billy), Fernand Liesse (John), Yvonne de Bray (Alice Brent), Renée Cogé (Madge Orlebar), Jeanne Even (Mistress Brent), Madeleine Farna (Thérèse).

5275. ———. ———. Paris: Pierre Lafitte, [1907]. 284 p. illus.

GERMAN

5276. Bonn, Ferdinand. *Der Hund von Baskerville: Schauspiel in vier Aufzügen aus dem schottischen Hochland.* Frei nach Motiven aus Poes und Doyles Novellen. Leipzig: Philipp Reclam jun., [1907]. 87 p. (Universal-Bibliothek, Nr. 4888)

First performed in Berlin at the Ferdinand Bonns Berliner Theater on January 17, 1907.

5277. ———. *Sherlock Holmes: Detektivkomödie in vier Aufzügen.* Frei nach Motiven aus Conan Doyles Roman-serie. Einrichtung des Berliner Theaters. Leipzig: Philipp Reclam jun., [1906]. 78 p. (Universal-Bibliothek, Nr. 4839)

First performed in Berlin at the Ferdinand Bonns Berliner Theater on July 2, 1906.

5278. Bozenhard, Albert. *Sherlock Holmes: Detektiv-Komödie in vier Akten nach Conan Doyle und Gillette.* Munich: Münchener Volkstheater, July 24-? 1906.

Credits: Director, Lothar Mayring.

Cast: Lothar Mayring (Sherlock Holmes), Otto Kustermann (Dr. Watson), Caesar Beck (Professor Moriarty), Hermann Pfanz (James Larrabee), Alexandrine Malten (Madge Larrabee), Marga Tornegg (Alice Faulkner), Grete Konrad (Mrs. Smeedley), Rudolf Brunner (Sidney Prince), Max Baer (Craigin), Fritz Freisler (Alf Bassick), Anton Trenk (Tim Leary), Ludwig Robert (McTague), Bruno Kretschmar (Benj. Forman), Rosa Lindner (Thérèse), Mary Holm (Billy), Josef Bertoli (Parsons).

5279. Marcellus, [Hermann]. *Der blaue Klub: Sherlock-Holmes-Komödie in zwei Akten.* Leipzig: C. Glaser, [1909]. 75 p. (Glaser's Theater-Bibliothek, Nr. 131)

NORWEGIAN

5280. Gillette, William. *Sherlock Holmes og forbrydernes konge: Detektivkomedie i 5 Akter.* Kristiania (Oslo): Centralteatret, February 12-? 1902.

Partial cast: Ingolf Schanche (Sherlock Holmes), Stub Wiberg (Professor Moriarty).

5281. Svendsen, Lauritz. *Sherlock Holmes: Detektivkomedie i 7 Afdelinger.* Kristiania (Oslo): Centralteatret, February 16-March 12, 1902.

Cast: Ingolf Schanche (Sherlock Holmes), Jac. von der Lippe (Dr. Watson and Brigham Young [sic]), David Lunde (John Ferrier), Ragnhild Fredriksen (Lucy, Ferrier's adopted daughter; Countess Talbot), Halvor Urdahl (James Hope, Ferrier's step-son), Fredrik Wingar (Stangerson; Tobias Gregson), Erling Holck (Drebber), Inga Olsen (Mrs. Hudson), Rolf Lorentzen (Lestrade), Wilhelm Ringe (Barclay, a banker), Eugen Hovind (Arthur, son of Barclay; P. C. Rance), Helene Andersen (Edith Ward), Jenny Gronner (a maid).

RUSSIAN

5282. Bonn, Ferdinand. [*A Hellish Dog: "Baskerville Hound": A Play-Episode from the Adventures of Sherlock Holmes in 4 Acts.* Tr. from the German by E. Mattern and I. Marko. Moscow: The Theatre Library of M. A. Soklova, 1907.] 68 p.

5283. Decourcelle, Pierre. [*The King of Thieves: From the Latest Adventures of Sherlock Holmes: A Play in 5 Acts and 6 Scenes.* Tr. from the French by E. Ya. Berlinraut and D. D. Yazykov. Moscow: Literary Moscow Theatre Library of C. F. Rossokhin, 1908.] 110 p.

5284. Dinglestedt, N. F. ["The Baskerville Mystery (The Devil-Dog): A Drama in 5 Acts and 11 Scenes, from the Adventures of Sherlock Holmes," Based on the novel by Conan Doyle. *A Collection of Plays.* With drawings. St. Petersburg: Generalov Pub. House, 1908] 117 p.

SPANISH

5285. Bonet, José Salvador. *El traficante en cadáverse; o, Astucias de un detective: Traji-comedia en 7 actos, dividida en ocho cuadros, inspirada en una novela inglesa.* Barcelona: Viuda de J. Solé y Piqué, 1908. 101 p.

5286. Graells Soler, Emilio, and Enrique Casanovas. *Hazañas de Sherlock Holmes: Melodrama en seis actos.* Barcelona: Biblioteca Theatro popvlar, [191-]. 114 p.

5287. Jóver, Gonzalo, and Enrique Arryo. *La tragedia de Baskerville: Drama policiaco en cinco actos, el último dividido en dos cuadros, arreglo de la novela El Perro de Baskerville.* Bilbao: Teatro Trueba, April 7-? 1915.
   Cast: Sr. Comes (Sherlock Holmes), Sr. Socías (Dr. Watson), Srta. Ziu (Beryl), Sra. Camarero (Señora Barrymore), Srts. Larrea (M.) (Clara Lyons), Sr. Del Cerro (Enrique de Baskerville), Sr. Farnós (Stapleton), Sr. H. del Río (El Doctor Mortimer), Sr. Sender (Barrymore), Sr. Camarero (Franckland), Sr. Ratia (Seldon), Sr. Martí (Un cochero), Sr. Ratia (Un ordenanza de telégrafos), Sr. Santander (Un criado).

5288. ———. ———. Barcelona: Biblioteca "Teatro Mundial," 1915. 79 p.
   On cover: Madrid, Soc. de autores españoles.

5289. Millá [Gacio], Luis, and Guillermo X. Roura. *La captura de Raffles: ó, El triunfo de Sherlock Holmes: Melodrama moderno, en un prólogo cinco actos y once cuadros.* Barcelona: Establecimiento Tipográfico de Félix Costa, 1912. 83 p.
   On cover: Madrid, Sociedad de autores españoles.
   First performed in Barcelona at the Teatro Moderno on November 29, 1908.

5290. ———. *Nadie más fuerte que Sherlock-Holmes: Segunda parte de La capture de Raffles: Drama en seis actos.* Barcelona: Establecimiento Tipográfico de Félix Costa, 1913. 92 p.
   On cover: Madrid, Sociedad de autores españoles.
   First performed in Barcelona at the Teatro Arnau on February 27, 1909.

5291. Sierra Montoya, Miguel. *El robo del millón; o, De potencia a potencia* [*Holmes y Rafles* [sic] *burlados*]: *Comedia dramática en cuatro actos y seis cuadros.* Melilla: 1916. 1 v.

5292. Sucarrats, M. S. *El vendedor de cadáveres; o, El timo a 'la Gresham': Melodrama en siete actos y ocho cuadros.* Barcelona: Biblioteca "Teatro Mundial," 1916. 78 p.
   On cover: Madrid, Sociedad de autores españoles.
   First performed at the Teatro Balear in December 1915.

5293. Viteri, Heraclio S., and Enrique Grimau de Mauro. *Le aguja hueca* (*Lupin y Holmes*). Madrid: Coliseo Imperial, May 10-? 1912.
   Based on the novel with the same title, in French, by Maurice Leblanc.

SWEDISH

5294. Fröberg, Einar. *Sherlock Holmes på Stoke Moran.* Adapted and staged by Einar Fröberg. Gothenburg: Stora Teatern, October 21-November 9, 1912; March 29, 1913. 8 performances.
   Cast: Einar Fröberg (Sherlock Holmes), Henric Ljungberg (Dr. Watson), Hugo Björne (Lestrade), Richard Lund (Dr. Grimesby Roylott), A-L Fröberg, A. Sandels, F. Pilo, U. Lindholm, A. Ervall, O. Olson.
   Based on Doyle's play *The Speckled Band.*

5295. Gillette, William. *Sherlock Holmes.* Folkskådespel i 5 akter af A. Conan Doyle [sic] och William Gillette. Musiken efter engelska originalet. Stockholm: Folkets Hus' Amatör-Teater, April 5-May 19, 1902. 12 performances.
   Credits: Settings, Leonard Pettersson.
   Partial cast: Hr. Bergendorff (Sherlock Holmes), Hr. Lagerman (Moriarty), Frk. Sundell (Mrs. Larrabee), H. Bodin (Billy), Frk. S. Borgström.
   This was the first portrayal of Holmes on the Swedish stage.
   Reviews: Dagens Nyheter (April 6, 1902); *Svenska Dagbladet* (April 6, 1902).

5296. ———. ———. Folkskådespel i fem akter i bearbetning af Bob. Stockholm: Folk-Teatern, April 21-27, 1902. 7 performances.
   Partial cast: Hr. Bergvall (Sherlock Holmes), Hr. Strandberg (Moriarty), Hr.

Blom (Mr. Larrabee), Frk. Carlsson (Mrs. Larrabee), Frk. Hjort (Miss Alice Faulkner), Hr. Fastbom, Frk. Rydqvist.
Reviews: Dagens Nyheter (April 22, 1902); *Svenska Dagbladet* (April 22, 1902).

5297. ———. ———. Folkskådespel i 5 akter af Walter Christmas. (Fritt efter Conan Doyle.) Öfversättnig af Frans Hedberg. Stockholm: Svenska Teatern, April 24- May 29, 1902. 24 performances.
Partial cast: Knut Nyblom (Sherlock Holmes), Hr. Barcklind (Dr. Watson), Justus Hagman (Moriarty), Hr. Lavén (Mr. Larrabee), Fru Fahlman (Mrs. Larrabee), Maria Johansson (Miss Alice Faulkner), Victor Lundberg (Mikkel Shark), Fru Lambert.
Reviews: Dagens Nyheter (April 25, 1902); *Svenska Dagbladet* (April 25, 1902).

5298. ———. ———. Gothenburg: Folkteatern, October 28-November 25, 1902. 16 performances.
Cast: Emil Ljungqvist (Sherlock Holmes), Alfred Andersson (Dr. Watson), Albin Widberg (Moriarty), John Borg (Mr. Larrabee), Ida Östergren (Mrs. Larrabee), Gerda Thomé (Miss Alice Faulkner), E. Lindeberg, T. Jasson, H. Ljungqvist, Z. Eklund, I. Kalling, W. Mattsson, C. Westermark, B. Dahlström, H. Hartman, F. Hellström.

5299. ———. ———. Gothenburg: Stora Teatern, March 25, 1903. 1 performance.
Cast: Hugo Rönnblad's Company.

5300. ———. ———. Malmö: Malmö Teater, March 19-April 2, 1905. 7 performances.
Partial cast: Hugo Rönnblad (Sherlock Holmes), Victor Sjöström (Moriarty).
Review: Sydsvenska Dagbladet Snällposten (March 21, 1905).

5301. ———. ———. Öfversättning af Harald Thornberg. Hälsingborg: Helsingborgs Teater, January 26-28, 1906. 2 performances.
Partial cast: Hugo Rönnblad (Sherlock Holmes), Eric Zachrison (Moriarty), Mauritz Stiller (Mr. Larrabee), Ingeborg Rönnblad (Mrs. Larrabee), Louise Eneman (Miss Alice Faulkner).
Review: Helsingborgs Dagblad (January 27, 1906).

5302. ———. ———. Gothenburg: Stora Teatern, December 1-7, 1908. 7 performances.
Cast: Hugo Rönnblad (Sherlock Holmes), Alfred Andersson (Dr. Watson), Karl Borin (Moriarty), Erland Colliander (Mr. Larrabee), Ingeborg Rönnlund (Mrs. Larrabee), Gulli Ericson (Miss Alice Faulkner), Hilda Rosenqvist, S. Bratt, E. Romlin, Hugo Rosenqvist, A. Ervall, M.

Sterner, J. Finnman, J. Westin, G. Rönnblad.
Review: Ridå. No. 19-20 (1908) (A. G-g).

5303. ———. ———. Borås: Borås Teater, January 2, 1910. 1 performance.
Cast: Hugo Rönnblad (Sherlock Holmes), Alfred Andersson (Dr. Watson), Gunnar Rönnblad (Benjamin Forman), Lucie Semb (Billy), Karl Borin (Moriarty), Ernst Öberg (James Larrabee), Arwid Erwall (Sidney Prince), Martin Sterner (Alfred Bassick), Bror Sjöqvist (McTague), Anna Johansson (Alice Faulkner), John Vestin (Tim Leary and Parsons), Ellen Ädelstam (Mary Larrabee), Signe Bratt (Thérèse), Elsa Löwendahl (Mrs. Smeedley).

5304. ———. ———. Hälsingborg: Helsingborgs Stads Teater, March 20, 1910. 1 performance.
Partial cast: Hugo Rönnblad (Sherlock Holmes), Karl Borin (Moriarty).
Review: Ridå, No. 6 (1910), 56.

5305. ———. ———. Malmö: Hippodromens Teater, December 17-18, 1911. 2 performances.
Partial cast: Hugo Rönnblad (Sherlock Holmes), Hr. Fischer (Moriarty), Frk. Ebbesen (Billy).

5306. ———. ———. Östermalms-Teatern, March 15-31, 1913. 15 performances.
Credits: Director, Wennersten; Settings, Carl Grabow; Background music, Jean Sibelius.
Partial cast: William Larsson (Sherlock Holmes), Frk. Anna Taflin, Frk. Hedvig Nenzén, Frk. Lizzie Sondell, Frk. Svea Ahman; Herrar Engborg, Fernquist, Borin, Borg, Wallin.
Reviews: Stockholmstidningen (March 17, 1913) (D. F.); *Svenska Dagbladet* (March 16, 1913) (X. O.); (November 11, 1963); *Thalia*, Nr. 12-13 (1913), 104.

5307. ———. ———. Gothenburg: Folkteatern, April 5-6, 1913. 2 performances.
Partial cast: Hugo Rönnblad (Sherlock Holmes), Olof Hillberg (Moriarty).

5308. Gordon, Jack. *Sherlock Holmes.* Stockholm: Södra Teatern, January 28-March 30, 1928. 64 performances.
Partial cast: Thure Alfe (Sherlock Holmes), Bertil Brusewitz (Dr. Watson).

F Radio

Most of the information for Sections F and G was obtained by laborious checking of the daily radio and television schedules published in *The Times* of London and *The New York Times*. Fortunately, the Colorado State University Library has a complete run of both these newspapers on microfilm. Detailed information for the British programs was gathered from the BBC's *Radio Times*, and therefore the information on the programs in England should be fairly complete. The only publication comparable to the *Radio Times* in this country is *TV Guide*, and it does not give full credits and cast for every television program. There is no publication that has provided full coverage for radio programs in the United States.

Edith Meiser, who wrote all the Sherlock Holmes radio programs in the U.S. between 1930 and 1943 (many of the programs were repeated in these and later years), has been a valuable source of information for this Bibliography. In addition to writing hundreds of radio scripts, she collaborated with Frank Giacoia on a series of Sherlock Holmes comic strips for the *New York Herald Tribune* from 1954 to 1956. Many women have been honored by the Baker Street Irregulars with the title of *The Woman*, the title Holmes reserved for Irene Adler; in the compiler's opinion, Edith Meiser is the woman above all others who deserves this honor. Her many accomplishments are noted in *The Biographical Encyclopaedia & Who's Who of the American Theatre* and in *Who's Who in America*.

All the radio series in this country originated in Hollywood; but in order to give a specific date and time of broadcast for each series and, when possible, for each story in a series, only the broadcasts in New York City are listed. These series, of course, were broadcast over many stations in all parts of the country.

A discussion of the Japan Broadcasting Company's reproductions of the Sherlock Holmes series of BBC programs appears in Japanese in Dr. Kohki Naganuma's book, *Greetings from Sherlock Holmes* (item 2138).

It is curious that so much has been written and said about the fourteen films in which Basil Rathbone and Nigel Bruce played between 1939 and 1946, but only scant attention has been paid to their weekly radio broadcasts during the same period. In a series of six Sherlock Holmes adventures, they made 218 programs (some of these may have been repeats). Nigel Bruce then appeared in one additional series of 39 programs with Tom Conway of Falcon fame the following year. Basil Rathbone also portrayed Holmes in a teleplay in 1953, in his wife's stage play later that year, and made several recordings between 1958 and 1967. One of the radio broadcasts has been released on both a record and a cassette, and it is hoped that others will follow. Perhaps no other actor portrayed the Master so per-

fectly, bringing him into the homes of many millions of people both here and abroad.

DENMARK

1943 POUL REUMERT AND BJARNE FORCHHAMMER

5309. "Sherlock Holmes," Friday, September 17, 1943, 2040-2150.
Credits: Director, Sigird Wantzin; Conductor, Ejnar Ferslev; Translator, Walter Christmas.
Cast: Poul Reumert (Sherlock Holmes), Bjarne Forchhamer (Dr. Watson), Tavs Neiiendam (John Forman, alias Smith), Elith Pio (James Larrabee), Else Højgaard (Lissy Larrabee), Anna Borg (Alice Faulkner), Emma Wiehe (Mrs. Faulkner), Adelhaid Nielsen (Thérèse), Valdemar Møller (Professor Moriarty), Einar Juhl (Alfred Bassick), Knud Heglund (Mikkel Shark), Povl Vendelbo (Thomas Long, "the Leech"), Peter Nielsen (Jim Kricker), Hugo Bruun (Bob McLuth), Viggo Wiehe (Porter), Vera Lense Møller (Billy), Victor Montell (Lord Balluster).

1959 BENDT ROTHE AND EMIL HASS CHRISTENSEN

5310. "Bruce Partington-planerne," Friday, December 18, 1959, 2055-2215.
Credits: Director, Kaj Wilton; Adapter, Felix Felton; Translator, Henrik V. Ringsted.
Cast: Bendt Rothe (Sherlock Holmes), Emil Hass Christensen (Dr. Watson), Gerda Flagsted (the housekeeper), Asbjørn Andersen (Mycroft Holmes), Freddy Koch (Lestrade), Einer Reim (the railwayman), Bjørn Spiro (the butler), Kjeld Jacobsen (Valentine Walter), Lone Luther (Miss Violet Westbury), Olaf Ussing (Sidney Johnson), Valsø Holm (the clerk in the ticket office).

1964 EBBE RODE AND HELGE KJAERULFF-SCHMIDT

5311. "Baskervilles hund," Tuesday, January 14, 1964, 1950-2130.
Credits: Director, Carlo M. Pedersen; Adapter, Felix Felton.
Cast: Ebbe Rode (Sherlock Holmes), Helge Kjaerulff-Schmidt (Dr. Watson), Holder Juul Hansen (Mr. Stapleton), Kjeld Jacobsen (Sir Henry Baskerville), Peter Poulsen (Dr. Mortimer), Marguerite Viby (Beryl Stapleton), Berthe Qvistgaard (Laura Lyons), Elith Pio (Barrymore), Karen Berg

(Eliza Barrymore), Mogens Brandt (Lestrade), Henry Jessen (Perkins), Børge Møller Grimstrup (the postmaster).

1968 JORGEN REENBERG AND KELD MARKUSLUND

5312. "De fires tegn," Monday, June 10, 1968, 2035-2200.
Credits: Director, Sam Besekow; Adapter, Michael Hardwick; Translator, Henrik V. Ringsted.
Cast: Jørgen Reenberg (Sherlock Holmes), Keld Markuslund (Dr. Watson), Grethe Mogensen (Mary Morstan), Ingolf David (Sholto), Poul Müller (Major Sholto), Knud Hallest (Athelney Jones), Ego Brønnum-Jacobsen (Sherman), Rigmor, Hvidtfeldt (Mrs. Smith), Miskow Makwarth (Jonathan Small).

1965-1968 HENRIK BENTZON

5313. "Prioratskolen," Sunday. July 18; Wednesday, July 21, 1965 (Aftenføljeton)
Cast: Henrik Bentzon (reader).

5314. "En Studie i rødt," August 1968. (Radiøfoljeton)
Cast: Henrik Bentzon (reader).

ENGLAND

1938

5315. "Sherlock Holmes and the Adventure of Silver Blaze," Empire and National Services, Tuesday, April 12, 1938, 12:15-12:45 p.m. (Detectives in Fiction, No. 1)
Credits: Producer, Leslie Stokes; Adapter, Pascoe Thornton.
Cast: F. Wyndham Goldie, Hugh Harben, Bramber Wills, John Moody, Betty Jardine, Cyril Gardener, Douglas Burbridge, Stanley Groode, Lilian Ward.

1943 ARTHUR WONTNER AND CARLETON HOBBS

5316. "The Boscombe Valley Mystery," BBC Home Service, Saturday, July 3, 1943, 9:35-10:25 p.m. (Saturday-Night Theatre)
Credits: Producer, Howard Rose; Adapter, Ashley Sampson.
Cast: Arthur Wontner (Sherlock Holmes), Carleton Hobbs (Dr. Watson), Foster Carlin (Cab-Driver), Ronald Kerr (Charles McCarthy), Alan Blair (James McCarthy), Juliet Mansel (Mrs. Moran), Lucille Lisle (Patience), Arthur Ridley (Coroner), Arthur Bush (Inspector Lestrade), Moira Lister (Miss Turner), Deryck Guyler (John Turner).

1945 SIR CEDRIC HARDWICKE AND FINLAY CURRIE

5317. "The Adventure of the Speckled Band,"

BBC Home Service, Thursday, May 17, 1945, 10:45-11:15 p.m.
Credits: Producer, Martyn C. Webster; Adapter, John Dickson Carr.
Cast: Sir Cedric Hardwicke (Sherlock Holmes), Finlay Currie (Dr. Watson), Thea Wells (Helen Stoner), Richard George (Dr. Grimesby Roylott), Dora Gregory (Mrs. Hudson).

1945 LAIDMAN BROWNE AND NORMAN SHELLEY

5318. "Silver Blaze," BBC Home Service, Thursday, August 3, 1945, 9:30-10:00 p.m. (Corner in Crime, No.1)
Credits: Producer, Walter Rilla; Editor, John Dickson Carr; Adapter, C. Gordon Glover.
Cast: Laidman Browne (Sherlock Holmes), Norman Shelley (Dr. Watson), Richard Williams (Inspector Gregory), Heron Carvic (Fitzroy Simpson), Gladys Spencer (Mrs. Straker), Bryan Powley (Mr. Straker), Freda Falconer (Edith), Arthur Ridley (Colonel Ross), and other members of the BBC Repertory Company.

1948 HOWARD MARION-CRAWFORD AND FINLAY CURRIE

5319. "The Adventure of the Speckled Band," BBC Home Service, Monday, December 27, 1948, 4:00-4:30 p.m.
Credits: Producer, David H. Godfrey; Adapter, John Dickson Carr.
Cast: Howard Marion-Crawford (Sherlock Holmes), Finlay Currie (Dr. Watson), Grizelda Hervey (Helen Stoner), Olive Gregg (Julia Stoner), Francis de Wolff (Dr. Roylott), Susan Richards (Mrs. Hudson).

1949 LAIDMAN BROWNE

5320. "The Speckled Band," BBC Light Programme, Monday-Friday, August 8-12, 1949, 11:00-11:15 p.m. 5 episodes. (A Book at Bedtime)
Cast: Laidman Browne (reader).

5321. "The Norwood Builder," BBC Light Programme, Monday-Friday, August 15-19, 1949, 11:00-11:15 p.m. 5 episodes. (A Book at Bedtime)
Cast: Laidman Browne (reader).

5322. "The Bruce-Partington Plans," BBC Light Programme, Monday-Friday, August 22-26, 1949, 11:00-11:15 p.m. 5 episodes. (A Book at Bedtime)
Cast: Laidman Browne (reader).

1949-1951

5323. "The Speckled Band," BBC Home

Service, Monday, October 3, 1949, 2:25-2:50 p.m. (Senior English I, No. 3)

Credits: Adapter, Philippa Pearce.

5324. "The Red-Headed League," BBC Home Service, Monday, September 18, 1950, 2:25-2:50 p.m. (Senior English I)

Credits: Adapter, Philippa Pearce.

5325. "The Hound of the Baskervilles," BBC Home Service, Mondays, January 22 and 29, 1951, 2:25-2:50 p.m. 2 episodes. (Senior English I)

Credits: Adapter, Philippa Pearce.

1953 CARLETON HOBBS AND NORMAN SHELLEY

5326. "Sherlock Holmes," by William Gillette. BBC Home Service, Saturday, January 3, 1953, 9:15-10:45 p.m. (Saturday-Night Theatre) Repeated: HS, Thursday, January 8, 1953, 2:45-4:15 p.m.

Credits: Producer and Adapter, Raymond Raikes.

Cast: Carleton Hobbs (Sherlock Holmes), Norman Shelley (Dr. Watson), Jonathan Field (Billy), Frederick Valk (Professor Moriarty), Allan Jeayes (John Forman), Valentine Dyall (James Larrabee), Catherine Salkeld (Madge Larrabee), Sarah Leigh (Alice Faulkner), Tony Quinn ("Lightfoot" McTague), Michael O'Halloran (Thomas Leary), Wyndham Milligan (Jim Craigin), Norman Claridge (Alfred Bassick), John Cazabon (Parsons), William Fox (Sir Edward Leighton), Victor Fairley (Count von Stalburg).

Review: *Radio Times*, 117 (December 26, 1952), 4 (S. C. Roberts).

1954 SIR JOHN GIELGUD AND SIR RALPH RICHARDSON

5327. "Dr. Watson Meets Mr. Sherlock Holmes," BBC Light Programme, Tuesday, October 5, 1954, 9:00-9:30 p.m. (The Adventures of Sherlock Holmes, No. 1)

Credits: Producer, Harry Alan Towers; Director, Val Gielgud; Adapter, John Keir Cross.

Cast: John Gielgud (Sherlock Holmes), Ralph Richardson (Dr. Watson), Norman Claridge (Stamford), Philip Leaver (Milverton), Monica Grey (Unknown Woman), John Cazabon (Inspector Lestrade).

5328. "A Scandal in Bohemia," BBC Light Programme, Tuesday, October 12, 1954, 9:00-9:30 p.m. (The Adventures of Sherlock Holmes, No. 2)

Credits: Producer, Harry Alan Towers; Director, Val Gielgud; Adapter, John Keir Cross.

Cast: John Gielgud (Sherlock Holmes), Ralph Richardson (Dr. Watson), Margaret Ward (Irene Adler), Olaf Pooley (King of Bohemia).

5329. "The Red-Headed League," BBC Light Programme, Tuesday, October 19, 1954, 9:00-9:30 p.m. (The Adventures of Sherlock Holmes, No. 3)

Credits: Producer, Harry Alan Towers; Director, Martyn C. Webster; Adapter, John Keir Cross.

Cast: John Gielgud (Sherlock Holmes), Ralph Richardson (Dr. Watson), Stanley Groome (Mr. Jabez Wilson), Denis Goacher (Vincent Spaulding), Duncan McIntyre (Duncan Ross), Lewis Stringer (Athelney Jones), Ivan Samson (Mr. Merryweather).

5330. "The Bruce-Partington Plans," BBC Light Programme, Tuesday, October 26, 1954, 9:00-9:30 p.m. (The Adventures of Sherlock Holmes, No. 4)

Credits: Producer, Harry Alan Towers; Director, Martyn C. Webster; Adapter, John Keir Cross.

Cast: John Gielgud (Sherlock Holmes), Ralph Richardson (Dr. Watson), Val Gielgud (Mycroft Holmes), John Cazabon (Inspector Lestrade), William Fox (Col. Valentine Walter).

5331. "A Case of Identity," BBC Light Programme, Tuesday, November 2, 1954, 9:00-9:30 p.m. (The Adventures of Sherlock Holmes, No. 5)

Credits: Producer, Harry Alan Towers; Director, Val Gielgud; Adapter, John Keir Cross.

Cast: John Gielgud (Sherlock Holmes), Ralph Richardson (Dr. Watson), Monica Grey (Mary Sutherland), Geoffrey Wincott (Hosmer Angel and James Windibank).

5332. "The Dying Detective," BBC Light Programme, Tuesday, November 9, 1954, 9:00-9:30 p.m. (The Adventures of Sherlock Holmes, No. 6)

Credits: Producer, Harry Alan Towers; Director, Martyn C. Webster; Adapter, John Keir Cross.

Cast: John Gielgud (Sherlock Holmes), Ralph Richardson (Dr. Watson), Anthony Jacobs (Culberton Smith), Elizabeth Maude (Mrs. Hudson), Frank Atkinson (Cabby), Hugh Manning (Inspector Morton).

5333. "The Second Stain," BBC Light Programme, Tuesday, November 16, 1954, 9:00-9:30 p.m. (The Adventures of Sherlock Holmes, No. 7)

Credits: Producer, Harry Alan Towers; Director, Martyn C. Webster; Adapter, John Keir Cross.

Cast: John Gielgud (Sherlock Holmes), Ralph Richardson (Dr. Watson), Elizabeth Maude (Mrs. Hudson), Marjorie Mars (Lady Hilda Trelawney Hope), John Cazabon (Inspector Lestrade), Raf de la Torre (Lord Bellinger), Guy Verney (The Rt. Hon.

383

Trelawney Hope), Michael Finlayson (Constable MacPherson).

5334. "The Norwood Builder," BBC Light Programme, Tuesday, November 23, 1954, 9:00-9:30 p.m. (The Adventures of Sherlock Holmes, No. 8)
Credits: Producer, Harry Alan Towers; Director, Val Gielgud; Adapter, John Keir Cross.
Cast: John Gielgud (Sherlock Holmes), Ralph Richardson (Dr. Watson), John Cazabon (Inspector Lestrade), Arthur Lawrence (John Hector McFarlane), Jean Stuart (Mrs. McFarlane), Arthur Ridley (Jonas Oldacre).

5335. "The Solitary Cyclist," BBC Light Programme, Tuesday, November 30, 1954, 9:00-9:30 p.m. (The Adventures of Sherlock Holmes, No. 9)
Credits: Producer, Harry Alan Towers; Director, Martyn C. Webster; Adapter, John Keir Cross.
Cast: John Gielgud (Sherlock Holmes), Ralph Richardson (Dr. Watson), Marjorie Westbury (Miss Violet Smith), John Bushelle (Carruthers), John Carson (Woodley), Malcolm Hayes (Williamson).

5336. "The Six Napoleons," BBC Light Programme, Tuesday, December 7, 1954, 9:00-9:30 p.m. (The Adventures of Sherlock Holmes, No. 10)
Credits: Producer, Harry Alan Towers; Director, Martyn C. Webster; Adapter, John Keir Cross.
Cast: John Gielgud (Sherlock Holmes), Ralph Richardson (Dr. Watson), John Cazabon (Inspector Lestrade). Other parts played by Robert Rietty and Denis Goacher.

5337. "The Blue Carbuncle," BBC Light Programme, Tuesday, December 14, 1954, 9:00-9:30 p.m. (The Adventures of Sherlock Holmes, No. 11)
Credits: Producer, Harry Alan Towers; Director Martyn C. Webster; Adapter, John Keir Cross.
Cast: John Gielgud (Sherlock Holmes), Ralph Richardson (Dr. Watson), John Carson (Peterson), James Thomason (Henry Baker), Charles Leno (Breckinridge), Alan Reid (Ryder).

5338. "The Final Problem," BBC Light Programme, Tuesday, December 21, 1954, 9:00-9:30 p.m. (The Adventures of Sherlock Holmes, No. 12)
Credits: Producer, Harry Alan Towers; Director, Martyn C. Webster; Adapter, John Keir Cross.
Cast: John Gielgud (Sherlock Holmes), Ralph Richardson (Dr. Watson), Orson Welles (Professor Moriarty).

The above series was repeated twice in the United States on WRCA-NBC, Sundays, January 2-June 5, 1955, 9:00-9:30 p.m.

1957 NOEL JOHNSON

5339. "The Hound of the Baskervilles," BBC Light Programme, April 23-May 10, 1957, 2:45-3:00 p.m. 14 episodes. (Woman's Hour)
Credits: Adapter, Neville Teller.
Cast: Noel Johnson (reader), Marjorie Anderson (introduction).

1958

5340. "The Blue Carbuncle," BBC Home Service, Friday, June 20, 1958, 2:40-3:00 p.m. (Senior English I)
Credits: Adapter, Aelred Horn.

1959 RICHARD HURNDALL AND BRYAN COLEMAN

5341. "The Sign of Four," BBC Light Programme, Sundays, May 17-June 14, 1959, 4:30-5:00 p.m. 5 episodes.
Credits: Producer, Archie Campbell; Adapter, Felix Felton.
Cast: Richard Hurndall (Sherlock Holmes), Bryan Coleman (Dr. Watson), Barbara Mitchell (Mary Hudson and Mary Morstan), Henry Kay (Williams), Edgar Norfolk (Cab driver and Hindu servant), John Moffatt (Thaddeus Sholto), Norman Claridge (Major John Sholto), Duncan McIntyre (McMurdo), Ella Milne (Mrs. Bernstone), Haydn Jones (Athelney Jones), Dorothy Black (Mrs. Cecil Forrester), Charles Lamb (Sherman), Doris Yorke (Mrs. Mordecai Smith), Lane Macnamara (Jack, her small son), John Graham (Cab driver and Toby, the dog), Elsa Palmer (Mrs. Hudson), Paul Taylor (Wiggins), Leigh Crutchley (Jonathan Small), Tom Bowman (Abdullah Khan, a Sikh), Ishaq Bux (Achmet, an Indian servant), Keith Williams (Captain Morstan).
Review: Radio Times, 143 (May 15, 1959), 3 (Felix Felton).

1968 NORMAN SHELLEY

5342. "The Blue Carbuncle," BBC Radio 4 (Home), Tuesday, October 22, 1968, 5:25-5:55 p.m. (Stories of Crime and Detection)
Credits: Producer, Herbert Smith; Adapter, Neville Teller.
Cast: Norman Shelley (reader).

1952-1969 CARLETON HOBBS AND NORMAN SHELLEY

5343. "The Naval Treaty," BBC Home Service, Wednesday, October 15, 1952, 5:10-5:50 p.m. (No. 1) (Children's Hour)
Credits: Producer, David Davis; Adapter, Felix Felton.
Cast: Carleton Hobbs (Sherlock Holmes),

Norman Shelley (Dr. Watson), Preston Lockwood (Percy Phelps), Olive Kirby (Annie Harrison), Eric Anderson (Joseph Harrison), Felix Felton (Lord Holdhurst), Antony Kearey (Forbes).

Review: Radio Times, 117 (October 10, 1952), 15.

5344. "The Five Orange Pips," BBC Home Service, Wednesday, November 12, 1952, 5:10-5:50 p.m. (No. 2) (Children's Hour)

Credits: Producer, David Davis; Adapter, Felix Felton.

Cast: Carleton Hobbs (Sherlock Holmes), Norman Shelley (Dr. Watson), John Clarke-Smith (John Openshaw), Macdonald Parke (Elias Openshaw), Felix Felton (Joseph Openshaw).

5345. "The Blue Carbuncle," BBC Home Service, Wednesday, December 10, 1952, 5:10-5:50 p.m. (No. 3) (Children's Hour)

Credits: Producer, David Davis; Adapter Felix Felton.

Cast: Carleton Hobbs (Sherlock Holmes), Norman Shelley (Dr. Watson), David Kossoff (Peterson), Felix Felton (Henry Baker), Richard Goolden (John Ryder), Janet Bruce (Mrs. Oakshott).

5346. "The Red-Headed League," BBC Home Service, Wednesday, January 7, 1953, 5:10-5:50 p.m. (No. 4) (Children's Hour)

Credits: Producer, David Davis; Adapter, Felix Felton.

Cast: Carleton Hobbs (Sherlock Holmes), Norman Shelley (Dr. Watson), Humphrey Morton (Jabez Wilson and Peter Jones), Felix Felton (Duncan Ross and Mr. Merryweather), Martin Starkie (Vincent Spaulding).

5347. "The Three Students," BBC Home Service, Wednesday, February 4, 1953, 5:10-5:50 p.m. (No. 5) (Children's Hour)

Credits: Producer, David Davis; Adapter, Felix Felton.

Cast: Carleton Hobbs (Sherlock Holmes), Norman Shelley (Dr. Watson), Felix Felton (Hilton Soames), Ernest Jay (Bannister), David Page (Gilchrist).

5348. "The Norwood Builder," BBC Home Service, Thursday, October 7, 1954, 5:15-5:55 p.m. (No. 1) (Children's Hour) Repeated: HS, Friday, April 15, 1955, 1:10-1:50 p.m.

Credits: Producer, David Davis; Adapter, Felix Felton.

Cast: Carleton Hobbs (Sherlock Holmes), Norman Shelley (Dr. Watson), Felix Felton (Inspector Lestrade), Leslie Heritage (John McFarlane), Hilda Schroder (Mrs. McFarlane), John Turnbull (Jonas Oldacre), Joan Clement Scott (Mrs. Lexington).

Review: Radio Times, 125 (October 1, 1954), 21 (Felix Felton).

5349. "The Bruce-Partington Plans," BBC Home Service, Thursday, November 4, 1954, 5:15-5:55 p.m. (No. 2) (Children's Hour) Repeated: HS, Friday, April 22, 1955, 1:10-1:50 p.m.

Credits: Producer, David Davis; Adapter, Felix Felton.

Cast: Carleton Hobbs (Sherlock Holmes), Norman Shelley (Dr. Watson), Malcolm Graeme (Mycroft Holmes), Felix Felton (Inspector Lestrade), Howard Lang (Col. Valentine Walter), Shirley Cooklin (Violet Westbury), Donovan O'Shiell (Railway Official), Ernest Jay (Sidney Johnson).

5350. "The Mazarin Stone," BBC Home Service, Thursday, December 2, 1954, 5:15-5:55 p.m. (No. 3) (Children's Hour) Repeated: HS, Friday, April 29, 1955, 1:10-1:50 p.m.

Credits: Producer, Josephine Plummer; Adapter, Felix Felton; Violinist, Eugene Pini.

Cast: Carleton Hobbs (Sherlock Holmes), Norman Shelley (Dr. Watson), Wilfrid Downing (Billy), Ralph Truman (Count Negretto Sylvius), Ivan Samson (Sam Merton), Mark Dignam (Lord Cantlemere).

5351. "The Missing Three-Quarter," BBC Home Service, Thursday, January 6, 1955, 5:15-5:55 p.m. (No. 4) (Children's Hour) Repeated: HS, Friday, May 6, 1955, 1:10-1:50 p.m.

Credits: Producer, David Davis; Adapter, Felix Felton.

Cast: Carleton Hobbs (Sherlock Holmes), Norman Shelley (Dr. Watson), John Clarke-Smith (Cyril Overton), Felix Felton (Lord Mount-James), Ronald Simpson (Dr. Leslie Armstrong), Humphrey Morton (A London Hotel Porter), Grace Rigby (A Post Office Girl).

5352. "The Copper Beeches," BBC Home Service, Thursday, February 3, 1955, 5:15-5:55 p.m. (No. 5) (Children's Hour) Repeated: HS, Friday, May 13, 1955, 1:10-1:50 p.m.

Credits: Producer, David Davis; Adapter, Felix Felton.

Cast: Carleton Hobbs (Sherlock Holmes), Norman Shelley (Dr. Watson), Hilda Schroder (Miss Violet Hunter), Harry Lockwood West (Mr. Jephro Rucastle), Natalie Moya (Miss Stoper), Dorothy Black (Mrs. Toller).

5353. "The Final Problem," BBC Home Service, Thursday, March 3, 1955, 5:15-5:55 p.m. (No. 6) (Children's Hour) Repeated: HS, Friday, May 20, 1955, 1:10-1:50 p.m.

Credits: Producer, David Davis; Adapter, Felix Felton.

Cast: Carleton Hobbs (Sherlock Holmes), Norman Shelley (Dr. Watson), Ralph Truman (Professor Moriarty), Humphrey

Morton (A Railway Porter), Felix Felton (Peter Steiler), Malcolm Graeme (Mycroft Holmes).

5354. "The Naval Treaty," BBC Home Service, Friday, October 11, 1957, 5:15-5:55 p.m. (No. 1) (Children's Hour)
Credits: Producer, Martyn C. Webster; Adapter, Felix Felton.
Cast: Carleton Hobbs (Sherlock Holmes), Norman Shelley (Dr. Watson), Peter Coke (Percy Phelps), Annabel Maule (Annie Harrison), James Thomason (Joseph Harrison), Felix Felton (Lord Holdhurst), Alan Reid (Forbes).

5355. "The Five Orange Pips," BBC Home Service, Friday, October 18, 1957, 5:15-5:55 p.m. (No. 2) (Children's Hour)
Credits: Producer, Martyn C. Webster; Adapter, Felix Felton.
Cast: Carleton Hobbs (Sherlock Holmes), Norman Shelley (Dr. Watson), Brian McDermott (John Openshaw), Macdonald Parke (Elias Openshaw), Felix Felton (Joseph Openshaw).

5356. "The Blue Carbuncle," BBC Home Service Friday, October 25, 1957, 5:15-5:55 p.m. (No. 3) (Children's Hour)
Credits: Producer, Martyn C. Webster; Adapter, Felix Felton.
Cast: Carleton Hobbs (Sherlock Holmes), Norman Shelley (Dr. Watson), Hamilton Dyce (Peterson), James Thomason (Breckinridge), Felix Felton (Henry Baker), Hamilton Dyce (Windigate), Hugh David (John Ryder), Janet Morrison (Mrs. Oakshott).

5357. "The Red-Headed League," BBC Home Service, Friday November 1, 1957, 5:15-5:55 p.m. (No. 4) (Children's Hour)
Credits: Producer, Martyn C. Webster; Adapter, Felix Felton.
Cast: Carleton Hobbs (Sherlock Holmes), Norman Shelley (Dr. Watson), Felix Felton (Jabez Wilson), Humphrey Morton (Peter Jones), Simon Lack (Duncan Ross), Ian Holm (Vincent Spaulding), George Hagen (Mr. Merryweather).

5358. "The Three Students," BBC Home Service, Friday, November 8, 1957, 5:15-5:55 p.m. (No. 5) (Children's Hour)
Credits: Producer, Martyn C. Webster; Adapter, Felix Felton.
Cast: Carleton Hobbs (Sherlock Holmes), Norman Shelley (Dr. Watson), Felix Felton (Hilton Soames), James Thomason (Bannister), Gordon Gardner (Gilchrist), Alan Reid (McLaren).

5359. "The Final Problem," BBC Home Service, Friday, November 15, 1957, 5:15-5:55 p.m. (No. 6) (Children's Hour)
Credits: Producer, Martyn C. Webster; Adapter, Felix Felton.

Cast: Carleton Hobbs (Sherlock Holmes), Norman Shelley (Dr. Watson), Felix Felton (Professor Moriarty), Humphrey Morton (A Railway Porter), Rolf Lefebvre (Peter Steiler), Malcolm Graeme (Mycroft Holmes).

5360. "The Hound of the Baskervilles," BBC Light Programme, Sundays, April 6-May 11, 1958, 4:30-5:00 p.m. 6 episodes. Repeated: HS, Thursdays, July 24-August 28, 1958, 11:30-12:00 a.m.
Credits: Producer, Patrick Dromgoole; Adapter, Felix Felton.
Cast: Carleton Hobbs (Sherlock Holmes), Norman Shelley (Dr. Watson), Paul Eddington (Dr. Mortimer), Ronald Wilson (Sir Henry Baskerville), Lewis Gedge (Barrymore), Rolf Lefebvre (Stapleton), Pamela Alan (Beryl Stapleton), Hedley Goodall (Mr. Frankland), June Barrie (Laura Lyons), Paul Lorraine (Inspector Lestrade), David Baron, Nicholas Selby, Frank Shelley, Edgar Harrison, Norman Kendall, Denis Raymond, Constance Chapman.
Review: *Radio Times*, 139 (April 4, 1958), 2 (Felix Felton); *SHJ*, 4, No. 1 (Winter 1958), 15-16 (Anthony Howlett and Humphrey Morton).

5361. "The Man with the Twisted Lip," BBC Light Programme, Tuesday, May 12, 1959, 8:30-9:00 p.m. (No. 1) (Thirty-Minute Theatre) Repeated: HS, Wednesday, January 18, 1961, 3:30-4:00 p.m.
Credits: Producer, Frederick Bradnum; Adapter, Michael Hardwick.
Cast: Carleton Hobbs (Sherlock Holmes), Norman Shelley (Dr. Watson), Sylvia Coleridge (Mrs. Watson), Eva Stuart (Mrs. Whitney), Robert Sansom (Isa Whitney), Hilda Schroder (Mrs. St. Clair), Garard Green (Lascar), Robert Sansom (An Inspector), Joe Sterne (A Constable), Ronald Baddiley (Inspector Bradstreet), Frederick Treves (Boone).

5362. "The Beryl Coronet," BBC Light Programme, Tuesday, June 30, 1959, 9:00-9:30 p.m. (No. 2) (Thirty-Minute Theatre) Repeated: HS, Wednesday, February 8, 1961, 3:30-4:00 p.m.
Credits: Producer, Frederick Bradnum; Adapter, Michael Hardwick.
Cast: Carleton Hobbs (Sherlock Holmes), Norman Shelley (Dr. Watson), Robert Sansom (Alexander Holder), Godfrey Kenton (His Grace), Frederick Treves (Arthur Holder), Eva Huszar (Mary Holder). Other parts played by Hilda Schroder and Ronald Baddiley.

5363. "The Blanched Soldier," BBC Light Programme, Tuesday, August 4, 1959, 9:00-9:30 p.m. (No. 3) (Thirty-Minute Theatre) Repeated: HS, Saturday, March 11, 1961, 2:40-3:10 p.m.

Credits: Producer, Frederick Bradnum; Adapter, Michael Hardwick.

Cast: Carleton Hobbs (Sherlock Holmes), Norman Shelley (Dr. Watson), Frederick Treves (James M. Dodd), Robert Sansom (Colonel Emsworth), Frank Atkinson (Ralph, the Butler), William Eedle (Mr. Kent), Denis Goacher (Godfrey Emsworth), Norman Claridge (Sir James Saunders).

5364. "The Cooper Beeches," BBC Light Programme, Tuesday, August 11, 1959, 9:00-9:30 p.m. (No. 4) (Thirty-Minute Theatre)

Credits: Producer, Frederick Bradnum; Adapter, Michael Hardwick.

Cast: Carleton Hobbs (Sherlock Holmes), Norman Shelley (Dr. Watson), Hilda Schroder (Violet Hunter), Eva Stuart (Miss Stoper and Mrs. Rucastle), Frederick Treves (Mr. Rucastle), Fanny Carby (Mrs. Toller).

5365. "The Noble Bachelor," BBC Light Programme, Tuesday, August 18, 1959, 9:00-9:30 p.m. (No. 5) (Thirty-Minute Theatre)

Credits: Producer, Frederick Bradnum; Adapter, Michael Hardwick.

Cast: Carleton Hobbs (Sherlock Holmes), Norman Shelley (Dr. Watson), William Eedle (Lord St. Simon), Frederick Treves (Inspector Lestrade), Jane Jordan Rogers (Mrs. Moulton), Jerold Wells (Francis Hay Moulton).

5366. "Shoscombe Old Place," BBC Light Programme, Tuesday, August 25, 1959, 9:00-9:30 p.m. (No. 6) (Thirty-Minute Theatre)

Credits: Producer, Frederick Bradnum; Adapter, Michael Hardwick.

Cast: Carleton Hobbs (Sherlock Holmes), Norman Shelley (Dr. Watson), Frederick Treves (John Mason), Ronald Baddiley (Josiah Barnes), Godfrey Kenton (Sir Robert Norberton), Fanny Carby (Mrs. Norlett), Robert Sansom (Mr. Norlett), Frank Atkinson (Stephens).

Review of above series: *Radio Times*, 143 (May 8, 1959), 5.

5367. "The Stockbroker's Clerk," BBC Light Programme, Tuesday, February 23, 1960, 8:30-9:00 p.m. (No. 1) (Thirty-Minute Theatre) Repeated: HS, Wednesday, March 2, 1960, 3:30-4:00 p.m.

Credits: Producer, Martyn C. Webster; Adapter, Michael Hardwick.

Cast: Carleton Hobbs (Sherlock Holmes), Norman Shelley (Dr. Watson), Desmond Carrington (Pycroft), Kathleen Helme (Landlady), Hugh Manning (Pinner).

5368. "The Naval Treaty," BBC Light Programme, Tuesday, March 22, 1960, 10:00-10:30 p.m. (No. 2) (Thirty-Minute Theatre) Repeated: HS, Wednesday, August 17, 1960, 3:30-4:00 p.m.

Credits: Producer, Martyn C. Webster; Adapter, Michael Hardwick.

Cast: Carleton Hobbs (Sherlock Holmes), Norman Shelley (Dr. Watson), Robert Corder (Joseph Harrison), Hamilton Dyce (Percy Phelps), George Hagan (Lord Holdhurst), Charles Simon (Tangey), Freda Dowie (Ada Tangey), Kenneth Dight (Detective Forbes), June Tobin (Mrs. Tangey), Cécile Chevreau (Annie Harrison), Kathleen Helme (Mrs. Hudson).

5369. "The Greek Interpreter," BBC Light Programme, Tuesday, April 5, 1960, 9:30-10:00 p.m. (No. 3) (Thirty-Minute Theatre) Repeated: HS, Wednesday, April 13, 1960, 3:30-4:00 p.m.

Credits: Producer, Martyn C. Webster; Adapter, Michael Hardwick.

Cast: Carleton Hobbs (Sherlock Holmes), Norman Shelley (Dr. Watson), Keith Williams (Mycroft Holmes), Jeffrey Segal (Melas), Brian McDermott (Harold Latimer), James Thomason (Kenp), Michael Turner (Inspector Gregson). Other parts played by members of the BBC Drama Repertory Company.

5370. "The Cardboard Box," BBC Light Programme, Tuesday, April 19, 1960, 9:30-10:00 p.m. (No. 4) (Thirty-Minute Theatre) Repeated: HS, Wednesday, April 27, 1960, 3:30-4:00 p.m.

Credits: Producer, Martyn C. Webster; Adapter, Michael Hardwick.

Cast: Carleton Hobbs (Sherlock Holmes), Norman Shelley (Dr. Watson), David Bird (Inspector Lestrade), Janet Burnell (Susan Cushing), Tom Watson (Jim Browner), Hugh Manning (Police Constable), Eva Stuart (Mary Browner), Cécile Chevreau (Sarah Cushing).

5371. "The Disappearance of Lady Frances Carfax," BBC Light Programme, Tuesday, May 3, 1960, 9:30-10:00 p.m. (No. 5) (Thirty-Minute Theatre) Repeated: HS, Wednesday, May 11, 1960, 3:30-4:00 p.m.

Credits: Producer, Martyn C. Webster; Adapter, Michael Hardwick.

Cast: Carleton Hobbs (Sherlock Holmes), Norman Shelley (Dr. Watson), John Hollis (Jules Vibart), Cécile Chevreau (Marie Devine), John Humphry (The Hon. Philip Green), George Merritt (Herr Dietrich), Michael Turner (Peters). Other parts played by members of the BBC Drama Repertory Company.

5372. "The Engineer's Thumb," BBC Light Programme, Tuesday, May 17, 1960, 9:30-10:00 p.m. (No. 6) (Thirty-Minute Theatre) Repeated: HS, Wednesday, May 25, 1960, 3:30-4:00 p.m.

Credits: Producer, Martyn C. Webster; Adapter, Michael Hardwick.

Cast: Carleton Hobbs (Sherlock Holmes), Norman Shelley (Dr. Watson), Harold Reese

(Victor Hatherley), Julian Somers (Colonel Lysander Stark), Stella Textor (Elise), Geoffrey Wincott (Mr. Ferguson), Edgar Norfolk (Inspector Bradsheet). Other parts played by Janet Morrison, Ian Sadler, and John Scott.

5373. "The Illustrious Client," BBC Light Programme, Tuesday, May 31, 1960, 8:30-9:00 p.m. (No. 7) (Thirty-Minute Theatre) Repeated: HS, Wednesday, June 8, 1960, 3:30-4:00 p.m.
Credits: Producer, Martyn C. Webster; Adapter, Michael Hardwick.
Cast: Carleton Hobbs (Sherlock Holmes), Norman Shelley (Dr. Watson), John Humphry (Sir James Damery), John G. Heller (Baron Gruner), Anthony Viccars (Shinwell Johnson), Eva Stuart (Kitty Winter), Nicholas Edmett (Newsvendor).

Review of above series: SHJ, 4, No. 4 (Spring 1960), 135, 140 (Anthony Howlett).

5374. "The Valley of Fear," BBC Home Service, Saturday, December 31, 1960, 8:30-10:00 p.m. Repeated: HS, Monday, January 2, 1961, 3:00-4:30 p.m.; Radio 4 (Home), Saturday, February 3, 1968, 8:30-10:00 p.m.; Radio 4 (Home), Monday, February 5, 1968, 3:15-4:45 p.m.
Credits: Producer, Robin Midgley; Adapter, Michael Hardwick.
Cast: Carleton Hobbs (Sherlock Holmes), Norman Shelley (Dr. Watson), Penelope Lee (Mrs. Hudson), Duncan McIntyre (Inspector Macdonald), Garard Green (Inspector Mason), Julian Somers (Sergeant Wilson), George Hagan (Cecil Barker), Robert Hartley (Ames), Humphrey Morton (Dr. Wood), June Tobin (Mrs. Allen), Valerie Hanson (Ivy Douglas), Lee Fox (John).
Review: Radio Times, 149 (December 29, 1960), 4 (Michael Hardwick), and reprinted in *CPBook,* 5, No. 17 (March 1969), 340.

5375. "Black Peter," BBC Light Programme, Sunday, March 5, 1961, 7:05-7:35 p.m.
Credits: Producer, Archie Campbell; Adapter, Alan Wilson.
Cast: Carleton Hobbs (Sherlock Holmes), Norman Shelley (Dr. Watson), Michael Turner (Inspector Hopkins), Kenneth Fortescue (John Hopley Neligan), Wilfred Babbage (James Lancaster), John Bryning (Henry Pattins), Eric Woodburn (Patrick Cairns).

5376. "The Hound of the Baskervilles," BBC Home Service, Saturday, August 5, 1961, 8:30-10:00 p.m. Repeated: HS, Monday, August 28, 1961, 3:00-4:30 p.m.; HS, Sunday, April 11, 1965, 2:30-4:00 p.m.; Radio 4, Saturday, February 13, 1971, 8:30-10:00 p.m.; Radio 4, Monday, February 15, 1971, 3:00-4:30 p.m.
Credits: Producer, Robin Midgley; Adapter, Felix Felton.

Cast: Carleton Hobbs (Sherlock Holmes), Norman Shelley (Dr. Watson), Kenneth Dight (Dr. Mortimer), Manning Wilson (Sir Henry Baskerville), Charles Simon (Barrymore), Gladys Spencer (Eliza Barrymore), Michael Bilton (Mr. Stapleton), Dorit Welles (Beryl Stapleton), Shirley Cooklin (Laura Lyons), Humphrey Morton (Inspector Lestrade), William Eedle (Perkins), Anthony Hall (Postmaster).

5377. "The Empty House," BBC Light Programme, Monday, November 27, 1961, 7:31-8:00 p.m. (No. 1)
Credits: Producer, Robin Midgley; Adapter, Michael Hardwick.
Cast: Carleton Hobbs (Sherlock Holmes), Norman Shelley (Dr. Watson), Humphrey Morton (Inspector Lestrade), David Terence (Constable), Noel Johnson (Colonel Moran), Eva Huszar (Jessie), Gudrun Ure (Mrs. Hudson).

5378. "The Reigate Squires," BBC Light Programme, Monday, December 4, 1961, 7:31-8:00 p.m. (No. 2) Repeated: HS, Thursday, July 19, 1962, 3:00-3:30 p.m.
Credits: Producer, Robin Midgley; Adapter, Michael Hardwick.
Cast: Carleton Hobbs (Sherlock Holmes), Norman Shelley (Dr. Watson), Ivan Samson (Colonel Hayter), Philip Leaver (Butler), Anthony Woodruff (Inspector Forrester), Wilfred Babbage (Cunningham), Malcolm Hayes (Alec Cunningham), Martin Lewis (Acton).

5379. "The Resident Patient," BBC Light Programme, Monday, December 11, 1961, 7:31-8:00 p.m. (No. 3)
Credits: Producer, Robin Midgley; Adapter, Michael Hardwick.
Cast: Carleton Hobbs (Sherlock Holmes), Norman Shelley (Dr. Watson), Hamilton Dyce (Dr. Trevelyan), Anthony Viccars (Blessington), John Bryning (Ivan), Earle Grey (Count Egrovitch), Godfrey Kenton (Inspector Lanner).

5380. "Charles Augustus Milverton," BBC Light Programme, Monday, December 18, 1961, 7:31-8:00 p.m. (No. 4)
Credits: Producer, Robin Midgley; Adapter, Michael Hardwick.
Cast: Carleton Hobbs (Sherlock Holmes), Norman Shelley (Dr. Watson), Tony Church (Milverton), Dudy Nimmo (Susan), Humphrey Morton (Inspector Lestrade and Gardener).

5381. "The Blue Carbuncle," BBC Light Programme, Monday, December 25, 1961, 7:31-8:00 p.m. (No. 5)
Credits: Producer, Robin Midgley; Adapter, Michael Hardwick.
Cast: Carleton Hobbs (Sherlock Holmes), Norman Shelley (Dr. Watson), Will Leighton (Peterson), Kenneth Dight (Henry

Baker), Derek Birch (Windigate), Wilfred Babbage (Breckinridge), Keith Buckley (Bill), John Pullen (James Ryder), Pauline Wynn (Maggie).

5382. "Thor Bridge," BBC Light Programme, Monday, January 1, 1962, 7:31-8:00 p.m. (No. 6) Repeated: HS, Thursday, July 12, 1962, 3:00-3:30 p.m.

Credits: Producer, Robin Midgley; Adapter, Michael Hardwick.

Cast: Carleton Hobbs (Sherlock Holmes), Norman Shelley (Dr. Watson), Robert Ayres (J. Neil Gibson), Humphrey Morton (Sergeant Coventry), Beryl Calder (Grace Dunbar and Mrs. Hudson).

5383. "The Priory School," BBC Light Programme, Monday, January 8, 1962, 7:31-8:00 p.m. (No. 7) Repeated: HS, Monday, June 11, 1962, 11:35-12:00 p.m.

Credits: Producer, Robin Midgley; Adapter, Michael Hardwick.

Cast: Carleton Hobbs (Sherlock Holmes), Norman Shelley (Dr. Watson), Eric Anderson (Dr. Huxtable), Peter Hutton (Roberts), Victor Lucas (Reuben Hayes), Wilfrid Grantham (Duke of Holdernesse), David Spenser (James Wilder).

Reviews of above series: Radio Times, 153 (November 23, 1961), 22; *The Times* (December 5, 1961), 15.

5384. "The Speckled Band," BBC Light Programme, Tuesday, July 17, 1962, 7:31-8:00 p.m. (Sherlock Holmes, No. 1) Repeated: HS, Thursday, December 27, 1962, 11:30-12:00 a.m.; LP, Monday, December 23, 1963, 8:00-8:30 p.m.

Credits: Producer, Robin Midgley; Adapter, Michael Hardwick.

Cast: Carleton Hobbs (Sherlock Holmes), Norman Shelley (Dr. Watson), Liane Aukin (Helen Stoner), Felix Felton (Dr. Grimesby Roylott), Miranda Connell (Julia Stoner).

5385. "Silver Blaze," BBC Light Programme, Tuesday, July 24, 1962, 7:31-8:00 p.m. (Sherlock Holmes, No. 2)

Credits: Producer, Robin Midgley; Adapter, Michael Hardwick.

Cast: Carleton Hobbs (Sherlock Holmes), Norman Shelley (Dr. Watson), Peter Pratt (John Straker), Elizabeth Weaver (Edith Baxter), John Baddeley (Jack), Michael Deacon (Charlie), Nigel Anthony (Hunter), Peggy Butt (Mrs. Straker), Peter Claughton (Fitzroy Simpson), Humphrey Morton (Inspector Gregory), George Curzon (Colonel Ross), George Hagan (Silas Brown).

5386. "The Musgrave Ritual," BBC Light Programme, Tuesday, July 31, 1962, 7:31-8:00 p.m. (Sherlock Holmes, No. 3) Repeated: HS, Thursday, January 10, 1963, 11:30-12:00 a.m.

Credits: Producer, Robin Midgley; Adapter, Michael Hardwick.

Cast: Carleton Hobbs (Sherlock Holmes), Norman Shelley (Dr. Watson), Roger Snowdon (Reginald Musgrave), Kenneth Hyde (Brunton), Vivienne Chatterton (Nurse), Humphrey Morton (Policeman), Patricia Mort (Rachel Howells).

5387. "The Golden Pince-Nez," BBC Light Programme, Tuesday, August 7, 1962, 7:31-8:00 p.m. (Sherlock Holmes, No. 4)

Credits: Producer, Robin Midgley; Adapter, Michael Hardwick.

Cast: Carleton Hobbs (Sherlock Holmes), Norman Shelley (Dr. Watson), Hugh Dickson (Stanley Hopkins), Grizelda Hervey (Anna), Humphrey Morton (Constable), Louida Vaughan (Susan), Jocelyn Page (Mrs. Marker), Andreas Malandrinos (Professor Coram).

5388. "The Missing Three-Quarter," BBC Light Programme, Tuesday, August 14, 1962, 7:31-8:00 p.m. (Sherlock Holmes, No. 5) Repeated: HS, Thursday, January 3, 1963, 11:30-12:00 a.m.

Credits: Producer, Robin Midgley; Adapter, Michael Hardwick.

Cast: Carleton Hobbs (Sherlock Holmes), Norman Shelley (Dr. Watson), Harvey Ashby (Cyril Overton), Blaise Wyndham (Hotel Porter), Keith Williams (Lord Mount-James and Godfrey Staunton), Dorit Welles (Lady Clerk), Eric Anderson (Dr. Leslie Armstrong).

5389. "The Abbey Grange," BBC Light Programme, Tuesday, August 21, 1962, 7:31-8:00 p.m. (Sherlock Holmes, No. 6) Repeated: LP, Friday 7, 1964, 7:31-8:00 p.m.

Credits: Producer, Robin Midgley; Adapter, Michael Hardwick.

Cast: Carleton Hobbs (Sherlock Holmes), Norman Shelley (Dr. Watson), Hugh Dickson (Stanley Hopkins), Josephine Price (Lady Brackenstall), Coral Fairweather (Thérèse), Peter Claughton (Croker), Douglas Storm (Manager).

5390. "The Devil's Foot," BBC Light Programme, Tuesday, August 28, 1962, 7:31-8:00 p.m. (Sherlock Holmes, No. 7)

Credits: Producer, Robin Midgley; Adapter, Michael Hardwick.

Cast: Carleton Hobbs (Sherlock Holmes), Norman Shelley (Dr. Watson), Humphrey Morton (Rev. Roundhay), George Hagan (Mortimer Tregennis), Grizelda Hervey (Mrs. Porter), Finlay Currie (Leon Sterndale).

5391. "The Mazarin Stone," BBC Light Programme, Tuesday, September 4, 1962, 7:31-8:00 p.m. (Sherlock Holmes, No. 8) Repeated: LP, Friday, August 14, 1964, 7:31-8:00 p.m.; HS, Thursday, March 16, 1967), 12:25-12:55 p.m.

Credits: Producer, Robin Midgley;

Adapter, Michael Hardwick; Violinist, Sydney Humphreys.

Cast: Carleton Hobbs (Sherlock Holmes), Norman Shelley (Dr. Watson), John Baddeley (Billy), Francis de Wolff (Count Sylvius), Peter Pratt (Sam Merton), James Thomason (Constable), Noel Iliff (Lord Cantlemere).

Review of above series: SHJ, 6, No. 1 (Winter 1962), 22-23 (Anthony Howlett).

5392. "A Study in Scarlet," BBC Home Service, Saturday, December 22, 1962, 8:30-10:00 p.m. (Saturday-Night Theatre) Repeated: HS, Monday, January 27, 1964, 3:00-4:30 p.m.

Credits: Producer, Norman Wright; Adapter, Michael Hardwick.

Cast: Carleton Hobbs (Sherlock Holmes), Norman Shelley (Dr. Watson), Barbara Mitchell (Mrs. Hudson), Timothy West (Commissionaire), Humphrey Morton (Inspector Gregson), Godgrey Kenton (Inspector Lestrade), Donald McKillop (Constable John Rance), David Valla (Wiggins), Vivienne Chatterton (Madame Charpentier), Stuart Nichol (Jefferson Hope), Tom Whyte (Joseph Stangerson), Errol MacKinnon (Enoch J. Drebber), John Graham (Arthur Charpentier). Other parts played by members of the BBC Drama Repertory Company.

Review: Radio Times, 157 (December 20, 1962), 8.

5393. "The Sign of the Four," BBC Home Service, Saturday, March 2, 1963, 8:30-10:00 p.m. (Saturday-Night Theatre) Repeated: HS, Monday, March 4, 1963, 3:00-4:30 p.m.; HS, Sunday, November 20, 1966, 2:30-4:00 p.m.

Credits: Producer, Val Gielgud; Adapter, Michael Hardwick.

Cast: Carleton Hobbs (Sherlock Holmes), Norman Shelley (Dr. Watson), Grizelda Hervey (Mrs. Hudson), Elizabeth Morgan (Mary Morstan), Philip Leaver (Thaddeus Sholto), George Curzon (Major Sholto), Duncan McIntyre (McMurdo), Harriet Petworth (Mrs. Bernstone), George Merritt (Inspector Athelney Jones), Will Leighton (Sergeant), Norman Claridge (Sherman), Carmen Hill (Mrs. Smith), Charles Eley (Jacky), Glyn Dearman (Wiggins), Malcolm Hayes (Jonathan Small), Robert Dodson, Timothy Palmer, Anthony Paul, Ronald Williams (Baker Street Irregulars).

Review: Radio Times, 158 (February 28, 1963), 7 (Michael Hardwick).

5394. "The Abbey Grange," BBC Light Programme, Friday, August 7, 1964, 7:31-8:00 p.m. (Sherlock Holmes Returns, No. 1) Recorded repeat of August 21, 1962.

5395. "The Speckled Band," BBC Light Programme, Friday, August 14, 1964, 7:31-8:00 p.m. (Sherlock Holmes Returns, No. 2) Recorded repeat of September 4, 1962.

5396. "The Solitary Cyclist," BBC Light Programme, Friday, August 21, 1964, 7:31-8:00 p.m. (Sherlock Holmes Returns, No. 3) Repeated: HS, Thursday, February 16, 1967, 12:25-12:55 p.m.

Credits: Producer, Graham Gauld; Adapter, Michael Hardwick.

Cast: Carleton Hobbs (Sherlock Holmes), Norman Shelley (Dr. Watson), Jane Wenham (Violet Smith), Norman Claridge (Carruthers), Gladys Spencer (Mrs. Smith), Malcolm Hayes (Woodley), Janet Morrison (Mrs. Hudson), Peter O'Shaughnessy (Landlord), George Merritt (Williamson).

5397. "The Bruce-Partington Plans," BBC Light Programme, Friday, August 28, 1964, 7:31-8:00 p.m. (Sherlock Holmes Returns, No. 4) Repeated: HS, Thursday, December 24, 1964, 10:30-11:00 a.m.; HS, Thursday, March 9, 1967, 12:25-12:55 p.m.

Credits: Producer, Graham Gauld; Adapter, Michael Hardwick.

Cast: Carleton Hobbs (Sherlock Holmes), Norman Shelley (Dr. Watson), Janet Morrison (Mrs. Hudson), Felix Felton (Mycroft Holmes), Humphrey Morton (Inspector Lestrade), Philip Cunningham (Colonel Walter), Mary Chester (Violet Westbury), John Boxer (Sidney Johnson).

5398. "The Three Garridebs," BBC Light Programme, Friday, September 4, 1964, 7:31-8:00 p.m. (Sherlock Holmes Returns, No. 5) Repeated: HS, Monday, December 28, 1964, 10:30-11:00 a.m.; HS, Thursday, March 30, 1967, 12:25-12:55 p.m.

Credits: Producer, Graham Gauld; Adapter, Michael Hardwick.

Cast: Carleton Hobbs (Sherlock Holmes), Norman Shelley (Dr. Watson), Janet Morrison (Mrs. Hudson), Eric Anderson (John Garrideb), Charles E. Stidwill (Nathan Garrideb), Harold Reese (Holloway), Humphrey Morton (Inspector Lestrade).

5399. "The Norwood Builder," BBC Light Programme, Friday, September 11, 1964, 7:31-8:00 p.m. (Sherlock Holmes Returns, No. 6) Repeated: HS, Tuesday, December 29, 1964, 10:30-11:00 a.m.; HS, Thursday, February 23, 1967, 12:25-12:55 p.m.

Credits: Producer, Graham Gauld; Adapter, Michael Hardwick.

Cast: Carleton Hobbs (Sherlock Holmes), Norman Shelley (Dr. Watson), Henry Stamper (McFarlane), Humphrey Morton (Inspector Lestrade), Eva Stuart (Mrs. Lexington), Hamlyn Benson (Jonas Oldacre), Molly Weir (Mrs. McFarlane), Janet Morrison (Mrs. Hudson), Alaric Cotter and Fraser Kerr (Constables).

5400. "The Sussex Vampire," BBC Light

Programme, Friday, September 18, 1964, 7:31-8:00 p.m. (Sherlock Holmes Returns, No. 7) Repeated: HS, Wednesday, December 30, 1964, 10:30-11:00 a.m.

Credits: Producer, Graham Gauld; Adapter, Michael Hardwick.

Cast: Carleton Hobbs (Sherlock Holmes), Norman Shelley (Dr. Watson), Stephen Jack (Ferguson), Gladys Spencer (Delores), Josefina Ray (Mrs. Ferguson), Peter Bartlett (Jack), Margaret Wolfit (Mrs. Mason).

5401. "The Red-Headed League," BBC Light Programme, Friday, September 25, 1964, 7:31-8:00 p.m. (Sherlock Holmes Returns, No. 8) Repeated: HS, Thursday, December 31, 1964, 10:30-11:00 a.m.; HS, Thursday, March 2, 1967, 12:25-12:55 p.m.

Credits: Producer, Graham Gauld; Adapter, Michael Hardwick.

Cast: Carleton Hobbs (Sherlock Holmes), Norman Shelley (Dr. Watson), Victor Lucas (Jabez Wilson), Peter Marinker (Vincent Spaulding), Frank Dunne (Duncan Ross), Gabriel Woolf (Inspector Jones), Eric Anderson (Merryweather).

5402. "The Three Gables," BBC Light Programme, Friday, October 2, 1964, 7:31-8:00 p.m. (Sherlock Holmes Returns, No. 9) Repeated: HS, Friday, January 1, 1965, 10:30-11:00 a.m.; HS, Thursday, March 2, 1967, 12:25-12:55 p.m.

Credits: Producer, Graham Gauld; Adapter, Michael Hardwick.

Cast: Carleton Hobbs (Sherlock Holmes), Norman Shelley (Dr. Watson), Frank Singuineau (Steve Dixie), Grizelda Hervey (Mary Maberley), Nicolette Bernard (Susan), Humphrey Morton (Inspector Lestrade), Selma Vaz Dias (Isadora Klein).

5403. "The Retired Colourman," BBC Light Programme, Friday, October 9, 1964, 7:31-8:00 p.m. (Sherlock Holmes Returns, No. 10)

Credits: Producer, Graham Gauld; Adapter, Michael Hardwick.

Cast: Carleton Hobbs (Sherlock Holmes), Norman Shelley (Dr. Watson), Denis Goacher (Barker), John Ruddock (Josiah Amberley), Garard Green (The Rev. Elman), Michael Kilgarriff (Inspector MacKinnon), Janet Morrison (Mrs. Hudson).

Review of above series: SHJ, 7, No. 1 (Winter 1964), 22 (Anthony Howlett).

5404. "A Scandal in Bohemia," BBC Light Programme, Monday, November 21, 1966, 8:00-8:30 p.m. (Sherlock Holmes Again, No. 1)

Credits: Producer, Martyn C. Webster; Adapter, Michael Hardwick.

Cast: Carleton Hobbs (Sherlock Holmes), Norman Shelley (Dr. Watson), Rolf Lefebvre (King of Bohemia), LeRoy Lingwood (Godfrey Norton), Gudrun Ure (Irene Adler), Noel Hood (Housekeeper). Other parts played by Anthony Viccars, Jonathan Scott, and Kim Grant.

Review: Radio Times, 173 (November 17, 1966), 29 (Michael Hardwick).

5405. "The Five Orange Pips," BBC Light Programme, Monday, November 28, 1966, 8:00-8:30 p.m. (Sherlock Holmes Again, No. 2)

Credits: Producer, Martyn C. Webster; Adapter, Michael Hardwick.

Cast: Carleton Hobbs (Sherlock Holmes), Norman Shelley (Dr. Watson), Barbara Mitchell (Mrs. Hudson), William Eedle (John Openshaw), Bruce Beeby (Elias Openshaw), James Thomason (Joseph Openshaw), Jonathan Scott (Shipping Clerk).

5406. "The Six Napoleons," BBC Light Programme, Monday, December 5, 1966, 8:00-8:30 p.m. (Sherlock Holmes Again, No. 3)

Credits: Producer, Martyn C. Webster; Adapter, Michael Hardwick.

Cast: Carleton Hobbs (Sherlock Holmes), Norman Shelley (Dr. Watson), Humphrey Morton (Inspector Lestrade), Alan Dudley (Horace Harker), Leroy Lingwood Harding), Allan McClelland (Morse Hudson), Geoffrey Wincott (Gelder), Arthur Lawrence (Sandeford).

5407. "The Boscombe Valley Mystery," BBC Light Programme, Monday, December 12, 1966, 8:00-8:30 p.m. (Sherlock Holmes Again, No. 4)

Credits: Producer, Martyn C. Webster; Adapter, Michael Hardwick.

Cast: Carleton Hobbs (Sherlock Holmes), Norman Shelley (Dr. Watson), Nigel Graham (James McCarthy), Geoffrey Wincott (Coroner), Humphrey Morton (Inspector Lestrade), Sheila Grant (Alice Turner), Bruce Beeby (John Turner).

5408. "The Crooked Man," BBC Light Programme, Monday, December 19, 1966, 8:00-8:30 p.m. (Sherlock Holmes Again, No. 5)

Credits: Producer, Martyn C. Webster; Adapter, Michael Hardwick.

Cast: Carleton Hobbs (Sherlock Holmes), Norman Shelley (Dr. Watson), Allan McClelland (Corporal Wood), Douglas Hankin (Sergeant Barclay), Alan Dudley (Major Murphy), Eva Stuart (Miss Morrison), William Eedle (William Flinn), Beth Boyd (Jane Stewart).

5409. "Wisteria Lodge," BBC Light Programme, Monday, December 26, 1966, 8:00-8:30 p.m. (Sherlock Holmes Again, No. 6)

Credits: Producer, Martyn C. Webster; Adapter, Michael Hardwick.

Cast: Carleton Hobbs (Sherlock Holmes),

Norman Shelley (Dr. Watson), John Baddeley (John Scott Eccles), Geoffrey Wincott (Inspector Gregson), Allan McClelland (Inspector Baynes), Gladys Spencer (Miss Burnet).

5410. "The Dying Detective," BBC Light Programme, Monday, January 2, 1967, 8:00-8:30 p.m. (Sherlock Holmes Again, No. 7)

Credits: Producer, Martyn C. Webster:Adapter, Michael Hardwick.

Cast: Carleton Hobbs (Sherlock Holmes), Norman Shelley (Dr. Watson), Barbara Mitchell (Mrs. Hudson), Alan Dudley (Inspector Morton), Arthur Lawrence (Staples), David March (Culverton Smith).

5411. "The Second Stain," BBC Light Programme, Monday, January 9, 1967, 8:00-8:30 p.m. (Sherlock Holmes Again, No. 8)

Credits: Producer, Martyn C. Webster; Adapter, Michael Hardwick.

Cast: Carleton Hobbs (Sherlock Holmes), Norman Shelley (Dr. Watson), Geoffrey Wincott (Lord Bellinger), Simon Lack (The Rt. Hon. Trelawney Hope), Barbara Mitchell (Mrs. Hudson), Hilda Schroder (Lady Hope), Humphrey Morton (Inspector Lestrade), Arthur Lawrence (Constable MacPherson).

5412. "The Final Problem," BBC Light Programme, Monday, January 16, 1967, 8:00-8:30 p.m. (Sherlock Holmes Again, No. 9)

Credits: Producer, Martyn C. Webster; Adapter, Michael Hardwick.

Cast: Carleton Hobbs (Sherlock Holmes), Norman Shelley (Dr. Watson), Rolf Lefebvre (Professor Moriarty), Alan Dudley (Peter Steiler), Gordon Gardner (Swiss Boy).

5413. "The Dancing Men," BBC Radio 2 (Light Programme), Tuesday, June 24, 1969, 8:15-8:45 p.m. (Sherlock Holmes, No. 1)

Credits: Producer, Graham Gauld; Adapter, Michael Hardwick.

Cast: Carleton Hobbs (Sherlock Holmes), Norman Shelley (Dr. Watson), Humphrey Morton (Hilton Cubitt), Ann Murray (Elsie Cubitt), John Cray (Hunt), Janet Morrison (Mrs. Hudson), Fred Yule (Inspector Martin), Janet Hitchman (Mrs. King), John Bentley (Abe Slaney).

5414. "A Case of Identity," BBC Radio 2 (Light Programme), Thursday, June 26, 1969, 8:15-8:45 p.m. (Sherlock Holmes, No. 2)

Credits: Producer, Graham Gauld; Adapter, Michael Hardwick.

Cast: Carleton Hobbs (Sherlock Holmes), Norman Shelley (Dr. Watson), Terry Raven (Billy), Ysanne Churchman (Mary Sutherland), Eva Haddon (Mrs. Sutherland), Lewis Stringer (Hosmer Angel), Humphrey Morton (Cabby).

5415. "Black Peter," BBC Radio 2 (Light Programme), Tuesday, July 1, 1969, 8:15-8:45 p.m. (Sherlock Holmes, No. 3)

Credits: Producer, Graham Gauld; Adapter, Michael Hardwick.

Cast: Carleton Hobbs (Sherlock Holmes), Norman Shelley (Dr. Watson), Arnold Peters (Inspector Hopkins), Gladys Spencer (Mrs. Carey), Mary Chester (Miss Carey), John Levitt (Neligan), Carl Oatley (Lancaster), Brian Haines (Pattins), Henry Stamper (Cairns).

5416. "The Red Circle," BBC Radio 2 (Light Programme), Thursday, July 3, 1969, 8:15-8:45 p.m. (Sherlock Holmes, No. 4)

Credits: Producer, Graham Gauld; Adapter, Michael Hardwick.

Cast: Carleton Hobbs (Sherlock Holmes), Norman Shelley (Dr. Watson), Grace Allardyce (Mrs. Warren), Robert Rietty (Gennaro), Humphrey Morton (Inspector Gregson), Robert Howay (Leverton), Gigi Gatti (Emilia).

5417. "The Lion's Mane," BBC Radio 2 (Light Programme), Tuesday, July 8, 1969, 8:15-8:45 p.m. (Sherlock Holmes, No. 5)

Credits: Producer, Graham Gauld; Adapter, Michael Hardwick.

Cast: Carleton Hobbs (Sherlock Holmes), Norman Shelley (Dr. Watson), Garard Green (Stackhurst), Henry Davies (Murdoch), Humphrey Morton (Bellamy), Pat Pleasance (Maud Bellamy), Janet Morrison (Mrs. Hudson).

5418. "His Last Bow," BBC Radio 2 (Light Programme), Thursday, July 10, 1969, 8:15-8:45 p.m. (Sherlock Holmes, No. 6)

Credits: Producer, Graham Gauld; Adapter, Michael Hardwick.

Cast: Carleton Hobbs (Sherlock Holmes), Norman Shelley (Dr. Watson), Francis de Wolff (Von Herling), Denis Goacher (Von Bork), Janet Morrison (Mrs. Hudson).

1969 NIGEL STOCK

5419. "The Hound of the Baskervilles," BBC Radio 4, Monday, October 20-November 7, 1969, 11:02-11:15 p.m. 15 episodes. (A Book at Bedtime)

Credits: Producer, John Cardy; Adapter, Michael Hardwick.

Cast: Nigel Stock (reader).

NORWAY

1958-1959 KNUT M. HANSSON AND WILLIE HOEL

5420. "De tre studentene" (3Stu), Norsk Rikskringkasting (Norwegian State Broadcasting Corporation), Tuesday, December 16, 1958, 1720-1750.

Credits: Director, Bjørn; Bryn; Adapter, Gunnar Lie.

Cast: Knut M. Hansson (Sherlock Holmes), Willie Hoel (Dr. Watson), Stig Egede-Nissen (Hilton Soames), Eilif Armand (Bannister), Knut Risan (Gilchrist).

5421. "Gull-lorgnetten" (Gold), Tuesday, January 20, 1959, 1705-1735.

Credits: Director, Bjørn Bryn; Adapter, Gunnar Lie.

Cast: Knut M. Hansson (Sherlock Holmes), Willie Hoel (Dr. Watson), Erling Lindahl (Stanley Hopkins), Folkman Schaaning (Professor Coram), Irene Thomsen (Mrs. Marker), Arne Rygg (Constable Wilson), Ragnhild Michelsen (Anna).

1959-1964 FRIDTJOF MJØEN AND ARNE BANG-HANSEN

5422. "Sherlock Holmes' vanskeligste sak," Saturday, May 23, 1959, 2035-2120.

Credits: Author, Arne Hirdman; Translator, Odd Refsdal; Director, Paul Skoe.

Cast: Fridtjof Mjøen (Sherlock Holmes), Arne Bang-Hansen (Dr. Watson), Else Heiberg (Mary Foley), Finn Bernhoft (George Newnes), Jon Lennart Mjøen (Sir Arthur Conan Doyle).

5423. "Rekreasjonsoppholdet" (Reig), Saturday, October 26, 1963, 2030-2105.

Credits: Director, Paul Skoe; Adapter, Michael Hardwick; Translator, Hans Heiberg.

Cast: Fridtjof Mjøen (Sherlock Holmes), Arne Bang-Hansen (Dr. Watson), Eilif Armand (Colonel Hayter), Tore Foss (Inspector Forrester), Rolf Just Nilsen (Butler), Helge Essmar (Squire Cunningham), Ståle Bjørnhaug (Alex Cunningham), Gisle Straume (Squire Acton).

5424. "Thornybroen" (Thor), Saturday, November 2, 1963, 2110-2145. Repeated: January 8, 1971, 1930-2005.

Credits: Director, Paul Skoe; Adapter, Michael Hardwick; Translator, Hans Heiberg.

Cast: Fridtjof Mjøen (Sherlock Holmes), Arne Bang-Hansen (Dr. Watson), Ola Isene (J. Neil Gibson), Wilfred Breistrand (Sergeant Coventry), Bab Christensen (Grace Dunbar).

5425. "Den prominente klienten" (Illu), Saturday, November 9, 1963, 2030-2110.

Credits: Director, Paul Skoe; Adapter, Michael Hardwick; Translator, Hans Heiberg.

Cast: Fridtjof Mjøen (Sherlock Holmes), Arne Bang-Hansen (Dr. Watson), Kolbjørn Buøen (Sir James Damery), Alfred Solaas (Baron Gruner), Ingeborg Cook (Kitty Winter), Henry Nyren (Shinwell Johnson).

5426. "Drapet på herregården" (Abbe), Saturday, November 16, 1963, 2035-2120.

Credits: Director, Paul Skoe; Adapter, Michael Hardwick; Translator, Hans Heiberg.

Cast: Fridtjof Mjøen (Sherlock Holmes), Anre Bang-Hansen (Dr. Watson), Tore Foss (Stanley Hopkins), Mona Hofland (Lady Brackenstall), Astrid Sommer (Theresa Wright), Øyvind Øyen (Ship's Office Clerk), Tor Stokke (Captain Jack Croker).

5427. "Musgrave-ritualet" (Musg), Saturday, November 23, 1963, 2030-2110.

Credits: Director, Paul Skoe; Adapter, Michael Hardwick; Translator, Hans Heiberg.

Cast: Fridtjof Mjøen (Sherlock Holmes), Arne Bang-Hansen (Dr. Watson), Rolf Berntsen (Reginald Musgrave), Per Lillo-Stenberg (Brunton), Lillemor Hoel (Rachel Howells), Gudrun Waadeland (Nurse), Finn Bernhoft (Constable).

5428. "Den vansirete tiggeren" (Twis), Saturday, November 30, 1963, 2040-2115.

Credits: Director, Paul Skoe; Adapter, Michael Hardwick; Translator, Hans Heiberg.

Cast: Fridtjof Mjøen (Sherlock Holmes), Arne Bang-Hansen (Dr. Watson), Helga Holdhus (Mrs. Watson), Anne Mari Dale (Kate Whitney), Dan Fosse (Isa Whitney and Indian Sailor), Britta Lech-Hansen (Mrs. St. Clair), Carsten Winger (Hugh Boone), Bjarne Bø (Inspector Bradstreet), Gerhard Bjelland (Constable).

5429. "Gullorgnetten" (Gold), Saturday, December 7, 1963, 2105-2145.

Credits: Director, Paul Skoe; Adapter, Michael Hardwick; Translator, Hans Heiberg.

Cast: Fridtjof Mjøen (Sherlock Holmes), Arne Bang-Hansen (Dr. Watson), Tore Foss (Stanley Hopkins), Hans Stormoen (Professor Coram), Nancy Schiefloe (Mrs. Marker), Bjørg Engh (Susan), Erik Øksnes (Constable Wilson), Gøril Havrevold (Anna).

5430. "Charles Augustus Milverton," Saturday, December 14, 1963, 2030-2105.

Credits: Director, Paul Skoe; Adapter, Michael Hardwick; Translator, Hans Heiberg.

Cast: Fridtjof Mjøen (Sherlock Holmes), Arne Bang-Hansen (Dr. Watson), Astrid Folstad (Agatha), Erling Lindahl (C. A. Milverton), Arne Rygg (Gardener), Sverre Wilberg (Inspector Lestjade).

5431. "Shoscombe herregård," Saturday, December 21, 1963, 2050-2130.

Credits: Director, Paul Skoe; Adapter,

Michael Hardwick; Translator, Hans Heiberg.

Cast: Fridtjof Mjøen (Sherlock Holmes), Arne Bang-Hansen (Dr. Watson), Harald Heide Steen (John Mason), Oscar Egede Nissen (Fred Stephens), Leif Enger (Barnes), Bjarne Andersen (Sir Robert Norburton), Ragnhild Kristiansen (Mrs. Norlett).

Radio

5432. "Smaragd-kronen" (Bery), Saturday, December 28, 1963, 2045-2120.

Credits: Director, Paul Skoe; Adapter, Michael Hardwick; Translator, Hans Heiberg.

Cast: Fridtjof Mjøen (Sherlock Holmes), Arne Bang-Hansen (Dr. Watson), Knut M. Hansson (Alexander Holder), Thorleif Reiss (His Excellency), Anne-Lise Tangstad (Mary Holder), Per Christensen (Arthur Holder), Marit Lund (Miss Parker), Jan Pande-Rolfsen (Roberts).

5433. "Det kataleptiske anfallet" (Resi), Saturday, January 4, 1964, 1925-2000.

Credits: Director, Paul Skoe; Adapter, Michael Hardwick; Translator, Hans Heiberg.

Cast: Fridtjof Mjøen (Sherlock Holmes), Arne Bang-Hansen (Dr. Watson), Knut Risan (Percy Trevelyan), Toralf Sandø (Mr. Blessington), Carl Struve (Count Egrovitch), Helge Reiss (Ivan Egrovitch), Frimann Falck Claussen (Inspector Lanner).

5434. "Det stripete båndet" (Spec), Saturday, January 11, 1964, 2040-2120. Repeated: January 15, 1971, 1930-2005.

Credits: Director, Hans Heiberg; Adapter, Michael Hardwick; Translator, Hans Heiberg.

Cast: Fridtjof Mjøen (Sherlock Holmes), Anre Bang-Hansen (Dr. Watson), Ingerid Vardund (Helen Stoner), Inger Teien (Julia Stoner), Jack Fjeldstad (Dr. Grimesby Roylott).

5435. "Det tomme huset" (Empt), Saturday, January 18, 1964, 2100-2135.

Credits: Director, Paul Skoe; Adapter, Michael Hardwick; Translator, Hans Heiberg.

Cast: Fridtjof Mjøen (Sherlock Holmes), Arne Bang-Hansen (Dr. Watson), Jon Lennart Mjøen (Mycroft Holmes), Bjørg Svendsen (Maidservant), Rolf Sand (First Man), Børseth Rasmussen (Colonel Moran and Second Man), Tore Foss (Inspector Forrester), Ingrid Øwre (Mrs. Hudson).

1961-1962 ERLING LINDAHL AND EINAR VAAGE

5436. "Den forsvunne gåsesteken" (Blue), Tuesday, January 17, 1961, 1730-1800. Repeated: December 28, 1967, 1700-1730.

Credits: Director, Barthold Halle; Adapter, Gunnar Lie.

Cast: Lars Nordrum (Narrator), Erling Lindahl (Sherlock Holmes), Einar Vaage (Dr. Watson), Bjarne Bø (Breckinridge), Helge Reiss (Peterson), Per Gjersøe (Henry Baker), Øyvind Johnsen (Breckinridge), Henrik Anker Steen (James Ryder).

5437. "De rødhåredes forening" (RedH), Tuesday, March 21, 1961, 1730-1800.

Credits: Director, Barthold Halle; Adapter, Gunnar Lie.

Cast: Lars Nordrum (Narrator), Erling Lindahl (Sherlock Holmes), Einar Vaage (Dr. Watson), Stig Egede-Nissen (Jabez Wilson), Magne Bleness (John Clay), Frank Robert (Peter Jones), Folkman Schaaning (Mr. Merryweather), Arne Rygg (Archie).

5438. "Den mystiske leieboeren" (RedC), Tuesday, June 6, 1961, 1710-1740. Repeated: June 23, 1969, 1710-1740.

Credits: Director, Barthold Halle; Adapter, Gunnar Lie.

Cast: Thor Hjort-Jensen (Narrator), Erling Lindahl (Sherlock Holmes), Einar Vaage (Dr. Watson), Edel Eckblad (Mrs. Warren), Gunnar Simenstad (Tobias Gregson), Astrid Folstad (Emilia Lucca).

5439. "Det forsvunne dokument" (Nava), Tuesday, September 12, 1961, 1730-1800.

Credits: Director, Barthold Halle; Adapter, Gunnar Lie.

Cast: Thor Hjort-Jensen (Narrator), Erling Lindahl (Sherlock Holmes), Einar Vaage (Dr. Watson), Øyvind Øyen (Percy Phelps), Ragnhild Hiorthøy (Annie Harrison), Joachim Calmeyer (Joseph Harrison), Folkman Schaaning (Lord Holdhurst), Magne Bleness (Inspector Forbes).

5440. "Et sjeldent navn" (3Gar), Tuesday, January 4, 1962, 1730-1800.

Credits: Director, Barthold Halle; Adapter, Gunnar Lie.

Cast: Lars Nordrum (Narrator), Erling Lindahl (Sherlock Holmes), Einar Vaage (Dr. Watson), Øyvind Øyen (John Garrideb), Sverre Hansen (Nathan Garrideb), Ragnhild Michelsen (Mrs. Hudson).

5441. "De seks Napoleonsbystene," Thursday, October 25, 1962, 1730-1800.

Credits: Director, Magne Bleness; Adapter, Gunnar Lie.

Cast: Lars Nordrum (Narrator), Erling Lindahl (Sherlock Holmes), Einar Vaage (Dr. Watson), Frank Robert (Inspector Lestrade), Per Gjersøe (Horace Harker), Carsten Winger (Morse Hudson), Wilfred Breistrand (Gelder), Tor Stokke (Harding), Sverre Holm (Beppo).

1968 JENS GUNDERSEN AND ARNE BANG-HANSEN

5442. Scenes from "Gullorgnetten," Saturday,

February 24, 1968, 2225-2305. ("En hestedrosje i Baker Street")
Credits: Adapter, Tor Edvin Dahl; Translator, Lotte Holmboe.
Cast: Jens Gundersen (Sherlock Holmes), Arne Bang-Hansen (Dr. Watson), Ola Isene (Professor Coram).

SWEDEN

1959-1960 GEORG ÅRLIN AND RAGNAR FALCK

5443. "De tre studenterna," Sveriges Radio, Ch. 1, Saturday, December 27, 1959, 1600-1630. (Ungdomsteatern)
Credits: Director, Ingrid Luterkort; Adapter, Gunnar Lie.
Cast: Georg Årlin (Sherlock Holmes), Ragnar Falck (Dr. Watson), Toivo Pawlo (Soames), Ivar Wahlgren (Bannister), Lars Edström (Gilchrist), Bernt Callenbo, Olof Brostedt (Students).

5444. "Den guldbågade pincenén," Syeriges Radio, Ch. 1, Sunday, January 3, 1960, 1600-1635. (Ungdomsteatern)
Credits: Director, Ingrid Luterkort; Adapter, Gunnar Lie.
Cast: Georg Årlin (Sherlock Holmes), Ragnar Falck (Dr. Watson), Ivar Wahlgren (Detective Hopkins), Gunnar Olsson (Professor Coram), Nina Scenna (Mrs. Coram), Dagmar Bentzen (Mrs. Marker), Britt Olofsson (Susan Tarlton), Bernt Callenbo (Constable Wilson).

1967 JÖRGEN CEDERBERG

5445. "Ur Baskervilles hund," Sveriges Radio, Ch. 1, Monday, April 24, 1967, 1615-1645.
Cast: Jörgen Cederberg (reader).

5446. "Det spräckliga bandet," Sveriges Radio, Ch. 1, Monday-Tuesday, April 24-25, 1967, 1615-1645.
Credits: Translator, Nils Holmberg.
Cast: Jörgen Cederberg (reader).

1967 HANS LINDGREN

5447. "Scenes from De fyras tecken," Sveriges Radio, Ch. 1, Tuesday, Thursday, September 26, 28, 1967, 1630-1700. (Mästerdetektiver och andra skärpta)
Cast: Hans Lindgren (reader), Stig Ericsson, Jörgen Cederberg.

1971 GEORG ÅRLIN AND GÖSTA PRÜZELIUS

5448. "Baskervilles hund," Radioteatern, Ch. 1, Saturdays, January 9-February 6, 1971, 0900-0930. 5 episodes.
Credits: Translator, Nils Holmberg; Adapter, Ittla Frodi; Director, Lars-Erik Liedholm.

Cast: Georg Årlin (Sherlock Holmes), Gösta Prüzelius (Dr. Watson), Börje Ahlstedt (Sir Henry Baskerville), Christian Berling (Dr. Mortimer), Henrik Schildt (Mr. Barrymore), Annika Tretow (Mrs. Barrymore), Björn Gustafson (Mr. Stapleton), Manne Grünberger (Mr. Frankland), Lena Granhagen (Beryl Stapleton), Nisse Söderlund (Cartwright), Einar Axelsson (Hotel-porter), Åke Lindström (Clayton), Sven-Eric Gamble (Lestrade).

UNITED STATES

1930 WILLIAM GILLETTE AND LEIGH LOVELL

5449. "The Adventure of the Speckled Band," New York: WEAF-NBC, Monday, October 20, 1930, 10:00-10:30 p.m. (Adventures of Sherlock Holmes)
Credit: Sponsor, G. Washington Coffee; Writer, Edith Meiser; Announcer, Joseph Bell.
Cast: William Gillette (Sherlock Holmes), Leigh Lovell (Dr. Watson).
The first dramatization of Sherlock Holmes on radio.
Review: New York Times (October 26, 1930) IX, 8, and reprinted in *VH*, 6, No. 3 (September 1972), 7-8.

1930-1933 RICHARD GORDON AND LEIGH LOVELL

5450. *Adventures of Sherlock Holmes.* New York: WEAF-NBC, Mondays, October 27, 1930-June 15, 1931, 10:00-10:30 p.m. 34 programs.
Cast: Richard Gordon (Sherlock Holmes), Leigh Lovell (Dr. Watson).
Credits: Sponsor, G. Washington Coffee; Writer, Edith Meiser; Announcer, Joseph Bell.
Contents: October 27: Scan. - November 3· RedH. - 10: Copp. - 17: Bosc. - 24: Twis. - December 1: Stoc. . 8: Silv. - 15: Croo. - 22: Nobl. - 29: Reig. - January 5: Musg. - 12: Resi. - 19: Nava. - 26: Gree. - February 2: Cree. - 9: Maza. - 16: Suss. - 23: Illu. - March 2: Blan. - 9: Five. - 16: Thor. - 23: Lion. - 30: Shos. - April 6: Reti. - 25: SixN. - June 1: Gold. - 8: Miss. - 15: Abbe 20: Danc. - 27: Sopi. - May 4: Prio . - 11: Blac. -

5451. ———. New York: WEAF-NBC, Thursdays, September 17-December 17, 1931, 9:30-10:00 p.m.; WJZ-NBC, Wednesdays, December 30, 1931-April 27, 1932, 9:00-9:30 p.m.; WEAF-NBC, Thursdays, May 5-June 23, 1932. 40 programs.
Credits: Sponsor, G. Washington Coffee; Writer, Edith Meiser; Announcer, Joseph Bell.

Actors, Performances, & Recordings

Radio

Edith Meiser, who wrote many Sherlock Holmes radio scripts (5450.5460) and comic strips (6196-6200).

Cast: Richard Gordon (Sherlock Holmes), Leigh Lovell (Dr. Watson).
Contents: [Unknown].

5452. ———. New York: WJZ-NBC, Wednesdays, September 28, 1932-May 31, 1933, 9:00-9:30 p.m. 36 programs.
Credits: Sponsor, G. Washington Coffee; Writer, Edith Meiser; Announcer, Joseph Bell.
Partial cast: Richard Gordon (Sherlock Holmes), Leigh Lovell (Dr. Watson).
Contents: September 28: Seco. - October 5: Empt. - 12: Last. - 19: 3Stu. - 26: Sign (pt. 1). - November 2: Sign (pt. 2). - 9: Sign (pt. 3). - 16: Sign (pt. 4). - 23: Sign (pt. 5). - 30: Sign (pt. 6). - December 7: Blue. - 14: Death in the Club Window. - 21: The Haunted Bagpipes. - 28: Murder by Proxy. - January 4: The Adventure of the Dying Rose Bush. - 11: The Adventure of the Missing Black Bag. - 18: Her Majesty's Wine Cellar. - 25: The Adventure of the Missing Dancer. - February 1: Death at Stonehenge. - 8: Mr. Pottle's Secret Profession. - 15: The Adventure of the Voodoo Curse. - 22: Death Holds the Prompt Book. - March 1: The Adventure of the Typewritten Will. - 8: The Adventure of the Aristocratic Model. - 15: The Adventure of the Poison Keg. - 22: The Corpse in the Cab. - 29: The Jewish Breast Plate. - April 5: The Lost Train. - 12: Shos. - 19: The Case of the Sealed Room. - 26: The Case of Vamberry, the Wine Merchant. - May 3: The Case of the Walking Corpse. - 10: The Case of the Poisoned Stick. - 17: The Case with Two Solutions. - 24: The Singular Affair of the Aluminum Crutch. - 31: The Armchair Solution.

1934-1935 LOUIS HECTOR AND LEIGH LOVELL

5453. ———. New York: WJZ-NBC, Sundays, November 11-December 30, 1934, 4:00-4:30 p.m.; January 6-May 26, 1935, 9:45-10:15 p.m. 29 programs.
Credits: Sponsor, G. Washington Coffee; Writer, Edith Meiser.
Partial cast: Louis Hector (Sherlock Holmes) Leigh Lovell (Dr. Watson).
Contents: November 11: The Jewish Breastplate. - November 18: The Case of the Lost Special. - November 25: The Adventure of the Syrian Mummy. - December 2: The Case of the Sealed Room. - December 9: The Case of Vamberry, the Wine Merchant. - December 16: [Unknown]. - December 23: The Case of the Poisoned Stick. - December 30, January 6: [Unknown]. - January 13: The Armchair Solution. - January 20: The Case of Dual Personality. - January 27: [Unknown]. - February 3: Cherchez la Femme. - February 10-May 26: [Unknown].

1935 WILLIAM GILLETTE

5454. "Sherlock Holmes," New York: WABC, Monday, November 18, 1935, 9:00-10:00 p.m. (Lux Radio Theatre).
Credits: Writer, William Gillette; Adapter, Edith Meiser.
Partial cast: William Gillette (Sherlock Holmes).
Review: New York Times (November 24, 1935), IX, 15, and reprinted in *VH*, 6, No. 3 (September 1972), 8-9.

1936 RICHARD GORDON AND HARRY WEST

5455. *Sherlock Holmes.* New York: WOR-MBS, Saturdays, February 1-March 28, 1936, 10:30-11:00 p.m.; Saturdays, April 4-July 25, 1936, 7:30-8:00 p.m.; Saturdays, August 1-September 26, 1936, 8:30-9:00 p.m. 35 programs.
Credits: Sponsor, Household Finance Corp.; Writer, Edith Meiser; Announcer, Joseph Bell.
Partial cast: Richard Gordon (Sherlock Holmes), Harry West (Dr. Watson).
Contents: February 1: Spec. - 8: RedH. - 15: Scan. - 22: Twis. - 29: Reig. - March 7: Suss. - 14: Resi. - 21: Cree. - 28: Dyin. - April 4: The Hindoo in the Wicker Basket. - 11: Silv. - 18: Illu. - 25: Death in the Club Window. - May 2: Blan. - 9: Danc. - 16: Death at Stonehenge. - 23: Maza. - 30: Devi. - June 6: The Armchair Solution. - 13: Thor. - 20: Soli - 27: Musg. - July 4: The Adventure of the Typewritten Will. - 11: Stoc. - 18: The Giant Rat of Sumatra. - 25:

Nobl. - August 1: Lion. - 8: Norw. - 15: Nava. - 22: Murder in the Waxworks. - 29 Scan - September 5: [Unknown]. - 12: Miss. - 19: Bery. - 26: Wist.

Review: Radio Stars (August 1936), 47, 64 (Lester Gottlieb).

5456. ———. New York: WEAF-NBC, Thursdays, October 1- December 24, 1936, 11:15-11:45 p.m. 13 programs.

Credits: Sponsor, Household Finance Corp.; Writer, Edith Meiser; Announcer, Joseph Bell.

Partial cast: Richard Gordon (Sherlock Holmes), Harry West (Dr. Watson).

Contents: October 1: The Case of the Sealed Room. - 8: The Adventure of the Voodoo Curse. - 15: Empt. - 22: The Haunted Bagpipes. - 29: The Adventure of the Dying Rose Bush. - November 5: [Unknown]. - 12: Seco. - 19: Gold. - 26: Blac. - December 3: SixN. - 10: Reti. - 17: Card. - 24: Blue.

1939-1946 BASIL RATHBONE AND NIGEL BRUCE

5457. *Adventures of Sherlock Holmes.* New York: WJZ-NBC, Mondays, October 2, 1939-March 11, 1940, 8:00-8:30 p.m. 24 programs. Originated from Hollywood. Hookup, 29 stations.

Credits: Sponsor, Grove Laboratories (Bromo Quinine); Producer, Harold Kemp; Adapter, Edith Meiser; Announcer, John Conte; Music, Lou Kosloff.

Partial cast: Basil Rathbone (Sherlock Holmes), Nigel Bruce (Dr. Watson).

Contents: October 2: Suss. - 9: Silv. - 16: Spec. - 23: Twis. - 30: Devi. - November 6: Bruc. - 13: Lion. - 20: Dyin. - 27: Cree. - December 4: Chas. - 11: Musg. - 18: Wist. - 25: 3Gar. - January 1: Blue. - 8: Prio. - 15: Gree. - 22: Card. - 29: Seco. - February 5; Abbe. - 12: Shos. - 19: Blan. - 26: Reig. - March 4: Bery. - 11: Reti.

Reviews: Billboard, 51 (October 14, 1939), 7 (Franken); *Radio Daily,* 9 (October 4, 1939), 7; *Variety,* 136 (October 4, 1939), 26.

5458. *Sherlock Holmes.* New York: WJZ-NBC, Sundays, September 29, 1940-March 9, 1941, 8:30-9:00 p.m. 24 programs. Originated from Hollywood. Hookup, 53 stations.

Credits: Sponsor, Grove Laboratories (Bromo Quinine); Producer, Tom McKnight; Adapter, Edith Meiser; Announcer and Interlocutor, Knox Manning; Music, Lou Kosloff.

Partial cast: Basil Rathbone (Sherlock Holmes), Nigel Bruce (Dr. Watson).

Contents: September 29: Empt. - October 6: Copp. - 13: Nobl. - 20: Engr. - 28: RedH.- November 3: Thor. - 10: Croo. - 17: The Norwood Hills Mystery. - 24: 3Stu. -

December 1: Danc. - 8: Blac. - 15: The Adventure of the Lost Naval Treaty. - 22: Bosc. - 29: Miss. - January 5: Maza. - 12: Houn (pt. 1). - 12: Houn (pt. 2). - 26: Houn (pt. 3). - February 2: Houn (pt. 4). - 9: Houn (pt. 5). - 16: Houn (pt. 6). - 23: Resi. - March 2: Spec. - 9: Shos.

Reviews: Billboard, 52 (October 19, 1940), 28 (Weiss); *New York Times* (October 6, 1940), IX, 10 (Lanfranco Rasponi); *New York Times* (March 2, 1941), IX, 12 (R. W. Stewart); *Variety,* 140 (October 2, 1940), 33.

5459. *Sherlock Holmes.* New York: WEAF-NBC, Sundays, October 5, 1941-March 1, 1942, 10:30-11:00 p.m. 22 programs. Originated from Hollywood.

Credits: Sponsor, Grove Laboratories (Bromo Quinine); Producer, Russell Seeds; Writer and Adapter, Edith Meiser; Announcer and Interlocutor, Knox Manning; Music, Lou Kosloff.

Partial cast: Basil Rathbone (Sherlock Holmes), Nigel Bruce (Dr. Watson).

Contents: October 5: Illu. - 12: SixN. - 19: Devi. - 26: Soli. - November 2: The Case of the Walking Corpse. - 9: Stoc. - 16: The Adventure of the Missing Papers. - 23: The Mystery of the Magician. - 30: Iden. - December 7: The Mystery of Mrs. Warren's Key. - 14: The Mystery of the Dark Gentleman. - 21: The Mystery of Donald's Death. - 28: The Mystery of the Gloria Scott. - January 4: Seco. - 11: The Haunted Bagpipes. - 18: 3 Gab. - 25: Lion. - February 1: Five. - 8: The Voodoo Mystery. - 15: The Dark Tragedy of the Circus. - 22: Suss. - March 1: The Giant Rat of Sumatra.

Review: Variety, 144 (October 8, 1941), 28.

5460. *Sherlock Holmes.* New York: WOR-MBS, Fridays, April 30-October 1, 1943, 8:30-8:55 p.m. 23 programs. Originated from Hollywood.

Credits: Sponsor, Petri Wine; Director, Glenn Heisch; Writer and Adapter, Edith Meiser; Announcer and Interlocutor, Owen Babby.

Partial cast: Basil Rathbone (Sherlock Holmes), Nigel Bruce (Dr. Watson).

Contents: April 30: [Unknown]. - May 7: Copp. - 14: Twis. - 21: Devi. - 28: RedH. - June 4: Engr. - 11: Silv. - 18: Dyin. - 25: Wist. - July 2: Prio. - 9: Cree. - 16: Musg. - 23: Gree. - 30: Murder in the Wax Works. - August 6: The Missing Leonardo da Vinci. - 13: The Syrian Mummy. - 20: The Missing Dancer [Scan]. - 27: Card. - September 3: Reti. - 10: Bruc. - 17: The Case of the Dying Rosebush. - 24: The Missing Black Bag (with Ronald Colman). - October 1: Spec.

Review: Variety, 150 (May 19, 1943), 30.

5461. *Sherlock Holmes.* New York: WOR-MBS, Mondays, October 4, 1943-May 28,

1945, 8:30-9:00 p.m. 87 programs. Originated from Hollywood.

Credits: Sponsor, Petri Wine; Producer, Glenhall Taylor; Writers, Bruce Taylor (Leslie Charteris), Denis Green, Anthony Boucher.

Partial cast: Basil Rathbone (Sherlock Holmes), Nigel Bruce (Dr. Watson).

Contents: October 4, 11, 18: [Unknown]. - 25: Ricoletti of the Club Foot. - November 1: The Brother's Footsteps. - 8: The Shocking Affair of the S. S. Friesland. - 15: The Apparition at Sadler's Wells. - 22: Murder at the Park. - 29: The Case of Mrs. Farintosh's Opal Tiara. - December 6: The Camberwell Poisoning Case. - 13: The Adventure of the Jumping Jack. - 20: The Adventure of the Missing Black Dog. - 27: The Adventure of the Tired Captain. - January 3, 10: [Unknown]. - 17: The Case of the Departed Banker. - 24: The Amateur Mendicant Society. - 31: The Dog That Howled in the Night. - February 7: Death At Cornwall. - 14: The Case of the Red Leeches - 21: The Adventure of Doctor Moore Agar. - 28: The Case of the Missing Bullion. - March 6: Death on the Scottish Express. - 13: The Peculiar Persecution of John Vincent Hardin. - 20: The Man Who Drowned in Paddington Station. - 27: The Haunted Bagpipes. - April 3: The Fingerprints That Couldn't Lie. - 10: The Man Who Was Hanged. - 17: The Singular Contents of the Ancient British Barrow. - 24: The Dentist Who Used Wolfbane. - May 1: Holmes and the Half Man. - 8: The Adventure of the Phantom Iceberg. - 15: The Adventure of the Missing Bloodstains. - 22: The Adventure of the Superfluous Pearl. - 29: The Adventure of Skull and Bones. - June 5: The Adventure of the Corpse in a Trunk. - 12: The Monster of Gyre. - 19: The Man with the Twisted Lip. - 26: The Adventure of the Dissimilar Body. - July 3: The Adventure of the Amateur Mendicant Society. - 10: The Adventure of the Devil's Foot. - 17: The Adventure of the Bruce-Partington Plans. - 24: The Strange Case of the Aluminum Crutch. - 31: The Case of the Giant Rat of Sumatra. -August 7: The Case of the Lighthouse, Frightened Politician, and Trained Cormorant. - 14: Murder by Remote Control. - 21: The Case of the Missing Corpse. - 28: The Adventure of the African Leopard Men.- September 4: Dimitrios, the Divine. - 11: Guardian of the Dead. - 18: The Invisible Necklace. - 25: The Vampire of Cadiz. - October 2: 200-Year-Old Murderer. - 9: The Third Hunchback. - 16: The Missing Treaty. - 23: League of Unhappy Orphans. - 30: The Haunted Chateau. - November 6: Murder Under the Big Top. - 13: Strange Case of the Veiled Horseman. - 20: Secret of Glaive. - 27: The Steamship Friesland. - December 4: Case of the Tell-Tale Bruises. - 11: The Island of

Uffa. - 18: The Wandering Miser. - 25: The Blue Carbuncle. - January 1: Should Auld Acquaintance Be Forgot? - 8: The Play's the Thing. - 15: Dr. Anselmo. - 22: The Elusive Umbrella. - 29: The Werewolf of Vair. - February 5: The Dead Adventuress. - 12: The Newmarket Killers. - 19: Mystery of the Surrey Inn. - 26: Lady Francis Carfax. - March 5: The Doomed Sextet. - 12: The Erratic Windmill - 19: Secret of Stonehenge. - 26: Book of Tobit. - April 2: Amateur Mendicant Society. - 9: The Viennese Strangler. - 16: The Remarkable Worm. - 23: The Notorious Canary Trainer. - 30: The Unfortunate Tobacconist. - May 7: The Purloined Ruby. - 14: On the Flanders. - 21: The Paradol Chamber. - 28: Dance of Death.

5462. *Sherlock Holmes.* New York: WOR-MBS, Mondays, September 3, 1945-May 27, 1946, 8:30-9:00 p.m. 39 programs. Originated from Hollywood.

Credits: Sponsor, Petri Wine; Producer, Edna Best; Supervisor, Glenwall Taylor; Writers, Denis Green and Anthony Boucher; Announcer and Interlocutor, Harry Bartell.

Partial cast: Basil Rathbone (Sherlock Holmes), Nigel Bruce (Dr. Watson).

Contents: September 3: The Limping Ghost (with Joe Kerns, Paul Freeze, Elizabeth Harrover, Gloria Jordan). - 10: Col. Warburton's Madness. - 17: Out of Date Murder. - 23: The Eyes of Mr. Leyton. - October 1: The Problem of Thor Bridge. - 8: The Vanishing Elephant. - 15: The Manor House Case. - 22: The Great Gandolfo. - 29: Murder in the Moonlight. - November 5: The Fifth of November. - 12: The Speckled Band. - 19: The Case of the Double Zero. - 26: The Case of the Accidental Murderess. - December 3: Murder in the Casbah. - 10: A Scandal in Bohemia. - 17: The Second Generation. - 24: The Night Before Christmas. - 31: The Strange Case of the Iron Box. - January 7: The Hampton Heath Killer. - 14: Murder in the Himalayas. - 21: The Telltale Pigeon Feathers. - 28: Sweeney Todd, the Demon Barber. - February 4: The Cross of Damascus. - 11: [Unknown]. - 18: The Camberwell Poisoning Case. - 25: Murder At the Opera. - March 4: [Unknown]. - 11: The Adventure of the Living Doll. - 18: The Adventure of the Blarney Stone. - 25: The Girl with the Gazelle. - April 1: The April Fool's Adventure. - 8: The Vanishing Scientists. - 15, 22: [Unknown]. - 29: Waltz of Death. - May 6: The Man with the Twisted Lip. - 13: The Case of the Uneasy Chair. - 20: The Haunting of Sherlock Holmes. - 27: The Singular Affair of the Baconian Cipher.

Review: Variety, 159 (September 5, 1945), 26.

1946-1947 TOM CONWAY AND NIGEL BRUCE

5463. *New Adventures of Sherlock Holmes.* New York: WJZ-ABC, Saturdays, October 12, 1946-January 4, 1947, 9:30-10:00 p.m.; Mondays, January 13-July 7, 1947, 8:30-9:00 p.m. 39 programs. Originated from Hollywood.

Credits: Sponsor, Kreml; Producer, Tom McKnight; Writers, Anthony Boucher and Denis Green; Announcer and Interlocutor, Joseph Bell; Music, Lou Kosloff.

Partial cast: Tom Conway (Sherlock Holmes), Nigel Bruce (Dr. Watson).

Contents: October 12: [Unknown]. - 19: The Case of the Black Angus. - 26: The Clue of the Hungry Cat. - November 2, 9: [Unknown]. - 16: The Mystery of the Murdered Violinist. - 23: [Unknown]. - 30: The Strange Death of Mrs. Abernetty. - December 7: The Case of the Coptic Compass. - 14: The Vanishing Emerald. - 21: [Unknown], 28: The White Cockerel. - January 4, 13: [Unknown], - 20: The Babbling Butler. - 27: [Unknown]. - February 3: The Adventure of the Dying Detective. - 10: The Persecuted Millionaire. - 17: The Haunted Bagpipes. - 24: The Horseless Carriage. - March 3: Queue For Murder. - 10: The Egyptian Curse. - 17: - [Unknown]. - 24: The Scarlet Worm - 31: [Unknown]. - 14: The Carpathian Horror. - 21: [Unknown]. - 28: The Island of Death. - May 5: The Pointless Robbery. - 12: The Voodoo Curse. - 19: [Unknown]. - 26: The Adventure of a Submerged Baronet. - June 2: The Red-Headed League. - 9, 16: [Unknown]. - 23: The Adventure of the Speckled Band. - 30; July 7: [Unknown].

Review: Variety, 164 (October 16, 1946), 30 (Cars).

1947-1948 JOHN STANLEY AND ALFRED SHIRLEY

5464. *Sherlock Holmes.* New York: WOR-MBS, Sundays, September 28, 1947-June 20, 1948, 7:00-7:30 p.m. 39 programs. Originated from Hollywood.

Credits: Sponsor, Trimount Clothing Co. (Clipper Craft Clothes); Producer and Director, Basil Loughrane; Writer, Edith Meiser; Announcer, Cy Harrice; Engineer, Don Williamson; Sound, Hal Reid; Music, Albert Buhrman.

Partial cast: John Stanley (Sherlock Holmes), Alfred Shirley (Dr. Watson).

Contents: September 28: The Case of the Dog Who Changed His Mind. - October 5: The Case of the Missing Heiress. - 12: The Adventure of the Red Headed League. - 19: The Affair of the Politician, the Lighthouse, and the Trained Cormorant. - 26: The Laughing Lemur of High Tower Heath. -

November 2: The Adventure of the Copper Beeches. - 9: The Cadaver in the Roman Toga. - 16: The Case of the Well-Staged Murder. - 23: The Case of the Stolen Naval Treaty. - 30: The Case of the Cradle That Rocked Itself. - December 7: The Case of Professor Moriarty and the Diamond Jubilee. - 14: The Sussex Vampire. - 21: The Adventure of the Christmas Bride. - 28: New Year's Eve Off the Scilly Isles. - January 4: The Mazarin Stone. - 11: The Case of Sudden Senility. 18: The Case of the Lucky Shilling. - 25: The Case of the Engineer's Thumb. - February 1: The Case of the Avenging Blade. - 8: The Case of the Sanguinary Specter. - 15: The Adventure of Shoscombe Old Place. - 22: The Adventure of the Wooden Claw. - 29: The Case of King Philip's Golden Salver. - March 7: The Adventure of the Six Napoleons. - 14: The Adventure of the Serpent God. - 21: Death Is a Golden Arrow. - 28: The Disappearance of Lady Frances Carfax. - April 4: The Return of the Monster. - 11: [Unknown]. - 18: The Case of the Very Best Butter. - 25: The Return of the Jack of Diamonds. - May 2, 9: [Unknown]. - 16: The Case of the Ever-blooming Roses. - 23: The Case of the Accommodating Valise. - 30: The Case of Identity. - June 6: The Complicated Poisoning at Eel Pie Island. - 13: [Unknown]. - 20: The Adventure of the Veiled Lodger.

Review: Variety, 168 (October 1, 1947), 24 (Herm).

1948-1949 JOHN STANLEY AND IAN MARTIN

5465. ———. New York: WOR-MBS, Sundays, September 12-December 26, 1948, 7:00-7:30 p.m.; Mondays, January 3-June 6, 1949, 8:30-9:00 p.m. 39 programs.

Credits: Sponsor, Trimount Clothing Co. (Clipper Craft Clothes); Producer and Director, Basil Loughrane; Writers, Howard Merrill *et al;* Announcer, Cy Harrice; Music, Albert Buhrman.

Cast: John Stanley (Sherlock Holmes), Ian Martin (Dr. Watson).

Contents: September 12: The Case of the Unwelcome Ambassador (with Barry Thompson, Charles D. Penman, Julie Bennett, Anthony Kemble Cooper). - 19: The Black Guardsman of Braddock Castle. - 26, October 3: [Unknown]. - 10: The Adventure of the Guy Fawkes Society. - 17: Black Peter. - 24: [Unknown]. - 31: The Adventure of the Uddington Witch. - November 7: The Logic of Murder. - 14: The Ancient Queen. - 21, 28: [Unknown]. - December 5: Island of the Dead. - 12: The Adventure of London Tower. - 19: [Unknown]. - 26: The Adventure of the Blue Carbuncle. - January 3: The Adventure of the Malicious Moor. - 10: The Knife of

Vengeance. - 17: The Adventure of the Fabulous Celebrities. - 24: The Guest in the Coffin. - 31: The Adventure of the Devil's Foot. - February 7: The Adventure of the Blood-Stained Goddess. 14: The Guest in the Coffin. - 21: [Unknown]. - 28: The Adventure of the East-End Strangler. - March 7: Murder on a Wager. - 14: The Adventure of the Unfortunate Valet. - 21: The Adventure of the Elusive Agent (pt. 1). - 28: The Adventure of the Elusive Agent (pt. 2). - April 4: The Adventure of the Elusive Agent (pt. 3). - 11: The Adventure of the Mad Miners of Cardiff. - 18: The Burmese Goddess. - 25: The Adventure of the Pince-Nez. - May 2: The Adventure of the Blood-Soaked Wagon. - 9: [Unknown]. - 16: The Adventure of the Gray Pasha. - 23: Dr. Winthrop's Notorious Carriage. - 30, June 6: [Unknown].

1949-1950 BEN WRIGHT AND ERIC SNOWDEN

5466. *Adventures of Sherlock Holmes.* New York: WJZ-ABC, Wednesdays, September 21, 1949-January 18, 1950, 8:30-8:55 p.m.; January 25-June 14, 1950, 9:00-9:25 p.m. 39 programs. Originated from Hollywood.

Credits: Sponsor, Petri Wine; Producer and Director, Ted Bliss and Ken Manson; Writer, Denis Green; Announcer, Herb Allen; Organist, Dean Fossler.

Partial cast: Ben Wright (Sherlock Holmes), Eric Snowden (Dr. Watson).

Contents: [Unknown].

Reviews: *Billboard*, 61 (October 8, 1949), 12 (June Bundy); *Variety*, 176 (September 28, 1949), 28 (Herm).

PUBLISHED RADIO SCRIPTS

5467. Eckerson, Olive. "The Adventure of the Lion's Mane: A Radio Play," *The Adventures of Sherlock Holmes.* Adapted by Olive Eckerson. Edited by Wallace R. Murray. New York: Globe Book Co., [1950]. p. 188-205

5468. Green, Denis. "The Disappearance of Lady Frances Carfax," Adapted for radio by Denis Green. *The Saint's Choice of Radio Thrillers.* Edited by Leslie Charteris. Hollywood, Calif.: Saint Enterprises Inc., [1946]. p. 51-66.

First performed on February 26, 1945, with Basil Rathbone and Nigel Bruce.

5469. Horowitz, Floyd. "Hairlock Holmes, Detective, Solves an Anachronistic Mystery," *BSJ*, 14, No. 4 (December 1964), 223-229.

"A script in the series *The World of Story* written for youngsters and produced by the Iowa School of the Air."

5470. Olfson, Lewy. "Sherlock Holmes and the Red-Headed League," Adapted by Lewy Olfson. *Plays.* 19, No. 1 (October 1959), 87-96.

5471. ———. "Sherlock Holmes and the Stockbroker's Clerk," A radio-style adaptation by Lewy Olfson. *Plays*, 23, No. 1 (October 1963), 85-95.

5472. Queen, Ellery. "The Disappearance of Mr. James Phillimore," *The Misadventures of Sherlock Holmes.* Edited by Ellery Queen. Boston: Little, Brown and Co., 1944. p. 89-107.

Characters: Mr. James Phillimore, Biggs, Coal Man, Telegraph Messenger, Nikki Porter, Inspector Queen, Sergeant Velie, Ellery Queen.

5473. [Steinbrunner, Chris.] *From Baker Street with Love: Spies and Sherlock Holmes.* [New York: Privately Produced, 1970.] [33] p.

A dramatization of two espionage cases: Seco and Bruc.

Presented by the Priory Scholars on June 28, 1970, over WFUV-FM, Fordham University Radio.

Credits: Producer, Chris Steinbrunner; Associate Producer, Peter Blau; Director, Charles M. Collins; Announcer, Don McCallion.

Cast for Seco: Robert Vierengel (Sherlock Holmes), Chris Steinbrunner (Dr. Watson), Jim Saunders (Inspector Lestrade), Ann Licari (Mrs. Hudson), Peter Blau (Trelawney Hope), Bobbie Ghidalia (Lady Hilda Hope), Charles Kane (Lord Bellinger), Vic Ghidalia (Constable McPherson).

Cast for Bruc: Robert Vierengel (Sherlock Holmes), Chris Steinbrunner (Dr. Watson), Jim Saunders (Inspector Lestrade), Ann Licarti (Mrs. Hudson), Charles Foster Kane (Mycroft Holmes), Peter Blau (Colonel Valentine Walter), Evelyn Herzog (Violet Westbury), Vic Ghidalia (Sidney Johnson).

G *Television*

ENGLAND

1951 ALAN WHEATLEY AND RAYMOND FRANCIS

5474. "The Empty House," BBC Television, Saturday, October 20, 1951, 8:00-8:30 p.m. (Sherlock Holmes, No. 1)

Credits: Producer, Ian Atkins; Adapter, C. A. Lejeune.

Cast: Alan Wheatley (Sherlock Holmes), Raymond Francis (Dr. Watson), Bill Owen (Inspector Lestrade), Eric Maturin (Colonel Moran), Iris Vandeleur (Mrs. Hudson),

Clement Hamelin (Tall Thin Man), Sam Kydd (Unimpressed Onlooker), Pamela Barnard (First Nursemaid), Iris Williams (Second Nursemaid), Tony Burton (First Errand Boy), Eddie Sutch (Second Errand Boy).

Review: *The Times* (October 23, 1951), 6.

5475. "A Scandal in Bohemia," BBC Television, Saturday, October 27, 1951, 8:00-8:30 p.m. (Sherlock Holmes, No. 2)

Credits: Producer, Ian Atkins; Adapter, C. A. Lejeune.

Cast: Alan Wheatley (Sherlock Holmes), Raymond Francis (Dr. Watson), Alan Judd (The King of Bohemia), Olga Edwards (Irene Adler), John Stevens (Godfrey Norton), Iris Vandeleur (Mrs. Hudson), Betty Turner (Housekeeper), Michael Raghan (Old Cabby), Donald Kemp (Young Cabby), Meadows White, John Fitzgerald, Vernon Gibb (Ostlers).

5476. "The Dying Detective," BBC Television, Saturday, November 3, 1951, 8:00-8:30 p.m. (Sherlock Holmes, No. 3)

Credits: Producer, Ian Atkins; Adapter, C. A. Lejeune.

Cast: Alan Wheatley (Sherlock Holmes), Raymond Francis (Dr. Watson), Bill Owen (Inspector Lestrade), Henry Oscar (Mr. Culverton Smith), Iris Vandeleur (Mrs. Hudson), A. G. Dennett (Staples).

5477. "The Reigate Squires," BBC Television Saturday, November 17, 1951, 8:00-8:30 p.m. (Sherlock Holmes, No. 4)

Credits: Producer, Ian Atkins; Adapter, C. A. Lejeune.

Cast: Alan Wheatley (Sherlock Holmes), Raymond Francis (Dr. Watson), H. G. Stoker (Colonel Hayter), Stanley Van Beers (Inspector Forrester), Beckett Bould (Mr. Cunningham), Thomas Heathcote (Alec Cunningham), John Vere (Butler), Iris Vandeleur (Cook), Pamela Barnard (Tweeny), Victor Platt (P. C. Perkins), Donald Kemp (P. C. Barker), Gordon Phillott (Mr. Acton).

5478. "The Red-Headed League," BBC Television, Saturday, November 24, 1951, 8:00-8:30 p.m. (Sherlock Holmes, No. 5)

Credits: Producer, Ian Atkins; Adapter, C. A. Lejeune.

Cast: Alan Wheatley (Sherlock Holmes), Raymond Francis (Dr. Watson), Bill Owen (Inspector Lestrade), Sebastian Cabot (Jabez Wilson), Martin Starkie (Vincent Spaulding), Larry Burns (Duncan Ross), Arthur Goulett (Mr. Merryweather), Christopher Hodge (Rejected Applicant), Nicolas Tannar (Hopeful Applicant).

5479. "The Second Stain," BBC Television, Saturday, December 1, 1951, 8:00-8:30 p.m. (Sherlock Holmes, No. 6)

Credits: Producer, Ian Atkins; Adapter, C. A. Lejeune.

Cast: Alan Wheatley (Sherlock Holmes), Raymond Francis (Dr. Watson), Bill Owen (Inspector Lestrade), John Robinson (Mr. Trelawney Hope), Alvys Maben (Lady Hilda Trelawney Hope), J. Leslie Frith (The Premier), Iris Vandeleur (Mrs. Hudson), John le Mesurier (Eduardo Lucas), Donald Kemp (P. C. Macpherson), Clarence Bigge (Butler).

1964-1965 DOUGLAS WILMER AND NIGEL STOCK

5480. "The Speckled Band," BBC (Ch. 1), Monday, May 18, 1964, 9:25-10:15 p.m. Repeated: BBC 2 (Ch. 33), Friday, September 25, 1964, 8:00-8:50 p.m.

Credits: Producer, David Goddard; Director, Robin Midgley; Adapter, Giles Cooper; Introduction, Rupert Davies; Detective theme music, John Addison; Incidental music, Max Harris; Script editor, Max Marquis; Assistant, John Gould; Designer, Charles Carroll; Animals from Colchester Zoo.

Cast: Douglas Wilmer (Sherlock Holmes), Nigel Stock (Dr. Watson), Liane Aukin (Helen Stoner), Marian Diamond (Julia Stoner), Felix Felton (Dr. Grimesby Roylott), Donald Douglas (Percy Armitage), Mary Holder (Mrs. Hudson), Nan Marriott-Watson (Annie).

Reviews: *Globe & Mail* [Toronto] (November 19, 1964) (Bruce West), and reprinted in *CPBook*, 1, No. 3 (Winter 1965), 64; *Radio Times*, 163 (May 14, 1964), 27; *SHJ*, 7, No. 1 (Winter 1964), 22 (Anthony Howlett).

5481. "The Illustrious Client," BBC 1 (Ch. 1), Saturday, February 20, 1965, 7:55-8:45 p.m. (Sherlock Holmes, No. 1)

Credits: Producer, David Goddard; Director, Peter Sasdy; Adapter, Giles Cooper; Music, Max Harris; Cameraman, James Balfour; Costume supervisor, Sheila Glassford; Make-up supervisor, Shirley Boakes; Designer, Roy Oxley.

Cast: Douglas Wilmer (Sherlock Holmes), Nigel Stock (Dr. Watson), Jimmy Ashton (Billy), Ballard Berkeley (Sir James Damery), Norman Mitchell (Shinwell Johnson), Rosemary Leach (Kitty Winter), Jennie Linden (Violet de Merville), Peter Wyngarde (Baron Gruner), Martin Gordon (Footman), Billy Cornelius (Leary), Anne Hart (Music-Hall Singer).

5482. "The Devil's Foot," BBC 1 (Ch. 1), Saturday, February 27, 1965, 8:40-9:30 p.m. (Sherlock Holmes, No. 2)

Credits: Producer, David Goddard; Director, Max Varnel; Adapter, Giles Cooper; Music, Max Harris; Cameraman, James Balfour; Editor, David Taylor;

Costume supervisor, Sheila Glassford; Make-up supervisor, Shirley Boakes; Designer, Sally Hulke.

Cast: Douglas Wilmer (Sherlock Holmes), Nigel Stock (Dr. Watson), Drank Crawshaw (Owen Tregennis), Derek Birch (George Tregennis), Camilla Hasse (Brenda Tregennis), Nora Gordon (Mrs. Porter), John Glyn-Jones (Vicar), Patrick Troughton (Mortimer Tregennis), Carl Bernard (Dr. Sterndale).

5483. "The Copper Beeches," BBC (Ch. 1), Saturday, March 6, 1965, 8:35-9:25 p.m. (Sherlock Holmes, No. 3)

Credits: Producer, David Goddard; Director, Gareth Davies; Adapter, Vincent Tilsley; Music, Max Harris; Cameraman, James Balfour; Editor, Geoffrey Fry; Costume supervisor, Ena Nickalls; Make-up supervisor, Shirley Boakes; Script editor, Anthony Read; Designer, Roy Oxley.

Cast: Douglas Wilmer (Sherlock Holmes), Nigel Stock (Dr. Watson), Hector (Carlos), Patrick Wymark (Jephro Rucastle), Alethea Charlton (Mrs. Rucastle), Norma Vogan (Alice Rucastle), Paul Harris (Mr. Fowler), Michael Robbins (Mr. Toller), Suzanne Neve (Violet Hunter), Anna Perry (Erica Thompson), Ross Clear (Page Boy), Sheila Keith (Miss Stoper), Margaret Diamond (Mrs. Toller), Garry Mason (Edward Rucastle).

5484. "The Red-Headed League," BBC 1 (Ch. 1), Saturday, March 13, 1965, 8:35-9:25 p.m. (Sherlock Holmes, No. 4)

Credits: Producer, David Goddard; Director, Peter Duguid; Adapter, Anthony Read; Music, Max Harris; Costume supervisor, Sheila Glassford; Make-up supervisor, Shirley Boakes; Designer, Roy Oxley.

Cast: Douglas Wilmer (Sherlock Holmes), Nigel Stock (Dr. Watson), Geoffrey Wincott (Merryweather), John Barcroft (Inspector Hopkins), Toke Townley (Jabez Wilson), Christopher Greatorex (Sgt. Jones), Beatrice Shaw (Old Woman), David Andrews (Vincent Spaulding), Carla Challoner (Mary Jane), Trevor Martin (Duncan Ross), Audrey O'Flynn (Mrs. Shaw).

5485. "The Abbey Grange," BBC 1 (Ch. 1), Saturday, March 20, 1965, 8:10-9:00 p.m. (Sherlock Holmes, No. 5)

Credits: Producer, David Goddard; Director, Peter Cregeen; Adapter, Clifford Witting; Music, Max Harris; Cameraman, Charles Lagus; Editor, Stephen Cross; Costume supervisor, Vanessa Clarke; Make-up supervisor, Shirley Boakes; Script editor, Anthony Read; Designer, Archie Clark.

Cast: Douglas Wilmer (Sherlock Holmes), Nigel Stock (Dr. Watson), Ronald Adams (Tom Randall), Pierce McAvoy (Frank Randall), David Harrison (William Randall), Peggy Thorpe-Bates (Theresa Wright), Michael Gover (Sir Eustace Brackenstall), Nyree Dawn Porter (Lady Brackenstall), Douglas Ives (Porter), John Barcroft (Det.-Insp. Hopkins), Keneth Thornett (Sgt. Mitchell), Ian Anders (Cabbie), Peter Jesson (Capt. Croker).

5486. "The Six Napoleons," BBC 1 (Ch. 1), Saturday, March 27, 1965, 8:10-9:00 p.m. (Sherlock Holmes, No. 6)

Credits: Producer, David Goddard; Director, Gareth Davies; Adapter, Giles Cooper; Music, Max Harris; Costume supervisor, Sheila Glassford; Make-up supervisor, Shirley Boakes; Script editor, Anthony Read; Designer, Stephen Bundy.

Cast: Douglas Wilmer (Sherlock Holmes), Nigel Stock (Dr. Watson), Terry Leigh (Venucci), Peter Madden (Inspector Lestrade), James Bree (Dr. Barnicot), Donald Hewlett (Horace Harker), Desmond Cullum-Jones (Police Constable), Martin Wyldeck (Morse Hudson), Raymond Witch (Inspector Hill), Norman Scace (Mr. Gelder), Jimmy Ashton (Billy), Arthur Hewlett (Josiah Brown), Betty Romaine (Mrs. Brown), Andreas Markos (Beppo), Lloyd Pearson (Mr. Sandeford).

5487. "The Man with the Twisted Lip," BBC 1 (Ch. 1), Saturday, April 3, 1965, 8:10-9:00 p.m. (Sherlock Holmes, No. 7)

Credits: Producer, David Goddard; Director, Eric Tayler; Adapter, Jan Read; Music, Max Harris; Cameraman, Dick Bush; Editor, Stephen Cross; Costume supervisor, Sheila Glassford; Make-up supervisor, Shirley Boakes; Script editor, Anthony Read; Designer, Roy Oxley; Fights arranged by Peter Diamond.

Cast: Douglas Wilmer (Sherlock Holmes), Nigel Stock (Dr. Watson), Anton Rodgers (Hugh Boone), Norman Pitt (City Gentleman), Manning Wilson (Police Sergeant), Bernard Shine (Police Constable), Robin Parkinson (Shipping Clerk), Anna Cropper (Mrs. St. Clair), John A. Tinn (Malay Attendant), Olaf Pooley (Lascar), Victor Brooks (Inspector Bradstreet), Peter Madden (Inspector Lestrade).

5488. "The Beryl Coronet," BBC 1 (Ch. 1), Saturday, April 10, 1965, 7:55-8:45 p.m. (Sherlock Holmes, No. 8)

Credits: Producer, David Goddard; Director, Max Varnel; Adapter, Nicholas Palmer; Music, Max Harris; Cameraman, James Balfour; Editor, Stephen Cross; Costume supervisor, Sheila Glassford; Make-up supervisor, Shirley Boakes; Script editor, Anthony Read; Designer, Richard Wilmot.

Cast: Douglas Wilmer (Sherlock Holmes), Nigel Stock (Dr. Watson), Sandra Hampton (Lucy Parr), Leonard Sachs (Holder),

Richard Carpenter (Arthur), Mark Singleton (Hector), David Burke (Sir George Burnwell), Suzan Farmer (Mary), Denis Shaw (Gregory).

5489. "The Bruce-Partington Plans," BBC 1 (Ch. 1), Saturday, April 17, 1965, 9:55-10:45 p.m. (Sherlock Holmes, No. 9)
Credits: Producer, David Goddard; Director, Shaun Sutton; Adapter, Giles Cooper; Music, Max Harris; Cameraman, A. A. Englander; Editor, Geoffrey Fry; Costume supervisor, Sheila Glassford; Make-up supervisor, Shirley Boakes; Script editor, Anthony Read; Designer, Stephen Bundy.
Cast: Douglas Wilmer (Sherlock Holmes), Nigel Stock (Dr. Watson), Bart Allison (Platelayer), Enid Lindsey (Mrs. Hudson), Derek Francis (Mycroft Holmes), Peter Madden (Inspector Lestrade), John Woodnutt (Station Master), Allan Cuthbertson (Colonel Valentine Walter), Walter Horsbrugh (Butler), Sandra Payne (Violet Westbury), Gordon Gostelow (Sydney Johnson), Erik Chitty (Waiter), Carl Duering (Herr Oberstein).

5490. "Charles Augustus Milverton," BBC 1 (Ch. 1), Saturday, April 24, 1965, 8:10-9:00 p.m. (Sherlock Holmes, No. 10)
Credits: Producer, David Goddard; Director, Philip Dudley; Adapter, Clifford Witting; Music, Max Harris; Cameraman, Stanley Speel; Editor, Geoffrey Fry; Costume supervisor, Sheila Glassford; Make-up supervisor, Shirley Boakes; Script editor, Anthony Read; Designer, Roy Oxley.
Cast: Douglas Wilmer (Sherlock Holmes), Nigel Stock (Dr. Watson), Ralph Tovey (Footman), Stephanie Bidmead (Lady Farningham), Tony Steedman (Lord Farningham), Len Jones (Newsboy), Barry Jones (Milverton), Derek Smee (Captain Fitzallen), Penelope Horner (Lady Eva Brackwell), Ann Penfold (Agatha), Jimmy Ashton (Billy), John Murray Scott (Footman), Edward Brooks (Under-gardener), Peter Madden (Inspector Lestrade).

5491. "The Retired Colourman," BBC 1 (Ch. 1), Saturday, May 1, 1965, 8:20-9:10 p.m. (Sherlock Holmes, No. 11)
Credits: Producer, David Goddard; Director, Michael Hayes; Adapter, Jan Read; Music, Max Harris; Cameraman, Dave Mason; Editor, Geoffrey Fry; Costume supervisor, Sheila Glassford; Make-up supervisor, Shirley Boakes; Script editor, Anthony Read; Designer, Roy Oxley.
Cast: Douglas Wilmer (Sherlock Holmes), Nigel Stock (Dr. Watson), Maurice Denham (Josiah Amberley), William Wilde (Dr. Ray Ernest), Lesley Saweard (Ellen Amberley), Peter Henchie (Barker), Enid Lindsey (Mrs. Hudson), Arthur R. Webb (Porter), Paul Martin (Choir-boy), Christopher Banks (The

Rev. J. C. Elman), Peter Madden (Inspector Lestrade), Robert Croudace (Constable).

5492. "Lady Frances Carfax," BBC 1 (Ch. 1), Saturday, May 8, 1965, 8:30-9:20 p.m. (Sherlock Holmes, No. 12)
Credits: Producer, David Goddard; Director, Shaun Sutton; Adapter, Vincent Tilsley; Music, Max Harris; Cameraman, James Balfour; Editor, Geoffrey Fry; Costume supervisor, Sheila Glassford; Make-up supervisor, Shirley Boakes; Script editor, Anthony Read; Designer, Roy Oxley; Fight arranged by Peter Diamond.
Cast: Douglas Wilmer (Sherlock Holmes), Nigel Stock (Dr. Watson), Roger Delgado (Moser), Ronald Radd (Dr. Shlessinger), Diana King (Mrs. Shlessinger), Sheila Shand Gibbs (Lady Frances Carfax), Neil Stacy (Jules), Marian MacCarthy (Marie), Joss Ackland (The Hon. Philip Green), Enid Lindsey (Mrs. Hudson), Peter Madden (Inspector Lestrade), John Woodnutt (Pawnbroker), Ivor Salter (Police Sergeant).

Reviews of above series: *Radio Times*, 166 (February 18, 1965), 3; 166 (February 25, 1965), 3; 166 (March 4, 1965), 3; 166 (March 11, 1965), 3; 167 (April 1, 1965), 3; 167 (April 8, 1965), 5; 167 (April 15, 1965), 5; 167 (April 29, 1965), 4; *SHJ*, 7, No. 2 (Spring 1965), 56-57 (Michael Pointer); *Stage and Television Today*, No. 4376 (February 25, 1965), 14 (Bill Edmund), *The Times* (February 27, 1965), 12, and reprinted in *CPBook*, 1, No. 4 (Spring 1965), 68; *The Times* (March 15, 1965), 13, and reprinted in *CPBook*, 1, No. 4 (Spring 1965), 68; *Variety*, 238 (March 3, 1965), 49 (Otta.); *Woman's Own* (October 22, 1966), 43 (Beverley Nichols).

1968 PETER CUSHING AND NIGEL STOCK

5493. "The Second Stain," BBC 1 (Ch. 1), Monday, September 9, 1968, 9:05-9:55 p.m. (Sherlock Holmes, No. 1)
Credits: Producer, William Sterling; Director, Henri Safran; Adapter, Jennifer Stuart; Script editor, John Barber; Costumes, Betty Aldiss; Make-up, Heather Stewart; Designer, Tom Carter.
Cast: Peter Cushing (Sherlock Holmes), Nigel Stock (Dr. Watson), Daniel Massey (Trelawney Hope), Cecil Parker (Lord Bellinger), Penelope Horner (Lady Hilda), Joane Crane (Renate), Alicia Deane (Madame Fournaye), Derek Waring (Henri Fournaye), Freddie Earlle (John Milton), Sandra June Williams (Lucy), Cheri Lunghi (Emily), Ronald Forfar (Ticket Clerk), William Lucas (Inspector Lestrade), Clifford Cox (P. C. Macpherson).

5494. "A Study in Scarlet," BBC 1 (Ch. 1),

Actors, Performances, & Recordings

Television

Monday, September 16, 1968, 9:05-9:55 p.m. (Sherlock Holmes, No. 2) Repeated: BBC 2, Tuesday, September 15, 1970, 8:00-8:50 p.m.

Credits: Producer, William Sterling; Director, Henri Safran; Adapter, Hugh Leonard; Script editor, John Barber; Designer, Stanley Morris.

Cast: Peter Cushing (Sherlock Holmes), Nigel Stock (Dr. Watson), Joe Melia (Joey Daly), Edward Bishop (Joseph Stangerson), Craig Hunter (Enoch Drebber), Dorothy Edwards (Madame Charpentier), Edina Ronay (Alice Charpentier), Larry Dann (Arthur Charpentier), Michael Segal (P. C. Rance), Michael Goldie (P. C. Murcher), Henry Kate (Commissionaire), George A. Cooper (Inspector Gregson), William Lucas (Inspector Lestrade), Grace Arnold (Mrs. Hudson), Freddie Earlle (Cabby), Tony McLaren (Wiggins), Larry Cross (Jefferson Hope).

5495. "The Dancing Men," BBC 1 (Ch. 1), Monday, September 23, 1968, 9:05-9:55 p.m. (Sherlock Holmes, No. 3) Repeated: BBC 2, Tuesday, September 22, 1970, 8:00-8:50 p.m.

Credits: Producer, William Sterling; Adapters, Michael and Mollie Hardwick; Script editors, John Barber and Donald Tosh; Designer, Stanley Morris.

Cast: Peter Cushing (Sherlock Holmes), Nigel Stock (Dr. Watson), Maxwell Reed (Hilton Cubitt), Judee Morton (Elsie Cubitt), Edward Brayshaw (Hunt), Grace Arnold (Mrs. Hudson), Gwen Nelson (Mrs. King), Richardson Morgan (Inspector Martin), Norman Caley (Bearded Constable), Henry Gilbert (Dr. Armstrong), Annabella Johnston (Maid), Frank Mann (Abe Slaney), David Simeon (Constable).

5496. "The Hound of the Baskervilles," BBC 1 (Ch. 1), Mondays, September 30, October 7, 1968, 9:05-9:55 p.m. 2 episodes, (Sherlock Holmes, No. 4) Repeated: BBC 2, Tuesdays, July 7, 14, 1970, 8:00-8:50 p.m.

Credits: Producer, William Sterling; Director, Graham Evans; Adapter, Hugh Leonard; Script editor, John Barber; Designer, Tom Carter;

Cast: Peter Cushing (Sherlock Holmes), Nigel Stock (Dr. Watson), Gary Raymond (Sir Henry Baskerville), Gabriella Licudi (Beryl Stapleton), Philip Bond (Stapleton), Gerald Flood (Sir Hugo Baskerville), Susan Lefton (Girl), Ballard Berkeley (Sir Charles Baskerville), David Leland (Dr. Mortimer), George Howe (Squire Frankland), Alan Meadows (Servant), Bob Harris (Coachman), David Trevena (Manager), Christopher Burgess (Barrymore), June Watson (Mrs. Barrymore), Tony Rohr (Convict), Penelope Lee (Laura Lyons), Edward Higgens (Landlord).

404 **5497.** "The Boscombe Valley Mystery," BBC 1

(Ch. 1), Monday, October 14, 1968, 9:05-9:55 p.m. (Sherlock Holmes, No. 5) Repeated: BBC 2, Tuesday, July 21, 1970, 8:00-8:50 p.m.

Credits: Producer, William Sterling; Director, Viktors Ritelis; Adapter, Bruce Stewart; Script editors, John Barber and Donald Tosh; Designer, Tom Carter.

Cast: Peter Cushing (Sherlock Holmes), Nigel Stock (Dr. Watson), John Tate (Turner), Nick Tate (James McCarthy), Jack Woolgar (Moran), Peter Madden (Bill McCarthy), Caroline Ellis (Patience), Gertan Klauber (Fat Man), Heather Kyd (Alice), Michael Godfrey (Inspector Lanner), Vernon Joyner (Matlock), Victor Brooks (Cowper), Sally Sanders (Bella).

5498. "The Greek Interpreter," BBC 1 (Ch. 1), Monday, October 21, 1968, 9:05-9:55 p.m. (Sherlock Holmes, No. 6)

Credits: Producer, William Sterling; Director, David Saire; Adapter, John Gould; Script editors, John Barber and Donald Tosh; Designer, James Bould.

Cast: Peter Cushing (Sherlock Holmes), Nigel Stock (Dr. Watson), Peter Woodthorpe (Wilson Kemp), Nigel Terry (Harold Latimer), Ronald Adam (Mycroft Holmes), Steve Plytas (Crito Manikuros), Edward Hardwicke (Davenport), George A. Cooper (Inspector Gregson), Evie Kyrol (Sophy), Alexis Mann (Paul), Clive Cazes (Melas), Doros Kamenos (Greek Priest).

5499. "The Naval Treaty," BBC 1 (Ch. 1), Monday, October 28, 1968, 9:05-9:55 p.m. (Sherlock Holmes, No. 7) Repeated: BBC 2, Tuesday, August 11, 1970, 8:00-8:50 p.m.

Credits: Producer, William Sterling; Director, Antony Kearey; Adapter, John Gould; Script editors, John Barber and Donald Tosh; Designer, Roger Cheveley.

Cast: Peter Cushing (Sherlock Holmes), Nigel Stock (Dr. Watson), Dennis Price (Lord Holdhurst), Corin Redgrave (Percy Phelps), Peter Bowles (Joseph Harrison), Roger Maxwell (Ambassador), Patrick Tull (Charles Gorot), Robin Wentworth (Tangey), Lane Meddick (Peters), Lucy Griffiths (Mrs. Tangey), Humphrey Heathcote (Constable), Donald Tandy (Inspector Forbes), Grace Arnold (Mrs. Hudson), Jane Lapotaire (Annie Harrison).

5500. "Thor Bridge," BBC 1 (Ch. 1), Monday, November 4, 1968, 9:05-9:55 p.m. (Sherlock Holmes, No. 8) Repeated: BBC 2, Tuesday, July 28, 1970, 8:00-8:50 p.m.

Credits: Producer, William Sterling; Director, Antony Kearey; Adapter, Harry Moore; Script editors, John Barber and Donald Tosh; Designer, John Cooper.

Cast: Peter Cushing (Sherlock Holmes), Nigel Stock (Dr. Watson), Juliet Mills (Grace Dunbar), Isa Miranda (Dolores), Grant Taylor (Neil Gibson), Henry Oscar (Bates), Willoughby Gray (Sergeant

Coventry), Anne Ogden (Rose), Grace Arnold (Mrs. Hudson), Gillian Hayes (Emily), Erin Geraghty (Sarah).

5501. "The Musgrave Ritual," BBC 1 (Ch. 1), Monday, November 11, 1968, 9:05-9:55 p.m. (Sherlock Holmes, No. 9) Repeated: BBC 2, Tuesday, August 4, 1970, 8:00-8:50 p.m.

Credits: Producer, William Sterling; Director, Viktors Ritelis; Adapter, Alexander Baron; Script editors, John Barber and Donald Tosh; Designer, Stanley Morris.

Cast: Peter Cushing (Sherlock Holmes), Nigel Stock (Dr. Watson), Georgia Brown (Rachel), Brian Jackson (John Brunton), Norman Wooland (Reginald Musgrave), Elizabeth Hughes (Janet), Norman Florence (Dick Darrell), Grace Arnold (Mrs. Hudson), Sheelah Wilcocks (Ellen), Dominic Allan (Sergeant).

5502. "Black Peter," BBC 1 (Ch. 1), Monday, November 18, 1968, 9:05-9:55 p.m. (Sherlock Holmes, No. 10)

Credits: Producer, William Sterling; Director, Antony Kearey; Adapter, Richard Harris; Script editor, John Barber; Designer, Spencer Chapman.

Cast: Peter Cushing (Sherlock Holmes), Nigel Stock (Dr. Watson), James Kenney (Inspector Hopkins), Ilona Rodgers (Rachel Carey), John Tate (Peter Carey), Ilona Ference (Mrs. Carey), John Baskcomb (Landlord), Brian Hayes (Slater), Wilfrid Downing (John Neligan), Grace Arnold (Mrs. Hudson), Fred Hugh (Allardyce), John de Marco (Lancaster), Jerold Wells (Patrick Cairns).

5503. "Wisteria Lodge," BBC 1 (Ch. 1), Monday, November 25, 1968, 9:05-9:55 p.m. (Sherlock Holmes, No. 11) Repeated: BBC 2, Tuesday, August 18, 1970, 8:00-8:50 p.m.

Credits: Producer, William Sterling; Director, Roger Jenkins; Adapter, Alexander Baron; Script editors, John Barber and Donald Tosh; Designer, Roy Oxley.

Cast: Peter Cushing (Sherlock Holmes), Nigel Stock (Dr. Watson), Richard Pearson (Inspector Baynes), Derek Francis (John Scott Eccles), Tutte Lemjow (Jose), Carlos Pierre (Garcia), Walter Gotell (Henderson), Grace Arnold (Mrs. Hudson), Philip Anthony (P. C. Walters), Desmond Stokes (Warner), Christopher Carlos (Lucas), Roy Stewart (Mulatto), Tanya Robinson (Miss Burnet).

5504. "Shoscombe Old Place," BBC 1 (Ch. 1), Monday, December 2, 1968, 9:05-9:55 p.m. (Sherlock Holmes, No. 12) Repeated: BBC 1 (Ch. 1), Sunday, July 13, 1969, 5:05-5:50 p.m. (Star Choice) BBC 2, Tuesday, August 25, 1970, 8:00-8:50 p.m.

Credits: Producer, William Sterling; Director, Bill Bain; Script editor, Donald Tosh; Designer, Tom Carter.

Cast: Peter Cushing (Sherlock Holmes), Nigel Stock (Dr. Watson), Nigel Green (Sir Robert Norberton), Edward Woodward (Mason), Yvonne Ball (Josie Bootle), Jim Collier, Maurice Quick, and John Lawrence (Racegoers), Peter Miles (Sam Brewer), David Bird (Stephens), Carol Macready (Carrie), Kevin Lindsay (George Norlett), Michael Beint (Barnes).

5505. "The Solitary Cyclist," BBC 1 (Ch. 1), Monday, December 9, 1968, 9:05-9:55 p.m. (Sherlock Holmes, No. 13) Repeated: BBC 2, Tuesday, September 1, 1970, 8:00-8:50 p.m.

Credits: Producer, William Sterling; Director, Viktors Ritelis; Adapter, Stanley Miller; Script editors, John Barber and Donald Tosh; Designer, Stanley Morris.

Cast: Peter Cushing (Sherlock Holmes), Nigel Stock (Dr. Watson), Carole Potter (Violet Smith), Charles Tingwell (Carruthers), David Butler (Woodley), Gillian Bailey (Lucy), Ysanne Churchman (Mrs. Bainbridge), Alan Tucker (Clerk), Clyde Pollitt (Mr. Trivett), Peter Miles (Williamson), Harry Webster (Landlord), Dean Harris (Peter).

5506. "The Sign of Four," BBC 1 (Ch. 1), Monday, December 16, 1968, 9:05-9:55 p.m. (Sherlock Holmes, No. 14) Repeated: BBC 2, Tuesday, September 8, 1970, 8:00-8:50 p.m.

Credits: Producer and Director, William Sterling; Adapters, Michael and Mollie Hardwick; Script editors, John Barber and Donald Tosh; Costumes, Sue Taylor; Make-up, Heather Stewart; Designer, Sally Hulke.

Cast: Peter Cushing (Sherlock Holmes), Nigel Stock (Dr. Watson), Ann Bell (Mary Morstan), Paul Daneman (Thaddeus and Bartholomew Sholto), John Stratton (Inspector Athelney Jones), Ailsa Grahame (Mrs. Forrester), Howard Goorney (Jonathan Small), Grace Arnold (Mrs. Hudson), Ahmed Khalil (Lal Rao), Sydney Conabere (McMurdo), Tony McLaren (Wiggins), Annabella Johnston (Mrs. Mordecai Smith), Davis S. Bolivar (Mr. Mordecai Smith), Ann Way (Mrs. Bernstone), Zen Keller (Tonga), Sara Clee (Alice), John Dunbar (John Sholto), Ves Dalahunt, David James, Kenneth Hale, and Tony Leary (Policemen).

5507. "The Blue Carbuncle," BBC 1 (Ch. 1), Monday, December 23, 1968, 9:05-9:55 p.m. (Sherlock Holmes, No. 15)

Credits: Producer, William Sterling; Director, Bill Bain; Adapter, Stanley Miller, Script editor, Donald Tosh; Lighting, Gerry Millerson; Sound and music, Alan Fogg; Costumes, Ian Adley; Make-up, Heather Stewart; Designer, Ian Watson.

Cast: Peter Cushing (Sherlock Holmes), Nigel Stock (Dr. Watson), Madge Ryan (Lady Morcar), James Beck (James Ryder),

Diana Chappel (Catherine Cusack), Neil Fitzpatrick (John Horner), Richard Butler (Mr. Baker), Ernest Hare (Windigate), Frank Middlemass (Peterson), Grace Arnold (Mrs. Hudson), Clyde Pollitt (Police Sergeant), Michael Robbins (Breckinridge), Edna Dore (Mrs. Oakshott).

Reviews of above series: Armchair Detective, 2 (January 1969), 122-123 (Veronica M. S. Kennedy); *Radio Times,* 180 (September 5, 1968), 30; 180 (September 19, 1968), 36-37 (Russell Twisk), and reprinted in *CPBook.* 5, No. 17 (Winter 1969), 324-325; 188 (July 2, 1970), 6 (Rosemary Collins); *SHJ,* 9, No. 1 (Winter 1968), 34 (Percy Metcalfe); 9, No. 2 (Summer 1969), 64-65 (Anthony Howlett); *Sherlockiana,* 14, Nr. 1 (1969), 1-2 (Brink Abrahamsen); *Stage and Television Today,* No. 4561 (September 12, 1968), 12 (Ann Purser); *Telegraph* (September 8, 1968) (T. S. Ferguson), and reprinted in *Sherlockiana,* 13, Nr. 3 (1968), 9; *TV Insight* (Kenneth Baily), and reprinted in *CPBook,* 5, No. 19 (June 1969), 374.

Thirty-one photographs of scenes from this series appear in the Dutch two-volume omnibus edition, *Meesterwerken van Sir Arthur Conan Doyle* (item 1039).

UNITED STATES

1937 LOUIS HECTOR AND WILLIAM PODMORE

5508. "The Three Garridebs," New York: Radio City, November 27, 1937.
Credits: Adapter, Thomas H. Hutchinson.
Cast: Louis Hector (Sherlock Holmes), William Podmore (Dr. Watson), Arthur Maitland (John Garrideb), James Spottswood (Nathan Garrideb), Violet Besson (Mrs. Hudson), Selma Hall (Mrs. Saunders), Eustace Wyatt (Inspector Lestrade).
The first dramatization of Sherlock Holmes on television.
Review: New York Times (November 28, 1937), XI, 12.

1953 BASIL RATHBONE AND MARTYN GREEN

5509. "The Adventure of the Black Baronet," by Adrian Conan Doyle and John Dickson Carr. New York: WCBS-TV (Ch. 2), Tuesday, May 26, 1953, 9:30-10:00 p.m.
Partial cast: Basil Rathbone (Sherlock Holmes), Martyn Green (Dr. Watson).

1954-1955 RONALD HOWARD AND HOWARD MARION CRAWFORD

5510. "The Case of the Cunningham Heritage," WRCA-TV (Ch. 4) NBC, Monday, October 18, 1954, 7:00-7:30 p.m.

(The New Adventures of Sherlock Holmes, No. 1)
Credits: Sponsor, Chase National Bank; Producer and Writer, Sheldon Reynolds; Director, Jack Gage; Music, Claude Durant.
Partial cast: Ronald Howard (Sherlock Holmes), H. Marion Crawford (Dr. Watson), Archie Duncan (Inspector Lestrade), Meg Lemonnier, Ursula Howells, Pierre Gay, Richard Larke.

5511. "The Case of Lady Beryl," WRCA-TV (Ch. 4) NBC, Monday, October 25, 1954, 7:00-7:30 p.m. (The New Adventures of Sherlock Holmes, No. 2)
Credits: Producer and Director, Sheldon Reynolds.
Partial cast: Ronald Howard (Sherlock Holmes), H. Marion Crawford (Dr. Watson), Paulette Goddard (Lady Beryl).

5512. "The Case of the Pennsylvania Gun," WRCA-TV (Ch. 4) NBC, November 1, 1954, 7:00-7:30 p.m. (The New Adventures of Sherlock Holmes, No. 3)
Credits: Producer and Director, Sheldon Reynolds.
Partial cast: Ronald Howard (Sherlock Holmes), H. Marion Crawford (Dr. Watson).

5513. "The Case of the Texas Cowgirl," WRCA-TV (Ch. 4) NBC Monday, November 8, 1954, 7:00-7:30 p.m. (The New Adventures of Sherlock Holmes, No. 4)
Credits: Producer and Director, Sheldon Reynolds.
Partial cast: Ronald Howard (Sherlock Holmes), H. Marion Crawford (Dr. Watson).

5514. "The Case of the Belligerent Ghost," WRCA-TV (Ch. 4) NBC, Monday, November 15, 1954, 7:00-7:30 p.m. (The New Adventures of Sherlock Holmes, No. 5)
Credits: Producer and Director, Sheldon Reynolds.
Partial Cast: Ronald Howard (Sherlock Holmes), H. Marion Crawford (Dr. Watson).

5515. "The Case of the Shy Ballerina," WRCA-TV (Ch. 4) NBC, Monday, November 22, 1954, 7:00-7:30 p.m. (The New Adventures of Sherlock Holmes, No. 6)
Credits: Producer and Director, Sheldon Reynolds.
Partial cast: Ronald Howard (Sherlock Holmes), H. Marion Crawford (Dr. Watson).

5516. "The Case of the Winthrop Legend," WRCA-TV (Ch. 4) NBC, Monday, November 29, 1954, 7:00-7:30 p.m. (The New Adventures of Sherlock Holmes, No. 7)
Credits: Producer and Director, Sheldon Reynolds.
Partial cast: Ronald Howard (Sherlock Holmes), H. Marion Crawford (Dr. Watson).

5517. "The Case of Blind Man's Bluff,"

WRCA-TV (Ch. 4) NBC, Monday, December 6, 1954, 7:00-7:30 p.m. (The New Adventures of Sherlock Holmes, No. 8) Repeated: August 1, 1955.

Credits: Producer and Director, Sheldon Reynolds.

Partial cast: Ronald Howard (Sherlock Holmes), H. Marion Crawford (Dr. Watson), Archie Duncan (Inspector Lestrade).

5518. "The Case of Harry Crocker," WRCA-TV (Ch. 4) NBC, Monday, December 13, 1954, 7:00-7:30 p.m. (The New Adventures of Sherlock Holmes, No. 9)

Credits: Producer and Director, Sheldon Reynolds.

Partial cast: Ronald Howard (Sherlock Holmes), H. Marion Crawford (Dr. Watson).

5519. "The Mother Hubbard Case," WRCA-TV (Ch. 4) NBC, Monday, December 20, 1954, 7:00-7:30 p.m. (The New Adventures of Sherlock Holmes, No. 10)

Credits: Producer and Director, Sheldon Reynolds.

Partial cast: Ronald Howard (Sherlock Holmes), H. Marion Crawford (Dr. Watson).

5520. "The Case of the Red-Headed League," WRCA-TV (Ch. 4) NBC, Monday, December 27, 1954, 7:00-7:30 p.m. (The New Adventures of Sherlock Holmes), No. 11) Repeated: August 8, 1955.

Credits: Producer and Director, Sheldon Reynolds.

Partial cast: Ronald Howard (Sherlock Holmes), H. Marion Crawford (Dr. Watson), Alexander Gauge, Eugene Deckers, Colin Drake, Richard Fitzgerald.

5521. "The Case of the Shoeless Engineer," WRCA-TV (Ch. 4) NBC, Monday, January 3, 1955, 7:00-7:30 p.m. (The New Adventures of Sherlock Holmes, No. 12)

Credits: Producer and Director, Sheldon Reynolds.

Partial cast: Ronald Howard (Sherlock Holmes), H. Marion Crawford (Dr. Watson).

5522. "The Case of the Split Ticket," WRCA-TV (Ch. 4) NBC, Monday, January 10, 1955, 7:00-7:30 p.m. (The New Adventures of Sherlock Holmes, No. 13) Repeated: August 15, 1955.

Credits: Producer and Director, Sheldon Reynolds.

Partial cast: Ronald Howard (Sherlock Holmes), H. Marion Crawford (Dr. Watson).

5523. "The Case of the French Interpreter," WRCA-TV (Ch. 4) NBC, Monday, January 17, 1955, 7:00-7:30 p.m. (The New Adventures of Sherlock Holmes, No. 14)

Credits: Producer and Director, Sheldon Reynolds.

Partial cast: Ronald Howard (Sherlock Holmes), H. Marion Crawford (Dr. Watson).

5524. "The Case of the Singing Violin," WRCA-TV (Ch. 4) NBC, Monday, January 24, 1955, 7:00-7:30 p.m. (The New Adventures of Sherlock Holmes, No. 15) Repeated: August 22, 1955.

Credits:Producer and Director, Sheldon Reynolds.

Cast: Ronald Howard (Sherlock Holmes), H. Marion Crawford (Dr. Watson), Delphine Seyrig (Betty), Arnold Bell (Guy Durham), Colin Mann (Jimmy), Ben Omanoff (Dr. Moreno).

5525. "The Case of the Greystone Inscription," WRCA-TV (Ch. 4) NBC, Monday, January 31, 1955, 7:00-7:30 p.m. (The New Adventures of Sherlock Holmes, No. 16) Repeated: August 29, 1955.

Credits: Producer, Sheldon Reynolds.

Partial cast: Ronald Howard (Sherlock Holmes), H. Marion Crawford (Dr. Watson), Archie Duncan (Inspector Lestrade), Martina Mayne, Eric Micklewood.

5526. "The Case of the Laughing Mummy," WRCA-TV (Ch. 4) NBC, Monday, February 7, 1955, 7:00-7:30 p.m. (The New Adventures of Sherlock Holmes, No. 17) Repeated: September 5, 1955.

Credits: Producer, Sheldon Reynolds.

Cast: Ronald Howard (Sherlock Holmes), H. Marion Crawford (Dr. Watson), Barry Mackay (Reggie Taunton), June Elliott (Rowena), Lois Perkins Marechal (Aunt Agatha), Frederick O'Brady (Prof. Caulkins), Colin Maun (Porter).

5527. "The Thistle Killer," WRCA-TV (Ch. 4) NBC, Monday, February 14, 1955, 7:00-7:30 p.m. (The New Adventures of Sherlock Holmes, No. 18)

Credits: Producer, Sheldon Reynolds.

Partial cast: Ronald Howard (Sherlock Holmes), H. Marion Crawford (Dr. Watson).

5528. "The Case of the Vanished Detective," WRCA-TV (Ch. 4) NBC, Monday, February 21, 1955, 7:00-7:30 p.m. (The New Adventures of Sherlock Holmes, No. 19)

Credits: Producer, Sheldon Reynolds.

Partial cast: Ronald Howard (Sherlock Holmes), H. Marion Crawford (Dr. Watson).

5529. "The Case of the Careless Suffragette," WRCA-TV (Ch. 4) NBC, Monday, February 28, 1955, 7:00-7:30 p.m. (The New Adventures of Sherlock Holmes, No. 20)

Credits: Producer, Sheldon Reynolds; Director, Jack Gage and Sheldon Reynolds; Writers, Charles and Joseph Early.

Cast: Ronald Howard (Sherlock Holmes), H. Marion Crawford (Dr. Watson), Archie Duncan (Inspector Lestrade), Dawn Addams (Doreen), Kenneth Richards (Sergeant), David Thomson (Henry), Margaret Russell (Agatha), Frederick O'Brady (Boris Turgoff).

5530. "The Case of the Reluctant Carpenter," WRCA-TV (Ch. 4) NBC, Monday, March 7, 1955, 7:00-7:30 p.m. (The New Adventures of Sherlock Holmes, No. 21) Repeated: September 12, 1955.

Credits: Producer, Sheldon Reynolds.

Cast: Ronald Howard (Sherlock Holmes), H. Marion Crawford (Dr. Watson), Pierre Gay (Bricker), Kenneth Richards (Sergeant), Henry Hubner (Guard), Donald Kotite (Chemist).

5531. "The Deadly Prophecy," WRCA-TV (Ch. 4) NBC, Monday, March 14, 1955, 7:00-7:30 p.m. (The New Adventures of Sherlock Holmes, No. 22)

Credits: Producer and Director, Sheldon Reynolds.

Partial cast: Ronald Howard (Sherlock Holmes), H. Marion Crawford (Dr. Watson).

5532. "The Christmas Pudding," WRCA-TV (Ch. 4) NBC, Monday, April 4, 1955, 7:00-7:30 p.m. (The New Adventures of Sherlock Holmes, No. 23) Repeated: September 26, 1955.

Credits: Producer and Director, Sheldon Reynolds.

Partial cast: Ronald Howard (Sherlock Holmes), H. Marion Crawford (Dr. Watson).

5533. "The Night-Train Riddle," WRCA-TV (Ch. 4) NBC, Monday, April 11, 1955, 7:00-7:30 p.m. (The New Adventures of Sherlock Holmes, No. 24) Postponed from March 28. Repeated: October 3, 1955.

Credits: Producer and Director, Sheldon Reynolds.

Partial cast: Ronald Howard (Sherlock Holmes), H. Marion Crawford (Dr. Watson), Roberta Haynes, Sonny Doran, Richard Watson.

5534. "The Case of the Violent Suitor," WRCA-TV (Ch. 4) NBC, Monday, April 18, 1955, 7:00-7:30 p.m. (The New Adventures of Sherlock Holmes, No. 25) Postponed from March 21.

Credits: Producer and Director, Sheldon Reynolds.

Partial cast: Ronald Howard (Sherlock Holmes), H. Marion Crawford (Dr. Watson).

5535. "The Case of the Baker Street Nursemaids," WRCA-TV (Ch. 4) NBC, Monday, April 25, 1955, 7:00-7:30 p.m. (The New Adventures of Sherlock Holmes, No. 26).

Credits: Producer and Director, Sheldon Reynolds.

Partial cast: Ronald Howard (Sherlock Holmes), H. Marion Crawford (Dr. Watson).

5536. "The Case of the Perfect Husband," WRCA-TV (Ch. 4) NBC, Monday, May 2, 1955, 7:00-7:30 p.m. (The New Adventures of Sherlock Holmes, No. 27) Postponed from January 17. Repeated: July 25 and October 10, 1955.

Credits: Producer and Director, Sheldon Reynolds.

Partial cast: Ronald Howard (Sherlock Holmes), H. Marion Crawford (Dr. Watson), Mary Sinclair (Janet Partridge), Michael Gough (Russel Partridge), Carl Saroyan.

5537. "The Case of the Jolly Hangman," WRCA-TV (Ch. 4) NBC, Monday, May 9, 1955, 7:00-7:30 p.m. (The New Adventures of Sherlock Holmes, No. 28)

Credits: Producer and Director, Sheldon Reynolds.

Partial cast: Ronald Howard (Sherlock Holmes), H. Marion Crawford (Dr. Watson).

5538. "The Case of the Imposter Mystery," WRCA-TV (Ch. 4) NBC, Monday, May 16, 1955, 7:00-7:30 p.m. (The New Adventures of Sherlock Holmes, No. 29)

Credits: Producer and Director, Sheldon Reynolds.

Partial cast: Ronald Howard (Sherlock Holmes), H. Marion Crawford (Dr. Watson).

5539. "The Case of the Eiffel Tower," WRCA-TV (Ch. 4) NBC, Monday, May 23, 1955, 7:00-7:30 p.m. (The New Adventures of Sherlock Holmes, No. 30)

Credits: Producer and Director, Sheldon Reynolds; Writer, Roger E. Garris.

Partial cast: Ronald Howard (Sherlock Holmes), H. Marion Crawford (Dr. Watson), Martine Alexis (Singer), Sacha Piteoff.

5540. "The Case of the Exhumed Client," WRCA-TV (Ch. 4) NBC, Monday, May 30, 1955, 7:00-7:30 p.m. (The New Adventures of Sherlock Holmes, No. 31)

Credits: Producer and Director, Sheldon Reynolds; Writers, Charles and Joseph Early.

Partial cast: Ronald Howard (Sherlock Holmes), H. Marion Crawford (Dr. Watson), Alvys Maben.

5541. "The Case of the Impromptu Performance," WRCA-TV (Ch. 4) NBC, Monday, June 6, 1955, 7:00-7:30 p.m. (The New Adventures of Sherlock Holmes, No. 32)

Credits: Producer and Director, Sheldon Reynolds; Writer, Joe Morhaim.

Partial cast: Ronald Howard (Sherlock Holmes), H. Marion Crawford (Dr. Watson), Richard Larke, Richard O'Sullivan.

5542. "The Case of the Baker Street Bachelors," WRCA-TV (Ch. 4) NBC, Monday, June 20, 1955, 7:00-7:30 p.m. (The New Adventures of Sherlock Holmes, No. 33)

Credits: Producer and Director, Sheldon Reynolds; Writer, Joseph Victor.

Partial cast: Ronald Howard (Sherlock Holmes), H. Marion Crawford (Dr. Watson).

5543. "The Case of the Royal Murder,"

WRCA-TV (Ch. 4) NBC, Monday, June 27, 1955, 7:00-7:30 p.m. (The New Adventures of Sherlock Holmes, No. 34)

Credits: Producer and Director, Sheldon Reynolds; Writers, Charles and Joseph Early.

Cast: Ronald Howard (Sherlock Holmes), H. Marion Crawford (Dr. Watson), Jacques Decqmine (King Conrad), Lise Dourdin (Princess Antonia), Maurice Teynac (Prince Stephan), Jacques Francois (Count Magor), Christine Paray (Gypsy).

5544. "The Case of the Haunted Gainsborough," WRCA-TV (Ch. 4) NBC, Monday, July 4, 1955, 7:00-7:30 p.m. (The New Adventures of Sherlock Holmes, No. 35)

Credits: Producer and Director, Sheldon Reynolds.

Cast: Ronald Howard (Sherlock Holmes), H. Marion Crawford (Dr. Watson), Archie Duncan (Inspector Lestrade), Cleo Rose, John Buckmaster, Zac Matalon, Roger E. Garris.

5545. "The Case of the Neurotic Detective," WRCA-TV (Ch. 4) NBC, Monday, July 11, 1955, 7:00-7:30 p.m. (The New Adventures of Sherlock Holmes, No. 36)

Credits: Producer and Director, Sheldon Reynolds; Writer, Joe Morhaim.

Cast: Ronald Howard (Sherlock Holmes), H. Marion Crawford (Dr. Watson), Kenneth Richards (Wilkins), Seymour Green (Commissioner), June M. Crawford (Jennifer Ames), Russ Caprio (Toby Judson), Eugene Deckers (Dr. A. Fishblade), James R. Richman (Young Man).

5546. "The Case of the Unlucky Gambler," WRCA-TV (Ch. 4) NBC, Monday, July 18, 1955, 7:00-7:30 p.m. (The New Adventures of Sherlock Holmes, No. 37)

Credits: Producer and Director, Sheldon Reynolds; Writer, Joe Morhaim.

Cast: Ronald Howard (Sherlock Holmes), H. Marion Crawford (Dr. Watson), Richard Larke (Wilkins), Richard O'Sullivan (Andy Fenwick), Duncan Elliot (Jack Driscoll), John Buckmaster (Bartender), Zach Matalone (Briggs), Russ Caprio (Manager), Rowland Bartrop (Herbert Fenwick), J. Seyfort (Patron).

5547. "The Case of the Diamond Tooth," WRCA-TV (Ch. 4) NBC, Monday, September 19, 1955, 7:00-7:30 p.m. (The New Adventures of Sherlock Holmes, No. 38)

Credits: Producer and Director, Sheldon Reynolds.

Partial cast: Ronald Howard (Sherlock Holmes), H. Marion Crawford (Dr. Watson).

5548. "The Case of the Tyrant's Daughter," WRCA-TV (Ch. 4) NBC, Monday, October 17, 1955, 7:00-7:30 p.m. (The New Adventures of Sherlock Holmes, No. 39)

Credits: Producer and Director, Sheldon Reynolds.

Partial cast: Ronald Howard (Sherlock Holmes), H. Marion Crawford (Dr. Watson).

Reviews of above series: BSJ, 4, No. 4 (October 1954), 249-250 (Edgar W. Smith); *Billboard,* 66 (October 30, 1954), 11 (Jack Singer); *Detroit Free Press* (November 2, 1954), 17 (Dick Osgood), and reprinted in *CPBook,* 1, No. 1 (Summer 1964), 4; *Look,* 18 (September 21, 1954), 59-60; *New York Herald Tribune* (January 30, 1955), IV, 1 (John Crosby), and reprinted in *CPBook,* 2, No. 5-6 (Summer-Fall 1965), 84 and 115; *New York Herald Tribune* (March 13, 1955), IV, 6 (Don Ross), and reprinted in *CPBook,* 5, No. 17 (Winter 1969), 323; *New York Times* (October 22, 1954), 36 (Jack Gould); *SHJ,* 10, No. 2 (Summer 1971), 48-49 (Michael Pointer); *TV Guide,* 2 (December 18, 1954), 20-22; *TV Guide,* 3 (January 29, 1955), 13; *Variety,* 196 (October 1954), 38 (Chan.).

1972 STEWART GRANGER AND BERNARD FOX

5549. "The Hound of the Baskervilles," New York: ABC-TV (Ch. 7), Saturday, February 12, 1972, 8:30-10:00 p.m. color.

Credits: Producer, Stanley Kallis; Director, Barry Crane; Writer, Robert E. Thompson; Associate Producer, Arthur D. Hilton; Director of Photography, Harry Wolf; Art Director, Howard E. Johnson; Set Decorations, Arthur Jeph Parker; Assistant Director, Donald Roberts; Unit Manager, Joe Cramer; Film Editor, Bill Mosher; Sound, James Alexander; Special Photographic Effects, Albert Whitlock; Editorial Supervision, Richard Belding; Music Supervision, Hal Mooney; Costumes, Richard Hopper.

Cast: Stewart Granger (Sherlock Holmes), Bernard Fox (Dr. Watson), William Shatner (Stapleton), Anthony Zerbe (Dr. Mortimer), Sally Ann Howes (Laura), Jane Merrow (Beryl Stapleton), Ian Ireland (Sir Henry), John Williams (Frankland), Alan Caillou (Lestrade), Brendan Dillon (Barrymore), Arline Anderson (Mrs. Barrymore), Liam Dunn (Messenger), Michael St. Clair (Constable), Barry Bernard (Manager), Constance Cavendish (Eel Monger), Billy Bowles (Cartwright), Arthur Malet (Higgins), Karen Kondan (Mrs. Mortimer), Elaine Church (Maid Servant), Jenifer Shaw (Peasant Girl), Terence Pushman (Chestnut Salesman), Eric Brotherson (Porter).

Reviews: Armchair Detective, 5 (April 1972), 158 (Dick Lochte); *BSJ,* 22, No. 2 (June 1972), 68-70 (Howard Lachtman); 22, No. 3 (September 1972), 185-188 (Robert A. Lanier) (Lloyd Fradkin) (Randolph Cox) (Donald A. Webster) (Margaret F. Morris) (Garrett Van Essen III) (Allen J. Severn); *DCC,* 8, No. 4-5 (September 1972), 12-13

(Frank Rhode); *HO,* 2, No. 2 (April 1972), 2 (Andrew Page); 2, No. 3 (June 1972), 14-15 (Glenn J. Shea); *Variety,* 266 (February 16, 1972), 43.

PUBLISHED TELEVISION SCRIPTS

5550. Hutchinson, Thomas H. "The Three Garridebs: A Typical Television Script with Production Directions," Adapted for television by Thos. H. Hutchinson. *Television Broadcasting: Production, Economics, Technique,* by Lenox R. Lohr. New York and London: McGraw-Hill Book Co., 1940. p. 50, 58-59, 87; Appendix I, p. 225-265.

The script, with commentary and seventeen photographs, for the historic performance on November 27, 1937. The play was presented during field tests of the NBC system prior to the beginning of public service.

5551. McLauchlin, Russell. "Tea Time in Baker Street," *BSJ* [OS], 3, No. 3 (July 1948), 317-329.

————. ————, *Ellery Queen's Mystery Magazine,* 59, No. 2 (February 1972), 92-106.

The audio-video script for what was thought to be the first televised dramatization of Sherlock Holmes. The event took place on March 12, 1948, over Station WWJ-TV of Detroit, Michigan, to honor the Amateur Mendicant Society on the occasion of its annual meeting.

H *Records*

5552. *"The Actual Voices of" Kipling, Conan Doyle and Shaw.* Audio Rarities, [n.d.] 2 s. 12 in. 33 rpm. (No. 2460)

Partial contents: Side 2, band 1. Sir Arthur Conan Doyle Talks on "Sherlock Holmes" and Spiritualism. 1930.

5553. *Adventures of Sherlock Holmes.* Complete and unabridged. Read by Basil Rathbone. St. Joseph, Mich.: Audio Book Co., 1958. 10 s. 7 in. 16 rpm. (Audio Books, GL 611)

Contents: Scan. - RedH. - Spec. - Blue.

5554. *The Adventures of Sherlock Holmes.* Croton-on-Hudson, N. Y.: The Radiola Co., February 1971. 2 s. 12 in. 33 rpm. (Release No. 5. Crime Series No. 1)

Limited to 1000 numbered copies.

Contents: Side 1. "The Adventure of the Missing Submarine Plans" (Bruc), broadcast over NBC, November 6, 1939, with Basil Rathbone and Nigel Bruce (item 5457). - Side 2. Mr. Chameleon Solves "The Perfect Maid Murder Case."

5555. *"Aunt Clara."* Sung by James Montgomery. "Sherlock Holmes," A Reminiscence by the Literary Agent. Philadelphia: The Sons of the Copper Beeches, 1961. 2 s. 7 in. 45 rpm. (No. 4289) Limited edition.

5556. *Baker Street: A Musical Adventure of Sherlock Holmes.* Book by Jerome Coopersmith. Music and lyrics by Marian Grudeff and Raymond Jessel. Adapted from the stories by Sir Arthur Conan Doyle. MGM Records, 1965. 2 s. 12 in. 33 rpm. (E-7000-OC) (S-7000-OC)

"The Baker Street Story," by Alexander H. Cohen on slipcase.

Contents: Side 1. Overture. - It's So Simple (Fritz Weaver, Peter Sallis, Patrick Horgan, Daniel Keyes). - I'm in London Again (Inga Swenson & Company). - Leave It to Us, Gov (Teddy Green & The Irregulars). - Letters (Inga Swenson). - Cold Clear World (Fritz Weaver). - Finding Words for Spring (Inga Swenson). - Side 2. What a Night This Is Going to Be (Fritz Weaver, Inga Swenson, Peter Sallis, Virginia Vestoff). - I Shall Miss You (Martin Gabel). - Roof Space (Teddy Green & The Irregulars). - A Married Man (Peter Sallis). - I'd Do It Again (Inga Swenson). - Pursuit (Fritz Weaver). - Jewelry (Martin Wolfson & The Company).

5557. *Baker Street Suite for Violin and Piano,* by Harvey Officer. In four movements, with Harvey Officer at the piano and Harold Kohon on the violin. Summit, N. J.: The Pamphlet House, 1944. 4 s. 12 in. 78 rpm.

Privately recorded in 1943.

Contents: A Study in Scarlet. - The Irene Adler Waltz. - The Dancing Men. - Finale.

5558. *Ben Abramson Discusses the Baker Street Irregulars with Martin Maloney on the Northwestern Radio Series.* Chicago: United Film and Recording Studios, 1956. 2 s. 12 in. 33 rpm. (UB 55-800 / 801)

Broadcast on March 1, 1954.

5559. *Conan Doyle Speaking.* London: The Gramophone Co., 1930. 2 s. 12 in. 78 rpm. (G-C1983)

Much of the record is about his spiritual research, but there are also some two minutes of stimulating talk about Sherlock Holmes. See also items 5552 and 5573.

5560. *Doctor Watson Meets Sherlock Holmes.* Produced by Harry Alan Towers. Dramatization of the stories by John Keir Cross. Original music by Sidney Torch played by Campoli. Read by Sir John Gielgud (Sherlock Holmes), Sir Ralph Richardson (Dr. Watson), and Orson Welles (Professor Moriarty). London: Decca Record Co., 1956 (LK 4164); 1957 (LL 1568). 2 s. 12 in. 33 rpm.

Contents: Stud (opening). - Chas. - Fina. First broadcast of Stud portion over BBC

Stewart Granger portraying Sherlock Holmes on television (**5549**).

on October 5, 1954 (item 5327), and Fina on December 21, 1954 (item 5338).
Review: New York Herald Tribune Book Review (September 15, 1957), 11 (Herbert Kupferberg).

5561. *"The Golden Age of the Theatre."* [Introduction by Mary Jo Devlin.] Audio Rarities, [n.d.] 2 s. 12 in. 33 rpm. (No. 2465)
Partial contents: William Gillette in a scene from Sherlock Holmes.

5562. " 'The Great Detective' Ballet Suite, Op. 68," by Richard Arnell. Pro Arte Orchestra conducted by Richard Arnell. *English Light Music*. London: Pye Records Ltd., 1958 [c. 1966]. Side 2, band 2. 12 in. 33 rpm. (Golden Guinea Collector Series, GSGC 14048)
See also item 5099.

5563. *Hit Songs from Baker Street and Other Broadway Musicals*. MGM Records, 1965. 2 s. 12 in. 33 rpm. (E-4293) (SE-4293)
Partial contents: Side 1. A Married Man (Richard Burton). - Finding Words for Spring (Felicia Sanders). - Jewelry (Richard Hayman). - What a Night This Is Going to Be (Felicia Sanders). - I'd Do It Again (Fran Jeffries). - Baker Street Mystery (Kai Winding).

5564. *Rawhide 2*. Performed by Max Ferguson. New York: Folkways Records, 1957. 2 s. 12 in. 33 rpm. (FS-3872)
Partial contents: Side 2, band 1. Sherlock

Holmes in "The Case of the Speckled Band."

5565. *The Red-Headed League*. Read by John Brewster. Old Greenwich, Conn.: Listening Library, 1966. 2 s. 12 in. 33 rpm. (Audio Arts, AA-3302)

5566. *Sherlock Holmes: Charles Augustus Milverton. Black Peter*. Dramatised and produced by Michael and Mollie Hardwick. Tunbridge Wells, Kent: Discourses, 1970. 2 s. 12 in. 33 rpm. (DCO 1210)
Cast for Chas (Side 1): Robert Hardy (Sherlock Holmes), Nigel Stock (Dr. Watson), Cecile Chevreau (Mrs. Hudson and the Veiled Woman), Judith Coke (Lady Eva), Brendan Barry (Milverton), Alan Dudley (Inspector Lestrade).
Cast for Blac (Side 2): Robert Hardy (Sherlock Holmes), Nigel Stock (Dr. Watson), Geoffrey Collins (Inspector Hopkins), Jonathan Bury (Neligan), Brendan Barry (Patrick Cairns).
Review: SHJ, 10, No. 1 (Winter 1970), 28-29 (Anthony Howlett).

5567. *Sherlock Holmes: The Speckled Band. The Blue Carbuncle*. Dramatised and produced by Michael and Mollie Hardwick. Tunbridge Wells, Kent: Discourses, 1970. 2 s. 12 in. 33 rpm. (DCO 1211)
Cast for Spec (Side 1): Robert Hardy (Sherlock Holmes), Nigel Stock (Dr. Watson), Valerie Kirkbright (Helen Stoner),

411

Alan Dudley (Dr. Grimesby Roylott), Judith Coke (Juliet Stoner).

Cast for Blue (Side 2): Robert Hardy (Sherlock Holmes), Nigel Stock (Dr. Watson), Alan Dudley (Peterson and Breckinridge), Brendan Barry (Henry Baker and Windigate), Geoffrey Collins (James Ryder).

5568. *Sherlock Holmes: The Norwood Builder. The Disappearance of Lady Frances Carfax.* Dramatised and produced by Michael and Mollie Hardwick. Tunbridge Wells, Kent: Discourses, 1971. 2 s. 12 in. 33 rpm. (DCO 1212)

Cast for Norw (Side 1): Robert Hardy (Sherlock Holmes), Nigel Stock (Dr. Watson), Edmund Pegge (McFarlane), Alan Dudley (Inspector Lestrade), Preston Lockwood (Jonas Oldacre), Gladys Spencer (Mrs. McFarlane).

Cast for Lady (Side 2): Robert Hardy (Sherlock Holmes), Nigel Stock (Dr. Watson), Roger Sansom (Monsieur Moser), John Graham (Herr Dietrich), Cecile Chevreau (Marie Devine), Garard Green (The Hon. Philip Green), Anthony Vicars (Peters).

5569. *Sherlock Holmes: Shoscombe Old Place. The Illustrious Client.* Dramatised and produced by Michael and Mollie Hardwick. Tunbridge Wells, Kent: Discourses, 1971. 2 s. 12 in. 33 rpm. (DCO 1213)

Cast for Shos (Side 1): Robert Hardy (Sherlock Holmes), Nigel Stock (Dr. Watson), Michael Spice (John Mason), Bernard Davies (Stephens and Norlett), John Baker (Josiah Barnes), Norman Claridge (Sir Robert Norberton).

Cast for Illu (Side 2): Robert Hardy (Sherlock Holmes), Nigel Stock (Dr. Watson), Richard Hurndall (Sir James Damery), Wolfe Morris (Baron Grüner), Daphne Rogers (Kitty Winter).

5570. *Sherlock Holmes Explained by His Creator Sir Arthur Conan Doyle and Presented in Action by William Gillette.* The National Vocarium, 1939. 2 s. 12 in. 78 rpm. (TNV-109)

Contains an excerpt from the Gramophone recording of 1930 (item 5559) and a private recording made in 1936 by Gillette and an anonymous Watson of the famous deductive sequence in Act II, Scene II of Gillette's play.

5571. *Silver Blaze.* Rockhill Recording, 1951. 2 s. 12 in. 78 rpm. (No. 2278 / 2280)

A transcription of the Wessex Plate by Red Smith and Joe H. Palmer, with an introductory poem by Tom Stix.

5572. ———. New York: National Broadcasting Co., March 3, 1956. 2 s. 12 in. 78 rpm. (Reference Recording)

5573. *Sir Arthur Conan Doyle—1930.* New York: Rare Record Guild, [n.d.] 1 s. 6 in. 33 rpm. (Collector's Item Series) (Catalogue No. W 123)

"A rare discussion of 'Sherlock Holmes and Spiritualism.' An unusual insight into the author." (Subtitle)

5574. *Songs from Baker Street.* Rudolf Statler Orchestra and Chorus. Philadelphia: Wyncote, 1965. 2 s. 12 in. 33 rpm. (W-9092) (SW-9092)

Contents: Side 1. Married Man. - I'd Do It Again. - Side 2. What a Night This Is Going to Be. - Jewelry.

5575. *Songs of Baker Street.* Sung by James Montgomery. [The Baker Street Irregulars, 1950.] 6 s. 12 in. 78 rpm.

Cover decorated by Bruce Montgomery. Limited to 100 copies.

Contents: The Adventure of the Irene Adler Recording, told and sung by James Montgomery. - An Irregular Song (with apologies to Thomas Moore and A. Conan Doyle), words by James Montgomery; traditional old Irish air, sung by James Montgomery. - Sitting on the Stile, Mary (as sung by Birdy Edwards at Lodge 341, Vermissa, U.S.A.), sung by James Montgomery. - On the Banks of Allan Water (as sung by Birdy Edwards at Lodge 341, Vermissa, U.S.A.), sung by James Montgomery.

5576. ———. Sung by James Montgomery. *Baker Street Suite for Violin and Piano,* by Harvey Officer. In four movements, with Harvey Officer at the piano and Harold Kohon on the violin. Morristown, N.J.: The Baker Street Irregulars, 1959. 2 s. 10 in. 33 rpm. (KO8L-2820 / 2821)

Limited to 200 copies.

Contents: Side 1. Songs of Baker Street: The Adventure of the Irene Adler Recording. - I'm Sitting on the Stile, Mary. - On the Banks of Allan Water. - An Irregular Song. - Side 2. Baker Street Suite.

5577. *The Stories of Sherlock Holmes.* [Vol. 1.] *The Adventure of the Speckled Band. The Final Problem.* Read by Basil Rathbone. Directed by Howard Sackler. New York: Caedmon Records, 1963. 2 s. 12 in. 33 rpm. (TC-1172)

Critical notes by Rex Stout on slipcase. Also available on a cassette (CDL-51172).

5578. ———. Vol. 2. *The Redheaded League.* Read by Basil Rathbone. New York: Caedmon Records, 1966. 2 s. 12 in. 33 rpm. (TC-1208)

"In Memoriam Sherlock Holmes," by Christopher Morley on slipcase. Also available on a cassette (CDL-51208).

5579. ———. Vol. 3. *A Scandal in Bohemia.*

Read by Basil Rathbone. New York: Caedmon Records, 1967. 2 s. 12 in. 33 rpm. (TC-1220)

Introduction by Basil Rathbone ˙ on slipcase.

Also available on a cassette (CDL-51220).

5580. ———. Vol. 4. *Silver Blaze.* Read by Basil Rathbone. New York: Caedmon Records, 1967. 2 s. 12 in. 33 rpm. (TC-1240)

"The Voice of Sherlock Holmes," by Robert N. Brodie on slipcase.

Also available on a cassette (CDL-51240).

5581. *A Study in Terror* (Sound Track from Columbia Pictures' *A Study in Terror*). Music composed, arranged and conducted by John Scott (Published by South Mountain Music-BMI). England: Roulette Records, 1966. 2 s. 12 in. 33 rpm. (OS-801) (OSS-801)

Contents: Side 1. Theme. - Shires (1st Section). - Annie Takes a Walk. - Angela Osborne. - Pub Music. - Sally and the Tramp. - Side 2. Fire. - Osborne. - Key. - Shires (2nd Section). - Walking with Thugs. - Liz.

5582. *Tales of Sherlock Holmes.* Read by John Brewster. Old Greenwich, Conn.: Listening Library, [n.d.] 4 s. 12 in. 16 rpm. (A-1608)

Contents: Side 1. Scan. - Side 2. RedH. - Side 3. Spec. - Side 4. Fina.

5583. *Voices from Baker Street,* 1. Ferndale, Mich.: The Old Soldiers of Baker Street, December 1961. 2 s. 12 in. 33 rpm. (Top Secret LP 221B)

"Rerecorded from original tape recording furnished by W. T. Rabe."

Custom pressed by Recorded Publications Co., Camden, N.J. (A32M-90882)

Photograph of 22nd Anniversary Dinner, Baker Street Irregulars, Cavanagh's, January 11, 1957, on album.

Contents: Side 1. 221B (Vincent Starrett). - Sonnet: To Sherlock Holmes (Anthony Boucher). - Lower Vault Address, and An Irregular Song (James Montgomery). - James Montgomery Sings of His Female Relative. - Baker Street Rubaiyat (Nathan Bengis). - Russell McLauchlin and Friends. - A Toast to Christopher Morley (Basil Davenport). - Side 2. BBC Broadcast of the Wessex Plate (Red Smith, Joe Palmer). -

Internal Research Group Prospectus (Rex Stout). - Exhortation to Clarity of Scholarship (Dr. John C. McCabe). - On the Terrace (Edgar Smith, Dr. John C. McCabe, Whit Vernon).

5584. *Voices from Baker Street,* 2. Ferndale, Mich.: The Old Soldiers of Baker Street, July 1965. 2 s. 12 in. 33 rpm. (LP 221C) (Z 54151, Z 54152)

"Rerecorded from client's furnished tape."

Custom pressed by Recorded Publications Co., Camden, N.J.

Contents: Side 1. Constitution and Buy Laws (Frank Waters, Basil Davenport, Rex Stout, etc.). - The Road to Baker Street (Cavanagh Choraleers). - The Final Problem (Russell McLauchlin, Henry Schneidewind). - Are You There, Arthur? (Herb Brean). - The Musgrave Ritual (Basil Davenport). - Side 2. The Canonical Toasts (The Amateur Mendicant Society). - Critics Who Have Panned for Gould (William S. Baring-Gould). - Remarkable, Lesh! Simply Remarkable! (Richard Lesh). - They Were the Footprints of What Hound? (Frederic Hayes, Harvey Barcus, Ray King). - Si! Si! Sherlock! (Frank Rhode). - The Return of Aunt Clara (James Montgomery, Bruce Montgomery).

I *Tapes*

5585. *Sherlock Holmes.* Houston, Texas: Pastime Products, [1971]. Cassette.(No. 225)

Contents: Side 1. The Blanched Soldier (with Carleton Hobbs and Norman Shelley).- Side 2. The Renegade Squire [sic The Reigate Squires] (with Carleton Hobbs and Norman Shelley).

See also items 5363 and 5378.

5586. ———. Houston, Texas: Pastime Products, [1971]. Cassette. (No. 228)

Contents: Side 1. Stolen Sub Plans [Bruc] (with Basil Rathbone and Nigel Bruce). - Side 2. The Final Problem (with Sir John Gielgud, Sir Ralph Richardson, and Orson Welles).

See also items 5554 and 5560.

Frank Giacoia, artist, and Edith Meiser, writer, collaborated on
these Sherlock Holmes comic strips (**6196 - 6200**).

414

X | Parodies, Pastiches, Burlesques, Travesties, and Satires

There seems to be no end to the imitations and caricatures of the Master Detective. Many persons have tried, with varying degrees of success, to write stories that are either serious imitations of .Watson's narratives or are episodes in which Holmes and Watson are treated in a humorous or farcical fashion. Many are based upon one of the untold adventures. Since some combine the two literary styles, it is not always possible to make a clear distinction between the pastiche and the parody. For this reason, all such stories are listed together in one alphabetical arrangement. The only exceptions are the pastiches or parodies (together with the translations of them) written by August Derleth, Adrian Conan Doyle and John Dickson Carr, and Robert L. Fish, which are given first because of these authors' numerous contributions. Stories that originally appeared in another language are listed in Part IV. Those in dramatic form are given in Part IX.

A. General and Miscellaneous Criticism

5587. Baring-Gould, William S. " 'He Is Now Translating My Small Works into French,' " *The Annotated Sherlock Holmes*. New York: Clarkson N. Potter, [1967]. Vol. 1, chap. 2, p. 19-22. illus.
A brief discussion of the translations, parodies and pastiches.

5588. Boucher, Anthony. "An Aborted Avatar," *BSJ*, 9, No. 3 (July 1959), 133-135.
Tha author reveals an incident in the second act of L. Frank Baum's *The King of Gee-Whiz* (1905) involving a character named "Willie Cook" who declares he is Sherlock Holmes.

5589. ———. "Introduction," *The Incredible Schlock Homes*, by Robert L. Fish. New York: Simon and Schuster, [1966]. p. 9-14.
An informative commentary on the mock-Sherlockian literature, including the Schlock Homes stories.

5590. [Fish, Robert L.] ["Letter"], *PD*, 2, No. 2 (April 1969), 1, 3. (Pontine Patter)
A letter from "John H. Watney" of 222-B Bagel Street criticizing the many crude imitators of his friend Schlock Homes—including Sherlock Holmes by someone named Boyle or Coyle!

5591. Fowke, Edith. "The One Hundred Authors of Sherlock Holmes," *The Canadian Forum*, 29, No. 343 (August 1949), 110-111.

5592. Pattrick, Robert R. "A Holmes by Any Other Name," *CR*, 1, No. 4 (September 1960), 6-8.
A supplementary list to Ellery Queen's (item 5593) containing nineteen variations on the names *Sherlock Holmes* and *Dr. Watson*.

5593. Queen, Ellery. "Introduction," *The Memoirs of Solar Pons*, by August Derleth. Sauk City, Wis.: Mycroft & Moran, 1951. p. ix-xxii.
In addition to a commentary on the origin of the names *Ellery Queen, Sherlock Holmes*, and *Solar Pons*, the authors (Frederic A. Dannay and Manfred B. Lee) have provided a nine-page list of the pastiches, parodies, and burlesques of Sherlock Holmes in which his name (and Watson's) has been altered.

5594. ———. "Introduction," *The Misadventures of Sherlock Holmes*. Edited by Ellery Queen. Boston: Little, Brown and Co., 1944. p. v-xviii.
An account of how one of the Queens first met Sherlock Holmes, the origin of the name, his aliases, and comments on the parodies and pastiches.

5595. Redmond, Chris. "Pastiches," *BSP*, No. 34 (April 1968), 2. (Editorial)

"Sherlock Holmes is not a Harlequin. He is a detective. People who write pastiches should try to keep that in mind."

5596. Skene-Melvin, David. "A Study in Literary Influence," *SHJ*, 6, No. 1 (Winter 1962), 16-17.

The author has discovered within the pages of Kenneth Grahame's *The Wind in the Willows* what he considers to be one of the first parodies of Holmes—"The Singular Adventure of the Unexpected Doorscraper." A summary of the incident and quotations of the pertinent sections follow his introductory remarks.

5597. Smith, Edgar W. "Introduction," *The Return of Solar Pons*, by August Derleth. Sauk City, Wis.: Mycroft & Moran, 1958. p. vii-xiii.

An excellent essay on the Sherlockian pastiches, including *The Exploits of Sherlock Holmes* (or Sherlock Holmes Exploited!) by Doyle and Carr, "The Case of the Man Who Was Wanted" by Arthur Whitaker, and the Solar Pons stories.

5598. [———.] "On Canonicity," *BSJ*, 6, No. 3 (July 1956), 131-132. (The Editor's Gas-Lamp)

A scathing criticism of those who "prostitute the Canon to a degree beyond speech or description."

5599. [———.] "Re: Pastiches," *BSJ*, 3, No. 4 (October 1953), 195-196. (The Editor's Gas-Lamp)

"Pastiches are made to be written but not to be read. They are the stuff of dreams, the projection of our fancies, the release of our repressed desires, in which we, but not others, should be expected to take delight."

5600. Starrett, Vincent, "Sherlock Holmes in Parody and Burlesque," *The Private Life of Sherlock Holmes.* New York: The Macmillan Co., 1933. p. 161-175.

B Solar Pons and Dr. Parker (August Derleth)

THE WRITINGS

Stories

5601. "The Adventure of the Aluminum Crutch," *The Chronicles of Solar Pons.* Sauk City, Wis.: Mycroft & Moran, 1973.

5602. "The Amateur Philologist," *Alfred Hitchcock's Mystery Magazine*, 9, No. 9 (September 1964), 118-130.

"The Adventure of the Amateur Philologist," *The Casebook of Solar Pons.* Sauk City, Wis.: Mycroft & Moran, 1965. p. 211-225.

"The Amateur Philologist," *Coffin Corner.* [Compiled by] Alfred Hitchcock. [New York: Dell Pub. Co., November 1969.] p. 129-142. (A Dell Book, No. 1323)

5603. "The Adventure of the Ascot Scandal," *The Casebook of Solar Pons.* Sauk City, Wis.: Mycroft & Moran, 1965. p. 138-153.

5604. "The Adventure of the Ball of Nostradamus," by August Derleth and Mack Reynolds. *The Magazine of Fantasy and Science Fiction*, 8, No. 6 (June 1955), 42-51.

———, *The Science-Fictional Sherlock Holmes.* Denver, Colo.: The Council of Four, 1960. p. 93-104.

———, *A Praed Street Dossier.* Sauk City, Wis.: Mycroft & Moran, 1968. p. 95-108.

5605. "The Adventure of the Benin Bronze," *The Chronicles of Solar Pons.* Sauk City, Wis.: Mycroft & Moran, 1973.

5606. "The Adventure of the Bishop's Companion," *The Chronicles of Solar Pons.* Sauk City, Wis.: Mycroft & Moran, 1973.

5607. "The Adventure of the Black Cardinal," *Gangster Stories*, 2, No. 1 (March 1930), 109-132.

———, *The Reminiscences of Solar Pons.* Sauk City, Wis.: Mycroft & Moran, 1961. p. 130-154.

5608. "The Adventure of the Black Narcissus," *The Dragnet Magazine*, 2, No. 1 (February 1929), 69-75.

———, *"In Re: Sherlock Holmes."* Sauk City, Wis.: Mycroft and Moran, 1945. p. 49-63.

———. *Maiden Murders.* [Edited by] Mystery Writers of America. Introduction by John Dickson Carr. New York: Harper & Brothers, [1952]. p. 161-173.

———, ———. London: Hammond & Co., [1953]. p. 161-173.

5609. "The Adventure of the Blind Clairaudient," *The Saint Mystery Magazine*, 15, No. 1 (September 1961), 16-28.

———, *The Reminiscences of Solar Pons.* Sauk City, Wis.: Mycroft & Moran, 1961. p. 176-193.

5610. "The Adventure of the Bookseller's Clerk," *A Praed Street Dossier.* Sauk City, Wis.: Mycroft & Moran, 1968. p. 64-75.

5611. "The Adventure of the Broken

Chessman," *The Dragnet Magazine*, 3, No. 4 (September 1929), 347-360.

————, *The Memoirs of Solar Pons*. Sauk City, Wis.: Mycroft & Moran, 1951. p. 44-64.

————, *The Saint Mystery Magazine*, 15, No. 4 (February 1962), 38-52.

5612. "The Adventure of the Camberwell Beauty," *Three Problems for Solar Pons*. Sauk City, Wis.: Mycroft & Moran, 1952. p. 69-112.

————, *The Return of Solar Pons*. Sauk City, Wis.: Mycroft & Moran, 1958. p. 197-222.

5613. "The China Cottage," *Alfred Hitchcock's Mystery Magazine*, 10, No. 3 (March 1965), 55-73.

"The Adventure of the China Cottage," *The Casebook of Solar Pons*. Sauk City, Wis.: Mycroft & Moran, 1965. p. 113-137.

"The China Cottage," *Alfred Hitchcock's Games Killers Play*. [New York: Dell Pub. Co., April 1968.] p. 11-29. (No. 2790)

5614. "The Adventure of the Circular Room," *BSJ* [OS], 1, No. 3 (July 1946), 340-360.

————, *The Memoirs of Solar Pons*. Sauk City, Wis.: Mycroft & Moran, 1951. p. 3-27.

In *BSJ* the names of Solar Pons and Dr. Parker were changed to Sherlock Holmes and Dr. Watson.

5615. "The Adventure of the Cloverdale Kennels," *The Saint Mystery Magazine*, 13, No. 6 (June 1960), 54-71.

————, *The Reminiscences of Solar Pons*. Sauk City, Wis.: Mycroft & Moran, 1961. p. 108-129.

5616. "The Adventure of the Crouching Dog," *The Saint Mystery Magazine*, 21, No. 1 (July 1964), 12-30.

————, *The Casebook of Solar Pons*. Sauk City, Wis.: Mycroft & Moran, 1965. p. 154-177.

5617. "The Adventure of the Devil's Footprints," *Double-Action Detective Stories*, 1, No. 4 (1956), 28-45.

————, *The Return of Solar Pons*. Sauk City, Wis. : Mycroft & Moran, 1958. p. 23-43.

5618. "The Adventure of the Dog in the Manger," *The Memoirs of Solar Pons*. Sauk City, Wis.: Mycroft & Moran, 1951. p. 65-84.

5619. "The Dorrington Inheritance," *The Saint Detective Magazine*, 9, No. 3 (March 1958), 24-38.

"The Adventure of the Dorrington Inheritance," *The Return of Solar Pons*. Sauk City, Wis.: Mycroft & Moran, 1958. p. 44-66.

5620. "The Adventure of the Fatal Glance," *The Saint Mystery Magazine*, 18, No. 3 (March 1963), 31-40.

————, *The Casebook of Solar Pons*. Sauk City, Wis.: Mycroft Moran, 1965. p. 54-66.

5621. "The Adventure of the Five Royal Coachmen," *The Memoirs of Solar Pons*. Sauk City, Wis.: Mycroft & Moran, 1951. p. 201-220.

5622. "The Adventure of the Frightened Baronet," *"In Re: Sherlock Holmes."* Sauk City, Wis.: Mycroft and Moran, 1945. p. 3-30.

5623. "The Adventure of the Golden Bracelet," *The Chronicles of Solar Pons*. Sauk City, Wis.: Mycroft & Moran, 1973.

5624. "The Curse of Grice-Paterson," *The Pursuit Detective Story Magazine*, 1, No. 18 (November 1956), 89-119.

"The Adventure of the Grice-Paterson Curse," *The Return of Solar Pons*. Sauk City, Wis.: Mycroft & Moran, 1958. p. 108-131.

————, *Alfred Hitchcock's Daring Detectives*. Illustrations by Arthur Shilstone. New York: Random House, [1969]. p. 120-139.

5625. "The Adventure of the Stolen Hats," *The Saint Mystery Magazine*, 11, No. 1 (January 1959), 4-20.

"The Adventure of the Hats of M. Dulac," *The Reminiscences of Solar Pons*. Sauk City, Wis.: Mycroft & Moran, 1961. p. 22-43.

5626. "The Adventure of the Haunted Library," *Alfred Hitchcock's Mystery Magazine*, 8, No. 11 (November 1963), 109-127.

————, *The Casebook of Solar Pons*. Sauk City, Wis.: Mycroft & Moran, 1965. p. 30-53.

5627. "The Adventure of the Innkeeper's Clerk," *The Saint Mystery Magazine*, 23, No. 2 (January 1966), 72-91.

————, *The Casebook of Solar Pons*. Sauk City, Wis.: Mycroft & Moran, 1965. p. 252-276.

5628. "The Adventure of the Intarsia Box," *Alfred Hitchcock's Mystery Magazine*, 9, No. 3 (March 1964), 138-159.

————, *The Casebook of Solar Pons*. Sauk City, Wis.: Mycroft & Moran, 1965. p. 67-93.

5629. "The Adventure of the Late Mr. Faversham," *The Dragnet Magazine*, 4, No. 3 (December 1929), 338-350.

————. *"In Re: Sherlock Holmes."* Sauk City, Wis.: Mycroft and Moran, 1945. p. 31-48.

Solar Pons and Dr. Parker

5630. "The Adventure of the Limping Man," *Detective Trails*, 1, No. 2 (December 1929), 195-210.
——, "*In Re: Sherlock Holmes.*" Sauk City, Wis.: Mycroft and Moran, 1945. p. 153-178.
——, [Picture strip by Frank Utpatel]. *Praed Street Papers.* New York: The Candlelight Press, 1965. p. 40-59.

5631. "The Adventure of the Little Hangman," *The Saint Detective Magazine,* 8, No. 3 (September 1957), 46-62.
——, *The Return of Solar Pons.* Sauk City, Wis.: Mycroft & Moran, 1958. p. 223-244.

5632. "The Case of the Lost Dutchman," *The Pursuit Detective Story Magazine*, 1, No. 7 (January 1955), 77-94.
"The Adventure of the Lost Dutchman," *The Return of Solar Pons.* Sauk City, Wis.: Mycroft & Moran, 1958. p. 3-22.

5633. "The Adventure of the Lost Holiday," "*In Re: Sherlock Holmes.*" Sauk City, Wis.: Mycroft and Moran, 1945. p. 197-218.

5634. "The Adventure of the Lost Locomotive," *The Memoirs of Solar Pons.* Sauk City, Wis.: Mycroft & Moran, 1951, p. 156-175.

5635. "The Adventure of the Man with the Broken Face," "*In Re: Sherlock Holmes.*" Sauk City, Wis.: Mycroft and Moran, 1945. p. 219-238.

5636. "The Thirteenth Coffin," *Hunted*, 1, No. 10 (June 1956), 53-68.
"The Adventure of the Mazarine Blue," *The Reminiscences of Solar Pons.* Sauk City, Wis.: Mycroft & Moran, 1961. p. 3-21.

5637. "The Adventure of the Missing Huntsman," *The Saint Mystery Magazine,* 22, No. 5 (September 1965), 12-37.
——, *The Casebook of Solar Pons.* Sauk City, Wis.: Mycroft & Moran, 1965. p. 178-210.

5638. "The Adventure of the Missing Tenants," *The Dragnet Magazine*, 4, No. 1 (June 1929), 67-76.
——, *The Chronicles of Solar Pons.* Sauk City, Wis.: Mycroft & Moran, 1973.
——, [Picture strip by Frank Utpatel]. *Praed Street Papers.* New York: The Candlelight Press, 1965. p. 60-78.

5639. *Mr. Fairlie's Final Journey.* Sauk City, Wis.: Mycroft & Moran, 1968. 131 p.
Contents: 1. The Last of Jonas Fairlie. - 2. Farway Hall. - 3. The Poor Cousins. - 4. Mr. Abercrombie's Reticence. - 5. An Attempt at Murder. - 6. Inquest. - 7. A Visit to Cheltenham. - 8. Jonas Fairlie's Retreat. - 9. The Second Secret.

5640. "The Adventure of the Mosaic Cylinders," *The Saint Mystery Magazine*, 12, No. 2 (August 1959), 65-97.
——, *The Reminiscences of Solar Pons.* Sauk City, Wis.: Mycroft & Moran, 1961. p. 44-88.

5641. "The Adventure of the Norcross Riddle," *The Misadventures of Sherlock Holmes.* Edited by Ellery Queen. Boston: Little, Brown and Co., 1944. p. 261-274.
——,"*In Re: Sherlock Holmes.*" Sauk City, Wis.: Mycroft and Moran, 1945. p. 64-79.

5642. "The Adventure of the Obrisset Snuff Box," *The Chronicles of Solar Pons.* Sauk City, Wis.: Mycroft & Moran, 1973.

5643. *The Adventure of the Orient Express.* With illustrations by Henry Lauritzen. New York: The Candlelight Press, 1965. 60 p.
——, *The Chronicles of Solar Pons.* Sauk City, Wis.: Mycroft & Moran, 1973.

5644. "The Adventure of the Paralytic Mendicant," *The Memoirs of Solar Pons.* Sauk City, Wis.: Mycroft & Moran, 1951. p. 221-245.

5645. "The Adventure of the Penny Magenta," *The Saint Detective Magazine*, 2, No. 5 (November 1954), 101-110.
——, *The Return of Solar Pons.* Sauk City, Wis.: Mycroft & Moran, 1958. p. 165-178.

5646. "The Adventure of the Perfect Husband," *The Memoirs of Solar Pons.* Sauk City, Wis.: Mycroft & Moran, 1951. p. 28-43.
——, *Illustrious Client's Third Case-Book.* Edited by J. N. Williamson and H. B. Williams. [Indianapolis, Ind.: The Illustrious Clients, 1953.] p. 169-190.

5647. "The Adventure of the Praed Street Irregulars," *The Reminiscences of Solar Pons.* Sauk City, Wis.: Mycroft & Moran, 1961. p. 89-107.

5648. "The Adventure of the Proper Comma," *The Memoirs of Solar Pons.* Sauk City, Wis.: Mycroft & Moran, 1951. p. 85-103.

5649. "The Adventure of the Purloined Periapt," "*In Re: Sherlock Holmes.*" Sauk City, Wis.: Mycroft and Moran, 1945. p. 132-152.
——, *Four-&-Twenty Bloodhounds.* Edited and with introductions by Anthony Boucher. New York: Simon and Schuster, 1950. p. 277-296. (Mystery Writers of America)

5650. "The Adventure of the Red Leech," *Alfred Hitchcock's Mystery Magazine*, 11, No. 10 (October 1966), 62-76.

——, *Best Detective Stories of the Year: 22nd Annual Collection.* Edited by Anthony Boucher. New York: E. P. Dutton & Co., 1967. p. 39-59.

——, *Boucher's Choicest: A Collection of Anthony Boucher's Favorites from Best Detective Stories of the Year.* Selected by Jeanne F. Bernkopf. Introduction by Allen J. Hubin. New York: E. P. Dutton & Co., 1969. p. 185-200.

——, *The Menace Masters: Tales from Boucher's Choicest.* Selected by Jeanne F. Bernkopf. Introduction by Allen J. Hubin. [New York: Dell Pub. Co., December 1971.] p. 109-129. (No. 5537)

——, *The Chronicles of Solar Pons.* Sauk City, Wis.: Mycroft & Moran, 1973.

5651. "The Adventure of the Remarkable Worm," *Three Problems for Solar Pons.* Sauk City, Wis.: Mycroft & Moran, 1952. p. 41-68.

——, *The Return of Solar Pons.* Sauk City, Wis.: Mycroft & Moran, 1958. p. 148-164.

"The Case of the Remarkable Worm," *The Saint Mystery Magazine*, 17, No. 2 (August 1962), 49-61.

5652. "The Adventure of the Retired Novelist," *"In Re: Sherlock Holmes."* Sauk City, Wis.: Mycroft & Moran, 1945. p. 80-93.

5653. "The Adventure of Ricoletti of the Club Foot," *The Memoirs of Solar Pons.* Sauk City, Wis.: Mycroft & Moran, 1951. p. 104-130.

5654. "The Adventure of the Rydberg Numbers," *Three Problems for Solar Pons.* Sauk City, Wis.: Mycroft & Moran, 1952. p. 1-40.

——, *The Return of Solar Pons.* Sauk City, Wis.: Mycroft & Moran, 1958. p. 84-107.

5655. "The Adventure of the Seven Passengers," *"In Re: Sherlock Holmes."* Sauk City, Wis.: Mycroft and Moran, 1945. p. 179-196.

5656. "The Adventure of the Seven Sisters," *The Chronicles of Solar Pons.* Sauk City, Wis.: Mycroft & Moran, 1973.

5657. "The Adventure of the Shaplow Millions," *The Chronicles of Solar Pons.* Sauk City, Wis.: Mycroft & Moran, 1973.

5658. "The Six Silver Spiders," *Ellery Queen's Mystery Magazine*, 16, No. 83 (October 1950), 65-80.

"The Adventure of the Six Silver Spiders," *The Memoirs of Solar Pons.* Sauk City, Wis.: Mycroft & Moran, 1951. p. 131-155.

Awarded a special prize for the best

Sherlockiana in *EQMM'S* 5th annual detective short-story contest.

5659. "The Adventure of the Snitch in Time," by August Derleth and Mack Reynolds. *The Magazine of Fantasy and Science Fiction*, 5, No. 1 (July 1953), 17-24.

——, *The Science-Fictional Sherlock Holmes.* Denver, Colo.: The Council of Four, 1960. p. 84-92.

——, *A Praed Street Dossier.* Sauk City, Wis.: Mycroft & Moran, 1968. p. 85-94.

5660. "The Adventure of the Sotheby Salesman," *"In Re: Sherlock Holmes."* Sauk City, Wis.: Mycroft and Moran, 1945. p. 113-131.

5661. "The Adventure of the Spurious Tamerlane," *The Saint Mystery Magazine*, 21, No. 4 (December 1964), 38-51.

——, *The Casebook of Solar Pons.* Sauk City, Wis.: Mycroft & Moran, 1965. p. 94-112.

5662. "The Adventure of the Stone of Scone," *The Return of Solar Pons.* Sauk City, Wis.: Mycroft & Moran, 1958. p. 132-147.

5663. "Adventures of the Sussex Archers," *Alfred Hitchcock's Mystery Magazine*, 7, No. 10 (October 1962), 53-70.

"The Adventure of the Sussex Archers," *The Casebook of Solar Pons.* Sauk City, Wis.: Mycroft & Moran, 1965. p. 3-29.

"Adventures of the Sussex Archers," *Skull Session.* Edited by Alfred Hitchcock. [New York: Dell Pub. Co., October 1968.] p. 156-175. (No. 8016)

5664. "The Adventure of the Swedenborg Signatures," *Nero Wolfe Mystery Magazine*, 1, No. 3 (June 1954), 4-14.

——, *The Return of Solar Pons.* Sauk City, Wis.: Mycroft & Moran, 1958. p. 245-261.

5665. "The Adventure of the Three Red Dwarfs," *"In Re: Sherlock Holmes."* Sauk City, Wis.: Mycroft and Moran, 1945. p. 94-112.

5666. "The Adventure of the Tottenham Werewolf," *The Memoirs of Solar Pons.* Sauk City, Wis.: Mycroft & Moran, 1951. p. 176-200.

——, *Startling Mystery Stories*, 1, No. 4 (Spring 1967), 8-27.

5667. "The Adventure of the Trained Cormorant," *The Saint Detective Magazine*, 6, No. 4 (October 1956), 37-50.

——, *The Return of Solar Pons.* Sauk City, Wis.: Mycroft & Moran, 1958. p. 179-196.

5668. "The Adventure of the 'Triple Kent,' "

Parodies, Pastiches

Solar Pons and Dr. Parker

Solar Pons and
Dr. Parker

The Saint Detective Magazine, 7, No. 4 (April 1957), 98-111.

———,*The Return of Solar Pons*. Sauk City, Wis.: Mycroft & Moran, 1958. p. 67-83.

5669. "Others Deal in Death," *Alfred Hitchcock's Mystery Magazine*, 6, No. 2 (February 1961), 62-97.

"The Adventure of the Troubled Magistrate," *The Reminiscences of Solar Pons*. Sauk City, Wis.: Mycroft & Moran, 1961. p. 155-175.

"Manche Manchen in Mord," Übersetzt von Margarete Rauchenberger. *Alfred Hitchcocks Kriminalmagazin*. Band 12. West Berlin: Ullstein Bücher, [1964]. p. 7-29. (Ullstein Buch, Nr. 981)

"Others Deal in Death," *Alfred Hitchcock's Noose Report*. [New York: Dell Pub. Co., August 1966.] p. 69-86. (A Dell Mystery, No. 6455)

5670. *The Adventure of the Unique Dickensians*. With illustrations by Frank Utpatel. Sauk City, Wis.: Mycroft & Moran, 1968. 38 p.

———, *The Chronicles of Solar Pons*. Sauk City, Wis.: Mycroft & Moran, 1973.

5671. "The Adventure of the Whispering Knights," *The Saint Mystery Magazine*, 19, No. 3 (September 1963), 20-39.

———, *The Casebook of Solar Pons*. Sauk City, Wis.: Mycroft & Moran, 1965. p. 226-251.

Collected Stories and Essays

5672. *The Casebook of Solar Pons*. With a foreword by Vincent Starrett and a monograph by Michael Harrison. Sauk City, Wis.: Mycroft & Moran, 1965. xviii, 281 p. Limited to 3000 copies.

Contents: SusA. - Haun. - Fata. - Inta. - Spur. - Chin. - Asco. - Crou. - MisH. - Amat. - Whis. - Innk. - Afterword. - Endpaper map by Luther Norris.

5673. *The Chronicles of Solar Pons*. Sauk City, Wis.: Mycroft & Moran, 1973.

Contents: RedL. - Orie. - GolB. - Shap. - Beni. - MisT. - Alum. - 7Sis. - Bish. - Uniq.

5674. *"In Re: Sherlock Holmes": The Adventures of Solar Pons*. With an introduction by Vincent Starrett. Sauk City, Wis.: Mycroft and Moran, 1945. xv, 238 p. Limited to 3000 copies.

Contents: A Word from Dr. Lyndon Parker. - FriB. - Late. - BlkN. - Norc. - RetN. - 3Red. - Soth. - Purl. - Limp. - 7Pas. - LosH. - ManB.

5675. *The Memoirs of Solar Pons*. With an introduction by Ellery Queen. Sauk City, Wis.: Mycroft & Moran, 1951. xii, 245 p.

Limited to 2000 copies.

———, *The Beautiful Stranger*, by Bernice Carey; *Fish Lane*, by Louis Corkill; *The Memoirs of Solar Pons*, by August Derleth; *Hangman's Hat*, by Paul Ernst. New York: Published for the Unicorn Mystery Book Club by Unicorn Press, 1951. [896] p. [Reproduced by offset from the original plates.]

Contents: Circ. - Perf. - Brok. - DogM. - Prop. - Rico. - 6Sil. - LosL. - Tott. - 5Roy. - Para.

5676. *A Praed Street Dossier*. With illustrations by Frank Utpatel. Sauk City, Wis.: Mycroft & Moran, 1968. 108 p.

Contents: *Solar Pons: Marginalia*: The Beginnings of Solar Pons. - The Sources of the Tales. - Concerning Dr. Parker's Background. - The Favorite Pastiches. - *From the Notebooks of Dr. Lyndon Parker*. - The Adventure of the Bookseller's Clerk. - *Solar Pons, Off-Trail*. - The Adventure of the Snitch in Time. - The Adventure of the Ball of Nostradamus.

5677. *Praed Street Papers*. With panels by Frank Utpatel. New York: The Candlelight Press, 1965. 82 p.

Contents: A Weekend with August Derleth: An Introduction, by Peter Ruber. - The Beginnings of Solar Pons. - The Sources of the Tales. - The Favorite Pastiches. - Concerning Dr. Parker's Background. - From the Notebooks of Dr. Lyndon Parker. - The Pictured Pons. - The Adventure of the Limping Man [picture strip by Frank Utpatel]. - The Adventure of the Missing Tenants [picture strip by Frank Utpatel]. - A Tentative Chronology of Solar Pons.

5678. *The Reminiscences of Solar Pons*. With an introduction by Anthony Boucher and a chronology by Robert Pattrick. Sauk City, Wis.: Mycroft & Moran, 1961. xi, 199 p. Limited to 2000 copies.

Contents: MazB. - Hats. - Mosa. - Prae. - Clov. - BlkC. - Trou. - Blin.

5679. *The Return of Solar Pons*. With an introduction by Edgar W. Smith. Sauk City, Wis.: Mycroft & Moran, 1958. xiii, 261 p. Limited to 2000 copies.

Contents: LosD. - DevF. - Dorr. - Trip. - Rydb. - Gric. - Ston. - Rema. - Penn. - Trai. - Camb. - Litt. - Swed.

5680. *Three Problems for Solar Pons*. Sauk City, Wis.: Mycroft & Moran, 1952. 112 p. Limited to 996 copies.

Contents: Rydb. - Rema. - Camb.

5681. *"In Re: Sherlock Holmes": Le avventure di Solar Pons seguite dalle Memorie di Solar Pons*. [The Adventures of Solar Pons Followed by The Memoirs of Solar Pons.] Prefazione di Ellery Queen. Traduzione di

Maria Basaglia. Milano: Longanesi & C., [1970]. [624] p. (La gaja scienza, Vol. 315)

Miscellany

5682. "A Word from Dr. Lyndon Parker." *"In Re: Sherlock Holmes."* Sauk City, Wis.: Mycroft and Moran, 1945. p. xiii-xv.

Parker recalls his historic meeting with Pons and how he came to record the cases in which he and his friend have taken part.

5683. "From the Notebooks of Dr. Lyndon Parker," *Praed Street Papers*. New York: The Candlelight Press, 1965. p. 32-38.

————, [Revised and enlarged] *A Praed Street Dossier*. Sauk City, Wis.: Mycroft & Moran, 1968. p. 27-80.

Random jottings from Parker's notebooks, covering the period August 17, 1919, to January 23, 1920, and including "The Adventure of the Bookseller's Clerk," dated January 14, 1920.

5684. "Some Further Jottings from the Notebooks of Dr. Lyndon Parker," Illustrated by Frank Utpatel. *PD Annual*, 1, No. 1 (1970), 3-8.

These cover the period February 1-11, 1920.

5685. "More from Dr. Parker's Notebooks," Illustrated by Henry Lauritzen. *PD Annual*, 1, No. 2 (1971), 43-48.

The last notes, from February 15-24, 1920, written about Pons and Parker before the author's death on July 4, 1971.

THE WRITINGS ABOUT THE WRITINGS, THE AGENT, AND THE PRAED STREET IRREGULARS

5686. Bengis, Nathan L. "Sherlocko-Pontine Parallels," *PD*, 1, No. 4 (September 1968), 1, 3-4.

A discussion of six unpublished adventures mentioned by Watson to which Parker tells Pontine solutions. They are Late, Rico, Gric, Rema, Trai, and RedL.

5687. Bloch, Robert. ["The Agent, August Derleth"], *The Arkham Collector*, No. 2 (Winter 1968), 32-39.

"With all these editorial restrictions and taboos, we who cherish the classic tale of detection can well pay homage to our Agent, who has adhered to the eternal verities. In his presentation of the detective Solar Pons he has given us the sleuth, the whole sleuth, and nothing but the sleuth. He has delivered us from James Bondage."

5688. ————. "Crumbs for a Toast to Solar Pons," Illustrated by William Dixon. *PD Annual*, 1, No. 2 (1971), 42.

"But we salute a sleuth / Who dignifies, in truth, The mantle of the master that he

dons; / All the others, irrespective, / Must defer to our detective— / So, gentlemen—I give you—Solar Pons!"

5689. Boucher, Anthony. "Introduction," *The Reminiscences of Solar Pons*. Sauk City, Wis.: Mycroft & Moran, 1961. p. vii-xi.

An informative introduction to the fourth volume of Solar Pons stories in which the late author points out some of the differences between Solar Pons and his prototype, Sherlock Holmes.

5690. Christopher, J. R. "A Sherlocko-Pontine Addendum," *PD*, 2, No. 1 (December 1968), 1, 3-4.

The author discusses a double case (Whis and Spur) which he thinks should be added to Mr. Bengis's list (item 5686).

5691. Cochran, Leonard. "Readers in Search of an Author," *PD*, 1, No. 3 (March 1968), 1, 4.

A report on the literary pilgrimage that Bob Hahn, Bill Goodrich, Mike Whelan, Fr. John Schwind, and Leonard Cochran took on August 20, 1966, to "Place of Hawks" (the home of August Derleth).

5692. Cox, Jean. "Dogging the Footsteps of Solar Pons," Illustrated by Tom Walker. *PD Annual*, 1, No. 1 (1970), 9-15.

A dog, not Miss Ethel Coster, was responsible for the death of Edward Horton, manager of the Cloverdale Kennels.

5693. Derleth, August. "Afterword," *The Casebook of Solar Pons*. Sauk City, Wis.: Mycroft & Moran, 1965. p. 277-281.

A brief commentary on the origin of Solar Pons and a list of fifty-six Pontine tales that have been collected and published in five books.

5694. ————. "The Beginnings of Solar Pons," *BSG*, 1, No. 4 (April 1962), 20-26.

————. ————, [Revised] *Praed Street Papers*. New York: The Candlelight Press, 1965. p. 17-22.

————. ————, *A Praed Street Dossier*. Sauk City, Wis.: Mycroft & Moran, 1968. p. 1-8.

"Solar Pons came into being out of Sherlock Holmes, just as Holmes came out of C. Auguste Dupin, all chronicled data about Dr. Joseph Bell of Edinburgh University to the contrary. In a sense, Sherlock Holmes *is* C. Auguste Dupin. In the same sense, Solar Pons is Sherlock Holmes."

5695. ————. "Concerning Dr. Parker's Background," *Praed Street Papers*. New York: The Candlelight Press, 1965. p. 30-32.

————. ————, [Revised] *A Praed Street Dossier*. Sauk City, Wis.: Mycroft & Moran, 1968. p. 15-17.

A supplement to Michael Harrison's biographical sketch of Dr. Parker (item 5710).

5696. ———. "The Favorite Pastiches," *Praed Street Papers*. New York: The Candlelight Press, 1965. p. 26-30.
———. ———, [Revised] *A Praed Street Dossier*. Sauk City, Wis.: Mycroft & Moran, 1968. p. 18-23.
The agent discusses his favorite Solar Pons stories, as well as the favorites of some other notable persons.

5697. ———. "The Sources of the Tales," *Praed Street Papers*. New York: The Candlelight Press, 1965. p. 22-26.
———. ———, [Revised] *A Praed Street Dossier*. Sauk City, Wis.: Mycroft & Moran, 1968. p. 9-14.

5698. ———. "A Tentative Chronology of Solar Pons," *Praed Street Papers*. New York: The Candlelight Press, 1965. p. 79-82.
"Based on the Robert Pattrick Chronology" (item 5729).

5699. Dettman, Bruce. "In the Master's Footsteps," *PD*, 1, No. 2 (December 1967), 1, 3.
"After the Master had gone to his bee keeping in Sussex, William Pons [Billy the page boy], having long before decided on a career modeled after Holmes. . . set off to make his own name as a consulting detective."

5700. ———. "The Praed Street Irregulars," *SOS*, No. 3 (February 1967), 10-11.
A knowledgeable article about the agent, the Pontine tales, and the PSI.

5701. ———. "Singular Malady of Septimus Grayle," *PD*, 2, No. 3 (August 1969), 1, 3.
An examination of Mr. Septimus Grayle's or the "Tottenham Werewolf's" condition known as lycanthropy.

5702. De Waal, Ronald Burt. "Solar Pons and Dr. Parker: A Bibliography, 1929-1969," *The American Book Collector*, 20, No. 7 (May 1970), 19-26. illus.
All the items in the bibliography are included in the present bibliography.

5703. Enright, Robert. " 'Sherlock Holmes' of Praed Street," *SIS*, 1, No. 2 (December 1965), 24-27.

5704. Farmer, Philip José. "Oft Have I Travelled," *PD*, 2, No. 2 (April 1969), 1, 3.
An appreciation for having been able to dwell in the world of Solar Pons and Dr. Parker.

5705. "First Annual PSI Dinner," *PD*, 1, No. 2 (December 1967), 1, 3.

An account of this historic dinner held April 30, 1967, at Andre's in Beverly Hills.

5706. Galerstein, David. "The Curious Case of the Croyden Crossing," Illustrated by Tom Walker. *PD Annual*, 1, No. 1 (1970), 18.
A discussion of the discrepancy between the reported and actual time it took Pons, Parker, and Jamison to reach the S.S. *Sheffield* in LosD.

5707. Germeshausen, Alvin F. "Call to Conclave," *PD*, 1, No. 1 (February 1967), 1, 3.
"An address by Toastmaster Alvin F. Germeshausen at the founding of The Praed Street Irregulars, June 12, 1966, at Ivory Towers, Hollywood, Calif."

5708. Halbach, Helan. "Exquisite Perquisite," *PD*, 2, No. 5 (March 1970), 4.
"Who shall he have do it—and why? / What method, what villainy devious—/ When Pons acts will Parker decry? / Where to next, will our heroes be previous?"

5709. Harrison, Michael. "Chant Royal of the Sodality of Praed-Street Irregulars," Words by Michael Harrison. Music by Haydn (to be sung to the Air of *Glorious Things*). *PD Annual*, 1, No. 1 (1970), 2.
A song in twelve stanzas and refrain praising Praed Street's great detective.

5710. ———. "(Cuthbert) Lyndon Parker," *The Casebook of Solar Pons*. Sauk City, Wis.: Mycroft & Moran, 1965. p. xiii-xviii.
About the ancestry and background of the man who made the Pontine tales possible.

5711. ———. "The Language of the Praed Street Irregulars," *PD*, 2, No. 4 (November 1969), 1, 3.
Parker edited the nearly incomprehensible Cockney rhyming slang spoken by the Praed Street Irregulars so that the adventures would be understood by a larger audience.

5712. ———. "May I Say a Few Well-Chosen Words?" by Alfred Peake. *PD*, 2, No. 5 (March 1970), 1-2, 4.
Alfred Peake tells, in his own words, how he came to be the first recruit to the Praed Street Irregulars.

5713. ———. "The Praed of Praeds," *PD*, 1, No. 1 (February 1967), 1, 3.
A biographical sketch of the English lawyer-poet Winthrop Mackworth Praed.

5714. [Henriksen, A. D.] "A Second-Generation Sherlock?" *Sherlockiana*, 11, Nr. 2 (1966), 7.
Extracts, in Danish, from the introductions to the Solar Pons stories.

5715. Johnson, Roger. "Concerning the Problem of *The Man with the Broken Face*," *PD Annual*, 1, No. 1 (1970), 32-35.

The house of Captain Hyatt Norton and his daughter Sylvia was not located on the Essex coast but on the coast of Cornwall between Padstow and Wadebridge, on the estuary of the River Camel.

5716. ———. "Trifling Monograph Concerning Mr. Solar Pons," *SHJ*, 9, No. 4 (Summer 1970), 135-137.

An informative article on Derleth, Pons, the PSI and its two scion societies—The Old Soldiers of Praed Street and The Solar Pons Society of London.

5717. Kennedy, Bruce. "A Latter Holmes," *PD*, 1, No. 3 (March 1968), 1, 4.

The Master came out of retirement in 1921 and assumed the name of Solar Pons to conceal his identity from the criminal underworld.

5718. Latchman, Howard. "The Second Master (On the passing of August Derleth, 4 July 1971)," *BSJ*, 21, No. 4 (December 1971), 195.

"The Second Master and his Agent pass / To that Celebrated Detective Kingdom above, / Imitative figures who performed / Original labours of love."

5719. Levy, Mark. "The Most Wanted Man," *PD*, 2, No. 4 (November 1969), 1, 3.

Only a great detective like Solar Pons could commit a crime without leaving any clues, but he would be discovered for this very reason.

5720. Lobdell, Jared C. "Addenda to the Canon," *The National Review*, 21, No. 29 (July 29, 1969), 758-759.

A review of *The Adventure of the Unique Dickensians*, *A Praed Street Dossier*, and *Mr. Fairlie's Final Journey*; with a brief discussion of the agent and other Solar Pons stories.

5721. [Lowndes, Robert A. W.] "The Cauldron" and "The Editor's Page," *Startling Mystery Stories*, 1, No. 4 (Spring 1967), 121-123; 1, No. 6 (Fall 1967), 116-117; 2, No. 5 (Winter 1968 / 69), 4-5 [Reprinted in *CPBook*, 5, No. 18 (Spring 1969), 361-362].

Excellent editorial commentaries on the Pontine tales and the PSI.

5722. Marx, George J. "My Auctorial Friend, August Derleth," *PD*, 1, No. 1 (February 1967), 4.

A brief article on some recent activities of the agent by a man who knew him for over twenty-five years.

5723. McGoldrick, John. "Jamison and Lestrade: A Comparative Study," *PD*, 1, No. 4 (September 1968), 1, 3.

"Though these two men are only lesser detectives in comparison to Holmes and Pons, where would these two great detectives be without the 'little problems' brought to them by Inspectors Jamison and Lestrade of the Yard?"

5724. ———. "Sherlock Holmes and Solar Pons: A Comparative Essay," *Transition* [Oak Park, Ill.: Fenwich High School] (1966-67), 4-6.

"The main differences between Holmes and Pons exist not in, but outside of their methods."

5725. McSherry, Frank D. "Now It Can Be Told: The Secret of the Pons," Illustrated by the author. *PD Annual*, 1, No. 2 (1971), 57-65.

A remarkable and noble identification of Solar Pons's brother Bancroft as the former Home Secretary and Prime Minister of Great Britain, Sir Winston S. Churchill. Biographers of Churchill please take note!

5726. Newsom, Jim. "Sherlock, Pons Fans Convene," *Citizen-News* [Hollywood] (May 10, 1967), A-8.

———. ———, *CPBook*, 3, No. 11 (Winter 1967), 216.

An article on the PSI and their second annual dinner. Includes a photograph of Robert Block, guest speaker at the meeting; Alvin F. Germeshausen, emcee; and Luther Norris, founder.

5727. Norris, Luther. "The London Map of Solar Pons," *The Casebook of Solar Pons*. Sauk City, Wis.: Mycroft & Moran, 1965. End papers (10 x 7-1 / 4 in.)

5728. ———. "Pontine Patter from the Desk of the Lord Warden," *PD*, 2, No. 1 (December 1968), 4, 3.

A report on the third annual conclave of the PSI held November 20, 1968, at the Corsican Restaurant in Hollywood. Illustrated with photographs by Chuck Ries.

5729. Pattrick, Robert. "A Chronology of Solar Pons," *The Reminiscences of Solar Pons*. Sauk City, Wis.: Mycroft & Moran, 1961. p. 194-199.

Contents: Canons of the Chronology. - The Chronology. - Untold Tales. - Notes on the Chronology.

5730. Power, Charles R. L. "The Old Doctor of Limehouse," *PD*, 2, No. 2 (April 1969), 4.

On the mysterious Dr. F. mentioned in Prae and Camb.

5731. "The Praed Street Irregulars" and "*The Pontine Dossier*," *The Arkham Collector*, No. 1 (Summer 1967), 10-11.

Sherlock Holmes
and Dr. Watson

———, *The Mystery Lover's Newsletter,* 1, No. 2 (December 1967), 7-8.

Information on the formation of this Society and its official publication (items 4198-4199).

5732. Price, Kay. " 'Praed Street Irregulars' Owe Their Identities to Derleth's Mystery Tales," *The Capital Times Green* [Madison, Wis.] (April 24, 1969).

———. ———, *PD Annual,* 1, No. 1 (1970), 16-17. (Pontine Patter)

An illustrated article about Luther Norris and a Sherlockian (Pontine) society that includes some six-hundred members.

5733. ["Reviews of *'In Re: Sherlock Holmes'* "], *New York Times Book Review* (December 2, 1945), 32 (Howard Haycraft), and reprinted in *CPBook,* 2, No. 5-6 (Summer-Fall 1965), 121; *Springfield Republican* (December 23, 1945), 4; *Time,* 46 (November 19, 1945), 108; *Wisconsin Library Bulletin,* 41 (December 1945), 126.

5734. ["Reviews of *The Memoirs of Solar Pons*"], *Chicago Sunday Tribune* (August 26, 1951), 2 (Ney MacMinn); *New York Herald Tribune Book Review* (September 30, 1951), 14 (James Sandoe); *New York Times Book Review* (August 26, 1951), 20 (Anthony Boucher); *San Francisco Chronicle* (September 2, 1951), 18 (L. G. Offord); *Wisconsin Library Bulletin,* 46 (September 1951), 215.

5735. ["Reviews of *A Praed Street Dossier*"], *New York Times Book Review* (July 14, 1968), 38 (Allen J. Hubin); *SOS,* 3, No. 2 (July 1969), 5-6 (Bruce Dettman); *Startling Mystery Stories,* 2, No. 5 (Winter 1968 / 69), 4-5 (Robert A. W. Lowndes).

5736. ["Review of *The Reminiscences of Solar Pons*"], *SHJ,* 6, No. 1 (Winter 1962), 30 (Lord Donegall).

5737. ["Reviews of *The Return of Solar Pons*"], *New York Herald Tribune Book Review* (April 12, 1959), 11 (James Sandoe); *New York Times Book Review* (January 4, 1959), 20 (Anthony Boucher); *San Francisco Chronicle* (February 1, 1959), 26 (L. G. Offord).

5738. ["Review of *Three Problems for Solar Pons*"], *New York Times Book Review* (January 11, 1953), 28 (Anthony Boucher).

5739. Ruber, Peter A. "The Pontine Canon: Key to the Story Names," *PD,* 1, No. 2 (December 1967), 4.

Four-letter abbreviations patterned after Professor Christ's to fifty-eight short stories. For a revised listing of the seventy-one stories, see Appendix I.

5740. ———. "A Weekend with August Derleth: An Introduction," *Praed Street Papers.* New York: The Candlelight Press, 1965. p. 8-14.

5741. Shroyer, Frederick. "August Derleth: Pre-Romantic," Photo by Edgar L. Obma. *PD Annual,* 1, No. 2 (1971), 49-51.

A tribute to the writer and man who was able to reconcile moonlight with the human predicament.

5742. Starrett, Vincent. "Foreword," *The Casebook of Solar Pons.* Sauk City, Wis.: Mycroft & Moran, 1965. p. ix-xi.

A brief commentary on Solar Pons, the best of all Sherlock Holmes's pupils.

5743. ———. "In Re: Solar Pons," *"In Re: Sherlock Holmes."* Sauk City, Wis.: Mycroft and Moran, 1945. p. ix-xii.

An introduction by the doyen of Sherlockians to the first appearance in book form of Solar Pons and Dr. Parker.

5744. Van Vogt, A. E. "The Adventure of the Pastiche Craftsman," *PD,* 2, No. 1 (December 1958), 1-3.

Derleth's pastiches of Sherlock Holmes have succeeded, where others have failed, because he was not afraid to create a genuine imitation and to be the unashamed equal of Doyle.

5745. ———. "Being an Examination of the Ponsian and Holmesian Secret Deductive Systems," Illustrated by Roy Hunt. *PD Annual,* 1, No. 2 (1971), 52-56.

Analyzes "What goes on in the brain of a person (Pons, or Holmes, or any lesser being) who is capable of making astounding analyses on that level of genius."

C *Sherlock Holmes and Dr. Watson (Adrian Conan Doyle & John Dickson Carr)*

Short Stories

5746. "The Adventure of the Abbas Ruby," by Adrian Conan Doyle. Illustrated by Robert Fawcett. *Collier's,* 132, No. 6 (August 21, 1953), 78-83.

———, Illustrated by Paul Granger. *Summertime* [Scholastic Magazines], 12, No. 6 (July 30, 1965), 13-15; 12, No. 7 (August 6, 1965), 13-15.

5747. "The Adventure of the Black Baronet," by Adrian Conan Doyle and John Dickson Carr. Illustrated by Robert Fawcett. *Collier's*, 131, No. 21 (May 23, 1953), 19-21, 54-59.

5748. "The Adventure of the Demon Angeles," by Adrian Conan Doyle. Illustrated by Robert Fawcett. *Collier's*, 132, No. 5 (August 7, 1953), 70-76.
   Retitled "The Adventure of the Dark Angeles" in *The Exploits of Sherlock Holmes*.

5749. "The Adventure of the Deptford Horror," by Adrian Conan Doyle. Illustrated by Robert Fawcett. *Collier's*, 132, No. 8 (September 18, 1953), 44-54.
   ———, *Seventeen Steps to 221B*. [Edited by] James Edward Holroyd. London: George Allen & Unwin Ltd., [1967]. p. 106-125.

5750. "The Adventure of Foulkes Rath," by Adrian Conan Doyle. Illustrated by Robert Fawcett. *Collier's*, 131, No. 26 (June 27, 1953), 26-31.

5751. "The Adventure of the Gold Hunter," by Adrian Conan Doyle and John Dickson Carr. Illustrated by Robert Fawcett. *Collier's*, 131, No. 22 (May 30, 1953), 26-33.

5752. "The Adventure of the Highgate Miracle," by Adrian Conan Doyle and John Dickson Carr. Illustrated by Robert Fawcett. *Collier's*, 131, No. 23 (June 6, 1953), 54-61.

5753. "The Adventure of the Red Widow," by Adrian Conan Doyle. Illustrated by Robert Fawcett. *Collier's*, 132, No. 9 (October 2, 1953), 106-111.

5754. "The Adventure of the Sealed Room," by Adrian Conan Doyle and John Dickson Carr. Illustrated by Robert Fawcett. *Collier's*, 131, No. 24 (June 13, 1953), 60-65.

5755. "The Adventure of the Seven Clocks," by Adrian Conan Doyle and John Dickson Carr. Drawings by Adolf Hallman. *Life*, 33, No. 26 (December 29, 1952), 54-61.

5756. "The Adventure of the Two Women," by Adrian Conan Doyle. Illustrated by Robert Fawcett. *Collier's*, 132, No. 7 (September 4, 1953), 50-59.

5757. "The Adventure of the Wax Gamblers," by Adrian Conan Doyle and John Dickson Carr. Illustrated by Robert Fawcett. *Collier's*, 131, No. 25 (June 20, 1953), 46-53.

Collected Stories

5758. *The Exploits of Sherlock Holmes*, by Adrian Conan Doyle and John Dickson

Carr. [Designed and illustrated by Jerome Kuhl.] New York: Random House, [1954]. xii, 338 p.
   ———. London: John Murray, [1954]. x, 313 p.
   ———. New York: Ace Books, [c. 1954]. 320 p. (Ace Double-Size Books, D-181)
   ———. Freeport, N.Y.: Books for Libraries Press, [1971]. xii, 338 p. (Short Story Index Reprint Series)
   Las hazanas de Sherlock Holmes. [Traducción de Vicente de Artadi.] Buenos Aires: Jackson, 1955. 322 p.
   ———. [Traducción de Vincente de Artadi.] México, D.F.: Editorial Cumbre, S.A., [1955]. 322 p.
   Exploits de Sherlock Holmes. Traduction de Gilles Vauthier. [Paris]: Robert Laffont, [1956]. 376 p. (Le Livre de Poche policier, 2423)
   ———, Traduction de Gilles Vauthier. *Oeuvres complètes*, [par] Sir Arthur Conan Doyle. Paris: Robert Laffont, 1958. Vol. 10, p. 353-660.
   [*Sherlock Holmes no kôseki*. Tr. by Yasuo Ôkubo. Tokyo: Hayakawashobô, 1958.] 352 p.
   Novas aventuras de Sherlock Holmes. [Traduçao portuguese de Natividade Gaspar.] Lisboa: Editorial Minerva, [1958]. [221] p.
   Contents: Publisher's Note [Always Holmes]. - Seven. - GoldH. - WaxGa. - Highg. - BlacB. - Seald. by Adrian Conan Doyle and John Dickson Carr. Foulk. - Abbas. - 2 Womn. - DarkA. - Deptf. - RedWi. by Adrian Conan Doyle.

5759. *The Exploits of Sherlock Holmes*, by Adrian Conan Doyle. London: John Murray, [1963]. 158 p.
   Sherlock Holmes sidste bedrifter. [Preface by A. D. Henriksen.] På dansk ved Georg Brandt. København: Martins Forlag, 1966. 141 p.
   Sherlock Holmes' Nachlass 2. [Deutsch von Alheit Kocher und Eva Thöl.] [Gütersloh]: C. Bertelsmann Verlag, [1966]. 186 p. (Sir Arthur Conan Doyle Gesammelte Werke in Einzelausgaben. Herausgegeben von Nino Erné. Band 18)
   Le imprese di Sherlock Holmes. Traduzione di Alberto Tedeschi e Paola Forti. [Milano; Verona]: Arnoldo Mondadori Editore, [1966]. 193 p. (N. 13)
   Contents: Publisher's Note. - Foulk. - Abbas. - 2Womn. - DarkA. - Deptf. - RedWi.

5760. *More Exploits of Sherlock Holmes*, by Adrian Conan Doyle and John Dickson Carr. London: John Murray, [1964]. ix, 146 p.
   Sherlock Holmes' bedrifter. På dansk ved Georg Brandt. København: Martins Forlag, 1966. 133 p.
   Sherlock Holmes' Nachlass 1. [Deutsch

Sherlock Holmes and Dr. Watson

von Arno Dohm, Alheit Kocher und Eva Thöl.] Hamburg: Mosaik Verlag, [1966]. 190 p. (Sir Arthur Conan Doyle Gesammelte Werke in Einzelausgaben. Herausgegeben von Nino Erné. Band 17)

Sherlock Holmes' Kriminalfälle 8: Kriminalstories. [Deutsch von Arno Dohm, Alheit Kocher und Eva Thöl.] München: Wilhelm Heyne Verlag, 1968. [158] p. (Heyne-Bücher, 1319)

Nuove imprese di Sherlock Holmes. Traduzione di Alberto Tedeschi. [Milano; Verona]: Arnoldo Mondadori Editore, [1966]. 222 p. (N. 14)

Contents: Publisher's Note. - Seven. - GoldH. - WaxGa. - Highg. - BlacB. - Seald.

Reviews and Criticism

Chicago Sunday Tribune (April 4, 1954), 6 (Vincent Starrett); *New York Times Book Review* (April 11, 1954), 27 (Anthony Boucher); *San Francisco Chronicle* (March 17, 1954), 19 (J. H. Jackson); *Time*, 63 (April 5, 1954), 110.

5761. Brean, Herbert. "How Holmes Was Reborn: A Unique Literary Partnership Engineered His Second Return," *Life*, 33, No. 26 (December 29, 1952), 62-66.

5762. Buxton, E. Timothy-Howe, Jr. "The Holmesiana Apocrypha," *BSJ*, 12, No. 3 (September 1962), 142-145.

A comparative analysis of the Exploits and the Canonical tales.

5763. Harris, M. "The Composite Doyle: A New Critique by an Unread Critic," *EL*, 1, No. 2 (August 1953), 9-10, 14.

A critical estimate of the Exploits by someone who did not read the stories lest his judgment be impaired!

5764. [Holroyd, James Edward.] " 'Any Views Watson?' " by Horace Harker [pseud.] *SHJ*, 2, No. 1 (July 1954), 14-16.

———. "The 'Exploits,' " *Baker Street Byways*. London: George Allen & Unwin Ltd., [1959]. p. 153-158.

"Not least among the fascinations of the new collection is the study of how far the stories conform to and how far they depart from the originals."

5765. Lawyer, A. Penang [pseud.] "The Name's the Same," *SHJ*, 2, No. 1 (July 1954), 11-13.

"Read them [the Exploits] with tongue in your cheek, as just another exercise in the great Sherlock Holmes Game which we all love to play, and you will find many moments in which the authentic portrait obtrudes itself through the new-fangled frame."

426

5766. Ward, Norman W. "Report of a Recent Conversation in a Remote Cottage on the South Downs," *The Best of the Pips.* Westchester County, N. Y.: The Five Orange Pips, 1955. p. 75-77.

Eavesdropping on the Master's observations of his alleged Exploits.

_____

D Schlock Homes and Dr. Watney (Robert L. Fish)

Short Stories

5767. "The Adventure of the Adam Bomb," *Ellery Queen's Mystery Magazine*, 36, No. 9 (September 1960), 81-89.

———, *Crimes and Misfortunes: The Anthony Boucher Memorial Anthology of Mysteries.* Edited by J. Francis McComas. New York: Random House, [1970]. p. 132-142.

"A aventura da bomba de adam," *Mistério Magazine de Ellery Queen* [Rio de Janeiro], No. 143 (June 1961), 85-94.

[———], *Ellery Queen's Mystery Magazine* [Japanese Edition] [Tokyo], No. 10 (October 1963).

5768. "The Adventure of the Artist's Mottle," *Ellery Queen's Mystery Magazine*, 38, No. 5 (November 1961), 90-98.

———, *To Be Read Before Midnight: 21 Stories from Ellery Queen's Mystery Magazine.* Edited by Ellery Queen. New York: Random House, [1962]. p. 144-156. (Ellery Queen's 17th Mystery Annual)

[———], *Ellery Queen's Mystery Magazine* [Japanese Edition] [Tokyo], No. 4 (April 1969).

5769. "The Adventure of the Ascot Tie," *Ellery Queen's Mystery Magazine*, 35, No. 2 (February 1960), 82-90.

"A aventura do pareo dobrado," *Mistério Magazine de Ellery Queen* [Rio de Janeiro], No. 135 (October 1960), 87-95.

[———], *Ellery Queen's Mystery Magazine* [Japanese Edition] [Tokyo], No. 10 (October 1963).

"Schlock Homes der hat-Trick," *Ellery Queen's Kriminalmagazin 23. 36. Auswahlband.* Deutsche Erstveröffentlichung. München: Wilhelm Heyne Verlag, [1970]. p. 46-56. (Heyne-Buch, Nr. 1406)

5770. "The Adventure of the Big Plunger," *Ellery Queen's Mystery Magazine*, 45, No. 2 (February 1965), 49-57.

"La aventura del gran salto," *Mystery*

Magazine (*Ellery Queen's*) [Barcelona] (June 1965), 51-59.

5771. "The Adventure of the Counterfeit Sovereign," *Ellery Queen's Mystery Magazine*, 41, No. 6 (June 1963), 67-74.
————, *Ellery Queen's 1971 Anthology.* Edited by Ellery Queen. New York: Davis Publications, Inc. [1970]. p. 114-122.

5772. "The Adventure of the Disappearance of Whistler's Mother," *Ellery Queen's Mystery Magazine*, 51, No. 2 (February 1968), 140-149.
"Schlock Homes: Auf den Spuren von Whistlers Mutter," *Ellery Queen's Kriminalmagazin 18.* 31. Auswahlband. Deutsche Erstveröffentlichung. [Deutsche Übersetzung von Elisabeth Simon.] München: Wilhelm Heyne Verlag, [1969]. p. 59-68. (Heyne-Buch, Nr. 1343)
[————], *Ellery Queen's Mystery Magazine* [Japanese Edition] [Tokyo], No. 6 (June 1969).

5773. "The Adventure of the Dog in the Knight," *Ellery Queen's Mystery Magazine*, 55, No. 2 (February 1970), 88-97.
"O caso do cachorro-quente e do cavaleiro," *Mistério Magazine de Ellery Queen* [Rio de Janeiro], No. 251 (June 1970), 47-56.

5774. "The Adventure of the Double-Bogey Man," *Ellery Queen's Mystery Magazine*, 39, No. 2 (February 1962), 81-89.
————, *Best Detective Stories of the Year: 18th Annual Collection.* Edited by Anthony Boucher. New York: E. P. Dutton & Co., 1963. p. 99-113.
————, *Boucher's Choicest: A Collection of Anthony Boucher's Favorites from Best Detective Stories of the Year.* Selected by Jeanne F. Bernkopf. Introduction by Allen J. Hubin. New York: E. P. Dutton & Co., 1969. p. 42-52.
————, *The Cream of Crime: More Tales from Boucher's Choicest.* Edited by Jeanne F. Bernkopf and with an introduction by Allen J. Hubin. [New York: Dell Pub. Co., March 1972.] p. 1-15. (No. 1571)
[————], *Ellery Queen's Mystery Magazine* [Japanese Edition] [Tokyo], No. 10 (October 1963).
————, *New Short Detective Stories, 10.* Edited, with Notes, by Shigeru Koike. [Tokyo]: Kenkyusha, [1967]. p. 13-32.
"A aventure do super-lobisomem," *Mistério Magazine de Ellery Queen* [Rio de Janeiro], No. 159 (October 1962), 82-90.
"Die Hand des Teufels," *Ellery Queen's Kriminalmagazin 22.* 35. Auswahlband. Deutsche Erstveröffenlichung. [Deutsche Übersetzung von Klaus von Schwarze.] München: Wilhelm Heyne Verlag, [1970]. p. 56-67. (Henye-Buch, Nr. 1398)

5775. "The Adventure of the Final Problem,"

Ellery Queen's Mystery Magazine, 43, No. 2 (February 1964), 44-53.
————, *Ellery Queen's 20th Anniversary Annual: 20 Stories from Ellery Queen's Mystery Magazine.* Edited by Ellery Queen. New York: Random House, [1965]. p. 104-115.
————, ————. New York: Popular Library, 1965. p. 101-112.
————, *New Short Detective Stories, 10.* Edited, with Notes, by Shigeru Koike. [Tokyo]: Kenkyusha, [1967]. p. 33-52.
"La aventura del problema final," *Mystery Magazine* (*Ellery Queen's*) [Barcelona], No. 10 (March 1964), 69-78.
"A aventura do problema final," *Mistério Magazine de Ellery Queen* [Rio de Janeiro], No. 181 (August 1964), 40-48.
Retitled "The Final Problem" in *The Incredible Schlock Homes.*

5776. "The Adventure of the Missing Cheyne-Stroke," *Ellery Queen's Mystery Magazine*, 38, No. 2 (August 1961), 70-78.
[————], *Ellery Queen's Mystery Magazine* [Japanese Edition] [Tokyo], No. 4 (April 1969).

5777. "The Adventure of the Missing Prince," *Ellery Queen's Mystery Magazine*, 40, No. 1 (July 1962), 100-107.
"A aventura do príncipe perdido," *Mistério Magazine de Ellery Queen* [Rio de Janeiro], No. 164 (March 1963), 97-104.
[————], *Ellery Queen's Mystery Magazine* [Japanese Edition] [Tokyo], No. 10 (October 1963).
Retitled "The Adventure of the Lost Prince" in *The Incredible Schlock Homes.*

5778. "The Adventure of the Missing Three-Quarters," *Ellery Queen's Mystery Magazine*, 50, No. 9 (September 1967), 59-66.
————, *Ellery Queen's Mystery Parade: 19 Stories from Ellery Queen's Mystery Magazine.* Edited by Ellery Queen. [New York]: The New American Library, [1968]. p. 147-155. (23rd EQMM Annual)
[————], *Ellery Queen's Mystery Magazine* [Japanese Edition] [Tokyo], No. 1 (January 1968).

5779. "The Adventure of the Perforated Ulster," *Ellery Queen's Mystery Magazine*, 49, No. 2 (February 1967), 67-76.
[————], *Ellery Queen's Mystery Magazine* [Japanese Edition] [Tokyo], No. 5 (May 1967).

5780. "The Adventure of the Printer's Inc.," *Ellery Queen's Mystery Magazine*, 35, No. 5 (May 1960), 51-60.
————, *Ellery Queen's 15th Mystery Annual.* New York: Random House, [1960]. p. 191-202.
[————], *Ellery Queen's Mystery Magazine*

[Japanese Edition] [Tokyo], 95, No. 5 (May 1964), 18-27.

5781. "The Return of Schlock Homes," *Ellery Queen's Mystery Magazine*, 43, No. 6 (June 1964), 90-98.

————, *Best Detective Stories of the Year: 20th Annual Collection*. Edited by Anthony Boucher. New York: E. P. Dutton & Co., 1965. p. 75-88.

"El retorno de Schlock Homes," *Mystery Magazine (Ellery Queen's)* [Barcelona] (August 1964), 47-56.

"A volta de Schlock Homes," *Mistério Magazine de Ellery Queen* [Rio de Janeiro], No. 185 (December 1964), 55-64.

"Schlock Homes' Rückkehr," *Ellery Queen's Kriminalmagazin 20. 33. Auswahlband. Deutsche Erstveröffentlichung.* [Deutsche Übersetzung von Elisabeth Simon.] München: Wilhelm Heyne Verlag, [1969]. p. 63-73. (Heyne-Buch, Nr. 1374)

5782. "The Adventure of the Snared Drummer," *Ellery Queen's Mystery Magazine*, 42, No. 3 (September 1963), 50-57.

"La aventura del tambor," *Mystery Magazine (Ellery Queen's)* [Barcelona], No. 4 (September 1963), 62-69.

[————], *Ellery Queen's Mystery Magazine* [Japanese Edition] [Tokyo], 109, No. 6 (June 1965), 21-28.

5783. "The Adventure of the Spectacled Band," *Ellery Queen's Mystery Magazine*, 36, No. 11 (November 1960), 29-37.

————, *A Pride of Felons: Twenty Stories*, by members of the Mystery Writers of America. Edited by the Gordons. New York: The Macmillan Co., [1963]. p. 104-115.

————, *Ellery Queen's Anthology, 1968 Mid-Year Edition.* New York: Davis Publications, Inc., [1968]. p. 69-77.

"A aventura dos musicistas disfarçados," *Mistério Magazine de Ellery Queen* [Rio de Janeiro], No. 145 (August 1961), 53-60.

[————], *Ellery Queen's Mystery Magazine* [Japanese Edition] [Tokyo], 97, No. 7 (July 1964), 44-52.

"Schlock Homes: Die musizierenden Brillenträger," *Ellery Queen's Kriminalmagazin 19. 32. Auswahlband, Deutsche Erstveröffentlichung.* [Deutsche Übersetzung von Bruni Sautter.] München: Wilhelm Heyne Verlag, [1969]. p. 83-94. (Heyne-Buch, Nr. 1359)

5784. "The Adventure of the Stockbroker's Clark," *Ellery Queen's Mystery Magazine*, 37, No. 3 (March 1961), 85-94.

[————], *Ellery Queen's Mystery Magazine* [Japanese Edition] [Tokyo], No. 10 (October 1963).

5785. "The Adventure of the Widow's

Weeds," *Ellery Queen's Mystery Magazine*, 48, No. 2 (August 1966), 90-98.

————, *Ellery Queen's All-Star Lineup: 22 Stories from Ellery Queen's Mystery Magazine.* Edited by Ellery Queen. [New York]: The New American Library, [1967]. p. 129-138.

[————], *Ellery Queen's Mystery Magazine* [Japanese Edition] [Tokyo], No. 11 (November 1966).

Collected Stories

5786. *The Incredible Schlock Homes.* With an introduction by Anthony Boucher. [Jacket and end-paper drawings by Edward Sorel.] New York: Simon and Schuster, [1966]. 217 p.

[————.] Tr. by Mariko Fukamachi. Tokyo: Hayakawa Shobo & Co., [1969]. 224 p. (Hayakawa Pocket Mystery Books, No. 1079)

Contents: AscT. - Prin. - Adam. - SpeB. - StoC. - MisC. - Arti. - Doub. - Snar. - Coun. - LosP. - FinA.

Reviews and Criticism

Best Sellers, 26 (May 15, 1966), 81; *Book Week* (August 14, 1966), 10 (D. B. Hughes); *Chicago Tribune* (April 24, 1966), 12 (Vincent Starrett); *New York Times Book Review* (May 8, 1966), 20 (Anthony Boucher); *SOS*, 1, No. 3 (February 1967), 2-3 (Bruce Dettman).

5787. Bensen, D. R. "S. H.," *Ellery Queen's Mystery Magazine*, 51, No. 2 (February 1968), 149 (Criminalimericks)

"Schlock Homes isn't loath to embrace / No matter how complex a case."

5788. [Holland, Glenn.] "Sherlockian Humour: Schlock Homes: A Pastiche Review," [by] Cartwright. *BSP* (NS), 1, No. 2 (August-September 1971), 3.

E *Other Stories*

5789. "The Adventure of the Clawed Horrors of Limehouse!" *Naked* [San Diego: Phenix Publishers Ltd.], No. 8 (November-December 1968). [66] p.

On cover: "A naked tribute to the world's greatest detective!"

The second most scandalous publication ever to appear on Sherlock Holmes and Dr. Watson. (For the first, see item 6127.) The brief text is accompanied by ninety-three photographs of the "Naked Street Irregulars" enacting their simpleminded adventure. Fortunately, the portrayers of Holmes, Watson, and Moriarty are fully clothed!

5790. "The Adventure of the Missing Bit," by B. Conan Doylie. *Datamation*, 10, No. 10 (October 1964), 46, 53; 10, No. 11 (November 1964), 57-58, 60.

————, *Faith, Hope and Parity.* Edited by Jack Moshman. Washington, D.C.: Thompson Book Co., 1966. p. 95-110.

Holmes solves a mystery involving a computer that turns out to be the murderer.

5791. "The Adventure of the Rubber Pipe," *Twenty-Five Detective Stories.* London: George Newnes Ltd., [1910] p. 217-222.

————, *Sherlockiana*, 11, Nr. 1 (1966), 2-4. "Shilah Coombes and Dr. Thatson."

5792. "The Adventures of Sheerluck Ohms," as related by Doctor Watts Ion. *The Anaconda Wire* (June 1947; February, March, April, June 1948; February, April 1949; May, October, November, December 1950; March 1951). 12 issues. illus.

Contents: The Case of the Alphabetical Vandal. - The Case of the Chain Reaction. - The Case of "Eye-Strained" Door. - The Case of the Account That Got Away. - The Case of the Fish That Wouldn't Keep. - The Case of the Limping Man. - The Case of the Persian Parsnip. - The Case of the Counterfeit Cent. - The Case of the Gushwell Ghost. - The Case of the Cummuppance Cup. - The Case of the Second Santa. - The Case of the Tootsbury Typist.

5793. Anderson, Poul. "The Martian Crown Jewels," *Ellery Queen's Mystery Magazine*, 31, No. 2 (February 1958), 74-88.

————. ————, *The Magazine of Fantasy and Science Fiction*, 16, No. 4 (April 1959), 94-107.

————. ————, *A Treasury of Great Science Fiction.* Edited by Anthony Boucher. Garden City, N.Y.: Doubleday & Co., 1959. Vol. 1, p. 400-412.

————. ————, *The Science-Fictional Sherlock Holmes.* Denver: The Council of Four, 1960. p. 15-31.

————. ————, *Tales of Time and Space.* Edited by Ross R. Olney. Illustrated by Harvey Kidder. Racine, Wis.: Whitman Pub. Co., [1969]. p. 161-188.

A futuristic tale involving a bird-like inhabitant named Syaloch of the red planet, who solves the disappearance of some precious gems. Syaloch smokes a curved pipe, wears a tirstoker cap, and has some remarkable deductive powers. The tale is cleverly done, especially the solution to the whereabouts of the jewels.

5794. ————. "Time Patrol," *Fantasy and Science Fiction*, 8, No. 5 (May 1955), 3-34.

————. ————, *Guardians of Time*, by Poul Anderson. London: Victor Gollancz Ltd., 1961.

————. ————, ————. London: Pan Books Ltd., [1964]. p. 7-45.

————. ————, *Hüter der Zeiten. Ein Utopisch-Technischer. Roman.* München: Wilhelm Goldmann Verlag, [1961]. p. 5-52. (Goldmanns Zukunftsromane, Band Z 21)

"Incidental revelations concerning the tragedy at Addleton and the singular contents of an ancient British barrow." (Edgar W. Smith)

5795. ————, and Gordon R. Dickson. "The Adventure of the Misplaced Hound," Illustrated by Ed Cartier. *Universe Science Fiction*, No. 3 (December 1953), 50-74.

————, ————. ————, *Earthman's Burden*, by Poul Anderson and Gordon R. Dickson. New York: Gnome Press, [1957]. p. 89-115.

————, ————. ————, *The Science-Fictional Sherlock Holmes.* Denver: The Council of Four, 1960. p. 35-61.

"In all the universe there is no planet with a more imitative people than Ioka. Subject them to Space Patrol television programs, and they become Space Patrol addicts. They live their fiction in reality. What happens when the complete works of Conan Doyle reaches the planet and Sherlock Holmes becomes the idol of the little teddy-bear race is the biggest belly-laugh from here to Vega." (*Universe Science Fiction*)

5796. Andrews, Charlton. "The Bound of the Astorbilts: A Modern Detective Story," *The Bookman*, 15, No. 4 (June 1902), 344-346.

5797. Anyhow. "An Ideal Interview with Sherlock Holmes," by "Anyhow." *The Bohemian*, 1, No. 5 (October 1893).

————. ————. Jamaica, N.Y.: House of El Dieff, Lew D. Feldman, [January 5, 1951]. [8] p.

Limited to 60 copies.

5798. Arnold, A. F. "Sherlock Watson's Last Case," *The Amateur Mart*, 9 (March 1935), 31-32; 9 (May 1935), 42, 47.

5799. Arthur, Robert. "The Adventure of the Single Footprint," *Ellery Queen's Mystery Magazine*, 12 (July 1948), 4-21.

————. ————, *The Queen's Awards, 1948.* Edited by Ellery Queen. Boston: Little, Brown and Co., 1948. p. 205-228.

————. ————, *Mystery and More Mystery*, by Robert Arthur. Illustrated by Saul Lambert. New York: Random House, [1966]. p. 139-169.

A pastiche within a mystery story that was awarded the *EQMM* special prize for the best Sherlockiana in the 3rd annual detective short-story contest.

5800. Ashmore, Constance. "Holmes at the Reference Desk," *RQ* [American Library Association], 9, No. 3 (Spring 1970), 239-240.

5801. Ashton, Ralph A. "The Adventure of the Pius Missal," *BSJ*, 7, No. 3 (July 1957), 149-152.

The author reports on his incredible discovery, in the barrel of a battered express rifle (not tin-dispatch box!), of some torn sheets of a manuscript in the handwriting of Rodolph von Esche and Dr. Watson relating the heretofore untold adventure of "The Politician, the Lighthouse, and the Trained Cormorant."

5802. Athey, Forrest. "The Adventure of the Soporific Cipher (Friday, 6 November 1896)," *BSJ*, 19, No. 2 (June 1969), 68-78.

5803. Austin, Bliss. "The Final Problem," *The Queen's Awards, 1946: The Winners of the First Annual Detective Short-Story Contest Sponsored by Ellery Queen's Mystery Magazine.* Edited by Ellery Queen. Boston: Little, Brown and Co., 1946. p. 359-380.

"Holmesian methods, exerted by Christopher Morley and Howard Haycraft, and abetted by much familiar Holmesian text, solve the murder of Ellery Queen by Colonel Moran." (Edgar W. Smith)

5804. Baker, Richard M. *The Green-Eyed Skeleton: Another Adventure of Sherlock Holmes.* [Kent, Conn.]: September 1916. 57 p. Unpublished typescript.

Location: Toronto Central Library.

5805. The Baker Street Pageboys. "The Adventure of the Ingsoc Diamond," *BSP*, No. 42 (December 1968), 2-5.

A pastiche written as a round-robin by five Pageboys.

5806. Ball, John. "The Ripe Moment," *BSJ*, 18, No. 3 (September 1968), 134-138.

An ingenious story in which Mr. James Phillimore is extracted from a time machine.

5807. Bamford, Francis. "The Case of the Crippled Bridegroom," *Return to Cottington.* London; New York; Toronto: Longmans, Green and Co., [1946]. p. 92-97.

A pastiche in which Dr. Watson solves a baffling 18th-century murder.

5808. Bangs, John Kendrick. "Mr. Homes Solves a Question of Authorship," *The New York Herald,* Literary Section (March 8, 1903), 7. (Shylock Homes: His Posthumous Memoirs)

————. ————, *The Misadventures of Sherlock Holmes.* Edited by Ellery Queen. Boston: Little, Brown and Co., 1944. p. 208-217.

"In this adventure Homes acts in behalf of three famous and / or infamous ladies—Lucretia Borgia, Mme. du Barry, and Portia. He reveals to them his great powers as a cipherologist, and in solving one of the most baffling mysteries of all time, Homes proves himself not only a detective but a literary detective to boot!" (Ellery Queen)

5809. ————. "The Mystery of Pinkham's Diamond Stud: Being the Tale Told by the Holder of the Eleventh Ball, Mr. Fulton Street," *Harper's Bazaar,* 32 (April 1, 1899), 288.

————. ————, *The Dreamers: A Club. Being a More or Less Faithful Account of the Literary Exercises of the First Regular Meeting of That Organization,* reported by John Kendrick Bangs. With illustrations by Edward Penfield. New York and London: Harper and Brothers, 1899. Chap. 10, p. 185-206.

————. ————, ————. Freeport, N.Y.: Books for Libraries Press, [1969]. Chap. 10, p. 185-206.

5810. ————. "A Pragmatic Enigma: Being a Chapter from 'The Failures of Sherlock Holmes' by A. Conan Watson, M.D.," *The New York Herald,* Magazine Section (April 19, 1908), 2.

————. ————, *Potted Fiction: Being a Series of Extracts from the World's Best Sellers, Put Up in Thin Slices for Hurried Consumers,* [by] The United States Literary Canning Co. New York: Doubleday, Page & Co., 1908. p. 76-89.

————. ————, ————. Freeport, N.Y.: Books for Libraries Press, [1971]. p. 76-89.

"A gazoozle reporter disguised as a Harvard professor calls on Sherlock Holmes, Esq., and gets away with two suitcases full of the Great Detective's personal effects, while Dr. Watson's hero tells what he does not know about Pragmatism."

5811. ————. "The Pursuit of the House-Boat: Being Some Further Account of the Divers Doings of the Associated Shades, Under the Leadership of Sherlock Holmes, Esq.," Illustrated by Peter Newell. *Harper's Weekly,* 41 (February 6, 1897), 136-137; (February 13, 1897), 159-160; (February 20, 1897), 183-184; (February 27, 1897), 202-203; (March 6, 1897), 231-232; (March 13, 1897), 269-270; (March 20, 1897), 295-296; (March 27, 1897), 318-320; (April 3, 1897), 343-344; (April 10, 1897), 369-370; (April 17, 1897), 381-382; (April 24, 1897), 413-414.

————. ————. Illustrated by Peter Newell. New York and London: Harper & Brothers, 1897. viii, 204 p.

————. ————. London: Osgood, McIlvaine & Co., 1897. viii, 204 p.

————. First two chapters with title: "The Stranger Unravels a Mystery," *The Misadventures of Sherlock Holmes.* Edited by Ellery Queen. Boston: Little, Brown and Co., 1944. p. 190-207.

————. ————. New York: AMS Press,

[1969]. viii, 204 p. illus. (Reprint of first ed.)
————. ————. New York: Harper, 1897. St. Clair Shores, Mich.: Scholarly Press. 1970. viii, 204 p.

Contents: 1. The Associated Shades Take Action. - 2. The Stranger Unravels a Mystery Himself. - 3. The Search-Party Is Organized. - 4. On Board the House-Boat. - 5. A Conference on Deck. - 6. A Conference Below-Stairs. - 7. The "Gehenna" Is Chartered. - 8. On Board the "Gehenna". - 9. Captain Kidd Meets with an Obstacle. - 10. A Warning Accepted. - 11. Marooned. - 12. The Escape and the End.

"Here is one of the earliest—if not actually the earliest—American parodies of Sherlock Holmes. . . .In this parody you will meet Sherlock Holmes in Hades. . .in company with other great and glittering personages—The Associated Shades, including Sir Walter Raleigh, Socrates, Dr. Livingstone, Confucius, Shakespeare, Noah, Dr. Samuel Johnson and Boswell, Solomon, Caesar, Napoleon, among others equally famous, all involved in a truly 'hellish' mystery." (Ellery Queen)

5812. ————. "The Remarkable Adventures of Raffles Holmes," Illustrated by Sydney Adamson. *Harper's Weekly*, 49 (July 22, 1905), 1060, 1062-1063) July 29, 1905), 1096-1099; (August 5, 1905), 1132, 1134-1135; (August 12, 1905), 1168, 1170-1171; (August 19, 1905), 1204, 1206-1207; (August 26, 1905), 1240-1243.
————. *R. Holmes & Co.: Being the Remarkable Adventures of Raffles Holmes, Esq., Detective and Amateur Cracksman by Birth*. Illustrated by Sydney Adamson. New York and London: Harper & Brothers, 1906. 230 p.
————. ————. Upper Saddle River, N.J.: Literature House / Gregg Press, [1969]. 230 p. (American Humorists Series, No. 2)

Contents: 1. Introducing Mr. Raffles Holmes. - 2. The Adventure of the Dorrington Ruby Seal. - 3. The Adventure of Mrs. Burlingame's Diamond Stomacher. - 4. The Adventure of the Missing Pendants. - 5. The Adventure of the Brass Check. - 6. The Adventure of the Hired Burglar. - 7. The Redemption of Young Billington Rand. - 8. "The Nostalgia of Nervy Jim the Snatcher". - 9. The Adventure of Room 407. - 10. The Major-General's Pepper-Pots.

"The conflicting traits and characteristics of Raffles and of Sherlock Holmes are strangely blended in this new hero, Raffles Holmes, who introduces himself as the son of the great detective. His history and adventures as recorded by Jenkins, who is his Dr. Watson and his Bunny in one, are highly amusing. In the double capacity of thief and detective he enjoys a successful and spectacular career, for while the Raffles in him perpetually cries 'Take,' the Holmes in him

thunders 'Restore' and he does both to his own advantage." (*Book Review Digest*)

5813. ————. "Sherlock Holmes Again," Illustrated by Peter Newell. *Harper's Weekly*, 43 (September 2, 1899), 863-864.
————. ————, *The Enchanted Typewriter*. Illustrated by Peter Newell. New York and London: Harper & Brothers, 1899. Chap. 9, p. 131-156.
————. ————, ————. Freeport, N.Y.: Books for Libraries Press, [1969]. Chap. 9, p. 131-156.
————. ————, ————. Upper Saddle River, N.J.: Literature House / Gregg Press, [1970]. Chap. 9, p. 131-156.

5814. ————. "Shylock Homes: His Posthumous Memoirs," *The New York Herald*, Literary Section (February 1-April 5, 1903).

Contents: 1. Mr. Homes Radiates a Wireless Message. - 2. Mr. Homes Makes an Important Confession. - 3. Mr. Homes Foils a Conspiracy and Gains a Fortune. - 4. Mr. Homes Reaches an Unhistorical Conclusion. - 5. Mr. Homes Shatters an Alibi. - 6. Mr. Homes Solves a Question of Authorship. - 7. Mr. Homes Tackles a "Hard Case". - 8. Mr. Homes Acts as Attorney for Solomon. - 9. Mr. Homes Shatters a Tradition. - 10. Shylock Homes: His Posthumous Memoirs.

5815. Baring, Maurice. "From the Diary of Sherlock Holmes," *The Eye-Witness* [London], 1, No. 23 (November 23, 1911), 717-718. (Lost Diaries)
————. ————, *The Living Age*, 272, (January 20, 1912), 185-187.
————. ————, *Lost Diaries*, by Maurice Baring. London: Duckworth & Co., 1913. Chap. 8, p. 74-84.
————. ————, ————. Boston and New York: Houghton Mifflin Co., 1913. Chap. 8, p. 74-84.
————. ————, *BSJ* [OS], 2, No. 4 (October 1947), 461-464. (Incunabulum)
————. ————, *Seventeen Steps to 221B*. [Edited by] James Edward Holroyd. London: George Allen & Unwin Ltd., [1967]. p. 21-24.

5816. [Barr, Robert.] "Detective Stories Gone Wrong: The Adventures of Sherlaw Kombs," by Luke Sharp [pseud.] Illustrated by George Hutchinson. *The Idler Magazine*, 1 (May 1892), 413-424.
————. "The Great Pegram Mystery," *The Face and the Mask*, by Robert Barr. Illustrated by A. Hencke. London: Hutchinson & Co., 1894.
————. ————, ————. New York: Frederick A. Stokes Co., 1895. Chap. 10, p. 111-123.
————. ————, *The Misadventures of Sherlock Holmes*. Edited by Ellery Queen. Boston: Little, Brown and Co., 1944 p. 3-13.

"Sherlaw Kombs and Whatson."
The first and one of the funniest Sherlockian parodies ever written.

5817. Barr, Stephen. "The Procurator of Justice," *Ellery Queen's Mystery Magazine*, 15, No. 2 (February 1950), 116-127.
———. ———. New York: Triggs Color Printing Corp., January 20, 1954 [12] p.
Winner of a special prize in *EQMM*'s 1948 short-story contest.
A clever takeoff on Antole France's "The Procurator of Judea," revealing the circumstances behind Mr. James Phillimore's strange disappearance.

5818. Barrie, Sir James M. "The Adventure of the Two Collaborators," *Memoirs and Adventures*, by Sir Arthur Conan Doyle. London: Hodder and Stoughton, [1924]. Chap. 11, p. 97-100.
———. ———, ———. Boston: Little, Brown and Co., 1924. Chap. 11, p. 97-100.
———. ———, *Arthur Conan Doyle: A Memoir*, by John Lamond. London: John Murray, [1931]. p. 46-50.
———. ———, *The Misadventures of Sherlock Holmes*. Edited by Ellery Queen. Boston: Little, Brown and Co., 1944. p. 119-122.
———. ———, *BSJ*, 7, No. 4 (October 1957), 221B-224.
A parody inspired by the failure of the Barrie-Doyle comic opera *Jane Annie*. It was Doyle's nomination for "the best of all the numerous parodies" of Sherlock Holmes.

5819. Barzun, Jacques. "Prolegomena to Dr. Watson's Ninth Marriage," by Giovanni Antipasto, as told to Jacques Barzun. *BSJ*, 5, No. 1 (January 1955), 43-50.

5820. Baury, Louis. "After Conan Doyle," *The Smart Set*, 28, No. 3 (July 1909), 158-159. (As They Would Have Told It)

5821. [Bedford-Jones, H.] "The Affair of the Aluminum Crutch," *Palm Springs News* (January 16-February 20, 1936). Published in five weekly installments.
———. ———, *BSJ* [OS], 1, No. 1 (January 1946), 71-87.

5822. Beerbohm, Max. "At the St. James's Theatre," *The Saturday Review* [London], 99 (May 6, 1905), 588-589.
———. ———, *Around Theatres*, by Max Beerbohm. London: William Heinemann, 1924. Vol. 2, p. 133-139.
———. ———, ———. New York: Alfred A. Knopf, 1930. Vol. 2, p. 480-484.
———. ———, ———. New York: Simon and Schuster, 1954. p. 373-376.
———. ———, ———. New York: Greenwood Press, [1968]. p. 373-376.
———. ———, ———. New York: Taplinger Pub. Co., [1969]. p. 373-376.

———. ———, Introductory note by James M. Sandoe. *BSJ*, 13, No. 2 (June 1963), 108-111. (Incunabulum)
———. An excerpt with title: *A Reminiscence of Sherlock Holmes*. [With a note by Vincent Starrett.] Tempe: Edwin B. Hill, 1948. [4] p. (Sherlockiana)
Limited to 36 copies.
A review, done in terms of a Sherlock Holmes adventure, of *John Chilcote, M. P.*, a play in four acts, by E. Temple Thurston, adapted from a story by Katherine Cecil Thurston, and produced at the St. James's Theatre on May 1, 1905.

5823. Bengis, Nathan L. "A Course of Miss Violet de Merville: A Sherlock Holmes Playlet in One Scene," *SHJ*, 3, No. 4 (Summer 1958), 14-16.
A dramatized reconstruction of the interview between Holmes and Violet de Merville (Illu). The skit was enacted by Mr. and Mrs. Bengis at the 5th annual meeting of the Musgrave Ritualists on March 12, 1954.

5824. ———. " 'Sorry, Mr. Sherlock Is Engaged Just Now,' " *SHJ*, 6, No. 3 (Winter 1963), 91.
A skit in which the author has reconstructed the first meeting of Holmes and Miss Agatha, the housemaid of Appledore Towers (Chas).

5825. Berkeley, Reginald. "The Adventure of the Chuckle-Headed Doctor: A Positively Final Story of Sherlock Holmes," *Decorations and Absurdities*, by Bohun Lynch and Reginald Berkeley. London: W. Collins Sons & Co. Ltd., [1923]. p. 77-80.

5826. Berman, Ruth. "Daniel Retold, or Sherlock Holmes Slightly Misquoted," *BSJ*, 8, No. 2 (April 1958), 87-89.
Lord Daniel, Premier of Babylon, investigates a case for King Belshazzar.

5827. ———. "Sherlock Holmes in Oz," Illustrated by Damon Ralph. *Oziana*, No. 1 [The International Wizard of Oz Club] (1971), 18-24.
———. ———, *The SHsf Fanthology* 3. Edited by Ruth Berman. Minneapolis, Minn.: The Professor Challenger Society, February 1972. p. 25-37.
"The Master is brought to the land of Oz to solve the mystery of the missing pearl—which he does, of course." (Julian Wolff)

5828. Boardman, John. "The Adventure of the Sinister American," *Double Action Detective and Mystery Stories*, No. 19 (November 1959), 91-98.
"Comrade Sherslav Golmsky and Dr. Ivan Vatsov solve the case of the vanished football player with the help of Finland

Yard and Inspectors Gregsov and Lestradsky." (Edgar W. Smith)

5829. Bonney, Joseph L. *Murder Without Clues*. New York: Carrick & Evans, Inc., [1940]. 303 p.

"A detective novel whose hero Simon Rolfe apes Sherlock Holmes in all but his processes of detection." (Edgar W. Smith) The story is narrated by Henry F. Watson.

5830. Boswell, Rolfe. "Colonel Warburton's Madness," *BSJ*, 12, No. 2 (June 1962), 85-98.

One of two cases that Watson brought to the attention of Holmes. The other was Engr.

5831. Boucher, Anthony. "The Adventure of the Bogle-Wolf," *Illustrious Client's Second Case-Book*. Edited by J. N. Williamson. [Indianapolis, Ind.: The Illustrious Clients, 1949.] p. 88-95.

"While assisting Dr. Watson in baby-sitting Kate Whitney's son, Holmes shows that Red Riding Hood's grandmother was a werewolf." (*VH*)

5832. ———. "The Adventure of the Illustrious Imposter," *The Misadventures of Sherlock Holmes*. Edited by Ellery Queen. Boston: Little, Brown and Co., 1944. p. 84-88.

"In a conversation with Dr. Watson in May of 1941, Holmes concludes that the Rudolph Hess captured in Scotland is an imposter." (*VH*)

5833. ———. "The Anomaly of the Empty Man," *The Magazine of Fantasy and Science Fiction*, 3, No. 2 (April 1952), 43-56.
———. ———, *Crooks' Tour*, by Members of the Mystery Writers of America. Edited by Bruno Fischer. New York: Dodd, Mead & Co., 1953. p. 145-163.
———. ———, *Far and Away: Eleven Fantasy and Science-Fiction Stories*, by Anthony Boucher. New York: Ballantine Books, [1955]. p. 3-21. (No. 109)
———. ———, *The Science-Fictional Sherlock Holmes*. Denver: The Council of Four, 1960. p. 62-79.
———. ———, *Cream of the Crime*. With a foreword by Hugh Pentecost. New York; Chicago; San Francisco: Holt, Rinehart and Winston, [1962]. p. 272-288. (The 15th Mystery Writers of America Anthology)
———. "The Empty Man," *Shock Magazine* (May 1960).

"Set in San Francisco in current times, it concerns Dr. Verner, a cousin of Holmes who supplies the answers to a strange series of disappearances where the individuals in question actually do leave the world never to be seen again." (Bruce Dettman)

5834. ———. *The Case of the Baker Street Irregulars*. New York: Simon and Schuster,
1940. 336 p. (An Inner Sanctum Mystery)
———. ———. New York: The World Pub. Co., [1942]. 336 p. (Tower Books)
———. ———. New York: Collier Books, [1962]. 252 p. (AS147)
———. *Blood on Baker Street*. Abridged edition. New York: Mercury Publications, [1953]. 127 p. (Mercury Mysteries, No. 179)
———. *Treffpunkt: Baker Street. Kriminalroman*. München: Die Mitternachtsbücher, Verlag Kurt Desch Müchen Wien Basel, 1963. 172 p. (Die Mitternachtsbücher, 172)

A group of Sherlock Holmes enthusiasts get together in Hollywood to keep tabs on the filming of Spec and to check up on the villainous scriptwriter who does not have the proper respect for the Holmes tradition.

Reviews: New York Herald Tribune Books (April 28, 1940), 16 (Will Cuppy); *New York Times Book Review* (May 5, 1940), 27 (Isaac Anderson); *Springfield Republican* (June 2, 1940), 7; *VH*, 5, No. 2 (April 1971), 2 (D. W. Dickensheet and J. R. Christopher).

5835. ———. "The Greatest Tertian," *Invaders of Earth*. Edited by Groff Conklin. New York: Vanguard Press, [1952]. p. 330-333.
———. ———, ———. New York: Grosset & Dunlap, 1962. p. 378-382. (Tempo Books, T6)
———. ———, *Illustrious Client's Third Case-Book*. Edited by J. N. Williamson and H. B. Williams. [Indianapolis, Ind.: The Illustrious Clients, 1953.] p. 74-78.
———. ———, *The Science-Fictional Sherlock Holmes*. Denver: The Council of Four, 1960. p. 80-83.

"An amusing short-shock mock report by a Martian on the past Tertian civilization, and particularly dealing with the genius known variously as Sherk Oms and Sherk Sper." (*VH*)

5836. Bradley, Worthen. "Bad Day on Baker Street," *BSJ*, 9, No. 3 (July 1959), 154-156.

5837. Brean, Herbert. *Wilders Walk Away*. New York: William Morrow & Co., 1948. 244 p.
———. ———. New York: Collier Books, 1962. 219 p. (AS234X)

Chapter headings from this mystery thriller are quoted texts from the Canon.

5838. Breitman, Gregory, "The Marriage of Sherlock Holmes," Tr. from the Russian by Benjamin Block. *Beau: The Man's Magazine*, 1, No. 3 (December 1926), 127-130.

5839. Brend, Gavin. "The Conk-Singleton Forgery Case," *SHJ*, 1, No. 4 (December 1953), 2-4.

One of three winners in the Christmas

Prooimion Competition for the best imaginary opening paragraphs to a typical Holmes and Watson adventure. For the other winners, see items 5846 and 6090.

5840. [Bretnor, Reginald.] "Through Time and Space with Ferdinand Feghoot," by Grendel Briarton [pseud.] *BSJ*, 17, No. 2 (June 1967), 101.

————. ————, *Best Detective Stories of the Year: 23rd Annual Collection.* Edited by Anthony Boucher. New York: E. P. Dutton & Co., 1968. p. 172-174.

————. ————, *Special Wonder: The Anthony Boucher Memorial Anthology of Fantasy and Science Fiction.* Edited by J. Francis McComas. New York: Random House, 1970. p. 49-50.

"Ferdinand Feghoot and Dr. Picasso Corstone-Corby."

5841. Brindley, Fred G. "The Adventures of a Holmesian," *BSJ*, [OS], 4, No. 1 (January 1949), 123-126.

A clever use of Canonical titles to relate the author's adventures at the Priory School.

5842. British Overseas Airways Corp. *The Case of the Disappearing Business Traveller,* [New York: November 1967.] [8] p.

An illustrated advertising booklet in the form of a parody with Sherwood Homes and Dr. Whartson.

5843. Brittain, William. "The Man Who Read Sir Arthur Conan Doyle," *Ellery Queen's Mystery Magazine*, 52, No. 2 (August 1968), 59-66.

The reader is asked to solve the problem before reading the last two lines of the story.

5844. Bromley, Albert J. "The Grate Fur Koat Mistery," *Snowshoe Al's Bed Time Storries (and uther times),* by Albert J. Bromley (Illustraited by the saim hombre). With an interduction by Richard Henry Little. New York: Minton, Balch & Co., 1926. p. 87-88.

————. ————, ————. Chicago: The Contributors' Guild, 1926. p. 87-88.

————. ————, *Illustrious Client's Third Case-Book.* Edited by J. N. Williamson and H. B. Williams. [Indianapolis, Ind.: The Illustrious Clients, 1953.] p. 192-194.

"Rex Homes and Dr. Hotbun."

5845. Bryan, C. D. S. "The Jefferson Nickel: An Astonishing Sherlock Holmes Adventure," *Monocle,* 5, No. 3 (Winter 1963-64), 46-55.

A pastiche in which the CIA appeals to the cryptanalytic ability of Holmes.

5846. Bryan-Brown, F. D. "Some Inferences from Colour," *SHJ*, 1, No. 4 (December 1953), 5-8.

One of three winners in the Christmas Prooimion Competition for the best imaginary opening paragraphs to a typical Holmes and Watson adventure. For the other winners, see items 5839 and 6090.

5847. Campbell, John F. "The Adventure of the Purloined Passport," *Foreign Service Journal*, 46, No. 9 (August 1969), 24-29, 40-41.

5848. Capes, Bernard. *The Great Skene Mystery. Chapter XXXI. A Notable Interlude.* [N.p., n.d.] 7 p. Unpublished typescript.

Location: Toronto Central Library.

5849. Carr, John Dickson. *The 9 Wrong Answers: A Novel for the Curious.* New York: Harper & Brothers, 1952. viii, 331 p.

————. ————. London: William Heinemann Ltd., 1952. 350 p.

"A novel of detection and suspense, replete with Holmesian references. The *dénouement* takes place in the room at the Sherlock Holmes Exhibition in London." (Edgar W. Smith)

5850. Cascade Natural Gas Corporation. *Sherlock Homes in the Curious Adventure of "Heating the House."* [Seattle, Wash.: 1964.] 31 p.

An illustrated advertising booklet extolling the advantages of heating with gas.

5851. [Casson, Mel.] "The Mysterious Note," *Angel* [Dell Pub. Co.], 1, No. 14 (May-July 1958), 18.

5852. Castier, Jules. "The Footprints on the Ceiling," *Rather Like. . .Some Endeavours to Assume the Mantles of the Great.* With a publisher's note embodying the opinions of the great. London: Herbert Jenkins Ltd., 1920. p. 91-104.

————. ————, *The Misadventures of Sherlock Holmes.* Edited by Ellery Queen. Boston: Little, Brown and Co., 1944. p. 245-255.

"Being an account of an adventure of Professor George E. Challenger, Lord John Roxton, Mr. Sherlock Holmes, Dr. Watson, M.D., and Mr. E. D. Malone." (Subtitle)

5853. Chandler, A. Bertram. "The Kinsolving's Planet Irregulars," Illustrated by Reese. *Galaxy Magazine*, 28, No. 5 (July 1969), 119-153.

5854. Chester, S. Beach. "The Arsène Lepine-Herlock Soames Affair," *Dîners, à Deux: Memoirs of a Maître d'Hôtel.* London: 1912.

"Herlock Soames and Dr. Watts."

5855. Chin, Frank. "Sherlock Holmes," *The California Pelican* [University of California] (January 7, 1959), 16.

"A new story of the master detective of Bacon St. as found by Frank Chin in the recently discovered notebooks of Sir Arthur Conning Tower."

5856. Christie, Agatha. "Blunt's Brilliant Detectives," *Ellery Queen's Mystery Magazine*, 35, No. 4 (April 1960), 40-52.

Not a parody, but a story in which Holmes is mentioned several times.

5857. ———. "The Case of the Missing Lady," *Partners in Crime*. London: William Collins Sons & Co., 1929.

———. ———, ———. New York: Dodd, Mead and Co., [1929]. Chap. 9, p. 84-100.

———. ———, ———. New York: Grosset and Dunlap, 1930. Chap. 9, p. 84-100.

———. ———, ———. London: Pan Books, 1962.

———. ———, ———. [New York: Dell Pub. Co., February 1963.] p. 73-85.

———. ———, ———. London: Published for The Crime Club, [1967]. Chap. 9, p. 60-71.

———. ———, *The Misadventures of Sherlock Holmes*. Edited by Ellery Queen. Boston: Little, Brown and Co., 1944. p. 70-83.

A Tommy and Tuppence Beresford takeoff on Sherlock Holmes.

5858. Chujoy, Anatole. "The Adventure of the Turned Worm," as (if) told by Dr. John H. Watson. *BSJ*, 5, No. 3 (July 1955), 176-181.

5859. Cillié, F. P. "The Adventure of the Second Stain," *Sunday Times News Magazine* (December 3, 1967).

One of two winning entries in a contest conducted by the Johannesburg *Sunday Times* whose editors believe that Seco is not the same story as the one described in Nava. For the other winner, see item 6025.

5860. Clark, Benjamin S. "Sunshine, Sunshine," *BSJ Christmas Annual*, No. 5 (1960), 289-292.

An explanation of the circumstances surrounding the untold adventure of Mr. James Phillimore's disappearance.

5861. Clarke, Richard W. "The Dreadful Business of the Abernetty Family," *BSJ*, 11, No. 1 (March 1961), 13-26.

5862. Clarkson, Steven. *The Kimberley Diamond Mine Substitution Scandal*. [Owings Mills, Md.: Privately Produced, 1970.] 12 p.

"Shearlock Combs and Dr. Witsend."

5863. Clendening, Logan. *The Case of the Missing Patriarchs*. Translated from the thyroid. [With a note by Vincent Starrett.] Ysleta, [Texas]: Edwin B. Hill, 1934. [4] p. (Sherlockiana)

Limited to 30 copies.

———. ———, *The Misadventures of Sherlock Holmes*. Edited by Ellery Queen. Boston: Little, Brown and Co., 1944. p. 330-331.

———. ———, *Profile by Gaslight*. Edited by Edgar W. Smith. New York: Simon and Schuster, 1944. p. 135-136.

———. ———, *MD Medical News Magazine*, 8, No. 12 (December 1964), 151.

———. ———, "Arthur Conan Doyle, Detective-Doctor," [by] C. Frederick Kittle. *University of Minnesota Medical Bulletin*, 36, No. 8 (April 1965), 286-287.

———. ———, *American Book Collector*, 18, No. 3 (November 1967), 22-23.

Facsimile reprint of Edwin B. Hill's leaflet.

———. ———, *Ellery Queen's Minimysteries*. Edited by Ellery Queen. New York and Cleveland: The World Pub. Co., [1969]. p. 194-195.

Dr. Clendening recounts an adventure of Holmes after he has died: Consternation reigned in Heaven because Adam and Eve had been missing for several eons. Holmes, whose astuteness was known in Heaven, was assigned to the search. He alone knew all others from Adam and could speedily pick out the missing pair, for he alone of all the myriads who preceded him through the pearly gates knew that they would be the only two without navels!

5864. Clouston, J. Storer. "The Truthful Lady," *Carrington's Cases*. Edinburgh and London: William Blackwood and Sons, 1920. Chap. 10, p. 147-160.

A parody about Watson in which Holmes is present but invisible.

5865. Cohen, Allen. "The Adventure of Vigor, the Hammersmith Wonder," *BSP Christmas Annual*, No. 1 (1966), 16-21.

5866. Collins, Howard. "The Affair of the Politician, the Lighthouse, and the Trained Cormorant," *BSJ* [OS], 2, No. 2 (April 1947), 195-204.

5867. Columbus Recording Lock Co., Columbus, Ohio. "Sherlock Holmes and the Sleepless Watchman," *Collier's Weekly*, 34, No. 5 (October 29, 1904), 27.

———. ———, *Shots from the Canon*, by James Montgomery. [Philadelphia: Privately Printed, 1953.] p. 26.

An advertisement in which Holmes tells Watson about the advantages of a recording lock.

5868. Conklin, Bill. "Caught in the Act," *The Saturday Evening Post*, 240, No. 17 (August 26, 1967), 18.

A gigantic rooster is slain in front of the Palladium, providing Fellock Holmes and Dr. Watso with an electrifying adventure.

5869. Cooke, Alistair. "The Case of the

November Sun-Tan," *Letters from America.* London: Rupert Hart-Davis, 1951. p. 179-190.

———. ———, *One Man's America.* New York: Alfred A. Knopf, 1952. p. 181-193.

"A satirical Baker Street colloquy in which Holmes describes to Watson the rise of the John Robert Powers model." (Edgar W. Smith)

5870. Cooper, J. Alston. "Dr. Watson's Wedding Present: The Partial Solution of a Mystery," *The Bookman*, 16, No. 6 (February 1903), 573-574.

5871. Courtney, J. W. "Dr. Watson and Mr. Holmes, or The Worm That Turned," *The Boston Medical and Surgical Journal*, 150, No. 21 (May 19, 1904), 553-555.

5872. Cox, A. B. "Holmes and the Dasher," *Jugged Journalism.* With thirty-two illustrations by George Morrow. London: Herbert Jenkins Ltd., 1925. Lesson 19, p. 258-263.

———. ———, by Anthony Berkeley [pseud.] *The Misadventures of Sherlock Holmes.* Edited by Ellery Queen. Boston: Little, Brown and Co., 1944. p. 66-69.

"Sherlock Holmes and Bertie Watson."

5873. Crawfurd, Oswald. "Our Mr. Smith," *The Revelations of Inspector Morgan.* New York: Dodd, Mead & Co., 1907. p. ix-xvii.

———. ———, *The Misadventures of Sherlock Holmes.* Edited by Ellery Queen. Boston: Little, Brown & Co., 1944. p. 238-244.

A parody, in the introduction, written especially for the American edition of the *Revelations* and absent from the Chapman & Hall edition (London: 1906).

"Purlock Hone and Jobson."

5874. Currie, Bob. "The Missing Motor Bicyclist," [Illustrated by Laurence Shrimpton]. *Motor Cycle*, 109 (December 20, 1962), 794-795.

"A story after—long way after—Sir Arthur Conan Doyle."

5875. Cutter, Robert A. "A Tall Adventure of Sherlock Holmes," *Sherlockian Studies.* Edited by Robert A. Cutter. [Jackson Heights, N.Y.: The Baker Street Press, 1947.] p. 25-31.

5876. Dahlinger, Susan Elizabeth. "The Adventure of the Aluminum Crutch," *BSJ*, 19, No. 1 (March 1969), 17-22.

5877. ———. "The Cask of Amontillado: Chapter Two," *A Curious Collection.* Edited by William J. Walsh. [Suffern, N.Y.]: The Musgrave Ritualists Beta, 1971. p. 12-18.

Holmes offers a solution to Poe's tale by the same name.

5878. [Dannay. Frederic.] "The Boy and the Book," *The Golden Summer*, by Daniel Nathan [pseud.] Boston: Little, Brown and Co., [1953]. Chap. 6-7, p. 51-68.

———. "The Adventures of Danny: The Boy and the Book," Introduction by Anthony Boucher. *Ellery Queen's Mystery Magazine*, 27, No. 6 (June 1956), 106-118.

"All about the ecstasies and agonies of a youthful Sherlockian who covets, secures, loses and regains a precious volume of the Canon." (Edgar W. Smith)

5879. Darvas, Robert, Norman De V. Hart, and Paul Stern. "Elememtary, My Dear Watson (The Tale of the Four Clubs)," *Right Through the Pack.* Drawings by Stanley Meltzoff. New York: Stuyvesant House, [1948]. p. 129-141.

A pastiche based on a hand of bridge.

5880. [Davis, James Francis.] *Frenological Finance: Being a True History of the Life and Adventures of Mortimer Kensington Queen*, by Nick Sherlock Collier [pseud.] Boston, Mass.: The C. M. Clark Pub. Co., 1907. [60] p. illus.

5881. [Donegall, Lord.] "The Case from Marseilles," *SHJ*, 3, No. 3 (Autumn 1957), 19-20; 3, No. 4 (Summer 1958), 18-19.

A hypothetical introduction to an adventure mentioned by Holmes in Iden and a further development of the story by Percy Metcalfe.

5882. ———. "The Case of the Missing Bodies," *SHJ*, 2, No. 2 (December 1954), 16-18. (The Curtain Rises at 221B)

An entry from the Prooimion Competition in which contestants wrote the introduction to an imaginary Holmesian adventure.

5883. "Doom at the Top, or The Ladies Have Designs," *Women's Wear Daily*, 122 (June 22, 1966), 1, 16.

"A Sherlockian pastiche concerned with happenings in the field of fashions; evidently more intelligible to those engaged in that field than to outsiders." (Julian Wolff)

5884. Douglass, Don. "The Case of the Sunburned Peer," *West by One and by One.* San Francisco: Privately Printed, 1965. p. 51-60.

5885. [Dunne, Finley Peter.] "Sherlock Holmes," *Observations by Mr. Dooley.* New York: R. H. Russell, 1902. p. 23-29.

———. ———, ———. New York: R. H. Russell, 1906. Grosse Pointe, Mich.: Scholarly Press, 1968. p. 23-29.

———. ———, ———. New York: Greenwood Press, [1969]. p. 23-29.

———. ———, *Mr. Dooley on Ivrything and Ivrybody.* Selected and with an introduction by Robert Hutchinson. New York: Dover Publications, [1963]. p. 173-177.

5886. Eustace, Frank J. "The Adventure of the Highest Beast," *BSJ*, 11, No. 1 (March 1961), 5-12.

A highly entertaining story of a climbing expedition to Everest during which Sigerson (an alias of Holmes's) solves the mystery of the Abominable Snowman.

5887. ———. "A Commission to the Sultan of Turkey," *BSJ*, 15, No. 1 (March 1965), 3-7.

5888. Ferguson, Rachel. " 'Home!' Sweet Holmes!" *Nymphs and Satires*. London: Ernest Benn Ltd., [1932]. p. 199-204.
———. "His Last Scrape, or Holmes, Sweet Holmes!" *The Misadventures of Sherlock Holmes*. Edited by Ellery Queen. Boston: Little, Brown and Co., 1944. p. 301-305.

5889. Fisher, Charles. "A Christmas Episode," *BSJ Christmas Annual*, No. 1 (1956), 62-64.

5890. ———. *Some Unaccountable Exploits of Sherlock Holmes*. Philadelphia: [Privately Printed], 1956. [28] p.

Contents: The Adventure of the Masked Caller. - The Problem of the Importunate Landlady. - The Case of the Haunted Ball Park. - The Case of the Beleaguered Detective. - The Adventure of the Foiled Revenge. - The Problem of the Empty Magnums. - The Adventure of the Mysterious Client. - The Puzzle of the Strange Visage.

These eight short pastiches originally appeared in the late *Philadelphia Record* in 1939 and 1940.

5891. [Foley, Francine.] "The Case of the Careless Suffragette," *Screen Stories* (February 1955), 47, 54-55. (Best TV Story of the Month)

A fictionalized adaptation of the teleplay (item 5529). Illustrated with scenes from the production.

5892. Ford, Corey. "The Rollo Boys with Sherlock in Mayfair, or Keep It Under Your Green Hat," *Three Rousing Cheers for the Rollo Boys*. Illustrated by Gluyas Williams. New York: George H. Doran Co., 1925. Chap. 19, p. 221-237.
———. ———, *The Bookman*, 62, No. 5 (January 1926), 583-588.

A triple-barreled parody of the Rover Boys, Sherlock Holmes, and Michael Arlen.

5893. Ford, James L. "The Story of Bishop Johnson," *The Pocket Magazine*, 1, No. 1 (November 1895), 85-93.

5894. Forkosch, Morris D. "The Case of the Curious Kerchief," *BSJ*, 20, No. 4 (December 1970), 234-238.

5895. Forrest, G. F. "The Adventure of the Diamond Necklace," *Misfits: A Book of Parodies*. Oxford: Frank Harvey, 1905. p. 67-70.

A jewel theft in which Warlock Bones is the culprit!

5896. "From the Diary of Dr. Watson," *G. K.'s Weekly*, 1, No. 22 (August 15, 1925), 486.
———, *CPBook*, 1, No. 4 (Spring 1965), 75-76.

5897. Fuller, William O. *A Night with Sherlock Holmes: A Paper Read Before the 12mo Club*. [Cambridge, Mass.]: Privately Printed [at the Riverside Press], 1929. vii, 30 p.

Limited to 200 copies.
———. "The Mary Queen of Scots Jewel," *The Misadventures of Sherlock Holmes*. Edited by Ellery Queen. Boston: Little, Brown and Co., 1944. p. 275-290.

5898. Gardner, Martin. "The Missing Walnuts," *Ellery Queen's Mystery Magazine*, 27, No. 2 (February 1956), 78-80.

5899. George, Isaac S. "The Sudden Death of Cardinal Tosca," *BSJ* [OS] 3, No. 1 (January 1948), 73-82.

5900. Gibson, Theodore W. "The Adventure of the Thinking (?) Machine," *BSJ*, 14, No. 4 (December 1964), 200.

5901. ———. "Watson's No. 8 in B Minor," *BSJ Christmas Annual*. No. 5 (1960), 277-280.

An "unfinished" tale of Moriarty's desperate game of check and countercheck against Holmes's rapier attack.

5902. Goldman, James. *They Might Be Giants*. New York: Lancer Books, [1970]. 152 p.

Illustrated with scenes from the film starring George C. Scott and Joanne Woodward (item 5165).

Review: HO, 1, No. 8 (October 1971), 5 (Dan Morrow).

5903. [Grainger, Francis Edward.] *Zambra the Detective: Some Clues from His Notebook*, by Headon Hill [pseud.] London: Chatto & Windus, 1894. 259 p.
———. *Sherlock Holmes' overmand*. [Sherlock Holmes' Superior.] Oversat af M. Laursen. København: E. Jespersens Forlag, 1909.
———. *O Rival de Sherlock-Holmes: Na pista do crime. . . .* Traducção de Celia Roma. Lisboa: Livraria Ferreira, 1911. 194 p. illus. (Memorias de um policia amador)
———. *Den ny Sherlock Holmes*. [The New

Sherlock Holmes.] Oversat af M. Laursen. København: E. Jespersens Forlag, 1920. 188 p.

Review: *Armchair Detective*, 1, No. 4 (July 1968), 116-117. (Nathan L. Bengis).

5904. [Grazebrook, O. F.] *Something of Dr. Watson*, by R-- --d K-- --g. [London: Privately Printed, 1949.] 24 p. (Studies in Sherlock Holmes, No. 6)

A double pastiche in which the young Rudyard Kipling has just returned from India and meets Holmes and Watson.

5905. The Greek Interpreters of East Lansing, Michigan. "The Singular Affair of Mr. Phillip Phot," compiled by Page Heldenbrand. *BSJ* [OS], 2, No. 1 (January 1947), 67-74, 77-84.

5906. Green, Charles. "The Adventure of the Twelve Toucans," *Ellery Queen's Mystery Magazine*, 38, No. 4 (October 1961), 10-27.

A young admirer of Holmes and the BSI solves the mystery by using the Master's methods.

5907. [Gross, E. Tudor.] "The Kidnapping of Mr. Chasebrook: A Kerlock Shomes Mystery," recorded by Dr. Warsaw. *Stamps*, 45, No. 10 (December 4, 1943), 331-332, 354.

5908. ———. "The Mystery of the 10-20-Thirt," *Stamps*, 48, No. 4 (July 22, 1944), 115-116, 137.

———. ———, *Sherlockian Studies*. Edited by Robert A. Cutter. [Jackson Heights, N.Y.: The Baker Street Press, 1947.] p. 15-21.

A philatelic parody with Kerlock Shomes and Dr. Warsaw.

5909. ———, "The Theft of the World's Rarest Stamp: A Kerlock Shomes Mystery," as reported by Dr. Warsaw. *Stamps*, 44, No. 11 (September 11, 1943), 380-383.

5910. [Hahn, Robert W., and John H. Nieminski.] "The Adventure of the Copper's Breeches," by A. Con and O. Yle. *DCC*, 3, No. 3 (April 1967), 2-3; 3, No. 4 (June 1967), 2-3; 3, No. 5 (August 1967), 2-4.

———. ———. Chicago, Ill.: B.S.I., [n.d.] [12] p.

5911. Halbach, Helan. "Caedmon, Caedmonk," *BSJ*, 15, No. 4 (December 1965), 202-205.

The first published fictional gambit experienced by Homonymous and Dr. N. Earnest Whopper, in which Homonymous lures his old friend into believing that his odd ramblings and gestures constitute prima facie senility, where he is really perversely conveying the news that their joint adventures have been contracted for by Caedmon Records—and that not only is the game afoot once more, but their monetary lapses will soon be a thing of the past.

5912. ———. "A Whale of a Tale (It Being a Concurrent and Synchronical Chronicle)," *VH*, 3, No. 1 (January 1969), 7-8.

A further adventure of Homonymous and Dr. Earnest Whopper.

5913. Hall, Vernon. "Sherlock Holmes and the Wife of Bath," *BSJ* [OS], 3, No. 1 (January 1948), 84-93.

During a visit to his old friend in Sussex, Watson listens while Holmes relates the circumstances surrounding a murder he has uncovered in Chaucer's *Wife of Bath's Prologue*.

5914. Hammond, Thomas. "Crimson Fog," *BSP*, No. 38 (August 1968), 2-4; No. 39 (September 1968), 1-2; No. 40 (October 1968), 2-3; No. 41 (November 1968), 3-5; No. 43 (January 1969), 3-4; No. 44 (February 1969), 2-3.

5915. ———. "The Singular Affair of the Tintype Woman," *SOS*, 3, No. 2 (July 1969), 17-18.

5916. Hardenbrook, Don. "Sam Small and Sherlock Holmes," *BSJ*, 10, No. 2 (April 1960), 83-85.

5917. ———. "Translation of 'Another Bird in a Gilded Cage,' " by Gaston Huret III. *West by One and by One*. San Francisco: Privately Printed, 1965. p. 102-106.

5918. Hardwick, Michael and Mollie. *The Private Life of Sherlock Holmes*. [London: Mayflower Books, 1970.] 175 p.

———. ———. New York: Bantam Books, [April 1971]. 154 p. (S5877)

———. *Sherlock Holmes' privatliv*. [Forord af A. D. Henriksen.] På dansk ved Peter Jerndorff Jessen. København: Martins Forlag, 1971. 154 p.

Contents: 1. The Man from Canada. - 2. A Racing Engine. - 3. The Singular Affair of the Russian Ballerina. - 4. The Girl from the River. - 5. Gabrielle. - 6. The Duchess. - 7. Mr. Mycroft Holmes. - 8. Three Boxes to Glennahurich. - 9. The Monster. - 10. The Red Runner. - 11. V. R. - 12. Ilse von Hoffmannsthal.

Based on the film by the same name (item 5164).

5919. Harmon, Jim. "Confidence Game," Illustrated by Epstein. *Galaxy Science Fiction*, 14, No. 2 (June 1957), 128-143.

5920. Harte, Bret. "The Stolen Cigar Case," by A. Co-n D-le. *Condensed Novels. Second Series. New Burlesques*, by Bret Harte.

Boston and New York: Houghton, Mifflin and Co., 1902. p. 37-61.

———. ———, *Condensed Novels. New Burlesques*. London: Chatto and Windus, 1902. p. 33-55.

———. ———, ———. New York: P. F. Collier & Son, [1902]. p. 39-61. ("Argonaut Edition" of The Works of Bret Harte, Vol. 5)

———. ———, *American Detective Stories*. Chosen by Carolyn Wells. New York: Oxford University Press, 1927. p. 238-250.

———. ———, *The Misadventures of Sherlock Holmes*. Edited by Ellery Queen. Boston: Little, Brown and Co., 1944. p. 164-174.

———. ———, *Stories to Remember*. Edited by Joyce McMaster. Vancouver: The Copp Clark Pub. Co., [1957]. p. 72-82.

———. ———, *The Condensed Novels of Bret Harte*. Upper Saddle River, N.J.: Literature House / Gregg Press, [1969]. Pt. 2 (Second Series), p. 37-61. (American Humorists Series, No. 10)

———. ———, *Horizons*. Vol. 3. *In Silent Rooms*. [Compiled by] Patricia A. Guthrie, Anne Patricia Campbell, [and] C. Helen Pielmeier. Revised edition. [Boston]: Ginn and Co., [1970]. p. 94-106. illus. (Faith and Freedom Basic Readers)

———. ———, *Workbook and Tests to Accompany Horizons*. p. 61-62.

"Bret Harte was a shrewd parodist. He was not content with mere exaggeration. He backboned his satire with a novel plot-idea. For in this tale Hemlock Jones, the Great Detective, is himself the victim of a crime! Yes, 'The Terror of Peculators' has himself been robbed! Probably the best parody of Sherlock Holmes." (Ellery Queen)

5921. Hartman, Harry. "The Adventure of the Pickled Hand (First Monthly Installment)," by John H. Henchika, M.D. *The Holy Quire*. [Culver City, Calif.: Luther Norris, December 1970.] p. 31-32.

An irreverent spoof on the Writings, and a glaring example of how it should not be done.

5922. Haunert, William C., and John H. Watson. "Crime in the Kentish Coach," *VH*, 2, No. 1 (January 1968), 6-9.

5923. Heard, H. F. "The Adventure of Mr. Montalba, Obsequist," *Ellery Queen's Mystery Magazine*, 6, No. 3 (September 1945), 98-114.

———. "Mr. Montalba, Obsequist," *To the Queen's Taste*. The first supplement to *101 Years' Entertainment* consisting of the best stories published in the first four years of *Ellery Queen's Mystery Magazine*. Edited by Ellery Queen. Boston: Little, Brown and Co., 1946. p. 322-343.

———. "L'Aventure de Mr. Montalba, obséquiste," *Ellery Queen's Mystère-Magazine*, No. 3 (March 1948), 37-60.

"It is, if it pleases your fancy, a pastiche of He-Who-Cannot-Be-Named, with Mr. Mycroft playing the role of The One and Only to the hilt, and Mr. Sidney Silchester doubling for the muddleheaded medico." (Ellery Queen)

5924. ———. "The Enchanted Garden," *Ellery Queen's Mystery Magazine*, 13, No. 3 (March 1949), 95-117.

5925. ———. *The Notched Hairpin: A Mycroft Mystery*. New York: The Vanguard Press, [1949]. 226 p.

———. ———. London: Cassell and Co. Ltd., 1951. 226 p.

Contents: 1. The Red-Brick Twins. - 2. The Inspector's "Who?" - 3. Mr. Millum's "Why?" - 4. Mr. Mycroft's "How?"

5926. ———. *Reply Paid: A Mystery*. New York: The Vanguard Press, [1942]. 274 p.

———. ———. London: Cassell and Co. Ltd., 1943. 199 p.

———. ———. New York: Dell Pub. Co., [n.d.] 237 p. (Dell Book, No. 44)

The name *Mr. Mycroft* has been changed to *Mr. Bowcross* in the Cassell edition.

5927. ———. *A Taste for Honey*. New York: The Vanguard Press, [1941]. viii, 234 p.

———. ———. New York: The American Mercury, [c.1941]. 125 p. (A Mercury Book, No. 70)

———. ———. London: Cassell and Co. Ltd., 1943. 153 p.

———. ———. New York: Avon Book Co., [1946]. 186 p. (No. 108)

———. ———, *Murder with a Difference: Three Unusual Crime Novels*. Selected and with an introduction by Christopher Morley. New York: Random House, [1946]. p. 175-306.

———. ———. New York: Lancer Books, [1964]. 142 p. (Lancer 72-752)

———. *A Taste for Murder*. New York: Avon Publications, [January 1947]. 127 p. (No. 625)

A detective novel with Mr. Mycroft.

5928. Heidenfeld, W. "The True Adventure of the Second Stain," *Ellery Queen's Mystery Magazine*, 53, No. 2 (February 1969), 105-120.

One of the non-winning pastiches entered in the Johannesburg *Sunday Times* short-story contest. For the winners, see items 5859 and 6025.

5929. ———. "The Unpleasantness at the Stooges Club," *Ellery Queen's Mystery Magazine*, 21, No. 2 (February 1953), 81-92.

"Watson and the other 'stooges' show their straightmen how a crime should be solved—and at the bottom of this crime is Professor Moriarty." (Edgar W. Smith)

5930. Heinlein, Robert A. "The Moon Is a Harsh Mistress," Illustrated by Gray Morrow. *Worlds of If Science Fiction,* 15-16 (December 1965-April 1966). 5 parts.
————. ————. New York: G. P. Putnam's Sons, [1966]. 383 p.
————. ————. [New York]: Berkley Pub. Corp., [1968]. 302 p. (A Berkley Medallion Book, N1601)
One of the main characters is a computer called Mycroft who comes to think of himself as being Mycroft in reality. As a result, the story is laced with Sherlockian references.

5931. [Heldenbrand, Page.] "The Man with the Monogrammed Middle," *Heldenbrand's Christmas Perennial.* New York: Appledore Towers Letter Press, 1954. p. 7-11.

5932. Helling, Cornelis. "The Adventure of the Squeaking Radio," *BSJ,* 17, No. 2 (June 1967), 95.
A parody from a Dutch newspaper, translated and altered "to bring it more in keeping with the true Baker Street atmosphere."

5933. Henry, O. "The Adventures of Shamrock Jolnes," *Sixes and Sevens.* Garden City, N.Y.: Doubleday, Page & Co., 1911. Chap. 18, p. 204-213.
————. ————, *The Misadventures of Sherlock Holmes.* Edited by Ellery Queen. Boston: Little, Brown and Co., 1944. p. 175-181.
————. ————, *The Saint's Choice of Humorous Crime.* Edited by Leslie Charteris. [Pasadena, Calif.]: The Shaw Press, [1945]. p. 118-125.
————. "Shamrock Jolnes' Eventyr," Oversat af Ellen Aaris Raae. *Kalifen og Sjoveren,* af O. Henry. [København]: Martins Forlag, 1920. p. 40-46.
"Shamrock Jolnes and Watsup."

5934. ————. "The Detective Detector," *Waifs and Strays: Twelve Stories.* Together with a representative selection of critical and biographical comment. Garden City, N.Y.: Doubleday, Page & Co., 1917. p. 82-89.
Shamrock Jolnes appears briefly, but the tale is a parody of the Master Criminal rather than the Master Detective.

5935. ————. "The Sleuths," *Sixes and Sevens.* Garden City, N.Y.: Doubleday, Page & Co., 1911. Chap. 2, p. 21-31.
————. ————. The first separate edition issued in 1914 as one of "The World's Best Short Stories now presented with Egyptienne 'Straights' Cigarettes, Piccadilly Little Cigars, and Sovereign Cigarettes—One Story accompanying each package." 2-7/8 x 2-1/8 in.

In this parody Jolnes shares the spotlight with another detective named Juggins.

5936. "Herlock Shomes at It Again," *The Wipers Times* [London], 1 (February 12-May 1, 1916). 6 chapters.
————, *The Wipers Times, Including for the First Time in One Volume a Facsimile Reproduction of the Complete Series of the Famous Wartime Trench Magazines.* Edited by F. J. Roberts and J. H. Pearson. London: Eveleigh Nash & Grayson Ltd., [June 1930]. [unpaged]
In the last two chapters "Shomes" is changed to "Sholmes."

5937. Herst, Herman, "Dirty Pool," *BSJ,* 16, No. 2 (June 1966), 82-87.
————. ————, *Stories to Collect Stamps By.* New York: Philatelic Book Publishers, Inc., [1968]. p. 9-16.

5938. Herzog, Evelyn. "The Second Case of the Speckled Band," *Albertinum* [New Haven, Conn.: Albertus Magnus College], 29, No. 2 (Spring 1966), 34-39.
"Holmes is almost taken in by some college students, but he foils the would-be deceivers and even manages to emerge with some profit." (Julian Wolff)

5939. Hinder, J. E. "Heartbeat in Baker Street," *Punch,* 241 (August 2, 1961), 177-178.
————. ————, *CPBook,* 4, No. 15 (August 1968), 282.

5940. Hoff, Ebbe Curtis and Phebe M. "A New Holmesian Treasure Trove," *BSJ,* 14, No. 3 (September 1964), 172-181; 14, No. 4 (December 1964), 239-245.
Acting as literary agents for John H. Watson, Dr. and Mrs. Hoff present the first in a series of completed stories found in Watson's battered tin dispatch-box. The story is entitled "The Problem of Biffley Vicarage."

5941. ————. "Another Tale from the Box at Cox and Company," *BSJ,* 16, No. 1 (March 1966), 33-49.
The second in a series of completed stories by John H. Watson from his famous tin dispatch-box. This one is entitled "The Adventure of the Hadderly Formula."

5942. Hoffmann, Banesh. "Shakespeare the Physicist," *Scientific American,* 184, No. 4 (April 1951), 52-53.
————. ————, *Sherlockiana,* 9, Nr. 1-2 (1964), 6-7.
————. Enlarged with title: "Sherlock, Shakespeare and the Bomb," *BSJ,* 10, No. 2 (April 1960), 69-79.
————. Longer version with title: "Sherlock, Shakespeare, and the Bomb," *Ellery Queen's Mystery Magazine,* 47, No. 2 (February 1966), 88-98.

"A little-known investigation by Sherlock Holmes reveals that the Bard anticipated wireless, relativity and the atomic bomb."

5943. Hogan, John C. "The Adventure of the Calabash Pipe," *BSJ*, 18, No. 3 (September 1968), 166-169.
———. ———, *Hongkong Standard* (April 6, 1969).

5944. ———. "A Sherlock Holmes Christmas Story," *The RANDom News* [Santa Monica, Calif.: The Rand Corp.], 7, No. 8 (November-December 1961), 5-7.
———. ———, *BSJ*, 11, No. 4 (December 1961), 222-224.
An ingenious use of Canonical titles to relate how Professor Moriarty sent Holmes the giant rat of Sumatra for a Christmas present.

5945. ———. "Sherlock Holmes in Hongkong," *Hongkong Standard* (March 30; April 6, 13, 20, 1969).
Contents: The Giant Rat of Sumatra. - The Adventure of the Calabash Pipe. - The Hound of the Basket-Maker. - The Persian Slipper.

5946. Holmes Electric Protective Co. *The Case of the Purloined Key: Pages from the Diary of Sherlock Holmes.* New York: [n.d.]
An illustrated advertising leaflet.

5947. ———. *The Case of the Safety Slide: Pages from the Diary of Sherlock Holmes.* New York: [n.d.]

5948. ———. *The Case of the Battering Bandits: Pages from the Diary of Sherlock Holmes.* New York: [n.d.]

5949. ———. *The Case of the Human Fly: Pages from the Diary of Sherlock Holmes.* New York: [n.d.]

5950. Horowitz, Floyd R. "The Case of the Schweinitz Portrait," *BSJ*, 15, No. 4 (December 1965), 236-244.

5951. Hubbard, P. M. "Last of the Line," *Punch*, 223 (December 31, 1952), 791-792.

5952. Iraldi, James C. *The Problem of the Purple Maculas: A Sherlock Holmes Adventure.* Illustrated by Henry Lauritzen. Culver City, Calif.: Luther Norris, April 1968. 41 p.
Limited to 500 copies.
A novelette that is not a parody or burlesque, but a serious study on the part of the author to recapture the style, settings, and atmosphere of the Canonical tales. The plot is based on a remark by Holmes in Miss concerning Henry Staunton, the man he "helped to hang."
Reviews: BSP, No. 40 (October 1968), 5 (Chris Redmond); SOS, 3, No. 1 (January

1969), 4-5 (Bruce Dettman). *SHJ*, 8, No. 4 (Summer 1968), 135-136 (Lord Donegall); *Startling Mystery Stories*, 2, No. 5 (Winter 1968 / 69), 5, 124 (Robert A. W. Lowndes).

5953. Jackson, Donald W. "Dénouement," *BSJ*, 16, No. 4 (December 1966), 198-201.
Holmes uses his powers of observation and deduction to explain what Christmas gift Watson purchased for him.

5954. Jackson, Henry Hollister. "Extracts from the Posthumous Papers of John H. Watson, M.D.," *Random Muse* (London: Institute of Actuaries Students' Society) (July 1947).
———. "Something About S. Holmes," *Fragments* [Montpelier, Vt.: National Life Insurance Co], [n.d.] p. 185-194.
The Master exposes some shortcomings of Edmund Halley, discoverer of the comet named after him and compiler of the first important mortality table. An anonymous commentary entitled "Actuary Henry H. Jackson Becomes a Sherlock Holmes" appears in the *National Messenger* [Montpelier, Vt.: National Life Insurance Co.], 31, No. 10 (October 1947), 27-28.

5955. Jacobson, John. "The Adventure of the Spot of Tea: A Tide Pooles, Dr. Harcourt Mystery," *BSJ*, 17, No. 1 (March 1967), 20-24.

5956. ———. "The Adventure of the Stone of Henge," *Astounding Deductions* [Rockford, Ill.] (September 1970), 1, 3-8. illus.
"Tide Pooles and Dr. Harcourt."

5957. ———. "Inspector Kirchner's Own Case," *BSP*, No. 48 (June 1969), 4-5; No. 49-50 (July-August 1969), 6.
"Tide Pooles and Dr. Harcourt."

5958. ———. "The Opera Murder," *SOS*, 1, No. 5 (June 1967), 8-10; 1, No. 6 (August 1967), 6-8; 2, No. 1 (October 1967), 12-15.
"Tide Pooles and Dr. Harcourt."

5959. ———. "The Phantom Anarchist," *BSP*, No. 20 (February 1967), 2.

5960. ———. "The Return of the Redheaded League," *SOS Annual*, No. 1 (January 1967), 5-15.
"Tide Pooles and Dr. Harcourt."

5961. Jameson, Colin G. "Singular Lady," *The Saturday Evening Post*, 215, No. 52 (June 26, 1943), 23, 42, 44-46.
"A short story about a lady whose thoughts and deeds were poured in the Sherlockian mold." (Edgar W. Smith)

5962. Johnston, J. Jeremy. "The Giant Rat of Sumatra: A Story for Which the World Is Now, At Last, Prepared," *The Harvard*

Lampoon, 152, No. 6-7 (November 14, 1962), 15-22. (Mystery Issue)

———. ———, *CPBook*, 3, No. 11 (Winter 1967), 204-209.

5963. Jones, P. H. "Master Minds at Play," *Bridge Quarterly*, 2, No. 2 (1958), 274-277.

"Sherlock Holmes performs a *tour de force* in making a contract of four spades against two fictional detectives—Hercule Poirot and Charlie Chan." (Edgar W. Smith)

5964. Kahn, William B. "More Adventures of Oilock Combs: The Succored Beauty," *The Smart Set*, 17, No. 2 (October 1905), 93-95.

———. *An Adventure of Oilock Combs: The Succored Beauty*. [San Francisco: The Beaune Press, December 1964.] [8] p. (Vintage No. 1)

Limited to 222 copies.

"Hand set and printed, mostly in M & H Monotype Baskerville, by Shirley & Dean Dickensheet."

"Oilock Combs and Spotson."

5965. Karlson, Katherine E. "A Case of Identity II, or Art in the Soup Can Take the Strangest Forms!" *BSJ*, 20, No. 3 (September 1970), 140-141.

"Cerlocio Olmez and Átsonez."

5966. ———. "The Case of the Restless Rooks," *A Curious Collection*. Edited by William J. Walsh. [Suffern, N.Y.]: The Musgrave Ritualists Beta, 1971. p. 22-27.

5967. Kayess, Walter. "The Land of the Wonderful Co.: A Story for Children," *Harry Furniss's Christmas Annual*. [Illustrated by Harry Furniss.] London: Anthony Treherne & Co. Ltd., 1905. p. 88-126.

Holmes appears as one of the characters in a burlesque of *Alice in Wonderland*.

5968. Kennedy, Bruce. "The Adventure of the Amesbury Disappearance," *BSP Christmas Annual*, No. 1 (1966), 4-7.

5969. ———. "The Adventure of the Carved Knife," *BSP*, No. 6 (December 1965), 2-3.

5970. ———. "The Adventure of the Dover Ghost," *SOS Annual*, No. 1 (January 1967), 17-20.

5971. ———. "The Adventure of the Headless Torso," *BSP*, No. 9-10 (March-April 1966), 3-5.

5972. ———. "The Adventure of the Prophetic Poet," *SOS Annual*, No. 2 (January 1968), 12-14.

5973. Kessel, D. H. "The Resurrection of Sherlock Holmes: Case 1. Dr. Watson's Caper," *The Gargoyle* [University of Michigan], 48, No. 5 (1955), 6-7.

5974. KEX Industrial Services. *The Case of the Missing Footprints*. [London: n.d.] [4] p.

An illustrated advertising leaflet.

5975. [Kimball, Elliot.] "The First Man Who Beat Holmes," by Llabmik Toille [pseud.] *BSG*, 1, No. 4 (April 1962), 47-50.

Little Sherlock is birched for his "impudence" by his maternal grandfather, Sir Edward Sherrinford.

5976. Kingsmill, Hugh. "The Ruby of Khitmandu: A Serial Story Told in Alternate Chapters by Arth-r C-n-n D-yle and E. W. H-rn-ng," *The Bookman*, 75, No. 1 (April 1932), 10-15.

———. ———, *The Misadventures of Sherlock Holmes*. Edited by Ellery Queen. Boston: Little, Brown and Co., 1944. p. 291-300.

"The Maharajah of Khitmandu, who is staying at Claridge's, is robbed of the famous Ruby of Khitmandu. Sherlock Holmes traces the theft to Raffles, who agrees to hand over the ruby to Holmes, on condition that he and his confederate Bunny are not proceeded against."

5977. Kjell, Bradley. "The Adventure of the Bored Professor: A Tide Pooles, Dr. Harcourt Mystery," *BSJ*, 17, No. 2 (June 1967), 92-94.

Professor Mortality hides a centipede in Poole's violin.

5978. ———. "The Adventure of the Misleading Murder," *BSP*, No. 28 (October 1967), 3-6.

"Tide Pooles and Dr. Harcourt."

5979. ———. "The Adventure of the Missing Scuttle," *SOS*, No. 2 (November 1966), 4-8.

"Tide Pooles and Dr. Harcourt."

5980. ———. "The Adventure of the Mowed Lawn," *SOS*, No. 3 (February 1967), 7-8.

"Tide Pooles and Dr. Harcourt."

5981. ———. "The Adventure of the Perilous Protoplasm," *Astounding Deductions* [Rockford, Ill.] (September 1970), 2, 9-12. illus.

"Tide Pooles and Dr. Harcourt."

5982. ———. "The Adventure of the Psychedelic Sleuth," *The Loft* [Rock Valley College], 1, No. 1 (January 1968), 29-34.

———. ———, *SOS*, 2, No. 5-6 (June-August 1968), 9-12.

The detective appears as Shrock Holmes in *The Loft* and as Tide Pooles in *SOS*.

5983. ———. "The Adventure of the Sick

Sleuth," *BSP Christmas Annual*, No. 1 (1966), 10-12.

"Tide Pooles and Dr. Harcourt."

5984. ———. "The Adventure of the Synthetic Soup," *SOS Annual*, No. 2 (January 1968), 3-8.

"Tide Pooles and Dr. Harcourt."

5985. ———. "The Adventure of the Unstrung Fiddler," *BSP*, No. 23 (May 1967), 7-10.

"Tide Pooles and Dr. Harcourt."

5986. [Knox, E. V.] "Conan Doyle in Space," by Evoe [pseud.] *Punch*, 239 (November 23, 1960), 744-746.

"Holmes serves his country by worming his way into the good graces of an 'Alien Power' and becoming their Orbiter Number One, the first spaceman." (Julian Wolff)

5987. [———.] "Me, or The Strange Episode of the Reincarnated Greek," *Fiction As She Is Wrote*, by E. V. Knox ("Evoe" of *Punch*). With 20 illustrations by George Morrow. London: Methuen & Co., [1923]. p. 98-116.

———. ———, ———. New York: Dial Press, 1924. p. 98-116.

"Written in collaboration by Cunning Rider and Haggard Toyle. In this the only story which has ever been written in conjunction by these two great masters of popular fiction, the strange attraction of the spirit-world is blended with the excitement of detective romance. Happiness comes at last to a character whose nobility has endeared him to every English reader's heart."

5988. Knox, Ronald A. "The Apocryphal Sherlock Holmes: The Adventure of the First Class Carriage," Illustrated by Tom Purvis. *The Strand Magazine*, 112 (February 1947), 42-52.

5989. ———. "A Decalogue Symposium," *Juxta Salices*. Oxford: Alden & Co. Ltd., Bocardo Press, 1910. p. 57-88.

Dramatis Personae: The Chairman (almost any XIXth Century Liberal), Hippoclides, Socrates, Aristotle, Cicero, S. Francis, Charles II, Dr. Johnson, Mrs. Malaprop, *Sherlock Holmes*, *Adimantus Boswell Watson*, Mr. B-rn-rd Sh-w, The March Hare, Sir Roger de Coverley, Peter Pan, Sir John Falstaff, Sam Weller, Chorus of Virtues, Chorus of Vices.

5990. Kummer, Frederic Arnold. "The Adventure of the Queen Bee," *The Mystery Magazine* [Dunellen, N. J.], 8, No. 1 (July 1933), 19-23, 108-113; No. 2 (August 1933), 19-23, 134-138; No. 3 (September 1933), 22-26, 114-118; No. 4 (October 1933), 24-26, 96-102.

A pastiche adapted from the play *The Holmeses of Baker Street* by Basil Mitchell

(items 5248-5249). The stars are Shirley Holmes and Joan Watson.

5991. ———, and Basil Mitchell. "The Canterbury Cathedral Murder," *The Mystery Magazine*, 8, No. 6 (December 1933), 24-26, 114-119.

———, ———. ———, *The Misadventures of Sherlock Holmes*. Edited by Ellery Queen. Boston: Little, Brown and Co., 1944. p. 313-329.

Another adventure with the daughters of Holmes and Watson.

5992. Lahey, John P. " 'We Three Kings of Orient Are,' " *BSJ Christmas Annual*, No. 4 (1959), 311-314.

"An excerpt from the Christmas story as retold by the late John H. Watson, M.D., extracted from his works and now revealed to a world which is prepared to receive it."

5993. Lallou, William J. "The Adventure of the Cardinal's Ring," *BSJ*, 14, No. 2 (June 1964), 77-79.

5994. Leacock, Stephen. "The Great Detective," *Laugh with Leacock: An Anthology of the Best Works of Stephen Leacock*. New York: Dodd, Mead and Co., 1930. p. 25-44.

———. ———, ———. New York: Pocket Books, Inc., [December 1946]. p. 25-44.

———. ———, ———. Toronto; Montreal: McClelland and Stewart Ltd., [1968]. p. 25-44. (Canadian Best-Seller Library, No. 41)

"The Great Detective and Poor Nut."

5995. ———. "An Irreducible Detective Story," *Further Foolishness: Sketches and Satires of the Follies of the Day*. London; New York: John Lane, 1916. p. 223-225.

———. ———, ———. Introduction: D. W. Cole. General Editor: Malcolm Ross. [Toronto]: McClelland and Stewart Ltd., [1968]. p. 18-19. (New Canadian Library, No. 60)

———. ———, *The Misadventures of Sherlock Holmes*. Edited by Ellery Queen. Boston: Little, Brown and Co., 1944. p. 227-228.

———. ———, With subtitle: "Hanged by a Hair, or A Murder Mystery Minimized," *Ellery Queen's Mystery Magazine*, 18, No. 95 (October 1951), 65.

———. ———, *Ellery Queen's Minimysteries*. Edited by Ellery Queen. New York and Cleveland: The World Pub. Co., [1969]. p. 188-189.

5996. ———. "Maddened by Mystery, or The Defective Detective," *Nonsense Novels*. London; New York: John Lane Co., 1911. Chap. 1, p. 11-27.

———, ———. Illustrated by John Kettelwell. London; New York: John Lane Co., 1921. Chap. 1, p. 11-27.

———. ———, ———. New York: Dodd, Mead and Co., 1922. Chap. 1, p. 11-27.

———. ———, ———. New York: Dover Publications, Inc., [1971]. p. 1-9.

———. ———, *The Misadventures of Sherlock Holmes.* Edited by Ellery Queen. Boston: Little, Brown and Co., 1944. p. 218-226.

———. ———, *Murder Without Tears: An Anthology of Crime.* Edited by Will Cuppy. New York: Sheridan House, [1946]. p. 553-561.

———. "The Great Detective," *The Second Century of Detective Stories.* Edited by E. C. Bentley. London: Hutchinson & Co., [1938]. p. 751-761.

5997. Lehmann, R. C. "The Bishop's Crime," by Cunnin Toil [pseud.] *Punch,* 105 (August 12, 1893), 69. (The Adventures of Picklock Holes, No. 1)

5998. ———. "The Duke's Feather," by Cunnin Toil. *Punch,* 105 (August 19, 1893), 76. (The Adventures of Picklock Holes, No. 2)

5999. ———. "The Escape of the Bull-Dog," by Cunnin Toil. *Punch,* 105 (September 2, 1893), 100. (The Adventures of Picklock Holes, No. 4)

6000. ———. "The Hungarian Diamond," by Cunnin Toil. *Punch,* 105 (October 14, 1893), 168 (The Adventures of Picklock Holes, No. 5)

6001. ———. "Lady Hilda's Mystery," by Cunnin Toil. *Punch,* 105 (August 26, 1893), 85. (The Adventures of Picklock Holes, No. 3)

6002. ———. "Picklock's Disappearance," by Cunnin Toil. *Punch,* 106 (January 13, 1894), 16. (The Adventures of Picklock Holes, No. 8)

———. ———, *EL,* 1, No. 1 (April 1953), 7.

6003. ———. "The Stolen March," by Cunnin Toil. *Punch,* 105 (December 23, 1893), 289; 105 (December 30, 1893), 301. (The Adventures of Picklock Holes, No. 7)

6004. ———. "The Umbrosa Burglary," by Cunnin Toil. *Punch,* 105 (November 4, 1893), 213. (The Adventures of Picklock Holes, No. 6)

———. ———, *The Misadventures of Sherlock Holmes.* Edited by Ellery Queen. Boston: Little, Brown and Co., 1944. p. 185-189.

6005. ———. *The Adventures of Picklock Holes, Together with a Perversion and a Burlesque.* With illustrations by E. T. Reed

and E. J. Wheeler. London: Bradbury, Agnew & Co., 1901. 172 p.

Partial contents: 1. The Bishop's Crime. - 2. The Duke's Feather. - 3. Lady Hilda's Mystery. - 4. The Escape of the Bull-Dog. - 5. The Hungarian Diamond. - 6. The Umbrosa Burglary. - 7. The Stolen March. - 8. The Stolen March (cont'd). - 9. Picklock's Disappearance.

"Picklock Holes and Dr. Potson."

6006. Leiber, Fritz. "The Moriarty Gambit," *Chess Review,* 30, No. 2 (February 1962), 45-47.

———. ———, *West by One and by One.* San Francisco: Privately Printed, 1965. p. 133-144.

Holmes tells Watson how he defeated Moriarty in the first round of chess at the London International Tournament of 1883.

6007. Lennon, John. "The Singularge Experience of Miss Anne Duffield," *A Spaniard in the Works.* [Drawings by John Lennon.] New York: Simon and Schuster, 1965. p. 24-33.

"Shamrock Womlbs and Doctored Whopper."

6008. Lewis, Arthur H. *Copper Beeches.* New York: Trident Press, [1971]. 317 p.

———. ———. New York: Pocket Books, [1972]. 245 p. (No. 77568)

"A novel in which the leading characters (as well as the author) are members of The Sons of the Copper Beeches. Not only is it of great interest in its own right, but is doubly so because so many Irregulars are closely identified with it." (Julian Wolff)

Reviews: Armchair Detective, 5 (October 1971), 40 (R. W. Hahn); *Best Sellers,* 31 (October 15, 1971), 316 (C. P. Collier); *Boston Globe* (December 19, 1971) (H. A. Kennedy); *Chicago Tribune* (January 12, 1972) (Bob Cromie), and reprinted in *DCC,* 8, No. 2 (February 1972), 10; *DCC,* 7, No. 6 (August 1971), 12-13 (R. W. Hahn); *Harper's Magazine,* 243 (October 1971), 120 (John Thompson); *HO,* 2, No. 3 (June 1972), 6 (Dan Morrow); *Library Journal,* 96 (September 1, 1971), 2674 (M. K. Grant); *Mystery Reader's Newsletter,* 5 (November-December 1971), 39 (Stanley Carlin); *New York Times Book Review* (November 14, 1971), 48, 50 (Newgate Callendar); *Providence Sunday Journal Leisure Weekly* (October 10, 1971) (G. D. Byrnes); *Saturday Review,* 54 (October 30, 1971), 56 (Haskel Frankel); *Sherlockiana,* 16, Nr. 3-4 (1971), 14.

6009. Limoli, Thomas J. "The Adventure of Stormy Cleopatra," *BSJ,* 19, No. 1 (March 1969), 23-31.

While sitting out the hurricane Cleo at Pompano Beach, Florida, Alex Wingood presents some convincing evidence that his friend Myron Homze is the grandson of Irene Adler and Sherlock Holmes.

6010. ———. "Dupin's Last Case," *BSJ*, 20, No. 1 (March 1970), 6-13.

A pastiche depicting the death of fictional sleuth C. Auguste Dupin, one of the models used by Doyle in creating Sherlock Holmes. Over the years Dupin's companion and chronicler has been progressively annoyed by the French detective's eccentricities and boastfulness. Eventually Dupin hurls an insult of such an intimately personal nature that for his companion there remains no redress but to accomplish Dupin's death. This he achieves by using methods described in several of Poe's stories. Finally, the companion's guilt is revealed by a talking raven, a pet recently acquired by Dupin.

6011. Lloyd-Taylor A. "The Wine Merchant: A Hitherto Unpublished Case of Sherlock Holmes as Recorded by Dr. Watson," transcribed and edited by A. Lloyd-Taylor. *SHJ*, 4, No. 3 (Winter 1959), 91-96; 4, No. 4 (Spring 1960), 121-124.

6012. Lofting, Hugh. ["The Food Mystery Story"], *Gub Gub's Book*. New York: Frederick A. Stokes Co., 1932. Chap. 4-5, p. 67-109.

The main character is a man called Sherbert Scones, the famous Icebox Detective.

6013. Loomis, Charles Battell. "A la Sherlock Holmes," *The Four-Masted Cat-Boat and Other Truthful Tales*. With illustrations by Florence Scovel Shinn. New York: The Century Co., 1899. Chap. 6, p. 25-29.

———. ———, ———. Freeport, N.Y.: Books for Libraries Press, [1970]. Chap. 6, p. 25-29. (Short Story Index Reprint Series).

6014. Ludwig, Edward. "The Martian Who Hated People," *Inside and Science Fiction Advertiser*, No. 7 (January 1955), 10-16, 29.

———. ———, *The SHsf Fanthology 2*. Edited by Ruth Berman. Minneapolis, Minn.: The Professor Challenger Society, September 1971. p. 4-12.

A parody in which an alien visitor is detected by Surly Homes and Dr. Watchson.

6015. Macmillan, W. R. Duncan. "Holmes in Scotland," *Blackwood's Magazine*, 274 (September 1953), 193-209.

A pastiche giving plausibility to the untold tale of "The Politician, the Lighthouse, and the Trained Cormorant."

6016. MacNamara, Brinsley. "The Man Who Knew Sherlock Holmes," Illustrations by Bernard Golden. *Tomorrow*, 5, No. 11 (July 1946), 9-11.

"A third-person pastiche in the form of an Irish tall tale." (Edgar W. Smith)

6017. Mallett, Richard. "The Case of the Diabolical Plot," *Punch*, 188 (June 12, 1935), 684-685.

———. ———, *The Misadventures of Sherlock Holmes*. Edited by Ellery Queen. Boston: Little, Brown and Co., 1944. p. 332-335.

"Garnished with thick satire sauce, the Great Detective again foils his ancient enemy, the Master Criminal. This time the Master Criminal is head of a secret society (the Hippy Hops) whose plot strikes at the very roots of the British Empire. How otherwise explain the singular and ubiquitous thefts of piano keys, circus elephants, and billiard balls?" (Ellery Queen)

6018. ———. "The Case of the Impersonation," *Punch*, 188 (May 8, 1935), 552-553.

"The Great Detective and J. Smith."

6019. ———. "The Case of the Pearls," *Punch*, 187 (November 21, 1934), 582-583.

"The Great Detective and J. Smith."

6020. ———. "The Case of the Pursuit," *Punch*, 188 (January 23, 1935), 88.

"The Great Detective and J. Smith."

6021. ———. "The Case of the Traveller," *Punch*, 187 (December 26, 1934), 704-705.

"The Great Detective and J. Smith."

6022. Malone, Ted. "The Case of the Ninety-Two Candles," *Ellery Queen's Mystery Magazine*, 9, No. 39 (February 1947), 54-57.

A pastiche in the form of a New Year's letter from Dr. Watson that was first broadcast on January 7, 1946, over the ABC network.

6023. Mannion, Rodney A. "The Case of the Twenty-Five Cent Electronic, Etc., Etc.," *BSJ*, 16, No. 2 (June 1966), 74-76.

6024. Masterman, J. C. "The Case of the Gifted Author," *MacKill's Mystery Magazine*, 1, No. 4 (December 1952), 59-66.

———. "The Case of the Gifted Amateur," *The Evening Standard* [London] January 18, 1954), 8.

———. ———, *The Saint Detective Magazine*, 2, No. 3 (September 1954), 142-150.

———. ———, *Seventeen Steps to 221B*. [Edited by] James Edward Holroyd. London: George Allen & Unwin Ltd., [1967]. p. 90-99.

Inspector Lestrade explains how Holmes was vastly overrated as a criminologist.

6025. Masters, Miles. "The Adventure of the Second Stain," *Sunday Times News Magazine* [Johannesburg] (December 10, 1967), 1, 14-16.

Subtitled "Sherlock Holmes accused of Jack the Ripper murders," this is one of two prize-winning entries in the *Sunday Times* short-story contest. For the other winner, see item 5859.

6026. McComas, Stanley. "The Case of the Crazy Americans," *Illustrious Client's Second Case-Book.* Edited by J. N. Williamson. [Indianapolis, Ind.: The Illustrious Clients, 1949.] p. 65-71.

6027. McGoldrick, John. "The Adventure of the Artissium Murderer," *SOH*, 1, No. 3 (1967), 4-6.
"Hemlock Holmes and Dr. Watts."

6028. McLauchlin, Russell. "The Adventure of the Paradol Chamber," *BSJ*, 15, No. 3 (September 1965), 131-135.
A case recorded by Watson in 1887, but as yet unpublished (Five). Mr. McLauchlin has written his own version of the tale.

6029. ————. " 'Her Death Was Doubtful,' " *BSJ*, 14, No. 2 (June 1964), 67-72.
————. " 'Hendes død var tvivlsom,' " Oversat af Peter Jerndorff. *Sherlockiana*, 9, Nr. 1-2 (1964), 1-5.
The exploring Norwegian named Sigerson (an alias of Holmes's) proves to the King of Denmark that the death of Ophelia in *Hamlet* was planned by Uncle Claudius!

6030. McMorris, Robert. "Caravan Cigarets Present: A Dramatic Reading," *BSJ*, 18, No. 3 (September 1968), 156-163.
A transatlantic telephone conversation between Watson and Barney Flank, a Madison Avenue advertising agent, concerning a new American television series, "Sherlock Holmes, Private Eye."

6031. [Mengert, Tom.] "The Adventure of the Albany Street Tobacconists," *VJ*, 1, No. 3 [June 1971], 4-5.
"A solve-it-yourself mystery pastiche."

6032. [————.] "A Study in Stagnation," *VJ*, 1, No. 2 [March 1971], 2-5.
"Sharlock Holmes and Dr. Nigel Watson."

6033. Michell, H. "The Adventure of the Giant Rat of Sumatra," *SHJ*, 2, No. 2 (December 1954), 19-20. (The Curtain Rises at 221B)
An entry from the Prooimion Competition in which contestants wrote the introduction to an imaginary Holmesian adventure.

6034. Miksch, W. F. "The Last Word on Holmes," [Illustration by Carl Rose]. *Collier's*, 127, No. 6 (February 10, 1951), 53.
————. ————, *CPBook*, 1, No. 1 (Summer 1964), 7.
Watson out deduces Holmes in "The Singular Case of the Plural Twosome."

6035. Miller, Roy S. "Inspector Lestrade Lets the Cat out of the Bag," *The London Mystery Selection*, 17, No. 75 (December 1967), 74-77.

6036. ————. "The Truth at Last: An Authentic Account of Some Baker Street Irregularities. . . ," *Courier* [London], 40, No. 1 (January 1963), 44-45.
A satire in which Watson complains about Holmes's selfishness and inconsiderateness, ending, "Holmes was never a friend of mine. Why, I hardly knew the fellow."

6037. Milne, Angela. "The Postmaster-General: A Further Adventure of Sherlock Holmes," *Punch*, 253 (November 1, 1967), 671-673.

6038. Mitchell, Gladys. *Watson's Choice.* London: Michael Joseph, [1955]. 239 p.
————. ————. Harmondsworth, Middlesex: Penguin Books, [1957]. [190] p. (No. 1194)
"Sir Bohun Chantrey, who was both wealthy and eccentric, numbered among his enthusiasms an absorbing admiration for Sherlock Holmes. To celebrate that great man's Anniversary, he gave a party at which the guests were invited to impersonate characters from the Holmes stories." (Dust jacket)

6039. Morley, Christopher. "The Adventure of the F. W. L.," *Sherlock Holmes and Dr. Watson: A Textbook of Friendship.* Edited by Christopher Morley. New York: Harcourt, Brace and Co., [1944]. Printed on dust jacket.
————. ————, *BSJ*, 9, No. 4 (October 1959), 227-229.
————. ————, *The Adventure of the F. W. L. by Christopher Morley and A Correspondence with F. D. R.* [Pittsfield, Mass.: The Spermaceti Press, 1969.] p. [4-5].
A parody written as a plug for the Fourth War Loan.

6040. ————. "A Scandal in Bohemia," *Ellery Queen's Mystery Magazine*, 5, No. 14 (January 1944), 116-117.
A playlet-pastiche adapted from the Sacred Writings as a New Year's Eve pastime.

6041. ————. *Thorofare.* New York: Harcourt, Brace and Co., [1942]. 469 p.
"A novel containing frequent and loving references to Sherlock Holmes." (Edgar W. Smith)

6042. Morley, Frank V. *Death in Dwelly Lane.* New York: Harper & Brothers, [1952]. 256 p.
————. *Dwelly Lane.* London: Eyre & Spottiswoode Ltd., 1952. 256 p.

A murder mystery in which the hero is a mathematician and retired gangster, as well as a nephew of Professor Moriarty.

6043. Morton, Humphrey. "The Emerald Tie-Pin: An Extravaganza," With acknowledgments to the late Laurence Housman. *SHJ*, 7, No. 1 (Winter 1964), 10-13.

———. "Smaragd-slipsnålen: En fantasi," Oversat af A. D. Henriksen. *Sherlock Holmes Årbog* I (1965), 29-41.

6044. Munkittrick, R. L. "The Sign of the '400': Being a Continuation of the Adventures of Sherlock Holmes," [by] Conan Doyle, per R. L. M. *Puck*, 37 (October 24, 1894), 148.

———. ———, *The Misadventures of Sherlock Holmes*. Edited by Ellery Queen. Boston: Little, Brown and Co., 1944. p. 235-237.

———. ———, *VH*, 4, No. 3 (September 1970), 5-6.

6045. Norris, Margaret. "A Case of Identities," *Ellery Queen's Mystery Magazine*, 47, No. 4 (April 1966), 135-138.

———. ———, *Ellery Queen's Minimysteries*. Edited by Ellery Queen. New York and Cleveland: The World Pub. Co., [1969]. p. 195-199.

A parody-pastiche to end all Sherlock Holmes parody-pastiches.

6046. Offord, Lenore Glen. "On the Wall," *BSJ*, 15, No. 1 (March 1965), 37-46.

It concerns, and is narrated by, a woman called Rachel, whose sister keeps a lodging house in Lauriston Gardens. Jefferson Hope is one of the lodgers. Rachel is also in contact with Enoch Drebber, who insults her. She tells Hope about this; and when the murder of Drebber is discovered, she is convinced that it was for her sake and that Hope had actually written part of her name on the wall. If the police had really looked for a Rachel and found her, she might have been forced against her will to reveal her knowledge of the crime.

6047. ———. "Three Monologues, or Possible Sidelights on Unwritten Stories," *VH*, 4, No. 1 (January 1970), 2-3.

6048. P., A. E. "The End of Sherlock Holmes," *The Manchester Guardian* (July 7, 1927).

———. ———, *The Living Age*, 333 (August 15, 1927), 355-357.

———. ———, *The Misadventures of Sherlock Holmes*. Edited by Ellery Queen. Boston: Little, Brown and Co., 1944. p. 256-260.

Holmes appears as the father of a three-year-old child prodigy.

6049. Palmer, Stuart. "The Adventure of the Marked Man," *Ellery Queen's Mystery Magazine*, 5, No. 17 (July 1944), 5-19.

6050. ———. "The Adventure of the Remarkable Worm," *The Misadventures of Sherlock Holmes*. Edited by Ellery Queen. Boston: Little, Brown and Co., 1944. p. 108-115.

A pastiche based on the untold tale of Isadora Persano (Thor).

6051. Pentecost, Hugh. "My Dear Uncle Sherlock," *Ellery Queen's Mystery Magazine*, 35, No. 1 (January 1960), 5-12.

———. ———, *Ellery Queen's 1968 Anthology*. Edited by Ellery Queen. New York: Davis Publications, Inc., [1967]. p. 34-41.

———. "Cher Oncle Sherlock," Traduction de Arlette Rosenblum. *Ellery Queen's Mystère-Magazine* [Paris] (February 1961).

"Uncle George had been reading the *Memoirs of Sherlock Holmes* to twelve-year-old Joey Trimble, and then Mrs. Leggett was murdered, and there was a dog in the nighttime. . . ."

6052. Perelman, S. J. " 'The Adventure of the Razor's Edge,' " *Diplomat Magazine*, 17, No. 188 (January 1966), 30-33.

6053. [Peterson, Robert C., ed.] *The Science-Fictional Sherlock Holmes*. Denver, Colo.: The Council of Four, 1960. 137 p.

Contents: Sherlock Holmes and Science Fiction, by Anthony Boucher. - The Martian Crown Jewels, by Poul Anderson. - Half a Hoka—Poul Anderson: An Appreciation, by Gordon R. Dickson. - The Adventure of the Misplaced Hound, by Poul Anderson and Gordon R. Dickson. - The Anomaly of the Empty Man, by Anthony Boucher. - The Greatest Tertian, by Anthony Boucher. - The Adventure of the Snitch in Time, by Mack Reynolds and August Derleth. - The Adventure of the Ball of Nostradamus, by Mack Reynolds and August Derleth. - The Return, by H. Beam Piper and John J. McGuire.

"Since Sherlock Holmes. . .lived surrounded by, and occasionally in the very thick of science fiction, science fiction writers are ever happy to pay tribute to him—as in these stories of his impact upon Americans in the future and upon the furry denizens of a remote planet, of his successor Solar Pons, his cousin Dr. Verner, and his Martian counterpart Syaloch (of the Street of Those Who Prepare Nourishment in Ovens), and of his triumphant survival when almost all else of human culture has perished." (Anthony Boucher)

Review: SOS. 2, No. 5-6 (June-August 1968), 2-3 (Bruce Dettman).

6054. [Peterson, West.] "Sherlock Holmes,"

Screen Romances, 18, No. 125 (October 1939), 42-44, 60-62.

A fictionalized adaptation of *The Adventures of Sherlock Holmes* (item 5147). Illustrated with scenes from the film.

6055. [Philips, Anita.] "Sherlock Holmes and the Secret Weapon," *Screen Romances*, 28, No. 165 (February 1943), 38-39, 89-90.

A fictionalized adaptation of the Universal Pictures production (item 5149). Illustrated with scenes from the film.

6056. Phillpotts, Eden. "Peters, Detective," *Ellery Queen's Mystery Magazine*, 23, No. 125 (April 1954), 46-58.

"A story about some minor feats of detection by an English schoolboy whose motive in life was to 'try to be like Sherlock Holmes in every possible way.' " (Edgar W. Smith)

6057. Piper, H. Beam, and John J. McGuire. "The Return," Illustrated by Kelly Freas. *Astounding Science Fiction*, 52, No. 5 (January 1954), 70-95.

————. ————, [Longer version] *The Science-Fictional Sherlock Holmes*. Denver: The Council of Four, 1960. p. 105-137.

"One of the most remarkable pastiches ever penned. Holmes and Watson are not in it; but their presences pervade a strange religion which has come to flourish, in the 22nd century, in one of the backwaters of civilization left by the devastation of the Atomic Wars." (Edgar W. Smith)

6058. Porges, Arthur. "Her Last Bow, or An Adventure of Stately Homes," *Ellery Queen's Mystery Magazine*, 29, No. 159 (February 1957), 26-30.

An outrageous tale of a grotesque murder in a "locked room."

6059. ————. "Another Adventure of Stately Homes," *The Saint Mystery Magazine*, 21, No. 2 (September 1964), 127-133.

A second tale narrated by Sun Wat in which Homes and his elder brother Tract lead Sir Henry Merrivale to the solution of the locked-room murder of Inspector French.

6060. ————. "Stately Homes. . .and the Box: A Mystery," *Diners Club Magazine*, 16, No. 8W (October 1965), 50-51.

"Stately Homes and Sun Wat."

6061. Pronzini, Bill. "Who's Afraid of Sherlock Holmes?" *Mike Shayne Mystery Magazine*, 22, No. 5 (April 1968), 60-69.

6062. Puhl, Gayle Lange. "The Adventure of Rasil Bathbone," *SOS*, 6, No. 1 (January 6, 1972), 10-21.

"Sheercrocked Moans and Dr. Watsdotter of 221B Borscht Street."

6063. ————. "The Adventure of Stocksen Bonds: A Sheercrocked Moans and Doctor Watsdotter Adventure," *BSJ*, 18, No. 2 (June 1968), 78-84.

Moans helps Bonds, a famous international spy, overthrow SMASM and bring about the downfall of its evil head, Professor Artymore.

6064. Queen, Ellery, ed. *The Misadventures of Sherlock Holmes*. Boston: Little, Brown and Co., 1944. xxii, 363 p. illus.

————. ————. 125 numbered copies with a special presentation page were distributed to those who attended the BSI dinner at the Murray Hill Hotel on March 31, 1944.

Contents: Introduction. - *Part One: By Detective-Story Writers.* 1892. The Great Pegram Mystery, by Robert Barr. - 1902. Holmlock Shears Arrives Too Late, by Maurice Leblanc. - 1915. The Adventures of the Clothes-Line, by Carolyn Wells. - -1920. The Unique Hamlet, by Vincent Starrett. - 1925. Holmes and the Dasher, by Anthony Berkeley. - 1929. The Case of the Missing Lady, by Agatha Christie. - 1942. The Adventure of the Illustrious Impostor, by Anthony Boucher. - 1943. The Disappearance of Mr. James Phillimore, by Ellery Queen. - 1943. The Adventure of the Remarkable Worm, by Stuart Palmer. - *Part Two: By Famous Literary Figures.* 1893. The Adventure of the Two Collaborators, by Sir James M. Barrie. - 1902. A Double-Barrelled Detective Story, by Mark Twain. - 1902. The Stolen Cigar Case, by Bret Harte. - 1911. The Adventures of Shamrock Jolnes, by O. Henry. - *Part Three: By Humorists.* 1893. The Umbrosa Burglar, by R. C. Lehmann. - 1897. The Stranger Unravels a Mystery, by John Kendrick Bangs. - 1903. Shylock Homes: His Posthumous Memoirs, by John Kendrick Bangs. - 1911. Maddened by Mystery: or, The Defective Detective, by Stephen Leacock. - 1916. An Irreducible Detective Story, by Stephen Leacock. - *Part Four: By Devotees and Others.* 1894. The Adventure of the Table Foot, by Zero (Allan Ramsay). - 1894. The Sign of the "400," by R. K. Munkittrick. - 1907. Our Mr. Smith, by Oswald Crawfurd. - 1920. The Footprints on the Ceiling, by Jules Castier. - 1927. The End of Sherlock Holmes, by A. E. P. - 1928. The Adventure of the Norcross Riddle, by August Derleth. - 1929. The Mary Queen of Scots Jewel, by William O. Fuller. - 1932. The Ruby of Khitmandu, by Hugh Kingsmill. - 1932. His Last Scrape: or, Holmes, Sweet Holmes! by Rachel Ferguson. - 1933. The Adventure of the Murdered Art Editor, by Frederic Dorr Steele. - 1933. The Canterbury Cathedral Murder, by Frederic Arnold Kummer and Basil Mitchell. - 1934. The Case of the Missing Patriarchs, by Logan Clendening. - 1935. The Case of the Diabolical Plot, by Richard Mallett. - 1936. Christmas Eve, by

S. C. Roberts. - 1941. The Man Who Was Not Dead, by Manly Wade Wellman. - Acknowledgments. - Bibliography. - Index.

Reviews: Chicago Tribune (April 9, 1944), VII, 10 (Vincent Starrett); *New York Herald Tribune Weekly Book Review* (April 9, 1944), 4 (M. L. Becker); *New York Times Book Review* (April 2, 1944), 15 (Howard Haycraft); *New Yorker*, 20 (April 8, 1944), 90; *Springfield Republican* (April 9, 1944), 4.

6065. ———. *A Study in Terror.* New York: Lancer Books, [1966]. 173 p. (Lancer 73-469)
———. *Sherlock Holmes Versus Jack the Ripper: A Novel.* London: Victor Gollancz Ltd., 1967. 156 p.
———. *En studie i mord: Ellery Queen og Sherlock Holmes løser Jack the Ripper mysteriet.* [Oversat af Bibba Jørgen Jensen.] [København]: Lademann, [1968]. [190] p.

"This is an enjoyable Holmes pastiche by a great American partnership of the detective story. It is also a pastiche-with-a-difference in that it is Inspector Queen who, in the final chapter, solves the mystery of the Ripper's identity, naturally proving that Holmes had been right and poor Watson, as usual, wrong." (Lord Donegall)
Reviews: BSP, No. 13 (July 1966), 4 (Michael Walsh); *BSP*, No. 19 (January 1967), 3-4 (Steve Tomashefsky); *SHJ*, 8, No. 2 (Spring 1967), 65 (Lord Donegall); *Sherlockiana*, 12, Nr. 1-2 (1967), 4.

6066. Rabe, W. T. "The Final Adventure," Read by Russell McLauchlin and Henry Schneidewind. *Voices from Baker Street*, 2. Ferndale, Mich.: The Old Soldiers of Baker Street, 1965. Side 1, band 3.
A parody written in 1950 and broadcast on "U of D Showtime," WJBK.

6067. [Ramsay, Allan.] "The Adventure of the Table Foot," by Zero [pseud.] *The Bohemian*, 2, No. 1 (January 1894), 39-41.
———. ———, *The Misadventures of Sherlock Holmes.* Edited by Ellery Queen. Boston: Little, Brown and Co., 1944. p. 231-234.
"Thinlock Bones and Whatsoname."

6068. Ratner, Edward. "The Baker Street Irregular," *Vox Vet Literary Supplement* [New York University, Washington Square College, Veterans Collegiate Association], No. 3 (Winter 1948), 3-5.
"A G.I. in London calls on Mr. Moriarty of Baker Street, with interesting complications." (Edgar W. Smith)

6069. [Reese, K. M.] "The Adventure of the Dancing Teeny-Bopper," *Chemical & Engineering News*, 45, No. 36 (August 28, 1967), 150.
———. ———, *BSJ*, 17, No. 4 (December 1967), 243.

———. ———, *CPBook*, 4, No. 14 (Winter 1968), 280.

6070. Reppert, Ralph. "Gone to the Bowwows," *The Sunday Sun Magazine* [Baltimore] (January 3, 1954), 4.
"How Sherlock Reppert solved the Case of the Barking Dog." (Subtitle)

6071. Reynolds, Mack. "The Adventure of the Extraterrestrial," Illustrated by John Schoenherr. *Analog Science Fiction / Science Fact*, 75, No. 5 (July 1965), 104-129.
"In which the Immortal Detective, despite his great age, proves the advantages of native wit in solving problems. . . ."

6072. Rhinelander, Philip H. *The Arrest of Wilson, the Notorious Canary Trainer.* Songs, words and music by Philip H. Rhinelander [Boston]: The Tavern Club, 1939. [8] p.
Contents: Butler's Song. - A Cat May Look at a King. - Riding Around in a Hansom. - Entrance of Police. - Finale, Act. I. - It's Very Unwise to Kill the Goose. - The Fog Hangs Deep in Baker Street. - Schnapps. - Finale, Act. III.

6073. Richardson, Frank. *The Secret Kingdom.* London: Duckworth & Co., 1905. xii, 340 p. (Duckworth's Colonial Library)
Partial contents: 12. The Humility of Holmes. - 13. The Dull Thud in the Dining-Room. - 14. Mainly About Sherlock. - 15. The Truth About Watson.

6074. Richardson, Maurice. "The Last Detective Story in the World," *Lilliput*, 18 (May 1946), 373-378.
———. ———, *Crusader: The British Forces Weekly* (June 2, 1946).
———. ———, *Ellery Queen's Mystery Magazine*, 9, No. 39 (February 1947), 63-69.
"The Armageddon of the detective story—the final battle between the powers of good and evil. . .the Grand Field Marshals in charge of strategy and tactics are none other than Sherlock Holmes and Professor Moriarty." (Ellery Queen)

6075. Roberts, Bechhofer. "The Persistent House-Hunters," *Ellery Queen's Mystery Magazine*, 22, No. 1 (July 1954), 51-64.
"A. B. C. Hawkes and Johnstone."

6076. Roberts, S. C. *Christmas Eve: An Unrecorded Adventure of Sherlock Holmes.* Newly edited from the MS by S. C. R. and privately printed at the University Press, Cambridge, 1936. [22] p.
Limited to 100 copies.
———. ———, *The Misadventures of Sherlock Holmes.* Edited by Ellery Queen. Boston: Little, Brown and Co., 1944. p. 336-347.

Other Stories

———. ———, *Holmes and Watson: A Miscellany*, by S. C. Roberts. London: Oxford University Press, 1953. p. 111-123.

6077. ———. "The Death of Cardinal Tosca," *SHJ*, 1, No. 3 (June 1953), 3-6, 18. (The Personality of Sherlock Holmes, pt. 2)
———. ———, *Holmes and Watson: A Miscellany*, by S. C. Roberts. London: Oxford University Press, 1953. p. 22-28.

6078. ———. "The Missing Quarto," *SHJ*, 6, No. 2 (Spring 1963), 40-42.
In this pastiche Holmes is called in to recover a rare copy of *Othello*.

6079. ———. *The Strange Case of the Megatherium Thefts: A Further Memoir of Sherlock Holmes.* Edited from an unpublished Ms. of Dr. Watson by S. C. R. Cambridge: [The University Press], 1945. 14 p. illus.
Limited to 125 copies.
———. ———, *Holmes and Watson: A Miscellany*, by S. C. Roberts. London: Oxford University Press, 1953. p. 124-137.

6080. Robertson, David. "The Abominable Affair of the Fireside Five (Minus Six), or I Might Enjoy Kippling (But How Do You Kipple?)," *SOH*, 3, No. 2 (1969), 4-8.
"Walter Ego and Dr. Weston."

6081. Rosenkjar, Pat. "The Adventure of the Persecuted Millionaire," *SIS*, 1, No. 2 (December 1965), 5-13.

6082. ———. "The Little Affair of the Vatican Cameos," *BSP*, No. 2 (August 1965), 3-4; No. 3 (September 1965), 1-2.

6083. Rosso, Anne Oakins. "The Adventure of the Tired Housewife," *Sherlock Holmes: Master Detective.* Edited by Theodore C. Blegen & E. W. McDiarmid. La Crosse: Printed for the Norwegian Explorers, St. Paul & Minneapolis, 1952. p. 54-61.
Holmes and Watson visit Mrs. Irene Norton.

6084. Rubens, Jeff. "The Doctor's Diagnosis," *The Bridge World*, 33, No. 8 (May 1961), 9-13.

6085. Ruber, P. A. *Dr. Watson Gets a Bow.* [New York: The Candlelight Press, 1962.] [4] p.
Limited to 200 copies.

6086. Russell, Ray. "The Murder of Conan Doyle," *Playboy*, 2, No. 5 (May 1955), 15-16, 39.
A satirical pastiche featuring Foames, Squatson, and Professor Goryarty.

6087. Salo, Paula. "Two Partial Pastiches," *West by One and by One.* San Francisco: Privately Printed, 1965. p. 82-87.

"As told respectively by an advertising copywriter and a hip member of the hard-boiled school." (Subtitle)
Contents: The Adventure of the Giant Rat of Sumatra. - The Caper of the Politician, the Lighthouse, and the Trained Cormorant.

6088. Sellers, Crighton. "The Dilemma of the Distressed Savoyard," *BSJ* [OS], 1, No. 4 (October 1946), 481-495.

6089. Shalet, Stephen A. "The Adventure of the Three Golden Chessmen," *BSJ*, 11, No. 3 (September 1961), 168-173.

6090. Sherbrooke-Walker, R. D. "The Wiltshire Farmer," *SHJ*, 1, No. 4 (December 1953), 4-5.
One of three winners in the Christmas Prooimion Competition for the best imaginary opening paragraphs to a typical Holmes and Watson adventure. For the other winners, see items 5839 and 5846.

6091. "Sherlock Holmes Meets 'The Bohemian': The Adventure of the Editorial Shoe," by A. Nother Doyle [pseud.] *Life*, 50 (October 31, 1907), 521.
———, *BSJ*, 19, No. 4 (December 1969). Printed on back cover.
An advertisement for *The Bohemian* in form of a Sherlockian parody.

6092. *Sherlock Ohms and Dr. Watts Illuminate 'The Case of the Unknown Quantity.'* New York: Promotional Pub. Co., 1958. [16] p.

6093. Shore, Viola Brothers. "A Case of Facsimile," *Ellery Queen's Mystery Magazine*, 12, No. 59 (October 1948), 82-93.
"Shirley Holmes and Jean Watson."

6094. Sikorski, John. "The Adventure of the Five Green Gasogenes," *SOH*, 3, No. 1 (1968), 3-5.

6095. Skinder, Bob. "The Cats of Erstwhileshire," *The Beacon* [Hyannis, Mass.: Cape Cod Community College], 1962.

6096. Smith, Edgar W. "The Disappearance of Mr. James Phillimore: A Pastiche," *A Baker Street Four-Wheeler.* Edited by Edgar W. Smith. [Maplewood, N.J., and New York: The Pamphlet House, 1944.] p. 58-70.
———. ———, *Baker Street and Beyond: Together with Some Trifling Monographs*, by Edgar W. Smith. Morristown, N.J.: The Baker Street Irregulars, 1957. [unpaged]

6097. [Smith, Ernest Bramah.] "S. Holmes," *A Little Flutter*, by Ernest Bramah [pseud.] London: Cassell and Co., [1930]. Chap. 15, p. 165-175.

6098. Smith, George Hudson. "The Adventure of the Wrong Time," *Famous Detective Stories* (October 1955).

"In which a John Watson, M.D., of 1956 receives a cryptic telephone announcement that the game is afoot." (Edgar W. Smith)

6099. Smith, H. Allen. "Friday, 21 September," *Smith's London Journal*. Garden City, N.Y.: Doubleday & Co., 1952. p. 166-170.

————. "I Met Sherlock Holmes," *Mystery Digest*, 3, No. 8 (September-October 1959), 71-75.

A visit to the London Sherlock Holmes Exhibition and an amusing daydream in which the great detective creates havoc while hiding out from Professor Moriarty in the author's home.

6100. Soklow, Jeffrey. "The Adventure of the Expatriate Zebra Collector, or The Cold War Service of Sherlock Holmes," *The Horace Mann Review of Russian Literature* [New York: Horace Mann High School], 1, No. 2 (1964), 9-12.

Part one of a story in which Holmes is involved with a cryptic message and politics.

6101. Sovine, J. W. "The Adventure of the Brimstone Chalice," by Dr. Hill Barton [pseud.] *BSJ Christmas Annual*, No. 4 (1959), 281-291.

6102. ————. "The Adventure of the Command Performance," *BSJ*, 8, No. 1 (January 1958), 17-28.

Holmes is tried in heaven on several counts and then sentenced to return to earth for a thousand years! "And that is why London, today, and the whole wide world are the sweeter for his presence."

6103. Sprague, Jane. "The Jukebox Mystery," Illustrated by Rick Brown. *Scholastic Scope*, 14, No. 1 (February 1, 1971), 8-9.

A high-school student named after his father's favorite detective (Sherlock Holmes) solves the case of the missing records and guitar.

6104. Stafford, T. P. "Misadventures of Sheerluck Gnomes. Misadventure XXCIVL. The Bars of Soap, or The Jew au Jus," *The Modern Detective* [London], 1, No. 1 (March 9, 1898), 8.

"Sheerluck Gnomes and Dr. Potson."

6105. Stanley, Donald. "Holmes Meets 007," *People: The California Weekly* [San Francisco Examiner] (November 29, 1964), 14-15.

————. ————. [San Francisco: The Beaune Press, December 1967.] [8] p. (Vintage No. 3)

"This edition is in two limited series; 222 copies numbered 1 to 221B and 25 copies numbered I to XXV for friends of Donald Stanley."

"Hand set and printed, in Baskerville type, by Shirley & Dean Dickensheet."

6106. Starrett, Vincent. "In Lieu of a Foreword," *Illustrious Client's Case-Book*. Edited by J. N. Williamson and H. B. Williams. [Indianapolis, Ind.: The Illustrious Clients, 1948] p. 1-3.

An anecdote told to the author one afternoon in London by Inspector Stanley Hopkins.

6107. ————. "Monologue in Baker Street," *BSJ Christmas Annual*, No. 1 (1956), 5-6.

————. ————. [New York]: The Mermaid Press [Fridolf Johnson], [1960]. [4] p.

Limited to 150 copies.

————. ————, "Christmases Remembered," by Vincent Starrett. *Gourmet*, 26, No. 12 (December 1966), 122-124.

Holmes retraces Watson's thought sequence during a fireside chat on Christmas Eve.

6108. ————. *The Unique Hamlet: A Hitherto Unchronicled Adventure of Mr. Sherlock Holmes*. Chicago, Ill.: Privately printed for the friends of Walter H. Hill, Christmas 1920. 39 p.

Limited to 33 copies.

————. "The Adventure of the Unique Hamlet," *221B: Studies in Sherlock Holmes*. Edited by Vincent Starrett. New York: The Macmillan Co., 1940. p. 88-108.

————. "The Unique Hamlet," *The Misadventures of Sherlock Holmes*. Edited by Ellery Queen. Boston: Little, Brown and Co., 1944. p. 48-65.

————. *Den Forsvundne Hamlet: Sherlock Holmes løser et bibliofilt problem*. Oversat af Grete Jacobsen. Med forord af Tage la Cour. København: Rosenkilde og Bagger, 1952. [48] p.

————. "The Adventure of the Unique 'Hamlet': Being an Unrecorded Adventure of Mr. Sherlock Holmes," *The Private Life of Sherlock Holmes*, by Vincent Starrett. Revised and enlarged. The University of Chicago Press, [1960]. p. 137-155.

————. "The Adventure of the Unique 'Hamlet' " *The Saint Mystery Magazine*, 21, No. 1 (July 1964), 31-47.

" 'The Unique Hamlet' is Vincent Starrett's most devout achievement in a lifelong 'career of Conan Doyle idolatry.' It is unanimously considered one of the finest pure pastiches of Sherlock Holmes ever written." (Ellery Queen)

6109. Steele, Frederic Dorr. *The Adventure of the Missing Artist: Sherlock Holmes Solves a Mystery and Discovers Something New*. [Illustrated by the author.] Pittsburgh, Pa.: Hydraulic Press, 1967. [6] p. (A Baker Street Christmas Stocking, No. 13)

6110. ———. "The Adventure of the Missing Hatrack: A Story of Mr. Sherlock Holmes," by F. D. S., with illustrations by the author. *The Players Bulletin* [New York] (October 15, 1926), 1-5.
———. ———, *The Players' Book: A Half-Century of Fact, Feeling, Fun and Folklore.* Edited by Henry Wysham Lanier. New York: The Players, 1938. p. 189-195.
———. ———, *BSJ*, 13, No. 4 (December 1963), 238-241. (Incunabulum)

6111. ———. "The Adventure of the Murdered Art Editor: A Reminiscence of Mr. Sherlock Holmes," *Spoofs.* Edited by Richard Butler Glaenzer. New York: Robert M. McBride & Co., 1933. p. 133-142.
———. ———, *The Misadventures of Sherlock Holmes.* Edited by Ellery Queen. Boston: Little, Brown and Co., 1944. p. 306-312.

6112. ———. "The Attempted Murder of Malcolm Duncan: A Reminiscence of Mr. Sherlock Holmes," by John Watson, M.D., plus F. D. S. *The Players Bulletin* [New York] (June 1, 1932), 15-18.

6113. [Stein, Aaron Marc.] *Drop Dead*, by George Bagby [pseud.] Garden City, N.Y.: Published for the Crime Club by Doubleday & Co., 1949. 189 p.
"A mystery novel, one of whose leading characters is an eleven-year-old amateur detective, Richard Holmes, with the blood of his grandfather hot in his veins." (Edgar W. Smith)

6114. Stevens, Shane. "The Final Adventure," *Ellery Queen's Mystery Magazine*, 53, No. 2 (February 1969), 99-104.
"A sacrilegious and rather gruesome (to Irregulars) tale of Holmes and Watson, possibly intended to put an end to the literature on the subject." (Julian Wolff)

6115. Stock, Robert T. "The Bungling Detective," Illustrated by Don Wolfe. *The Scholastic* [Notre Dame University], 91, No. 9 (November 4, 1949), 14-16, 29.

6116. Stone, Daniel B. ["Review of *The Diabetic's Handbook* (2nd Edition)"], *A.M.A. Archives of Internal Medicine*, 105 (March 1960), 500-501.
———, *BSJ*, 10, No. 4 (October 1960), 254.
Holmes and Watson review the above book by Anthony M. Sindoni, Jr.

6117. *A Study in Scarlet and Pink: Being the Chronicle of How the Mark of Joseph Magnin Was Left.* [San Francisco]: Joseph Magnin, [August 1962]. [7] p.
A Sherlockian advertisement prepared for those attending the American Bar Association meeting in San Francisco.

6118. Sutherland, John. "The Struldbrugg

Reaction," *The Magazine of Fantasy and Science Fiction*, 27, No. 1 (July 1964), 91-108.
"Haricot Bones and Dr. Dawson."

6119. Taylor, Bert Leston. "The Adventure of the Double Santa Claus," *Illustrious Client's Second Case-Book.* Edited by J. N. Williamson. [Indianapolis, Ind.: The Illustrious Clients, 1949.] p. 15-18.
Written in 1904 by B. L. T. and discovered by H. B. Williams.

6120. Temple, Michael. "Misdirected Martyrs," *Shallowdale: Ourselves, Our Friends and Our Village.* London: Herbert Jenkins Ltd., 1922. Chap. 17, p. 271-290.
Mr. Holmes, the village schoolmaster, tries to emulate Sherlock in a village where the most serious crime is stealing chickens.

6121. Thierry, James Francis. *The Adventure of the Eleven Cuff-Buttons.* New York: The Neale Pub. Co., 1918. 190 p.
"Being one of the exciting episodes in the career of the famous detective Hemlock Holmes, as recorded by his friend Dr. Watson." (Subtitle)

6122. Thrasher, Harry. "Case of the Worn Riding Crop," *Campus Detroiter: The Student Magazine of the University of Detroit*, 5, No. 4 (April 1964), 14-15.
"The sleuth of Baker Street discovers the inside dope on U-D's Riding Club."

6123. Todd, Peter. "The Missing Millionaire: An Adventure of Herlock Sholmes," *Tom Merry's Own.* London: Mandeville Publications, [n.d.] p. 56-61.
"Herlock Sholmes and Dr. Jotson of Shaker Street."

6124. Tomashefsky, Steven. "The Adventure of Isadora Persano," *BSJ*, 16, No. 4 (December 1966), 209-214.
"Sherlock Ohms and Dr. Watts."

6125. [———.] "The Colossal Schemes of Baron Maupertuis," by S'ian Lemming [pseud.] *BSP*, No. 9-10 (March-April 1966), 5-6; No. 11 (May 1966), 3-4; No. 12 (June 1966), 2-3; No. 13 (July 1966), 1-2; No. 14 (August 1966), 3; No. 15 (September 1966), 5; No. 16 (October 1966), 3-4.
———. ———. Kingston, Ontario: The Remarkable Invention Press, 1967. [18] p.
"Sherlock Ohms and Dr. Watts."

6126. [———.] "Doctor Negative: An Adventure of Sherlock Ohms and Dr. Watts," by S'ian Lemming [pseud.] *SIS*, 1, No. 2 (December 1965), 28-34.

6127. [Townsend, Larry.] *The Sexual Adventures of Sherlock Holmes*, [by] J. Watson. [New York: The Traveller's Companion (The Olympia Press), 1971.]

[220] p. (The Other Traveller, TC-511)
Contents: Introduction. - A Study in Lavender Lace. - The Queer Affair of the Greek Interpreter. - The Final Solution.
Reviews: *Screw*, No. 151 (January 24, 1972), 17 (Michael Perkins); *SHJ*, 10, No. 3 (Winter 1971), 101 (Lord Donegall).

6128. Twain, Mark. "A Double-Barrelled Detective Story," [Illustrated by Lucius Hitchcock]. *Harper's Monthly Magazine*, 104 (January 1902), 254-270; (February 1902), 429-441.
———. ———. Illustrated by Lucius Hitchcock. New York and London: Harper & Brothers, 1902. 179 p.
———. ———, ["Slightly condensed version"] *The Misadventures of Sherlock Holmes*. Edited by Ellery Queen. Boston: Little, Brown and Co., 1944. p. 123-163.
———. *Plus fort que Sherlock Holmès*. Traduit par François de Gail. Paris: Société dv Mercvre de France, 1907. p. 1-128. (Collection d'Auteurs Etrangers)
———. *En indiviklet Detektivhistorie og andre Fortaellinger*. Frederiksberg Biblioteks Forlag, 1914. p. 7-98.
———. "En skarpladt Detektivhistorie," *Muntre Historier*. Oversat af Kurt Kreutzfeld. København: Carit Andersens Forlag, [n.d.] p. 46-108.
———. "Sherlock Holmes, derrotado," *Revista Literaria Novelas y Cuentos* [Madrid], No. 176 (May 1932), 3-16.
"Mark Twain wrote *A Double Barrelled Detective Story* as a partial satire on the melodramatic detective fiction of his day. Apparently, he was greatly amused at the casual manner in which the renowned mystery writer, Conan Doyle, 'killed off' the celebrated Sherlock Holmes in one book, only to bring the great detective back to life again in the next. He must also have been slightly irritated at times by the smug manner in which Sherlock Holmes always confounded his enemies and emerged omnipotently triumphant at the end of each story. So Mr. Twain sat down and wrote *A Double Barrelled Detective Story*, in which he placed Detective Holmes in a most uncomfortable but highly amusing situation and confounds *him* for a change!" (Robert St. Clair)
For a stage adaptation by Robert St. Clair, see item 5262.

6129. Upward, Allen. "The Adventure of the Stolen Doormat," *The Wonderful Career of Ebenezer Lobb*, related by himself. Edited, with an appreciation by Allen Upward. London: Hurst and Blackett Ltd., 1900. p. 235-248.

6130. Utechin, Nicholas. "The Adventures of Porlock Moans," *SOS*, 4, No. 2 (July 1970), 6-10.
"Porlock Moans and Potsdam of Bacon Street."

6131. Walsh, William J. "The Adventure of the Harassed Prussian," *SOS*, 3, No. 2 (July 1969), 7-14.

6132. Ward, Norman W. "Colonel Warburton's Madness," *The Best of the Pips*. Westchester County, N.Y.: The Five Orange Pips, 1955. p. 59-73.

6133. Watkins, Alan. "Holmes in Whitehall," *New Statesman*, 75 (March 15, 1968), 322. (Spotlight on Politics)

6134. Watt, T. S. "The Adventure of the Missing Laureate," *Punch*, 223 (November 19, 1952), 623-624.

6135. ———. "The Adventure of Missing Laureate: II. In the Shadow of Thomas Hardy," *Punch*, 223 (December 10, 1952), 707-708.

6136. ———. "Giants in These Days—A Fantasy," *Punch*, 225 (July 6, 1953), 7-9.
A pastiche satirizing Watson's preoccupation with socialized medicine.

6137. Weiss, David A. "The Celestial Pastiche," *BSJ*, [OS], 3, No. 2 (April 1948), 218-223.
An account of the Avenging Angels' annual meeting in "The Land of the Saints" during which the Scion Society president, Angel No. 1 (also known as Gabriel), announces that Angel No. 103, author of such historical novels as *The White Company* and *Micah Clarke*, is the winner of the annual pastiche contest.

6138. Wellman, Manly Wade. "But Our Hero Was Not Dead," *Argosy* [New York], 309, No. 6 (August 9, 1941), 62-65.
———. "The Man Who Was Not Dead," *The Misadventures of Sherlock Holmes*. Edited by Ellery Queen. Boston: Little, Brown and Co., 1944. p. 348-356.
"One of the last adventures of Mr. Sherlock Holmes in which the author tells how England was saved by the insight of an old gentleman who trapped a gang of Nazi spies who had parachuted into England. They had the misfortune to call at the house where old Mr. Holmes was living in retirement." (Edith Fowke)

6139. ———, and Wade Wellman. "The Adventure of the Martian Client," *Fantasy and Science Fiction*, 37, No. 6 (December 1969), 62-72.
During H. G. Wells's Martian invasion, Holmes, Watson, and Professor Challenger lure one of the invaders to 221B.

6140. Wells, Carolyn, "The Adventure of the Clothes-Line," *Century Magazine*, 90 (May 1915), 153-158.
———. ———, *The Misadventures of Sherlock Holmes*. Edited by Ellery Queen.

Boston: Little, Brown and Co., 1944. p. 39-47.

A burlesque detective story introducing Holmes as president of the Society of Infallible Detectives.

6141. Wells, J. W. "His First Bow," *Ellery Queen's Mystery Magazine*, 18, No. 97 (December 1951), 47-60.

6142. [Whitaker, Arthur.] ["The Man Who Was Wanted: A Fragment," by Sir Arthur Conan Doyle], *Conan Doyle: His Life and Art*, by Hesketh Pearson. London: Methuen & Co., [1943]. p. 98-100.
———. ———, *A Baker Street Four-Wheeler*. Edited by Edgar W. Smith. [Maplewood, N.J., and New York: The Pamphlet House, 1944.] p. 11-13.
Extracts from the "lost" manuscript whose authorship was mistakenly attributed to Dr. Watson's literary agent.

6143. [———.] "The Case of the Man Who Was Wanted," by Sir Arthur Conan Doyle [sic]. Illustrated by Robert Fawcett. *Cosmopolitan*, 125, No. 2 (August 1948), 48-51, 92-99.
———. ———, *The Sunday Dispatch* [London, Manchester, and Edinburgh] (January 2, 9, 16, 1949). illus.
———. ———. [Pittsburgh: Privately produced by Robert H. Schutz, 1966.] 14 p.
Reviews: *BSJ* [OS], 3, No. 4 (October 1948), 399-400, 444, 447-448, 459-462 (Edgar W. Smith) (Christopher Morley) (Russell McLauchlin); (NS), 3, No. 2 (April 1953), 121-123 (Edgar W. Smith); *Chicago Tribune* (August 15 and September 19, 1948) (Vincent Starrett); *London Dispatch* (February 27, 1949) (John Bingham), and reprinted in *CPBook*, 1, No. 2 (Fall 1964), 36; *New York Times* (September 13, 1942), 16, and reprinted in *CPBook*, 2, No. 7-8 (Winter-Spring 1966), 159-160; *New York Times* (September 28, 1942), 16, and reprinted in *CPBook*, 2, No. 7-8 (Winter-Spring 1966), 157-158; *The Public Papers of a Bibliomaniac*, by Charles Honce (Mount Vernon: The Golden Eagle Press, 1942), 159-164; *San Francisco Chronicle, This World* (November 29, 1942), 19 (Anthony Boucher); *SHJ*, 6, No. 2 (Spring 1963), 62-63 (Dennis L. Bird) (Nathan L. Bengis); *SHJ*, 6, No. 3 (Winter 1963), 96 (Adrian M. Conan Doyle); *The Trib* [*Chicago Tribune*], 30 (March 1949), 4, and reprinted in *CPBook*, 1, No. 1 (Summer 1964), 13; *VH*, 3, No. 2 (April 1969), 12 (Francis C. Brown).

6144. White, Alain C. "The Adventure of the Strange Sound," Problem by Murray Marble. *The Good Companion Chess Problem Club* [Philadelphia], 1, No. 6 (April 1, 1914). [8] p.
———. ———, *Flights of Fancy in the Chess World*. Leeds, England: Whitehead & Miller, 1919.

———. ———, *BSP*, No. 8 (February 1966), 1-4.
A chess problem presented through a pastiche. Dr. Watson (without reference to the game!) has been knighted.

6145. White, Frank Marshall. "The Recrudescence of Sherlock Holmes," *Life*, 24 (October 18, 1894), 250-251.
———. ———, With an introduction by E. R. Hagemann. *BSJ*, 19, No. 4 (December 1969), 224-226.
A pastiche describing the meeting of Holmes and Watson in New York.

6146. White, Richard W. "The Affair of the Spindled Manager," *Bell Telephone Magazine*, 46, No. 4 (July-August 1967), 26-29.
———. ———, *Records Management Journal*, 5, No. 4 (Winter 1967), 16-20.
"One man's reaction to the increasing volume of paper work."

6147. Wilde, Percival. *Design for Murder: A Novel*. New York: Random House, [1941]. 274 p.
———. ———. London: Victor Gollancz Ltd., [1942]. 152 p.
A mystery novel with Sherlockian flavorings.

6148. Williams, Stephen Daniel. *The Adventures of Shylar Homes*. New York: Carlton Press, Inc., [1966]. 52 p. (A Geneva Book)
Contents: Introduction. - The Adventure of the Bradley Tragedy. - The Adventure of the Pendleton Jewels. - The Adventure of the Missing Bullet.
Three tales about Shylar Homes and Dr. John Whatley of 21B Barlow Street, Houston, Texas.
The second tale was also published in *BSJ*, 17, No. 4 (December 1967), 226-232.
Reviews: *BSP*, No. 24 (June 1967), 5 (Bruce Kennedy); *SHJ*, 8, No. 1 (Winter 1966), 29 (Lord Donegall); *SOS*, 1, No. 5 (June 1967), 2-3 (Bruce Dettman).

6149. Williamson, Jerry Neal. "The Adventure of the Bugged Bird: A Christmas Story Like Without Slush," *BSJ Christmas Annual*, No. 5 (1960), 261-264.
"Sheerback Tones and Bopson."
Winner of the 3rd annual Morley-Montgomery Memorial Award for the best contribution to *BSJ* in 1960.

6150. ———. "The Adventure of the Politician, the Lighthouse, and the Trained Cormorant," *Illustrious Client's Second Case-Book*. Edited by J. N. Williamson. [Indianapolis, Ind.: The Illustrious Clients, 1949.] p. 55-61.

6151. ———. "Bopping It in Bohemia, or Sheerbach Tones in Basin Street," *Ellery*

Queen's Mystery Magazine, 37, No. 1 (January 1961), 40-42.

"The most irreverent, blasphemous, and sacrilegious pastiche ever written of Sherlock Holmes." (Ellery Queen)

6152. ———. "The Gig of the Man (with the Twist)," *BSJ,* 16, No. 1 (March 1966), 10-17.

"Apologies to John H. Watson, M.D., *Et Cetera*—It's What's Happening!"

Includes a three-page glossary to the teen-age terms used in the story "for those who may think young, but not *that* young."

"Sure-They-Lock Homez and Doc Whooson."

6153. ———. "The Terrible Death of Crosby, the Banker: A Sherlock Holmes Pastiche," *Illustrious Client's Case-Book.* Edited by J. N. Williamson and H. B. Williams. [Indianapolis, Ind.: The Illustrious Clients, 1948.] p. 58-66.

6154. [Willock, A. Dewar.] "A Study in Red," by A. Donan Coyle [pseud.] *Fun,* 56 (July 6, 1892), 8.

———. ———, [With an introduction by Edward S. Lauterbach]. *BSJ,* 15, No. 1 (March 1965), 34-36.

6155. [Wilmunen, Jon.] "The Adventure of Sir Edward Pins: An Adventure of Neville Boyles and Dr. Watchpot," by Acorn N. Doyle [pseud.] Illustrated by Jon Wilmunen. *BSJ,* 15, No. 3 (September 1965), 139-141.

6156. ———. "The Adventure of the Speckled Hand: Another Watchpot-Neville Boyles Adventure," by Acorn N. Doyle. [Illustrated by Jon Wilmunen.] *BSJ,* 16, No. 1 (March 1966), 30-32.

6157. ———. "The Adventure of the Tarred Captain: A New Watchpot-Neville Boyles Story," by Acorn N. Doyle. *The Gamebag,* No. 2 (1966), 11-13.

6158. Wilson, Alan. "The Adventure of the Tired Captain," *SHJ,* 4, No. 1 (Winter 1958), 8-11; 4, No. 2 (Spring 1959), 48-51.

6159. ———. " 'The Adventure of the Paradal Chamber': A Further Problem of Sherlock Holmes," *SHJ,* 5, No. 2 (Spring 1961), 45-50; 5, No. 3 (Winter 1961), 78-83.

6160. Wilson, David. "Sherlock Holmes in a Wood," *Anecdotes of Big Cats and Other Beasts.* London: Methuen & Co., [1910]. p. 19-26.

6161. Wilson, John A. "The Case of the Two Coptic Patriarchs," *BSJ* [OS], 4, No. 1 (January 1949), 74-85.

6162. Wolff, Julian. *A Case of Scotch.* New York: [Privately Produced], 1959. [12] p. illus.

"A delectable blend of the distillations of Sherlock Holmes and Colin St. Andrew MacThrockle Glencannon, to be washed down for Christmas by Duggan's Dew of Kirkintilloch." (Edgar W. Smith)

6163. [———.] *Still Waters.* [New York: Privately Printed, 1960.] [8] p.

"A trifling brochure containing a previously unrecorded account of Sherlock Holmes's involvement with spirits."

6164. Yell, E. M. "The Lost Professor," by Sir A. Donan Coyle. *The Shriek & Other Stories,* by E. M. Yell, Sir A. Donan Coyle, Henry O. [and] Kudyard Ripling. London: Stanley Paul & Co., 1923. p. 23-35.

"Herlock Sholmes and Dr. Potson."

6165. Zimler, Robert and Michael. "Home Office: 221B Baker Street, or A Study in Cement," *Ellery Queen's Mystery Magazine,* 41, No. 2 (February 1963), 61-77.

"An actor, qualified by having played the part, sets up in business as Sherlock Holmes—complete with Watson." (Julian Wolff)

F Children's Stories and Picture Books

6166. Brooks, Walter R. *Freddy, the Detective.* With illustrations by Kurt Wiese. New York: Alfred A. Knopf, 1932. 263 p.

———. ———. New York: Scholastic Book Services, 1963. 153 p. (Tab Books, TX162)

"A delightful detective story about the beloved characters on Mr. Bean's farm. The pig, Freddy, stimulated by reading about Sherlock Holmes, sets up in business as a detective. Recommended for young Sherlockians." (Peter E. Blau)

6167. Fulton, Mary J. *Detective Arthur on the Scent.* Pictures by Aurelius Battaglia. New York: Golden Press, [1971]. [unpaged] (A Golden Fragrance Book)

6168. Heath, Lester. *The Case of the Aluminum Crutch.* New York: Dell Pub. Co., [September 1963]. 119 p. (Dell Seal Books, No. 1110)

At head of title: The Casebook of Sherlock Jones.

6169. Holding, James. *Sherlock on the Trail.* Illustrated by Aliki. New York: William Morrow & Co., 1964. [30] p. (Morrow Junior Books)

"When Sherlock the bloodhound got a whiff of something, such as an old sneaker, he could follow the scent for miles. His biggest test came the day his mistress

Marjory discovered that her piggy bank was missing, and he had to use his wonderful smeller to help her and a policeman find the robber's lair." (Dust jacket)

6170. Merow, Erva. *Sherlock Bones: Dogtective and His Many Disguises Solves...The Case of the Stolen Pearls.* [New York: James & Jonathan, Inc., 1961.] [14] p. illus. (Peek-a-Book, No. 3363)
———. *Sherlock Bones and His Many Disguises.* [London: W. Foulsham & Co., n.d.] [14] p. illus. (Bonnie Novelty Books, No. 53)

6171. Platt, Kin. *Big Max: An I Can Read Mystery.* With pictures by Robert Lopshire. New York, Evanston, and London: Harper & Row, [1965]. 64 p.
Big Max, the world's greatest detective (a caricature of Sherlock Holmes), travels by umbrella to help the King of Pooka Pooka find Jumbo, his prize elephant who has mysteriously disappeared. For seven- and eight-year-olds *and* Sherlockians.

6172. Titus, Eve. *Basil of Baker Street.* Illustrated by Paul Galdone. New York: McGraw-Hill Book Co., [1958]. 96 p.
———. ———. New York: Washington Square Press, [August 1970]. 112 p. illus. (An Archway Paperback, No. 29303)
"A delightful book for children (four to seven) and for Baker Street Irregulars (seven to eighty-four) about a detective mouse who lives with his friend Dr. Dawson in the cellar of 221B." (Edgar W. Smith) Miss Titus claims that the book was actually written by Basil's colleague and close associate, Dr. David Q. Dawson, and that she was merely the translator.

6173. ———. *Basil and the Lost Colony: A Basil of Baker Street Mystery.* Illustrated by Paul Galdone. New York: McGraw-Hill Book Co., [1964]. [96] p.
"Another adventure of the Mouster, a shaggy mouse story, suitable for young Irregulars from six to eighty-six, featuring the Adorable Snowmouse and mentioning several thinly-disguised Irregulars." (Julian Wolff)

6174. ———. *Basil and the Pygmy Cats: A Basil of Baker Street Mystery.* Illustrated by Paul Galdone. New York: McGraw-Hill Book Co., [1971]. 96 p.
Review: Horn Book Magazine, 48 (April 1972), 149-150 (V. H.).

G *Comic Books and Strips*

6175. *The Adventure of the Baker Street*

Spirit, by Jon Wilmunen. [Buhl, Minn.: The Gamekeepers of Northern Minnesota, December 1970.] 1 p.
Issued in place of the author's annual *Gamebag* (item 4215).

6176. "The Adventures of Chubb-Lock Homes," *Comic Cuts* [London] (November 18, 1893-September 1894). 33 issues.
Reviews: SHJ, 10, No. 3 (Winter 1971), 94-96 (Michael Pointer).

6177. "Baker Street Mysteriet," af Dr. Watsons optengnelser, ved Kaj Engholm. *Årbog 1966.* Udgivet af Poe-Klubben. København: Spektrum. 1966. p. 50-53.

6178. "Captain Marvel and Mr. Tawny's Detective Case," *Captain Marvel Adventures,* 18, No. 108 (May 1950), 37-45.
"Mr. Tawny, the talking tiger, leads a quite ordinary life as a worker and home owner. And like you and I, yearning to break up the monotony, he takes up a new role as a modern Sherlock Holmes. With Captain Marvel as his 'Doctor Watson,' Mr. Tawny plays the part of a mastermind sleuth, courting thrilling adventure and danger."

6179. *Daffydils,* by Tad. New York: Cupples & Leon Co., 1911. [41] p.
Reprinted from *The New York Evening Journal.*
"Quick Watson the needle!"

6180. "If Sherlock Holmes Were to Investigate...That Barber Shop Murder," *Sick,* 1, No. 2 (October 1960), 19-21.
A twenty-panel cartoon strip.

6181. *Hawkshaw the Detective,* by Gus Mager. Akron, Ohio: The Saalfield Pub. Co., 1917 [Press Pub. Co., New York World, c.1916]. [24] p.
Contents: He Takes Pity on a Poor Old Invalid and Drives Him to His Destination. - The Strange Case of the Lost Letter and the Postponed Journey to Rio de Janeiro. - He Has to Have a Vacation Once in a While, So Why Not Now? - The Amusing Episode of the Unexpected Letter and the Altered Diagram. - When You Are in Prison There's Nothing Like Having Good Friends on the Outside. - The Strange Case of the Forged Letter of Recommendation and the Musical Convict. - The Thrilling Narrative of the Escaping Prisoners and the Missing Row Boat.

6182. "Hawkshaw the Detective," by Watso. *The Captain and the Kids,* 4, No. 4 (March 1943), 1-36.
Contents: The Odd Affair of the Dummy Cracksman. - A Lesson in Vigilance. - The Unwritten Story or Maiden Beware!- Hawkshaw's Triumph! - The Peculiar Circumstance of the Scattered Toothpicks. - The End of the Case of the Scattered Tooth-

picks. - The Phonograph Test. - The Affair of the Miser. - The Affair of the Bootleg Oil. - The Droll Dénouement of the Basher Social. - The Affair of the Basher Social. - The Case of the Dummy Hands. - Taking Sugar off a Baby. - The Peculiar Episode of the Snoozer. - The Circumstance of the Watchful Guinea Fowl. - The Episode of the Telescope. - Extra! The Great Hawkshaw Foiled! - Bingo! - The Incident of the Erratic Weather-Vane. - The Hilarious Interlude of the Wonder Ape. - The Morganbilt Case. - The Baffling Episode of the Midget Twins. - The Supernatural Raider. - The Episode of the Gallivanting Bath-tub. - The Incident at the Exposition Grounds. - Somebody Always Pays. - The Odd Dénouement of the Shackamaxon Plot. - The Strange Case of the Ambitious Watchman. - Hounding the Phantom. - The Amateur Star Gazer.

6183. ———, by Watso. *The Captain and the Kids. Comics on Parade*, 5, No. 1 (June 1945), 8-9.
    Contents: A Lesson in Caution. - The Getaway.

6184. ———, by Watso. *The Captain and the Kids. Comics on Parade*, Special Issue (July 1946). Inside of front and back covers.
    Contents: Winners. - Tweet-Tweet. - The Absent-Minded Professor.

6185. "The Hound of the Basketville, Starring Sherlock Mouse and Doctor Goofy," *Walt Disney's Comics and Stories*, 25, No. 12 (September 1965), 1-10 (The Walt Disney Theater)

6186. *The Hound of the Baskervilles.* [Illustrated by H. C. Kiefer.] *Classics Illustrated*, No. 33 (January 1947). [48] p.
    Cover title: The Adventures of Sherlock Holmes.

6187. "Hugh Dunnit—in the Case of the Missing Ink Blot!" *Madhouse*, 1, No. 3 (October 1957), 15-18.

6188. "Mickey Mouse in The Mysterious Pill Plot," *Walt Disney's Comics and Stories*, 12, No. 11 (August 1952), 43-48.

6189. *New Adventures of Sherlock Holmes.* [Illustrated by Frank Giacoia.] *Dell Exciting Adventure*, No. 1169 (March-May 1961). [32] p.
    Title from cover.
    Contents: The Case of the Deadly Inheritance. - The Tunnel Scheme.

6190. ———. [Illustrated by Frank Giacoia.] *Dell Exciting Adventure*, No. 1245 (January 1962).
    Title from cover.
    Contents: The Derelict Ship. - The Safe Robber. - The Cunning Assassin.

6191. "Peanuts," by Charles Schulz. *The New York Herald Tribune* (August 28, 1964).
    ———, *CPBook*, 1, No. 2 (Fall 1964), 23.
    Two comic strips centering on Houn and an adaptation of another Holmes story.

6192. ———, *The New York Post* (August 27, 1968).
    ———, *CPBook*, 4, No. 16 (February 1969), 322.
    A "blanket-carrying" Sherlock Holmes.

6193. "Sherlock," by Gahan Wilson. *Playboy*, 6, No. 12 (December 1959), 91-94.
    ———. Reprinted "with the compliments of Peter E. Blau." [4] p.
    Cartoons and vignettes relating "some little-known misadventures of the great detective."

6194. [———], by Gahan Wilson. *Playboy*, 15, No. 4 (April 1968), 193.
    A full-page colored cartoon of Holmes trying on a new outfit.

6195. "Sherlock Hoax with Dr. Puton in The Final Problem," by Jon V. Wilmunen. *The Gamebag*, No. 4 (December 1968), 16-17.

6196. "Sherlock Holmes," Written by Edith Meiser and illustrated by Frank Giacoia. *New York Herald Tribune* (March 1-April 18, 1954).
    Based on Thor.
    Review: *BSJ*, 4, No. 2 (April 1954), 127-128 (Edgar W. Smith)

6197. ———, Written by Edith Meiser and illustrated by Frank Giacoia. *New York Herald Tribune* (March 26-May 31, 1956). 67 comic strips.
    Based on Silv.

6198. ———, Written by Edith Meiser and illustrated by Frank Giacoia. *New York Herald Tribune* (June 1-July 15, 1956). 41 comic strips.
    Based on Bery.

6199. ———, Written by Edith Meiser and illustrated by Frank Giacoia. *New York Herald Tribune* (July 16-September 12, 1956). 58 comic strips.
    Based on Devi.

6200. ———, Written by Edith Meiser and illustrated by Frank Giacoia. *New York Herald Tribune* (September 13-November 17, 1956). 66 comic strips.
    Based on Fina.

6201. *Sherlock Holmes.* Vol. 1, No. 1 (October 1955). [32] p. (Charlton Comics Group)
    Contents: Sherlock Holmes in the Final Curtain. - Sherlock Holmes in Love Thy Neighbor. - Sherlock Holmes and the Star of the East.

Comic Books

6202. *Sherlock Holmes and the Hound of the Baskervilles.* [London: The Amalgamated Press Ltd., 1956?] 64 p. (Super Detective Library, No. 78)
Also contains: Sherlock Holmes and the Missing Heiress.

6203. *Sherlock Holmes and the Mystery of the Red-Headed League.* [London: The Amalgamated Press Ltd., 1956] 64 p. (Super Detective Library, No. 65)
Also contains: Sherlock Holmes and the Case of the Greek Interpreter.

6204. *Sherlock Holmes and the Mystery of the Thames Afire.* [London: The Amalgamated Press Ltd., 1956?] 64 p. (Super Detective Library, No. 74)
Also contains: Sherlock Holmes and a Scandal in Bohemia.

6205. "Sherlock Holmes: The Adventure of the Haunted House," by Jon V. Wilmunen. *The Gamebag,* No. 3 (1967), 1-18.

6206. "Sherlock Holmes: The Adventure of the Murdered Duke," by Jon V. Wilmunen. *The Gamebag,* No. 1 (1965), 1-13.

6207. "Sherlock Holmes: The Adventure of the Pierce-Randall Report," by Jon V. Wilmunen. *The Gamebag,* No. 2 (1966), 1-10.

6208. "Sherlock Holmes: The Adventure of the Remarkable Worm," by Jon V. Wilmunen. *The Gamebag,* No. 4 (1968), 1-15.

6209. "Sherlock Holmes: The Adventure of the Whitechapel Madonna," by Jon V. Wilmunen. *The Gamebag,* No. 5 (1969), 1-10.

6210. "Sherlock Holmes: The Strange Case of the Queen's Pupils," by Charles O'Hegarty and Michel Choquette. With engravings by Frank Spring. *National Lampoon,* 1, No. 16 (July 1971), 52-58.
———, *The Best of National Lampoon,* No. 1 (1972), [unpaged].

6211. *Sherlock Holmes und das Geheimnis der blauen Erbse* [Sherlock Holmes and the Secret of the Blue Carbuncle], von Volker Ernsting. [Frankfurt]: Verlag Bärmeier und Nikel, [1971]. 53 p. (B & N Comic)
A series of thirty-five comic strips that first appeared in the German TV magazine *Hör Zu.*

6212. "Sherlock Holmes: Walter Marino. . . Death at the Opera," *Spectacular Stories Magazine.* No. 4 (July 1950), 22-31.
"Walter Marino led one of the strangest criminal careers ever recorded in the crime annals scrupulously kept by the master detective, Sherlock Holmes!"

6213. "Sherlock, the Monk, and Chuck in 'Confidence No End,' " *Fawcett's Funny Animals,* 9, No. 53 (September 1947), 21-26.

6214. "Sherlock, the Monk, and Chuck [in] 'Entrance to an Exit,' " *Fawcett's Funny Animals,* 7, No. 41 (August 1946), 35-38.

6215. "Sherlock, the Monk, and Chuck [in] 'Jump to Conclusions,' " *Fawcett's Funny Animals,* 9, No. 49 (May 1947), 18-24.

6216. "Shermlock Shomes!" Written by Harvey Kurtzman. Drawn by Bill Elder. *Mad,* 1, No. 2 (1953), 1-8.
———, *Inside Mad.* New York: Ballantine Books, 1955. p. 158-181. (No. 124)

6217. "Shermlock Shomes in The Hound of the Basketballs!" by Bill Elder. *Mad,* 1, No. 7 (October-November 1953), 1-8.
———, *Mad,* 1, No. 16 (October 1954), 1-8.
———, *William M. Gaines' The Brothers Mad.* New York: Ballantine Books, October 1958. p. 52-57. (No. 494K)
———, ———. Revised ed. New York: Ballantine Books, December 1963. p. 52-75. (No. U2105)
"Shermlock Shomes and Dr. Whatsit of 2-1 / 2 Baker Street."

6218. *Shylar Homes* [*in*] *The Adventure of the Missing Bullet,* from *The Adventures of Shylar Homes,* by Stephen D. Williams. [New York: Carlton Press, 1966.] 8 p.

6219. " 'The Sign of the 4,' " Illustrated by Zansky. *3 Famous Mysteries. Classics Illustrated,* No. 21 [n.d.], 1-29.
Also contains: The Flayed Hand. - The Murders in the Rue Morgue.

6220. "Spylot Bones," *Leading Comics,* No. 15 (Summer 1945), 10-16.

6221. *A Study in Scarlet.* [Illustrated by Seymour Moskowitz.] *Classics Illustrated,* No. 110 (August 1953). [48] p.
Also contains: The Adventure of the Speckled Band.
Also published in a Greek edition (Classics Illustrated, No. 98).

Appendix

Indexes

Appendix

Hats	Hats of M. Dulac
Haun	Haunted Library
Innk	Innkeeper's Clerk
Inta	Intarsia Box
Late	Late Mr. Faversham
Limp	Limping Man
Litt	Little Hangman
LosD	Lost Dutchman
LosH	Lost Holiday
LosL	Lost Locomotive
ManB	Man with the Broken Face
MazB	Mazarine Blue
MisH	Missing Huntsman
MisT	Missing Tenants
MrFa	Mr. Fairlie's Final Journey
Mosa	Mosaic Cylinders
Norc	Norcross Riddle
Obri	Obrisset Snuff Box
Orie	Orient Express
Para	Paralytic Mendicant
Penn	Penny Magenta
Perf	Perfect Husband
Prae	Praed Street Irregulars
Prop	Proper Comma
Purl	Purloined Periapt
RedL	Red Leech
Rema	Remarkable Worm
RetN	Retired Novelist
Rico	Ricoletti of the Club Foot
Rydb	Rydberg Numbers
7Pas	Seven Passengers
7Sis	Seven Sisters
Shap	Shaplow Millions
6Sil	Six Silver Spiders
Snit	Snitch in Time
Soth	Sotheby Salesman
Spur	Spurious *Tamerlane*
Ston	Stone of Scone
SusA	Sussex Archers
Swed	Swedenborg Signatures
3Red	Three Red Dwarfs
Tott	Tottenham Werewolf
Trai	Trained Cormorant
Trip	"Triple Kent"
Trou	Troubled Magistrate
Uniq	Unique Dickensians
Whis	Whispering Knights

THE EXPLOITS OF SHERLOCK HOLMES

by Chris Redmond

Abbas	Abbas Rubby
BlacB	Black Baronet
DarkA	Dark Angeles
Deptf	Deptford Horror
Foulk	Foulkes Rath
GoldH	Gold Hunter
Highg	Highgate Miracle

RedWi	Red Widow
Seald	Sealed Room
Seven	Seven Clocks
2 Womn	Two Women
WaxGa	Wax Gamblers

SCHLOCK HOMES

by Ronald De Waal

Adam	Adam Bomb
Arti	Artist's Mottle
AscT	Ascot Tie
BigP	Big Plunger
Coun	Counterfeit Sovereign
Disa	Disappearance of Whistler's Mother
DogK	Dog in the Knight
Doub	Double-Bogey Man
FinA	Final Adventure
LosP	Lost Prince
MisC	Missing Cheyne-Stroke
MisQ	Missing Three-Quarters
PerU	Perforated Ulster
Prin	Printer's Inc.
Retu	Return of Schlock Homes
Snar	Snared Drummer
SpeB	Spectacled Band
StoC	Stockbroker's Clark
Wido	Widow's Weeds

ABBREVIATIONS OF SHERLOCKIAN PERIODICALS

BSC	*Baker Street Collecting*
BSCL	*The Baker Street Cab Lantern*
BSG	*The Baker Street Gasogene*
BSJ	*The Baker Street Journal* (New Series)
BSJ [OS]	*The Baker Street Journal* [Old Series]
BSP	*Baker Street Pages*
BSP (NS)	*The Baker Street Pages* (New Series)
—	*Bulletin*
CPBook	*The Commonplace Book*
CR	*The Cormorants' Ring*
DCC	*The Devon County Chronicle*
EL	*Encyclical Letter*
HO	*The Holmesian Observer*
—	*Investigations*
IR	*Irregular Report*
PD	*The Pontine Dossier*
SHJ	*The Sherlock Holmes Journal*
—	*Sherlockiana*
SIS	*Studies in Scarlet*
SOH	*Sidelights on Holmes*
SOS	*Shades of Sherlock*
SS	*The Scandal Sheet*
VH	*The Vermissa Herald* (New Series)
VH [OS]	*Vermissa Herald* [Old Series]
VJ	*The Victorian Journal*

PRIVATE COLLECTORS

Carl H. Anderson
Gate House, State Road
Penn Valley,
Narberth, Pa.

An excellent collection of first and other editions of the tales, including some manuscript material. Mr. Anderson's original library was destroyed by fire. His present collection was, in part, formerly owned by the late Edgar W. Smith. See also item 4790.

James Bliss Austin
114 Buckingham Road
Pittsburgh, Pa.

A collection, unsurpassed in the United States, that includes all the first and other important editions of the Canon, the writings, periodicals, and manuscripts. Dr. Austin has described some of his Sherlockian rarities in a letter to Lord Donegall (item 3791).

Nathan L. Bengis
658 West 188th Street
New York, N.Y.

A fine collection, including over 200 variant editions of Sign. Mr. Bengis has discussed his library and "Signs" in bibliographies and essays listed under items 2468, 2684-2685, and 3793-3795. The items in his collection have since been sold to other Sherlockians, including Peter E. Blau, John P. Crotty, Adrian Homer Goldstone, Norman Nolan, Otto Penzler, John Schrandt, Theodore G. Schulz, and John Bennett Shaw.

Ronald Burt De Waal
719 South Washington
Apt. 221B
Fort Collins, Colo.

From an initial "collection"—a two-volume omnibus edition of the stories—at the beginning of the compilation of this bibliography, the compiler, by choice and necessity, has accumulated several hundred items, including complete sets of all the Sherlockian periodicals and many foreign-language editions of the Canon. Although modest when compared to the other private libraries listed here, it is by now the largest collection in the Rocky Mountain States. See also items 4795 and 4801.

Dean W. Dickensheet
2430 Lake St., Apt. 7
San Francisco, Ca.

One of the best collections on the West Coast, containing most of the writings about the Writings and numerous editions of the tales.

Irving Fenton
1655 Flatbush Avenue
Brooklyn, N.Y.

An outstanding library that contains the largest collection of foreign translations in this and perhaps any other country.

James C. Iraldi
33-65 14th Street
Long Island City, N.Y.

An important collection of Sherlockiana representing an accumulation of more than 35 years. See also item 3721. (The collection has been - purchased by the University of Minnesota Library.)

John Bennett Shaw
1917 Fort Union Drive
Santa Fe, N.M.

Quite possibly the largest Sherlock Holmes library in the world. It includes a virtually complete collection of the writings and ephemeral material. For further information, see items 3735, 4796, and 4798.

Julian Wolff, M.D.
33 Riverside Drive
New York, N.Y.

The editor of *The Baker Street Journal* and Commissionaire of the Baker Street Irregulars since 1960 naturally has an impressive collection of books and articles about Holmes.

LIBRARIES

British Museum
London

A library that is especially strong in Sherlockiana published in England and other European countries. For a list of its holdings, see the *British Museum General Catalogue of Printed Books*. Loan policy: non-circulating.

Colorado State University
The Libraries
Fort Collins, Colo.

The largest institutional collection in the Rocky Mountain States. Loan policy: circulating.

Library of Congress
Washington, D.C.

The largest library in the world has, of course, most of the books and periodicals published in this country. As would be expected, it does not have many of the Sherlockian ephemeras or privately produced publications. For a list of its holdings, as well as those reported to the Library of Congress by several hundred participating libraries, see *The National Union Catalog* (item 3737). Loan policy: non-circulating, although many books are available on interlibrary loan, and periodicals will be photoduplicated upon request.

Appendix

New York Public Library:
Library & Museum of the
Performing Arts at Lincoln
Center

This collection has a vast amount of material concerning the Sherlock Holmes plays, film adaptations, and the radio and television productions. The files include clippings, programs, photographs, still books, reviews, playbills, prompt books, etc.

San Francisco Public Library

An expanding collection based upon the bequest to The Scowrers and Molly Maguires of Anthony Boucher's library. It is especially rich in translations, pastiches, and commentaries in Spanish. See Mr. Boucher's bibliography "Holmesiana Hispanica" (item 3705). The collection may eventually contain the bequests of other Scowrers, and shows promise of becoming the best Sherlockian collection in the Western States. Loan policy: non-circulating.

Toronto Central Library
Ontario, Canada

The nucleus of this outstanding Arthur Conan Doyle Collection was formed in 1969 with the acquisition of the Arthur Baillie Collection, which included a number of first editions and writings about the Writings. This paved the way for the purchase of a collection from the London bookseller Harold Mortlake (see item 3727). In 1970 the Library acquired another monumental collection—that of S. Tupper Bigelow. For information on his collection and index, see items 4270 and 4271.

Miss Mary McMahon, Head of the Literature Section, and her staff are to be commended for establishing what is now the largest and most important institutional collection of Sherlockiana-Doyliana. See also item 4791.

DIRECTORY OF SHERLOCK HOLMES SOCIETIES
Revised April 27, 1977
ALPHABETICAL LISTING

The Abbey Grangers of Chislehurst
Colin Prestige
34 Pont St.
London, SW1, England

The Adventuresses of Sherlock Holmes
Pat Moran
12 W. 19th St.
New York, NY 10011

The Afghanistan Perceivers
Stafford G. Davis
2144 N. Elwood
Tulsa, OK 74106
(918) 584-0794

The Amateur Mendicant Society of Detroit
Gene Leeb
1420 Harvard Rd.
Grosse Pointe Park, MI 48230
(313) 885-2300

The Andaman Islanders
Marcia C. Walsh
700 Richards St., No. 703
Honolulu, HI 96913

The Anderson Murderers (sic)
J. David Kiser
P. O. Box 84
Skyland, NC 28776

The Arcadia Mixture
David K. Maxfield
2217 Manchester Rd.
Ann Arbor, MI 48104
(313) 971-6573

The Arkansas Valley Investors, Ltd.
Jason Rouby
P. O. Box 2233
Little Rock, AR 72203
(501) 664-4468

The Arnsworth Castle
Robert H. Schutz
1375 Anderson Ave.
Morgantown, WV 26505
(304) 599-2566

The Avenging Angels
Linda L. De Waal
615 Fourth Ave.
Salt Lake City, UT 84103
(801) 322-2222

The Bagatelle Card Club of Milwaukee
Sue Flaherty
N62 W15127 Tepee Ct.
Menomonee Falls, WI 53051
(414) 252-3276

The Baker Street Irregulars
Dr. Julian Wolff, M.D.
33 Riverside Dr.
New York, NY 10023
(212) TR 7-7173

The Baker Street Students
Russell McDermott
1310 E. 30th
Texarkana, AR 75502
(501) 772-9459

The Baker Street Underground
Andrew Jay Peck
2974 Perry Ave.
Bronx, NY 10458

The Ballarat Bushrangers
Jennifer E. Chorley
32 Wrecclesham Hill
Farnham, Surrey, England

The Baritsu Chapter of
The Baker Street Irregulars
Richard Hughes
Shepherd Court
33 Conduit Rd., Apt. D-2
Hong Kong

The Bee-Keepers
Thomas Storck
780 W. Brice Ave.
Lima, OH 45801

The Beekeepers of Sussex
August Whiteside
505 N. Washington Ave.
Brownsville, TN 38012

The Birdy Edwards Society
J. Randolph Cox
Rolvaag Memorial Library
Saint Olaf College
Northfield, MN 55057
(507) 663-3224

The Board-School Beacons
Steve Clarkson
3612 Briarstone Rd.
Randallstown, MD 21133
(301) 922-7131

The Bootmakers of Toronto
Cameron Hollyer
Metropolitan Toronto Central Library
214 College St.
Toronto, Ontario, Canada M5T 1R3
(416) 924-9511

The Brothers Three of Moriarty
John Bennett Shaw
1917 Fort Union Dr.
Santa Fe, NM 87501
(505) 982-2947

The Bruce-Partington Planners
Cheri Hochberg
3700 Mandeville Canyon Rd.
Los Angeles, CA 90049
(213) 476-4211

The Bruce-Partington Planners of
The Baker Street Irregulars
in the Military-Industrial Complex
Jon L. Lellenberg
5027 Fillmore Ave.
Alexandria, VA 22311
(703) 379-1455

The Carlton Club
Ralph Edwards
3024 N. Calvert St., Apt. A-1
Baltimore, MD 21218
(301) 889-7036

The Cavendish Squares, Ltd.
Rosie Vogel
1041 Camelot Gardens Dr.
St. Louis, MO 63125

The Cimbrian Friends of Baker Street
Henry Lauritzen
Vesterbro 60
Dk-9000 Aalborg, Denmark
(08) 12 39 13

The Confederates of Wisteria Lodge
(Atlanta)
Robert S. Gellerstedt, Jr.
1035 Wedgewood Dr.
Fayetteville, GA 30214
(404) 461-3166

The Cornish Horrors
Rev. Henry T. Folsom
338 Main St.
Old Saybrook, CT 06475
(203) 388-3332

The Council of Four
Robert C. Peterson
2845 S. Gilpen St.
Denver, CO 80210
(303) 756-8516

The Country of the Saints
Kevin John
637 N. 2nd West
Brigham, UT 84302
(801) 723-3142

The Creeping Men of Cleveland
William McCullam
Fairmont Rd.
Newbury, OH 44065
(216) 338-3253

The Crew of the Barque *Gloria Scott*
Scott Forester
492 Careswell St.
Green Harbor, Marshfield, MA 02050
(617) 837-0052

The Crew of the Barque *Lone Star*
William B. Beeson
108 S. Bowser, Apt. 7
Richardson, TX 75081
(214) 238-9737

The Crew of the S.S. *Friesland*
Cornelis Helling
Toutenburgh 36
Emmeloord N.O.P., Holland

The Criterion Bar Association
Janet Null
1928 N. Kenmore
Chicago, IL 60614
(312) 528-4040

The Diogenes Club of Gothenburg
Engström
Västes gata 60
S-421 53 V Frölunda, Sweden

The Diogenes Club of New York
Dr. Charles Goodman
601 W. 174th St.
New York, NY 10033
(212) WA 3-6181

Dr. Watson's Neglected Patients
Ronald B. De Waal
5020 Hogan Dr.
Ft. Collins, CO 80521
(303) 491-5911

The Double-Barrelled Tiger Cubs
George H. Scheetz
409½ W. Vine St.
Champaign, IL 61820
(217) 351-2196

The Elmstalker
John L. Krumm
1705 E. Nevada St.
Marshalltown, IA 50158
(515) 752-4981

The Eyford Engineers
Pat Pierce
2475 Vantage Way
Del Mar, CA 92014

The Fifth Northumberland Fusiliers
James J. Zunic
611 Suffolk St.
Pittsburgh, PA 15214
(412) 322-7230

The Five Orange Pips of Westchester
County
Richard W. Clarke
Holly Branch Rd.
Katonah, NY 10536
(914) 232-3737

The Fortescue Scholarship Examiners
Carol Fishbaugh
4601 Valdez Dr.
Des Moines, IA 50310
(515) 278-5975

The Friends of Irene Adler
Daniel Posnansky
Gutman Library
Harvard University
Cambridge, MA 02138
(617) 495-4225

The Gamekeepers of Northern Minnesota
Jon V. Wilmunen
P.O. Box 7
Buhl, MN 55713
(218) 258-3783

The Giant Rats of Sumatra
Robert A. Lanier
635 West Dr.
Memphis, TN 38112
(901) 452-4667

Appendix

The Goose Club of the Alpha Inn
John Sohl
2645 4th St.
Santa Monica, CA 90405
(213) 396-1644

The Great Alkali Plainsmen
of Greater Kansas City
Jon L. Lellenberg
4501 W. 90th St.
Shawnee Mission, KS 66207
(913) 648-5560

The Greek Interpreters of East Lansing
Donald A. Yates
Department of Romantic Languages
Michigan State University
East Lansing, MI 48824
(517) 353-3286

The Hansom Wheels
E. Wayne Wall
28 Carroll Ct.
West Columbia, SC 29169
(803) 794-3989

The Hansoms of John Clayton
Philip José Farmer
4106 Devon Ln.
Peoria, IL 61614
(309) 688-5701

The High Tors
Dr. Paul G. Ashdown
Ridgeview Dr.
Bowling Green, KY 42101
(502) 781-9126

The Hollywood Hounds
Sir Alvin F. Germeshausen
2720 Woodhaven Dr.
Hollywood, CA 90068
(213) 467-8091

The Hounds of the Baskerville (sic)
Robert W. Hahn
509 S. Ahrens
Lombard, IL 60148
(312) 620-0694

The Hudson Valley Sciontists
Glenn Laxton
Orchard Rd.
Poughkeepsie, NY 12603
(914) 471-9680

Hugo's Companions
Ely Liebow
Department of English
Northeastern Illinois University
Chicago, IL 60625
(312) 583-8120

The Illustrious Clients
Michael F. Whelan
5522A Rue de Ville
Indianapolis, IN 46220
(367) 253-9285

The Inner Brotherhood of the Holy Four
Colin Prestige
34 Pont St.
London, SW1, England

Institute of Sherlock Holmes Studies
Nicholas C. Denyer
Corpus Christi College
Oxford, England

The Inverness Capers
Michael Senuta
881 Columbine Dr.
Barberton, OH 44203
(216) 753-8320

An Irish Secret Society at Buffalo
Prof. Frank A. Hoffmann
Department of English
State University College at Buffalo
1300 Elmwood Ave.
Buffalo, NY 14222
(716) 862-5517

The Islanders of Uffa
Jeff Clow
3501 Mayberry
Enid, OK 73701
(405) 234-5791

The Legends of the West Country
Howard Lachtman
926 W. Mendocino Ave.
Stockton, CA 95204
(209) 465-8660

The Maiwand Jezails
Richard D. Lesh
505 E. 10th St.
Wayne, NE 68787
(402) 375-3793

The Master's Class of Philadelphia
Dr. Michael H. Kean
264 Forrest Rd.
Merion Station, PA 19066
(215) MO 4-9673

The Men on the Tor
Harold E. Niver
142 W. Meadow Rd.
Rocky Hill, CT 06067

The Mexborough Lodgers
William C. McGaw
138 Gibbs St.
El Paso, TX 79907
(915) 859-9859

The Milvertonians of Hampstead
Peter Richard
2 Leeside Crescent
London, NW 11, England
01-455 2905

The Missing Three-Quarters
David Greeney
292 Anfield Rd.
Liverpool 4, England

Mrs. Hudson's Cliff Dwellers
Norman Schatell
81 Columbia Ave.
Cliffside Park, NJ 07010
(201) 943-8967

Mrs. Hudson's Lodgers
Donald E. Novorsky
15606 Norway Ave.
Cleveland, OH 44111
(216) 476-2459

Moulton's Prospectors
Matt Fairlie
10263 102nd Ave.
Sun City, AZ 85351
(602) 933-4970

The Musgrave Ritualists
Nathan L. Bengis
15 W. Fairview Ave.
Dover, NJ 07801
(201) 361-6706

The Mycroft Holmes Society
Gerald R. Clark
103 Frederick Dr.
Liverpool, NY 13088
(315) 457-0588

Mycroft's Isolated Companions
Dennis S. Kluk
7241 N. Ridge Blvd.
Chicago, IL 60645
(312) 262-0628

The Napoleons of Crime (Michigan)
Mark McPherson
2438 Lake in the Woods Blvd., Apt. 913
Ypsilanti, MI 48197

The Napoleons of Crime (New York)
Leonard Picker
119 81st Ave.
Kew Gardens, NY 11415
(212) LI 4-8757

The New Zealand Stocks
David Skene Melvin
7 Oakley Ave.
Hamilton, New Zealand

The Noble and Most Singular Order
of the Blue Carbuncle
Betty Jo Graves
7033 NE Flanders
Portland, OR 97213
(506) 253-7243

The Noble Bachelors (and Concubines)
of St. Louis
Philip A. Shreffler
827 W. Rose Hill
Kirkwood, MO 63122
(314) 822-2428

The Non-Canonical Calabashes of
Los Angeles
Sean M. Wright
5542 Romaine St.
Hollywood, CA 90038
(213) HOLMES-4

The Nonpareil Club
Brian D. Taylor
Rt. 1, Box 156-A
Jamul, CA 92035

The Norwegian Explorers
E. W. McDiarmid
1473 Fulham St.
St. Paul, MN 55108
(612) 645-2358

The Norwood Builders of Burlington
A. L. Brue
R.F.D. 2
Broad Lake Rd.
Winooski, VT 05404

The Notorious Canary-Trainers
Sue Flaherty
N62 W15127 Tepee Ct.
Menomonee Falls, WI 53051
(414) 252-3276

The Old Soldiers of Baker Street
W. T. Rabe
909 Prospect
Sault Sainte Marie, MI 49783
(906) 635-5085

The Old Soldiers of Praed Street
Lt. Col. Theodore G. Schulz
180 Mt. Lassen Dr.
San Rafael, CA 94903
(415) 479-6554

The Outpatients, A Department of
Dr. Watson's Neglected Patients
Jill Stone
55 S. Hoyt St.
Lakewood, CO 80226
(303) 233-6296

The Pawky Humorists
Peter G. Ashman
15 Kenlawn Ct.
Towson, MD 21204

The Pleasant Places of Florida
Rev. Dr. Benton Wood
4408 Gulf Dr.
Holmes Beach, FL 33510
(813) 778-1638

The Praed Street Irregulars
Luther Norris
3844 Watseka Ave.
Culver City, CA 90230
(213) 837-6628 (listed under
Pons, Solar)

The Priory Scholars
Chris Steinbrunner
62-52 82nd St.
Elmhurst, NY 11379
(212) NE 9-9057

The Priory Scholars of
Fenwick High School
Rev. Leonard Cochran
505 Washington Blvd.
Oak Park, IL 60302
(312) 386-0127

The Rascally Lascars of Beverly Hills
Laurence Wright
P.O. Box 46-215
Los Angeles, CA 90046

The Red Circle of Washington, D.C.
Peter E. Blau
4107 W St., NW
Washington, D.C. 20007
(202) 338-1808

The Reluctant Scholars
Scion of The Praed Street Irregulars
David Irwin
6797 Satinwood Cove
Memphis, TN 38138
(901) 754-7573

The Resident Patients of Baker Street
Valerie Hill
6760 SW 76th Terrace
South Miami, FL 33143

The Retired Colourmen of Dayton
Frederick M. Avolio
58 Frank St.
Dayton, OH 45409
(513) 224-5286

Appendix

The Saxe-Coburg Squares of
Mecklenburg County
Fred Mende
1214 Tarrington Ave.
Charlotte, NC 28205
(704) 537-3640

The Scandalous Bohemians of New Jersey
Norman S. Nolan
68 Crest Rd.
Middletown, NJ 07748
(201) 671-0820

The Scion of the Four
Andrew G. Fusco
158 Hoffman Ave.
Morgantown, WV 26505
(304) 599-9454

The Scowrers and Molly Maguires
Dean W. Dickensheet
2430 Lake St., Apt. 7
San Francisco, CA 94121
(415) 387-5930

The Seventeen Steps of Columbus
Patricia Rockwell
4163 Squires Ln.
Columbus, OH 43220
(614) 457-5473

S.H.E.R.L.O.C.K.
(Sherlock Holmes Enthusiastic
Readers League of Criminal Knowledge)
Dr. Martin Arbagi
Department of History
Wright State University
Dayton, OH 45431
(513) 873-2909

The Sherlock Holmes Cipher Society
Gerald R. Clark
103 Frederick Dr.
Liverpool, NY 13088
(315) 457-0588

Sherlock Holmes Klubben i Danmark
(The Danish Baker Street Irregulars)
Henry Lauritzen
Vesterbro 60
Dk-9000 Aalborg, Denmark
(08) 12 39 13

The Sherlock Holmes Society of London
Capt. W. R. Michell, R.N.
5 Manor Close
Warlingham, Surrey CR3 9SF, England

The Sherlock Holmes Wireless Society
David Galerstein
51 Fall Ln.
Jericho, NY 11753
(516) WE 8-5788

Sherlock Holmes's Varied Correspondence (sic)
Desmond Tyler
162 Leybridge Ct.
Eltham Rd.
London SE12 8 TL, England
01-852 0919

The Silver Blazers
Larry DeKay
P.O. Box 20275
Louisville, KY 40220

The Sir James Saunders Society
Dr. Edgar B. Smith, M.D.
School of Medicine
University of New Mexico
Albuquerque, NM 87131
(505) 277-4757

The Six Napoleons of Baltimore
Philip Sherman
1102 Blaustein Bldg.
One North Charles St.
Baltimore, MD 21201
(301) 727-5020

The Society for the Prevention
of Cruelty to Canonical Criminals
(address withheld)

The Society of Solitary Cyclists
William F. Connelly
6803 Vinewood Pl.
Cincinnati, OH 45227

The Solar Pons Society of London
Roger Johnson
38, North House
Bush Fair
Harlow, Essex, England

The Solitary Cyclists of South Bend
Prof. Michael J. Crowe
53155 Oakmont Park West Dr.
South Bend, IN 46637
(219) 272-3426

The Solitary Cyclists of Sweden
Ted Bergman
Storkvägen 10
S-181 35 Lidingö, Sweden
08/767 2009

The Sons of the Copper Beeches
John B. Koelle
244 Haverford Ave.
Swarthmore, PA 19081
(215) KI 3-5190

The Speckled Band of Boston
James Keddie, Jr.
28 Laurel Ave.
Wellesley Hills, MA 02181
(617) 235-1038

The Stapletons of Merripit House
David Galerstein, Faculty Adviser
Hillside Junior High School 172, Queens
81-14 257th St.
Floral Park, NY 11004
(212) 343-4897

The Stormy Petrels of Maumee Bay
Dr. Chuck Terbille
2134 Alvin
Toledo, OH 43606
(419) 536-3227

The Strange Old Book Collectors
Lucy Green
8502 Ahern, Apt. 202
San Antonio, TX 78216
(512) 342-2409

The Students in Scarlet of
Clark University
Dr. Paul S. Clarkson
3 Lowell Ave.
Holden, MA 01520
(617) 829-4076

468

The Sub-Librarians Scion of
The Baker Street Irregulars in
The American Library Association
Margaret Francine Morris
3010 Wisconsin Ave., NW
Washington, D.C. 20016
(202) 966-5773

The Sub-Librarians Scion of
The Sherlock Holmes Society of London
Within the Canadian Library Association
Cameron Hollyer
Metropolitan Toronto Central Library
214 College St.
Toronto, Ontario, Canada M5T 1R3
(416) 924-9511

The Sussex Vampires
William S. Mandel
437 Arlington Rd.
Cedarhurst, NY 11516

The Tankerville Club
Paul D. Herbert
4565 Harrison Ave.
Cincinnati, OH 45236
(513) 791-5404

The Three Garridebs
Bruce Kennedy
200 Diplomat Dr., Apt. 8P
Mount Kisco, NY 10549
(914) 666-4905

The Three Students of Camford
Colin Prestige
34 Pont St.
London, SW1, England

The Tidewaiters of San Francisco Bay
William A. Berner
4712 17th St.
San Francisco, CA 94117
(415) 564-6297

The Tigers of San Pedro
John Farrell
1367 W. 6th St.
San Pedro, CA 90732
(213) 832-4412

The Travellers for Nevada
William E. Dudley
Box 2020
Las Vegas, NV 89101
(702) 385-6424

The Trichinopoly Society of Long Island
Arthur L. Levine
463 Dunster Ct.
West Hempstead, NY 11552
(516) IV 5-0481

The Trifling Monographs
Lucy Chase Williams
1466 N. Glengarry Rd.
Birmingham, MI 48010

The Unanswered Correspondents
Jack Tracy
709 W. 6th St.
Bloomington, IN 47401
(812) 332-5169

The Unanswered Correspondents (sic)
Bruce R. Beaman
727 Second St.
Stevens Point, WI 54481
(715) 344-7050

Unravellers of the Scarlet Thread
Alfred H. Curtis III
4529 E. 9th
Tucson, AZ 85711

"VR"
Dr. Charles S. Petty, M.D.
5230 Medical Center Dr.
P.O. Box 35728
Dallas, TX 75235
(214) 356-6588

The Veiled Lodgers
2625 Nubgaard Rd.
Ferndale, WA 98248

The Victorian Gentlemen
Tom Mengert
9102 Lake Steilacoom Point
Tacoma, WA 98498
(206) 584-0994

The Wastrels of Watson
Roberta Sklower
11888 Longridge Dr., Apt. 2078
Baton Rouge, LA 70816
(504) 293-0819

The William Gillette Memorial Luncheon
Lisa McGaw
392 Central Park West, Apt. 4-G
New York, NY 10025
(212) 666-9134

The Women's Auxiliary to
The Baker Street Irregulars
Sue Dahlinger
135 Orchard Pl.
Maywood, NJ 07607

The Young Sherlockian Corresponding
Society
Charles O'Boyle
Box 567
Hollis, NH 03049
(603) 465-7614

GEOGRAPHICAL LISTING

CANADA
The Bootmakers of Toronto
The Sub-Librarians Scion of
The Sherlock Holmes Society of London
Within the Canadian Library Association

DENMARK
The Cimbrian Friends of Baker Street
Sherlock Holmes Klubben i Danmark

ENGLAND
The Abbey Grangers of Chislehurst
The Ballarat Bushrangers
The Inner Brotherhood of the Holy Four
Institute of Sherlock Holmes Studies
The Milvertonians of Hampstead
The Missing Three-Quarters
The Sherlock Holmes Society of London
Sherlock Holmes Varied Correspondents
(sic)
The Solar Pons Society of London
The Three Students of Camford

HOLLAND
The Crew of the S.S. *Friesland*

Appendix

HONG KONG
The Baritsu Chapter of
The Baker Street Irregulars

NEW ZEALAND
The New Zealand Stocks

SWEDEN
The Diogenes Club of Gothenburg
The Solitary Cyclists of Sweden

UNITED STATES

Arizona
Moulton's Prospectors
Unravellers of the Scarlet Thread

Arkansas
The Arkansas Valley Investors, Ltd.
The Baker Street Students

California
The Bruce-Partington Planners
The Eyford Engineers
The Goose Club of the Alpha Inn
The Hollywood Hounds
The Legends of the West Country
The Non-Canonical Calabashes of
Los Angeles
The Nonpareil Club
The Old Soldiers of Praed Street
The Praed Street Irregulars
The Rascally Lascars of Beverly Hills
The Scowrers and Molly Maguires
The Tidewaiters of San Francisco Bay
The Tigers of San Pedro

Colorado
The Council of Four
Dr. Watson's Neglected Patients
The Outpatients

Connecticut
The Cornish Horrors
The Men on the Tor

District of Columbia
The Bruce-Partington Planners of
The Baker Street Irregulars
in the Military-Industrial Complex
The Red Circle of Washington, D.C.
The Sub-Librarians Scion of
The Baker Street Irregulars in
The American Library Association

Florida
The Pleasant Places of Florida
The Resident Patients of Baker Street

Georgia
The Confederates of Wisteria Lodge

Hawaii
The Andaman Islanders

Illinois
The Criterion Bar Association
The Double-Barrelled Tiger Cubs
The Hansoms of John Clayton
The Hounds of the Baskerville (sic)
Hugo's Campanions
Mycroft's Isolated Companions
The Priory Scholars of
Fenwick High School

Indiana
The Solitary Cyclists of South Bend
The Unanswered Correspondents

Iowa
The Elmstalker
The Fortescue Scholarship Examiners

Kansas
The Great Alkali Plainsmen

Kentucky
The High Tors
The Silver Blazers

Louisiana
The Wastrels of Watson

Maryland
The Board-School Beacons
The Carlton Club
The Pawky Humorists
The Six Napoleons of Baltimore

Massachusetts
The Crew of the Barque *Gloria Scott*
The Friends of Irene Adler
The Speckled Band of Boston
The Students in Scarlet

Michigan
The Amateur Mendicant Society of Detroit
The Arcadia Mixture
The Greek Interpreters of East Lansing
The Napoleons of Crime (Michigan)
The Old Soldiers of Baker Street
The Solitary Cyclists of South Bend
The Trifling Monographs

Minnesota
The Birdy Edwards Society
The Gamekeepers of Northern Minnesota
The Norwegian Explorers

Missouri
The Cavendish Squares, Ltd.
The Great Alkali Plainsmen of
Greater Kansas City
The Noble Bachelors (and Concubines)

Nebraska
The Maiwand Jezails

Nevada
The Travellers for Nevada

New Hampshire
The Young Sherlockian Corresponding Society

New Jersey
Mrs. Hudson's Cliff Dwellers
The Musgrave Ritualists
The Scandalous Bohemians of New Jersey
The Women's Auxiliary to
The Baker Street Irregulars

New Mexico
The Brothers Three of Moriarty
The Sir James Saunders Society

New York
The Adventuresses of Sherlock Holmes
The Baker Street Irregulars
The Baker Street Underground
The Diogenes Club of New York
The Five Orange Pips of Westchester County
The Hudson Valley Sciontists

An Irish Secret Society at Buffalo
The Mycroft Holmes Society
The Napoleons of Crime (New York)
The Priory Scholars
The Sherlock Holmes Cipher Society
The Sherlock Holmes Wireless Society
The Stapletons of Merripit House
The Sussex Vampires
The Three Garridebs
The Trichinopoly Society of Long Island
The William Gillette Memorial Luncheon

North Carolina
The Anderson Murderers (sic)
The Saxe-Coburg Squares of
Mecklenburg County

Ohio
The Bee-Keepers
The Creeping Men of Cleveland
The Inverness Capers
Mrs. Hudson's Lodgers
The Retired Colourmen
The Seventeen Steps of Columbus
S.H.E.R.L.O.C.K.
The Society of Solitary Cyclists
The Stormy Petrels of Maumee Bay
The Tankerville Club

Oklahoma
The Afghanistan Perceivers
The Islanders of Uffa

Oregon
The Noble and Most Singular Order
of the Blue Carbuncle

Pennsylvania
The Fifth Northumberland Fusiliers
The Master's Class of Philadelphia
The Sons of the Copper Beeches

Rhode Island
The Cornish Horrors

South Carolina
The Hansom Wheels

Tennessee
The Beekeepers of Sussex
The Giant Rats of Sumatra
The Reluctant Scholars

Texas
The Crew of the Barque *Lone Star*
The Mexborough Lodgers
The Strange Old Book Collectors
"VR"

Utah
The Avenging Angels
The Country of the Saints

Vermont
The Norwood Builders of Burlington

Washington
The Veiled Lodgers
The Victorian Gentlemen

West Virginia
The Arnsworth Castle
The Scion of the Four

Wisconsin
The Bagatelle Card Club of Milwaukee
The Notorious Canary-Trainers
The Unanswered Correspondents (sic)

Index of Names

486

Index
of
Names

Index of Titles

Index
of
Titles

Index
of
Titles

Index of Titles

Index of Titles

382

3143
"Trade Relations," 4939
"The Trail of Scarlet," 3960
Trailing the Counterfeiter, 5116
A Tramp Abroad, 2780
"Transactions of the Sherlock
   Holmes Society of London,"
   4767
"Translation of 'Another Bird in
   a Gilded Cage,' " 5917
"Travels of a Donkey," 4780
"Travels with a Pumpkin," 4708
Treasure Island, 2708
*A Treasury of Great Science
   Fiction*, 5793
A Treasury of Short Stories, 212
Treasury of Snake Lore, 400
"A Treatise on the Binomial
   Theorem,". 3538
"A Treaty for Breakfast," 1986
"A Tremor at the Edge of the
   Web," 3548
"Trent's Last Case," 1927
"The Therapeutic Doctor
   Watson," 4127
"A Trifle Trying," 2896
"Trifling Monograph Concerning
   Mr. Solar Pons," 5716
"Triolet: J. H. W. to S. H.," 4410
"Triolet on Frederic Dorr Steele,"
   3899
"Triolet: On the Immortality of
   Sherlock Holmes and Doctor
   Watson," 4494
"The Trip That Was," 2403
*The Triumph of Sherlock
   Holmes*, 5138
"The True Adventure of the
   Second Stain," 5928
"The True and Proper Coat of
   Arms of Mr. Sherlock
   Holmes," 3869
"The True Author of Last and
   Maza," 3452
"The True Blue: A Case of
   Identification," 2283
The True Conan Doyle, 3921
"The True Story of Sherlock
   Holmes," 2022
"The True Story of the Dancing
   Men," 2342
"True Tales of 'Sherlock
   Holmes,' " 3974
"The Trusty Servant," 3309
"The Truth About Moriarty,"
   3547
"The Truth About Nero Wolfe,"
   4042
"The Truth About Professor
   Moriarty," 3564
"The Truth About Sherlock
   Holmes," 2381, 3927
"The Truth About the Speckled
   Band," 2738
"The Truth About Watson,"
   3359
"The Truth at Last," 6036
"The Truthful Lady," 5864

"Tsutsugamushi," 1987
"Tsutsugamushi to You, Dr.
   Ober," 2363
"Tune in Again for Sherlock
   Holmes," 5034
" 'Twas the Second Morning
   After Christmas," 2287
"The 'Twelve Best,' " 4249
Twentieth Century Authors, 3966
"Twnety-First Birthday," 4753
Twenty-Five Detective Stories,
   5791
"21 Baker Street Is the Real
   221B," 3689
"Twenty Questions on Animals
   Found in 'The Adventure of the
   Devil's Foot,' " 5004
*Twenty Thousand Leagues Under
   the Sea*, 3584
"The Twenty-Three Deductions,"
   2624
"Twenty Years After," 4771
Two Baker Street Akronisms,
   1914
*Two Ballads in Praise of Sherlock
   Holmes*, 4510
"Two Bibliographical Foot-
   notes," 3277, 4328
"Two Bits from Boston," 4146
"Two Canonical Problems
   Solved," 3533
" 'Two Good Men,' " 2845
Two Irregular Sonnets, 4411
"The Two Moriarties," 3585
"Two Partial Pastiches," 6087
"The Two-Shilling Award," 4648
Two Sonnets, 4464
"Two Southern Exposures of
   Sherlock Holmes," 2455, 2861
"Two Suppressed Holmes
   Episodes," 3625
"221B," 3677, 3690, 4504, 5583
"221B Baker Street," 2042, 3677
"221B Baker Street?" 3682
"221B Baker Street: Certain
   Physical Details," 3665
*221B Baker Street: Sherlock
   Holmes' Privatliv*, 2037
"221B Baker Street: Where
   Sherlock Holmes Lived," 3692
"221B in Retrospect," 4809
221B Lapel Pin, 4821
"221B Madison Avenue," 3035
*221B: Studies in Sherlock
   Holmes*, 2230
Types of English Fiction, 446

*Über die Rauchgewohnheiten
   Sherlock Holmes'*, 3248
"Den udodelige Sherlock
   Holmes," 2087
"The Ultimate Source of
   Sherlock Holmes," 3008
"The Umbrosa Burglary," 6004
"Un-Christmaslike Thoughts on
   The Blue Carbuncle," 2289
"Uncle Jeremy's Household,"
   4071

"The Uncrowned Queen of
   Horror," 2550
"The Un-Curious Incident of the
   Baker Street Bathroom," 3672
Under the Clock, 5182
"The Underground," 4355
*An 'Undiscerning Critic'
   Discerned*, 3934
"The Undying Detective," 2174
"Unending Speculation About
   Poor Mozart," 4161
Ungdomsskeppen, 1916
"The Unique Hamlet," 6108
The Universal Holmes, 5041
The Unknown Murderer, 2995
"The Unknown Watson," 3395
"The Unmasking of Sherlock
   Holmes," 4024
"The Unpleasantness at the
   Stooges Club," 5929
Unpopular Opinions, 2182
*The Unrecorded Adventures of
   Sherlock Holmes in Their
   Relation to the Mental
   Processes of Dr. John H.
   Watson*, 4371
"An Unrecorded Incident," 4687
"An Unsolved Baskerville
   Puzzle," 4909
"An Unsolved Puzzle in the
   Writings," 2045
"An Unsung Heroine," 3433
"The Untidy Holmes?" 3646
"The Untold Tales of Dr.
   Watson," 4379
"Up from the Needle," 3097
"Up in the Attic," 4455
"Upon the Dating of the Master's
   Birth," 2945
*"Upon the Distinction Between
   the Ashes of the Various
   Tobaccos,"* 3298
"Upon the Identification of
   Cardinal Tosca," 4401
"Upon the Identity of Bisulphate
   of Baryta," 2512
"Upon the Probable Number of
   Cases of Mr. Sherlock
   Holmes," 4381
"Upon the Tracing of Footprints
   by Sherlock Holmes," 4935

"Vale," 4606
"A Valentine to Sherlock," 2665
"The Valley of Cheer," 2885
The Valley of Fear, 5124, 5138
"The Valley of Fear
   Bibliographically Considered,"
   2855
"The Valley of Fear Revisited,"
   2853
"Valuable Sherlockian Hunting-
   Ground," 2272
Vanity Fair, 2480
"Var Sherlock Holmes fram-
   staende idrottsman?" 3177
Varia: Essays om Boger, 3289
"Variations on a Casual

Index of Titles